THE NORTON
SHAKESPEARE

BASED ON THE OXFORD EDITION

Romances and Poems

*The original Oxford Text on which this
edition is based was prepared by*

Stanley Wells
Gary Taylor
General Editors

John Jowett
William Montgomery

THE NORTON
SHAKESPEARE

BASED ON THE OXFORD EDITION

Romances and Poems

Stephen Greenblatt, *General Editor*
HARVARD UNIVERSITY

Walter Cohen
CORNELL UNIVERSITY

Jean E. Howard
COLUMBIA UNIVERSITY

Katharine Eisaman Maus
UNIVERSITY OF VIRGINIA

With an essay on the Shakespearean stage
by Andrew Gurr

W · W · NORTON & COMPANY · NEW YORK · LONDON

Copyright © 1997 by W. W. Norton & Company, Inc.
Text and some commentaries copyright © 1986, 1988 by Oxford University Press.
A *Funeral Elegy* (text): copyright © 1997 by Donald W. Foster.
All rights reserved.
Printed in the United States of America.

The text of this book is composed in Electra with the display set in Centaur.
Composition by Binghamton Valley Composition.
Manufacturing by R. R. Donnelley & Sons.
Book design by Antonina Krass.

The Library of Congress has cataloged the one-volume edition as follows:
Shakespeare, William, 1564–1616.
The Norton Shakespeare / Stephen Greenblatt, general editor ;
Walter Cohen, Jean E. Howard, Katharine Eisaman Maus [editors] ;
with an essay on the Shakespearean stage by Andrew Gurr.
p.   cm.
"Based on the Oxford edition."
Includes bibliographical references and index.

ISBN 0-393-97087-6. — ISBN 0-393-04107-7

I. Greenblatt, Stephen Jay.   II. Cohen, Walter, 1949–   .
III. Howard, Jean E. (Jean Elizabeth), 1948–   .   IV. Maus,
Katharine Eisaman, 1955–   .   V. Title.
PR2754.G74   1997
822.3'3—DC21

97-7083
CIP
Rev.

Romances and Poems: ISBN 0-393-97673-4 (pbk.)

W. W. Norton & Company, Inc., 500 Fifth Avenue, New York, N.Y. 10110
www.wwnorton.com

W. W. Norton & Company Ltd., 10 Coptic Street, London WC1A 1PU

2 3 4 5 6 7 8 9 0

Contents

Romances

Poems

Appendices

Preface

Since Shakespeare's principal medium, the drama, was thoroughly collaborative, it seems appropriate that this edition of his works is itself the result of a sustained collaboration. Two lists of editors' names on the title-page spread hint at the collaboration that has brought to fruition *The Norton Shakespeare*. But the title page does not tell the full history of this project. The text on which *The Norton Shakespeare* is based was published in both modern-spelling and original-spelling versions by Oxford University Press, in 1986. Under the general editorship of Stanley Wells and Gary Taylor, the Oxford text was a thorough rethinking of the entire body of Shakespeare's works, the most far-reaching and innovative revision of the traditional canon in centuries. When many classroom instructors who wanted to introduce their students to the works of Shakespeare through a modern text expressed a need for the pedagogical apparatus they have come to expect in an edition oriented toward students, Norton negotiated with Oxford to assemble an editorial team of its own to prepare the necessary teaching materials around the existing Oxford text. Hence ensued a collaboration of two publishers and two editorial teams.

To what extent is this the *Norton Shakespeare* and to what extent the Oxford text? Since the Norton contributions appear here for the first time, the many pages that follow will provide the answer to the first part of the question. Introductions (both the General Introduction and those to individual plays and poems), footnotes, glosses, bibliographies, genealogies, annals, documents, and illustrations have all been the responsibility of the Norton team. We also asked Andrew Gurr of the University of Reading to contribute to this edition an essay on the London theater in Shakespeare's time, and we asked Donald W. Foster of Vassar College to introduce, edit, and gloss *A Funeral Elegy*, a poem, included here in an appendix, that raises important questions about the attribution of works to Shakespeare.

The textual notes and variants derive for the most part from the work of the Oxford team, especially as represented in *William Shakespeare: A Textual Companion* (Oxford University Press, 1987), a remarkably comprehensive explanation of editorial decisions that is herewith strongly recommended to instructors as a valuable companion to this volume. Some of the annotations spring from the never-published commentaries of the Oxford team, who have graciously allowed the Norton editors full use of them.

The Oxford text is widely available and already well-known to scholars. A few words here may help clarify the extent of our fidelity to that text and the nature of the collaboration that has brought about this volume. The Oxford editors have profited from the massive and sustained attention accorded their edition by Shakespeare scholars across the globe, and of course they have continued to participate actively in the ongoing scholarly discussion about the nature of Shakespeare's text. In the reprintings of the Oxford volumes and in various articles over the past years, the Oxford editors have made a number of refinements of the edition they originally published. Such changes have been incorporated silently here. A small number of other changes made by the Norton team, however, were not part of the Oxford editors' design and were only accepted by them after we reached, through lengthy consultation, a mutual understanding about the nature, purpose, and intended audience of this volume. In all such changes, our main concern was for the classroom; we wished to make fully and clearly available the scholarly innovation and freshness of the Oxford text, while at the same time making certain that this was a superbly useful teaching text. It is a pleasure here to record, on behalf of the Norton team, our gratitude for the personal and professional generosity of the Oxford editors in offering advice and entertaining arguments in our common goal of providing the best student Shakespeare for our times. The Norton changes to the Oxford text are various, but in only a few instances are they major. The following brief notes are sufficient to summarize all of these changes, which are also indicated in appropriate play introductions, footnotes, or textual notes.

1. The Oxford editors, along with other scholars, have strenuously argued—in both the Oxford text and elsewhere—that the now-familiar text of *King Lear*, so nearly omnipresent in our classrooms as to seem unquestionably authoritative but in reality dating from the work of Alexander Pope (1723) and Lewis Theobald (1733), represents a wrong-headed conflation of two distinct versions of the play: Shakespeare's original creation as printed in the 1608 Quarto and his substantial revision as printed in the First Folio (1623). The Oxford text, therefore, prints both *The History of King Lear* and *The Tragedy of King Lear*. Norton follows suit, but where Oxford presents these two texts sequentially, we print them on facing pages. While each version may be read independently, and to ensure this we have provided glosses and footnotes for each, the substantial points of difference between the two are immediately apparent and available for comparison. But even many who agree with the scholarly argument for the two texts of *Lear* nevertheless favor making available a conflated text, the text on which innumerable performances of the play have been based and on which a huge body of literary criticism has been written. With the reluctant acquiescence, therefore, of the Oxford editors, we have included a conflated *Lear*, a text that has no part in the Oxford canon and that has been edited by Barbara K. Lewalski of Harvard University rather than by Gary Taylor, the editor of the Oxford *Lears*.

    The Norton Shakespeare, then, includes three separate texts of *King Lear*. The reader can compare them, understand the role of editors in constructing the texts we now call Shakespeare's, explore in considerable detail the kinds of decisions that playwrights, editors, and printers make and remake, witness first-hand the historical transformation of what might at first glance seem fixed and unchanging. *The Norton Shakespeare* offers extraordinary access to this supremely brilliant, difficult, compelling play.

2. *Hamlet* (along with several other plays, including *Richard II, Troilus and Cressida*, and *Othello*) offers similar grounds for objections to the traditional conflation, but both the economics of publishing and the realities of bookbinding—not to mention our recognition of the limited time in the typical undergraduate syllabus—preclude our offering three (or even four) *Hamlets* to match three *Lears*.

    The Oxford text of *Hamlet* was based upon the Folio text, with an appended list of Additional Passages from the Second Quarto (Q2). These additional readings total more than two hundred lines, a significant number, among which are lines that have come to seem very much part of the play as widely received, even if we may doubt that they belong with all the others in any single one of Shakespeare's *Hamlets*. The Norton team, while following the Oxford text, has moved the Q2 passages from the appendix to the body of the play. But in doing so, we have not wanted once again to produce a conflated text. We have therefore indented the Q2 passages, printed them in a different typeface, and numbered them in such a way as to make clear their provenance. Those who wish to read the Folio version of *Hamlet* can thus simply skip over the indented Q2 passages, while at the same time it is possible for readers to see clearly the place that the Q2 passages occupy. We have adopted a similar strategy with several other plays: passages printed in Oxford in appendices are generally printed here in the play texts, though clearly demarcated and not conflated. In the case of *The Taming of the Shrew* and the related quarto text, *The Taming of a Shrew*, however, we have followed Oxford's procedure and left the quarto passages in an appendix, since we believe the texts reflect two distinct plays rather than a revision of one. We have similarly reproduced Oxford's brief appendices to A *Midsummer Night's Dream* and *Henry V*, enabling readers to consider alternative revisions of certain passages.

3. For reasons understood by every Shakespearean (and rehearsed at some length in this volume), the Oxford editors chose to restore the name "Sir John Oldcastle" to the character much better known as Falstaff in *1 Henry IV*. (They made comparable changes in the names of the characters known as Bardolph and Peto.) But for reasons understood by everyone who has presented this play to undergraduates or sampled the centuries of enthusiastic criticism, the Norton editors, with the Oxford editors' gracious agreement, have for this classroom edition opted for the familiar name "Falstaff " (and those of his boon companions), properly noting the change and its significance in the play's introduction.

4. The Oxford editors chose not to differentiate between those stage directions that appeared in the early editions up to and including the Folio and those that have been added by subsequent editors. Instead, in *A Textual Companion* they include separate lists of the original stage directions. These lists are not readily available to readers of the Norton text, whose editors opted instead to bracket all stage directions that derive from editions published after the Folio. Readers can thus easily see which stage directions derive from texts that may bear at least some relation to performances in Shakespeare's time, if not to Shakespeare's own authorship. The Norton policy is more fully explained in the General Introduction.

It has long been the dream of the publisher, W.W. Norton, to bring out a Shakespeare edition. The task proved to be a complex one, with many players. The initial efforts of the late John Benedict at Norton were followed, with the crucial encouragement of the firm's chairman, Donald S. Lamm, by the efforts of Barry Wade, who brought together with patience, tact, and goodwill the scholars who eventually carried the project to fruition. To our deep sadness and regret, Barry Wade did not live to see the completion of the work to which he devoted so much energy. He was succeeded in overseeing the project by Julia Reidhead, whose calm intelligence, common sense, and steady focus have been essential in enabling us to reach the end of the long road. We were blessed with the exceptionally thoughtful and scrupulous developmental editing of Marian Johnson and with the assistance of an extraordinary group of Norton staffers: head manuscript editor Susan Gaustad, who was assisted by copyeditor Alice Falk and project editor Kurt Wildermuth; editorial assistant Tara Parmiter, who, among many other things, coordinated the art program; production manager Diane O'Connor; in-house editor of the *Norton Shakespeare Workshop* CD-ROM Anna Karvellas; and proofreaders Carol Walker and Rich Rivellese.

The Norton Shakespeare editors have, in addition, had the valuable, indeed indispensable support of a host of undergraduate and graduate research assistants, colleagues, friends, and family. Even a partial listing of those to whom we owe our heartfelt thanks is very long, but we are all fortunate enough to live in congenial and supportive environments, and the edition has been part of our lives for a long time. We owe special thanks for sustained dedication and learning to our principal research assistants: Pat Cahill, Jody Greene, Nate Johnson, Jesse Liu, Joseph Nugent, Beth Quitslund, Henry Turner, and Michael Witmore. Particular thanks are due to Noah Heringman for his work on the texts assembled in the documents section and for the prefatory notes and comments on those texts; to Philip Schwyzer for preparing the genealogies and the glossary and for conceiving and preparing the Shakespearean Chronicle; and to Young Jean Lee for a variety of complex editorial tasks. In addition, we are deeply grateful to Jim, Kate, and Caleb Baker, Gen Beckman, Aimée Boutin, Dan Brayton, Laura Brown, Francesca Coppelli, Adam Feldman, Margaret Ferguson, William Flesch, Elizabeth Gardner, Ellen Greenblatt, Josh and Aaron Greenblatt, Mark Hazard, David Kastan, Dennis Kezar, Shawn Kirschner, Jeffrey Knapp, Baty Landis, Wendy Lesser, Laurie Maguire, Fred Everett Maus, Stephen

Orgel, Phyllis Rackin, James Shapiro, Debora Shuger, Melissa Wiley Stickney, Ramie Targoff, Elda Tsou, and the staff of the Wissenschaftskolleg zu Berlin. All of these companions, and many more besides, have helped us find in this long collective enterprise what the Dedicatory Epistle to the First Folio promises to its readers: delight. We make the same promise to the readers of our edition and invite them to continue the great Shakespearean collaboration.

STEPHEN GREENBLATT
WALTER COHEN
JEAN E. HOWARD
KATHARINE EISAMAN MAUS

Acknowledgments

Among our many critics, advisers, and friends, the following were of special help in providing critiques of particular plays or of the project as a whole: Barry Adams (Cornell University), Richard Adams (California State University, Sacramento), Denise Albanes (George Mason University), Mark Anderson (SUNY Brockport), Herman Asarnow (University of Portland), John H. Astington (Erindale, University of Toronto), Jonathan Baldo (University of Rochester), Jonathan Bate, Leonard Barkan (New York University), John Baxter (Dalhousie University), D. A. Beecher (Carleton University), S. Berg (University of Alberta), Paula Berggren (CUNY), Edward Berry (University of Victoria), Walter Blanco (Lehman, CUNY), Thomas L. Blanton (Central Washington University), Al Braunmuller (UCLA), Stephen Brown (Trent University), Douglas Bruster (University of Chicago), Kate Buckley (Pontifical College, Josephinum), Joseph Candido (University of Arkansas), William Carroll (Boston University), Thomas Cartelli (Muhlenberg College), Sheila Cavanaugh (Emory University), Susan Cerasano (Colgate University), Gerald N. Chapman (University of Denver), Lois Chapman (South Suburban College), Maurice Charney (Rutgers University), Thomas Clayton (University of Minnesota), Peter J. Connelly (Grinnell College), Barbara Correll (Cornell University), Jonathan Crewe (Dartmouth College), Earl Dachslager (University of Houston), Roger Deakins (New York University), Kenneth L. Deal (Huntingdon College), Margreta de Grazia (University of Pennsylvania), H. Delisle (Bridgewater State University), Alan Dessen (University of North Carolina, Chapel Hill), Nirmal Singh Dhesi (Sonoma State University), William R. Drennan (University of Wisconsin, Center Baraboo), Heather Dubrow (University of Wisconsin), Sara Eaton (North Central College), Katherine Eggert (University of Colorado), Charles R. Forker (Indiana University), Donald Foster (Vassar College), Michael Frachmann (California State University, Bakersfield), Lisa Freinkel (University of Oregon), Charles Frey (University of Washington), Lloyd G. Gibbs (University of South Carolina), Dominique Goy-Blanquet (University of Amiens), Hugh Grady (Beaver College), Anthony Graham-White (University of Illinois, Chicago), Peter Greenfield (University of Puget Sound), R. Chris Hassel Jr. (Vanderbilt University), David Haley (University of Minnesota), Jay Halio (University of Delaware), Richard Helgerson (University of California, Santa Barbara), Richard Hillman (York University), Barbara Hodgdon (Drake University), Peter Holland (Cambridge University), Trevor Howard-Hill (University of South Carolina), Clark Hulse (University of Illinois, Chicago), Gabriele Bernhard Jackson (Temple University), Henry D. Janzen (University of Windsor), Barbara Kachur (University of Missouri, St. Louis), Coppelia Kahn (Brown University), Michael H. Keefer (Université Sainte Anne), Robert Knapp (Reed College), Mary Kramer (University of Lowell), James Lake (Louisiana State University, Shreveport), Ian Lancashire (New College, University of Toronto), Judiana Lawrence (St. John Fisher College), Alexander Leggatt (University College, University of Toronto), Ted Leinwand (University of Maryland, College Park), Carol Leventen (Adrian College), Murray J. Levith (Skidmore College), Barbara Lewalski (Harvard University), Cynthia Lewis (Davidson College), Arthur Little (UCLA), M. Loyola (University of Saskatchewan), J. M. Lyon (University of Bristol), Joyce MacDonald (University of Kentucky), Irene R. Makaryk (University of Ottawa), Eric Mallin (University of Texas, Austin), Leah Marcus (University of Texas, Austin), Arthur Marotti (Wayne State University), Cynthia Marshall (Rhodes College), Steven Marx (Cal Poly State University, San Luis Obispo), Margaret Maurer (Colgate University), M. A. McDonald (Belmont College), Nan Morrison (College of Charleston), Richard E. Morton (McMaster University), Steven Mullaney (University of Michigan), Ronnie Mulryne (University of Warwick), Carol Thomas Neely

(University of Illinois), Malcolm A. Nelson (SUNY Fredonia), Karen Newman (Brown University), M. Noble (Defiance College), John O'Connor (George Mason University), Gail Paster (George Washington University), Donald Peet (Indiana University), Lois Potter (University of Delaware), Phyllis Rackin (University of Pennsylvania), Constance Relihan (Auburn University), Neil Rhodes (University of St. Andrews), Jeremy Richard (University of Connecticut, Stamford), Gilbert Robinson (San Francisco State University), D. S. Rodes (UCLA), Mark Rose (University of California, Santa Barbara), David Rosen (University of Maine, Machias), Kiernan Ryan (Cambridge University), Peter Saccio (Dartmouth College), Nadine S. St. Louis (University of Wisconsin, Eau Claire), Naheeb Shaheen (Memphis State University), J. W. Shaw (University of Massachusetts), William P. Shaw (LeMoyne College), John W. Sider (Westmont College), Jim Siemon (Boston University), W. W. E. Slights (University of Saskatchewan), Molly Smith (Aberdeen University), Edward V. Stackpoole (University of San Francisco), Lisa Starks (East Texas State University), Michael J. Taylor (University of New Brunswick), Richard C. Tobias (University of Pittsburgh), Robert K. Turner (University of Wisconsin), Virginia Mason Vaughan (Clark University), Wendy Wall (Northwestern University), Robert N. Watson (UCLA), Valerie Wayne (University of Hawaii, Manoa), Herbert S. Weil, Jr. (University of Manitoba), Barry Weller (University of Utah), Paul Werstine (King's College), R. L. Widmann (University of Colorado, Boulder), Inga Wiehl (Yakina Valley Community College), Douglas B. Wilson (University of Denver).

Mr. WILLIAM
SHAKESPEARES
COMEDIES,
HISTORIES, &
TRAGEDIES.

Published according to the True Originall Copies.

Martin Droeshout sculpsit London.

L O N D O N
Printed by Isaac Iaggard, and Ed. Blount. 1623.

Engraving of Shakespeare by Martin Droeshout. Title page of the 1623 First Folio. (The Documents appendix, below, reproduces the front matter to the Folio, including Ben Jonson's poem "To the Reader.")

General Introduction
by
STEPHEN GREENBLATT

"He was not of an age, but for all time!"

The celebration of Shakespeare's genius, eloquently initiated by his friend and rival Ben Jonson, has over the centuries become an institutionalized rite of civility. The person who does not love Shakespeare has made, the rite implies, an incomplete adjustment not simply to a particular culture—English culture of the late sixteenth and early seventeenth centuries—but to "culture" as a whole, the dense network of constraints and entitlements, dreams and practices that links us to nature. Indeed, so absolute is Shakespeare's achievement that he has himself come to seem like great creating nature: the common bond of humankind, the principle of hope, the symbol of the imagination's power to transcend time-bound beliefs and assumptions, peculiar historical circumstances, and specific artistic conventions.

The near-worship Shakespeare inspires is one of the salient facts about his art. But we must at the same time acknowledge that this art is the product of peculiar historical circumstances and specific conventions, four centuries distant from our own. The acknowledgment is important because Shakespeare the working dramatist did not typically lay claim to the transcendent, visionary truths attributed to him by his most fervent admirers; his characters more modestly say, in the words of the magician Prospero, that their project was "to please" (*The Tempest*, Epilogue, line 13). The starting point, and perhaps the ending point as well, in any encounter with Shakespeare is simply to enjoy him, to savor his imaginative richness, to take pleasure in his infinite delight in language.

"If then you do not like him," Shakespeare's first editors wrote in 1623, "surely you are in some manifest danger not to understand him." Over the years, accommodations have been devised to make liking Shakespeare easier for everyone. When the stage sank to melodrama and light opera, Shakespeare—in suitably revised texts—was there. When the populace had a craving for hippodrama, plays performed entirely on horseback, *Hamlet* was dutifully rewritten and mounted. When audiences went mad for realism, live frogs croaked in productions of *A Midsummer Night's Dream*. When the stage was stripped bare and given over to stark exhibitions of sadistic cruelty, Shakespeare was our contemporary. And when the theater itself had lost some of its cultural centrality, Shakespeare moved effortlessly to Hollywood and the sound stages of the BBC.

This virtually universal appeal is one of the most astonishing features of the Shakespeare phenomenon: plays that were performed before glittering courts thrive in junior high school auditoriums; enemies set on destroying one another laugh at the same jokes and weep at the same catastrophes; some of the richest and most complex English verse ever written migrates with spectacular success into German and Italian, Hindi, Swahili, and Japanese. Is there a single, stable, continuous object that underlies all of these migrations and metamorphoses? Certainly not. The fantastic diffusion and long life of Shakespeare's works depends on their extraordinary malleability, their protean capacity to elude definition and escape secure possession. At the same time, they are not without identifiable shared features: across centuries and continents, family resemblances link many of the wildly diverse manifestations of plays such as *Romeo and Juliet*, *Hamlet*, and *Twelfth Night*. And if there is no clear limit or end point, there is a reasonably clear beginning, the

1

England of the late sixteenth and early seventeenth centuries, when the plays and poems collected in this volume made their first appearance.

An art virtually without end or limit but with an identifiable, localized, historical origin: Shakespeare's achievement defies the facile opposition between transcendent and time-bound. It is not necessary to choose between an account of Shakespeare as the scion of a particular culture and an account of him as a universal genius who created works that continually renew themselves across national and generational boundaries. On the contrary: crucial clues to understanding his art's remarkable power to soar beyond its originary time and place lie in the very soil from which that art sprang.

Shakespeare's World

Life and Death

Life expectation at birth in early modern England was exceedingly low by our standards: under thirty years old, compared with over seventy today. Infant mortality rates were extraordinarily high, and it is estimated that in the poorer parishes of London only about half the children survived to the age of fifteen, while the children of aristocrats fared only a little better. In such circumstances, some parents must have developed a certain detachment—one of Shakespeare's contemporaries writes of losing "some three or four children"—but there are many expressions of intense grief, so that we cannot assume that the frequency of death hardened people to loss or made it routine.

Still, the spectacle of death, along with that other great threshold experience, birth, must have been far more familiar to Shakespeare and his contemporaries than to ourselves. There was no equivalent in early modern England to our hospitals, and most births and deaths occurred at home. Physical means for the alleviation of pain and suffering were extremely limited—alcohol might dull the terror, but it was hardly an effective anesthetic—and medical treatment was generally both expensive and worthless, more likely to intensify suffering than to lead to a cure. This was a world without a concept of antiseptics, with little actual understanding of disease, with few effective ways of treating earaches or venereal disease, let alone the more terrible instances of what Shakespeare calls "the thousand natural shocks that flesh is heir to."

The worst of these shocks was the bubonic plague, which repeatedly ravaged England, and particularly English towns, until the third quarter of the seventeenth century. The plague was terrifyingly sudden in its onset, rapid in its spread, and almost invariably lethal. Physicians were helpless in the face of the epidemic, though they prescribed amulets, preservatives, and sweet-smelling substances (on the theory that the plague was carried by

Bill recording plague deaths in London, 1609.

noxious vapors). In the plague-ridden year of 1564, the year of Shakespeare's birth, some 254 people died in Stratford-upon-Avon, out of a total population of 800. The year before, some 20,000 Londoners are thought to have died; in 1593, almost 15,000; in 1603, 36,000, or over a sixth of the city's inhabitants. The social effects of these horrible visitations were severe: looting, violence, and despair, along with an intensification of the age's perennial poverty, unemployment, and food shortages. The London plague regulations of 1583, reissued with modifications in later epidemics, ordered that the infected and their households should be locked in their homes for a month; that the streets should be kept clean; that vagrants should be expelled; and that funerals and plays should be restricted or banned entirely.

The plague, then, had a direct and immediate impact on Shakespeare's own profession. City officials kept records of the weekly number of plague deaths; when these surpassed a certain number, the theaters were peremptorily closed. The basic idea was not only to prevent contagion but also to avoid making an angry God still angrier with the spectacle of idleness. While restricting public assemblies may in fact have slowed the epidemic, other public policies in times of plague, such as killing the cats and dogs, may have made matters worse (since the disease was spread not by these animals but by the fleas that bred on the black rats that infested the poorer neighborhoods). Moreover, the playing companies, driven out of London by the closing of the theaters, may have carried plague to the provincial towns.

Even in good times, when the plague was dormant and the weather favorable for farming, the food supply in England was precarious. A few successive bad harvests, such as occurred in the mid-1590s, could cause serious hardship, even starvation. Not surprisingly, the poor bore the brunt of the burden: inflation, low wages, and rent increases left large numbers of people with very little cushion against disaster. Further, at its best, the diet of most people seems to have been seriously deficient. The lower classes then, as throughout most of history, subsisted on one or two foodstuffs, usually low in protein. The upper classes disdained green vegetables and milk and gorged themselves on meat. Illnesses that we now trace to vitamin deficiencies were rampant. Some but not much relief from pain was provided by the beer that Elizabethans, including children, drank almost incessantly. (Home brewing aside, enough beer was sold in England for every man, woman, and child to have consumed forty gallons a year.)

Wealth

Despite rampant disease, the population of England in Shakespeare's lifetime was steadily growing, from approximately 3,060,000 in 1564 to 4,060,000 in 1600 and 4,510,000 in 1616. Though the death rate was more than twice what it is in England today, the birthrate was almost three times the current figure. London's population in particular soared, from 60,000 in 1520 to 120,000 in 1550, 200,000 in 1600, and 375,000 a half-century later, making it the largest and fastest-growing city not only in England but in all of Europe. Every year in the first half of the seventeenth century, about 10,000 people migrated to London from other parts of England—wages in London tended to be around 50 percent higher than in the rest of the country—and it is estimated that one in eight English people lived in London at some point in their lives. The economic viability of Shakespeare's profession was closely linked to this extraordinary demographic boom: between 1567 and 1642, a theater historian has calculated, the London playhouses were paid close to 50 million visits.

As these visits to the theater indicate, in the capital city and elsewhere a substantial number of English men and women, despite hardships that were never very distant, had money to spend. After the disorder and dynastic wars of the fifteenth century, England in the sixteenth and early seventeenth centuries was for the most part a nation at peace, and with peace came a measure of enterprise and prosperity: the landowning classes busied themselves building great houses, planting orchards and hop gardens, draining marshlands, bringing untilled "wastes" under cultivation. The artisans and laborers who actually accomplished these tasks, though they were generally paid very little, often managed to accumulate something, as did the small freeholding farmers, the yeomen, who are repeatedly celebrated in the period as the backbone of English national independence and well-being. William Harrison's *Description of Britaine* (1577) lovingly itemizes the yeoman's precious possessions: "fair garnish of pewter on his cupboard, with so much more odd vessel going about the house, three or four featherbeds, so many coverlets and carpets of tapestry, a silver salt[cellar], a bowl for wine (if not a whole nest) and a dozen of spoons." There are comparable accounts of the hard-earned acquisitions of the city dwellers—masters and apprentices in small workshops, shipbuilders, wool merchants, cloth makers, chandlers, tradesmen, shopkeepers, along with lawyers, apothecaries, schoolteachers, scriveners, and the like—whose pennies from time to time enriched the coffers of the players.

The chief source of England's wealth in the sixteenth century was its textile industry, an industry that depended on a steady supply of wool. In *The Winter's Tale*, Shakespeare provides a richly comic portrayal of a rural sheepshearing festival, but the increasingly intensive production of wool had in reality its grim side. When a character in Thomas More's *Utopia* (1516) complains that "the sheep are eating the people," he is referring to the practice of enclosure: throughout the sixteenth and early seventeenth centuries, many acres of croplands once farmed in common by rural communities were enclosed with fences by wealthy landowners and turned into pasturage. The ensuing misery, displacement, and food shortages led to repeated riots, some of them violent and bloody, along with a series of government proclamations, but the process of enclosure was not reversed.

The economic stakes were high, and not only for the domestic market. In 1565, woolen cloth alone made up more than three-fourths of England's exports. (The remainder consisted mostly of other textiles and raw wool, with some trade in lead, tin, grain, and skins.) The Merchant Adventurers Company carried cloth to distant ports on the Baltic and Mediterranean, establishing links with Russia and Morocco (each took about 2 percent of London's cloth in 1597–98). English lead and tin, as well as fabrics, were sold in Tuscany and Turkey, and merchants found a market for Newcastle coal on the island of Malta. In the latter half of the century, London, which handled more than 85 percent of all exports, regularly shipped abroad more than 100,000 woolen cloths a year, at a value of at least £750,000. This figure does not include the increasingly important and profitable trade in so-called New Draperies, including textiles that went by such exotic names as bombazines, callamancoes, damazellas, damizes, mockadoes, and virgenatoes. When the Earl of Kent in *King Lear* insults Oswald as a "filthy worsted-stocking knave" (2.2.14–15) or when the aristocratic Biron in *Love's Labour's Lost* declares that he will give up "taffeta phrases, silken terms precise, / Three-piled hyperboles" and woo henceforth "in russet yeas, and honest kersey noes" (5.2.406–07, 413), Shakespeare is assuming that a substantial portion of his audience will be alert to the social significance of fabric.

There is amusing confirmation of this alertness from an unexpected source: the report of a visit made to the Fortune playhouse in London in 1614 by a foreigner, Father Orazio Busino, the chaplain of the Venetian embassy. Father Busino neglected to mention the name of the play he saw, but like many foreigners, he was powerfully struck by the presence of gorgeously dressed women in the audience. In Venice, there was a special gallery for courtesans, but socially respectable women would not have been permitted to attend plays, as they could in England. In London, not only could middle- and upper-class women go to the theater, but they could also wear masks and mingle freely with male spectators and women of ill repute. The bemused cleric was uncertain about the ambiguous social situation in which he found himself:

> These theatres are frequented by a number of respectable and handsome ladies, who come freely and seat themselves among the men without the slightest hesitation. On the evening in question his Excellency and the Secretary were pleased to play me a trick by placing me amongst a bevy of young women. Scarcely was I seated ere a very elegant dame, but in a mask, came and placed herself beside me. . . . She asked me for my address both in French and English; and, on my turning a deaf ear, she determined

to honour me by showing me some fine diamonds on her fingers, repeatedly taking off not fewer than three gloves, which were worn one over the other. . . . This lady's bodice was of yellow satin richly embroidered, her petticoat of gold tissue with stripes, her robe of red velvet with a raised pile, lined with yellow muslin with broad stripes of pure gold. She wore an apron of point lace of various patterns: her head-tire was highly perfumed, and the collar of white satin beneath the delicately-wrought ruff struck me as extremely pretty.

Father Busino may have turned a deaf ear on this "elegant dame" but not a blind eye: his description of her dress is worthy of a fashion designer and conveys something of the virtual clothes cult that prevailed in England in the late sixteenth and early seventeenth centuries, a cult whose major shrine, outside the royal court, was the theater.

Imports, Patents, and Monopolies

England produced some luxury goods, but the clothing on the backs of the most fashionable theatergoers was likely to have come from abroad. By the late sixteenth century, the English were importing substantial quantities of silks, satins, velvets, embroidery, gold and silver lace, and other costly items to satisfy the extravagant tastes of the elite and of those who aspired to dress like the elite. The government tried to put a check on the sartorial ambitions of the upwardly mobile by passing sumptuary laws—that is, laws restricting to the ranks of the aristocracy the right to wear certain of the most precious fabrics. But the very existence of these laws, in practice almost impossible to enforce, only reveals the scope and significance of the perceived problem.

Sumptuary laws were in part a conservative attempt to protect the existing social order from upstarts. Social mobility was not widely viewed as a positive virtue, and moralists repeatedly urged people to stay in their place. Conspicuous consumption that was tolerated, even admired, in the aristocratic elite was denounced as sinful and monstrous in less exalted social circles. English authorities were also deeply concerned throughout the period about the effects of a taste for luxury goods on the balance of trade. One of the principal English imports was wine: the "sherris" whose virtues Falstaff extols in 2 *Henry IV* came from Xeres in Spain; the malmsey in which poor Clarence is drowned in *Richard III* was probably made in Greece or in the Canary Islands (from whence came Sir Toby Belch's "cup of canary" in *Twelfth Night*); and the "flagon of rhenish" that Yorick in *Hamlet* had once poured on the Gravedigger's head came from the Rhine region of Germany. Other imports included canvas, linen, fish, olive oil, sugar, molasses, dates, oranges and lemons, figs, raisins, almonds, capers, indigo, ostrich feathers, and that increasingly popular drug tobacco.

Joint stock companies were established to import goods for the burgeoning English market. The Merchant Venturers of the City of Bristol (established in 1552) handled great shipments of Spanish sack, the light, dry wine that largely displaced the vintages of Bordeaux and Burgundy when trade with France was disrupted by war. The Muscovy Company (established in 1555) traded English cloth and manufactured goods for Russian furs, oil, and beeswax. The Venice Company and the Turkey Company—uniting in 1593 to form the wealthy Levant Company—brought silk and spices home from Aleppo and carpets from Constantinople. The East India Company (founded in 1600), with its agent at Bantam in Java, brought pepper, cloves, nutmeg, and other spices from east Asia, along with indigo, cotton textiles, sugar, and saltpeter from India. English privateers "imported" American products, especially sugar, fish, and hides, in huge quantities, along with more precious cargoes. In 1592, a privateering expedition principally funded by Sir Walter Ralegh captured a huge Portuguese carrack (sailing ship), the *Madre de Dios*, in the Azores and brought it back to Dartmouth. The ship, the largest that had ever entered any English port, held 536 tons of pepper, cloves, cinnamon, cochineal, mace, civet, musk, ambergris, and nutmeg, as well as jewels, gold, ebony, carpets, and silks. Before order could be established, the English seamen began to pillage this immensely rich prize, and witnesses said

Cannoneer. From *Edward Webbe, His Travailes* (1590).

they could smell the spices on all the streets around the harbor. Such piratical expeditions were rarely officially sanctioned by the state, but the queen had in fact privately invested £1,800, for which she received about £80,000.

In the years of war with Spain, 1586–1604, the goods captured by the privateers annually amounted to 10–15 percent of the total value of England's imports. But organized theft alone could not solve England's balance-of-trade problems. Statesmen were particularly worried that the nation's natural wealth was slipping away in exchange for unnecessary things. In his *Discourse of the Commonweal* (1549), the prominent humanist Sir Thomas Smith exclaims against the importation of such trifles as mirrors, paper, laces, gloves, pins, inkhorns, tennis balls, puppets, and playing cards. And more than a century later, the same fear that England was trading its riches for trifles and wasting away in idleness was expressed by the Bristol merchant John Cary. The solution, Cary argues in "An Essay on the State of England in Relation to Its Trade" (1695), is to expand productive domestic employment. "People are or may be the Wealth of a Nation," he writes, "yet it must be where you find Employment for them, else they are a Burden to it, as the Idle Drone is maintained by the Industry of the laborious Bee, so are all those who live by their Dependence on others, as Players, Ale-House Keepers, Common Fiddlers, and such like, but more particularly Beggars, who never set themselves to work."

Stage players, all too typically associated here with vagabonds and other idle drones, could have replied in their defense that they not only labored in their vocation but also exported their skills abroad: English acting companies routinely traveled overseas and performed as far away as Bohemia. But their labor was not regarded as a productive contribution to the national wealth, and plays were in truth no solution to the trade imbalances that worried authorities.

The government attempted to stem the flow of gold overseas by establishing a patent system initially designed to encourage skilled foreigners to settle in England by granting them exclusive rights to produce particular wares by a patented method. Patents were granted for such things as the making of hard white soap (1561), ovens and furnaces (1563), window glass (1567), sailcloths (1574), drinking glasses (1574), sulphur, brimstone, and oil (1577), armor and horse harness (1587), starch (1588), white writing paper made from rags (1589), aqua vitae and vinegar (1594), playing cards (1598), and mathematical instruments (1598).

Although their ostensible purpose was to increase the wealth of England, encourage technical innovation, and provide employment for the poor, the effect of patents was often the enrichment of a few and the hounding of poor competitors by wealthy monopolists, a group that soon extended well beyond foreign-born entrepreneurs to the favorites of the monarch who vied for the huge profits to be made. "If I had a monopoly out" on folly, the Fool in *King Lear* protests, glancing at the "lords and great men" around him, "they would have part on't." The passage appears only in the quarto version of the play (*History of King Lear* 4.135–36); it may have been cut for political reasons from the Folio. For the issue of monopolies provoked bitter criticism and parliamentary debate for decades. In 1601, Elizabeth was prevailed upon to revoke a number of the most hated monopolies, including aqua vitae and vinegar, bottles, brushes, fish livers, the coarse sailcloth known as poldavis and mildernix, pots, salt, and starch. The whole system was revoked during the reign of James I by an act of Parliament.

Haves and Have-Nots

When in the 1560s Elizabeth's ambassador to France, the humanist Sir Thomas Smith, wrote a description of England, he saw the commonwealth as divided into four sorts of people: "gentlemen, citizens, yeomen artificers, and laborers." At the forefront of the class of gentlemen was the monarch, followed by a very small group of nobles—dukes, marquesses, earls, viscounts, and barons—who either inherited their exalted titles, as the eldest male heirs of their families, or were granted them by the monarch. Under Elizabeth, this aristocratic peerage numbered between 50 and 60 individuals; James's promotions increased the number to nearer 130. Strictly speaking, Smith notes, the younger sons of the nobility were only entitled to be called "esquires," but in common speech they were also called "lords."

Below this tiny cadre of aristocrats in the social hierarchy of gentry were the knights, a title of honor conferred by the monarch, and below them were the "simple gentlemen." Who was a gentleman? According to Smith, "whoever studieth the laws of the realm, who studieth in the universities, who professeth liberal sciences, and to be short, who can live idly and without manual labor, and will bear the port, charge and countenance of a gentleman, he shall be called master . . . and shall be taken for a gentleman." To "live idly and without manual labor": where in Spain, for example, the crucial mark of a gentleman was "blood," in England it was "idleness," in the sense of sufficient income to afford an education and to maintain a social position without having to work with one's hands.

For Smith, the class of gentlemen was far and away the most important in the kingdom. Below were two groups that had at least some social standing and claim to authority: the citizens, or burgesses, those who held positions of importance and responsibility in their cities, and yeomen, farmers with land and a measure of economic independence. At the bottom of the social order was what Smith calls "the fourth sort of men which do not rule." The great mass of ordinary people have, Smith writes, "no voice nor authority in our commonwealth, and no account is made of them but only to be ruled." Still, even they can bear some responsibility, he notes, since they serve on juries and are named to such positions as churchwarden and constable.

In everyday practice, as modern social historians have observed, the English tended to divide the population not into four distinct classes but into two: a very small empowered group—the "richer" or "wiser" or "better" sort—and all the rest who were without much social standing or power, the "poorer" or "ruder" or "meaner" sort. References to the "middle sort of people" remain relatively rare until after Shakespeare's lifetime; these people are absorbed into the rulers or the ruled, depending on speaker and context.

The source of wealth for most of the ruling class, and the essential measure of social status, was land ownership, and changes to the social structure in the sixteenth and seventeenth centuries were largely driven by the land market. The property that passed into private hands as the Tudors and early Stuarts sold off confiscated monastic estates and then their own crown lands for ready cash amounted to nearly a quarter of all the land in England. At the same time, the buying and selling of private estates was on the rise throughout the period. Land was bought up not only by established landowners seeking to enlarge their estates but by successful merchants, manufacturers, and urban professionals; even if the taint of vulgar moneymaking lingered around such figures, their heirs would be taken for true gentlemen. The rate of turnover in land ownership was great; in many counties, well over half the gentle families in 1640 had appeared since the end of the fifteenth century. The class that Smith called "simple gentlemen" was expanding rapidly: in the fifteenth century, they had held no more than a quarter of the land in the country, but by the later seventeenth, they controlled almost half. Over the same period, the land held by the great aristocratic magnates held steady at 15–20 percent of the total.

Riot and Disorder

London was a violent place in the first half of Shakespeare's career. There were thirty-five riots in the city in the years 1581–1602, twelve of them in the volatile month of June

1595. These included protests against the deeply unpopular lord mayor Sir John Spencer, attempts to release prisoners, anti-alien riots, and incidents of "popular market regulation." There is an unforgettable depiction of a popular uprising in *Coriolanus*, along with many other glimpses in Shakespeare's works, including John Cade's grotesque rebellion in *The First Part of the Contention (2 Henry VI)*, the plebeian violence in *Julius Caesar*, and Laertes' "riotous head" in *Hamlet*.

The London rioters were mostly drawn from the large mass of poor and discontented apprentices who typically chose as their scapegoats foreigners, prostitutes, and gentlemen's servingmen. Theaters were very often the site of the social confrontations that sparked disorder. For two days running in June 1584, disputes between apprentices and gentlemen triggered riots outside the Curtain Theatre involving up to a thousand participants. On one occasion, a gentleman was said to have exclaimed that "the apprentice was but a rascal, and some there were little better than rogues that took upon them the name of gentlemen, and said the prentices were but the scum of the world." These occasions culminated in attacks by the apprentices on London's law schools, the Inns of Court.

The most notorious and predictable incidents of disorder came on Shrove Tuesday (the Tuesday before the beginning of Lent), a traditional day of misrule when apprentices ran riot. Shrove Tuesday disturbances involved attacks by mobs of young men on the brothels of the South Bank, in the vicinity of the Globe and other public theaters. The city authorities took precautions to keep these disturbances from getting completely out of control, but evidently did not regard them as serious threats to public order.

Of much greater concern throughout the Tudor and early Stuart years were the frequent incidents of rural rioting against the enclosure of commons and waste land by local landlords (and, in the royal forests, by the crown). This form of popular protest was at its height during Shakespeare's career: in the years 1590–1610, the frequency of anti-enclosure rioting doubled from what it had been earlier in Elizabeth's reign.

Although they often became violent, anti-enclosure riots were usually directed not against individuals but against property. Villagers—sometimes several hundred, often fewer than a dozen—gathered to tear down newly planted hedges. The event often took place in a carnival atmosphere, with songs and drinking, that did not prevent the participants from acting with a good deal of political canniness and forethought. Especially in the Jacobean period, it was common for participants to establish a common fund for legal defense before commencing their assault on the hedges. Women were frequently involved, and on a number of occasions wives alone participated in the destruction of the enclosure,

"The Peddler." From Jost Amman, *The Book of Trades* (1568).

since there was a widespread, though erroneous, belief that married women acting without the knowledge of their husbands were immune from prosecution. In fact, the powerful Court of Star Chamber consistently ruled that both the wives and their husbands should be punished.

Although Stratford was never the scene of serious rioting, enclosure controversies turned violent more than once in Shakespeare's lifetime. In January 1601, Shakespeare's friend Richard Quiney and others leveled the hedges of Sir Edward Greville, lord of Stratford manor. Quiney was elected bailiff of Stratford in September of that year but did not live to enjoy the office for long. He died from a blow to the head struck by one of Greville's men in a tavern brawl. Greville, responsible for the administration of justice, neglected to punish the murderer.

There was further violence in January 1615,

when William Combe's men threw to the ground two local aldermen who were filling in a ditch by which Combe was enclosing common fields near Stratford. The task of filling in the offending ditch was completed the next day by the women and children of Stratford. Combe's enclosure scheme was eventually stopped in the courts. Though he owned land whose value would have been affected by this controversy, Shakespeare took no active role in it, since he had previously come to a private settlement with the enclosers insuring him against personal loss.

Most incidents of rural rioting were small, localized affairs, and with good reason: when confined to the village community, riot was a misdemeanor; when it spread outward to include multiple communities, it became treason. The greatest of the anti-enclosure riots, those in which hundreds of individuals from a large area participated, commonly took place on the eve of full-scale regional rebellions. The largest of these disturbances, Kett's Rebellion, involved some 16,000 peasants, artisans, and townspeople who rose up in 1549 under the leadership of a Norfolk tanner and landowner, Robert Kett, to protest economic exploitation. The agrarian revolts in Shakespeare's lifetime were on a much smaller scale. In the abortive Oxfordshire Rebellion of 1596, a carpenter named Bartholomew Steere attempted to organize a rising against enclosing gentlemen. The optimistic Steere promised his followers that "it was but a month's work to overrun England" and informed them "that the commons long since in Spain did rise and kill all gentlemen . . . and since that time have lived merrily there." Steere expected several hundred men to join him on Enslow Hill on November 21, 1596, for the start of the rising; no more than twenty showed up. They were captured, imprisoned, and tortured. Several were executed, but Steere apparently died in prison.

Rebellions, most often triggered by hunger and oppression, continued into the reign of James I. The Midland Revolt of 1607, which may be reflected in *Coriolanus*, consisted of a string of agrarian risings in the counties of Northamptonshire, Warwickshire, and Leicestershire, involving assemblies of up to five thousand rebels in various places. The best-known of their leaders was John Reynolds, called "Captain Powch" because of the pouch he wore, whose magical contents were supposed to defend the rebels from harm. (According to the chronicler Edmund Howes, when Reynolds was captured and the pouch opened, it contained "only a piece of green cheese.") The rebels, who were called by themselves and others both "Levelers" and "Diggers," insisted that they had no quarrel with the king but only sought an end to injurious enclosures. But Robert Wilkinson, who preached a sermon against the leaders at their trial, credited them with the intention to "level all states as they leveled banks and ditches." Most of the rebels got off relatively lightly, but, along with other ringleaders, Captain Powch was executed.

The Legal Status of Women

Though England was ruled for over forty years by a powerful woman, the great majority of women in the kingdom had very restricted social, economic, and legal standing. To be sure, a tiny number of influential aristocratic women, such as the formidable Countess of Shrewsbury, Bess of Hardwick, wielded considerable power. But, these rare exceptions aside, women were denied any rightful claim to institutional authority or personal autonomy. When Sir Thomas Smith thinks of how he should describe his country's social order, he declares that "we do reject women, as those whom nature hath made to keep home and to nourish their family and children, and not to meddle with matters abroad, nor to bear office in a city or commonwealth." Then, with a kind of glance over his shoulder, he makes an exception of those few for whom "the blood is respected, not the age nor the sex": for example, the queen.

English women were not under the full range of crushing constraints that afflicted women in some countries in Europe. Foreign visitors were struck by their relative freedom, as shown, for example, by the fact that respectable women could venture unchaperoned into the streets and attend the theater. Single women, whether widowed or unmarried, could, if they were of full age, inherit and administer land, make a will, sign a contract, possess property, sue and be sued, without a male guardian or proxy. But married women had no such rights under the common law.

Early modern writings about women and the family constantly return to a political model of domination and submission, in which the father justly rules over wife and children as the monarch rules over the state. This conception of a woman's role conveniently ignores the fact that a *majority* of the adult women at any time in Shakespeare's England were not married. They were either widows or spinsters (a term that was not yet pejorative), and thus for the most part managing their own affairs. Even within marriage, women typically had more control over certain spheres than moralizing writers on the family cared to admit. For example, village wives oversaw the production of eggs, cheese, and beer, and sold these goods in the market.

Women were not in practice as bereft of economic power and property as, according to English common law, they should have been. Demographic studies indicate that the inheritance system called primogeniture, the orderly transmission of property from father to eldest male heir, was more often an unfulfilled wish than a reality. Some 40 percent of marriages failed to produce a son, and in such circumstances fathers often left their land to their daughters, rather than to brothers, nephews, or male cousins. In many families, the father died before his male heir was old enough to inherit property, leaving the land, at least temporarily, in the hands of the mother. And while they were less likely than their brothers to inherit land ("real property"), daughters normally inherited a substantial share of their father's personal property (cash and movables).

In fact, the legal restrictions upon women, though severe in Shakespeare's time, actually worsened in subsequent decades. The English common law, the system of law based on court decisions rather than on codified written laws, was significantly less egalitarian in its approach to wives and daughters than were alternative legal codes (manorial, civil, and ecclesiastical) still in place in the late sixteenth century. The eventual triumph of common law stripped women of many traditional rights, slowly driving them out of economically productive trades and businesses.

Limited though it was, the economic freedom of Elizabethan and Jacobean women far exceeded their political and social freedom—the opportunity to receive a grammar school or university education, to hold office in church or state, to have a voice in public debates, or even simply to speak their mind fully and openly in ordinary conversation. Women who asserted their views too vigorously risked being perceived as shrewish and labeled "scolds." Both urban and rural communities had a horror of scolds. In the Elizabethan period, such women came to be regarded as a threat to public order, to be dealt with by the local authorities. The preferred methods of correction included public humiliation—of the sort Katherine endures in *The Taming of the Shrew*—and such physical abuse as slapping, bridling, and soaking by means of a contraption called the "cucking stool" (or "ducking stool"). This latter punishment originated in the Middle Ages, but its use spread in the sixteenth century, when it became almost exclusively a punishment for women. From 1560 onward, cucking stools were built or renovated in many English provincial towns; between 1560 and 1600, the contraptions were installed by rivers or ponds in Norwich, Bridport, Shrewsbury, Kingston-upon-Thames, Marlborough, Devizes, Clitheroe, Thornbury, and Great Yarmouth.

Such punishment was usually intensified by a procession through the town to the sound of "rough music," the banging together of pots and pans. The same cruel festivity accompanied the "carting" or "riding" of those accused of being whores. In some parts of the country, villagers also took the law into their own hands, publicly shaming women who married men much younger than themselves or who beat or otherwise domineered over their husbands. One characteristic form of these charivaris, or rituals of shaming, was known in the West Country as the Skimmington Ride. Villagers would rouse the offending couple from bed with rough music and stage a raucous pageant in which a man, holding a distaff, would ride backward on a donkey, while his "wife" (another man dressed as a woman) struck him with a ladle. In these cases, the collective ridicule and indignation was evidently directed at least as much at the henpecked husband as at his transgressive wife.

Women and Print

Books published for a female audience surged in popularity in the late sixteenth century, reflecting an increase in female literacy. (It is striking how many of Shakespeare's women are shown reading.) This increase is probably linked to a Protestant longing for direct access to the Scriptures, and the new books marketed specifically for women included devotional manuals and works of religious instruction. But there were also practical guides to such subjects as female education (for example, Giovanni Bruto's *Necessary, Fit, and Convenient Education of a Young Gentlewoman*, 1598), midwifery (James Guillemeau's *Child-birth; or, the Happy Delivery of Women*, 1612), needlework (Federico di Vinciolo's *New and Singular Patterns and Works of Linen*, 1591), cooking (Thomas Dawson's *The Good Housewife's Jewel*, 1587), gardening (Pierre Erondelle, *The French Garden*, 1605), and married life (Patrick Hanney's *A Happy Husband; or, Directions for a Maid to Choose Her Mate*, 1619). As the authors' names suggest, many of these works were translations, and almost all were written by men.

Starting in the 1570s, writers and their publishers increasingly addressed works of recreational literature (romance, fiction, and poetry) partially or even exclusively to women. Some books, such as Robert Greene's *Mamillia, a Mirror or Looking-Glass for the Ladies of England* (1583), directly specified in the title their desired audience. Others, such as Sir Philip Sidney's influential and popular romance *Arcadia* (1590–93), solicited female readership in their dedicatory epistles. The ranks of Sidney's followers eventually included his own niece, Mary Wroth, whose romance *Urania* was published in 1621.

In the literature of Shakespeare's time, women readers were not only wooed but also frequently railed at, in a continuation of a popular polemical genre that had long inspired heated charges and countercharges. Both sides in the polemic generally agreed that it was the duty of women to be chaste, dutiful, shamefast, and silent; the argument was whether women fulfilled or fell short of this proper role. Ironically, then, a modern reader is more likely to find inspiring accounts of courageous women not in the books written in defense of female virtue but in attacks on those who refused to be silent and obedient.

The most famous English skirmish in this controversy took place in a rash of pamphlets at the end of Shakespeare's life. Joseph Swetnam's crude *Arraignment of Lewd, Idle, Froward, and Unconstant Women* (1615) provoked three fierce responses attributed to women: Rachel Speght's *A Muzzle for Melastomus*, Esther Sowernam's *Esther Hath Hang'd Haman*, and Constantia Munda's *Worming of a Mad Dog*, all 1617. There was also an anonymous play, *Swetnam the Woman-hater Arraigned by Women* (1618), in which Swetnam, depicted as a braggart and a lecher, is put on trial by women and made to recant his misogynistic lies.

Prior to the Swetnam controversy, only one English woman, "Jane Anger," had published a defense of women (*Jane Anger Her Protection for Women*, 1589). Learned women writers in the sixteenth century tended not to become involved in public debate but rather to undertake a project to which it was difficult for even obdurately chauvinistic males to object: the translation of devotional literature into English. Thomas More's daughter Margaret More Roper translated Erasmus (*A Devout Treatise upon the Pater Noster*, 1524); Francis Bacon's mother, Anne Cooke Bacon, translated Bishop John Jewel (*An Apology or Answer in Defence of the Church of England*, 1564); Anne Locke Prowse, a friend of John Knox, translated the *Sermons of John Calvin* in 1560; and Mary Sidney, the Countess of Pembroke, completed the metrical version of the Psalms that her brother Sir Philip Sidney had begun. Elizabeth Tudor (the future queen) herself translated, at the age of eleven, Marguerite de Navarre's *Le Miroir de l'âme pécheresse* (*The Glass of the Sinful Soul*, 1544). The translation was dedicated to her stepmother, Katherine Parr, herself the author of a frequently reprinted book of prayers.

There was in the sixteenth and early seventeenth centuries a social stigma attached to print. Far from celebrating publication, authors, and particularly female authors, often apologized for exposing themselves to the public gaze. Nonetheless, a number of women ventured beyond pious translations. Some, including Elizabeth Tyrwhitt, Anne Dowriche,

Title page of *Swetnam the Woman-Hater Arraigned by Women*
(1620), a play written in response to Joseph Swetnam's *The
Arraignment of Lewd, Idle, Froward and Unconstant Women*
(1615); the woodcut depicts the trial of Swetnam in Act 4.

Isabella Whitney, Mary Sidney, and Aemilia Lanyer, composed and published their own
poems. Aemilia Lanyer's *Salve Deus Rex Judaeorum*, published in 1611, is a poem in praise
of virtuous women, from Eve and the Virgin Mary to her noble patron, the Countess of
Cumberland. "A Description of Cookeham," appended to the poem, may be the first
English country house poem.

The first Tudor woman to translate a play was the learned Jane Lumley, who com-
posed an English version of Euripides' *Iphigenia at Aulis* (c. 1550). The first known origi-
nal play in English by a woman was by Elizabeth Cary, Viscountess Falkland, whose
Tragedy of Mariam, the Fair Queen of Jewry was published in 1613. This remarkable play,
which was not intended to be performed, includes speeches in defense of women's equal-
ity, though the most powerful of these is spoken by the villainous Salome, who schemes to
divorce her husband and marry her lover. Cary, who bore eleven children, herself had a
deeply troubled marriage, which effectively came to an end in 1625 when, defying her
husband's staunchly Protestant family, she openly converted to Catholicism. Her biogra-
phy was written by one of her four daughters, all of whom became nuns.

Henry VIII and the English Reformation

There had long been serious ideological and institutional tensions in the religious life
of England, but officially, at least, England in the early sixteenth century had a single
religion, Catholicism, whose acknowledged head was the pope in Rome. In 1517, drawing

upon long-standing currents of dissent, Martin Luther, an Augustinian monk and professor of theology at the University of Wittenberg, challenged the authority of the pope and attacked several key doctrines of the Catholic Church. According to Luther, the Church, with its elaborate hierarchical structure centered in Rome, its rich monasteries and convents, and its enormous political influence, had become hopelessly corrupt, a conspiracy of venal priests who manipulated popular superstitions to enrich themselves and amass worldly power. Luther began by vehemently attacking the sale of indulgences—certificates promising the remission of punishments to be suffered in the afterlife by souls sent to purgatory to expiate their sins. These indulgences were a fraud, he argued; purgatory itself had no foundation in the Bible, which in his view was the only legitimate source of religious truth. Christians would be saved not by scrupulously following the ritual practices fostered by the Catholic Church—observing fast days, reciting the ancient Latin prayers, endowing chantries to say prayers for the dead, and so on—but by faith and faith alone.

This challenge, which came to be known as the Reformation, spread and gathered force, especially in northern Europe, where major leaders like the Swiss pastor Ulrich Zwingli and the French theologian John Calvin established institutional structures and elaborated various and sometimes conflicting doctrinal principles. Calvin, whose thought came to be particularly influential in England, emphasized the obligation of governments to implement God's will in the world. He advanced too the doctrine of predestination, by which, as he put it, "God adopts some to hope of life and sentences others to eternal death." God's "secret election" of the saved made Calvin uncomfortable, but his study of the Scriptures had led him to conclude that "only a small number, out of an incalculable multitude, should obtain salvation." It might seem that such a conclusion would lead to passivity or even despair, but for Calvin predestination was a mystery bound up with faith, confidence, and an active engagement in the fashioning of a Christian community.

The Reformation had a direct and powerful impact on those territories, especially in northern Europe, where it gained control. Monasteries were sacked, their possessions seized by princes or sold off to the highest bidder; the monks and nuns, expelled from their cloisters, were encouraged to break their vows of chastity and find spouses, as Luther and his wife, a former nun, had done. In the great cathedrals and in hundreds of smaller churches and chapels, the elaborate altarpieces, bejeweled crucifixes, crystal reliquaries holding the bones of saints, and venerated statues and paintings were attacked as "idols" and often defaced or destroyed. Protestant congregations continued, for the most part, to celebrate the most sacred Christian ritual, the Eucharist, or Lord's Supper, but they did so in a profoundly different spirit from that of the Catholic Church—more as commemoration than as miracle—and they now prayed not in the old liturgical Latin but in the vernacular.

The Reformation was at first vigorously resisted in England. Indeed, with the support of his ardently Catholic chancellor, Thomas More, Henry VIII personally wrote (or at least lent his name to) a vehement, often scatological attack on Luther's character and views, an attack for which the pope granted him the honorific title "Defender of the Faith." Protestant writings, including translations of the Scriptures into English, were seized by officials of the church and state and burned. Protestants who made their views known were persecuted, driven to flee the country, or arrested, put on trial, and burned at the stake. But the situation changed drastically and decisively when in 1527 Henry decided to seek a divorce from his first wife, Catherine of Aragon, in order to marry Anne Boleyn.

Catherine had given birth to six children, but since only a daughter, Mary, survived infancy, Henry did not have the son he craved. Then as now, the Catholic Church did not ordinarily grant divorce, but Henry's lawyers argued on technical grounds that the marriage was invalid (and therefore, by extension, that Mary was illegitimate and hence unable to inherit the throne). Matters of this kind were far less doctrinal than diplomatic: Catherine, the daughter of Ferdinand of Aragon and Isabella of Castile, had powerful allies in Rome, and the pope ruled against Henry's petition for a divorce. A series of momentous events followed, as England lurched away from the Church of Rome. In 1531, Henry charged the entire clergy of England with having usurped royal authority in the

"The Pope as Antichrist riding the Beast of the Apocalypse." From *Fierie Tryall of God's Saints* (1611; author unknown).

administration of canon law (the ecclesiastical law that governed faith, discipline, and morals, including such matters as divorce). Under extreme pressure, including the threat of mass confiscations and imprisonment, the Convocation of the Clergy begged for pardon, made a donation to the royal coffers of over £100,000, and admitted that the king was "supreme head of the English Church and clergy" (modified by the rider "as far as the law of Christ allows"). On May 15 of the next year, the convocation submitted to the demand that the king be the final arbiter of canon law; on the next day, Thomas More resigned his post.

In 1533, Henry's marriage to Catherine was officially declared null and void, and on June 1 Anne Boleyn was crowned queen (a coronation Shakespeare depicts in *All Is True*). The king was promptly excommunicated by the pope, Clement VII. In the following year, the parliamentary Act of Succession confirmed the effects of the divorce and required an oath from all adult male subjects confirming the new dynastic settlement. Thomas More and John Fisher, the Bishop of Rochester, were among the small number who refused. The Act of Supremacy, passed later in the year, formally declared the king to be "Supreme Head of the Church in England" and again required an oath to this effect. In 1535 and 1536, further acts made it treasonous to refuse the oath of royal supremacy or, as More had tried to do, to remain silent. The first victims were three Carthusian monks who rejected the oath—"How could the king, a layman," said one of them, "be Head of the Church of England?"—and in May 1535, they were duly hanged, drawn, and quartered. A few weeks later, Fisher and More were convicted and beheaded. Between 1536 and 1539, the monasteries were suppressed and their vast wealth seized by the crown.

Royal defiance of the authority of Rome was a key element in the Reformation but did not by itself constitute the establishment of Protestantism in England. On the contrary, in the same year that Fisher and More were martyred for their adherence to Roman Catholicism, twenty-five Protestants, members of a sect known as Anabaptists, were burned for heresy on a single day. Through most of his reign, Henry remained an equal-opportunity persecutor, ruthless to Catholics loyal to Rome and hostile to many of those who espoused Reformation ideas, though many of these ideas gradually established themselves on English soil.

Even when Henry was eager to do so, it proved impossible to eradicate Protestantism, as it would later prove impossible for his successors to eradicate Catholicism. In large part this tenacity arose from the passionate, often suicidal heroism of men and women who felt that their souls' salvation depended on the precise character of their Christianity. It arose too from a mid-fifteenth-century technological innovation that made it almost impossible to suppress unwelcome ideas: the printing press. Early Protestants quickly grasped that with a few clandestine presses they could defy the Catholic authorities and flood the country with their texts. "How many printing presses there be in the world," wrote the Protestant polemicist John Foxe, "so many blockhouses there be against the high castle" of the pope in Rome, "so that either the pope must abolish knowledge and printing or printing at length will root him out." By the century's end, it was the Catholics who were using the clandestine press to propagate their beliefs in the face of Protestant persecution.

The greatest insurrection of the Tudor age was not over food, taxation, or land but over religion. On Sunday October 1, 1536, stirred up by their vicar, the traditionalist parishioners of Louth in Lincolnshire, in the north of England, rose up in defiance of the ecclesiastical visitation sent to enforce royal supremacy. The rapidly spreading rebellion, which became known as the Pilgrimage of Grace, was led by the lawyer Robert Aske. The city of Lincoln fell to the rebels on October 6, and though it was soon retaken by royal forces, the rebels seized cities and fortifications throughout Yorkshire, Durham, Northumberland, Cumberland, Westmoreland, and northern Lancashire. Carlisle, Newcastle, and a few castles were all that were left to the king in the north. The Pilgrims soon numbered 40,000, led by some of the region's leading noblemen. The Duke of Norfolk, representing the crown, was forced to negotiate a truce, with a promise to support the rebels' demands that the king restore the monasteries, shore up the regional economy, suppress heresy, and dismiss his evil advisers.

The Pilgrims kept the peace for the rest of 1536, on the naive assumption that their demands would be met. But Henry moved suddenly early in 1537 to impose order and capture the ringleaders; 130 people, including lords, knights, heads of religious houses, and, of course, Robert Aske, were executed.

In 1549, two years after the death of Henry VIII, the west and the north of England were the sites of further unsuccessful risings for the restoration of Catholicism. The Western Rising is striking for its blend of Catholic universalism and intense regionalism among people who did not yet regard themselves as English. One of the rebels' articles, protesting against the imposition of the English Bible and religious service, declares, "We the Cornish men (whereof certain of us understand no English) utterly refuse this new English." The rebels besieged but failed to take the city of Exeter. As with almost all Tudor rebellions, the number of those executed in the aftermath of the failed rising was far greater than those killed in actual hostilities.

Henry VIII's Children: Edward, Mary, and Elizabeth

Upon Henry's death in 1547, his ten-year-old son, Edward VI, came to the throne, with his maternal uncle Edward Seymour named as Lord Protector and Duke of Somerset. Both Edward and his uncle were staunch Protestants, and reformers hastened to transform the English church accordingly. During Edward's reign, Archbishop Thomas Cranmer formulated the forty-two articles of religion that became the core of Anglican orthodoxy and wrote the first *Book of Common Prayer*, which was officially adopted in 1549 as the basis of English worship services.

Somerset fell from power in 1549 and was replaced as Lord Protector by John Dudley, later Duke of Northumberland. When Edward fell seriously ill, probably of tuberculosis, Northumberland persuaded him to sign a will depriving his half-sisters, Mary (the daughter of Catherine of Aragon) and Elizabeth (the daughter of Anne Boleyn), of their claim to royal succession. The Lord Protector was scheming to have his daughter-in-law the Protestant Lady Jane Grey, a granddaughter of Henry VII, ascend to the throne. But when Edward died in 1553, Mary marshaled support, quickly secured the crown from Lady Jane (who had been titular queen for nine days), and had Lady Jane executed, along with her husband and Northumberland.

Queen Mary immediately took steps to return her kingdom to Roman Catholicism. Though she was unable to get Parliament to agree to restore church lands seized under

The Family of Henry VIII: An Allegory of the Tudor Succession. By Lucas de Heere (c. 1572). Henry, in the middle, is flanked by Mary to his right, and Edward and Elizabeth to his left.

Henry VIII, she restored the Catholic Mass, once again affirmed the authority of the pope, and put down a rebellion that sought to depose her. Seconded by her ardently Catholic husband, Philip II, King of Spain, she initiated a series of religious persecutions that earned her (from her enemies) the name "Bloody Mary." Hundreds of Protestants took refuge abroad in cities such as Calvin's Geneva; almost three hundred less fortunate Protestants were condemned as heretics and burned at the stake.

Mary died childless in 1558, and her younger half-sister Elizabeth became queen. Elizabeth's succession had been by no means assured. For if Protestants regarded Henry VIII's marriage to Catherine as invalid and hence deemed Mary illegitimate, so Catholics regarded his marriage to Anne Boleyn as invalid and deemed Elizabeth illegitimate. Henry VIII himself seemed to support both views, since only three years after divorcing Catherine, he beheaded Anne Boleyn on charges of treason and adultery and urged Parliament to invalidate the marriage. Moreover, though during her sister's reign Elizabeth outwardly complied with the official Catholic religious observance, Mary and her advisers were deeply suspicious, and the young princess's life was in grave danger. Poised and circumspect, Elizabeth warily evaded the traps that were set for her. As she ascended the throne, her actions were scrutinized for some indication of the country's future course. During her coronation procession, when a girl in an allegorical pageant presented her with a Bible in English translation—banned under Mary's reign—Elizabeth kissed the book, held it up reverently, and laid it to her breast; when the abbot and monks of Westminster Abbey came to greet her in broad daylight with candles (a symbol of Catholic devotion) in their hands, she briskly dismissed them with the telling words "Away with those torches! we can see well enough." England had returned to the Reformation.

Many English men and women, of all classes, remained loyal to the old Catholic faith, but English authorities under Elizabeth moved steadily, if cautiously, toward ensuring at least an outward conformity to the official Protestant settlement. Recusants, those who refused to attend regular Sunday services in their parish churches, were fined heavily.

Anyone who wished to receive a university degree, to be ordained as a priest in the Church of England, or to be named as an officer of the state had to swear an oath to the royal supremacy. Commissioners were sent throughout the land to confirm that religious services were following the officially approved liturgy and to investigate any reported backsliding into Catholic practice or, alternatively, any attempts to introduce more radical reforms than the queen and her bishops had chosen to embrace. For the Protestant exiles who streamed back were eager not only to undo the damage Mary had done but to carry the Reformation much further. They sought to dismantle the church hierarchy, to purge the calendar of folk customs deemed pagan and the church service of ritual practices deemed superstitious, to dress the clergy in simple garb, and, at the extreme edge, to smash "idolatrous" statues, crucifixes, and altarpieces. Throughout her long reign, however, Elizabeth herself remained cautiously conservative and determined to hold in check religious zealotry.

In the space of a single lifetime, England had gone officially from Roman Catholicism, to Catholicism under the supreme headship of the English king, to a guarded Protestantism, to a more radical Protestantism, to a renewed and aggressive Roman Catholicism, and finally to Protestantism again. Each of these shifts was accompanied by danger, persecution, and death. It was enough to make some people wary. Or skeptical. Or extremely agile.

The English Bible

Luther had undertaken a fundamental critique of the Catholic Church's sacramental system, a critique founded on the twin principles of salvation by faith alone (*sola fide*) and the absolute primacy of the Bible (*sola scriptura*). *Sola fide* contrasted faith with "works," by which was meant primarily the whole elaborate system of rituals sanctified, conducted, or directed by the priests. Protestants proposed to modify or reinterpret many of these rituals or, as with the rituals associated with purgatory, to abolish them altogether. *Sola scriptura* required direct lay access to the Bible, which meant in practice the widespread availability of vernacular translations. The Roman Catholic Church had not always and everywhere opposed such translations, but it generally preferred that the populace encounter the Scriptures through the interpretations of the priests, trained to read the Latin translation known as the Vulgate. In times of great conflict, this preference for clerical mediation hardened into outright prohibition of vernacular translation and into persecution and book burning.

Zealous Protestants set out, in the teeth of fierce opposition, to put the Bible into the hands of the laity. A remarkable translation of the New Testament, by an English Lutheran named William Tyndale, was printed on the continent and smuggled into England in 1525; Tyndale's translation of the Pentateuch, the first five books of the Hebrew Bible, followed in 1530. Many copies of these translations were seized and burned, as was the translator himself, but the printing press made it extremely difficult for authorities to eradicate books for which there was a passionate demand. The English Bible was a force that could not be suppressed, and it became, in its various forms, the single most important book of the sixteenth century.

Tyndale's translation was completed by an associate, Miles Coverdale, whose rendering of the Psalms proved to be particularly influential. Their joint labor was the basis for the Great Bible (1539), the first authorized version of the Bible in English, a copy of which was ordered to be placed in every church in the kingdom. With the accession of Edward VI, many editions of the Bible followed, but the process was sharply reversed when Mary came to the throne in 1553. Along with people condemned as heretics, English Bibles were burned in great bonfires.

Marian persecution was indirectly responsible for what would become the most popular as well as most scholarly English Bible, the translation known as the Geneva Bible, prepared, with extensive, learned, and often fiercely polemical marginal notes, by English exiles in Calvin's Geneva and widely diffused in England after Elizabeth came to the throne. In addition, Elizabethan church authorities ordered a careful revision of the Great Bible, and this version, known as the Bishops' Bible, was the one read in the churches. The success of the Geneva Bible in particular prompted those Elizabethan Catholics who now in turn found themselves in exile to bring out a vernacular translation of their own in order to counter the Protestant readings and glosses. This Catholic translation, known as the Rheims Bible, may have been known to Shakespeare, but he seems to have been far better acquainted with the Geneva Bible, and he would also have repeatedly heard the Bishops' Bible read aloud. Scholars have identified over three hundred references to the Bible in Shakespeare's work; in one version or another, the Scriptures had a powerful impact on his imagination.

A Female Monarch in a Male World

In the last year of Mary's reign, 1558, the Scottish Calvinist minister John Knox thundered against what he called "the monstrous regiment of women." When the Protestant Elizabeth came to the throne the following year, Knox and his religious brethren were less inclined to denounce female rulers, but in England as elsewhere in Europe there remained a widespread conviction that women were unsuited to wield power over men. Many men seem to have regarded the capacity for rational thought as exclusively male; women, they assumed, were led only by their passions. While gentlemen mastered the arts of rhetoric and warfare, gentlewomen were expected to display the virtues of silence and good housekeeping. Among upper-class males, the will to dominate others was acceptable and indeed admired; the same will in women was condemned as a grotesque and dangerous aberration.

Apologists for the queen countered these prejudices by appealing to historical prece-

The Armada portrait: note Elizabeth's hand on the globe.

dent and legal theory. History offered inspiring examples of just female rulers, notably Deborah, the biblical prophetess who judged Israel. In the legal sphere, crown lawyers advanced the theory of "the king's two bodies." As England's crowned head, Elizabeth's person was mystically divided between her mortal "body natural" and the immortal "body politic." While the queen's natural body was inevitably subject to the failings of human flesh, the body politic was timeless and perfect. In political terms, therefore, Elizabeth's sex was a matter of no consequence, a thing indifferent.

Elizabeth, who had received a fine humanist education and an extended, dangerous lesson in the art of survival, made it immediately clear that she intended to rule in more than name only. She assembled a group of trustworthy advisers, foremost among them William Cecil (later named Lord Burghley), but she insisted on making many of the crucial decisions herself. Like many Renaissance monarchs, Elizabeth was drawn to the idea of royal absolutism, the theory that ultimate power was properly concentrated in her person and indeed that God had appointed her to be His deputy in the kingdom. Opposition to her rule, in this view, was not only a political act but also a kind of impiety, a blasphemous grudging against the will of God. Apologists for absolutism contended that God commands obedience even to manifestly wicked rulers whom He has sent to punish the sinfulness of humankind. Such arguments were routinely made in speeches and political tracts and from the pulpits of churches, where they were incorporated into the *Book of Homilies*, which clergymen were required to read out to their congregations.

In reality, Elizabeth's power was not absolute. The government had a network of spies, informers, and *agents provocateurs*, but it lacked a standing army, a national police force, an efficient system of communication, and an extensive bureaucracy. Above all, the queen had limited financial resources and needed to turn periodically to an independent and often recalcitrant Parliament, which by long tradition had the sole right to levy taxes and to grant subsidies. Members of the House of Commons were elected from their boroughs, not appointed by the monarch, and though the queen had considerable influence over their decisions, she could by no means dictate policy. Under these constraints, Elizabeth ruled through a combination of adroit political maneuvering and imperious command, all the while enhancing her authority in the eyes of both court and country by means of an extraordinary cult of love.

"We all loved her," Elizabeth's godson Sir John Harington wrote, with just a touch of irony, a few years after the queen's death, "for she said she loved us." Ambassadors, courtiers, and parliamentarians all submitted to Elizabeth's cult of love, in which the queen's gender was transformed from a potential liability into a significant asset. Those who approached her generally did so on their knees and were expected to address her with extravagant compliments fashioned from the period's most passionate love poetry; she in turn spoke, when it suited her to do so, in the language of love poetry. The court moved in an atmosphere of romance, with music, dancing, plays, and the elaborate, fancy-dress entertainments called masques. The queen adorned herself in gorgeous clothes and rich jewels. When she went on one of her summer "progresses," ceremonial journeys through her land, she looked like an exotic, sacred image in a religious cult of love, and her noble hosts virtually bankrupted themselves to lavish upon her the costliest pleasures. England's leading artists, such as the poet Edmund Spenser and the painter Nicholas Hilliard, enlisted themselves in the celebration of Elizabeth's mystery, likening her to the goddesses and queens of mythology: Diana, Astraea, Gloriana. Her cult drew its power from cultural discourses that ranged from the secular (her courtiers could pine for her as a cruel Petrarchan mistress) to the sacred (the veneration that under Catholicism had been due to the Virgin Mary could now be directed toward England's semidivine queen).

There was a sober, even grim aspect to these poetical fantasies: Elizabeth was brilliant at playing one dangerous faction off against another, now turning her gracious smiles on one favorite, now honoring his hated rival, now suddenly looking elsewhere and raising an obscure upstart to royal favor. And when she was disobeyed or when she felt that her prerogatives had been challenged, she was capable of an anger that, as Harington put it, "left no doubtings whose daughter she was." Thus when Sir Walter Ralegh, one of the queen's glittering favorites, married without her knowledge or consent, he found himself promptly imprisoned in the Tower of London. And when the Protestant polemicist John Stubbs ventured to publish a pamphlet stridently denouncing the queen's proposed marriage to the French Catholic Duke of Alençon, Stubbs and his publisher were arrested and had their right hands chopped off. (After receiving the blow, the now prudent Stubbs lifted his hat with his remaining hand and cried, "God save the Queen!")

The queen's marriage negotiations were a particularly fraught issue. When she came to the throne at twenty-five years old, speculation about a suitable match, already widespread, intensified and remained for decades at a fever pitch, for the stakes were high. If Elizabeth died childless, the Tudor line would come to an end. The nearest heir was her cousin Mary, Queen of Scots, a Catholic whose claim was supported by France and by the papacy and whose penchant for sexual and political intrigue confirmed the worst fears of English Protestants. The obvious way to avert the nightmare was for Elizabeth to marry and produce an heir, and the pressure upon her to do so was intense.

More than the royal succession hinged on the question of the queen's marriage; Elizabeth's perceived eligibility was a vital factor in the complex machinations of international diplomacy. A dynastic marriage between the Queen of England and a foreign ruler would forge an alliance powerful enough to alter the balance of power in Europe. The English court hosted a steady stream of ambassadors from kings and princes eager to win the hand of the royal maiden, and Elizabeth, who prided herself on speaking fluent French and Italian (and on reading Latin and Greek), played her romantic part with exemplary skill, sighing and spinning the negotiations out for months and even years. Most probably, she never meant to marry any of her numerous foreign (and domestic) suitors. Such a decisive act would have meant the end of her independence, as well as the end of the marriage game by which she played one power off against another. One day she would seem to be on the verge of accepting a proposal; the next, she would vow never to forsake her virginity. "She is a Princess," the French ambassador remarked, "who can act any part she pleases."

The Kingdom in Danger

Beset by Catholic and Protestant extremists, Elizabeth contrived to forge a moderate compromise that enabled her realm to avert the massacres and civil wars that poisoned France and other countries on the Continent. But menace was never far off, and there were constant fears of conspiracy, rebellion, and assassination. Many of the fears swirled around Mary, Queen of Scots, who had been driven from her own kingdom in 1568 by a powerful faction of rebellious nobles and had taken refuge in England. Her presence, under a kind of house arrest, was the source of intense anxiety and helped generate continual rumors of plots. Some of these plots were real enough, others imaginary, still others traps set in motion by the secret agents of the government's intelligence service under the direction of Sir Francis Walsingham. The situation worsened greatly after the St. Bartholomew's Day Massacre of Protestants (Huguenots) in France (1572), after Spanish imperial armies invaded the Netherlands in order to stamp out Protestant rebels, and after the assassination there of Europe's other major Protestant leader, William of Orange (1584).

The queen's life seemed to be in even greater danger after Pope Gregory XIII's proclamation in 1580 that the assassination of the great heretic Elizabeth (who had been excommunicated a decade before) would not constitute a mortal sin. The immediate effect of the proclamation was to make existence more difficult for English Catholics, most of whom were loyal to the queen but who fell under grave suspicion. Suspicion was intensified by the clandestine presence of English Jesuits, trained at seminaries abroad and smuggled back into England to serve the Roman Catholic cause. When Elizabeth's spymaster Walsingham unearthed an assassination plot in the correspondence between the Queen of Scots and the Catholic Anthony Babington, the wretched Mary's fate was sealed. After vacillating, a very reluctant Elizabeth signed the death warrant in February 1587, and her cousin was beheaded.

The long-anticipated military confrontation with Catholic Spain was now unavoidable.

Elizabeth learned that Philip II, her former brother-in-law and onetime suitor, was preparing to send an enormous fleet against her island realm. It was to sail to the Netherlands, where a Spanish army would be waiting to embark and invade England. Barring its way was England's small fleet of well-armed and highly maneuverable fighting vessels, backed up by ships from the merchant navy. The Invincible Armada reached English waters in July 1588, only to be routed in one of the most famous and decisive naval battles in European history. Then, in what many viewed as an act of God on behalf of Protestant England, the Spanish fleet was dispersed and all but destroyed by violent storms.

As England braced itself to withstand the invasion that never came, Elizabeth appeared in person to review a detachment of soldiers assembled at Tilbury. Dressed in a white gown and a silver breastplate, she declared that though some among her councillors had urged her not to appear before a large crowd of armed men, she would never fail to trust the loyalty of her faithful and loving subjects. Nor did she fear the Spanish armies. "I know I have the body of a weak and feeble woman," Elizabeth declared, "but I have the heart and stomach of a king, and of England too." In this celebrated speech, Elizabeth displayed many of her most memorable qualities: her self-consciously histrionic command of grand public occasion, her subtle blending of magniloquent rhetoric and the language of love, her strategic appropriation of traditionally masculine qualities, and her great personal courage. "We princes," she once remarked, "are set on stages in the sight and view of all the world."

The English and Otherness

Shakespeare's London had a large population of resident aliens, mainly artisans and merchants and their families, from Portugal, Italy, Spain, Germany, and above all France and the Netherlands. Many of these people were Protestant refugees, and they were accorded some legal and economic protection by the government. But they were not always welcome by the local populace. Throughout the sixteenth century, London was the site of repeated demonstrations and, on occasion, bloody riots against the communities of foreign artisans, who were accused of taking jobs away from Englishmen. There was widespread hostility as well toward the Welsh, the Scots, and especially the Irish, whom the English had for centuries been struggling unsuccessfully to subdue. The kings of England claimed to be rulers of Ireland, but in reality they effectively controlled only a small area known as the Pale, extending north from Dublin. The great majority of the Irish people remained stubbornly Catholic and, despite endlessly reiterated English repression, burning of villages, destruction of crops, and massacres, incorrigibly independent.

Shakespeare's *Henry V* (1598–99) seems to invite the audience to celebrate the conjoined heroism of English, Welsh, Scots, and Irish soldiers all fighting together as a "band of brothers" against the French. But such a way of imagining the national community must be set against the tensions and conflicting interests that often set these brothers at each other's throats. As Shakespeare's King Henry realizes, a feared or hated foreign enemy helps at least to mask these tensions, and indeed, in the face of the Spanish Armada, even the bitter gulf between Catholic and Protestant Englishmen seemed to narrow significantly. But the patriotic alliance was only temporary.

Another way of partially masking the sharp differences in language, belief, and custom among the peoples of the British Isles was to group these people together in contrast to the Jews. Medieval England's Jewish population, the recurrent object of persecution, extortion, and massacre, had been officially expelled by King Edward I in 1290, but Elizabethan England harbored a tiny number of Jews or Jewish converts to Christianity who were treated with suspicion and hostility. One of these was Elizabeth's own physician, Roderigo Lopez, who was tried in 1594 for an alleged plot to poison the queen. Convicted and condemned to the hideous execution reserved for traitors, Lopez went to his death, in the words of the Elizabethan historian William Camden, "affirming that he loved the Queen as well as he loved Jesus Christ; which coming from a man of the Jewish profession moved

A Jewish man depicted poisoning a well. From Pierre Boaistuau, *Certaine Secrete Wonders of Nature* (1569).

no small laughter in the standers-by." It is difficult to gauge the meaning here of the phrase "the Jewish profession," used to describe a man who never as far as we know professed Judaism, just as it is difficult to gauge the meaning of the crowd's cruel laughter.

Elizabethans appear to have been fascinated by Jews and Judaism but quite uncertain whether the terms referred to a people, a foreign nation, a set of strange practices, a living faith, a defunct religion, a villainous conspiracy, or a messianic inheritance. Protestant Reformers brooded deeply on the Hebraic origins of Christianity; government officials ordered the arrest of those "suspected to be Jews"; villagers paid pennies to itinerant fortune-tellers who claimed to be descended from Abraham or masters of cabalistic mysteries; and London playgoers, perhaps including some who laughed at Lopez on the scaffold, enjoyed the spectacle of the downfall of the wicked Barabas in Christopher Marlowe's *Jew of Malta* (c. 1592) and the forced conversion of Shylock in Shakespeare's *Merchant of Venice* (1596–97). Few if any of Shakespeare's contemporaries would have encountered on English soil Jews who openly practiced their religion, though England probably harbored a small number of so-called Marranos, Spanish or Portuguese Jews who had officially converted to Christianity but secretly continued to observe Jewish practices. Jews were not officially permitted to resettle in England until the middle of the seventeenth century, and even then their legal status was ambiguous.

Shakespeare's England also had a small African population whose skin color was the subject of pseudo-scientific speculation and theological debate. Some Elizabethans believed that Africans' blackness resulted from the climate of the regions in which they lived, where, as one traveler put it, they were "so scorched and vexed with the heat of the sun, that in many places they curse it when it riseth." Others held that blackness was a curse inherited from their forefather Chus, the son of Ham, who had, according to Genesis, wickedly exposed the nakedness of the drunken Noah. George Best, a proponent of this theory of inherited skin color, reported that "I myself have seen an Ethiopian as black as coal brought into England, who taking a fair English woman to wife, begat a son in all respects as black as the father was, although England were his native country, and an English woman his mother: whereby it seemeth this blackness proceedeth rather of some natural infection of that man."

As the word "infection" suggests, Elizabethans frequently regarded blackness as a physical defect, though the blacks who lived in England and Scotland throughout the sixteenth century were also treated as exotic curiosities. At his marriage to Anne of Denmark, James I entertained his bride and her family by commanding four naked black youths to dance before him in the snow. (The youths died of exposure shortly afterward.) In 1594, in the festivities celebrating the baptism of James's son, a "Black-Moor" entered pulling an elaborately decorated chariot that was, in the original plan, supposed to be drawn in by a lion. There was a black trumpeter in the courts of Henry VII and Henry VIII, while Elizabeth had at least two black servants, one an entertainer and the other a page. Africans became increasingly popular as servants in aristocratic and gentle households in the last decades of the sixteenth century.

Some of these Africans were almost certainly slaves, though the legal status of slavery in England was ambiguous. In Cartwright's Case (1569), the court ruled "that England was too Pure an Air for Slaves to breathe in," but there is evidence that black slaves were owned in Elizabethan and Jacobean England. Moreover, by the mid-sixteenth century, the English had become involved in the profitable trade that carried African slaves to the New World. In 1562, John Hawkins embarked on his first slaving voyage, transporting some three hundred blacks from the Guinea coast to Hispaniola, where they were sold for £10,000. Elizabeth is reported to have said of this venture that it was "detestable, and would call down the Vengeance of Heaven upon the Undertakers." Nevertheless, she invested in Hawkins's subsequent voyages and loaned him ships.

English men and women of the sixteenth century experienced an

Man with head beneath his shoulders. From a Spanish edition of Mandeville's *Travels*. See *Othello* 1.3.144–45: "and men whose heads / Do grow beneath their shoulders." Such men were occasionally reported by medieval travelers to the East.

unprecedented increase in knowledge of the world beyond their island, for a number of reasons. Religious persecution compelled both Catholics and Protestants to live abroad; wealthy gentlemen (and, in at least a few cases, ladies) traveled in France and Italy to view the famous cultural monuments; merchants published accounts of distant lands such as Turkey, Morocco, and Russia; and military and trading ventures took English ships to still more distant shores. In 1496, a Venetian tradesman living in Bristol, John Cabot, was granted a license by Henry VII to sail on a voyage of exploration; with his son Sebastian, he discovered Newfoundland and Nova Scotia. Remarkable feats of seamanship and reconnaissance soon followed: on his ship the *Golden Hind*, Sir Francis Drake circumnavigated the globe in 1579 and laid claim to California on behalf of the queen; a few years later, a ship commanded by Thomas Cavendish also completed a circumnavigation. Sir Martin Frobisher explored bleak Baffin Island in search of a Northwest Passage to the Orient; Sir John Davis explored the west coast of Greenland and discovered the Falkland Islands off the coast of Argentina; Sir Walter Ralegh ventured up the Orinoco Delta, in what is now Venezuela, in search of the mythical land of El Dorado. Accounts of these and other exploits were collected by a clergyman and promoter of empire, Richard Hakluyt, and published as *The Principal Navigations* (1589; expanded edition 1599).

"To seek new worlds for gold, for praise, for glory," as Ralegh characterized such enterprises, was not for the faint of heart: Drake, Cavendish, Frobisher, and Hawkins all died at sea, as did huge numbers of those who sailed under their command. Elizabethans sensible enough to stay at home could do more than read written accounts of their fellow countrymen's far-reaching voyages. Expeditions brought back native plants (including, most famously, tobacco), animals, cultural artifacts, and, on occasion, samples of the native

An Indian dance. From Thomas Hariot, A *Briefe and True Report of the New Found Land of Virginia* (1590).

peoples themselves, most often seized against their will. There were exhibitions in London of a kidnapped Eskimo with his kayak and of Virginians with their canoes. Most of these miserable captives, violently uprooted and vulnerable to European diseases, quickly perished, but even in death they were evidently valuable property: when the English will not give one small coin "to relieve a lame beggar," one of the characters in *The Tempest* wryly remarks, "they will lay out ten to see a dead Indian" (2.2.30–31).

Perhaps most nations learn to define what they are by defining what they are not. This negative self-definition is, in any case, what Elizabethans seemed constantly to be doing, in travel books, sermons, political speeches, civic pageants, public exhibitions, and theatrical spectacles of otherness. The extraordinary variety of these exercises (which include public executions and urban riots, as well as more benign forms of curiosity) suggests that the boundaries of national identity were by no means clear and unequivocal. Even peoples whom English writers routinely, viciously stigmatize as irreducibly alien—Italians, Indians, Turks, and Jews—have a surprising instability in the Elizabethan imagination and may appear for brief, intense moments as powerful models to be admired and emulated before they resume their place as emblems of despised otherness.

James I and the Union of the Crowns

Though under great pressure to do so, the aging Elizabeth steadfastly refused to name her successor. It became increasingly apparent, however, that it would be James Stuart, the son of Mary, Queen of Scots, and by the time Elizabeth's health began to fail, several of her principal advisers, including her chief minister, Robert Cecil, had been for several years in secret correspondence with him in Edinburgh. Crowned King James VI of Scotland in 1567 when he was but one year old, Mary's son had been raised as a Protestant by his powerful guardians, and in 1589 he married a Protestant princess, Anne of Denmark. When Elizabeth died on March 24, 1603, English officials reported that on her deathbed the queen had named James to succeed her.

Upon his accession, James—now styled James VI of Scotland and James I of England—made plain his intention to unite his two kingdoms. As he told Parliament in 1604, "What God hath conjoined then, let no man separate. I am the husband, and all of the whole isle is my lawful wife; I am the head and it is my body; I am the shepherd and it is my flock." But the flock was less perfectly united than James optimistically envisioned: English and Scottish were sharply distinct identities, as were Welsh and Cornish and other peoples who were incorporated, with varying degrees of willingness, into the realm.

Fearing that to change the name of the kingdom would invalidate all laws and institutions established under the name of England, a fear that was partly real and partly a cover for anti-Scots prejudice, Parliament balked at James's desire to be called "King of Great Britain" and resisted the unionist legislation that would have made Great Britain a legal reality. Though the English initially rejoiced at the peaceful transition from Elizabeth to her successor, there was a rising tide of resentment against James's advancement of Scots friends and his creation of new knighthoods. Lower down the social ladder, English and Scots occasionally clashed violently on the streets: in July 1603, James issued a proclamation against Scottish "insolencies," and in April 1604, he ordered the arrest of "swaggerers" waylaying Scots in London. The ensuing years did not bring the amity and docile obedience for which James hoped, and, though the navy now flew the Union Jack, combining the Scottish cross of St. Andrew and the English cross of St. George, the unification of the kingdoms remained throughout his reign an unfulfilled ambition.

Funeral procession of Queen Elizabeth. From a watercolor sketch by an unknown artist (1603).

The Jacobean Court

With James as with Elizabeth, the royal court was the center of diplomacy, ambition, intrigue, and an intense jockeying for social position. As always in monarchies, proximity to the king's person was a central mark of favor, so that access to the royal bedchamber was one of the highest aims of the powerful, scheming lords who followed James from his sprawling London palace at Whitehall to the hunting lodges and country estates to which he loved to retreat. A coveted office, in the Jacobean as in the Tudor court, was the Groom of the Stool, the person who supervised the disposal of the king's wastes. The officeholder was close to the king at one of his most exposed and vulnerable moments and enjoyed the further privilege of sleeping on a pallet at the foot of the royal bed and putting on the royal undershirt. Another, slightly less privileged official, the Gentleman of the Robes, dressed the king in his doublet and outer garments.

The royal life-style was increasingly expensive. Unlike Elizabeth, James had to maintain separate households for his queen and for the heir apparent, Prince Henry. (Upon Henry's death at the age of eighteen in 1612, his younger brother, Prince Charles, became heir, eventually succeeding his father in 1625.) James was also extremely generous to his friends, amassing his own huge debts in the course of paying off theirs. As early as 1605, he told his principal adviser that "it is a horror to me to think of the height of my place, the greatness of my debts, and the smallness of my means." This smallness notwithstanding, James continued to lavish gifts upon handsome favorites such as the Earl of Somerset, Robert Carr, and the Duke of Buckingham, George Villiers.

The attachment James formed for these favorites was highly romantic. "God so love me," the king wrote to Buckingham, "as I desire only to live in the world for your sake,

James I. By Marc Gheeraerts II, court painter.

and that I had rather live banished in any part of the earth with you than live a sorrowful widow's life without you." Such sentiments, not surprisingly, gave rise to widespread rumors of homosexual activities at court. The rumors are certainly plausible, though the surviving evidence of same-sex relationships, at court or elsewhere, is extremely difficult to interpret. A statute of 1533 made "the detestable and abominable vice of buggery committed with mankind or beast" a felony punishable by death. (English law declined to recognize or criminalize lesbian acts.) The effect of the draconian laws against buggery and sodomy seems to have been to reduce actual prosecutions to the barest minimum: for the next hundred years, there are no known cases of trials resulting in a death sentence for homosexual activity alone. If the legal record is therefore unreliable as an index of the extent of homosexual relations, the literary record (including, most famously, the majority of Shakespeare's sonnets) is equally opaque. Any poetic avowal of male-male love may simply be a formal expression of affection based on clas-

Two Young Men. By Crispin van den Broeck.

sical models, or, alternatively, it may be an expression of passionate physical and spiritual love. The interpretive difficulty is compounded by the absence in the period of any clear reference to a homosexual "identity," though there are many references to same-sex acts and feelings. What is clear is that male friendships at the court of James and elsewhere were suffused with a potential eroticism, at once delightful and threatening, that subsequent periods policed more anxiously.

In addition to the extravagant expenditures on his favorites, James was also the patron of ever more elaborate feasts and masques. Shakespeare's work provides a small glimpse of these in *The Tempest*, with its exotic banquet and its "majestic vision" of mythological goddesses and dancing nymphs and reapers, but the actual Jacobean court masques, designed by the great architect, painter, and engineer Inigo Jones, were spectacular, fantastic, technically ingenious, and staggeringly costly celebrations of regal magnificence. With their exquisite costumes and their elegant blend of music, dancing, and poetry, the masques, generally performed by the noble lords and ladies of the court, were deliberately ephemeral exercises in conspicuous expenditure and consumption: by tradition, at the end of the performance, the private audience would rush forward and tear to pieces the gorgeous scenery. And though masques were enormously sophisticated entertainments, often on rather esoteric allegorical themes, they could on occasion collapse into grotesque excess. In a letter of 1606, Sir John Harington describes a masque in honor of the visiting Danish king in which the participants, no doubt toasting their royal majesties, had had too much to drink. A lady playing the part of the Queen of Sheba attempted to present precious gifts, "but, forgetting the steps arising to the canopy, overset her caskets into his Danish Majesty's lap. . . . His Majesty then got up and would dance with the Queen of Sheba; but he fell down and humbled himself before her, and was carried to an inner chamber and laid on a bed." Meanwhile, Harington writes, the masque continued with a pageant of Faith, Hope, and Charity, but Charity could barely keep her balance, while Hope and Faith "were both sick and spewing in the lower hall." This was, we can hope, not a typical occasion.

While the English seem initially to have welcomed James's free-spending ways as a change from the parsimoniousness of Queen Elizabeth, they were dismayed by its consequences. Elizabeth had died owing £400,000. In 1608, the royal debt had risen to

£1,400,000 and was increasing by £140,000 a year. The money to pay off this debt, or at least to keep it under control, was raised by various means. These included customs farming (leasing the right to collect customs duties to private individuals); the highly unpopular impositions (duties on the import of nonnecessities, such as spices, silks, and currants); the sale of crown lands; the sale of baronetcies; and appeals to an increasingly grudging and recalcitrant Parliament. In 1614, Parliament demanded an end to impositions before it would relieve the king and was angrily dissolved without completing its business.

James's Religious Policy and the Persecution of Witches

Before his accession to the English throne, the king had made known his view of Puritans, the general name for a variety of Protestant sects that were agitating for a radical reform of the church, the overthrow of its conservative hierarchy of bishops, and the rejection of a large number of traditional rituals and practices. In a book he wrote, *Basilikon Doron* (1599), James denounced "brainsick and heady preachers" who were prepared "to let King, people, law and all be trod underfoot." Yet he was not entirely unwilling to consider religious reforms. In religion, as in foreign policy, he was above all concerned to maintain peace.

On his way south to claim the throne of England in 1603, James was presented with the Millenary Petition (signed by one thousand ministers), which urged him as "our physician" to heal the disease of lingering "popish" ceremonies. He responded by calling a conference on the ceremonies of the Church of England, which duly took place at Hampton Court Palace in January 1604. The delegates who spoke for reform were moderates, and there was little in the outcome to satisfy Puritans. Nevertheless, while the Church of England continued to cling to such remnants of the Catholic past as wedding rings, square caps, bishops, and Christmas, the conference did produce some reform in the area of

The "swimming" of a suspected witch.

ecclesiastical discipline. It also authorized a new English translation of the Bible, known as the King James Bible, which was printed in 1611, too late to have been extensively used by Shakespeare. Along with Shakespeare's works, the King James Bible has probably had the profoundest influence on the subsequent history of English literature.

Having arranged this compromise, James saw his main task as ensuring conformity. He promulgated the 1604 Canons (the first definitive code of canon law since the Reformation), which required all ministers to subscribe to three articles. The first affirmed royal supremacy; the second confirmed that there was nothing in the Book of Common Prayer "contrary to the Word of God" and required ministers to use only the authorized services; the third asserted that the central tenets of the Church of England were "agreeable to the Word of God." There were strong objections to the second and third articles from those of Puritan leanings inside and outside the House of Commons. In the end, many ministers refused to conform or subscribe to the articles, but only about ninety of them, or 1 percent of the clergy, were deprived of their livings. In its theology and composition, the Church of England was little changed from what it had been under Elizabeth. In hindsight, what is most striking are the ominous signs of growing religious divisions that would by the 1640s burst forth in civil war and the execution of James's son Charles.

James seems to have taken seriously the official claims to the sacredness of kingship, and he certainly took seriously his own theories of religion and politics, which he had printed for the edification of his people. He was convinced that Satan, perpetually warring against God and His representatives on earth, was continually plotting against him. James thought moreover that he possessed special insight into Satan's wicked agents, the witches, and in 1597, while King of Scotland, he published his *Demonology,* a learned exposition of their malign threat to his godly rule. Hundreds of witches, he believed, were involved in a 1590 conspiracy to kill him by raising storms at sea when he was sailing home from Denmark with his new bride.

In the 1590s, Scotland embarked on a virulent witch craze of the kind that had since the fifteenth century repeatedly afflicted France, Switzerland, and Germany, where many thousands of women (and a much smaller number of men) were caught in a nightmarish web of wild accusations. Tortured into lurid confessions of infant cannibalism, night flying, and sexual intercourse with the devil at huge, orgiastic "witches' Sabbaths," the victims had little chance to defend themselves and were routinely burned at the stake.

In England too there were witchcraft prosecutions, though on a much smaller scale and with significant differences in the nature of the accusations and the judicial procedures. Witch trials began in England in the 1540s; statutes against witchcraft were enacted in 1542, 1563, and 1604. English law did not allow judicial torture, stipulated lesser punishments in cases of "white magic," and mandated jury trials. Juries acquitted more than half of the defendants in witchcraft trials; in Essex, where the judicial records are particularly extensive, some 24 percent of those accused were executed, while the remainder of those convicted were pilloried and imprisoned or sentenced and reprieved. The accused were generally charged with *maleficium,* an evil deed—usually harming neighbors, causing destructive storms, or killing farm animals—but not with worshipping Satan.

After 1603, when James came to the English throne, he somewhat moderated his enthusiasm for the judicial murder of witches, for the most part defenseless, poor women resented by their neighbors. Though he did nothing to mitigate the ferocity of the ongoing witch-hunts in his native Scotland, he did not try to institute Scottish-style persecutions and trials in his new realm. This relative waning of persecutorial eagerness principally reflects the differences between England and Scotland, but it may also bespeak some small, nascent skepticism on James's part about the quality of evidence brought against the accused and about the reliability of the "confessions" extracted from them. It is sobering to reflect that plays like Shakespeare's *Macbeth* (1606), Thomas Middleton's *Witch* (before 1616), and Thomas Dekker, John Ford, and William Rowley's *Witch of Edmonton* (1621) seem to be less the allies of skepticism than the exploiters of fear.

The Playing Field

Cosmic Spectacles

The first permanent, freestanding public theaters in England date only from Shakespeare's own lifetime: a London playhouse, the Red Lion, is mentioned in 1567, and James Burbage's playhouse, The Theatre, was built in 1576. (The innovative use of these new stages, crucial to a full understanding of Shakespeare's achievement, is the subject of a separate essay in this volume, by the theater historian Andrew Gurr.) But it is quite misleading to identify English drama exclusively with these specially constructed playhouses, for in fact there was a rich and vital theatrical tradition in England stretching back for centuries. Many towns in late medieval England were the sites of annual festivals that mounted elaborate cycles of plays depicting the great biblical stories, from the creation of the world to Christ's Passion and its miraculous aftermath. Most of these plays have been lost, but the surviving cycles, such as those from York, are magnificent and complex works of art. They are sometimes called "mystery plays," either because they were performed by the guilds of various crafts (known as "mysteries") or, more likely, because they represented the mysteries of the faith. The cycles were most often performed on the annual feast day instituted in the early fourteenth century in honor of the Corpus Christi, the sacrament of the Lord's Supper, which is perhaps the greatest of these religious mysteries.

The feast of Corpus Christi, celebrated on the Thursday following Trinity Sunday, helped give the play cycles their extraordinary cultural resonance, but it also contributed to their downfall. For along with the specifically liturgical plays traditionally performed by religious confraternities and the "saints' plays, which depicted miraculous events in the lives of individual holy men and women, the mystery cycles were closely identified with the Catholic Church. Protestant authorities in the sixteenth century, eager to eradicate all remnants of popular Catholic piety, moved to suppress the annual procession of the Host, with its gorgeous banners, pageant carts, and cycle of visionary plays. In 1548, the Feast of Corpus Christi was abolished. Towns that continued to perform the mysteries were under increasing pressure to abandon them. It is sometimes said that the cycles were already dying out from neglect, but recent research has shown that many towns and their guilds were extremely reluctant to give them up. Desperate offers to strip away any traces of Catholic doctrine and to submit the play scripts to the authorities for their approval met with unbending opposition from the government. In 1576, the courts gave York permission to perform its cycle but only if

> in the said play no pageant be used or set forth wherein the Majesty of God the Father, God the Son, or God the Holy Ghost or the administration of either the Sacraments of baptism or of the Lord's Supper be counterfeited or represented, or anything played which tend to the maintenance of superstition and idolatry or which be contrary to the laws of God . . . or of the realm.

Such "permission" was tantamount to an outright ban. The local officials in the city of Norwich, proud of their St. George and the Dragon play, asked if they could at least parade the dragon costume through the streets, but even this modest request was refused. It is likely that as a young man Shakespeare had seen some of these plays: when Hamlet says of a noisy, strutting theatrical performance that it "out-Herods Herod," he is alluding to the famously bombastic role of Herod of Jewry in the mystery plays. But by the century's end, the cycles were no longer performed.

Early English theater was by no means restricted to these civic and religious festivals. Payments to professional and amateur performers appear in early records of towns and aristocratic households, though the terms—"ministralli," "histriones," "mimi," "lusores," and so forth—are not used with great consistency and make it difficult to distinguish among minstrels, jugglers, stage players, and other entertainers. Performers acted in town halls and the halls of guilds and aristocratic mansions, on scaffolds erected in town squares

Panorama of London, showing two theaters, both round and
both flying flags: a flying flag indicated that a performance was
in progress. The Globe is in the foreground, and the Beargar-
den or Hope is to the left.

and marketplaces, on pageant wagons in the streets, and in inn yards. By the fifteenth
century, and probably earlier, there were organized companies of players traveling under
noble patronage. Such companies earned a living providing amusement, while enhancing
the prestige of the patron.

A description of a provincial performance in the late sixteenth century, written by one
R. Willis, provides a glimpse of what seems to have been the usual procedure:

> In the City of Gloucester the manner is (as I think it is in other like corporations) that
> when the Players of Interludes come to town, they first attend the Mayor to inform him
> what nobleman's servant they are, and so to get licence for their public playing; and if
> the Mayor like the Actors, or would show respect to their Lord and Master, he appoints
> them to play their first play before himself and the Aldermen and common Council of
> the City and that is called the Mayor's play, where everyone that will come in without
> money, the Mayor giving the players a reward as he thinks fit to show respect unto
> them.

In addition to their take from this "first play," the players would almost certainly have
supplemented their income by performing in halls and inn yards, where they could pass
the hat after the performance or even on some occasions charge an admission fee. It was
no doubt a precarious existence.

The "Interludes" mentioned in Willis's description of the Gloucester performances are
likely plays that were, in effect, staged dialogues on religious, moral, and political themes.
Such works could, like the mysteries, be associated with Catholicism, but they were also
used in the sixteenth century to convey polemical Protestant messages, and they reached
outside the religious sphere to address secular concerns as well. Henry Medwall's *Fulgens
and Lucrece* (c. 1490–1501), for example, pits a wealthy but dissolute nobleman against a
virtuous public servant of humble origins, while John Heywood's *Play of the Weather* (c.
1525–33) stages a debate among social rivals, including a gentleman, a merchant, a forest
ranger, and two millers. The structure of such plays reflects the training in argumentation
that students received in Tudor schools and, in particular, the sustained practice in exam-
ining all sides of a difficult question. Some of Shakespeare's amazing ability to look at
critical issues from multiple perspectives may be traced back to this practice and the dra-
matic interludes it helped to inspire.

Another major form of theater that flourished in England in the fifteenth century and
continued on into the sixteenth was the morality play. Like the mysteries, moralities
addressed questions of the ultimate fate of the soul. They did so, however, not by rehears-

ing scriptural stories but by dramatizing allegories of spiritual struggle. Typically, a person named Human or Mankind or Youth is faced with a choice between a pious life in the company of such associates as Mercy, Discretion, and Good Deeds and a dissolute life among riotous companions like Lust or Mischief. Plays like *Mankind* (c. 1465–70) and *Everyman* (c. 1495) show how powerful these unpromising-sounding dramas could be, in part because of the extraordinary comic vitality of the evil character, or Vice, and in part because of the poignancy and terror of an individual's encounter with death. Shakespeare clearly grasped this power. The hunchbacked Duke of Gloucester in *Richard III* gleefully likens himself to "the formal Vice, Iniquity." And when Othello wavers between Desdemona and Iago (himself a Vice figure), his anguished dilemma echoes the fateful choice repeatedly faced by the troubled, vulnerable protagonists of the moralities.

If such plays sound a bit like sermons, it is because they were. Clerics and actors shared some of the same rhetorical skills. It would be misleading to regard churchgoing and playgoing as comparable entertainments, but in attacking the stage, ministers often seemed to regard the professional players as dangerous rivals. The players themselves were generally too discreet to rise to the challenge; it would have been foolhardy to present the theater as the church's direct competitor. Yet in its moral intensity and its command of impassioned language, the stage frequently emulates and outdoes the pulpit.

Music and Dance

Playacting took its place alongside other forms of public expression and entertainment as well. Perhaps the most important, from the perspective of the theater, were music and dance, since these were directly and repeatedly incorporated into plays. Many plays, comedies and tragedies alike, include occasions that call upon the characters to dance: hence Beatrice and Benedick join the other masked guests at the dance in *Much Ado About Nothing*; in *Twelfth Night*, the befuddled Sir Andrew, at the instigation of the drunken Sir Toby Belch, displays his skill, such as it is, in capering; Romeo and Juliet first see each other at the Capulet ball; the witches dance in a ring around the hideous caldron and perform an "antic round" to cheer Macbeth's spirits; and, in one of Shakespeare's strangest and most wonderful scenes, the drunken Antony in *Antony and Cleopatra* joins hands with Caesar, Enobarbus, Pompey, and others to dance "the Egyptian Bacchanals."

Moreover, virtually all plays in the period, including Shakespeare's, apparently ended with a dance. Brushing off the theatrical gore and changing their expressions from woe to pleasure, the actors in plays like *Hamlet* and *King Lear* would presumably have received the audience's applause and then bid for a second round of applause by performing a stately pavane or a lively jig. Indeed, jigs, with their comical leaping dance steps often accompanied by scurrilous ballads, became so popular that they drew not only large crowds but also official disapproval. A court order of 1612 complained about the "cut-purses and other lewd and ill-disposed persons" who flocked to the theater at the end of every play to be entertained by "lewd jigs, songs, and dances." The players were warned to suppress these disreputable entertainments on pain of imprisonment.

The displays of dancing onstage clearly reflected a widespread popular interest in dancing outside the walls of the playhouse as well. Renaissance intellectuals conjured up visions of the universe as a great cosmic dance, poets figured relations between men and women in terms of popular dance steps, stern moralists denounced dancing as an incitement to filthy lewdness, and, perhaps as significant, men of all classes evidently spent a great deal of time worrying about how shapely their legs looked in tights and how gracefully they could leap. Shakespeare assumes that his audience will be quite familiar with a variety of dances. "For, hear me, Hero," Beatrice tells her friend, "wooing, wedding, and repenting is as a Scotch jig, a measure, and a cinquepace" (2.1.60–61). Her speech dwells on the comparison a bit, teasing out its implications, but it still does not make much sense if you do not already know something about the dances and perhaps occasionally venture to perform them yourself.

Closely linked to dancing and even more central to the stage was music, both instrumental and vocal. In the early sixteenth century, the Reformation had been disastrous for sacred music: many church organs were destroyed, choir schools were closed, the glorious polyphonal liturgies sung in the monasteries were suppressed. But by the latter part of the century, new perspectives were reinvigorating English music. Latin masses were reset in English, and tunes were written for newly translated, metrical psalms. More important for the theater, styles of secular music were developed that emphasized music's link to humanist eloquence, its ability to heighten and to rival rhetorically powerful texts.

This link is particularly evident in vocal music, at which Elizabethan composers excelled. Renowned composers William Byrd, Thomas Morley, John Dowland, and others wrote a rich profusion of madrigals (part songs for two to eight voices unaccompanied) and ayres (songs for solo voice, generally accompanied by the lute). These works, along with hymns, popular ballads, rounds, catches, and other forms of song, enjoyed immense popularity, not only in the royal court, where musical skill was regarded as an important accomplishment, and in aristocratic households, where professional musicians were employed as entertainers, but also in less

Richard Tarlton. Tarlton was the lead comedian of the Queen's Company from 1583, the year of its founding, until 1588, when he died.

exalted social circles. In his *Plain and Easy Introduction to Practical Music* (1597), Morley tells a story of social humiliation at a failure to perform that suggests that a well-educated Elizabethan was expected to be able to sing at sight. Even if this is an exaggeration in the interest of book sales, there is evidence of impressively widespread musical literacy, reflected in a splendid array of music for the lute, viol, recorder, harp, and virginal, as well as the marvelous vocal music.

Whether it is the aristocratic Orsino luxuriating in the dying fall of an exquisite melody or bully Bottom craving "the tongs and the bones," Shakespeare's characters frequently call for music. They also repeatedly give voice to the age's conviction that there was a deep relation between musical harmony and the harmonies of the well-ordered individual and state. "The man that hath no music in himself," warns Lorenzo in *The Merchant of Venice*, "nor is not moved with concord of sweet sounds, / Is fit for treasons, stratagems, and spoils" (5.1.82–84). This conviction in turn reflects a still deeper link between musical harmony and the divinely created harmony of the cosmos. When Ulysses in *Troilus and Cressida* wishes to convey the image of universal chaos, he speaks of the untuning of a string (1.3.109).

The playing companies must have regularly employed trained musicians, and many actors (like the actor who in playing Pandarus in *Troilus and Cressida* is supposed to accompany himself on the lute) must have possessed musical skill. Unfortunately, we possess the original settings for very few of Shakespeare's songs, possibly because many of them may have been set to popular tunes of the time that everyone knew and no one bothered to write down.

Alternative Entertainments

Plays, music, and dancing were by no means the only shows in town. There were jousts, tournaments, royal entries, religious processions, pageants in honor of newly installed civic officials or ambassadors arriving from abroad; wedding masques, court masques, and costumed entertainments known as "disguisings" or "mummings"; juggling acts, fortune-tellers, exhibitions of swordsmanship, mountebanks, folk healers, storytellers, magic shows; bearbaiting, bullbaiting, cockfighting, and other blood sports; folk festivals such as Maying, the Feast of Fools, Carnival, and Whitsun Ales. For several years, Elizabethan Londoners were delighted by a trained animal—Banks's Horse—that could, it was thought, do arithmetic and answer questions. And there was always the grim but compelling spectacle of public shaming, mutilation, and execution.

Most English towns had stocks and whipping posts. Drunks, fraudulent merchants, adulterers, and quarrelers could be placed in carts or mounted backward on asses and paraded through the streets for crowds to jeer and throw refuse at. Women accused of being scolds could be publicly muzzled by an iron device called a "brank" or tied to a cucking stool and dunked in the river. Convicted criminals could have their ears cut off, their noses slit, their foreheads branded. Public beheadings (generally reserved for the elite) and hangings were common. In the worst cases, felons were sentenced to be "hanged by the neck, and being alive cut down, and your privy members to be cut off, and your bowels to be taken out of your belly and there burned, you being alive."

Shakespeare occasionally takes note of these alternative entertainments: at the end of *Macbeth*, for example, with his enemies closing in on him, the doomed tyrant declares, "They have tied me to a stake. I cannot fly, / But bear-like I must fight the course" (5.7.1–2). The audience is reminded then that it is witnessing the human equivalent of a popular spectacle—a bear chained to a stake and attacked by fierce dogs—that they could have paid to watch at an arena near the Globe. And when, a few moments later, Macduff enters carrying Macbeth's head, the audience is seeing the theatrical equivalent of the execution of criminals and traitors that they could have also watched in the flesh, as it were, nearby. In a different key, the audiences who paid to see *A Midsummer Night's Dream* or *The Winter's Tale* got to enjoy the comic spectacle of a Maying and a Whitsun Pastoral, while

An Elizabethan hanging.

the spectators of *The Tempest* could gawk at what the Folio list of characters calls a "salvage and deformed slave" and to enjoy an aristocratic magician's wedding masque in honor of his daughter.

The Enemies of the Stage

In 1624, a touring company of players arrived in Norwich and requested permission to perform. Permission was denied, but the municipal authorities, "in regard of the honorable respect which this City beareth to the right honorable the Lord Chamberlain," gave the players twenty shillings to get out of town. Throughout the sixteenth and early seventeenth centuries, there are many similar records of civic officials prohibiting performances and then, to appease a powerful patron, paying the actors to take their skills elsewhere. As early as the 1570s, there is evidence that the London authorities, while mindful of the players' influential protectors, were energetically trying to drive the theater out of the city.

Why should what we now regard as one of the undisputed glories of the age have aroused so much hostility? One answer, curiously enough, is traffic: plays drew large audiences—the public theaters could accommodate thousands—and residents objected to the crowds, the noise, and the crush of carriages. Other, more serious concerns were public health and crime. It was thought that numerous diseases, including the dreaded bubonic plague, were spread by noxious odors, and the packed playhouses were obvious breeding grounds for infection. (Patrons often tried to protect themselves by sniffing nosegays or stuffing cloves into their nostrils.) The large crowds drew pickpockets, cutpurses, and other scoundrels. On one memorable afternoon, a pickpocket was caught in the act and tied for the duration of the play to one of the posts that held up the canopy above the stage. The theater was, moreover, a well-known haunt of prostitutes, and, it was alleged, a place where innocent maids were seduced and respectable matrons corrupted. It was darkly rumored that "chambers and secret places" adjoined the theater galleries, and in any case, taverns, disreputable inns, and whorehouses were close at hand.

There were other charges as well. Plays were performed in the afternoon and therefore drew people, especially the young, away from their work. They were schools of idleness, luring apprentices from their trades, law students from their studies, housewives from their kitchens, and potentially pious souls from the sober meditations to which they might otherwise devote themselves. Wasting their time and money on disreputable shows, citizens exposed themselves to sexual provocation and outright political sedition. Even when the content of plays was morally exemplary—and, of course, few plays were so gratify-

Syphilis victim in tub. Frontispiece to the play *Cornelianum Dolium* (1638), possibly authored by Thomas Randolph. The tub inscription translates as "I sit on the throne of love, I suffer in the tub"; and the banner as "Farewell O sexual pleasures and lusts."

ingly high-minded—the theater itself, in the eyes of most mayors and aldermen, was inherently disorderly.

The attack on the stage by civic officials was echoed and intensified by many of the age's moralists and religious leaders, especially those associated with Puritanism. While English Protestants earlier in the sixteenth century had attempted to counter the Catholic mystery cycles and saints' plays by mounting their own doctrinally correct dramas, by the century's end a fairly widespread consensus, even among those mildly sympathetic toward the theater, held that the stage and the pulpit were in tension with one another. After 1591, a ban on Sunday performances was strictly enforced, and in 1606, Parliament passed an act imposing a fine of £10 on any person who shall "in any stage-play, interlude, show, May-game, or pageant, jestingly or profanely speak or use the holy name of God, or of Christ Jesus, or of the Holy Ghost, or of the Trinity (which are not to be spoken but with fear and reverence)." If changes in the printed texts are a reliable indication, the players seem to have complied at least to some degree with the ruling. The Folio (1623) text of *Richard III*, for example, omits the quarto's (1597) four uses of "zounds" (for "God's wounds"), along with a mention of "Christ's dear blood shed for our grievous sins"; "God's my judge" in *The Merchant of Venice* becomes "well I know"; "By Jesu" in *Henry V* becomes a very proper "I say"; and in all the plays, "God" is from time to time metamorphosed to "Jove."

But for some of the theater's more extreme critics, these modest expurgations were tiny bandages on a gaping wound. In his huge book *Histriomastix* (1633), William Prynne regurgitates a half-century of frenzied attacks on the "sinful, heathenish, lewd, ungodly Spectacles." In the eyes of Prynne and his fellow antitheatricalists, stage plays were part of a demonic tangle of obscene practices proliferating like a cancer in the body of society. It is "manifest to all men's judgments," he writes, that

> effeminate mixed dancing, dicing, stage-plays, lascivious pictures, wanton fashions, face-painting, health-drinking, long hair, love-locks, periwigs, women's curling, powdering and cutting of their hair, bonfires, New-year's gifts, May-games, amorous pastorals, lascivious effeminate music, excessive laughter, luxurious disorderly Christmas-keeping, mummeries . . . [are] wicked, unchristian pastimes.

Given the anxious emphasis on effeminacy, it is not surprising that denunciations of this kind obsessively focused on the use of boy actors to play the female parts. The enemies of the stage charged that theatrical transvestism excited illicit sexual desires, both heterosexual and homosexual.

Since cross-dressing violated a biblical prohibition (Deuteronomy 22:5), religious antitheatricalists attacked it as wicked regardless of its erotic charge; indeed, they often seemed to consider any act of impersonation as inherently wicked. In their view, the theater itself was Satan's domain. Thus a Cambridge scholar, John Greene, reports the sad fate of "a Christian woman" who went to the theater to see a play: "She entered in well and sound, but she returned and came forth possessed of the devil. Whereupon certain godly brethren demanded Satan how he durst be so bold, as to enter into her a Christian. Whereto he answered, that *he found her in his own house*, and therefore took possession of her as his own" (italic in original). When the "godly brethren" came to power in the mid-seventeenth century, with the overthrow of Charles I, they saw to it that the playhouses, temporarily shut down in 1642 at the onset of the Civil War, remained closed. The theater did not resume until the restoration of the monarchy in 1660.

Faced with enemies among civic officials and religious leaders, Elizabethan and Jacobean playing companies relied on the protection of their powerful patrons. As the liveried servants of aristocrats or of the monarch, the players could refute the charge that they were mere vagabonds, and they claimed, as a convenient legal fiction, that their public performances were necessary rehearsals in anticipation of those occasions when they would be called upon to entertain their noble masters. But harassment by the mayor and aldermen continued unabated, and the players were forced to build their theaters outside the immediate jurisdiction of the city authorities, either in the suburbs or in the areas known as the "liberties." A liberty was a piece of land within the City of London itself that was not directly subject to the authority of the lord mayor. The most significant of these from the point of view of the theater was the area near St. Paul's Cathedral called "the Blackfriars," where, until the dissolution of the monasteries in 1538, there had been a Dominican monastery. It was here that in 1608 Shakespeare's company, then called the King's Men, built the indoor playhouse in which they performed during the winter months, reserving the open-air Globe in the suburb of Southwark for their summer performances.

Censorship and Regulation

In addition to those authorities who campaigned to shut down the theater, there were others whose task was to oversee, regulate, and censor it. Given the outright hostility of the former, the latter may have seemed to the London players equivocal allies rather than enemies. After all, plays that passed the censor were at least licensed to be performed and hence conceded to have some limited legitimacy. In April 1559, at the very start of her reign, Queen Elizabeth drafted a proposal that for the first time envisaged a system for the prior review and regulation of plays throughout her kingdom:

> The Queen's Majesty doth straightly forbid all manner interludes to be played either openly or privately, except the same be notified beforehand, and licensed within any city or town corporate, by the mayor or other chief officers of the same, and within any shire, by such as shall be lieutenants for the Queen's Majesty in the same shire, or by two of the Justices of Peace inhabiting within that part of the shire where any shall be played. . . . And for instruction to every of the said officers, her Majesty doth likewise charge every of them, as they will answer: that they permit none to be played wherein either matters of religion or of the governance of the estate of the commonweal shall be handled or treated upon, but by men of authority, learning and wisdom, nor to be handled before any audience, but of grave and discreet persons.

This proposal, which may not have been formally enacted, makes an important distinction between those who are entitled to address sensitive issues of religion and politics—authors "of authority, learning and wisdom" addressing audiences "of grave and discreet persons"—and those who are forbidden to do so.

The London public theater, with its playwrights who were the sons of glovers, shoemakers, and bricklayers and its audiences in which the privileged classes mingled with rowdy apprentices, masked women, and servants, was clearly not a place to which the government wished to grant freedom of expression. In 1581, the Master of the Revels, an official in the lord chamberlain's department whose role had hitherto been to provide entertainment at court, was given an expanded commission. Sir Edmund Tilney, the functionary who held the office, was authorized

> to warn, command, and appoint in all places within this our Realm of England, as well within franchises and liberties as without, all and every player or players with their playmakers, either belonging to any nobleman or otherwise . . . to appear before him with all such plays, tragedies, comedies, or shows as they shall in readiness or mean to set forth, and them to recite before our said Servant or his sufficient deputy, whom we ordain, appoint, and authorize by these presents of all such shows, plays, players, and playmakers, together with their playing places, to order and reform, authorize and put down, as shall be thought meet or unmeet unto himself or his said deputy in that behalf.

What emerged from this commission was in effect a national system of regulation and censorship. One of its consequences was to restrict virtually all licensed theater to the handful of authorized London-based playing companies. These companies would have to submit their plays for official scrutiny, but in return they received implicit, and on occasion explicit, protection against the continued fierce opposition of the local authorities. Plays reviewed and allowed by the Master of the Revels had been deemed fit to be performed before the monarch; how could mere aldermen legitimately claim that such plays should be banned as seditious?

The key question, of course, is how carefully the Master of the Revels scrutinized the plays brought before him either to hear or, more often from the 1590s onward, to peruse. What was Tilney, who served in the office until his death in 1610, or his successor, Sir George Buc, who served from 1610 to 1621, looking for? What did they insist be cut before they would release what was known as the "allowed copy," the only version licensed for performance? Unfortunately, the office books of the Master of the Revels in Shakespeare's time have been lost; what survives is a handful of scripts on which Tilney, Buc, and their assistants jotted their instructions. These suggest that the readings were rather painstaking, with careful attention paid to possible religious, political, and diplomatic repercussions. References, directly or strongly implied, to any living Christian prince or any important English nobleman, gentleman, or government official were particularly sensitive and likely to be struck. Renaissance political life was highly personalized; people in power were exceptionally alert to insult and zealously patrolled the boundaries of their prestige and reputation.

Moreover, the censors knew that audiences and readers were quite adept at applying theatrical representations distanced in time and space to their own world. At a time of riots against resident foreigners, Tilney read *Sir Thomas More*, a play in which Shakespeare probably had a hand, and instructed the players to cut scenes that, though set in 1517, might have had an uncomfortable contemporary resonance. "Leave out the insurrection wholly," Tilney's note reads, "and the cause thereof and begin with Sir Thomas More at the Mayor's sessions, with a report afterwards of his good service done being sheriff of London upon a mutiny against the Lombards only by a short report and not otherwise at your own perils. E. Tilney." Of course, as Tilney knew perfectly well, most plays succeed precisely by mirroring, if only obliquely, their own times, but this particular reflection evidently seemed to him too dangerous or provocative.

The topical significance of a play depends in large measure on the particular moment in which it is performed, and on certain features of the performance—for example, a striking resemblance between one of the characters and a well-known public figure—that the script itself will not necessarily disclose to us at this great distance or even to the censor at the time. Hence the Master of the Revels noted angrily of one play performed in 1632 that "there were diverse personated so naturally, both of lords and others of the court, that I took it ill." Hence too a play that was deemed allowable when it was first written and performed could return, like a nightmare, to haunt a different place and time. The most famous instance of such a return involves Shakespeare, for on the day before the Earl of Essex's attempted coup against Queen Elizabeth in 1601, someone paid the Lord Chamberlain's Men (the name of Shakespeare's company at the time) forty shillings to revive their old play about the deposition and murder of Richard II. "I am Richard II," the queen declared. "Know ye not that?" However distressed she was by this performance, the queen significantly did not take out her wrath on the players: neither the playwright nor his company was punished, nor was the Master of the Revels criticized for allowing the play in the first place. It was Essex and several of his key supporters who lost their heads.

Evidence suggests that the Master of the Revels often regarded himself not as the strict censor of the theater but as its friendly guardian, charged with averting catastrophes. He was a bureaucrat concerned less with subversive ideas per se than with potential trouble. That is, there is no record of a dramatist being called to account for his heterodox beliefs; rather, plays were censored if they risked offending influential people, including important foreign allies, or if they threatened to cause public disorder by exacerbating religious or other controversies. The distinction is not a stable one, but it helps to explain the intellectual boldness, power, and freedom of a censored theater in a society in which the perceived enemies of the state were treated mercilessly. Shakespeare could have Lear articulate a searing indictment of social injustice—

Robes and furred gowns hide all. Plate sin with gold,
And the strong lance of justice hurtless breaks;
Arm it in rags, a pygmy's straw does pierce it.
(4.5.155–57)

—and evidently neither the Master of the Revels nor the courtiers in their robes and furred gowns protested. But when the Spanish ambassador complained about Thomas Middleton's anti-Spanish allegory A Game at Chess, performed at the Globe in 1624, the whole theater was shut down, the players were arrested, and the king professed to be furious at his official for licensing the play in the first place and allowing it to be performed for nine consecutive days.

In addition to the system for the licensing of plays for performance, there was also a system for the licensing of plays for publication. At the start of Shakespeare's career, such press licensing was the responsibility of the Court of High Commission, headed by the Archbishop of Canterbury and the Bishop of London. Their deputies, a panel of junior clerics, were supposed to review the manuscripts, granting licenses to those worthy of publication and rejecting any they deemed "heretical, seditious, or unseemly for Christian ears." Without a license, the Stationers' Company, the guild of the book trade, was not supposed to register a manuscript for publication. In practice, as various complaints and attempts to close loopholes attest, some playbooks were printed without a license. In 1607, the system was significantly revised when Sir George Buc began to license plays for the press. When Buc succeeded to the post of Master of the Revels in 1610, the powers to license plays for the stage and the page were vested in one man.

Theatrical Innovations

The theater continued to flourish under this system of regulation after Shakespeare's death; by the 1630s, as many as five playhouses were operating daily in London. When the theater reemerged after the eighteen-year hiatus imposed by Puritan rule, it quickly resumed its cultural importance, but not without a number of significant changes. Major innovations in staging resulted principally from continental influences on the English artists who accompanied the court of Charles II into exile in France, where they supplied it with masques and other theatrical entertainments.

The institutional conditions and business practices of the two companies chartered by Charles after the Restoration in 1660 also differed from those of Shakespeare's theater. In place of the more collective practice of Shakespeare's company, the Restoration theaters were controlled by celebrated actor-managers who not only assigned themselves starring roles, in both comedy and tragedy, but also assumed sole responsibility for many business decisions, including the setting of their colleagues' salaries. At the same time, the power of the actor-manager, great as it was, was limited by the new importance of outside capital. No longer was the theater, with all of its properties from script to costumes, owned by the "sharers," that is, by those actors who held shares in the joint-stock company. Instead, entrepreneurs would raise capital for increasingly fantastic sets and stage machinery that could cost as much as £3,000, an astronomical sum, for a single production. This investment in turn not only influenced the kinds of new plays written for the theater but helped to transform old plays that were revived, including Shakespeare's.

In his diary entry for August 24, 1661, Samuel Pepys notes that he has been "to the Opera, and there saw Hamlet, Prince of Denmark, done with scenes very well, but above all, Betterton did the prince's part beyond imagination." This is Thomas Betterton's first review, as it were, and it is typical of the enthusiasm he would inspire throughout his fifty-year career on the London stage. Pepys's brief and scattered remarks on the plays he voraciously attended in the 1660s are precious because they are among the few records from the period of concrete and immediate responses to theatrical performances. Modern readers might miss the significance of Pepys's phrase "done with scenes": this production of *Hamlet* was only the third play to use the movable sets first introduced to England by its producer, William Davenant. The central historical fact that makes the productions of this period so exciting is that public theater had been banned altogether for eighteen years until the Restoration of Charles II.

A brief discussion of theatrical developments in the Restoration period will enable us at least to glance longingly at a vast subject that lies outside the scope of this introduction: the rich performance history that extends from Shakespeare's time to our own, involving tens of thousands of productions and adaptations for theater, opera, Broadway musicals, and of course films. The scale of this history is vast in space as well as time: as early as 1607, there is a record of a *Hamlet* performed on board an English ship, HMS *Dragon*, off the coast of Sierra Leone, and troupes of English actors performed in the late sixteenth and early seventeenth centuries as far afield as Poland and Bohemia.

William Davenant, who claimed to be Shakespeare's bastard son, had become an expert on stage scenery while producing masques at the court of Charles I, and when the theaters reopened, he set to work on converting an indoor tennis court into a new kind of theater. He designed a broad open platform like that of the Elizabethan stage, but he replaced the relatively shallow space for "discoveries" (tableaux set up in an opening at the center of the stage, revealed by drawing back a curtain) and the "tiring-house" (the players' dressing room) behind this space with one expanded interior, framed by a proscenium arch, in which scenes could be displayed. These elaborately painted scenes could be moved on and off, using grooves on the floor. The perspectival effect for a spectator of one central painted panel with two "wings" on either side was that of three sides of a room. This effect anticipated that of the familiar "picture frame" stage, developed fully in the nineteenth century, and began a subtle shift in theater away from the elaborate verbal descriptions that are so central to Shakespeare and toward the evocative visual poetry of the set designer's art.

Another convention of Shakespeare's stage, the use of boy actors for female roles, gave way to the more complete illusion of women playing women's parts. The king issued a decree in 1662 forcefully permitting, if not requiring, the use of actresses. The royal decree is couched in the language of social and moral reform: the introduction of actresses will require the "reformation" of scurrilous and profane passages in plays, and this in turn will help forestall some of the objections that shut the theaters down in 1642. In reality, male theater audiences, composed of a narrower range of courtiers and aristocrats than in Shakespeare's time, met this intended reform with the assumption that the new actresses were fair game sexually; most actresses (with the partial exception of those who married male members of their troupes) were regarded as, or actually became, whores. But despite the social stigma, and the fact that their salaries were predictably lower than those of their male counterparts, the stage saw some formidable female stars by the 1680s.

The first recorded appearance of an actress was that of a Desdemona in December 1660. Betterton's Ophelia in 1661 was Mary Saunderson (c. 1637–1712), who became Mrs. Betterton a year later. The most famous Ophelia of the period was Susanna Mountfort, who appeared in that role for the first time at the age of fifteen in 1705. The performance by Mountfort that became legendary occurred in 1720, after a disappointment in love, or so it was said, had driven her mad. Hearing that *Hamlet* was being performed, Mountfort escaped from her keepers and reached the theater, where she concealed herself until the scene in which Ophelia enters in her state of insanity. At this point, Mountfort rushed onto the stage and, in the words of a contemporary, "was in truth Ophelia herself, to the amazement of the performers and the astonishment of the audience."

That the character Ophelia became increasingly and decisively identified with the mad scene owes something to this occurrence, but it is also a consequence of the text used for Restoration performances of *Hamlet*. Having received the performance rights to a good number of Shakespeare's plays, Davenant altered them for the stage in the 1660s, and many of these acting versions remained in use for generations. In the case of *Hamlet*, neither Davenant nor his successors did what they so often did with other plays by Shakespeare, that is, alter the plot radically and interpolate other material. But many of the lines were cut or "improved." The cuts included most of Ophelia's sane speeches, such as her spirited retort to Laertes' moralizing; what remained made her part almost entirely an emblem of "female love melancholy."

Thomas Betterton (1635–1710), the prototype of the actor-manager, who would be the dominant figure in Shakespeare interpretation and in the theater generally through the nineteenth century, made Hamlet his premier role. A contemporary who saw his last performance in the part (at the age of seventy-four, a rather old Prince of Denmark) wrote that to *read* Shakespeare's play was to encounter "dry, incoherent, & broken sentences," but that to see Betterton was to "prove" that the play was written "correctly." Spectators especially admired his reaction to the Ghost's appearance in the Queen's bedchamber: "his Countenance . . . thro' the violent and sudden Emotions of Amazement and Horror, turn[ed] instantly on the Sight of his fathers Spirit, as pale as his Neckcloath, when every Article of his Body seem's affected with a Tremor inexpressible."

The Spanish Tragedie:

OR,

Hieronimo is mad againe.

Containing the lamentable end of *Don Horatio*, and *Belimperia*; with the pittifull death of *Hieronimo*.

Newly corrected, amended, and enlarged with new Additions of the *Painters* part, and others, as it hath of late been diuers times acted.

LONDON,
Printed by W. White, for I. White and T. Langley, and are to be sold at their Shop ouer against the Sarazens head without New-gate. 1615.

Title page of Thomas Kyd's *Spanish Tragedy* (1615). The first known edition dates from 1592.

A piece of stage business in this scene, Betterton's upsetting his chair on the Ghost's entrance, became so thoroughly identified with the part that later productions were censured if the actor left it out. This business could very well have been handed down from Richard Burbage, the star of Shakespeare's original production, for Davenant, who had coached Betterton in the role, had known the performances of Joseph Taylor, who had succeeded Burbage in it. It is strangely gratifying to notice that Hamlets on stage and screen still occasionally upset their chairs.

Shakespeare's Life and Art

Playwrights, even hugely successful playwrights, were not ordinarily the objects of popular curiosity in early modern England, and few personal documents survive from Shakespeare's life of the kind that usually give the biographies of artists their appeal: no diary, no letters, private or public, no accounts of his childhood, almost no contemporary gossip, no scandals. Shakespeare's exact contemporary the great playwright Christopher Marlowe, lived a mere twenty-nine years—he was murdered in 1593—but he left behind tantalizing glimpses of himself in police documents, the memos of high-ranking government officials, and detailed denunciations by sinister double agents. Ben Jonson recorded his opinions and his reading in a remarkable published notebook, *Timber; or, Discoveries made upon men and matter*, and he also shared his views of the world (including some criticisms of his fellow playwright Shakespeare) with a Scottish poet, William Drummond of Hawthornden, who had the wit to jot them down for posterity. From Shakespeare, there is nothing comparable, not even a book with his name scribbled on the cover and a few marginal notes such as we have for Jonson, let alone working notebooks.

Yet Elizabethan England was a record-keeping society, and centuries of archival labor have turned up a substantial number of traces of its greatest playwright and his family. By themselves the traces would have relatively little interest, but in the light of Shakespeare's plays and poems, they have come to seem like precious relics and manage to achieve a considerable resonance.

Shakespeare's Family

William Shakespeare's grandfather Richard farmed land by the village of Snitterfield, near the small, pleasant market town of Stratford-upon-Avon, about ninety-six miles north-west of London. The playwright's father, John, moved in the mid-sixteenth century to Stratford, where he became a successful glover, landowner, moneylender, and dealer in wool and other agricultural goods. In or about 1557, he married Mary Arden, the daughter of a prosperous and well-connected farmer from the same area, Robert Arden of Wilmcote.

John Shakespeare was evidently highly esteemed by his fellow townspeople, for he held a series of important posts in local government. In 1556, he was appointed ale taster, an office reserved for "able persons and discreet," in 1558 was sworn in as a constable, and in 1561 was elected as one of the town's fourteen burgesses. As burgess, John served as one of the two chamberlains, responsible for administering borough property and revenues. In 1567, he was elected bailiff, Stratford's highest elective office and the equivalent of mayor. Though John Shakespeare signed all official documents with a cross or other sign, it is likely, though not certain, that he knew how to read and write. Mary, who also signed documents only with her mark, is less likely to have been literate.

According to the parish registers, which recorded baptisms and burials, the Shake-speares had eight children, four daughters and four sons, beginning with a daughter Joan born in 1558. A second daughter, Margaret, was born in December 1562 and died a few months later. William Shakespeare ("Gulielmus, filius Johannes Shakespeare"), their first son, was baptized on April 26, 1564. Since there was usually a few days' lapse between birth and baptism, it is conventional to celebrate Shakespeare's birthday on April 23, which happens to coincide with the feast of St. George, England's patron saint, and with the day of Shakespeare's death fifty-two years later.

William Shakespeare had three younger brothers, Gilbert, Richard, and Edmund, and

"Southeast Prospect of Stratford-upon-Avon, 1746." From *The Gentleman's Magazine* (December 1792).

two younger sisters, Joan and Anne. (It was often the custom to recycle a name, so the first-born Joan must have died before the birth in 1569 of another daughter christened Joan, the only one of the girls to survive childhood.) Gilbert, who died in his forty-fifth year in 1612, is described in legal records as a Stratford haberdasher; Edmund followed William to London and became a professional actor, though evidently of no particular repute. He was only twenty-eight when he died in 1607 and was given an expensive funeral, perhaps paid for by his successful older brother.

At the high point of his public career, John Shakespeare, the father of this substantial family, applied to the Herald's College for a coat of arms, which would have marked his (and his family's) elevation from the ranks of substantial middle-class citizenry to that of the gentry. But the application went nowhere, for soon after he initiated what would have been a costly petitioning process, John apparently fell on hard times. The decline must have begun when William was still living at home, a boy of twelve or thirteen. From 1576 onward, John Shakespeare stopped attending council meetings. He became caught up in costly lawsuits, started mortgaging his land, and incurred substantial debts. In 1586, he was finally replaced on the council; in 1592, he was one of nine Stratford men listed as absenting themselves from church out of fear of being arrested for debt.

The reason for the reversal in John Shakespeare's fortunes is unknown. Some have speculated that it may have stemmed from adherence to Catholicism, since those who remained loyal to the old faith were subject to increasingly vigorous and costly discrimination. But if John Shakespeare was a Catholic, as seems quite possible, it would not necessarily explain his decline, since other Catholics (and Puritans) in Elizabethan Stratford and elsewhere managed to hold on to their offices. In any case, his fall from prosperity and local power, whatever its cause, was not absolute. In 1601, the last year of his life, his name was included among those qualified to speak on behalf of Stratford's rights. And he was by that time entitled to bear a coat of arms, for in 1596, some twenty years after the application to the Herald's office had been initiated, it was successfully renewed. There is no record of who paid for the bureaucratic procedures that made the grant possible, but it is likely to have been John's oldest son William, by that time a highly successful London playwright.

Education

Stratford was a small provincial town, but it had long been the site of an excellent free school, originally established by the church in the thirteenth century. The main purpose of such schools in the Middle Ages had been to train prospective clerics; since many aristocrats could neither read nor write, literacy by itself conferred no special distinction and was not routinely viewed as desirable. But the situation began to change markedly in the sixteenth century. Protestantism placed a far greater emphasis upon lay literacy: for the sake of salvation, it was crucially important to be intimately acquainted with the Holy Book, and printing made that book readily available. Schools became less strictly bound up with training for the church and more linked to the general acquisition of "literature," in the sense both of literacy and of cultural knowledge. In keeping with this new emphasis on reading and with humanist educational reform, the school was reorganized during the reign of Edward VI (1547–53). School records from the period have not survived, but it is almost certain that William Shakespeare attended the King's New School, as it was renamed in Edward's honor.

Scholars have painstakingly reconstructed the curriculum of schools of this kind and have even turned up the names and rather impressive credentials of the schoolmasters who taught there when Shakespeare was a student. (Shakespeare's principal teacher was Thomas Jenkins, an Oxford graduate, who received £20 a year and a rent-free house.) A child's education in Elizabethan England began at age four or five with two years at what was called the "petty school," attached to the main grammar school. The little scholars carried a "hornbook," a sheet of paper or parchment framed in wood and covered, for protection, with a transparent layer of horn. On the paper was written the alphabet and the Lord's Prayer, which were reproduced as well in the slightly more advanced *ABC with the Catechism,* a combination primer and rudimentary religious guide.

The Cholmondeley sisters, c. 1600–1610. This striking image brings to mind Shakespeare's fascination with twinship, both identical (notably in *The Comedy of Errors*) and fraternal (in *Twelfth Night*).

After students demonstrated some ability to read, the boys could go on, at about age seven, to the grammar school. Shakespeare's images of the experience are not particularly cheerful. In his famous account of the Seven Ages of Man, Jaques in *As You Like It* describes

> the whining schoolboy with his satchel
> And shining morning face, creeping like snail
> Unwillingly to school.
>
> (2.7.144–46)

The schoolboy would have crept quite early: the day began at 6:00 A.M. in summer and 7:00 A.M. in winter and continued until 5:00 P.M., with very few breaks or holidays.

At the core of the curriculum was the study of Latin, the mastery of which was in effect a prolonged male puberty rite involving much discipline and pain as well as pleasure. A late sixteenth-century Dutchman (whose name fittingly was Batty) proposed that God had created the human buttocks so that they could be severely beaten without risking permanent injury. Such thoughts dominated the pedagogy of the age, so that even an able young scholar, as we might imagine Shakespeare to have been, could scarcely have escaped recurrent flogging.

Shakespeare evidently reaped some rewards for the miseries he probably endured: his works are laced with echoes of many of the great Latin texts taught in grammar schools. One of his earliest comedies, *The Comedy of Errors,* is a brilliant variation on a theme by the Roman playwright Plautus, whom Elizabethan schoolchildren often performed as well as read; and one of his earliest tragedies, *Titus Andronicus,* is heavily indebted to Seneca. These are among the most visible of the classical influences that are often more subtly and pervasively interfused in Shakespeare's works. He seems to have had a particular fondness for *Aesop's Fables*, Apuleius's *Golden Ass*, and above all Ovid's *Metamorphoses*. His learned contemporary Ben Jonson remarked that Shakespeare had "small Latin and less Greek," but from this distance what is striking is not the limits of Shakespeare's learning but rather the unpretentious ease, intelligence, and gusto with which he draws upon what he must have first encountered as laborious study.

Traces of a Life

In November 1582, William Shakespeare, at the age of eighteen, married twenty-six-year-old Anne Hathaway, who came from the village of Shottery near Stratford. Their first daughter, Susanna, was baptized six months later. This circumstance, along with the fact that Anne was eight years Will's senior, has given rise to a mountain of speculation, all the more lurid precisely because there is no further evidence. Shakespeare depicts in several plays situations in which marriage is precipitated by a pregnancy, but he also registers, in *Measure for Measure* (1.2.125ff.), the Elizabethan belief that a "true contract" of marriage could be legitimately made and then consummated simply by the mutual vows of the couple in the presence of witnesses.

On February 2, 1585, the twins Hamnet and Judith Shakespeare were baptized in Stratford. Hamnet died at the age of eleven, when his father was already living for much of the year in London as a successful playwright. These are Shakespeare's only known children, though the playwright and impressario William Davenant in the mid-seventeenth century claimed to be his bastard son. Since people did not ordinarily advertise their illegitimacy, the claim, though impossible to verify, at least suggests the unusual strength of the Shakespeare's posthumous reputation.

William Shakespeare's father, John, died in 1601; his mother died seven years later. They would have had the satisfaction of witnessing their eldest son's prosperity, and not only from a distance, for in 1597 William purchased New Place, the second largest house in Stratford. In 1607, the playwright's daughter Susanna married a successful and well-known physician, John Hall. The next year, the Halls had a daughter, Elizabeth, Shakespeare's first grandchild. In 1616, the year of Shakespeare's death, his daughter Judith married a vintner, Thomas Quiney, with whom she had three children. Shakespeare's widow, Anne, died in 1623, at the age of sixty-seven. His first-born, Susanna, died at the age of sixty-six in 1649, the year that King Charles I was beheaded by the parliamentary army. Judith lived through Cromwell's Protectorate and on to the Restoration of the monarchy; she died in February 1662, at the age of seventy-seven. By the end of the century, the line of Shakespeare's direct heirs was extinct.

Patient digging in the archives has turned up other traces of Shakespeare's life as a family man and a man of means: assessments, small fines, real estate deeds, minor actions in court to collect debts. In addition to his fine Stratford house and a large garden and cottage facing it, Shakespeare bought substantial parcels of land in the vicinity. When in *The Tempest* the wedding celebration conjures up a vision of "barns and garners never empty," Shakespeare could have been glancing at what the legal documents record as his own "tithes of corn, grain, blade, and hay" in the fields near Stratford. At some point after 1610, Shakespeare seems to have begun to shift his attention from the London stage to his Stratford properties, though the term "retirement" implies a more decisive and definitive break than appears to have been the case. By 1613, when the Globe Theatre burned down during a performance of *All Is True* (*Henry VIII*), Shakespeare was probably residing for the most part in Stratford, but he retained his financial interest in the rebuilt playhouse and probably continued to have some links to his theatrical colleagues. Still, by this point, his career as a playwright was substantially over. Legal documents from his last years show him concerned to protect his real estate interests in Stratford.

A half-century after Shakespeare's death, a Stratford vicar and physician, John Ward, noted in his diary that Shakespeare and his fellow poets Michael Drayton and Ben Jonson "had a merry meeting, and it seems drank too hard, for Shakespeare died of a fever there contracted." It is not inconceivable that Shakespeare's last illness was somehow linked, if only coincidentally, to the festivities on the occasion of the wedding in February 1616 of his daughter Judith (who was still alive when Ward made his diary entry). In any case, on March 25, 1616, Shakespeare revised his will, and on April 23 he died. Two days later, he was buried in the chancel of Holy Trinity Church beneath a stone bearing an epitaph he is said to have devised:

> Good friend for Jesus' sake forbear,
> To dig the dust enclosed here:
> Blest be the man that spares these stones,
> And curst be he that moves my bones.

The verses are hardly among Shakespeare's finest, but they seem to have been effective: though bones were routinely dug up to make room for others—a fate imagined with unforgettable intensity in the graveyard scene in *Hamlet*—his own remains were undisturbed. Like other vestiges of sixteenth- and early seventeenth-century Stratford, Shakespeare's grave has for centuries now been the object of a tourist industry that borders on a religious cult.

Shakespeare's will has been examined with an intensity befitting this cult; every provision and formulaic phrase, no matter how minor or conventional, has borne a heavy weight of interpretation, none more so than the bequest to his wife, Anne, of only "my second-best bed." Scholars have pointed out that Anne would in any case have been provided for by custom and that the terms are not necessarily a deliberate slight, but the absence of the customary words "my loving wife" or "my well-beloved wife" is difficult to ignore.

Portrait of the Playwright as Young Provincial

The great problem with the surviving traces of Shakespeare's life is not that they are few but that they are a bit dull. Christopher Marlowe was a double or triple agent, accused of brawling, sodomy, and atheism. Ben Jonson, who somehow clambered up from bricklayer's apprentice to classical scholar, served in the army in Flanders, killed a fellow actor in a duel, converted to Catholicism in prison in 1598, and returned to the Church of England in 1610. Provincial real estate investments and the second-best bed cannot compete with such adventurous lives. Indeed, the relative ordinariness of Shakespeare's social background and life has contributed to a persistent current of speculation that the glover's son from Stratford-upon-Avon was not in fact the author of the plays attributed to him.

The anti-Stratfordians, as those who deny Shakespeare's authorship are sometimes called, almost always propose as the real author someone who came from a higher social class and received a more prestigious education. Francis Bacon, the Earl of Oxford, the Earl of Southampton, even Queen Elizabeth, have been advanced, among many others, as glamorous candidates for the role of clandestine playwright. Several famous people, including Mark Twain and Sigmund Freud, have espoused these theories, though very few scholars have joined them. Since Shakespeare was quite well-known in his own time as the author of the plays that bear his name, there would need to have been an extraordinary conspiracy to conceal the identity of the real master who (the theory goes) disdained to appear in the vulgarity of print or on the public stage. Like many conspiracy theories, the extreme implausibility of this one only seems to increase the fervent conviction of its advocates.

To the charge that a middle-class author from a small town could not have imagined the lives of kings and nobles, one can respond by citing the exceptional qualities that Ben Jonson praised in Shakespeare: "excellent *Phantsie*; brave notions, and gentle expressions." Even in ordinary mortals, the human imagination is a strange faculty; in Shakespeare, it seems to have been uncannily powerful, working its mysterious, transforming effects on everything he encountered. It is possible to study this power in his reworking of books by Raphael Holinshed, Plutarch, Ovid, Plautus, Seneca, and others. But books were clearly not the only objects of Shakespeare's attention; like most artists, he drew upon the whole range of his life experiences.

To integrate some of the probable circumstances of Shakespeare's early years with the particular shape of the theatrical imagination associated with his name, let us indulge briefly in the biographical daydreams that modern scholarship is supposed to have rendered forever obsolete. The vignettes that follow are conjectural, but they may suggest ways in which his life as we know it found its way into his art.

1. THE GOWN OF OFFICE

Shakespeare was a very young boy—not quite four years old—when his father was chosen by the Stratford council as the town bailiff. The bailiff of an Elizabethan town was a significant position; he served the borough as a justice of the peace and performed a variety of other functions, including coroner and clerk of the market. He dealt routinely with an unusually wide spectrum of local society, for on the one hand he distributed alms and on the other he negotiated with the lord of the manor. More to the point, for our purposes, the office was attended with considerable ceremony. The bailiff and his deputy were entitled to appear in public in furred gowns, attended by sergeants bearing maces before them. On Rogation Days (three days of prayer for the harvest, before Ascension Day), they would solemnly pace out the parish boundaries, and they would similarly walk in processions on market and fair days. On Sundays, the sergeants would accompany the bailiff to church, where he would sit with his wife in a front pew, and he would have a comparable seat of honor at sermons in the Guild Chapel. On special occasions, there would also be plays in the Guildhall, at which the bailiff would be seated in the front row.

On a precocious child (or even, for that matter, on an ordinary child), the effect of this ceremony would be at least threefold. First, the ceremony would convey irresistibly the power of clothes (the ceremonial gown of office) and of symbols (the mace) to transform identity as if by magic. Second, it would invest the father with immense power, distinction, and importance, awakening what we may call a lifelong dream of high station. And third, pulling slightly against this dream, it would provoke an odd feeling that the father's clothes do not fit, a perception that the office is not the same as the man, and an intimate, first-hand knowledge that when the robes are put off, their wearer is inevitably glimpsed in a far different, less exalted light.

2. PROGRESSES AND ELECTIONS

This second biographical fantasy, slightly less plausible than the first but still quite likely, involves a somewhat older child witnessing two characteristic forms of Elizabethan political ceremony, both of which were well-known in the provinces. Queen Elizabeth was fond of going on what were known as "Progresses," triumphant ceremonial journeys around her kingdom. Let us imagine that the young Shakespeare—say, in 1574, when he was ten years old—went with his kinsfolk or friends to Warwick, some eight miles distant, to witness a Progress. He would thus have participated as a spectator in an elaborate celebration of charismatic power: the courtiers in their gorgeous clothes, the nervous local officials bedecked in velvets and silks, and at the center, carried in a special litter like a painted idol, the bejeweled queen. Let us imagine further that in addition to being struck by the overwhelming force of this charisma, the boy was struck too by the way this force depended paradoxically on a sense that the queen was after all quite human. Elizabeth was in fact fond of calling attention to this peculiar tension between near-divinization and human ordinariness. For example, on this occasion at Warwick (and what follows really happened), after the trembling Recorder, presumably a local civil official of high standing, had made his official welcoming speech, Elizabeth offered her hand to him to be kissed: "Come hither, little Recorder," she said. "It was told me that you would be afraid to look upon me or to speak boldly; but you were not so afraid of me as I was of you; and I now thank you for putting me in mind of my duty." Of course, the charm of this royal "confession" of nervousness depends on its manifest implausibility: it is, in effect, a theatrical performance of humility by someone with immense confidence in her own histrionic power.

A royal Progress was not the only form of spectacular political activity that Shakespeare might well have seen in the 1570s; it is still more likely that he would have witnessed parliamentary elections, particularly since his father was qualified to vote. In 1571, 1572, 1575, and 1578, there were shire elections conducted in nearby Warwick, elections that would certainly have attracted well over a thousand voters. These were often memorable events: large crowds came together; there was usually heavy drinking and carnivalesque festivity; and at the same time, there was enacted, in a very different register from that of the monarchy, a ritual of empowerment. The people, those entitled to vote by virtue of meeting the property and residence requirements, chose their own representatives by giving their votes—their voices—to candidates for office. Here, legislative sovereignty was conferred not by God but by the consent of the community, a consent marked by shouts and applause.

Recent cultural historians have been so fascinated by the evident links between the spectacles of the absolutist monarchy and the theater that they have largely ignored the significance of this alternative public arena, one that generated intense excitement throughout the country. A child who was a spectator at a parliamentary election in the 1570s might well have found the occasion enormously compelling. It is striking, in any case, how often the adult Shakespeare returns to scenes of acclamation and mass consent, and striking too how much the theater depends on the soliciting of popular voices.

3. EXORCISMS

A third and final Shakespearean fantasy is even more speculative than the second and involves a controversial discovery. It is a fact that in April 1757, the owner of Shakespeare's birthplace in Stratford decided to retile the roof. One of the workmen, described as of "very honest, sober, industrious character," found an old document between the rafters and the tiling. The document, six leaves stitched together, was a profession of faith in fourteen articles, conspicuously Catholic in form; it was, if genuine (for the original has disappeared), by John Shakespeare. The clear implication of this find, that the playwright was probably brought up in a Roman Catholic household in a time of official suspicion and persecution of recusancy, has found support in a recent biographical study by E. A. J. Honigmann. Honigmann has turned up a network of interlinked Catholic families in Lancashire with whom one "William Shakeshafte," possibly a young schoolmaster or player, was connected in the late 1570s or early 1580s.

Accepting for the moment that William Shakespeare was raised in the recusant faith of his father, let us imagine that one day in the early 1580s the young man attended a strange and extraordinary event: an exorcism conducted in secret in the house of a member of the Catholic gentry. These events, though illegal and potentially dangerous, were fairly common in the period and are known to have drawn substantial crowds. The rituals were generally conducted by Jesuits, living in hiding and under constant threat of torture and execution, and centered on the spectacular struggle between the sacred authority of the church and the obscene, blasphemous, and tenacious demons lodged deep within the demoniacs' tortured bodies. Elizabethan authorities were alarmed by the compelling power of exorcisms, which they regarded, not without some justification, as highly self-conscious Catholic propaganda. (The demons, speaking from within the possessed, had the disquieting habit of declaring their admiration for Martin Luther and John Calvin.) Official spokesmen repeatedly stigmatized the rituals as a form of illicit theater: a "play of sacred miracles," a "wonderful pageant," a "devil Theater."

Exorcism: Nicole Aubry, in the Cathedral at Laon, 1566.

The young Shakespeare, whether

true believer or skeptic or something in between ("So have I heard, and do in part believe it," says Hamlet's friend Horatio [1.1.146]), might have carried away from such an occasion several impressions: an awareness that strange, alien voices may speak from within ordinary, familiar bodies; a sense of the irresistible power of illusion; an intimation of immense, cosmic forces that may impinge upon human life; a belief in the possibility of making contact with these forces and compelling them to speak.

These imaginary portraits of the playwright as a young provincial introduce us to several of the root conditions of the Elizabethan theater. Biographical fantasies, though entirely speculative and playful, are useful in part because some people have found it difficult to conceive how Shakespeare, with his provincial roots and his restricted range of experience, could have so rapidly and completely mastered the central imaginative themes of his times. Moreover, it is sometimes difficult to grasp how seeming abstractions such as market society, monarchical state, and theological doctrine were actually experienced directly by peculiar, distinct individuals. Shakespeare's plays were social and collective events, but they also bore the stamp of a particular artist, one endowed with a remarkable capacity to craft lifelike illusions (what Jonson called "excellent *Phantsie*"), a daring willingness to articulate an original vision ("brave notions"), and a loving command, at once precise and generous, of language ("gentle expressions"). These plays are stitched together from shared cultural experiences, inherited dramatic devices, and the pungent vernacular of the day, but we should not lose sight of the extent to which they articulate an intensely personal vision, a bold shaping of the available materials. Four centuries of feverish biographical speculation, much of it foolish, bears witness to a basic intuition: the richness of these plays, their inexhaustible openness, is the consequence not only of the auspicious collective conditions of the culture but also of someone's exceptional skill, inventiveness, and courage at taking those conditions and making of them something rich and strange.

The Theater of the Nation

What precisely are the collective conditions highlighted by these vignettes? First, the growth of Stratford-upon-Avon, the bustling market town of which John Shakespeare was bailiff, is a small version of a momentous sixteenth-century development that made Shakespeare's career possible: the making of an urban "public." That development obviously depended on adequate numbers; the period experienced a rapid and still unexplained growth in population. With it came an expansion and elaboration of market relations: markets became less periodic, more continuous, and more abstract—centered, that is, not on the familiar materiality of goods but on the liquidity of capital and goods. In practical terms, this meant that it was possible to conceive of the theater not only as festive entertainment for special events—lord mayor's pageants, visiting princes, seasonal festivals, and the like—but as a permanent, year-round business venture. The venture relied on ticket sales—it was an innovation of this period to have money advanced in the expectation of pleasure rather than offered to servants afterward as a reward—and counted on habitual playgoing with a concomitant demand for new plays from competing theater companies: "But that's all one, our play is done," sings Feste at the end of *Twelfth Night* and adds a glance toward the next afternoon's proceeds: "And we'll strive to please you every day" (5.1.394–95.

Second, the royal Progress is an instance of what the anthropologist Clifford Geertz has called the Theater State, a state that manifests its power and meaning in exemplary public performances. Professional companies of players, like the one Shakespeare belonged to, understood well that they existed in relation to this Theater State and would, if they were fortunate, be called upon to serve it. Unlike Ben Jonson, Shakespeare did not, as far as we know, write royal entertainments on commission, but his plays were frequently performed before Queen Elizabeth and then before King James and Queen Anne, along with their courtiers and privileged guests. There are many fascinating glimpses of these performances, including a letter from Walter Cope to Robert Cecil, early in James's reign. "Burbage is come," Cope writes, referring to the leading actor of Shakespeare's company, "and says there is no new play that the queen hath not seen, but they have revived an old one, called *Love's Labours Lost*, which for wit and mirth he says will please her exceedingly. And this is appointed to be played tomorrow night at my Lord of Southampton's." Not only would such theatrical performances have given great pleasure—evidently, the queen had already exhausted the company's new offerings—but they conferred prestige upon those who commanded them and those in whose honor they were mounted.

Monarchical power in the period was deeply allied to spectacular manifestations of the ruler's glory and disciplinary authority. The symbology of power depended on regal magnificence, reward, punishment, and pardon, all of which were heavily theatricalized. Indeed, the conspicuous public display does not simply serve the interests of power; on many occasions in the period, power seemed to exist in order to make pageantry possible, as if the nation's identity were only fully realized in theatrical performance. It would be easy to exaggerate this perception: the subjects of Queen Elizabeth and King James were acutely aware of the distinction between shadow and substance. But they were fascinated by the political magic through which shadows could be taken for substantial realities, and the ruling elite was largely complicit in the formation and celebration of a charismatic absolutism. At the same time, the claims of the monarch who professes herself or himself to be not the representative of the nation but its embodiment were set against the counter-claims of the House of Commons. And this institution too, as we have glimpsed, had its own theatrical rituals, centered on the crowd whose shouts of approval, in heavily stage-managed elections, chose the individuals who would stand for the polity and participate in deliberations held in a hall whose resemblance to a theater did not escape contemporary notice.

Third, illicit exorcism points both to the theatricality of much religious ritual in the late Middle Ages and the Renaissance and to the heightened possibility of secularization. English Protestant authorities banned the medieval mystery plays, along with pilgrimages and other rituals associated with holy shrines and sacred images, but playing companies could satisfy at least some of the popular longings and appropriate aspects of the social energy no longer allowed a theological outlet. That is, official attacks on certain Catholic practices made it more possible for the public theater to appropriate and exploit their allure. Hence, for example, the plays that celebrated the solemn miracle of the Catholic Mass were banned, along with the most elaborate church vestments, but in *The Winter's Tale* Dion can speak in awe of what he witnessed at Apollo's temple:

> I shall report,
> For most it caught me, the celestial habits—
> Methinks I so should term them—and the reverence
> Of the grave wearers. O, the sacrifice—
> How ceremonious, solemn, and unearthly
> It was i'th' off'ring!
>
> (3.1.3–8)

And at the play's end, the statue of the innocent mother breathes, comes to life, and embraces her child.

The theater in Shakespeare's time, then, is intimately bound up with all three crucial cultural formations: the market society, the theater state, and the church. But it is important to note that the institution is not *identified* with any of them. The theater may be a market phenomenon, but it is repeatedly and bitterly attacked as the enemy of diligent, sober, productive economic activity. Civic authorities generally regarded the theater as a pestilential nuisance, a parasite on the body of the commonwealth, a temptation to students, apprentices, housewives, even respectable merchants to leave their serious business and lapse into idleness and waste. That waste, it might be argued, could be partially recuperated if it went for the glorification of a guild or the entertainment of an important dignitary, but the only group regularly profiting from the theater were the players and their disreputable associates.

For his part, Shakespeare made a handsome profit from the commodification of theatrical entertainment, but he seems never to have written "city comedy"—plays set in London and more or less explicitly concerned with market relations—and his characters express deep reservations about the power of money and commerce: "That smooth-faced gentleman, tickling commodity," Philip the Bastard observes in *King John*, "wins of all, / Of kings, of beggars, old men, young men, maids" (2.1.570–74). We could argue that the smooth-faced gentleman is none other than Shakespeare himself, for his drama famously mingles kings and clowns, princesses and panderers. But the mingling is set against a romantic current of social conservatism: in *Twelfth Night*, the aristocratic heiress Olivia falls in love with someone who appears far beneath her in wealth and social station, but it is revealed that he (and his sister Viola) are of noble blood; in *The Winter's Tale*, Leontes' daughter Perdita is raised as a shepherdess, but her noble nature shines through her humble upbringing, and she marries the Prince of Bohemia; the strange island maiden with whom Ferdinand, son of the King of Naples, falls madly in love in *The Tempest* turns out to be the daughter of the rightful Duke of Milan. Shakespeare pushes against this conservative logic in *All's Well That Ends Well*, but the noble young Bertram violently resists the unequal match thrust upon him by the King, and the play's mood is notoriously uneasy.

Similarly, Shakespeare's theater may have been patronized and protected by the monarchy—after 1603, his company received a royal patent and was known as the King's Men—but it was by no means identical in its interests or its ethos. To be sure, *Richard III* and *Macbeth* incorporate aspects of royal propaganda, but given the realities of censorship, Shakespeare's plays, and the period's drama as a whole, are surprisingly independent and complex in their political vision. There is, in any case, a certain inherent tension between kings and player kings: Elizabeth and James may both have likened themselves to actors onstage, but they were loath to admit their dependence on the applause and money, freely given or freely withheld, of the audience. The charismatic monarch insists that the sacredness of authority resides in the body of the ruler, not in a costume that may be worn and then discarded by an actor. Kings are not *representations* of power—or do not admit that they are—but claim to be the thing itself. The government institution that was actually based on the idea of representation, Parliament, had theatrical elements, as we have seen, but it significantly excluded any audience from its deliberations. And Shakespeare's oblique portraits of parliamentary representatives, the tribunes Sicinius Velutus and Junius Brutus in *Coriolanus*, are anything but flattering.

Finally, the theater drew significant energy from the liturgy and rituals of the late medieval church, but as Shakespeare's contemporaries widely remarked, the playhouse and the church were scarcely natural allies. Not only did the theater represent a potential competitor to worship services, and not only did ministers rail against prostitution and other vices associated with playgoing, but theatrical representation itself, even when ostensibly pious, seemed to many to empty out whatever it presented, turning substance into mere show. The theater could and did use the period's deep currents of religious feeling, but it had to do so carefully and with an awareness of conflicting interests.

Shakespeare Comes to London

How did Shakespeare decide to turn his prodigious talents to the stage? When did he make his way to London? How did he get his start? To these and similar questions we have a mountain of speculation but no secure answers. There is not a single surviving record of Shakespeare's existence from 1585, when his twins were baptized in Stratford church, until 1592, when a rival London playwright made an envious remark about him. In the late seventeenth century, the delightfully eccentric collector of gossip John Aubrey was informed that prior to moving to London the young Shakespeare had been a schoolteacher in the country. Aubrey also recorded a story that Shakespeare had been a rather unusual apprentice butcher: "When he killed a calf, he would do it in a high style, and make a speech."

These and other legends, including one that has Shakespeare whipped for poaching game, fill the void until the unmistakable reference in Robert Greene's *Groats-worth of Wit Bought with a Million of Repentaunce* (1592). An inspired hack writer with a university education, a penchant for self-dramatization, a taste for wild living, and a strong streak of resentment, Greene, in his early thirties, was dying in poverty when he penned his last farewell, piously urging his fellow dramatists Christopher Marlowe, Thomas Nashe, and George Peele to abandon the wicked stage before they were brought low, as he had been, by a new arrival: "For there is an upstart crow, beautified with our feathers, that with his 'Tiger's heart wrapped in player's hide' supposes he is as well able to bombast out a blank verse as the best of you, and, being an absolute *Johannes Factotum*, is in his own conceit the only Shake-scene in a country." If "Shake-scene" is not enough to identify the object of his attack, Greene parodies a line from Shakespeare's early play *Richard Duke of York (3 Henry VI)*: "O tiger's heart wrapped in a woman's hide!" (1.4.138). Greene is accusing Shakespeare of being an upstart, a plagiarist, an egomaniacal jack-of-all-trades—and, above all perhaps, a popular success.

By 1592, then, Shakespeare had already arrived on the highly competitive London theatrical scene. He was successful enough to be attacked by Greene and, a few months later, defended by Henry Chettle, another hack writer who had seen Greene's manuscript through the press (or, some scholars speculate, had written the attack himself and passed it off as the dying Greene's). Chettle expresses his regret that he did not suppress Greene's diatribe and spare Shakespeare "because myself have seen his demeanor no less civil than he excellent in the quality he professes." Besides, Chettle adds, "divers of worship have reported his uprightness of dealing, which argues his honesty and his facetious [polished] grace in writing that approves his art." "Divers of worship": not only was Shakespeare established as an accomplished writer and actor, but he evidently had aroused the attention and the approbation of several socially prominent people. In Elizabethan England, aristocratic patronage, with the money, protection, and prestige it alone could provide, was probably a professional writer's most important asset.

This patronage, or at least Shakespeare's quest for it, is most visible in the dedications in 1593 and 1594 of his narrative poems *Venus and Adonis* and *The Rape of Lucrece* to the young nobleman Henry Wriothesley, Earl of Southampton. It may be glimpsed as well, perhaps, in the sonnets, with their extraordinary adoration of the fair youth, though the identity of that youth has never been determined. What return Shakespeare got for his exquisite offerings is likewise unknown. We do know that among wits and gallants, the narrative poems won Shakespeare a fine reputation as an immensely stylish and accomplished poet. An amateur play performed at Cambridge University at the end of the sixteenth century, *The Return from Parnassus*, makes fun of this vogue, as a foolish character effusively declares, "I'll worship sweet Mr. Shakespeare, and to honour him will lay his *Venus and Adonis* under my pillow." Many readers at the time may have done so: the poem went through sixteen editions before 1640, more than any other work by Shakespeare.

Patronage was crucially important not only for individual artists but also for the actors, playwrights, and investors who pooled their resources to form professional theater companies. The public playhouses had enemies, especially among civic and religious authorities, who wished greatly to curb performances or to ban them altogether. An act of 1572 included players among those classified as vagabonds, threatening them therefore with the horrible punishments meted out to those regarded as economic parasites. The players' escape route was to be nominally enrolled as the servants of high-ranking noblemen. The legal fiction was that their public performances were a kind of rehearsal for the command performances before the patron or the monarch.

When Shakespeare came to London, presumably in the late 1580s, there were more than a dozen of these companies operating under the patronage of various aristocrats. We do not know for which of these companies, several of which had toured in Stratford, he originally worked, nor whether he began, as legend has it, as a prompter's assistant and then graduated to acting and playwriting. Shakespeare is listed among the actors in Ben Jonson's *Every Man in His Humour* (performed in 1598) and *Sejanus* (performed in 1603), but we do not know for certain what roles he played, nor are there records of any of his other performances. Tradition has it that he played Adam in *As You Like It* and the Ghost in *Hamlet*, but he was clearly not one of the leading actors of the day.

By the 1590s, the number of playing companies in London had been considerably reduced, in part through competition and in part through legislative restriction. (In 1572, knights and gentry lost the privilege of patronizing a troupe of actors; in 1598, justices of the peace lost the power to authorize performances.) By the early years of the seventeenth century, there were usually only three companies competing against one another in any season, along with two children's companies, which were often successful at drawing audiences away from the public playhouses. Shakespeare may initially have been associated with the Earl of Leicester's company or with the company of Ferdinando Stanley, Lord Strange; both groups included actors with whom Shakespeare was later linked. Or he may have belonged to the Earl of Pembroke's Men, since there is evidence that they performed *The Taming of a Shrew* and a version of *Richard Duke of York (3 Henry VI)*. At any event,

by 1594, Shakespeare was a member of the Lord Chamberlain's Men, for his name, along with those of Will Kempe and Richard Burbage, appears on a record of those "servants to the Lord Chamberlain" paid for performance at the royal palace at Greenwich on December 26 and 28. Shakespeare stayed with this company, which during the reign of King James received royal patronage and became the King's Men, for the rest of his career.

Many playwrights in Shakespeare's time worked freelance, moving from company to company as opportunities arose, collaborating on projects, adding scenes to old plays, scrambling from one enterprise to another. But certain playwrights, among them the most successful, wrote for a single company, often agreeing contractually to give that company exclusive rights to their theatrical works. Shakespeare seems to have followed such a pattern. For the Lord Chamberlain's Men, he wrote an average of two plays per year. His company initially performed in The Theatre, a playhouse built in 1576 by an entrepreneurial carpenter, James Burbage, the father of the actor Richard, who was to perform many of Shakespeare's greatest roles. When in 1597 their lease on this playhouse expired, the Lord Chamberlain's Men passed through a difficult and

Edward Alleyn (1566–1626). Artist unknown. Alleyn was the great tragic actor of the Lord Admiral's Men (the principal rival to Shakespeare's company). He was famous especially for playing the great Marlovian heroes.

legally perilous time, but they formed a joint-stock company, raising sufficient capital to lease a site and put up a splendid new playhouse in the suburb of Southwark, on the south bank of the Thames. This playhouse, the Globe, opened in 1599. Shakespeare is listed in the legal agreement as one of the principal investors, and when the company began to use Blackfriars as their indoor playhouse around 1609, he was a major shareholder in that theater as well. The Lord Chamberlain's Men, later the King's Men, dominated the theater scene, and the shares were quite valuable. Then as now, the theater was an extremely risky enterprise—most of those who wrote plays and performed in them made pathetically little money—but Shakespeare was a notable exception. The fine house in Stratford and the coat of arms he succeeded in acquiring were among the fruits of his multiple mastery, as actor, playwright, and investor of the London stage.

The Shakespearean Trajectory

Though Shakespeare's England was in many ways a record-keeping society, no reliable record survives that details the performances, year by year, in the London theaters. Every play had to be licensed by a government official, the Master of the Revels, but the records kept by the relevant officials from 1579 to 1621, Sir Edmund Tilney and Sir George Buc, have not survived. A major theatrical entrepreneur, Philip Henslowe, kept a careful account of his expenditures, including what he paid for the scripts he commissioned, but unfortunately Henslowe's main business was with the Rose and the Fortune theaters and not with the playhouses at which Shakespeare's company performed. A comparable ledger must have been kept by the shareholders of the Lord Chamberlain's Men, but it has not survived. Shakespeare himself apparently had no interest in preserving for posterity the sum of his writings, let alone in clarifying the chronology of his works or in specifying which plays he wrote alone and which with collaborators.

The principal source for Shakespeare's works is the 1623 Folio volume of *Mr. William Shakespeares Comedies, Histories, & Tragedies.* Most scholars believe that the editors were careful to include only those plays for which they knew Shakespeare to be the main author. Their edition does not, however, include any of Shakespeare's nondramatic poems, and it omits two plays in which Shakespeare is now thought to have had a significant hand, *Pericles, Prince of Tyre* and *The Two Noble Kinsmen,* along with his probable contribution to the multi-authored *Sir Thomas More.* (A number of other plays were attributed to Shakespeare, both before and after his death, but scholars have not generally accepted any of these into the established canon.) Moreover, the Folio edition does not print the plays in chronological order, nor does it attempt to establish a chronology. We do not know how much time would normally have

IF YOV KNOW NOT ME,
You know no body.
OR,
The troubles of Queene ELIZABETH.

LONDON.
Printed by B.A. and T.F. for *Nathanael Butter.* 1632.

Title page of *If You Know Not Me, You Know No Body; or, the Troubles of Queene Elizabeth* (1632).

elapsed between the writing of a play and its first performance, nor, with a few exceptions, do we know with any certainty the month or even the year of the first performance of any of Shakespeare's plays. The quarto editions of those plays that were published during Shakespeare's lifetime obviously establish a date by which we know a given play had been written, but they give us little more than an end point, because there was likely to be a substantial though indeterminate gap between the first performance of a play and its publication.

With enormous patience and ingenuity, however, scholars have gradually assembled a considerable archive of evidence, both external and internal, for dating the composition of the plays. Besides actual publication, the external evidence includes explicit reference to a play, a record of its performance, or (as in the case of Greene's attack on the "upstart crow") the quoting of a line, though all of these can be maddeningly ambiguous. The most important single piece of external evidence appears in 1598 in *Palladis Tamia*, a long book of jumbled reflections by Francis Meres that includes a survey of the contemporary literary scene. Meres finds that "the sweet, witty soul of Ovid lives in mellifluous and honey-tongued Shakespeare, witness his *Venus and Adonis*, his *Lucrece*, his sugered Sonnets among his private friends, etc." Meres goes on to list Shakespeare's accomplishments as a playwright as well:

> As Plautus and Seneca are accounted the best for Comedy and Tragedy among the Latins: so Shakespeare among the English is the most excellent in both kinds for the stage; for Comedy, witness his *Gentlemen of Verona*, his *Errors*, his *Love labors lost*, his *Love labours won*, his *Midsummers night dream*, & his *Merchant of Venice*: for Tragedy his *Richard the 2*, *Richard the 3*, *Henry the 4*, *King John*, *Titus Andronicus* and his *Romeo and Juliet*.

Meres thus provides a date by which twelve of Shakespeare's plays had definitely appeared (including one, *Love's Labour's Won*, that appears to have been lost). Unfortunately, Meres provides no clues about the order of appearance of these plays, and there are no other comparable lists.

Faced with the limitations of the external evidence, scholars have turned to a bewildering array of internal evidence, ranging from datable sources and topical allusions on the one hand to evolving stylistic features (ratio of verse to prose, percentage of rhyme to blank verse, colloquialisms, use of extended similes, and the like) on the other. Thus, for example, a cluster of plays with a high percentage of rhymed verse may follow closely upon Shakespeare's writing of the rhymed poems *Venus and Adonis* and *The Rape of Lucrece* and therefore be datable to 1594–95. Similarly, vocabulary overlap probably indicates proximity in composition, so if four or five plays share relatively "rare" vocabulary, it is likely that they were written in roughly the same period. Again, there seems to be a pattern in Shakespeare's use of colloquialisms, with a steady increase from *As You Like It* (1599–1600) to *Coriolanus* (1608), followed in the late romances by a retreat from the colloquial.

More sophisticated computer analysis should provide further guidance in the future, though the precise order of the plays, still very much in dispute, is never likely to be settled to universal satisfaction. Still, certain broad patterns are now widely accepted. These patterns can be readily grasped in the *Norton Shakespeare*, which presents the plays in the chronological order proposed by the Oxford editors.

Shakespeare began his career, probably in the early 1590s, by writing both comedies and history plays. The attack by Greene suggests that he made his mark with the series of theatrically vital but rather crude plays based on the foreign and domestic broils that erupted during the unhappy reign of the Lancastrian Henry VI. Modern readers and audiences are more likely to find the first sustained evidence of unusual power in *Richard III* (c. 1592), a play that combines a brilliantly conceived central character, a dazzling command of histrionic rhetoric, and an overarching moral vision of English history.

At virtually the same time that he was setting his stamp on the genre of the history play, Shakespeare was writing his first—or first surviving—comedies. Here, there are even fewer signs than in the histories of an apprenticeship: *The Comedy of Errors*, one of his early efforts in this genre, already displays a rare command of the resources of comedy: mistaken identity, madcap confusion, and the threat of disaster, giving way in the end to reconciliation, recovery, and love. Shakespeare's other comedies from the early 1590s, *The Taming of the Shrew*, *The Two Gentlemen of Verona*, and *Love's Labour's Lost*, are no less remarkable for their sophisticated variations on familiar comic themes, their inexhaustible rhetorical inventiveness, and their poignant intimation, in the midst of festive celebration, of loss.

Successful as are these early histories and comedies, and indicative of an extraordinary theatrical talent, Shakespeare's achievement in the later 1590s would still have been all but impossible to foresee. Starting with *A Midsummer Night's Dream* (c. 1595), Shakespeare wrote an unprecedented series of romantic comedies—*The Merchant of Venice*, *The Merry Wives of Windsor*, *Much Ado About Nothing*, *As You Like It*, and *Twelfth Night* (c. 1602)—whose poetic richness and emotional complexity remain unmatched. In the same period, he wrote a sequence of profoundly searching and ambitious history plays—*Richard II*, *1* and *2 Henry IV*, and *Henry V*—which together explore the death throes of feudal England and the birth of the modern nation-state ruled by a charismatic monarch. Both the comedies and histories of this period are marked by their capaciousness, their ability to absorb characters who press up against the outermost boundaries of the genre: the comedy *Merchant of Venice* somehow contains the figure, at once nightmarish and poignant, of Shylock, while the *Henry IV* plays, with their somber vision of crisis in the family and the state, bring to the stage one of England's greatest comic characters, Falstaff.

If in the mid to late 1590s Shakespeare reached the summit of his art in two major genres, he also manifested a lively interest in a third. As early as 1593, he wrote the crudely violent tragedy *Titus Andronicus*, the first of several plays on themes from Roman history, and a year or two later, in *Richard II*, he created in the protagonist a figure who achieves by the play's close the stature of a tragic hero. In the same year that Shakespeare wrote the wonderfully farcical "Pyramus and Thisbe" scene in *A Midsummer Night's Dream*, he probably also wrote the deeply tragic realization of the same story in *Romeo and Juliet*. But once again, the lyric anguish of *Romeo and Juliet* and the tormented self-revelation of *Richard II*, extraordinary as they are, could not have led anyone to predict the next phase of Shakespeare's career, the great tragic dramas that poured forth in the early years of the seventeenth century: *Hamlet*, *Othello*, *King Lear*, *Macbeth*, *Antony and Cleopatra*, and *Coriolanus*. These plays, written from 1601 to 1607, seem to mark a major shift in sensibility, an existential and metaphysical darkening that many readers think must have originated in a deep personal anguish, perhaps caused by the death of Shakespeare's father, John, in 1601.

Whatever the truth of these speculations—and we have no direct, personal testimony either to support or to undermine them—there appears to have occurred in the same period a shift as well in Shakespeare's comic sensibility. The comedies written between 1601 and 1604, *Troilus and Cressida*, *All's Well That Ends Well*, and *Measure for Measure*, are sufficiently different from the earlier comedies—more biting in tone, more uneasy with comic conventions, more ruthlessly questioning of the values of the characters and the resolutions of the plots—to have led many twentieth-century scholars to classify them as "problem plays" or "dark comedies." This category has recently begun to fall out of favor, since Shakespeare criticism is perfectly happy to demonstrate that *all* of the plays are "problem plays." But there is another group of plays, among the last Shakespeare wrote, that continue to constitute a distinct category. *Pericles*, *Cymbeline*, *The Winter's Tale*, and *The Tempest*, written between 1608 and 1611, when the playwright had developed a remarkably fluid, dreamlike sense of plot and a poetic style that could veer, apparently effortlessly, from the tortured to the ineffably sweet, are known as the "romances." These plays share an interest in the moral and emotional life less of the adolescents who dominate the earlier comedies than of their parents. The romances are deeply concerned with patterns of loss and recovery, suffering and redemption, despair and renewal. They have seemed to many critics to constitute a deliberate conclusion to a career that began in histories and comedies and passed through the dark and tormented tragedies.

One effect of the practice of printing Shakespeare's plays in a reconstructed chronological order, as this edition does, is to produce a kind of authorial plot, a progress from youthful exuberance and a heroic grappling with history, through psychological anguish and radical doubt, to a mature serenity built upon an understanding of loss. The ordering of Shakespeare's "complete works" in this way reconstitutes the figure of the author as the beloved hero of his own, lived romance. There are numerous reasons to treat this romance with considerable skepticism: the precise order of the plays remains in dispute, the obsessions of the earliest plays crisscross with those of the last, the drama is a collaborative art form, and the relation between authorial consciousness and theatrical representation is murky. Yet a longing to identify Shakespeare's personal trajectory, to chart his psychic and spiritual as well as professional progress, is all but irresistible.

The Fetishism of Dress

Whatever the personal resonance of Shakespeare's own life, his art is deeply enmeshed in the collective hopes, fears, and fantasies of his time. For example, throughout his plays, Shakespeare draws heavily upon his culture's investment in costume, symbols of authority, visible signs of status—the fetishism of dress he must have witnessed from early childhood. Disguise in his drama is often assumed to be incredibly effective: when Henry V borrows a cloak, when Portia dresses in a jurist's robes, when Viola puts on a young man's suit, it is as if each has become unrecognizable, as if identity resided in clothing. At the end of Twelfth Night, even though Viola's true identity has been disclosed, Orsino continues to call her Cesario; he will do so, he says, until she resumes her maid's garments, for only then will she be transformed into a woman:

> Cesario, come—
> For so you shall be while you are a man;
> But when in other habits you are seen,
> Orsino's mistress, and his fancy's queen.
> (5.1.372–75)

The pinnacle of this fetishism of costume is the royal crown, for whose identity-conferring power men are willing to die, but the principle is everywhere from the filthy blanket that transforms Edgar into Poor Tom to the coxcomb that is the badge of the licensed fool. Antonio, wishing to express his utter contempt, spits on Shylock's "Jewish gaberdine," as if the clothing were the essence of the man; Kent, pouring insults on the loathsome Oswald, calls him a "filthy worsted-stocking knave"; and innocent Innogen, learning that her husband has ordered her murder, thinks of herself as an expensive cast-off dress, destined to be ripped at the seams:

> Poor I am stale, a garment out of fashion,
> And for I am richer than to hang by th' walls
> I must be ripped. To pieces with me!
> (Cymbeline 3.4.50–52)

What can be said, thought, felt, in this culture seems deeply dependent on the clothes one wears—clothes that one is, in effect, *permitted* or *compelled* to wear, since there is little freedom in dress. Shakespearean drama occasionally represents something like such freedom: after all, Viola in Twelfth Night chooses to put off her "maiden weeds," as does Rosalind, who declares, "We'll have a swashing and a martial outside" (As You Like It 1.3.114). But these choices are characteristically made under the pressure of desperate circumstances, here shipwreck and exile. Part of the charm of Shakespeare's heroines is their ability to transform distress into an opportunity for self-fashioning, but the plays often suggest that there is less autonomy than meets the eye. What looks like an escape from cultural determinism may be only a deeper form of constraint. We may take, as an allegorical emblem of this constraint, the transformation of the beggar Christopher Sly in the playful Induction to *The Taming of the Shrew* into a nobleman. The transformation seems to suggest that you are free to make of yourself whatever you choose to be—the play begins with the drunken Sly indignantly claiming the dignity of his pedigree ("Look in the Chronicles" [Induction 1.3–4])—but in fact he is only the subject of the mischievous lord's experiment, designed to demonstrate the interwovenness of clothing and identity. "What think you," the lord asks his huntsman,

> if he were conveyed to bed,
> Wrapped in sweet clothes, rings put upon his fingers,
> A most delicious banquet by his bed,
> And brave attendants near him when he wakes—
> Would not the beggar then forget himself?

To which the huntsman replies, in words that underscore the powerlessness of the drunken beggar, "Believe me, lord, I think he cannot choose" (Induction 1.33–38).

Petruccio's taming of Katherine is similarly constructed around an imposition of identity, an imposition closely bound up with the right to wear certain articles of clothing. When the haberdasher arrives with a fashionable lady's hat, Petruccio refuses it over his wife's vehement objections: "This doth fit the time, / And gentlewomen wear such caps as these." "When you are gentle," Petruccio replies, "you shall have one, too, / And not till then" (4.3.69–72). At the play's close, Petruccio demonstrates his authority by commanding his tamed wife to throw down her cap: "Off with that bauble, throw it underfoot" (5.2.126). Here as elsewhere in Shakespeare, acts of robing and disrobing are intensely charged, a charge that culminates in the trappings of monarchy. When Richard II, in a scene that was probably censored during the reign of Elizabeth from the stage as well as the printed text, is divested of his crown and scepter, he experiences the loss as the eradication of his name, the symbolic melting away of his identity:

> Alack the heavy day,
> That I have worn so many winters out
> And know not now what name to call myself!
> O, that I were a mockery king of snow,
> Standing before the sun of Bolingbroke
> To melt myself away in water-drops!
>
> (4.1.255–60)

When Lear tears off his regal "lendings" in order to reduce himself to the nakedness of the Bedlam beggar, he is expressing not only his radical loss of social identity but the breakdown of his psychic order as well, expressing therefore his reduction to the condition of the "poor bare forked animal" that is the primal condition of undifferentiated existence. And when Cleopatra determines to kill herself in order to escape public humiliation in Rome, she magnificently affirms her essential being by arraying herself as she had once done to encounter Antony:

> Show me, my women, like a queen. Go fetch
> My best attires. I am again for Cydnus
> To meet Mark Antony.
>
> (5.2.223–25)

Such scenes are a remarkable intensification of the everyday symbolic practice of Renaissance English culture, its characteristically deep and knowing commitment to illusion: "I know perfectly well that the woman in her crown and jewels and gorgeous gown is an aging, irascible, and fallible mortal—she herself virtually admits as much—yet I profess that she is the virgin queen, timelessly beautiful, wise, and just." Shakespeare understood how close this willed illusion was to the spirit of the theater, to the actors' ability to work on what the chorus in *Henry V* calls the "imaginary forces" of the audience.

But there is throughout Shakespeare's works a counterintuition that, while it does not exactly overturn this illusion, renders it poignant, vulnerable, fraught. The "masculine usurp'd attire" that is donned by Viola, Rosalind, Portia, Jessica, and other Shakespeare heroines alters what they can say and do, reveals important aspects of their character, and changes their destiny, but it is, all the same, not theirs and not all of who they are. They have, the plays insist, natures that are neither transformed nor altogether concealed by their dress: "Pray God defend me," exclaims the frightened Viola. "A little thing would make me tell them how much I lack of a man" (*Twelfth Night* 3.4.268–69).

The Paradoxes of Identity

The gap between costume and identity is not simply a matter of what women supposedly lack; virtually all of Shakespeare's major characters, men and women, convey the sense of both a *self-division* and an *inward expansion*. The belief in a complex inward realm beyond costumes and status is a striking inversion of the clothes cult: we know perfectly well that the characters have no inner lives apart from what we see on the stage, and yet we believe that they continue to exist when we do not see them, that they exist apart from their represented words and actions, that they have hidden dimensions. How is this conviction aroused and sustained? In part, it is the effect of what the characters themselves say: "My grief lies all within," Richard II tells Bolingbroke,

> And these external manner of laments
> Are merely shadows to the unseen grief
> That swells with silence in the tortured soul.
> (4.1.294–96)

Similarly, Hamlet, dismissing the significance of his outward garments, declares, "I have that within which passeth show— / These but the trappings and the suits of woe" (1.2.85–86). And the distinction between inward and outward is reinforced throughout this play and elsewhere by an unprecedented use of the aside and the soliloquy.

The soliloquy is a continual reminder in Shakespeare that the inner life is by no means transparent to one's surrounding world. Prince Hal seems open and easy with his mates in Eastcheap, but he has a hidden reservoir of disgust:

> I know you all, and will a while uphold
> The unyoked humour of your idleness.
> Yet herein will I imitate the sun,
> Who doth permit the base contagious clouds
> To smother up his beauty from the world,
> That when he please again to be himself,
> Being wanted he may be more wondered at
> By breaking through the foul and ugly mists
> Of vapours that did seem to strangle him.
> (*I Henry IV* 1.2.173–81)

"When he please again to be himself": the line implies that identity is a matter of free choice—you decide how much of yourself you wish to disclose—but Shakespeare employs other devices that suggest more elusive and intractable layers of inwardness. There is a peculiar, recurrent lack of fit between costume and character, in fools as in princes, that is not simply a matter of disguise and disclosure. If Hal's true identity is partially "smothered" in the tavern, it is not completely revealed either in his soldier's armor or in his royal robes, nor do his asides reach the bedrock of unimpeachable self-understanding.

Identity in Shakespeare repeatedly slips away from the characters themselves, as it does from Richard II after the deposition scene and from Lear after he has given away his land and from Macbeth after he has gained the crown. The slippage does not mean that they retreat into silence; rather, they embark on an experimental, difficult fashioning of themselves and the world, most often through role-playing. "I cannot do it," says the deposed and imprisoned Richard II. "Yet I'll hammer it out" (5.5.5). This could serve as the motto for many Shakespearean characters: Viola becomes Cesario, Rosalind calls herself Ganymede, Kent becomes Caius, Edgar presents himself as Poor Tom, Hamlet plays the madman that he has partly become, Hal pretends that he is his father and a highwayman and Hotspur and even himself. Even in comedy, these ventures into alternate identities are rarely matters of choice; in tragedy, they are always undertaken under pressure and compulsion. And often enough it is not a matter of role-playing at all, but of a drastic transformation whose extreme emblem is the harrowing madness of Lear and of Leontes.

There is a moment in *Richard II* in which the deposed King asks for a mirror and then, after musing on his reflection, throws it to the ground. The shattering of the glass serves to remind us not only of the fragility of identity in Shakespeare but of its characteristic appearance in fragmentary mirror images. The plays continually generate alternative reflections, identities that intersect with, underscore, echo, or otherwise set off that of the principal character. Hence, Desdemona and Iago are not only important figures in Othello's world, they also seem to embody partially realized aspects of himself; Falstaff and Hotspur play a comparable role in relation to Prince Hal, Fortinbras and Horatio in relation to Hamlet, Gloucester and the Fool in relation to Lear, and so forth. In many of these plays, the complementary and contrasting characters figure in subplots, subtly interwoven with the play's main plot and illuminating its concerns. The note so conspicuously sounded by Fortinbras at the close of *Hamlet*—what the hero might have been, "had he been put on"—is heard repeatedly in Shakespeare and contributes to the overwhelming intensity, poignancy, and complexity of the characters. This is a world in which outward appearance is everything and nothing, in which individuation is at once sharply etched and continually blurred, in which the victims of fate are haunted by the ghosts of the possible, in which everything is simultaneously as it must be and as it need not have been.

Are these antinomies signs of a struggle between contradictory and irreconcilable perspectives in Shakespeare? In certain plays—notably, *Measure for Measure*, *All's Well That Ends Well*, *Coriolanus*, and *Troilus and Cressida*—the tension seems both high and entirely unresolved. But Shakespearean contradictions are more often reminiscent of the capacious spirit of Montaigne, who refused any systematic order that would betray his sense of reality. Thus, individual characters are immensely important in Shakespeare—he is justly celebrated for his unmatched skill in the invention of particular dramatic identities, marked with distinct speech patterns, manifested in social status, and confirmed by costume and gesture—but the principle of individuation is not the rock on which his theatrical art is founded. After the masks are stripped away, the pretenses exposed, the claims of the ego shattered, there is a mysterious remainder; as the shamed but irrepressible Paroles declares in *All's Well That Ends Well*, "Simply the thing I am / Shall make me live" (4.3.309–10). Again and again the audience is made to sense a deeper energy, a source of power that at once discharges itself in individual characters and seems to sweep right through them.

The Poet of Nature

In *The Birth of Tragedy*, Nietzsche called a comparable source of energy that he found in Greek tragedy "Dionysos." But the god's name, conjuring up Bacchic frenzy, does not seem appropriate to Shakespeare. In the late seventeenth and eighteenth centuries, it was more plausibly called Nature: "The world must be peopled," says the delightful Benedick in *Much Ado About Nothing* (2.3.213–14), and there are frequent invocations elsewhere of the happy, generative power that brings couples together—

> Jack shall have Jill,
> Naught shall go ill,
> the man shall have his mare again, and all shall be well.
> (*A Midsummer Night's Dream* 3.3.45–47)

—and the melancholy, destructive power that brings all living things to the grave: "Golden lads and girls all must, / As chimney-sweepers, come to dust" (*Cymbeline* 4.2.263–64).

But the celebration of Shakespeare as a poet of nature—often coupled with an inane celebration of his supposedly "natural" (that is, untutored) genius—has its distinct limitations. For Shakespearean art brilliantly interrogates the "natural," refusing to take for granted precisely what the celebrants think is most secure. His comedies are endlessly inventive in showing that love is not simply natural: the playful hint of bestiality in the line quoted above, "the man shall have his mare again," (from a play in which the Queen of the Fairies falls in love with an ass-headed laborer), lightly unsettles the boundaries between the natural and the perverse. These boundaries are called into question throughout Shakespeare's work, from the cross-dressing and erotic crosscurrents that deliciously complicate the lives of the characters in *Twelfth Night* and *As You Like It* to the terrifying violence that wells up from the heart of the family in *King Lear* or from the sweet intimacy of sexual desire in *Othello*. Even the boundary between life and death is not secure, as the ghosts in *Julius Caesar, Hamlet,* and *Macbeth* attest, while the principle of natural death (given its most eloquent articulation by old Hamlet's murderer, Claudius!) is repeatedly tainted and disrupted.

Disrupted too is the idea of order that constantly makes its claim, most insistently in the history plays. Scholars have observed the presence in Shakespeare's works of the so-called Tudor myth—the ideological justification of the ruling dynasty as a restoration of national order after a cycle of tragic violence. The violence, Tudor apologists claimed, was divine punishment unleashed after the deposition of the anointed king, Richard II, for God will not tolerate violations of the sanctified order. Traces of this propaganda certainly exist in the histories—Shakespeare may, for all we know, have personally subscribed to its premises—but a closer scrutiny of his plays has disclosed so many ironic reservations and qualifications and subversions as to call into question any straightforward adherence to a political line. The plays manifest a profound fascination with the monarchy and with the ambitions of the aristocracy, but the fascination is never simply endorsement. There is always at least the hint of a slippage between the great figures, whether admirable or monstrous, who stand at the pinnacle of authority and the vast, miscellaneous mass of soldiers, scriveners, ostlers, poets, whores, gardeners, thieves, weavers, shepherds, country gentlemen, sturdy beggars, and the like who make up the commonwealth. And the idea of order, though eloquently articulated (most memorably by Ulysses in *Troilus and Cressida*), is always shadowed by a relentless spirit of irony.

The Play of Language

If neither the individual nor nature nor order will serve, can we find a single comprehensive name for the underlying force in Shakespeare's work? Certainly not. The work is too protean and capacious. But much of the energy that surges through this astonishing body of plays and poems is closely linked to the power of language. Shakespeare was the supreme product of a rhetorical culture, a culture steeped in the arts of persuasion and verbal expressiveness. In 1512, the great Dutch humanist Erasmus published a work called *De copia* that taught its readers how to cultivate "copiousness," verbal richness, in discourse. (Erasmus obligingly provides, as a sample, a list of 144 different ways of saying "Thank you for your letter.") Recommended modes of variation include putting the subject of an argument into fictional form, as well as the use of synonym, substitution, paraphrase, metaphor, metonymy, synecdoche, hyperbole, diminution, and a host of other figures of speech. To change emotional tone, he suggests trying *ironia, interrogatio, admiratio, dubitatio, abominatio*—the possibilities seem infinite.

In Renaissance England, certain syntactic forms or patterns of words known as "figures" (also called "schemes") were shaped and repeated in order to confer beauty or heighten expressive power. Figures were usually known by their Greek and Latin names, though in an Elizabethan rhetorical manual, *The Arte of English Poesie*, George Puttenham made a valiant if short-lived attempt to give them English equivalents, such as "*Hyperbole*, or the

Overreacher," *"Ironia, or the Dry Mock,"* and *"Ploce, or the Doubler."* Those who received a grammar school education throughout Europe at almost any point between the Roman Empire and the eighteenth century probably knew by heart the names of up to one hundred such figures, just as they knew by heart their multiplication tables. According to one scholar's count, Shakespeare knew and made use of about two hundred.

As certain grotesquely inflated Renaissance texts attest, lessons from *De copia* and similar rhetorical guides could encourage mere prolixity and verbal self-display. But though he shared his culture's delight in rhetorical complexity, Shakespeare always understood how to swoop from baroque sophistication to breathtaking simplicity. Moreover, he grasped early in his career how to use figures of speech, tone, and rhythm not only to provide emphasis and elegant variety but also to articulate the inner lives of his characters. Take, for example, these lines from *Othello*, where, as scholars have noted, Shakespeare deftly combines four common rhetorical figures—*anaphora, parison, isocolon,* and *epistrophe*— to depict with painful vividness Othello's psychological torment:

> By the world,
> I think my wife be honest, and think she is not.
> I think that thou art just, and think thou art not.
> I'll have some proof.
>
> (3.3.388–91)

Anaphora is simply the repetition of a word at the beginning of a sequence of sentences or clauses ("I/I"). *Parison* is the correspondence of word to word within adjacent sentences or clauses, either by direct repetition ("think/think") or by the matching of noun with noun, verb with verb ("wife/thou"; "be/art"). *Isocolon* gives exactly the same length to corresponding clauses ("and think she is not/and think thou art not"), and *epistrophe* is the mirror image of *anaphora*, in that it is the repetition of a word at the end of a sequence of sentences or clauses ("not/not"). Do we need to know the Greek names for these figures in order to grasp the effectiveness of Othello's lines? Of course not. But Shakespeare and his contemporaries, convinced that rhetoric provided the most natural and powerful means by which feelings could be conveyed to readers and listeners, were trained in an analytical language that helped at once to promote and to account for this effectiveness. In his 1593 edition of *The Garden of Eloquence*, Henry Peacham remarks that *epistrophe* "serveth to leave a word of importance in the end of a sentence, that it may the longer hold the sound in the mind of the hearer," and in *Directions for Speech and Style* (c. 1599), John Hoskins notes that *anaphora* "beats upon one thing to cause the quicker feeling in the audience."

Shakespeare also shared with his contemporaries a keen understanding of the ways that rhetorical devices could be used not only to express powerful feelings but to hide them: after all, the artist who created Othello also created Iago, Richard III, and Lady Macbeth. He could deftly skewer the rhetorical affectations of Polonius in *Hamlet* or the pedant Holophernes in *Love's Labour's Lost*. He could deploy stylistic variations to mark the boundaries not of different individuals but of different social realms; in *A Midsummer Night's Dream*, for example, the blank verse of Duke Theseus is played off against the rhymed couplets of the well-born young lovers, and both in turn contrast with the prose spoken by the artisans. At the same time that he thus marks boundaries between both individuals and groups, Shakespeare shows a remarkable ability to establish unifying patterns of imagery that knit together the diverse strands of his plot and suggest subtle links among characters who may be scarcely aware of how much they share with one another.

One of the hidden links in Shakespeare's own works is the frequent use he makes of a somewhat unusual rhetorical figure called *hendiadys*. An example from the Roman poet Virgil is the phrase *pateris libamus et auro*, "we drink from cups and gold" (*Georgics* 2.192). Rather than serving as an adjective or a dependent noun, as in "golden cups" or "cups of gold," the word "gold" serves as a substantive joined to another substantive, "cups," by a conjunction, "and." Shakespeare uses the figure over three hundred times in all, and since it does not appear in ancient or medieval lists of tropes and schemes and is treated only briefly by English rhetoricians, he may have come upon it directly in Virgil. *Hendiadys* literally means "one through two," though Shakespeare's versions often make us quickly, perhaps only subliminally, aware of the complexity of what ordinarily passes for straightforward perceptions. When Othello, in his suicide speech, invokes the memory of "a malignant and a turbaned Turk," the figure of speech at once associates enmity with cultural difference and keeps them slightly apart. And when Macbeth speaks of his "strange and self-abuse," the *hendiadys* seems briefly to hold both "strange" and "self" up for scrutiny. It would be foolish to make too much of any single feature in Shakespeare's varied and diverse creative achievement, and yet this curious rhetorical scheme has something of the quality of a fingerprint.

But all of his immense rhetorical gifts, though rich, beautiful, and supremely useful, do not adequately convey Shakespeare's relation to language, which is less strictly functional than a total immersion in the arts of persuasion may imply. An Erasmian admiration for copiousness cannot fully explain Shakespeare's astonishing vocabulary of some 25,000 words. (His closest rival among the great English poets of the period was John Milton, with about 12,000 words, and most major writers, let alone ordinary people, have much smaller vocabularies.) This immense word hoard, it is worth noting, was not the result of scanning a dictionary; in the late sixteenth century, there were no English dictionaries of the kind to which we are now accustomed. Shakespeare seems to have absorbed new words from virtually every discursive realm he ever encountered, and he experimented boldly and tirelessly with them. These experiments were facilitated by the very fact that dictionaries as we know them did not exist and by a flexibility in grammar, orthography, and diction that the more orderly, regularized English of the later seventeenth and eighteenth centuries suppressed.

Owing in part to the number of dialects in London, pronunciation was variable, and there were many opportunities for phonetic association between words: the words "bear," "barn," "bier," "bourne," "born," and "barne" could all sound like one another. Homonyms were given greater scope by the fact that the same word could be spelled so many different ways—Christopher Marlowe's name appears in the records as Marlowe, Marloe, Marlen, Marlyne, Merlin, Marley, Marlye, Morley, and Morle—and by the fact that a word's grammatical function could easily shift, from noun to verb, verb to adjective, and so forth. Since grammar and punctuation did not insist on relations of coordination and subordination, loose, nonsyntactic sentences were common, and etymologies were used to forge surprising or playful relations between distant words.

It would seem inherently risky for a popular playwright to employ a vocabulary so far in excess of what most mortals could possibly possess, but Shakespeare evidently counted on his audience's linguistic curiosity and adventurousness, just as he counted on its general and broad-based rhetorical competence. He was also usually careful to provide a context that in effect explained or translated his more arcane terms. For example, when Macbeth reflects with horror on his murderous hands, he shudderingly imagines that even the sea could not wash away the blood; on the contrary, his bloodstained hand, he says, "will rather / The multitudinous seas incarnadine." The meaning of the unfamiliar word "incarnadine" is explained by the next line: "Making the green one red" (2.2.59–61).

What is most striking is not the abstruseness or novelty of Shakespeare's language but its extraordinary vitality, a quality that the playwright seemed to pursue with a kind of passionate recklessness. Perhaps Samuel Johnson was looking in the right direction when he complained that the "quibble," or pun, was "the fatal Cleopatra for which [Shakespeare] lost the world, and was content to lose it." For the power that continually discharges itself throughout the plays, at once constituting and unsettling everything it touches, is the polymorphous power of language, language that seems both costume and that which lies beneath the costume, personal identity and that which challenges the merely personal, nature and that which enables us to name nature and thereby distance ourselves from it.

Shakespeare's language has an overpowering exuberance and generosity that often resembles the experience of love. Consider, for example, Oberon's description in A *Mid-*

summer *Night's Dream* of the moment when he saw Cupid shoot his arrow at the fair vestal: "Thou rememb'rest," he asks Puck,

> Since once I sat upon a promontory
> And heard a mermaid on a dolphin's back
> Uttering such dulcet and harmonious breath
> That the rude sea grew civil at her song
> And certain stars shot madly from their spheres
> To hear the sea-maid's music?
>
> (2.1.149–54)

Here, Oberon's composition of place, lightly alluding to a classical emblem, is infused with a fantastically lush verbal brilliance. This brilliance, the result of masterful alliterative and rhythmical technique, seems gratuitous; that is, it does not advance the plot, but rather exhibits a capacity for display and self-delight that extends from the fairies to the playwright who has created them. The rich music of Oberon's words imitates the "dulcet and harmonious breath" he is intent on recalling, breath that has, in his account, an oddly contradictory effect: it is at once a principle of order, so that the rude sea is becalmed like a lower-class mob made civil by a skilled orator, and a principle of disorder, so that celestial bodies in their fixed spheres are thrown into mad confusion. And this contradictory effect, so intimately bound up with an inexplicable, supererogatory, and intensely erotic verbal magic, is the key to *A Midsummer Night's Dream*, with its exquisite blend of confusion and discipline, lunacy and hierarchical ceremony.

The fairies in this comedy seem to embody a pervasive sense found throughout Shakespeare's work that there is something uncanny about language, something that is not quite human, at least in the conventional and circumscribed sense of the human that dominates waking experience. In the comedies, this intuition is alarming but ultimately benign: Oberon and his followers trip through the great house at the play's close, blessing the bridebeds and warding off the nightmares that lurk in marriage and parenthood. But there is in Shakespeare an alternative, darker vision of the uncanniness of language, a vision also embodied in creatures that test the limits of the human—not the fairies of *A Midsummer Night's Dream* but the weird sisters of *Macbeth*. When in the tragedy's opening scene the witches chant, "Fair is foul, and foul is fair," they unsettle through the simplest and most radical act of linguistic equation (x is y) the fundamental antinomies through which a moral order is established. And when Macbeth appears onstage a few minutes later, his first words unconsciously echo what we have just heard from the witches' mouths: "So foul and fair a day I have not seen" (1.3.36). What is the meaning of this linguistic "unconscious"? On the face of things, Macbeth presumably means only that the day of fair victory is also a day of foul weather, but the fact that he echoes the witches (something that we hear but that he cannot know) intimates an occult link between them, even before their direct encounter. It is difficult, perhaps impossible, to specify exactly what this link signifies—generations of emboldened critics have tried without notable success—but we can at least affirm that its secret lair is in the play's language, like a half-buried pun whose full articulation will entail the murder of Duncan, the ravaging of his kingdom, and Macbeth's own destruction.

Macbeth is haunted by half-buried puns, equivocations, and ambiguous grammatical constructions known as amphibologies. They manifest themselves most obviously in the words of the witches, from the opening exchanges to the fraudulent assurances that deceive Macbeth at the close, but they are also present in his most intimate and private reflections, as in his tortured broodings about his proposed act of treason:

> If it were done when 'tis done, then 'twere well
> It were done quickly. If th'assassination
> Could trammel up the consequence, and catch
> With his surcease success: that but this blow

Might be the be-all and the end-all, here,
But here upon this bank and shoal of time,
We'd jump the life to come.

(1.7.1–7)

The dream is to reach a secure and decisive end, to catch as in a net (hence "trammel up") all of the slippery, unforeseen, and uncontrollable consequences of regicide, to hobble time as one might hobble a horse (another sense of "trammel up"), to stop the flow ("success") of events, to be, as Macbeth later puts it, "settled." But Macbeth's words themselves slip away from the closure he seeks; they slide into one another, trip over themselves, twist and double back and swerve into precisely the sickening uncertainties their speaker most wishes to avoid. And if we sense a barely discernible note of comedy in Macbeth's tortured language, a discordant playing with the senses of the word "done" and the hint of a childish tongue twister in the phrase "catch / With his surcease success," we are in touch with a dark pleasure to which Shakespeare was all his life addicted.

Look again at the couplet from *Cymbeline*: "Golden lads and girls all must, / As chimney-sweepers, come to dust."

The playwright who insinuated a pun into the solemn dirge is the same playwright whose tragic heroine in *Antony and Cleopatra*, pulling the bleeding body of her dying lover into the pyramid, says, "Our strength is all gone into heaviness" (4.16.34). He is the playwright whose Juliet, finding herself alone on the stage, says, "My dismal scene I needs must act alone" (*Romeo and Juliet* 4.3.19), and the playwright who can follow the long, wrenching periodic sentence that Othello speaks, just before he stabs himself, with the remark "O bloody period!" (5.2.366). The point is not merely the presence of puns in the midst of tragedy (as there are stabs of pain in the midst of Shakespearean comedy); it is rather the streak of wildness that they so deliberately disclose, the sublimely indecorous linguistic energy of which Shakespeare was at once the towering master and the most obedient, worshipful servant.

The Dream of the Master Text

Shakespeare and the Printed Book

Ben Jonson's famous tribute to Shakespeare—"He was not of an age, but for all time!"—comes in one of the dedicatory poems to the 1623 First Folio of *Mr. William Shakespeares Comedies, Histories, & Tragedies*. This large, handsome volume, the first collection of Shakespeare's plays, was not, as far as we know, the product of the playwright's own design. We do not even know if he would have approved of the Folio's division of each play into five acts or its organization of the plays into three loose generic categories, comedies, histories, and tragedies (to which modern editors have often added a fourth, the romances, to group together *Cymbeline*, *Pericles*, *The Winter's Tale*, and *The Tempest*). Published seven years after the playwright's death, the Folio was printed by the London printers William and Isaac Jaggard, who were joined in this expensive venture by Edward Blount, John Smethwicke, and William Apsley. It was edited by two of Shakespeare's old friends and fellow actors, John Heminges and Henry Condell, who claimed to be using "True Originall Copies" in the author's own hand. (None of these copies has survived, or, more cautiously, none has to date been found.) Eighteen plays included in the First Folio had already appeared individually in print in the small-format and relatively inexpensive texts called "quartos" (or, in one case, the still smaller format called "octavo"); to these, Heminges and Condell added eighteen others never before published: *All's Well That Ends Well, Antony and Cleopatra, As You Like It, The Comedy of Errors, Coriolanus, Cymbeline, All Is True (Henry VIII), Julius Caesar, King John, Macbeth, Measure for Measure, The Taming of the Shrew, The Tempest, Timon of Athens, Twelfth Night, The Two*

Sixteenth-century printing shop. Engraving by Jan van der Straet. From *Nova Reperta* (1580).

Gentlemen of Verona, *The Winter's Tale*, and *1 Henry VI*.* None of the plays included in the Folio has dropped out of the generally accepted canon of Shakespeare's works, and only two plays not included in the volume (*Pericles* and *The Two Noble Kinsmen*) have been allowed to join this select company, along with the nondramatic poems. Of the latter, *Venus and Adonis* (1593) and *The Rape of Lucrece* (1594) first appeared during Shakespeare's lifetime in quartos with dedications from the author to the Earl of Southampton. *Shakespeare's Sonnets* (1609) were apparently printed without his authorization, as were his poems in a collection called *The Passionate Pilgrim* (1599).

The plays were the property of the theatrical company in which Shakespeare was a shareholder. It was not normally in the interest of such companies to have their scripts circulating in print, at least while the plays were actively in repertory: players evidently feared competition from rival companies and thought that reading might dampen playgoing. Plays were generally sold only when the theaters were temporarily closed by plague, or when the company was in need of capital (four of Shakespeare's plays were published in 1600, presumably to raise money to pay the debts incurred in building the new Globe), or when a play had grown too old to revive profitably. There is no evidence that Shakespeare himself disagreed with this professional caution, no sign that he wished to see his plays in print. Unlike Ben Jonson, who took the radical step of rewriting his own plays for

*This sketch simplifies several complex questions such as the status of the 1594 Quarto called *The Taming of a Shrew*, sufficiently distinct from the similarly titled Folio text as to constitute for many editors a different play.

publication in the 1616 folio of his *Works*, Shakespeare evidently was not interested in constituting his plays as a canon. If in the sonnets he imagines his verse achieving a symbolic immortality, this dream apparently did not extend to his plays, at least through the medium of print.

Moreover, there is no evidence that Shakespeare had an interest in asserting authorial rights over his scripts, or that he or any other working English playwright had a public "standing," legal or otherwise, from which to do so. (Jonson was ridiculed for his presumption.) There is no indication whatever that he could, for example, veto changes in his scripts or block interpolated scenes or withdraw a play from production if a particular interpretation, addition, or revision did not please him. To be sure, in his advice to the players, Hamlet urges that those who play the clowns "speak no more than is set down for them," but—apart from the question of whether the Prince speaks for the playwright—the play-within-the-play in *Hamlet* is precisely an instance of a script altered to suit a particular occasion. It seems likely that Shakespeare would have routinely accepted the possibility of such alterations. Moreover, he would of necessity have routinely accepted the possibility, and in certain cases the virtual inevitability, of cuts in order to stage his plays in the two to two and one-half hours that was the normal performing time. There is an imaginative generosity in many of Shakespeare's scripts, as if he were deliberately offering his fellow actors more than they could use on any one occasion and hence giving them abundant materials with which to reconceive and revivify each play again and again, as they or their audiences liked it. The Elizabethan theater, like most theater in our own time, was a collaborative enterprise, and the collaboration almost certainly extended to decisions about selection, trimming, shifts of emphasis, and minor or major revision.

For many years, it was thought that Shakespeare himself did little or no revising. Some recent editors—above all the editors of the *Oxford Shakespeare*, whose texts the *Norton* presents—have argued persuasively that there are many signs of authorial revision, even wholesale rewriting. But there is no sign that Shakespeare sought through such revision to bring each of his plays to its "perfect," "final" form. On the contrary, many of the revisions seem to indicate that the scripts remained open texts, that the playwright and his company expected to add, cut, and rewrite as the occasion demanded.

Ralph Waldo Emerson once compared Shakespeare and his contemporary Francis Bacon in terms of the relative "finish" of their work. All of Bacon's work, wrote Emerson, "lies along the ground, a vast unfinished city." Each of Shakespeare's dramas, by contrast, "is perfect, hath an immortal integrity. To make Bacon's work complete, he must live to the end of the world." Recent scholarship suggests that Shakespeare was more like Bacon than Emerson thought. Neither the Folio nor the quarto texts of Shakespeare's plays bear the seal of final authorial intention, the mark of decisive closure that has served, at least ideally, as the guarantee of textual authenticity. We want to believe, as we read the text, "This is the play as Shakespeare himself wanted it read," but there is no license for such a reassuring sentiment. To be "not of an age, but for all time" means in Shakespeare's case not that the plays have achieved a static perfection, but that they are creatively, inexhaustibly unfinished.

That we have been so eager to link certain admired scripts to a single known playwright is closely related to changes in the status of artists in the Renaissance, changes that led to a heightened interest in the hand of the individual creator. Like medieval painting, medieval drama gives us few clues as to the particular individuals who fashioned the objects we admire. We know something about the places in which these objects were made, the circumstances that enabled their creation, the spaces in which they were placed, but relatively little about the particular artists themselves. It is easy to imagine a wealthy patron or a civic authority in the late Middle Ages commissioning a play on a particular subject (appropriate, for example, to a seasonal ritual, a religious observance, or a political festivity) and specifying the date, place, and length of the performance, the number of actors, even the costumes to be used, but it is more difficult to imagine him specifying a particular playwright and still less insisting that the entire play be written by this dramatist alone. Only with the Renaissance do we find a growing insistence on the name of the maker, the signature that heightens the value and even the meaning of the work by implying that it is the emanation of a single, distinct shaping consciousness.

In the case of Renaissance painting, we know that this signature does not necessarily mean that every stroke was made by the master. Some of the work, possibly the greater part of it, may have been done by assistants, with only the faces and a few finishing touches from the hand of the illustrious artist to whom the work is confidently attributed. As the skill of individual masters became more explicitly valued, contracts began to specify how much was to come from the brush of the principal painter. Consider, for example, the Italian painter Luca Signorelli's contract of 1499 for frescoes in Orvieto Cathedral:

> The said master Luca is bound and promises to paint [1] all the figures to be done on the said vault, and [2] especially the faces and all the parts of the figures from the middle of each figure upwards, and [3] that no painting should be done on it without Luca himself being present. . . . And it is agreed [4] that all the mixing of colours should be done by the said master Luca himself.

Such a contract at once reflects a serious cash interest in the characteristic achievement of a particular artist and a conviction that this achievement is compatible with the presence of other hands, provided those hands are subordinate, in the finished work. For paintings on a smaller scale, it was more possible to commission an exclusive performance. Thus the contract for a small altarpiece by Signorelli's great teacher, Piero della Francesca, specifies that "no painter may put his hand to the brush other than Piero himself."

There is no record of any comparable concern for exclusivity in the English theater. Unfortunately, the contracts that Shakespeare and his fellow dramatists almost certainly signed have not, with one significant exception, survived. But plays written for the professional theater are by their nature an even more explicitly collective art form than paintings; they depend for their full realization on the collaboration of others, and that collaboration may well extend to the fashioning of the script. It seems that some authors may simply have been responsible for providing plots that others then dramatized; still others were hired to "mend" old plays or to supply prologues, epilogues, or songs. A particular playwright's name came to be attached to a certain identifiable style—a characteristic set of plot devices, a marked rhetorical range, a tonality of character—but this name may refer in effect more to a certain product associated with a particular playing company than to the individual artist who may or may not have written most of the script. The one contract whose details do survive, that entered into by Richard Brome and the actors and owners of the Salisbury Court Theatre in 1635, does not stipulate that Brome's plays must be written by him alone or even that he must be responsible for a certain specifiable proportion of each script. Rather, it specifies that the playwright "should not nor would write any play or any part of a play to any other players or playhouse, but apply all his study and endeavors therein for the benefit of the said company of the said playhouse." The Salisbury Court players want rights to everything Brome writes for the stage; the issue is not that the plays associated with his name be exclusively *his* but rather that he be exclusively *theirs*.

Recent textual scholarship, then, has been moving steadily away from a conception of Shakespeare's plays as direct, unmediated emanations from the mind of the author and toward a conception of them as working scripts, composed and continually reshaped as part of a collaborative commercial enterprise in competition with other, similar enterprises. One consequence has been the progressive weakening of the idea of the solitary, inspired genius, in the sense fashioned by Romanticism and figured splendidly in the statue of Shakespeare in the public gardens in Germany's Weimar, the city of Goethe and Schiller: the poet, with his sensitive, expressive face and high domed forehead sitting alone and brooding, a skull at his feet, a long-stemmed rose in his crotch. In place of this projection of German Romanticism, we have now a playwright and sometime actor who is also (to his considerable financial advantage) a major shareholder in the company—the Lord Chamberlain's Men, later the King's Men—to which he loyally supplies for most of his career an average of two plays per year.

These developments are salutary insofar as they direct attention to the actual conditions

in which the textual traces that the Folio calls Shakespeare's "Comedies, Histories, & Tragedies" came to be produced, reproduced, consumed, revised, and transmitted to future generations. They highlight elements that Shakespeare shared with his contemporaries, and they insistently remind us that we are encountering scripts written primarily for the stage and not for the study. They make us more attentive to such matters as business cycles, plague rolls, the cost of costumes, government censorship, and urban topography and less concerned with the elusive and enigmatic details of the poet's biography—his supposed youthful escapades and erotic yearnings and psychological crises.

All well and good. But the fact remains that in 1623, seven years after the playwright's death, Heminges and Condell thought they could sell copies of their expensive collection of Shakespeare's plays—"What euer you do," they urge their readers, "buy"—by insisting that their texts were "as he conceiued them." This means that potential readers in the early seventeenth century were already interested in Shakespeare's "conceits"—his "wit," his imagination, and his creative power—and were willing to assign a high value to the products of his particular, identifiable skill, one distinguishable from that of his company and of his rival playwrights. After all, Jonson's tribute praises Shakespeare not as the playwright of the incomparable King's Men but as the equal of Aeschylus, Sophocles, and Euripides. And if we now see Shakespeare's dramaturgy in the context of his contemporaries and of a collective artistic practice, readers continue to have little difficulty recognizing that most of the plays attached to his name tower over those of his rivals.

From Foul to Fair: The Making of the Printed Play

What exactly is a printed play by Shakespeare? Is it like a novel or a poem? Is it like the libretto or the score of an opera? Is it the trace of an absent event? Is it the blueprint of an imaginary structure that will never be completed? Is it a record of what transpired in the mind of a man long dead? We might say cautiously that it is a mechanically reproduced version of what Shakespeare wrote, but unfortunately, with the possible (and disputed) exception of a small fragment from a collaboratively written play called *Sir Thomas More*, virtually nothing Shakespeare actually wrote in his own hand survives. We might propose that it is a printed version of the script that an Elizabethan actor would have held in his hands during rehearsals, but here too no such script of a Shakespeare play survives; and besides, Elizabethan actors were evidently not given the whole play to read. To reduce the expense of copying and the risk of unauthorized reproduction, each actor received only his own part, along with the cue lines. (Shakespeare uses this fact to delicious comic effect in *A Midsummer Night's Dream* 3.1.80–88.) Nonetheless, the play certainly existed as a whole, either in the author's original manuscript or in the copy prepared for the government censor or for the company's prompter or stage manager, so we might imagine the text we hold in our hands as a printed copy of one of these manuscripts. But since no contemporary manuscript survives of any of Shakespeare's plays, we cannot verify this hypothesis. And even if we could, we would not have resolved the question of the precise relation of the printed text either to the playwright's imagination or to the theatrical performance by the company to which he belonged.

All of Shakespeare's plays must have begun their textual careers in the form of "foul papers," drafts presumably covered with revisions, crossings-out, and general "blotting." To be sure, Heminges and Condell remark that so great was the playwright's facility that they "have scarce received from him a blot in his papers." This was, however, a routine and conventional compliment in the period. The same claim, made for the playwright John Fletcher in an edition published in 1647, is clearly contradicted by the survival of Fletcher's far-from-unblotted manuscripts. It is safe to assume that, as Shakespeare was human, his manuscripts contained their share of second and third thoughts scribbled in the margins and between the lines. Once complete, this authorial draft would usually have to be written out again, either by the playwright or by a professional scribe employed by the theater company, as "fair copy."

In the hands of the theater company, the fair copy (or sometimes, it seems, the foul

papers themselves) would be annotated and transformed into "the book of the play" or the "playbook" (what we would now call a "promptbook"). Shakespeare's authorial draft presumably contained a certain number of stage directions, though these may have been sketchy and inconsistent. The promptbook clarified these and added others, noted theatrical properties and sound effects, and on occasion cut the full text to meet the necessities of performance. The promptbook was presented to the Master of the Revels for licensing, and it incorporated any changes upon which the master insisted. As the editors of the Oxford Shakespeare put it, the difference between foul papers and promptbook is the difference between "the text in an as yet individual, private form" and "a socialized text."

But the fact remains that for Shakespeare's plays, we have neither foul papers nor fair copies nor promptbooks. We have only the earliest printed editions of these texts in numerous individual quartos and in the First Folio. (Quartos are so called because each sheet of paper was folded twice, making four leaves or eight pages front and back; folio sheets were folded once, making two leaves or four pages front and back.) From clues embedded in these "substantive" texts—substantive because (with the exception of *The Two Noble Kinsmen*) they date from Shakespeare's own lifetime or from the collected works edited by his associates using, or claiming to use, his own manuscripts—editors attempt to reconstruct each play's journey from manuscript to print. Different plays took very different journeys.

Of the thirty-six plays included in the First Folio, eighteen had previously appeared in quarto editions, some of these in more than one printing. Generations of editors have distinguished between "good quartos," presumably prepared from the author's own draft or from a scribal transcript of the play (fair copy), and "bad quartos." The latter category, first formulated as such by A. W. Pollard in 1909, includes, by widespread though not universal agreement, the 1594 version of *The First Part of the Contention* (2 *Henry VI*), the 1595 *Richard Duke of York* (3 *Henry VI*), the 1597 *Richard III*, the 1597 *Romeo and Juliet*, the 1600 *Henry V*, the 1602 *Merry Wives of Windsor*, the 1603 *Hamlet*, and *Pericles* (1609). Some editors also regard the 1591 *Troublesome Reign of King John*, the 1594 *Taming of a Shrew*, and the 1608 *King Lear* as bad quartos, but others have strenuously argued that these are distinct rather than faulty texts, and the whole concept of the bad quarto has come under increasingly critical scrutiny. The criteria for distinguishing between "good" and "bad" texts are imprecise, and the evaluative terms seem to raise as many questions as they answer. Nevertheless, the striking mistakes, omissions, repetitions, and anomalies in a number of the quartos require some explanation beyond the ordinary fallibility of scribes and printers.

The explanation most often proposed for suspect quartos is that they are the products of "memorial reconstruction." The hypothesis, first advanced in 1910 by W. W. Greg, is that a series of features found in what seem to be particularly flawed texts may be traced to the derivation of the copy from the memory of one or more of the actors. Elizabethan actors, Greg observed, often found themselves away from the London theaters, for example on tour in the provinces during plague periods, and may not on those occasions have had access to the promptbooks they would ordinarily have used. In such circumstances, those in the company who remembered a play may have written down or dictated the text, as best they could, perhaps adapting it for provincial performance. Moreover, unscrupulous actors may have sold such texts to enterprising printers eager to turn a quick profit.

Memorially reconstructed texts tend to be much shorter than those prepared from foul papers or fair copy; they frequently paraphrase or garble lines, drop or misplace speeches and whole scenes, and on occasion fill in the gaps with scraps from other plays. In several cases, scholars think they can detect which roles the rogue actors played, since these parts (and the scenes in which they appear) are reproduced with greater accuracy than the rest of the play. Typically, these roles are minor ones, since the leading parts would be played by actors with a greater stake in the overall financial interest of the company and hence less inclination to violate its policy. Thus, for example, editors speculate that the bad quarto of *Hamlet* (Q1) was provided by the actor playing Marcellus (and doubling as Lucianus). What is often impossible to determine is whether particular differences between a bad quarto and a good quarto or Folio text result from the actor's faulty memory or from

changes introduced in performance, possibly with the playwright's own consent, or from both. Shakespearean bad quartos ceased to appear after 1609, perhaps as a result of greater scrutiny by the Master of the Revels, who after 1606 was responsible for licensing plays for publication as well as performance.

The syndicate that prepared the Folio had access to the manuscripts of the King's Men. In addition to the previously published editions of eighteen plays, they made use of scribal transcripts (fair copies), promptbooks, and (more rarely) foul papers. The indefatigable labors of generations of bibliographers, antiquaries, and textual scholars have recovered an extraordinary fund of information about the personnel, finances, organizational structure, and material practices of Elizabethan and Jacobean printing houses, including the names and idiosyncrasies of particular compositors who calculated the page length, set the type, and printed the sheets of the Folio. This impressive scholarship has for the most part intensified respect for the seriousness with which the Folio was prepared and printed, and where the Folio is defective, it has provided plausible readings from the quartos or proposed emendations to approximate what Shakespeare is likely to have written. But it has not succeeded, despite all its heroic efforts, in transforming the Folio, or any other text, into an unobstructed, clear window into Shakespeare's mind.

The dream of the master text is a dream of transparency. The words on the page should ideally give the reader unmediated access to the astonishing forge of imaginative power that was the mind of the dramatist. Those words welled up from the genius of the great artist, and if the world were not an imperfect place, they would have been set down exactly as he conceived them and transmitted to each of us as a precious inheritance. Such is the vision—at its core closely related to the preservation of the holy text in the great scriptural religions—that has driven many of the great editors who have for centuries produced successive editions of Shakespeare's works. The vision was not yet fully formed in the First Folio, for Heminges and Condell still felt obliged to apologize to their noble patrons for dedicating to them a collection of mere "trifles." But by the eighteenth century, there were no longer any ritual apologies for Shakespeare; instead, there was a growing recognition not only of the supreme artistic importance of his works but also of the uncertain, conflicting, and in some cases corrupt state of the surviving texts. Every conceivable step, it was thought, must be undertaken to correct mistakes, strip away corruptions, return the texts to their pure and unsullied form, and make this form perfectly accessible to readers.

Paradoxically, this feverishly renewed, demanding, and passionate editorial project has produced the very opposite of the transparency that was the dream of the master text. The careful weighing of alternative readings, the production of a textual apparatus, the writing of notes and glosses, the modernizing and regularizing of spelling and punctuation, the insertion of scene divisions, the complex calculation of the process of textual transmission from foul papers to print, the equally complex calculation of the effects that censorship, government regulation, and, above all, theatrical performance had on the surviving documents all make inescapably apparent the fact that we do not have and never will have any direct, unmediated access to Shakespeare's imagination. Every Shakespeare text, from the first that was published to the most recent, has been edited: it has come into print by means of a tangled social process and inevitably exists at some remove from the author.

Heminges and Condell, who knew the author and had access to at least some of his manuscripts, lament the fact that Shakespeare did not live "to have set forth and overseen his own writings." And even had he done so—or, alternatively, even if a cache of his manuscripts were discovered in a Warwickshire attic tomorrow—all of the editorial problems would not be solved, nor would all of the levels of mediation be swept away. Certainly the entire textual landscape would change. But the written word has strange powers: it seems to hold on to something of the very life of the person who has written it, but it also seems to pry that life loose from the writer, exposing it to vagaries of history and chance quite independent of those to which the writer was personally subject. Moreover, with the passing of centuries, the language itself and the whole frame of reference within which language and symbols are understood have decisively changed. The most learned modern scholar still lives at a huge experiential remove from Shakespeare's world and, even holding a precious copy of the First Folio in hand, cannot escape having to read across a vast chasm of time what is, after all, an edited text. The rest of us cannot so much as indulge in the fantasy of direct access: our eyes inevitably wander to the glosses and the explanatory notes.

The Oxford Shakespeare

The shattering of the dream of the master text is no cause for despair, nor should it lead us to throw our hands up and declare that one text is as good as another. What it does is to encourage the reader to be actively interested in the editorial principles that underlie the particular edition that he or she is using. It is said that the great artist Brueghel once told a nosy connoisseur who had come to his studio, "Keep your nose out of my paintings; the smell of the paint will poison you." In the case of Shakespeare, it is increasingly important to bring one's nose close to the page, as it were, and sniff the ink. More precisely, it is important to understand the rationale for the choices that the editors have made.

The text of the *Norton Shakespeare* is, with very few changes, that published in 1988 by the Oxford University Press. The *Oxford Shakespeare* was the extraordinary achievement of a team of editors, Stanley Wells, Gary Taylor, John Jowett, and William Montgomery, with Wells and Taylor serving as the general editors. The Oxford editors approached their task with a clear understanding that, as we have seen, all previous texts have been mediated by agents other than Shakespeare, but they regard this mediation not as a melancholy obstacle intervening between the reader and the "true" Shakespearean text but rather as a constitutive element of this text. The art of the playwright is thoroughly dependent on the craft of go-betweens.

Shakespeare's plays were not written to be circulated in manuscript or printed form among readers. They were written to be performed by the players and, as the preface to the quarto *Troilus and Cressida* indelicately puts it, "clapper-clawed with the palms of the vulgar." The public was thus never meant to be in a direct relationship with the author but in a "triangular relationship" in which the players gave voice and gesture to the author's words. As we have seen, Shakespeare was the master of the unfinished, the perpetually open. And even if we narrow our gaze and try to find only what Shakespeare himself might have regarded as a textual resting point, a place to stop and go on to another play, we have, the Oxford editors point out, a complex task. For whatever Shakespeare wrote was meant from the start to be supplemented by an invisible "para-text" consisting of words spoken by Shakespeare to the actors and by the actors to each other, concerning emphasis, stage business, tone, pacing, possible cuts, and so forth. To the extent that this para-text was ever written down, it was recorded in the promptbook. Therefore, in contrast to standard editorial practice, the Oxford editors prefer, when there is a choice, copy based on the promptbook to copy based on the author's own draft. They choose the text immersed in history, that is, in the theatrical embodiment for which it was intended by its author, over the text unstained by the messy, collaborative demands of the playhouse. The closest we can get to Shakespeare's "final" version of a play—understanding that for him as for us there is no true "finality" in a theatrical text—is the latest version of that play performed by his company during his professional life, that is, during the time in which he could still oversee and participate in any cuts and revisions.

This choice does not mean that the Oxford editors are turning away from the very idea of Shakespeare as author. On the contrary, Wells and Taylor are deeply committed to establishing a text that comes as close as possible to the plays as Shakespeare wrote them, but they are profoundly attentive to the fact that he wrote them as a member of a company of players, a company in which he was a shareholder and an actor as well as a writer. "Writing" for the theater, at least for Shakespeare, is not simply a matter of setting words to paper and letting the pages drift away; it is a social process as well as individual act. The Oxford editors acknowledge that some aspects of this social process may have been frustrating to Shakespeare: he may, for example, have been forced on occasion to cut lines and even whole scenes to which he was attached, or his fellow players may have insisted that

they could not successfully perform what he had written, compelling him to make changes he did not welcome. But compromise and collaboration are part of what it means to be in the theater, and Wells and Taylor return again and again to the recognition that Shakespeare was, supremely, a man of the theater.

Is there a tension between the Oxford editors' preference for the performed, fully socialized text and their continued commitment to recovering the text as Shakespeare himself intended it? Yes. The tension is most visible in their determination to strip away textual changes arising from circumstances, such as government censorship, over which Shakespeare had no control. ("We have, wherever possible," they write, put "profanities back in Shakespeare's mouth.") It can be glimpsed as well in the editors' belief, almost a leap of faith, that there was little revision of Shakespeare's plays in his company's revivals between the time of his death and the publication of the Folio. But the tension is mainly a creative one, for it forces them (and therefore us) to attend to the playwright's unique imaginative power as well as his social and historical entanglements.

The Oxford editors took a radical stance on a second major issue: the question of authorial revision. Previous editors had generally accepted the fact that Shakespeare practiced revision within individual manuscripts, that is, while he was still in the act of writing a particular play, but they generally rejected the notion that he undertook substantial revisions from one version of a play to another (and hence from one manuscript to another). Wells and Taylor point out that six major works (*Hamlet, Othello, 2 Henry IV, King Lear, Richard II,* and *Troilus and Cressida*) survive in two independent substantive sources, both apparently authoritative, with hundreds of significant variant readings. Previous editors have generally sought to deny authority to one edition or another ("faced with two sheep," the Oxford editors observe wryly, "it is all too easy to insist that one *must* be a goat") or have conflated the two versions into a single text in an attempt to reconstruct the ideal, definitive, complete, and perfect version that they imagine Shakespeare must have reached for each of his plays. But if one doubts that Shakespeare ever conceived of his plays as closed, finished entities, if one recalls that he wrote them for the living repertory of the commercial playing company to which he belonged, then the whole concept of the single, authoritative text of each play loses its force. In a startling departure from the editorial tradition, the *Oxford Shakespeare* printed two distinct versions of *King Lear*, quarto and Folio, and the editors glanced longingly at the impractical but alluring possibility of including two texts of *Hamlet, Othello,* and *Troilus.*

The *Oxford Shakespeare* was published in both old-spelling and modern-spelling editions. The former, the first of its kind ever published, raised some reviewers' eyebrows because the project, a critical edition rather than a facsimile, required the modern editors to invent plausible Elizabethan spellings for their emendations and to add stage directions. The modern-spelling edition, which is the basis for Norton's text, is noteworthy for taking the principles of modernization further than they had generally been taken. Gone are such words as "murther," "mushrump," "vild," and "porpentine," which confer on many modern-spelling editions a certain cozy, Olde-English quaintness; Oxford replaces them with "murder," "mushroom," "vile," and "porcupine."

The inclusion of two texts of *King Lear* aroused considerable controversy when the *Oxford Shakespeare* first appeared, though by now the arguments for doing so have received widespread, though not unanimous, scholarly support. Other features remain controversial: "Ancients" Pistol and Iago have been modernized to "Ensigns"; *Henry VIII* has reverted to its performance title *All Is True*; demonic spirits in *Macbeth* sing lyrics written by Thomas Middleton. The inclusion of a poem not usually considered part of Shakespeare's canon, "Shall I die?" provoked an enormous wave of charge and countercharge. The white-hot intensity of the debates triggered by the *Oxford Shakespeare*'s editorial choices casts an interesting light on the place of Shakespeare not only in the culture at large but in the psyches of millions of individuals: any alteration, however minor, in a deeply familiar and beloved text, even an alteration based on thoughtful and highly plausible scholarly principles, arouses genuine anxiety. The anxiety in this case was intensified not only by the boldness of certain crucial emendations but also by the fact that the editors'

explanations, arguments, and justifications for all their decisions were printed in a separate, massive volume, *William Shakespeare: A Textual Companion*. This formidable, dense volume is an astonishing monument to the seriousness, scholarly rigor, and immense labor of the Oxford editors. Anyone who is interested in pursuing why Shakespeare's words appear as they do in the current edition, anyone who wishes insight into the editors' detailed reasons for making the thousands of decisions required by a project of this kind, should consult the *Textual Companion*.

The Norton Shakespeare

The primary task that the editors of the *Norton Shakespeare* set themselves was to present the modern-spelling Oxford *Complete Works* in a way that would make the text more accessible to modern readers. The *Oxford Shakespeare* prints little more than the text itself: along with one-page introductions to the individual works, it contains a short general introduction, a list of contemporary allusions to Shakespeare, and a brief glossary. But while it is possible to enjoy a Shakespeare play on stage or screen without any assistance beyond the actors' own art, many readers at least since the eighteenth century have found it far more difficult to understand and to savor the texts without some more substantial commentary.

In addition to writing introductions, textual notes, and brief bibliographies for each of the works, the Norton editors provide glosses and footnotes designed to facilitate comprehension. Such is the staggering richness of Shakespeare's language that it is tempting to gloss everything, but there is a law of diminishing returns: too much explanatory whispering at the margins makes it difficult to enjoy what the reader has come for in the first place. Our general policy is to gloss only those words that cannot be found in an ordinary dictionary or whose meanings have altered out of recognition. The glosses attempt to be simple and straightforward, giving multiple meanings for words only when the meanings are essential for making sense of the passages in which they appear. We try not to gloss the same word over and over—it becomes distracting to be told three times on a single page that "an" means "if"—but we also assume that the reader does not have a perfect memory, so after an interval we will gloss the same word again.

Marginal glosses generally refer to a single word or a short phrase. The footnotes paraphrase longer units or provide other kinds of information, such as complex plays on words, significant allusions, textual cruxes, historical and cultural contexts. Here too, however, we have tried to check the impulse to annotate so heavily that the reader is distracted from the pleasure of the text, and we have avoided notes that provide interpretation, as distinct from information.

Following each of the works, the Norton editors have provided lists of textual variants. These are variants from the control text only; that is, they do not record all of the variants in all of the substantive texts, nor do they record all of the myriad shifts of meaning that may arise from modernization of spelling and repunctuation. Readers who wish to pursue these interesting, if complex, topics are encouraged to consult the *Textual Companion*, along with the old-spelling *Oxford Shakespeare*, the Norton facsimile of the First Folio, and the quarto facsimiles published by the University of California Press. The *Norton Shakespeare* does provide a convenient list for each play of the different ways the same characters are designated in the speech prefixes in the substantive texts. These variants (for example, Lady Capulet in *Romeo and Juliet* is called, variously, "Lady, "Mother," "Wife," "Old Woman," etc.) often cast an interesting light on the ways a particular character is conceived. Variants as they appear in this edition, as well as their line numbers, are printed in boldface; each is followed by the corresponding reading in the control text, and sometimes the source from which the variant is taken. Further information on readings in substantive texts is given in brackets.

Stage directions pose a complex set of problems for the editors of a one-volume Shakespeare. The printing conventions for the stage directions in sixteenth- and seventeenth-century plays were different from those of our own time. Often all of the entrances for a

particular scene are grouped together at the beginning, even though some of the characters clearly do not enter until later; placement in any case seems at times haphazard or simply incorrect. There are moments when the stage directions seem to provide stunning insight into the staging of the plays in Shakespeare's time, other moments when they are absent or misleading. It is difficult to gauge how much the stage directions in the substantive editions reflect Shakespeare's own words or at least decisions. It would seem that he was often relatively careless about them, understanding perhaps that these decisions in any precise sense would be the first to be made and unmade by different productions.

The Oxford editors, like virtually all modern editors, necessarily altered and supplemented the stage directions in their control texts. They decided to mark certain of the stage directions with a special sign to indicate a dubious action or placement, but they did not distinguish between the stage directions that came from the substantive texts and those added in later texts, from the seventeenth century to the present. They referred readers instead to the *Textual Companion*, which provides lists of the exact wording of the stage directions in the substantive texts.

The editors of the *Norton Shakespeare* share a sense of the limitations of the early stage directions and share as well some skepticism about how many of these should be attributed even indirectly to Shakespeare. Hence we do not routinely differentiate between quarto and Folio stage directions; we do so only when we think it is a significant point. But there is, it seems to us, a real interest in knowing which stage directions come from those editions of the plays published up to the 1623 Folio (and including *The Two Noble Kinsmen*, published shortly thereafter) and which were added when the editors were no longer in contact with Shakespeare's presence or his manuscripts. Therefore, we have placed brackets around all stage directions that were added after the First Folio. Unbracketed stage directions, then, all derive from editions up through the Folio.

The *Norton Shakespeare* has made several other significant departures from the Oxford text. The Oxford editors note that when *I Henry IV* was first performed, probably in 1596, the character we know as Sir John Falstaff was called Sir John Oldcastle. But in the wake of protests from Oldcastle's descendants, one of whom, William Brooke, Seventh Lord Cobham, was Elizabeth I's lord chamberlain, Shakespeare changed the name to "Falstaff" (and probably for similar reasons changed the names of Falstaff's companions, Russell and Harvey, to "Bardolph" and "Peto"). Consistent with their decision not to honor changes that Shakespeare was *compelled* to make by censorship or other forms of pressure, the Oxford editors changed the names back to their initial form. But this decision is a problem for several reasons. It draws perhaps too sharp a distinction between those things that Shakespeare did under social pressure and those he did of his own accord. More seriously, it pulls against the principle of a text that represents the latest performance version of a play during Shakespeare's lifetime: after all, even the earliest quarto title page advertises "the humorous conceits of Sir John Falstaff." And, of course, it asks the reader to ignore completely and radically centuries of response—elaboration, fascination, and love—all focused passionately on Sir John Falstaff. The response is not a modern phenomenon: it began with Shakespeare, who developed the character as Sir John Falstaff in *2 Henry IV* and *The Merry Wives of Windsor*. Norton thus restores the more familiar names.

Another major departure from the Oxford text is Norton's printing of the so-called Additional Passages, especially in *Hamlet*. Consistent with their decision not to conflate quarto and Folio texts, the Oxford editors adhere to their control text for *Hamlet*, the Folio, and print those passages that appear only in the Second Quarto in an appendix at the end of the play. As explained at length in the Textual Note to the play, the Norton editors decided not to follow this course, but instead chose a different way of demarcating the quarto and Folio texts (inserting the quarto passages, indented, in the body of the text), one that makes it easier to see how the quarto passages functioned in a version of the play that Shakespeare also authored.

The *Norton Shakespeare* follows Oxford in printing separate quarto and Folio texts of *King Lear*. But we have departed from Oxford in printing these on facing pages, so that their differences can be readily weighed, and we have added a conflated version of *King*

Lear, so that readers will have the opportunity to assess for themselves the effects of the traditional editorial practice.

Finally, the *Norton Shakespeare* includes, among its appendices, a poem called "A Funeral Elegy," edited by Donald Foster, who has recently made a case for Shakespeare's authorship. An introduction presents some of the arguments for and against this attribution. We should add that there are several other texts that have been with some plausibility attributed at least in part to Shakespeare—among the most interesting, a play entitled *Edward III*—and that more may be found in the years to come. This should surprise no one who has read this General Introduction: with Shakespeare, the boundaries are and must remain forever open.

ROMANCES

A Reconstructed Text of Pericles, Prince of Tyre

On paper, *Pericles, Prince of Tyre* (1607–8) has long seemed like the play from hell. Its plot is preposterous, its characters flat, its moralizing simplistic, its mode of representation old-fashioned and undramatic, its style uneven and often insipid, its authorship uncertain, and its text unreliable. Yet *Pericles* was one of the most popular plays of its time and has proven effective in modern productions as well. Possessed of a coherent and innovative design, it brought a new dramatic genre—romance—into Shakespeare's work and and, arguably, onto the English stage in general. Even so, the romance pattern does not entirely succeed in mastering the messiness of the play's materials. Moreover, despite *Pericles'* considerable structural and thematic unity, the play raises but does not resolve a series of social, political, and sexual anxieties.

Shakespeare's younger contemporary Ben Jonson spoke for many subsequent critics and audiences in disparaging *Pericles* as "a mouldy tale . . . and stale," and in attributing its success to its use of "scraps out of every dish." It is easy to see what Jonson is talking about. In *Pericles*, a king adorns his palace walls with the skulls of his victims. A princess commits incest with her father. Another princess is kidnapped by pirates and sold to a brothel. Famine brings a city to its knees. An entire crew is lost in a tumultuous storm. Two royal families are sent to fiery destruction. And Pericles is almost deposed by his restless nobility.

Characteristically, Pericles does not act; he is acted upon. Bad things (as well as good) just keep happening to him. Every member of his family narrowly escapes death: two evade assassins sent by murderous monarchs, and the third survives burial at sea. Each is reported dead, only to experience apparently miraculous rebirth. The play seems consciously to eschew the complex probing of the protagonist's psyche that marks Shakespeare's immediately preceding tragic period, in favor of clear-cut moral oppositions and an emphatic poetic justice. By the end of *Pericles*, the good have been rewarded and the bad annihilated.

But if the central characters only seem to be reborn, one person really does return from the dead, and he tells the story. This is Gower. As the onstage presence of this fourteenth-century author (John Gower) indicates, the most important direct source of *Pericles* is his major work, *Confessio Amantis*. The eighth book of this verse narrative is primarily devoted to the tale of Apollonius of Tyre, which, via medieval intermediaries dating all the way back to a fifth- or sixth-century Latin text, derives from a now-lost late classical Latin or, more probably, Greek romance influenced by *The Odyssey*. A different route through the medieval sources, this time incorporating the lives of early Christian saints who suffered persecution in brothels, leads to the other proximate source of the play, Laurence Twine's *Pattern of Painful Adventures* (written by 1576, published 1594?). *Pericles* is the first dramatization of these lengthy traditions. The shift in the protagonist's name from "Apollonius" to "Pericles" may derive from still other strains in the Apollonius tradition; from Sir Philip Sidney's *Arcadia* (1590), one of whose protagonists is named Pyrocles; or from one of Shakespeare's favorite sources, Plutarch's *Lives*, which may provide still other characters' names (in addition to praising the renowned fifth-century B.C. Athenian statesman Pericles, it harshly judges his rival and successor Cleon as well as the fourth-century general Lysimachus).

The play follows its sources more faithfully than many of Shakespeare's works do. One sign of this fidelity is the episodic plot. More striking still is the appearance of Gower

The true History of the Play of *Pericles*, as it was lately presented by the worthy and ancient Poet *John Gower*.

John Gower.

Woodcut of John Gower, from the title page of *The Painful Adventures of Pericles Prince of Tyre*, by George Wilkins (1608).

himself as a character. His role as chorus is anticipated in *Henry V*, but he is specifically designed to give a (pseudo) medieval feel to the action. He initially speaks in the rhymed tetrameter couplets in which the *Confessio Amantis* is written: "To sing a song that old was sung / From ashes ancient Gower is come" (1.1–2). The theatrical Gower's diction often echoes the medieval poet's and is deliberately antiquated as well ("iwis" for "certainly," for example, at 5.2). His moralizing speeches are often graced by an unrealistic theatrical device from Shakespeare's youth—the dumb show. Further, much of the action is recounted by Gower in his eight monologues, as if to emphasize that poet's authorship of what sometimes feels like essentially narrative, as opposed to dramatic, material.

The actual authorship of *Pericles* is beset by unresolved questions, which are treated at length in the Textual Note. Here it is worth mentioning only that George Wilkins probably wrote most of the first nine scenes and Shakespeare most of the remaining thirteen. Acknowledgment of dual authorship is tied to the long-standing recognition of stylistic differences in the two parts of the play. Wilkins's section of the dialogue is closer to Gower's language than is Shakespeare's. Though both playwrights regularly compose verse in iambic pentameter, Wilkins uses far more end-stopped rhyming couplets than does Shakespeare. And Shakespeare's predilection for blank-verse enjambment, in which the phrase or idea does not conclude at the end of the line, produces a tension between syntax and verse form.

Thus Wilkins's Pericles decorously repudiates the incestuous Daughter of Antiochus:

> Fair glass of light, I loved you, and could still,
> Were not this glorious casket stored with ill.
> . . . .
> For he's no man on whom perfections wait
> That, knowing sin within, will touch the gate.
> . . . .
> But, being played upon before your time,
> Hell only danceth at so harsh a chime.
>   (1.119–28)

Shakespeare's Pericles reacts to a storm in imagistically more complex but also more colloquial verse:

>   O still
> Thy deaf'ning dreadful thunders, gently quench
> Thy nimble sulph'rous flashes. . . .
> . . . .
>   The seaman's whistle
> Is as a whisper in the ears of death,
> Unheard.—Lychorida!—Lucina, O!
> Divinest patroness, and midwife gentle

> To those that cry by night, convey thy deity
> Aboard our dancing boat, make swift the pangs
> Of my queen's travails!—Now, Lychorida.
> (11.4–14)

As a result, Shakespeare's section of the play is theatrically livelier, the contrast with the increasingly frequent monologues by Gower correspondingly sharper. Pericles' meeting with the fishermen is the only episode by Wilkins that seems of a piece with such later parts of the play as the second tempest (quoted from above), the revival of Pericles' wife, Thaisa, the two brothel scenes, and the first recognition scene. And structurally, *Pericles* breaks neatly in two: in the first nine scenes, Pericles moves from felicity to misfortune and back to felicity; in the remaining thirteen, he simply repeats this pattern, though with greater intensity. Although critics have sometimes found a rationale for these dramaturgical shifts, the change in author is probably the central explanation.

Yet such distinctions are misleading. Many Renaissance plays were written collaboratively; Shakespeare collaborated on about a quarter of his plays, mostly near the beginning and end of his career. Especially in performance, such works do not necessarily seem any less unified than single-author pieces. Though its "feel" shifts, *Pericles* remains consistent throughout in motif—Pericles as a noble tree, his jewellike family, destructive eating, providential storms, divine music. Its episodes echo one another, within and across the two parts of the play. For example, the deadly skulls at Antiochus's palace are answered by the harmless jousting at Simonides' court, and the bad potential marriage to Antiochus's Daughter is echoed by the good real one to Simonides'. The incestuous relationship between Antiochus and his Daughter is contrasted with the lovingly innocent ones between Simonides and Thaisa, Pericles and Marina. Thaliart's foiled attempt to assassinate Pericles at Antiochus's behest anticipates Leonine's failed effort to murder Marina at Dionyza's. The storm that costs Pericles his men but leads him to Thaisa is paralleled by the later tempest that apparently disposes of Thaisa. The vigorous popular culture of the fishermen is set against the degraded popular culture of the brothel. The false vow of chastity Thaisa apparently takes when she wants to marry Pericles is fulfilled both in her genuine vow of chastity when she thinks him gone forever and in Marina's successful defense of her chastity in the brothel. And the apparent burial of Thaisa is duplicated in the apparent burial of her daughter.

Throughout, the play insists that the concatenation of miseries inflicted on Pericles and his family ultimately leads to a higher felicity. This is the structure of tragicomic romance, the genre of nearly all of Shakespeare's final plays. Though the adaptation of a traditionally narrative form last popular in the 1580s may be part of the nostalgia for Elizabeth that James's reign unintentionally inspired, Shakespearean romance is also influenced by contemporary Italian dramatic theory and practice. *Pericles* and its successors emphasize long periods of suffering and the concomitant necessity of patience, perilous sea journeys beset by storms, symbolic geography, near-death experiences followed by spiritual rebirths, the healing power of time, the eventual reunion of royal families whose children (primarily daughters) have been separated from their parents (primarily fathers) at birth, and complex plots whose unraveling reveals the working of a mysterious Christian providence often masquerading as the Greco-Roman gods. All of these motifs seem to glance—flatteringly, in most critics' view—at the royal family of James I, while giving the romance form a middle-aged (or older), retrospective view that nonetheless leaves room for the future in the concluding marriage of the royal daughter. In this respect, the romances recapitulate Shakespeare's previous work while reversing its chronology: in the unfolding of an individual romance, the tragic mood of the early seventeenth century precedes the comic tone of the 1590s. *Pericles*, for instance, echoes *King Lear* both in its storm scenes and in its reunion of ravaged father and redemptive daughter, who gives "another life / To Pericles thy father" (21.194–95); it then duplicates *The Comedy of Errors*, which draws on the same sources as *Pericles* in its concluding retrieval of the missing wife-turned-priestess from the temple of Diana at Ephesus.

Gower reassuringly emphasizes this larger pattern—"I'll show you those in trouble's reign, / Losing a mite, a mountain gain" (5.7–8)—which becomes especially prominent in Shakespeare's scenes through the presiding benevolence of Diana. She is first mentioned when, according to Simonides, Thaisa feints in the direction of continued virginity (9.9). Then Thaisa invokes her upon awakening in an opened coffin, as does Pericles when he vows not to cut his hair till his baby Marina is married (12.102, 13.28). Thaisa becomes her priestess, and Marina places her virginity in the goddess's protection (14.12, 15.4, 16.131). Finally, after Pericles is reunited with Marina, Diana appears to him in a dream, promising him happiness only if he goes to her temple in Ephesus and publicly recounts his loss of Thaisa (21.224–34). This supernatural moment recalls Thaisa's quasi-magical preservation by Cerimon (of whom Pericles says, "The gods can have no mortal officer / More like a god than you," 22.85–86), anticipates Pericles' actual meeting with her in the final scene (where Diana is repeatedly mentioned), and follows hard upon Pericles' per- haps unique ability to hear "the music of the spheres" (21.214), the sound of a heavenly harmony that extends to human affairs below. A special sensitivity to music has marked Pericles' family throughout. Pericles is "music's master," Thaisa awakens to "still and woe- ful music," and, most tellingly, Marina "sings like one immortal" (9.28, 12.86, 20.3).

Though these visual and auditory signs of a divine providence guiding the destiny of Pericles' family are pagan in form, they are Christian in content. Tragicomedy's movement from tribulation to triumph is modeled on the *felix culpa*, the fortunate fall of Adam and Eve that led to the redemptive coming of Christ. Antioch recalls the sinister side of Eden: Pericles will "taste the fruit of yon celestial tree / Or die in the adventure"; Antiochus praises the "golden fruit, but dang'rous to be touched" and later warns, "touch not, upon thy life" (1.64–65, 71, 130). More generally, the eastern Mediterranean of late Greek antiq- uity in which *Pericles* is set also carries connotations of Judaism and early Christianity. Tyre is connected with the reigns of David and Solomon, and was captured by the Chris- tian forces in the First Crusade. Antioch recalls the rebellion of the Maccabees; in addi- tion, both Peter and Paul preached there. Paul was born in Tarsus and had a lengthy ministry in Ephesus. Pentapolis has no such resonance, but the fishermen on its shore are literally, like St. Peter, fishers of men. Amid talk of devouring whales (5.63–80), they fish

Scenic view of the Temple of Diana, designed by Inigo Jones for the pastoral *Florentine* (1635).

out the Jonah-like figure of Pericles, whom "the sea hath cast upon [their] coast" (5.92). Similarly, at Mytilene, the Pander laments, "Neither is our profession any mystery; it's no calling" (16.32–33)—where both "mystery" and "calling" have religious reverberations.

In a final, typically moralistic, speech, Gower tells the audience,

> In Pericles, his queen, and daughter seen,
> Although assailed with fortune fierce and keen,
> Virtue preserved from fell destruction's blast,
> Led on by heav'n, and crowned with joy at last.
>   (22.110–13)

Though there is no ambiguity here, the play as a whole leaves room for doubts, on structural, social and political, and sexual grounds. First, despite the overarching pattern of the triumph over a pagan "fortune" by an implicitly Christian "heav'n," Pericles' sufferings feel arbitrary. It is hard to understand, except according to fairy tale logic, why his predecessors cannot solve Antiochus's obvious riddle or why the King advertises the very secret he wants to preserve. Similarly, the play does not explain why Pericles leaves his daughter at Tarsus or why Dionyza, eager to be rid of Marina, does not consider sending her home instead of murdering her. More important, the misfortunes in Pericles—as opposed, for instance, to those in The Winter's Tale—seem unrelenting, unconnected, and unrelated to the character or behavior of their victims. Yet this disjunction fails to inspire any Job-like reflections on injustice. In short, the triumph of divine providence is not fully integrated with the secular saga of misfortune.

Second, Pericles evades its own social and political material. The representation of popular culture provides some of Pericles' most engaging scenes without, however, consistently linking up to the larger movement of the plot. The initial storm leaves Pericles "bereft / Unfortunately both of ships and men" (7.79–80), a loss that apparently is his rather than the men's. The fishermen who then help him repeatedly receive his praise:

MASTER . . . I can compare our rich misers to nothing so fitly as to a whale: a plays and tumbles, driving the poor fry before him, and at last devours them all at a mouthful. . . .
PERICLES (aside) A pretty moral.

                                                                    (5.68–73)

This disabused account leads to a rebuke of the monarch: "if the good King Simonides were of my mind . . . We would purge the land of these drones that rob the bee of her honey" (5.80–84). But the complaint quickly disappears, leaving only the positive image of Pericles' future father-in-law. Similarly, though Pericles promises the fishermen, "if that ever my low fortune's better, / I'll pay your bounties, till then rest your debtor" (5.177–78), the debt, which is usually honored in previous tales of Apollonius (including Twine's), is not recalled when Pericles' fortunes quickly improve.

The anticommercial outlook implicit in the Master's denunciation of "rich misers" also informs the brothel scenes. Prostitution is the only commercial activity depicted in the play, and in that context the Bawd's advice to Marina distinctively develops the mercantile motif: "You have fortunes coming upon you. Mark me, you must seem to do that fearfully which you commit willingly, to despise profit where you have most gain. To weep that you live as ye do makes pity in your lovers. Seldom but that pity begets you a good opinion, and that opinion a mere profit" (16.101–6). Marina is thus urged to perform like an actor at one of London's professional theaters. With all commerce reduced to the oldest profession, Shakespeare undermines the institutional basis of his own career. This stance makes some sense in a play that often prefers narrative to drama. Yet it is oddly placed in a scene whose very effectiveness demonstrates the power of theater. Relatedly, perhaps because Marina's function is to resist her surroundings, the brothel scenes reveal her virtue without widening her experience. The same is true even after her graduation to an honest livelihood, which Gower simply reports.

Thus, despite successfully exploiting popular culture for theatrical effect, *Pericles* fails to incorporate that culture into the final reconciliation: the play concludes with a purely aristocratic and royal circle. Yet *Pericles* is the only one of Shakespeare's romances written before the King's Men began performing during the winter at Blackfriars, a "private," elite, commercial theater. It was acted at the Globe, the preeminent "public" theater, and its success in the early seventeenth century attests to the enduring, at least partly popular appeal of its traditional romance plot.

Further, the political value of aristocratic rule is questionable. Antioch has been ruled by an incestuous murderer, and there is no indication of his successor. The Governor of Tarsus lets his city slip into famine; his wife is a murderer. Though the inhabitants eventually kill the couple, their own earlier behavior does not inspire confidence: "All poverty was scorned, and pride so great / The name of help grew odious to repeat" (4.30–31). Under duress they are even worse:

> Those mothers who to nuzzle up their babes
> Thought naught too curious are ready now
> To eat those little darlings whom they loved.
> (4.42–44)

The passage echoes in reverse the riddle's equation of cannibalism with incest—"I feed / On mother's flesh" (1.107–8)—while also recalling numerous other moments where "to eat" is to devour. Ephesus's future remains unspecified: Lord Cerimon acts as a private figure. The Governor of Mytilene frequents a brothel until Marina converts him; at the end of the play, the brothel remains, while the Governor, betrothed to Marina, leaves Mytilene in uncertain hands and goes off to rule Tyre. Earlier, Pericles' departure from Tyre inspires aristocratic "mutiny" (10.29) and begins the practice of absentee landlordism that reaches its climax near the end of the play when his deputy, Helicanus, appoints Aeschines as *his* deputy and sets out with Pericles. Shortly thereafter, Pericles and Thaisa accede to the throne of Pentapolis, a society whose virtues and defects the fishermen dissect. The death of Thaisa's father, "the good Simonides," is treated not as an occasion for grief but as an opportunity to dole out kingdoms and, ironically, to break up a family that has only just been reunited. This outcome may parallel the isolation of the various members of James I's family, an isolation emblematized by James's failure to come to the deathbeds of two of his children. Pericles' absenteeism may also reflect on James's style of governing.

Finally, *Pericles* raises sexual doubts. Although the play subjects its protagonists to debased sexuality only to demonstrate their Diana-like purity, they may not escape unpolluted. In Gower's *Confessio Amantis*, Pericles' daughter is not Marina but Thaisa. Sexual relations with Thaisa, which in Gower would have been incest, are here converted into perfectly appropriate marital intimacy. It is almost as if the name change allows Pericles to have the very experience castigated in Antioch under the protection of the marriage bond. When the nearly catatonic Pericles arrives in Mytilene, Lysimachus agrees that Marina might be the cure:

> She questionless, with her sweet harmony
> And other choice attractions, would alarum [quarto has "allure"]
> And make a batt'ry through his deafened ports.
> (21.34–36)

"Alarum" in the second line works better with the last lines, but the quarto's reading goes well with "choice attractions"; thus, "allure" may be correct. If so, Lysimachus, ignorant of Marina's parentage, is suggesting a potentially unfamilial relationship between father and daughter. So too does Pericles. He addresses Marina as "thou that begett'st him that did thee beget" (21.182)—a line that may simply express gratitude for bringing him back to life. Yet the words uneasily recall the generational reversals of Antiochus's incestuous riddle: "He's father, son, and husband mild; / I mother, wife, and yet his child" (1.111–12). Tragicomic romance often provides a nontragic resolution to the tale of Oedipus, Pericles' predecessor in solving murderous riddles. Do Pericles' words to Marina reverse or repeat Antiochus's riddle? It is ambiguities such as this one that trouble the providential pattern.

They also trouble modern performances of *Pericles*. Although some productions attempt to create naturalistic settings and complex characters, most respect *Pericles*' relative indifference to such matters by exploiting what's unrealistic about the play and about Renaissance theater generally. First, the doubling of parts has led to the same actress playing Antiochus's Daughter and Marina, Marina and Thaisa, or Thaisa and Dionyza. This procedure can accentuate the differences between the paired characters; more often, however, it has generated an overtone of incest. Relatedly, when one actor plays all the Mediterranean kings, the stage can capture the underlying similarity, the repetitiousness of Pericles' adventures, and hence the formal, ritualistic quality of the work. Second, although the figure of Gower can establish intimacy between audience and action, the tendency has been to follow the German dramatist Bertolt Brecht in resisting empathy and identification. Gower's role is thus made to underscore the play's theatricality: it has at various times been sung, treated as a voice-over, and played by a street performer. The dramatized action itself has been represented as street theater, as the work of a traveling troupe, as Chinese opera, as an African-American boatswain's sea shanty to his fellow sailors aboard ship, as a child's picture book, as events in an asylum, as the floor show in a gay brothel. One consequence of these techniques has sometimes been an ironic, farcical approach to the absurdities of the plot. The price, however, is the failure of the climactic recognition scenes, which thrive on psychological nuance. Perhaps the solution, in reading as well as performance, is to refuse to level the unevenness of the play, remaining faithful to its various and incompatible registers.

WALTER COHEN

TEXTUAL NOTE

Pericles, Prince of Tyre poses insuperable textual problems. At some point between 1606 and 1608, most likely in late 1607 or early 1608, Shakespeare probably collaborated on a draft of *Pericles* with George Wilkins, a freelance playwright whose *Miseries of Enforced Marriage* had been successfully staged around 1606 by Shakespeare's company, the King's Men. The exact mechanism of the collaboration is unknown, but Wilkins seems to have composed most of Scenes 1–9 (Acts 1–2 in other modern editions) and Shakespeare most of Scenes 10–22 (Acts 3–5). Each dramatist may also have had a small share in the other's part: for instance, Shakespeare seems not to have written Scene 18 or Gower's epilogue at the end of Scene 22.

The central evidence for dual authorship and for the attribution to Wilkins is the stylistic disparity between the two sections of the play. The style of the first nine scenes shares a prosaic manner, end-stopped versification, and rhyming couplets with Wilkins's other works during these years. It does not resemble Shakespeare's style at any time (or that of anyone else proposed so far). By contrast, the final thirteen scenes are in Shakespeare's characteristically idiosyncratic late style, marked by complex imagery and, even more notably, by a radical use of enjambment. At various times, scholars have offered alternative explanations—that Shakespeare wrote the first part of *Pericles* early in his career and came back to it years later; that he wrote it all at once but that the two parts were differently mangled on the path from his manuscript to the printed page; that he deliberately shifted styles midway through the play for aesthetic effect; or that he did collaborate, but with someone other than Wilkins. None of these claims is as plausible as the assumption of joint authorship by Wilkins and Shakespeare.

The play was probably first performed between December 1607 and May 1608, and was apparently a commercial success at the Globe. The King's Men seem to have submitted the company's official promptbook of *Pericles* to the Stationers' Register May 20, 1608, ostensibly with intent to print. Since ownership of the play rested not with the playwright but with the company, however, their real purpose may have been to block Wilkins from illegally exploiting *Pericles'* popularity by selling it to a publisher himself—something he seems to have done the previous year with *The Miseries of Enforced Marriage*. In the event, the play was not printed in 1608; nonetheless, if the King's Men were trying to stop publication, their strategy failed in at least two respects.

First, Wilkins published a prose rendering of the story entitled *The Painful Adventures of Pericles, Prince of Tyre* sometime in 1608. Its title page advertises its indebtedness to the theatrical version, which for the most part, primarily in Scenes 1–9, it faithfully follows. Yet even in these early scenes, Wilkins's narrative is not as close to the play as might be expected. One purely speculative theory is that he was following not Shakespeare's *Pericles* but an earlier play. It is far more likely, however, that as a collaborating dramatist unattached to an acting company, he would not necessarily have retained a manuscript of the part he wrote and might never have had a personal copy of the entire, jointly authored piece. Indeed, given Wilkins's previous behavior, the King's Men may have made a point of keeping the text out of his hands. *The Painful Adventures* thus seems to record Wilkins's memory of the play he recently helped to write. That memory is less accurate, of course, in the parts he did not compose.

The King's Men may have been unable to prevent publication in another way as well. In 1609, one or more actors who had performed in *Pericles* may have sold it for publication. If so, he or they had to reassemble the text from memory, since an actor routinely possessed a written version of little more than his own part. Since the unauthorized publication of the manuscript would have hurt the interests of the company's actor-shareholders, such as Shakespeare, the actors most likely to have gone to press are thus to be found elsewhere. Perhaps the text was the work of the boy actor who played Lychorida and Marina, as well as some minor other parts, and of a hired man who may have been one of the fishermen and the Pander, among other small roles. These two actors also seem to have acquired a copy of Gower's speeches: perhaps the boy was apprenticed to the actor-shareholder who played Gower.

Almost inevitably, the actor(s)' report significantly differs not only from what Shakespeare wrote but also from what was actually performed. Evidence for this divergence is to be found especially in the large number of errors in meter, but perhaps also in the repeated confusion of verse and prose and in the high degree of verbal repetition. The conjectural identification of the actors who reconstructed the text is based on the relative absence of these defects from the speeches of the characters they presumably played and from the scenes in which they appear. Certainly, the process of reporting cannot account for the stylistic differences between the two parts of the play. The First Quarto (Q1) of *Pericles* was typeset in two printing houses: probably one compositor worked in the first shop, two in the second. But here again, the division between shops and among compositors does not correspond to the stylistic shift beginning in Scene 10. Neither can compositorial error explain most of the defects in the text. And although the title page names Shakespeare as the author, four other plays published in quarto before 1623 and attributed to William Shakespeare, as well as three more assigned to "W.S.," were clearly written by others.

Pericles remained popular in the early seventeenth century. It was revived several times through 1631—at the Globe, on tour in the countryside, and before a more elite audience. The print record is similarly extensive: the Second Quarto (Q2) appeared in the same year as the first, 1609, with subsequent quartos in 1611, 1619, 1630, and 1635. Each was based on the previous quarto, though Q6 also drew on Q4. But *Pericles* was excluded from the First Folio (F) in 1623, perhaps because the editors thought of it as a collaborative piece. It was published in the Third Folio (1663), which relied on Q6; again in the Fourth Folio (1685), which used the Third Folio; and in some major early eighteenth-century editions. But the play then largely dropped out of Shakespeare's works until 1780, when Edmund Malone successfully reintroduced it and provided it with act and scene divisions—both lacking in Q1—subsequent editors have basically accepted. The play has been routinely included in Shakespeare's canon since then.

Because all editions ultimately derive from Q1, *Pericles* occupies a unique status. For every other Shakespearean play with the ambiguous exception of *Richard III*, at least one early printed version apparently draws directly on either an authorial manuscript or a scribal transcript of it, such as a promptbook. (*Sir Thomas More* remained unpublished during the Renaissance and survives in an authorial manuscript.) Since no reasonably authoritative text of *Pericles* exists, even the claim that Q1 is a report of a performance cannot depend on comparison with a presumably more accurate version but must rely on internal evidence alone. Various unsatisfactory alternatives thus confront an editor. The most commonly adopted strategy in the last fifty years has been to emend the text only conservatively to increase its intelligibility. This approach has the obvious advantage of avoiding the introduction of many new deviations from the original play. On the other hand, it is unlikely to preserve the early printed version, the early performed version, or the authors' original version.

The Oxford editors have taken a different tack. In their original-spelling edition, they reprint Q1. In their modern-spelling edition, followed here, they take advantage of the probable dual authorship of the play and the survival of Wilkins's *Painful Adventures*, which they treat as a reported text, like Q1. Primarily in Wilkins's share of the play (Scenes 1–9), this edition draws on *The Painful Adventures* (PA) when the reporting in Q1 seems to be poor and when Wilkins's prose version seems superior in logic, language, or meter and is not invalidated as a report of the play by dependence on another printed source (Laurence Twine's *The Pattern of Painful Adventures*, 1594?). Although the rationale for this procedure is clearly strengthened by the assumption that Wilkins wrote the first nine scenes, it is not completely dependent on it.

Wilkins's prose is often metrical, as if he were remembering verse drama. Emendation based on PA regularly involves the conversion of prose into verse, as well as a wide variety of discretionary decisions. This policy improves the sense in many places (especially Scene 2). Further, Q1 lacks but apparently refers to a short passage displaying Pericles' musical talent that is reconstructed here (Scene 8a). In addition, by following Wilkins's prose, the rationale for Pericles' marriage to Thaisa is shifted from the nobility of his birth to the nobility of his soul (Scene 9). The same strategy of borrowing, in this instance inspired by the suspicion that Q1 reports a politically censored version of the dialogue between Marina and Lysimachus, initially places Lysimachus in a harsher light (Scene 19). Finally, because this edition's scene divisions often differ from those in other modern editions, the play is divided into scenes but not acts.

Although previous scholars and editors have drawn on PA and even engaged in conjectural reconstruction of long passages, this version of *Pericles* pursues such an approach more radically and is bound to remain controversial. It can be criticized not only if some of its underlying assumptions are faulty but even if all of them prove correct. The chance is nil that so many emendations, many of them major, will accurately reproduce what was originally written or performed. Yet this is to say no more than that the Oxford edition takes bigger risks than do its predecessors, but on a play where risk taking makes sense. As already noted, if Q1 is a reported text, other modern editions cannot possibly reproduce the original play at all accurately. This edition may deviate more widely than they do from the original version of *Pericles*; then again, it may well approximate that version more closely.

So that readers can form their own judgments on this question, for each scene the notes provide the act and scene equivalents in most modern texts of *Pericles*. Where scene division departs from the editorial norm, the deviation is explained. More important, the notes also record every emendation drawn from PA that significantly alters the meaning, and every emendation that is one line or longer in length. Rationales for most of these changes are supplied as well. The Textual Variants provide selected examples of the conversion in this edition of Q1's prose into verse and a complete record of the verbal borrowings from PA, with full quotation except where Wilkins's prose is exactly followed.

SELECTED BIBLIOGRAPHY

Archibald, Elizabeth. *Apollonius of Tyre: Medieval and Renaissance Themes and Variations, Including the Text of the "Historia Apollonii Regis Tyri" with an English Translation.* Cambridge, Eng.: D. S. Brewer, 1991.

Barber, C. L. " 'Thou that beget'st him that did thee beget': Transformation in *Pericles* and *The Winter's Tale.*" *Shakespeare Survey* 22 (1969): 59–67.

Felperin, Howard. *Shakespearean Romance.* Princeton: Princeton University Press, 1972. 143–76.

Knight, G. Wilson. *The Crown of Life: Essays in Interpretation of Shakespeare's Final Plays.* Oxford: Oxford University Press, 1947. 32–75.

Hoeniger, F. David. "Gower and Shakespeare in *Pericles.*" *Shakespeare Quarterly* 33 (1982): 461–79.

Lewis, Anthony J. " 'I feed on mother's flesh': Incest and Eating in *Pericles.*" *Essays in Literature* 15 (1988): 147–63.

Lomax, Marion. *Stage Images and Traditions: Shakespeare to Ford.* Cambridge, Eng.: Cambridge University Press, 1987. 70–98.

Mullaney, Steven. *The Place of the Stage: License, Play, and Power in Renaissance England.* Chicago: University of Chicago Press, 1987. 135–51.

Nevo, Ruth. "The Perils of Pericles." *The Undiscover'd Country: New Essays on Psychoanalysis and Shakespeare.* Ed. B. J. Sokol. London: Free Association Books, 1993. 150–78.

Relihan, Constance C. "Liminal Geography: *Pericles* and the Politics of Place." *Philological Quarterly* 71 (1992): 281–99.

A Reconstructed Text of Pericles, Prince of Tyre

The Persons of the Play

John GOWER, the Presenter
ANTIOCHUS, King of Antioch
His DAUGHTER
THALIART, a villain
PERICLES, Prince of Tyre
HELICANUS ⎱ two grave counsellors of Tyre
AESCHINES ⎰
MARINA, Pericles' daughter
CLEON, Governor of Tarsus
DIONYZA, his wife
LEONINE, a murderer
KING SIMONIDES, of Pentapolis
THAISA, his daughter
Three FISHERMEN, his subjects
Five PRINCES, suitors of Thaisa
A MARSHAL
LYCHORIDA, Thaisa's nurse
A ship MASTER
CERIMON, a physician of Ephesus
PHILEMON, his servant
LYSIMACHUS, Governor of Mytilene
A BAWD
A PANDER
BOULT, servant to Bawd and Pander
DIANA, goddess of chastity
Lords, ladies, pages, messengers, sailors, pirates, knights,
  gentlemen

Scene 1

Enter GOWER[1] [*as Prologue*]

GOWER To sing a song that old° was sung   *of old*
  From ashes ancient Gower is come,
  Assuming man's infirmities°   *Donning mortal flesh*
  To glad your ear and please your eyes.
5 It hath been sung at festivals,
  On ember-eves and holy-ales,[2]
  And lords and ladies in their lives
  Have read it for restoratives.°   *as a medicine*

Scene 1 (Q1 lacks act and scene divisions; the present edition numbers scenes consecutively throughout, omitting act divisions [see the Textual Note]. Other modern versions treat Gower's monologue as a prologue and start Act 1, Scene 1, at line 43. This edition, however, assumes that the row of heads referred to by Gower and Antiochus ["yon," lines 40, 77] is seen from roughly the same position both times and is first revealed after line 39. But the heads could be visible from the start. Further, Gower could be looking at them from the outside and Antiochus from the inside, in which case a scene division would be necessary. See the Introduction.)

Location: The palace at Antioch.

1. Fourteenth-century English poet, whose story of Apollonius of Tyre in the eighth book of his *Confessio Amantis* is an important source of the play. See the Introduction.
2. *ember-eves:* evenings before periods of religious fasting. *holy-ales:* country festivals.

The purchase° is to make men glorious,   *benefit*
10   *Et bonum quo antiquius eo melius.*³
     If you, born in these latter times
     When wit's more ripe,° accept my rhymes,   *poetry's more advanced*
     And that° to hear an old man sing   *And if*
     May to your wishes pleasure bring,
15   I life would wish, and that I might
     Waste° it for you like taper°-light.   *Use it up / candle*
     This'° Antioch, then; Antiochus the Great   *This is*
     Built up this city for his chiefest seat,°   *capital*
     The fairest in all Syria.
20   I tell you what mine authors° say.   *sources*
     This king unto him took a fere°   *mate*
     Who died, and left a female heir
     So buxom,° blithe, and full of face°   *lively / attractive?*
     As° heav'n had lent her all his° grace,   *As if / its*
25   With whom the father liking took,
     And her to incest did provoke.
     Bad child, worse father, to entice his own
     To evil should° be done by none.   *that should*
     By custom what they did begin
30   Was with long use account' no sin.⁴
     The beauty of this sinful dame
     Made many princes thither frame°   *go*
     To seek her as a bedfellow,
     In marriage pleasures playfellow,
35   Which to prevent he made a law
     To keep her still,° and men in awe,   *always*
     That whoso asked her for his wife,
     His riddle told not,⁵ lost his life.
     So for her many a wight° did die,   *fellow*
          [*A row of heads is revealed*]
40   As yon grim looks do testify.
     What now ensues, to th' judgement of your eye
     I give, my cause who best can justify.⁶   *Exit*
          [*Sennet.*]° Enter [*King*] ANTIOCHUS, *Prince* PERICLES,   *Trumpet*
          and [*lords and peers in their richest ornaments*]
ANTIOCHUS   Young Prince of Tyre, you have at large received°   *fully understood*
     The danger of the task you undertake.
45 PERICLES   I have, Antiochus, and with a soul
     Emboldened with the glory of her praise
     Think death no hazard in this enterprise.
ANTIOCHUS   Music!
          [*Music sounds*]
     Bring in our daughter, clothèd like a bride
50   Fit for th'embracements ev'n of Jove himself,
     At whose conception, till Lucina reigned,
     Nature this dowry gave to glad her presence:⁷

---

3. And the older something good is, the better (Latin).   best perceive the truth of my story.
4. *By . . . sin*: When what they started (incest) became a   7. *At . . . presence*: During pregnancy, until my daughter
habit, they no longer experienced it as a sin.   was born (Lucina was the Roman goddess of childbirth,
5. If he failed to explain Antiochus's riddle.   often equated with Diana), nature gave her this dowry to
6. *my . . . justify*: which (your eye's "judgement") will   make her presence welcome.

The senate-house of planets all did sit,
In her their best perfections to knit.[8]
Enter Antiochus' DAUGHTER
55 PERICLES   See where she comes, apparelled like the spring,
Graces her subjects,[9] and her thoughts the king
Of ev'ry virtue gives° renown to men;   *that gives*
Her face the book of praises,[1] where is read
Nothing but curious° pleasures, as from thence   *delicate*
60 Sorrow were ever razed and testy wrath
Could never be her mild companion.[2]
You gods that made me man, and sway° in love,   *hold sway*
That have inflamed desire in my breast
To taste the fruit of yon celestial tree
65 Or die in the adventure, be my helps,
As I am son and servant to your will,
To compass° such a boundless happiness.   *attain*
ANTIOCHUS   Prince Pericles—
PERICLES   That would be son to great Antiochus.
70 ANTIOCHUS   Before thee stands this fair Hesperides,
With golden fruit, but dang'rous to be touched,
  [*He gestures towards the heads*]
For death-like dragons here affright thee hard.[3]
  [*He gestures towards his* DAUGHTER]
Her heav'n-like face enticeth thee to view
Her countless° glory, which desert must gain;   *(like the stars)*
75 And which without desert, because thine eye
Presumes to reach, all the whole heap° must die.   *your whole body*
Yon sometimes° famous princes, like thyself   *at one time*
Drawn by report, advent'rous by° desire,   *taking a risk out of*
Tell thee with speechless tongues and semblants° bloodless *appearances*
80 That without covering save yon field of stars
Here they stand, martyrs slain in Cupid's wars,
And with dead cheeks advise thee to desist
From going on° death's net, whom none resist.   *into*
PERICLES   Antiochus, I thank thee, who hath taught
85 My frail mortality to know itself,
And by those fearful objects to prepare
This body, like to them, to what I must;[4]
For death remembered should be like a mirror
Who tells us life's but breath, to trust it error.
90 I'll make my will then, and, as sick men do,
Who know the world, see heav'n, but feeling woe
Grip not at earthly joys as erst° they did,   *previously*
So I bequeath a happy peace to you
And all good men, as ev'ry prince should do;
95 My riches to the earth from whence they came,
[*To the* DAUGHTER] But my unspotted fire of love to you.
[*To* ANTIOCHUS] Thus ready for the way of life or death,
I wait the sharpest blow, Antiochus.

---

8. *The . . . knit:* Astrological forces arranged to give her every perfection.
9. With mastery of all human graces.
1. The anthology of all that is commendable.
2. *as . . . companion:* as if sorrow were permanently blotted out (from her face) and anger were incompatible with her mildness.

3. *Before . . . hard:* the Hesperides (here representing Antiochus's Daughter) were daughters of Hesperus inhabiting a garden where golden apples grew, whose entrance was patrolled by a dragon. The "golden fruit, but dang'rous to be touched," like "the fruit of yon celestial tree" (line 64), also evokes Eden.
4. *to what I must:* for death.

ANTIOCHUS   Scorning advice, read the conclusion° then,   *riddle*
    [*He angrily throws down the riddle*]
100   Which read and not expounded, 'tis decreed,
    As these before thee, thou thyself shalt bleed.
DAUGHTER [*to* PERICLES]   Of all 'sayed° yet, mayst thou prove   *who have tried (assayed)*
    prosperous;
    Of all 'sayed yet, I wish thee happiness.
PERICLES   Like a bold champion I assume the lists,°   *enter combat*
105   Nor ask advice of any other thought
    But faithfulness and courage.
         [*He takes up and reads aloud*] *the riddle*
    I am no viper, yet I feed
    On mother's flesh which did me breed.[5]
    I sought a husband, in which labour
110   I found that kindness° in a father.   *kinship; affection*
    He's father, son, and husband mild;
    I mother, wife, and yet his child.
    How this may be and yet in two,°   *only two people*
    As you will live resolve it you.
115   Sharp physic is the last.[6] [*Aside*] But O, you powers
    That gives heav'n countless eyes° to view men's acts,   *(the stars)*
    Why cloud they not their sights perpetually
    If this be true which makes me pale to read it?
         [*He gazes on the* DAUGHTER]
    Fair glass° of light, I loved you, and could still,   *image*
120   Were not this glorious casket stored with ill.[7]
    But I must tell you now my thoughts revolt,
    For he's no man on whom perfections wait°   *(as servants)*
    That, knowing sin within, will touch the gate.
    You're a fair viol,[8] and your sense° the strings   *senses*
125   Who, fingered to make man his lawful music,
    Would draw heav'n down and all the gods to hearken,
    But, being played upon before your time,
    Hell only danceth at so harsh a chime.
    Good sooth,° I care not for you.   *Truly*
130   ANTIOCHUS   Prince Pericles, touch not,[9] upon thy life,
    For that's an article within our law
    As dang'rous as the rest. Your time's expired.
    Either expound now, or receive your sentence.
PERICLES   Great King,
135   Few love to hear the sins they love to act.
    'Twould braid° yourself too near° for me to tell it.   *upbraid / plainly*
    Who° has a book of all that monarchs do,   *Whoever*
    He's more secure to keep it shut than shown,
    For vice repeated, like the wand'ring wind,
140   Blows dust in others' eyes to spread itself;
    And yet the end of all is bought thus dear,
    The breath is gone, and the sore eyes see clear
    To stop the air would hurt them.[1] The blind mole casts

---

5. Vipers were thought to eat their way out of their mother's body at birth (again with Edenic associations).
6. This final threat is harsh medicine.
7. If your body weren't so sinful.
8. Stringed instrument; vial.
9. Perhaps Pericles makes some movement that Anti-

ochus misinterprets (further Edenic overtones).
1. *For vice . . . them*: For with the breath used to speak word of others' sins, one blows irritating dust in the eyes of the offenders. But the consequence is merely the speaker's death, since the offenders nevertheless see well enough to stop the news-spreading breath.

Copped° hills towards heav'n to tell° the earth is thronged   *Peaked / tell that*
145   By man's oppression, and the poor worm doth die for't.[2]
Kings are earth's gods; in vice their law's their will,
And if Jove stray, who dares say Jove doth ill?
It is enough you know,° and it is fit,   *(that I know)*
What being more known grows worse,[3] to smother° it.   *conceal*
150   All love the womb that their first being bred;[4]
Then give my tongue like leave to love my head.
ANTIOCHUS [*aside*]   Heav'n, that I had thy head! He's found the
     meaning.
But I will gloze° with him. —Young Prince of Tyre,   *dissemble*
Though by the tenor of our strict edict,
155   Your exposition misinterpreting,
We might proceed to cancel° of your days,   *to the termination*
Yet hope, succeeding from so fair a tree[5]
As your fair self, doth tune° us otherwise.   *move*
Forty days longer we do respite you,
160   If by which time our secret be undone,
This mercy shows we'll joy in such a son.
And until then your entertain° shall be   *entertainment*
As doth befit your worth and our degree.
        [*Flourish. Exeunt.*] *Manet* PERICLES *solus*°   *Pericles remains alone*
PERICLES   How courtesy would seem° to cover sin   *lie*
165   When what is done is like an hypocrite,
The which is good in nothing but in sight.°   *appearance*
If it be true that I interpret false,
Then were it certain you were not so bad
As with foul incest to abuse your soul,
170   Where now you're both a father and a son
By your uncomely claspings with your child—
Which pleasures fits a husband, not a father—
And she, an eater of her mother's flesh,
By the defiling of her parents' bed,
175   And both like serpents are, who though they feed
On sweetest flowers, yet they poison breed.
Antioch, farewell, for wisdom sees those men°   *men who*
Blush not in actions blacker than the night
Will 'schew no course° to keep them from the light.   *eschew no means*
180   One sin, I know, another doth provoke.
Murder's as near to lust as flame to smoke.
Poison and treason are the hands of sin,
Ay, and the targets° to put off the shame.   *shields*
Then, lest my life be cropped to keep you clear,°   *(of blame)*
185   By flight I'll shun the danger which I fear.   *Exit*
     Enter ANTIOCHUS
ANTIOCHUS   He hath found the meaning, for the which we mean
To have his head. He must not live
To trumpet forth my infamy, nor tell the world
Antiochus doth sin in such a loathèd manner,

---

2. *The blind . . . for't:* When we blindly protest against the injustice of our superiors, we die (with "mole" meaning "worm"), or innocent creatures suffer (here, the "mole" is different from the "worm" and may even feed on it).
3. Since bad deeds become worse for being known.
4. All love the daughter they raised when young. The obvious meaning—all love their mother's womb—gets the incest backward.
5. Hope of a correct answer (an heir), with the successful answer (succession) coming from such a fine specimen (Pericles' regal lineage).

190 And therefore instantly this prince must die,
For by his fall my honour must keep high.
Who attends us there?
      Enter THALIART
THALIART   Doth your highness call?
ANTIOCHUS   Thaliart, you are of our chamber,° Thaliart,   *my chamberlain*
And to your secrecy our mind partakes°   *imparts*
195 Her° private actions. For your faithfulness   *Its*
We will advance you, Thaliart. Behold,
Here's poison, and here's gold.
We hate the Prince of Tyre, and thou must kill him.
It fits° thee not to ask the reason. Why?   *befits*
200 Because we bid it. Say, is it done?
THALIART   My lord, 'tis done.
ANTIOCHUS   Enough.
      Enter a MESSENGER [*hastily*]
Let your breath cool yourself, telling your haste.[6]
MESSENGER   Your majesty, Prince Pericles is fled.   [*Exit*]
ANTIOCHUS [*to* THALIART]   As thou wilt live, fly after; like an
205   arrow
Shot from a well-experienced archer hits
The mark his eye doth level° at, so thou   *aim*
Never return unless it be to say
'Your majesty, Prince Pericles is dead.'
210 THALIART   If I can get him in my pistol's length°   *range*
I'll make him sure° enough. Farewell, your highness.   *unthreatening (dead)*
ANTIOCHUS   Thaliart, adieu.   [*Exit* THALIART]
      Till Pericles be dead
My heart can lend no succour to my head.
      [*Exit. The heads are concealed*]

Scene 2

Enter PERICLES [*distempered*] *with his lords*
PERICLES   Let none disturb us.   [*Exeunt lords*]
      Why should this change of thoughts,°   *changed state of mind*
The sad companion, dull-eyed melancholy,
Be my so used° a guest as not an hour   *accustomed*
In the day's glorious walk or peaceful night,
5 The tomb where grief should sleep, can breed me quiet?
Here pleasures court mine eyes, and mine eyes shun them,
And danger, which I feared, 's° at Antioch,   *is*
Whose arm seems far too short to hit me here.
Yet neither pleasure's art can joy my spirits,
10 Nor yet care's author's distance comfort me.
Then it is thus: the passions of the mind,°   *obsessions*
That have their first conception by misdread,°   *fear*
Have after-nourishment and life by care,°   *worry*
And what was first but fear what might be done
15 Grows elder now, and cares it be not done.[1]
And so with me. The great Antiochus,

---

6. Use your rapid breathing to cool yourself by explaining the reason for your haste.

Scene 2 (Act 1, Scene 2, in other modern editions)
Location: The palace at Tyre.
1. *And what . . . done:* And what starts out as simple fear matures into a more rational concern for safety.

'Gainst whom I am too little to contend,
Since he's so great can° make his will his act,   *that he can*
Will think me speaking though I swear to silence,
20   Nor boots it° me to say I honour him   *does it help*
If he suspect I may dishonour him.
And what may make him blush in being known,
He'll stop the course by which it might be known.
With hostile forces he'll o'erspread the land,
25   And with th'ostent° of war will look so huge   *display*
Amazement° shall drive courage from the state,   *Terror*
Our men be vanquished ere they do resist,
And subjects punished that ne'er thought offence,
Which care of them, not pity of myself,
30   Who am no more but as the tops of trees
Which fence° the roots they grow by and defend them,   *shield*
Makes both my body pine and soul to languish,
And punish that° before that he would punish.[2]   *(myself)*
            Enter all the LORDS, [*among them old* HELICANUS,] *to*
            PERICLES
FIRST LORD   Joy and all comfort in your sacred breast!
35   SECOND LORD   And keep your mind peaceful[3] and comfortable.
HELICANUS   Peace, peace, and give experience tongue.
    [*To* PERICLES] You[4] do not well so to abuse yourself,
    To waste your body here with pining sorrow,
    Upon whose safety doth depend the lives
40   And the prosperity of a whole kingdom.
    'Tis ill in you to do it, and no less
    Ill in your council not to contradict it.
    They do abuse the King that flatter him,
    For flatt'ry is the bellows blows° up sin;   *that blows*
45   The thing the which is flattered, but a spark,
    To which that wind gives heat and stronger glowing;
    Whereas reproof, obedient and in order,
    Fits kings as they are men, for they may err.
    When Signor Sooth[5] here does proclaim a peace
50   He flatters you, makes war upon your life.
            [*He kneels*]
    Prince, pardon me, or strike me if you please.
    I cannot be much lower than my knees.
PERICLES   All leave us else;° but let your cares o'erlook   *except Helicanus*
    What shipping and what lading's[6] in our haven,
    And then return to us.   [*Exeunt* LORDS]
55   Helicane, thou
    Hast movèd us. What seest thou in our looks?
HELICANUS   An angry brow, dread lord.
PERICLES   If there be such a dart° in princes' frowns,   *danger*
    How durst thy tongue move anger to our brows?
HELICANUS   How dares the plants look up to heav'n from
60   whence

---

2. *before . . . punish:* before he punishes me ("that").
3. Q1 has "And keep your mind till you return to us peaceful," a phrase that anticipates Pericles' "return to us" (line 55). The omission here eliminates the speaker's clairvoyance about a trip that no one else contemplates until line 111.

4. Lines 37–42 are not in Q1 but are adapted from Wilkins's *Painful Adventures* (PA). They explain why Helicanus thinks Pericles has been, but should not be, flattered.
5. Mock name for a flatterer, a soother of egos.
6. *let . . . lading's:* look carefully to find out what vessels are coming and going and what cargo is.

They have their nourishment?

PERICLES   Thou knowest I have pow'r to take thy life from thee.

HELICANUS   I have ground the axe myself; do you but strike the
    blow.

PERICLES [*lifting him up*]   Rise, prithee, rise. Sit down. Thou art
    no flatterer,
65 I thank thee for it, and the heav'ns forbid
    That kings should let their ears hear their faults hid.
    Fit counsellor and servant for a prince,
    Who by thy wisdom mak'st a prince thy servant,
    What wouldst thou have me do?

HELICANUS   To bear with patience
70 Such griefs as you do lay upon yourself.

PERICLES   Thou speak'st like a physician, Helicanus,
    That ministers a potion unto me
    That thou wouldst tremble to receive thyself.
    Attend me,° then. I went to Antioch,   Listen to me
75 Where, as thou know'st, against the face of death
    I sought the purchase° of a glorious beauty   acquisition
    From whence an issue I might propagate,
    As children are heav'n's blessings: to parents, objects;[7]
    Are arms° to princes, and bring joys to subjects.   weapons
80 Her face was to mine eye beyond all wonder,
    The rest—hark in thine ear—as black as incest,
    Which by my knowledge found, the sinful father
    Seemed not to strike, but smooth.° But thou know'st this,   reconcile
    'Tis time to fear when tyrants seems to kiss;
85 Which fear so grew in me I hither fled
    Under the covering of careful night,
    Who seemed my good protector, and being here
    Bethought me what was past, what might succeed.°   happen next
    I knew him tyrannous, and tyrants' fears
90 Decrease not, but grow faster than the years.
    And should he doubt°—as doubt no° doubt he doth—   suspect / as no
    That I should open° to the list'ning air   declare
    How many worthy princes' bloods were shed
    To keep his bed of blackness unlaid ope,
95 To lop that doubt he'll fill this land with arms,
    And make pretence of wrong that I have done him,
    When all for mine—if I may call—offence
    Must feel war's blow, who° spares not innocence;   which
    Which love to all, of which thyself art one,
    Who now reproved'st me for't—

100 HELICANUS   Alas, sir.

PERICLES   Drew sleep out of mine eyes, blood from my cheeks,
    Musings into my mind, with thousand doubts,
    How I might stop this tempest ere it came,
    And, finding little comfort to relieve them,°   (his subjects)
105 I thought it princely charity to grieve them.°   (by my sorrow)

HELICANUS   Well, my lord, since you have giv'n me leave to
        speak,
    Freely will I speak. Antiochus you fear,

---

7. Objects of affection. This line, added in the present edition, fills a long-recognized gap in Q1 between lines 77 and 79.

And justly too, I think, you fear the tyrant,
Who either by public war or private treason
110 Will take away your life.
Therefore, my lord, go travel for a while,
Till that his rage and anger be forgot,
Or destinies do cut his thread of life.[8]
Your rule direct° to any; if to me,   *assign*
115 Day serves not light more faithful than I'll be.
PERICLES   I do not doubt thy faith,
But should he in my absence wrong thy liberties?°   *jurisdictions*
HELICANUS   We'll mingle our bloods together in the earth
From whence we had our being and our birth.
120 PERICLES   Tyre, I now look from thee then, and to Tarsus
Intend° my travel, where I'll hear from thee,   *Direct*
And by whose letters I'll dispose myself.
The care I had and have of subjects' good
On thee I lay, whose wisdom's strength can bear it.
125 I'll take thy word for faith, not ask thine oath;
Who° shuns not to break one will sure crack both.   *He who*
But in our orbs° we'll live so round° and safe   *places / prudently*
That time of both this truth shall ne'er convince:°   *refute*
Thou showed'st a subject's shine, I a true prince.°   *Exeunt*   *prince's*

Scene 3

Enter THALIART

THALIART   So this is Tyre, and this the court. Here must I kill
King Pericles, and if I do it and am caught I am like to be
hanged abroad, but[1] if I do it not, I am sure to be hanged at
home. 'Tis dangerous. Well, I perceive he was a wise fellow
5 and had good discretion that, being bid to ask what he would
of the King, desired he might know none of his secrets.[2] Now
do I see he had some reason for't, for if a king bid a man be a
villain, he's bound by the indenture° of his oath to be one.   *servant's contract*
Hush, here comes the lords of Tyre.

     Enter HELICANUS [*and*] AESCHINES, *with*
     other lords

10 HELICANUS   You shall not need, my fellow peers of Tyre,
Further to question of your King's departure.
His sealed° commission left in trust with me   *(with royal wax)*
Does speak sufficiently he's gone to travel.
THALIART [*aside*]   How? The King gone?
15 HELICANUS   If further yet you will be satisfied
Why, as it were unlicensed of your loves,°   *without your approval*
He would depart, I'll give some light unto you.
Being at Antioch—
THALIART [*aside*]   What from Antioch?
HELICANUS   Royal Antiochus, on what cause I know not,
20 Took some displeasure at him—at least he judged so—
And doubting lest° that he had erred or sinned,   *And fearing*
To show his sorrow he'd correct° himself;   *he wished to punish*

---

8. In Greek mythology, a person died when the three
Fates "cut his thread of life."
Scene 3 (Act 1, Scene 3)
Location: The palace at Tyre.
1. *if . . . but:* this is a conjectural editorial addition that

semantically balances Thaliart's reflection on the conse-
quences of failure. *like:* likely. *abroad:* in Tyre.
2. According to Plutarch's *Lives* and Barnabe Riche in
Souldiers Wishe to Briton's Welfare (1604), the poet Phil-
ippides made this request of King Lysimachus of Thrace.

So puts himself unto the ship-man's toil,
With whom each minute threatens life or death.

25 THALIART   [aside]   Well, I perceive I shall not be hanged now,
Although I would.[3]
But since he's gone, the King's ears it must please
He scaped° the land to perish on the seas.   *escaped*
I'll present myself.—Peace to the lords of Tyre.
30 Lord Thaliart am I, of Antioch.[4]

HELICANUS   Lord Thaliart of Antioch is welcome.

THALIART   From King Antiochus I come
With message unto princely Pericles,
But since my landing I have understood
35 Your lord's betook himself to unknown travels.
Now my message must return from whence it came.

HELICANUS   We have no reason to enquire it,
Commended° to our master, not to us.   *Directed*
Yet ere you shall depart, this we desire:
40 As friends to Antioch, we may feast° in Tyre.   *Exeunt*   *prepare a feast for you*

Scene 4

Enter CLEON, *the Governor of Tarsus, with* [DIONYZA]
his wife, and others

CLEON   My Dionyza, shall we rest us here
And, by relating tales of others' griefs,
See if 'twill teach us to forget our own?

DIONYZA   That were to blow at fire in hope to quench it,
5 For who digs° hills because they do aspire   *whoever digs up*
Throws down one mountain to cast up a higher.
O my distressèd lord, e'en such our griefs are;
Here they're but felt and seen with midges' eyes,°   *as small matters*
But like to groves, being topped° they higher rise.   *pruned*

10 CLEON   O Dionyza,
Who wanteth food and will not say he wants it,
Or can conceal his hunger till he famish?
Our tongues our sorrows dictate to sound° deep   *proclaim; plumb*
Our woes into the air, our eyes to weep
15 Till lungs fetch breath that may proclaim them louder,
That, if heav'n slumber while their° creatures want,   *(heaven's)*
They° may awake their° helps to comfort them.   *(creatures) / (heaven's)*
I'll then discourse our woes, felt sev'ral years,
And, wanting° breath to speak, help me with tears.   *when I'm out of*

20 DIONYZA   As you think best, sir.

CLEON   This Tarsus o'er which I have the government,
A city o'er whom plenty held full hand,°   *generously presided*
For riches strewed herself ev'n in the streets,
Whose tow'rs bore heads so high they kissed the clouds,
25 And strangers ne'er beheld but wondered° at,   *without admiring*
Whose men and dames so jetted° and adorned°   *strutted / (themselves)*
Like one another's glass to trim them[1] by;
Their tables were stored full to glad the sight,
And not so much to feed on as delight.

---

3. Even if I return home (?); even if that's what I wanted.
4. This line, not in Q1, is added to explain how Helicanus knows who Thaliart is.

Scene 4 (Act 1, Scene 4)
Location: Tarsus.
1. Mirror to dress themselves. (Everyone was a model of fashion.)

30   All poverty was scorned, and pride so great
       The name of help grew odious to repeat.
    DIONYZA   O, 'tis too true.
    CLEON   But see what heav'n can do by this our change.
       Those mouths who but of late° earth, sea, and air   *just recently*
35   Were all too little to content and please,
       Although they gave their creatures in abundance,
       As houses are defiled for want° of use,   *by lack*
       They are now starved for want of exercise.
       Those palates who, not yet two summers younger,
40   Must have inventions° to delight the taste   *Demanded novel foods*
       Would now be glad of bread and beg for it.
       Those mothers who to nuzzle up° their babes   *raise*
       Thought naught too curious° are ready now   *exquisite*
       To eat those little darlings whom they loved.
45   So sharp are hunger's teeth that man and wife
       Draw lots who first shall die to lengthen life.°   *(of the other)*
       Here weeping stands a lord, there lies a lady dying,
       Here many sink, yet those which see them fall
       Have scarce strength left to give them burial.
50   Is not this true?
    DIONYZA   Our cheeks and hollow eyes do witness it.
    CLEON   O, let those cities that of plenty's cup
       And her prosperities so largely taste
       With their superfluous riots,° heed these tears!   *excessive indulgence*
55   The misery of Tarsus may be theirs.
          Enter a [fainting] LORD [*of Tarsus slowly*]
    LORD   Where's the Lord Governor?
    CLEON   Here. Speak out thy sorrows which thou bring'st in
       haste,
       For comfort is too far for us t'expect.
    LORD   We have descried upon our neighbouring shore
60   A portly sail° of ships make hitherward.   *stately fleet*
    CLEON   I thought as much.
       One sorrow never comes but brings an heir
       That may succeed as his inheritor,
       And so in ours. Some neighbour nation,
65   Taking advantage of our misery,
       Hath stuffed these hollow vessels with their power°   *soldiers*
       To beat us down, the which are down already,
       And make a conquest of unhappy men,
       Whereas no glory's got to overcome.²
70   LORD   That's the least fear,° for by the semblance   *not to be feared*
       Of their white flags displayed they bring us peace,
       And come to us as favourers, not foes.
    CLEON   Thou speak'st like him's untutored to repeat;³
       Who makes the fairest show means most deceit.
75   But bring they° what they will and what they can,   *let them bring*
       What need we fear?
       Our grave's the low'st,° and we are half-way there.   *lowest we can go*
       Go tell their gen'ral we attend° him here   *await*
       To know for what he comes, and whence he comes.

---

2. Where there's no glory in winning.
3. Like him who hasn't learned (the following lesson) by heart.

80 LORD I go, my lord.   [*Exit*]
   CLEON Welcome is peace, if he on peace consist;°   *resolve*
      If wars, we are unable to resist.
         Enter [the LORD *again conducting]* PERICLES *with atten-*
            dants
   PERICLES [*to* CLEON] Lord Governor, for so we hear you are,
      Let not our ships and number of our men
85   Be like a beacon fixed t'amaze° your eyes.   *to terrify*
      We have heard your miseries as far as Tyre,
      Since entering your unshut gates have witnessed
      The widowed⁴ desolation of your streets;
      Nor come we to add sorrow to your hearts,
90   But to relieve them of their heavy load;
      And these our ships, you happily° may think   *perhaps*
      Are like the Trojan horse was fraught within
      With bloody veins importing overthrow,⁵
      Are stored with corn to make your needy bread,
95   And give them life whom hunger starved half dead.
   ALL OF TARSUS [*falling on their knees and weeping*] The gods of
         Greece protect you, and we'll pray for you!
   PERICLES Arise, I pray you, rise.
      We do not look for reverence but for love,
      And harbourage for me, my ships and men.
100 CLEON The which when any shall not gratify,
      Or pay you with unthankfulness in thought,
      Be it our wives, our children, or ourselves,
      The curse of heav'n and men succeed° their evils!   *follow from*
      Till when—the which I hope shall ne'er be seen—
105   Your grace is welcome to our town and us.
   PERICLES Which welcome we'll accept, feast here a while,
      Until our stars that frown lend us a smile.   *Exeunt*

Scene 5

         Enter GOWER
   GOWER Here have you seen a mighty king
      His child, iwis,° to incest bring;   *certainly*
      A better prince° and benign lord   *(Pericles)*
      Prove awe-full° both in deed and word.   *worthy of respect*
5   Be quiet then, as men should be,
      Till he hath passed necessity.¹
      I'll show you those° in trouble's reign,   *those who*
      Losing a mite, a mountain gain.
      The good in conversation,²
10   To whom I give my benison,°   *blessing*
      Is still at Tarsus where each man
      Thinks all is writ he speken can,³
      And to remember what he does

4. *Since . . . widowed*: this line, adapted from *PA*, replaces
Q1's "And seene the"; the substitution prevents the infer-
ence that Pericles has "seen" Tarsus's "desolation" "as far
as Tyre."
5. *was . . . overthrow*: was laden ("fraught") with Greek
soldiers ("bloody veins") who sacked the city.
Scene 5 (Other editions treat Gower's monologue as a
prologue to Act 2 and start Act 2, Scene 1, at line 41. The
present edition, however, interprets "here he comes" [line

39] as evidence that the scene does not change.)
Location: The seashore at Pentapolis, which was the
coastal area of Cyrenaica, in the northeast corner of what
is now Libya. This scene locates it in Greece, however
(line 100).
1. *necessity*: the suffering that is his lot.
2. The good man (Pericles) in conduct.
3. Archaic (as often in Gower's speeches): Thinks all Per-
icles says is holy scripture ("writ").

His statue build to make him glorious.
15   But tidings to the contrary
Are brought your eyes. What need speak I?
                    Dumb show.[4]

> *Enter at one door* PERICLES *talking with* CLEON, *all the*
> *train with them. Enter at another door a gentleman with*
> *a letter to* PERICLES. PERICLES *shows the letter to* CLEON.
> PERICLES *gives the messenger a reward, and knights him.*
> *Exeunt [with their trains]* PERICLES *at one door and*
> CLEON *at another*

Good Helicane that stayed at home,
Not to eat honey like a drone
From others' labours, for that he strive
20   To killen bad, keep good alive,
And to fulfil his prince' desire
Sent word of all that haps in Tyre;
How Thaliart came full bent with° sin   *intent on*
And hid intent to murdren him,
25   And that in Tarsus was not best
Longer for him to make his rest.
He deeming so put forth to seas,
Where when men been° there's seldom ease,   *are*
For now the wind begins to blow;
30   Thunder above and deeps below
Makes such unquiet that the ship
Should° house him safe is wrecked and split,   *Which should*
And he, good prince, having all lost,
By waves from coast to coast is tossed.
35   All perishen of man, of pelf,°   *goods*
Ne aught escapend° but himself,   *Nothing escaping*
Till fortune, tired with doing bad,
Threw him ashore to give him glad.°   *joy*
            Enter PERICLES *wet [and half-naked]*
And here he comes. What shall be next
40   Pardon old Gower; this 'longs[5] the text.   [*Exit*]
            [*Thunder and lightning*]
PERICLES   Yet cease your ire, you angry stars of heaven!
Wind, rain, and thunder, remember earthly man
Is but a substance that must yield to you,
And I, as fits my nature, do obey you.
45   Alas, the seas hath cast me on the rocks,
Washed me from shore to shore, and left my breath
Nothing to think on but ensuing death.
Let it suffice the greatness of your powers
To have bereft a prince of all his fortunes,
50   And, having thrown him from your wat'ry grave,
Here to have death in peace is all he'll crave.
            [*He sits.*]
            Enter [two poor] FISHERMEN [*one the* MASTER, *the other*
            his man]
MASTER [*calling*]   What ho, Pilch![6]

---

4. In Renaissance drama, a brief pantomime perfor-
mance used to advance the plot.
5. Continuing would lengthen Gower's speech too
much; or, *'longs:* belongs to.

6. Nickname derived from a rustic leather garment. The
nicknames, homely references, and social critiques in this
scene have a distinctively English feel.

SECOND FISHERMAN [*calling*]   Ha, come and bring away the nets.
MASTER [*calling*]   What, Patchbreech,° I say!   (*another nickname*)
[*Enter a* THIRD FISHERMAN *with a hood upon his head
and a filthy leathern pelt upon his back, unseemly clad,
and homely to behold. He brings nets to dry and repair*]

55   THIRD FISHERMAN   What say you, master?
MASTER   Look how thou stirrest now. Come away, or I'll fetch
th' with a wanion.[7]
THIRD FISHERMAN   Faith, master, I am thinking of the poor men
that were cast away before us° even now.   *in our sight*
60   MASTER   Alas, poor souls, it grieved my heart to hear what pitiful
cries they made to us to help them when, well-a-day,° we could   *alas*
scarce help ourselves.
THIRD FISHERMAN   Nay, master, said not I as much when I saw
the porpoise how he bounced and tumbled?° They say they're   (*predictive of storms*)
65   half fish, half flesh. A plague on them, they ne'er come but I
look to be washed.° Master, I marvel how the fishes live in the sea.   (*by a storm*)
MASTER   Why, as men do a-land°— the great ones eat up the   *on land*
little ones. I can compare our rich misers to nothing so fitly as
to a whale: a° plays and tumbles, driving the poor fry before   *he*
70   him, and at last devours them all at a mouthful. Such whales
have I heard on° o'th' land, who never leave gaping° till they   *of / close their mouths*
swallowed the whole parish: church, steeple, bells, and all.
PERICLES [*aside*]   A pretty moral.
THIRD FISHERMAN   But, master, if I had been the sexton, I would
75   have been that day in the belfry.
SECOND FISHERMAN   Why, man?
THIRD FISHERMAN   Because he should have swallowed me, too,
and when I had been in his belly I would have kept such a
jangling of the bells that he should never have left till he cast°   *vomited*
80   bells, steeple, church, and parish up again. But if the good
King Simonides were of my mind—
PERICLES [*aside*]   Simonides?
THIRD FISHERMAN   We would purge the land of these drones that
rob the bee of her honey.
85   PERICLES [*aside*]   How from the finny subject° of the sea   *citizens*
These fishers tell th'infirmities of men,
And from their wat'ry empire recollect°   *gather*
All that may men approve or men detect!°   *expose*
[*Coming forward*] Peace be at your labour, honest fishermen.
90   SECOND FISHERMAN   Honest, good fellow? What's that? If it be a
day fits you, scratch't out of the calendar, and nobody look after it.[8]
PERICLES   May° see the sea hath cast upon your coast—   *You may*
SECOND FISHERMAN   What a drunken knave was the sea to cast
thee in our way![9]
95   PERICLES   A man, whom both the waters and the wind
In that vast tennis-court hath made the ball
For them to play upon,° entreats you pity him.   *with*
He asks of you that never used to beg.

7. *Look . . . wanion:* Look how quick you are (ironic).
Hurry along, or I'll beat you with a vengeance.
8. *Honest . . . after it:* If "honest" were a day in the calen-
dar that suited someone in your sorry state, you could
remove it without anyone noticing; honesty is so rare
already, no one would notice its departure. (Perhaps a

line is missing before line 89, in which Pericles wishes
the fishermen good day.)
9. Like St. Peter, the fishermen are literally fishers of
men, who help save Pericles from the sea. Their discus-
sion of whales also evokes the tale of Jonah. The scene is
full of biblical echoes.

MASTER   No, friend, cannot you beg? Here's them° in our coun-   *There are those*
100   try of Greece gets° more with begging than we can do with   *who get*
working.
SECOND FISHERMAN   Canst thou catch any fishes, then?
PERICLES   I never practised it.
SECOND FISHERMAN   Nay, then thou wilt starve, sure; for here's
105   nothing to be got nowadays unless thou canst fish for't.°   *get it by deception*
PERICLES   What I have been, I have forgot to know,
But what I am, want teaches me to think on:
A man thronged up° with cold; my veins are chill,   *overwhelmed*
And have no more of life than may suffice
110   To give my tongue that heat to crave your help,
Which if you shall refuse, when I am dead,
For that° I am a man, pray see me buried.   *Because*
      [*He falls down*]
MASTER   Die, quotha?° Now, gods forbid't an° I have a gown   *says he / if*
here! [*To* PERICLES, *lifting him up from the ground*] Come, put
115   it on, keep thee warm. Now, afore me,° a handsome fellow!   *on my word*
Come, thou shalt go home, and we'll have flesh for holidays,
fish for fasting-days, and moreo'er puddings° and flapjacks, and   *sausages*
thou shalt be welcome.
PERICLES   I thank you, sir.
120   SECOND FISHERMAN   Hark you, my friend, you said you could
not beg?
PERICLES   I did but crave.
SECOND FISHERMAN   But crave? Then I'll turn craver too, an so I
shall scape whipping.°   *(for begging)*
125   PERICLES   Why, are all your beggars whipped, then?
SECOND FISHERMAN   O, not all, my friend, not all; for if all your°   *the*
beggars were whipped I would wish no better office than to be
beadle.[1]
MASTER[2]   Thine office, knave—
130   SECOND FISHERMAN   Is to draw up the other nets. I'll go.
               [*Exit with* THIRD FISHERMAN]
PERICLES [*aside*]   How well this honest mirth becomes their
labour!
MASTER [*seating himself by* PERICLES]   Hark you, sir, do you
know where ye are?
135   PERICLES   Not well.
MASTER   Why, I'll tell you. This is called Pentapolis, and our
king the good Simonides.
PERICLES   'The good Simonides' do you call him?
MASTER   Ay, sir, and he deserves so to be called for his peaceable
140   reign and good government.
PERICLES   He is a happy king, since from his subjects
He gains the name of good by his government.
How far is his court distant from this shore?
MASTER   Marry,° sir, some half a day's journey. And I'll tell you,   *To be sure*
145   he hath a fair daughter, and tomorrow is her birthday, and
there are princes and knights come from all parts of the world
to joust and tourney for her love.

---

1. Court official who administered corporal punishment.   continuation of the Second Fisherman's speech: "But
2. To improve the motivation of the Second Fisherman's   Master, I'll go draw up the net."
exit, this edition substitutes "MASTER . . . I'll go" for Q1's

PERICLES Were but my fortunes answerable
    To my desires I could wish to make one° there.   *be one of the princes*
150 MASTER O, sir, things must be as they may, and what a man
    cannot get himself, he may lawfully deal for with his wife's soul.[3]
        Enter the [other] two FISHERMEN *drawing up a net*
SECOND FISHERMAN Help, master, help! Here's a fish hangs in
    the net like a poor man's right in the law; 'twill hardly come out.
        [Before help comes, up comes their prize]
    Ha, bots on't,° 'tis come at last, and 'tis turned to a rusty armour.   *a pox (plague) on it*
155 PERICLES An armour, friends? I pray you let me see it.
    [Aside] Thanks, fortune, yet that after all thy crosses°   *hardships*
    Thou giv'st me somewhat to repair my losses,
    And though° it was mine own, part of my heritage   *Even though*
    Which my dead father did bequeath to me
160 With this strict charge ev'n as he left his life:
    'Keep it, my Pericles; it hath been a shield
    'Twixt me and death,' and pointed to this brace,°   *arm armor*
    'For that° it saved me, keep it. In like necessity,   *Because*
    The which the Gods forfend,° the same may defend thee.'   *forbid*
165 It kept° where I kept, I so dearly loved it,   *remained*
    Till the rough seas that spares not any man
    Took it in rage, though calmed have giv'n't again.
    I thank thee for't. My shipwreck now's no ill,
    Since I have here my° father gave in 's° will.   *what my / his*
170 MASTER What mean you, sir?
PERICLES To beg of you, kind friends, this coat of worth,
    For it was sometime target° to a king.   *once a shield*
    I know it by this mark. He loved me dearly,
    And for his sake I wish the having of it,
175 And that you'd guide me to your sov'reign's court,
    Where with't I may appear a gentleman.
    And if that ever my low fortune's better,
    I'll pay your bounties,° till then rest your debtor.   *repay your generosity*
MASTER Why, wilt thou tourney for the lady?
180 PERICLES I'll show the virtue I have learned in arms.
MASTER Why, d'ye take it, and the gods give thee good on't!
SECOND FISHERMAN Ay, but hark you, my friend, 'twas we that
    made° up this garment through the rough seams of the waters.   *raised*
    There are certain condolements,[4] certain vails.° I hope, sir, if   *tips*
185 you thrive, you'll remember from whence you had this.
PERICLES Believe't, I will.
    By your furtherance I'm clothed in steel,
    And spite of all the rapture° of the sea   *plundering*
    This jewel holds his building° on my arm.   *its place*
190 Unto thy° value I will mount myself   *(the jewel's)*
    Upon a courser° whose delightsome steps   *a horse*
    Shall make the gazer joy to see him tread.
    Only, my friends, I yet am unprovided
    Of a pair of bases.[5]
195 SECOND FISHERMAN We'll sure provide. Thou shalt have my

---

3. *what . . . soul:* probably ironic: when a man can no longer "get" (make a living; have children), he can legitimately do so by persuading his "wife's soul" (her conscience; also, "his wife's hole") to trade (prostitute) herself (with men who will "get"—beget—children with her).

The additions of "himself" and "with" (line 151) in this edition make the meaning more accessible.
4. Blunder for "dole."
5. Skirts for armored knights on horseback.

best gown to make thee a pair, and I'll bring thee to the court
myself.
PERICLES   Then honour be but equal to my will,
This day I'll rise, or else add ill to ill.

[Exeunt with nets and armour]

Scene 6

[Sennet.] Enter KING SIMONIDES *and* THAISA *with*
*[*LORDS *in] attendance [and sit on two thrones]*
KING SIMONIDES   Are the knights ready to begin the triumph?°   *tournament*
FIRST LORD   They are, my liege,
And stay° your coming to present themselves.   *await*
KING SIMONIDES   Return° them we are ready; and our daughter,   *Answer*
5   In honour of whose birth these triumphs are,
Sits here like beauty's child, whom nature gat°   *conceived*
For men to see and, seeing, wonder at.

[Exit one]

THAISA   It pleaseth you, my father, to express
My commendations great, whose merit's less.
10   KING SIMONIDES   It's fit it should be so, for princes° are   *rulers*
A model which heav'n makes like to itself.
As jewels lose their glory if neglected,
So princes their renown, if not respected.
'Tis now your office, daughter, to entertain°   *review*
15   The labour of each knight in his device.[1]
THAISA   Which, to preserve mine honour, I'll perform.
[Flourish.] The first knight passes by [richly armed, and
his page before him, bearing his device on his shield,
delivers it to the Lady THAISA]
KING SIMONIDES   Who is the first that doth prefer° himself?   *present*
THAISA   A knight of Sparta, my renownèd father,
And the device he bears upon his shield
20   Is a black Ethiop reaching at the sun.
The word, *Lux tua vita mihi.*[2]
[She presents it to the KING]
KING SIMONIDES   He loves you well that holds his life of° you.   *receives his life from*
[He returns it to the page, who exits with the first
knight.]
[Flourish.] The second knight [passes by richly armed,
and his page before him, bearing his device on his
shield, delivers it to the Lady THAISA]
Who is the second that presents himself?
THAISA   A prince of Macedon, my royal father,
25   And the device he bears upon his shield
An armèd knight that's conquered by a lady.
The motto thus: *Piùe per dolcezza che per forza.*[3]
[She presents it to the KING]
KING SIMONIDES   You win him more by lenity than force.[4]

Scene 6 (Act 2, Scene 2)
Location: Pentapolis, area near the tournament arena,
including a reviewing stand.
1. An emblem in heraldry, which concerns the right to
bear coats of arms.
2. Your light is my life (Latin).

3. More by gentleness than by force (Italian). Q1 pre-
cedes this phrase with the words "in Spanish"—probably
an error by the reporter. (See the Textual Note.)
4. Not in Q1; adapted from *PA.* Simonides comments on
three of the other five mottoes.

[*He returns it to the page, who exits with the second knight.*]
[*Flourish. The*] *third knight* [*passes by richly armed, and his page before him, bearing his device on his shield, delivers it to the Lady* THAISA]

And what's the third?

THAISA   The third of Antioch,
30   And his device a wreath of chivalry.[5]
      The word, *Me pompae provexit apex.*[6]
      [*She presents it to the* KING]

KING SIMONIDES   Desire of renown he doth devise,
      The which hath drawn him to this enterprise.[7]
      [*He returns it to the page, who exits with the third knight.*]
      [*Flourish. The*] *fourth knight* [*passes by richly armed, and his page before him, bearing his device on his shield, delivers it to the Lady* THAISA]

What is the fourth?

THAISA   A knight of Athens bearing[8]
35   A burning torch that's turnèd upside down.
      The word, *Qui me alit me extinguit.*[9]
      [*She presents it to the* KING]

KING SIMONIDES   Which shows that beauty hath this power and will,
      Which can as well inflame as it can kill.
      [*He returns it to the page, who exits with the fourth knight.*]
      [*Flourish. The*] *fifth knight* [*passes by richly armed, and his page before him, bearing his device on his shield, delivers it to the Lady* THAISA]

And who the fifth?

THAISA   The fifth, a prince of Corinth,
40   Presents[1] an hand environèd with clouds,
      Holding out gold that's by the touchstone[2] tried.
      The motto thus: *Sic spectanda fides.*[3]
      [*She presents it to the* KING]

KING SIMONIDES   So faith is to be looked into.[4]
      [*He returns it to the page, who exits with the fifth knight.*]
      [*Flourish. The*] *sixth knight* [PERICLES, *in a rusty armour, who, having neither page to deliver his shield nor shield to deliver, presents his device unto the Lady* THAISA]

And what's the sixth and last, the which the knight himself
45   With such a graceful courtesy° delivereth?   bow

THAISA   He seems to be a stranger, but his present° is   presented object
      A withered branch that's only green at top.
      The motto, *In hac spe vivo.*°   I live in this hope

KING SIMONIDES   From the dejected state wherein he is
50   He hopes by you his fortunes yet may flourish.

---

5. (Heraldic term): twisted band that joins the crest and the knight's helmet.
6. The summit of glory has led me on (Latin).
7. Lines 32–33 are not in Q1; adapted from *PA*.
8. Not in Q1; adapted from *PA*.
9. Who nourishes me extinguishes me.
1. Lines 39–40, adapted from *PA*, replace Q1's "The fift";

the substitution produces symmetry with the other knights' introductions.
2. Black stone used to check the purity of gold and silver; symbol of fidelity.
3. Thus is faith to be examined.
4. Not in Q1; adapted from *PA*.

FIRST LORD   He had need mean° better than his outward show   *must intend something*
　　　　Can any way speak in his just commend,°   *on his behalf*
　　　　For by his rusty outside he appears
　　　　T'have practised more the whipstock than the lance.[5]
55　SECOND LORD   He well may be a stranger,° for he comes   *foreigner*
　　　　Unto an honoured triumph strangely furnished.°   *bizarrely equipped*
　　THIRD LORD   And on set purpose let his armour rust
　　　　Until this day, to scour it in the dust.[6]
　　KING SIMONIDES   Opinion's but a fool, that makes us scan
60　　The outward habit° for the inward man.   *costume*
　　　　　　[*Cornetts*]°   *Ceremonial trumpets*
　　　　But stay, the knights are coming. We will withdraw
　　　　Into the gallery.   [*Exeunt*]
　　　　　　[*Cornetts and*] *great shouts* [*within*]*, and all cry 'The*
　　　　　　mean° knight!'   *impoverished*

Scene 7

[*A stately banquet is brought in.*] *Enter* KING [SIMON-
IDES, THAISA *and their train at one door, and at another
door a* MARSHAL *conducting* PERICLES] *and* [*the other*]
KNIGHTS *from tilting*
　KING SIMONIDES [*to the* KNIGHTS]   To say you're welcome were
　　　　superfluous.
　　To place upon the volume of your deeds
　　As in a title page[1] your worth in arms
　　Were more than you expect, or more than's fit,
5　　Since every worth in show° commends itself.   *in practice*
　　Prepare for mirth, for mirth becomes a feast.
　　You're princes, and my guests.
　THAISA [*to* PERICLES]   But you, my knight and guest;
　　To whom this wreath of victory I give,
　　And crown you king of this day's happiness.
10　PERICLES   'Tis more by fortune, lady, than my merit.
　KING SIMONIDES   Call it by what you will, the day is yours,
　　　And here I hope is none that envies it.
　　In framing° artists art hath thus decreed,   *making*
　　To make some good, but others to exceed.
　　You are her laboured scholar.[2] [*To* THAISA] Come, queen
15　　　o'th' feast—
　　For, daughter, so you are—here take your place.
　　　[*To* MARSHAL]   Marshal the rest as they deserve their grace.[3]
　KNIGHTS   We are honoured much by good Simonides.
　KING SIMONIDES   Your presence glads our days; honour we love,
20　　For who hates honour hates the gods above.
　MARSHAL [*to* PERICLES]   Sir, yonder is your place.
　PERICLES   Some other is more fit.
　FIRST KNIGHT   Contend not, sir, for we are gentlemen
　　Have° neither in our hearts nor outward eyes   *Who've*
　　Envied the great, nor shall the low despise.

---

5. *he appears . . . lance:* he looks more like a manual
laborer (a "whipstock" was the handle of a whip used to
drive workhorses) than a knight.
6. To polish it in the dust (when he loses).
Scene 7 (Act 2, Scene 3)
Location: The palace at Pentapolis.

1. Renaissance publishers often advertised the contents
on the title page of a book ("volume").
2. Art (creative power) worked hard to make you.
3. Arrange the others according to the honor they
deserve.

PERICLES You are right courteous knights.

25 KING SIMONIDES   Sit, sir, sit.

[PERICLES *sits directly over against*° *the* KING *and*   across from
THAISA. *The guests feed apace.* PERICLES *sits still and*
eats nothing]

[*Aside*] By Jove I wonder, that is king of thoughts,
These cates distaste me, he but thought upon.[4]

THAISA [*aside*] By Juno, that is queen of marriage,
I am amazed all viands that I eat

30 Do seem unsavoury, wishing him my meat.
[*To the* KING] Sure he's a gallant gentleman.

KING SIMONIDES He's but a country gentleman.
He's done no more than other knights have done.
He's broke a staff° or so, so let it pass.   an opponent's lance

35 THAISA [*aside*] To me he seems like diamond to glass.

PERICLES [*aside*] Yon king's to me like to my father's picture,
Which tells me in what glory once he was—
Had princes sit like stars about his throne,
And he the sun for them to reverence.

40 None that beheld him but like lesser lights
Did vail° their crowns to his supremacy;   lower
Where now his son's a glow-worm in the night,
The which hath fire in darkness, none in light;
Whereby I see that time's the king of men;

45 He's both their parent and he is their grave,
And gives them what he will, not what they crave.

KING SIMONIDES What, are you merry, knights?

THE OTHER KNIGHTS Who can be other in this royal presence?

KING SIMONIDES Here with a cup that's stored unto the brim,

50 As you do love, full[5] to your mistress' lips,
We drink this health to you.

THE OTHER KNIGHTS   We thank your grace.

KING SIMONIDES Yet pause a while. Yon knight doth sit too melancholy,
As if the entertainment in our court
Had not a show might countervail° his worth.   that might equal
Note it not you, Thaisa?

55 THAISA   What is't to me, my father?

KING SIMONIDES O, attend, my daughter. Princes in this
Should live like gods above, who freely give
To everyone that come to honour them.
And princes not so doing are like gnats

60 Which make a sound but, killed, are wondered at.[6]
Therefore to make his entertain° more sweet,   entertainment
Here bear this standing-bowl° of wine to him.   bowl on a pedestal

THAISA Alas, my father, it befits not me
Unto a stranger knight to be so bold.

65 He may my proffer take for an offence,
Since men take women's gifts for impudence.

KING SIMONIDES How? Do as I bid you, or you'll move° me else.   anger

THAISA [*aside*] Now, by the gods, he could not please me better.

---

4. *These . . . upon:* (I'm so taken with him that, merely)
thinking of him, I lose my appetite for delicacies.
5. Just as you love fully, all the way.

6. Which, when dead, appear surprisingly small for all
the noise they made alive.

KING SIMONIDES   Furthermore, tell him we desire to know
70   Of whence he is, his name and parentage.
           [THAISA *bears the cup to* PERICLES]
THAISA   The King my father, sir, has drunk to you,
     Wishing it so much blood unto your life.
PERICLES   I thank both him and you, and pledge° him freely.   *drink to*
           [*He pledges the* KING]
THAISA   And further he desires to know of you
75   Of whence you are, your name and parentage.
PERICLES   A gentleman of Tyre, my name Pericles,
     My education been in arts° and arms,   *liberal arts*
     Who, looking for adventures in the world,
     Was by the rough unconstant seas bereft
80   Unfortunately both of ships and men,
     And after shipwreck driven upon this shore.
           [THAISA *returns to the* KING]
THAISA   He thanks your grace, names himself Pericles,
     A gentleman of Tyre, who, seeking adventures,
     Was solely by misfortune of the seas
85   Bereft of ships and men, cast on this shore.
KING SIMONIDES   Now by the gods I pity his mishaps,
     And will awake him from his melancholy.
           [SIMONIDES, *rising from his state, goes forthwith and*
             embraces PERICLES]
     Be⁷ cheered, for what misfortune hath impaired° you of,   *deprived*
     Fortune by my help can repair° to you.   *restore*
90   My self and country both shall be your friends,
     And presently° a goodly milk-white steed   *directly*
     And golden spurs I first bestow upon you,
     The prizes due your merit, and ordained
     For this day's enterprise.
95 PERICLES   Your kingly courtesy I thankfully accept.
KING SIMONIDES   Come, gentlemen, we sit° too long on trifles,   *dwell*
     And waste the time which looks for other revels.
     Ev'n in your armours, as you are addressed,°   *dressed*
     Your limbs will well become a soldier's dance.
100   I will not have excuse with saying this,
     'Loud music° is too harsh for ladies' heads',   *The sound of armor*
     Since they love men in arms as well as beds.
           [*The* KNIGHTS] *dance*
     So° this was well asked, 'twas so well performed.   *Just as*
     Come, here's a lady that wants breathing° too.   *exercise*
105   [*To* PERICLES] And I have heard, sir, that the knights of Tyre
     Are excellent in making ladies trip,°   *dance; go astray*
     And that their measures° are as excellent.   *dances; means*
PERICLES   In those that practise them they are, my lord.
KING SIMONIDES   O, that's as much as you would be denied
110   Of your fair courtesy.⁸ Unclasp,° unclasp.   *Disclose*
           They dance
     Thanks, gentlemen, to all. All have done well,
     [*To* PERICLES] But you the best.—Lights, pages, to conduct

---

7. Lines 88–95 are not in Q1; they are adapted from *PA*   8. *that's . . . courtesy:* that's just what your modesty dic-
to improve the transition between lines 87 and 96.   tates you should say.

These knights unto their sev'ral° lodgings.—Yours, sir,   *separate*
We have giv'n order should be next our own.
115 PERICLES   I am at your grace's pleasure.
KING SIMONIDES   Princes, it is too late to talk of love,
And that's the mark I know you level° at.   *aim*
Therefore each one betake him to his rest;
Tomorrow all for speeding do their best.⁹   [*Exeunt severally*]°   *separately*

Scene 8

Enter HELICANUS *and* AESCHINES
HELICANUS   No, Aeschines, know this of me:
Antiochus from incest lived not free,
For which the most high gods, not minding° longer   *wishing*
To hold the vengeance that they had in store
5 Due to this heinous capital offence,
Even in the height and pride of all his glory,
When he was seated in a chariot
Of an inestimable value, and
His daughter with him, both apparelled all in jewels,¹
10 A fire from heaven came and shrivelled up
Their bodies e'en to loathing, for they so stunk
That all those eyes adored° them ere their fall   *that adored*
Scorn now their° hands should give them burial.   *that their*
AESCHINES   'Twas very strange.
HELICANUS   And yet but justice, for though
15 This king were great, his greatness was no guard
To bar heav'n's shaft, but sin had his° reward.   *its*
AESCHINES   'Tis very true.
Enter three LORDS [*and stand aside*]
FIRST LORD   See, not a man in private conference
Or council has respect° with him but he.°   *influence / (Aeschines)*
20 SECOND LORD   It shall no longer grieve° without reproof.   *cause us grief*
THIRD LORD   And cursed be he that will not second it.
FIRST LORD   Follow me, then.—Lord Helicane, a word.
HELICANUS   With me? And welcome. Happy day, my lords.
FIRST LORD   Know that our griefs° are risen to the top,   *grievances*
25 And now at length they overflow their banks.
HELICANUS   Your griefs? For what? Wrong not your prince you love.
FIRST LORD   Wrong not yourself, then, noble Helicane,
But if the prince do live, let us salute him
Or know what ground's made happy by his step,
30 And be resolved° he lives to govern us,   *reassured*
Or dead, give 's° cause to mourn his funeral   *us*
And leave us to our free election.
SECOND LORD   Whose death indeed's the strongest° in our   *(likelihood)*
      censure,°   *judgment*
And knowing this—kingdoms without a head,
35 Like goodly buildings left without a roof,
Soon fall to utter ruin—your noble self,
That best know how to rule and how to reign,
We thus submit unto as sovereign.

---

9. Each one do his best to succeed (in wooing the Prin-   **Scene 8** (Act 2, Scene 4)
cess).   Location: Tyre, the Governor's house.
                                                                                        1. *both . . . jewels:* not in Q1; taken from *PA*.

ALL [*kneeling*]   Live, noble Helicane!
40 HELICANUS   By honour's cause, forbear your suffrages.°   *voting (for me)*
     If that you love Prince Pericles, forbear.
          [*The* LORDS *rise*]
     Take I° your wish I leap into the seas   *If I accept*
     Where's° hourly trouble for a minute's ease,   *Where there is*
     But if I cannot win you to this love,[2]
45   A twelvemonth longer then let me entreat you
     Further to bear the absence of your king;
     If in which time expired he not return,
     I shall with agèd patience bear your yoke.
     Go, seek your noble prince like noble subjects,
50   And in your search spend your adventurous worth,
     Whom if you find and win unto° return,   *persuade to*
     You shall like diamonds sit about his crown.
     FIRST LORD   To wisdom he's a fool that will not yield,
     And since Lord Helicane enjoineth us,
55   We with our travels will endeavour us.
     If in the world he live we'll seek him out;
     If in his grave he rest, we'll find him there.[3]
     HELICANUS   Then you love us, we you, and we'll clasp hands.
     When peers thus knit, a kingdom ever stands.   *Exeunt*

Scene 8a
          [*Enter* PERICLES *with* GENTLEMEN *with lights*]
     FIRST GENTLEMAN   Here is your lodging, sir.
     PERICLES   Pray leave me private.
     Only for instant solace pleasure me
     With[1] some delightful instrument, with which,
     And with my former practice,° I intend   *(of music)*
5   To pass away the tediousness of night,
     Though slumbers were more fitting.
     FIRST GENTLEMAN   Presently.°   *At once*
                    [*Exit* FIRST GENTLEMAN]
     SECOND GENTLEMAN   Your will's obeyed in all things, for our
          master
     Commanded you be disobeyed in nothing.
          [*Enter* FIRST GENTLEMAN *with a stringed instrument*]
     PERICLES   I thank you. Now betake you to your pillows,
10   And to the nourishment of quiet sleep.   [*Exeunt* GENTLEMEN]
          [PERICLES *plays and sings*]
     Day—that hath still that sovereignty to draw back
     The empire of the night, though for a while
     In darkness she usurp—brings morning on.
     I will go give his grace that salutation
15   Morning requires of me.   [*Exit with instrument*]

---

2. Love of Pericles (line 41). This line appears in Q1 after line 48, thereby rendering incomprehensible the First Lord's willingness to "yield" (line 53) to the suggestion of searching for Pericles.
3. Lines 56–57 appear after line 29 in Q1. There, they make lines 30–32 problematic and, as in note 2, undermine the First Lord's agreement to travel.

Scene 8a (This scene is not in Q1 or other modern editions. It was adapted from *PA* and provides a reference point for Simonides' compliments in Scene 9, lines 23–28. See the Textual Note.)
Location: The palace at Pentapolis.
1. *pleasure me / With*: grant me.

Scene 9

Enter KING [SIMONIDES] *at one door reading of a letter,
the* KNIGHTS [*enter at another door and*] *meet him*

FIRST KNIGHT   Good morrow to the good Simonides.

KING SIMONIDES   Knights, from my daughter this I let you know:
That for this twelvemonth she'll not undertake
A married life. Her reason to herself
5   Is only known, which from her none can get.

SECOND KNIGHT   May we not have access to her, my lord?

KING SIMONIDES   Faith, by no means. It is impossible,
She hath so strictly tied her to her chamber.
One twelve moons more she'll wear Diana's liv'ry.[1]
10   This by the eye of Cynthia[2] hath she vowed,
And on her virgin honour will not break it.

THIRD KNIGHT   Loath to bid farewell, we take our leaves.
                              [*Exeunt* KNIGHTS]

KING SIMONIDES   So, they are well dispatched. Now to my
         daughter's letter.
She tells me here she'll wed the stranger knight,
15   Or never more to view nor° day nor light.[3]   neither
I like that well. Nay, how absolute she's in't,
Not minding whether I dislike or no!
Mistress, t'is well, I do commend your choice,
And will no longer have it be delayed.
         Enter PERICLES
20   Soft, here he comes. I must dissemble that
In show, I have determined on in heart.[4]

PERICLES   All fortune to the good Simonides.

KING SIMONIDES   To you as much, sir. I am beholden to you
For your sweet music this last night. My ears,
25   I do protest, were never better fed
With such delightful pleasing harmony.

PERICLES   It is your grace's pleasure to commend,
Not my desert.

KING SIMONIDES   Sir, you are music's master.

PERICLES   The worst of all her scholars, my good lord.

KING SIMONIDES   Let me ask you one thing. What think you of
30   my daughter?

PERICLES   A most virtuous princess.

KING SIMONIDES   And fair, too, is she not?

PERICLES   As a fair day in summer; wondrous fair.

KING SIMONIDES   My daughter, sir, thinks very well of you;
So well indeed that you must be her master
35   And she will be your scholar;° therefore look to it.°   student / be prepared

PERICLES   I am unworthy for her schoolmaster.

KING SIMONIDES   She thinks not so. Peruse this writing else.°   if you doubt me
         [*He gives the letter to* PERICLES, *who reads*]

PERICLES [*aside*]   What's here? —a letter that she loves the knight
         of Tyre?
'Tis the King's subtlety to have my life.

Scene 9 (Act 2, Scene 5)
Location: The palace at Pentapolis.
1. She'll serve Diana, goddess of chastity.
2. Diana, also goddess of the moon.
3. After this line, Q1 has " 'Tis well Mistress, your choice

agrees with mine," which is omitted in this edition
because the same thoughts are expressed in lines 16 and
18.
4. *that . . . heart:* replace Q1's "it" (adapted from *PA*).
that / In show: outwardly what.

[*He prostrates himself at the King's feet*]

40 O, seek not to entrap me, gracious lord,
A stranger and distressèd gentleman
That never aimed so high to° love your daughter,   *as to*
But bent all offices to honour her.⁵
Never did thought of mine levy° offence,   *give*
45 Nor never did my actions yet commence
A deed might° gain her love or your displeasure.   *that might*
KING SIMONIDES   Thou liest like a traitor.
PERICLES   Traitor?
KING SIMONIDES   Ay, traitor,
That thus disguised art stol'n into my court
With witchcraft of thy actions to bewitch
50 The yielding spirit of my tender child.
PERICLES [*rising*]   Who calls me traitor, unless it be the King,
Ev'n in his bosom I will write the lie.°   *(with my sword)*
KING SIMONIDES [*aside*]   Now, by the gods, I do applaud his
     courage.
PERICLES   My actions are as noble as my blood,
55 That never relished of° a base descent.   *gave a hint of*
I came unto your court in search of honour,
And not to be a rebel to your state;
And he that otherwise accounts of me,
This sword shall prove he's honour's enemy.
60 KING SIMONIDES   I shall prove otherwise, since both your practice° *actions*
And her consent therein is evident
There, by my daughter's hand, as she can witness.⁶
     Enter THAISA
PERICLES [*to* THAISA]   Then as you are as virtuous as fair,
By what you hope of heaven or desire
65 By your best wishes here i'th' world fulfilled,⁷
Resolve° your angry father if my tongue   *Inform*
Did e'er solicit, or my hand subscribe
To any syllable made° love to you.   *that made*
THAISA   Why, sir, say if you had,
70 Who takes offence at that° would make me glad?   *what*
KING SIMONIDES   How, minion, are you so peremptory?°   *determined*
[*Aside*] I am glad on't.—Is⁸ this a fit match for you?
A straggling Theseus, born we know not where,⁹
One that hath neither blood nor merit
75 For thee to hope for, or himself to challenge
Of thy perfections e'en the least allowance.°   *share*
THAISA [*kneeling*]   Suppose his birth were base, when that° his life *even though*
Shows that he is not so, yet he hath virtue,
The very ground of all nobility,
80 Enough to make him noble. I entreat you
To remember that I am in love,

5. After this line, Q1 has

KING Thou hast bewitched my daughter,
    And thou art a villain.
PERICLES By the Gods I have not.

This passage breaks up what is a single speech in *PA*. It is omitted here and replaced by Simonides' speech at lines 47–50, which is adapted from *PA* and is more powerful. *bent all offices*: performed all services.
6. Except for "she can witness," lines 60–62 are adapted

from *PA*; they replace Q1's "No? here comes my daughter, she can witness it," which echoes *Othello*, 1.3.169. The reporter of this passage may have played Desdemona.
7. *By what . . . fulfilled*: not in Q1; adapted from *PA*.
8. Lines 72–96, adapted from *PA*, replace Q1's "with all my heart"; inclusion of this passage shifts the emphasis from nobility of birth to nobility of soul.
9. Theseus was an Athenian hero of ambiguous parentage who sometimes mistreated women.

The power of which love cannot be confined
By th' power of your will. Most royal father,
What with my pen I have in secret written
85 With my tongue now I openly confirm,
Which is I have no life but in his love,
Nor any being but in joying of his worth.
KING SIMONIDES   Equals to equals, good to good is joined.
This not being so, the bavin° of your mind   firewood
90 In rashness kindled must again be quenched,
Or purchase° our displeasure.—And for you, sir,   provoke
First learn to know I banish you my court,
And yet I scorn our rage should stoop so low.
For your ambition, sir, I'll have your life.
95 THAISA [to PERICLES]   For every drop of blood he sheds of yours
He'll draw another from his only child.
KING SIMONIDES   I'll tame you, yea, I'll bring you in subjection.
Will you not having my consent
Bestow your love and your affections
100 Upon a stranger?—[aside] who for aught I know
May be, nor can I think the contrary,
As great in blood as I myself.
        [He catches THAISA rashly by the hand]
Therefore hear you, mistress: either frame° your will to mine—   mold
        [He catches PERICLES rashly by the hand]
And you, sir, hear you: either be ruled by me—
Or I shall make you
        [He claps their hands together]
105   man and wife.
Nay, come, your hands and lips must seal it too,
        [PERICLES and THAISA kiss]
And being joined, I'll thus your hopes destroy,
        [He parts them]
And for your further grief, God give you joy.
What, are you pleased?
THAISA   Yes, [to PERICLES] if you love me, sir.
110 PERICLES   Ev'n as my life° my blood that fosters it.   as my life loves
KING SIMONIDES   What, are you both agreed?
PERICLES and THAISA   Yes, if't please your majesty.
KING SIMONIDES   It pleaseth me so well that I will see you wed,
Then with what haste you can, get you to bed.   Exeunt

Scene 10

        Enter GOWER
GOWER   Now sleep y-slackèd hath the rout,[1]
No din but snores the house about,
Made louder by the o'erfed breast
Of this most pompous° marriage feast.   lavish
5 The cat with eyne° of burning coal   eyes
Now couches fore the mouse's hole,
And crickets sing at th'oven's mouth
As the blither for their drouth.[2]
Hymen° hath brought the bride to bed,   god of marriage

Scene 10 (Act 3, Chorus)   2. As if happier for being dry.
1. Sleep has rendered everyone inactive.

10 Where by the loss of maidenhead
A babe is moulded. Be attent,°   *attentive*
And time that is so briefly spent°   *spent onstage*
With your fine fancies quaintly eche.°   *skillfully fill out*
What's dumb in show, I'll plain° with speech.   *clarify*

[Dumb show.]

Enter PERICLES *and* SIMONIDES *at one door with atten-
dants. A messenger [comes hastily in to] them, kneels,
and gives* PERICLES *a letter.* PERICLES *shows it* SIMON-
IDES; *the lords kneel to him. Then enter* THAISA *with
child, with* LYCHORIDA, *a nurse. The* KING *shows her the
letter. She rejoices. She and* PERICLES *take leave of her
father and depart [with* LYCHORIDA *at one door;* SIMON-
IDES *and attendants depart at another]*

15 By many a dern° and painful perch°   *wild / patch of land*
Of Pericles the care-full search,
By the four opposing coigns°   *corners*
Which the world together joins,
Is made with all due diligence
20 That horse and sail and high expense
Can stead° the quest. At last from Tyre   *sustain in*
Fame° answering the most strange enquire,°   *Rumor / distant queries*
To th' court of King Simonides
Are letters brought, the tenor these:
25 Antiochus and his daughter dead,
The men of Tyrus on the head
Of Helicanus would set on
The crown of Tyre, but he will° none.   *desires*
The mutiny there he hastes t'appease,
30 Says to 'em if King Pericles
Come not home in twice six moons
He, obedient to their dooms,°   *judgments*
Will take the crown. The sum of this
Brought hither to Pentapolis
35 Y-ravishèd° the regions round,   *Enraptured*
And everyone with claps can° sound   *started to*
'Our heir-apparent is a king!
Who dreamt, who thought of such a thing?'
Brief° he must hence depart to Tyre;   *In short; quickly*
40 His queen with child makes her desire—
Which who shall cross?—along to go.
Omit we all their dole and woe.
Lychorida her nurse she takes,
And so to sea. Their vessel shakes
45 On Neptune's billow. Half the flood°   *voyage*
Hath their keel cut, but fortune's mood
Varies again. The grizzled° north   *grisly*
Disgorges such a tempest forth
That as a duck for life that dives,
50 So up and down the poor ship drives.
The lady shrieks, and well-a-near°   *alas*
Does fall in travail° with her fear,   *Goes into labor*
And what ensues in this fell° storm   *cruel*
Shall for itself itself perform;
55 I nill° relate; action may   *will not*

Conveniently the rest convey,
Which might not what by me is told.[3]
In your imagination hold°   think
This stage the ship, upon whose deck
60 The sea-tossed Pericles appears to speke.   [*Exit*]

Scene 11
[*Thunder and lightning.*] *Enter* PERICLES *a-shipboard*
PERICLES   The god of this great vast° rebuke these surges   vast sea
Which wash both heav'n and hell; and thou that hast
Upon the winds command, bind them in brass,
Having called them from the deep. O still°   quiet
5   Thy deaf'ning dreadful thunders, gently quench
Thy nimble sulph'rous flashes.—O, ho, Lychorida!
How does my queen?—Thou stormest venomously.
Wilt thou spit all thyself? The seaman's whistle
Is as a whisper in the ears of death,°   of a dead person
10 Unheard.—Lychorida!—Lucina,° O!   goddess of childbirth
Divinest patroness, and midwife gentle
To those that cry by night, convey thy deity
Aboard our dancing boat, make swift the pangs
Of my queen's travails!—Now, Lychorida.
Enter LYCHORIDA [*with an infant*]
15 LYCHORIDA   Here is a thing too young for such a place,
Who, if it had conceit,° would die, as I   understanding
Am like° to do. Take in your arms this piece   likely
Of your dead queen.
PERICLES   How, how, Lychorida?
LYCHORIDA   Patience, good sir, do not assist the storm.°   (by ranting and tears)
20 Here's all that is left living of your queen,
A little daughter. For the sake of it
Be manly, and take comfort.
PERICLES   O you gods!
Why do you make us love your goodly gifts,
And snatch them straight away? We here below
25 Recall° not what we give, and therein may   Demand back
Use honour with you.[1]
LYCHORIDA   Patience, good sir,
E'en for this charge.[2]
                    [*She gives him the infant.* PERICLES, *looking mournfully
                    upon it, shakes his head, and weeps*]
PERICLES   Now mild may be thy life,
For a more blust'rous birth had never babe;
Quiet and gentle thy conditions,° for   circumstances
30 Thou art the rudeliest welcome to this world
That e'er was prince's child; happy° what follows.   let be happy
Thou hast as chiding° a nativity   upsetting
As fire, air, water, earth, and heav'n can make
To herald thee from th' womb. Poor inch of nature,
35 Ev'n at the first thy loss is more than can

3. Which could not easily "convey" what I've related so
far.
Scene 11 (Act 3, Scene 1)
Location: At sea.

1. *therein . . . you:* so we can criticize you by this standard
of honor.
2. For the sake of this child.

Thy partage quit with all thou canst find here.[3]
Now the good gods throw their best eyes° upon't.   *look favorably*
   Enter [the MASTER *and a]* SAILOR
MASTER What, courage, sir! God save you.
PERICLES Courage enough, I do not fear the flaw;°   *squall*
40 It hath done to me its worst. Yet for the love
Of this poor infant, this fresh new seafarer,
I would it would be quiet.
MASTER *[calling]* Slack the bow-lines, there.—Thou° wilt not,   *(the storm)*
 wilt thou? Blow, and split thyself.
45 SAILOR But searoom,[4] an° the brine and cloudy billow kiss the   *if*
 moon, I care not.
MASTER *[to* PERICLES*]* Sir, your queen must overboard. The sea
 works° high, the wind is loud, and will not lie° till the ship be   *surges / lie still*
 cleared of the dead.
50 PERICLES That's but your superstition.
MASTER Pardon us, sir; with us at sea it hath been still° observed,   *always*
 and we are strong in custom. Therefore briefly° yield 'er, for   *quickly*
 she must overboard straight.
PERICLES As you think meet. Most wretched queen!
LYCHORIDA   Here she lies, sir.
   [She draws the curtains and discovers the body of Thaisa
   in a bed. PERICLES *gives* LYCHORIDA *the infant]*
55 PERICLES *[to* THAISA*]* A terrible childbed hast thou had, my dear,
No light, no fire. Th'unfriendly elements
Forgot thee utterly, nor have I time
To give thee hallowed to thy grave, but straight
Must cast thee, scarcely coffined, in the ooze,°   *seabed*
60 Where, for° a monument upon thy bones   *in place of*
And aye-remaining° lamps, the belching whale   *ever-burning*
And humming water must o'erwhelm thy corpse,
Lying with simple shells.—O Lychorida,
Bid Nestor bring me spices, ink, and paper,
65 My casket and my jewels, and bid Nicander
Bring me the satin coffer. Lay the babe
Upon the pillow. Hie° thee whiles I say   *Hurry*
A priestly farewell to her. Suddenly,° woman.   *Immediately*
        [Exit LYCHORIDA*]*
SAILOR Sir, we have a chest beneath the hatches caulked and
70 bitumed[5] ready.
PERICLES I thank thee. *[To the* MASTER*]* Mariner, say, what coast is this?
MASTER We are near Tarsus.
PERICLES   Thither, gentle mariner,
 Alter thy course from Tyre. When canst thou reach it?
MASTER By break of day, if the wind cease.
PERICLES   Make for Tarsus.
75 There will I visit Cleon, for the babe
Cannot hold out to Tyrus. There I'll leave it
At careful nursing. Go thy ways,° good mariner.   *Get to it*
I'll bring the body presently.
    *Exit [*MASTER *at one door and* SAILOR *beneath*
    the hatches. Exit PERICLES *to* THAISA,
    closing the curtains]

---

3. *than . . . here:* than your share of anything you find in
this life can make up for.
4. As long as we're at sea (safe from the rocks).
5. *bitumed:* caulked with pitch.

Scene 12

Enter Lord CERIMON *with a [poor man and a] servant*

CERIMON   Philemon, ho!

Enter PHILEMON

PHILEMON   Doth my lord call?

CERIMON   Get fire and meat for those poor men.[1]

[*Exit* PHILEMON]

'T'as been a turbulent and stormy night.

SERVANT   I have seen many, but such a night as this

5 Till now I ne'er endured.

CERIMON   Your master will be dead ere you return.

There's nothing can be ministered in nature

That can recover him. [*To poor man*] Give this to th' pothecary°   druggist

And tell me how it works.

[*Exeunt poor man and servant*]

Enter two GENTLEMEN

FIRST GENTLEMAN   Good morrow.

SECOND GENTLEMAN   Good morrow to your lordship.

10 CERIMON   Gentlemen,

Why do you stir so early?

FIRST GENTLEMAN   Sir,

Our lodgings, standing bleak upon° the sea,   exposed to

Shook as° the earth did quake.   as if

The very principals° did seem to rend   principal rafters

15 And all to topple. Pure surprise and fear

Made me to quit the house.

SECOND GENTLEMAN   That is the cause we trouble you so early;

'Tis not our husbandry.°   good work habits

CERIMON   O, you say well.

FIRST GENTLEMAN   But I much marvel that your lordship should,

20 Having rich tire° about you, at this hour   bed furniture

Shake off the golden slumber of repose. 'Tis most strange,

Nature to be so conversant with pain,[2]

Being thereto not compelled.

CERIMON   I held it ever;°   always believed

Virtue and cunning° were endowments greater   knowledge

25 Than nobleness and riches. Careless heirs

May the two latter darken and dispend,°   expend

But immortality attends the former,

Making a man a god. 'Tis known I ever°   always

Have studied physic,° through which secret art,   medicine

30 By turning o'er authorities,° I have,   reading learned texts

Together with my practice, made familiar

To me and to my aid° the blest infusions   assistant

That dwells in vegetives,[3] in metals, stones,

And so can speak of the disturbances

35 That nature works, and of her cures, which doth give me

A more content° and cause of true delight   greater happiness

Than to be thirsty after tott'ring° honour,   unstable

Or tie my pleasure up in silken bags°   (of money)

To glad the fool and death.[4]

Scene 12 (Act 3, Scene 2)
Location: Cerimon's house in Ephesus.
1. Offstage supplicants. Q1s "these poor men" might refer to characters onstage.

2. That your nature should be so accustomed to labor.
3. Beneficial substances in plants.
4. To gladden the fool who trusts in wealth, which death inherits.

SECOND GENTLEMAN　　　　　Your honour has
40　　Through Ephesus poured forth your charity,
　　　And hundreds call themselves your creatures[5] who by you
　　　Have been restored. And not alone your knowledge,
　　　Your personal pain,° but e'en your purse still° open　　　　　　　　*labor / always*
　　　Hath built Lord Cerimon such strong renown
45　　As time shall never—
　　　　　　　　Enter [PHILEMON *and one*] *or two*[6] *with a chest*
PHILEMON　So, lift there.
CERIMON　What's that?
PHILEMON　Sir, even now
　　　The sea tossed up upon our shore this chest.
　　　'Tis off some wreck.
50　CERIMON　　　　　　　　Set't down. Let's look upon't.
SECOND GENTLEMAN　'Tis like a coffin, sir.
CERIMON　　　　　　　　　　Whate'er it be,
　　　'Tis wondrous heavy.—Did the sea cast it up?
PHILEMON　I never saw so huge a billow, sir,
　　　Or a more eager.[7]
CERIMON　　　　　　　　Wrench it open straight.
　　　　　　　[*The others start to work*]
55　If the sea's stomach be o'ercharged with gold
　　　'Tis by a good constraint of queasy fortune[8]
　　　It belches upon us.
SECOND GENTLEMAN　'Tis so, my lord.
CERIMON　How close° 'tis caulked and bitumed!　　　　　　　　　　*tightly*
　　　　　　　[*They force the lid*]
　　　　　　　　　　　　　Soft,° it smells　　　　　　　　　　*But wait*
　　　Most sweetly in my sense.
SECOND GENTLEMAN　　　　　A delicate odour.
60　CERIMON　As ever hit my nostril. So, up with it.
　　　　　　　[*They take the lid off*]
　　　O you most potent gods! What's here—a corpse?
SECOND GENTLEMAN
　　　Most strange.
CERIMON　　　　　　Shrouded in cloth of state,° and crowned,　　　*royal fabric*
　　　Balmed and entreasured with full bags of spices.
　　　A passport,° too!　　　　　　　　　　　　　　　　*An identification paper*
　　　　　　　[*He takes a paper from the chest*]
65　Apollo perfect me i'th' characters.[9]
　　　'Here I give to understand,
　　　If e'er this coffin drives a-land,
　　　I, King Pericles, have lost
　　　This queen worth all our mundane cost.°　　　　　　　　　*earthly wealth*
70　Who° finds her, give her burying;　　　　　　　　　　　　*Whoever*
　　　She was the daughter of a king.
　　　Besides this treasure for a fee,

5. *call . . . creatures:* owe their lives to you.
6. "Philemon" replaces Q1's "two or three" here, "Servant" in the speech prefixes to lines 46–53, and "one" in the stage direction to line 84, in accord with the emphasis on one of Cerimon's assistants in Twine's *Pattern of Painful Adventures* and in order to make sense of Philemon's appearance at the beginning of the scene.
7. *Did . . . eager:* In Q1, these lines appear after "bitumed" (line 58), where the question seems inappro-

priate. The passage is then followed by "Wrench it open," which repeats line 54. Here, "Or a more eager," adapted from *PA*, replaces Q1's "as tossed it upon shore" (which repeats Q1's "toss up upon our shore," line 49). These changes seek to remedy the possibly faulty memory of the reporters.
8. By a forced act of nauseous good luck that.
9. Apollo (patron of both scholars and physicians) help me read the writing correctly.

The° gods requite his charity.'   *May the*
If thou liv'st, Pericles, thou hast a heart
75   That even cracks for woe. This chanced tonight.°   *occurred last night*
SECOND GENTLEMAN   Most likely, sir.
CERIMON   Nay, certainly tonight,
For look how fresh she looks. They were too rash
That threw her in the sea. Make a fire within.
Fetch hither all my boxes in my closet.   [*Exit* PHILEMON]
80   Death may usurp on nature many hours,
And yet the fire of life kindle again
The o'erpressed° spirits. I have heard   *overcome*
Of an Egyptian nine hours dead
Who was by good appliances° recovered.   *medical treatments*
        Enter [PHILEMON] *with napkins and fire*
85   Well said, well said, the fire and cloths.
The still° and woeful music that we have,   *soft*
Cause it to sound, beseech you.
        [*Music*]
                    The vial° once more.   *(of medicine)*
How thou stirr'st,[1] thou block! The music there!
I pray you give her air. Gentlemen,
90   This queen will live. Nature awakes, a warmth
Breathes out of her. She hath not been entranced°   *unconscious*
Above five hours. See how she 'gins to blow°   *bloom*
Into life's flow'r again.
FIRST GENTLEMAN   The heavens
Through you increase our wonder, and set up
Your fame for ever.
95 CERIMON   She is alive. Behold,
Her eyelids, cases to those heav'nly jewels
Which Pericles hath lost,
Begin to part their fringes of bright gold.
The diamonds of a most praisèd water°   *luster*
100 Doth appear to make the world twice rich.[2]—Live,
And make us weep to hear your fate, fair creature,
Rare° as you seem to be.   *Exquisite*
        She moves
THAISA   O dear Diana,
Where am I? Where's my lord? What world is this?
SECOND GENTLEMAN
Is not this strange?
FIRST GENTLEMAN   Most rare.
CERIMON   Hush, gentle neighbours.
105 Lend me your hands. To the next chamber bear her.
Get linen. Now this matter must be looked to,
For her relapse is mortal.° Come, come,   *would be fatal*
And Aesculapius° guide us.   *They carry her away. Exeunt*   *god of healing*

Scene 13

Enter PERICLES *at Tarsus, with* CLEON *and* DIONYZA
[*and* LYCHORIDA *with a babe*]
PERICLES   Most honoured Cleon, I must needs be gone.
My twelve months are expired, and Tyrus stands

1. How lively you are (ironic).
2. Once by the precious gold of her eyelids and again by the jewels they conceal.

In a litigious° peace. You and your lady   *conflict-ridden*
Take from my heart all thankfulness. The gods
Make up the rest upon you!¹

5   CLEON   Your strokes of fortune,
Though they hurt you mortally, yet glance
Full woundingly on us.

   DIONYZA   O your sweet queen!
That the strict fates had pleased you'd brought her hither
T'have blessed mine eyes with her!

   PERICLES   We cannot but obey

10 The pow'rs above us. Should° I rage and roar   *Even if*
As doth the sea she lies in, yet the end
Must be as 'tis. My gentle babe Marina,
Whom for° she was born at sea I have named so,   *because*
Here I charge° your charity withal,° and leave her   *saddle / with*
15 The infant of your care, beseeching you
To give her princely training, that she may be
Mannered° as she is born.   *Instructed in manners*

   CLEON   Fear not, my lord, but think
Your grace, that fed my country with your corn —
For which the people's pray'rs still fall upon you —
20 Must in your child be thought on. If neglection
Should therein make me vile, the common body°   *the people*
By you relieved would force me to my duty.
But if to that° my nature need a spur,   *that duty*
The gods revenge it upon me and mine
To th' end of generation.

25   PERICLES   I believe you.
Your honour and your goodness teach me to't°   *to do so*
Without your vows. — Till she be married, madam,
By bright Diana, whom we honour all,
Unscissored shall this hair of mine remain,
30 Though I show ill° in't. So I take my leave.   *look bad*
Good madam, make me blessèd in your care
In bringing up my child.

   DIONYZA   I have one myself,
Who shall not be more dear to my respect°   *attention*
Than yours, my lord.

   PERICLES   Madam, my thanks and prayers.
35   CLEON   We'll bring your grace e'en to the edge o'th' shore,
Then give you up to th' masted Neptune° and   *ship-conveying sea*
The gentlest winds of heaven.

   PERICLES   I will embrace your offer. — Come, dear'st madam. —
O, no tears, Lychorida, no tears.
40 Look to your little mistress, on whose grace°   *favor*
You may depend hereafter. — Come, my lord.   [*Exeunt*]

Scene 14

Enter CERIMON *and* THAISA
   CERIMON   Madam, this letter and some certain jewels
Lay with you in your coffer, which are all
At your command. Know you the character?°   *handwriting*

Scene 13 (Act 3, Scene 3)   1. Give you the rest of what you deserve.
Location: The Governor's house in Tarsus.

THAISA   It is my lord's. That I was shipped° at sea   *on a ship*
5   I well remember, ev'n on my eaning° time,   *birthing*
    But whether there delivered, by th' holy gods
    I cannot rightly say. But since King Pericles,
    My wedded lord, I ne'er shall see again,
    A vestal liv'ry[1] will I take me to,
10 And never more have joy.
CERIMON   Madam, if this you purpose° as ye speak,   *intend*
    Diana's temple is not distant far,
    Where till your date° expire you may abide.   *time of life*
    Moreover, if you please a niece of mine
15 Shall there attend you.
THAISA   My recompense is thanks, that's all,
    Yet my good will is great, though the gift small.   *Exeunt*

Scene 15

Enter GOWER
GOWER   Imagine Pericles arrived at Tyre,
    Welcomed and settled to his own desire.
    His woeful queen we leave at Ephesus,
    Unto Diana there 's a votaress.°   *as a devotee*
5   Now to Marina bend your mind,
    Whom our fast-growing scene must find
    At Tarsus, and by Cleon trained
    In music, letters; who hath gained
    Of education all the grace,
10 Which makes her both the heart and place°   *focal point*
    Of gen'ral wonder. But, alack,
    That monster envy, oft the wrack°   *ruin*
    Of earnèd praise, Marina's life
    Seeks to take off by treason's knife,
15 And in this kind° our Cleon has   *connection*
    One daughter, and a full-grown lass
    E'en ripe for marriage-rite. This maid
    Hight° Philoten, and it is said   *Is called*
    For certain in our story she
20 Would ever° with Marina be,   *always*
    Be't when they weaved the sleided° silk   *divided into filaments*
    With fingers long, small, white as milk;
    Or when she would with sharp nee'le° wound   *needle*
    The cambric° which she made more sound   *fine linen*
25 By hurting it, or when to th' lute
    She sung, and made the night bird° mute,   *nightingale*
    That still records° with moan; or when   *always sings*
    She would with rich and constant pen
    Vail° to her mistress Dian. Still   *Inscribe praises*
30 This Philoten contends in skill
    With absolute° Marina; so   *perfect*
    With dove of Paphos might the crow

Scene 14 (Act 3, Scene 4)
Location: Cerimon's house in Ephesus.
1. Vestal virgin's uniform of religious chastity.
Scene 15 (Other modern editions treat Gower's mono-
logue as a prologue to Act 4 and start Act 4, Scene 1, at
line 53. This edition assumes that the grave Marina goes

"to strew" [line 66] "is revealed" during Gower's speech
[stage direction after line 42], that Dionyza and Leonine
enter near, rather than [as in Q1] at the end of that
speech, and hence that the scene does not change.)
Location: Tarsus, near the seashore.

Vie feathers white.[1] Marina gets
All praises which are paid as debts,
35 And not as given.[2] This so darks°   *(by comparison)*
In Philoten all graceful marks
That Cleon's wife with envy rare°   *extreme*
A present murder does prepare
For good Marina, that her daughter
40 Might stand peerless by° this slaughter.   *by means of*
The sooner her vile thoughts to stead°   *help*
Lychorida, our nurse, is dead,
       [*A tomb is revealed*]
And cursèd Dionyza hath
The pregnant instrument of wrath
45 Pressed for this blow.[3] Th'unborn event°   *outcome*
I do commend to your content,°   *(viewing) pleasure*
Only I carry wingèd Time
Post° on the lame feet of my rhyme,   *Quickly*
Which never could I so convey
50 Unless your thoughts went on my way.
       Enter DIONYZA *with* LEONINE
Dionyza does appear,
With Leonine, a murderer.   *Exit*
DIONYZA   Thy oath remember. Thou hast sworn to do't.
   'Tis but a blow, which never shall be known.
55 Thou canst not do a thing i'th' world so soon°   *quickly*
   To yield thee so much profit. Let not conscience,
   Which is but cold, or fanning love thy bosom
   Unflame[4] too nicely,° nor let pity, which   *scrupulously*
   E'en women have cast off, melt thee; but be
   A soldier to thy purpose.
60 LEONINE   I will do't;
   But yet she is a goodly creature.
DIONYZA   The fitter then the gods should have her.
       Enter MARINA [*to the tomb*] *with a basket of flowers*
   Here she comes, weeping her only nurse's death.
   Thou art resolved.
LEONINE   I am resolved.
65 MARINA   No, I will rob Tellus of her weed°   *earth of its garment*
   To strew thy grave with flow'rs. The yellows, blues,
   The purple violets and marigolds
   Shall as a carpet hang upon thy tomb
   While summer days doth last. Ay me, poor maid,
70 Born in a tempest when my mother died,
   This world to me is but a ceaseless storm
   Whirring° me from my friends.   *Hurrying*
DIONYZA   How now, Marina, why do you keep alone?
   How chance° my daughter is not with you?   *Why is it*
75 Do not consume your blood with sorrowing.[5]
   Have you a nurse of me.[6] Lord, how your favour°   *appearance*
   Is changed with this unprofitable woe!

---

1. *so . . . white:* so might the crow try to be whiter than
the dove. Paphos was a city sacred to Venus.
2. *Marina . . . given:* Marina's virtues compel praise,
whether or not one wants to.
3. Has prepared a ready means for the murder.

4. *or . . . / Unflame:* or cooling love blow out the murder-
ous flame in your bosom. Editors variously emend Q1's
"in flaming, thy love bosom, enslave."
5. Sighs were thought to consume one's blood.
6. Let me be your nurse.

Give me your flowers. Come, o'er the sea margin°   *seashore*
Walk with Leonine. The air is piercing there,
80   And quick;° it sharps the stomach.° Come, Leonine,   *refreshing / appetite*
Take her by th' arm. Walk with her.
MARINA   No, I pray you,
I'll not bereave you of your servant.
DIONYZA   Come, come,
I love the King your father and yourself
With more than foreign heart.° We ev'ry day   *As if we were kin*
85   Expect him here. When he shall come and find
Our paragon to all reports thus blasted,[7]
He will repent the breadth of his great voyage,
Blame both my lord and me, that we have taken
No care to your best courses.° Go, I pray you,   *courses of action*
90   Walk and be cheerful once again; resume
That excellent complexion which did steal
The eyes of young and old. Care not for me.
I can go home alone.
MARINA   Well, I will go,
But truly I have no desire to it.
95 DIONYZA   Nay, I know 'tis good for you. Walk half an hour,
Leonine, at the least; remember
What I have said.
LEONINE   I warr'nt° you, madam.   *guarantee*
DIONYZA [*to* MARINA]   I'll leave you, my sweet lady, for a while.
Pray you walk softly, do not heat your blood.
What, I must have care of you!
100 MARINA   My thanks, sweet madam.
                        [*Exit* DIONYZA]
Is this wind westerly that blows?
LEONINE   South-west.
MARINA   When I was born the wind was north.
LEONINE   Was't so?
MARINA   My father, as nurse says, did never fear,
But cried 'Good seamen' to the mariners,
105 Galling° his kingly hands with haling° ropes,   *Irritating / pulling*
And, clasping to the mast, endured a sea
That almost burst the deck.
LEONINE   When was this?
MARINA   When I was born.
110 Never was waves nor wind more violent.
Once from the ladder tackle washes off
A canvas-climber.° 'Ha!' says one, 'wolt out?'[8]   *sailor in the rigging*
And with a dropping° industry they skip   *dripping-wet*
From stem to stern. The boatswain whistles, and
115 The master calls and trebles their confusion.
LEONINE   Come, say your prayers.
MARINA   What mean you?
LEONINE   If you require a little space for prayer
I grant it. Pray, but be not tedious.°   *drawn out*
120 The gods are quick of ear, and I am sworn
To do my work with haste.

---

7. Our universally admired paragon of beauty so   8. So you want to get off ship? (a cruel joke).
blighted.

MARINA	Why would you kill me?	
LEONINE To satisfy my lady.		
MARINA	Why would she have me killed?	

Now, as I can remember, by my troth°   *faith*
I never did her hurt in all my life.
125   I never spake bad word, nor did ill turn
To any living creature. Believe me, la.°   *(exclamation)*
I never killed a mouse nor hurt a fly.
I trod once on a worm against my will,
But I wept for it. How have I offended
130   Wherein my death might yield her any profit
Or my life imply her danger?

LEONINE   My commission
Is not to reason of the deed, but do't.

MARINA   You will not do't for all the world, I hope.
You are well favoured, and your looks foreshow
135   You have a gentle heart. I saw you lately
When you caught° hurt in parting two that fought.   *got*
Good sooth,° it showed well in you. Do so now.   *Truly*
Your lady seeks my life. Come you between,
And save poor me, the weaker.

LEONINE *[drawing out his sword]* I am sworn,
140   And will dispatch.

Enter PIRATES *[running]*

FIRST PIRATE   Hold, villain.

*[*LEONINE *runs away and hides behind the tomb]*

SECOND PIRATE   A prize,° a prize.   *Booty (Marina)*

THIRD PIRATE   Half-part,° mates, half-part. Come, let's have her   *To be shared*
aboard suddenly.°   *quickly*

*Exeunt [*PIRATES *carrying* MARINA*]*

LEONINE *[steals back]*

145   LEONINE   These roguing° thieves serve the great pirate Valdes.[9]   *law-breaking*
An° they have seized Marina, let her go.   *If*
There's no hope she'll return. I'll swear she's dead
And thrown into the sea; but I'll see further.
Perhaps they will but please themselves upon her,°   *will only rape her*
150   Not carry her aboard. If she remain,
Whom they have ravished must by me be slain.

Exit. [The tomb is concealed]

Scene 16

[A brothel sign.] Enter [the PANDER, *his wife] the* BAWD
[and their man BOULT*]*[1]

PANDER   Boult.

BOULT   Sir.

PANDER   Search the market narrowly.° Mytilene is full of gal-   *carefully*
lants. We lose too much money this mart° by being wenchless.   *market time*
5   BAWD   We were never so much out of creatures.° We have but   *prostitutes*
poor three, and they can do no more than they can do, and
they with continual action are even as good as rotten.°   *have venereal disease*
PANDER   Therefore let's have fresh ones, whate'er we pay for

---

9. Probably named after an admiral in the Spanish
Armada.
Scene 16 (Act 4, Scene 2)
Location: Mytilene, on the island of Lesbos; before a

brothel.
1. *Pander*: sexual go-between, after Pandarus in *Troilus
and Cressida. Bawd*: supplier of prostitutes. The name
"Boult" may have phallic connotations.

them. If there be not a conscience to be used[2] in every trade,
10   we shall never prosper.
BAWD   Thou sayst true. 'Tis not our bringing up of poor bas-
tards°—as I think I have brought up some eleven—   *(that enriches us)*
BOULT   Ay, to eleven, and brought them down again.[3] But shall
I search the market?
15   BAWD   What else, man? The stuff we have, a strong wind will
blow it to pieces, they are so pitifully sodden.[4]
PANDER   Thou sayst true. They're too unwholesome, o' con-
science.° The poor Transylvanian is dead that lay with the little   *on my conscience*
baggage.°   *prostitute*
20   BOULT   Ay, she quickly pooped° him, she made him roast meat   *overcame (by disease)*
for worms. But I'll go search the market.   *Exit*
PANDER   Three or four thousand chequins° were as pretty a pro-
portion° to live quietly, and so give over.°   *gold coins*
                                                    sum / retire
BAWD   Why to give over, I pray you? Is it a shame to get° when
25   we are old?   *earn*
PANDER   O, our credit comes not in like the commodity, nor the
commodity wages not with the danger.[5] Therefore if in our
youths we could pick up some pretty estate, 'twere not amiss to
keep our door hatched.° Besides, the sore terms we stand upon   *closed for business*
30   with the gods[6] will be strong° with us for giving o'er.   *a strong argument*
BAWD   Come, other sorts offend as well as we.
PANDER   As well as we? Ay, and better too; we offend worse. Nei-
ther is our profession any mystery,[7] it's no calling.° But here   *(religious) vocation*
comes Boult.
        Enter BOULT *with the* PIRATES *and* MARINA
35   BOULT [*to the* PIRATES]   Come your ways,° my masters,° you say   *Come along / gentlemen*
she's a virgin?
A PIRATE   O sir, we doubt it not.
BOULT [*to* PANDER]   Master, I have gone through° for this piece°   *bargained / (of flesh)*
you see. If you like her, so;° if not, I have lost my earnest.°   *fine / deposit*
40   BAWD   Boult, has she any qualities?°   *accomplishments*
BOULT   She has a good face, speaks well, and has excellent good
clothes. There's no farther necessity of qualities can° make her   *whose absence can*
be refused.
BAWD   What's her price, Boult?
45   BOULT   I cannot be bated one doit of[8] a hundred sesterces.
PANDER [*to* PIRATES]   Well, follow me, my masters. You shall
have your money presently.° [*To* BAWD] Wife, take her in,   *immediately*
instruct her what she has to do, that she may not be raw in her
entertainment.[9]   [*Exeunt* PANDER *and* PIRATES]
50   BAWD   Boult, take you the marks of her, the colour of her hair,
complexion, height, her age, with warrant of her virginity, and
cry 'He that will give most shall have her first.' Such a maiden-
head were no cheap thing if men were as they have been. Get
this done as I command you.

---

2. If we don't proceed diligently; if conscience can't be economically exploited; perhaps a comic blunder for "if conscience is involved."
3. And corrupted them when they turned eleven.
4. Overboiled in the sweating tub as treatment for vene-real disease.
5. Our reputation doesn't accumulate like our profit, nor does the profit justify the danger (with extended eco-nomic wordplay: "credit," "commodity," "wages"). For

the anticommercial bias implicit in the equation of com-merce with prostitution, see the Introduction.
6. This out-of-character admission is part of the religious undercurrent of the scene.
7. Any secret; any (holy) trade.
8 I cannot get the price reduced a penny (*doit*: small coin) from.
9. May not be unprepared to entertain customers.

55 BOULT Performance shall follow.   *Exit*

MARINA Alack that Leonine was so slack, so slow.
     He should have struck, not spoke; or that° these pirates,   *if only*
     Not enough barbarous, had but o'erboard thrown me
     To seek my mother.

60 BAWD Why lament you, pretty one?

MARINA That I am pretty.

BAWD Come, the gods have done their part in you.

MARINA I accuse them not.

BAWD You are light° into my hands, where you are like° to live.   *arrived / likely*

65 MARINA The more my fault°   *misfortune*
     To scape his hands where I was like to die.

BAWD Ay, and you shall live in pleasure.

MARINA No.

BAWD Yes, indeed shall you, and taste gentlemen of all fashions.
70   You shall fare well. You shall have the difference of all com-
     plexions.[1] What, do you stop your ears?

MARINA Are you a woman?

BAWD What would you have me be an I be not a woman?

MARINA An honest° woman, or not a woman.   *A chaste*

75 BAWD Marry, whip the gosling! I think I shall have something to
     do° with you. Come, you're a young foolish sapling, and must   *some trouble*
     be bowed as I would have you.

MARINA The gods defend me!

BAWD If it please the gods to defend you by men, then men
80   must comfort you, men must feed you, men must stir you up.
          Enter BOULT
     Now, sir, hast thou cried° her through the market?   *advertised*

BOULT I have cried her almost to° the number of her hairs. I   *down to*
     have drawn her picture with my voice.

BAWD And I prithee tell me, how dost thou find the inclination
85   of the people, especially of the younger sort?

BOULT Faith, they listened to me as they would have hearkened
     to their fathers' testament.° There was a Spaniard's mouth   *will*
     watered as he went to bed to her very description.

BAWD We shall have him here tomorrow with his best ruff° on.   *collar*

90 BOULT Tonight, tonight. But mistress, do you know the French
     knight that cowers i' the hams?[2]

BAWD Who, Monsieur Veroles?

BOULT Ay, he. He offered to cut a caper[3] at the proclamation,
     but he made a groan at it, and swore he would see her
95   tomorrow.

BAWD Well, well, as for him, he brought his disease hither.[4]
     Here he does but repair° it. I know he will come in our shadow   *renew*
     to scatter his crowns of the sun.[5]

BOULT Well, if we had of every nation a traveller, we should
100   lodge them all with this sign.[6]

BAWD [*to* MARINA] Pray you, come hither a while. You have for-

---

1. The variety of appearances (temperaments; ethnici-
ties).
2. Who crouches (from venereal disease).
3. He prepared to leap up and clap his heels together.
4. Englishmen called syphilis "the French disease." This
allusion is one indication of the distinctively English feel
of the scene; see also Scene 5.

5. He will come inside our house to spend his French
crowns; to lose hair from syphilis; to spend his money on
Marina ("sun," if Q1's "in the sun" is retained). With a
play on "shadow" and "sun."
6. We would draw them all here by my pictorial descrip-
tion of Marina.

tunes coming upon you.⁷ Mark me, you must seem to do that
fearfully which you commit willingly, to despise profit where
you have most gain. To weep that you live as ye do° makes pity   *(by prostitution)*
105   in your lovers. Seldom but that pity begets you a good opinion,
and that opinion a mere° profit.   *clear*

MARINA   I understand you not.

BOULT [*to* BAWD]   O, take her home,° mistress, take her home.   *inside; to task*
These blushes of hers must be quenched with some present
110   practice.

BAWD   Thou sayst true, i'faith, so they must, for your bride goes
to that with shame which is her way to go with warrant.°   *legitimately*

BOULT   Faith, some do and some do not. But mistress, if I have
bargained for the joint°—   *cut of meat*

115 BAWD   Thou mayst cut a morsel off the spit.°   *deflower her*

BOULT   I may so.

BAWD   Who should deny it? [*To* MARINA] Come, young one, I
like the manner of your garments well.

BOULT   Ay, by my faith, they shall not be changed yet.⁸

120 BAWD   [*giving him money*]   Boult, spend thou that in the town.
Report what a sojourner we have. You'll lose nothing by cus-
tom.⁹ When nature framed this piece° she meant thee a good   *(of work); (of flesh)*
turn. Therefore say what a paragon she is, and thou reapest the
harvest out of thine own setting forth.

125 BOULT   I warrant you, mistress, thunder shall not so awake the
beds of eels¹ as my giving out her beauty stirs up the lewdly
inclined. I'll bring home some tonight.   [*Exit*]

BAWD   Come your ways, follow me.

MARINA   If fires be hot, knives sharp, or waters deep,
130   Untied I still my virgin knot will keep.
Diana° aid my purpose.   *goddess of chastity*

BAWD   What have we to do with Diana? Pray you, will you go
with me?   *Exeunt.* [*The sign is removed*]

Scene 17

Enter [*in mourning garments*] CLEON *and* DIONYZA

DIONYZA   Why, are you foolish? Can it be undone?

CLEON   O Dionyza, such a piece of slaughter
The sun and moon ne'er looked upon.

DIONYZA   I think you'll turn a child again.

5 CLEON   Were I chief lord of all this spacious world
I'd give it to undo the deed. A lady°   *(Marina)*
Much less in blood than virtue, yet a princess
To equal any single crown o'th' earth
I'th' justice of compare.° O villain Leonine,   *In a fair comparison*
10   Whom thou hast poisoned too,
If thou hadst drunk to him 't'ad been a kindness
Becoming well thy fact.¹ What canst thou say
When noble Pericles demands his child?

DIONYZA   That she is dead. Nurses are not the fates.

---

7. You have prosperity (wealthy men) about to come to
(have an orgasm on top of) you.
8. Exchanged or sold (for a prostitute's wardrobe), since
they proclaim her virginity and social status.
9. Perhaps: Your costs as a customer (of taverns and such)
spreading the word will come back in your commission

on the customers who come here.
1. Eels were supposedly roused by thunder.
Scene 17 (Act 4, Scene 3)
Location: The Governor's house in Tarsus.
1. *If . . . fact:* If you had drunk his health (from the same
poison), the self-punishment would have fit the crime.

15	To foster is not ever° to preserve.	*always*
	She died at night. I'll say so. Who can cross° it,	*deny*
	Unless you play the pious innocent	
	And, for an honest attribute,° cry out	*reputation*
	'She died by foul play.'	
	CLEON O, go to.° Well, well,	*(contemptuous)*
20	Of all the faults beneath the heav'ns the gods	
	Do like this worst.	
	DIONYZA Be one of those that thinks	
	The petty wrens of Tarsus will fly hence	
	And open° this to Pericles. I do shame	*disclose*
	To think of what a noble strain° you are,	*bloodline*
	And of how cowed a spirit.	
25	CLEON To such proceeding	
	Whoever but his approbation added,	
	Though not his prime° consent, he did not flow	*prior*
	From honourable sources.	
	DIONYZA Be it so, then.	
	Yet none does know but you how she came dead,	
30	Nor none can know, Leonine being gone.	
	She did distain° my child, and stood between	*stain (by comparison)*
	Her and her fortunes. None would look on her,	
	But cast their gazes on Marina's face	
	Whilst ours was blurted at,° and held a malkin°	*scorned / dirty peasant*
35	Not worth the time of day. It pierced me through,	
	And though you call my course unnatural,	
	You not your child well loving, yet I find	
	It greets° me as an enterprise of kindness	*strikes*
	Performed to your sole daughter.	
40	CLEON Heavens forgive it.	
	DIONYZA And as for Pericles,	
	What should he say? We wept after her hearse,	
	And yet° we mourn. Her monument	*still*
	Is almost finished, and her epitaphs	
45	In glitt'ring golden characters express	
	A gen'ral praise to her and care in us,	
	At whose expense 'tis done.	
	CLEON Thou art like the harpy,[2]	
	Which, to betray, dost, with thine angel face,	
	Seize in thine eagle talons.	
50	DIONYZA Ye're like one that superstitiously	
	Do swear to th' gods that winter kills the flies,[3]	
	But yet I know you'll do as I advise. *Exeunt*	

Scene 18

Enter GOWER

GOWER	Thus time we waste,° and long leagues make we short,	*pass quickly*
	Sail seas in cockles,° have and wish but for't,[1]	*seashells*
	Making to take° imagination	*Proceeding by*
	From bourn° to bourn, region to region.	*border*

---

2. Monstrous creature with a woman's face and an eagle's talons.

3. *Ye're . . . flies*: perhaps, You're so afraid of the gods that you'd feel it necessary to tell them insignificant and unalterable things they already know (that winter killed the flies).

Scene 18 (Act 4, Scene 4)
Location: Before Marina's tomb in Tarsus.
1. Get something merely by wishing for it.

5   By you being pardoned, we commit no crime
    To use one language in each sev'ral clime°   *separate region*
    Where our scene seems to live. I do beseech you
    To learn of me, who stand i'th' gaps° to teach you   *(between scenes)*
    The stages of our story: Pericles
10   Is now again thwarting° the wayward seas,   *crossing*
    Attended on by many a lord and knight,
    To see his daughter, all his life's delight.
    Old Helicanus goes along. Behind
    Is left to govern, if you bear in mind,
15   Old Aeschines, whom Helicanus late°   *recently*
    Advanced in Tyre to great and high estate.°   *rank*
    Well sailing ships and bounteous winds have brought
    This king to Tarsus—think his pilot thought;[2]
    So with his steerage shall your thoughts go on—
20   To fetch his daughter home, who first° is gone.   *already*
    Like motes and shadows[3] see them move a while;
    Your ears unto your eyes I'll reconcile.
                      [Dumb show.]
     Enter PERICLES *at one door with all his train,* CLEON
     and DIONYZA *[in mourning garments] at the other.*
     CLEON *[draws the curtain and] shows* PERICLES *the*
     tomb, whereat PERICLES *makes lamentation, puts on*
     sack-cloth, and in a mighty passion° departs [followed by   *sorrow*
     his train. CLEON *and* DIONYZA *depart at the other door]*
    See how belief may suffer by foul show.°   *false appearances*
    This borrowed passion stands for true-owed woe,[4]
25   And Pericles, in sorrow all devoured,
    With sighs shot through, and biggest tears o'ershow'red,
    Leaves Tarsus, and again embarks. He swears
    Never to wash his face nor cut his hairs.
    He puts on sack-cloth, and to sea. He bears
30   A tempest which his mortal vessel tears,[5]
    And yet he rides it out. Now please you wit°   *know*
    The epitaph is° for Marina writ   *that is*
    By wicked Dionyza.
          [He reads Marina's epitaph[6] on the tomb]
    'The fairest, sweetest, best lies here,
35   Who withered in her spring of year.°   *early in life*
    In nature's garden, though by growth a bud,
    She was the chiefest flower: she was good.'
    No visor does become black villainy
    So well as soft and tender flattery.
40   Let Pericles believe his daughter's dead
    And bear his courses to be orderèd[7]
    By Lady Fortune, while our scene must play
    His daughter's woe and heavy well-a-day°   *lamentation*
    In her unholy service. Patience then,
45   And think you now are all in Mytilene.

                       Exit

---

2. Think that his pilot is swiftly traveling thought.
3. Like specks of dust in a sunbeam and like (theatrical) illusions.
4. Cleon and Dionyza's "woe" is "borrowed," not "true-owed" (owned).
5. *He bears . . . tears*: His suffering assaults his body.

(Note the internalization of the earlier storms.)
6. The four-line epitaph is from *PA*, which may preserve the author's revised version of this passage. Q1's ten-line version (see the Additional Passage at the end of the play) includes the first two lines here.
7. And allow his fate to be arranged.

Scene 19

[*A brothel sign.*] *Enter two* GENTLEMEN
FIRST GENTLEMAN   Did you ever hear the like?
SECOND GENTLEMAN   No, nor never shall do in such a place as
this, she being once gone.
FIRST GENTLEMAN   But to have divinity preached there—did you
5   ever dream of such a thing?
SECOND GENTLEMAN   No, no. Come, I am for no more bawdy
houses. Shall 's go hear the vestals sing?[1]
FIRST GENTLEMAN   I'll do anything now that is virtuous, but I am
out of the road of rutting° for ever.   *Exeunt*   *fornication*
Enter [PANDER,] BAWD [*and* BOULT]
10 PANDER   Well, I had rather than twice the worth of her she had
ne'er come here.
BAWD   Fie, fie upon her, she's able to freeze the god Priapus and
undo the whole of generation.[2] We must either get her ravished
or be rid of her. When she should do for clients her fitment°   *duty*
15   and do me the kindness of our profession, she has° me her   *gives*
quirks, her reasons, her master reasons, her prayers, her knees,°   *(kneeling to plead)*
that she would make a puritan of the devil if he should
cheapen° a kiss of her.   *bargain for*
BOULT   Faith, I must ravish her, or she'll disfurnish us of all our
20   cavalleria° and make our swearers[3] priests.   *gentlemen customers*
PANDER   Now, the pox upon her green-sickness[4] for me.
BAWD   Faith, there's no way to be rid on't but by the way to the pox.°   *venereal disease*
Enter LYSIMACHUS [*disguised*]
Here comes the Lord Lysimachus, disguised.
BOULT   We should have both lord and loon° if the peevish bag-   *lowborn*
25   gage° would but give way to custom.[5]   *whore*
LYSIMACHUS   How now, how° a dozen of virginities?   *how much for*
BAWD   Now, the gods to-bless your honour!
BOULT   I am glad to see your honour in good health.
LYSIMACHUS   You may so. 'Tis the better for you that your resort-
30   ers stand upon sound legs.[6] How now, wholesome iniquity°   *healthy whore*
have you, that a man may deal withal° and defy the surgeon?°   *with / avoid the doctor*
BAWD   We have here one, sir, if she would—but there never
came her like in Mytilene.
LYSIMACHUS   If she'd do the deed of darkness, thou wouldst say.
35 BAWD   Your honour knows what 'tis to say° well enough.   *what I mean*
LYSIMACHUS   Well, call forth, call forth.   [*Exit* PANDER]
BOULT   For flesh and blood, sir, white and red, you shall see a
rose. And she were a rose indeed, if she had but—[7]
LYSIMACHUS   What, prithee?
40 BOULT   O sir, I can be modest.

Scene 19 (Other modern editions divide this scene in
two: Act 4, Scene 5 [lines 1–9] and Scene 6 [lines 10–
211]. But the location remains in or around the brothel
throughout. This edition assumes both that there is no
gap in time between the two parts and that the modest
shifts in locale within the scene do not violate the rela-
tively unspecific notion of place on the early seventeenth-
century stage.)
Location: The brothel in Mytilene.
1. Shall we go hear the vestal virgins (religious devotees)
sing?

2. Able to stop the "whole" (hole) work of breeding. Pria-
pus was the god of procreation, especially of male virility
and lechery. "The whole of" emends Q1's "a hole."
3. Loyal (blasphemous) customers.
4. Moody stubbornness, supposedly caused by anemia in
young women; queasiness from lack of experience.
5. Customers; customary behavior. Q1 has "customers."
6. Rather than upon legs bent from venereal disease.
7. If she had but a thorn; if she were sexually experi-
enced.

LYSIMACHUS   That dignifies the renown of a bawd no less than it
gives a good report to a noble to be chaste.[8]
                        Enter [PANDER *with*] MARINA
BAWD   Here comes that which grows to° the stalk, never plucked   *affixed to*
yet, I can assure you. Is she not a fair creature?
45   LYSIMACHUS   Faith, she would serve after a long voyage at sea.
Well, there's for you. Leave us.
                        [*He pays the* BAWD]
BAWD   I beseech your honour give me leave: a word, and I'll
have done presently.°   *be done soon*
LYSIMACHUS   I beseech you, do.
50   BAWD [*aside to* MARINA]   First, I would have you note this is an
honourable man.
MARINA   I desire to find him so, that I may honourably know him.
BAWD   Next, he's the governor of this country, and a man whom
I am bound to.
55   MARINA   If he govern the country you are bound to him indeed,
but how honourable he is in that, I know not.
BAWD   Pray you, without any more virginal fencing, will you use
him kindly? He will line your apron with gold.
MARINA   What he will do graciously I will thankfully receive.
60   LYSIMACHUS [*to* BAWD]   Ha' you done?
BAWD   My lord, she's not paced° yet. You must take some pains   *trained (like a horse)*
to work her to your manège.[9] [*To* BOULT *and* PANDER] Come,
we will leave his honour and hers together. Go thy ways.°   *Come along*
                        Exeunt [PANDER,] BAWD [*and* BOULT]
LYSIMACHUS   Fair one, how long have you been at this trade?
65   MARINA   What trade, sir?
LYSIMACHUS   I cannot name it but I shall offend.
MARINA   I cannot be offended with my trade.
Please you to name it.
LYSIMACHUS   How long have you been
Of this profession?
MARINA   E'er since I can remember.
70   LYSIMACHUS   Did you go to't° so young? Were you a gamester°   *copulate / loose woman*
At five, or seven?
MARINA   Earlier too, sir,
If now I be one.
LYSIMACHUS   Why, the house you dwell in
Proclaimeth you a creature of sale.
MARINA   And do you know this house to be a place
75   Of such resort° and will come into it?   *purpose*
I hear say you're of honourable blood,
And are the governor of this whole province.
LYSIMACHUS   What, hath your principal° informed you who I am?   *employer*
MARINA   Who is my principal?
LYSIMACHUS   Why, your herb-woman;
80   She that sets seeds of shame, roots of iniquity.
                        [MARINA *weeps*]
O, you've heard something of my pow'r, and so
Stand off aloof for a more serious wooing.

8. Than it gives a noble(wo)man a (falsely) good reputa-   9. To bring her under your control (from horsemanship).
tion for being chaste. Q1 has "number" for "noble."

But I protest to thee,
Pretty one, my authority can wink
85   At blemishes,[1] or can on faults look friendly;
Or my displeasure punish at my pleasure,
From which displeasure, not thy beauty shall
Privilege thee, nor my affection,° which   *lust*
Hath drawn me here, abate with further ling'ring.
90   Come bring me to some private place. Come, come.
MARINA   Let not authority, which teaches you
To govern others, be the means to make you
Misgovern much yourself.[2]
If you were born to honour,° show it now;   *high status; virtue*
95   If put upon you,[3] make the judgement good
That thought you worthy of it. What[4] reason's in
Your justice, who hath power over all,
To undo any? If you take from me
Mine honour, you're like him that makes a gap
100   Into forbidden ground, whom after
Too many enter, and of all their evils
Yourself are guilty. My life is yet unspotted;°   *still free of sin*
My chastity unstainèd ev'n in thought.
Then if your violence deface this building,°   *body*
105   The workmanship of heav'n, you do kill your honour,
Abuse your justice, and impoverish me.
My yet good lord, if there be fire before me,
Must I straight fly° and burn myself? Suppose this house—   *go immediately*
Which too too many feel such houses are—
110   Should be the doctor's patrimony, and
The surgeon's feeding;° follows it, that I   *livelihood*
Must needs infect myself to give them maint'nance?
LYSIMACHUS   How's this, how's this? Some more. Be sage.
MARINA [*kneeling*]   For me
That am a maid, though most ungentle fortune
115   Have franked° me in this sty, where since I came   *shut*
Diseases have been sold dearer than physic—[5]
That the gods would set me free from this unhallowed place,
Though they did change me to the meanest° bird   *humblest*
That flies i'th' purer air!
LYSIMACHUS [*moved*]   I did not think
120   Thou couldst have spoke so well, ne'er dreamt thou couldst.
[*He lifts her up with his hands*]
Though I brought hither a corrupted mind,
Thy speech hath altered it,
[*He wipes the wet from her eyes*]
                         and my foul thoughts
Thy tears so well hath laved° that they're now white.   *cleansed*
I came here meaning but to pay the price,

---

1. *can wink / At blemishes:* can refuse to see moral short-comings. Lines 84–89 are adapted from *PA* and replace Q1's "my authority shall not see thee, or else look friendly upon thee," which doesn't reflect as badly on Lysimachus. Here and in subsequent passages in this scene, *PA* may preserve Shakespeare's original words, while Q1 records the politically censored version that was actually performed.
2. *Let . . . yourself:* not in Q1 adapted from *PA.*
3. If you were granted rank not by birth but by merit.
4. Lines 96–112 are not in Q1 but were adapted from *PA.* Q1's lines 94–96 ("If . . . it") and 113–19 ("For . . . air") seem inadequate to produce Lysimachus's response at line 113 and dramatic conversion at lines 119–20.
5. Sold at a higher price than medical treatment.

125 A piece of gold for thy virginity;
Here's twenty to relieve thine honesty.[6]
Persever still° in that clear way thou goest,   *always*
And the gods strengthen thee.
MARINA   The good gods preserve you!
LYSIMACHUS The[7] very doors and windows savour vilely.
130 Fare thee well. Thou art a piece of virtue,
The best wrought up° that ever nature made,[8]   *created*
And I doubt not thy training hath been noble.
A curse upon him, die he° like a thief,   *may he die*
That robs thee of thy honour. Hold, here's more gold.
135 If thou dost hear from me, it shall be for thy good.
               [*Enter* BOULT *standing ready at the door, making his*
               obeisance unto him as LYSIMACHUS *should go out*]
BOULT I beseech your honour, one piece for me.
LYSIMACHUS Avaunt,° thou damnèd door-keeper!   *Begone*
Your house, but for this virgin that doth prop it,
Would sink and overwhelm you. Away.   [*Exit*]
140 BOULT How's this? We must take another course with you. If
your peevish chastity, which is not worth a breakfast in the
cheapest country under the cope,° shall undo a whole house-   *sky*
hold, let me be gelded like a spaniel. Come your ways.
MARINA Whither would you have me?
145 BOULT I must have your maidenhead taken off, or the common
executioner shall do it.[9] We'll have no more gentlemen driven
away. Come your ways, I say.
               Enter BAWD [*and* PANDER]
BAWD How now, what's the matter?
BOULT Worse and worse, mistress, she has here spoken holy
150 words to the Lord Lysimachus.
BAWD O, abominable!
BOULT She makes our profession as it were to stink afore the
face of the gods.
BAWD Marry° hang her up for ever!   (*expresses irritation*)
155 BOULT The nobleman would have dealt with her like a noble-
man,[1] and she sent him away as cold as a snowball, saying his
prayers, too.
PANDER Boult, take her away. Use her at thy pleasure. Crack the
ice of her virginity, and make the rest malleable.
160 BOULT An if° she were a thornier piece of ground than she is,   *Even if*
she shall be ploughed.
MARINA Hark, hark, you gods!
BAWD She conjures.° Away with her! Would she had never   *calls on the gods*
come within my doors.—Marry, hang you!—She's born to
165 undo us.—Will you not go the way of womenkind? Marry,
come up, my dish of chastity with rosemary and bays.[2]
               Exeunt [BAWD *and* PANDER]
BOULT [*catching her rashly by the hand*] Come, mistress, come
your way with me.

6. To assist your chastity. Lines 124–26, adapted from
PA, replace Q1's "Hold here's gold for thee."
7. Q1 precedes these lines with "For me be you
thoughten [understand], that I came with no ill intent, for
to me."
8. Line 131 not in Q1; adapted from PA.

9. "Executioner shall do" replaces Q1's "hāg-man shall
execute," producing wordplay on "maidenhead" and
"executioner" (one who chops off heads).
1. Would have used her and rewarded her well.
2. The Bawd chides Marina for thinking herself to exqui-
site a dish (for making too much of her chastity).

MARINA   Whither wilt thou have me?

170 BOULT   To take from you the jewel you hold so dear.

MARINA   Prithee, tell me one thing first.

BOULT   Come, now, your one thing.

MARINA   What canst thou wish thine enemy to be?[3]

BOULT   Why, I could wish him to be° my master, or rather my   *(as bad as)*

175 mistress.

MARINA   Neither of these can be so bad as thou art,
Since they do better thee in their command.[4]
Thou hold'st a place the painèd'st° fiend of hell   *most tortured*
Would not in reputation change with thee,

180 Thou damnèd doorkeeper to ev'ry coistrel°   *scoundrel*
That comes enquiring for his Tib.°   *loose woman*
To th' choleric fisting of ev'ry rogue
Thy ear is liable.[5] Thy food is such
As hath been belched on by infected lungs.

185 BOULT   What would you have me do? Go to the wars, would
you, where a man may serve seven years for the loss of° a leg,   *only to lose*
and have not money enough in the end to buy him a wooden one?

MARINA   Do anything but this thou dost. Empty
Old receptacles or common sew'rs of filth,

190 Serve by indenture° to the public hangman —   *as apprentice*
Any of these are yet better than this.
For what thou professest a baboon, could he speak,
Would own a name too dear.[6] Here's gold for thee.
If that thy master would make gain by me,

195 Proclaim that I can sing, weave, sew, and dance,
With other virtues° which I'll keep from boast,   *accomplishments*
And I will undertake all these to teach.
I doubt not but this populous city will
Yield many scholars.°   *pupils*

200 BOULT   But can you teach all this you speak of?

MARINA   Prove° that I cannot, take me home again   *If you prove*
And prostitute me to the basest groom°   *lowest servant*
That doth frequent your house.

BOULT   Well, I will see what I can do for thee. If I can place

205 thee, I will.

MARINA   But amongst honest women.

BOULT   Faith, my acquaintance lies little amongst them; but
since my master and mistress hath bought you, there's no going
but by their consent. Therefore I will make them acquainted

210 with your purpose, and I doubt not but I shall find them tracta-
ble enough. Come, I'll do for thee what I can. Come your ways.

Exeunt. [The sign is removed]

Scene 20

Enter GOWER

GOWER   Marina thus the brothel scapes, and chances
Into an honest house, our story says.

---

3. What is the worst thing you could wish on your enemy?

4. Since they can command you to do what even they wouldn't do themselves.

5. *To . . . liable:* Even the lowest rogue would box your ear if angry.

6. Would consider beneath him. Q1 follows this sentence with "That the gods would safely deliver me from this place: here"—a repetition of line 117 that is out of place here.

She sings like one immortal, and she dances
As goddess-like to her admirèd lays.°   *songs*
5   Deep clerks she dumbs,[1] and with her nee'le° composes   *needle*
Nature's own shape, of bud, bird, branch, or berry,
That e'en her art sisters° the natural roses.   *equals*
Her inkle,° silk, twin with the rubied cherry;   *linen thread*
That° pupils lacks she none of noble race,   *So that*
10   Who pour their bounty on her, and her gain
She gives the cursèd Bawd. Here we her place,
And to her father turn our thoughts again.
We left him on the sea. Waves there him tossed,
Whence, driven tofore° the winds, he is arrived   *before*
15   Here where his daughter dwells, and on this coast
Suppose him now at anchor. The city strived°   *surpassed itself*
God Neptune's annual feast to keep, from whence
Lysimachus our Tyrian ship espies,
His° banners sable,° trimmed with rich expense;   *Its / black*
20   And to him° in his barge with fervour hies.   *it*
In your supposing° once more put your sight;   *imagination*
Of heavy° Pericles think this the barque,°   *sad / ship*
Where what is done in action, more if might,
Shall be discovered.[2] Please you sit and hark.   *Exit*

Scene 21

Enter HELICANUS [*above; below, enter*] *to him* [*at the
first door*] *two* SAILORS [*one* OF TYRE, *the other* OF MYTI-
LENE]
SAILOR OF TYRE [*to* SAILOR OF MYTILENE]   Lord Helicanus can
    resolve[1] you, sir.
[*To* HELICANUS]   There is a barge put off from Mytilene.
In it, Lysimachus, the governor,
Who craves to come aboard. What is your will?
HELICANUS   That he have his.
                [*Exit* SAILOR OF MYTILENE *at first door*]
5   Call up some gentlemen.
                    [*Exit* HELICANUS *above*]
SAILOR OF TYRE   Ho, my lord calls!
    Enter [*from below the stage*] *two or three*
    GENTLEMEN[; *to them, enter* HELICANUS]
FIRST GENTLEMAN   What is your lordship's pleasure?
HELICANUS   Gentlemen, some of worth° would come aboard.   *some noble visitor*
I pray you, greet him fairly.
    Enter LYSIMACHUS [*at first door, with the* SAILOR *and*
    LORDS OF MYTILENE]
SAILOR OF MYTILENE [*to* LYSIMACHUS]   This is the man that can
    in aught resolve° you.   *answer anything for*
10 LYSIMACHUS [*to* HELICANUS]   Hail, reverend sir; the gods preserve you!
HELICANUS   And you, sir, to outlive the age I am,
And die as I would do.

Scene 20 (Act 5, Chorus)
1. Her wisdom reduces learned men to silence.
2. *Where . . . discovered:* Where the stage action, which
would show more if it could, will reveal what happens.

Scene 21 (Act 5, Scene 1)
Location: Pericle's ship, off Mytilene.
1. Answer. This line replaces Q1's "Where is Lord Heli-
canus? He can resolve you, / O here he is sir."

LYSIMACHUS   You wish me well.
  I am the governor of Mytilene;[2]
  Being on shore, honouring of Neptune's triumphs,[3]
15 Seeing this goodly vessel ride before us,
  I made to it to know of whence you are.
HELICANUS Our vessel is of Tyre, in it our king,
  A man who for this three months hath not spoken
  To anyone, nor taken sustenance
20 But to prorogue° his grief.   *extend*
LYSIMACHUS Upon what ground grew his distemp'rature?°   *emotional disturbance*
HELICANUS 'Twould be too tedious to tell it over,
  But the main grief springs from the precious loss
  Of a belovèd daughter and a wife.
LYSIMACHUS May we not see him?
25 HELICANUS   See him, sir, you may,
  But bootless° is your sight. He will not speak   *pointless*
  To any.
LYSIMACHUS Let me yet obtain my wish.
HELICANUS Behold him.
      [HELICANUS *draws a curtain, revealing* PERICLES *lying*
      upon a couch with a long overgrown beard, diffused°   *disorderly*
      hair, undecent nails on his fingers, and attired in sack-
      cloth]
           This was a goodly person
  Till the disaster of one mortal° night   *fatal*
  Drove him to this.
30 LYSIMACHUS [*to* PERICLES] Sir, King, all hail. Hail, royal sir.
      [PERICLES *shrinks himself down upon his pillow*]
HELICANUS It is in vain. He will not speak to you.
LORD OF MYTILENE Sir, we have a maid in Mytilene I durst wager
  Would win some words of him.
LYSIMACHUS   'Tis well bethought.
  She questionless, with her sweet harmony
35 And other choice attractions, would alarum[4]
  And make a batt'ry through his deafened ports,
  Which now are midway stopped.° She in all happy,°   *half closed / skillful*
  As the fair'st of all, among her fellow maids
  Dwells now i'th' leafy shelter that abuts
40 Against the island's side. Go fetch her hither.   [*Exit* LORD]
HELICANUS Sure, all effectless; yet nothing we'll omit
  That bears recov'ry's name.° But since your kindness   *That might cure him*
  We have stretched thus far, let us beseech you
  That for our gold we may provision have,
45 Wherein we are not destitute for want,
  But weary for the staleness.
LYSIMACHUS   O sir, a courtesy
  Which if we should deny, the most just gods
  For every graft° would send a caterpillar,   *cultivated plant*
  And so inflict° our province. Yet once more   *afflict (with famine)*

---

2. This line replaces Q1's
  HELICANUS First what is your place?
  LYSIMACHUS I am the Governor of this place you lie
    before,
which appears after line 16, where it interrupts the dia-
logue and attributes to Helicanus a rudeness that is gratu-

itous, since he already knows who Lysimachus is (see line
3).
3. Observing Neptune's festival. •
4. Awaken (as a trumpet). Q1 has "allure," which intro-
duces a sexual innuendo (see the Introduction).

50 Let me entreat to know at large° the cause   *in detail*
Of your king's sorrow.
HELICANUS   Sit, sir. I will recount it.
          [*Enter* LORD *with* MARINA *and another* MAID]
But see, I am prevented.
LYSIMACHUS   O, here's the lady that I sent for.—
Welcome, fair one.—Is't not a goodly presence?°   *Isn't she attractive*
55 HELICANUS   She's a gallant° lady.   *fine*
LYSIMACHUS   She's such a one that, were I well assured
Came of gentle kind° or noble stock, I'd wish   *a gentry family*
No better choice to think me rarely° wed.—   *superbly*
Fair one, all goodness that consists in bounty
60 Expect e'en here, where is a kingly patient;
If that thy prosperous and artificial feat°   *artful skill*
Can draw him but to answer thee in aught,
Thy sacred physic° shall receive such pay   *treatment*
As thy desires can wish.
MARINA   Sir, I will use
65 My utmost skill in his recure,° provided   *cure*
That none but I and my companion maid
Be suffered° to come near him.   *permitted*
LYSIMACHUS [*to the others*]   Let us leave her,
And the gods prosper her.   [*The men stand aside*]
          The Song⁵
LYSIMACHUS [*coming forward*] Marked° he your music?   *Noticed*
MAID   No, nor looked on us.
LYSIMACHUS [*to the others*]   See, she will speak to him.
70 MARINA [*to* PERICLES]   Hail, sir; my lord, lend ear.
PERICLES   Hmh, ha!
          [*He roughly repulses her*]
MARINA   I am a maid,
My lord, that ne'er before invited eyes,
But have been gazed on like a comet.° She speaks,   *in awe*
75 My lord, that maybe hath endured a grief
Might° equal yours, if both were justly weighed.   *That might*
Though wayward fortune did malign my state,°   *reduce my status*
My derivation was from ancestors
Who stood equivalent with mighty kings,
80 But time hath rooted out⁶ my parentage,
And to the world and awkward casualties°   *adverse events*
Bound me in servitude. [*Aside*] I will desist.
But there is something glows upon my cheek,
And whispers in mine ear 'Stay till he speak.'
85 PERICLES   My fortunes, parentage, good parentage,
To equal mine? Was it not thus? What say you?
MARINA   I said if you did know my parentage,
My lord, you would not do me violence.
PERICLES   I do think so. Pray you, turn your eyes upon me.
90 You're like something that—what countrywoman?°   *what nationality*
Here of these shores?
MARINA   No, nor of any shores,

5. The song is given in *PA*, which takes it from Twine's   6. Uprooted me from; obscured; killed.
Pattern of Painful Adventures.

Yet I was mortally° brought forth, and am   *fatally*
No other than I seem.
PERICLES [*aside*]   I am great° with woe, and shall deliver   *pregnant*
    weeping.
95   My dearest wife was like this maid, and such
    My daughter might have been. My queen's square brows,
    Her stature to an inch, as wand-like straight,
    As silver-voiced, her eyes as jewel-like,
    And cased as richly, in pace° another Juno,   *stride*
100   Who starves the ears she feeds, and makes them hungry
    The more she gives them speech.—Where do you live?
MARINA   Where I am but a stranger.° From the deck   *foreigner*
    You may discern the place.
PERICLES   Where were you bred,
    And how achieved you these endowments which
    You make more rich to owe?°   *by your owning them*
105   MARINA   If I should tell
    My history, it would seem like lies
    Disdained in the reporting.°   *as soon as told*
PERICLES   Prithee speak.
    Falseness cannot come from thee, for thou look'st
    Modest as justice, and thou seem'st a palace
110   For the crowned truth to dwell in. I will believe thee,
    And make my senses credit thy relation°   *trust your story*
    To° points that seem impossible. Thou show'st   *Even to*
    Like one I loved indeed. What were thy friends?°   *kin*
    Didst thou not say, when I did push thee back—
115   Which was when I perceived thee—that thou cam'st
    From good descending?
MARINA   So indeed I did.
PERICLES   Report thy parentage. I think thou said'st
    Thou hadst been tossed from wrong to injury,
    And that thou thought'st thy griefs might equal mine,
    If both were opened.°   *revealed*
120   MARINA   Some such thing I said,
    And said no more but what my circumstance
    Did warrant° me was likely.   *assure*
PERICLES   Tell thy story.
    If thine considered prove the thousandth part
    Of my endurance,° thou art a man, and I   *suffering*
125   Have suffered like a girl. Yet thou dost look
    Like patience gazing on kings' graves, and smiling
    Extremity out of act.[7] What were thy friends?
    How lost thou them? Thy name, my most kind[8] virgin?
    Recount, I do beseech thee. Come, sit by me.
        [*She sits*]
MARINA   My name, sir, is Marina.
130   PERICLES   O, I am mocked,
    And thou by some incensèd god sent hither
    To make the world to laugh at me.

---

7. *Yet . . . act:* Yet you seem able to bear even the deaths of kings (like statues of patience personified, perhaps on royal tombs) and to face down the worst extremities (espe- cially suicidal despair) with a smile.
8. Sympathetic; related by blood ("kind" also meant "kin").

MARINA   Patience, good sir,
  Or here I'll cease.
PERICLES   Nay, I'll be patient.
  Thou little know'st how thou dost startle me
  To call thyself Marina.
135   MARINA   The name
  Was given me by one that had some power:
  My father, and a king.
PERICLES   How, a king's daughter,
  And called Marina?
MARINA   You said you would believe me,
  But not to be a troubler of your peace
  I will end here.
140   PERICLES   But are you flesh and blood?
  Have you a working pulse and are no fairy?
  Motion° as well? Speak on. Where were you born,   *(of life)*
  And wherefore called Marina?
MARINA   Called Marina
  For I was born at sea.
PERICLES   At sea? What mother?
145   MARINA   My mother was the daughter of a king,
  Who died when I was born, as my good nurse
  Lychorida hath oft recounted weeping.
PERICLES   O, stop there a little! [*Aside*] This is the rarest dream
  That e'er dulled sleep did mock sad fools withal.°   *with*
150   This cannot be my daughter, buried. Well.
  [*To* MARINA] Where were you bred? I'll hear you more to th'
      bottom°   *the end*
  Of your story, and never interrupt you.
MARINA   You will scarce believe me. 'Twere best I did give o'er.°   *stop*
PERICLES   I will believe you by the syllable
155   Of what you shall deliver. Yet give me leave.°   *(to ask)*
  How came you in these parts? Where were you bred?
MARINA   The King my father did in Tarsus leave me,
  Till cruel Cleon, with his wicked wife,
  Did seek to murder me, and wooed a villain
160   To attempt the deed; who having drawn to do't,
  A crew of pirates came and rescued me.
  To Mytilene they brought me. But, good sir,
  What will you° of me? Why do you weep? It may be   *What do you want*
  You think me an impostor. No, good faith,
165   I am the daughter to King Pericles,
  If good King Pericles be.°   *live*
PERICLES [*rising*]   Ho, Helicanus!
HELICANUS [*coming forward*]   Calls my lord?
PERICLES   Thou art a grave and noble counsellor,
170   Most wise in gen'ral. Tell me if thou canst
  What this maid is, or what is like° to be,   *likely*
  That thus hath made me weep.
HELICANUS   I know not.
  But here's the regent, sir, of Mytilene
  Speaks° nobly of her.   *Who speaks*
LYSIMACHUS   She would never tell
175   Her parentage. Being demanded that,
  She would sit still and weep.

PERICLES   O Helicanus, strike me, honoured sir,
  Give me a gash, put me to present° pain,   *immediate*
  Lest this great sea of joys rushing upon me
180 O'erbear° the shores of my mortality   *Overflow*
  And drown me with their sweetness! [*To* MARINA] O, come hither,
     [MARINA *stands*]
  Thou that begett'st him that did thee beget,[9]
  Thou that wast born at sea, buried at Tarsus,
  And found at sea again!—O Helicanus,
185 Down on thy knees, thank the holy gods as loud
  As thunder threatens us, this is Marina!
  [*To* MARINA] What was thy mother's name? Tell me but that,
  For truth can never be confirmed enough,
  Though doubts did ever sleep.[1]
MARINA   First, sir, I pray,
  What is your title?
190 PERICLES   I am Pericles
  Of Tyre. But tell me now my drowned queen's name.
  As in the rest thou hast been godlike perfect,°   *have been omniscient*
  So prove but true in that, thou art my daughter,[2]
  The heir of kingdoms, and another life
  To Pericles thy father.
195 MARINA [*kneeling*]   Is it no more
  To be your daughter than to say my mother's name?
  Thaisa was my mother, who did end
  The minute I began.
PERICLES Now blessing on thee! Rise. Thou art my child.
     [MARINA *stands. He kisses her*]
200 [*To attendants*] Give me fresh garments.—Mine own, Helicanus!
  Not dead at Tarsus, as she should have been[3]
  By savage Cleon. She shall tell thee all,
  When thou shalt kneel and justify in knowledge° *satisfy yourself that*
  She is thy very princess. Who is this?
205 HELICANUS Sir, 'tis the governor of Mytilene,
  Who, hearing of your melancholy state,
  Did come to see you.
PERICLES [*to* LYSIMACHUS] I embrace you, sir.—
  Give me my robes.
     [*He is attired in fresh robes*]
         I am wild in my beholding.[4]
  O heavens, bless my girl!
     [*Celestial music*]
        But hark, what music?
210 Tell Helicanus, my Marina, tell him
  O'er point by point, for yet he seems to doubt,
  How sure you are my daughter. But what music?
HELICANUS My lord, I hear none.
PERICLES None? The music of the spheres![5] List,° my Marina. *Listen*
LYSIMACHUS [*aside to the others*] It is not good to cross him. Give

---

9. The possible sexual complications here, including incest, can be highlighted in performance by doubling the part of Marina with that of Thaisa or Antiochus's Daughter. (For the possible relevance of doubling the part of Marina to the transmission of the text, see the Textual Note.)
1. Even in the absence of doubts.

2. Line is not in Q1; it was added to fill a suspected gap.
3. As she was believed (intended) to be.
4. Unkempt in my appearance, ecstatic at what I see.
5. A sign of celestial harmony, brought about by the proper movement of the heavenly bodies around earth (hence a sign of divine order).

215   him way.

PERICLES Rar'st sounds. Do ye not hear?

LYSIMACHUS Music, my lord?

PERICLES I hear most heav'nly music.

It raps° me unto list'ning, and thick slumber   *compels*

220   Hangs upon mine eyelids. Let me rest.

      [*He sleeps*]

LYSIMACHUS A pillow for his head.

    [*To* MARINA *and others*]   Companion friends,

If this but answer to my just belief

I'll well remember° you. So leave him all.   *reward; recall*

                [*Exeunt all but* PERICLES]

    DIANA [*descends from the heavens*]

DIANA My temple stands in Ephesus. Hie thee thither,

225   And do upon mine altar sacrifice.

There when my maiden priests are met together,

At large discourse thy fortunes in this wise:

With a full voice[6] before the people all,

Reveal how thou at sea didst lose thy wife.

230   To mourn thy crosses,° with thy daughter's, call   *losses*

And give them repetition to the life.[7]

Perform my bidding, or thou liv'st in woe;

Do't, and rest happy, by my silver bow.[8]

Awake, and tell thy dream.   [DIANA *ascends into the heavens*]

235 PERICLES Celestial Dian, goddess argentine,°   *silver (like the moon)*

I will obey thee. [*Calling*] Helicanus!

    [*Enter* HELICANUS, LYSIMACHUS, *and* MARINA]

HELICANUS   Sir?

PERICLES My purpose was for Tarsus, there to strike

Th'inhospitable Cleon, but I am

For other service first. Toward Ephesus

240   Turn our blown° sails. Eftsoons° I'll tell thee why.   *inflated / Later*

                [*Exit* HELICANUS]

Shall we refresh us, sir, upon your shore,

And give you gold for such provision

As our intents will need?

LYSIMACHUS   With all my heart, sir,

And when you come ashore I have a suit.

245 PERICLES You shall prevail, were it to woo my daughter,

For it seems you have been noble towards her.

LYSIMACHUS Sir, lend me your arm.

PERICLES   Come, my Marina.

    Exit [PERICLES *with* LYSIMACHUS *at one arm,*

        MARINA *at the other*]

Scene 22

    Enter GOWER

GOWER Now our sands are almost run;

More a little, and then dumb.°   *silent*

This my last boon give me,

---

6. *At . . . voice:* not in Q1; added to fill a suspected gap. *At large discourse:* tell in detail (in public). *wise:* way.
7. *call . . . life:* speak loudly and repeat exactly what happened.
8. A crescent moon. Diana was goddess of the moon and a renowned hunter.

Scene 22 (Other modern editions divide this scene in two: Act 5, Scene 2 [Gower's monologue, lines 1–20] and Scene 3 [lines 21–125]. But they anomalously keep Thaisa and the temple of Diana onstage across the scene break. Even Gower may remain.)
Location: The temple of Diana in Ephesus.

	For such kindness must relieve me,	
5	That you aptly will suppose°	*readily will imagine*
	What pageantry, what feats, what shows,	
	What minstrelsy and pretty din	
	The regent° made in Mytilene	*Lysimachus*
	To greet the King. So well he° thrived	*(Lysimachus)*
10	That he is promised to be wived	
	To fair Marina, but in no wise°	*way*
	Till he° had done his sacrifice	*(Pericles)*
	As Dian bade, whereto being bound	
	The int'rim, pray you, all confound.°	*skip*
15	In feathered° briefness sails are filled,	*winged*
	And wishes fall out as they're willed.	
	At Ephesus the temple see:	

[*An altar,* THAISA *and other vestals are revealed*]

Our king, and all his company.

Enter PERICLES, MARINA, LYSIMACHUS, HELICANUS[, CER-
IMON, *with attendants*]

	That he can hither come so soon	
20	Is by your fancies' thankful doom.[1]	

[GOWER *stands aside*]

PERICLES	Hail, Dian. To perform thy just° command	*precise*
	I here confess myself the King of Tyre,	
	Who, frighted from my country, did espouse	
	The fair Thaisa	

[THAISA *starts*]

	at Pentapolis.	
25	At sea in childbed died she, but brought forth	
	A maid° child called Marina, who, O goddess,	*girl*
	Wears yet thy silver liv'ry.[2] She at Tarsus	
	Was nursed with° Cleon, whom at fourteen years	*by*
	He sought to murder, but her better stars	
30	Bore her to Mytilene, 'gainst whose shore riding[3]	
	Her fortunes brought the maid aboard our barque,	
	Where, by her own most clear remembrance, she	
	Made known herself my daughter.	
THAISA	Voice and favour°—	*appearance*
	You are, you are—O royal Pericles!	

[*She falls*]

35	PERICLES What means the nun? She dies. Help, gentlemen!	
CERIMON	Noble sir,	
	If you have told Diana's altar true,	
	This is your wife.	
PERICLES	Reverend appearer,° no.	*reverend-looking man*
	I threw her overboard with these same arms.	
CERIMON	Upon this coast, I warr'nt you.	
40	PERICLES 'Tis most certain.	
CERIMON	Look to the lady. O, she's but o'erjoyed.	
	Early one blustering morn this lady	
	Was thrown upon this shore. I oped the coffin,	
	Found there rich jewels, recovered° her, and placed her	*revived*

---

1. Thanks to your imaginations' agreement.
2. Still wears your uniform (remains a virgin).

3. *'gainst . . . riding*: where, as we rode at anchor.

Here in Diana's temple.

45 PERICLES   May we see them?

CERIMON   Great sir, they shall be brought you to° my house,   *at*
     Whither I invite you. Look, Thaisa is
     Recoverèd.

THAISA   O, let me look upon him!
     If he be none of mine, my sanctity
50   Will to my sense bend no licentious ear,
     But curb it, spite of seeing.[4] O, my lord,
     Are you not Pericles? Like him you spake,
     Like him you are. Did you not name a tempest,
     A birth and death?

55 PERICLES   The voice of dead Thaisa!

THAISA   That Thaisa
     Am I, supposèd dead and drowned.

PERICLES *[taking Thaisa's hand]*   Immortal Dian!

THAISA   Now I know you better.
60   When we with tears parted° Pentapolis,   *departed*
     The King my father gave you such a ring.

PERICLES   This, this! No more, you gods. Your present kindness
     Makes my past miseries sports;° you shall do well   *trifles (of the gods)*
     That° on the touching of her lips I may   *If*
65   Melt, and no more be seen.—O come, be buried
     A second time within these arms.
          [They embrace and kiss]

MARINA *[kneeling to* THAISA*]*   My heart
     Leaps to be gone into my mother's bosom.

PERICLES   Look who kneels here: flesh of thy flesh, Thaisa,
     Thy burden at the sea, and called Marina
     For she was yielded° there.   *Because she was born*

70 THAISA *[embracing* MARINA*]*   Blessed, and mine own!

HELICANUS *[kneeling to* THAISA*]*
     Hail, madam, and my queen.

THAISA   I know you not.

PERICLES   You have heard me say, when I did fly from Tyre,
     I left behind an ancient substitute.
     Can you remember what I called the man?
75   I have named him oft.

THAISA   'Twas Helicanus then.

PERICLES   Still confirmation.
     Embrace him, dear Thaisa; this is he.
     Now do I long to hear how you were found,
80   How possibly preserved, and who to thank—
     Besides the gods—for this great miracle.

THAISA   Lord Cerimon, my lord. This is the man
     Through whom the gods have shown their pow'r, that can
     From first to last resolve° you.   *answer everything for*

PERICLES *[to* CERIMON*]*   Reverend sir,
85   The gods can have no mortal officer
     More like a god than you. Will you deliver°   *explain*
     How this dead queen re-lives?

CERIMON   I will, my lord.
     Beseech you, first go with me to my house,

---

4. *my sanctity . . . seeing:* my religious vows will forbid my sense to feel desire, in spite of what I see.

Where shall be shown you all was° found with her, *that was*
90 And told how in this temple she came° placed, *came to be*
No needful thing omitted.
PERICLES   Pure Diana,
I bless thee for thy vision,° and will offer *(in Scene 21)*
Nightly oblations° to thee.—Beloved Thaisa, *offerings*
This prince, the fair betrothèd of your daughter,
95 At Pentapolis shall marry her.
[*To* MARINA] And now this ornament° *this hair that*
Makes me look dismal will I clip to form,
And what this fourteen years no razor touched,
To grace thy marriage day I'll beautify.
100 THAISA Lord Cerimon hath letters of good credit,° *trustworthiness*
Sir, from Pentapolis: my father's dead.
PERICLES Heav'n make a star of him! Yet there, my queen,
We'll celebrate their nuptials, and ourselves
Will in that kingdom spend our following days.
105 Our son and daughter shall in Tyrus reign.—
Lord Cerimon, we do our longing stay° *delay our desire*
To hear the rest untold. Sir, lead 's the way.
        Exeunt [*all but*] GOWER
GOWER In Antiochus and his daughter you have heard
Of monstrous lust the due and just reward;
110 In Pericles, his queen, and daughter seen,° *you have seen*
Although assailed with fortune fierce and keen,
Virtue preserved from fell° destruction's blast, *cruel*
Led on by heav'n, and crowned with joy at last.
In Helicanus may you well descry
115 A figure of truth, of faith, of loyalty.
In reverend Cerimon there well appears
The worth that learnèd charity aye° wears. *always*
For wicked Cleon and his wife, when fame° *rumor*
Had spread their cursèd deed to° th' honoured name *against*
120 Of Pericles, to rage the city turn,° *turned*
That° him and his they in his palace burn. *So that*
The gods for murder seemèd so content
To punish that, although not done, but meant.
So on your patience evermore attending,
125 New joy wait on you. Here our play has ending. [*Exit*]

Additional Passage

Q gives this more expansive version of Marina's Epitaph (18.34–37):

'The fairest, sweetest, best lies here,
Who withered in her spring of year.
She was of Tyrus the King's° daughter, *the King of Tyre's*
On whom foul death hath made this slaughter.
5 Marina was she called, and at her birth
Thetis,[1] being proud, swallowed° some part o'th' earth; *flooded*
Therefore the earth, fearing to be o'erflowed,

Additional Passage
1. A sea nymph here confused with Tethys, wife of Oceanus (in Greek myth, the ruler of a river that encir-cled the earth). The image in this passage is of the ocean (because of Thetis / Tethys) surging happily in response to Marina's birth and angrily in response to her death.

Hath Thetis' birth-child on the heav'ns bestowed,
Wherefore she° does, and swears she'll never stint, *(Thetis)*
10 Make raging batt'ry upon shores of flint."° *rocky shores*

TEXTUAL VARIANTS

Control text: Q1

Q1: The Quarto of 1609
Q2: The Quarto of 1609
Q3: The Quarto of 1611
Q4: The Quarto of 1619
Q5: The Quarto of 1630
Q6: The Quarto of 1635
Qa, Qb: Successive states of Q1 incorporating various print-shop corrections and changes
PA: George Wilkins, THE Painfull Aduentures of *Pericles* Prince of Tyre. *Being* The true History of the Play of *Pericles*, as it was lately presented by the worthy and ancient Poet *Iohn Gower*

Title: Pericles, Prynce of Tyre [Stationers' Register entry] THE LATE, / And much admired Play, / Called / Pericles, Prince of Tyre. / With the true Relation of the whole Historie, / aduentures, and fortunes of the said Prince: / As also, / The no lesse strange, and worthy accidents, / in the Birth and Life, of his Daughter / MARIANA. [Q1 title page] The Play of Pericles / Prince of Tyre. &c. [Q1 head title] *The Play of Pericles Prince of Tyre* [Q1 running titles]

Scene 1 [not in Q1; see note to Scene 1] 6 **holy-ales** Holydayes 11 **these** [Q2] those 17 **This'** This 21 **fere** Peere 29 **By** But 30 **account'** account'd 39 **a wight** of wight 42 s.d. *lords and peers in their richest ornaments* [PA] fellowers 50 **Fit for th'** For 54 **In her their best perfections to knit** To knit in her, their best perfections 60 **razed** racte 67 **boundless** bondlesse 73 **heav'n-like face** face like Heauen 79 **semblants** semblance **bloodless** pale 83 **From** For 99 s.p. ANTIOCHUS [not in Q1] s.d. *He . . . riddle* [not in Q1] which the tyrant receiuing with an angry brow, threw downe the Riddle [PA] 102 **'sayed** sayd 107 s.d. *He . . . riddle* [not in Q1] which the Prince taking vp, read aloude [PA] 113 **this** [PA] they 139 **like** is like 152 **He's** he ha's 154 **our** your 156 **cancel** counsell 163 **your worth and our degree** our honour and your worth 170 **you're** you 171 **uncomely** vntimely 179 **'schew** shew 186 **the which** which 194–95 **And . . . your** And our minde pertakes her priuat actions, / To your secrecie; and for your 202 s.d. *hastily* [PA; not in Q1] 204 **Your majesty** My Lord 205 **after; like** after, and like 208 **it be to say** thou say 209 **Your majesty** [not in Q1] 210–11 **If . . . highness** My Lord, if I can get him within my Pistols length, Ile make him sure enough, so farewell to your highnesse. [prose] 212 s.p. ANTIOCHUS [Q4; not in Q1]

Scene 2 [not in Q1] s.d. *distempered* [not in Q1] Princes distemperature [PA] 3 **Be my** By me 7 **feared, 's** fearde is 10 **care's** author's the others 20 **honour him** honour 25 **th'ostent** the stint 30 **am** once 33 s.d. *among them old* HELICANUS [not in Q1] olde [PA, describing Helicanus] 37–42 **You . . . contradict it** [not in Q1] he did not wel so to abuse himselfe, to waste his body there with pyning sorrow, vpon whose safety depended the liues and proserity of a whole kingdome, that it was ill in him to doe it, and no lesse in his counsell to suffer him, without contradicting it [PA; Helicanus to Pericles] 46 **wind** sparke 49 **a** [not in Q1] 55 **Helicane** Hellicanus 59 **brows** face 63 **you but** [Q4] but you 64 s.d. *lifting him up* [PA; not in Q1] 65 **for it** [Q4] fort the **heav'ns** heauē 68 **mak'st** makes 70 **you** you your selfe 75 **Where, as** [Q2] Whereas 78 **As children are heav'n's blessings: to parents, objects** [not in Q1] 86 **of** of a 88 me [not in Q1] 89 fears feare 91 doubt—as doubt no doubt doo't, as no doubt 105 grieve griue for 113 Or or til the 117 in my absence wrong thy liberties wrong my liberties in my absence 120 Tarsus *Tharsus* 126 sure crack cracke 127 we'll will

Scene 3 [not in Q1] 2–3 and am caught . . . but if I do it [not in Q1] 10–40 You . . . Tyre [prose in Q1] 11 question question mee 21 lest that he lest hee 27 King's ears it Kings seas 28 on the seas at the Sea 30 Lord Thaliart am I, of Antioch [not in Q1] 31 s.p. HELICANUS [Q4; not in Q1] of Antioch from *Antiochus* 32 King Antiochus him 35 lord's Lord has betoke [Q2] betake 36 Now my now 37 enquire desire

Scene 4 [not in Q1] 8 they're they are midges' mischiefs 13 our sorrows and sorrowes 15 lungs toungs 17 helps helpers 20 As you think best Ile doe my best 22 o'er on 23 the [Q3] her 34 Those These 36 they [Q2] thy 39 two summers [PA] too sauers 47 Here weeping stands a lord, there lies a lady dying Heere stands a Lord, and there a Ladie weeping; heere standes one weeping, and there lies another dying [PA] 54 heed heare 55 s.d. *fainting . . . slowly* a fainting messenger came slowely into them [PA] 57 thou [Q4] thee 58 t'expect to expect 64 neighbour [PA] neighbouring 66 Hath That these the 68 men mee 72 not not as 73 him's himnes 77 grave's grounds 79 whence he comes. whence he comes, and what he craues? 82 s.d. *the* LORD *again conducting* [not in Q1] he demaunded of the fellow where the Gouernour was, and foorthwith to be conducted to him [PA] 87–88 Since entering your unshut gates have witnessed / The widowed desolation And seene the desolation; Pericles . . . no sooner entred into their unshut gates, but his princely eies were partaking witnesses of their widowed desolation [PA] 89 hearts teares 92 fraught stuft; fraughted [PA] 93 importing expecting 96 s.p. ALL OF TARSUS *Omnes.* s.d. *falling . . . weeping* [not in Q1] the feeble soules . . . fell on their knees, and wept [PA] 99 me, my our selfe, our 104 ne'er neare

Scene 5 [not in Q1] 4 Prove That Will prove 11 Tarsus *Tharstill* 12 speken spoken 14 His statue build Build his Statue 17 Helicane [Q3] *Helicon* 19 for that for though 22 Sent word Sau'd one 24 hid intent to murden hid in Tent to murdred [Qa] had intent to murder [Qb] 25 Tarsus *Tharsis* 27 deeming doing 36 aught ought 51 s.d. *two poor* three; pore Fishermen [PA; in this edition, the Third Fisherman enters after the first two.] 52 s.p. MASTER I.; the maister Fisherman [PA; changed throughout, except at line 80, where "I." is changed to "THIRD FISHERMAN"] What ho, Pilch What, to pelch 54 s.d. *He . . . repair* [not in Q1] certayne *Fishermen* . . . were come out from their homely cottages to dry and repaire their nettes [PA] 56–72, 74–75, 77–81, 83–84, 90–92, 93–94, 99–101, 123, 136–37, 139–40, 144–47, 152–54, 195–97 [verse in Q1] 70 devours deuowre 77 s.p. THIRD FISHERMAN [Q4] 3. FISHER-MAN I. 110 crave aske 112 pray [Q4] pray you 113 quotha ke-tha an and 114 s.d. *To . . . ground* the chiefe of these fishermen . . . lifting him vp from the ground [PA] 116 holidays all day 117 moreo'er more; or 123 an and 124 all your you 128–30 beadle. MASTER Thine office, knave— SECOND FISHERMAN Is to draw up the other nets. I'll go Beadle: But Maister, Ile goe draw vp the Net; goe dragge vp some other nettes [PA; the Master commanding his servants—hence, this edition introduces an interjection by the Master into the Second Fisherman's speech.] 133 s.d. *seating . . . Pericles* [not in Q1] the maister . . . seated himselfe by him [PA] 136 is [Q2] I 141–42 from his subjects / He gains he gaines from / His subjects 144 some half [PA] halfe 148 Were but [PA] Were answerable [PA] equall 151 get himself get for with for 153 s.d. *Before . . . prize* [not in Q1] before helpe came, vp came the Fish expected, but prooued indeede to be a rusty armour. [PA] 155 pray [Qb] pary [Qa] 156 thy [not in Q1] all her crosses [PA] 157 losses selfe 164 forfend, the same may protect thee, Fame may 169 in 's [Q4] in his 176 with't with it 180 learned [PA] borne 185 this them 187 I'm I am 188 rapture rupture 191 delightsome delight 193 friends friend 198 equal a Goale

Scene 6 [not in Q1] s.d. *and sit on two thrones* [not in Q1] They thus seated [PA] 4 daughter daughter heere 8 my my royall 13 renown Renownes 14 office honour 16

s.d. *richly* . . . THAISA [not in Q1] richly armed, their Pages before them bearing their Deuices on their shields being by the knights Page deliuered to the Lady [*PA*; repeated for each knight in this edition] **21 s.d. *She* . . . KING** [not in Q1] from her presented to the King her father [*PA*; repeated for each knight in this edition] **22 s.d.** [See note to 6.16.] **26 An armèd** Is an Armed **27 thus** thus in Spanish *Piùe per dolcezza che per forza Pue Per doleera kee per forsa* **s.d.** [See note to 6.21.] **28 You . . . force** [not in Q1] more by lenitie than by force [*PA*] **s.d.** [See note to 6.16.] **29 what's** [Q4] with **31 pompae** Pompey; *pompa* [*PA*] **s.d.** [See note to 6.21.] **32–33 Desire . . . enterprise** [not in Q1] desire of renowne drew him to this enterprise [*PA*] **33 s.d.** [See note to 6.16.] **34 A knight of Athens bearing** [not in Q1] The fift of *Athens*, and his Deuice was [*PA*] **36 s.d.** [See note to 6.21.] **37 this** his **38 s.d.** [See note to 6.16.] **39 And who the fifth?** [not in Q1] **39–40 a prince of Corinth / Presents** [not in Q1] a prince of *Corinth* [*PA*] **43 So . . . into** [*PA*; not in Q1] **s.d. PERICLES . . . THAISA** [not in Q1] The sixt and last was *Pericles*, Prince of *Tyre*, who hauing neither Page to deliuer his shield, nor shield to deliuer . . . Himselfe with a most gracefull curtesie presented it vnto her . . . being himselfe in a rusty Armour [*PA*] **45 delivereth** deliuered **49 From** A pretty morrall frō **54 T'have** To haue **56 Unto** To **60 for** by

Scene 7 [not in Q1] **s.d. A *stately banquet is brought in*** [not in Q1] a most stately banquet [*PA*] *a* **MARSHAL** *conducting* [not in Q1] by the Kings Marshall conducted [*PA*] **1 to the KNIGHTS To say** Knights, to say **2 To I 7 You're** You are **11 yours** [Q4] your **13 artists** an Artist **15 You are** And you are **24 Envied** Enuies **25 s.d. PERICLES . . . THAISA** placed directly ouer-against where the king and his daughter sate [*PA* (said of Pericles)] **27 distaste** resist **but not 29 I am amazed** [not in Q1] **34 broke** broken **36 Yon** [Q2] You **37 me** [Q4; not in Q1] **what** that **42 son's** sonne **a** like a **48 s.p. THE OTHER KNIGHTS** *Knights* **49 stored** stur'd **50 you do** [Q4] do you **full** fill **51 s.p. THE OTHER KNIGHTS** *Knight.* **59 so doing** doing so **like** like to **61 entertain** entraunce **62 bear** say **wee** drinke **69 Furthermore** And furthermore **know** know of him **71–72 THAISA The King . . . Wishing** *Tha.* The king my father (sir) has drunke to you / *Peri.* I thanke him / *Tha.* Wishing **79 unconstant** [not in Q1] and vnconstant [*PA*] **79–80 bereft / Unfortunately** both reft [Q1] most vnfortunately bereft both [*PA*] **83–84 seeking adventures / Was** [not in Q1] **83–84 A gentleman . . . seas** A Gentleman of *Tyre*: who onely by misfortune of the seas **84 solely** onely **86 mishaps** misfortune **87 s.d.– 95 SIMONIDES . . . accept** [not in Q1] Which mishaps of his the king vnderstanding of, hee was strucke with present pitty to him, and rising from his state, he came foorthwith and imbraced him, bade him be cheered, and tolde him, that whatsoeuer misfortune had impayred him of, fortune, by his helpe, could repayre to him, for both himselfe and Countrey should be his friendes, and presently calling for a goodly milke white Steede, and a payre of golden spurres, them first hee bestowed vppon him, telling him, they were the prises due to his merite, and ordained for that dayes enterprise: which kingly curtesie Pericles as thankefully accepting. Much time beeing spent in dauncing and other reuells [*PA*] **99 Your limbs will** Will **104 Come** Come sir **105 sir, that the you 112 Lights, pages, to** Pages and lights to **114 should** [not in Q1] **116 s.p. KING SIMONIDES** [Q3; not in Q1, where the speech continues as Pericles']

Scene 8 [not in Q1] **4 hold** with-hold **9 both apparelled all in jewels** [*PA*; not in Q1] **11 Their** those **13 hands** hand **29 step** breath **33 death indeed's** death in deed, **34 this—kingdoms** this Kingdome is **36 utter** [not in Q1] **38 unto** as vnto our **40 By** Try **44 But . . . love** [follows line 48 in Q1] **45 longer then let me** longer, let me **46 Further to bear** To forbeare **49 seek your noble prince** search like nobles, **55 us** [not in Q1] **56–57 If . . . out / If . . . there** [after line 29 in Q1]

Scene 8a [not in Q1] Prince *Pericles* hauing had (as before is mentioned) his lodging directed next adioyning to the kings bed-chamber, whereas all the other Princes vppon their comming to their lodgings betooke themselues to their pillowes, and to the nourishment of a quiet sleepe, he of the Gentlemen that attended him, (for it is to be noted, that vpon the grace that the king had bestowed on him, there was of his Officers toward him no attendance wanting) hee desired that hee might be left priuate, only that for his instant solace they would pleasure him with some delightfull Instrument, with which, and his former practise hee intended to passe away the tediousnesse of the night insteade of more fitting slumbers. His wil was presently obeyed in all things since their master had commaunded he should be disobeyed in nothing: the Instrument is brought him, and as hee had formerly wished, the Chamber is disfurnished of any other company but himselfe [PA, from which this scene is reconstructed] **8 s.d.** *a stringed instru-ment* [implied by PA, which refers to the "fingering" of the instrument and describes Pericles singing as he plays] **9–10 Now . . . sleep** all the other Princes . . . betooke themselues to their pillowes [PA] **10 s.d.** PERICLES *plays and sings* [PA elaborately describes the performance.] **11–13 Day . . . on.** But day that hath still that soueraigntie to drawe backe the empire of the night, though a while shee in darkenesse vsurpe, brought the morning on [PA] **14–15 I . . . me** euen in the instant came in *Pericles*, to giue his Grace that salutation which the morning required of him [PA]

Scene 9 [not in Q1] **5 none can** by no meanes can I **6 have** get **7–8 It . . . chamber** she hath so strictly / Tyed her to her Chamber, that t'is impossible **15 light light** / T'is well Mistris, your choyce agrees with mine **18 Mistress, 'tis well** Well, your her **20–21 that / In show, I have determined on in heart** it; the king intending to dissemble that in shew, which hee had determined on in heart [PA] **24–25 night. My ears, / I do protest** night: / I do protest, my eares **30 think you of my daughter** do you thinke of my Daughter, sir **31 And** And she is **33 My daughter, sir** Sir, my Daughter **34 So well indeed** I so well **39 s.d. He . . . feet** [not in Q1] foorthwith prostrating himselfe at the kings feete [PA] **43 her** her. / *king.* Thou has bewicht my daughter, / And thou art a villaine. / *Peri.* By the Gods I haue not **47 Thou liest like a traitor** Traytor, thou lyest **48–50 That . . . child** [not in Q1] I, traytour, quoth the king, that thus disguised, art stolne into my Court, with the witchcraft of thy actions to bewitch, the yeelding spirit of my tender Childe [PA] **51–52 Who calls me traitor, unless it be the King, / Ev'n in his bosom I will write the lie** Even in his throat, vnlesse it be the King, / That cals me Traytor, I returne the lye [Q1] were it any in his Court, except himselfe, durst call him traytor, even in his bosome he would write the lie [PA] **54 blood** thoughts **56 in search of honour** [PA] for Honours cause **57 your state** her state [Q1] his State [PA] **60–62 I . . . witness** No? heere comes my Daughter, she can witnesse it [Q1] answered, he should prooue it otherwise, since by his daughters hand, it there was euident, both his practise and her consent therein [PA] **64–65 By what . . . fulfilled** [not in Q1] demaunded of her by the hope she had of heauen, or the desire she had to haue her best wished fulfilled heere in the worlde [PA] **68 made** that made **71 How, minion** [PA] Yea Mistris **72–96 I am glad on't . . . only child** I am glad on't with all my heart [Q1] How minion, quoth her Father (taking her off at the very word, who dare be displeased withalle) Is this a fit match for you? a stragling *Theseus* borne we knowe not where, one that hath neither bloud nor merite for thee to hope for, or himselfe to challenge euen the least allowaunce of thy perfections, when she humbling her princely knees before her Father, besought him to consider, that suppose his birth were base (when his life shewed him not to be so) yet hee had vertue, which is the very ground of all nobilitie, enough to make him noble: she intreated him to remember that she was in loue, the power of which loue was not to be confined by the power of his will. And my most royall Father, quoth shee, what with my penne I haue in secret written vnto you, with my tongue now I openly confirme, which is, that I have no life but his loue, neither any being but in the enioying of his worth. But daughter (quoth *Symonides*) equalles to equalls, good to good is ioyned, this not being so, the bauine of your minde in rashnesse kindled, must againe be quenched, or purchase our displeasure, And for you sir (speaking to prince *Pericles*) first learne to know, I banish you my Court, and yet scorning that our kingly inragement should stoope so lowe, for that your ambition sir, Ile haue your life. Be constant quoth *Thaysa*, for euerie droppe of blood hee sheades of yours, he shall draw an other from his onely childe [PA] **97 yea** [not in Q1] **102 s.d. He . . . hand** [not in Q1] catching them both rashly by the handes [PA] **103 s.d. He . . . hand** [not in Q1; see note to line 102 s.d.] **105 I shall** Ile s.d. *He . . . together* [not in Q1] heclapt them hand in hand [PA] **106 s.d. PERICLES and THAISA kiss** [not in Q1] while they as louingly ioyned lip to lip [PA] **108 your further** further you you both **112 s.p. PERICLES and THAISA** *Ambo.* **113 Then** And then

Scene 10 [not in Q1] **2 the house about** about the house **6 fore** from **7 crickets** Cricket **8 As** Are **10 Where by** [Q2] Whereby **13 eche** each **14 s.d. comes hastily in to meetes;** came hastily in to them [PA] **17 coigns** Crignes **21 stead** steed **29 mutiny there he** mutanie, hee there **t'appease** t'oppresse **46 fortune's mood** fortune mou'd **60 sea-tossed** seas tost **speke** speake

Scene 11 [not in Q1] **7 Thou stormest** then storme **8 spit** speat **11 patroness** [Q4] patrioness **midwife** my wife **27 s.d. She . . . infant** [not in Q1] vp comes *Lycorida* the Nurse . . . and into his armies deliuers his Sea-borne Babe [PA] **s.d. PERICLES . . . weeps** [not in Q1] *Pericles* looking mournfully vpon it, shooke his head, and wept [PA] **34 Poor inch of nature** [PA; not in Q1] **36 partage** portage **37 s.d. the MASTER and a SAILOR** two *Saylers* **38, 43, 47, 51 s.p. MASTER** 1. *Sayl.* **40 its worst** the worst **43–53** [verse in Q1] **43 Slack** Slacke [Qb] Slake [Qa] **bow-lines** bolins **45 s.p. SAILOR** 2. *Sayl.* **an** and **50 but** [not in Q1] **52 custom** easterne **52–54 yield 'er . . . queen!** yeeld'er, / *Per.* As you thinke meet; for she must ouer board straight: / Most wretched Queene. **59 ooze** oare **61 And** The **aye-remaining** ayre remayning **64 paper** [Q2] Taper **66 coffer** coffin **69 s.p. SAILOR** 2. **72, 74 s.p. MASTER** 2. **73 from** for **74 Make** O make

Scene 12 [not in Q1] **s.d. poor man and a** some that came to him both for helpe for themselues, and reliefe for others [PA] **2 those** these **4 seen** been in **5 ne'er** neare **7 in to** to th' **8 to th'** to the **19–20 lordship should, / Having . . . you, at** Lordship, / Hauing . . . you, should at **20 this hour** these early howers **22 to** should **23 held** hold **26 dispend** [PA] expend **34 so** [not in Q1] **36 and cause** in course **39 glad** please **42 alone** [not in Q1] **46 48, 53 s.p. PHILEMON** Seru⟨ant⟩ [variously abbreviated] **49 The sea tossed up** did the sea tosse vp **52–53 Did . . . sir** [Question and answer occur after "bitumed" at line 58 in Q1.] **54 Or a more eager** as tost it vpon shore **s.p. CERIMON** [not in Q1; see last note to line 58] **56 by** [not in Q1] queasy [not in Q1] **58 bitumed** bottomed **soft** *Cer.* Wrench it open soft. **62 and crowned** [not in Q1] crowned [PA] **65 i'th'** in the **75 even** [Q4] euer **77 rash** rough **82 have heard** heard **83 nine hours dead** that had 9. howers lien dead **84 appliances** applyaunce **84 s.d. PHILEMON** one **86 still** rough **87 vial** Violl **90–91 warmth / Breathes** warmth breath **94 set** sets **104 gentle** my gentle

Scene 13 [not in Q1] **5 strokes** shakes **6 hurt** hant **7 woundingly** wondringly **8 you'd** you had **9 T'have** to haue **10 Should** Could **14 and leave** leauing **25 th'** the **29 Unscissored** vncisserd [PA] vnsisterd **29 hair** heyre **32 s.p. DIONYZA** I [Q1] *Cler.* I [Q1 catchword] **35 s.p. CLEON** [Q4] *Cler.* **36 th'** masted the mask'd

Scene 14 [not in Q1] **s.d. THAISA** *Tharsa* **2 are all** are **5 eaning** learning **6 th'** the **11 s.p. CERIMON** *Cler.* **13 till your date expire you may abide** you may abide till your date expire **16 s.p. THAISA** [Q4] *Thin.*

Scene 15 [not in Q1] **8 music** Musicks **10 her** hie **the heart** the art **14 Seeks** Seeke **15 has** hath **16 lass** wench **17 ripe** [Q2] right **rite** sight **26 bird** bed **32 With dove of Paphos might the** The Doue of *Paphos* might with the **38 murder** murderer **42 s.d. A tomb is revealed** a monument in remembrance [PA] **47 carry** carried **55 i'th'** in the **57–58 or fanning love thy bosom / Unflame** in flaming, thy loue bosome, enflame **63 weeping** weeping for **nurse's** Mistresse **66 grave** greene **68 tomb** graue **71 but** [not in Q1] **ceaseless** lasting **76–77 favour / Is changed** fauours / Changd **78 Give me your flowers. Come** Come giue me your flowers o'er ere **margin** marre it **79 is piercing** is quicke **80 And quick; it sharps** And it perces and sharpens **81 th'** the **81–151 No . . . slain** [prose in Q1; many of the following emendations help create metrical verse lines] **90 resume** reserue **94 truly** yet **95 Nay** Come, come **99 Pray you** pray **104 mariners** Saylers **105 with** [not in Q1] **111 Once** and **114 stem** stern **120 The** for the **121 would** will **128 once on a worm** vpon a worme **129 for it** [Q4] fort **131 danger** any danger **139**

s.d. *drawing out his sword* [PA] 140 s.d. *running* [PA] 144 s.d. PIRATES *carrying* MARINA the pyrates who had thus rescued *Marina*, carried her to their shippes [PA] LEONINE *steals back Enter Leonine*; he secretly stole back [PA] 146 An and 147 **she'll** shee will

Scene 16 [not in Q1] 4 **lose** lost **too much** [Q2] too much much 4 **wenchless** too wenchlesse 17 **They're too** ther's two 33 **mystery** trade 37 s.p. A PIRATE *Sayler.* 45 **hundred sesterces** [PA] thousand peeces 58 **had but** had not 59 **To** for to 66 **like** [Q4; not in Q1] 80 **must stir** [Q4] stir 88 **watered as** watred, and 92 **Veroles** *Verollus* 98 **of** in 100 **all** [not in Q1] 103 **to despise** despise 111 s.p. BAWD *Mari⟨na⟩* 123–24 **reapest the harvest out of thine own setting forth** hast the haruest out of thine owne report 133 **with me** with vs

Scene 17 [not in Q1] s.d. *in mourning garments* mourning garments [PA] 1 **are** ere 5–47 **Were ... done** [prose in Q1] 6 **A lady** O Ladie 12 **fact** face 13 **demands** shall demaund 15 **is not** it, not 17 **pious** [PA] impious 25 **cowed** coward 27 **prime** prince 28 **sources** courses 31 **distain** disdaine 33 **Marina's** [Q2] *Marianas* 34 **malkin** Mawkin 48 **angel** Angells 49 **in thine eagle talons** with thine Eagles talents

Scene 18 [not in Q1] 1 **make we** make 3 **take** take our 7 **scene** sceanes 8 **i'th'** with 10 **the** [Q2] thy 14 **govern, if** gouerne it, 16 **Tyre** time 18 **his** this 19 **go on** grone 24 **true-owed** true olde 29 **puts** put 34 **sweetest, best** *sweetest, and best* 36–37 **In ... good** [PA; not in Q1. For the eight lines from Q1 omitted here, see Additional Passage.] 42 **scene** Steare

Scene 19 [not in Q1] 2 s.p. SECOND GENTLEMAN [Qa, Qb, Qb catchword] *Gower.* [Qa catchword] 13 **the whole of** a whole 24 **loon** Lowne 25 **custom** customers 27 **tobless** to blesse 34 **deed** deedes 41 **dignifies** dignities 42 **noble** number 52 **honourably know** worthilie note 63 **hers** her 64–139 **Fair ... Away** [prose in Q1; many of the following emendations help create metrical verse lines] 64 **Fair** Now prittie 66 **I** Why I **name it but** name but 71 **or** or at 73 **Proclaimeth you** proclaimes you to be 74 **And** [not in Q1] 75 **into it** intoo't 76 **blood** parts 77 **whole province** place 78 **What** Why **informed** made knowne vnto 80 **seeds of shame, roots of** seeds and rootes of shame and s.d. MARINA *weeps* [not in Q1] teares [PA] 81 **you've** you haue 82 **off** aloof **for a** aloft for 85–89 **can ... ling'ring** shall not see thee, or else looke friendly vpon thee; vrging her, that he was the Gouernour, whose authoritie coulde wincke at those blemishes, her selfe, and that sinnefull house could cast vppon her, or his displeasure punish at his owne pleasure, which displeasure of mine, thy beauty shall not priuiledge thee from, nor my affection, which hath drawen me vnto this place abate, if thou with further lingering withstand me [PA] 85 **or can on faults look friendly** or else looke friendly vpon thee [not in PA] 91–93 **Let ... yourself** [not in Q1] If as you say (my Lorde) you are the Gouernour, let not your authoritie, which should teach you to rule others, be the meanes to make you misgouerne your selfe [PA] 96–106 **What ... impoverish me** [not in Q1] What reason is there in your Justice, who hath power ouer all, to vndoe any? If you take from mee mine honour, you are like him, that makes a gappe into forbidden ground, after whome too many enter, and you are guiltie of all their euilles: my life is yet vnspotted, my chastitie vnstained in thought. Then if your violence deface this building, the workemanship of heauen, made vp for good, and not to be the exercise of sinnes intemperaunce, you do kill your owne honour, abuse your owne iustice, and impouerish me. . . . Is there a necessitie (my yet good Lord) if there be fire before me, that I must strait then thither flie and burne my selfe? Or if suppose this house, (which too too many feele such houses are) should be the Doctors patrimony, and Surgeons feeding; folowes it therefore, that I must needs infect my self to giue them maintenaunce? [PA] 114 s.d. *kneeling* [not in Q1] which wordes (being spoken vpon her knees) [PA] 115 **franked** plac't 119 s.d. *moved* [PA; not in Q1] 120 s.d. *He ... hands* [not in Q1] hee lift her vp with his hands [PA] 121 **Though** Had 122 **hath** had s.d. *He ... eyes* [not in Q1] in steede of willing her to drie her eyes, he wiped the wet himselfe off [PA] **and my foul thoughts** [not in Q1] I hither came with thoughte intemperate, foule and deformed [PA] 123 **Thy ... white** [not in Q1] the which your paines so well hath laued, that they are now white [PA] **124–26 I** . . . **honesty** holde, heeres golde for thee [Q1] and for my parte, who hither came but to haue payd the price, a peece of golde for your virginitie, now giue you twenty to releeue your honesty [PA] **127 Persever still** perseuer **128 The** For me be you thoughten, that I came with no ill intent, for to me the **131 The** . . . **made** [PA; not in Q1] **132 not** not but **noble** noble, hold, heeres more golde for thee **134 honour. Hold, here's more gold. / If** goodnes, if [A shorter version of the words omitted at line 132 is reintroduced here.] **135 s.d. Enter** . . . **out** [not in Q1] the bawde standing ready at the doore, as hee should go out, making his obeysaunce vnto him as hee should returne [PA] **146 executioner shall do** hãg-man shal execute **We'll** come your way, weele **152 She** He **158 s.p. PANDER** Bawd. **159 ice** glass **167 s.d. catching** . . . **hand** [PA; not in Q1] **176–84 Neither** . . . **lungs** [prose in Q1; many of the following emendations help create metrical verse lines] **176 can be** are **178 place** place for which **179 change with thee** change **180 Thou** Thou art the **182 To th'** To the ev'ry euery **190 sew'rs** shores **190 public** common **191 these** these wayes **193 dear** deere, that the gods wold safely deliuer me from this place **Here's** here, heers **194 make** gain gaine **197 I will** will **206 women** [Q4] woman

Scene 20 [not in Q1] **8 twin** Twine **13 We** Where wee **Waves there him tossed** wee there him left **14 Whence** Where **tofore** before **20 fervour** [Qb] former [Qa] **22 the** his

Scene 21 [not in Q1] **1 s.p. SAILOR OF TYRE** 1 Say. **1–53 Where** . . . **prevented** [prose in Q1] **1 Lord Helicanus can resolve you, sir** Where is Lord *Helicanus*? hee can resolue you, O here he is Sir **3 In it** and in it is **6 s.p. SAILOR OF TYRE** 2 Say. **6 Ho** Ho **Gentlemen What is your lordship's pleasure** Doeth your Lordship call **7 some there is some 8 you** [not in Q1] **9 s.p. SAILOR OF MYTILENE** Hell. [Qa] 1 Say [Qb] This Sir, this **aught** ought you would **11 sir** [not in Q1] **12–16 You wish me well. / I** . . . **Mytilene; / Being** . . . **are** Li⟨simachus⟩ You wish mee well, beeing . . . are. Hell⟨icanus⟩ First what is your place? Ly⟨simachus⟩ I . . . this place you lie before [Helicanus's question in Q1 is omitted, and an emended version of Lysimachus's reply ("I . . . before") is moved to an earlier position, after "You wish me well."] **17 Our** Syr our **our king** the King **21 grew** is **22 tell it ouer** repeat **23 precious** [not in Q1] **25 See him, sir, you may** You may **26 sight. He** [Qb] sight see [Qa] **27 any. LYSIMACHUS** Let me yet any, yet let me [speech continued by Helicanus in Q1, with different word order] **28 s.p. HELICANUS** [Q4] Lys⟨imachus⟩ **s.d. lying** . . . **sack-cloth** [not in Q1] so attired from the ordinary habite of other men, as with a long ouer-growne beard, diffused hayre, vndecent nayles on his fingers, and himselfe lying vppon his cowch groueling on his face [PA; when Pericles first learns of Marina's death, PA reports that "hee apparrelles himselfe in sacke-cloth."] **28–29 person, / Till** [Q4] person. / Hell⟨icanus⟩ Till [In this edition, Helicanus is already speaking.] **29 of that night** wight **30 all hail** all haile, the Gods preserue you **s.d. PERICLES** . . . **pillow** hee shruncke himselfe downe vppon his pillow [PA] **35 choice** chosen **alarum** allure **36 deafened ports** defend parts **37 in all** is all **38 among** and **39 Dwells now i'th'** now vpon the **40 Go fetch her hither** [not in Q1] **47 gods** God **51 it** it to you **54 presence** present **57 of** of a **or and I'd** [Q4] I do **58 to** and **wed** [Q4] to wed **59 one** on **bounty** beautie **60 feat** fate **64–140 Sir** . . . **end here** [prose in Q1; many of the following emendations help to create metrical verse lines] **65 recure** recouerie **67 Let** Come, let **68 prosper her** make her prosperous **Marked** [Q4] Marke **69 s.p. MAID** Mar⟨ina⟩ **84 Stay** go not **88 My lord** [after "said," line 87, in Q1] **90–91 what** . . . **shores?** what Countrey women heare of these shewes? **93 seem** appeare **95 such** sucha one **99 cased** caste **109 palace** Pallas **111 make my senses** [Q4] makes senses **112 Thou show'st** for thou lookest **114 say** stay **121 circumstance** thoughts **123 thousandth** thousand **128 lost thou them?** Thy name lost thou thy name **130 sir,** [not in Q1] **142 Motion as well?** Motion well **146 when** the minute **147 recounted** deliuered **153 You will scarce believe me** You scorne, beleeue me **159 wooed** hauing wood **160 the deed** it **162 To Mytilene they brought me** Brought me to *Metaline* **163 What will you of me** whither wil you haue me? **164**

impostor imposture 167 **s.p. PERICLES** *Hell⟨icanus⟩* 174 **would never** neuer would 192 **rest** rest you sayd 193 **So prove but true in that, thou art my daughter** [not in Q1] 194 **life** like 196 **name?** name was *Thaisa* 199 **Thou art** [Q4] th'art **s.d.** *He kisses her* he falls on hir necke, and kisses her [PA] 201 **Not** shee is not 207 **sir** [not in Q1] 211 **doubt** doat 217–18 **LYSIMACHUS Music, my lord? /** **PERICLES I hear most** *Lys.* Musicke my Lord? I heare. / *Per.* Most 219 **raps** nips 220 **eyelids** eyes **s.d.** *He sleeps* he fell into a slumber [PA] 221 **A . . . head. Companion** A Pillow for his head, so leaue him all. / Well my companion 223 **So leave him all** [after "head" (line 222) in Q1] 227–28 **At large . . . voice** [not in Q1] 231 **life** like 232 **Perform** or performe 233 **rest** [not in Q1] 238 **Th'** The

Scene 22 [not in Q1] 9 **well** [not in Q1] 23 **espouse** [PA] wed 24 **The fair Thaisa . . . at Pentapolis** at *Pentapolis*, the faire *Thaisa* **s.d. THAISA** *starts* At the naming of whome, she her selfe being by, could not choose but starte [PA] 26 **who** whom 28 **whom** who 30 **Bore** brought 31 **our barque** vs 35 **nun** mum 39 **same** verie 42 **one** in 48 **upon him** [not in Q1] 70 **s.d.** *embracing* **MARINA** [not in Q1] giuing his daughter to her armes to embrace her as a child [PA] 72 **s.p. PERICLES** [Q4] *Hell⟨icanus⟩* 82 **is the** [not in Q1] 90 **And told how in this temple she came placed** How shee came plac'ste heere in the Temple [Q1] for in this Temple was she placed [PA] 91 **Diana** *Dian* 92 **I** [not in Q1] 93 **Nightly** Night **Beloved** [not in Q1] 95 **At Pentapolis shall marry her** shall marrie her at *Pentapolis* 101 **from Pentapolis** [not in Q1] 102 **Heav'n** Heauens [Q1] Heauen [Q1 catchword] 112 **preserved** preferd 113 **Led** [Q2] Led 119 **their** [Q4] his **deed to th'** deede, the 123 **that** [not in Q1]

The Winter's Tale

In his induction to *Bartholomew Fair* (1614), Ben Jonson complained of plays that "make nature afraid" and "beget Tales, Tempests, and such like drolleries." His remarks seem aimed directly at his contemporary William Shakespeare, who, in the last years of his theatrical career, had written a number of plays, including *The Winter's Tale* (1609–11) and *The Tempest* (1611), that by some accounts might be said to "make nature afraid." Jonson implies that such plays, eschewing realism, present fantastic or impossible events that defy the laws of nature. While Jonson found such concoctions unpalatable, most of Shakespeare's contemporaries did not. In prose romances popular throughout the period, characters regularly undertake impossible quests, encounter marvels, and are unexpectedly reunited with lost children. Shakespeare's late plays participate fully in this taste for the marvelous, reveling in, rather than being embarrassed by, the strange and the improbable. In the case of *The Winter's Tale*, we possess a rather full description of the play by Simon Forman, a London astrologer and doctor, who saw it performed on May 15, 1611, and described its complicated plot with no hint that he found either its events absurd or the play defective. On the contrary, Forman's detailed description suggests him to have been fully absorbed by what he saw. Concluding with an account of the deceptive tricks of the play's rogue, Autolycus, Forman moralized: "Beware trusting feigned beggars or fawning fellows."

Modern editors often group *Pericles*, *The Winter's Tale*, *Cymbeline*, and *The Tempest* together under the label "romances," though this is not a category used in the Folio (1623). There Shakespeare's plays are divided into comedies, tragedies, and histories. *Pericles* is not included in the Folio; *Cymbeline* is placed at the end of the tragedies; *The Tempest* appears as the first of the comedies and *The Winter's Tale* as the last. These placements are suggestive of the mixed tragicomic nature of these particular dramas. Like Shakespeare's earlier comedies, they all end happily, with families reunited and marriages in prospect; but the late plays also engage with the tragic dimensions of human life to a degree not customary for the early comedies. Before the characters in these plays reach safe harbor, they encounter tyranny, incest, the loss of wives and children, and the treachery of brothers. The protagonists suffer intensely, both because of fortune's blows and because of their own folly. Only by what is experienced as miracle does tragedy turn to mirth and suffering cease. While the miraculous quality of these reversals binds these plays together as a group, it is also at the heart of Jonson's objections. Improbable occurrences and unexpected transformations of sorrow into joy can affront sober common sense, but they also make romance emotionally and theatrically appealing. In defiance of probability, these plays construct a world in which (at least for some fortunate characters) second chances are possible.

By its very title *The Winter's Tale* signals its affiliations with popular storytelling. Within the play, Mamillius, the King of Sicilia's young son, informs his mother that "a sad tale's best for winter" (2.1.27) and offers to tell her one "of sprites and goblins" (2.1.28). The only sprites and goblins in Shakespeare's play turn out to be the internal demons of jealousy and suspicion that erupt in the mind of its protagonist, King Leontes, but *The Winter's Tale* is permeated by sadness, even during its festive conclusion, and its plot is full of wonders. Its starting point is King Leontes' sudden certainty that his wife, Hermione, is pregnant not with his own child, but with that of his childhood friend, King Polixenes of Bohemia, a visitor at Leontes' Sicilian court. Warned of Leontes' jealousy, Polixenes flees back to Bohemia, leaving the King to vent his wrath on Hermione. Imprisoned, she gives birth to a daughter, Perdita, whom Leontes orders to be abandoned in the countryside far from

In the early seventeenth century, popular pamphlet literature circulated sensational stories of parents, especially unmarried women, who murdered or abandoned their children. In this title page from *The Bloody Mother* (1609), a serving woman and her master bury the illegitimate child she has killed. On the right, for his part in begetting and disposing of the child, the master is consumed by lice and worms.

Sicilia. Even when the oracle of Apollo subsequently declares Hermione innocent, Leontes continues to insist on her guilt. As he does, the death of his only son, Mamillius, is announced, and Hermione appears to die of grief. The first three acts of *The Winter's Tale* thus enact a miniature tragedy (not unlike Shakespeare's tragedy of the jealous Othello) in which Leontes' actions result in the loss of wife, daughter, and son. His personal tragedy also affects his kingdom. The oracle proclaims: "the King shall live without an heir if that which is lost be not found" (3.2.133–34). A kingdom without an heir to the throne is a kingdom in danger.

But then something extraordinary happens. The character Time appears onstage, informing the audience that sixteen years have passed and that Perdita, abandoned on the seacoast of Bohemia, has survived. Suddenly, instead of the wintry world of Leontes' Sicilian court, the play bursts with the energies of a Bohemian spring. The Old Shepherd who rescued Perdita is about to hold a sheepshearing festival, and Florizel, King Polixenes' son, has fallen in love with Perdita. A series of extraordinary events returns the young couple to Leontes' court, where Perdita's true status as his child and heir is revealed. More wonders follow. Taken to see what they believe to be a statue of the long-dead Hermione, the King and his newly recovered daughter witness the seeming miracle of the statue's transformation into flesh and blood.

Shakespeare's chief source for this tale was Robert Greene's popular prose romance *Pandosto*, first published in 1588. Greene provided Shakespeare with the story of a jealous king who loses queen and daughter but eventually has his daughter restored to him. But the differences between Shakespeare's play and Greene's prose tale are as striking as the similarities. For example, Shakespeare carefully changed the names of most of the characters he borrowed from Greene. In *Pandosto* the king's lost daughter is Fawnia, but Shakespeare names her Perdita, a word that in Latin means "that which is lost." In Shakespeare's hands, Perdita's lover ceases to be Dorastus and becomes, instead, Florizel, which suggests the young prince's connection with the flowers of spring. Greene's protagonist, Pandosto, is transformed into Leontes, evoking the leonine or lionlike nature of his wrath. Shakespeare also reversed the kingdoms ruled by Greene's kings. In *Pandosto* the protagonist is King of Bohemia and his childhood friend rules Sicilia. In *The Winter's Tale* the reverse is true, and one reason may be the association of Sicilia with the myth of Proserpina, the beautiful daughter of Ceres abducted by Dis, the god of the underworld, as she was picking flowers. Her mother attempted to free Proserpina, but she was allowed to return to the upper world only six months of each year. During that period, spring and summer came to the earth, but winter reigned when Proserpina returned to Dis's kingdom. The sixteen years of mourning Leontes undergoes in Perdita's absence provide a counterpart to aspects of this myth.

Shakespeare, however, made much larger changes in Greene's romance. For example, he enhanced the role of Leontes' son, who is barely mentioned by Greene; he added the characters of Paulina, Emilia, Antigonus, Autolycus, Clown, Time, and rustics such as Dorcas and Mopsa (in *Pandosto* Mopsa was the name of the Old Shepherd's wife; in *The Winter's Tale* that wife is long dead). The magnificent sheepshearing festival is Shakespeare's invention; nothing like it exists in *Pandosto*. Most importantly, Greene's romance ends on a tragic note. Though the King and his daughter are finally reunited, Pandosto's wife is never restored to him, and overcome with desire for his grown daughter, he attempts incest and later takes his own life.

Shakespeare clearly saw in Greene's rather grim tale the basis for a much more resonant narrative of loss and redemption. The play is a diptych of winter and summer, hinged by the appearance of Time. It is probably a mistake to account for this structure by using only one interpretive framework, for the play's deliberate primitivism resonates with many narratives of renewal. Some have read the play in Christian terms, seeing Leontes as a sinner who after a period of suffering and repentance receives the gift of God's grace through the return of his daughter and the Christ-like resurrection of his wife. The play loosely traces the liturgical calendar, moving from the hospitality associated with Christmas to the Lenten period of deprivation and repentance to the joyous celebration of Easter and the Maying festivals associated with Whitsuntide, which occurs seven weeks after Easter. Other critics have stressed the mythic qualities of the play, its resemblance, for example, to the myth of Proserpina, or to fertility rites in which the coming of spring and sexual fulfillment depend on the sacrifice of a winter king. In *The Winter's Tale* Leontes does not die, but he does mourn for sixteen years; and his servant Antigonus, who takes the babe to Bohemia, and there names her Perdita, becomes Leontes' sacrificial substitute. Once he has deposited Perdita, Antigonus is mauled and eaten by a bear. As the Old Shepherd who rescues Perdita says to his son, who has witnessed this death, "Thou metst with things dying, I with things new-born" (3.3.104–05), the latter event seemingly dependent on the former. Other critics stress the pattern of generational renewal informing the play as the sins of the father, Leontes, are displaced by the innocent goodness of Florizel and Perdita. In some productions, the actress playing Hermione also plays Perdita (though a double usually has to be used for Perdita in the statue scene), deepening the sense that it is through their children that parents have a second life. Resonating with all these interpretive paradigms, *The Winter's Tale* draws richly on the many narratives and structures of belief through which Western culture has produced and sustained its desire for transcendence and renewal.

In modern productions, the symbolic power of the play's diptych structure is often highlighted by contrasts in the costumes and sets used to distinguish Sicilia and Bohemia. Sicilia, for example, is often the snow kingdom, dominated by white clothing and metallic props; Bohemia is the summer kingdom, the stage carpeted in green, the characters at the sheepshearing festival a riot of variegated colors. When the Bohemian party comes to Sicilia, the winter landscape is literally overwritten with the colorful clothes associated with Whitsuntide.

The play, however, is not simply about the triumph of the young, the rebirth of a world of possibility. *The Winter's Tale,* as befits a tragicomedy, moves from sorrow to joy, but that joy is bittersweet. However important the younger generation is to this old tale, the focus in this and the other romances stays resolutely on the older generation. It is Leontes who sins and must repent; Leontes whose family is reconstituted. Crucially, that reconstitution is only partial and imperfect. Mamillius, the young son, dies, the ultimate sacrifice to Leontes' tyrannous actions, and in the play's last scene, the playwright is at pains to stress that the "statue" of Hermione has wrinkles, the mark of time on her body. Traduced while a fertile wife and mother, Hermione returns as a woman past childbearing. Time, whose appearance marks the hinge of the play, may heal old sorrows and bring new births to pass, but it also shuts down possibilities and destroys youth and strength. The ending of Shakespeare's old tale induces wonder and joy, but it cannot make an old man young or erase all the consequences of rash deeds. Shakespeare's late plays achieve their rich emotional effects from the deep strains of melancholia that underwrite their measured celebrations of the return of love and hope to a chastened social order.

Nor, despite the archaic quality that permeates these plays, are they simple enactments of timeless patterns and narratives. The precipitating event of the play—the eruption of Leontes' jealousy—is a symptom of the faultlines in a particular patriarchal culture. Often said to be "irrational," this jealousy in actuality has its roots in the cultural practices which in Jacobean England made men the heads of families, lineages, and kingdoms, but at the same time made them crucially dependent on women's reproductive powers to generate legitimate heirs. As *The Winter's Tale* opens, Leontes asks Polixenes to extend his stay in Sicilia. Polixenes refuses, but when Hermione entreats him, he agrees. This event, and the sight of his pregnant wife conversing with his friend and holding him by the hand, triggers in Leontes so deep a suspicion of his wife's fidelity that he plans to have Polixenes killed and doubts the legitimacy of his son, as well. In part, what disturbs Leontes is the unknowability of the biological origins of his children. Men theoretically had dominion over their wives, but as Leontes says, "No barricado for a belly" (1.2.205)—that is, no absolute defense of a woman's chastity but her own honor, and that lies in her control, not her husband's.

A deep ambivalence toward women and sexuality, moreover, surfaces earlier in the same scene when, reminiscing about his boyhood friendship with Leontes, Polixenes describes the two of them as twinned lambs who experienced a fall from paradise only when they felt sexual passion and had their first encounters with women. In this conversation, the two men echo a strand of early modern thought that viewed men's friendships with men as of greater worth than what were seen as men's more dangerous and unpredictable relations with women, an idea examined as early in Shakespeare's work as *The Two Gentlemen of Verona*. Construed as physically imperfect and as intellectually inferior to men, women were supposedly ruled by their passions and could in turn evoke dangerous and degrading emotions in men. Yet men were enjoined to marry these irrational creatures to procreate and to continue family lineage. Leontes' rage at Hermione seems to stem in part from his dependence on her to give him legitimate heirs.

Other tensions permeate the opening scenes. If in their younger days Polixenes and Leontes were like twinned lambs, in adulthood their friendship is tinged with competitiveness, with Hermione gradually becoming the focus of their rivalry. Polixenes' attendant Archidamus opens the play expressing uneasiness about repaying the generous hospitality provided by Leontes, and suggesting rivalry as well as friendship between the two kingdoms; in 1.2 Leontes asks Polixenes if he loves *his* son as dearly as Leontes loves Mamillius, again suggesting competitiveness between the two kings at the level of paternal affection for their sons. In this general context of subterranean rivalry, Leontes' command that Hermione entreat Polixenes to stay not only expresses his ostentatious generosity (he will even share his wife's attentions with his friend), but also calls forth his rivalrous jealousy (perhaps his friend has taken advantage of his generosity and assumed Leontes' place in Hermione's bed).

Once his jealousy has been triggered, Leontes gives the rein to a deadly rage that finds its chief object in Hermione's pregnant body. This anger is played out in part through Leontes' increasing identification with his young son, Mamillius. In Mamillius Leontes sees himself as he once was, a young boy not yet wearing either the breeches or the sharp phallic dagger associated with adult manhood (1.2.157–58). It is an image of innocence but also of vulnerability. The name Mamillius, another of Shakespeare's brilliant inventions, suggests one source of that vulnerability. *Mamilla* is the word for the nipple on a breast or a diminutive form of *mamma*, the Latin word for the breast itself. His name thus connects Mamillius to the lactating breast and to the world of women, who in early modern culture presided over childbirth and the early years of children's lives. In a culture in which baby formula did not exist, infants depended utterly on women, either wet nurses or mothers, to provide the crucial sustenance, breast milk. As was often true of women from the upper class, Hermione does not herself seem to have nursed Mamillius. As Leontes bitterly exclaims: "I am glad you did not nurse him" (2.1.58). Nonetheless, the young boy's name and his appearance in 2.1 with his pregnant mother and her waiting women clearly associate him with the feminine sphere of birth, lactation, and early childhood. In identifying with Mamillius, a boy so young his nurse's milk is scarcely out of him, Leontes seems to feel both the vulnerability of the infant dependent on the lactating body of woman and the vulnerability of the adult husband dependent on the pregnant body and the chastity of his wife for legitimate offspring. As if to deny these dependencies, Leontes banishes Mamillius from his mother's presence, and he banishes Hermione to prison. Mamillius dies; Leontes appears to lose all that would link him to the future: wife, son, daughter.

The Winter's Tale makes Leontes unmistakably a villain and portrays his anger and paranoia as forces that torture his speech and profoundly isolate him. In the first three acts, Leontes' most characteristic action is to turn away from those who love or attempt to help him. He sends his wife to prison; casts out his infant daughter; refuses the good counsel of his courtiers; rages in misogynistic fury at Paulina, who brings Perdita to him from prison; and finally defies the oracle of Apollo. Lacking trust in his wife and in all those around him, Leontes condemns himself to deathlike isolation. As in Shakespeare's other late plays, much of the language of *The Winter's Tale* is difficult and dense. Normal word order is inverted; speeches begin and end in the middle of a line; figurative language is given elliptical expression. During his period of intense jealousy, Leontes' language becomes even more dense and compressed than is typical of the rest of the play. Looking at his son, he exclaims:

> Can thy dam—may't be?—
> Affection, thy intention stabs the centre.
> Thou dost make possible things not so held,
> Communicat'st with dreams—how can this be?—
> With what's unreal thou coactive art,
> And fellow'st nothing. Then 'tis very credent

> Thou mayst co-join with something, and thou dost—
> And that beyond commission; and I find it—
> And that to the infection of my brains
> And hard'ning of my brows.

(1.2.139–48)

In this difficult passage, Leontes wrestles with the knowledge that his "affection" (the passions of rage, jealousy, and suspicion released in him) wounds him and perhaps leads him to imagine things to be true that are not. On the other hand, his suspicions *may* be justified; he may already be a cuckold. In this horrible state of uncertainty, Leontes' speech verges on incoherence. He interrupts the flow of his own thoughts with questions and ejaculations; his mind darts from boy to mother to his own pain; he realizes he may be wrong, but returns, obsessively, to the coarse and shameful image of his forehead disfigured with the horns of a cuckold.

The inner disorder suggested by this language finds its outward manifestation in Leontes' increasingly tyrannical actions. In the early modern period, the ruler of a kingdom was often compared to the head of a family. Good order in the commonwealth had its foundation in a well-ordered domestic realm. In *The Winter's Tale* Leontes oversteps his just authority in both domains, refusing to take counsel from his courtiers, defying the gods, and condemning his wife for adultery with no evidence but his own suspicions. Nowhere, however, does he more certainly exceed his patriarchal authority than when he

Childbirth was largely a women's affair in the early modern period. In this picture from Jacob Rüff's *De conceptu et generatione hominis* (*Concerning the conception and birth of man*) (1580), several women attend to a woman in labor while, in the background, two men cast the child's horoscope.

orders Hermione to stand trial before the proper period of her lying-in has passed. In the Renaissance, childbirth was recognized as an event both important and dangerous. Women gave birth surrounded by other women, usually a hired midwife, as well as by neighbors and female family members. The laboring female body, opened to let the child pass into the world, was considered to be in a particularly vulnerable state, needing to be protected from the unhealthful air that might enter the open womb. Consequently, birthing took place in a closed chamber, and after birth had occurred, women lay in their chambers for an extended period, recovering strength and purging their bodies of the blood and other fluids associated with pregnancy. At the end of this period, often lasting a month but sometimes longer, the woman came out of her house and returned to her normal routines. This occasion was marked by a "churching" ceremony, a rite of purification and celebration in which thanks were given for the safe delivery of a child and the woman's body declared cleansed of the impurities of pregnancy and birth.

When Hermione is made to stand trial, the pathos of her dignified defense of herself is heightened by her weakened state. In many productions she appears on stage unattended, almost unable to stand. Among the wrongs done her, she accuses Leontes of having "with immodest hatred / The childbed privilege denied, which 'longs / To women of all fashion; lastly, hurried / Here, to this place, i'th open air, before / I have got strength of limit" (3.2.100–04). Leontes' fury against the maternal body extends to denying that body the privileges of the lying-in period and exposing it to the dangers of the open air of a public place. This is domestic tyranny of a hideous sort.

After such cruelty, what recovery? Bohemia seems to be the place of hope in the play, and that feeling is conveyed in part by the vast expansion of character and event in that pastoral locale. After the claustrophobic focus on Leontes, the action unfolds to encompass the tricks of a wily rogue, Autolycus (whose name links him to the Autolycus of classical myth, a crafty thief and grandfather of Ulysses; Autolycus' own father, Mercury, was the god of thieves); the sports of a sheepshearing festival; the courtship of Florizel and Perdita; and the intrigues which take many of these players back to Sicilia. The scene depicting the festival at the Old Shepherd's farm, 4.4, is one of the longest in Shakespeare's canon (810 lines), is entirely his own invention, and is a great feast of languages and events. It includes the singing of ballads, a dance of twelve satyrs, Perdita's lyrical catalog of the flowers appropriate to each stage of life, and the painful moment when Polixenes forbids his son's marriage.

As this last moment shows, though Bohemia is a place of healing, it is not a paradise. In Bohemia, "great creating nature" for a time replaces Apollo as the deity who presides over the action. The fertility of the earth and, by extension, the fertility of woman may here seem to be redeemed from the curse laid upon them by Leontes' suspicion of his wife; and Florizel's staunch commitment to Perdita in the face of mounting obstacles to their love augers well. But Polixenes just as staunchly opposes their union, threatening to use his patriarchal power in a way that, as with Leontes, would separate him from his son and from the possibility of future lineage. Bohemia also contains the rogue Autolycus, picking the pockets of country bumpkins and hiding his identity by a series of disguises; and Bohemian life is marked by enormous disparities of wealth. The Old Shepherd is rich, helped by the money he found beside Perdita, but also probably because of the profitability of raising sheep. Throughout the sixteenth and seventeenth centuries, land was increasingly enclosed—that is, fenced off for grazing sheep rather than available for communal use in raising food and feeding cattle. These enclosures were popularly blamed for perceived increases in rural poverty and for the creation of masterless men, poor folk who roamed the countryside without fixed places of residence and who were believed to feign sickness or deformity in order to enforce charity from those they met. Autolycus, pretending to have lost his clothes to a highwayman, is a comic version of such a masterless man, yet his presence in the play, juxtaposed to that of the rich shepherd, is a reminder of the social tensions and economic stratifications that permeate the rural landscape with the advent of increasingly entrepreneurial economic practices. Some of the ingredients Perdita needs for her sheepshearing feast—raisins, rice, and spices, for example—were exotic lux-

In this late-seventeenth-century woodcut from the Pepysian collection of early modern ballads, a pedlar carries a huge pack and holds several rabbits, or conies, which suggests that he is also a cony-catcher—that is, a con man (like Autolycus), whose victims were popularly called conies.

ury goods, foodstuffs quite in excess of the subsistence diet of bread, beer, and cheese that was still the staple for many.

Bohemia is also the locale of one of the great set pieces of the play—the debate between Polixenes and Perdita concerning the relative values of art and nature and the relationship between them. This was an ancient debate and one that could give off a decidedly musty odor, even though it was dusted off by a number of Shakespeare's contemporaries. At the heart of this debate lay the question of artifice. Was it a good thing? Did it distort or enhance nature? Given the imperfections of the fallen world and humankind's weaknesses, could art be instrumental in calling into being a better world, or was it merely a temptation to pride or to competition with the divine creator? The refreshing thing about the handling of these issues in *The Winter's Tale* is that the play comes to no abstract resolution concerning them. Rather, it encases the actual debate between Polixenes and Perdita in multiple ironies, and it complexly connects this debate to the actions of characters who seemingly have no involvement with it. For Perdita, product of the pastoral landscape, art is a bad thing. She wants no grafted or hybrid flowers in her garden. Yet even as she speaks her condemnation of art, Perdita is reluctantly dressed as queen of the sheepshearing feast, a bit of artifice that reveals a truth she herself cannot know: namely, that she is a queen's daughter. Polixenes, for his part, champions art, declaring that the practice of mixing wild and cultivated plants produces sturdy hybrids and that the art of grafting is itself a gift of nature. Yet when his son wishes to graft himself to a shepherd's daughter, Polixenes finds such a practice abhorrent.

Besides making the obvious point that people don't always act on their stated beliefs, this exchange shows the extreme pressure the play puts on the art-nature dichotomy. In Perdita's case, her "natural" condition as princess is revealed only by means of two kinds of artifice: her dress as queen of the feast and the role Camillo creates for her as Florizel's Libyan princess when he devises a way for the two young lovers to return to Leontes' court. Camillo even goes so far as to provide lines for the two to speak. His goal is ameliorative: to satisfy the desires of the young (as well as his own deep longings to again see his homeland) and to heal the breach between the two disseeered kingdoms. The point seems to be not whether in some abstract sense "art" violates "nature," but how artfulness, defined broadly as the representation of the world through painting, statuary, plays, and song, can open new possibilities for imagining what nature is or could be.

This is not an inconsequential point, for in the badly flawed world depicted in *The Winter's Tale* art gradually emerges as one of the resources people can use, either badly or well, to affect the world around them: to correct old mistakes and to forge new realities. Its effects are determined and limited, of course, by the skill and intentions of the artist and by the receptiveness of the audience. Autolycus is a subversive con man who uses disguises and deceptions to fleece money from gulls. By contrast, in the play's final movement, Paulina emerges as the chief representative of the ameliorative artist who uses her skills to make better the world around her. Once reviled by Leontes as a witch, Paulina becomes the King's spiritual guide in the last half of the play (her name linking her to the New Testament evangelist, St. Paul). This strikingly outspoken woman spends sixteen years preparing Leontes to be a fit spectator to the tableau of resurrection and renewal enacted in the last scene. When she had first brought the infant to Leontes from prison, Paulina had seemed to believe in the self-evident nature of truth. Laying the babe at Leontes' feet, she proclaimed that the "good goddess Nature" (2.3.104) had made it an exact copy of the father. Leontes had only to read what nature had written in the face of his child. But distorting jealousy and rage at his wife had bleared the King's vision. He would not or could not see himself in the female child he had helped beget. So for sixteen years Paulina worked another way, fueling Leontes' remorse and artfully withholding both from him and from the theater audience the knowledge that Hermione lived. When the disguised princess returns to Sicilia, Leontes gets a second chance. Looking at Perdita, he is finally able to see—not so much himself as the unslandered image of his wife in the young girl before him. Having admired Perdita, Leontes says to Paulina, "I thought of her [Hermione] / Even in these looks I made" (5.1.226–27). When he can believe in the potential goodness of women, and specifically in the chastity of the young woman who is the simulacrum of his wife, then Leontes can help to create the reality in which Perdita is truly a princess and his wife a living being rather than the corpse into which his rage and distrust had transformed her.

The statue scene itself is one of the most moving dramatic moments in any of Shakespeare's plays. Like Leontes, the untutored audience does not know that Hermione lives. Consequently, under Paulina's careful guidance, the spectators both onstage and off seem to participate in willing the statue into life. When Hermione descends from her pedestal, the audience can feel itself present at the miraculous resurrection of the dead. And so the old tale ends happily, or mostly so. At the end of the play, patriarchy has been reformed, but its potential for abuses has hardly been eradicated. In the final scene, the highly charged image of the pregnant female body is nowhere to be seen. Perdita is not yet a wife; Paulina and Hermione are too old for childbearing. For Perdita and Florizel perhaps the greatest tests of faith and mutuality lie ahead, when Perdita's transformation from maid into wife and mother will present new occasions for jealousy and distrust. Moreover, in The Winter's Tale the remembrance of things that were lost and can never be regained intrudes even on the celebration of the return of Perdita and of Hermione. Paulina pointedly recalls her husband, Antigonus, lost in carrying Perdita to Bohemia; Hermione speaks to Perdita of the sixteen long years of their separation; her wrinkles attest to other losses; Mamillius is gone forever. The point of The Winter's Tale hardly seems to be that folly has no consequences or that earthly paradise is possible. Those claims would indeed make nature afraid. Rather, the play celebrates the true miracle of partial restorations, of moments of exquisite joy wrested by work, art, and good fortune from the pains of the imperfect world men and women have made.

JEAN E. HOWARD

TEXTUAL NOTE

The Winter's Tale was first printed in the Folio of 1623 at the end of the group of comedies. Simon Forman, a London doctor, saw a performance at the Globe on May 15, 1611, and it was performed at court on November 11 of that year. Its exact date of composition, however, is unknown. Largely on stylistic evidence and because The Winter's Tale is at several points indebted to Plutarch, a principal source for Shakespeare's classical tragedies such as Coriolanus (1608), the Oxford editors place the date of composition in 1609, before Cymbeline. Other editors believe the play was written late in 1610 or early in 1611 before the May performance witnessed by Forman. In Act 4, Scene 4, working men at the sheepshearing festival perform a satyr dance that resembles a dance in Ben Jonson's Masque of Oberon, which was performed at court on January 1, 1611. In Shakespeare's play the Old Shepherd remarks that three of the performers had "danced before the King" (4.4.324). This reference has been used to suggest that Shakespeare either was writing The Winter's

Tale in January of 1611, and so incorporated a contemporary court event into his play, or that he composed the bulk of the play after that date. It is also possible that Shakespeare—or someone else—added this dance to *The Winter's Tale* after the play had already been written and was in performance in order to capitalize on the glamour attached to court occasions, especially if, as the Old Shepherd indicates, members of Shakespeare's company performed in Jonson's masque. If so, the dance would have been recorded in the promptbook, but not necessarily in Shakespeare's original manuscript.

The Folio text of the play was probably set from a transcript prepared by Ralph Crane, a scrivener who transcribed a number of plays associated with the King's Men. In many of the manuscripts prepared by Crane, and this is true for *The Winter's Tale*, all the characters who appear in certain scenes, regardless of when they actually come on stage, are listed in the opening stage direction. Crane sometimes modified stage directions in the interest of clarity and imposed his own punctuation and spelling on the playscripts, showing a decided preference for the heavy use of parentheses, hyphens, and apostrophes. The changes Crane made while copying the plays make it difficult to recognize what kind of manuscript lay behind his transcriptions: promptbook or foul papers. As with other plays set from Crane's transcriptions, the Folio *Winter's Tale* is a relatively clean text. Act and scene divisions are carefully and consistently noted, though stage directions are sparse. There are only forty-three in the Folio, and they are regularly supplemented in modern editions.

SELECTED BIBLIOGRAPHY

Adelman, Janet. "Masculine Authority and the Maternal Body: The Return to Origins in the Romances." *Suffocating Mothers: Fantasies of Maternal Origins in Shakespeare's Plays, "Hamlet" to "The Tempest."* Routledge: London, 1992. 193–238.

Bristol, Michael. "In Search of the Bear: Spatiotemporal Form and the Heterogeneity of Economies in *The Winter's Tale*." *Shakespeare Quarterly* 42 (1991): 145–67.

Dolan, Frances. "Finding What Has Been 'Lost': Representations of Infanticide and *The Winter's Tale*." *Dangerous Familiars: Representations of Domestic Crime in England, 1550–1700.* Ithaca, N.Y.: Cornell University Press, 1994. 121–70.

Egan, Robert. " 'The Art Itself Is Nature': *The Winter's Tale*." *Drama Within Drama: Shakespeare's Sense of His Art in "King Lear," "The Winter's Tale," and "The Tempest."* New York: Columbia University Press, 1975. 56–89.

Erickson, Peter. "The Limitations of Reformed Masculinity in *The Winter's Tale*." *Patriarchal Structures in Shakespeare's Drama.* Berkeley: University of California Press, 1985. 148–72.

Felperin, Howard. " 'Our Carver's Excellence': *The Winter's Tale*." *Shakespearean Romance.* Princeton: Princeton University Press, 1972. 211–45.

Frey, Charles. *Shakespeare's Vast Romance: A Study of "The Winter's Tale."* Columbia, Mo.: University of Missouri Press, 1980.

Frye, Northrop. "The Triumph of Time." *A Natural Perspective: The Development of Shakespearean Comedy and Romance.* New York: Columbia University Press, 1965. 72–117.

Mowat, Barbara A. "Rogues, Shepherds, and the Counterfeit Distressed: Texts and Infracontexts of *The Winter's Tale* 4.3." *Shakespeare Studies* 22 (1994): 58–76.

Paster, Gail Kern. "Quarreling with the Dug, *or I Am Glad You Did Not Nurse Him.*" *The Body Embarrassed: Drama and the Disciplines of Shame in Early Modern Europe.* Ithaca, N.Y.: Cornell University Press, 1993. 215–80.

The Winter's Tale

THE PERSONS OF THE PLAY

LEONTES, King of Sicilia
HERMIONE, his wife
MAMILLIUS, his son
PERDITA, his daughter
CAMILLO ⎫
ANTIGONUS ⎪ Lords at Leontes' court
CLEOMENES ⎪
DION ⎭
PAULINA, Antigonus's wife
EMILIA, a lady attending on Hermione
A JAILER
A MARINER
Other Lords and Gentlemen, Ladies, Officers, and Servants at
    Leontes' court
POLIXENES, King of Bohemia
FLORIZEL, his son, in love with Perdita; known as Doricles
ARCHIDAMUS, a Bohemian lord
AUTOLYCUS, a rogue, once in the service of Florizel
OLD SHEPHERD
CLOWN, his son
MOPSA ⎫ shepherdesses
DORCAS ⎭
SERVANT of the Old Shepherd
Other Shepherds and Shepherdesses
Twelve countrymen disguised as satyrs
TIME, as chorus

1.1

Enter CAMILLO *and* ARCHIDAMUS

ARCHIDAMUS If you shall chance, Camillo, to visit Bohemia on
    the like occasion whereon my services are now on foot,[1] you
    shall see, as I have said, great difference betwixt our Bohemia
    and your Sicilia.

5 CAMILLO I think this coming summer the King of Sicilia means
    to pay Bohemia the visitation which he justly owes him.

ARCHIDAMUS Wherein our entertainment shall shame us, we
    will be justified in our loves;[2] for indeed—

CAMILLO Beseech you—

10 ARCHIDAMUS Verily, I speak it in the freedom of my knowledge.
    We cannot with such magnificence—in so rare— I know not
    what to say.— We will give you sleepy drinks,° that your senses,   *drinks to make you drowsy*
    unintelligent of our insufficience,[3] may, though they cannot
    praise us, as little accuse us.

15 CAMILLO You pay a great deal too dear for what's given freely.

1.1 Location: Sicilia. The palace of Leontes.
1. On an occasion similar to the one in which I am now
engaged (that is, as attendant lord to a visiting king).

2. Insofar as our less elaborate hospitality will put us to
shame, we will compensate by (the depth of) our love.
3. Unaware of our inadequacy.

ARCHIDAMUS Believe me, I speak as my understanding instructs
me, and as mine honesty puts it to utterance.

CAMILLO Sicilia cannot show himself over-kind to Bohemia.
They were trained together in their childhoods, and there
20   rooted betwixt them then such an affection which cannot
choose but branch[4] now. Since their more mature dignities
and royal necessities made separation of their society,° their   *forced them apart*
encounters—though not personal— hath been royally attor-
neyed[5] with interchange of gifts, letters, loving embassies, that°   *so that*
25   they have seemed to be together, though absent; shook hands
as over a vast;° and embraced as it were from the ends of   *wide expanse*
opposed winds.[6] The heavens continue their loves.

ARCHIDAMUS I think there is not in the world either malice or
matter to alter it. You have an unspeakable° comfort of° your   *inexpressible / in*
30   young prince, Mamillius. It° is a gentleman of the greatest   *(He)*
promise that ever came into my note.

CAMILLO I very well agree with you in the hopes of him. It is a
gallant child; one that, indeed, physics the subject,[7] makes old
hearts fresh. They that went on crutches ere he was born desire
35   yet their life° to see him a man.   *hope to live long enough*

ARCHIDAMUS Would they else be content to die?

CAMILLO Yes—if there were no other excuse why they should
desire to live.

ARCHIDAMUS If the King had no son they would desire to live on
40   crutches till he had one.   *Exeunt*

1.2

Enter LEONTES, HERMIONE, MAMILLIUS, POLIXENES, *and*
CAMILLO[1]

POLIXENES Nine changes of the wat'ry star hath been
The shepherd's note[2] since we[3] have left our throne
Without a burden.° Time as long again   *an occupant*
Would be filled up, my brother, with our thanks,
5   And yet we should for perpetuity
Go hence in debt.[4] And therefore, like a cipher,
Yet standing in rich place,[5] I multiply
With one 'We thank you' many thousands more
That go before it.

LEONTES   Stay° your thanks a while,   *Postpone*
And pay them when you part.

10   POLIXENES   Sir, that's tomorrow.
I am questioned by my fears° of what may chance[6]   *I am afraid*
Or breed upon° our absence, that may blow   *develop because of*
No sneaping winds at home to make us say

---

4. Flourish and spread (as a tree does when it puts forth
branches); divide.
5. Performed by deputies.
6. From opposite ends of the earth. Early modern atlases
often showed the four "corners" of the earth as the source
of the winds.
7. Restores the health of the king's subjects.
1.2 Location: Sicilia. The palace of Leontes.
1. Though listed in the stage direction in F, Camillo has
no part in this scene until line 210, when Leontes says,
"What, Camillo there!" Camillo may be a silent observer

for the first 210 lines, or, as some editors believe, his first
entrance may be marked by Leontes' exclamation.
2. The shepherd has observed nine changes of the moon
(that is, nine months). The moon is "the wat'ry star"
because it governs the tides.
3. Both kings employ the royal "we," speaking of them-
selves in the plural.
4. And even then we would depart forever in your debt.
5. Like a zero ("cipher"), which is worthless in itself, but
valuable when it follows another number.
6. Happen by chance.

'This is put forth too truly.'[7] Besides, I have stayed
To tire your royalty.
15 LEONTES   We are tougher, brother,
Than you can put us to't.[8]
POLIXENES   No longer stay.
LEONTES   One sennight° longer.   *week*
POLIXENES   Very sooth,° tomorrow.   *In truth (a mild oath)*
LEONTES   We'll part the time° between's, then; and in that   *split the difffference*
I'll no gainsaying.°   *allow no contradiction*
POLIXENES   Press me not, beseech you, so.
20 There is no tongue that moves, none, none i'th' world
So soon as yours, could win me. So it should now,
Were there necessity in your request, although
'Twere needful I denied it. My affairs
Do even drag me homeward; which to hinder
25 Were, in your love, a whip to me;[9] my stay
To you a charge and trouble. To save both,
Farewell, our brother.
LEONTES   Tongue-tied, our queen? Speak you.
HERMIONE   I had thought, sir, to have held my peace until
You had drawn oaths from him not to stay. You, sir,
30 Charge him too coldly. Tell him you are sure
All in Bohemia's well. This satisfaction
The bygone day proclaimed.[1] Say this to him,
He's beat from his best ward.[2]
LEONTES   Well said, Hermione!
HERMIONE   To tell° he longs to see his son were strong.   *assert*
35 But let him say so then, and let him go.
But let him swear so and he shall not stay,
We'll thwack him hence with distaffs.[3]
[*To* POLIXENES] Yet of your royal presence I'll adventure°   *risk*
The borrow° of a week. When at Bohemia   *loan*
40 You take my lord, I'll give him my commission°   *permission*
To let him there a month behind the gest
Prefixed for's parting.[4]—Yet, good deed,° Leontes,   *indeed*
I love thee not a jar° o'th' clock behind   *tick*
What lady she her lord.[5]—You'll stay?
POLIXENES   No, madam.
45 HERMIONE   Nay, but you will?
POLIXENES   I may not, verily.
HERMIONE   Verily?
You put me off with limber° vows. But I,   *weak*
Though you would seek t'unsphere the stars[6] with oaths,
50 Should yet say 'Sir, no going.' Verily
You shall not go. A lady's 'verily' 's
As potent as a lord's. Will you go yet?

---

7. *"that may . . . too truly,"*: an obscure passage. Fearing the worst, Polixenes hopes that no biting ("sneaping") winds may blow (that is, no envious forces be active) at home to make him conclude that his worries were justified.
8. Than any test you put us to.
9. That is, "To hinder me from going home, though lovingly done, would be a punishment ('whip') to me."
1. This good news was announced yesterday.
2. He's forced to relinquish his strongest position. A fenc-

ing metaphor.
3. Wooden sticks, usually about three feet long, which were used in spinning wool. Proverbially, they were female tools and symbols of female authority.
4. To remain there a month longer than the time ("gest") appointed in advance for his departure.
5. That is, "I love you no less than any noblewoman loves her husband."
6. To disorder the cosmos. Alluding to the idea that the stars move in fixed orbits around the earth.

Force me to keep you as a prisoner,
Not like a guest: so you shall pay your fees
When you depart,[7] and save your thanks. How say you?
My prisoner? or my guest? By your dread 'verily',
One of them you shall be.
POLIXENES   Your guest then, madam.
To be your prisoner should import offending,°   *mean I have offended you*
Which is for me less easy to commit
Than you to punish.
HERMIONE   Not your jailer then,
But your kind hostess. Come, I'll question you
Of my lord's tricks and yours when you were boys.
You were pretty lordings° then?   *young lords*
POLIXENES   We were, fair Queen,
Two lads that thought there was no more behind°   *(in the future)*
But such a day tomorrow as today,
And to be boy eternal.
HERMIONE   Was not my lord
The verier wag° o'th' two?   *greater mischief-maker*
POLIXENES   We were as twinned° lambs that did frisk i'th' sun,   *identical*
And bleat the one at th'other. What we changed°   *exchanged*
Was innocence for innocence. We knew not
The doctrine of ill-doing, nor dreamed
That any did. Had we pursued that life,
And our weak spirits ne'er been higher reared
With stronger blood,° we should have answered heaven *With more mature passions*
Boldly, 'Not guilty', the imposition cleared
Hereditary ours.[8]
HERMIONE   By this we gather
You have tripped° since.   *sinned*
POLIXENES   O my most sacred lady,
Temptations have since then been born to's; for
In those unfledged[9] days was my wife a girl.
Your precious self had then not crossed the eyes
Of my young playfellow.
HERMIONE   Grace to boot!°   *Heaven help me!*
Of this make no conclusion,[1] lest you say
Your queen and I are devils. Yet go on.
Th'offences we have made you do we'll answer,°   *answer for*
If you first sinned with us, and that with us
You did continue fault, and that you slipped not
With any but with us.
LEONTES   Is he won yet?
HERMIONE   He'll stay, my lord.
LEONTES   At my request he would not.
Hermione, my dearest, thou never spok'st
To better purpose.
HERMIONE   Never?
LEONTES   Never but once.
HERMIONE   What, have I twice said well? When was't before?

---

7. In early modern England prisoners were required to pay fees to jailers both for provisions and upon their release.
8. Freed even of the charge of original sin. The doctrine of original sin held that everyone at birth was tainted by sin because the first humans, Adam and Eve, disobeyed God in the Garden of Eden.
9. Youthful. An unfledged, or young, bird is one as yet lacking the feathers necessary for flight.
1. Do not follow out this line of reasoning.

I prithee tell me. Cram's° with praise, and make's   *Stuff us; overfeed us*
As fat as tame things. One good deed dying tongueless
95   Slaughters a thousand waiting upon that.[2]
Our praises are our wages. You may ride's
With one soft kiss a thousand furlongs ere
With spur we heat° an acre.[3] But to th' goal.°   *race over / purpose*
My last good deed was to entreat his stay.
100   What was my first? It has an elder sister,
Or I mistake you. O, would her name were Grace![4]
But once before I spoke to th' purpose? When?
Nay, let me have't. I long.
LEONTES   Why, that was when
Three crabbèd° months had soured themselves to death   *bitter*
105   Ere I could make thee open thy white hand
And clap° thyself my love. Then didst thou utter,   *pledge*
'I am yours for ever.'
HERMIONE   'Tis grace indeed.
Why lo you now; I have spoke to th' purpose twice.
The one for ever earned a royal husband;
Th'other, for some while a friend.[5]
    [*She gives her hand to* POLIXENES.[6]
    They stand aside]
110   LEONTES [*aside*]   Too hot, too hot:
To mingle friendship farre is mingling bloods.°   *uniting in passion*
I have *tremor cordis*[7] on me. My heart dances,
But not for joy, not joy. This entertainment°   *hospitality*
May a free° face put on, derive a liberty   *innocent*
115   From heartiness, from bounty, fertile bosom,°   *generous affection*
And well become the agent.[8] 'T may, I grant.
But to be paddling° palms and pinching fingers,[9]   *caressing*
As now they are, and making practised smiles
As in a looking-glass; and then to sigh, as 'twere
120   The mort o'th' deer[1]—O, that is entertainment
My bosom likes not, nor my brows.[2]—Mamillius,
Art thou my boy?
MAMILLIUS   Ay, my good lord.
LEONTES   I'fecks,°   *In faith (a mild oath)*
Why, that's my bawcock.° What? Hast smutched° thy nose?   *fine fellow / dirtied*
They say it is a copy out of mine. Come, captain,
125   We must be neat—not neat,[3] but cleanly, captain.
And yet the steer, the heifer, and the calf

---

2. If one virtuous act goes unremarked, then the thousand more that might have been inspired by it will not come to be.
3. That is, "You'll go much farther with us if you will treat us kindly," with a pun on "ride" as meaning "enjoy us sexually."
4. Would that my first good act were virtuous (full of God's Grace). Hermione may be countering Leontes' earlier suggestion that she first caused him to sin. With a possible allusion to the Three Graces (Aglaia, Euphrosyne, and Thalia) of classical myth. Usually depicted nude and dancing in a circle, the three women represented the epitome of earthly beauty and harmony.
5. "Friend" could also mean "lover," a meaning that Leontes takes up in his next speech.
6. It is not certain when Hermione and Polixenes join hands, but by line 117 Leontes remarks that they are

"paddling palms and pinching fingers." Joined hands—or hands separated from one another—are an important and recurring visual motif in the play, culminating at 5.3.107, when Paulina commands Leontes to "present your hand" to Hermione as she ceases to appear a statue.
7. A malady marked by an erratic heart rate.
8. And makes the actor of these deeds (Hermione) appear attractive.
9. Early modern texts often represent hands as erotic body parts. Moist palms were believed to be signs of sexual arousal; finger games may suggest sexual penetration.
1. To sigh as loudly as the horn blast that proclaims the death of a hunted deer.
2. Alluding to the proverbial notion that a cuckold sprouted horns from his brow.
3. Punning on neat as meaning both "clean" and "cattle with horns."

Are all called neat. — Still virginalling
Upon his palm?[4] — How now, you wanton° calf— *playful*
Art thou my calf?
MAMILLIUS   Yes, if you will, my lord.
130 LEONTES   Thou want'st a rough pash° and the shoots° that I have,   *shaggy head / horns*
To be full° like me. Yet they say we are   *entirely, fully*
Almost as like as eggs. Women say so,
That will say anything. But were they false
As o'er-dyed blacks,[5] as wind, as waters, false
135 As dice are to be wished by one that fixes
No bourn° 'twixt his and mine, yet were it true   *boundary, limit*
To say this boy were like me. Come, sir page,
Look on me with your welkin° eye. Sweet villain,   *sky blue*
Most dear'st, my collop!°[6] Can thy dam°—may't be?—   *mother*
140 Affection, thy intention stabs the centre.[7]
Thou dost make possible things not so held,°   *things held as impossible*
Communicat'st with dreams—how can this be?—
With what's unreal thou coactive art,°   *you collaborate*
And fellow'st° nothing. Then 'tis very credent°   *are companion to / believable*
145 Thou mayst co-join with something, and thou dost—
And that beyond commission;° and I find it—   *what is permitted*
And that to the infection of my brains
And hard'ning of my brows.°   *(with cuckold's horns)*
POLIXENES   What means Sicilia?
HERMIONE   He something seems° unsettled.   *seems somewhat*
POLIXENES   How, my lord!
LEONTES   What cheer? How is't with you, best brother?
150 HERMIONE   You look
As if you held a brow of much distraction.
Are you moved,° my lord?   *angry*
LEONTES   No, in good earnest.
How sometimes nature will betray its folly,
Its tenderness, and make itself a pastime°   *source of amusement*
155 To harder bosoms! Looking on the lines
Of my boy's face, methoughts I did recoil°   *go back*
Twenty-three years, and saw myself unbreeched,[8]
In my green velvet coat; my dagger muzzled,°   *in its sheath; blunted*
Lest it should bite its master, and so prove,
160 As ornament oft does, too dangerous.
How like, methought, I then was to this kernel,
This squash,° this gentleman.—Mine honest friend,   *unripe peapod*
Will you take eggs for money?[9]
MAMILLIUS   No, my lord, I'll fight.
LEONTES   You will? Why, happy man be's dole![1]—My brother,

---

4. Still caressing his hand as if playing the virginal, a leg-less keyboard instrument played on the lap; still acting chastely (like a virgin).
5. Referring to Africans, whose black skin was said to result from overexposure to the sun or to textiles made artificially black. It was a commonplace that Africans were prone to licentiousness and thus sexually "false." Black clothing was said to be rendered "false" or weakened by the harsh chemicals used to make the dye.
6. That is, "my own flesh." A "collop" is a portion of meat.
7. Passion (probably the passion of jealousy), your inten-

sity ("intention") pierces my heart or to the core of my being.
8. Not yet old enough to wear men's clothing ("breeches"). Before about the age of six, both girls and boys in early modern England wore a dresslike garment. Giving a boy breeches was a sign of his passage out of childhood and out of the care of women into the world of men.
9. A proverbial expression meaning "Will you accept a trifle in place of something valuable?"
1. Proverbial for "May you have good luck!"

165 Are you so fond of your young prince as we
Do seem to be of ours?
POLIXENES   If at home, sir,
He's all my exercise, my mirth, my matter;°   *concern*
·Now my sworn friend, and then mine enemy;
My parasite, my soldier, statesman, all.
170 He makes a July's day short as December,
And with his varying childness° cures in me   *youthful ways*
Thoughts that would thick my blood.[2]
LEONTES   So stands this squire
Officed with me.[3] We two will walk, my lord,
And leave you to your graver steps. Hermione,
175 How thou lov'st us show in our brother's welcome.
Let what is dear in Sicily be cheap.
Next to thyself and my young rover, he's
Apparent° to my heart.   *Heir apparent*
HERMIONE   If you would seek us,
We are yours i'th' garden. Shall's attend you there?
180 LEONTES   To your own bents° dispose you. You'll be found,   *inclinations*
Be you beneath the sky. [*Aside*] I am angling° now,   *fishing; scheming*
Though you perceive me not how I give line.
Go to, go to!
How she holds up the neb, the bill to him,[4]
185 And arms her° with the boldness of a wife   *herself*
To her allowing° husband!   *approving*
                          [*Exeunt* POLIXENES *and* HERMIONE]
                          Gone already.
Inch-thick, knee-deep, o'er head and ears a forked° one!—   *horned*
Go play, boy, play. Thy mother plays,° and I   *dallies sexually*
Play° too; but so disgraced a part, whose issue[5]   *Play a role*
190 Will hiss me to my grave. Contempt and clamour
Will be my knell. Go play, boy, play. There have been,
Or I am much deceived, cuckolds ere now,
And many a man there is, even at this present,
Now, while I speak this, holds his wife by th'arm,
195 That little thinks she has been sluiced[6] in's absence,
And his pond[7] fished by his next neighbour, by
Sir Smile, his neighbour.[8] Nay, there's comfort in't,
Whiles other men have gates,[9] and those gates opened,
As mine, against their will. Should all despair
200 That have revolted° wives, the tenth of mankind   *rebellious; unfaithful*
Would hang themselves. Physic° for't there's none.   *Medicine*
It is a bawdy planet, that will strike
Where 'tis predominant;[1] and 'tis powerful. Think it:

2. Ideas that would make me melancholy, a physical and
emotional malady connected with a supposed excess of
"thick blood."
3. So this young man performs the same duty for me.
4. How she holds up her face, her mouth to him (to be
kissed).
5. Outcome, with puns on "issue" as also meaning "off-
spring" and "the exit an actor makes from a stage."
Leontes' words imply that in playing the part of a cuckold,
the result of his role will be disgrace; the illegitimate off-
spring produced by his wife will bring him disgrace; and
his exit from the stage (at death) will be a disgraceful one.
6. Little thinks she has had sexual relations. A sluice was
a trough or channel through which water could be

directed. To be sluiced was to have water poured down
one's "channel," here probably referring to the vagina
where sperm entered.
7. Slang term for the sexual organs of his wife.
8. It is possible that "Sir Smile" is a reference to Poli-
xenes, who may be laughing or smiling in his conversa-
tion with Hermione.
9. Another slang term for female genitalia. Leontes imag-
ines the vulva as a gateway that ought to be entered only
by a husband.
1. Alluding to the notion that planets control human
actions and may exercise malign influences ("strike")
when they are in certain "predominant" positions.

From east, west, north, and south, be it concluded,
205   No barricado for a belly.² Know't,
        It will let in and out the enemy
        With bag and baggage.³ Many thousand on's°   *of us*
        Have the disease and feel't not.—How now, boy?
MAMILLIUS   I am like you, they say.
LEONTES   Why, that's some comfort.
        What, Camillo there!
210   CAMILLO [*coming forward*] Ay, my good lord.
LEONTES   Go play, Mamillius, thou'rt an honest man.
                                            [*Exit* MAMILLIUS]
        Camillo, this great sir will yet stay longer.
CAMILLO   You had much ado to make his anchor hold.
        When you cast out, it still came home.°   *always failed to hold*
LEONTES   Didst note it?
215   CAMILLO   He would not stay at your petitions, made
        His business more material.°   *important*
LEONTES   Didst perceive it?
        [*Aside*] They're here with me⁴ already, whisp'ring, rounding,°   *murmuring*
        'Sicilia is a so-forth'. 'Tis far gone
        When I shall gust° it last.—How came't, Camillo,   *perceive; taste*
        That he did stay?
220   CAMILLO   At the good Queen's entreaty.
LEONTES   'At the Queen's' be't. 'Good' should be pertinent,
        But so° it is, it is not. Was this taken°   *as / perceived*
        By any understanding pate but thine?
        For thy conceit is soaking,° will draw in   *you are quick-witted*
225   More than the common blocks.° Not noted, is't,   *dimwits*
        But of° the finer natures? By some severals°   *by / individuals*
        Of head-piece° extraordinary? Lower messes⁵   *intellect*
        Perchance are to this business purblind?° Say.   *blind*
CAMILLO   Business, my lord? I think most understand
230   Bohemia stays here longer.
LEONTES   Ha?
CAMILLO   Stays here longer.
LEONTES   Ay, but why?
—   CAMILLO   To satisfy your highness, and the entreaties
        Of our most gracious mistress.
235   LEONTES   Satisfy?⁶
        Th'entreaties of your mistress? Satisfy?
        Let that suffice. I have trusted thee, Camillo,
        With all the near'st things to my heart, as well
        My chamber-counsels,° wherein, priest-like, thou   *secret matters*
240   Hast cleansed my bosom, I from thee departed
        Thy penitent reformed. But we have been
        Deceived in thy integrity, deceived
        In that which seems so.
CAMILLO   Be it forbid, my lord.
LEONTES   To bide° upon't: thou art not honest; or   *dwell*
245   If thou inclin'st that way, thou art a coward,

---

2. No means of defending a womb.
3. With full military (or sexual) equipment.
4. They know my secret.
5. Those of lower social status at the dining table. A

"mess" refers to a group of four people who share meals together.
6. Punning on "satisfy" as meaning both "appease" and "give sexual pleasure to."

Which hoxes honesty behind,[7] restraining
From course required.[8] Or else thou must be counted
A servant grafted in my serious trust[9]
And therein negligent, or else a fool
250 That seest a game played home,° the rich stake drawn,°   *in earnest / won*
And tak'st it all for jest.
CAMILLO   My gracious lord,
I may be negligent, foolish, and fearful.
In every one of these no man is free,°   *guiltless*
But that his negligence, his folly, fear,
255 Among the infinite doings of the world
Sometime puts forth.° In your affairs, my lord,   *reveals itself*
If ever I were wilful-negligent,
It was my folly. If industriously°   *deliberately*
I played the fool, it was my negligence,
260 Not weighing well the end. If ever fearful
To do a thing where I the issue° doubted,   *outcome*
Whereof the execution did cry out
Against the non-performance,[1] 'twas a fear
Which oft infects the wisest. These, my lord,
265 Are such allowed infirmities that honesty
Is never free of. But beseech your grace
Be plainer with me, let me know my trespass
By its own visage. If I then deny it,
'Tis none of mine.
LEONTES   Ha' not you seen, Camillo—
270 But that's past doubt; you have, or your eye-glass°   *the lens of your eye*
Is thicker than a cuckold's horn—or heard—
For, to a vision° so apparent, rumour   *sight*
Cannot be mute—or thought—for cogitation
Resides not in that man that does not think—
275 My wife is slippery? If thou wilt confess—
Or else be impudently negative°   *shamelessly deny*
To have nor eyes, nor ears, nor thought—then say
My wife's a hobby-horse,[2] deserves a name
As rank° as any flax-wench[3] that puts to°   *indecent / has sexual relations*
280 Before her troth-plight.° Say't, and justify't.   *betrothal*
CAMILLO   I would not be a stander-by to hear
My sovereign mistress clouded so without
My present° vengeance taken. 'Shrew° my heart,   *immediate / Curse*
You never spoke what did become you less
285 Than this, which to reiterate° were sin   *repeat*
As deep as that, though true.[4]
LEONTES   Is whispering nothing?
Is leaning cheek to cheek? Is meeting noses?
Kissing with inside lip? Stopping the career°   *full gallop*
Of laughter with a sigh?—a note° infallible   *sign*

---

7. Which ensures that frankness is shackled.
8. Keeping (honesty) from the path it must take (to find out truth).
9. A servant who has grown into my confidence as a cutting is grafted onto a plant.
1. Even when the need to do the deed protested against its nonperformance.
2. Whore. The image is of a woman, who, like a horse,
can be mounted. F has "Holy-Horse," an obscure phrase nearly all modern editors emend to "hobby-horse."
3. A girl or woman, usually of low social status, who worked with flax, a fibrous plant used to make candle-wicks, clothing, and linen.
4. That is, "As grave as is the sin that you accuse your wife of, even if it were true (which it is not)."

290　　Of breaking honesty.° Horsing foot on foot?[5]　　　　　　*violating chastity*
　　　　Skulking in corners? Wishing clocks more swift,
　　　　Hours minutes, noon midnight? And all eyes
　　　　Blind with the pin and web° but theirs, theirs only,　　　　*cataract disease*
　　　　That would unseen be wicked? Is this nothing?
295　　Why then the world and all that's in't is nothing,
　　　　The covering sky is nothing, Bohemia nothing,
　　　　My wife is nothing, nor nothing have these nothings[6]
　　　　If this be nothing.
CAMILLO　　　　　　　Good my lord, be cured
　　　　Of this diseased opinion, and betimes,°　　　　　　　　*quickly*
　　　　For 'tis most dangerous.
300　LEONTES　　　　　　　Say it be, 'tis true.
CAMILLO　No, no, my lord.
LEONTES　　　　　　　It is. You lie, you lie.
　　　　I say thou liest, Camillo, and I hate thee,
　　　　Pronounce thee a gross lout, a mindless slave,
　　　　Or else a hovering° temporizer, that　　　　　　　　　*irresolute*
305　　Canst with thine eyes at once see good and evil,
　　　　Inclining to them both. Were my wife's liver
　　　　Infected as her life, she would not live
　　　　The running of one glass.°　　　　　　　　　　　　*hourglass*
CAMILLO　　　　　　　Who does infect her?
LEONTES　Why, he that wears her like her medal,[7] hanging
310　　About his neck, Bohemia, who, if I
　　　　Had servants true about me, that bare° eyes　　　　*possessed*
　　　　To see alike mine honour as their profits,
　　　　Their own particular thrifts,° they would do that　　　*personal gain*
　　　　Which should undo° more doing.° Ay, and thou　　*stop / sexual acts*
315　　His cupbearer,[8] whom I from meaner form°　　　*lower rank or place*
　　　　Have benched, and reared to worship,[9] who mayst see
　　　　Plainly as heaven sees earth and earth sees heaven,
　　　　How I am galled,° mightst bespice a cup　　　　　*sorely vexed*
　　　　To give mine enemy a lasting wink,[1]
　　　　Which draught to me were cordial.[2]
320　CAMILLO　　　　　　　　　　　Sir, my lord,
　　　　I could do this, and that with no rash° potion,　　　*quick-acting*
　　　　But with a ling'ring° dram, that should not work　　　*slow-working*
　　　　Maliciously,° like poison. But I cannot　　　　　　　*Violently*
　　　　Believe this crack° to be in my dread mistress,　　　*flaw*
325　　So sovereignly being honourable.
　　　　I have loved thee—
LEONTES　　　　　　　Make that thy question,° and go rot!　　*concern*
　　　　Dost think I am so muddy, so unsettled,
　　　　To appoint° myself in this vexation?　　　　　　　*put*
　　　　Sully the purity and whiteness of my sheets—
330　　Which to preserve is sleep, which being spotted
　　　　Is goads, thorns, nettles, tails of wasps—

5. Mounting or rubbing one foot on another. A sexually titillating pastime.
6. Alluding to the proverbial notion that nothing can come of nothing.
7. As though she were a miniature portrait of herself. Ornate lockets containing miniature portraits were popular love tokens among courtiers.
8. In a noble household a male servant whose responsibilities included serving wine to his master.
9. Given authority and elevated to a dignified position. Referring to his "bench" or place at the dining table as a sign of his high rank.
1. To close my enemy's eyes forever.
2. Which drink would be medicinal to me; which drink would cure my heartsickness (perhaps the *"tremor cordis"* to which Leontes referred at 1.2.112).

Give scandal to the blood o'th' prince, my son —
Who I do think is mine, and love as mine —
Without ripe moving° to't? Would I do this?   *good reason*
Could man so blench?°   *stray (from sense)*

335 CAMILLO   I must believe you, sir.
I do, and will fetch off° Bohemia for't,   *kill; rescue*
Provided that when he's removed your highness
Will take again your queen as yours at first,
Even for your son's sake, and thereby for sealing°   *silencing*
340 The injury of tongues in courts and kingdoms
Known and allied to yours.
LEONTES   Thou dost advise me
Even so as I mine own course have set down.
I'll give no blemish to her honour, none.
CAMILLO   My lord, go then, and with a countenance as clear
345 As friendship wears at feasts, keep° with Bohemia   *associate*
And with your queen. I am his cupbearer.
If from me he have wholesome beverage,
Account me not your servant.
LEONTES   This is all.
Do't, and thou hast the one half of my heart;
Do't not, thou splitt'st thine own.
350 CAMILLO   I'll do't, my lord.
LEONTES   I will seem friendly, as thou hast advised me.   *Exit*
CAMILLO   O miserable lady. But for me,
What case stand I in? I must be the poisoner
Of good Polixenes, and my ground to do't
355 Is the obedience to a master — one
Who in rebellion with himself, will have
All that are his so too. To do this deed,
Promotion follows. If I could find example
Of thousands that had struck anointed kings
360 And flourished after, I'd not do't. But since
Nor° brass, nor stone, nor parchment³ bears not one,   *Neither*
Let villainy itself forswear't.° I must   *swear not to do it*
Forsake the court. To do't, or no, is certain
To me a break-neck.°   *(death)*
            Enter POLIXENES
                        Happy° star reign now!   *Lucky*
Here comes Bohemia.
365 POLIXENES [*aside*]   This is strange. Methinks
My favour here begins to warp. Not speak? —
Good day, Camillo.
CAMILLO   Hail, most royal sir.
POLIXENES   What is the news i'th' court?
CAMILLO   None rare,° my lord.   *noteworthy*
POLIXENES   The King hath on him such a countenance
370 As° he had lost some province, and a region   *As if*
Loved as he loves himself. Even now I met him
With customary compliment, when he,
Wafting his eyes to th' contrary,° and falling   *Shifting his gaze away*
A lip of much contempt,° speeds from me, and   *sneering*

---

3. That is, since no form of historical record (brass monuments, stone markers, or paper manuscripts) shows an example of a man who flourished after killing a king.

375 So leaves me to consider what is breeding
That changes thus his manners.
CAMILLO   I dare not know, my lord.
POLIXENES   How, 'dare not'? Do not? Do you know, and dare not?
Be intelligent° to me. 'Tis thereabouts.[4]   *informative*
For to yourself what you do know you must,°   *(know)*
380 And cannot say you 'dare not'. Good Camillo,
Your changed complexions are to me a mirror
Which shows me mine changed, too; for I must be
A party in this alteration,° finding   *(of Leontes' manner)*
Myself thus altered with't.
CAMILLO   There is a sickness
385 Which puts some of us in distemper, but
I cannot name th' disease, and it is caught
Of you that yet are well.
POLIXENES   How caught of me?
Make me not sighted like the basilisk.[5]
I have looked on thousands who have sped° the better   *fared*
390 By my regard, but killed none so. Camillo,
As you are certainly a gentleman, thereto
Clerk-like experienced,[6] which no less adorns
Our gentry° than our parents' noble names,   *status as gentlemen*
In whose success we are gentle:[7] I beseech you,
395 If you know aught which does behove my knowledge
Thereof to be informed,[8] imprison't not
In ignorant concealment.[9]
CAMILLO   I may not answer.
POLIXENES   A sickness caught of me, and yet I well?
I must be answered. Dost thou hear, Camillo,
400 I conjure thee, by all the parts° of man   *duties*
Which honour does acknowledge, whereof the least
Is not this suit of mine, that thou declare
What incidency° thou dost guess of harm   *event*
Is creeping toward me; how far off, how near,
405 Which way to be prevented, if to be;
If not, how best to bear it.
CAMILLO   Sir, I will tell you,
Since I am charged in honour, and by him
That I think honourable. Therefore mark my counsel,
Which must be e'en as swiftly followed as
410 I mean to utter it; or both yourself and me
Cry lost, and so good night!°   *goodbye forever*
POLIXENES   On, good Camillo.
CAMILLO   I am appointed him to murder you.
POLIXENES   By whom, Camillo?
CAMILLO   By the King.
POLIXENES   For what?
CAMILLO   He thinks, nay, with all confidence he swears
415 As he had seen't, or been an instrument
To vice° you to't, that you have touched his queen   *force*
Forbiddenly.

---

4. That is, "I'm more or less right (that you are afraid to
tell me)."
5. A mythical serpent whose glance was said to be fatal.
6. Also having the experience of an educated man.

7. By succession from whom we are made noble.
8. Which it is necessary for me to know.
9. In concealment that keeps me ignorant; in conceal-
ment on the pretense that you are ignorant.

POLIXENES   O, then my best blood turn
To an infected jelly, and my name
Be yoked with his° that did betray the Best!°   *(Judas') name / Christ*
420   Turn then my freshest reputation to
A savour° that may strike the dullest nostril   *foul odor*
Where I arrive, and my approach be shunned,
Nay hated, too, worse than the great'st infection
That e'er was heard or read.
CAMILLO   Swear his thought over[1]
425   By each particular star in heaven, and
By all their influences,[2] you may as well
Forbid the sea for to obey the moon
As or° by oath remove or counsel shake   *either*
The fabric of his folly, whose foundation
430   Is piled upon his faith, and will continue
The standing of his body.°   *As long as he lives*
POLIXENES   How should this grow?°   *come to be*
CAMILLO   I know not, but I am sure 'tis safer to
Avoid what's grown than question how 'tis born.
If therefore you dare trust my honesty,
435   That lies enclosèd in this trunk° which you   *body*
Shall bear along impawned,[3] away tonight!
Your followers I will whisper to the business,
And will by twos and threes at several posterns°   *city gates*
Clear them o'th' city. For myself, I'll put
440   My fortunes to your service, which are here
By this discovery° lost. Be not uncertain,   *revelation*
For by the honour of my parents, I
Have uttered truth; which if you seek to prove,
I dare not stand by; nor shall you be safer
445   Than one condemnèd by the King's own mouth,
Thereon his execution sworn.
POLIXENES   I do believe thee,
I saw his heart in's face. Give me thy hand.
Be pilot to me, and thy places° shall   *your position*
Still neighbour° mine. My ships are ready, and   *Always be near*
450   My people did expect my hence departure
Two days ago. This jealousy
Is for a precious creature. As she's rare
Must it be great; and as his person's mighty
Must it be violent; and as he does conceive
455   He is dishonoured by a man which ever
Professed° to him, why, his revenges must   *Professed love*
In that be made more bitter. Fear o'ershades me.
Good expedition° be my friend and comfort   *Let speed (in leaving)*
The gracious Queen, part of his theme, but nothing
460   Of his ill-ta'en suspicion.[4] Come, Camillo,
I will respect thee as a father if
Thou bear'st my life off hence. Let us avoid.°   *be gone*

---

1. You may swear that his allegations are false.
2. Substances which, according to contemporary astrological theories, were emitted by stars and helped to shape human destiny.
3. Shall carry with you as a pledge (of my faith).
4. And make easier the situation of the virtuous queen, who is a part of Leontes' accusation, but who is not guilty of his unjustified suspicion.

CAMILLO It is in mine authority to command
The keys of all the posterns. Please your highness
465 To take the urgent hour.° Come, sir, away. *Exeunt* *seize the moment*

2.1

Enter HERMIONE, MAMILLIUS, [*and*] LADIES

HERMIONE Take the boy to you. He so troubles me
'Tis past enduring.
FIRST LADY   Come, my gracious lord,
Shall I be your play-fellow?
MAMILLIUS No, I'll none of you.
5 FIRST LADY Why, my sweet lord?
MAMILLIUS You'll kiss me hard, and speak to me as if
I were a baby still. [*To* SECOND LADY] I love you better.
SECOND LADY And why so, my lord?
MAMILLIUS   Not for because
Your brows° are blacker—yet black brows they say *eyebrows*
10 Become some women best, so that there be not
Too much hair there, but in a semicircle,
Or a half-moon made with a pen.
SECOND LADY   Who taught° 'this? *taught you*
MAMILLIUS I learned it out of women's faces. Pray now,
What colour are your eyebrows?
FIRST LADY   Blue, my lord.
15 MAMILLIUS Nay, that's a mock. I have seen a lady's nose
That has been blue,[1] but not her eyebrows.
FIRST LADY   Hark ye,
The Queen your mother rounds apace.° We shall *grows round quickly*
Present our services to a fine new prince
One of these days, and then you'd wanton° with us, *play*
If we would have you.
20 SECOND LADY   She is spread of late
Into a goodly bulk, good time encounter her.° *good fortune be with her*
HERMIONE What wisdom stirs amongst you? Come sir, now
I am for you again. Pray you sit by us,
And tell's a tale.
25 MAMILLIUS Merry or sad shall't be?
HERMIONE As merry as you will.
MAMILLIUS A sad tale's best for winter. I have one
Of sprites and goblins.
HERMIONE   Let's have that, good sir.
Come on, sit down, come on, and do your best
30 To fright me with your sprites. You're powerful at it.
MAMILLIUS There was a man—
HERMIONE   Nay, come sit down, then on.
MAMILLIUS [*sitting*] Dwelt by a churchyard.—I will tell it softly,
Yon crickets° shall not hear it. *(the other women)*
HERMIONE Come on then, and give't me in mine ear.
[*Enter apart* LEONTES, ANTIGONUS, *and* LORDS][2]

2.1 Location: Sicilia. The palace of Leontes.
1. It is unclear whether Mamillius is making a joke here or possibly referring to noses made "blue" by the cold or disfigured by venereal disease.
2. As with many scenes in this play, Ralph Crane, the scrivener who probably prepared the manuscript for the printer, massed all the entrances for 2.1 in the initial stage direction, regardless of when individual characters actually appeared on stage. Though it is clear that Leontes, Antigonus, and the other Lords enter only at 2.1.34, in F no entrance is marked for them here, and their names are included in the direction preceding 2.1.1.

35	LEONTES Was he met there? His train?° Camillo with him?	*retinue*
	A LORD Behind the tuft of pines I met them. Never	
	Saw I men scour° so on their way. I eyed them	*hurry*
	Even to their ships.	
	LEONTES How blest am I	
	In my just censure,° in my true opinion!	*judgment*
40	Alack, for lesser knowledge°—how accursed	*Would I knew less*
	In being so blest! There may be in the cup	
	A spider steeped, and one may drink, depart,	
	And yet partake no venom, for his knowledge	
	Is not infected;³ but if one present	
45	Th'abhorred ingredient to his eye, make known	
	How he hath drunk, he cracks his gorge,° his sides,	*throat*
	With violent hefts.° I have drunk, and seen the spider.	*retching*
	Camillo was his help in this, his pander.	
	There is a plot against my life, my crown.	
50	All's true that is mistrusted.° That false villain	*suspected*
	Whom I employed was pre-employed by him.	
	He has discovered° my design, and I	*revealed*
	Remain a pinched° thing, yea, a very trick	*tormented*
	For them to play at will. How came the posterns	
	So easily open?	
55	A LORD By his great authority,	
	Which often hath no less prevailed than so	
	On your command.	
	LEONTES I know't too well.	
	[*To* HERMIONE] Give me the boy. I am glad you did not nurse him.⁴	
	Though he does bear some signs of me, yet you	
	Have too much blood in him.	
60	HERMIONE What is this? Sport?	
	LEONTES [*to a* LORD] Bear the boy hence. He shall not come about her.	
	Away with him, and let her sport herself	
·	With that she's big with, [*to* HERMIONE] for 'tis Polixenes	
·	Has made thee swell thus. [*Exit one with* MAMILLIUS]	
	HERMIONE But I'd say he had not,	
65	And I'll be sworn you would believe my saying,	
	Howe'er you lean to th' nayward.°	*the contrary*
	LEONTES You, my lords,	
	Look on her, mark her well. Be but about	
	To say she is a goodly lady, and	
	The justice of your hearts will thereto add	
70	' 'Tis pity she's not honest,° honourable.'	*chaste*
	Praise her but for this her without-door° form—	*external*
	Which on my faith deserves high speech—and straight°	*immediately*
	The shrug, the 'hum' or 'ha', these petty brands°	*expressions; stigmas*
	That calumny° doth use—O, I am out,°	*slander / wrong*
75	That mercy does, for calumny will sear°	*stigmatize*
	Virtue itself⁵—these shrugs, these 'hum's' and 'ha's',	
	When you have said she's goodly, come between	
	Ere you can say she's honest. But be't known	

3. Alluding to the belief that a spider consumed with food or drink would be poisonous only if its presence were known to the consumer.
4. Women who breast-fed infants were believed to shape an infant's character by substances transmitted in their milk.
5. Leontes seems to mean that calumny (slander) will openly attack virtue, and since Hermione is not virtuous, it is not calumny to attack her. Rather, it is mercy who speaks in indirect "hum's" and "ha's" about her behavior.

From him that has most cause to grieve it should be,
She's an adultress.
80 HERMIONE   Should a villain say so,
The most replenished° villain in the world,   *complete*
He were as much more° villain. You, my lord,   *by so much more a*
Do but mistake.
    LEONTES   You have mistook,° my lady—   *erred; improperly taken*
Polixenes for Leontes. O, thou thing,
85 Which I'll not call a creature of thy place[6]
Lest barbarism,° making me the precedent,   *uncivilized rudeness*
Should a like° language use to all degrees,°   *the same / all ranks*
And mannerly distinguishment° leave out   *proper distinction*
Betwixt the prince and beggar. I have said
90 She's an adultress, I have said with whom.
More, she's a traitor, and Camillo is
A federary° with her, and one that knows   *confederate*
What she should shame to know herself,
But with her most vile principal:° that she's   *partner*
95 A bed-swerver,° even as bad as those   *adultress*
That vulgars give bold'st titles;[7] ay, and privy
To this their late° escape.   *recent*
HERMIONE   No, by my life,
Privy to none of this. How will this grieve you
When you shall come to clearer knowledge, that
100 You thus have published° me? Gentle my° lord,   *proclaimed / My noble*
You scarce can right me throughly° then to say   *fully do me justice*
You did mistake.
    LEONTES   No. If I mistake
In those foundations which I build upon,
The centre° is not big enough to bear   *earth*
105 A schoolboy's top.—Away with her to prison!
He who shall speak for her is afar-off° guilty,   *indirectly*
But that he speaks.°   *Merely for speaking*
HERMIONE   There's some ill planet reigns.
I must be patient till the heavens look
With an aspect more favourable.[8] Good my° lords,   *My good*
110 I am not prone to weeping, as our sex
Commonly are; the want of which vain dew
Perchance shall dry your pities. But I have
That honourable grief lodged here which burns
Worse than tears drown. Beseech you all, my lords,
115 With thoughts so qualified° as your charities   *tempered*
Shall best instruct you, measure me; and so
The King's will be performed.
LEONTES   Shall I be heard?
HERMIONE   Who is't that goes with me? Beseech your highness
My women may be with me, for you see
120 My plight requires it.—Do not weep, good fools,°   *dear ones*
There is no cause. When you shall know your mistress
Has deserved prison, then abound in tears
As I come out. This action I now go on

---

6. To whom I'll not give the title of your (high) social position.
7. That common people call by the coarsest names.

8. Another allusion to the belief that planets can have an evil effect or "aspect" when situated in certain positions.

Is for my better grace.[9]—Adieu, my lord.
125   I never wished to see you sorry; now
       I trust I shall. My women, come, you have leave.°   permission
LEONTES   Go, do our bidding. Hence!

             [*Exit* HERMIONE, *guarded, with* LADIES]

A LORD   Beseech your highness, call the Queen again.
ANTIGONUS [*to Leontes*]   Be certain what you do, sir, lest your justice
130   Prove violence, in the which three great ones suffer—
       Yourself, your queen, your son.
A LORD [*to* LEONTES]   For her, my lord,
       I dare my life lay down, and will do't, sir,
       Please you t'accept it, that the Queen is spotless
       I'th' eyes of heaven and to you—I mean
       In this which you accuse her.
135 ANTIGONUS [*to* LEONTES]   If it prove
       She's otherwise, I'll keep my stables where
       I lodge my wife,[1] I'll go in couples with her;[2]
       Than when I feel and see her, no farther trust her.
       For every inch of woman in the world,
140   Ay, every dram° of woman's flesh is false   smallest piece
       If she be.
LEONTES   Hold your peaces.
A LORD   Good my lord—
ANTIGONUS [*to* LEONTES]   It is for you we speak, not for ourselves.
       You are abused, and by some putter-on°   instigator
       That will be damned for't. Would I knew the villain—
145   I would land-damn him.[3] Be she honour-flawed—
       I have three daughters: the eldest is eleven;
       The second and the third nine and some five;
       If this prove true, they'll pay for't. By mine honour,
       I'll geld 'em all.[4] Fourteen they shall not see,
150   To bring false generations.° They are co-heirs,   illegitimate children
       And I had rather glib° myself than they   castrate
       Should not produce fair issue.°   legitimate offspring
LEONTES   Cease, no more!
       You smell this business with a sense as cold
       As is a dead man's nose. But I do see't and feel't
155   As you feel doing thus;[5] and see withal
       The instruments that feel.[6]
ANTIGONUS   If it be so,
       We need no grave to bury honesty;°   chastity
       There's not a grain of it the face to sweeten°   to sweeten the face
       Of the whole dungy° earth.   foul
LEONTES   What? Lack I credit?
160 A LORD   I had rather you did lack than I, my lord,
       Upon this ground;° and more it would content me   In this affair

---

9. This trial I am enduring is for my greater honor (when vindicated); *or* this suffering I am enduring is to refine and purge me, leading to greater virtue.
1. An obscure passage, meaning that he'll guard his wife's lodgings as vigilantly as he guards his horses *or* that he will treat his wife's lodgings as he does his stables, where mares are separated from stallions.
2. Have her tied to me (as hounds were leashed together for the hunt).
3. A term of abuse whose exact meaning is unclear. It

may be a dialect form of "lamback" or "lambaste," which means "thrash."
4. I'll make them all barren. Literally, I'll cut out their organs of generation.
5. Leontes here probably does some action (touching a courtier or rubbing his hands together) that shows the immediacy of his sensory reactions.
6. I see the fingers ("instruments") with which I touch things; I see the sinners, Hermione and Polixenes, who touch one another.

To have her honour true than your suspicion,
Be blamed for't how you might.

LEONTES   Why, what need we
Commune with you of this, but rather follow
165   Our forceful instigation?° Our prerogative   *Our own powerful impulse*
Calls not your counsels,[7] but our natural goodness
Imparts this;° which, if you—or° stupefied   *this information / either*
Or seeming so in skill°—cannot or will not   *cunningly*
Relish° a truth like us, inform yourselves   *Appreciate*
170   We need no more of your advice. The matter,
The loss, the gain, the ord'ring on't,° is all   *of it*
Properly ours.

ANTIGONUS   And I wish, my liege,
You had only in your silent judgement tried it
Without more overture.°   *public disclosure*

LEONTES   How could that be?
175   Either thou art most ignorant by age
Or thou wert born a fool. Camillo's flight
Added to their familiarity,
Which was as gross as ever touched conjecture
That lacked sight only, naught for approbation
180   But only seeing,[8] all other circumstances
Made up to th' deed°—doth push on this proceeding.[9]   *Pointed to the deed*
Yet for a greater confirmation—
For in an act of this importance 'twere
Most piteous to be wild°—I have dispatched in post°   *rash / haste*
185   To sacred Delphos,[1] to Apollo's temple,
Cleomenes and Dion, whom you know
Of stuffed sufficiency.° Now from the oracle   *ample competence*
They will bring all, whose spiritual counsel had°   *obtained*
Shall stop or spur me. Have I done well?

190   A LORD   Well done, my lord.

LEONTES   Though I am satisfied, and need no more
Than what I know, yet shall the oracle
Give rest to th' minds of others such as he,
Whose ignorant credulity will not
195   Come up to th' truth. So have we thought it good
From our free° person she should be confined,   *openly accessible*
Lest that the treachery of the two fled hence
Be left her to perform. Come, follow us.
We are to speak in public; for this business
Will raise° us all.   *rouse (to action)*

200   ANTIGONUS [*aside*]   To laughter, as I take it,
If the good truth were known.   *Exeunt*

2.2

Enter PAULINA, *a Gentleman* [*and attendants*]

PAULINA   The keeper of the prison, call to him.
Let him have knowledge who I am.   [*Exit Gentleman*]

7. My privileges as king do not require that I seek your advice.
8. As obvious ("gross") as any suspicion ("conjecture") ever was that only lacked eyewitnesses ("sight" and "seeing") to confirm its truth.
9. Does urge on this course of action.

1. Delos, often called Delphos by Renaissance writers, was the island where Apollo, the sun god, was supposedly buried. It is here conflated with Delphi, the Greek mainland town where the oracle of Apollo could be consulted.
2.2 Location: Sicilia. A prison.

Good lady,
No court in Europe is too good for thee.
What dost thou then in prison?
      [*Enter* JAILER *and Gentleman*]
                       Now, good sir,
You know me, do you not?

5 JAILER   For a worthy lady,
And one who much I honour.

PAULINA   Pray you then,
Conduct me to the Queen.

JAILER   I may not, madam. To the contrary
I have express commandment.

10 PAULINA   Here's ado,°   *Here's such a fuss*
To lock up honesty and honour from
Th'access of gentle° visitors. Is't lawful, pray you,   *noble; kind*
To see her women? Any of them? Emilia?

JAILER   So please you, madam,
15 To put apart these your attendants, I
Shall bring Emilia forth.

PAULINA   I pray now call her. —
Withdraw yourselves.   [*Exeunt Gentleman and attendants*]

JAILER   And, madam,
20 I must be present at your conference.

PAULINA   Well, be't so, prithee.   [*Exit* JAILER]
  Here's such ado, to make no stain a stain
As passes colouring.[1]
      [*Enter* JAILER *and* EMILIA]
              Dear gentlewoman,
How fares our gracious lady?

25 EMILIA   As well as one so great and so forlorn
May hold together. On° her frights and griefs,   *Because of*
Which never tender lady hath borne greater,
She is, something° before her time, delivered.   *somewhat*

PAULINA   A boy?

EMILIA   A daughter, and a goodly babe,
30 Lusty,° and like° to live. The Queen receives   *Vigorous / likely*
Much comfort in't; says, 'My poor prisoner,
I am innocent as you.'

PAULINA   I dare be sworn.
These dangerous, unsafe lunes° i'th' King, beshrew them!   *fits of lunacy*
He must be told on't, and he shall. The office°   *job*
35 Becomes a woman best. I'll take't upon me.
If I prove honey-mouthed, let my tongue blister,[2]
And never to my red-looked° anger be   *red-faced*
The trumpet[3] any more. Pray you, Emilia,
Commend° my best obedience to the Queen.   *Send*
40 If she dares trust me with her little babe
I'll show't the King, and undertake to be
Her advocate to th' loud'st. We do not know
How he may soften at the sight o'th' child.

---

1. To make from no stain at all a stain that exceeds what the art of dyeing can do; to make of no sin a sin that surpasses all attempts to justify it.
2. Alluding to the proverb that deceitfulness causes blisters on the tongue.

3. In early modern warfare, a "trumpet" was a soldier who, bearing a trumpet, went before the red-coated herald who carried messages, often angry ones, to the enemy camp.

The silence often of pure innocence
Persuades when speaking fails.

45 EMILIA   Most worthy madam,
Your honour and your goodness is so evident
That your free° undertaking cannot miss   *generous*
A thriving issue.⁴ There is no lady living
So meet° for this great errand. Please your ladyship   *suitable*
50 To visit the next room, I'll presently
Acquaint the Queen of your most noble offer,
Who but today hammered of° this design   *mused upon*
But durst not tempt a minister of honour⁵
Lest she should be denied.

PAULINA   Tell her, Emilia,
55 I'll use that tongue I have. If wit flow from't
As boldness from my bosom, let't not be doubted
I shall do good.

EMILIA   Now be you blest for it!
I'll to the Queen. Please you come something° nearer.   *somewhat*

JAILER   Madam, if't please the Queen to send the babe
60 I know not what° I shall incur to pass it,⁶   *what (risk)*
Having no warrant.

PAULINA   You need not fear it, sir.
This child was prisoner to the womb, and is
By law and process of great nature thence
Freed and enfranchised, not a party to
65 The anger of the King, nor guilty of—
If any be—the trespass of the Queen.

JAILER   I do believe it.

PAULINA   Do not you fear. Upon mine honour,
I will stand twixt you and danger.   *Exeunt*

2.3

Enter LEONTES

LEONTES   Nor° night nor day, no rest! It is but weakness   *Neither*
To bear the matter thus, mere weakness. If
The cause were not in being°—part o'th' cause,   *alive*
She, th'adultress; for the harlot° King   *lewd*
5 Is quite beyond mine arm, out of the blank°   *target*
And level° of my brain, plot-proof; but she   *aim*
I can hook to me. Say that she were gone,
Given to the fire,¹ a moiety° of my rest   *portion*
Might come to me again. Who's there?
[*Enter a* SERVANT]

SERVANT   My lord.

LEONTES   How does the boy?

10 SERVANT   He took good rest tonight.
'Tis hoped his sickness is discharged.

LEONTES   To see his nobleness!
Conceiving° the dishonour of his mother   *Realizing*
He straight° declined, drooped, took it deeply,   *immediately*
15 Fastened and fixed the shame on't° in himself;   *of it*

---

4. A successful outcome, with a pun on "issue" as "off-
spring."
5. But dared not risk asking a person of higher rank.

6. To let it pass (out of the prison).
2.3 Location: Sicilia. The palace of Leontes.
1. Burned at the stake (for treason against the king).

Threw off his spirit, his appetite, his sleep,
And downright languished. Leave me solely.° Go,   *alone*
See how he fares.   [*Exit* SERVANT]
          Fie, fie, no thought of him.°   *(Polixenes)*
The very thought of my revenges that way
20 Recoil upon me. In himself too mighty,
And in his parties,° his alliance.° Let him be   *supporters / allies*
Until a time may serve. For present vengeance,
Take it on her. Camillo and Polixenes
Laugh at me, make their pastime at my sorrow.
25 They should not laugh if I could reach them, nor
Shall she, within my power.
      Enter PAULINA [*carrying a babe, with* ANTIGONUS,
      LORDS, *and the* SERVANT, *trying to restrain her*]
A LORD   You must not enter.
PAULINA   Nay rather, good my lords, be second to me.°   *help me*
Fear you his tyrannous passion more, alas,
Than the Queen's life?—a gracious, innocent soul,
More free° than he is jealous.   *innocent*
30 ANTIGONUS   That's enough.
SERVANT   Madam, he hath not slept tonight, commanded
None should come at him.
PAULINA   Not so hot, good sir.
I come to bring him sleep. 'Tis such as you,
That creep like shadows by him, and do sigh
35 At each his needless heavings, such as you
Nourish the cause of his awaking.° I   *wakefulness*
Do come with words as medicinal as true,
Honest as either, to purge him of that humour°   *mental disorder*
That presses him from sleep.
LEONTES   What noise there, ho?
40 PAULINA   No noise, my lord, but needful conference
About some gossips[2] for your highness.
LEONTES   How?
Away with that audacious lady! Antigonus,
I charged thee that she should not come about me.
I knew she would.
ANTIGONUS   I told her so, my lord,
45 On your displeasure's peril° and on mine,   *At the risk of your anger*
She should not visit you.
LEONTES   What, canst not rule her?
PAULINA   From all dishonesty he can. In this,
Unless he take the course that you have done—
Commit° me for committing honour—trust it,   *Imprison*
He shall not rule me.
50 ANTIGONUS   La you now, you hear.
When she will take the rein I let her run,
But she'll not stumble.
PAULINA [*to* LEONTES]   Good my liege, I come—
And I beeseech you hear me, who professes
Myself your loyal servant, your physician,
55 Your most obedient counsellor; yet that dares
Less appear so in comforting° your evils   *condoning*

2. Godparents or sponsors at a child's baptism.

Than such as most seem yours[3] —I say, I come
From your good queen.
LEONTES   Good queen?

60 PAULINA   Good queen, my lord, good queen, I say good queen,
And would by combat make her good,[4] so were I
A man, the worst about° you.   *lowest in rank of*
LEONTES *[to LORDS]*   Force her hence.
PAULINA   Let him that makes but trifles of his eyes
First hand° me. On mine own accord, I'll off.   *touch*
65 But first I'll do my errand. The good Queen—
For she is good—hath brought you forth a daughter—
Here 'tis—commends it to your blessing.
            [She lays down the babe]
LEONTES   Out!
A mankind° witch! Hence with her, out o'door—   *manlike*
A most intelligencing bawd.°   *spying go-between*
PAULINA   Not so.
70 I am as ignorant in that as you
In so entitling me,° and no less honest   *In calling me that*
Than you are mad, which is enough, I'll warrant,
As this world goes, to pass for honest.
LEONTES *[to LORDS]*   Traitors,
Will you not push her out?
[To ANTIGONUS]   Give her the bastard.
75 Thou dotard, thou art woman-tired,[5] unroosted
By thy Dame Partlet here.[6] Take up the bastard,
Take't up, I say. Give't to thy crone.°   *old woman*
PAULINA *[to ANTIGONUS]*   For ever
Unvenerable° be thy hands if thou   *Unworthy of respect*
Tak'st up the princess by that forcèd baseness[7]
Which he has put upon't.
80 LEONTES   He dreads° his wife.   *fears*
PAULINA   So I would you did. Then 'twere past all doubt
You'd call your children yours.
LEONTES   A nest of traitors.
ANTIGONUS   I am none, by this good light.
PAULINA   Nor I, nor any
But one that's here, and that's himself, for he
85 The sacred honour of himself, his queen's,
His hopeful son's, his babe's, betrays to slander,
Whose sting is sharper than the sword's; and will not—
For as the case now stands, it is a curse
He cannot be compelled to't—once remove
90 The root of his opinion, which is rotten
As ever oak or stone was sound.
LEONTES *[to LORDS]*   A callat°   *scold; harlot*
Of boundless tongue, who late° hath beat her husband,   *recently*
And now baits° me! This brat is none of mine.   *provokes*
It is the issue° of Polixenes.   *offspring*

3. Than those who (wrongly) seem most loyal.
4. Prove her to be innocent. Alluding to the chivalric tri-
als by combat in which knights would establish inno-
cence or guilt by means of duels.
5. You are pecked at by women. A metaphor from fal-

conry.
6. Expelled from your "roost" or "perch," the position of
domestic authority assigned to men. In medieval tales,
"Partlett" is a traditional name for a hen.
7. Under that wrongful name of bastard.

95 Hence with it, and together with the dam
Commit them to the fire.
PAULINA   It is yours,
And might we lay th'old proverb to your charge,°   *apply the proverb to you*
So like you 'tis the worse. Behold, my lords,
Although the print° be little, the whole matter   *copy*
100 And copy of the father: eye, nose, lip,
The trick° of's frown, his forehead, nay, the valley,[8]   *distinctive character*
The pretty dimples of his chin and cheek, his smiles,
The very mould and frame of hand, nail, finger.
And thou good goddess Nature, which hast made it
105 So like to him that got° it, if thou hast   *begot*
The ordering of the mind too, 'mongst all colours
No yellow[9] in't, lest she suspect, as he does,
Her children not her husband's.
—▷ LEONTES [*to* ANTIGONUS]   A gross hag!—
And lozel,° thou art worthy to be hanged,   *scoundrel*
That wilt not stay her tongue.
110 ANTIGONUS   Hang all the husbands
That cannot do that feat, you'll leave yourself
Hardly one subject.
LEONTES   Once more, take her hence.
PAULINA   A most unworthy and unnatural lord
Can do no more.
LEONTES   I'll ha' thee burnt.
PAULINA   I care not.
115 It is an heretic that makes the fire,
Not she which burns in't.[1] I'll not call you tyrant;
But this most cruel usage of your queen—
Not able to produce more accusation
Than your own weak-hinged fancy—something savours
120 Of tyranny, and will ignoble make you,
Yea, scandalous to the world.
LEONTES [*to* ANTIGONUS]   On your allegiance,
Out of the chamber with her! Were I a tyrant,
Where were her life? She durst not call me so
If she did know me one. Away with her!
125 PAULINA   I pray you do not push me, I'll be gone.
Look to your babe, my lord; 'tis yours. Jove°   *(King of the gods)*
A better guiding spirit. What needs these hands?[2]
You that are thus so tender o'er° his follies   *gentle with*
Will never do him good, not one of you.
130 So, so. Farewell, we are gone.   *Exit*
LEONTES [*to* ANTIGONUS]   Thou, traitor, hast set on thy wife to this.
My child? Away with't! Even thou, that hast
A heart so tender o'er it, take it hence
And see it instantly consumed with fire.
135 Even thou, and none but thou. Take it up straight.°   *at once*
Within this hour bring me word 'tis done,
And by good testimony,° or I'll seize thy life,   *with good evidence*

---

8. Referring to an indentation in the lip or a cleft in the chin.
9. Proverbially, the color of jealousy.
1. The heretic is the one who unjustly makes the fire

(Leontes), not the woman who burns in it (Hermione).
2. Why is it necessary for you to push me out? (spoken to Leontes' attendant lords).

With what thou else call'st thine. If thou refuse
And wilt encounter with my wrath, say so.
140 The bastard brains with these my proper° hands   *own*
Shall I dash out. Go, take it to the fire;
For thou set'st on thy wife.
ANTIGONUS   I did not, sir.
These lords, my noble fellows, if they please
Can clear me in't.
LORDS   We can. My royal liege,
145 He is not guilty of her coming hither.
LEONTES   You're liars all.
A LORD   Beseech your highness, give us better credit.°   *think us more honorable*
We have always truly served you, and beseech
So to esteem of us. And on our knees we beg,
150 As recompense of our dear services
Past and to come, that you do change this purpose
Which, being so horrible, so bloody, must
Lead on to some foul issue. We all kneel.
LEONTES   I am a feather for each wind that blows.
155 Shall I live on, to see this bastard kneel
And call me father? Better burn it now
Than curse it then. But be it. Let it live.
It shall not neither.
[*To* ANTIGONUS]   You, sir, come you hither,
You that have been so tenderly officious
160 With Lady Margery[3] your midwife there,
To save this bastard's life—for 'tis a bastard,
So sure as this beard's grey. What will you adventure°   *risk*
To save this brat's life?
ANTIGONUS   Anything, my lord,
That my ability may undergo,
165 And nobleness impose. At least thus much,
I'll pawn the little blood which I have left[4]
To save the innocent; anything possible.
LEONTES   It shall be possible. Swear by this sword
Thou wilt perform my bidding.
ANTIGONUS   I will, my lord.
170 LEONTES   Mark, and perform it. Seest thou? For the fail°   *failure*
Of any point in't shall not only be
Death to thyself but to thy lewd-tongued wife,
Whom for this time we pardon. We enjoin thee,
As thou art liegeman° to us, that thou carry   *loyal servant*
175 This female bastard hence, and that thou bear it
To some remote and desert place, quite out
Of our dominions; and that there thou leave it,
Without more mercy, to it° own protection   *its*
And favour of the climate. As by strange fortune[5]
180 It came to us, I do in justice charge thee,
On thy soul's peril and thy body's torture,
That thou commend it strangely to some place[6]
Where chance may nurse° or end it. Take it up.   *nurture; help*

3. A contemptuous name (like "Dame Partlett") for a dis-
orderly woman. "Margery-prater" is a slang term for
"hen."
4. Aging was thought to reduce the amount of blood in
the body.
5. Since by some unusual chance; since by the act of a
foreigner (Polixenes).
6. That you take it to some foreign land.

ANTIGONUS   I swear to do this, though a present death
185   Had been more merciful. Come on, poor babe,
Some powerful spirit instruct the kites° and ravens   *birds of prey*
To be thy nurses. Wolves and bears, they say,
Casting their savageness aside, have done
Like° offices of pity. Sir, be prosperous   *Similar*
190   In more than this deed does require;[7] [*to the babe*] and blessing
Against° this cruelty, fight on thy side,   *To counteract*
Poor thing, condemned to loss.°   *Exit [with the babe]*   *ruin*
LEONTES   No, I'll not rear
Another's issue.
          Enter a SERVANT
SERVANT   Please your highness, posts°   *messengers*
From those you sent to th'oracle are come
195   An hour since. Cleomenes and Dion,
Being well arrived from Delphos, are both landed,
Hasting to th' court.
A LORD [*to* LEONTES]   So please you, sir, their speed
Hath been beyond account.°   *without precedent*
LEONTES   Twenty-three days
They have been absent. 'Tis good speed, foretells
200   The great Apollo suddenly° will have   *at once*
The truth of this appear. Prepare you, lords.
Summon a session,° that we may arraign   *trial*
Our most disloyal lady; for as she hath
Been publicly accused, so shall she have
205   A just and open trial. While she lives
My heart will be a burden to me. Leave me,
And think upon my bidding.   *Exeunt [severally]°*   *separately*

3.1

          Enter CLEOMENES *and* DION
CLEOMENES   The climate's delicate, the air most sweet;
Fertile the isle,[1] the temple much surpassing
The common praise it bears.
DION   I shall report,
For most it caught° me, the celestial habits—°   *charmed / garments*
5   Methinks I so should term them—and the reverence
Of the grave wearers. O, the sacrifice—
How ceremonious, solemn, and unearthly
It was i'th' off'ring!
CLEOMENES   But of all, the burst°   *blast (of thunder)*
And the ear-deaf'ning voice o'th' oracle,
10   Kin to Jove's thunder, so surprised my sense
That I was nothing.
DION   If th'event° o'th' journey   *outcome*
Prove as successful to the Queen—O, be't so!—
As it hath been to us rare, pleasant, speedy,
The time is worth the use on't.[2]
CLEOMENES   Great Apollo

---

7. To a greater extent or in more ways than this action
deserves.
3.1 Location: A road in Sicilia.
1. The island of Delphos, Apollo's birthplace, here con-
flated with Delphi, where Apollo's oracle was located. See
note to 2.1.185.
2. The time will have been well spent.

15 Turn all to th' best! These proclamations,
So forcing faults upon Hermione,
I little like.
DION   The violent carriage of it[3]
Will clear or end the business. When the oracle,
Thus by Apollo's great divine° sealed up,   *priest*
20 Shall the contents discover,° something rare   *reveal*
Even then will rush to knowledge. Go. Fresh horses!
And gracious be the issue.°   *Exeunt*   *result; the child*

3.2

Enter LEONTES, LORDS, [*and*] OFFICERS
LEONTES   This sessions, to our great grief we pronounce,
Even pushes 'gainst our heart: the party tried
The daughter of a king, our wife, and one
Of us° too much beloved. Let us be cleared   *By us*
5 Of being tyrannous since we so openly
Proceed in justice, which shall have due course
Even to the guilt or the purgation.°   *acquittal*
Produce the prisoner.
OFFICER   It is his highness' pleasure
That the Queen appear in person here in court.
[*Enter* HERMIONE *guarded, with* PAULINA *and Ladies*]
10 Silence.[1]
LEONTES   Read the indictment.
OFFICER [*reads*]   Hermione, queen to the worthy Leontes, King
of Sicilia, thou art here accused and arraigned of high treason
in committing adultery with Polixenes, King of Bohemia, and
15 conspiring with Camillo to take away the life of our sovereign
lord the King, thy royal husband; the pretence° whereof being   *purpose*
by circumstances partly laid open, thou, Hermione, contrary to
the faith and allegiance of a true subject, didst counsel and aid
them for their better safety to fly away by night.
20 HERMIONE   Since what I am to say must be but° that   *only*
Which contradicts my accusation, and
The testimony on my part no other
But what comes from myself, it shall scarce boot° me   *profit*
To say 'Not guilty'. Mine integrity
25 Being counted falsehood shall, as I express it,
Be so received. But thus: if powers divine
Behold our human actions—as they do—
I doubt not then but innocence shall make
False accusation blush, and tyranny
30 Tremble at patience. You, my lord, best know—
Who least will seem to do so—my past life
Hath been as continent, as chaste, as true
As I am now unhappy; which° is more   *which unhappiness*
Than history can pattern,[2] though devised
35 And played to take° spectators. For behold me,   *captivate*
A fellow of the royal bed, which owe°   *who owns*
A moiety° of the throne; a great king's daughter,   *A portion*

---

3. The rash way in which it is being carried out.
3.2 Location: Sicilia. A court of justice.
1. In F the word "Silence" is printed in italics and set as
a stage direction. Here it is treated as an imperative and

assigned to the Officer who announces the Queen's
entrance.
2. Than story or drama can show a precedent for.

The mother to a hopeful prince, here standing
To prate and talk for life and honour, fore°   *before*
40 Who please to come and hear. For° life, I prize° it   *As for / value*
As I weigh° grief, which I would spare.° For honour,   *value / do without*
'Tis a derivative³ from me to mine,°   *(my children)*
And only that I stand° for. I appeal   *fight*
To your own conscience, sir, before Polixenes
45 Came to your court how I was in your grace,
How merited to be so; since he came,
With what encounter so uncurrent° I   *conduct so unacceptable*
Have strained° t'appear thus.° If one jot beyond   *transgressed / (on trial)*
The bound of honour, or in act or will
50 That way inclining, hardened be the hearts
Of all that hear me, and my near'st of kin
Cry 'Fie' upon my grave.
LEONTES   I ne'er heard yet
That any of these bolder vices wanted
Less° impudence to gainsay° what they did   *Were more lacking in / deny*
Than to perform it first.
55 HERMIONE   That's true enough,
Though 'tis a saying, sir, not due° to me.   *relevant*
LEONTES You will not own it.
HERMIONE   More than mistress of
Which comes to me in name of fault, I must not
At all acknowledge.⁴ For Polixenes,
60 With whom I am accused, I do confess
I loved him as in honour he required;°   *was his due*
With such a kind of love as might become
A lady like me; with a love, even such,
So, and no other, as yourself commanded;
65 Which not to have done I think had been in me
Both disobedience and ingratitude
To you and toward your friend, whose love had spoke
Even since it could speak, from an infant, freely
That it was yours. Now for conspiracy,
70 I know not how it tastes, though it be dished°   *served*
For me to try how. All I know of it
Is that Camillo was an honest man;
And why he left your court, the gods themselves,
Wotting° no more than I, are ignorant.   *If they know*
75 LEONTES You knew of his departure, as you know
What you have underta'en to do in's absence.
HERMIONE Sir,
You speak a language that I understand not.
My life stands in the level of your dreams,⁵
Which I'll lay down.
80 LEONTES   Your actions are my 'dreams'.
You had a bastard by Polixenes,
And I but° dreamed it. As you were past all shame—   *merely*
Those of your fact° are so—so past all truth;   *(guilty) of your crime*

---

3. Something handed on.
4. I must not answer for ("acknowledge") more than
those faults that I actually possess (am "mistress of"). Her-
mione is denying she possesses the "bolder vices" of

which Leontes accuses her in line 53.
5. As the target ("level") of your delusions. A metaphor
from archery.

Which to deny concerns more than avails;[6] for as
85 Thy brat hath been cast out, like to itself,°   *as it should be*
No father owning it—which is indeed
More criminal in thee than it—so thou
Shalt feel our justice, in whose easiest passage
Look for no less than death.[7]

HERMIONE   Sir, spare your threats.
90 The bug° which you would fright me with, I seek.   *horrible object*
To me can life be no commodity.°   *profit; comfort*
The crown and comfort of my life, your favour,
I do give° lost, for I do feel it gone   *reckon*
But know not how it went. My second joy,°   *(Mamillius)*
95 And first fruits of my body, from his presence
I am barred, like one infectious. My third comfort,
Starred most unluckily,[8] is from my breast,
The innocent milk in it° most innocent mouth,   *its*
Haled° out to murder; myself on every post[9]   *Dragged*
100 Proclaimed a strumpet, with immodest° hatred   *excessive*
The childbed privilege[1] denied, which 'longs°   *belongs*
To women of all fashion;° lastly, hurried   *ranks*
Here, to this place, i'th' open air,[2] before
I have got strength of limit.[3] Now, my liege,
105 Tell me what blessings I have here alive,
That I should fear to die. Therefore proceed.
But yet hear this—mistake me not—no life,
I prize it not a straw; but for mine honour,
Which I would free:° if I shall be condemned   *vindicate*
110 Upon surmises, all proofs sleeping else°   *except*
But what your jealousies awake, I tell you
'Tis rigour, and not law.[4] Your honours all,
I do refer me° to the oracle.   *appeal*
Apollo be my judge.
A LORD   This your request
115 Is altogether just. Therefore bring forth,
And in Apollo's name, his oracle.   *[Exeunt certain Officers]*
HERMIONE   The Emperor of Russia[5] was my father.
O that he were alive, and here beholding
His daughter's trial; that he did but see
120 The flatness° of my misery—yet with eyes   *boundlessness*
Of pity, not revenge.
            [Enter OFFICERS with CLEOMENES and DION]
OFFICER   You here shall swear upon this sword of justice
That you, Cleomenes and Dion, have
Been both at Delphos, and from thence have brought
125 This sealed-up oracle, by the hand delivered

---

6. Your denial of the truth costs you more effort than it's worth.
7. In the mildest course of justice, you can expect death. The implication is that death may well be preceded by torture.
8. Born under most unlucky stars.
9. Alluding to the early modern practice of nailing proclamations to posts in public places.
1. The right to enjoy a period of bedrest and seclusion after childbirth.
2. Exposure to air outside the domestic space was consid-

ered unsafe for women weakened by childbirth.
3. Before I have the strength that follows the customary period of confinement.
4. Playing on the expression "the rigor of the law," Hermione implies that judgment against her would be mere tyranny ("rigor") and not law.
5. Possibly a reference to the legendary Tsar Ivan the Terrible, who died in 1584. Many London merchants were interested in trade with Russia, especially after the formation of the Muscovy Company in 1553.

Of great Apollo's priest; and that since then
You have not dared to break the holy seal,
Nor read the secrets in't.
CLEOMENES *and* DION   All this we swear.
130 LEONTES   Break up the seals, and read.
OFFICER [*reads*]   Hermione is chaste, Polixenes blameless, Ca-
   millo a true subject, Leontes a jealous tyrant, his innocent babe
   truly begotten, and the King shall live without an heir if that
   which is lost be not found.
LORDS   Now blessèd be the great Apollo!
135 HERMIONE   Praised!
LEONTES   Hast thou read truth?
OFFICER   Ay, my lord, even so as it is here set down.
LEONTES   There is no truth at all i'th' oracle.
   The sessions shall proceed. This is mere falsehood.
        [*Enter a* SERVANT]
SERVANT   My lord the King! The King!
140 LEONTES   What is the business?
SERVANT   O sir, I shall be hated to report it.
   The prince your son, with mere conceit° and fear   thought
   Of the Queen's speed,° is gone.   fortune
LEONTES   How, 'gone'?
SERVANT   Is dead.
LEONTES   Apollo's angry, and the heavens themselves
   Do strike at my injustice.
        [HERMIONE *falls to the ground*]
145   How now there?
PAULINA   This news is mortal to the Queen. Look down
   And see what death is doing.
LEONTES   Take her hence.
   Her heart is but o'ercharged.° She will recover.   overburdened (by emotion)
   I have too much believed mine own suspicion.
150 Beseech you, tenderly apply to her
   Some remedies for life.
        [*Exeunt* PAULINA *and Ladies, carrying* HERMIONE]
                  Apollo, pardon
   My great profaneness 'gainst thine oracle.
   I'll reconcile me to Polixenes,
   New woo my queen, recall the good Camillo,
155 Whom I proclaim a man of truth, of mercy;
   For being transported by my jealousies
   To bloody thoughts and to revenge, I chose
   Camillo for the minister to poison
   My friend Polixenes, which had° been done,   would have
160 But that the good mind of Camillo tardied°   delayed
   My swift command. Though I with death and with
   Reward did threaten and encourage him,
   Not doing it, and being done,[6] he, most humane
   And filled with honour, to my kingly guest
165 Unclasped my practice,° quit his fortunes here—   Revealed my plot
   Which you knew great—and to the certain hazard
   Of all incertainties himself commended,°   consigned himself

6. That is, "Though I threatened him with death if he did not do it and encouraged him with the promise of reward
if he did do it."

No richer than his honour.[7] How he glisters
Through my rust![8] And how his piety
Does my deeds make the blacker!
    [*Enter* PAULINA]

170 PAULINA   Woe the while!
O cut my lace,[9] lest my heart, cracking it,
Break too.
A LORD   What fit is this, good lady?
PAULINA [*to* LEONTES]   What studied° torments, tyrant, hast for me?   *expertly devised*
What wheels, racks, fires? What flaying, boiling
175 In leads or oils?[1] What old or newer torture
Must I receive, whose every word deserves
To taste of thy most worst? Thy tyranny,
Together working with thy jealousies—
Fancies too weak for boys, too green and idle°   *immature and foolish*
180 For girls of nine—O think what they have done,
And then run mad indeed, stark mad, for all
Thy bygone fooleries were but spices° of it.   *slight tastes*
That thou betrayed'st Polixenes, 'twas nothing.
That did but show thee, of° a fool, inconstant,   *for*
185 And damnable° ingrateful. Nor was't much   *damnably; cursedly*
Thou wouldst have poisoned good Camillo's honour
To have him kill a king—poor° trespasses,   *minor*
More monstrous standing by,[2] whereof I reckon
The casting forth to crows thy baby daughter
190 To be or° none or little, though a devil   *either*
Would have shed water out of fire ere done't.[3]
Nor is't directly laid to thee the death
Of the young prince, whose honourable thoughts—
Thoughts high for one so tender°—cleft the heart   *young*
195 That could conceive a gross° and foolish sire   *stupid*
Blemished his gracious dam.° This is not, no,   *mother*
Laid to thy answer.[4] But the last—O lords,
When I have said,° cry woe! The Queen, the Queen,   *finished speaking*
The sweet'st, dear'st creature's dead, and vengeance for't
Not dropped down yet.
200 A LORD   The higher powers forbid!
PAULINA   I say she's dead. I'll swear't. If word nor oath
Prevail not, go and see. If you can bring
Tincture° or lustre in her lip, her eye,   *Color*
Heat outwardly or breath within, I'll serve you
205 As I would do the gods. But O thou tyrant,
Do not repent these things, for they are heavier
Than all thy woes° can stir.° Therefore betake thee   *grief / remove*
To nothing but despair. A thousand knees,
Ten thousand years together, naked, fasting,
210 Upon a barren mountain, and still° winter   *always*

---

7. Possessing no fortune but his honor.
8. How he shines ("glisters") in comparison with my rust. The image alludes to polished and rusty armor.
9. It was believed that fainting might be prevented by cutting the stays on the tight bodices characteristic of female dress in this period.
1. A list of early modern forms of torture. The wheel was a device to which a person was tied and his or her limbs broken, usually by beating. The rack typically consisted of a frame with a roller at each end; a person was attached to this frame and his or her limbs stretched by turning the rollers. To "flay" was to strip off someone's skin while he or she was still alive.
2. In comparison with more monstrous ones near at hand.
3. A devil would have shed tears from his fiery eyes (or from hellfires) before he had done it.
4. Presented as a charge you must answer.

In storm perpetual, could not move the gods
To look that way thou wert.°   *in your direction*
LEONTES   Go on, go on.
  Thou canst not speak too much. I have deserved
  All tongues to talk their bitt'rest.
A LORD [*to* PAULINA]   Say no more.
215 Howe'er the business goes, you have made fault
  I'th' boldness of your speech.
PAULINA   I am sorry for't.
  All faults I make, when I shall come to know them
  I do repent. Alas, I have showed too much
  The rashness of a woman. He is touched
220 To th' noble heart. What's gone and what's past help
  Should be past grief.
  [*To* LEONTES]   Do not receive affliction
  At my petition.° I beseech you, rather   *Because of my injunction*
  Let me be punished, that have minded° you   *reminded*
  Of what you should forget. Now, good my liege,
225 Sir, royal sir, forgive a foolish woman.
  The love I bore your queen—lo, fool again!
  I'll speak of her no more, nor of your children.
  I'll not remember you of my own lord,
  Who is lost too. Take your patience to you,°   *Be patient*
  And I'll say nothing.
230 LEONTES   Thou didst speak but well
  When most the truth, which I receive much better
  Than to be pitied of° thee. Prithee bring me   *by*
  To the dead bodies of my queen and son.
  One grave shall be for both. Upon them shall
235 The causes of their death appear, unto
  Our shame perpetual. Once a day I'll visit
  The chapel where they lie, and tears shed there
  Shall be my recreation.[5] So long as nature°   *my bodily being*
  Will bear up with this exercise, so long
240 I daily vow to use it. Come, and lead me
  To these sorrows.   *Exeunt*

3.3

Enter ANTIGONUS, [*carrying the*] *babe*, [*with*] *a* MARINER
ANTIGONUS Thou art perfect° then our ship hath touched upon   *certain*
  The deserts of Bohemia?
MARINER   Ay, my lord, and fear
  We have landed in ill time. The skies look grimly
  And threaten present blusters.° In my conscience,°   *impending storms / opinion*
5 The heavens with that we have in hand are angry,
  And frown upon's.
ANTIGONUS Their sacred wills be done. Go get aboard.
  Look to thy barque.° I'll not be long before   *ship*
  I call upon thee.
MARINER   Make your best haste, and go not
10 Too far i'th' land. 'Tis like to be loud° weather.   *stormy*

---

5. My only diversion; my spiritual renewal or re-creation.
3.3 Location: Bohemia. The seacoast. This play, as does
Greene's *Pandosto*, credits Bohemia with a coast. Only

for two brief periods in the late Middle Ages may Bohe-
mia have controlled a small piece of territory on the Adri-
atic Sea, but it was otherwise landlocked.

Besides, this place is famous for the creatures
Of prey that keep° upon't.   *live*

ANTIGONUS   Go thou away.
I'll follow instantly.
MARINER   I am glad at heart
To be so rid o'th' business.   *Exit*
ANTIGONUS   Come, poor babe.
15   I have heard, but not believed, the spirits o'th' dead
May walk again. If such thing be, thy mother
Appeared to me last night, for ne'er was dream
So like a waking. To me comes a creature,
Sometimes her head on one side, some another.
20   I never saw a vessel° of like sorrow,   *person; receptacle*
So filled and so becoming.[1] In pure white robes
Like very sanctity she did approach
My cabin where I lay, thrice bowed before me,
And, gasping to begin some speech, her eyes
25   Became two spouts. The fury spent, anon°   *soon*
Did this break from her: 'Good Antigonus,
Since fate, against thy better disposition,
Hath made thy person for the thrower-out
Of my poor babe according to thine oath,
30   Places remote enough are in Bohemia.
There weep, and leave it crying; and for° the babe   *because*
Is counted lost for ever, Perdita[2]
I prithee call't. For this ungentle° business   *unkind; ignoble*
Put on thee by my lord, thou ne'er shalt see
35   Thy wife Paulina more.' And so with shrieks
She melted into air. Affrighted much,
I did in time collect myself, and thought
This was so, and no slumber. Dreams are toys,°   *trifles*
Yet for this once, yea superstitiously,
40   I will be squared° by this. I do believe   *ruled*
Hermione hath suffered death, and that
Apollo would—this being indeed the issue°   *child*
Of King Polixenes—it should here be laid,
Either for life or death, upon the earth
45   Of its right father. Blossom, speed° thee well!   *fare*
       [*He lays down the babe and a scroll*]
There lie, and there thy character.[3]
       [*He lays down a box*]
                    There these,[4]
Which may, if fortune please, both breed thee, pretty,
And still rest thine.[5]
       [*Thunder*]
              The storm begins. Poor wretch,
That for thy mother's fault art thus exposed
50   To loss and what may follow! Weep I cannot,
But my heart bleeds, and most accursed am I
To be by oath enjoined to this. Farewell.

---

1. So filled with sorrow and so beautiful.
2. Latin for "lost one."
3. The written account of your history and parentage.
4. The gold and jewels with which the Old Shepherd grows rich and which are later used to identify the Prin-

cess.
5. Which may, if you are lucky, be sufficient to pay for your upbringing, pretty child, and still leave you with something besides.

The day frowns more and more. Thou'rt like to have
A lullaby too rough. I never saw
55 The heavens so dim by day. A savage clamour!
Well may I get aboard. This is the chase.°   *hunt*
I am gone for ever!   *Exit, pursued by a bear*[6]
        [*Enter an* OLD SHEPHERD]

OLD SHEPHERD I would there were no age between ten and
three-and-twenty, or that youth would sleep out the rest; for
60 there is nothing in the between but getting wenches with child,
wronging the ancientry,° stealing, fighting—hark you now,   *elderly people*
would any but these boiled-brains° of nineteen and two-and-   *lunatics*
twenty hunt this weather? They have scared away two of my
best sheep, which I fear the wolf will sooner find than the mas-
65 ter. If anywhere I have them, 'tis by the seaside, browsing of°   *on*
ivy. Good luck, an't° be thy will!   *if it*
        [*He sees the babe*]
What have we here? Mercy on's, a bairn!° A very pretty bairn. *child*
A boy or a child,° I wonder? A pretty one, a very pretty one. *girl*
Sure some scape.[7] Though I am not bookish,° yet I can read   *not familiar with books*
70 'waiting-gentlewoman' in the scape. This has been some stair-
work, some trunk-work, some behind-door-work.[8] They were
warmer that got° this than the poor thing is here. I'll take it up *begot*
for pity; yet I'll tarry till my son come. He hallooed but even
now. Whoa-ho-hoa!
        Enter CLOWN°   *Bumpkin*
75 CLOWN Hilloa, loa!

OLD SHEPHERD What, art so near? If thou'lt see a thing to talk
on° when thou art dead and rotten, come hither. What ail'st   *about*
thou, man?

CLOWN I have seen two such sights, by sea and by land! But I
80 am not to say it is a sea, for it is now the sky. Betwixt the fir-
mament and it you cannot thrust a bodkin's° point.   *needle's*

OLD SHEPHERD Why, boy, how is it?

CLOWN I would you did but see how it chafes, how it rages, how
it takes up the shore. But that's not to the point. O, the most
85 piteous cry of the poor souls! Sometimes to see 'em, and not to
see 'em; now the ship boring° the moon with her mainmast,   *piercing*
and anon swallowed with yeast° and froth, as you'd thrust a cork *foam*
into a hogshead.° And then for the land-service,[9] to see how the *cask of liquor*
bear tore out his shoulder-bone, how he cried to me for help,
90 and said his name was Antigonus, a nobleman! But to make an
end of the ship—to see how the sea flap-dragoned it![1] But first,
how the poor souls roared, and the sea mocked them, and how

---

6. One of the most famous stage directions in English drama. A real bear, rather than a man in a bear suit, might have been used in this scene, perhaps discreetly led on a rope by the fleeing Antigonus. There were reports of tame bears in Shakespeare's London, and bearbaiting (setting dogs on chained bears) was a popular Elizabethan sport, sometimes occurring in the same amphitheaters used at other times for stage plays. It is more likely, however, that the bear was impersonated by an actor in a bear costume. Modern productions vary significantly in their representation of the bear. Some strive for realism, having a bearskin-clad actor or a mechanical likeness of a bear pass across a darkened stage illuminated only by the occasional lightning bolt. Others productions are more styl-
ized, suggesting a bear by the obvious artifice of a mask or symbol.
7. Sexual transgression. English ballads and other popular literature of the period offer numerous accounts of female servants who abandon or kill children born out of wedlock.
8. Some secret sexual affair conducted on back stairs, in chests, or behind doors.
9. Punning on the military and culinary meanings of "service" to suggest both "combat on land" and "food to be served up on land."
1. Devoured it as if it were a flapdragon, a raisin floating on flaming brandy.

the poor gentleman roared, and the bear mocked him, both
roaring louder than the sea or weather.

95 OLD SHEPHERD Name of mercy, when was this, boy?

CLOWN Now, now. I have not winked° since I saw these sights.   *blinked an eye*
The men are not yet cold under water, nor the bear half dined
on the gentleman. He's at it now.

OLD SHEPHERD Would I had been by to have helped the old
100 man!

CLOWN I would you had been by the ship side, to have helped
her. There your charity would have lacked footing.[2]

OLD SHEPHERD Heavy° matters, heavy matters. But look thee   *Sad*
here, boy. Now bless thyself. Thou metst with things dying, I
105 with things new-born. Here's a sight for thee. Look thee, a bear-
ing-cloth[3] for a squire's child.
[*He points to the box*]
Look thee here, take up, take up, boy. Open't. So, let's see. It
was told me I should be rich by the fairies. This is some
changeling.[4] Open't. What's within, boy?

110 CLOWN [*opening the box*] You're a made° old man. If the sins of   *prosperous*
your youth are forgiven you, you're well to live.° Gold, all gold!   *well off; virtuous*

OLD SHEPHERD This is fairy gold,[5] boy, and 'twill prove so. Up
with't, keep it close.° Home, home, the next° way. We are   *secret / nearest*
lucky, boy, and to be so still° requires nothing but secrecy. Let   *always*
115 my sheep go. Come, good boy, the next way home.

CLOWN Go you the next way with your findings. I'll go see if the
bear be gone from the gentleman, and how much he hath
eaten. They are never curst° but when they are hungry. If there   *vicious*
be any of him left, I'll bury it.

120 OLD SHEPHERD That's a good deed. If thou mayst discern by that
which is left of him what he is,° fetch me to th' sight of him.   *his identity or rank*

CLOWN Marry[6] will I; and you shall help to put him i'th' ground.

OLD SHEPHERD 'Tis a lucky day, boy, and we'll do good deeds
on't.   *Exeunt*

4.1

Enter TIME,[1] *the Chorus*

TIME I that please some, try° all; both joy and terror   *test*
Of good and bad; that makes and unfolds error,
Now take upon me in the name° of Time   *with the authority*
To use my wings. Impute it not a crime
5 To me or my swift passage that I slide
O'er sixteen years and leave the growth untried°   *development unexamined*
Of that wide gap, since it is in my power
To o'erthrow law, and in one self-born° hour   *self-same*
To plant and o'erwhelm° custom. Let me pass   *establish and overthrow*
10 The same I am ere ancient'st order was

---

2. There you would not have had a secure place to stand,
with a pun on "footing" as meaning "a foundation" (upon
which a charity might be founded).
3. The blanket used to wrap an infant in preparation for
baptism. A squire's child, being of a fairly high social posi-
tion, would have a rich bearing-cloth.
4. A child secretly substituted for another by fairies. The
term could apply to the abducted child (usually beautiful)
or to the one (often ugly or deformed) left in its place.
5. Riches left by fairies were unreliable. If not kept secret,
they brought bad luck.

6. A mild oath derived from the name of the Virgin
Mary.
4.1 Location: Scene continues.
1. In early modern texts, Time was conventionally repre-
sented as an old bald man with wings, signifying how
swiftly time passes. He often carried an hourglass and a
scythe, symbol of the power of time to destroy life. A com-
mon saying was that Time was the revealer of Truth, or
that Truth was the daughter of Time. Robert Greene's
Pandosto, Shakespeare's chief source for *The Winter's
Tale*, was subtitled *The Triumph of Time*.

Or what is now received.[2] I witness to
The times that brought them in; so shall I do
To th' freshest things now reigning, and make stale
The glistering° of this present as my tale   *glittering shine*
15 Now seems to it.[3] Your patience this allowing,
I turn my glass,° and give my scene such growing   *hourglass*
As° you had slept between. Leontes leaving   *As if*
Th'effects of his fond° jealousies, so grieving   *foolish*
That he shuts up himself, imagine me,
20 Gentle spectators, that I now may be
In fair Bohemia, and remember well
I mentionèd a son o'th' King's, which Florizel
I now name to you; and with speed so pace°   *proceed*
To speak of Perdita, now grown in grace
25 Equal with wond'ring.[4] What of her ensues
I list not° prophesy, but let Time's news   *do not wish to*
Be known when 'tis brought forth. A shepherd's daughter
And what to her adheres,° which follows after,   *pertains*
Is th'argument° of Time. Of this allow,   *subject matter*
30 If ever you have spent time worse ere now.
If never, yet that Time himself doth say
He wishes earnestly you never may.   *Exit*

4.2

Enter POLIXENES *and* CAMILLO

POLIXENES   I pray thee, good Camillo, be no more importunate.
'Tis a sickness denying° thee anything, a death to grant this.   *to deny*
CAMILLO   It is sixteen[1] years since I saw my country. Though I
have for the most part been aired abroad,° I desire to lay my   *breathed foreign air*
5 bones there. Besides, the penitent King, my master, hath sent
for me, to whose feeling° sorrows I might be some allay°—or I   *deeply felt / relief*
o'erween° to think so—which is another spur to my departure.   *am bold enough*
POLIXENES   As thou lov'st me, Camillo, wipe not out the rest of
thy services by leaving me now. The need I have of thee thine
10 own goodness hath made. Better not to have had thee than thus
to want° thee. Thou, having made me businesses[2] which none   *be without*
without thee can sufficiently manage, must either stay to exe-
cute them thyself or take away with thee the very services thou
hast done; which if I have not enough considered°—as too   *rewarded*
15 much I cannot—to be more thankful to thee shall be my study,
and my profit therein, the heaping friendships.[3] Of that fatal° *deadly*
country Sicilia, prithee speak no more, whose very naming
punishes me with the remembrance of that penitent—as thou
callest him—and reconciled King my brother, whose loss of his
20 most precious queen and children are even now to be afresh°   *newly*
lamented. Say to me, when sawest thou the Prince Florizel,
my son? Kings are no less unhappy, their issue° not being gra-   *children*
cious,° than they are in losing them when they have ap-   *not proving virtuous*
proved° their virtues.   *demonstrated*

---

2. Let me remain as I have been from before the begin-
nings of civilization even to the time of present customs.
3. As my tale now seems stale in comparison with the
present.
4. Now grown so gracious as to inspire admiration.
4.2 Location: Bohemia. The palace of Polixenes.

1. F reads "fifteene." At 4.1.6 Time says that sixteen years
have passed. This apparent error may be due to care-
lessness on Shakespeare's part or to a misreading of a
Roman numeral by a compositor or scribe.
2. Performed services for me.
3. The accumulation of your kindnesses.

25 CAMILLO   Sir, it is three days since I saw the Prince. What his
happier affairs may be are to me unknown; but I have missingly
noted° he is of late much retired from court, and is less fre-   *noted by his absence*
quent to° his princely exercises than formerly he hath   *less often engaged in*
appeared.
30 POLIXENES   I have considered so much, Camillo, and with some
care, so far that I have eyes under my service° which look upon   *spies in my employ*
his removedness,° from whom I have this intelligence: that he   *retirement (from court)*
is seldom from the house of a most homely° shepherd, a man,   *simple*
they say, that from very nothing, and beyond the imagination
35 of his neighbours, is grown into an unspeakable estate.°   *untold wealth*
CAMILLO   I have heard, sir, of such a man, who hath a daughter
of most rare note.° The report of her is extended more than can   *quality*
be thought to begin° from such a cottage.   *originate*
POLIXENES   That's likewise part of my intelligence; but, I fear,
40 the angle° that plucks our son thither. Thou shalt accompany   *fish hook*
us to the place, where we will, not appearing what we are, have
some question with the shepherd; from whose simplicity I
think it not uneasy° to get the cause of my son's resort thither.   *difficult*
Prithee, be my present partner in this business, and lay aside
45 the thoughts of Sicilia.
CAMILLO   I willingly obey your command.
POLIXENES   My best Camillo! We must disguise ourselves.
                                                              Exeunt

4.3

Enter AUTOLYCUS *singing*

AUTOLYCUS
     When daffodils begin to peer,
          With heigh, the doxy° over the dale,   *beggar's wench*
     Why then comes in the sweet° o'the year,   *sweetest part*
          For the red blood reigns in the winter's pale.°   *skin made pale by winter*

5   The white sheet bleaching on the hedge,[1]
          With heigh, the sweet birds, O how they sing!
     Doth set my pugging° tooth on edge,   *thieving*
          For a quart of ale is a dish for a king.

     The lark, that tirra-lirra chants,
10   With heigh, with heigh, the thrush and the jay,
     Are summer songs for me and my aunts[2]
          While we lie tumbling in the hay.

     I have served Prince Florizel, and in my time wore three-pile,[3]
     but now I am out of service.

15   But shall I go mourn for that, my dear?
                    The pale moon shines by night,
               And when I wander here and there
                    I then do most go right.

               If tinkers[4] may have leave° to live,   *permission*
20   And bear the sow-skin budget,[5]

4.3 Location: Bohemia. Near the cottage where the Old
Shepherd, the Clown, and Perdita live.
1. It was common practice to set clothes out to dry on
hedges.
2. Another slang term for women who take beggars or
vagabonds for lovers.

3. A rich velvet cloth with a thick nap or "pile."
4. Menders of metal pots and kettles. The term was also
applied to itinerant beggars and thieves.
5. Pigskin bag. Bag in which a tinker carried his tools;
hence, a sign of his trade.

Then my account I well may give,
And in the stocks avouch it.°   *acknowledge (my crime)*
My traffic° is sheets. When the kite builds, look to lesser linen.[6]   *trade*
My father named me Autolycus,[7] who being, as I am, littered
25 under Mercury,[8] was likewise a snapper-up of unconsidered
trifles. With die and drab° I purchased this caparison, and my   *dice and whores*
revenue is the silly cheat.[9] Gallows and knock° are too powerful   *beatings*
on the highway.[1] Beating and hanging are terrors to me. For°   *As for*
the life to come, I sleep out the thought of it. A prize, a prize!
     Enter CLOWN
30 CLOWN   Let me see. Every 'leven wether tods,[2] every tod yields
pound and odd° shilling. Fifteen hundred shorn, what comes   *one*
the wool to?
AUTOLYCUS [*aside*]   If the springe° hold, the cock's[3] mine.   *trap*
CLOWN   I cannot do't without counters.[4] Let me see, what am I
35 to buy for our sheep-shearing feast?[5] Three pound of sugar, five
pound of currants, rice—what will this sister of mine do with
rice? But my father hath made her mistress of the feast, and she
lays it on. She hath made me four-and-twenty nosegays for the
shearers— three-man-song-men,[6] all, and very good ones—but
40 they are most of them means° and basses, but one Puritan   *tenors*
amongst them, and he sings psalms to hornpipes.[7] I must have
saffron to colour the warden° pies; mace; dates, none—that's   *winter pear*
out of my note;° nutmegs, seven; a race° or two of ginger—but   *not on my list / root*
that I may beg; four pound of prunes, and as many of raisins
45 o'th' sun.°   *sun-dried*
AUTOLYCUS   [*grovelling on the ground*] O, that ever I was born!
CLOWN   I'th' name of me!
AUTOLYCUS   O help me, help me! Pluck but off these rags, and
then death, death!
50 CLOWN   Alack, poor soul, thou hast need of more rags to lay on
thee rather than have these off.
AUTOLYCUS   O sir, the loathsomeness of them offend me more
than the stripes° I have received, which are mighty ones and   *blows*
millions.
55 CLOWN   Alas, poor man, a million of beating may come to a
great matter.[8]
AUTOLYCUS   I am robbed, sir, and beaten; my money and apparel
ta'en from me, and these detestable things put upon me.
CLOWN   What, by a horseman, or a footman?°   *man on foot*
60 AUTOLYCUS   A footman, sweet sir, a footman.
CLOWN   Indeed, he should be a footman, by the garments he has
left with thee. If this be a horseman's coat it hath seen very hot

6. The kite, a small bird of prey, supposedly stole small pieces of linen to make its nest. Autolycus steals sheets, larger pieces of linen.
7. In classical myth a crafty thief and grandfather of Ulysses; Autolycus's own father, Mercury, was the god of thieves.
8. Fathered by Mercury; born when the planet Mercury was ascendant.
9. I was reduced to wearing this garb, and my income derives from petty swindles.
1. Autolycus fears the penalties meted out to highwaymen. He would rather be a petty thief.
2. Every eleven rams will yield 28 pounds (a "tod") of wool. The Clown and his father could expect to earn a substantial amount of money (almost 150 pounds) for

their wool.
3. Woodcock, a bird easily caught and hence proverbial for its stupidity.
4. Disks used in calculating sums.
5. In rural England a traditional summer event in which people of different ranks took part in feasting and revelry.
6. Men who sing three-part songs.
7. Shrill-sounding musical instruments often played at country dances and hardly appropriate to accompany the singing of psalms. Shakespeare may here be satirizing Puritans, who were notorious for their opposition to music and dancing.
8. A million blows can be a serious affair, with a pun on "matter" as "pus," the sign of an infection caused by open wounds.

service. Lend me thy hand, I'll help thee. Come, lend me thy
hand.
    [*He helps* AUTOLYCUS *up*]
65 AUTOLYCUS O, good sir, tenderly. O!
CLOWN Alas, poor soul!
AUTOLYCUS O, good sir, softly,° good sir! I fear, sir, my shoulder-   *gently*
blade is out.
CLOWN How now? Canst stand?
70 AUTOLYCUS Softly, dear sir. Good sir, softly.
    [*He picks the* CLOWN'*s pocket*][9]
You ha' done me a charitable office.°   *service*
CLOWN [*reaching for his purse*] Dost lack any money? I have a
little money for thee.
AUTOLYCUS No, good sweet sir, no, I beseech you, sir.[1] I have a
75 kinsman not past three-quarters of a mile hence, unto whom I
was going. I shall there have money, or anything I want. Offer
me no money, I pray you. That kills° my heart.   *touches*
CLOWN What manner of fellow was he that robbed you?
AUTOLYCUS A fellow, sir, that I have known to go about with
80 troll-madams.° I knew him once a servant of the Prince. I can-   *whores*
not tell, good sir, for which of his virtues it was, but he was
certainly whipped out of the court.
CLOWN His vices, you would say. There's no virtue whipped out
of the court. They cherish it to make it stay there; and yet it
85 will no more but abide.°   *stay there only briefly*
AUTOLYCUS Vices, I would say, sir. I know this man well. He
hath been since an ape-bearer,[2] then a process-server— a bai-
liff—then he compassed a motion° of the Prodigal Son,[3] and   *devised a puppet show*
married a tinker's wife within a mile where my land and living°   *property*
90 lies, and having flown over many knavish professions, he settled
only in rogue. Some call him Autolycus.
CLOWN Out upon him! Prig,° for my life, prig! He haunts   *Thief*
wakes,° fairs, and bear-baitings.   *festivals*
AUTOLYCUS Very true, sir. He, sir, he. That's the rogue that put
95 me into this apparel.
CLOWN Not a more cowardly rogue in all Bohemia. If you had
but looked big and spit at him, he'd have run.
AUTOLYCUS I must confess to you, sir, I am no fighter. I am false
of heart° that way, and that he knew, I warrant him.   *without courage*
100 CLOWN How do you now?
AUTOLYCUS Sweet sir, much better than I was. I can stand, and
walk. I will even take my leave of you, and pace softly towards
my kinsman's.
CLOWN Shall I bring thee° on the way?   *escort you*
105 AUTOLYCUS No, good-faced sir, no, sweet sir.
CLOWN Then fare thee well. I must go buy spices for our sheep-
shearing.
AUTOLYCUS Prosper you, sweet sir.   *Exit* [*the* CLOWN]

---

9. It is uncertain when Autolycus actually picks the
Clown's pocket, but it adds to the humor if Autolycus's
next line, "You ha' done me a charitable office," can refer
both to the kindness the Clown has knowingly shown
Autolycus *and* to the kindness the Clown has unwittingly
done him in making available a purse for the wily rogue
to steal.
1. Autolycus does not want the Clown to find out he has

picked his pocket and so left him with no money. He may
here restrain the Clown from putting his hand into his
pocket.
2. One who carried about a trained monkey.
3. Alluding to the New Testament story of a spendthrift
son who squandered his money only to be forgiven by his
father.

Your purse is not hot° enough to purchase your spice. I'll be   *full*
110 with you at your sheep-shearing, too. If I make not this cheat°   *deception*
bring out° another, and the shearers prove sheep, let me be   *lead to*
unrolled[4] and my name put in the book of virtue.
[*Sings*]   Jog on, jog on, the footpath way,
          And merrily hent° the stile[5]-a.   *grab (to leap over)*
115   A merry heart goes all the day,
        Your sad tires in a mile-a.   *Exit*

4.4

Enter FLORIZEL [*dressed as Doricles a countryman*],
[*and*] PERDITA [*as Queen of the Feast*][1]

FLORIZEL   These your unusual weeds° to each part of you   *garments*
Does give a life; no shepherdess, but Flora°   *goddess of flowers*
Peering in April's front.[2] This your sheep-shearing
Is as a meeting of the petty gods,
And you the queen on't.°   *of it*
5 PERDITA   Sir, my gracious lord,
To chide at your extremes° it not becomes me—   *extravagances*
O, pardon that I name them! Your high self,
The gracious mark o'th' land,[3] you have obscured
With a swain's wearing,° and me, poor lowly maid,   *shepherd's costume*
10 Most goddess-like pranked up.° But that our feasts   *adorned*
In every mess[4] have folly, and the feeders°   *those who eat*
Digest it with a custom,[5] I should blush
To see you so attired; swoon, I think,
To show myself a glass.°   *mirror*
FLORIZEL   I bless the time
15 When my good falcon made her flight across
Thy father's ground.
PERDITA   Now Jove afford you cause!
To me the difference° forges dread; your greatness   *(in rank)*
Hath not been used to fear. Even now I tremble
To think your father by some accident
20 Should pass this way, as you did. O, the fates!
How would he look to see his work,° so noble,   *offspring; writings*
Vilely bound up?[6] What would he say? Or how
Should I, in these my borrowed flaunts,° behold   *rich garments*
The sternness of his presence?
FLORIZEL   Apprehend
25 Nothing but jollity. The gods themselves,
Humbling their deities to love, have taken
The shapes of beasts upon them. Jupiter
Became a bull, and bellowed; the green Neptune
A ram, and bleated; and the fire-robed god,
30 Golden Apollo, a poor humble swain,

---

4. Let my name be taken off the list (of thieves and vaga-
bonds).
5. Steps by which people pass over a fence or hedge.
4.4 Location: Bohemia. In front of the cottage where the
Old Shepherd, the Clown, and Perdita live.
1. Again, F lists in the initial stage direction all the major
characters who appear in this very long scene. Florizel
and Perdita seem, however, to have a private conversation
before the Old Shepherd, Polixenes, and others enter to

them at line 54.
2. Peeping out in early April.
3. The one whose graces make him admired by all.
4. A group of four served at table together. See note to
1.2.227.
5. Tolerate it because they have grown used to it.
6. Outfitted in such an inferior way. A bookbinding met-
aphor.

As I seem now.[7] Their transformations
Were never for a piece° of beauty rarer,   *person*
Nor in a way so chaste,[8] since my desires
Run not before mine honour, nor my lusts
Burn hotter than my faith.

35 PERDITA   O, but sir,
Your resolution cannot hold when 'tis
Opposed, as it must be, by th' power of the King.
One of these two must be necessities,
Which then will speak that you must change this purpose,
Or I my life.[9]

40 FLORIZEL   Thou dearest Perdita,
With these forced° thoughts I prithee darken not   *unnatural; farfetched*
The mirth o'th' feast. Or° I'll be thine, my fair,   *Either*
Or not my father's. For I cannot be
Mine own, nor anything to any, if
45 I be not thine. To this I am most constant,
Though destiny say no. Be merry, gentle;
Strangle such thoughts as these with anything
That you behold the while. Your guests are coming.
Lift up your countenance as° it were the day   *as if*
50 Of celebration of that nuptial which
We two have sworn shall come.

PERDITA   O Lady Fortune,[1]
Stand you auspicious!

FLORIZEL   See, your guests approach.
Address° yourself to entertain them sprightly,   *Prepare*
And let's be red with mirth.

> [*Enter the* OLD SHEPHERD, *with* POLIXENES *and* CA-
> MILLO, *disguised, the* CLOWN, MOPSA, DORCAS, *and*
> *others*]

55 OLD SHEPHERD [*to* PERDITA]   Fie, daughter, when my old wife lived, upon
This day she was both pantler,° butler, cook,   *pantry maid*
Both dame° and servant, welcomed all, served all,   *mistress of the house*
Would sing her song and dance her turn, now here
At upper end o'th' table, now i'th' middle,
60 On his° shoulder, and his,° her face afire   *one person's / another's*
With labour, and the thing she took to quench it
She would to each one sip. You are retired
As if you were a feasted one and not
The hostess of the meeting. Pray you bid
65 These unknown friends to's welcome, for it is
A way to make us better friends, more known.
Come, quench your blushes, and present yourself
That which you are, mistress o'th' feast. Come on,
And bid us welcome to your sheep-shearing,
As your good flock shall prosper.

70 PERDITA [*to* POLIXENES]   Sir, welcome.
It is my father's will I should take on me

---

7. In classical myth, Jupiter transformed himself into a
bull and abducted Europa; Neptune took on the shape of
a ram to carry off Theopane; and the sun god Apollo dis-
guised himself as a shepherd to court Alcestis.
8. Nor ever conducted with so chaste a purpose.

9. One of two things will become necessary: either you
must change your plans or I must change my life (that is,
risk death).
1. In classical myth, a woman of fickle disposition whose
favors cannot be relied upon.

The hostess-ship o'th' day.
[*To* CAMILLO] You're welcome, sir.
Give me those flowers there, Dorcas. Reverend sirs,
For you there's rosemary and rue. These keep°   *retain*
75 Seeming° and savour° all the winter long.   *Color / scent*
Grace and remembrance[2] be to you both,
And welcome to our shearing.
POLIXENES   Shepherdess,
A fair one are you. Well you fit our ages
With flowers of winter.
PERDITA   Sir, the year growing ancient,
80 Not yet on summer's death, nor on the birth
Of trembling winter, the fairest flowers o'th' season
Are our carnations and streaked gillyvors,[3]
Which some call nature's bastards. Of that kind
Our rustic garden's barren, and I care not
To get slips of them.
85 POLIXENES   Wherefore, gentle maiden,
Do you neglect them?
PERDITA   For I have heard it said
There is an art[4] which in their piedness° shares   *streaked color*
With great creating nature.
POLIXENES   Say there be,
Yet nature is made better by no mean°   *means*
90 But nature makes that mean. So over that art
Which you say adds to nature is an art
That nature makes. You see, sweet maid, we marry
A gentler scion to the wildest stock,
And make conceive a bark of baser kind
95 By bud of nobler race.[5] This is an art
Which does mend nature—change it rather; but
The art itself is nature.
PERDITA   So it is.
POLIXENES Then make your garden rich in gillyvors,
And do not call them bastards.
PERDITA   I'll not put
100 The dibble° in earth to set° one slip of them,   *trowel / plant*
No more than, were I painted,° I would wish   *wearing cosmetics*
This youth should say 'twere well, and only therefore
Desire to breed by me. Here's flowers for you:
Hot[6] lavender, mints, savory, marjoram,
105 The marigold, that goes to bed wi'th' sun,
And with him rises, weeping.[7] These are flowers
Of middle summer, and I think they are given
To men of middle age. You're very welcome.
[*She gives them flowers*]

---

2. Grace ("repentance") and remembrance are qualities associated with rue and rosemary, respectively.
3. Gillyflowers or multicolored carnations. Their variations in color were thought to result from cross-breeding with other flowers, which may be why Perdita calls them "nature's bastards." They were proverbially associated with sexual license.
4. The art of cross-breeding or grafting.
5. We unite a cutting from a highly cultivated plant to the stem of a lesser one and cause the lesser plant to bring

forth a highly cultivated flower, with puns on "gentler scion," "wildest stock," "baser kind," and "nobler race" to suggest a successful union between a high-born heir and a member of the lower social orders.
6. Herbs were divided into "hot" and "cold" varieties based on their supposed temperatures.
7. The marigold, sometimes called "the spouse of the sun," supposedly closed at sunset and opened, filled with dew, in the morning when the sun came up.

CAMILLO   I should leave grazing were I of your flock,
  And only live by gazing.
110 PERDITA   Out, alas,
  You'd be so lean that blasts of January
  Would blow you through and through.
  [*To* FLORIZEL]   .   Now, my fair'st friend,
  I would I had some flowers o'th' spring that might
  Become your time of day; [*to* MOPSA *and* DORCAS] and yours, and yours,
115   That wear upon your virgin branches yet
  Your maidenheads growing. O Proserpina,[8]
  For the flowers now that, frighted, thou letst fall
  From Dis's wagon!° — daffodils,   *chariot*
  That come before the swallow dares, and take°   *charm*
120   The winds of March with beauty; violets, dim,°   *with hanging head*
  But sweeter than the lids of Juno's eyes
  Or Cytherea's breath;[9] pale primroses,
  That die unmarried ere they can behold
  Bright Phoebus° in his strength — a malady   *the sun god*
125   Most incident to maids;[1] bold oxlips, and
  The crown imperial;[2] lilies of all kinds,
  The flower-de-luce[3] being one. O, these I lack,
  To make you garlands of, and my sweet friend,
  To strew him o'er and o'er.
FLORIZEL   What, like a corpse?
130 PERDITA   No, like a bank, for love to lie and play on,
  Not like a corpse — or if, not to be buried,
  But quick° and in mine arms. Come, take your flowers.   *living*
  Methinks I play as I have seen them do
  In Whitsun pastorals.[4] Sure this robe of mine
  Does change my disposition.
135 FLORIZEL   What you do
  Still° betters what is done. When you speak, sweet,   *Always*
  I'd have you do it ever; when you sing,
  I'd have you buy and sell so, so give alms,
  Pray so; and for the ord'ring° your affairs,   *arranging for*
140   To sing them too. When you do dance, I wish you
  A wave o'th' sea, that you might ever do
  Nothing but that, move still, still so,
  And own° no other function. Each your doing,°   *have / Each thing you do*
  So singular° in each particular,   *distinctive*
145   Crowns what you are doing in the present deeds,
  That all your acts are queens.
PERDITA   O Doricles,[5]
  Your praises are too large. But that your youth
  And the true blood which peeps so fairly through't

---

8. In Ovid's *Metamorphoses* Proserpina, the daughter of Ceres, is abducted by Dis, or Pluto, as she gathers flowers and is taken in his chariot ("wagon") to his underworld kingdom.
9. Juno was queen of the gods; "Cytherea" was another name for Venus, the goddess of love.
1. Alluding to the superstition that women who died of a kind of anemia known as green sickness would be transformed into primroses. Green sickness was especially associated with young virginal women; vigorous sexual

activity was sometimes advocated as a cure.
2. A lily first imported into England from Turkey in the late sixteenth century.
3. Fleur-de-lis, the national flower of France.
4. English rural festivities traditionally held at Whitsuntide, a religious feast day occurring in the spring, seven weeks after Easter. The festivities, often organized under a festival king and queen, included morris dances and Robin Hood plays.
5. The name Florizel has assumed.

Do plainly give you out an unstained shepherd,
150 With wisdom I might fear, my Doricles,
You wooed me the false way.

FLORIZEL   I think you have
As little skill° to fear as I have purpose   *reason*
To put you to't. But come, our dance, I pray;
Your hand, my Perdita. So turtles[6] pair,
That never mean to part.

155 PERDITA   I'll swear for 'em.

POLIXENES [*to* CAMILLO]   This is the prettiest low-born lass that ever
Ran on the greensward.° Nothing she does or seems   *grassy turf*
But smacks of something greater than herself,
Too noble for this place.

CAMILLO   He tells her something
160 That makes her blood look out.° Good sooth, she is   *makes her blush*
The queen of curds and cream.[7]

CLOWN   Come on, strike up!

DORCAS   Mopsa must be your mistress. Marry, garlic to mend
her kissing with![8]

MOPSA   Now, in good time!

165 CLOWN   Not a word, a word, we stand upon our manners. Come,
strike up!

[*Music.*] *Here a dance of shepherds and shepherdesses*

POLIXENES   Pray, good shepherd, what fair swain is this
Which dances with your daughter?

OLD SHEPHERD   They call him Doricles, and boasts himself°   *he boasts*
170 To have a worthy feeding;° but I have it   *good pasture land*
Upon his own report, and I believe it.
He looks like sooth.° He says he loves my daughter.   *appears to be honest*
I think so, too, for never gazed the moon
Upon the water as he'll stand and read,
175 As 'twere, my daughter's eyes; and to be plain,
I think there is not half a kiss to choose
Who loves another° best.   *the other*

POLIXENES   She dances featly.°   *nimbly*

OLD SHEPHERD   So she does anything, though I report it
That° should be silent. If young Doricles   *Who*
180 Do light upon her, she shall bring him that
Which he not dreams of.

Enter [a] SERVANT

SERVANT   O, master, if you did but hear the pedlar at the door,
you would never dance again after a tabor and pipe.[9] No, the
bagpipe could not move you. He sings several° tunes faster than   *different*
185 you'll tell° money. He utters them as he had eaten ballads,[1]   *count*
and all men's ears grew° to his tunes.   *listened intently*

CLOWN   He could never come better.° He shall come in. I love   *at a better time*
a ballad but even too well, if it be doleful matter merrily set
down, or a very pleasant thing indeed, and sung lamentably.

190 SERVANT   He hath songs for man or woman, of all sizes. No milli-
ner[2] can so fit his customers with gloves. He has the prettiest

6. Turtledoves, which proverbially mate for life.
7. Referring perhaps to a cream custard known as "white
pot." In some May games a woman was chosen as queen
of white-pot cream.
8. To make her breath sweet (said ironically).
9. A small drum and fife used for morris dancing.

1. Alluding to the broadside ballads which were sung and
sold by peddlers who traveled throughout the country.
2. One who sells fashionable articles of clothing such as
hats and gloves. Originally, the word meant one who sells
items imported from Milan.

love songs for maids, so without bawdry, which is strange, with
such delicate burdens° of dildos and fadings, 'Jump her, and   *refrains*
thump her';[3] and where some stretch-mouthed° rascal would,   *obscene*
195 as it were, mean mischief and break a foul gap into the matter,[4]
he makes the maid to answer, 'Whoop, do me no harm, good
man'; puts him off, slights him, with 'Whoop, do me no harm,
good man!'

POLIXENES This is a brave° fellow.   *fine*

200 CLOWN Believe me, thou talkest of an admirable conceited° fel-   *very witty*
low. Has he any unbraided° wares?   *new; not shopworn*

SERVANT He hath ribbons of all the colours i'th' rainbow; points[5]
more than all the lawyers in Bohemia can learnedly handle,
though they come to him by th' gross; inkles, caddises, cam-
205 brics, lawns[6] — why, he sings 'em over as they were gods or god-
desses. You would think a smock° were a she-angel, he so   *a woman's undergarment*
chants to the sleeve-hand° and the work about the square on't.[7]   *wristband*

CLOWN Prithee bring him in, and let him approach singing.

PERDITA Forewarn him that he use no scurrilous words in's
210 tunes.   [*Exit* SERVANT]

CLOWN You have of these° pedlars that have more in them than   *There are some*
you'd think, sister.

PERDITA Ay, good brother, or go about° to think.   *intend*

Enter AUTOLYCUS [*wearing a false beard, carrying his*
pack, and] *singing*

AUTOLYCUS Lawn as white as driven snow,
215   Cypress[8] black as e'er was crow,
         Gloves as sweet° as damask roses,   *perfumed*
         Masks for faces, and for noses;[9]
         Bugle-bracelet,[1] necklace amber,
         Perfume for a lady's chamber;
220   Golden coifs,° and stomachers[2]   *caps*
         For my lads to give their dears;
         Pins and poking-sticks of steel,[3]
         What maids lack from head to heel
         Come buy of me, come, come buy, come buy,
225   Buy, lads, or else your lasses cry. Come buy!

CLOWN If I were not in love with Mopsa thou shouldst take no
money of me, but being enthralled as I am, it will also be the
bondage of certain ribbons and gloves.[4]

MOPSA I was promised them against° the feast, but they come   *in time for*
230 not too late now.

DORCAS He hath promised you more than that,[5] or there be
liars.

---

3. Though the servant claims the songs are without
bawdiness, the refrains are in fact full of sexual puns
which the servant may not understand. "Dildos" are arti-
ficial penises; "fadings" can mean "orgasms"; and "jump
her and thump her" denotes sexual relations with a
woman.
4. Would interrupt the song with an indecent insertion.
5. Laces for fastening garments, with a pun on "points"
as meaning "legal arguments."
6. "Inkles" were linen tapes; "caddises" were worsted
tapes used for garters; "cambrics" and "lawns" were heavy
and sheer linens.
7. The stitching about the yoke of the garment.
8. A crepe material imported from Cyprus and used for

mourning clothes.
9. Many upper-class English women wore masks to pro-
tect their skin from exposure to the sun. Some women's
noses were eaten away by syphilis, and masks would also
cover this deformity.
1. A bracelet of shiny black beads.
2. Embroidered bodices for dresses.
3. Metal rods used to iron the ruffs or stiff collars worn by
both men and women. The term is also slang for "penis."
4. Because I am the prisoner of love, certain ribbons and
gloves must also be put in bondage (bound up in a
parcel).
5. (Perhaps he has promised marriage.)

MOPSA He hath paid° you all he promised you. Maybe he has   *given; had sex with*
    paid you more, which will shame you to give him again.[6]
235 CLOWN Is there no manners left among maids? Will they wear
    their plackets where they should bear their faces?[7] Is there not
    milking-time, when you are going to bed, or kiln-hole,° to whis-   *fireplace*
    tle of these secrets, but you must be tittle-tattling before all our
    guests? 'Tis well they are whispering. Clammer your tongues,[8]
240   and not a word more.
MOPSA I have done. Come, you promised me a tawdry-lace[9] and
    a pair of sweet gloves.
CLOWN Have I not told thee how I was cozened by the way,°   *cheated on the road*
    and lost all my money?
245 AUTOLYCUS And indeed, sir, there are cozeners abroad, therefore
    it behoves men to be wary.
CLOWN Fear not thou, man, thou shalt lose nothing here.
AUTOLYCUS I hope so, sir, for I have about me many parcels of
    charge.°   *valuable goods*
250 CLOWN What hast here? Ballads?
MOPSA Pray now, buy some. I love a ballad in print, alife,° for   *on my life*
    then we are sure they are true.
AUTOLYCUS Here's one to a very doleful tune, how a usurer's
    wife was brought to bed of twenty money-bags at a burden,° and   *in one childbirth*
255   how she longed to eat adders' heads and toads carbonadoed.°   *cut and grilled*
MOPSA Is it true, think you?
AUTOLYCUS Very true, and but a month old.
DORCAS Bless me from marrying a usurer!
AUTOLYCUS Here's the midwife's name to't, one Mistress Tail-
260   Porter,[1] and five or six honest° wives' that were present. Why   *truthful; chaste*
    should I carry lies abroad?
MOPSA [*to* CLOWN] Pray you now, buy it.
CLOWN Come on, lay it by, and let's first see more ballads. We'll
    buy the other things anon.
265 AUTOLYCUS Here's another ballad, of a fish that appeared upon
    the coast on Wednesday the fourscore° of April, forty thousand   *eightieth day*
    fathom° above water, and sung this ballad against the hard   *measurement of six feet*
    hearts of maids. It was thought she was a woman, and was
    turned into a cold fish for she would not exchange flesh° with   *have sex*
270   one that loved her. The ballad is very pitiful, and as true.
DORCAS Is it true too, think you?
AUTOLYCUS Five justices' hands at it,° and witnesses more than   *signatures on it*
    my pack will hold.
CLOWN Lay it by, too. Another.
275 AUTOLYCUS This is a merry ballad, but a very pretty one.
MOPSA Let's have some merry ones.
AUTOLYCUS Why, this is a passing° merry one, and goes to the   *very*
    tune of 'Two Maids Wooing a Man'. There's scarce a maid
    westward° but she sings it. 'Tis in request, I can tell you.   *in the west*

---

6. "More" may allude to a pregnancy that will result in an illegitimate child which she will give to the Clown.
7. That is, "Will they reveal their most private affairs in public?" There is a pun on "placket," which refers to both an opening in a petticoat and female genitals.
8. An obscure phrase. The Clown clearly means they are to be quiet. "To clammer" is a term from bell-ringing that means "to make the jangling sound characteristic of bells before they grow silent. In F the phrase is printed as "clamor your tongues." Many emendations have been proposed.
9. A cheap, brightly colored scarf associated with St. Audrey's Fair. St. Audrey was the founder of Ely Cathedral; she died of a throat tumor that she believed was a punishment for wearing gay neckerchiefs in her youth.
1. The name punningly suggests one who reports gossip ("tales") as well as one who handles genitalia (slang meaning of "tail").

280 MOPSA We can both sing it. If thou'lt bear a part² thou shalt
hear; 'tis in three parts.
DORCAS We had the tune on't° a month ago.   *of it*
AUTOLYCUS I can bear my part, you must know, 'tis my occupa-
tion.° Have at it with you.   *job; act of copulation*
     [*They sing*]
285 AUTOLYCUS Get you hence, for I must go³
                  Where it fits not you to know.
     DORCAS   Whither?
     MOPSA   O whither?
     DORCAS   Whither?
     MOPSA   It becomes thy oath full well
                  Thou to me thy secrets tell.
290 DORCAS   Me too. Let me go thither.
     MOPSA   Or thou go'st to th' grange° or mill,   *farm*
     DORCAS   If to either, thou dost ill.
     AUTOLYCUS   Neither.
     DORCAS   What neither?
     AUTOLYCUS   Neither.
     DORCAS   Thou hast sworn my love to be.
295 MOPSA   Thou hast sworn it more to me.
                  Then whither goest? Say, whither?
CLOWN We'll have this song out anon by ourselves. My father
and the gentlemen are in sad° talk, and we'll not trouble them.   *serious*
Come, bring away thy pack after me. Wenches, I'll buy for you
300 both. Pedlar, let's have the first choice. Follow me, girls.
                  [*Exit with* DORCAS *and* MOPSA]
AUTOLYCUS And you shall pay well for 'em.
     [*Sings*]   Will you buy any tape,
                  Or lace for your cape,
                My dainty duck, my dear-a?
305   Any silk, any thread,
                  Any toys° for your head,   *small ornaments*
               Of the new'st and fin'st, fin'st wear-a?
                  Come to the pedlar,
                  Money's a meddler,
310   That doth utter° all men's ware-a.   *Exit*   *put on sale*
          [*Enter* SERVANT]
SERVANT Master, there is three carters,° three shepherds, three   *drivers of carts*
neatherds,° three swineherds that have made themselves all   *keepers of cows*
men of hair.⁴ They call themselves saultiers,° and they have a   *jumpers*
dance which the wenches say is a gallimaufry of gambols,°   *jumble of jumps*
315 because they are not in't. But they themselves are o'th' mind,
if it be not too rough for some that know little but bowling,° it   *(a more sedate sport)*
will please plentifully.
OLD SHEPHERD Away. We'll none on't. Here has been too much
homely° foolery already. [*To* POLIXENES] I know, sir, we weary   *rough*
320 you.
POLIXENES You weary those that° refresh us. Pray, let's see these   *who*
four threes° of herdsmen.   *trios*
SERVANT One three of them, by their own report, sir, hath

---

2. Sing a part in the song; play a role (in a sexual encoun-
ter with the two women).
3. F prints "Song" before this line and "Autolycus" before
the next.

4. Probably they have disguised themselves in animal
skins in order to resemble satyrs—mythical woodland
figures, part man, part beast, having the pointed ears, legs,
and short horns of a goat.

danced before the King,[5] and not the worst of the three but
325   jumps twelve foot and a half by th' square.°   *exactly*
OLD SHEPHERD   Leave your prating. Since these good men are
    pleased, let them come in—but quickly, now.
SERVANT   Why, they stay at door, sir.
        Here a dance of twelve satyrs
POLIXENES [*to the* OLD SHEPHERD]   O, father, you'll know more of that hereafter.
330   [*To* CAMILLO] Is it not too far gone? 'Tis time to part them.
    He's simple, and tells much.
    [*To* FLORIZEL]   How now, fair shepherd,
    Your heart is full of something that does take
    Your mind from feasting. Sooth, when I was young
    And handed love° as you do, I was wont   *pledged love*
335   To load my she with knacks.° I would have ransacked   *small gifts; trifles*
    The pedlar's silken treasury, and have poured it
    To her acceptance.° You have let him go,   *For her to choose*
    And nothing marted° with him. If your lass   *bought from*
    Interpretation should abuse,° and call this   *Should misinterpret*
340   Your lack of love or bounty, you were straited°   *hard-pressed*
    For a reply, at least if you make a care
    Of happy holding her.°   *Of keeping her happy*
FLORIZEL   Old sir, I know
    She prizes not such trifles as these are.
    The gifts she looks° from me are packed and locked   *expects*
345   Up in my heart, which I have given already,
    But not delivered.
    [*To* PERDITA]   O, hear me breathe my life°   *make vows of eternal love*
    Before this ancient sir, who, it should seem,
    Hath sometime loved. I take thy hand, this hand
    As soft as dove's down, and as white as it,
350   Or Ethiopian's tooth, or the fanned snow that's bolted°   *sifted*
    By th' northern blasts twice o'er.
POLIXENES   What follows this?
    How prettily the young swain seems to wash
    The hand was° fair before! I have put you out.°   *that was / interrupted you*
    But to your protestation. Let me hear
    What you profess.
355 FLORIZEL   Do, and be witness to't.
POLIXENES   And this my neighbour too?
FLORIZEL   And he, and more
    Than he; and men, the earth, the heavens, and all,
    That were I crowned the most imperial monarch,
    Thereof most worthy, were I the fairest youth
360   That ever made eye swerve,° had force and knowledge   *commanded attention*
    More than was ever man's, I would not prize them
    Without her love; for her employ them all,
    Commend them and condemn them to her service
    Or to their own perdition.[6]
POLIXENES   Fairly offered.
CAMILLO   This shows a sound affection.

---

5. This may be a reference to a court performance of Ben Jonson's *Masque of Oberon*, which included a dance of twelve satyrs. It was first put on in January of 1611.

6. Either dedicate my attributes to her service or sentence them to destruction, with a pun on "perdition" and "Perdita."

365 OLD SHEPHERD   But, my daughter,
    Say you the like to him?
    PERDITA   I cannot speak
    So well, nothing so well, no, nor mean better.
    By th' pattern of mine own thoughts I cut out
    The purity of his.[7]
    OLD SHEPHERD   Take hands, a bargain;
370   And, friends unknown, you shall bear witness to't.
    I give my daughter to him, and will make
    Her portion° equal his.   *dowry*
    FLORIZEL   O, that must be
    I'th' virtue of your daughter. One° being dead,   *Someone*
    I shall have more than you can dream of yet,
375   Enough then for your wonder. But come on,
    Contract us fore these witnesses.[8]
    OLD SHEPHERD   Come, your hand;
    And, daughter, yours.
    POLIXENES   Soft,° swain, a while, beseech you.   *Go slowly*
    Have you a father?
    FLORIZEL   I have. But what of him?
380 POLIXENES   Knows he of this?
    FLORIZEL   He neither does nor shall.
    POLIXENES   Methinks a father
    Is at the nuptial of his son a guest
    That best becomes the table. Pray you once more,
385   Is not your father grown incapable
    Of reasonable affairs?[9] Is he not stupid
    With age and alt'ring rheums?° Can he speak, hear,   *debilitating disease*
    Know man from man? Dispute° his own estate?°   *Discuss / condition*
    Lies he not bed-rid, and again does nothing
    But what he did being childish?
390 FLORIZEL   No, good sir.
    He has his health, and ampler strength indeed
    Than most have of his age.
    POLIXENES   By my white beard,
    You offer him, if this be so, a wrong
    Something unfilial.° Reason my son[1]   *Somewhat unbecoming a son*
395   Should choose himself a wife, but as good reason
    The father, all whose joy is nothing else
    But fair posterity, should hold some counsel
    In such a business.
    FLORIZEL   I yield° all this;   *grant*
    But for some other reasons, my grave sir,
400   Which 'tis not fit you know, I not acquaint
    My father of this business.
    POLIXENES   Let him know't.
    FLORIZEL   He shall not.
    POLIXENES   Prithee let him.
    FLORIZEL   No, he must not.
    OLD SHEPHERD   Let him, my son. He shall not need to grieve
    At knowing of thy choice.

---

7. By my pure thoughts I recognize the purity of his. A
dressmaking metaphor.
8. A pledge of marriage spoken before two witnesses was
legally binding.

9. Unfit to handle matters requiring reason and good
sense.
1. It is reasonable that my son.

FLORIZEL   Come, come, he must not.
   Mark our contract.
405 POLIXENES [*removing his disguise*]   Mark your divorce, young sir,
   Whom son I dare not call. Thou art too base
   To be acknowledged. Thou a sceptre's heir,
   That thus affects° a sheep-hook?   *desires*
   [*To the* OLD SHEPHERD]   Thou, old traitor,
   I am sorry that by hanging thee I can but
   Shorten thy life one week.
410 [*To* PERDITA]   And thou, fresh piece
   Of excellent witchcraft,[2] who of force° must know   *of necessity*
   The royal fool thou cop'st° with —   *you deal; you have sex*
OLD SHEPHERD   O, my heart!
POLIXENES   I'll have thy beauty scratched with briers and made
   More homely than thy state.
   [*To* FLORIZEL]   For thee, fond° boy,   *foolish*
415 If I may ever know thou dost but sigh
   That thou no more shalt see this knack,° as never   *worthless thing*
   I mean thou shalt, we'll bar thee from succession,
   Not hold thee of our blood, no, not our kin,
   Farre than Deucalion off.[3] Mark thou my words.
   Follow us to the court.
420 [*To the* OLD SHEPHERD]   Thou churl, for this time,
   Though full of our displeasure, yet we free thee
   From the dead° blow of it.   *deadly*
   [*To* PERDITA]   And you, enchantment,
   Worthy enough a herdsman—yea, him° too,   *(Florizel)*
   That makes himself, but for our honour therein,
425 Unworthy thee[4]—if ever henceforth thou
   These rural latches to his entrance open,
   Or hoop° his body more with thy embraces,   *encircle*
   I will devise a death as cruel for thee
   As thou art tender to't.   *Exit*
PERDITA   Even here undone.
430 I was not much afeard, for once or twice
   I was about to speak, and tell him plainly
   The selfsame sun that shines upon his court
   Hides not his visage from our cottage, but
   Looks on alike.° Will't please you, sir, be gone?   *both alike*
435 I told you what would come of this. Beseech you,
   Of your own state take care. This dream of mine
   Being now awake, I'll queen it no inch farther,°   *play the queen no further*
   But milk my ewes and weep.
CAMILLO [*to the* OLD SHEPHERD]   Why, how now, father?
   Speak ere thou diest.
OLD SHEPHERD   I cannot speak, nor think,
   Nor dare to know that which I know.
440 [*To* FLORIZEL]   O sir,
   You have undone a man of fourscore-three,°   *eighty-three*

---

2. You beautiful young woman skilled in witchcraft.
Some people believed that witches could induce love by
potions.
3. Less linked in kinship than Deucalion, who according
to classical myth was the ancestor of humankind and thus
the most distant relation one might have.

4. A difficult passage. Polixenes seems to mean that Flor-
izel by his actions has made himself unworthy of even a
shepherd's daughter were it not for the fact that he is a
king's son and so would harm his father's honor by such
a marriage.

That thought to fill his grave in quiet, yea,
To die upon the bed my father died,
To lie close by his honest bones. But now
445 Some hangman must put on my shroud, and lay me
Where no priest shovels in dust.[5]
[*To* PERDITA]   O cursed wretch,
That knew'st this was the Prince, and wouldst adventure
To mingle faith° with him. Undone, undone!   exchange vows
If I might die within this hour, I have lived
To die when I desire.   *Exit*
450 FLORIZEL [*to* PERDITA] Why look you so upon me?
I am but sorry, not afeard; delayed,
But nothing altered. What I was, I am,
More straining on for plucking back,[6] not following
My leash unwillingly.[7]
CAMILLO   Gracious my lord,
455 You know your father's temper. At this time
He will allow no speech—which I do guess
You do not purpose° to him; and as hardly°   intend / unwillingly
Will he endure your sight as yet, I fear.
Then till the fury of his highness settle,
Come not before him.
460 FLORIZEL   I not purpose it.
I think, Camillo?[8]
CAMILLO   Even he, my lord.
PERDITA [*to* FLORIZEL] How often have I told you 'twould be thus?
How often said my dignity would last
But° till 'twere known?   Only
FLORIZEL   It cannot fail but by
465 The violation of my faith, and then
Let nature crush the sides o'th' earth together
And mar the seeds° within. Lift up thy looks.   sources of life
From my succession wipe me, father! I
Am heir to my affection.
CAMILLO   Be advised.°   prudent
470 FLORIZEL I am, and by my fancy.° If my reason   love
Will thereto be obedient, I have reason.[9]
If not, my senses, better pleased with madness,
Do bid it° welcome.   (madness)
CAMILLO   This is desperate, sir.
FLORIZEL So call it. But it does fulfil my vow.
475 I needs must think it honesty. Camillo,
Not for Bohemia, nor the pomp that may
Be thereat gleaned; for all the sun sees, or
The close° earth wombs,° or the profound seas hides   secret / holds in her womb
In unknown fathoms, will I break my oath
480 To this my fair beloved. Therefore, I pray you,
As you have ever been my father's honoured friend,
When he shall miss me—as, in faith, I mean not
To see him any more—cast your good counsels

---

5. As a criminal, he would be buried without ritual under
the gallows. In regular funeral rites, the priest customarily
placed the first shovelful of dirt on the grave.
6. More eager to go forward because of being pulled
back.

7. Not following this course of action unwillingly (like a
dog dragged by its leash).
8. Camillo may here have taken off his disguise or been
recognized by Florizel even with it on.
9. If my reason will obey love, I will embrace reason.

	Upon his passion.° Let myself and fortune	*anger*
485	Tug° for the time to come. This you may know,	*Contend*
	And so deliver:° I am put to sea	*report*
	With her who here I cannot hold on shore;	
	And most opportune to her need, I have	
	A vessel rides fast by,° but not prepared	*anchored nearby*
490	For this design. What course I mean to hold	
	Shall nothing benefit your knowledge, nor	
	Concern me the reporting.[1]	

CAMILLO   O my lord,
I would your spirit were easier for advice,°   *to advise*
Or stronger for your need.
FLORIZEL   Hark, Perdita—
[*To* CAMILLO]   I'll hear you by and by.
CAMILLO [*aside*]   He's irremovable,°   *unyielding*
Resolved for flight. Now were I happy if
His going I could frame to serve my turn,
Save him from danger, do him love and honour,
Purchase the sight again of dear Sicilia
And that unhappy king, my master, whom
I so much thirst to see.
FLORIZEL   Now, good Camillo,
I am so fraught with curious business° that   *matters requiring care*
I leave out ceremony.
CAMILLO   Sir, I think
You have heard of my poor services i'th' love
That I have borne your father?
FLORIZEL   Very nobly
Have you deserved. It is my father's music
To speak your deeds, not little of his care
To have them recompensed as thought on.[2]
CAMILLO   Well, my lord,
If you may please to think I love the King,
And through him what's nearest to him, which is
Your gracious self, embrace but my direction,°   *simply follow my advice*
If your more ponderous° and settled project   *weighty*
May suffer° alteration. On mine honour,   *permit*
I'll point you where you shall have such receiving
As shall become your highness, where you may
Enjoy your mistress—from the whom I see
There's no disjunction° to be made but by,   *separation*
As heavens forfend,° your ruin—marry her,   *forbid*
And with my best endeavours in your absence
Your discontenting° father strive to qualify°   *discontented / appease*
And bring him up to liking.°   *to giving approval*
FLORIZEL   How, Camillo,
May this, almost a miracle, be done?—
That I may call thee something more than man,
And after that trust to thee.
CAMILLO   Have you thought on°   *of*
A place whereto you'll go?
FLORIZEL   Not any yet.

---

1. Would not benefit you to know nor me to report.
2. And no small matter among his affairs to reward your deeds as fully as he values them.

But as th'unthought-on accident is guilty
To what we wildly do,[3] so we profess
Ourselves to be the slaves of chance, and flies
Of every wind that blows.[4]

CAMILLO   Then list to me.
530 This follows, if you will not change your purpose
But undergo this flight: make for Sicilia,
And there present yourself and your fair princess,
For so I see she must be, fore Leontes.
She shall be habited° as it becomes   *dressed*
535 The partner of your bed. Methinks I see
Leontes opening his free° arms and weeping   *generous*
His welcomes forth; asks thee there 'Son, forgiveness!'
As 'twere i'th' father's person,[5] kisses the hands
Of your fresh princess; o'er and o'er divides him
540 'Twixt his unkindness and his kindness.[6] Th'one
He chides° to hell, and bids the other grow   *rebukes*
Faster than thought or time.

FLORIZEL   Worthy Camillo,
What colour° for my visitation shall I   *pretext*
Hold up before him?

CAMILLO   Sent by the King your father
545 To greet him, and to give him comforts. Sir,
The manner of your bearing towards him, with
What you, as from your father, shall deliver—°   *say*
Things known betwixt us three—I'll write you down,
The which shall point you forth° at every sitting   *direct you*
550 What you must say, that he shall not perceive
But that you have your father's bosom° there,   *trust*
And speak his very heart.

FLORIZEL   I am bound to you.
There is some sap° in this.   *life*

CAMILLO   A course more promising
Than a wild dedication of yourselves
555 To unpathed waters, undreamed shores; most certain,
To miseries enough—no hope to help you,
But as you shake off one, to take another;
Nothing so certain° as your anchors, who   *certain (to detain you)*
Do their best office if they can but stay° you   *keep*
560 Where you'll be loath to be. Besides, you know,
Prosperity's the very bond of love,
Whose fresh complexion and whose heart together
Affliction alters.°   *changes for the worse*

PERDITA   One of these is true.
I think affliction may subdue the cheek°   *make one pale*
But not take in° the mind.   *conquer*
565 CAMILLO   Yea, say you so?
There shall not at your father's house these seven years[7]
Be born another such.

FLORIZEL   My good Camillo,

---

3. But as the unexpected event (Polixenes' discovery of
our love) is responsible for our rash behavior now.
4. And like flies blown about by the winds.
5. As if he were your father; *or* as if you were your father.

6. That is, he divides his speech between his past un-
kindness to your father and the kindness he is eager to
perform now.
7. Proverbial expression meaning "for a long time."

She's as forward of her breeding as
She is i'th' rear our birth.[8]

CAMILLO   I cannot say 'tis pity
570 She lacks instructions,° for she seems a mistress°   *schooling / teacher*
To most that teach.

PERDITA   Your pardon, sir. For this
I'll blush you thanks.

FLORIZEL   My prettiest Perdita!
But O, the thorns we stand upon! Camillo,
Preserver of my father, now of me,
575 The medicine of our house, how shall we do?
We are not furnished° like Bohemia's son,   *dressed; equipped*
Nor shall appear so in Sicilia.

CAMILLO   My lord,
Fear none of this. I think you know my fortunes
580 Do all lie there. It shall be so my care
To have you royally appointed° as if   *outfitted*
The scene you play were mine.° For instance, sir,   *written by me*
That you may know you shall not want—one word.
[*They speak apart.*]
Enter AUTOLYCUS

AUTOLYCUS   Ha, ha! What a fool honesty is, and trust—his sworn
585 brother—a very simple gentleman! I have sold all my trumpery;
not a counterfeit stone, not a ribbon, glass, pomander,[9] brooch,
table-book,° ballad, knife, tape, glove, shoe-tie, bracelet, horn-   *notebook*
ring[1] to keep my pack from fasting.° They throng who should   *from going empty*
buy first, as if my trinkets had been hallowed,° and brought a   *blessed; made sacred*
590 benediction to the buyer; by which means I saw whose purse
was best in picture;° and what I saw, to my good use I remem-   *looked best (to steal)*
bered. My clown, who wants but something° to be a reasonable   *lacks only one thing*
man, grew so in love with the wenches' song that he would not
stir his pettitoes° till he had both tune and words, which so   *feet (pigs' toes)*
595 drew the rest of the herd to me that all their other senses stuck
in ears.° You might have pinched a placket, it was sense-   *were devoted to hearing*
less.° 'Twas nothing to geld a codpiece of a purse.[2] I could have   *felt nothing*
filed keys off that hung in chains. No hearing, no feeling but
my sir's song, and admiring the nothing of it.[3] So that in this
600 time of lethargy I picked and cut most of their festival purses,
and had not the old man come in with a hubbub against his
daughter and the King's son, and scared my choughs° from the   *jackdaws (silly birds)*
chaff, I had not left a purse alive in the whole army.
[CAMILLO, FLORIZEL, *and* PERDITA *come forward*]

CAMILLO   Nay, but my letters by this means being there
605 So soon as you arrive shall clear that doubt.

FLORIZEL   And those that you'll procure from King Leontes—

CAMILLO   Shall satisfy your father.

PERDITA   Happy be you!
All that you speak shows fair.

CAMILLO [*seeing* AUTOLYCUS]   Who have we here?

---

8. That is, "She is as superior to her lowly upbringing as
she is inferior to our noble birth."
9. A mixture of sweet-smelling substances made into a
ball and carried about for ornament or to prevent infec-
tion.
1. A ring made from horn, which was said to possess mag-
ical qualities.
2. It was easy to cut a purse loose from a codpiece, the
baglike article of dress attached to the front of a man's
hose and covering his genitals.
3. The silliness of it, with a pun on "nothing" and "not-
ing" (meaning "tune"), which were similarly pronounced.

We'll make an instrument of this, omit
610 Nothing° may give us aid.   *Nothing that*
AUTOLYCUS [*aside*] If they have overheard me now—why,
    hanging!
CAMILLO   How now, good fellow? Why shakest thou so? Fear
    not, man. Here's no harm intended to thee.
615 AUTOLYCUS   I am a poor fellow, sir.
CAMILLO   Why, be so still.° Here's nobody will steal that from   *always*
    thee. Yet for the outside of thy poverty,° we must make an   *your ragged clothes*
    exchange. Therefore disease° thee instantly— thou must think   *undress*
    there's a necessity in't—and change garments with this gentle-
620 man. Though the pennyworth° on his side be the worst, yet   *bargain*
    hold thee, [*giving him money*] there's some boot.°   *something more*
AUTOLYCUS   I am a poor fellow, sir. [*Aside*] I know ye well
    enough.
CAMILLO   Nay prithee, dispatch°—the gentleman is half flayed[4]   *hurry*
625 already.
AUTOLYCUS   Are you in earnest,[5] sir? [*Aside*] I smell the trick on't.
FLORIZEL   Dispatch, I prithee.
AUTOLYCUS   Indeed, I have had earnest, but I cannot with con-
    science take it.
630 CAMILLO   Unbuckle, unbuckle.
        [FLORIZEL *and* AUTOLYCUS *exchange clothes*]
    [*To* PERDITA] Fortunate mistress—let my prophecy
    Come home to ye![6]—you must retire yourself
    Into some covert,° take your sweetheart's hat   *hiding place*
    And pluck it o'er your brows, muffle your face,
635 Dismantle you,° and, as you can, disliken°   *Take off your cloak / disguise*
    The truth of your own seeming,° that you may—   *appearance*
    For I do fear eyes°—over to shipboard   *spies*
    Get undescried.
PERDITA   I see the play so lies
    That I must bear a part.
CAMILLO   No remedy.
    [*To* FLORIZEL] Have you done there?
640 FLORIZEL   Should I now meet my father
    He would not call me son.
CAMILLO   Nay, you shall have no hat.
        [*He gives the hat to* PERDITA]
    Come, lady, come. Farewell, my friend.
AUTOLYCUS   Adieu, sir.
FLORIZEL   O Perdita, what have we twain forgot!
    Pray you, a word.
        [*They speak aside*]
645 CAMILLO [*aside*]   What I do next shall be to tell the King
    Of this escape, and whither they are bound;
    Wherein my hope is I shall so prevail
    To force him after, in whose company
    I shall re-view Sicilia, for whose sight
    I have a woman's longing.[7]

---

4. Half undressed (skinned).
5. "Serious," with a pun on "earnest" as meaning both
"sincere" and "an advance payment." See line 628.

6. Let my prophecy (that she be fortunate) be fulfilled.
7. Women, especially pregnant women, were said to be
vulnerable to irrational and very intense cravings.

650 FLORIZEL   Fortune speed us!
    Thus we set on, Camillo, to th' seaside.
  CAMILLO   The swifter speed the better.
                Exeunt [FLORIZEL, PERDITA, *and* CAMILLO][8]
  AUTOLYCUS   I understand the business, I hear it. To have an open
    ear, a quick eye, and a nimble hand is necessary for a cutpurse.
655   A good nose is requisite also, to smell out work for th'other
    senses. I see this is the time that the unjust man doth thrive.
    What an exchange had this been without boot!° What a boot[9]   *even without payment*
    is here with this exchange! Sure the gods do this year connive
    at° us, and we may do anything extempore.° The Prince him-   *indulge / spontaneously*
660   self is about a piece of iniquity, stealing away from his father
    with his clog° at his heels. If I thought it were a piece of honesty   *encumbrance (Perdita)*
    to acquaint the King withal,° I would not do't. I hold it the   *with it*
    more knavery to conceal it, and therein am I constant° to my   *faithful*
    profession.
            Enter [*the*] CLOWN *and* [*the* OLD] SHEPHERD[, *carrying*
            a fardel° *and a box*]   *bundle*
665   Aside, aside! Here is more matter for a hot brain. Every lane's
    end, every shop, church, session,° hanging, yields a careful   *court session*
    man work.
  CLOWN   See, see, what a man you are now! There is no other
    way but to tell the King she's a changeling,[1] and none of your
670   flesh and blood.
  OLD SHEPHERD   Nay, but hear me.
  CLOWN   Nay, but hear *me*.
  OLD SHEPHERD   Go to,° then.   *Go ahead*
  CLOWN   She being none of your flesh and blood, your flesh and
675   blood has not offended the King, and so your flesh and blood
    is not to be punished by him. Show those things you found
    about her, those secret things, all but what she has with her.
    This being done, let the law go whistle, I warrant you.
  OLD SHEPHERD   I will tell the King all, every word, yea, and his
680   son's pranks, too, who, I may say, is no honest man, neither to
    his father nor to me, to go about to make me the King's brother-
    in-law.
  CLOWN   Indeed, brother-in-law was the farthest off° you could   *most remote relation*
    have been to him, and then your blood had been the dearer by
685   I know not how much an ounce.
  AUTOLYCUS [*aside*]   Very wisely, puppies.
  OLD SHEPHERD   Well, let us to the King. There is that in this
    fardel will make him scratch his beard.
  AUTOLYCUS [*aside*]   I know not what impediment this complaint
690   may be to the flight of my master.°   *(Florizel)*
  CLOWN   Pray heartily he be at'° palace.   *at the*
  AUTOLYCUS [*aside*]   Though I am not naturally honest, I am so
    sometimes by chance. Let me pocket up my pedlar's excre-
    ment.°   *hair*
            [*He removes his false beard*]
695   —How now, rustics, whither are you bound?
  OLD SHEPHERD   To th' palace, an° it like your worship.   *if*

---

8. F marks a single "*Exit*" here for Camillo, but Florizel   9. Benefit; shoe.
and Perdita undoubtedly exit also, leaving Autolycus   1. A child left or abducted by fairies. See note to 3.3.109.
alone on stage to comment on what he has witnessed.

AUTOLYCUS Your affairs there? What? With whom? The condition of that fardel?° The place of your dwelling? Your names? Your ages? Of what having,° breeding,° and anything that is fitting to be known, discover.°   *nature of that bundle / property / upbringing / reveal*

CLOWN We are but plain° fellows, sir.   *simple; smooth*

AUTOLYCUS A lie, you are rough and hairy. Let me have no lying. It becomes none but tradesmen, and they often give us soldiers the lie,[2] but we pay them for it with stamped coin, not stabbing steel, therefore they do not *give* us the lie.[3]

CLOWN Your worship had like to have given us one° if you had not taken yourself with the manner.[4]   *(the lie)*

OLD SHEPHERD Are you a courtier, an't like you, sir?

AUTOLYCUS Whether it like me or no, I am a courtier. Seest thou not the air of the court in these enfoldings?° Hath not my gait in it the measure° of the court? Receives not thy nose court odour from me? Reflect I not on thy baseness court-contempt? Thinkest thou, for that I insinuate° to toze° from thee thy business, I am therefore no courtier? I am courtier cap-à-pie,° and one that will either push on or pluck back thy business there. Whereupon I command thee to open° thy affair.   *garments / stately walk / subtly work / tease out / from head to foot / reveal*

OLD SHEPHERD My business, sir, is to the King.

AUTOLYCUS What advocate hast thou to him?

OLD SHEPHERD I know not, an't like you.

CLOWN [aside to the OLD SHEPHERD] 'Advocate''s the court word for a pheasant.[5] Say you have none.

OLD SHEPHERD None, sir. I have no pheasant, cock nor hen.

AUTOLYCUS [aside] How blessed are we that are not simple men! Yet nature might have made me as these are, Therefore I will not disdain.

CLOWN This cannot be but° a great courtier.   *anyone but*

OLD SHEPHERD His garments are rich, but he wears them not handsomely.

CLOWN He seems to be the more noble in being fantastical.° A great man, I'll warrant. I know by the picking on's teeth.[6]   *eccentric*

AUTOLYCUS The fardel there, what's i'th' fardel? Wherefore that box?

OLD SHEPHERD Sir, there lies such secrets in this fardel and box which none must know but the King, and which he shall know within this hour, if I may come to th' speech of him.

AUTOLYCUS Age,° thou hast lost thy labour.   *Old man*

OLD SHEPHERD Why, sir?

AUTOLYCUS The King is not at the palace, he is gone aboard a new ship to purge° melancholy and air himself; for if thou beest capable of° things serious, thou must know the King is full of grief.   *rid himself of / can understand*

OLD SHEPHERD So 'tis said, sir; about his son, that should have married a shepherd's daughter.

AUTOLYCUS If that shepherd be not in handfast,° let him fly. The   *arrested*

---

2. They call us soldiers liars; they cheat us soldiers.
3. Punning on "give the lie" as meaning both "cheat" and "insult me in a way that requires a challenge to a duel." The point seems to be that since soldiers pay with good currency rather than by stabbing (the appropriate response to an insult), vendors can't claim to have given anything—including the lie—to anyone, and a duel can be successfully avoided.

4. If you had not stopped yourself in the middle.
5. The Clown thinks "advocate" means "bribe" or "gift," of which a pheasant would be an example. He is confusing the king's court with a law court in which game birds were supposedly given as bribes to local magistrates.
6. Ornate toothpicks were considered fashionable accessories.

745   curses he shall have, the tortures he shall feel, will break the
back of man, the heart of monster.
CLOWN   Think you so, sir?
AUTOLYCUS   Not he alone shall suffer what wit can make heavy
and vengeance bitter, but those that are germane° to him,   *related*
750   though removed fifty times, shall all come under the hangman,
which, though it be great pity, yet it is necessary. An old sheep-
whistling rogue,[7] a ram-tender, to offer to have his daughter
come into grace!° Some say he shall be stoned; but that death   *favor (at court)*
is too soft for him, say I. Draw our throne into a sheepcote?°   *pen for sheep*
755   All deaths are too few, the sharpest too easy.
CLOWN   Has the old man e'er a son, sir, do you hear, an't like
you, sir?
AUTOLYCUS   He has a son, who shall be flayed alive, then
'nointed over with honey, set on the head of a wasps' nest, then
760   stand till he be three-quarters-and-a-dram° dead, then recov-   *a tiny bit*
ered again with aqua-vitae,° or some other hot infusion, then,   *brandy*
raw as he is, and in the hottest day prognostication° proclaims,   *almanac prediction*
shall he be set against a brick wall, the sun looking with a
southward eye upon him, where he is to behold him with flies
765   blown° to death. But what talk we of these traitorly rascals,   *swollen*
whose miseries are to be smiled at, their offences being so capi-
tal? Tell me, for you seem to be honest plain men, what you
have° to the King. Being something gently considered,[8] I'll   *have to say*
bring you where he is aboard, tender° your persons to his pres-   *deliver*
770   ence, whisper him in your behalfs, and if it be in man, besides
the King, to effect your suits, here is man shall do it.
CLOWN *[to the* OLD SHEPHERD*]*   He seems to be of great author-
ity. Close° with him, give him gold; and though authority be a   *Make a deal*
stubborn bear, yet he is oft led by the nose with gold. Show the
775   inside of your purse to the outside of his hand, and no more
ado. Remember—'stoned', and 'flayed alive'.
OLD SHEPHERD   An't please you, sir, to undertake the business
for us, here is that° gold I have. I'll make it as much more, and   *what*
leave this young man in pawn° till I bring it you.   *as security*
780 AUTOLYCUS   After I have done what I promised?
OLD SHEPHERD   Ay, sir.
AUTOLYCUS   Well, give me the moiety.° *[To the* CLOWN*]* Are you   *half*
a party in this business?
CLOWN   In some sort, sir. But though my case° be a pitiful one,   *condition; skin*
785   I hope I shall not be flayed out of it.
AUTOLYCUS   O, that's the case of the shepherd's son. Hang him,
he'll be made an example.
CLOWN *[to the* OLD SHEPHERD*]*   Comfort, good comfort. We
must to the King, and show our strange sights. He must
790   know 'tis none of your daughter, nor my sister. We are gone°   *lost (dead)*
else.° *[To* AUTOLYCUS*]* Sir, I will give you as much as this old   *otherwise*
man does when the business is performed, and remain, as he
says, your pawn till it be brought you.
AUTOLYCUS   I will trust you. Walk before° toward the seaside. Go   *ahead of me*
795   on the right hand. I will but look upon the hedge,[9] and follow
you.

---

7. An old rascal who whistles while he tends sheep.   will give me a bribe worthy of my high rank.
8. As I am a highly regarded gentleman at court; if you   9. Slang for "relieve myself."

CLOWN [*to the* OLD SHEPHERD]   We are blessed in this man, as I
may say, even blessed.

OLD SHEPHERD   Let's before, as he bids us. He was provided to
800   do us good.   [*Exit with the* CLOWN]

AUTOLYCUS   If I had a mind to be honest, I see fortune would
not suffer° me. She drops booties° in my mouth. I am courted   *permit / prizes*
now with a double occasion:° gold, and a means to do the   *opportunity*
Prince my master good, which who knows how that may turn
805   back to my advancement? I will bring these two moles, these
blind ones, aboard him.° If he think it fit to shore them[1] again,   *(his ship)*
and that the complaint they have to the King concerns him
nothing, let him call me rogue for being so far officious, for I
am proof against° that title, and what shame else belongs to't.   *impervious to*
810   To him will I present them. There may be matter in it.   *Exit*

5.1

Enter LEONTES, CLEOMENES, DION, [*and*] PAULINA

CLEOMENES [*to* LEONTES]   Sir, you have done enough, and have performed
A saint-like sorrow. No fault could you make
Which you have not redeemed, indeed, paid down
More penitence than done trespass.[1] At the last
5   Do as the heavens have done, forget your evil.
With them, forgive yourself.

LEONTES   Whilst I remember
Her and her virtues I cannot forget
My blemishes in them,° and so still think of   *in relation to them*
The wrong I did myself, which was so much
10   That heirless it hath made my kingdom, and
Destroyed the sweet'st companion that e'er man
Bred his hopes out of. True?

PAULINA   Too true, my lord.
If one by one you wedded all the world,
Or from the all that are took something good
15   To make a perfect woman, she you killed
Would be unparalleled.

LEONTES   I think so. Killed?
She I killed? I did so. But thou strik'st me
Sorely to say I did; it is as bitter
Upon thy tongue as in my thought. Now, good now,°   *if you would*
Say so but seldom.

20   CLEOMENES   Not at all,° good lady.   *Never (say these things)*
You might have spoke a thousand things that would
Have done the time more benefit,[2] and graced°   *showed*
Your kindness better.

PAULINA   You are one of those
Would have him wed again.

DION   If you would not so
25   You pity not the state,° nor the remembrance   *kingdom*
Of his most sovereign name,[3] consider little
What dangers, by his highness' fail of issue,°   *lack of offspring*
May drop upon his kingdom and devour

---

1. Put them ashore.
5.1 Location: Sicilia. The palace of Leontes.
1. Performed more penance than your sin warranted.

2. That would have been more useful in these times.
3. Nor the perpetuation of his royal lineage (through a new child).

Incertain lookers-on.[4] What were more holy
30   Than to rejoice the former queen is well?°   (in heaven)
What holier, than for royalty's repair,
For present comfort and for future good,
To bless the bed of majesty again
With a sweet fellow to't?
PAULINA   There is none worthy
35   Respecting° her that's gone. Besides, the gods   In comparison to
Will have fulfilled their secret purposes.[5]
For has not the divine Apollo said?
Is't not the tenor of his oracle
That King Leontes shall not have an heir
40   Till his lost child be found? Which that it shall
Is all as monstrous° to our human reason   incredible
As my Antigonus to break his grave
And come again to me, who, on my life,
Did perish with the infant. 'Tis your counsel
45   My lord should to the heavens be contrary,
Oppose against their wills.
[To LEONTES]   Care not for issue.
The crown will find an heir. Great Alexander
Left his to th' worthiest,[6] so his successor
Was like to be the best.
LEONTES   Good Paulina,
50   Who hast the memory of Hermione,
I know, in honour—O, that ever I
Had squared me° to thy counsel! Then even now   conformed my actions
I might have looked upon my queen's full eyes,
Have taken treasure from her lips.
PAULINA   And left them
More rich for what they yielded.
55   LEONTES   Thou speak'st truth.
No more such wives, therefore no wife. One worse,
And better used,° would make her sainted spirit   treated
Again possess her° corpse, and on this stage,   (Hermione's)
Where we offenders mourn, appear soul-vexed,°   with troubled soul
And begin, 'Why° to me?'   Why offer this insult
60   PAULINA   Had she such power
She had just cause.
LEONTES   She had, and would incense me
To murder her I married.
PAULINA   I should so.
Were I the ghost that walked I'd bid you mark
Her eye, and tell me for what dull part in't
65   You chose her. Then I'd shriek that even your ears
Should rift° to hear me, and the words that followed   split
Should be, 'Remember mine'.°   (my eyes)
LEONTES   Stars, stars,
And all eyes else,° dead coals! Fear thou no wife.   all other eyes
I'll have no wife, Paulina.

4. And destroy those subjects who are bewildered (by the matter of his successor).
5. Will ensure that their secret purposes are fulfilled.
6. Alexander the Great (356–323 B.C.), conqueror of Greece, Persia, and Egypt, died before his own son was born and reportedly urged his followers simply to choose the worthiest man as his successor.

PAULINA   Will you swear
70   Never to marry but by my free leave?
LEONTES   Never, Paulina, so be blest my spirit.
PAULINA   Then, good my lords, bear witness to his oath.
CLEOMENES   You tempt him over-much.
PAULINA   Unless another
    As like Hermione as is her picture
    Affront° his eye—   *Confront*
75   CLEOMENES   Good madam, I have done.[7]
PAULINA   Yet if my lord will marry—if you will, sir;
    No remedy but you will—give me the office
    To choose your queen. She shall not be so young
    As was your former, but she shall be such
80   As, walked your first queen's ghost,[8] it should take joy
    To see her in your arms.
LEONTES   My true Paulina,
    We shall not marry till thou bidd'st us.
PAULINA   That
    Shall be when your first queen's again in breath.°   *alive*
    Never till then.
             Enter a SERVANT
85   SERVANT   One that gives out himself° Prince Florizel,   *claims to be*
    Son of Polixenes, with his princess—she
    The fairest I have yet beheld—desires access
    To your high presence.
LEONTES   What° with him? He comes not   *Who comes*
    Like to° his father's greatness. His approach,   *As befits*
90   So out of circumstance° and sudden, tells us   *informal*
    'Tis not a visitation framed,° but forced   *planned*
    By need and accident. What train?°   *retinue*
SERVANT   But few,
    And those but mean.°   *of low rank*
LEONTES   His princess, say you, with him?
SERVANT   Ay, the most peerless piece of earth, I think,
    That e'er the sun shone bright on.
95   PAULINA   O, Hermione,
    As every present time doth boast itself
    Above a better, gone, so must thy grave
    Give way to what's seen now![9]
    [*To the* SERVANT]   Sir, you yourself
    Have said and writ so; but your writing now
100   Is colder than that theme. She had not been
    Nor was not to be equalled—thus your verse
    Flowed with her beauty once. 'Tis shrewdly° ebbed   *grievously*
    To say you have seen a better.
SERVANT   Pardon, madam.
    The one° I have almost forgot—your pardon!   *(Hermione)*
105   The other, when she has obtained your eye,
    Will have your tongue too. This is a creature,

---

7. Many editors emend this line to assign "I have done" to Paulina, rather than Cleomenes. As it stands, the line suggests Cleomenes' exasperation that Paulina will not listen to him. If emended to assign the last three words to Paulina, the exchange may suggest that Paulina is at least minimally responsive to the pleas of Leontes' courtiers that she mitigate her opposition to his remarriage.
8. If Hermione appeared as a ghost.
9. As each present time boasts itself to be superior to a time better than itself, but gone from view, so you, in your grave, must be superseded by what is now seen.

Would she begin a sect, might quench the zeal
Of all professors else;[1] make proselytes°   *converts*
Of who° she but bid follow.   *Of those who*
PAULINA   How? Not women!
110 SERVANT Women will love her that she is a woman
More worth° than any man; men, that she is   *worthy*
The rarest of all women.
LEONTES   Go, Cleomenes.
Yourself, assisted with your honoured friends,
Bring them to our embracement.   *Exit* [CLEOMENES]
                        Still 'tis strange
He thus should steal upon us.
115 PAULINA   Had our prince,
Jewel of children, seen this hour, he had paired
Well with this lord. There was not full a month°   *a full month*
Between their births.
LEONTES   Prithee no more, cease. Thou know'st
He dies to me again when talked of. Sure,
120 When I shall see this gentleman thy speeches
Will bring me to consider that which may
Unfurnish me of reason.° They are come.   *Make me go mad*
    Enter FLORIZEL, PERDITA, CLEOMENES, *and others*
Your mother was most true to wedlock, Prince,
For she did print your royal father off,[2]
125 Conceiving you. Were I but twenty-one,
Your father's image is so hit° in you,   *exact*
His very air, that I should call you brother,
As I did him, and speak of something wildly
By us performed before. Most dearly welcome,
130 And your fair princess—goddess! O, alas,
I lost a couple that 'twixt heaven and earth
Might thus have stood, begetting wonder, as
You, gracious couple, do; and then I lost—
All mine own folly—the society,
135 Amity too, of your brave° father, whom,   *stout-hearted*
Though bearing misery, I desire my life[3]
Once more to look on him.
FLORIZEL   By his command
Have I here touched Sicilia, and from him
Give you all greetings that a king at friend°   *in friendship*
140 Can send his brother; and but° infirmity,   *were it not that*
Which waits upon worn times,° hath something seized *accompanies old age*
His wished ability,[4] he had himself
The lands and waters 'twixt your throne and his
Measured° to look upon you, whom he loves— *Journeyed across*
145 He bade me say so—more than all the sceptres,
And those that bear them, living.
LEONTES   O, my brother!
Good gentleman, the wrongs I have done thee stir
Afresh within me, and these thy offices,°   *greetings*
So rarely° kind, are as interpreters   *extraordinarily*

---

1. Of all those who professed other religions.
2. Made an exact copy of Polixenes, as a printer produces a book.

3. Whom, though I am suffering, I wish to live long enough.
4. Has somewhat deprived him of his desired strength.

150   Of my behindhand slackness.[5] Welcome hither,
   As is the spring to th'earth! And hath he too
   Exposed this paragon to th' fearful usage—
   At least ungentle—of the dreadful Neptune°   *god of the sea*
   To greet a man not worth her pains, much less
   Th'adventure° of her person?   *risk*
155 FLORIZEL   Good my lord,
   She came from Libya.
LEONTES   Where the warlike Smalus,[6]
   That noble honoured lord, is feared and loved?
FLORIZEL   Most royal sir, from thence; from him whose daughter
   His tears proclaimed his, parting with her. Thence,
160   A prosperous south wind friendly, we have crossed,
   To execute the charge my father gave me
   For visiting your highness. My best train
   I have from your Sicilian shores dismissed;
   Who for Bohemia bend,° to signify   *make their way*
165   Not only my success in Libya, sir,
   But my arrival, and my wife's, in safety
   Here where we are.
LEONTES   The blessèd gods
   Purge all infection from our air whilst you
   Do climate° here! You have a holy father,   *reside*
170   A graceful gentleman, against whose person,
   So sacred as it is, I have done sin,
   For which the heavens, taking angry note,
   Have left me issueless; and your father's blessed,
   As he from heaven merits it, with you,
175   Worthy his goodness. What might I have been,
   Might I a son and daughter now have looked on,
   Such goodly things as you?
            Enter a LORD
LORD   Most noble sir,
   That which I shall report will bear no credit
   Were not the proof so nigh. Please you, great sir,
180   Bohemia greets you from himself by me;
   Desires you to attach° his son, who has,   *arrest*
   His dignity and duty[7] both cast off,
   Fled from his father, from his hopes, and with
   A shepherd's daughter.
LEONTES   Where's Bohemia? Speak.
185 LORD   Here in your city. I now came from him.
   I speak amazedly,° and it becomes°   *confusedly / befits*
   My marvel° and my message. To your court   *astonishment*
   Whiles he was hast'ning—in the chase, it seems,
   Of this fair couple—meets he on the way
190   The father of this seeming° lady and   *apparent; false*
   Her brother, having both their country quitted
   With this young prince.
FLORIZEL   Camillo has betrayed me,

---

5. Are reminders of my slowness (in greeting you).
6. An obscure allusion. The name may be a misprint for "Synalus," a soldier from Carthage mentioned by Plu-tarch.
7. His royal status and his duty to his father.

Whose honour and whose honesty till now
Endured all weathers.
LORD   Lay't so to his charge.°   *Accuse him directly*
He's with the King your father.
195 LEONTES   Who, Camillo?
LORD   Camillo, sir. I spake with him, who now
Has these poor men in question. Never saw I
Wretches so quake. They kneel, they kiss the earth,
Forswear° themselves as often as they speak.   *Perjure*
200 Bohemia stops his ears, and threatens them
With divers deaths in death.°   *With diverse tortures*
PERDITA   O, my poor father!
The heaven sets spies upon us, will not have
Our contract celebrated.
LEONTES   You are married?
FLORIZEL   We are not, sir, nor are we like to be.
205 The stars, I see, will kiss the valleys first.
The odds for high and low's alike.[8]
LEONTES   My lord,
Is this the daughter of a king?
FLORIZEL   She is,
When once she is my wife.
LEONTES   That 'once', I see, by your good father's speed
210 Will come on very slowly. I am sorry,
Most sorry, you have broken from his liking
Where you were tied in duty; and as sorry
Your choice is not so rich in worth° as beauty,   *rank*
That you might well enjoy her.
FLORIZEL [*to* PERDITA]   Dear, look up.
215 Though fortune, visible an enemy,
Should chase us with my father, power no jot
Hath she to change our loves.[9]—Beseech you, sir,
Remember since you owed no more to time
Than I do now.° With thought of such affections,   *when you were my age*
220 Step forth mine advocate. At your request
My father will grant precious things as trifles.
LEONTES   Would he do so, I'd beg your precious mistress,
Which he counts but a trifle.
PAULINA   Sir, my liege,
Your eye hath too much youth in't. Not a month
225 Fore your queen died she was more worth such gazes
Than what you look on now.
LEONTES   I thought of her
Even in these looks I made.
[*To* FLORIZEL]   But your petition
Is yet unanswered. I will to your father.
Your honour not o'erthrown by your desires,[1]
230 I am friend to them and you. Upon which errand
I now go toward him. Therefore follow me,
And mark what way I make. Come, good my lord.   *Exeunt*

---

8. That is, "Chance treats those of high and low rank identically."
9. Even if Lady Fortune were to make herself apparent as our enemy and join my father in pursuit, she would remain powerless to change our love.
1. So long as you have not allowed passion to destroy your virtue.

5.2

Enter AUTOLYCUS *and a* GENTLEMAN

AUTOLYCUS Beseech you, sir, were you present at this relation?° *when this was told*

FIRST GENTLEMAN I was by at the opening of the fardel, heard
the old shepherd deliver the manner how he found it; where-
upon, after a little amazedness, we were all commanded out of
5 the chamber. Only this, methought I heard the shepherd say
he found the child.

AUTOLYCUS I would most gladly know the issue° of it. *outcome*

FIRST GENTLEMAN I make a broken delivery° of the business, but *confused report*
the changes I perceived in the King and Camillo were very
10 notes of admiration.[1] They seemed almost, with staring on one
another, to tear the cases° of their eyes. There was speech in *burst the sockets*
their dumbness, language in their very gesture. They looked as° *as if*
they had heard of a world ransomed, or one destroyed. A nota-
ble passion of wonder appeared in them, but the wisest
15 beholder, that knew no more but seeing, could not say if
th'importance were joy or sorrow. But in the extremity of the
one,° it must needs be. *of the one or the other*

Enter another GENTLEMAN

Here comes a gentleman that happily° knows more. The news, *perhaps*
Ruggiero!

20 SECOND GENTLEMAN Nothing but bonfires. The oracle is ful-
filled. The King's daughter is found. Such a deal° of wonder is *a great quantity*
broken out within this hour, that ballad-makers cannot be able
to express it.[2]

Enter another GENTLEMAN

Here comes the Lady Paulina's steward. He can deliver you
25 more.—How goes it now, sir? This news which is called true is
so like an old tale that the verity of it is in strong suspicion. Has
the King found his heir?

THIRD GENTLEMAN Most true, if ever truth were pregnant by cir-
cumstance.° That which you hear you'll swear you see, there is *proven by evidence*
30 such unity in the proofs. The mantle of Queen Hermione's,
her jewel about the neck of it, the letters of Antigonus found
with it, which they know to be his character;° the majesty of *handwriting*
the creature, in resemblance of the mother; the affection of° *instinct toward*
nobleness which nature shows above° her breeding,° and many *in excess of / upbringing*
35 other evidences proclaim her with all certainty to be the King's
daughter. Did you see the meeting of the two kings?

SECOND GENTLEMAN No.

THIRD GENTLEMAN Then have you lost a sight which was to be
seen, cannot be spoken of. There might you have beheld one
40 joy crown another, so and in such manner that it seemed sor-
row wept to take leave of them, for their joy waded in tears.
There was casting up of eyes, holding up of hands, with counte-
nance° of such distraction[3] that they were to be known by gar- *face*
ment, not by favour.° Our king being ready to leap out of *features*
45 himself for joy of his found daughter, as if that joy were now
become a loss cries, 'O, thy mother, thy mother!', then asks
Bohemia forgiveness, then embraces his son-in-law, then again

---

5.2 Location: Sicilia. The palace of Leontes.
1. Were the very marks of wonder.
2. Ballads often provided accounts of contemporary scan-

dals and sensations.
3. So altered by emotion.

worries he° his daughter with clipping° her. Now he thanks the   *he agitates / embracing*
old shepherd, which stands by like a weather-bitten conduit of
50 many kings' reigns.[4] I never heard of such another encounter,
which lames report to follow it,[5] and undoes° description to do°   *defies / express*
it.

SECOND GENTLEMAN   What, pray you, became of Antigonus, that
carried hence the child?

55 THIRD GENTLEMAN   Like an old tale still, which will have matter
to rehearse° though credit° be asleep and not an ear open. He   *relate / belief*
was torn to pieces with a bear. This avouches° the shepherd's   *vows*
son, who has not only his innocence,° which seems much, to   *simplemindedness*
justify him, but a handkerchief and rings of his,° that Paulina   *(of Antigonus)*
60 knows.

FIRST GENTLEMAN   What became of his barque° and his fol-   *ship*
lowers?

THIRD GENTLEMAN   Wrecked the same instant of their master's
death, and in the view of the shepherd; so that all the instru-
65 ments which aided to expose the child were even then lost
when it was found. But O, the noble combat that 'twixt joy and
sorrow was fought in Paulina! She had one eye declined for
the loss of her husband, another elevated[6] that the oracle was
fulfilled. She lifted the Princess from the earth, and so locks
70 her in embracing as if she would pin her to her heart, that she
might no more be in danger of losing.°   *of being lost*

FIRST GENTLEMAN   The dignity of this act was worth the audi-
ence of kings and princes, for by such was it acted.

THIRD GENTLEMAN   One of the prettiest touches of all, and that
75 which angled for mine eyes—caught the water,° though not   *(my tears)*
the fish—was when at the relation of the Queen's death, with
the manner how she came to't bravely confessed and lamented
by the King, how attentiveness° wounded his daughter till from   *intent listening*
one sign of dolour° to another she did, with an 'Alas,' I would   *grief*
80 fain say bleed tears; for I am sure my heart wept blood. Who
was most marble° there changed colour. Some swooned, all   *unfeeling*
sorrowed. If all the world could have seen't, the woe had been
universal.

FIRST GENTLEMAN   Are they returned to the court?

85 THIRD GENTLEMAN   No. The Princess, hearing of her mother's
statue, which is in the keeping of Paulina, a piece many years
in doing, and now newly performed° by that rare Italian master   *completed*
Giulio Romano,[7] who, had he himself eternity and could put
breath into his work, would beguile° nature of her custom,° so   *cheat / business*
90 perfectly he is her ape.° He so near to Hermione hath done   *imitator*
Hermione that they say one would speak to her and stand in
hope of answer. Thither with all greediness of affection are they
gone, and there they intend to sup.

SECOND GENTLEMAN   I thought she had some great matter there
95 in hand, for she hath privately twice or thrice a day, ever since
the death of Hermione, visited that removed° house. Shall we   *distant; hidden*
thither, and with our company piece° the rejoicing?   *join*

---

4. Who stands by weeping like a waterspout that has been
around for the reigns of many kings. Some large buildings
had "conduits" or waterpipes in the form of gargoyles or
gnarled human faces.
5. Which makes any account of it seem deficient.

6. That is, Paulina simultaneously cried and laughed.
7. An Italian painter and sculptor, a follower of Raphael,
who died in 1546. It is not clear why Shakespeare chose
to lavish such praise upon this particular artist or whether,
in fact, he had ever seen any of his work.

FIRST GENTLEMAN   Who would be thence, that has the benefit
of access? Every wink of an eye some new grace will be born.
100   Our absence makes us unthrifty to our knowledge.[8] Let's
along.   *Exeunt* [GENTLEMEN]
AUTOLYCUS   Now, had I not the dash° of my former life in me,   *stain; touch*
would preferment° drop on my head. I brought the old man   *royal favor*
and his son aboard the° Prince; told him I heard them talk of a   *aboard the ship of the*
105   fardel, and I know not what. But he at that time over-fond of
the shepherd's daughter—so he then took her to be—who
began to be much sea-sick, and himself little better, extremity
of weather continuing, this mystery remained undiscovered.
But 'tis all one to me, for had I been the finder-out of this secret
110   it would not have relished° among my other discredits.   *appeared well*
          Enter [the OLD] SHEPHERD *and* [the] CLOWN [*dressed as
          gentlemen*]
Here come those I have done good to against my will, and
already appearing in the blossoms of their fortune.
OLD SHEPHERD   Come, boy; I am past more children, but thy
sons and daughters will be all gentlemen born.
115   CLOWN [*to* AUTOLYCUS]   You are well met, sir. You denied to
fight with me this other° day because I was no gentleman born.   *the other*
See you these clothes? Say you see them not, and think me
still no gentleman born. You were best say these robes are not
gentlemen born. Give me the lie,[9] do, and try whether I am
120   not now a gentleman born.
AUTOLYCUS   I know you are now, sir, a gentleman born.
CLOWN   Ay, and have been so any time these four hours.
OLD SHEPHERD   And so have I, boy.
CLOWN   So you have; but I was a gentleman born before my
125   father, for the King's son took me by the hand and called me
brother; and then the two kings called my father brother; and
then the Prince my brother and the Princess my sister called
my father father; and so we wept; and there was the first gentle-
man-like tears that ever we shed.
130   OLD SHEPHERD   We may live, son, to shed many more.
CLOWN   Ay, or else 'twere hard luck, being in so preposterous
estate[1] as we are.
AUTOLYCUS   I humbly beseech you, sir, to pardon me all the
faults I have committed to your worship, and to give me your
135   good report to the Prince my master.
OLD SHEPHERD   Prithee, son, do, for we must be gentle° now we   *act nobly*
are gentlemen.
CLOWN   Thou wilt amend thy life?
AUTOLYCUS   Ay, an it like your good worship.
140   CLOWN   Give me thy hand. I will swear to the Prince thou art as
honest a true fellow as any is in Bohemia.
OLD SHEPHERD   You may say it, but not swear it.
CLOWN   Not swear it now I am a gentleman? Let boors° and   *peasants*
franklins° say it; I'll swear it.   *small farmers*
145   OLD SHEPHERD   How if it be false, son?
CLOWN   If it be ne'er so false,° a true gentleman may swear it in   *Even if it is false*

8. Makes us squander an opportunity to add to our
knowledge.
9. Insult me so that I must respond with the challenge of
a duel.

1. The Clown probably means "prosperous," but "prepos-
terous" is a nice blunder for it suggests that their new
status as gentlemen preposterously inverts the customary
social order.

the behalf of his friend, [*to* AUTOLYCUS] and I'll swear to the
Prince thou art a tall fellow of thy hands° and that thou wilt not   *a brave man of action*
be drunk; but I know thou art no tall fellow of thy hands and
150   that thou wilt be drunk; but I'll swear it, and I would thou
wouldst be a tall fellow of thy hands.
AUTOLYCUS   I will prove so, sir, to my power.°   *as well as I can*
CLOWN   Ay, by any means prove a tall fellow. If I do not wonder
how thou dar'st venture to be drunk, not being a tall fellow,
155   trust me not.
　　　[*Flourish within*]
Hark, the kings and princes, our kindred, are going to see the
Queen's picture.° Come, follow us. We'll be thy good masters.   *likeness*
　　　　　　　　　　　　　　　　　　　　Exeunt

5.3

Enter LEONTES, POLIXENES, FLORIZEL, PERDITA, CA-
MILLO, PAULINA, LORDS [*and attendants*][1]
LEONTES   O grave and good Paulina, the great comfort
That I have had of thee!
PAULINA　　　　　　　　　What,° sovereign sir,   *Whatever*
I did not well, I meant well. All my services
You have paid home,° but that you have vouchsafed°   *fully rewarded / vowed*
5   With your crowned brother and these young contracted
Heirs of your kingdoms my poor house to visit,
It is a surplus° of your grace which never   *an additional sign*
My life may last to answer.
LEONTES　　　　　　　　　O Paulina,
We honour you with trouble.[2] But we came
10   To see the statue of our queen. Your gallery
Have we passed through, not without much content
In many singularities;° but we saw not   *In seeing many rarities*
That which my daughter came to look upon,
The statue of her mother.
PAULINA　　　　　　　　As she lived peerless,
15   So her dead likeness I do well believe
Excels what ever yet you looked upon,
Or hand of man hath done. Therefore I keep it
Lonely,° apart. But here it is. Prepare   *Alone*
To see the life as lively mocked° as ever   *realistically imitated*
20   Still° sleep mocked death. Behold, and say 'tis well.   *Quiet*
　　　[*She draws a curtain and reveals the figure of* HERMI-
　　　ONE, *standing like a statue*]
I like your silence; it the more shows off
Your wonder. But yet speak; first you, my liege.
Comes it not something° near?   *somewhat*
LEONTES　　　　　　　　　Her natural posture.
Chide me, dear stone, that I may say indeed
25   Thou art Hermione; or rather, thou art she
In thy not chiding, for she was as tender

5.3 Location: Sicilia. Paulina's house.
1. In F the stage direction reads: *Enter Leontes, Polixenes,*
Florizell, Perdita, Camillo, Paulina: Hermione (like a
Statue:) Lords, etc. For a reader of the play, this direction
suggests that Hermione is a living character pretending to
be a statue. For a theatergoer unacquainted with the play,
by contrast, the immobile female figure seen on stage is
probably first assumed to be an actual statue of the dead
queen.
2. The honor we pay to you demands much of you (by
way of hospitality).

As infancy and grace. But yet, Paulina,
Hermione was not so much wrinkled, nothing°   *not at all*
So agèd as this seems.
POLIXENES   O, not by much.
30 PAULINA   So much the more our carver's excellence,
Which lets go by some sixteen years, and makes her
As° she lived now.   *As if*
LEONTES   As now she might have done,
So much to my good comfort as it is
Now piercing to my soul. O, thus she stood,
35 Even with such life of majesty—warm life,
As now it coldly stands—when first I wooed her.
I am ashamed. Does not the stone rebuke me
For being more stone° than it? O royal piece!°   *hard-hearted / work of art*
There's magic in thy majesty, which has
40 My evils conjured to remembrance, and
From thy admiring° daughter took the spirits,   *wondering*
Standing like stone with thee.
PERDITA   And give me leave,
And do not say 'tis superstition, that
I kneel and then implore her blessing. Lady,
45 Dear Queen, that ended when I but began,
Give me that hand of yours to kiss.
PAULINA   O, patience!
The statue is but newly fixed;° the colour's   *painted*
Not dry.
CAMILLO [*to* LEONTES]   My lord, your sorrow was too sore° laid on,   *painfully*
50 Which sixteen winters cannot blow away,
So many summers dry.[3] Scarce any joy
Did ever so long live; no sorrow
But killed itself much sooner.
POLIXENES [*to* LEONTES]   Dear my brother,
Let him that was the cause of this have power
55 To take off so much grief from you as he
Will piece up in himself.[4]
PAULINA [*to* LEONTES]   Indeed, my lord,
If I had thought the sight of my poor image
Would thus have wrought you°—for the stone is mine—   *made you distraught*
I'd not have showed it.
         [*She makes to draw the curtain*]
LEONTES   Do not draw the curtain.
60 PAULINA   No longer shall you gaze on't, lest your fancy
May think anon it moves.
LEONTES   Let be, let be!
Would I were dead but that methinks already.[5]
What was he that did make it? See, my lord,
Would you not deem it breathed, and that those veins
Did verily bear blood?
65 POLIXENES   Masterly done.
The very life seems warm upon her lip.
LEONTES   The fixture of her eye has motion in't,[6]

---

3. And an equal number of summers cannot dry up.   6. The setting ("fixture") of her eye gives the appearance
4. Will make a part of himself.   of motion.
5. May die if I do not think it already moves.

	As° we are mocked with art.		*In such a way that*
	PAULINA I'll draw the curtain.		
	My lord's almost so far transported that		
	He'll think anon it lives.		
70	LEONTES O sweet Paulina,		

As° we are mocked with art.   *In such a way that*
PAULINA   I'll draw the curtain.
  My lord's almost so far transported that
  He'll think anon it lives.
70   LEONTES   O sweet Paulina,
  Make me to think so twenty years together.
  No settled senses° of the world can match   *calm state of mind*
  The pleasure of that madness. Let't alone.
  PAULINA   I am sorry, sir, I have thus far stirred you; but
  I could afflict you farther.
75   LEONTES   Do, Paulina,
  For this affliction has a taste as sweet
  As any cordial° comfort. Still methinks   *restorative*
  There is an air comes from her.° What fine chisel   *she seems to breathe*
  Could ever yet cut breath? Let no man mock me,
  For I will kiss her.   *
80   PAULINA   Good my lord, forbear.
  The ruddiness upon her lip is wet.
  You'll mar it if you kiss it, stain your own
  With oily painting.° Shall I draw the curtain?   *paint*
  LEONTES   No, not these twenty years.
  PERDITA   So long could I
  Stand by, a looker-on.
85   PAULINA   Either forbear,
  Quit presently° the chapel, or resolve you   *immediately*
  For more amazement. If you can behold it,
  I'll make the statue move indeed, descend,
  And take you by the hand. But then you'll think—
90   Which I protest against—I am assisted
  By wicked powers.
  LEONTES   What you can make her do
  I am content to look on; what to speak,
  I am content to hear; for 'tis as easy
  To make her speak as move.
  PAULINA   It is required
95   You do awake your faith. Then, all stand still.
  Or those that think it is unlawful business
  I am about, let them depart.
  LEONTES   Proceed.
  No foot shall stir.
  PAULINA   Music; awake her; strike!°   *strike up!*
      [*Music*]
  [*To* HERMIONE] 'Tis time. Descend. Be stone no more. Approach.
100   Strike all that look upon with marvel. Come,
  I'll fill your grave up. Stir. Nay, come away.
  Bequeath to death your numbness, for from him°   *(death)*
  Dear life redeems you.
      [*To* LEONTES]   You perceive she stirs.
       [HERMIONE *slowly descends*]
  Start not. Her actions shall be holy as
105   You hear my spell is lawful. Do not shun her
  Until you see her die again, for then
  You kill her double.[7] Nay, present your hand.

---

7. That is, "If you were to shun her in this new life, you would kill her again."

When she was young, you wooed her. Now, in age,
Is she become the suitor?

LEONTES   O, she's warm!

110   If this be magic, let it be an art
Lawful as eating.

POLIXENES   She embraces him.

CAMILLO   She hangs about his neck.
If she pertain to life,° let her speak too.   *be truly alive*

115 POLIXENES   Ay, and make it manifest where she has lived,
Or how stol'n from the dead.

PAULINA   That she is living,
Were it but told you, should be hooted at
Like an old tale. But it appears she lives,
Though yet she speak not. Mark a little while.

120   [*To* PERDITA] Please you to interpose, fair madam. Kneel,
And pray your mother's blessing. — Turn, good lady,
Our Perdita is found.

HERMIONE   You gods, look down,
And from your sacred vials pour your graces
Upon my daughter's head. — Tell me, mine own,

125   Where hast thou been preserved? Where lived? How found
Thy father's court? For thou shalt hear that I,
Knowing by Paulina that the oracle
Gave hope thou wast in being,° have preserved   *alive*
Myself to see the issue.°   *the outcome; the child*

PAULINA   There's time enough for that,

130   Lest they desire upon this push to trouble
Your joys with like relation.[8] Go together,
You precious winners all; your exultation
Partake° to everyone. I, an old turtle,   *Spread your happiness*
Will wing me to some withered bough, and there

135   My mate, that's never to be found again,
Lament till I am lost.°   *dead*

LEONTES   O peace, Paulina!
Thou shouldst a husband take by my consent,
As I by thine a wife. This is a match,
And made between's by vows. Thou hast found mine,

140   But how is to be questioned, for I saw her,
As I thought, dead, and have in vain said many
A prayer upon her grave. I'll not seek far —
For him, I partly know his mind — to find thee
An honourable husband. Come, Camillo,

145   And take her by the hand, whose worth and honesty
Is richly noted, and here justified°   *testified to*
By us, a pair of kings. Let's from this place.
[*To* HERMIONE] What, look upon my brother. Both your pardons,
That e'er I put between your holy looks

150   My ill suspicion. This'° your son-in-law   *This is*
And son unto the King, whom heavens directing
Is troth-plight° to your daughter. Good Paulina,   *betrothed*
Lead us from hence, where we may leisurely
Each one demand and answer to his part

155   Performed in this wide gap of time since first
We were dissevered. Hastily lead away.   *Exeunt*

---

8. Lest they (bystanders?) desire at this crucial moment to trouble your happiness with similar stories.

TEXTUAL VARIANTS

Control text: F
F: The Folio of 1623

s.p. OLD SHEPHERD [F's use of *"Shep⟨heard⟩."* has been changed throughout.]
s.p. FIRST LADY [F's use of *"Lady"* has been changed at 2.1.2, 5, 14, 16.]
s.p. A LORD [F's use of *"Lord"* has been changed throughout 2.1; at 2.3.26, 147, and 197; and at 3.2.114, 172, 200, and 214.

1.2.106 And A   **160 ornament** Ornaments   **209 they** [not in F]   **278 hobby-horse** Holy-Horse
2.2.56 let't le't   **69 twixt** betwixt
2.3.39 What Who
3.2.10 Silence. [italicized and set as stage direction in F]   **31 Who** Whom   **166 certain** [not in F]
3.3.67 bairn Barne   **73 hallooed** hallow'd   **110 made** mad
4.2.3 sixteen fifteene
4.3.10 With heigh, with heigh, *With heigh,*
4.4.12 it [not in F]   **13 swoon** sworne   **98 your** you   **148 so** [not in F]   **160 out** on't   **237 kiln-hole** kill-hole   **239 Clammer** clamor   **298 gentlemen** Gent.   **347 who** whom   **407 acknowledged** acknowledge   **411 who** whom   **416 see** neuer see   **427 hoop** hope   **455 your** my   **577 so** [not in F]   **597 could** would   **685 know not** know   **713 to** at
5.1.21 spoke spoken   **58–59 stage, / Where ... mourn, appear** Stage / (Where ... now appeare)   **61 just** iust such   **78 your** you a
5.3.5 young contracted your contracted   **18 Lonely** Louely   **67 fixture** fixure   **96 Or those** On: those   **150 This'** This

Cymbeline

Toward the end of *Cymbeline*, one of the chief characters, Posthumus Leonatus, awakens from a dream vision to find a tablet on his chest, left there by Jupiter, king of the gods. In the dream, Jupiter had promised that the tablet would explain Posthumus's future fortunes. But when Posthumus reads the writing on the tablet, it is incomprehensible to him:

> 'Tis still a dream, or else such stuff as madmen
> Tongue, . . .
> Or senseless speaking, or a speaking such
> As sense cannot untie.

Yet he concludes: "Be what it is, / The action of my life is like it" (5.5.238–42). By his own estimation, Posthumus's life is a senseless riddle. As he speaks, Posthumus—a British soldier crucial to the Britons' recent victory over Rome but now disguised as a Roman—is himself a prisoner of the victorious British forces. And unbeknownst to him, his wife, Innogen, whom he believes dead by his own order (an order given because of false accusations of sexual infidelity), is alive, disguised as a Roman boy named Fidele.

Such plot complexities are typical of *Cymbeline*. In this play, an inordinate number of characters assume disguises, have more than one name, don't know who their "real" parents are, or find themselves unable to decipher the complicated events around them. In one of the play's most famous (or infamous) scenes, Innogen, traveling in a page's disguise to find Posthumus, wakes up from a drug-induced sleep to find herself lying beside the body of a headless man dressed in her husband's clothing. The man is really Cloten, the wicked son of Innogen's evil stepmother, who is Posthumus's rival for her hand. Seeing the headless body, Innogen breaks into a lament for the man she believes to be her husband. Her grief is genuine and affecting, but it is prompted by a profound misreading of the object before her.

The improbabilities and complexities of *Cymbeline*'s plot have given some critics pause, as has the freedom with which times and places are handled. Ostensibly set in Roman Britain at the time of Christ's birth (which, according to the chronicles, occurred during the reign of Cymbeline), the play also contains scenes that appear to take place in contemporary sixteenth-century Italy. It is in this modern Italy, for example, that Posthumus is tricked into believing that Innogen is sexually unfaithful to him. Reacting to the play's unusual features, the eighteenth-century critic Samuel Johnson complained:

> This play has many just sentiments, some natural dialogues, and some pleasing scenes, but they are obtained at the expense of much incongruity. To remark the folly of the fiction, the absurdity of the conduct, the confusion of the names, and manners of different times, and the impossibility of the events in any system of life, were to waste criticism upon unresisting imbecility, upon faults too evident for detection, and too gross for aggravation.

This response, however, may say more about Johnson's neoclassical tastes than about the ultimate value of Shakespeare's play. In *Cymbeline*, the complexity of the action seems deliberate rather than inadvertent or unskillful. It creates in the audience both a longing for clarity and control and an anxiety that the play may afford neither. The pleasure of the final act, therefore, stems from the relief experienced when—after a dizzying whirl of events, reversals, revelations, and disguises—peace descends, all identities revealed and all riddles expounded. The sense of wonder produced by this miraculous untangling of complicated events is one of the signal effects of Shakespeare's late plays: amazement that after astonishing suffering can come new hope, after labyrinthine confusions the solace of questions answered.

This feature of the play is one of the reasons that in modern criticism *Cymbeline* is usually called a romance or sometimes a tragicomedy, though in the First Folio of 1623 it was grouped with the tragedies. The plays written late in Shakespeare's theatrical career that emphasize the miraculous transformation of suffering to joy include, besides *Cymbeline, The Winter's Tale, Pericles*, and *The Tempest*. Verging on tragedy, they all nonetheless win through to bittersweet conclusions in which shattered families are reconstituted and plot complexities untangled—but always at a cost. Mistakes have consequences in these plays. Sons die; years are lost in exile and wandering; women suffer from unjust slander. If, in the end, good fortune returns to the sufferers, it does not cancel their former pain but provides a miraculous contrast to it.

The date of *Cymbeline* is uncertain, though it is usually given as 1609 or 1610. Scholars differ as to whether it proceeded or followed *The Winter's Tale*. We know that it was in performance by 1611, because Simon Forman, a London doctor and astrologer, wrote about seeing it, probably between April 20 and April 30 of that year. It is not clear whether he saw the play at the Globe, the outdoor theater Shakespeare's company used after 1599, or at Blackfriars, the indoor theater they also began to use in 1608. The spectacular scenic effects possible in staging this play, such as the descent of Jupiter on the back of an eagle in Act 5, may have been designed with the more elaborate technical capacities of the Blackfriars venue in mind. Some critics have tried to date the play by relating it to the

The eagle, king of birds and emblem of the Roman god Jupiter; according to myth, it could stare at the sun without blinking and fly into the sun in order to burn off its old feathers. From Joachim Camerarius, *Symbola et Emblemata* (1605).

investiture of Henry, King James's oldest son, as Prince of Wales in 1610, since a number of the key scenes of the play take place in Wales. We have no record of a court performance of the play until 1634, however, when it was played before King Charles, who liked it. Other critics have tried to determine the play's relationship to Beaumont and Fletcher's popular tragicomedy *Philaster*, usually dated 1609, to which *Cymbeline* bears some resemblances. But though the two plays are related, it is not clear which influenced the other.

Whatever its exact date, *Cymbeline* belongs to Shakespeare's late period, and because of its setting it allowed Shakespeare simultaneously to address his long-standing interests both in British and in Roman history. The play intertwines three plot lines and draws on a variety of source materials. The main plot involves Innogen, the daughter and apparently the only living heir of Cymbeline, King of Britain, and her thwarted attempts to live with her chosen husband, Posthumus. Angry that Innogen loves a man of lesser social rank than herself and that she has not married Cloten, his second wife's son, Cymbeline banishes Posthumus from Britain. Posthumus goes to Italy, where he wagers on his wife's chastity with the villain Giacomo, who ultimately makes Posthumus believe Innogen unfaithful. Whether the love of Innogen and Posthumus can be restored is one of the key questions of this plot. This wager story draws on two sources: Boccacio's *Decameron*, a series of prose tales first translated into English in 1620 but available in a French translation in the sixteenth century, and *Frederick of Jennen*, an English translation of a German version of the same story.

A second plot strand deals with Britain's relationship with Rome, especially Rome's demand that the Britons pay the tribute pledged to Julius Caesar upon his conquest of the isle. For this part of the story, Shakespeare drew primarily on the brief account of Cymbeline's reign in Raphael Holinshed's *Chronicles of England, Scotland, and Ireland* (second edition, 1587). Cymbeline was King when the Roman Emperor Augustus Caesar ushered in the famous time of peace known as the *pax Romana*. In most of the sources, it was Cymbeline's son Guiderius who refused to pay Rome tribute. Shakespeare modified the story, however, so that Cymbeline, urged on by his Queen and her son, is the one who withholds the tribute and provokes a Roman invasion.

The third plot line has to do with two sons of Cymbeline, stolen from their nursery by a wrongly defamed courtier, Belarius, who raises them in the mountains of Wales. By chance, their sister Innogen, disguised as a boy, stumbles upon their mountain cave on her flight from her father's court in pursuit of Posthumus. Near this cave, Cloten, wearing Posthumus's clothes, is killed by one of these sons; also near this cave, Innogen awakes from her sleep to find herself beside his headless body. For the play to reach its resolution, Cymbeline's sons must be reunited with their father. This reunion occurs, but only after the sons play a decisive role in the final battle against the Roman invaders. Their heroic actions in this battle are modeled on quite another part of Holinshed, *The History of Scotland*, which recounts the story of a farmer named Hay and his two sons, who routed Danish invaders at the Battle of Luncarty in A.D. 976.

From these complex and diverse materials, Shakespeare wove a play whose rich allusiveness has invited many kinds of topical interpretations. One line of criticism has focused on *Cymbeline*'s relationship to events and ideas connected to the reign of King James I. James was interested in linking imperial Rome and the Roman emperors to modern Britain and to his own kingship. He had himself painted crowned with laurel leaves, in the Roman manner, and had coins stamped with his laurel-crowned profile. Like Augustus Caesar, James presented himself as the great peacemaker after Elizabeth's reluctant involvement in wars in Ireland and in defending the Protestant countries of the Continent against Catholic powers, especially Spain. Moreover, just as Augustus ruled over a vast empire, James aspired to unite Scotland and England (along with the already incorporated Wales) into a single entity with one church and one set of laws. His project failed, but he exerted much effort in promoting this union during the first years of his reign. *Cymbeline* uncannily echoes some of James's preoccupations. Sometimes called Shakespeare's last Roman play, *Cymbeline* dramatizes ancient Britain's attempts to come to terms with imperial Rome. Names of Roman gods—particularly Diana, Apollo, and Jupiter—abound (Jupiter

James I liked to present himself as heir to Roman greatness. In this 1613 engraving, Crispin van de Passe portrays him in the laurel wreath worn by Roman emperors.

alone is mentioned over thirty times); and figures from Roman myth and history, such as Tarquin, Philomela, and Aeneas, are often evoked. The play's title character, like James, is a British monarch respectful of Rome, even when asserting his independence in the matter of the tribute. The final word of the play, spoken by the King, is "peace." The analogies between the play and the Stuart court, however, have their limits. Cymbeline is also a King duped by his wicked Queen and her doltish son—hardly a compliment to James and the royal family if events in the play are seen literally to mirror their circumstances.

Other allusions expand the play's possible range of meanings. Much is made, for example, of Milford Haven, the port in southern Wales where the Romans come ashore for their invasion of England. This port was famous to Shakespeare's audience as the place where Henry Richmond landed in 1485 to begin his assault on the forces of Richard III. Having defeated Richard, Richmond was crowned Henry VII, first of the Tudor kings; Henry's daughter Margaret married James IV of Scotland, grandfather to the James who assumed the English throne in 1603. When the Romans land at Milford Haven, they in effect precipitate a transformation of the kingdom much as Henry Richmond was to do fifteen hundred years later. At the time of their arrival, Cymbeline believes his two sons dead, and his daughter and Cloten have both fled the court. Britain is without an heir. But through the battle with the Romans, the lost sons of Cymbeline are discovered and the kingdom renewed. So too James fancied himself an agent of renewal, a second Henry VII arriving from Scotland to unite the whole island under his rule.

Wales itself is an important symbolic location in this play. Though officially incorporated into England in the 1530s, Wales remained quite distinct, often stigmatized as rude and uncivilized. The Welsh language, banned from use in public contexts, was taken to symbolize the barbarity of this borderland region. On the other hand, in some narratives, Wales was also the place from which the legitimate rulers of England sprang. The stories surrounding the mythical King Arthur give him a Welsh origin, and traditionally the eldest son of the British monarch was (and still is) given the title Prince of Wales. In *Cymbeline*, Wales is imagined as a harsh pastoral landscape in which Belarius and the King's sons live in a cave, hunt the food they eat, and have little contact with other human beings. These sons, Guiderius and Arviragus, frequently complain that they know nothing of the world and its customs and manners. But Wales shelters these sons as they grow to manhood and protects them from the vices of court life. In fact, as is traditional in pastoral literature, the Welsh scenes contain a good deal of anticourt satire. In the play's spatial and symbolic economies, Wales is the place where true British manhood is preserved. In part, the Welsh material can be seen as a compliment to Prince Henry, who was a staunch champion of the Protestant cause in Europe and showed every promise of being a more martial figure than his peace-loving father.

There can be little doubt that *Cymbeline* works with material imbued with a new kind of significance under the reign of James. Yet it may be a mistake to tie the play too closely to the royal family or to particular events. The play doesn't just reflect the world around it; it transforms the materials from that world into a powerful imaginative and ideological structure. In the largest sense, *Cymbeline* works to define both Britain and proper British manhood by constructing a complex narrative about national origins. The wager plot, with its story of sexual slander and threatened rape, is central to that narrative, not only because Innogen often seems to stand for Britain itself (she is several times addressed as "Britain," and she bears the name of the wife of Brute, the legendary ancient King of Britain), but also because the realignment of gender relations plays a crucial role in the "renewal" of Britain and in the play's turn from tragedy to comedy.

Strikingly, this play about Britain's past never mentions the word "England." In the history plays written in the 1590s, the reverse tends to be true: "Britain" is seldom employed, "England" is invoked with great frequency. There are several reasons for Shakespeare's choice in this later play. He is, of course, deliberately evoking the world of the ancient Britons, the early inhabitants of the island who provide the starting point for his creation of a fictive national past. At the same time, he is to some extent reflecting, and helping to create, the Stuart monarch's sense of the entity over which he ruled. James, after all, was not an "Englander" in the same way Elizabeth had been. He was a Scotsman who spoke with an accent and aspired to bring the entire island into a new political alignment.

Setting the play in the reign of Cymbeline allowed Shakespeare to imagine a primitive Britain that was also the cosmopolitan heir to the westward movement of empire. The treatment of Rome is particularly interesting in *Cymbeline*. Partly, the Romans are figured as an invading force, threatening the island. Yet the British characters most eager to repel the Romans and to treat them as an enemy are the evil Queen and her evil son. Cymbeline himself, while defending Britain's right to live free and under its own laws, is more disposed to come to terms with his great opponents and invariably treats them with respect. There is, in fact, a pronounced tension in the play between Britain's desires to defeat the Romans and to emulate them. This tension is managed in part through the splitting of the Romans into the noble figure of Lucius and the devilish figure of Giacomo, who in his deceit and misogyny embodies sixteenth-century stereotypes concerning the villainous Italian.

When Giacomo comes to Britain to test Innogen's fidelity, he fails in his initial attempt to portray Posthumus as a philanderer upon whom Innogen should seek sexual revenge. He then proceeds more secretly; he has himself conveyed in a trunk into her bedroom, from which he issues in the dead of night to survey her sleeping body and the contents of her room. His stealthy act is framed by references to infamous acts of rape. As he steps from the trunk, Giacomo compares himself to Tarquin, the Roman tyrant who raped Lucrece (a story told in Shakespeare's lengthy poem *The Rape of Lucrece*, written in the 1590s). Furthermore, the book Innogen had been reading when she fell asleep is opened to the story of Tereus, who raped Philomela and cut out her tongue. Though Giacomo does not literally rape Innogen, he violates the privacy of her body with his peering eyes and rapes her honor by lying successfully to Posthumus about her infidelity. At one level, this incident is about the unjust sufferings of a slandered woman. At another level, Innogen is Britain, threatened by a skillful invader. Giacomo penetrates Innogen's bedchamber, and later he penetrates the ear of Posthumus with his poisonous slander.

In the play's denouement, the threat of foreign penetration is graphically repelled when Belarius and the sons of Cymbeline come from the Welsh mountains, joined by Posthumus disguised as a British peasant, and take a stand "in a narrow lane," putting the Romans to flight and instilling courage in the British. The vulnerable vaginal passage is thus barricaded against outsiders by the phallic sons of Cymbeline crying, "Stand, stand" (5.5.28); "stand" is a slang term for "have an erection." This event proves pivotal, lending itself equally well to aphorism and to Posthumus's mocking rhyme: "Two boys, an old man twice a boy, a lane, / Preserved the Britons, was the Romans' bane" (5.5.57–58). In the play's symbolic economy, the threat of penetration initiated by Giacomo is thus repulsed, and in the final scene Giacomo kneels to Posthumus, asking his forgiveness—the Italian subdued by the Briton.

Something quite different occurs with Lucius, the Roman military leader, who embodies the laudable virtues of ancient Rome rather than the hideous vices of sixteenth-century Italy. Though the Roman army is defeated, Cymbeline decides to resume paying tribute, and in his final speech the King says: "let / A Roman and a British ensign wave / Friendly together" (5.6.479–81). This rapprochment of warring powers is ratified by one of the play's several mysterious visions. Before the battle, a Roman soothsayer told Lucius what the gods had revealed to him:

> I saw Jove's bird, the Roman eagle, winged
> From the spongy south to this part of the west,
> There vanished in the sunbeams; which portends,
> Unless my sins abuse my divination,
> Success to th' Roman host.
>
> (4.2.350–54)

In this play, not even soothsayers have perfect interpretive skills. The outcome of the battle requires some revisions in the exegesis of the vision. Now the soothsayer says:

> For the Roman eagle,
> From south to west on wing soaring aloft,
> Lessened herself, and in the beams o'th' sun
> So vanished; which foreshowed our princely eagle
> Th'imperial Caesar should again unite
> His favour with the radiant Cymbeline,
> Which shines here in the west.
>
> (5.6.470–76)

Conquest has been transformed into concord as the Roman eagle and the British sun merge and as Cymbeline celebrates this peace within the temple of Jupiter.

In stressing the final union of Britain and Rome, the play's conclusion makes Britain the heir of Rome's imperial legacy even as Britain proclaims the integrity of her own land, laws, and customs. In the early modern period, the course of empire was thought to move westward. When Troy fell, the Trojan hero Aeneas bore his father on his back from the fires of the burning city and eventually fulfilled his destiny by establishing a new kingdom in Italy in what was to become the center of the Roman Empire. In the soothsayer's vision, the Roman eagle journeys even farther west, renewing itself, as eagles were believed to do, by enduring the burning fires of Britain's sun to purge away old feathers in preparation for the growth of new.

The play's culminating vision of a Britain separate unto itself but also the cosmopolitan heir of an imperial tradition is anticipated in the actions of Innogen and Posthumus. In the final act, both are partly Roman in their dress and sympathies. Posthumus Leonatus comes to Britain in the company of the Italian gentry, but then dresses as a British peasant and fights with Belarius in the narrow lane before reassuming his Italian garb. Innogen is present at the battle as page to Lucius, the Roman general who had found her weeping over the headless corpse of Cloten. In the final moments of reconciliation, Cymbeline's daughter and her husband stand before the British King in foreign clothes. Innogen, more-

The Trojan hero Aeneas bearing his father, Anchises, from the burning city of Troy. From Andrea Alciati, *Omnia Emblemata* (1577).

over, earlier makes a telling speech about Britain's place in the world when discussing with a trusted servant where she would live after Posthumus had come to believe her unchaste. Her father's court, with Cloten present, she finds unthinkable. She then asks:

> Hath Britain all the sun that shines? Day, night,
> Are they not but in Britain? I'th' world's volume
> Our Britain seems as of it but not in't,
> In a great pool a swan's nest.
>
> (3.4.136–39)

Innogen nicely captures the play's most complex view of Britain. Eschewing an insular patriotism associated with Cloten and the Queen, she recognizes a vast world beyond the shores of Britain. That world is a huge book (volume) in which Britain is but a detached page, or a great pool in which Britain is a swan's nest. As the image of the swan's nest indicates, Britain remains the special seat of grace and beauty. But it is also connected to something larger than itself. There are other pages in the volume to which, even if detached, Britain belongs.

The play, then, seems to be negotiating a new vision of the nation suited for the Stuart moment, a vision resulting from the richly suggestive concatenation of discursive traditions Shakespeare brought together in this play. Reaching back into the chronicle materials of ancient Britain, he provides a genealogy for modern Britain that (1) insists on the integrity and freedom of the island kingdom but (2) presents it as purged—largely through the efforts of the King's "Welsh" sons—of the corruptions of modern court life as embodied in figures such as Giacomo or Cloten, and (3) aligns Britain with the cosmopolitan values of Rome and positions the island kingdom as the appropriate heir of Roman greatness: both warlike and peace-loving.

The renewed Britain has a fourth striking characteristic, and that is its decidedly masculine coloration. The wager plot makes plain the role of gender in configuring British national identity. Consider first the changing fortunes of Innogen. At the beginning of the play, she is a beloved and important figure in her father's court. Cymbeline's only living heir, the Princess is also strong-willed and decisive. She chooses Posthumus for her husband even though he has little money and is not of royal birth. By the end of the play, Innogen has been displaced from the succession by her two rediscovered brothers; she has also been ordered killed by her husband, threatened with rape, knocked unconscious by a drug she believes to be medicine, and struck by her husband when, in her page's attire, she steps forward to reveal her identity to him in the last scene. Though cross-dressed for much of the second half of the play, she does not, like Portia in *The Merchant of Venice* and Rosalind in *As You Like It*, use that disguise aggressively to shape her own destiny. Rather, burdened by the knowledge that her husband unjustly and inexplicably desires her death, Innogen grows less powerful and more passive as the play progresses. Her decline can be summarized in the pun on "heir" and "air." Innogen begins as the former and ends as the latter. The mysterious tablet laid on Posthumus's breast contained a riddling prophecy: "Whenas a lion's whelp shall, to himself unknown, without seeking find, and be embraced by a piece of tender air; and when from a stately cedar shall be lopped branches which, being dead many years, shall after revive, be jointed to the old stock, and freshly grow; then shall Posthumus end his miseries, Britain be fortunate and flourish in peace and plenty" (5.5.232–37). When the soothsayer finally untangles this riddle, he declares Posthumus Leonatus to be the lion's offspring; Cymbeline the cedar tree; his lost sons the lopped branches; and Innogen the tender air, because "tender air" in Latin translates as *mollis aer*, which (by a stretch of the imagination) derives from *mulier*, Latin for "wife." When Posthumus is embraced by the "tender air" (no longer an "heir"), his miseries will cease. Apparently because she is now less important to the succession, Innogen is allowed to live with her chosen husband, his masculinity affirmed by his pivotal role in the British victory over the Roman forces.

Victorian critics loved Innogen, idealizing her as a paragon of selfless and long-suffering womanhood. For example, the Princess never protests her demotion from the position of heir apparent; in fact, she says that she considers finding her brothers worth the loss of the kingdom. To many contemporary critics, however, her role in the play's narrative of nation is a troubling one. Britain renews itself as women are disempowered or disappear. Cymbeline's Queen is an embodiment of hypocritical viciousness (Shakespeare does not even bother to give her a name), and her son, a figure whose father is never mentioned or seen, bears her taint. The play's happy resolution occurs only after all traces of this Queen and her offspring have been erased. When finally united with his children, Cymbeline articulates the fantasy of having himself given birth to all three: "O, what am I? / A mother to the birth of three? Ne'er mother / Rejoiced deliverance more" (5.6.369–71). This is the dream of androgenesis, reproduction without union with women.

Much earlier in the play, Posthumus, believing himself cuckolded by Innogen, voices a similar wish: "Is there no way for men to be, but women / Must be half-workers?" (2.5.1–2). In one of the most deeply misogynist speeches in the Shakespeare canon, Posthumus then blames all the vices of the world on "the woman's part" (line 20)—on woman herself and on that part of woman lodged in man, Eve's mark upon the human race. This mistaken projection onto woman of responsibility for evil is one reason why the androgenesis fantasy appears in the play and why, in the last scene, no persons appareled as women are to be seen (Innogen is still dressed as a page). The happy union of Britain and Rome and Wales is overwhelmingly a union of men.

The play's own counterpoint to its exclusion of women from public power is its demonization of the slanderous Giacomo and its depiction of Posthumus's gradual recovery of faith in Innogen. When Posthumus receives a bloody cloth signifying (falsely) that his order to murder Innogen has been fulfilled, he is overcome with remorse and berates husbands like himself for murdering wives "for wrying but a little" (5.1.5). At this point, Posthumus still believes his wife to have been sexually unfaithful to him, yet he castigates himself for having ordered her punished. His words form a remarkable exception to the more usual patriarchal assumption that female chastity is the primary marker of a woman's value and virtue and that loss of chastity is an unforgivable crime. Critics differ as to how much weight to assign this speech. Posthumus makes it when he believes Innogen to be dead; and generally it is easier to forgive the dead than the living. By the time he is finally reconciled to the living, breathing woman, Giacomo's lies have been exposed and Posthumus takes to himself a wife whose chastity is not in question.

The play, however, overtly punishes violence against women when the evil Cloten, who had fantasized raping Innogen, is beheaded, and it punishes misogynous lies when Giacomo must submit to Posthumus in the final scene. Posthumus, who had formerly himself believed slander against Innogen and had attempted to have her killed, repents and becomes the play's image of the proper husband. After Posthumus's performance in battle and when Innogen is no longer heir apparent, Cymbeline withdraws his objections to Posthumus's union with her. Nevertheless, Innogen's formerly dominant position in that marriage now seems to belong to Posthumus, with Jupiter himself providing the warrant for this reversal. In prison, Posthumus has a dream that not only reconnects him to his familial origins but also provides an image of his own future family. As he sleeps, Posthumus's two warlike brothers and his warlike father appear to him. The father is described as "leading in his hand an ancient matron, his wife, and mother to Posthumus" (stage direction following 5.5.123). After this dream, sent by Jupiter, Posthumus recovers his "true" identity as Innogen's husband and Britain's warrior hero. As he assumes his position in the honored line of Leonati men, the place marked for Innogen is that of Roman / British wife, "led in his hand." In its narratives of nation, *Cymbeline* seems able to reprove the most virulent forms of misogyny only when it simultaneously removes women from public power, transforms them into chaste, domesticated wives, and reaffirms the dominance of husbands.

Samuel Johnson was right when he said that *Cymbeline* is a play with many incongruities of time, place, and circumstance. And yet it is not an incoherent play but rather one that richly interweaves the history of the nation with the stories of the figures who take up their positions in that nation. What is eerie about *Cymbeline* is that its characters often understand so little about what is happening to them, and yet each appears to play out the part assigned to him or her by some higher power: Jupiter, destiny, time. But fictions of inevitability can be deceiving. One should remember that the soothsayer had to revise his interpretation of his vision of the eagle and the sun to make his narrative square with events as they actually happened. And to decipher Posthumus's tablet, he could make the prophecy tally with the facts only by means of a tortuous transformation of "tender air" into "wife." This might suggest that in this play, at least, the higher powers determine less than they appear to do; rather, the forms taken by family, nation, and empire are the result of human efforts, interventions, and narratives. Shakespeare's play is one such narrative. The resolution of its complex plot may invite relieved assent to its culminating vision, but the very artifice of that resolution also reveals its contingency, suggesting that there is nothing either natural or inevitable about the familial and political arrangements that are the objects of negotiation and struggle in this tragicomic play.

JEAN E. HOWARD

TEXTUAL NOTE

Cymbeline was first printed in the First Folio (F) of 1623. Its heavy punctuation suggests that it was prepared for printing by a professional scribe—perhaps by Ralph Crane, who is believed to have prepared five of Shakespeare's other plays for the print shop. While not every feature associated with a Crane manuscript is displayed, the use of parentheses, hyphens, and apostrophes in the Folio text of *Cymbeline* is consistent with Crane's practice. Because the scribe regularized the manuscript he copied, it is hard to determine the exact nature of that manuscript. It may or may not have been a promptbook. Though the Folio text contains almost no stage directions relating to sounds, such as trumpet flourishes to mark ceremonial entrances and exits or the noises associated with battle or with hunting parties, this elision of clues to performance practice is characteristic of "literary" transcripts of the sort associated with Crane.

In this edition, several names have been changed from the versions that appear in F. F's "Iachimo" has been modernized to "Giacomo," the Italian name for "James," on the grounds that a modernized text of Shakespeare should also give personal names in modernized forms. Other editors have proposed "Jackimo" as an alternative modernization. F's "Philario" has also been modernized to "Filario." In this instance, F itself uses the form "Filorio" at 1.1.98, though elsewhere it employs "Philario." Finally, the heroine's name, given as "Imogen" in F, is here changed to "Innogen." There are several reasons for this alteration. In Holinshed's *Chronicles*, one of Shakespeare's sources for the play, the wife of Brute (an early King of England) was named Innogen. Many scholars assume that this was Shakespeare's source for the name. In addition, Simon Forman, one of Shakespeare's contemporaries, who described a performance of the play in 1611, gave the name of the Princess as Innogen. Forman could have gotten the name wrong, but he might have been accurately recording a fact of performance lost in the printed text. Finally, in *Much Ado About Nothing*, Leonato has a wife called Innogen (who never makes a stage appearance); that couple might thus anticipate the Innogen and Leonatus of *Cymbeline*. The Oxford editors surmise that the compositors who set type for F misread the word "Innogen," mistaking "nn" for "m" and so printing "Imogen." Other scholars disagree, arguing that Shakespeare might well have changed a name he found in his sources and that Forman may have misheard what he observed on the stage or may have remembered the name from his own reading and mistakenly attributed it to the production.

Act and scene divisions in this text follow those employed in most editions since the eighteenth century, with several exceptions, all in Act 5. In most texts, the culminating battle between the Romans and Britons occurs in 5.2. The Oxford editors divide this battle sequence into three scenes—5.2, 5.3, and 5.4—because at two points the stage is momentarily cleared. On the other hand, most editions separate the action that immediately follows the battle into two scenes: Posthumus's arrest by the Britons after this battle, then the actual depiction of his captivity and the appearance of his family to him in a dream. This edition makes these events into one continuous scene, 5.5, since there is no evidence that Posthumus and his jailers ever leave the stage between these two actions.

SELECTED BIBLIOGRAPHY

Adelman, Janet. "Masculine Authority and the Maternal Body: The Return to Origins in the Romances." *Suffocating Mothers: Fantasies of Maternal Origins in Shakespeare's Plays, "Hamlet" to "The Tempest."* Routledge: London, 1992. 193–238.

Bergeron, David. "Shakespeare's Romances." *Shakespeare's Romances and the Royal Family.* Lawrence: University Press of Kansas, 1985. 113–222.

Harris, Bernard. " 'What's past is prologue': *Cymbeline* and *Henry VIII.*" *Later Shakespeare.* Ed. John Russell Brown and Bernard Harris. London: Edward Arnold, 1966. 203–34.

Jones, Emrys. "Stuart *Cymbeline.*" *Essays in Criticism* 11 (1961): 84–99.

Knight, George Wilson. "Cymbeline." *The Crown of Life: Essays in Interpretation of Shakespeare's Final Plays.* London: Oxford University Press, 1947. 129–202.

Marcus, Leah S. "James." *Puzzling Shakespeare: Local Reading and Its Discontents.* Berkeley: University of California Press, 1988. 106–59.

Mikalachki, Jodi. "The Masculine Romance of Roman Britain: *Cymbeline* and Early Modern Nationalism." *Shakespeare Quarterly* 46 (1995): 301–22.

Parker, Patricia. "Romance and Empire: Anachronistic *Cymbeline.*" *Unfolded Tales: Essays on Renaissance Romance.* Ed. George M. Logan and Gordon Teskey. Ithaca, N.Y.: Cornell University Press, 1989. 189–207.

Skura, Meredith. "Interpreting Posthumus' Dream from Above and Below: Families, Psychoanalysis, and Literary Critics." *Representing Shakespeare: New Psychoanalytic Essays.* Ed. Murray M. Schwartz and Coppélia Kahn. Baltimore: Johns Hopkins University Press, 1980. 203–16.

Warren, Roger, *Shakespeare in Performance: Cymbeline.* Manchester: Manchester University Press, 1989.

Cymbeline, King of Britain

The Persons of the Play

CYMBELINE, King of Britain
Princess INNOGEN, his daughter, later disguised as a man
   named Fidele
GUIDERIUS, known as Polydore ⎱ Cymbeline's sons, stolen by Belarius
ARVIRAGUS, known as Cadwal ⎰
QUEEN, Cymbeline's wife, Innogen's stepmother
Lord CLOTEN, her son
BELARIUS, a banished lord, calling himself Morgan
CORNELIUS, a physician
HELEN, a lady attending on Innogen
Two LORDS attending on Cloten
Two GENTLEMEN
Two British CAPTAINS
Two JAILERS
POSTHUMUS Leonatus, a poor gentleman, Innogen's husband
PISANIO, his servant
FILARIO, a friend of Posthumus
GIACOMO, an Italian ⎰
A FRENCHMAN ⎱
A DUTCHMAN ⎰ Filario's friends
A SPANIARD ⎰
Caius LUCIUS, ambassador from Rome, later General of the
   Roman forces
Two Roman SENATORS
Roman TRIBUNES
A Roman CAPTAIN
Philharmonus, a SOOTHSAYER
JUPITER
Ghost of SICILIUS Leonatus, father of Posthumus
Ghost of the MOTHER of Posthumus
Ghosts of the BROTHERS of Posthumus
Lords attending on Cymbeline, ladies attending on the Queen,
   musicians attending on Cloten, messengers, soldiers

1.1

Enter two GENTLEMEN

FIRST GENTLEMAN   You do not meet a man but frowns. Our bloods
  No more obey the heavens than our courtiers
  Still seem as does the King.[1]
SECOND GENTLEMAN   But what's the matter?
FIRST GENTLEMAN   His daughter, and the heir of 's kingdom, whom
5 He purposed to° his wife's sole son—a widow   *intended for*
  That late° he married—hath referred° herself   *recently / given*
  Unto a poor but worthy gentleman. She's wedded,

1.1 Location: Cymbeline's court, Britain.
1. *Our . . . King:* Our dispositions ("bloods") are not more
subject to planetary influences than our courtiers' moods
are determined by the King's. (The planets were believed
to affect human actions and emotions.)

Her husband banished, she imprisoned. All
Is outward sorrow, though I think the King
Be touched at very heart.

10 SECOND GENTLEMAN   None but the King?
FIRST GENTLEMAN   He° that hath lost her, too. So is the Queen,   *(the Queen's son)*
That most desired the match. But not a courtier—
Although they wear their faces to the bent
Of° the King's looks—hath a heart that is not   *In accordance with*
Glad of the thing they scowl at.

15 SECOND GENTLEMAN   And why so?
FIRST GENTLEMAN   He that hath missed the Princess is a thing
Too bad for bad report, and he that hath her—
I mean that married her—alack, good man,
And therefore banished!—is a creature such
20 As, to seek through the regions of the earth
For one his like, there would be something failing°   *lacking*
In him that should compare.² I do not think
So fair an outward and such stuff° within   *substance; fabric*
Endows a man but he.
SECOND GENTLEMAN   You speak him far.°   *praise him greatly*
25 FIRST GENTLEMAN   I do extend him, sir, within himself;³
Crush him together rather than unfold
His measure duly.⁴
SECOND GENTLEMAN   What's his name and birth?
FIRST GENTLEMAN   I cannot delve him to the root.⁵ His father
Was called Sicilius, who did join his honour°   *prowess (as a soldier)*
30 Against the Romans with Cassibelan
But had his titles by Tenantius,⁶ whom
He served with glory and admired success,
So gained the sur-addition 'Leonatus';⁷
And had, besides this gentleman in question,
35 Two other sons who in the wars o'th' time
Died with their swords in hand; for which their father,
Then old and fond of issue,° took such sorrow   *of his offspring*
That he quit being, and his gentle lady,
Big of° this gentleman, our theme, deceased   *Pregnant with*
40 As he was born. The King, he takes the babe
To his protection, calls him Posthumus⁸ Leonatus,
Breeds him,° and makes him of his bedchamber;⁹   *Brings him up*
Puts to him° all the learnings that his time   *Offers him*
Could make him the receiver of, which he took
45 As we do air, fast as 'twas ministered,
And in 's spring became a harvest; lived in court—
Which rare it is to do—most praised, most loved;
A sample° to the youngest, to th' more mature   *An example*
A glass that feated them,¹ and to the graver
50 A child that guided dotards.° To his mistress,   *foolish old men*

---

2. In any man selected for comparison.
3. I set forth his virtues, sir, within the boundaries of his own merit.
4. *rather . . . duly:* rather than reveal what he is really worth. The metaphor picks up on the sense of "stuff" as "fabric" in line 23. Fabric can be crushed together or unfolded and accurately measured.
5. I cannot completely account for his lineage.
6. Tenantius was Cymbeline's father and the brother of Cassibelan, who in 3.1.5 is described as Cymbeline's uncle.
7. The additional name "Leonatus" (born of a lion).
8. In Latin, the word means "after death." As applied to a child, it means "one born after his or her father's death."
9. Makes him a personal servant.
1. A mirror that furnished ("feated") them with images of virtue or elegance.

For whom he now is banished, her own price
Proclaims how she esteemed him and his virtue.[2]
By her election° may be truly read   *choice (of him)*
What kind of man he is.
SECOND GENTLEMAN   I honour him
55   Even out° of your report. But pray you tell me,   *Even beyond the limits*
Is she sole child to th' King?
FIRST GENTLEMAN   His only child.
He had two sons—if this be worth your hearing,
Mark it: the eld'st of them at three years old,
I'th' swathing° clothes the other, from their nursery   *swaddling*
60   Were stol'n, and to this hour no guess in knowledge°   *no informed conjecture*
Which way they went.
SECOND GENTLEMAN   How long is this ago?
FIRST GENTLEMAN   Some twenty years.
SECOND GENTLEMAN   That a king's children should be so conveyed,
65   So slackly guarded, and the search so slow
That could not trace them!
FIRST GENTLEMAN   Howsoe'er 'tis strange,
Or that the negligence may well be laughed at,
Yet is it true, sir.
SECOND GENTLEMAN   I do well believe you.
      Enter the QUEEN, POSTHUMUS, *and* INNOGEN[3]
FIRST GENTLEMAN   We must forbear.° Here comes the gentleman,   *withdraw*
70   The Queen and Princess.   *Exeunt [the two* GENTLEMEN]*[4]
QUEEN   No, be assured you shall not find me, daughter,
After the slander of[5] most stepmothers,
Evil-eyed unto you. You're my prisoner, but
Your jailer shall deliver you the keys
75   That lock up your restraint. For you, Posthumus,
So soon as I can win th'offended King
I will be known your advocate. Marry,[6] yet
The fire of rage is in him, and 'twere good
You leaned unto° his sentence with what patience   *You obeyed*
Your wisdom may inform° you.   *instill in*
80 POSTHUMUS   Please your highness,
I will from hence today.
QUEEN   You know the peril.
I'll fetch a turn about the garden, pitying
The pangs of barred affections, though the King
Hath charged you should not speak together.   *Exit*
85 INNOGEN   O dissembling courtesy! How fine this tyrant
Can tickle° where she wounds! My dearest husband,   *flatter*
I something° fear my father's wrath, but nothing—   *somewhat*
Always reserved my holy duty—what

---

2. *her . . . virtue:* the price she paid (for loving him) dem-
onstrates how much she valued him and his virtue; her
own worth ("price") shows the high esteem in which she
held him and his virtues.
3. In F, the name of the Princess is Imogen; but in Holin-
shed's *Chronicles,* the wife of the ancient English king
Brute is called Innogen. A number of scholars have
concluded that Shakespeare took the name from Holin-
shed. For a fuller discussion of the Innogen/Imogen de-

bate, see the Textual Note.
4. F marks *Scena Secunda* (second scene) after the gen-
tlemen exit. Then the Queen, Posthumus, and Innogen
enter. There is, however, no change of time or place, and
the Queen and the lovers are probably in view at line 69
when the First Gentleman announces their entrance.
Most previous editors do not indicate a new scene here.
5. In accordance with the slanderous things said about.
6. A mild oath, from the name of the Virgin Mary.

His rage can do on me.[7] You must be gone,
90 And I shall here abide the hourly shot
Of angry eyes, not comforted to live
But that there is this jewel in the world
That I may see again.

POSTHUMUS   My queen, my mistress!
O lady, weep no more, lest I give cause
95 To be suspected of more tenderness
Than doth become a man. I will remain
The loyal'st husband that did e'er plight troth;°   pledge marriage
My residence in Rome at one Filario's,
Who to my father was a friend, to me
100 Known but by letter; thither write, my queen,
And with mine eyes I'll drink the words you send
Though ink be made of gall.°   bile, bitter liquid
        Enter QUEEN
QUEEN   Be brief, I pray you.
If the King come, I shall incur I know not
How much of his displeasure. [Aside] Yet I'll move him
105 To walk this way. I never do him wrong
But he does buy my injuries, to be friends,[8]
Pays dear for my offences.   [Exit]
POSTHUMUS   Should we be taking leave
As long a term° as yet we have to live,   time
The loathness° to depart would grow. Adieu.   unwillingness
110 INNOGEN   Nay, stay a little.
Were you but riding forth to air yourself
Such parting were too petty. Look here, love:
This diamond was my mother's. Take it, heart;
        [She gives him a ring]
But keep it till you woo another wife
When Innogen is dead.
115 POSTHUMUS   How, how? Another?
You gentle gods, give me but this I have,
And cere up[9] my embracements from a next°   another wife
With bonds of death! Remain, remain thou here
        [He puts on the ring]
While sense° can keep it on; and, sweetest, fairest,   the ability to feel
120 As I my poor self did exchange for you
To your so infinite loss, so in our trifles°   love tokens
I still win of you.[1] For my sake wear this.
        [He gives her a bracelet]
It is a manacle of love. I'll place it
Upon this fairest prisoner.
INNOGEN   O the gods!
When shall we see again?
        Enter CYMBELINE and lords
125 POSTHUMUS   Alack, the King!
CYMBELINE   Thou basest° thing, avoid hence,° from my sight!   most lowborn / be off

---

7. but . . . me: an ambiguous phrase. My holy duty of obedience to my father excepted (a bond put in jeopardy by Cymbeline's act), I do not at all ("nothing") fear what Cymbeline's rage can do to me. Or: My holy duty to my husband excepted (which Cymbeline could disrupt by interfering with the marriage), I do not at all fear what Cymbeline's rage may do to me.

8. But he does endure the consequences of ("buy") my injuries in order to be friends.
9. And wrap up (in the cerecloth, or waxed linen, used in burial shrouds).
1. I still am enriched by you. Posthumus suggests that he is unequal in rank and wealth to Innogen. Correspondingly, his love token is of less value than hers.

If after this command thou fraught° the court   *burden*
With thy unworthiness, thou diest. Away.
Thou'rt poison to my blood.
POSTHUMUS   The gods protect you,
130   And bless the good remainders of° the court!   *people remaining at*
I am gone.   *Exit*
INNOGEN   There cannot be a pinch° in death   *pain*
More sharp than this is.
CYMBELINE   O disloyal thing,
That shouldst repair° my youth, thou heap'st   *restore*
A year's age on me.
INNOGEN   I beseech you, sir,
135   Harm not yourself with your vexation.
I am senseless of° your wrath. A touch° more rare   *unable to feel / An emotion*
Subdues all pangs, all fears.
CYMBELINE   Past grace,° obedience—   *all sense of duty*
INNOGEN   Past hope and in despair: that way past grace.²
CYMBELINE   That mightst have had the sole son of my queen!
140   INNOGEN   O blessèd that I might not! I chose an eagle
And did avoid a puttock.³
CYMBELINE   Thou took'st a beggar, wouldst have made my throne
A seat for baseness.
INNOGEN   No, I rather added
A lustre to it.
CYMBELINE   O thou vile one!
INNOGEN   Sir,
145   It is your fault that I have loved Posthumus.
You bred him as my playfellow, and he is
A man worth any woman, over-buys me
Almost the sum he pays.⁴
CYMBELINE   What, art thou mad?
INNOGEN   Almost, sir. Heaven restore me! Would I were
150   A neatherd's° daughter, and my Leonatus   *cowherd's*
Our neighbour shepherd's son.
Enter QUEEN
CYMBELINE   Thou foolish thing.
[*To* QUEEN] They were again together; you have done
Not after° our command. [*To lords*] Away with her,   *according to*
And pen her up.
QUEEN   Beseech° your patience, peace,   *I beseech*
155   Dear lady daughter, peace. Sweet sovereign,
Leave us to ourselves, and make yourself some comfort
Out of your best advice.
CYMBELINE   Nay, let her languish
A drop of blood a day,⁵ and, being aged,
Die of this folly.   *Exit [with lords]*
QUEEN   Fie, you must give way.
Enter PISANIO
160   Here is your servant. How now, sir? What news?

---

2. Redemption. Alluding to the Christian belief that those who despair distrust God and are beyond the reach of grace.
3. A kite, or common predatory bird.
4. *over-buys . . . pays:* pays too much for me by almost the amount he gives for me. (Posthumus both gives himself

to Innogen in marriage and also pays the price of banishment.) Innogen insists that Posthumus's worth equals her own and that their marriage consequently does not degrade her.
5. Referring to the popular belief that one lost a drop of blood with each sigh.

PISANIO My lord your son drew° on my master.   *drew a sword*
QUEEN   Ha!
No harm, I trust, is done?
PISANIO   There might have been,
But that my master rather played than fought,
And had no help of anger. They were parted
By gentlemen at hand.
165 QUEEN   I am very glad on't.
INNOGEN Your son's my father's friend; he takes his part
To draw upon an exile°—O brave sir!   *(Posthumus)*
I would they were in Afric° both together,   *Africa*
Myself by with a needle, that I might prick°   *urge on*
The goer-back.° [*To* PISANIO] Why came you from your   *swordsman who retreated*
170   master?
PISANIO On his command. He would not suffer° me   *allow*
To bring him to the haven, left these notes
Of what commands I should be subject to
When't pleased you to employ me.
QUEEN   This hath been
175 Your faithful servant. I dare lay mine honour
He will remain so.
PISANIO I humbly thank your highness.
QUEEN Pray walk a while.   [*Exit*]⁶
INNOGEN About some half hour hence, pray you speak with me.
180 You shall at least go see my lord aboard.
For this time leave me.   *Exeunt* [*severally*]°   *separately*

1.2

Enter CLOTEN *and two* LORDS
FIRST LORD Sir, I would advise you to shift° a shirt. The violence   *change*
of action hath made you reek° as a sacrifice. Where air comes   *emit vapors; stink*
out, air comes in. There's none abroad so wholesome as that
you vent.¹
5 CLOTEN If my shirt were bloody, then to shift it.° Have I hurt   *then I would change it*
him?
SECOND LORD [*aside*] No, faith, not so much as his patience.
FIRST LORD Hurt him? His body's a passable° carcass if he be   *pretty good; penetrable*
not hurt. It is a thoroughfare for steel if he be not hurt.
10 SECOND LORD [*aside*] His steel was in debt—it went o'th' back-
side the town.²
CLOTEN The villain would not stand° me.   *confront; stay still for*
SECOND LORD [*aside*] No, but he fled forward still,° toward your   *always*
face.
15 FIRST LORD Stand you? You have land enough of your own, but
he added to your having, gave you some ground.°   *fell back before you*
SECOND LORD [*aside*] As many inches as you have oceans.° Pup-   *(i.e., no inches)*
pies!
CLOTEN I would they had not come between us.

---

6. F does not mark a separate exit for the Queen here, but Innogen appears to be speaking privately to Pisanio, and only Pisanio, in the following three lines.
1.2 Location: Cymbeline's court.
1. The First Lord flatters Cloten by saying that the odorous vapors he is giving off are more healthful than the

outside ("abroad") air that is being exchanged for them.
2. Cloten's sword, like a debtor avoiding creditors, kept to the backstreets, that is, avoided the thoroughfare or main street of Posthumus's body (with a possible allusion to anal penetration).

20   SECOND LORD [*aside*]   So would I, till you had measured how
    long a fool you were upon the ground.
  CLOTEN   And that she should love this fellow and refuse me!
  SECOND LORD [*aside*]   If it be a sin to make a true election,³ she
    is damned.
25   FIRST LORD   Sir, as I told you always, her beauty and her brain
    go not together. She's a good sign,° but I have seen small   *she has a good appearance*
    reflection of her wit.
  SECOND LORD [*aside*]   She shines not upon fools lest the reflec-
    tion should hurt her.
30   CLOTEN   Come, I'll to my chamber. Would there had been some
    hurt done.
  SECOND LORD [*aside*]   I wish not so, unless it had been the fall
    of an ass, which is no great hurt.
  CLOTEN [*to* SECOND LORD]   You'll go with us?
35   FIRST LORD   I'll attend your lordship.
  CLOTEN   Nay, come, let's go together.
  SECOND LORD   Well, my lord.   *Exeunt*

1.3

Enter INNOGEN *and* PISANIO

INNOGEN   I would thou grew'st unto the shores o'th' haven
  And questionedst every sail. If he should write
  And I not have it, 'twere a paper lost
  As offered mercy is.¹ What was the last
  That he spake to thee?
5   PISANIO   It was his queen, his queen.
  INNOGEN   Then waved his handkerchief?
  PISANIO   And kissed it, madam.
  INNOGEN   Senseless° linen, happier therein than I!   *Unfeeling*
  And that was all?
  PISANIO   No, madam. For so long
  As he could make me with this eye or ear
10   Distinguish him from others he did keep
  The deck, with glove or hat or handkerchief
  Still waving, as the fits and stirs of 's mind
  Could best express how slow his soul sailed on,
  How swift his ship.
  INNOGEN   Thou shouldst have made him
15   As little as a crow, or less, ere left
  To after-eye him.²
  PISANIO   Madam, so I did.
  INNOGEN   I would have broke mine eye-strings,³ cracked them, but
  To look upon him till the diminution
  Of space had pointed him sharp as my needle;⁴
20   Nay, followed him till he had melted from
  The smallness of a gnat to air, and then
  Have turned mine eye and wept. But, good Pisanio,
  When shall we hear from him?

---

3. A proper choice; with a pun on the Christian doctrine that certain souls are "elected," or predestined for salvation.
1.3 Location: Cymbeline's palace.
1. *'twere . . . is:* the lost letter would be a document written in vain, like an offer of mercy that is not accepted or received (for example, a judge's reprieve that comes too

late).
2. *ere . . . him:* before ceasing to gaze after him.
3. The muscles of the eye, which were supposed to break at death or from overuse.
4. *till . . . needle:* until the distance between us had made him seem as small as the point on my needle.

PISANIO   Be assured, madam,
25   With his next vantage.°   *his first opportunity*
INNOGEN   I did not take my leave of him, but had
        Most pretty things to say. Ere I could tell him
        How I would think on him at certain hours,
        Such thoughts and such, or I could make him swear
30   The shes° of Italy should not betray   *women*
        Mine interest° and his honour, or have charged him   *My entitlement (to him)*
        At the sixth hour of morn, at noon, at midnight
        T'encounter me with orisons⁵—for then
        I am in heaven for him—or ere I could
35   Give him that parting kiss which I had set
        Betwixt two charming words,⁶ comes in my father,
        And, like the tyrannous breathing of the north,°   *north wind*
        Shakes all our buds from growing.
                        Enter a LADY
LADY   The Queen, madam,
        Desires your highness' company.
40   INNOGEN [*to* PISANIO]   Those things I bid you do, get them dispatched.
        I will attend the Queen.
PISANIO   Madam, I shall.
        Exeunt [INNOGEN *and* LADY *at one door,* PISANIO *at another*]

                              1.4
        [*A table brought out, with a banquet upon it.*]¹ *Enter*
        FILARIO, GIACOMO, *a* FRENCHMAN, *a* DUTCHMAN, *and a*
        SPANIARD
GIACOMO   Believe it, sir, I have seen him in Britain. He was then
        of a crescent note,° expected to prove so worthy as since he   *growing reputation*
        hath been allowed the name of. But I could then have looked
        on him without the help of admiration,° though the catalogue   *wonder*
5   of his endowments had been tabled° by his side and I to peruse   *listed*
        him by items.°   *part by part*
FILARIO   You speak of him when he was less furnished than now
        he is with that which makes° him both without and within.   *constitutes*
FRENCHMAN   I have seen him in France. We had very many
10   there could behold the sun with as firm eyes as he.²
GIACOMO   This matter of marrying his king's daughter, wherein
        he must be weighed rather by her value than his own, words
        him, I doubt not, a great deal from the matter.³
FRENCHMAN   And then his banishment.
15   GIACOMO   Ay, and the approbation of those that weep this
        lamentable divorce under her colours⁴ are wonderfully to
        extend him,° be it but to fortify her judgement, which else an   *exaggerate his worth*
        easy battery° might lay flat for taking a beggar without less qual-   *a slight assault*

---

5. To join me in prayers ("orisons"); to assail me (as an
object of devotion) with prayers.
6. Between two words carrying a charm to ward off dan-
ger.
1.4 Location: Filario's house, Rome.
1. No banquet—a light meal of fruit, sweetmeats, and
wine following the main meal—is specified in F, but in
other texts, such as Boccacio's *Decameron*, parallel wager
scenes occur during a meal; and at 5.6.155, Giacomo,

retelling the tale of the wager, says it occurred "at a feast."
2. Alluding to the popular belief that only eagles could
gaze directly on the sun. At 1.1.140, Innogen described
Posthumus as an eagle.
3. *words . . . matter:* causes his reputation, I am sure, to
be amplified beyond what is true.
4. That is, on Innogen's side (with a pun on "colours" as
meaning both "a military banner" and "pretexts").

20 ity.° But how comes it he is to sojourn with you? How creeps *of no rank or merit*
acquaintance?[5]

FILARIO   His father and I were soldiers together, to whom I have
been often bound for no less than my life.

Enter POSTHUMUS

Here comes the Briton. Let him be so entertained amongst you
as suits with gentlemen of your knowing° to a stranger of his *knowledge*
25 quality.° I beseech you all, be better known to this gentleman, *foreigner of his rank*
whom I commend to you as a noble friend of mine. How wor-
thy he is I will leave to appear hereafter rather than story° him *give an account of*
in his own hearing.

FRENCHMAN [*to* POSTHUMUS]   Sir, we have known together° in *been acquainted*
30 Orléans.

POSTHUMUS   Since when I have been debtor to you for courtesies
which I will be ever to pay, and yet pay still.

FRENCHMAN   Sir, you o'er-rate my poor kindness. I was glad I did
atone° my countryman and you. It had been pity you should *reconcile*
35 have been put together° with so mortal° a purpose as then each *(in a duel) / deadly*
bore, upon importance° of so slight and trivial a nature. *matters*

POSTHUMUS   By your pardon, sir, I was then a young traveller,
rather shunned to go even° with what I heard than[6] in my every *refused to agree*
action to be guided by others' experiences; but upon my
40 mended° judgement—if I offend not to say it is mended—my *improved*
quarrel was not altogether slight.

FRENCHMAN   Faith, yes, to be put to the arbitrement of swords,° *settlement by duel*
and by such two that would by all likelihood have confounded° *destroyed*
one the other, or have fallen both.

45 GIACOMO   Can we with manners ask what was the difference?

FRENCHMAN   Safely, I think. 'Twas a contention in public, which
may without contradiction suffer° the report. It was much like *permit*
an argument that fell out last night, where each of us fell in
praise of our country mistresses,[7] this gentleman at that time
50 vouching—and upon warrant of bloody affirmation°—his to be *affirming it with blood*
more fair, virtuous, wise, chaste, constant, qualified,° and less *having notable qualities*
attemptable[8] than any the rarest of our ladies in France.

GIACOMO   That lady is not now living, or this gentleman's opin-
ion by this° worn out. *by now*

55 POSTHUMUS   She holds her virtue still, and I my mind.

GIACOMO   You must not so far prefer her fore ours of Italy.

POSTHUMUS   Being so far provoked as I was in France I would
abate her nothing,[9] though I profess myself her adorer, not her
friend.° *lover; spouse*

60 GIACOMO   As fair and as good—a kind of hand-in-hand compari-
son[1]—had been something too fair and too good for any lady
in Britain. If she went before° others I have seen—as that dia- *she surpassed*
mond of yours outlustres many I have beheld—I could not but
believe she excelled many; but I have not seen the most pre-
65 cious diamond that is, nor you the lady.

POSTHUMUS   I praised her as I rated° her; so do I my stone. *valued*

GIACOMO   What do you esteem it at?

---

5. How does he claim a connection to you? Giacomo
implies that Posthumus cunningly insinuated himself
into Filario's friendship.
6. Than to appear.
7. The women of our country.

8. Less open to sexual solicitation.
9. I would subtract nothing from my estimation of her.
1. A comparison claiming equality (not superiority); with
a possible pun on the "handfast" by which couples
pledged their duty to one another at their betrothal.

POSTHUMUS More than the world enjoys.°   *possesses*

GIACOMO Either your unparagoned mistress is dead, or she's
70   outprized° by a trifle.   *exceeded in value*
                                                                              (the ring)

POSTHUMUS You are mistaken. The one° may be sold or given,   *(the ring)*
or if° there were wealth enough for the purchase or merit for   *if either*
the gift. The other° is not a thing for sale, and only the gift of   *(his mistress)*
the gods.

75   GIACOMO Which the gods have given you?

POSTHUMUS Which, by their graces, I will keep.

GIACOMO You may wear her in title yours;² but, you know,
strange fowl light upon neighbouring ponds.³ Your ring⁴ may
be stolen too; so your brace of unprizable estimations,⁵ the one
80   is but frail, and the other casual.⁶ A cunning thief or a that-way
accomplished courtier⁷ would hazard° the winning both of first   *venture*
and last.

POSTHUMUS Your Italy contains none so accomplished a court-
ier to convince° the honour of my mistress if in the holding or   *overcome*
85   loss of that you term her frail. I do nothing doubt you have
store° of thieves; notwithstanding, I fear not⁸ my ring.   *an abundance*

FILARIO Let us leave° here, gentlemen.   *stop the conversation*

POSTHUMUS Sir, with all my heart. This worthy signor, I thank
him, makes no stranger of me. We are familiar at first.

90   GIACOMO With five times so much conversation I should get
ground of⁹ your fair mistress, make her go back° even to the   *relent*
yielding, had I admittance and opportunity to friend.°   *to assist me*

POSTHUMUS No, no.

GIACOMO I dare thereupon pawn the moiety° of my estate to   *one half*
95   your ring, which in my opinion o'ervalues it something. But I
make my wager rather against your confidence than her reputa-
tion, and, to bar your offence¹ herein too, I durst attempt it
against any lady in the world.

POSTHUMUS You are a great deal abused in too bold a persua-
100   sion,² and I doubt not you sustain° what you're worthy of by   *will receive*
your attempt.

GIACOMO What's that?

POSTHUMUS A repulse; though your attempt, as you call it,
deserve more—a punishment, too.

105   FILARIO Gentlemen, enough of this. It came in too suddenly.
Let it die as it was born; and, I pray you, be better acquainted.

GIACOMO Would I had put my estate and my neighbour's on
th'approbation° of what I have spoke.   *the proof*

POSTHUMUS What lady would you choose to assail?

110   GIACOMO Yours, whom in constancy you think stands so safe. I
will lay° you ten thousand ducats to your ring that, commend   *wager*
me to the court where your lady is, with no more advantage
than the opportunity of a second conference, and I will bring
from thence that honour of hers which you imagine so
115   reserved.

2. You may claim her as your legal possession (with a pun
on "wear" as meaning "enjoy her sexually").
3. *strange . . . ponds*: strangers may come upon your prop-
erty (with a pun on "pond" as referring to female genitals).
4. Punning on "ring" as another slang term for "female
genitals."
5. So of the two ("brace of") objects you deem invalu-
able.

6. And the other subject to accident (referring to the
ring).
7. A courtier skilled in that way (in the arts of seduction
and theft).
8. Am not anxious about.
9. Get the advantage of.
1. To prevent you from feeling personally affronted.
2. A great deal deceived in your too bold belief.

POSTHUMUS   I will wage against your gold, gold to it;° my ring I   *gold equal to it*
hold dear as my finger, 'tis part of it.
GIACOMO   You are a friend, and therein the wiser.³ If you buy
ladies' flesh at a million a dram,⁴ you cannot preserve it from
120   tainting. But I see you have some religion in you, that° you   *since*
fear.
POSTHUMUS   This is but a custom in your tongue.⁵ You bear a
graver purpose, I hope.
GIACOMO   I am the master of my speeches, and would undergo°   *undertake*
125   what's spoken, I swear.
POSTHUMUS   Will you? I shall but lend my diamond till your
return. Let there be covenants° drawn between 's. My mistress   *agreements*
exceeds in goodness the hugeness of your unworthy thinking. I
dare you to this match. Here's my ring.
130   FILARIO   I will have it no lay.°   *wager*
GIACOMO   By the gods, it is one. If I bring you no sufficient testi-
mony that I have enjoyed the dearest bodily part of your mis-
tress, my ten thousand ducats are yours; so is your diamond too.
If I come off and leave her in such honour as you have trust in,
135   she your jewel, this your jewel, and my gold are yours, provided
I have your commendation for my more free entertainment.⁶
POSTHUMUS   I embrace these conditions; let us have articles
betwixt us. Only thus far you shall answer: if you make your
voyage upon her and give me directly° to understand you have   *plainly*
140   prevailed, I am no further your enemy; she is not worth our
debate. If she remain unseduced, you not making it appear
otherwise, for your ill opinion and th'assault you have made to
her chastity you shall answer me with your sword.
GIACOMO   Your hand, a covenant. We will have these things set
145   down by lawful counsel, and straight away° for Britain, lest the   *depart at once*
bargain should catch cold and starve.° I will fetch my gold and   *die*
have our two wagers recorded.
POSTHUMUS   Agreed.   [*Exit with* GIACOMO]
FRENCHMAN   Will this hold, think you?
150   FILARIO   Signor Giacomo will not from it. Pray let us follow 'em.
Exeunt. [*Table is removed*]

1.5

Enter QUEEN, LADIES, *and* CORNELIUS [*a doctor*]
QUEEN   Whiles yet the dew's on ground, gather those flowers.
Make haste. Who has the note° of them?   *list*
A LADY   I, madam.
QUEEN   Dispatch.°   *Exeunt* LADIES   *Make haste*
Now, Master Doctor, have you brought those drugs?
5   CORNELIUS   Pleaseth° your highness, ay. Here they are, madam.   *If it please*
[*He gives her a box*]
But I beseech your grace, without offence —
My conscience bids me ask — wherefore° you have   *why*
Commanded of me these most poisonous compounds,

---

3. Implying that Posthumus's intimacy with Innogen ("friend" means "lover" or "husband") makes him wise enough not to risk his ring in a wager on her chastity or wise enough to know the danger of this wager.
4. Even if you pay a large amount of money for a very small amount (a "dram") of female flesh.
5. This is merely a conventional way for you to speak.
6. Provided I have your introduction (to Innogen) to ensure a generous reception.
1.5 Location: Cymbeline's court, Britain.

Which are the movers of a languishing death,
But though slow, deadly.
10 QUEEN   I wonder, doctor,
Thou ask'st me such a question. Have I not been
Thy pupil long? Hast thou not learned° me how   taught
To make perfumes, distil, preserve—yea, so
That our great King himself doth woo me oft
15 For my confections?° Having thus far proceeded,   medical compounds
Unless thou think'st me devilish, is't not meet°   fitting
That I did amplify my judgement in
Other conclusions?° I will try° the forces   experiments / test
Of these thy compounds on such creatures as
20 We count not worth the hanging, but none human,
To try the vigour of them, and apply
Allayments to their act,¹ and by them° gather   (these experiments)
Their several virtues² and effects.
CORNELIUS   Your highness
Shall from this practice but make hard your heart.
25 Besides, the seeing these effects will be
Both noisome° and infectious.   offensive
QUEEN   O, content thee.
        Enter PISANIO
[*Aside*] Here comes a flattering rascal; upon him
Will I first work. He's factor° for his master,   an agent
And enemy to my son. [*Aloud*] How now, Pisanio?—
30 Doctor, your service for this time is ended.
Take your own way.
CORNELIUS [*aside*]   I do suspect you, madam.
But you shall do no harm.
QUEEN [*to* PISANIO]   Hark thee, a word.
CORNELIUS [*aside*] I do not like her. She doth think she has
Strange ling'ring poisons. I do know her spirit,
35 And will not trust one of her malice with
A drug of such damned nature. Those she has
Will stupefy and dull the sense a while,
Which first, perchance, she'll prove° on cats and dogs,   test
Then afterward up higher; but there is
40 No danger in what show of death it makes
More than the locking up the spirits a time,³
To be more fresh, reviving. She is fooled
With a most false effect, and I the truer
So to be false with her.
QUEEN   No further service, doctor,
Until I send for thee.
45 CORNELIUS   I humbly take my leave.   *Exit*
QUEEN [*to* PISANIO]   Weeps she still, sayst thou? Dost thou think in time
She will not quench,° and let instructions° enter   grow cool / good advice
Where folly now possesses? Do thou work.
When thou shalt bring me word she loves my son
50 I'll tell thee on the instant thou art then
As great as is thy master—greater, for
His fortunes all lie speechless, and his name°   reputation

---

1. *apply . . . act:* apply antidotes to their operation.
2. Their (the compounds') individual powers.

3. Other than the temporary suspension of the vital func-
tions.

Is at last gasp. Return he cannot, nor
Continue where he is. To shift his being°   change his abode
55 Is to exchange one misery with another,
And every day that comes comes to decay°   destroy
A day's work in him. What shalt thou expect
To be depender on a thing that leans,[4]
Who cannot be new built nor has no friends
So much as but to prop him?
        [*She drops her box. He takes it up*]
60   Thou tak'st up
Thou know'st not what; but take it for thy labour.
It is a thing I made which hath the King
Five times redeemed from death. I do not know
What is more cordial.° Nay, I prithee take it.   restorative
65 It is an earnest° of a farther good   initial payment
That I mean to thee. Tell thy mistress how
The case stands with her; do't as from thyself.
Think what a chance thou changest on,[5] but think
Thou hast thy mistress still; to boot,° my son,   in addition
70 Who shall take notice of thee.° I'll move the King   give attention to you
To any shape of thy preferment,° such   any kind of advancement
As thou'lt desire; and then myself, I chiefly,
That set thee on to this desert,° am bound   action deserving reward
To load thy merit richly. Call my women.
75 Think on my words.   *Exit* PISANIO
                    A sly and constant knave,
Not to be shaked; the agent for his master,
And the remembrancer of her° to hold   the one who reminds her
The hand-fast° to her lord. I have given him that[6]   marriage contract
Which, if he take, shall quite unpeople her
80 Of liegers for her sweet,[7] and which she after,
Except she bend her humour,[8] shall be assured
To taste of too.
        Enter PISANIO *and* LADIES
                    So, so; well done, well done.
The violets, cowslips, and the primroses
Bear to my closet.° Fare thee well, Pisanio.   private chamber
Think on my words, Pisanio.
85 PISANIO   And shall do.
        Exeunt QUEEN *and* LADIES
But when to my good lord I prove untrue,
I'll choke myself—there's all I'll do for you.   *Exit*

1.6

Enter INNOGEN
INNOGEN   A father cruel and a stepdame false,
A foolish suitor to a wedded lady
That hath her husband banished.[1] O, that husband,
My supreme crown of grief, and those repeated[2]
5 Vexations of it! Had I been thief-stol'n,

---

4. To be dependent on a thing that is about to fall.
5. Consider what opportunity you have to change your
service (and become my servant).
6. The box supposedly containing poison.
7. Of ambassadors for her sweetheart.

8. Unless she changes her disposition.
1.6 Location: Cymbeline's court.
1. Who has a banished husband.
2. Those already enumerated. Innogen has already complained of her father, stepmother, and foolish suitor.

As my two brothers, happy;[3] but most miserable
Is the desire that's glorious.[4] Blest be those,
How mean soe'er,[5] that have their honest wills,°   simple desires
Which seasons comfort.[6]
       Enter PISANIO *and* GIACOMO
                     Who may this be? Fie!
10 PISANIO   Madam, a noble gentleman of Rome
Comes from my lord with letters.
GIACOMO   Change you,° madam?   *Do you turn pale*
The worthy Leonatus is in safety,
And greets your highness dearly.
       [*He gives her the letters*]
INNOGEN   Thanks, good sir.
       [*She reads the letters*]
15 GIACOMO [*aside*]   All of her that is out of door° most rich!   *is visible*
If she be furnished with a mind so rare
She is alone, th'Arabian bird,[7] and I
Have lost the wager. Boldness be my friend;
Arm me audacity from head to foot,
20 Or, like the Parthian, I shall flying fight;[8]
Rather, directly fly.
INNOGEN *reads* [*aloud*] 'He is one of the noblest note,° to whose   *reputation*
kindnesses I am most infinitely tied. Reflect° upon him accord-   *Bestow attention*
ingly, as you value
25   Your truest
                     Leonatus.'
[*To Giacomo*] So far I read aloud,
But even the very middle of my heart
Is warmed by th' rest, and takes it thankfully.
30 You are as welcome, worthy sir, as I
Have words to bid you, and shall find it so
In all that I can do.
GIACOMO   Thanks, fairest lady.
What, are men mad? Hath nature given them eyes
To see this vaulted arch° and the rich crop°   *the sky / harvest*
35 Of sea and land, which can distinguish 'twixt
The fiery orbs above and the twinned° stones   *identical*
Upon th'unnumbered beach,[9] and can we not
Partition make with spectacles[1] so precious
'Twixt fair and foul?
INNOGEN   What makes your admiration?°   *causes you wonder*
40 GIACOMO   It cannot be i'th' eye—for apes and monkeys,
'Twixt two such shes,° would chatter this way[2] and   *women*
Contemn with mows° the other; nor i'th' judgement,   *Scorn with grimaces*
For idiots in this case of favour° would   *question of preference*
Be wisely definite; nor i'th' appetite—
45 Sluttery,° to such neat° excellence opposed,   *Sluttishness / elegant*

---

3. *happy:* I would have been glad or fortunate.
4. But most wretched is the longing for what is exalted
(in her case, a longing for Posthumus).
5. However low in status.
6. Which adds spice to their comfort.
7. The phoenix, only one of which existed at any given
time. This mythical bird consumed itself in fire every five

hundred years but then rose from its own ashes.
8. The mounted archers of Parthia were famous for their
tactics in warfare, which included shooting arrows behind
them as they retreated.
9. Upon the beach whose grains of sand are uncounted.
1. Make distinction with organs of sight.
2. Would make their preference (for Innogen) clear.

Should make desire vomit emptiness,
Not so allured to feed.[3]

INNOGEN   What is the matter, trow?°   *in truth*

GIACOMO   The cloyèd will,°   *sated sexual desire*

50   That satiate° yet unsatisfied desire, that tub   *glutted*
Both filled and running,° ravening° first the lamb,   *emptying itself / devouring*
Longs after for the garbage.

INNOGEN   What, dear sir,
Thus raps° you? Are you well?   *transports*

GIACOMO   Thanks, madam, well. [*To* PISANIO] Beseech° you, sir,   *I ask*

55   Desire° my man's abode where I did leave him.   *Seek out*
He's strange° and peevish.°   *a foreigner / irritable*

PISANIO   I was going, sir,
To give him welcome.   *Exit*

INNOGEN   Continues well my lord?
His health, beseech you?

GIACOMO   Well, madam.

INNOGEN   Is he disposed to mirth? I hope he is.

60 GIACOMO   Exceeding pleasant, none a stranger° there   *none of the foreigners*
So merry and so gamesome.[4] He is called
The Briton Reveller.

INNOGEN   When he was here
He did incline to sadness,° and oft-times   *seriousness*
Not knowing why.

GIACOMO   I never saw him sad.

65 There is a Frenchman his companion, one
An eminent monsieur that, it seems, much loves
A Gallian° girl at home. He furnaces[5]   *French*
The thick sighs from him, whiles the jolly° Briton—   *lively; lustful*
Your lord, I mean—laughs from 's free° lungs, cries 'O,   *unconstrained*

70 Can my sides hold, to think that man, who knows
By history, report or his own proof
What woman is, yea, what she cannot choose
But must be, will 's free hours languish°   *pine away*
For assurèd bondage?'

INNOGEN   Will my lord say so?

75 GIACOMO   Ay, madam, with his eyes in flood with laughter.
It is a recreation to be by
And hear him mock the Frenchman. But heavens know
Some men are much to blame.

INNOGEN   Not he, I hope.

GIACOMO   Not he; but yet heaven's bounty towards him might

80 Be used more thankfully. In himself 'tis much;
In you, which I count his, beyond all talents.[6]
Whilst I am bound to wonder, I am bound
To pity too.

INNOGEN   What do you pity, sir?

GIACOMO   Two creatures heartily.

INNOGEN   Am I one, sir?

---

3. *Should . . . feed:* Should destroy sexual desire, not
arouse it (literally, should make desire vomit until it is
empty, not tempt it to eat).
4. Sportive; sexually playful.
5. He exhales like a furnace.

6. *In himself . . . talents:* As regards his own qualities,
heaven's generosity is considerable. In giving him you,
whom I consider his, heaven's generosity surpasses all
abundance.

85 You look on me; what wreck° discern you in me   *downfall*
Deserves your pity?
GIACOMO   Lamentable! What,
To hide me from the radiant sun, and solace°   *take comfort*
I'th' dungeon by a snuff?°   *candle end*
INNOGEN   I pray you, sir,
Deliver with more openness your answers
90 To my demands. Why do you pity me?
GIACOMO   That others do—
I was about to say enjoy your—but
It is an office° of the gods to venge° it,   *a duty / revenge*
Not mine to speak on't.°   *of it*
INNOGEN   You do seem to know
95 Something of me, or what concerns me. Pray you,
Since doubting° things go ill often hurts more   *suspecting*
Than to be sure they do—for certainties
Either are past remedies, or, timely knowing,
The remedy then born[7]—discover° to me   *reveal*
What both you spur and stop.[8]
100 GIACOMO   Had I this cheek
To bathe my lips upon; this hand whose touch,
Whose every touch, would force the feeler's soul
To th'oath of loyalty; this object which
Takes prisoner the wild motion of mine eye,
105 Firing° it only here: should I, damned then,   *Enflaming*
Slaver with lips as common as the stairs
That mount the Capitol;[9] join grips with hands
Made hard with hourly falsehood—falsehood as
With labour;[1] then by-peeping° in an eye   *glancing coyly*
110 Base and illustrous° as the smoky light   *lacking luster*
That's fed with stinking tallow—it were fit
That all the plagues of hell should at one time
Encounter° such revolt.°   *Confront / infidelity*
INNOGEN   My lord, I fear,
Has forgot Britain.
GIACOMO   And himself. Not I
115 Inclined to this intelligence pronounce
The beggary of his change,[2] but 'tis your graces
That from my mutest conscience° to my tongue   *most quiet inner being*
Charms this report out.
INNOGEN   Let me hear no more.
GIACOMO   O dearest soul, your cause doth strike my heart
120 With pity that doth make me sick. A lady
So fair, and fastened to an empery°   *empire*
Would make the great'st king double,° to be partnered   *twice as great*
With tomboys hired with that self exhibition[3]
Which your own coffers yield; with diseased ventures°   *prostitutes; vendors*
125 That play with all infirmities for gold

---

7. *or . . . born:* or, they being known about in time, the remedy is then brought about.
8. *What you both* urge on and restrain (as one commands a horse).
9. *Slaver . . . Capitol:* Offer drooling kisses to whores who, like the stairs to the Roman Capitol building, are available to everyone.
1. *join . . . labour:* clasp hands made as hard with hourly

lies or sexual infidelities as they might have been made hard with work.
2. *Not . . . change:* It is not because I am disposed to give this information that I report the contemptible nature of his change.
3. With whores ("tomboys") hired with that same payment.

Which rottenness can lend to nature; such boiled stuff[4]
As well might poison poison! Be revenged,
Or she that bore you was no queen, and you
Recoil° from your great stock.   *Degenerate*

INNOGEN   Revenged?
130 How should I be revenged? If this be true—
As I have such a heart that both mine ears
Must not in haste abuse[5]—if it be true,
How should I be revenged?

GIACOMO   Should he make me
Live like Diana's priest[6] betwixt cold sheets
135 Whiles he is vaulting variable ramps,[7]
In your despite, upon your purse[8]—revenge it.
I dedicate myself to your sweet pleasure,
More noble than that runagate° to your bed,   *renegade*
And will continue fast° to your affection,   *constant*
Still close as sure.[9]

140 INNOGEN   What ho, Pisanio!

GIACOMO   Let me my service tender on your lips.

INNOGEN   Away, I do condemn mine ears that have
So long attended thee. If thou wert honourable
Thou wouldst have told this tale for virtue, not
145 For such an end thou seek'st, as base as strange.
Thou wrong'st a gentleman who is as far
From thy report as thou from honour, and
Solicit'st here a lady that disdains
Thee and the devil alike. What ho, Pisanio!
150 The King my father shall be made acquainted
Of thy assault. If he shall think it fit
A saucy stranger in his court to mart°   *do business*
As in a Romish stew,° and to expound   *Roman brothel*
His beastly mind to us, he hath a court
155 He little cares for, and a daughter who
He not respects at all. What ho, Pisanio!

GIACOMO   O happy Leonatus! I may say
The credit° that thy lady hath of° thee   *trust / in*
Deserves thy trust, and thy most perfect goodness
160 Her assured credit.[1] Blessèd live you long,
A lady to the worthiest sir that ever
Country called his;° and you his mistress, only   *its own*
For the most worthiest fit. Give me your pardon.
I have spoke this to know if your affiance°   *faith*
165 Were deeply rooted, and shall make your lord
That which he is new o'er;[2] and he is one
The truest mannered,[3] such a holy witch°   *a charming person*
That he enchants societies into° him;   *crowds of people to*
Half all men's hearts are his.

---

4. Such diseased prostitutes. Sweating, usually induced by the steam from boiling water, was a common treatment for syphilis.
5. *a heart . . . abuse:* a heart that my ears must not abuse by too hastily accepting what they hear.
6. That is, live chastely. Diana was the Roman goddess of the hunt known for her chastity and her circle of virgin followers.
7. While he is having sexual intercourse with whores ("ramps") of all kinds.

8. In contempt of you, with your money.
9. Always as secret as I am true.
1. *and . . . credit:* and your most perfect goodness deserves her absolute trust.
2. *and . . . o'er:* and I (by this news of your fidelity) shall make your lord feel afresh what he already is (that is, your lord).
3. *he . . . mannered:* he is above all others the most perfect in conduct.

INNOGEN   You make amends.

170 GIACOMO   He sits 'mongst men like a descended god.
      He hath a kind of honour sets him off
      More than a mortal seeming.[4] Be not angry,
      Most mighty princess, that I have adventured°   *dared*
      To try° your taking of a false report, which hath   *test*
175   Honoured with confirmation your great judgement
      In the election of a sir so rare
      Which° you know cannot err. The love I bear him   *Whom*
      Made me to fan[5] you thus, but the gods made you,
      Unlike all others, chaffless.° Pray, your pardon.   *without chaff; perfect*
180 INNOGEN   All's well, sir. Take my power i'th' court for yours.

     GIACOMO   My humble thanks. I had almost forgot
      T'entreat your grace but in a small request,
      And yet of moment° too, for it concerns   *importance*
      Your lord; myself and other noble friends
      Are partners in the business.

185 INNOGEN   Pray what is't?

     GIACOMO   Some dozen Romans of us, and your lord—
      Best feather of our wing—have mingled sums
      To buy a present for the Emperor,
      Which I, the factor° for the rest, have done   *agent*
190   In France. 'Tis plate[6] of rare device, and jewels
      Of rich and exquisite form; their value's great,
      And I am something curious,° being strange,°   *somewhat anxious / foreign*
      To have them in safe stowage. May it please you
      To take them in protection?

     INNOGEN   Willingly,
195   And pawn mine honour for their safety; since
      My lord hath interest° in them, I will keep them   *a stake*
      In my bedchamber.

     GIACOMO   They are in a trunk
      Attended by my men. I will make bold
      To send them to you, only for this night.
      I must aboard tomorrow.

200 INNOGEN   O, no, no!

     GIACOMO   Yes, I beseech, or I shall short° my word   *break*
      By length'ning my return. From Gallia°   *France*
      I crossed the seas on purpose and on promise
      To see your grace.

     INNOGEN   I thank you for your pains;
      But not away tomorrow!

205 GIACOMO   O, I must, madam.
      Therefore I shall beseech you, if you please
      To greet your lord with writing, do't tonight.
      I have outstood° my time, which is material   *overstayed*
      To th' tender° of our present.   *the offering*

     INNOGEN   I will write.
210   Send your trunk to me, it shall safe be kept,
      And truly yielded° you. You're very welcome.   *faithfully returned to*

                         Exeunt [severally]

---

4. So that he appears more than mortal.
5. Winnow. When grain was harvested, wheat was win-
nowed from the chaff; metaphorically, the good was win-
nowed from the bad.
6. Objects, often tableware, either made of precious met-
als or covered ("plated") with them.

2.1

Enter CLOTEN *and the two* LORDS

CLOTEN   Was there ever man had such luck? When I kissed the
jack[1] upon an upcast,° to be hit away! I had a hundred pound   *on a final throw*
on't, and then a whoreson jackanapes° must take me up[2] for   *an idiotic bastard*
swearing, as if I borrowed mine oaths of him, and might not
5   spend them at my pleasure.
FIRST LORD   What got he by that? You have broke his pate with
your bowl.
SECOND LORD [*aside*]   If his wit had been like him that broke it,
it would have run all out.
10   CLOTEN   When a gentleman is disposed to swear it is not for any
standers-by to curtail[3] his oaths, ha?
SECOND LORD   No, my lord [*aside*]—nor crop the ears of them.
CLOTEN   Whoreson dog! I give him satisfaction? Would he had
been one of my rank.[4]
15   SECOND LORD [*aside*]   To have smelled like a fool.
CLOTEN   I am not vexed more at anything in th'earth. A pox
on't,[5] I had rather not be so noble as I am. They dare not fight
with me because of the Queen, my mother. Every jack-slave°   *lowborn fellow*
hath his bellyful of fighting, and I must go up and down like a
20   cock that nobody can match.°   *equal; fight with*
SECOND LORD [*aside*]   You are cock and capon too an you crow
cock with your comb on.[6]
CLOTEN   Sayst thou?
SECOND LORD   It is not fit your lordship should undertake° every   *take on*
25   companion° that you give offence to.   *fellow*
CLOTEN   No, I know that, but it is fit I should commit offence
to[7] my inferiors.
SECOND LORD   Ay, it is fit for your lordship only.
CLOTEN   Why, so I say.
30   FIRST LORD   Did you hear of a stranger° that's come to court   *foreigner*
tonight?
CLOTEN   A stranger, and I not know on't?°   *of it*
SECOND LORD [*aside*]   He's a strange fellow himself and knows it
not.
35   FIRST LORD   There's an Italian come, and, 'tis thought, one of
Leonatus' friends.
CLOTEN   Leonatus? A banished rascal; and he's another, whatso-
ever he be. Who told you of this stranger?
FIRST LORD   One of your lordship's pages.
40   CLOTEN   Is it fit I went to look upon him? Is there no derogation°   *loss of dignity*
in't?
SECOND LORD   You cannot derogate,[8] my lord.
CLOTEN   Not easily, I think.

2.1 Location: Cymbeline's court, Britain.
1. In the game of bowls, the jack is the target ball. To
"kiss the jack" is to roll one's ball so that it touches the
jack.
2. Challenge me; rebuke me.
3. Shorten, as one bobbed the tails (and sometimes the
ears) of certain dogs. This leads the Second Lord to talk
of cropping the ears of oaths in line 12.
4. Social position. Gentlemen were only supposed to
fight ("give satisfaction" to) men of their own rank. The

Second Lord puns on "rank" as meaning "strong smell."
5. A mild oath meaning "a plague on it."
6. And a castrated cock too if you brag ("crow") that you
are a cock while wearing a fool's cap (coxcomb). There
are puns here on "capon" and "cap on," on "cock's comb"
and "coxcomb."
7. I should assault, with the perhaps unintended second-
ary meaning of "to defecate upon."
8. You cannot forfeit your dignity; you have no dignity to
lose.

SECOND LORD [*aside*]   You are a fool granted,° therefore your   *an acknowledged fool*
45   issues,° being foolish, do not derogate.   *deeds*
CLOTEN   Come, I'll go see this Italian. What I have lost today at
   bowls I'll win tonight of him. Come, go.
SECOND LORD   I'll attend your lordship.
                              Exeunt [CLOTEN *and* FIRST LORD]
   That such a crafty devil as is his mother
50   Should yield the world this ass!—a woman that
   Bears all down° with her brain, and this her son   *Overcomes everyone*
   Cannot take two from twenty, for his heart,°   *for the life of him*
   And leave eighteen. Alas, poor princess,
   Thou divine Innogen, what thou endur'st,
55   Betwixt a father by thy stepdame governed,
   A mother hourly coining plots, a wooer
   More hateful than the foul expulsion is
   Of thy dear husband, than that horrid act
   Of the divorce he'd make! The heavens hold firm
60   The walls of thy dear honour, keep unshaked
   That temple, thy fair mind, that thou mayst stand
   T'enjoy thy banished lord and this great land!   *Exit*

2.2

   [*A trunk and arras.*[1] *A*] *bed* [*is thrust forth with*] INNO-
   GEN [*in it, reading a book. Enter to her* HELEN], *a lady*[2]
INNOGEN   Who's there? My woman Helen?
HELEN   Please you, madam.
INNOGEN   What hour is it?
HELEN   Almost midnight, madam.
INNOGEN   I have read three hours then. Mine eyes are weak.
   Fold down the leaf where I have left. To bed.
5   Take not away the taper; leave it burning,
   And if thou canst awake by four o'th' clock,
   I prithee call me. Sleep hath seized me wholly.   [*Exit* HELEN]
   To your protection I commend me, gods.
   From fairies° and the tempters of the night   *evil beings*
10   Guard me, beseech ye.°   *I entreat you*
            [*She*] *sleeps.*
         GIACOMO [*comes*] *from the trunk*
GIACOMO   The crickets sing, and man's o'er-laboured sense
   Repairs itself by rest. Our Tarquin[3] thus
   Did softly press the rushes[4] ere he wakened
   The chastity he wounded. Cytherea,[5]
15   How bravely° thou becom'st thy bed! Fresh lily,   *splendidly*
   And whiter than the sheets! That I might touch,
   But kiss, one kiss! Rubies unparagoned,
   How dearly they do't![6] 'Tis her breathing that
   Perfumes the chamber thus. The flame o'th' taper

2.2 Location: Innogen's chambers.
1. Tapestry wall covering.
2. F's stage direction reads "Enter Imogen, in her Bed,
and a Lady." The trunk in which Giacomo is concealed
is probably brought onstage as the scene opens, either car-
ried on or raised up through the trapdoor in the stage
floor. Beds typically were "thrust forth" from a door at the
back of the stage. Giacomo mentions an arras in his ensu-
ing description of Innogen's bedroom. One may have

been hung up at the back of the stage for this scene.
3. The ancient Roman Sextus Tarquinius, whose rape of
Lucrece was the subject of a poem by Shakespeare.
4. Reeds commonly used as a floor covering.
5. A name for Aphrodite, or Venus, the goddess of beauty
and love, who first set foot on the island of Cytherea after
her birth from sea-foam.
6. How dearly do they (her ruby lips) kiss one another.

20 Bows toward her, and would underpeep her lids,
To see th'enclosèd lights, now canopied
Under these windows,° white and azure-laced   *eyelids*
With blue of heaven's own tinct.° But my design—   *hue*
To note the chamber. I will write all down.
        [*He writes in his tables*]°   *writing tablets*
25 Such and such pictures, there the window, such
Th'adornment of her bed, the arras, figures,
Why, such and such; and the contents o'th' story.[7]
Ah, but some natural notes° about her body   *marks*
Above ten thousand meaner movables[8]
30 Would testify t'enrich mine inventory.
O sleep, thou ape° of death, lie dull° upon her,   *mimic / heavy*
And be her sense but as a monument[9]
Thus in a chapel lying. Come off, come off;
As slippery as the Gordian knot was hard.[1]
        [*He takes the bracelet from her arm*]
35 'Tis mine, and this will witness outwardly,
As strongly as the conscience does within,[2]
To th' madding° of her lord. On her left breast   *maddening*
A mole, cinque-spotted,° like the crimson drops   *with five spots*
I'th' bottom of a cowslip. Here's a voucher°   *piece of evidence*
40 Stronger than ever law could make. This secret
Will force him think I have picked the lock and ta'en
The treasure of her honour.[3] No more. To what end?
Why should I write this down that's riveted,
Screwed to my memory? She hath been reading late,
45 The tale of Tereus.[4] Here the leaf's turned down
Where Philomel gave up. I have enough.
To th' trunk again, and shut the spring of it.
Swift, swift, you dragons of the night, that dawning
May bare the raven's eye![5] I lodge in fear.
50 Though this' a heavenly angel, hell is here.
        Clock strikes
One, two, three. Time, time!
        Exit [*into the trunk. The bed and trunk are removed*]

2.3

Enter CLOTEN *and* [*the two*] LORDS

FIRST LORD   Your lordship is the most patient man in loss, the
        most coldest° that ever turned up ace.[1]   *least passionate*
CLOTEN   It would make any man cold to lose.

---

7. The design on the tapestry (?). In 2.4.66–91, Giacomo
describes in more detail what he saw in Innogen's bed-
chamber: a tapestry depicting the story of Antony and
Cleopatra and a chimneypiece carving of Diana bathing.
He could here be referring to the "figures" and "contents"
of either the tapestry or chimneypiece.
8. Less important pieces of property, especially furniture
or furnishings.
9. And let her senses be like those of an effigy on a tomb.
1. As easy to open as the Gordian knot was difficult to
untie. Alluding to the myth of Gordius, King of Phrygia,
who tied an impossibly intricate knot and declared that
whoever untied it would reign over Asia; with a single
thrust of his sword, Alexander the Great cut through it.
Giacomo's unclasping of the bracelet has sexual implica-
tions. He is metaphorically violating Innogen's chastity

and, by stealing Posthumus's love token, is interfering in
the marriage bond that links Posthumus and Innogen.
2. As powerfully as does his inward consciousness.
3. Giacomo means his knowledge of the mole will make
Posthumus believe he has slept with Innogen. To "pick
the lock" is a euphemism for "to have sex."
4. In Greek myth, Tereus, King of Thrace, raped his
wife's sister Philomela and cut out her tongue so she
could not reveal what had happened. Philomela later
wove the story into a tapestry.
5. May cause the raven to wake. The bird supposedly
slept facing east and awakened at dawn.
2.3 Location: A room near Innogen's chambers.
1. *that . . . ace*: who ever threw the lowest score in a game
of dice, with a pun on "ass."

FIRST LORD   But not every man patient after° the noble temper   *according to*
5   of your lordship. You are most hot and furious when you win.

CLOTEN   Winning will put any man into courage. If I could get
this foolish Innogen I should have gold enough. It's almost
morning, is't not?

FIRST LORD   Day, my lord.

10 CLOTEN   I would this music would come. I am advised to give
her music o' mornings; they say it will penetrate.[2]

      Enter MUSICIANS

Come on, tune. If you can penetrate her with your fingering,
so; we'll try with tongue too.[3] If none will do,° let her remain;   *suffice*
but I'll never give o'er. First, a very excellent good-conceited°   *ingenious*
15 thing; after, a wonderful sweet air with admirable rich words to
it; and then let her consider.

      [Music]

MUSICIAN *[sings]*[4]   Hark, hark, the lark at heaven gate sings,
    And Phoebus gins° arise,   *Apollo (sun god) begins*
    His steeds to water at those springs
20   On chaliced flowers[5] that lies,
    And winking Mary-buds° begin to ope their golden eyes;   *closed marigold buds*
    With everything that pretty is, my lady sweet, arise,
      Arise, arise!

CLOTEN   So, get you gone. If this penetrate I will consider° your   *value*
25 music the better; if it do not, it is a vice° in her ears which   *defect*
horse hairs and calves' guts[6] nor the voice of unpaved[7] eunuch
to boot can never amend.   *[Exeunt* MUSICIANS]

      Enter CYMBELINE *and [the]* QUEEN

SECOND LORD   Here comes the King.

CLOTEN   I am glad I was up so late, for that's the reason I was up
30 so early. He cannot choose but take this service I have done
fatherly. Good morrow to your majesty, and to my gracious
mother.

CYMBELINE   Attend you here the door of our stern daughter?
Will she not forth?

35 CLOTEN   I have assailed her with musics, but she vouchsafes no
notice.

CYMBELINE   The exile of her minion° is too new.   *darling*
She hath not yet forgot him. Some more time
Must wear the print° of his remembrance out,   *imprint*
And then she's yours.

40 QUEEN *[to* CLOTEN]   You are most bound to th' King,
Who lets go by no vantages° that may   *opportunities*
Prefer° you to his daughter. Frame° yourself   *Recommend / Prepare*
To° orderly solicits,° and be friended   *With / solicitations*
With aptness of the season.[8] Make denials
45 Increase your services; so seem as if
You were inspired to do those duties which
You tender to her; that you in all obey her,

2. Affect her emotions; arouse her sexually.
3. If your instrumental music can move her, that's good.
We'll try to move her with song as well. These lines also
carry an explicitly sexual secondary meaning: If you can
insert your fingers inside her, that's good. We'll try oral
sex as well. It is unclear if Cloten understands the bawdy
import of his own words.
4. F does not attribute this song to a particular singer

but simply introduces it as "SONG." It also appears in a
seventeenth-century manuscript located in the Bodleian
Library at Oxford.
5. Flowers with cuplike blossoms.
6. Both were used as strings for musical instruments.
7. Castrated (lacking stones).
8. And be assisted by appropriate timing.

Save when command to your dismission tends,
And therein you are senseless.[9]
CLOTEN   Senseless? Not so.
          [*Enter a* MESSENGER]
50 MESSENGER [*to* CYMBELINE]   So like you,° sir, ambassadors from Rome;   *If you please*
     The one is Caius Lucius.
CYMBELINE   A worthy fellow,
     Albeit he comes on angry purpose now:
     But that's no fault of his. We must receive him
     According to the honour of his sender,
55 And towards himself, his goodness forespent on us,[1]
     We must extend our notice. Our dear son,
     When you have given good morning to your mistress,
     Attend the Queen and us. We shall have need
     T'employ you towards this Roman. Come, our queen.
                              Exeunt [*all but* CLOTEN]
60 CLOTEN   If she be up, I'll speak with her; if not,
     Let her lie still and dream.
          [*He knocks*]
                              By your leave, ho!—
     I know her women are about her; what
     If I do line° one of their hands? 'Tis gold   *fill (with gold)*
     Which buys admittance—oft it doth—yea, and makes
65 Diana's rangers false° themselves, yield up   *gamekeepers turn false*
     Their deer to th' stand o'th' stealer;[2] and 'tis gold
     Which makes the true man killed and saves the thief,
     Nay, sometime hangs both thief and true man. What
     Can it not do and undo? I will make
70 One of her women lawyer to° me, for   *advocate for*
     I yet not understand the case[3] myself.—
     By your leave.
          Knocks. Enter a LADY
LADY   Who's there that knocks?
CLOTEN   A gentleman.
LADY   No more?
CLOTEN   Yes, and a gentlewoman's son.
LADY   That's more
75 [*Aside*][4] Than some whose tailors are as dear° as yours   *expensive*
     Can justly boast of. [*To him*] What's your lordship's pleasure?
CLOTEN   Your lady's person. Is she ready?°   *dressed; prepared*
LADY   Ay.
     [*Aside*] To keep her chamber.
CLOTEN   There is gold for you.
     Sell me your good report.
80 LADY   How, my good name?°—or to report of you   *reputation*
     What I shall think is good?
          Enter INNOGEN
                         The Princess.   [*Exit*]

---

9. *Save . . . senseless:* Except what pertains to your dismissal ("dismission"), which you are incapable of understanding. Cloten, however, takes "senseless" to mean "stupid."
1. *his . . . us:* in view of the virtue he has shown in previous dealings with us.
2. *yield . . . stealer:* surrender their deer to the place where the thief stands to shoot; surrender what is most dear or valuable (their chastity) to the thief's erect penis ("th'

stand").
3. *for . . . case:* for I still do not know how to manage the matter (with wordplay on "stand under" as slang for "sexually penetrate" and on "case" as slang for "vagina").
4. The Lady's speaking all or part of this and her next speech in asides explains the outspokenness of her comments; it also follows the pattern of 2.1 and of later scenes in which Cloten's words are slyly subjected to derogatory commentary by those with whom he converses.

CLOTEN   Good morrow, fairest. Sister, your sweet hand.
INNOGEN   Good morrow, sir. You lay out too much pains
  For purchasing but trouble. The thanks I give
85 Is telling you that I am poor of thanks,
  And scarce can spare them.
CLOTEN   Still I swear I love you.
INNOGEN   If you but said so, 'twere as deep° with me.   *solemn; binding*
  If you swear still,° your recompense is still   *always*
  That I regard it not.
CLOTEN   This is no answer.
90 INNOGEN   But° that you shall not say I yield being silent,   *Except*
  I would not speak. I pray you, spare me. Faith,
  I shall unfold equal discourtesy[5]
  To your best kindness. One of your great knowing°   *knowledge*
  Should learn, being taught, forbearance.
95 CLOTEN   To leave you in your madness, 'twere my sin.
  I will not.
INNOGEN   Fools cure not mad folks.
CLOTEN   Do you call me fool?
INNOGEN   As I am mad, I do.
  If you'll be patient, I'll no more be mad;
  That cures us both. I am much sorry, sir,
100 You put me to forget a lady's manners
  By being so verbal;[6] and learn now for all
  That I, which know my heart, do here pronounce
  By th' very truth of it: I care not for you,
  And am so near the lack of charity
105 To accuse myself I hate you,[7] which I had rather
  You felt than make't my boast.°   *than I had to say it*
CLOTEN   You sin against
  Obedience which you owe your father. For°   *As for*
  The contract you pretend° with that base wretch,   *claim*
  One bred of alms and fostered with cold dishes,
110 With scraps o'th' court, it is no contract, none.
  And though it be allowed in meaner° parties—   *socially inferior*
  Yet who than he more mean?—to knit their souls,
  On whom there is no more dependency
  But brats and beggary,[8] in self-figured° knot,   *self-contracted*
115 Yet you are curbed from that enlargement° by   *freedom*
  The consequence o'th' crown,[9] and must not foil°   *defile*
  The precious note° of it with a base slave,   *reputation*
  A hilding for a livery,[1] a squire's cloth,°   *uniform*
  A pantler°—not so eminent.   *pantry servant*
INNOGEN   Profane fellow,
120 Wert thou the son of Jupiter,° and no more   *king of the gods*
  But what thou art besides, thou wert too base
  To be his° groom; thou wert dignified enough,[2]   ·   *(Posthumus's)*
  Even to the point of envy, if 'twere made
  Comparative for your virtues to be styled

---

5. I shall display discourtesy equal.
6. "Verbal" (talkative; plainspoken) may refer either to
Cloten or to Innogen.
7. And . . . you: And I am so near uncharitableness that I
can charge myself with hating you.
8. On . . . beggary: Upon whose marriage nothing de-
pends but worthless children and extreme poverty.

9. by . . . crown: by the importance of the crown; by the
consequences that flow from your inheritance of the
crown.
1. A worthless person fit only to wear the uniform ("liv-
ery") of his master's household.
2. You were raised in status sufficiently.

125 The under-hangman³ of his kingdom, and hated
　　For being preferred° so well.　　　　　　　　　　　　　　*advanced*
CLOTEN　　　　　　　　　The south-fog⁴ rot him!
INNOGEN　He never can meet more mischance than come
　　To be but named of° thee. His meanest garment　　　　　*by*
　　That ever hath but clipped° his body is dearer　　　　　*encircled*
130 In my respect than all the hairs above thee,°　　　　*on your head*
　　Were they all made such men. How now, Pisanio!

　　　　　Enter PISANIO

CLOTEN　His garment? Now the devil—
INNOGEN [*to* PISANIO]　To Dorothy, my woman, hie thee presently.°　　*at once*
CLOTEN　His garment?
INNOGEN [*to* PISANIO]　I am sprited with° a fool,　　　*am haunted by*
135 Frighted, and angered worse. Go bid my woman
　　Search for a jewel that too casually
　　Hath left mine arm. It was thy master's. 'Shrew me°　*Beshrew me (plague on me)*
　　If I would lose it for a revenue
　　Of any king's in Europe! I do think
140 I saw't this morning; confident I am
　　Last night 'twas on mine arm; I kissed it.
　　I hope it be not gone to tell my lord
　　That I kiss aught but he.
PISANIO　　　　　　　　　'Twill not be lost.
INNOGEN　I hope so. Go and search.　　　　[*Exit* PISANIO]
CLOTEN　　　　　　　　　You have abused me.
　　'His meanest garment'?
145 INNOGEN　　　　　　　Ay, I said so, sir.
　　If you will make't an action,° call witness to't.　　　*a lawsuit*
CLOTEN　I will inform your father.
INNOGEN　　　　　　　　Your mother too.
　　She's my good lady, and will conceive,° I hope,°　　*think / expect*
　　But the worst of me. So I leave you, sir,
　　To th' worst of discontent.　　　　　　*Exit*
150 CLOTEN　　　　　　　I'll be revenged.
　　'His meanest garment'? Well!　　　　　*Exit*

2.4

　　　　Enter POSTHUMUS *and* FILARIO
POSTHUMUS　Fear it not, sir. I would I were so sure
　　To win the King as I am bold her honour
　　Will remain hers.
FILARIO　　　　　What means° do you make to him?　　*intercessions*
POSTHUMUS　Not any; but abide the change of time,
5 Quake in the present winter's state, and wish
　　That warmer days would come. In these seared° hopes　*withered*
　　I barely gratify° your love; they failing,　　　　*repay*
　　I must die much your debtor.
FILARIO　　Your very goodness and your company
10 O'erpays all I can do. By this,° your king　　　　*By now*
　　Hath heard of great Augustus. Caius Lucius
　　Will do 's commission throughly.° And I think　　　*thoroughly*

3. *if 'twere . . . under-hangman:* if a comparison were
made between your virtues and those of Posthumus and
you were given the job of assistant hangman; if, in accor-
dance with your virtues, you were given the job of assis-
tant hangman.
4. A damp fog brought by the south wind and supposed
to breed infections.
2.4 Location: Filario's house, Rome.

He'll grant the tribute, send th'arrearages,°   *overdue payments*
Ere look upon our Romans, whose remembrance°   *the memory of whom*
Is yet fresh in their grief.[1]

15 POSTHUMUS   I do believe,
Statist° though I am none, nor like to be,   *Statesman*
That this will prove a war, and you shall hear
The legions now in Gallia sooner landed
In our not-fearing Britain than have tidings
20 Of any penny tribute paid. Our countrymen
Are men more ordered° than when Julius Caesar   *better disciplined*
Smiled at their lack of skill but found their courage
Worthy his frowning at. Their discipline,
Now wing-led[2] with their courage, will make known
25 To their approvers° they are people such   *those who would test them*
That mend upon the world.[3]
       Enter GIACOMO
FILARIO   See, Giacomo.
POSTHUMUS [*to* GIACOMO]   The swiftest harts° have posted° you   *deer / conveyed*
    by land,
And winds of° all the corners° kissed your sails   *from / (of the globe)*
To make your vessel nimble.
FILARIO [*to* GIACOMO]   Welcome, sir.
30 POSTHUMUS [*to* GIACOMO]   I hope the briefness of your answer made°   *caused*
The speediness of your return.
GIACOMO   Your lady is
One of the fair'st that I have looked upon—
POSTHUMUS   And therewithal the best, or let her beauty
Look through a casement[4] to allure false hearts,
And be false with them.
35 GIACOMO   Here are letters for you.
POSTHUMUS   Their tenor good, I trust.
GIACOMO   'Tis very like.
    [POSTHUMUS *reads the letters*]
FILARIO   Was Caius Lucius in the Briton court
When you were there?
GIACOMO   He was expected then,
But not° approached.   *had not*
POSTHUMUS   All is well yet.
40 Sparkles this stone as it was wont, or is't not
Too dull for your good wearing?
GIACOMO   If I had lost it
I should have lost the worth of it in gold.
I'll make a journey twice as far t'enjoy
A second night of such sweet shortness which
45 Was mine in Britain; for the ring is won.
POSTHUMUS   The stone's too hard to come by.
GIACOMO   Not a whit,
Your lady being so easy.
POSTHUMUS   Make not, sir,
Your loss your sport. I hope you know that we
Must not continue friends.

---

1. The Britons' grief; the grief inflicted by the Romans.
2. Carried aloft (as if on wings); led on each flank (each "wing"). The Second Folio (F2, printed in 1632) has "mingled," an emendation adopted by some editors.
3. *such . . . world*: who improve in the world's estimation.
4. Look out through a window (alluding to the manner in which prostitutes solicited customers).

GIACOMO	Good sir, we must,	
50	If you keep covenant. Had I not brought	
	The knowledge° of your mistress home I grant	*A sexual account*
	We were to question° farther, but I now	*dispute*
	Profess myself the winner of her honour,	
	Together with your ring, and not the wronger	
55	Of her or you, having proceeded but	
	By both your wills.	

GIACOMO   Good sir, we must,
50   If you keep covenant. Had I not brought
      The knowledge° of your mistress home I grant   *A sexual account*
      We were to question° farther, but I now   *dispute*
      Profess myself the winner of her honour,
      Together with your ring, and not the wronger
55   Of her or you, having proceeded but
      By both your wills.
      POSTHUMUS   If you can make't apparent
      That you have tasted her in bed, my hand
      And ring is yours. If not, the foul opinion
      You had of her pure honour gains or loses
60   Your sword or mine,⁵ or masterless leaves both°   *both swords*
      To who shall find them.
      GIACOMO   Sir, my circumstances,°   *detailed evidence*
      Being so near the truth as I will make them,
      Must first induce you to believe; whose strength
      I will confirm with oath, which I doubt not
65   You'll give me leave to spare° when you shall find   *omit*
      You need it not.
      POSTHUMUS   Proceed.
      GIACOMO   First, her bedchamber—
      Where I confess I slept not, but profess
      Had that was well worth watching°—it was hanged   *staying awake for*
      With tapestry of silk and silver; the story
70   Proud Cleopatra when she met her Roman,⁶
      And Cydnus⁷ swelled above the banks, or for°   *either because of*
      The press of boats or pride: a piece of work
      So bravely° done, so rich, that it did strive   *splendidly*
      In workmanship and value;⁸ which I wondered
75   Could be so rarely and exactly wrought,
      Such the true life on't was.
      POSTHUMUS   This is true,
      And this you might have heard of here, by me
      Or by some other.
      GIACOMO   More particulars
      Must justify° my knowledge.   *confirm*
      POSTHUMUS   So they must,
      Or do your honour injury.
80   GIACOMO   The chimney°   *fireplace*
      Is south the chamber, and the chimney-piece⁹
      Chaste Dian¹ bathing. Never saw I figures
      So likely to report themselves;² the cutter
      Was as another nature; dumb, outwent her,
      Motion and breath left out.³
85   POSTHUMUS   This is a thing
      Which you might from relation° likewise reap,   *report*

---

5. *gains . . . mine*: makes one of us the winner, the other the loser, of his sword in a duel.
6. Alluding to a meeting, described also in Shakespeare's play *Antony and Cleopatra*, between the Egyptian queen Cleopatra and Mark Antony, a Roman general who was her lover.
7. A river in Cilicia (now Turkey).
8. *that . . . value*: that craftmanship and monetary worth both competed for preeminence.

9. Ornament above the fireplace.
1. Another reference to the goddess associated in classical myth with hunting, childbirth, and chastity.
2. So lifelike that they could give an account of themselves.
3. *the cutter . . . out*: the sculptor ("cutter") was like a second nature in creative power. Speechless, the sculpture surpassed nature, apart from its lack of movement and breathing.

Being, as it is, much spoke of.

GIACOMO   The roof o'th' chamber
With golden cherubins is fretted.°   Her andirons—   *carved*
I had forgot them—were two winking Cupids[4]
90   Of silver, each on one foot standing, nicely°   *ingeniously*
Depending° on their brands.°   *Leaning / torches*

POSTHUMUS   This is her honour!
Let it be granted you have seen all this—and praise
Be given to your remembrance—the description
Of what is in her chamber nothing saves
The wager you have laid.

95   GIACOMO   Then, if you can
Be pale,° I beg but leave to air this jewel. See!   *Be unmoved*
        [*He shows the bracelet*]
And now 'tis up° again; it must be married   *put away*
To that your diamond. I'll keep them.

POSTHUMUS   Jove!°   *king of the gods*
Once more let me behold it. Is it that
Which I left with her?

100 GIACOMO   Sir, I thank her, that.
She stripped it from her arm. I see her yet.
Her pretty action did outsell° her gift,   *exceed in value*
And yet enriched it too. She gave it me,
And said she prized it once.

POSTHUMUS   Maybe she plucked it off
To send it me.

105 GIACOMO   She writes so to you, doth she?

POSTHUMUS   O, no, no, no—'tis true! Here, take this too.
        [*He gives* GIACOMO *his ring*]
It is a basilisk[5] unto mine eye,
Kills me to look on't. Let there be no honour
Where there is beauty, truth where semblance,° love   *the mere appearance of it*
110 Where there's another man. The vows° of women   *Let the vows*
Of no more bondage be to where they are made
Than they are° to their virtues, which is nothing!   *Than women are bound*
O, above measure false!

FILARIO   Have patience, sir,
And take your ring again; 'tis not yet won.
115 It may be probable she lost it, or
Who knows if one° her woman, being corrupted,   *one of*
Hath stol'n it from her?

POSTHUMUS   Very true,
And so I hope he came by't. Back my ring.
        [*He takes his ring again*]
Render to me some corporal sign about her
120 More evident° than this; for this was stol'n.   *conclusive*

GIACOMO   By Jupiter,[6] I had it from her arm.

POSTHUMUS   Hark you, he swears, by Jupiter he swears.
'Tis true, nay, keep the ring, 'tis true. I am sure
She would not lose it. Her attendants are
125 All sworn° and honourable. They induced to steal it?   *bound by oaths*

And by a stranger? No, he hath enjoyed her.
The cognizance° of her incontinency   *token*
Is this. She hath bought the name of whore thus dearly.
    [*He gives* GIACOMO *his ring*]
There, take thy hire,° and all the fiends of hell   *fee*
Divide themselves between you!

130 FILARIO   Sir, be patient.
This is not strong enough to be believed
Of one persuaded° well of.   *thought*
POSTHUMUS   Never talk on't.
She hath been colted° by him.   *sexually enjoyed*
GIACOMO   If you seek
For further satisfying, under her breast—

135 Worthy the pressing—lies a mole, right proud
Of that most delicate lodging. By my life,
I kissed it, and it gave me present° hunger   *immediate*
To feed again, though full. You do remember
This stain° upon her?   *mark*
POSTHUMUS   Ay, and it doth confirm

140 Another stain as big as hell can hold,
Were there no more but it.
GIACOMO   Will you hear more?
POSTHUMUS   Spare your arithmetic, never count the turns.°   *sexual acts*
Once, and a million![7]
GIACOMO   I'll be sworn.
POSTHUMUS   No swearing.
If you will swear you have not done't, you lie,

145 And I will kill thee if thou dost deny
Thou'st made me cuckold.
GIACOMO   I'll deny nothing.
POSTHUMUS   O that I had her here to tear her limb-meal!°   *limb from limb*
I will go there and do't i'th' court, before
Her father. I'll do something.   *Exit*
FILARIO   Quite besides°   *beyond*

150 The government° of patience! You have won.   *control*
Let's follow and pervert° the present wrath   *turn aside*
He hath against himself.
GIACOMO   With all my heart.   *Exeunt*

2.5

    Enter POSTHUMUS[1]
POSTHUMUS   Is there no way for men to be,° but women   *to exist*
Must be half-workers?° We are bastards all,   *be partners*
And that most venerable man which I
Did call my father was I know not where

5 When I was stamped.[2] Some coiner with his tools[3]
Made me a counterfeit; yet my mother seemed
The Dian of that time: so doth my wife
The nonpareil° of this. O vengeance, vengeance!   *one who has no equal*

---

7. That is, there is no difference between having been
unfaithful once and having done it a million times.
2.5 Location: Scene continues.
1. In F, Posthumus's soliloquy is part of 2.4. He is mak-
ing a reentry, however, after his departure at line 149, and

most modern editions mark the soliloquy as a separate
scene.
2. Conceived, as coins are stamped with images when
they are made.
3. With pun on "tool" as meaning "penis."

Me of my lawful pleasure[4] she restrained,
10 And prayed me oft forbearance;[5] did it with
A pudency° so rosy the sweet view on't°   modesty / of it
Might well have warmed old Saturn;[6] that I thought her
As chaste as unsunned snow. O all the devils!
This yellow° Giacomo in an hour—was't not?—   sallow
15 Or less—at first?° Perchance he spoke not, but   instantly
Like a full-acorned boar,[7] a German one,
Cried 'O!' and mounted; found no opposition
But what he looked for should oppose[8] and she
Should from encounter guard. Could I find out
20 The woman's part in me—for there's no motion°   impulse
That tends to vice in man but I affirm
It is the woman's part; be it lying, note it,
The woman's; flattering, hers; deceiving, hers;
Lust and rank thoughts, hers, hers; revenges, hers;
25 Ambitions, covetings, change of prides,° disdain,   varying extravagances
Nice° longing, slanders, mutability,   Lustful
All faults that man can name, nay, that hell knows,
Why, hers in part or all, but rather all—
For even to vice
30 They are not constant, but are changing still
One vice but of a minute old for one
Not half so old as that. I'll write against them,
Detest them, curse them, yet 'tis greater skill°   cleverness
In a true hate to pray they have their will.°   desire
35 The very devils cannot plague them better.   Exit

3.1

[*Flourish.*] *Enter in state* CYMBELINE, [*the*] QUEEN,
CLOTEN, *and lords at one door, and at another, Caius*
LUCIUS *and attendants*

CYMBELINE   Now say, what would Augustus Caesar with us?
LUCIUS   When Julius Caesar—whose remembrance yet
Lives in men's eyes, and will to ears and tongues
Be theme and hearing ever—was in this Britain
5 And conquered it, Cassibelan, thine uncle,
Famous in Caesar's praises no whit less
Than in his feats deserving it, for him
And his succession° granted Rome a tribute,   heirs
Yearly three thousand pounds, which by thee lately
Is left untendered.
10 QUEEN   And, to kill the marvel,[1]
Shall be so ever.
CLOTEN   There will be many Caesars
Ere such another Julius. Britain's a world
By itself, and we will nothing pay
For wearing our own noses.[2]

---

4. The sexual pleasure to which marriage entitled him.
5. And often begged me to defer sexual pleasures.
6. The Roman god of agriculture, usually characterized
as cold and melancholy.
7. A boar fed full of acorns (with a pun on "boor" as
meaning "a German or Dutch peasant").
8. *found . . . oppose:* found no opposition except the body
parts he expected to encounter.

3.1 Location: Cymbeline's court, Britain.
1. And, to put a stop to the amazement (which our non-
payment has caused).
2. Perhaps referring to contemporary theories of physiog-
nomy that identified specific physical features, such as
noses, with racial types. Roman noses were notoriously
prominent.

QUEEN   That opportunity

15   Which then they had to take from 's, to resume°   *take back*
     We have again. Remember, sir, my liege,°   *sovereign*
     The kings your ancestors, together with
     The natural bravery° of your isle, which stands   *splendor*
     As Neptune's park,[3] ribbed and paled in°   *enclosed and fenced in*
20   With banks unscalable and roaring waters,
     With sands that will not bear your enemies' boats,
     But suck them up to th' topmast. A kind of conquest
     Caesar made here, but made not here his brag
     Of 'came and saw and overcame'.[4] With shame—
25   The first that ever touched him—he was carried
     From off our coast, twice beaten; and his shipping,°   *ships*
     Poor ignorant° baubles, on our terrible seas   *silly*
     Like eggshells moved upon their surges, cracked
     As easily 'gainst our rocks; for joy whereof
30   The famed Cassibelan, who was once at point°—   *ready*
     O giglot° fortune!—to master Caesar's sword,   *fickle; whorish*
     Made Lud's town[5] with rejoicing fires bright,
     And Britons strut with courage.

CLOTEN   Come, there's no more tribute to be paid. Our king-
35   dom is stronger than it was at that time, and, as I said, there is
     no more such Caesars. Other of them may have crooked noses,
     but to owe° such straight° arms, none.   *possess / powerful*

CYMBELINE   Son, let your mother end.

CLOTEN   We have yet many among us can grip as hard as Cassi-
40   belan. I do not say I am one, but I have a hand. Why tribute?
     Why should we pay tribute? If Caesar can hide the sun from us
     with a blanket, or put the moon in his pocket, we will pay him
     tribute for light; else, sir, no more tribute, pray you now.

CYMBELINE [*to* LUCIUS]   You must know,
45   Till the injurious° Romans did extort   *insulting*
     This tribute from us we were free. Caesar's ambition,
     Which swelled so much that it did almost stretch
     The sides o'th' world, against all colour[6] here
     Did put the yoke upon 's, which to shake off
50   Becomes a warlike people, whom we reckon
     Ourselves to be. We do say then to Caesar,
     Our ancestor was that Mulmutius[7] which
     Ordained our laws, whose use the sword of Caesar
     Hath too much mangled, whose repair and franchise°   *free exercise*
55   Shall by the power we hold be our good deed,
     Though Rome be therefore angry. Mulmutius made our laws,
     Who was the first of Britain which did put
     His brows within a golden crown and called
     Himself a king.

LUCIUS   I am sorry, Cymbeline,
60   That I am to pronounce Augustus Caesar—

---

3. As grounds owned by Neptune, Roman god of the sea.
4. When Julius Caesar, leading an army into Asia, defeated King Pharnaces and his allies, Plutarch reports that Caesar wrote three words to his friend Anitius in Rome: *veni, vidi, vici* ("I came, I saw, I overcame"). See Plutarch's *Life of Julius Caesar* in his *Lives of the Noble Graecians and Romans* as translated by Thomas North

(1579).
5. London. Contemporary texts such as Holinshed's *Chronicles* erroneously asserted that "London" was derived from "Lud," the name of the mythological British king who was Cymbeline's grandfather.
6. Without any pretense of justice.
7. According to Holinshed, the first King of Britain.

Caesar, that hath more kings his servants than
Thyself domestic officers—thine enemy.
Receive it from me, then: war and confusion°   *destruction*
In Caesar's name pronounce I 'gainst thee. Look
65   For fury not to be resisted. Thus defied,
I thank thee for myself.
CYMBELINE   Thou art welcome, Caius.
Thy Caesar knighted me; my youth I spent
Much under him; of him I gathered honour,
Which he to seek of me again perforce
70   Behoves me keep at utterance.[8] I am perfect°   *fully aware*
That the Pannonians and Dalmatians[9] for
Their liberties are now in arms, a precedent
Which not to read would show the Britons cold;°   *lacking in spirit*
So Caesar shall not find them.
LUCIUS   Let proof° speak.   *the result*
75   CLOTEN   His majesty bids you welcome. Make pastime with us a
day or two or longer. If you seek us afterwards in other terms,
you shall find us in our salt-water girdle.[1] If you beat us out of
it, it is yours; if you fall in the adventure, our crows shall fare
the better for you; and there's an end.
80   LUCIUS   So, sir.
CYMBELINE   I know your master's pleasure, and he mine.
All the remain° is 'Welcome'.   [*Flourish.*] *Exeunt*   *All that is left to say*

3.2

Enter PISANIO, *reading of a letter*
PISANIO   How? Of adultery? Wherefore write you not
What monster's her accuser? Leonatus,
O master, what a strange infection
Is fall'n into thy ear! What false Italian,
5   As poisonous tongued as handed,[1] hath prevailed
On thy too ready hearing? Disloyal? No.
She's punished for her truth,° and undergoes,   *faithfulness*
More goddess-like than wife-like, such assaults
As would take in° some virtue. O my master,   *overcome*
10   Thy mind to° hers is now as low as were   *compared to*
Thy fortunes. How? That I should murder her,
Upon the love and truth and vows which I
Have made to thy command? I her? Her blood?
If it be so to do good service, never
15   Let me be counted serviceable. How look I,
That I should seem to lack humanity
So much as this fact° comes to? [*Reads*] 'Do't. The letter   *action*
That I have sent her, by her own command
Shall give thee opportunity.' O damned paper,[2]
20   Black as the ink that's on thee! Senseless bauble,

---

8. *Which . . . utterance:* His seeking that honor of me
again makes it necessary for me to defend ("keep") it to
the death.
9. Inhabitants of Hungary and Dalmatia, a region on the
Adriatic Sea.
1. In the sea that encircles us (as a girdle does the body).

3.2 Location: Cymbeline's court.
1. Having as many poisons (lies) in his tongue as in his
hands. Contemporary texts depicted Italians as infinitely
skilled in making and administering poisons.
2. O hellish object (referring to the letter).

Art thou a fedary° for this act, and look'st
                                                   an accomplice

So virgin-like without?
        Enter INNOGEN
                    Lo, here she comes.
I am ignorant in° what I am commanded.
                                  will pretend ignorance of

INNOGEN   How now, Pisanio?

25 PISANIO Madam, here is a letter from my lord.

INNOGEN Who, thy lord that is my lord, Leonatus?
  O learned indeed were that astronomer°   *astrologer*
  That knew the stars as I his characters°—   *handwriting*
  He'd lay the future open. You good gods,

30 Let what is here contained relish° of love,   *taste*
  Of my lord's health, of his content—yet not
  That we two are asunder; let that grieve him.
  Some griefs are med'cinable;° that is one of them,   *beneficial*
  For it doth physic love³—of his content

35 All but in that. Good wax,° thy leave. Blest be   *sealing wax*
  You bees that make these locks of counsel!° Lovers   *for private matters*
  And men in dangerous bonds⁴ pray not alike;
  Though forfeiters you cast in prison,⁵ yet
  You clasp° young Cupid's tables.° Good news, gods!   *lovingly embrace / tablets*
  [*She opens and reads the letter*]

40 'Justice and your father's wrath, should he take me in his
  dominion, could not be so cruel to me as° you, O the dearest   *but that*
  of creatures, would even renew me° with your eyes. Take   *would revive me*
  notice that I am in Cambria,° at Milford Haven.⁶ What your   *Wales*
  own love will out of this advise you, follow. So he wishes you

45 all happiness, that remains loyal to his vow, and your increasing
  in love,
                                  Leonatus Posthumus.'
  O for a horse with wings! Hear'st thou, Pisanio?
  He is at Milford Haven. Read, and tell me

50 How far 'tis thither. If one of mean affairs°   *with unimportant business*
  May plod it in a week, why may not I
  Glide thither in a day? Then, true Pisanio,
  Who long'st like me to see thy lord, who long'st—
  O let me bate°—but not like me—yet long'st   *moderate my speech*

55 But in a fainter kind—O, not like me,
  For mine's beyond beyond; say, and speak thick°—   *speak quickly*
  Love's counsellor should fill the bores of hearing,°   *the ears*
  To th' smothering of the sense⁷—how far it is
  To this same blessèd Milford. And by° th' way   *on*

60 Tell me how Wales was made so happy as
  T'inherit such a haven. But first of all,
  How we may steal from hence; and for the gap
  That we shall make in time from our hence-going
  Till our return, to excuse; but first, how get hence.

65 Why should excuse be born or ere begot?⁸

---

3. For it nurtures love; for it keeps love in good health.
4. Men bound by agreements imposing penalties (which are sealed with wax). Innogen is contrasting the fear with which men in legal trouble greet sealed documents to the joy with which lovers receive a sealed love letter.
5. Although you cast those who default on agreements in prison (because sealed bonds lead to indictments).
6. A port in southern Wales that became important in later British history when Henry Tudor landed there in 1485. Defeating the army of Richard III, he was crowned Henry VII, bringing to an end the civil strife known as the Wars of the Roses.
7. Until the sense of hearing is overwhelmed.
8. Why should an excuse be born even before it is conceived, that is, be manufactured before it is needed?

We'll talk of that hereafter. Prithee speak,
How many score of° miles may we well ride   *set of twenty*
'Twixt hour and hour?°   *In an hour*
PISANIO   One score 'twixt sun and sun,
Madam, 's enough for you, and too much too.

70 INNOGEN   Why, one that rode to 's execution, man,
Could never go so slow. I have heard of riding wagers
Where horses have been nimbler than the sands
That run i'th' clock's behalf.[9] But this is fool'ry.
Go bid my woman feign a sickness, say

75 She'll home to her father; and provide me presently°   *at once*
A riding-suit no costlier than would fit°   *suit*
A franklin's housewife.[1]
PISANIO   Madam, you're best° consider.   *you'd better*
INNOGEN   I see before° me, man. Nor here, nor here,   *straight ahead of*
Nor what ensues,[2] but have a fog in them

80 That I cannot look through. Away, I prithee,
Do as I bid thee. There's no more to say:
Accessible is none but Milford way.   *Exeunt*

3.3

Enter BELARIUS, [*followed by*] GUIDERIUS *and* ARVIRA-
GUS [*from a cave in the woods*][1]

BELARIUS   A goodly day not to keep house° with such   *stay home*
Whose roof's as low as ours. Stoop, boys; this gate
Instructs you how t'adore the heavens, and bows you°   *makes you bow down*
To a morning's holy office.° The gates of monarchs   *a morning prayer*

5 Are arched so high that giants may jet° through   *swagger*
And keep their impious turbans[2] on without
Good morrow to the sun. Hail, thou fair heaven!
We house i'th' rock, yet use thee not so hardly°   *badly*
As prouder livers° do.   *those living more grandly*
GUIDERIUS   Hail, heaven!
ARVIRAGUS   Hail, heaven!

10 BELARIUS   Now for our mountain sport. Up to yon hill,
Your legs are young; I'll tread these flats.° Consider,   *this plain*
When you above perceive me like a crow,
That it is place° which lessens and sets off,°   *position / enhances*
And you may then revolve° what tales I have told you   *consider*

15 Of courts, of princes, of the tricks in war;
That service is not service, so being done,
But being so allowed.[3] To apprehend thus
Draws us a profit from all things we see,
And often to our comfort shall we find

20 The sharded beetle[4] in a safer hold°   *refuge*

---

9. *than . . . behalf*: than the sands that run through the hourglass.
1. The wife of a landowning farmer whose social status was lower than that of the gentry. Early modern English sumptuary codes prescribed specific fabrics and styles of dress for people of different ranks.
2. *Nor here . . . ensues*: Neither (what is) on this side, nor on that, nor what will happen (after Milford Haven is reached).
3.3 Location: The cave of Belarius, Wales.
1. In his account of a performance of the play in 1611, Simon Forman wrote of "the Cave in the woods" and of

the "woods" where Innogen's supposedly dead body was laid. It is possible that some form of stage foliage surrounded the entrance to Belarius's cave.
2. The idea of giants wearing turbans may come from prose romances in which giants were often equated with Saracens, or followers of Islam, who wore turbans and were seen as impious enemies of Christians.
3. *That service . . . allowed*: That acts of service are not acts of service simply by being done, but rather by being acknowledged as such (by superiors).
4. The beetle who lives in dung. "Shard" means "patch of dung."

Than is the full-winged eagle. O, this life
Is nobler than attending for a check,[5]
Richer than doing nothing for a bauble,
Prouder than rustling in unpaid-for silk;
25 Such gain the cap of him that makes 'em fine,
Yet keeps his book uncrossed.[6] No life to ours.
GUIDERIUS Out of your proof° you speak. We, poor unfledged,[7]   *experience*
Have never winged from view o'th' nest, nor know not
What air's from° home. Haply° this life is best,   *away from / Perhaps*
30 If quiet life be best; sweeter to you
That have a sharper known; well corresponding
With your stiff age, but unto us it is
A cell of ignorance, travelling abed,°   *only while dreaming*
A prison for a debtor, that not dares
To stride a limit.[8]
35 ARVIRAGUS [*to* BELARIUS]   What should we speak of
When we are old as you? When we shall hear
The rain and wind beat dark December, how,
In this our pinching cave,[9] shall we discourse
The freezing hours away? We have seen nothing.
40 We are beastly:° subtle as the fox for prey,   *like beasts*
Like° warlike as the wolf for what we eat.   *As*
Our valour is to chase what flies; our cage
We make a choir, as doth the prisoned bird,
And sing our bondage freely.
BELARIUS   How you speak!
45 Did you but know the city's usuries,[1]
And felt them knowingly; the art o'th' court,
As hard to leave as keep,° whose top to climb   *dwell in*
Is certain falling, or so slipp'ry that
The fear's as bad as falling; the toil o'th' war,
50 A pain° that only seems to seek out danger   *labor*
I'th' name of fame and honour, which dies i'th' search
And hath as oft a sland'rous epitaph
As record of fair act; nay, many times
Doth ill deserve° by doing well; what's worse,   *earn ill treatment*
55 Must curtsy at the censure.[2] O boys, this story
The world may read in me. My body's marked
With Roman swords, and my report° was once   *reputation*
First with the best of note.° Cymbeline loved me,   *the most renowned*
And when a soldier was the theme my name
60 Was not far off. Then was I as a tree
Whose boughs did bend with fruit; but in one night
A storm or robbery, call it what you will,
Shook down my mellow hangings,° nay, my leaves,   *ripe fruit*
And left me bare to weather.
GUIDERIUS   Uncertain favour!
65 BELARIUS My fault being nothing, as I have told you oft,
But that two villains, whose false oaths prevailed

---

5. Than acting as a servant only to be rebuked.
6. *Such . . . uncrossed:* Such men win the deference (shown by removing "the cap") of the tailor who is the source of their grandeur, yet continue to have their debts standing ("uncrossed") in the tailor's account book.
7. Lacking the feathers necessary for flight (spoken of a young bird).

8. *that . . . limit:* who does not dare to leave a place of sanctuary (for fear of being arrested).
9. Our confining cave; our cave that pinches us with cold.
1. Financial practices whereby money was lent at excessive or illegal rates of interest.
2. Must defer to the person who finds fault.

Before my perfect honour, swore to Cymbeline
I was confederate with the Romans. So
Followed my banishment, and this twenty years
70 This rock and these demesnes° have been my world,   *regions*
Where I have lived at honest freedom, paid
More pious debts to heaven than in all
The fore-end° of my time. But up to th' mountains!   *early days*
This is not hunter's language. He that strikes
75 The venison first shall be the lord o'th' feast,
To him the other two shall minister,
And we will fear no poison which attends°   *is always present*
In place of greater state. I'll meet you in the valleys.
                    Exeunt [GUIDERIUS *and* ARVIRAGUS]
How hard it is to hide the sparks of nature!
80 These boys know little they are sons to th' King,
Nor Cymbeline dreams that they are alive.
They think they are mine, and though trained up thus meanly°   *in a humble style*
I'th' cave wherein they bow, their thoughts do hit
The roofs of palaces, and nature prompts them
85 In simple and low things to prince it° much   *to act like princes*
Beyond the trick° of others. This Polydore,   *custom*
The heir of Cymbeline and Britain, who
The King his father called Guiderius—Jove,
When on my three-foot stool I sit and tell
90 The warlike feats I have done, his spirits fly out
Into my story: say 'Thus mine enemy fell,
And thus I set my foot on 's neck', even then
The princely blood flows in his cheek, he sweats,
Strains his young nerves,° and puts himself in posture   *sinews*
95 That acts my words. The younger brother, Cadwal,
Once Arviragus, in as like a figure°   *acting the part as aptly*
Strikes life into my speech, and shows much more
His own conceiving.°   *imagination*
                    [*A hunting-horn sounds*]
                    Hark, the game is roused!
O Cymbeline, heaven and my conscience knows[3]
100 Thou didst unjustly banish me, whereon
At three and two years old I stole these babes,
Thinking to bar thee of succession as
Thou reft'st° me of my lands. Euriphile,   *deprived*
Thou wast their nurse; they took thee for their mother,
105 And every day do honour to her grave.
Myself, Belarius, that am Morgan called,
They take for natural father.
                    [*A hunting-horn sounds*]
                    The game is up.°   *Exit*   *roused*

3.4

Enter PISANIO, *and* INNOGEN [*in a riding-suit*]
INNOGEN   Thou told'st me when we came from horse° the place   *we dismounted*
Was near at hand. Ne'er longed my mother so

---

3. Editors have conjectured that lines 99–107 are either a non-Shakespearean addition or a section he added in revision. They stand apart from the rest of the speech, providing a hurried summary of information. Moreover, "the game is roused" (line 98) is repeated in "The game is up" (line 107).
3.4 Location: Wales, near Milford Haven.

To see me first as I have° now. Pisanio, man,   *do*

Where is Posthumus? What is in thy mind

5 That makes thee stare thus? Wherefore breaks that sigh

From th'inward of thee? One but painted thus

Would be interpreted a thing perplexed°   *bewildered*

Beyond self-explication. Put thyself

Into a haviour of less fear,[1] ere wildness°   *madness*

10 Vanquish my staider senses. What's the matter?

    [PISANIO *gives her a letter*]

Why tender'st thou that paper to me with

A look untender? If't be summer news,

Smile to't before; if winterly, thou need'st

But keep that count'nance still. My husband's hand?

15 That drug-damned Italy[2] hath out-craftied° him,   *outwitted*

And he's at some hard point.° Speak, man. Thy tongue   *in some crisis*

May take off some extremity° which to read   *reduce the horror*

Would be even mortal° to me.   *fatal*

PISANIO   Please you read,

And you shall find me, wretched man, a thing

20 The most disdained of fortune.

INNOGEN *reads* 'Thy mistress, Pisanio, hath played the strumpet

in my bed, the testimonies whereof lies bleeding in me. I speak

not out of weak surmises but from proof as strong as my grief

and as certain as I expect my revenge. That part thou, Pisanio,

25 must act for me, if thy faith be not tainted with the breach of

hers. Let thine own hands take away her life. I shall give thee

opportunity at Milford Haven. She hath my letter for the pur-

pose, where if thou fear to strike and to make me certain it is

done, thou art the pander to her dishonour and equally to me

30 disloyal.'

PISANIO [*aside*] What shall I need to draw my sword? The paper

Hath cut her throat already. No, 'tis slander,

Whose edge is sharper than the sword, whose tongue

Outvenoms all the worms of Nile,[3] whose breath

35 Rides on the posting° winds and doth belie°   *speeding / deceive*

All corners of the world. Kings, queens, and states,

Maids, matrons, nay, the secrets of the grave

This viperous slander enters. [*To* INNOGEN] What cheer, madam?

INNOGEN False to his bed? What is it to be false?

40 To lie in watch° there and to think on him?   *wakefulness*

To weep 'twixt clock and clock?° If sleep charge° nature,   *continually / overcome*

To break it with a fearful dream of° him   *a dream fearful for*

And cry myself awake? That's false to 's bed, is it?

PISANIO Alas, good lady.

45 INNOGEN I false? Thy conscience witness, Giacomo,

Thou didst accuse him of incontinency.

Thou then lookedst like a villain; now, methinks,

Thy favour's° good enough. Some jay° of Italy,   *appearance is / strumpet*

Whose mother was her painting,[4] hath betrayed him.

---

1. *Put . . . fear*: Adopt a less fearsome manner.
2. That country notorious for its poisons.
3. Alluding to the poisonous serpents associated with Egypt's Nile River. Slander was often personified as a woman with snakes issuing from her mouth. In early modern England, women frequently brought cases in the ecclesiastical courts against those who defamed or slan-

dered them; overwhelmingly, they were defending their reputations against claims that they had committed a sexual offense and were unchaste. Pisanio rightly assumes that Innogen is the victim of just such slanderous accusations.
4. Who is entirely the product of her cosmetics.

50	Poor I am stale,° a garment out of fashion,	*out of date; not new*
	And for I am richer than to hang by th' walls	
	I must be ripped.[5] To pieces with me! O,	
	Men's vows are women's traitors. All good seeming,°	*appearance*
	By thy revolt, O husband, shall be thought	
55	Put on for villainy; not born where't grows,	
	But worn a bait for ladies.	

PISANIO   Good madam, hear me.

	INNOGEN True honest men being heard like false Aeneas[6]	
	Were in his time thought false, and Sinon's[7] weeping	
	Did scandal° many a holy tear, took pity	*discredit*
60	From most true wretchedness. So thou, Posthumus,	
	Wilt lay the leaven on all proper men.[8]	
	Goodly° and gallant shall be false and perjured	*Admirable*
	From thy great fail.° [*To* PISANIO] Come, fellow, be thou honest,	*failure*
	Do thou thy master's bidding. When thou seest him,	
65	A little witness° my obedience. Look,	*Briefly attest to*
	I draw the sword myself. Take it, and hit	
	The innocent mansion of my love, my heart.	
	Fear not, 'tis empty of all things but grief.	
	Thy master is not there, who was indeed	
70	The riches of it. Do his bidding; strike.	
	Thou mayst be valiant in a better cause,	
	But now thou seem'st a coward.	

PISANIO   Hence, vile instrument,

Thou shalt not damn my hand!

INNOGEN   Why, I must die,

	And if I do not by thy hand thou art	
75	No servant of thy master's. Against self-slaughter	
	There is a prohibition so divine	
	That cravens° my weak hand. Come, here's my heart.	*makes cowardly*
	Something's afore't. Soft,° soft, we'll no defence;	*Gently*
	Obedient as the scabbard. What is here?	

[*She takes letters from her bosom*]

80	The scriptures° of the loyal Leonatus,	*writing; sacred texts*
	All turned to heresy? Away, away,	
	Corrupters of my faith, you shall no more	
	Be stomachers[9] to my heart. Thus may poor fools	
	Believe false teachers. Though those that are betrayed	
85	Do feel the treason sharply, yet the traitor	
	Stands in worse case of woe. And thou, Posthumus,	
	That didst set up° my disobedience 'gainst the King	*instigate*
	My father, and make me put into contempt the suits	
	Of princely fellows,° shalt hereafter find	*those equal to my rank*
90	It is no act of common passage but	
	A strain of rareness;[1] and I grieve myself	
	To think, when thou shalt be disedged° by her	*surfeited*

---

5. *And . . . ripped:* And because I am too valuable to be discarded (by being hung up and forgotten about), I must be torn apart (so that the material may be reused).
6. Being heard as though they were as false as the hero of Virgil's *Aeneid*, Aeneas, who deserted his love, Dido, the Queen of Carthage.
7. Another deceitful character from the *Aeneid*. Sinon betrayed Troy to the Greeks by inducing the Trojans to let into the city a wooden horse in which Greek warriors were concealed.
8. Will corrupt the reputations of all faithful men (as a portion of inferior dough spoils the rest).
9. Ornamented chest coverings worn by women under their bodices.
1. *It . . . rareness:* My choice was no commonplace action but the sign of exceptional qualities.

That now thou tirest on,[2] how thy memory
Will then be panged by° me. [*To* PISANIO] Prithee, dispatch.   *pierced by thoughts of*
95   The lamb entreats the butcher. Where's thy knife?
Thou art too slow to do thy master's bidding
When I desire it too.
PISANIO   O gracious lady,
Since I received command to do this business
I have not slept one wink.
INNOGEN   Do't, and to bed, then.
PISANIO   I'll wake mine eyeballs out first.[3]
100   INNOGEN   Wherefore then
Didst undertake it? Why hast thou abused
So many miles with a pretence?—this place,
Mine action, and thine own? Our horses' labour,
The time inviting thee? The perturbed court,
105   For my being absent, whereunto I never
Purpose° return? Why hast thou gone so far   *Intend*
To be unbent[4] when thou hast ta'en thy stand,°   *shooting position*
Th'elected° deer before thee?   *The chosen*
PISANIO   But to win time
To lose so bad employment, in the which
110   I have considered of a course. Good lady,
Hear me with patience.
INNOGEN   Talk thy tongue weary. Speak.
I have heard I am a strumpet, and mine ear,
Therein false struck, can take no greater wound,
Nor tent to bottom that.[5] But speak.
PISANIO   Then, madam,
I thought you would not back° again.   *go back (to court)*
115   INNOGEN   Most like,
Bringing me here to kill me.
PISANIO   Not so, neither.
But if I were as wise as honest, then
My purpose would prove well. It cannot be
But that my master is abused.° Some villain,   *deceived*
120   Ay, and singular° in his art, hath done you both   *unmatched*
This cursèd injury.
INNOGEN   Some Roman courtesan.
PISANIO   No, on my life.
I'll give but notice you are dead, and send him
125   Some bloody sign of it, for 'tis commanded
I should do so. You shall be missed at court,
And that will well confirm it.
INNOGEN   Why, good fellow,
What shall I do the while, where bide, how live,
Or in my life what comfort when I am
Dead to my husband?
130   PISANIO   If you'll back° to th' court—   *return*
INNOGEN   No court, no father, nor no more ado
With that harsh, churlish, noble, simple nothing,

---

2. Whom now you feed on (in the manner of a bird of   4. To be with bow unready.
prey).   5. Nor probe ("tent") the depths of that wound.
3. I'll stay awake until my eyes drop out before I'll do it.

That Cloten, whose love suit hath been to me
As fearful as a siege.
PISANIO   If not at court,
Then not in Britain must you bide.
135 INNOGEN   Where then?
Hath Britain all the sun that shines? Day, night,
Are they not but° in Britain? I'th' world's volume   *Do they exist only*
Our Britain seems as of it but not in't,[6]
In a great pool a swan's nest. Prithee, think
There's livers out of Britain.[7]
140 PISANIO   I am most glad
You think of other place. Th'ambassador,
Lucius the Roman, comes to Milford Haven
Tomorrow. Now if you could wear a mind
Dark° as your fortune is, and but disguise   *Secret; dismal*
145 That which t'appear itself must not yet be
But by self-danger,[8] you should tread a course
Pretty and full of view;[9] yea, haply° near   *perhaps*
The residence of Posthumus; so nigh, at least,
That though his actions were not visible, yet
150 Report should render° him hourly to your ear   *describe*
As truly as he moves.
INNOGEN   O, for such means,°   *a method of access*
Though peril° to my modesty, not death on't,°   *a danger / of it*
I would adventure.°   *take the risk*
PISANIO   Well then, here's the point:
You must forget to be a woman; change
155 Command[1] into obedience, fear and niceness°—   *daintiness*
The handmaids of all women, or more truly
Woman it pretty self[2]—into a waggish° courage,   *mischievous*
Ready in gibes, quick-answered, saucy and
As quarrelous° as the weasel. Nay, you must   *quarrelsome*
160 Forget that rarest treasure of your cheek,
Exposing it[3]—but O, the harder heart![4]—
Alack, no remedy—to the greedy touch
Of common-kissing Titan,[5] and forget
Your laboursome and dainty trims° wherein   *apparel*
You made great Juno° angry.   *queen of the gods*
165 INNOGEN   Nay, be brief.
I see into thy end,° and am almost   *purpose*
A man already.
PISANIO   First, make yourself but like one.
Forethinking° this, I have already fit°—   *Anticipating / at hand*
'Tis in my cloak-bag—doublet, hat, hose, all
170 That answer to° them. Would you in their serving,[6]   *go with*
And with what imitation you can borrow

---

6. Seems part of the world, yet distinct. The metaphor is of the world as a book in which Britain is a page, but one not bound into the volume.
7. *Prithee . . . Britain:* I pray you, believe that there are people living outside Britain.
8. *and but . . . self-danger:* and simply disguise your appearance, which if it were now to show itself for what it is would put you in danger.
9. Advantageous and with good prospects.
1. The commanding ways of a princess.

2. *or . . . self:* or, more accurately, womanhood itself.
3. In early modern England, English women of the upper classes shielded themselves from the sun and cultivated pale complexions, the "treasure" of their cheeks.
4. The "harder heart" probably refers to Innogen, who must harden her heart even as she tans her skin. It may refer to Posthumus's cruelty to Innogen or to Pisanio's cruelty in forcing these harsh facts upon Innogen.
5. The sun god who shines on ("kisses") everyone alike.
6. If you would with their help.

From youth of such a season,° fore° noble Lucius   *an age / before*
Present yourself, desire his service,° tell him   *to serve him*
Wherein you're happy[7] —which will make him know°   *convince him*
175 If that his head have ear in music—doubtless
With joy he will embrace you, for he's honourable,
And, doubling that, most holy. Your means° abroad—   *As for means of support*
You have me, rich, and I will never fail
Beginning nor supplyment.[8]
INNOGEN   Thou art all the comfort
180 The gods will diet° me with. Prithee away.   *feed*
There's more to be considered, but we'll even°   *keep pace with*
All that good time will give us. This attempt
I am soldier to,° and will abide it with   *committed to*
A prince's courage. Away, I prithee.
185 PISANIO Well, madam, we must take a short farewell
Lest, being missed, I be suspected of
Your carriage° from the court. My noble mistress,   *removal*
Here is a box. I had it from the Queen.
What's in't is precious. If you are sick at sea
190 Or stomach-qualmed° at land, a dram° of this   *nauseous / tiny portion*
Will drive away distemper. To some shade,
And fit you to your manhood.[9] May the gods
Direct you to the best.
INNOGEN   Amen. I thank thee. *Exeunt [severally]*

3.5

[*Flourish.*] *Enter* CYMBELINE, [*the*] QUEEN, CLOTEN,
   LUCIUS, *and lords*
CYMBELINE [*to* LUCIUS]   Thus far, and so farewell.
LUCIUS   Thanks, royal sir.
My emperor hath wrote I must from hence;
And am right sorry that I must report ye
My master's enemy.
CYMBELINE   Our subjects, sir,
5 Will not endure his yoke, and for ourself
To show less sovereignty than they must needs
Appear unkinglike.
LUCIUS   So, sir, I desire of you
A conduct° over land to Milford Haven.   *An escort*
[*To the* QUEEN] Madam, all joy befall your grace, [*to* CLOTEN] and you.
10 CYMBELINE My lords, you are appointed for that office.°   *duty*
The due of honour in no point omit.
So farewell, noble Lucius.
LUCIUS   Your hand, my lord.
CLOTEN Receive it friendly, but from this time forth
I wear it as your enemy.
LUCIUS   Sir, the event°   *outcome*
15 Is yet to name the winner. Fare you well.
CYMBELINE Leave not the worthy Lucius, good my lords,
Till he have crossed the Severn.[1] Happiness.
               Exeunt LUCIUS [*and lords*]

---

7. In which things you are skilled.   manhood.
8. In providing the initial amount nor in supplementing it.   3.5 Location: Cymbeline's court, Britain.
9. Dress yourself in accordance with your (pretended)   1. River flowing between Wales and England.

QUEEN   He goes hence frowning, but it honours us
    That we have given him cause.
CLOTEN   'Tis all the better.
20   Your valiant Britons have their wishes in it.
CYMBELINE   Lucius hath wrote already to the Emperor
    How it goes here. It fits° us therefore ripely°   *befits / quickly*
    Our chariots and our horsemen be in readiness.
    The powers° that he already hath in Gallia   *military forces*
25   Will soon be drawn to head,[2] from whence he moves
    His war for Britain.
QUEEN   'Tis not sleepy business,
    But must be looked to speedily and strongly.
CYMBELINE   Our expectation that it would be thus
    Hath made us forward.° But, my gentle queen,   *well prepared*
30   Where is our daughter? She hath not appeared
    Before the Roman, nor to us hath tendered
    The duty of the day. She looks us° like   *seems to us*
    A thing more made of malice than of duty.
    We have noted it. Call her before us, for
    We have been too slight in sufferance.°   [*Exit one or more*]   *mild in our tolerance*
35   QUEEN   Royal sir,
    Since the exile of Posthumus most retired
    Hath her life been, the cure whereof, my lord,
    'Tis time must do. Beseech your majesty
    Forbear sharp speeches to her. She's a lady
40   So tender of° rebukes that words are strokes,   *sensitive to*
    And strokes death to her.
        Enter a MESSENGER
CYMBELINE   Where is she, sir? How
    Can her contempt be answered?
MESSENGER   Please you, sir,
    Her chambers are all locked, and there's no answer
    That will be given to th' loud'st of noise we make.
45   QUEEN   My lord, when last I went to visit her
    She prayed me to excuse her keeping close,°   *staying confined*
    Whereto constrained by her infirmity,
    She should that duty leave unpaid to you
    Which daily she was bound to proffer. This
50   She wished me to make known, but our great court°   *court business*
    Made me to blame° in memory.   *at fault*
CYMBELINE   Her doors locked?
    Not seen of late? Grant heavens that which I
    Fear prove false.   *Exit*
QUEEN   Son, I say, follow the King.
CLOTEN   That man of hers, Pisanio, her old servant,
    I have not seen these two days.
55   QUEEN   Go, look after.   *Exit* [CLOTEN]
    Pisanio, thou that stand'st so for° Posthumus!   *so much takes the part of*
    He hath a drug of mine. I pray his absence
    Proceed by° swallowing that, for he believes   *Results from*
    It is a thing most precious. But for her,
60   Where is she gone? Haply° despair hath seized her,   *Perhaps*
    Or, winged with fervour of her love, she's flown

---

2. Be gathered to their full strength.

To her desired Posthumus. Gone she is
To death or to dishonour, and my end
Can make good use of either. She being down,
65 I have the placing of the British crown.

Enter CLOTEN

How now, my son?

CLOTEN   'Tis certain she is fled.
Go in and cheer the King. He rages, none
Dare come about him.

QUEEN   All the better. May
This night forestall him of the coming day.[3]   *Exit*

70 CLOTEN   I love and hate her. For° she's fair and royal,   *Because*
And that she hath all courtly parts° more exquisite   *features*
Than lady, ladies, woman—from every one
The best she hath, and she, of all compounded,
Outsells° them all—I love her therefore; but   *Exceeds in value*
75 Disdaining me, and throwing favours on
The low Posthumus, slanders° so her judgement   *discredits*
That what's else° rare is choked; and in that point   *otherwise*
I will conclude to hate her, nay, indeed,
To be revenged upon her. For when fools
Shall—

Enter PISANIO

80   Who is here? What, are you packing,° sirrah?[4]   *scheming*
Come hither. Ah, you precious pander! Villain,
Where is thy lady? In a word, or else
Thou art straightway with the fiends.

PISANIO   O good my lord!

CLOTEN   Where is thy lady?—or, by Jupiter,
85 I will not ask again. Close° villain,   *Secretive*
I'll have this secret from thy tongue or rip
Thy heart to find it. Is she with Posthumus,
From whose so many weights° of baseness cannot   *measures*
A dram of worth be drawn?

PISANIO   Alas, my lord,
90 How can she be with him? When was she missed?
He is in Rome.

CLOTEN   Where is she, sir? Come nearer.°   *Be more precise*
No farther halting. Satisfy me home°   *completely*
What is become of her.

PISANIO   O my all-worthy lord!

95 CLOTEN   All-worthy villain,
Discover° where thy mistress is at once,   *Reveal*
At the next word. No more of 'worthy lord'.
Speak, or thy silence on the instant is
Thy condemnation and thy death.

PISANIO   Then, sir,
100 This paper is the history of my knowledge
Touching her flight.

[*He gives* CLOTEN *a letter*]

CLOTEN   Let's see't. I will pursue her
Even to Augustus' throne.

PISANIO [*aside*]   Or° this or perish.   *Either*

---

3. That is, kill him. *forestall*: deprive.   4. Fellow (a common form of address to a social inferior).

She's far enough, and what he learns by this
May prove his travel,[5] not her danger.
CLOTEN   Hum!
105 PISANIO [aside] I'll write to my lord she's dead. O Innogen,
Safe mayst thou wander, safe return again!
CLOTEN   Sirrah, is this letter true?
PISANIO   Sir, as I think.
CLOTEN   It is Posthumus' hand; I know't. Sirrah, if thou wouldst
not be a villain but do me true service, undergo° those employ-   *undertake*
110 ments wherein I should have cause to use thee with a serious
industry—that is, what villainy soe'er I bid thee do, to perform
it directly and truly—I would think thee an honest man. Thou
shouldst neither want° my means for thy relief nor my voice for   *find lacking*
thy preferment.°   *advancement*
115 PISANIO   Well, my good lord.
CLOTEN   Wilt thou serve me? For since patiently and constantly
thou hast stuck to the bare fortune of that beggar Posthumus,
thou canst not in the course of gratitude but be a diligent fol-
lower of mine. Wilt thou serve me?
120 PISANIO   Sir, I will.
CLOTEN   Give me thy hand. Here's my purse. Hast any of thy
late° master's garments in thy possession?   *former*
PISANIO   I have, my lord, at my lodging the same suit he wore
when he took leave of my lady and mistress.
125 CLOTEN   The first service thou dost me, fetch that suit hither.
Let it be thy first service. Go.
PISANIO   I shall, my lord.   *Exit*
CLOTEN   Meet thee at Milford Haven! I forgot to ask him one
thing;[6] I'll remember't anon. Even there, thou villain Posthu-
130 mus, will I kill thee. I would these garments were come. She
said upon a time—the bitterness of it I now belch from my
heart—that she held the very garment of Posthumus in more
respect than my noble and natural person, together with the
adornment of my qualities. With that suit upon my back will I
135 ravish her—first kill him, and in her eyes; there shall she see
my valour, which will then be a torment to her contempt. He
on the ground, my speech of insultment° ended on his dead   *contemptuous triumph*
body, and when my lust hath dined—which, as I say, to vex her
I will execute in the clothes that she so praised—to the court
140 I'll knock° her back, foot° her home again. She hath despised   *beat / kick*
me rejoicingly, and I'll be merry in my revenge.
    Enter PISANIO [*with Posthumus' suit*]
Be those the garments?
PISANIO   Ay, my noble lord.
CLOTEN   How long is't since she went to Milford Haven?
PISANIO   She can scarce be there yet.
145 CLOTEN   Bring this apparel to my chamber. That is the second
thing that I have commanded thee. The third is that thou wilt
be a voluntary mute to° my design. Be but duteous, and true   *be quiet about*
preferment shall tender itself to thee. My revenge is now at
Milford. Would I had wings to follow it. Come, and be true.
                                                                    Exit

---

5. May turn out to be merely a long journey for him.
6. The "one thing" may be how long a time has passed
since Innogen set out for Milford Haven (see Cloten's
question at line 143).

150 PISANIO   Thou bidd'st me to my loss,° for true to thee   *perdition*
      Were to prove false, which I will never be
      To him that is most true. To Milford go,
      And find not her whom thou pursuest. Flow, flow,
      You heavenly blessings, on her. This fool's speed
155   Be crossed° with slowness; labour be his meed.°   *Exit*   *thwarted / reward*

3.6
Enter INNOGEN [*dressed as a man, before the cave*]
INNOGEN   I see a man's life is a tedious one.
      I have tired myself, and for two nights together
      Have made the ground my bed. I should be sick,
      But that my resolution helps me. Milford,
5   When from the mountain-top Pisanio showed thee,
      Thou wast within a ken.° O Jove, I think   *within sight*
      Foundations[1] fly the wretched—such, I mean,
      Where they should be relieved.[2] Two beggars told me
      I could not miss my way. Will poor folks lie,
10   That have afflictions on them, knowing 'tis
      A punishment or trial?[3] Yes. No wonder,
      When rich ones scarce tell true. To lapse in fullness°   *To do wrong when rich*
      Is sorer° than to lie for need, and falsehood   *worse*
      Is worse in kings than beggars. My dear lord,
15   Thou art one o'th' false ones. Now I think on thee
      My hunger's gone, but even before° I was   *just a moment ago*
      At point° to sink for° food. But what is this?   *Ready / for want of*
      Here is a path to't. 'Tis some savage hold.°   *refuge*
      I were best not call; I dare not call; yet famine,
20   Ere clean° it o'erthrow nature, makes it valiant.   *completely*
      Plenty and peace breeds cowards, hardness° ever   *hardship*
      Of hardiness is mother. Ho! Who's here?
      If anything that's civil, speak; if savage,
      Take or lend.[4] Ho! No answer? Then I'll enter.
25   Best draw my sword, and if mine enemy
      But fear the sword like me he'll scarcely look on't.
      Such a foe, good heavens![5]   *Exit* [*into the cave*]
            Enter BELARIUS, GUIDERIUS, *and* ARVIRAGUS[6]
BELARIUS   You, Polydore, have proved best woodman° and   *hunter*
      Are master of the feast. Cadwal and I
30   Will play the cook and servant; 'tis our match.°   *bargain*
      The sweat of industry would dry and die
      But for the end it works to. Come, our stomachs
      Will make what's homely° savoury. Weariness   *plain*
      Can snore upon the flint when resty° sloth   *lazy*
35   Finds the down pillow hard. Now peace be here,
      Poor house, that keep'st thyself.°   *goes untended*
GUIDERIUS   I am throughly weary.
ARVIRAGUS   I am weak with toil yet strong in appetite.

3.6 Location: Before the cave of Belarius, Wales.   3. *knowing . . . trial:* knowing that poverty is a punish-
1. Certainties; charitable institutions.   ment or a test of one's virtue.
2. *such . . . relieved:* such certainties, I mean, as should   4. Take everything I have, or help me.
give mental relief to the wretched; such charitable institu-   5. May it please heaven I meet such a timid foe.
tions as should give physical relief (food and rest) to the   6. F marks a new scene at this point, but the action is
wretched.   continuous.

GUIDERIUS There is cold meat i'th' cave. We'll browse° on that   *nibble*
   Whilst what we have killed be cooked.
BELARIUS [*looking into the cave*]   Stay, come not in.
40   But° that it eats our victuals I should think   *But for the fact*
   Here were a fairy.
GUIDERIUS   What's the matter, sir?
BELARIUS By Jupiter, an angel—or, if not,
   An earthly paragon. Behold divineness
   No elder than a boy.
       Enter INNOGEN [*from the cave, dressed as a man*]
INNOGEN   Good masters, harm me not.
45   Before I entered here I called, and thought°   *intended*
   To have begged or bought what I have took. Good truth,
   I have stol'n naught, nor would not, though I had found
   Gold strewed i'th' floor. Here's money for my meat.
   I would have left it on the board so° soon   *as*
50   As I had made my meal, and parted
   With prayers for the provider.
GUIDERIUS   Money, youth?
ARVIRAGUS All gold and silver rather turn to dirt,
   As 'tis no better reckoned but of° those   *better thought of but by*
   Who worship dirty gods.
INNOGEN   I see you're angry.
55   Know, if you kill me for my fault, I should
   Have died had I not made it.
BELARIUS   Whither bound?
INNOGEN To Milford Haven.
BELARIUS   What's your name?
INNOGEN Fidele,[7] sir. I have a kinsman who
   Is bound for Italy. He embarked at Milford,
60   To whom being going, almost spent with hunger,
   I am fall'n in° this offence.   *into*
BELARIUS   Prithee, fair youth,
   Think us no churls,° nor measure our good minds   *base fellows*
   By this rude° place we live in. Well encountered.   *wild*
   'Tis almost night. You shall have better cheer°   *provisions*
65   Ere you depart, and thanks to° stay and eat it.   *our gratitude if you*
   Boys, bid him welcome.
GUIDERIUS   Were you a woman, youth,
   I should woo hard but be° your groom in honesty,   *rather than fail to be*
   Ay, bid for you as I'd buy.[8]
ARVIRAGUS   I'll make't my comfort
   He is a man, I'll love him as my brother.
70   [*To* INNOGEN] And such a welcome as I'd give to him
   After long absence, such is yours. Most welcome.
   Be sprightly,° for you fall 'mongst friends.   *cheerful*
INNOGEN   'Mongst friends
   If brothers.[9] [*Aside*] Would it had been so that they
   Had been my father's sons. Then had my price°   *worth*

---

7. In French and Italian, the name means "faithful one."
8. Yes, make an offer for you with every intent to buy (that is, to marry you).

9. '*Mongst . . . brothers:* Yes, certainly I am among friends if you claim me as a brother.

75 Been less, and so more equal ballasting°   *equal in weight*
To thee, Posthumus.
[*The three men speak apart*]
BELARIUS   He wrings° at some distress.   *twists in pain*
GUIDERIUS Would I could free't.°   *remove it*
ARVIRAGUS   Or I, whate'er it be,
What° pain it cost, what danger. Gods!   *Whatever*
BELARIUS   Hark, boys.
[*They whisper*]
INNOGEN [*aside*] Great men
80 That had a court no bigger than this cave,
That did attend° themselves and had the virtue   *wait on*
Which their own conscience sealed° them, laying by°   *assured / disregarding*
That nothing-gift of differing multitudes,[1]
Could not outpeer° these twain. Pardon me, gods,   *surpass*
85 I'd change my sex to be companion with them,
Since Leonatus' false.
BELARIUS   It shall be so.
Boys, we'll go dress our hunt.° Fair youth, come in.   *game*
Discourse is heavy, fasting.[2] When we have supped
We'll mannerly demand thee of thy story,
So far as thou wilt speak it.
90 GUIDERIUS   Pray draw near.
ARVIRAGUS The night to th' owl and morn to th' lark less welcome.
INNOGEN Thanks, sir.
ARVIRAGUS I pray draw near.   *Exeunt [into the cave]*

3.7
Enter two Roman SENATORS, and TRIBUNES
FIRST SENATOR   This is the tenor of the Emperor's writ:
That since the common men are now in action
'Gainst the Pannonians and Dalmatians,
And that the legions now in Gallia are
5 Full weak° to undertake our wars against   *Too weak*
The fall'n-off° Britons, that we do incite   *rebelling*
The gentry to this business. He creates
Lucius pro-consul,[1] and to you the tribunes,
For this immediate levy, he commends°   *entrusts*
10 His absolute commission.° Long live Caesar!   *authority*
A TRIBUNE Is Lucius general of the forces?
SECOND SENATOR   Ay.
A TRIBUNE Remaining now in Gallia?
FIRST SENATOR   With those legions
Which I have spoke of, whereunto your levy
Must be supplyant.° The words of your commission   *auxiliary*
15 Will tie you to° the numbers and the time   *indicate to you*
Of their dispatch.
A TRIBUNE   We will discharge our duty.   *Exeunt*

---

1. That worthless gift offered by a public that cannot agree on anything.
2. Conversation is difficult when one is without food.

3.7 Location: A public place, Rome.
1. One who acted as governor or military commander in a Roman province.

4.1

Enter CLOTEN [*in Posthumus' suit*]

CLOTEN   I am near to th' place where they should meet, if
   Pisanio have mapped it truly. How fit° his garments serve me!   aptly
   Why should his mistress, who was made by him that made the
   tailor, not be fit° too?—the rather—saving reverence of the   apt; sexually compatible
5   word[1]—for 'tis said a woman's fitness comes by fits.[2] Therein I
   must play the workman. I dare speak it to myself, for it is not
   vainglory for a man and his glass° to confer in his own cham-   mirror
   ber. I mean the lines of my body are as well drawn as his: no
   less young, more strong, not beneath him in fortunes, beyond
10   him in the advantage of the time,[3] above him in birth, alike
   conversant in general services, and more remarkable in single
   oppositions.[4] Yet this imperceiverant° thing loves him in my   stupid
   despite.° What mortality[5] is! Posthumus, thy head which now   to spite me
   is growing upon thy shoulders shall within this hour be off, thy
15   mistress enforced,° thy garments cut to pieces before thy face;   raped
   and all this done, spurn her home to her father, who may haply
   be a little angry for my so rough usage; but my mother, having
   power of° his testiness, shall turn all into my commendations.   over
   My horse is tied up safe. Out, sword, and to a sore purpose!
20   Fortune, put them into my hand. This is the very description
   of their meeting-place, and the fellow dares not deceive me.

Exit

4.2

Enter BELARIUS, GUIDERIUS, ARVIRAGUS, *and* INNOGEN
[*dressed as a man,*] *from the cave*

BELARIUS [*to* INNOGEN]   You are not well. Remain here in the cave.
   We'll come to you from hunting.
ARVIRAGUS [*to* INNOGEN]   Brother, stay here.
   Are we not brothers?
INNOGEN   So man and man should be,
   But clay and clay[1] differs in dignity,°   social position
5   Whose dust[2] is both alike. I am very sick.
GUIDERIUS [*to* BELARIUS *and* ARVIRAGUS]   Go you to hunting.
   I'll abide with him.
INNOGEN   So sick I am not, yet I am not well;
   But not so citizen a wanton as
   To seem to die ere sick.[3] So please you, leave me.
10   Stick to your journal course.° The breach of custom   daily routine
   Is breach of all. I am ill, but your being by me
   Cannot amend me. Society is no comfort
   To one not sociable. I am not very sick,
   Since I can reason of° it. Pray you, trust me here.   talk about
15   I'll rob none but myself; and let me die,
   Stealing so poorly.[4]

4.1 Location: Near the cave of Belarius, Wales.
1. With apologies for my punning.
2. For it is said that a woman's inclination for sexual
intercourse comes intermittently.
3. In the favorable opportunities afforded by the times.
4. *alike . . . oppositions:* similarly acquainted with battle
tactics, and superior in single combat or duels (with puns
on "service" and "oppositions" as referring to sexual
exploits).

5. Life; humankind.
4.2 Location: Before the cave of Belarius.
1. Yet two humans (alluding to the biblical notion that
humans are formed out of clay).
2. The substance to which all humans return at death.
3. *But . . . sick:* But I am not so city-bred a weakling
("wanton") as to think I am dying even before I am sick.
4. Stealing only from one so poor as myself.

GUIDERIUS   I love thee: I have spoke it;
    How much the quantity,° the weight as much,   *As greatly*
    As I do love my father.
BELARIUS   What, how, how?
ARVIRAGUS   If it be sin to say so, sir, I yoke me°   *I share*
20   In my good brother's fault. I know not why
    I love this youth, and I have heard you say
    Love's reason's without reason. The bier⁵ at door
    And a demand who is't shall die, I'd say
    'My father, not this youth'.
BELARIUS [*aside*]   O noble strain!°   *inherited character*
25   O worthiness of nature, breed of greatness!
    Cowards father cowards, and base things sire base.
    Nature hath meal and bran,° contempt and grace.   *flour and husks*
    I'm not their father, yet who this should be
    Doth miracle itself, loved before me.⁶
    [*Aloud*] 'Tis the ninth hour o'th' morn.
30 ARVIRAGUS [*to* INNOGEN]   Brother, farewell.
INNOGEN   I wish ye sport.
ARVIRAGUS   You health. — So please you, sir.
INNOGEN [*aside*]   These are kind creatures. Gods, what lies I have heard!
    Our courtiers say all's savage but at court.
    Experience, O thou disprov'st report!
35   Th'imperious° seas breeds monsters; for the dish   *imperial*
    Poor tributary rivers as sweet fish.⁷
    I am sick still, heart-sick. Pisanio,
    I'll now taste of thy drug.
    [*She swallows the drug. The men speak apart*]
GUIDERIUS   I could not stir him.
    He said he was gentle° but unfortunate,   *a gentleman by birth*
40   Dishonestly afflicted but yet honest.
ARVIRAGUS   Thus did he answer me, yet said hereafter
    I might know more.
BELARIUS   To th' field, to th' field!
    [*To* INNOGEN] We'll leave you for this time. Go in and rest.
ARVIRAGUS [*to* INNOGEN]   We'll not be long away.
BELARIUS [*to* INNOGEN]   Pray be not sick,
    For you must be our housewife.
45 INNOGEN   Well or ill,
    I am bound° to you.   *Exit*   *indebted*
BELARIUS   And shalt be ever.
    This youth, howe'er distressed, appears° hath had   *apparently*
    Good ancestors.
ARVIRAGUS   How angel-like he sings!
50 GUIDERIUS   But his neat° cookery!   *dainty*
BELARIUS⁸   He cut our roots in characters,°   *alphabet shapes*
    And sauced our broths as° Juno had been sick   *as if*
    And he her dieter.°   *cook*
ARVIRAGUS   Nobly he yokes

---

5. The litter, or platform, on which a corpse was carried to the grave.
6. yet . . . me: yet who this may be who is loved more than me is a source of great wonder.
7. for . . . fish: but when it comes to eating, small tributaries breed fish as sweet as does the sea.

8. F assigns this speech to Arviragus, but he has the next one as well. One editorial solution has been to assign the lines to Guiderius as an extension of his prior speech. Another, as here, is to give the lines to Belarius, who thus joins his adopted sons in praising Innogen/Fidele.

A smiling with a sigh, as if the sigh
55 Was that° it was for not being such a smile;   *Was what*
The smile mocking the sigh that° it would fly   *because*
From so divine a temple to commix°   *join*
With winds that sailors rail at.
GUIDERIUS   I do note
That grief and patience, rooted in him both,
Mingle their spurs° together.   *roots*
60 ARVIRAGUS   Grow patience,
And let the stinking elder,[9] grief, untwine
His perishing° root with° the increasing vine.   *deadly / from*
BELARIUS   It is great morning.° Come away. Who's there? *full daylight*

Enter CLOTEN [*in Posthumus' suit*]

CLOTEN   I cannot find those runagates.° That villain   *runaways; fugitives*
Hath mocked me. I am faint.
65 BELARIUS [*aside to* ARVIRAGUS *and* GUIDERIUS]   'Those runagates'?
Means he not us? I partly know him; 'tis
Cloten, the son o'th' Queen. I fear some ambush.
I saw him not these many years, and yet
I know 'tis he. We are held as outlaws. Hence!
GUIDERIUS [*aside to* ARVIRAGUS *and* BELARIUS]   He is but one.
70   You and my brother search
What companies° are near. Pray you, away.   *companions*
Let me alone with him.   [*Exeunt* ARVIRAGUS *and* BELARIUS]
CLOTEN   Soft, what are you
That fly me thus? Some villain mountaineers?°   *lowborn mountain people*
I have heard of such. What slave art thou?
GUIDERIUS   A thing
75 More slavish did I ne'er than answering
A slave without a knock.°   *without striking him*
CLOTEN   Thou art a robber,
A law-breaker, a villain. Yield thee, thief.
GUIDERIUS   To who? To thee? What art thou? Have not I
An arm as big as thine, a heart as big?
80 Thy words, I grant, are bigger, for I wear not
My dagger in my mouth.[1] Say what thou art,
Why I should yield to thee.
CLOTEN   Thou villain base,
Know'st me not by my clothes?
GUIDERIUS   No, nor thy tailor, rascal,
Who is thy grandfather. He made those clothes,
Which, as it seems, make thee.[2]
85 CLOTEN   Thou precious varlet,°   *absolute scoundrel*
My tailor made them not.
GUIDERIUS   Hence, then, and thank
The man that gave them thee. Thou art some fool.
I am loath to beat thee.
CLOTEN   Thou injurious° thief,   *insulting*
Hear but my name and tremble.
GUIDERIUS   What's thy name?

---

9. A tree with strong-smelling leaves and flowers on
which Judas, the disciple who betrayed Jesus, is said to
have hanged himself.

1. *for . . . mouth:* for I don't let words substitute for wea-
pons.
2. Alluding to the proverb "The tailor makes the man."

90   CLOTEN   Cloten, thou villain.
  GUIDERIUS   Cloten, thou double villain, be thy name,
    I cannot tremble at it. Were it toad or adder, spider,
    'Twould move me sooner.
  CLOTEN   To thy further fear,
    Nay, to thy mere confusion,° thou shalt know   *absolute destruction*
    I am son to th' Queen.
95   GUIDERIUS   I am sorry for't, not seeming
    So worthy as thy birth.
  CLOTEN   Art not afeard?
  GUIDERIUS   Those that I reverence, those I fear, the wise.
    At fools I laugh, not fear them.
  CLOTEN   Die the death.
    When I have slain thee with my proper° hand   *own*
100   I'll follow those that even now fled hence,
    And on the gates of Lud's town° set your heads.[3]   *London*
    Yield, rustic mountaineer.   *Fight and exeunt*
      Enter BELARIUS *and* ARVIRAGUS
  BELARIUS   No company's abroad?°   *about*
  ARVIRAGUS   None in the world. You did mistake him, sure.
  BELARIUS   I cannot tell. Long is it since I saw him,
105   But time hath nothing blurred those lines of favour°   *facial features*
    Which then he wore. The snatches° in his voice   *hesitations*
    And burst° of speaking were as his. I am absolute°   *sudden rush / sure*
    'Twas very Cloten.°   *Cloten himself*
  ARVIRAGUS   In this place we left them.
    I wish my brother make good time with him,[4]
    You say he is so fell.°   *fierce*
110   BELARIUS   Being scarce made up,°   *barely full-grown*
    I mean to man, he had not apprehension°   *had no consciousness*
    Of roaring terrors; for defect of judgement
    Is oft the cause of fear.[5]
      Enter GUIDERIUS [*with Cloten's head*]
                    But see, thy brother.
  GUIDERIUS   This Cloten was a fool, an empty purse,
115   There was no money in't. Not Hercules[6]
    Could have knocked out his brains, for he had none.
    Yet I not doing this,° the fool had borne   *had I not done this*
    My head as I do his.
  BELARIUS   What hast thou done?
  GUIDERIUS   I am perfect° what: cut off one Cloten's head,   *certain*
120   Son to the Queen after his own report,
    Who called me traitor, mountaineer, and swore
    With his own single hand he'd take us in,°   *capture us*
    Displace our heads where—thanks, ye gods—they grow,
    And set them on Lud's town.
  BELARIUS   We are all undone.
125   GUIDERIUS   Why, worthy father, what have we to lose
    But that° he swore to take, our lives? The law   *what*

---

3. The heads of criminals were frequently displayed on poles on London Bridge and other places throughout the city.
4. I hope my brother is successful with him.
5. *for . . . fear*: an obscure passage. It may mean that Cloten's faulty judgment, which led him to know no fear, caused fear in others. A less likely meaning is that while defects in judgment cause fear, Cloten knew no fear because he had absolutely no judgment, being utterly witless.
6. Mythical hero of enormous strength.

Protects not us: then why should we be tender
To let[7] an arrogant piece of flesh threat us,
Play judge and executioner all himself,
130 For° we do fear the law? What company   *Because*
Discover you abroad?[8]
BELARIUS   No single soul
Can we set eye on, but in all safe reason
He must have some attendants. Though his humour°   *disposition*
Was nothing but mutation,° ay, and that   *changeableness*
135 From one bad thing to worse, not° frenzy,   *neither*
Not° absolute madness, could so far have raved°   *Nor / made him mad enough*
To bring him here alone. Although perhaps
It may be heard at court that such as we
Cave° here, hunt here, are outlaws, and in time   *Live in a cave*
140 May make some stronger head,° the which he hearing—   *raise a stronger force*
As it is like him—might break out, and swear
He'd fetch us in, yet is't not probable
To come° alone, either he so undertaking,   *That he would come*
Or they so suffering.[9] Then on good ground we fear
145 If we do fear this body hath a tail°   *rear end; followers*
More perilous than the head.
ARVIRAGUS   Let ord'nance°   *destiny*
Come as the gods foresay° it; howsoe'er,   *predict*
My brother hath done well.
BELARIUS   I had no mind
To hunt this day. The boy Fidele's sickness
Did make my way long forth.°   *my journey tedious*
150 GUIDERIUS   With his own sword,
Which he did wave against my throat, I have ta'en
His head from him. I'll throw't into the creek
Behind our rock, and let it to the sea
And tell the fishes he's the Queen's son, Cloten.
That's all I reck.°   *Exit [with Cloten's head]*   *care*
155 BELARIUS   I fear 'twill be revenged.
Would, Polydore, thou hadst not done't, though valour
Becomes thee well enough.
ARVIRAGUS   Would I had done't,
So the revenge alone pursued me.° Polydore,   *only pursued me*
I love thee brotherly, but envy much
160 Thou hast robbed me of this deed. I would revenges
That possible strength might meet would seek us through
And put us to our answer.[1]
BELARIUS   Well, 'tis done.
We'll hunt no more today, nor seek for danger
Where there's no profit. I prithee, to our rock.
165 You and Fidele play the cooks. I'll stay
Till hasty Polydore return, and bring him
To dinner presently.
ARVIRAGUS   Poor sick Fidele!
I'll willingly to him. To gain° his colour   *restore*

---

7. *be tender / To let:* be so meek as to allow.
8. What companions (of Cloten) did you find hereabouts?
9. *either . . . suffering:* either that he would undertake it or

that they would allow it.
1. *I would . . . answer:* I wish that revenges equal to all the power that we might muster would find us out and test our mettle.

I'd let a parish of such Clotens blood,[2]
And praise myself for charity.   *Exit [into the cave]*
170 BELARIUS   O thou goddess,
Thou divine Nature, how thyself thou blazon'st[3]
In these two princely boys! They are as gentle
As zephyrs° blowing below the violet,   *breezes from the west*
Not wagging his sweet head; and yet as rough,°   *violent*
175 Their royal blood enchafed,° as the rud'st wind   *enflamed*
That by the top doth take the mountain pine
And make him stoop to th' vale. 'Tis wonder
That an invisible instinct should frame° them   *shape*
To royalty unlearned, honour untaught,
180 Civility not seen from other,° valour   *not witnessed in others*
That wildly° grows in them, but yields a crop   *without cultivation*
As if it had been sowed. Yet still it's strange
What Cloten's being here to us portends,
Or what his death will bring us.
                    Enter GUIDERIUS
GUIDERIUS   Where's my brother?
185 I have sent Cloten's clotpoll° down the stream   *blockhead*
In embassy to his mother. His body's hostage
For his return.[4]
                    Solemn music
BELARIUS   My ingenious° instrument! —   *artfully crafted*
Hark, Polydore, it sounds. But what occasion
Hath Cadwal now to give it motion? Hark!
GUIDERIUS   Is he at home?
190 BELARIUS   He went hence even now.
GUIDERIUS   What does he mean? Since death of my dear'st mother
It did not speak before. All solemn things
Should answer° solemn accidents. The matter?   *correspond to*
Triumphs for nothing and lamenting toys
195 Is jollity for apes and grief for boys.[5]
Is Cadwal mad?
                    Enter [from the cave] ARVIRAGUS *with* INNOGEN, *dead,*
                    bearing her in his arms
BELARIUS   Look, here he comes,
And brings the dire occasion in his arms
Of what we blame him for.
ARVIRAGUS   The bird is dead
That we have made so much on.° I had rather   *of*
200 Have skipped from sixteen years of age to sixty,
To have turned my leaping time° into a crutch,°   *youth / (old age)*
Than have seen this.
GUIDERIUS [*to* INNOGEN]   O sweetest, fairest lily!
My brother wears thee not one half so well
As when thou grew'st thyself.
BELARIUS   O melancholy,
205 Who ever yet could sound thy bottom,° find   *measure your depths*
The ooze to show what coast thy sluggish crare°   *small ship*
Might easiliest harbour in? Thou blessèd thing,

2. I'd draw blood from a whole parish full of fools like
Cloten.
3. How you proclaim yourself (as in a coat of arms).
4. *His body's . . . return:* I will hold his body hostage until

his head returns (which will be never).
5. *Triumphs . . . boys:* Public celebrations for no reason
and showing great grief for trivial matters are foolish and
unmanly.

Jove knows what man thou mightst have made; but I,°   *I know*
Thou diedst a most rare boy, of melancholy.
[*To* ARVIRAGUS] How found you him?
210 ARVIRAGUS   Stark,° as you see,   *stiff*
Thus smiling as° some fly had tickled slumber,   *as if*
Not as death's dart being laughed at;[6] his right cheek
Reposing on a cushion.
GUIDERIUS   Where?
ARVIRAGUS   O'th' floor,
His arms thus leagued.° I thought he slept, and put   *linked together*
215 My clouted brogues° from off my feet, whose rudeness   *hobnailed boots*
Answered° my steps too loud.   *Rendered*
GUIDERIUS   Why, he but sleeps.
If he be gone he'll make his grave a bed.
With female fairies will his tomb be haunted,
[*To* INNOGEN] And worms will not come to thee.
ARVIRAGUS [*to* INNOGEN]   With fairest flowers
220 Whilst summer lasts and I live here, Fidele,
I'll sweeten thy sad grave. Thou shalt not lack
The flower that's like thy face, pale primrose, nor
The azured harebell,° like thy veins; no, nor   *blue hyacinth*
The leaf of eglantine,° whom not to slander   *honeysuckle*
225 Outsweetened not thy breath. The ruddock would
With charitable bill—O bill sore shaming
Those rich-left heirs that let their fathers lie
Without a monument!—bring thee all this,
Yea, and furred moss besides, when flowers are none,
To winter-gown thy corpse.[7]
230 GUIDERIUS   Prithee, have done,
And do not play in wench-like words[8] with that
Which is so serious. Let us bury him,
And not protract with admiration° what   *wonder*
Is now due debt. To th' grave.
ARVIRAGUS   Say, where shall 's° lay him?   *ought we to*
GUIDERIUS   By good Euriphile, our mother.
235 ARVIRAGUS   Be't so,
And let us, Polydore, though now our voices
Have got the mannish crack, sing him to th' ground
As once our mother; use like note° and words,   *a similar tune*
Save that 'Euriphile' must be 'Fidele'.
240 GUIDERIUS   Cadwal,
I cannot sing. I'll weep, and word° it with thee,   *speak*
For notes of sorrow out of tune are worse
Than priests and fanes° that lie.   *temples*
ARVIRAGUS   We'll speak it then.
BELARIUS   Great griefs, I see, medicine° the less, for Cloten   *cure*
245 Is quite forgot. He was a queen's son, boys,
And though he came our enemy, remember
He was paid° for that. Though mean° and mighty rotting   *punished / lowborn*
Together have one dust, yet reverence,

---

6. Not as if laughing at the approach of death. Death was often depicted carrying a spear ("dart").
7. *The ruddock . . . corpse:* referring to the belief that robins ("ruddocks") covered dead bodies with flowers and moss. *winter-gown:* clothe for winter.

8. Words appropriate to women. In Shakespeare's plays, speeches about flowers are often delivered by female characters, perhaps most notably in *Hamlet* and *The Winter's Tale*.

That angel of the world,[9] doth make distinction
250   Of place 'tween high and low. Our foe was princely,
  And though you took his life as being our foe,
  Yet bury him as a prince.
GUIDERIUS   Pray you, fetch him hither.
  Thersites' body is as good as Ajax'[1]
  When neither are alive.
ARVIRAGUS [to BELARIUS] If you'll go fetch him,
  We'll say our song the whilst.   [Exit BELARIUS]
255   Brother, begin.
GUIDERIUS   Nay, Cadwal, we must lay his head to th'east.[2]
  My father hath a reason for't.
ARVIRAGUS   'Tis true.
GUIDERIUS   Come on, then, and remove him.
ARVIRAGUS   So, begin.[3]
GUIDERIUS   Fear no more the heat o'th' sun,
260   Nor the furious winter's rages.
        Thou thy worldly task hast done,
            Home art gone and ta'en thy wages.
        Golden lads and girls all must,
            As° chimney-sweepers, come to dust.   *Like*
265 ARVIRAGUS   Fear no more the frown o'th' great,
            Thou art past the tyrant's stroke.
        Care no more to clothe and eat,
            To thee the reed is as the oak.[4]
        The sceptre, learning, physic,° must   *medical knowledge*
270   All follow this and come to dust.
GUIDERIUS   Fear no more the lightning flash,
ARVIRAGUS   Nor th'all-dreaded thunder-stone.°   *thunderbolt*
GUIDERIUS   Fear not slander, censure rash.
ARVIRAGUS   Thou hast finished joy and moan.
275 GUIDERIUS *and* ARVIRAGUS   All lovers young, all lovers must
            Consign to thee[5] and come to dust.
GUIDERIUS   No exorcisor° harm thee,   *conjurer of spirits*
ARVIRAGUS   Nor no witchcraft charm thee.
GUIDERIUS   Ghost unlaid forbear thee.[6]
280 ARVIRAGUS   Nothing ill come near thee.
GUIDERIUS *and* ARVIRAGUS   Quiet consummation° have,   *ending*
            And renownèd be thy grave.
    Enter BELARIUS *with the body of Cloten* [*in Posthumus'
    suit*]
GUIDERIUS   We have done our obsequies. Come, lay him down.
BELARIUS   Here's a few flowers, but 'bout midnight more;
285   The herbs that have on them cold dew o'th' night°   *of the night*
  Are strewings fitt'st for graves upon th'earth's face.
  You were as flowers, now withered; even so

9. Reverence (respect for someone because of his or her
social position) may here be called the "angel of the
world" because social hierarchy was thought by some to
imitate heavenly hierarchy.
1. Alluding to two Greeks present at the siege of Troy:
Thersites, a scurrilous coward, and Ajax, a mighty hero.
Both appear in Shakespeare's *Troilus and Cressida*.
2. An allusion to classical or Celtic burial practices. The
English custom was to lay the head to the west.
3. In F, the following duet is introduced as "SONG." Lines

240–43, in which the brothers say they cannot sing and
must speak the words, may have been added because the
particular actors who played Arviragus and Guiderius
were not good singers.
4. Referring to traditional symbols of weakness and
strength, respectively.
5. Submit to the same terms as you.
6. May spirits who have not been laid to rest leave you
alone.

These herblets shall,° which we upon you strow.   *shall wither*
Come on, away; apart upon our knees⁷
290 [   ]
The ground that gave them° first has them again.   *gave them life*
Their pleasures here are past, so is their pain.
                    Exeunt [BELARIUS, ARVIRAGUS, *and* GUIDERIUS]
INNOGEN *awakes*   Yes, sir, to Milford Haven. Which is the way?
I thank you. By yon bush? Pray, how far thither?
295 'Od's pitykins,° can it be six mile yet?   *By God's pity (mild oath)*
I have gone° all night. 'Faith, I'll lie down and sleep.   *walked*
        [*She sees* CLOTEN]
But soft,° no bedfellow! O gods and goddesses!   *wait*
These flowers are like the pleasures of the world,
This bloody man the care on't.⁸ I hope I dream,
300 For so° I thought I was a cavekeeper,   *For then*
And cook to honest creatures. But 'tis not so.
'Twas but a bolt° of nothing, shot of° nothing,   *an arrow / from*
Which the brain makes of fumes.⁹ Our very eyes
Are sometimes like our judgements, blind. Good faith,
305 I tremble still with fear; but if there be
Yet left in heaven as small a drop of pity
As a wren's eye, feared gods, a part of it!
The dream's here still. Even when I wake it is
Without me as within me; not imagined, felt.
310 A headless man? The garments of Posthumus?
I know the shape of 's leg; this is his hand,
His foot Mercurial, his Martial¹ thigh,
The brawns° of Hercules; but his Jovial² face—   *muscles*
Murder in heaven! How? 'Tis gone. Pisanio,
315 All curses madded Hecuba³ gave the Greeks,
And mine to boot, be darted on thee! Thou,
Conspired° with that irregulous° devil Cloten,   *Conspiring / lawless*
Hath here cut off my lord. To write and read
Be henceforth treacherous! Damned Pisanio
320 Hath with his forgèd letters—damned Pisanio—
From this most bravest° vessel of the world   *splendid*
Struck the main-top!° O Posthumus, alas,   *top of the mast; his head*
Where is thy head? Where's that? Ay me, where's that?
Pisanio might have killed thee at the heart
325 And left thy head on. How should this be? Pisanio?
'Tis he and Cloten. Malice and lucre° in them   *greed*
Have laid this woe here. O, 'tis pregnant,° pregnant!   *clear*
The drug he gave me, which he said was precious
And cordial° to me, have I not found it   *restorative*
330 Murd'rous to th' senses? That confirms it home.°   *completely*
This is Pisanio's deed, and Cloten—O,
Give colour to my pale cheek with thy blood,
That we the horrider° may seem to those   *more terrifying*
Which chance to find us!

---

7. Some other place ("apart"), let us pray (be "upon our knees"). Because the previous two lines rhyme, as do the next two lines, it is probable that a line is missing here. The sense of "apart upon our knees" also seems obscure, probably because the thought is truncated.
8. This bloody man is like the sorrow of the world.
9. "Fumes" (vapors) were thought to rise from the stom-
ach and cause dreams and distortions of the imagination.
1. Fashioned for battle, like that of Mars, the god of war. *Mercurial:* Like that of Mercury, the fleet-footed messenger of the gods.
2. Majestic like the face of Jove, king of the gods.
3. The Queen of Troy, Priam's wife, whose desire for revenge against the Greeks made her insane ("madded").

[*She smears her face with blood*]
                              O my lord, my lord!
[*She faints.*]
Enter LUCIUS, [*Roman*] *Captains, and a* SOOTHSAYER

A ROMAN CAPTAIN [*to* LUCIUS]   To them° the legions garrisoned   *In addition to them*
335   in Gallia
         After your will⁴ have crossed the sea, attending°   *waiting for*
         You here at Milford Haven with your ships.
         They are hence in readiness.
LUCIUS   But what from Rome?
A ROMAN CAPTAIN   The senate hath stirred up the confiners°   *inhabitants*
340   And gentlemen of Italy, most willing spirits
         That promise noble service, and they come
         Under the conduct of bold Giacomo,
         Siena's° brother.   *The Duke of Siena's*
LUCIUS   When expect you them?
A ROMAN CAPTAIN   With the next benefit o'th' wind.
LUCIUS   This forwardness°   *readiness*
345   Makes our hopes fair. Command our present numbers
         Be mustered; bid the captains look to't.   [*Exit one or more*]
         [*To* SOOTHSAYER]   Now, sir,
         What have you dreamed of late of this war's purpose?°   *outcome*
SOOTHSAYER   Last night the very gods showed me a vision—
         I fast,° and prayed for their intelligence°—thus: *fasted / information*
350   I saw Jove's bird, the Roman eagle, winged
         From the spongy° south to this part of the west,   *damp*
         There vanished in the sunbeams; which portends,
         Unless my sins abuse° my divination,   *falsify*
         Success to th' Roman host.
LUCIUS   Dream often so,
         And never false.°   *dream falsely*
         [*He sees Cloten's body*]
355   Soft, ho, what trunk is here
         Without his top? The ruin speaks that sometime°   *once*
         It was a worthy building. How, a page?
         Or° dead or sleeping on him? But dead rather,   *Either*
         For nature doth abhor to make his bed
360   With the defunct, or sleep upon the dead.
         Let's see the boy's face.
A ROMAN CAPTAIN   He's alive, my lord.
LUCIUS   He'll then instruct us of this body. Young one,
         Inform us of thy fortunes, for it seems
         They crave to be demanded. Who is this
365   Thou mak'st thy bloody pillow? Or who was he
         That, otherwise than noble nature did,⁵
         Hath altered that good picture? What's thy interest
         In this sad wreck?° How came't? Who is't?   *ruin*
         What art thou?
INNOGEN   I am nothing; or if not,
370   Nothing to be were better.⁶ This was my master,
         A very valiant Briton, and a good,
         That here by mountaineers lies slain. Alas,

---

4. According to your command.   6. It were better to be nothing.
5. Who, in a manner different from nature's workings.

There is no more such masters. I may wander
From east to occident, cry out for service,
375 Try many, all good; serve truly, never
Find such another master.
LUCIUS   'Lack,° good youth,   Alack
Thou mov'st no less with thy complaining than
Thy master in bleeding. Say his name, good friend.
INNOGEN   Richard du Champ.⁷ [Aside] If I do lie and do
380 No harm by it, though the gods hear I hope
They'll pardon it. [Aloud] Say you, sir?
LUCIUS   Thy name?
INNOGEN   Fidele, sir.
LUCIUS   Thou dost approve° thyself the very same.   show
Thy name well fits thy faith,° thy faith thy name.   fidelity
Wilt take thy chance with me? I will not say
385 Thou shalt be so well mastered, but be sure,
No less beloved. The Roman Emperor's letters
Sent by a consul to me should not sooner
Than thine own worth prefer° thee. Go with me.   recommend
INNOGEN   I'll follow, sir. But first, an't° please the gods,   if it
390 I'll hide my master from the flies as deep
As these poor pickaxes° can dig; and when   (her hands)
With wild-wood leaves and weeds I ha' strewed his grave
And on it said a century of° prayers,   a hundred
Such as I can, twice o'er I'll weep and sigh,
395 And leaving so his service, follow you,
So please you entertain° me.   employ
LUCIUS   Ay, good youth,
And rather father thee than master thee. My friends,
The boy hath taught us manly duties. Let us
Find out the prettiest daisied plot we can,
400 And make him with our pikes and partisans⁸
A grave. Come, arm° him. Boy, he is preferred°   lift / recommended
By thee to us, and he shall be interred
As soldiers can. Be cheerful. Wipe thine eyes.
Some falls are means the happier to arise.⁹
                          Exeunt [with Cloten's body]

4.3

Enter CYMBELINE, LORDS, and PISANIO
CYMBELINE   Again, and bring me word how 'tis with her.
                                        Exit one or more
A fever with° the absence of her son,   on account of
A madness of which her life's in danger—heavens,
How deeply you at once do touch° me! Innogen,   afflict
5 The great part of my comfort, gone; my queen
Upon a desperate bed,° and in a time   Extremely ill in bed
When fearful wars point at me; her son gone,
So needful for this present!° It strikes me past   So needed now
The hope of comfort. [To PISANIO] But for thee, fellow,

7. This French name translates as "Richard of the Field,"
perhaps an allusion to a well-known London printer
named Richard Field, who was born in Stratford-upon-
Avon and printed Shakespeare's Rape of Lucrece and
Venus and Adonis in the 1590s.

8. With our spears and our halberds (long-handled weap-
ons with axe-like blades).
9. Some falls are means by which good fortune arises.
4.3 Location: Cymbeline's court, Britain.

10 Who needs must know of her departure and
Dost seem so ignorant, we'll enforce it from thee
By a sharp torture.
PISANIO   Sir, my life is yours.
I humbly set it at your will. But for my mistress,
I nothing know° where she remains, why gone,   *know nothing about*
15 Nor when she purposes° return. Beseech° your highness,   *intends to / I beseech*
Hold me° your loyal servant.   *Regard me as*
A LORD   Good my liege,
The day that she was missing he was here.
I dare be bound he's true, and shall perform
All parts of his subjection° loyally. For Cloten,   *duty as a subject*
20 There wants° no diligence in seeking him,   *is lacking*
And will° no doubt be found.   *he will*
CYMBELINE   The time is troublesome.°   *dire*
[*To* PISANIO] We'll slip you° for a season, but our jealousy   *let you go*
Does yet depend.[1]
A LORD   So please your majesty,
The Roman legions, all from Gallia drawn,
25 Are landed on your coast with a supply
Of Roman gentlemen by the senate sent.
CYMBELINE   Now for° the counsel of my son and queen!   *If only I now had*
I am amazed° with matter.°   *overwhelmed / business*
A LORD   Good my liege,
Your preparation can affront no less
30 Than what you hear of.[2] Come more, for more you're ready.
The want° is but to put those powers in motion   *The only thing needed*
That long to move.
CYMBELINE   I thank you. Let's withdraw,
And meet the time as it seeks us. We fear not
What can from Italy annoy° us, but   *harm*
35 We grieve at chances° here. Away.   *events*
                    Exeunt [CYMBELINE *and* LORDS]
PISANIO   I heard no letter from my master since
I wrote him Innogen was slain. 'Tis strange.
Nor hear I from my mistress, who did promise
To yield me often tidings. Neither know I
40 What is betid° to Cloten, but remain   *has happened*
Perplexed in all. The heavens still must work.
Wherein I am false I am honest; not true, to be true.
These present wars shall find I love my country
Even to the note° o'th' King, or I'll fall in them.   *notice*
45 All other doubts, by time let them be cleared:
Fortune brings in some boats that are not steered.   *Exit*

4.4

Enter BELARIUS, GUIDERIUS, *and* ARVIRAGUS
GUIDERIUS   The noise is round about us.
BELARIUS   Let us from it.
ARVIRAGUS   What pleasure, sir, find we in life to lock it°   *shut it off*
From action and adventure?
GUIDERIUS   Nay, what hope

---

1. *but . . . depend*: but our suspicions still hold.
2. *Your . . . of*: Your forces can confront all those you have
heard of.
4.4 Location: Before the cave of Belarius, Wales.

Have we in hiding us? This way° the Romans   *By this course of action*
5   Must or° for Britains slay us, or receive us   *either*
  For barbarous and unnatural revolts°   *rebels*
  During their use,[1] and slay us after.
BELARIUS   Sons,
  We'll higher to the mountains; there secure us.
  To the King's party there's no going. Newness
10   Of Cloten's death—we being not known, not mustered
  Among the bands°—may drive us to a render°   *troops / an account*
  Where we have lived, and so extort from 's that
  Which we have done, whose answer would be death
  Drawn on° with torture.   *Prolonged*
GUIDERIUS   This is, sir, a doubt
15   In such a time nothing becoming you
  Nor satisfying us.
ARVIRAGUS   It is not likely
  That when they hear the Roman horses neigh,
  Behold their quartered files,° have both their eyes   *orderly troops*
  And ears so cloyed importantly[2] as now,
20   That they will waste their time upon our note,°   *in observing us*
  To know from whence we are.
BELARIUS   O, I am known
  Of° many in the army. Many years,   *By*
  Though Cloten then° but young, you see, not wore° him   *was then / did not wear*
  From my remembrance. And besides, the King
25   Hath not deserved my service nor your loves,
  Who find in my exile the want of breeding,
  The certainty of this hard life;[3] aye hopeless
  To have the courtesy your cradle promised,[4]
  But to be still° hot summer's tanlings,[5] and   *always*
  The shrinking slaves of winter.
30 GUIDERIUS   Than be so,
  Better to cease to be. Pray, sir, to th'army.
  I and my brother are not known; yourself
  So out of thought, and thereto° so o'ergrown,[6]   *in addition*
  Cannot be questioned.
ARVIRAGUS   By this sun that shines,
35   I'll thither. What thing is't[7] that I never
  Did see man die, scarce ever looked on blood
  But that of coward hares, hot° goats, and venison,   *lecherous*
  Never bestrid a horse save one that had
  A rider like myself, who ne'er wore rowel[8]
40   Nor iron on his heel! I am ashamed
  To look upon the holy sun, to have
  The benefit of his blest beams, remaining
  So long a poor unknown.
GUIDERIUS   By heavens, I'll go.
  If you will bless me, sir, and give me leave,
45   I'll take the better care;° but if you will not,   *be the more careful*

---

1. While they have need of us.
2. So completely taken up with important matters.
3. Who . . . life: (You) who experience as a result of my exile a lack of proper education, the enduring fact of this hard life.
4. aye . . . promised: yes, without hope to have the cultivated existence your noble birth promised.

5. People exposed to the sun. In England at this time, tanned skin denoted low social status.
6. So overgrown with hair or beard; so grown in years; so grown out of memory.
7. What a bad state of affairs it is.
8. Small rotating disk at the end of a spur. Wearing spurs was the privilege of gentlemen.

The hazard therefore due[9] fall on me by
The hands of Romans.

ARVIRAGUS   So say I, amen.

BELARIUS   No reason I, since of your lives you set
So slight a valuation, should reserve

50   My cracked° one to more care. Have with you,° boys!   weakened / Come then
If in your country° wars you chance to die,   country's
That is my bed, too, lads, and there I'll lie.
Lead, lead. [*Aside*] The time seems long. Their blood thinks scorn°   disdains itself
Till it fly out and show them princes born.   *Exeunt*

5.1

Enter POSTHUMUS [*dressed as an Italian
gentleman, carrying a bloody cloth*]

POSTHUMUS   Yea, bloody cloth, I'll keep thee, for I once wished
Thou shouldst be coloured thus. You married ones,
If each of you should take this course, how many
Must murder wives much better than themselves

5   For wrying° but a little! O Pisanio,   erring
Every good servant does not all commands,
No bond but° to do just ones. Gods, if you   No obligation except
Should have ta'en vengeance on my faults, I never
Had lived to put on this;° so had you saved   to undertake this deed

10   The noble Innogen to repent, and struck
Me, wretch, more worth your vengeance. But alack,
You snatch some hence for little faults; that's love,
To have them fall no more.[1] You some permit
To second° ills with ills, each elder° worse,   reinforce / later fault

15   And make them dread ill, to the doer's thrift.[2]
But Innogen is your own. Do your blest wills,
And make me blest to obey. I am brought hither
Among th'Italian gentry, and to fight
Against my lady's kingdom. 'Tis enough

20   That, Britain, I have killed thy mistress-piece;[3]
I'll give no wound to thee. Therefore, good heavens,
Hear patiently my purpose. I'll disrobe me
Of these Italian weeds, and suit° myself   dress
As does a Briton peasant.
[*He disrobes himself*]
So I'll fight

25   Against the part° I come with; so I'll die   side
For thee, O Innogen, even for whom my life
Is every breath a death; and, thus unknown,
Pitied° nor hated, to the face of peril   Neither pitied
Myself I'll dedicate. Let me make men know

30   More valour in me than my habits° show.   garments
Gods, put the strength o'th' Leonati in me.
To shame the guise° o'th' world, I will begin   customs; dress
The fashion—less without and more within.   *Exit*

---

9. May the danger due to me (as a result of my disobedience).
5.1 Location: The Roman camp, Britain.
1. *that's . . . more:* that is a sign of love, to have them no longer sin.
2. And make them fear punishment, to their own benefit.
3. Punning on "masterpiece." Most editions, following F,

read: " 'Tis enough / That, Britain, I have killed thy mistress; peace." "Mistress-piece," which can be found in other texts from the period, suggests the extraordinary excellence of Innogen. "Piece" could be spelled "peace" in the early modern period, and the unfamiliar compound might have been misread by the person setting type for the play.

5.2

[*A march.*] *Enter* LUCIUS, GIACOMO, *and the Roman
army at one door, and the Briton army at another, Leo-
natus* POSTHUMUS *following like a poor soldier. They
march over and go out.* [*Alarums.*] *Then enter again in
skirmish* GIACOMO *and* POSTHUMUS: *he vanquisheth and
disarmeth* GIACOMO, *and then leaves him*

GIACOMO   The heaviness and guilt within my bosom
  Takes off° my manhood. I have belied° a lady,   *Destroys / slandered*
  The princess of this country, and the air on't°   *of it*
  Revengingly enfeebles me; or° could this carl,°   *otherwise / peasant*
5   A very drudge° of nature's, have subdued me   *slave*
  In my profession? Knighthoods and honours borne
  As I wear mine are titles but° of scorn.   *merely*
  If that thy gentry, Britain, go before°   *surpass*
  This lout as he exceeds our lords, the odds
10   Is that we scarce are men and you are gods.   *Exit*

5.3[1]

The battle continues. [*Alarums. Excursions. The trum-
pets sound a retreat.*] *The Britons fly,* CYMBELINE *is
taken. Then enter to his rescue* BELARIUS, GUIDERIUS,
and ARVIRAGUS

BELARIUS   Stand, stand, we have th'advantage of the ground.
  The lane is guarded. Nothing routs us but
  The villainy of our fears.
GUIDERIUS *and* ARVIRAGUS   Stand, stand, and fight.
          Enter POSTHUMUS [*like a poor soldier*], *and seconds the
          Britons. They rescue* CYMBELINE *and exeunt*

5.4

[*The trumpets sound a retreat,*] *then enter* LUCIUS, GIA-
COMO, *and* INNOGEN

LUCIUS [*to* INNOGEN]   Away, boy, from the troops, and save thyself;
  For friends kill friends, and the disorder's such
  As war were hoodwinked.[1]
GIACOMO   'Tis their fresh supplies.
LUCIUS   It is a day turned strangely. Or betimes
5   Let's reinforce, or fly.[2]   *Exeunt*

5.5

Enter POSTHUMUS [*like a poor soldier*], *and a Briton
     LORD*

LORD   Cam'st thou from where they made the stand?
POSTHUMUS   I did,
  Though you, it seems, come from the fliers.
LORD   Ay.
POSTHUMUS   No blame be to you, sir, for all was lost,
  But° that the heavens fought. The King himself   *Had it not been*

5.2 Location: A field between the British and Roman camps, Britain.
5.3 Location: Scene continues.
1. In F and most modern editions, there is no new scene marked here or at 5.4, since 5.2, 5.3, and 5.4 form one continuous battle sequence. However, the stage is temporarily cleared where the Oxford editors have marked 5.3

and 5.4, and a cleared stage is the usual signal of a new scene on the Renaissance stage.
5.4 Location: Scene continues.
1. As if war were blindfolded.
2. *Or betimes . . . fly:* Let us either promptly reinforce our troops or flee.
5.5 Location: Scene continues.

5 Of his wings destitute,[1] the army broken,	
And but° the backs of Britons seen, all flying	*only*
Through a strait° lane; the enemy full-hearted,°	*narrow / bold*
Lolling the tongue with slaught'ring,[2] having work	
More plentiful than tools to do't, struck down	
10 Some mortally, some slightly touched,° some falling	*wounded*
Merely through fear, that the strait pass was dammed°	*clogged*
With dead men hurt behind,[3] and cowards living	
To die with lengthened shame.[4]	

LORD   Where was this lane?

POSTHUMUS Close by the battle, ditched, and walled with turf;	
15 Which gave advantage to an ancient soldier,	
An honest one, I warrant, who deserved	
So long a breeding as his white beard came to,[5]	
In doing this for 's country. Athwart° the lane	*Across*
He with two striplings—lads more like° to run	*likely*
20 The country base[6] than to commit such slaughter;	
With faces fit for masks,[7] or rather fairer	
Than those for preservation cased, or shame[8]—	
Made good° the passage, cried to those that fled	*Secured*
'Our Britain's harts die flying, not her men.	
25 To darkness fleet° souls that fly backwards. Stand,	*rush*
Or we are Romans,[9] and will give you that°	*(death)*
Like beasts which you shun beastly,° and may save	*in cowardly fashion*
But to look back in frown.[1] Stand, stand.' These three,	
Three thousand confident,[2] in act as many—	
30 For three performers are the file° when all	*entire force*
The rest do nothing—with this word 'Stand, stand',	
Accommodated° by the place, more charming[3]	*Assisted*
With their own nobleness, which could have turned	
A distaff to a lance,[4] gilded° pale looks;	*brought color to*
35 Part shame, part spirit renewed,[5] that some, turned coward	
But by example[6]—O, a sin in war,	
Damned in the first beginners![7]—gan° to look	*began*
The way that they° did and to grin[8] like lions	*(the three)*
Upon the pikes o'th' hunters. Then began	
40 A stop° i'th' chaser, a retire. Anon°	*halt / Soon*
A rout, confusion thick; forthwith they fly	
Chickens the way which they stooped eagles;[9] slaves,	
The strides they victors made;[1] and now our cowards,	
Like fragments° in hard voyages, became	*scraps of food*

---

1. Deprived of his wings (that is, the troops to either side of the main division of the army).
2. With their tongues hanging out either from the labor of slaughter or from eagerness to commit the slaughter.
3. Hurt on their backs (as they were fleeing).
4. To die later after a life of prolonged shame.
5. *who . . . to:* who deserved to live so long again as his white beard indicated he had already lived.
6. *to run . . . base:* to play a children's game (prisoner's house) that involves running between two bases.
7. Gentlewomen wore masks to protect their complexions from the elements.
8. *fairer . . . shame:* more delicate than those covered with masks for protection ("preservation") or out of modesty.
9. Or we will behave like Romans.
1. *and may . . . frown:* and may prevent only by turning back upon the enemy with threatening face.
2. As confident as if they were three thousand.
3. *more charming:* casting a spell on others.
4. *could . . . lance:* that is, could have made women fight. The distaff, an instrument used in spinning wool, was a proverbial symbol of womanhood.
5. Shame inspired some, courage others.
6. Because of the example set by others.
7. In those who first set the example (of cowardly behavior).
8. To bare their teeth.
9. *forthwith . . . eagles:* straightway they (the Romans) fled like chickens along the passage down which they had just swooped like eagles.
1. *slaves . . . made:* like slaves, they retrace the steps they had made as victors.

45 The life o'th' need.[2] Having found the back door open
Of the unguarded hearts,[3] heavens, how they wound!
Some slain before,[4] some dying, some their friends
O'erborne° i'th' former wave, ten chased by one,   *Overwhelmed*
Are now each one the slaughterman of twenty.
50 Those that would die or ere° resist are grown   *before they would*
The mortal bugs° o'th' field.   *deadly terrors*
LORD   This was strange chance:
A narrow lane, an old man, and two boys.
POSTHUMUS   Nay, do not wonder at it. Yet you are made
Rather to wonder at the things you hear
55 Than to work° any. Will you rhyme upon't,   *perform*
And vent it[5] for a mock'ry? Here is one:
'Two boys, an old man twice a boy,° a lane,   *in his second childhood*
Preserved the Britons, was the Romans' bane.'
LORD   Nay, be not angry, sir.
POSTHUMUS   'Lack,° to what end?   *Alas*
60 Who dares not stand° his foe, I'll be his friend,   *confront*
For if he'll do as he is made° to do,   *inclined*
I know he'll quickly fly my friendship too.
You have put° me into rhyme.   *forced*
LORD   Farewell; you're angry.   *Exit*
POSTHUMUS   Still going?° This a lord? O noble misery,[6]   *Still running away*
65 To be i'th' field and ask 'What news?' of me!
Today how many would have given their honours
To have saved their carcasses—took heel to do't,
And yet died too!° I, in mine own woe charmed,[7]   *anyway*
Could not find death where I did hear him groan,
70 Nor feel him where he struck. Being an ugly monster,
'Tis strange he hides him in fresh cups, soft beds,
Sweet words, or hath more ministers° than we   *other agents*
That draw his knives i'th' war. Well, I will find him;
For being now a favourer to the Briton,[8]
75 No more° a Briton, I have resumed again   *I am no more*
The part° I came in. Fight I will no more,   *role*
But yield me to the veriest hind° that shall   *peasant*
Once touch my shoulder.° Great the slaughter is   *try to arrest me*
Here made by th' Roman; great the answer be°   *great the retaliation*
80 Britons must take. For me, my ransom's death,
On either side I come to spend my breath,°   *give up my life*
Which neither here I'll keep nor bear° again,   *carry away*
But end it by some means for Innogen.
        Enter two [Briton] CAPTAINS, *and soldiers*
FIRST CAPTAIN   Great Jupiter be praised, Lucius is taken.
85 'Tis thought the old man and his sons were angels.
SECOND CAPTAIN   There was a fourth man, in a seely habit,°   *rustic garments*
That gave th'affront with them.
FIRST CAPTAIN   So 'tis reported,
But none of 'em can be found. Stand, who's there?
POSTHUMUS   A Roman,

2. Vital in the time of crisis.
3. *Having . . . hearts:* Having found unprotected the weak
spot of these undefended souls (that is, the Romans).
4. Some that earlier were as good as dead.

5. And circulate ("vent") your rhymes.
6. What noble wretchedness.
7. In my despair preserved, as if by a charm.
8. Since death is now looking kindly upon Britons.

90	Who had not now been drooping here if seconds°	*supporters*
	Had answered him.°	*followed him*
	SECOND CAPTAIN [*to soldiers*] Lay hands on him, a dog!	
	A leg of Rome shall not return to tell	
	What crows have pecked them here. He brags his service	
	As if he were of note.° Bring him to th' King.	*high rank*

[*Flourish.*] *Enter* CYMBELINE [*and his train*], BELARIUS,
GUIDERIUS, ARVIRAGUS, PISANIO, *and Roman captives.*
The CAPTAINS *present* POSTHUMUS *to* CYMBELINE, *who
delivers him over to a* JAILER. [*Exeunt all but* POSTHU-
MUS *and two* JAILERS *who lock gyves*° *on his legs*][9]   *fetters*

95	FIRST JAILER You shall not now be stol'n. You have locks upon you,	
	So graze as you find pasture.	
	SECOND JAILER Ay, or a stomach. [*Exeunt* JAILERS]	
	POSTHUMUS Most welcome, bondage, for thou art a way,	
	I think, to liberty. Yet am I better	
	Than one that's sick o'th' gout, since he had rather	
100	Groan so in perpetuity than be cured	
	By th' sure physician, death, who is the key	
	T'unbar these locks. My conscience, thou art fettered	
	More than my shanks° and wrists. You good gods give me	*legs*
	The penitent instrument to pick that bolt,	
105	Then free for ever.[1] Is't enough I am sorry?	
	So children temporal fathers do appease;	
	Gods are more full of mercy. Must I repent,	
	I cannot do it better than in gyves	
	Desired more than constrained.° To satisfy,°	*forced (upon me) / atone*
110	If of my freedom 'tis the main part,[2] take	
	No stricter render° of me than my all.	*repayment*
	I know you are more clement° than vile men	*merciful*
	Who of their broken° debtors take a third,	*bankrupt*
	A sixth, a tenth, letting them thrive again	
115	On their abatement.° That's not my desire.	*reduced amount*
	For Innogen's dear life take mine, and though	
	'Tis not so dear,° yet 'tis a life; you coined it.	*valuable*
	'Tween man and man they weigh not every stamp;	
	Though light, take pieces for the figure's sake;[3]	
120	You rather mine, being yours.[4] And so, great powers,	
	If you will make this audit,° take this life,	*settle this account*
	And cancel these cold bonds.[5] O Innogen,	
	I'll speak to thee in silence!	

---

9. F and most modern editions mark a new scene here.
Confusion arises because in F, no exit is marked for any
character after Posthumus is handed over to a Jailer.
Either everyone exits and Posthumus then reenters with
two Jailers, indicating a new scene, or, as here, Posthu-
mus and Jailers stay onstage continuously. The latter
option means that Posthumus is fettered in the open
fields, giving new point to the First Jailer's injunction to
"graze as you find pasture" (5.5.96). Usually, Posthumus
is assumed to be fettered inside a British prison.
1. *The . . . ever:* Give me penitence, the instrument to
pick that lock (the lock on his conscience, which is fet-
tered by guilt). Then (I am) free forever; then free me (by

death).
2. If it is the most important element in freeing me from
guilt.
3. *'Tween . . . sake:* In business dealings between men,
they do not weigh every coin ("stamp"). Though some
coins are deficient in weight ("light"), they accept them
because of the image (of the King) stamped on them.
4. You should be more inclined to accept my coin (me),
since your image is stamped on me. This line refers to the
Christian belief that humans are made in the image of
God.
5. These old legal agreements; these cruel links with life;
these harsh fetters.

[*He sleeps.*] *Solemn music. Enter, as in an apparition,*
SICILIUS *Leonatus (father to Posthumus, an old man),*
attired like a warrior, leading in his hand an ancient
matron, his wife, and MOTHER *to Posthumus, with music*
before them. Then, after other music, follows the two
young Leonati, BROTHERS *to Posthumus, with wounds as*
they died in the wars. They circle POSTHUMUS *round as*
he lies sleeping

SICILIUS   No more, thou thunder-master,[6] show

125   Thy spite on mortal flies.°   *frail creatures*
With Mars° fall out, with Juno° chide,   *god of war / Jove's wife*
That° thy adulteries   *Who*
Rates° and revenges.   *Berates*
Hath my poor boy done aught but well,

130   Whose face I never saw?
I died whilst in the womb he stayed,
Attending nature's law,[7]
Whose father then—as men report
Thou orphans' father art—

135   Thou shouldst have been, and shielded him
From this earth-vexing smart.[8]

MOTHER   Lucina° lent not me her aid,   *goddess of childbirth*
But took me in my throes,
That from me was Posthumus ripped,

140   Came crying 'mongst his foes,
A thing of pity.

SICILIUS   Great nature like his ancestry
Moulded the stuff° so fair   *substance*
That he deserved the praise o'th' world

145   As great Sicilius' heir.

FIRST BROTHER   When once he was mature for man,°   *had matured into manhood*
In Britain where was he
That could stand up his parallel,
Or fruitful° object be   *life-giving*

150   In eye of Innogen, that best
Could deem° his dignity?°   *judge / worth*

MOTHER   With marriage wherefore° was he mocked,   *why*
To be exiled, and thrown
From Leonati seat and cast

155   From her his dearest one,
Sweet Innogen?

SICILIUS   Why did you suffer Giacomo,
Slight° thing of Italy,   *Worthless*
To taint his nobler heart and brain

160   With needless jealousy,
And to become the geck° and scorn   *dupe*
O'th' other's villainy?

SECOND BROTHER   For this from stiller seats[9] we come,
Our parents and us twain,

165   That striking in our country's cause
Fell bravely and were slain,

---

6. Jupiter, or Jove, the king of the gods, often made him-
self known to humans through thunder and lightning.
7. Awaiting the decree of nature (for his birth).

8. From this suffering that afflicts all humans.
9. From calmer regions (alluding to the Elysian fields, in
classical myth the abode of the blessed after death).

Our fealty and Tenantius'° right   *(Cymbeline's father)*
 With honour to maintain.
FIRST BROTHER   Like hardiment° Posthumus hath   *Similar bold deeds*
170   To Cymbeline performed.
Then, Jupiter, thou king of gods,
 Why hast thou thus adjourned°   *deferred*
The graces for his merits due,
 Being all to dolours° turned?   *sorrows*
175 SICILIUS   Thy crystal window ope;° look out;   *open*
 No longer exercise
Upon a valiant race thy harsh
 And potent injuries.
MOTHER   Since, Jupiter, our son is good,
180   Take off his miseries.
SICILIUS   Peep through thy marble mansion. Help,
 Or we poor ghosts will cry
To th' shining synod° of the rest°   *assembly / rest of the gods*
 Against thy deity.°   *godhead*
185 BROTHERS   Help, Jupiter, or we appeal,
 And from thy justice fly.
    JUPITER *descends in thunder and lightning, sitting upon*
    an eagle. He throws a thunderbolt. The ghosts fall on
    their knees
JUPITER   No more, you petty spirits of region low,
Offend our hearing. Hush! How dare you ghosts
Accuse the thunderer, whose bolt, you know,
190   Sky-planted,° batters all rebelling coasts?   *Rooted in the heavens*
Poor shadows of Elysium, hence, and rest
 Upon your never-withering banks of flowers.
Be not with mortal accidents° oppressed;   *events*
 No care of yours it is; you know 'tis ours.
195 Whom best I love, I cross,° to make my gift,   *thwart*
 The more delayed, delighted.° Be content.   *the more pleasing*
Your low-laid son our godhead will uplift.
 His comforts thrive, his trials well are spent.°   *ended*
Our Jovial star° reigned at his birth, and in   *The planet Jupiter*
200   Our temple was he married. Rise, and fade.
He shall be lord of Lady Innogen,
 And happier much by his affliction made.
This tablet lay upon his breast, wherein
 Our pleasure his full fortune doth confine.[1]
    [*He gives the ghosts a tablet which they lay upon Posthu-*
    mus' breast]
205 And so away. No farther with your din
Express impatience, lest you stir up mine.
Mount, eagle, to my palace crystalline.   [*He*] *ascends* [*into the heavens*]
SICILIUS   He came in thunder. His celestial breath
 Was sulphurous to smell.[2] The holy eagle
210 Stooped, as to foot us.[3] His ascension is
More sweet than our blest fields. His royal bird

---

1. *wherein . . . confine:* wherein it is our pleasure his great fortune precisely to set forth.
2. Sulfur was popularly associated with thunder and lightning. As a constituent of gunpowder, its smell may have been detectable in the theater when gunpowder was used.
3. Swooped as if to seize us in its talons.

Preens the immortal wing and claws his beak
As when his god is pleased.

ALL THE GHOSTS   Thanks, Jupiter.

SICILIUS   The marble pavement⁴ closes, he is entered

215 His radiant roof. Away, and, to be blest,
Let us with care perform his great behest.   [*The ghosts*] *vanish*
                    [POSTHUMUS *awakes*]

POSTHUMUS   Sleep, thou hast been a grandsire, and begot
A father to me; and thou hast created
A mother and two brothers. But, O scorn,°   *bitter mockery*

220 Gone! They went hence so soon as they were born,
And so I am awake. Poor wretches that depend
On greatness' favour dream as I have done,
Wake and find nothing. But, alas, I swerve.°   *go astray*
Many dream not to find, neither deserve,

225 And yet are steeped in favours; so am I,
That have this golden chance and know not why.
What fairies haunt this ground? A book? O rare one,
Be not, as is our fangled world,⁵ a garment
Nobler than that it covers. Let thy effects

230 So follow to° be most unlike our courtiers,   *that they*
As good as promise.
                    [*He*] *reads*

'Whenas° a lion's whelp shall, to himself unknown, without   *When*
seeking find, and be embraced by a piece of tender air; and
when from a stately cedar shall be lopped branches which,

235 being dead many years, shall after revive, be jointed to the old
stock, and freshly grow; then shall Posthumus end his miseries,
Britain be fortunate and flourish in peace and plenty.'
'Tis still a dream, or else such stuff as madmen
Tongue,° and brain° not; either both, or nothing,   *Speak / understand*

240 Or senseless speaking,° or a speaking such   *Either meaningless speech*
As sense° cannot untie. Be what it is,   *reason*
The action of my life is like it, which I'll keep,
If but for sympathy.⁶
                    Enter JAILER

JAILER   Come, sir, are you ready for death?

245 POSTHUMUS   Over-roasted rather; ready long ago.

JAILER   Hanging⁷ is the word, sir. If you be ready for that, you
are well cooked.

POSTHUMUS   So, if I prove a good repast to the spectators, the
dish pays the shot.⁸

250 JAILER   A heavy reckoning for you, sir. But the comfort is, you
shall be called to no more payments, fear no more tavern bills,
which are as often the sadness of parting as the procuring of
mirth. You come in faint for want of meat, depart reeling with
too much drink, sorry that you have paid too much and sorry

255 that you are paid too much;⁹ purse and brain both empty: the
brain the heavier for being too light,° the purse too light, being   *foolish*

---

4. Referring to the closing of the trapdoor in the ceiling
above the stage, which represents the floor ("pavement")
of the heavens.
5. Our world so obsessed with fashions.
6. If only because of the similarity.
7. Death by hanging, with a pun on "hanging" as refer-

ring to the practice of hanging up raw meat before cook-
ing.
8. The food pays the reckoning; I am worth what it costs
to hang me.
9. Subdued by too much drink.

drawn of heaviness.[1] Of this contradiction you shall now be
quit. O, the charity of a penny cord! It sums up thousands in a
trice.° You have no true debitor and creditor[2] but it: of what's
past, is, and to come the discharge.° Your neck, sir, is pen,
book, and counters;[3] so the acquittance° follows.

an instant
release from debt
deliverance

POSTHUMUS   I am merrier to die than thou art to live.

JAILER   Indeed, sir, he that sleeps feels not the toothache; but a
man that were to° sleep your sleep, and a hangman to help him
to bed, I think he would change places with his officer;° for
look you, sir, you know not which way you shall go.

were about to
(the hangman)

POSTHUMUS   Yes, indeed do I, fellow.

JAILER   Your death has eyes in 's head, then. I have not seen him
so pictured.[4] You must either be directed by some that take
upon them° to know, or take upon yourself that which I am
sure you do not know, or jump° the after-enquiry on your own
peril; and how you shall speed° in your journey's end I think
you'll never return to tell on.°

some who profess
risk
succeed
of

POSTHUMUS   I tell thee, fellow, there are none want° eyes to
direct them the way I am going but such as wink° and will not
use them.

lacking
shut their eyes

JAILER   What an infinite mock is this, that a man should have
the best use of eyes to see the way of blindness!° I am sure
hanging's the way of winking.

the way to death

Enter a MESSENGER

MESSENGER   Knock off his manacles, bring your prisoner to the
King.

POSTHUMUS   Thou bring'st good news, I am called to be made
free.[5]

JAILER   I'll be hanged then.

POSTHUMUS   Thou shalt be then freer than a jailer; no bolts for
the dead.[6]

JAILER [*aside*]   Unless a man would marry a gallows and beget
young gibbets, I never saw one so prone.° Yet, on my con-
science, there are verier knaves desire to live, for all° he be a
Roman; and there be some of them, too, that die against their
wills; so should I if I were one. I would we were all of one
mind, and one mind good. O, there were desolation° of jailers
and gallowses! I speak against my present profit, but my wish
hath a preferment[7] in't.   *Exeunt*

eager
even though

the ruin

5.6

[*Flourish.*] *Enter* CYMBELINE, BELARIUS, GUIDERIUS,
ARVIRAGUS, PISANIO, *and lords*

CYMBELINE [*to* BELARIUS, GUIDERIUS, *and* ARVIRAGUS]   Stand by
    my side, you whom the gods have made
Preservers of my throne. Woe is my heart

1. Being emptied of the money that makes it heavy.
2. Account book.
3. Metal tokens used for making calculations.
4. So depicted (referring to visual representations of
death as a skeleton or skull with no eyes).
5. Posthumus means "set free by death." The Jailer thinks
he means "set free from prison."
6. Most editions, following F2, have everyone leave the
stage here except the Jailer. However, the Jailer himself

has been ordered to bring the prisoner to the King, which
would mean he must not be separated from Posthumus.
Rather than being a monologue, the ensuing speech may
be largely spoken in asides to the audience as the Jailer
unlocks Posthumus's fetters and prepares to take him to
Cymbeline.
7. Had a promotion in it (implying that a world without
the need for jailers could offer him better employment).
5.6 Location: The camp of Cymbeline, Britain.

That the poor soldier that so richly fought,
Whose rags shamed gilded arms, whose naked breast
5   Stepped before targs of proof,[1] cannot be found.
He shall be happy that can find him, if
Our grace can make him so.
BELARIUS   I never saw
Such noble fury in so poor a thing,
Such precious deeds in one that promised naught
But beggary and poor looks.
10 CYMBELINE   No tidings of him?
PISANIO   He hath been searched° among the dead and living,   sought
But no trace of him.
CYMBELINE   To my grief I am
The heir of his reward, which I will add
[*To* BELARIUS, GUIDERIUS, *and* ARVIRAGUS] To you, the liver,
heart, and brain of Britain,
15 By whom I grant she lives. 'Tis now the time
To ask of whence you are. Report it.
BELARIUS   Sir,
In Cambria° are we born, and gentlemen.   Wales
Further to boast were neither true nor modest,
Unless I add we are honest.
CYMBELINE   Bow your knees.
        [*They kneel. He knights them*]
20 Arise, my knights o'th' battle.[2] I create you
Companions to our person, and will fit° you   supply
With dignities becoming your estates.°   (new) rank
        [BELARIUS, GUIDERIUS, *and* ARVIRAGUS *rise.*]
        Enter CORNELIUS *and* LADIES
There's business in these faces. Why so sadly
Greet you our victory? You look like Romans,
And not o'th' court of Britain.
25 CORNELIUS   Hail, great King!
To sour your happiness I must report
The Queen is dead.
CYMBELINE   Who worse than a physician
Would this report become? But I consider
By medicine life may be prolonged, yet death
30 Will seize the doctor too. How ended she?
CORNELIUS   With horror, madly dying, like her life,
Which being cruel to the world, concluded
Most cruel to herself. What she confessed
I will report, so please you. These her women
35 Can trip me° if I err, who with wet cheeks   point out my mistakes
Were present when she finished.
CYMBELINE   Prithee, say.
CORNELIUS   First, she confessed she never loved you, only
Affected° greatness got by you, not you;   Desired
Married your royalty, was wife to your place,°   position
Abhorred your person.
40 CYMBELINE   She alone knew this,
And but° she spoke it dying, I would not   except that

---

1. *targs of proof*: shields whose strength had been tested.
2. A special group of knights who won their titles for extraordinary bravery on the battlefield.

Believe her lips in opening it. Proceed.
CORNELIUS Your daughter, whom she bore in hand° to love   *she pretended*
  With such integrity, she did confess
45 Was as a scorpion to her sight, whose life,
  But that her flight prevented it, she had
  Ta'en off° by poison.   *Ended*
CYMBELINE   O most delicate° fiend!   *subtle*
  Who is't can read a woman? Is there more?
CORNELIUS More, sir, and worse. She did confess she had
50 For you a mortal mineral° which, being took,   *a deadly poison*
  Should by the minute feed on life, and, ling'ring,
  By inches waste you. In which time she purposed
  By watching,° weeping, tendance,[3] kissing, to   *staying awake*
  O'ercome you with her show;° and in fine,°   *performance / finally*
55 When she had fit you with° her craft, to work   *shaped you by*
  Her son into th'adoption of the crown;[4]
  But failing of her end by his strange absence,
  Grew shameless-desperate, opened° in despite   *revealed*
  Of heaven and men her purposes, repented
60 The evils she hatched were not effected; so
  Despairing died.
CYMBELINE   Heard you all this, her women?
LADIES We did, so please your highness.
CYMBELINE   Mine eyes
  Were not in fault, for she was beautiful;
  Mine ears that heard her flattery, nor my heart
65 That thought her like her seeming.° It had been vicious°   *appearance / wrong*
  To have mistrusted her. Yet, O my daughter,
  That it was folly in me thou mayst say,
  And prove it in thy feeling.[5] Heaven mend all!
      Enter LUCIUS, GIACOMO, SOOTHSAYER, *and other Roman*
      prisoners, POSTHUMUS *behind, and* INNOGEN [*dressed as*
      a man, all guarded by Briton soldiers]
  Thou com'st not, Caius, now for tribute. That
70 The Britons have razed out,° though with the loss   *erased*
  Of many a bold one; whose kinsmen have made suit
  That their good souls° may be appeased with slaughter   *(of the dead Britons)*
  Of you, their captives, which ourself have granted.
  So think of your estate.°   *condition*
75 LUCIUS Consider, sir, the chance of war. The day
  Was yours by accident. Had it gone with us,
  We should not, when the blood was cool, have threatened
  Our prisoners with the sword. But since the gods
  Will have it thus, that nothing but our lives
80 May be called ransom, let it come. Sufficeth
  A Roman with a Roman's heart can suffer.
  Augustus lives to think on't;[6] and so much
  For my peculiar care.° This one thing only   *concern for myself*
  I will entreat:
      [*He presents* INNOGEN *to* CYMBELINE]
      my boy, a Briton born,

---

3. Showing attention to you.
4. *to work . . . crown:* to work her son into the position of heir to the crown.
5. And find it true by your experience.
6. Augustus lives and can consider what to do.

85   Let him be ransomed. Never master had
     A page so kind, so duteous, diligent,
     So tender over his occasions,° true,   *thoughtful of his needs*
     So feat,° so nurse-like; let his virtue join   *graceful*
     With my request, which I'll make bold your highness
90   Cannot deny. He hath done no Briton harm,
     Though he have served a Roman. Save him, sir,
     And spare no blood beside.°   *no one else*
  CYMBELINE   I have surely seen him.
     His favour° is familiar to me. Boy,   *face*
     Thou hast looked thyself into my grace,[7]
95   And art mine own. I know not why, wherefore,
     To say 'Live, boy'. Ne'er thank thy master. Live,
     And ask of Cymbeline what boon° thou wilt   *reward*
     Fitting my bounty and thy state,° I'll give it,   *rank*
     Yea, though thou do demand a prisoner
     The noblest ta'en.
100 INNOGEN   I humbly thank your highness.
  LUCIUS   I do not bid thee beg my life, good lad,
     And yet I know thou wilt.
  INNOGEN   No, no. Alack,
     There's other work in hand. I see a thing[8]
     Bitter to me as death. Your life, good master,
     Must shuffle° for itself.   *shift*
105 LUCIUS   The boy disdains me.
     He leaves me, scorns me. Briefly die their joys
     That place them on the truth of girls and boys.[9]
     Why stands he so perplexed?
  CYMBELINE [*to* INNOGEN]   What wouldst thou, boy?
     I love thee more and more; think more and more
110   What's best to ask. Know'st him thou look'st on? Speak,
     Wilt have him live? Is he thy kin, thy friend?
  INNOGEN   He is a Roman, no more kin to me
     Than I to your highness, who, being born your vassal,
     Am something nearer.
  CYMBELINE   Wherefore ey'st him so?
115 INNOGEN   I'll tell you, sir, in private, if you please
     To give me hearing.
  CYMBELINE   Ay, with all my heart,
     And lend my best attention. What's thy name?
  INNOGEN   Fidele, sir.
  CYMBELINE   Thou'rt my good youth, my page.
     I'll be thy master. Walk with me, speak freely.
        [CYMBELINE *and* INNOGEN *speak apart*]
  BELARIUS [*aside to* GUIDERIUS *and* ARVIRAGUS]   Is not this boy
       revived from death?
120 ARVIRAGUS   One sand° another   *One grain of sand*
     Not more resembles that° sweet rosy lad   *than he resembles that*
     Who died, and was Fidele. What think you?
  GUIDERIUS   The same dead thing alive.
  BELARIUS   Peace, peace, see further. He eyes us not. Forbear.

---

7. You have by your appearance gained my favor.
8. Referring to the ring that she gave to Posthumus and that is now on Giacomo's finger.

9. *Briefly . . . boys:* Quickly dies the happiness of those who depend on the fidelity of girls and boys.

125 Creatures may be alike. Were't he, I am sure
He would have spoke to us.
GUIDERIUS   But we see° him dead.   *saw*
BELARIUS   Be silent; let's see further.
PISANIO [*aside*]   It is my mistress.
Since she is living, let the time run on
To good or bad.
CYMBELINE [*to* INNOGEN]   Come, stand thou by our side,
130 Make thy demand aloud. [*To* GIACOMO]   Sir, step you forth.
Give answer to this boy, and do it freely,
Or, by our greatness and the grace of it,
Which is our honour, bitter torture shall
Winnow° the truth from falsehood.   *Separate*
[*To* INNOGEN]   On, speak to him.
135 INNOGEN   My boon is that this gentleman may render°   *declare*
Of whom he had this ring.
POSTHUMUS [*aside*]   What's that to him?
CYMBELINE [*to* GIACOMO]   That diamond upon your finger, say,
How came it yours?
GIACOMO   Thou'lt torture me to leave° unspoken that   *for leaving*
Which to be spoke would torture thee.
140 CYMBELINE   How, me?
GIACOMO   I am glad to be constrained to utter that°   *what*
Torments me to conceal. By villainy
I got this ring; 'twas Leonatus' jewel,
Whom thou didst banish; and, which more may grieve thee,
145 As it doth me, a nobler sir ne'er lived
'Twixt sky and ground. Wilt thou hear more, my lord?
CYMBELINE   All that belongs to this.
GIACOMO   That paragon thy daughter,
For whom my heart drops blood, and my false spirits
Quail to remember—give me leave, I faint.
150 CYMBELINE   My daughter? What of her? Renew thy strength.
I had rather thou shouldst live while nature will°   *as long as nature allows*
Than die ere I hear more. Strive, man, and speak.
GIACOMO   Upon a time—unhappy was the clock
That struck the hour—it was in Rome—accursed
155 The mansion where—'twas at a feast—O, would
Our viands had been poisoned, or at least
Those which I heaved to head!°—the good Posthumus—   *raised to my mouth*
What should I say?—he was too good to be
Where ill men were, and was the best of all
160 Amongst the rar'st of good ones—sitting sadly,
Hearing us praise our loves of Italy
For beauty that made barren the swelled boast[1]
Of him that best could speak; for feature laming
The shrine of Venus or straight-pitched Minerva,[2]
165 Postures beyond brief nature;[3] for condition,°   *character*
A shop of all the qualities that man
Loves woman for; besides that hook of wiving,°   *bait for marriage*
Fairness which strikes the eye—

---

1. For beauty so great that it rendered hollow even the
exaggerated boasts.
2. *for . . . Minerva:* for looks that rendered deficient even
the body of the goddess of love (Venus) and the magiste-
rial goddess of the arts (Minerva).
3. Forms surpassing those of mere mortals.

CYMBELINE I stand on fire.
Come to the matter.
GIACOMO All too soon I shall,
170 Unless thou wouldst grieve quickly. This Posthumus,
Most like a noble lord in love and one
That had a royal lover, took his hint,
And not dispraising whom we praised—therein
He was as calm as virtue—he began
175 His mistress' picture, which by his tongue being made,
And then a mind put in't, either our brags   *uttered in defense*
Were cracked° of kitchen-trulls, or his description   *fools incapable of speech*
Proved us unspeaking sots.°
CYMBELINE Nay, nay, to th' purpose.
GIACOMO Your daughter's chastity—there it begins.
180 He spake of her as° Dian had hot° dreams   *as if / lustful*
And she alone were cold,° whereat I, wretch,   *chaste*
Made scruple of° his praise, and wagered with him   *Disputed*
Pieces of gold 'gainst this which then he wore
Upon his honoured finger, to attain
185 In suit° the place of 's bed and win this ring   *By urging my suit*
By hers and mine adultery. He, true knight,
No lesser of her honour confident
Than I did truly find her, stakes this ring—
And would so had it been a carbuncle
190 Of Phoebus' wheel,[4] and might so safely had it
Been all the worth of 's car.° Away to Britain   *worth the entire chariot*
Post° I in this design. Well may you, sir,   *Hasten*
Remember me at court, where I was taught
Of° your chaste daughter the wide difference   *By*
195 'Twixt amorous and villainous. Being thus quenched
Of hope, not longing,° mine Italian brain   *though not of desire*
Gan° in your duller Britain[5] operate   *Began*
Most vilely; for my vantage,° excellent.   *profit*
And, to be brief, my practice° so prevailed   *deceit*
200 That I returned with simular° proof enough   *pretended; specious*
To make the noble Leonatus mad
By wounding his belief in her renown°   *reputation*
With tokens thus and thus; averring° notes   *confirming*
Of chamber-hanging, pictures, this her bracelet—
205 O cunning, how I got it!—nay, some marks
Of secret on her person, that he could not
But think her bond of chastity quite cracked,
I having ta'en the forfeit.[6] Whereupon—
Methinks I see him now—
POSTHUMUS [coming forward] Ay, so thou dost,
210 Italian fiend! Ay me, most credulous fool,
Egregious murderer, thief, anything
That's due[7] to all the villains past, in being,
To come! O, give me cord, or knife, or poison,
Some upright justicer!° Thou, King, send out   *judge*
215 For torturers ingenious. It is I

---

4. *had . . . wheel:* even if it had been a precious stone
from the wheel of the sun god's chariot.
5. Alluding to the belief that England's northern climate
made its inhabitants sluggish and slow of wit.
6. Believing I had taken what she gave up (her chastity).
7. *anything / That's due:* any name that's owed.

That all th'abhorrèd things o'th' earth amend[8]
By being worse than they. I am Posthumus,
That killed thy daughter—villain-like, I lie:
That caused a lesser villain than myself,
220 A sacrilegious thief, to do't. The temple
Of virtue was she; yea, and she herself.°   *she was virtue herself*
Spit and throw stones, cast mire upon me, set
The dogs o'th' street to bay me. Every villain
Be called Posthumus Leonatus, and
225 Be 'villain' less than 'twas![9] O Innogen!
My queen, my life, my wife, O Innogen,
Innogen, Innogen!
INNOGEN [*approaching him*]   Peace, my lord. Hear, hear.
POSTHUMUS   Shall 's have a play of this? Thou scornful page,
There lie thy part.°   *Your role is to lie there*
    [*He strikes her down*]
PISANIO [*coming forward*]   O gentlemen, help!
230 Mine and your mistress! O my lord Posthumus,
You ne'er killed Innogen till now. Help, help!
    [*To* INNOGEN] Mine honoured lady.
CYMBELINE   Does the world go round?
POSTHUMUS   How comes these staggers[1] on me?
PISANIO [*to* INNOGEN]   Wake, my mistress.
CYMBELINE   If this be so, the gods do mean to strike me
235 To death with mortal° joy.   *death-causing*
PISANIO [*to* INNOGEN]   How fares my mistress?
INNOGEN   O, get thee from my sight!
Thou gav'st me poison. Dangerous fellow, hence.
Breathe not where princes are.
CYMBELINE   The tune of Innogen.
240 PISANIO   Lady, the gods throw stones of sulphur° on me if   *thunderbolts*
That box I gave you was not thought by me
A precious thing. I had it from the Queen.
CYMBELINE   New matter still.
INNOGEN   It poisoned me.
CORNELIUS   O gods!
I left out one thing which the Queen confessed
245 [*To* PISANIO] Which must approve° thee honest. 'If Pisanio   *prove*
Have', said she, 'given his mistress that confection°   *compound*
Which I gave him for cordial, she is served
As I would serve a rat.'
CYMBELINE   What's this, Cornelius?
CORNELIUS   The Queen, sir, very oft importuned me
250 To temper° poisons for her, still° pretending   *mix / always*
The satisfaction of her knowledge only
In killing creatures vile, as cats and dogs
Of no esteem.° I, dreading that her purpose   *value*
Was of more danger, did compound for her
255 A certain stuff which, being ta'en, would cease
The present power of life, but in short time

---

8. Who makes all loathsome things seem better.
9. *Every . . . 'twas:* May the word "villain" be less abhor-
rent than it was, since "Posthumus Leonatus" has replaced
it.
1. A disease, usually of horses, that causes an unsteady
walk; dizziness.

All offices of nature° should again   *All natural faculties*
Do their due functions. [*To* INNOGEN] Have you ta'en of it?
INNOGEN   Most like° I did, for I was dead.   *likely*
BELARIUS [*aside to* GUIDERIUS *and* ARVIRAGUS]   My boys,
  There was our error.
260 GUIDERIUS   This is sure Fidele.
INNOGEN [*to* POSTHUMUS]   Why did you throw your wedded
      lady from you?
  Think that you are upon a lock,[2] and now
  Throw me again.
        [*She throws her arms about his neck*]
POSTHUMUS   Hang there like fruit, my soul,
  Till the tree die.
CYMBELINE [*to* INNOGEN]   How now, my flesh, my child?
265 What, mak'st thou me a dullard° in this act?   *sluggish performer*
  Wilt thou not speak to me?
INNOGEN [*kneeling*]   Your blessing, sir.
BELARIUS [*aside to* GUIDERIUS *and* ARVIRAGUS]   Though you did
      love this youth, I blame ye not.
  You had a motive° for't.   *reason*
CYMBELINE   My tears that fall
  Prove holy water on thee!
      [*He raises her*]
          Innogen,
  Thy mother's dead.
270 INNOGEN   I am sorry for't, my lord.
CYMBELINE   O, she was naught,° and 'long° of her it was   *worthless / because*
  That we meet here so strangely.° But her son   *like strangers*
  Is gone, we know not how nor where.
PISANIO   My lord,
  Now fear is from me I'll speak truth. Lord Cloten,
275 Upon my lady's missing,° came to me   *absence*
  With his sword drawn, foamed at the mouth, and swore
  If I discovered° not which way she was gone   *revealed*
  It was my instant death. By accident°   *chance*
  I had a feignèd letter of my master's[3]
280 Then in my pocket, which directed him
  To seek her on the mountains near to Milford,
  Where in a frenzy, in my master's garments,
  Which he enforced from me, away he posts°   *hastens*
  With unchaste purpose, and with oath to violate
285 My lady's honour. What became of him
  I further know not.
GUIDERIUS   Let me end the story.
  I slew him there.
CYMBELINE   Marry, the gods forfend!
  I would not thy good deeds° should from my lips   *(on the battlefield)*
  Pluck a hard sentence. Prithee, valiant youth,
290 Deny't again.°   *Take it back*
GUIDERIUS   I have spoke it, and I did it.
CYMBELINE   He was a prince.
GUIDERIUS   A most incivil° one. The wrongs he did me   *barbarous*

2. You are in a wrestling hold. This is a disputed passage;   3. Referring to the letter written by Posthumus to mislead
F here reads "rock."   Innogen.

Were nothing prince-like, for he did provoke me
295   With language that would make me spurn the sea
If it could so roar to me. I cut off 's head,
And am right glad he is not standing here
To tell this tale of mine.⁴
CYMBELINE   I am sorrow for thee.
By thine own tongue thou art condemned, and must
Endure our law. Thou'rt dead.
300 INNOGEN   That headless man
I thought had been my lord.
CYMBELINE [*to soldiers*]   Bind the offender,
And take him from our presence.
BELARIUS   Stay, sir King.
This boy is better than the man he slew,
As well descended as thyself, and hath
305   More of thee merited than a band of Clotens
Had ever scar for.⁵ Let his arms alone;
They were not born for bondage.
CYMBELINE   Why, old soldier,
Wilt thou undo the worth thou art unpaid for⁶
By tasting of our wrath? How of descent
As good as we?
310 ARVIRAGUS   In that he spake too far.
CYMBELINE [*to* BELARIUS]⁷   And thou shalt die for't.
BELARIUS   We will die all three
But I will prove° that two on 's° are as good   *Unless I prove / of us*
As I have given out him. My sons, I must
For mine own part unfold a dangerous speech,
Though haply° well for you.   *perhaps*
315 ARVIRAGUS   Your danger's ours.
GUIDERIUS   And our good his.
BELARIUS   Have at it then. By leave,⁸
Thou hadst, great King, a subject who
Was called Belarius.
CYMBELINE   What of him? He is
A banished traitor.
BELARIUS   He it is that hath
320   Assumed° this age. Indeed, a banished man;   *Reached*
I know not how a traitor.
CYMBELINE [*to soldiers*]   Take him hence.
The whole world shall not save him.
BELARIUS   Not too hot.°   *fast*
First pay me for the nursing of thy sons,
And let it° be confiscate all so soon   *(the payment)*
As I have received it.
325 CYMBELINE   Nursing of my sons?
BELARIUS   I am too blunt and saucy. [*Kneeling*] Here's my knee.
Ere I arise I will prefer° my sons,   *advance*
Then spare not the old father. Mighty sir,

---

4. To tell a tale of cutting off my head.
5. *than . . . for:* than an army of Clotens ever earned by
their battle scars.
6. The merit you are not yet rewarded for.
7. It is unclear to whom—Arviragus or Belarius—Cym-
beline speaks the next line. Arviragus has just addressed

Cymbeline, and one might expect the King's reply to be
directed to him. Belarius, however, made the offending
remark about Guiderius being of as good birth as Cloten,
and the threat of death probably applies to him.
8. Let's begin, then. With your permission.

These two young gentlemen that call me father
330 And think they are my sons are none of mine.
They are the issue° of your loins, my liege,   offspring
And blood of your begetting.
CYMBELINE   How, my issue?
BELARIUS   So sure as you your father's. I, old Morgan,[9]
Am that Belarius whom you sometime° banished.   once
335 Your pleasure was my mere offence,[1] my punishment
Itself, and all my treason. That I suffered
Was all the harm I did. These gentle princes—
For such and so they are—these twenty years
Have I trained up. Those arts° they have as I   accomplishments
340 Could put into them. My breeding was, sir,
As your highness knows. Their nurse Euriphile,
Whom for the theft I wedded, stole these children
Upon my banishment. I moved° her to't,   persuaded
Having received the punishment before
345 For that which I did then. Beaten° for loyalty   Having been beaten
Excited me to treason. Their dear loss,
The more of you 'twas felt, the more it shaped°   suited
Unto° my end° of stealing them. But, gracious sir,   With / purpose
Here are your sons again, and I must lose
350 Two of the sweet'st companions in the world.
The benediction of these covering heavens
Fall on their heads like dew, for they are worthy
To inlay heaven with stars.°   To become constellations
CYMBELINE   Thou weep'st, and speak'st.
The service that you three have done is more
355 Unlike° than this thou tell'st. I lost my children.   Improbable
If these be they, I know not how to wish
A pair of worthier sons.
BELARIUS [rising]   Be pleased a while.
This gentleman, whom I call Polydore,
Most worthy prince, as yours, is true Guiderius.
                    [GUIDERIUS kneels]
360 This gentleman, my Cadwal, Arviragus,
Your younger princely son.
                    [ARVIRAGUS kneels]
                              He, sir, was lapped°   wrapped
In a most curious° mantle wrought by th' hand   delicately fashioned
Of his queen mother, which for more probation°   proof
I can with ease produce.
CYMBELINE   Guiderius had
365 Upon his neck a mole, a sanguine° star.   blood-red
It was a mark of wonder.
BELARIUS   This is he,
Who hath upon him still that natural stamp.
It was wise nature's end in the donation°   purpose in giving it
To be his evidence now.
CYMBELINE   O, what am I?
370 A mother to the birth of three? Ne'er mother

---

9. Morgan was the Welsh name Belarius assumed during   1. What you pleased (to accuse me of) was my entire of-
the years he spent in Wales.   fense.

Rejoiced deliverance more.[2] Blest pray you be,
That, after this strange starting from your orbs,[3]
You may reign in them now!
　　　[GUIDERIUS *and* ARVIRAGUS *rise*]
　　　　　　　　　　　　　O Innogen,
Thou hast lost by this a kingdom.
INNOGEN　　　　　　　　　　　No, my lord,
375　I have got two worlds by't. O my gentle brothers,
Have we thus met? O, never say hereafter
But I am truest speaker. You called me brother
When I was but your sister; I you brothers
When ye were so indeed.
CYMBELINE　　　　　　　　Did you e'er meet?
ARVIRAGUS　Ay, my good lord.
380　GUIDERIUS　　　　　　　　And at first meeting loved,
Continued so until we thought he died.
CORNELIUS　By the Queen's dram she swallowed.
CYMBELINE　　　　　　　　　　　　　O rare instinct!
When shall I hear all through? This fierce° abridgement　　　　　*drastic*
Hath to it circumstantial branches which
385　Distinction should be rich in.[4] Where? How lived you?
And when came you to serve our Roman captive?
How parted with your brothers? How first met them?
Why fled you from the court? And whither? These,
And your three motives° to the battle, with　　　　*the motives of you three*
390　I know not how much more, should be demanded,
And all the other by-dependences,°　　　　　　　　*circumstances*
From chance° to chance. But nor° the time nor place　　*occurrence / neither*
Will serve our long inter'gatories.° See,　　　　*lengthy questioning*
Posthumus anchors upon Innogen,
395　And she, like harmless lightning, throws her eye
On him, her brothers, me, her master, hitting
Each object with a joy. The counterchange
Is severally in all.[5] Let's quit this ground,
And smoke° the temple with our sacrifices.　　　　*fill with smoke*
400　[*To* BELARIUS] Thou art my brother; so we'll hold thee ever.
INNOGEN [*to* BELARIUS]　　You are my father too, and did relieve° me　　*save*
To see this gracious season.
CYMBELINE　　　　　　　　All o'erjoyed,
Save these in bonds. Let them be joyful too,
For they shall taste our comfort.
INNOGEN [*to* LUCIUS]　　　　My good master,
I will yet do you service.
405　LUCIUS　　　　　　　　Happy be you!
CYMBELINE　The forlorn° soldier that so nobly fought,　　　*wretched*
He would have well becomed this place, and graced
The thankings of a king.
POSTHUMUS　　　　　　　I am, sir,
The soldier that did company these three

---

2. Never did giving birth cause a mother to rejoice more.
3. After this unnatural displacement from your rightful
positions. Referring to astrological theories that each heav-
enly body moved in its proper orb, or circle, around the
earth. For a planet to move outside its orb caused distur-
bances in the heavens.
4. *circumstantial . . . in:* many ramifications that will pro-
vide particulars in rich abundance.
5. *The . . . all:* The exchange (of glances) passes from
each to each.

410 In poor beseeming.° 'Twas a fitment[6] for   *appearance*
The purpose I then followed. That I was he,
Speak, Giacomo; I had you down, and might
Have made you finish.°   *die*
GIACOMO [*kneeling*]   I am down again,
But now my heavy conscience sinks my knee
415 As then your force did. Take that life, beseech you,
Which I so often owe;° but your ring first,   *owe so many times over*
And here the bracelet of the truest princess
That ever swore her faith.
POSTHUMUS [*raising him*]   Kneel not to me.
The power that I have on you is to spare you,
420 The malice towards you to forgive you. Live,
And deal with others better.
CYMBELINE   Nobly doomed!°   *sentenced*
We'll learn our freeness of a son-in-law.
Pardon's the word to all.
ARVIRAGUS [*to* POSTHUMUS]   You holp° us, sir,   *helped*
As° you did mean indeed to be our brother.   *As if*
425 Joyed are we that you are.
POSTHUMUS   Your servant, princes. [*To* LUCIUS] Good my lord of Rome,
Call forth your soothsayer. As I slept, methought
Great Jupiter, upon his eagle backed,°   *riding on his eagle*
Appeared to me with other spritely° shows   *ghostly*
430 Of mine own kindred. When I waked I found
This label° on my bosom, whose containing°   *tablet / contents*
Is so from sense in hardness that I can
Make no collection of it.[7] Let him show
His skill in the construction.°   *interpretation*
LUCIUS   Philharmonus.
SOOTHSAYER   Here, my good lord.
435 LUCIUS   Read, and declare the meaning.
SOOTHSAYER *reads* [*the tablet*] 'Whenas a lion's whelp shall, to
himself unknown, without seeking find, and be embraced by a
piece of tender air; and when from a stately cedar shall be
lopped branches which, being dead many years, shall after
440 revive, be jointed to the old stock, and freshly grow: then shall
Posthumus end his miseries, Britain be fortunate and flourish
in peace and plenty.'
Thou, Leonatus, art the lion's whelp.
The fit and apt construction of thy name,
445 Being *leo-natus*,° doth import so much.   *lion-born*
[*To* CYMBELINE] The piece of tender air thy virtuous daughter,
Which we call '*mollis aer*';[8] and '*mollis aer*'
We term it '*mulier*', [*to* POSTHUMUS] which '*mulier*' I divine
Is this most constant wife, who even now,
450 Answering the letter of the oracle,[9]
Unknown to you, unsought, were clipped about°   *embraced*
With this most tender air.
CYMBELINE   This hath some seeming.
SOOTHSAYER   The lofty cedar, royal Cymbeline,

---

6. A suitable disguise.
7. *Is . . . it:* Is so difficult to make sense of that I can draw no conclusion from it.
8. Latin for "gentle air." An ancient (and erroneous) etymology for *mulier*, Latin for "woman" or "wife."
9. Fulfilling the exact terms of the oracle.

Personates° thee, and thy lopped branches point   *Stands for*
455   Thy two sons forth, who, by Belarius stol'n,
For many years thought dead, are now revived,
To the majestic cedar joined, whose issue
Promises Britain peace and plenty.
CYMBELINE   Well,
My peace we will begin; and, Caius Lucius,
460   Although the victor, we submit to Caesar
And to the Roman empire, promising
To pay our wonted tribute, from the which
We were dissuaded by our wicked queen,
Whom° heavens in justice both on her and hers   *On whom*
465   Have laid most heavy hand.
SOOTHSAYER   The fingers of the powers above do tune
The harmony of this peace. The vision,
Which I made known to Lucius ere the stroke
Of this yet scarce-cold battle,[1] at this instant
470   Is full° accomplished. For the Roman eagle,   *entirely*
From south to west on wing soaring aloft,
Lessened herself,[2] and in the beams o'th' sun
So vanished; which foreshowed our princely eagle
Th'imperial Caesar should again unite
475   His favour with the radiant Cymbeline,
Which shines here in the west.
CYMBELINE   Laud we the gods,
And let our crookèd° smokes climb to their nostrils   *curling*
From our blest altars. Publish° we this peace   *Proclaim*
To all our subjects. Set we forward,° let   *Let us go forth*
480   A Roman and a British ensign° wave   *banner*
Friendly together. So through Lud's town march,
And in the temple of great Jupiter
Our peace we'll ratify, seal it with feasts.
Set on there.° Never was a war did cease,   *March forth*
485   Ere bloody hands were washed, with such a peace.
                [*Flourish.*] *Exeunt* [*in triumph*]

TEXTUAL VARIANTS

Control text: F

F: The Folio of 1623
Fa, Fb: Successive states of F incorporating various print-shop corrections and changes

Title: *Cymbeline King of Britaine* [F table of contents] *The Tragedie of Cymbeline* [F head title]

s.p. INNOGEN [F's use of *Imogen* is changed throughout.]
s.p. GIACOMO [F's use of *Iachimo* is modernized throughout.]
s.p. HELEN [In 2.2, F's use of *La.* is changed throughout.]
s.p. FILARIO [F's use of *Philario* is modernized throughout.]
s.p. A ROMAN CAPTAIN [F's *Captain* is changed at 4.2.335, 339, 344, and 361.]

---

1. *ere . . . battle:* before the action of this battle, which has only just ceased.   2. Made herself small (by flying into the distance).

s.p. A LORD [F's use of *Lord* is changed at 4.3.16, 23, 28.]
s.p. FIRST JAILER [F's use of *Gao* is changed at 5.5.95.]

1.1.3 King Kings 15 of at 30 Cassibelan *Cassibulan* 98 Filario's *Filorio's*
1.2.9 steel if he Steele if it
1.3.9 this his
1.4.40 not to to 62 Britain Britanie 63 not but not 72 purchase purchases 90 five [Fb] fine [Fa] 111 thousand thousands
1.5.28 factor for for 85 words, Pisanio words
1.6.7 desire desires 25 truest *trust.* 29 takes take 37 th'unnumbered the number'd 81 count account 126 lend to lend 163 me [Fb] ma [Fa] 169 men's men 170 descended defended 187 Best The best
2.1.21 an and 24 your you 31 tonight night 58 husband, than husband then.
2.2.2 hour houre [Fb] houe [Fa] 43 riveted riueted [Fb] riuete [Fa] 49 bare beare
2.3.6 s.p. CLOTEN [not in text] 17 s.p. MUSICIAN [not in F] heaven *Heauens* 24 s.p. CLOTEN [not in F] 25 vice voyce 27 amend amed 39 out on't 43 solicits solicity 96 cure are 116 foil foyle 132 garment Garments 149 you your
2.4.6 seared hopes fear'd hope 14 Ere Or 18 legions Legion 24 courage courages 34 through thorough 37 s.p. FILARIO *Post.* 41 had haue 47 not note 57 you yon 60 leaves leaue 76 Such since 116 her woman her women 135 the her 151 follow follow him
2.5.2 bastards all all Bastards 16 German one Iarmen on 27 man can name name
3.1.5 Cassibelan *Cassibulan* 11 There will There 20 banks Oakes 30, 39–40 Cassibelan *Cassibulan*
3.2.2 accuser accuse 10 to hers to her 14 to do good [Fb] to go do od [Fa] 22 here [Fb] her [Fa] 64 Till And 67 score store ride rid 78 Nor here, nor nor heere, not
3.3.2 Stoop Sleepe 15–16 war; / That Warre. / This 23 bauble Babe 25 'em him 28 know knowes 33 travelling abed trauailing a bed 34 prison for Prison, or 83 wherein they bow whereon the Bowe 86 Polydore *Poladour* 106 Morgan *Mergan*
3.4.78 afore't a-foot 88 make makes 100 out [not in F] 132 churlish, noble noble
3.5.32 looks looke 40 strokes, stroke; 44 loud'st lowd of 86 tongue heart
3.6.68 Ay I I'd I do 74 price prize
3.7.9 commends commands
4.2.2 from after 47 hath he hath 51 s.p. BELARIUS *Arui⟨ragus⟩.* 59 him them 60 patience patient 123 thanks, ye thanks the 133 humour Honor 171 how thou 187 ingenious ingenuous 203 not not the 206 crare care 207 Might Might'st 225 ruddock Raddocke 230 winter-gown winter-ground 238 once once to 258 begin. begin. / SONG. 286 th'earth's face their Faces 288 strow strew 292 is are 325 thy this 338 are hence are heere 392 wild-wood leaves wild wood-leaues 401 he is hee's
4.3.40 betid betide
4.4.2 find we we finde 17 the their 18 files Fires 27 hard heard
5.1.1 once wished am wisht 15 dread ill dread it 16 blest best 20 mistress-piece Mistris: Peace
5.5.2 Ay I did 24 harts hearts her our 42 stooped stopt 43 they the 53 Yet you you 64 This This is 121 make take 161 geck geeke 163 come came 175 look looke / looke 212 Preens Prunes claws cloyes 252 are as are 257 Of Oh, of 260 sir Sis 270 or take or to take 273 on one
5.6.54 and in fine and in time 55 fit fitted 62 s.p. LADIES *La.* 64 heard heare 134 On One 142 Torments Which torments 205 got it got 225 villain villany 261 from fro 262 lock Rocke 303 boy man 335 mere neere 352 like liks 379 you we 387 brothers Brother 393 inter'gatories Interrogatories 406 so no 469 this yet yet this

The Tempest

Near the close of *King Lear*, the ruined old King, stripped of the last vestiges of his power, dreams of being locked away happily in prison with his beloved Cordelia. Father and daughter have a more tragic fate in store for them, but Shakespeare returns to the dream in *The Tempest*. The play opens on a remote island of exile where Prospero, deposed from power and thrust out of Milan by his wicked brother, has found shelter with his only daughter, Miranda. Unlike many of Shakespeare's plays, *The Tempest* does not appear to have a single dominant source for its plot, but it is a kind of echo chamber of Shakespearean motifs. Its story of loss and recovery and its air of wonder link it closely to the group of late plays that modern editors generally call "romances" (*Pericles, The Winter's Tale, Cymbeline*), but it resonates as well with issues that haunted Shakespeare's imagination throughout his career: the painful necessity for a father to let his daughter go (*Othello, King Lear*); the treacherous betrayal of a legitimate ruler (*Richard II, Julius Caesar, Hamlet, Macbeth*); the murderous hatred of one brother for another (*Richard III, As You Like It, Hamlet, King Lear*); the passage from court society to the wilderness and the promise of a return (*A Midsummer Night's Dream, As You Like It*); the wooing of a young heiress in ignorance of her place in the social hierarchy (*Twelfth Night, Pericles, The Winter's Tale*); the dream of manipulating others by means of art, especially by staging miniature plays-within-plays (*I Henry IV, Much Ado About Nothing, Hamlet*); the threat of a radical loss of identity (*The Comedy of Errors, Richard II, King Lear*); the relation between nature and nurture (*Pericles, The Winter's Tale*); the harnessing of magical powers (*The First Part of the Contention [2 Henry VI], A Midsummer Night's Dream, Macbeth*).

Though it is the first play printed in the First Folio (1623), *The Tempest* is probably one of the last Shakespeare wrote. It can be dated fairly precisely: it uses material that was not available until late 1610, and there is a record of a performance before the king on Hallowmas Night, 1611. Since Shakespeare retired soon after to Stratford, *The Tempest* has seemed to many to be his valedictory to the theater. In this view, Prospero's strangely anxious and moving epilogue — "Now my charms are all o'erthrown, / And what strength I have's mine own" — is the expression of Shakespeare's own professional leave-taking. There are reasons to be skeptical: after finishing *The Tempest*, he collaborated on at least two other plays, *All Is True (Henry VIII)* and *The Two Noble Kinsmen*, and it is perilous to identify Shakespeare too closely with any of his characters, let alone an exiled, embittered, manipulative princely wizard. Yet the echo-chamber effect is striking, and when Prospero and others speak of his powerful "art," it is difficult not to associate the skill of the great magician with the skill of the great playwright. Near the end of the play, the association is made explicit when Prospero uses his magic powers to produce what he terms "some vanity of mine art" (4.1.41), a betrothal masque performed by spirits whom he calls forth "to enact / My present fancies" (4.1.121–22). The masque, a lavish courtly performance with music and dancing, may have seemed particularly appropriate on the occasion of another early performance: *The Tempest* was one of fourteen plays provided as part of the elaborate festivities in honor of the betrothal and marriage of King James's daughter Elizabeth to Frederick, the elector palatine. As Prospero's gift of the beautiful spectacle displays his magnificence and authority, so *The Tempest* and the other plays commanded by the king for his daughter's wedding would have enhanced his own prestige.

The Tempest opens with a spectacular storm that recalls *King Lear* not only in its violence but in its indifference to the ruler's authority: "What cares these roarers for the name of king?" (1.1.15–16), shouts the exasperated Boatswain at the aristocrats who are standing in his way. The Boatswain's outburst seems unanswerable: like the implacable

Magical storm. From Olaus Magnus, *Historia de Gentibus Septentrionalibus* (1555).

thunder in *King Lear*, the tempest marks the point at which exalted titles are revealed to be absurd pretensions, substanceless in the face of the elemental forces of nature and the desperate struggle for survival. But we soon learn that this tempest is not in fact natural and that it emphatically does hear and respond to human power, a power that is terrifying but, at least by its own account, benign: "The direful spectacle of the wreck," Prospero tells his daughter, "I have with such provision in mine art / So safely ordered" (1.2.26, 28–29) that no one on board has been harmed.

Shakespeare's contemporaries were fascinated by the figure of the *magus*, the great magician who by dint of deep learning, ascetic discipline, and patient skill could command the secret forces of the natural and supernatural world. Distinct from the village witch and "cunning man," figures engaged in local acts of healing and malice, and distinct too from alchemical experimenters bent on turning base metal into gold, the magus, cloaked in a robe covered with mysterious symbols, pronounced his occult charms, called forth spirits, and ranged in his imagination through the heavens and the earth, conjoining contemplative wisdom with virtuous action in order to confer great benefits upon his age. But there was a shiver of fear mingled with the popular admiration: when the person in Shakespeare's time most widely identified as a magus, the wizard John Dee, was away from his house, his library, one of the greatest private collections of books in England, was set on fire and burned to the ground.

Book, costume, powerful language, the ability to enact the fancies of the brain: these are key elements of both magic and theater. "I have bedimmed / The noontide sun," Prospero declares, beginning an enumeration of extraordinary accomplishments that culminates with the revelation that

> graves at my command
> Have waked their sleepers, oped, and let 'em forth
> By my so potent art.
>
> (5.1.41–50)

For the playwright who conjured up the ghosts of Caesar and old Hamlet, the claim does not seem extravagant, but for a magician it amounts to an extremely dangerous confession. Necromancy—communing with the spirits of the dead—was the very essence of black magic, the hated practice from which Prospero is careful to distinguish himself throughout the play. Before his exile, the island had been the realm of the "damned witch Sycorax," who was banished there "for mischiefs manifold and sorceries terrible" (1.2.265–66). The legitimacy of Prospero's power, including power over his slave Caliban, Sycorax's son, depends on his moral authority, but for one disturbing moment it is difficult to see the difference between "foul witch" and princely magician. Small wonder that as soon as he has disclosed that he has trafficked with the dead, Prospero declares that he abjures his "rough magic" (5.1.50).

Prospero does not give an explicit reason for this abjuration, but it appears to be a key stage in the complex process that has led, before the time of the play, to his overthrow and will lead, after the play's events are over, to his return to power. Together with his early *Comedy of Errors*, *The Tempest* is unusual among Shakespeare's plays in observing what literary critics of the age called the unities of time and place; unlike *Antony and Cleopatra*, for example, which ranges over a huge territory, or *The Winter's Tale*, which covers a huge span of time, the actions of *The Tempest* all take place in a single locale, the island, during the course of a single day. In a long scene of exposition just after the spectacular opening storm, Prospero tells Miranda that he is at a critical moment; everything depends on his seizing the opportunity that fortune has granted him. The whole play, then, is the spectacle of his timing, timing that might be cynically termed political opportunism or theatrical cunning but that Prospero himself associates with the working out of "providence divine" (1.2.160). The opportunity he seizes has its tangled roots in what he calls "the dark backward and abyss of time" (1.2.50). Many years before, when he was Duke of Milan, Prospero's preoccupation with "secret studies" gave his ambitious and unscrupulous brother Antonio the opportunity to topple him from power. Now those same studies, perfected during his long exile, have enabled Prospero to cause Antonio and his shipmates, sailing back to Italy from Tunis, to be shipwrecked on his island, where they have fallen unwittingly under his control. His magic makes it possible not only to wrest back his dukedom but to avenge himself for the terrible wrong that his brother and his brother's principal ally, Alonso, the King of Naples, have done him: "They now are in my power" (3.3.90). Audiences in Shakespeare's time would have had an all too clear image of how horrendous

The Conjurer. Engraving by Theodore de Bry after a drawing by John White. From Thomas Hariot, *A Briefe and True Report of the New Found Land of Virginia* (1590).

the vengeance of enraged princes usually was. That Prospero restrains himself from the full exercise of his power to harm his enemies, that he breaks his magic staff and drowns his book, is his highest moral achievement, a triumphant display of self-mastery: "The rarer action is / In virtue than in vengeance" (5.1.27–28).

All of those who are shipwrecked on the island undergo the same shock of terror and unexpected survival, but their experiences, as they cross the yellow sands and make their way toward the interior of the island, differ markedly. The least affected are the mariners, including the feisty Boatswain; after their exhausting labors in the storm, they have sunk into a strange, uneasy sleep, only to be awakened in time to sail the miraculously restored ship back to Italy. The others are put through more complex trials; they are in effect subjects in a psychological experiment, exposed to varying degrees of anxiety, temptation, grief, fear, and penitence. The most generously treated is Ferdinand, the only son of the King of Naples, whom Prospero, in what is essentially a carefully planned dynastic alliance, has secretly chosen to be his son-in-law. As Ferdinand bewails what he assumes is his father's death by drowning, he hears strange, haunting music, including the remarkable song of death and metamorphosis, "Full fathom five thy father lies" (1.2.400). Ferdinand is the only one of the shipwrecked company, until the play's final scene, to encounter Prospero directly; the magician makes the experience menacing, humiliating, and frustrating, but this is the modest, salutary price the young man must pay to win the hand of the beautiful Miranda, who seems to him a goddess and who, for her part, has fallen in love with him at first sight.

Prospero directs the experience of the rest as well, but not in person; instead they principally encounter his diligent servant, Ariel. Ariel is not human, though at a crucial moment he is able to imagine what he would feel "were I human" (5.1.20). He is, as the cast of characters describes him, an "airy spirit," capable of moving at immense speed, altering the weather, and producing vivid illusions. We learn that Ariel possesses an inherent moral "delicacy," a delicacy that in the past (that is, before the time depicted in the play) has brought him pain. For, as Prospero reminds him, he had been Sycorax's servant and was, for refusing "to act her earthy and abhorred commands" (1.2.275), imprisoned by the witch for many years in a cloven pine. Prospero freed him from confinement and now demands in return a fixed term of service, which Ariel provides with a mixture of brilliant alacrity and grumbling. Prospero responds in turn with mingled affection and anger, alternating warm praises and dire threats. Though Prospero's "art," through which he commands Ariel and the lesser spirits, seems to foresee and control everything, this control is purchased by constant discipline.

And, for all his godlike powers, there are limits to what Prospero can do. He can make the loathed Antonio and the others know something of the bitterness of loss and isolation; he can produce in them irresistible drowsiness and startled awakenings; he can command Ariel to lay before them a splendid banquet and then make it suddenly vanish; he can drive them to desperation and madness. But in the case of his own brother and Alonso's similarly wicked brother Sebastian, Prospero cannot reshape their inner lives and effect a moral transformation. The most he can do with these men without conscience is to limit through continual vigilance any further harm they might do and to take back what is rightfully his. When, with an obvious effort, Prospero declares that he forgives his brother's "rankest fault" (5.1.134), Antonio is conspicuously silent.

But the higher moral purpose of Prospero's art is not all a failure. With Alonso, the project of provoking repentance by generating intense grief and fear succeeds admirably: Alonso not only gives up his power over the dukedom of Milan but begs Prospero's pardon for the wrong he committed in conspiring to overthrow him. (Both rulers, Alonso and Prospero, can look forward to a unification of their states in the next generation, through the marriage of Ferdinand and Miranda.) Moreover, Prospero's carefully contrived scenarios succeed in confirming the decency, loyalty, and goodness of Alonso's counselor, Gonzalo, who had years before provided the exiled Duke and his daughter with the means necessary for their survival.

It is Gonzalo's goodness that at the end of the play enables him to grasp the providential pattern in the bewildering tangle of events—"Was Milan thrust from Milan, that his issue / Should become kings of Naples?" (5.1.208–9)—and that earlier inspires him to sense the miraculous nature of their survival. Indifferent to the contemptuous mockery of the cynical Antonio and Sebastian, Gonzalo responds to shipwreck on the strange island by speculating on how he would govern it were he responsible for its "plantation":

> I'th' commonwealth I would by contraries
> Execute all things. For no kind of traffic
> Would I admit, no name of magistrate;
> Letters should not be known; riches, poverty,
> And use of service, none; contract, succession,
> Bourn, bound of land, tilth, vineyard, none;
> No use of metal, corn, or wine, or oil;
> No occupation, all men idle, all.
>
> (2.1.147–54)

Shakespeare adapted Gonzalo's utopian speculations from a passage in "Of the Cannibals" (1580), a remarkably free-spirited essay by the French humanist Michel de Montaigne. The Brazilian Indians, Montaigne admiringly writes (in John Florio's 1603 translation), have "no kind of traffic, no knowledge of letters, no intelligence of numbers, no name of magistrate nor of politic superiority, no use of service, of riches or of poverty, no contracts, no successions . . . no occupation but idle, no respect of kindred but common, no apparel but natural, no manuring of lands, no use of wine, corn, or metal." For Montaigne, the European adventurers and colonists, confident in their cultural superiority, are the real barbarians, while the American natives, with their cannibalism and free love, live in accordance with nature.

The issues raised by Montaigne, and more generally by New World voyages, may have been particularly interesting to *The Tempest*'s early audiences as news reached London of the extraordinary adventures of the Virginia Company's colony at Jamestown. Shakespeare seems to have read a detailed account of these adventures in a letter written by the colony's secretary, William Strachey; though the letter was not printed until 1625, it was evidently

America. Engraving by Theodore Galle after a drawing by Jan van der Straet (c. 1580).

circulating in manuscript in 1610. In 1609, a fleet carrying more than four hundred persons sent out to reinforce the colony was struck by a hurricane near the Virginia coast. Two of the vessels reached their destination, but the third, the ship carrying the governor Sir Thomas Gates, ran aground on an uninhabited island in the Bermudas. Remarkably enough, all of the passengers and crew survived; but their tribulations were not over. By forcing everyone to labor side by side in order to survive, the violence of the storm had weakened the governor's authority, and both the natural abundance and the isolation of the island where they were shipwrecked weakened it further. Gates ordered the company to build new ships in order to sail to Jamestown, but his command met with ominous grumblings and threats of mutiny. According to Strachey's letter, the main troublemaker directly challenged Gates's authority: "therefore let the Governour (said he) kiss, etc." In response, Gates had the troublemaker shot to death. New ships were built, and in an impressive feat of navigation, the entire company reached Jamestown. The group found the settlement deeply demoralized: illness was rampant, food was scarce, and relations with the neighboring Indians, once amicable, had completely broken down. Only harsh military discipline kept the English colony from falling apart.

With the possible exception of some phrases from Strachey's description of the storm and a few scattered details, The Tempest does not directly use any of this vivid narrative. Prospero's island is evidently in the Mediterranean, and the New World is only mentioned as a far-off place, "the still-vexed Bermudas" (1.2.230), where the swift Ariel flies to fetch dew. Yet Shakespeare's play seems constantly to echo precisely the issues raised by the Bermuda shipwreck and its aftermath. What does it take to survive? How do men of different classes and moral character react during a state of emergency? What is the proper relation between theoretical understanding and practical experience or between knowledge and power? Is obedience to authority willing or forced? How can those in power protect themselves from the conspiracies of malcontents? Is it possible to detect a providential design in what looks at first like a succession of accidents? If there are natives to contend with, how should colonists establish friendly and profitable relations with them? What is to be done if relations turn sour? How can those who rule prevent an alliance between hostile natives and disgruntled or exploited colonists? And—Montaigne's more radical questions—what is the justification of one person's rule over another? Who is the civilized man and who is the barbarian?

The unregenerate nastiness of Antonio and Sebastian, conjoined with the goodness of Gonzalo, might seem indirectly to endorse Montaigne's critique of the Europeans and his praise of the cannibals, were it not for the menacing presence in The Tempest of the character whose name is almost an anagram for "cannibal," Caliban. Caliban, whose god Setebos is mentioned in accounts of Magellan's voyages as a Patagonian deity, is anything but a noble savage. Shakespeare does not shrink from the darkest European fantasies about the Wild Man. Indeed, he exaggerates them: Caliban is deformed, lecherous, evil smelling, treacherous, naive, drunken, lazy, rebellious, violent, and devil worshipping. According to Prospero, he is not even human: "A devil, a born devil, on whose nature / Nurture can never stick" (4.1.188–89). When he first came to the island, Prospero recalls, he treated Caliban with "human care" (1.2.349), lodging him in his own cell until the savage tried to rape Miranda. The arrival of the other Europeans brings out still worse qualities. Encountering the basest of the company, Alonso's jester, Trinculo, and drunken butler, Stefano, Caliban falls at their feet in brutish worship and then devises a conspiracy to murder Prospero in his sleep. Were the conspiracy to succeed, Caliban would get neither the girl for whom he lusts nor the freedom for which he shouts—he would become "King" Stefano's "foot-licker" (4.1.218)—but he would satisfy the enormous hatred he feels for Prospero.

Prospero's power, Caliban reasons, derives from his superior knowledge. "Remember / First to possess his books," he urges the louts, "for without them / He's but a sot as I am. ... Burn but his books" (3.2.86–90). The strategy is a canny one, but the problem is not only that Stefano and Trinculo are hopeless fools but also that Prospero, like all Renaissance princes, has a diligent spy network: the invisible Ariel overhears the conspirators and warns his master of the approaching danger. Prospero's sudden recollection of the warning leads him to break off the betrothal masque with one of the most famous speeches in all of Shakespeare, "Our revels now are ended" (4.1.148ff.). This brooding meditation on the theatrical insubstantiality of the entire world and the dreamlike nature of human existence has seemed to many the pinnacle of the play's visionary wisdom. But it does not subsume in its rich cadences the other voices in *The Tempest;* specifically, it does not silence the surprising power of Caliban's voice.

Caliban enters the play cursing, grumbling, and above all disputing Prospero's authority: "This island's mine, by Sycorax my mother, / Which thou tak'st from me" (1.2.334–35). By the close, his attempt to kill Prospero foiled and his body racked with cramps and bruises, Caliban declares that he will "be wise hereafter, / And seek for grace" (5.1.298–99). Yet it is not his mumbled reformation but his vehement protests that leave an indelible mark on *The Tempest.* The play may depict Caliban, in Prospero's ugly term, as "filth," but it gives him a remarkable, unforgettable eloquence. To Miranda's taunting reminder that she taught him to speak, Caliban retorts, "You taught me language, and my profit on't / Is I know how to curse" (1.2.366–67). It is not only in cursing, however, that Caliban is gifted: in richly sensuous poetry, he speaks of the island's natural resources and of his dreams. Caliban can be beaten into submission, but the master cannot eradicate his slave's desires, his pleasures, and his inconsolable pain. And across the vast gulf that divides the triumphant prince and the defeated savage, there is a momentary, enigmatic glimpse of a hidden bond: "This thing of darkness," Prospero says of Caliban, "I / Acknowledge mine" (5.1.278–79). The words need only be a claim of ownership, but they seem to hint at a deeper, more disturbing link between father and monster, legitimate ruler and savage, judge and criminal. Perhaps the link is only an illusion, a trick of the imagination on a strange island, but as Prospero leaves the island, it is he who begs for pardon.

STEPHEN GREENBLATT

TEXTUAL NOTE

The only authoritative printed text of *The Tempest* is in the First Folio of 1623 (F), where it appears as the first play, at the head of the comedies. The text seems to have been prepared with care. It includes a list of characters ("*Names of the Actors*") printed at the end of the play and supplies act and scene divisions that this edition follows. There are also unusually full stage directions, though scholars have argued about whether these were written entirely by Shakespeare or were supplied or elaborated by the person who transcribed the author's manuscript for the compositors. Certain features of this transcription have led scholars to the conclusion that it was done by Ralph Crane, an experienced scribe who was responsible for the preparation of at least four other Shakespeare plays.

Most of the songs in *The Tempest* are preserved in early-to-mid-seventeenth-century manuscripts. These manuscripts indicate repeats and refrains, which have accordingly been accepted in the text of this edition.

SELECTED BIBLIOGRAPHY

Barker, Francis, and Peter Hulme. "Nymphs and Reapers Heavily Vanish: The Discursive Con-texts of *The Tempest.*" *Alternative Shakespeares.* Ed. John Drakakis. London: Methuen, 1985. 206–27.

Berger, Harry, Jr. "Miraculous Harp: A Reading of Shakespeare's *Tempest.*" *Shakespeare Studies* 5 (1969): 253–83.

Brown, Paul. " 'This Thing of Darkness I Acknowledge Mine': *The Tempest* and the Discourse of Colonialism." *Political Shakespeare: New Essays in Cultural Materialism.* Ed. Jonathan Dollimore and Alan Sinfield. Ithaca, N.Y.: Cornell University Press, 1985. 48–71.

Fiedler, Leslie A. "The New World Savage as Stranger; or, 'Tis new to thee.' " *The Stranger in Shakespeare.* Frogmore, St. Albans: Paladin, 1974.

Greenblatt, Stephen. "Martial Law in the Land of Cockaigne." *Shakespearean Negotiations.* Berkeley: University of California Press, 1988. 129–63.

Orgel, Stephen. *The Illusion of Power: Political Theatre in the English Renaissance.* Berkeley: University of California Press, 1975.

Skura, Meredith. "Discourse and the Individual: The Case of Colonialism in *The Tempest.*" *Shakespeare Quarterly* 40 (1989): 42–69.

Sundelson, David. "So Rare a Wonder'd Father: Prospero's *Tempest.*" *Representing Shakespeare: New Psychoanalytic Essays.* Ed. Murray Schwartz and Coppélia Kahn. Baltimore: Johns Hopkins University Press, 1980. 33–53.

Spencer, Theodore. *Shakespeare and the Nature of Man.* New York: Macmillan, 1942.

Vaughan, Alden T., and Virginia Mason Vaughan. *Shakespeare's Caliban: A Cultural History.* Cambridge: Cambridge University Press, 1991.

The Tempest

THE PERSONS OF THE PLAY

PROSPERO, the rightful Duke of Milan
MIRANDA, his daughter
ANTONIO, his brother, the usurping Duke of Milan
ALONSO, King of Naples
SEBASTIAN, his brother
FERDINAND, Alonso's son
GONZALO, an honest old counsellor of Naples
ADRIAN ⎱
FRANCISCO ⎰ lords
ARIEL, an airy spirit attendant upon Prospero
CALIBAN, a savage and deformed native of the island, Prospero's slave
TRINCULO, Alonso's jester
STEFANO, Alonso's drunken butler
The MASTER of a ship
BOATSWAIN
MARINERS
SPIRITS
 The Masque
Spirits appearing as:
IRIS
CERES
JUNO
Nymphs, reapers

1.1

A tempestuous noise of thunder and lightning heard.
Enter a SHIPMASTER *and a* BOATSWAIN¹ [*at separate*
doors]

MASTER Boatswain!

BOATSWAIN Here, Master. What cheer?

MASTER Good,² speak to th' mariners. Fall to't yarely,° or we run   *promptly*
  ourselves aground. Bestir, bestir!   *Exit*
  Enter MARINERS

5 BOATSWAIN Heigh, my hearts!° Cheerly, cheerly, my hearts!   *hearties*
  Yare, yare! Take in the topsail!³ Tend° to th' Master's whistle!— *Attend*
  Blow till thou burst thy wind, if room enough.⁴
   Enter ALONSO, SEBASTIAN, ANTONIO, FERDINAND, GON-
   ZALO, *and others*

ALONSO Good Boatswain, have care. Where's the Master?
  [*To the* MARINERS] Play the men!°   *Act like men*

10 BOATSWAIN I pray now, keep below.

ANTONIO Where is the Master, Boatswain?

1.1 Location: A ship at sea.
1. The Boatswain probably enters after the shipmaster calls him; the latter is perhaps on the upper stage.
2. Acknowledging the Boatswain's presence; or perhaps short for "good man."

3. To reduce the surface area of the sail, and thereby lessen the force of the wind pushing the ship toward the island.
4. The wind may blow until it splits itself, provided there is enough sea room to maneuver in.

BOATSWAIN　Do you not hear him? You mar our labour. Keep
　　your cabins; you do assist the storm.
GONZALO　Nay, good,° be patient.　　　　　　　　　　　　　　　*good man*
15　BOATSWAIN　When the sea is. Hence! What cares these roarers
　　for the name of king?[5] To cabin! Silence; trouble us not.
GONZALO　Good, yet remember whom thou hast aboard.
BOATSWAIN　None that I more love than myself. You are a coun-
　　cillor;[6] if you can command these elements to silence and work
20　peace of the present,[7] we will not hand° a rope more. Use your　　　*handle*
　　authority. If you cannot, give thanks you have lived so long and
　　make yourself ready in your cabin for the mischance of the
　　hour, if it so hap. [*To the* MARINERS] Cheerly, good hearts! [*To*
　　GONZALO] Out of our way, I say!　　　　　　　　　　　*Exit*
25　GONZALO　I have great comfort from this fellow. Methinks he
　　hath no drowning mark[8] upon him; his complexion is perfect
　　gallows.[9] Stand fast, good Fate, to his hanging. Make the rope
　　of his destiny our cable,[1] for our own doth little advantage.° If　　　*use*
　　he be not born to be hanged, our case is miserable.
　　　　　　　　　　　　　　　　　　　　　　Exit [*Courtiers*]
　　　　　　Enter BOATSWAIN
30　BOATSWAIN　Down with the topmast![2] Yare! Lower, lower! Bring
　　her to try wi'th' main-course![3]
　　　　　　A cry within
　　A plague upon this howling! They are louder than the weather,
　　or our office.[4]
　　　　　　Enter SEBASTIAN, ANTONIO, *and* GONZALO
　　Yet again? What do you here? Shall we give o'er° and drown?　　　*up*
35　Have you a mind to sink?
SEBASTIAN　A pox o'your throat, you bawling, blasphemous,
　　incharitable dog!
BOATSWAIN　Work you, then.
ANTONIO　Hang, cur, hang, you whoreson insolent noisemaker.
40　We are less afraid to be drowned than thou art.
　　　　　　　　　　　　　　　　　[*Exeunt* MARINERS]
GONZALO　I'll warrant him for drowning,[5] though° the ship were　　　*even if*
　　no stronger than a nutshell and as leaky as an unstanched°　　　*a freely menstruating*
　　wench.
BOATSWAIN　Lay her a-hold, a-hold! Set her two courses![6] Off to
45　sea again! Lay her off!
　　　　　　Enter MARINERS, *wet*
MARINERS　All lost! To prayers, to prayers! All lost!
　　　　　　　　　　　　　　　　　[*Exeunt* MARINERS]
BOATSWAIN　What, must our mouths be cold?[7]
GONZALO　The King and Prince at prayers! Let's assist them,
　　For our case is as theirs.

---

5. "Roarers," referring here to the waves, was also a term
for riotous people.
6. Member of the King's council; also an adviser or per-
suader.
7. Of the present circumstances.
8. Birthmark whose position was held to portend death
by drowning. "He that was born to be hanged will never
be drowned" was proverbial.
9. His physiognomy, appearance, shows that he will cer-
tainly be hanged.
1. Anchor cable (an anchor is actually useless in a storm).
2. To reduce the top weight of the ship and make it more

stable.
3. Bring the ship close to the wind sailing only with the
mainsail. By sailing at an angle into the wind, the ship
can be maneuvered away from the shore.
4. Duties (in shouting orders).
5. I'll guarantee him against drowning.
6. Keep the vessel close to the wind, by setting the fore-
sail in addition to the mainsail.
7. To be cold in the mouth—to be dead—was proverbial;
may also suggest that the mariners warm their mouths
with liquor (line 50).

SEBASTIAN   I'm out of patience.

50 ANTONIO We are merely° cheated of our lives by drunkards.   *utterly*
 This wide-chopped° rascal—would thou mightst lie drowning *large-mouthed*
 The washing of ten tides.[8]

GONZALO   He'll be hanged yet,[9]
 Though every drop of water swear against it
 And gape at wid'st to glut° him.   *its widest to swallow*
   A *confused noise within*

MARINERS [*within*]   Mercy on us!

55 We split, we split! Farewell, my wife and children!
 Farewell, brother! We split, we split, we split![1]

         [*Exit* BOATSWAIN]

ANTONIO Let's all sink wi'th' King.

SEBASTIAN   Let's take leave of him.

     Exit [ANTONIO *and* SEBASTIAN]

GONZALO Now would I give a thousand furlongs of sea for an
 acre of barren ground: long heath, broom, furze,[2] anything.

60 The wills above be done, but I would fain die a dry death.

           Exit

1.2

 Enter PROSPERO [*in his magic cloak, with a staff*], *and*
  MIRANDA

MIRANDA[1] If by your art,[2] my dearest father, you have
 Put the wild waters in this roar, allay them.
 The sky, it seems, would pour down stinking pitch,
 But that the sea, mounting to th' welkin's° cheek,   *sky's*

5 Dashes the fire out. O, I have sufferèd
 With those that I saw suffer! A brave° vessel,   *splendid*
 Who had, no doubt, some noble creature in her,
 Dashed all to pieces! O, the cry did knock
 Against my very heart! Poor souls, they perished.

10 Had I been any god of power, I would
 Have sunk the sea within the earth, or ere°   *before*
 It should the good ship so have swallowed and
 The fraughting souls[3] within her.

PROSPERO[4]   Be collected.
 No more amazement.° Tell your piteous° heart *consternation / pitying*
 There's no harm done.

MIRANDA   O woe the day!

15 PROSPERO   No harm.
 I have done nothing but in care of thee,
 Of thee, my dear one, thee, my daughter, who
 Art ignorant of what thou art, naught knowing
 Of whence I am, nor that I am more better°   *higher in rank*

---

8. Pirates were hanged on the shore at low-water mark
and left there for the ebbing and flowing of three tides.
9. Apparently offered as an opinion differing from Anto-
nio's, suggesting that Gonzalo misses the point of Anto-
nio's allusion to a pirate's hanging.
1. *split*: break apart. If these cries are "confused," they
will have no verse meter; the effect may alternatively be a
stylized one.
2. Heather, yellow shrubs, and gorse—all shrubs that
grow in poor soil.

1.2 Location: The rest of the play is set in various parts
of Prospero's island.
1. "Miranda" in Latin means "admirable" or "wonder-
ful." Miranda uses the formal "you"; contrast with Pros-
pero's more familiar "thou."
2. Skill; magic; learning; science.
3. Souls constituting the freight; perhaps also suggesting
"burdened."
4. "Prospero" in Italian and Spanish means "fortunate"
or "prosperous."

20   Than Prospero, master of a full poor cell[5]
     And thy no greater father.
MIRANDA   More to know
     Did never meddle with° my thoughts.   *intrude upon*
PROSPERO   'Tis time
     I should inform thee farther. Lend thy hand,
     And pluck my magic garment from me.
         [MIRANDA *removes Prospero's cloak, and he lays it on the*
         ground]
                            So.
25   Lie there, my art.—Wipe thou thine eyes; have comfort.
     The direful spectacle of the wreck, which touched
     The very virtue of compassion in thee,
     I have with such provision° in mine art   *foresight*
     So safely ordered that there is no soul—
30   No, not so much perdition° as an hair   *loss*
     Betid° to any creature in the vessel,   *Happened*
     Which° thou heard'st cry, which thou saw'st sink. Sit down,   *Whom*
     For thou must now know farther.
         [MIRANDA *sits*]
MIRANDA   You have often
     Begun to tell me what I am, but stopped
35   And left me to a bootless inquisition,°   *profitless inquiry*
     Concluding 'Stay; not yet'.
PROSPERO   The hour's now come.
     The very minute bids thee ope° thine ear,   *open*
     Obey, and be attentive. Canst thou remember
     A time before we came unto this cell?
40   I do not think thou canst, for then thou wast not
     Out° three years old.   *Fully*
MIRANDA   Certainly, sir, I can.
PROSPERO   By° what? By any other house or person?   *About*
     Of anything the image tell me that
     Hath kept with thy remembrance.
MIRANDA   'Tis far off,
45   And rather like a dream than an assurance°   *a certainty*
     That my remembrance warrants.° Had I not   *guarantees is true*
     Four or five women once that tended me?
PROSPERO   Thou hadst, and more, Miranda. But how is it
     That this lives in thy mind? What seest thou else
50   In the dark backward° and abyss of time?   *past*
     If thou remileb'rest aught° ere thou cam'st here,   *anything*
     How thou cam'st here thou mayst.
MIRANDA   But that I do not.
PROSPERO   Twelve year since, Miranda, twelve year since,
     Thy father was the Duke of Milan,[6] and
     A prince of power—
55 MIRANDA   Sir, are not you my father?
PROSPERO   Thy mother was a piece° of virtue,° and   *perfect example / chastity*
     She said thou wast my daughter; and thy father
     Was Duke of Milan, and his only heir
     And princess no worse issued.°   *no less nobly born*

---

5. Suggesting a hermit's or a poor man's dwelling. *full:*   6. Pronounced with stress on the first syllable.
very.

MIRANDA   O the heavens!
60   What foul play had we that we came from thence?
      Or blessèd° was't we did?   *providential*
PROSPERO   Both, both, my girl.
      By foul play, as thou sayst, were we heaved thence,
      But blessedly holp° hither.   *helped*
MIRANDA   O, my heart bleeds
      To think o'th' teen° that I have turned you to,   *sorrow; trouble*
65   Which is from° my remembrance. Please you, farther.   *out of*
PROSPERO   My brother and thy uncle called Antonio—
      I pray thee mark me, that a brother should
      Be so perfidious—he whom next° thyself   *after*
      Of all the world I loved, and to him put
70   The manage° of my state—as at that time   *control*
      Through all the signories° it was the first,   *lordships*
      And Prospero the prime° duke—being so reputed   *foremost*
      In dignity, and for the liberal arts°   *abstract learning*
      Without a parallel—those being all my study,
75   The government I cast upon my brother,
      And to my state grew stranger, being transported[7]
      And rapt in secret studies. Thy false uncle—
      Dost thou attend me?
MIRANDA   Sir, most heedfully.
PROSPERO   Being once perfected how to grant suits,[8]
80   How to deny them, who t'advance and who
      To trash for over-topping,[9] new created
      The creatures° that were mine, I say—or changed 'em   *dependents*
      Or else new formed 'em;[1] having both the key°   *control*
      Of officer and office, set all hearts i'th' state
85   To what tune pleased his ear, that° now he was   *so that*
      The ivy which had hid my princely trunk
      And sucked my verdure° out on't. Thou attend'st not!   *vitality; power*
MIRANDA   O good sir, I do.
PROSPERO   I pray thee mark me.
      I, thus neglecting worldly ends, all dedicated
90   To closeness° and the bettering of my mind   *seclusion*
      With that which but° by being so retired   *merely*
      O'er-priced all popular rate,[2] in my false brother
      Awaked an evil nature; and my trust,
      Like a good parent,[3] did beget of him
95   A falsehood, in its contrary° as great   *inverse qualities*
      As my trust was, which had indeed no limit,
      A confidence sans° bound. He being thus lorded   *without*
      Not only with what my revenue yielded
      But what my power might else exact, like one
100   Who having into° truth, by telling oft,   *unto*
      Made such a sinner of his memory
      To credit his own lie,[4] he did believe
      He was indeed the Duke. Out o'th'° substitution,   *As a consequence of the*

---

7. Enraptured, with suggestions of "conveyed to another
place." *grew stranger:* grew alienated from; became a for-
eigner to.
8. Having become skillful in handling suitors.
9. For rising too high. *trash:* restrain, hold back (as by a
leash).
1. *changed . . . 'em:* changed the duties and allegiance of

existing officials, or created new ones.
2. Became too precious for the people to value, or under-
stand.
3. From the colloquial "Good parents breed bad chil-
dren."
4. *like one . . . lie:* like someone who comes to believe his
own repeatedly stated lie. *To:* So as to.

	And executing° th'outward face° of royalty	*portraying / image*
105	With all prerogative, hence his ambition growing—	
	Dost thou hear?	
	MIRANDA Your tale, sir, would cure deafness.	
	PROSPERO To have no screen between this part he played	
	And him he played it for, he needs will be	
	Absolute Milan.⁵ Me,° poor man—my library	*As for me*
110	Was dukedom large enough—of temporal royalties°	*rule*
	He thinks me now incapable; confederates,°	*(he) plots*
	So dry° he was for sway,° wi'th' King of Naples	*thirsty / power*
	To give him annual tribute, do him homage,	
	Subject his coronet to his crown,⁶ and bend	
115	The dukedom, yet unbowed—alas, poor Milan—	
	To most ignoble stooping.⁷	
	MIRANDA O the heavens!	
	PROSPERO Mark his condition° and th'event,° then tell me	*treaty / outcome*
	If this might be a brother.	
	MIRANDA I should sin	
	To think but° nobly of my grandmother.	*anything but*
	Good wombs have borne bad sons.⁸	
120	PROSPERO Now the condition.	
	This King of Naples, being an enemy	
	To me inveterate, hearkens my brother's suit;	
	Which was that he, in lieu o'th' premises⁹	
	Of homage and I know not how much tribute,	
125	Should presently extirpate me and mine	
	Out of the dukedom, and confer fair Milan,	
	With all the honours, on my brother. Whereon,	
	A treacherous army levied, one midnight	
	Fated to th' purpose did Antonio open	
130	The gates of Milan; and, i'th' dead of darkness,	
	The ministers° for th' purpose hurried thence	*agents*
	Me and thy crying self.	
	MIRANDA Alack, for pity!	
	I, not rememb'ring how I cried out then,	
	Will cry it o'er again; it is a hint°	*an occasion*
	That wrings mine eyes to't.	
135	PROSPERO [*sitting*] Hear a little further,	
	And then I'll bring thee to the present business	
	Which now's upon's, without the which this story	
	Were most impertinent.°	*irrelevant*
	MIRANDA Wherefore did they not	
	That hour destroy us?	
	PROSPERO Well demanded, wench;¹	
140	My tale provokes that question. Dear, they durst not,	
	So dear the love my people bore me; nor set	
	A mark so bloody on the business, but	
	With colours fairer painted their foul ends.	
	In few,° they hurried us aboard a barque,°	*short / ship*

5. *To have ... Milan:* He wanted to be the Duke of Milan in actual fact, rather than merely exercising power as the Duke's proxy. *screen:* partition, barrier
6. Subject Antonio's coronet to Alonso's crown. *coronet:* a lesser crown indicating the wearer's inferiority to the sovereign.
7. *and bend ... stooping:* by making Milan, previously free, a tributary subject of Naples.
8. Antonio's character need not imply that his mother committed adultery (see line 94).
9. In return for the conditions agreed upon.
1. A young woman; also term of endearment to wife, daughter, or sweetheart.

145 Bore us some leagues to sea, where they prepared
A rotten carcass of a butt,[2] not rigged,
Nor tackle, sail, nor mast—the very rats
Instinctively have quit it. There they hoist us,
To cry to th' sea that roared to us, to sigh
150 To th'winds, whose pity, sighing back again,
Did us but loving wrong.[3]
MIRANDA   Alack, what trouble
Was I then to you!
PROSPERO   O, a cherubin
Thou wast that did preserve me. Thou didst smile,
Infusèd with a fortitude from heaven,
155 When I have decked° the sea with drops full salt,   covered; adorned
Under my burden groaned;[4] which° raised in me   (Miranda's smile)
An undergoing stomach,° to bear up   A courage to endure
Against what should ensue.
MIRANDA   How came we ashore?
160 PROSPERO   By providence divine.
Some food we had, and some fresh water, that
A noble Neapolitan, Gonzalo,
Out of his charity—who being then appointed
Master of this design—did give us; with
165 Rich garments, linens, stuffs, and necessaries
Which since have steaded° much. So, of his gentleness,[5]   been useful
Knowing I loved my books, he furnished me
From mine own library with volumes that
I prize above my dukedom.
MIRANDA   Would I might
But ever see that man!
170 PROSPERO   Now I arise.[6]
          [He stands and puts on his cloak][7]
Sit still,° and hear the last of our sea-sorrow.   Continue to sit
Here in this island we arrived, and here
Have I thy schoolmaster made thee more profit°   profit more
Than other princes[8] can, that have more time
175 For vainer hours and tutors not so careful.°   caring
MIRANDA   Heavens thank you for't. And now I pray you, sir—
For still 'tis beating in my mind—your reason
For raising this sea-storm.
PROSPERO   Know thus far forth.
By accident most strange, bountiful Fortune,
180 Now my dear lady,[9] hath mine enemies
Brought to this shore; and by my prescience
I find my zenith[1] doth depend upon
A most auspicious star,[2] whose influence
If now I court not, but omit,° my fortunes   disregard

2. Cask or tub: here, deprecatory for "boat."
3. The winds, responding sympathetically to our sighs,
only blew us farther out to sea.
4. The secondary sense provides an image of giving birth.
5. Nobility; kindness.
6. Referring to the action of standing; or to Prospero's
rising fortunes (as in lines 179–85). The former might
visually reinforce the latter, especially if Prospero also
resumes his magical powers by putting on his cloak.

7. This direction, necessary before Prospero can charm
Miranda to sleep, follows naturally from the reference to
Prospero's books, his other source of power.
8. princes: a generic plural for "princes and princesses."
9. Traditional characterization of Fortune as a woman
changeable in her affections.
1. Highest point, as of a star in the sky.
2. Referring to the belief that celestial bodies had astro-
logical influence on people and events.

185 Will ever after droop. Here cease more questions.
Thou art inclined to sleep; 'tis a good dullness,°   *drowsiness*
And give it way. I know thou canst not choose.
    [MIRANDA *sleeps*]
Come away,° servant, come! I am ready now.   *Come here*
Approach, my Ariel,³ come!
    Enter ARIEL
190 ARIEL   All hail, great master, grave sir, hail. I come
To answer thy best pleasure. Be't to fly,
To swim, to dive into the fire, to ride
On the curled clouds, to thy strong bidding task
Ariel and all his quality.°   *cohorts; faculties*
PROSPERO   Hast thou, spirit,
195 Performed⁴ to point° the tempest that I bade thee?   *in detail*
ARIEL   To every article.
I boarded the King's ship. Now on the beak,°   *prow*
Now in the waste,° the deck,° in every cabin,   *midship / poop*
I flamed amazement.⁵ Sometime I'd divide,
200 And burn in many places;⁶ on the top-mast,
The yards, and bowsprit, would I flame distinctly;
Then meet and join. Jove's lightning, the precursors
O'th' dreadful thunderclaps, more momentary
And sight-outrunning° were not. The fire and cracks   *quicker than the eye*
205 Of sulphurous⁷ roaring the most mighty Neptune
Seem to besiege, and make his bold waves tremble,
Yea, his dread trident shake.
PROSPERO   My brave spirit!
Who was so firm, so constant, that this coil°   *turmoil*
Would not infect his reason?
ARIEL   Not a soul
210 But felt a fever of the mad,° and played   *such as madmen feel*
Some tricks of desperation. All but mariners
Plunged in the foaming brine and quit the vessel,
Then all afire with me. The King's son Ferdinand,
With hair upstaring°—then like reeds, not hair—   *standing on end*
215 Was the first man that leaped; cried 'Hell is empty,
And all the devils are here'.
PROSPERO   Why, that's my spirit!
But was not this nigh shore?
ARIEL   Close by, my master.
PROSPERO   But are they, Ariel, safe?
ARIEL   Not a hair perished.
On their sustaining⁸ garments not a blemish,
220 But fresher than before. And, as thou bad'st° me,   *commanded*
In troops° I have dispersed them 'bout the isle.   *groups*
The King's son have I landed by himself,
Whom I left cooling of° the air with sighs   *cooling*
In an odd angle° of the isle, and sitting,   *corner*
His arms in this sad knot.⁹

---

3. Ariel's name, along with sounding like "airy," also means in Hebrew "lion of God." The name appears as a magical spirit in various occult texts.
4. Presented; executed.
5. I appeared as flames, causing terror.
6. The phosphorescent effect of St. Elmo's fire, caused in a thunderstorm by the charge of static electricity that builds up particularly around metal projections.
7. Sulphur was popularly associated with thunder and lightning.
8. Buoying up, and thus suggesting "life-giving."
9. Folded sadly, like this (folded arms implied sorrow).

225 PROSPERO   Of the King's ship,
     The mariners, say how thou hast disposed,
     And all the rest o'th' fleet.
     ARIEL   Safely in harbour
     Is the King's ship, in the deep nook where once
     Thou called'st me up at midnight to fetch dew
230 From the still-vexed° Bermudas, there she's hid;   *ever-stormy*
     The mariners all under hatches stowed,
     Who, with° a charm joined to° their suffered labour,   *by virtue of / with*
     I have left asleep. And for the rest o'th' fleet,
     Which I dispersed, they all have met again,
235 And are upon the Mediterranean float°   *billow; sea*
     Bound sadly home for Naples,
     Supposing that they saw the King's ship wrecked,
     And his great person perish.
     PROSPERO   Ariel, thy charge
     Exactly is performed; but there's more work.
     What is the time o'th' day?
240 ARIEL   Past the mid season.°   *noon*
     PROSPERO   At least two glasses.° The time 'twixt six and now   *hourglasses*
     Must by us both be spent most preciously.
     ARIEL   Is there more toil? Since thou dost give me pains,°   *tasks*
     Let me remember° thee what thou hast promised   *remind*
     Which is not yet performed me.
245 PROSPERO   How now? Moody?
     What is't thou canst demand?
     ARIEL   My liberty.
     PROSPERO   Before the time be out? No more!
     ARIEL   I prithee,
     Remember I have done thee worthy service,
     Told thee no lies, made thee no mistakings, served
250 Without or° grudge or grumblings. Thou did promise   *either*
     To bate° me a full year.   *remit; excuse*
     PROSPERO   Dost thou forget
     From what a torment I did free thee?
     ARIEL   No.
     PROSPERO   Thou dost, and think'st it much to tread the ooze
     Of the salt deep,
255 To run upon the sharp wind of the north,
     To do me business in the veins¹ o'th' earth
     When it is baked° with frost.   *dried and hardened*
     ARIEL   I do not, sir.
     PROSPERO   Thou liest, malignant thing. Hast thou forgot
     The foul witch Sycorax, who with age and envy
260 Was grown into a hoop?° Hast thou forgot her?   *bent over with age*
     ARIEL   No, sir.
     PROSPERO   Thou hast. Where was she born? Speak, tell me!
     ARIEL   Sir, in Algiers.
     PROSPERO   O, was she so! I must
     Once in a month recount what thou hast been,
265 Which thou forget'st. This damned witch Sycorax,
     For mischiefs manifold and sorceries terrible
     To enter human hearing, from Algiers

---

1. Mineral veins or subterranean rivers.

Thou know'st was banished. For one thing she did
They would not take her life.[2] Is not this true?
270 ARIEL Ay, sir.
PROSPERO This blue-eyed[3] hag was hither brought with child,
And here was left by th' sailors. Thou, my slave,
As thou report'st thyself, was then her servant;
And for° thou wast a spirit too delicate   *because*
275 To act her earthy[4] and abhorred commands,
Refusing her grand hests,° she did confine thee   *commands*
By help of her more potent ministers,°   *agents; slaves*
And in her most unmitigable rage,
Into a cloven pine; within which rift
280 Imprisoned thou didst painfully remain
A dozen years, within which space she died
And left thee there, where thou didst vent thy groans
As fast as mill-wheels strike.° Then was this island—   *hit the water*
Save for the son that she did litter° here,   *give birth to*
285 A freckled whelp, hag-born—not honoured with
A human shape.
ARIEL   Yes, Caliban her son.
PROSPERO Dull thing, I say so:[5] he, that Caliban
Whom now I keep in service. Thou best know'st
What torment I did find thee in. Thy groans
290 Did make wolves howl, and penetrate° the breasts   *arouse sympathy in*
Of ever-angry bears; it was a torment
To lay upon the damned, which Sycorax
Could not again undo. It was mine art,
When I arrived and heard thee, that made gape
The pine and let thee out.
295 ARIEL   I thank thee, master.
PROSPERO If thou more murmur'st, I will rend an oak,
And peg thee in his° knotty entrails till   *its*
Thou hast howled away twelve winters.
ARIEL   Pardon, master.
I will be correspondent° to command,   *compliant*
300 And do my spriting gently.°   *graciously*
PROSPERO Do so, and after two days
I will discharge thee.[6]
ARIEL   That's my noble master!
What shall I do? Say what, what shall I do?
PROSPERO Go make thyself like to a nymph o'th' sea. Be subject
305 To no sight but thine and mine, invisible
To every eyeball else.[7] Go take this shape,°   *appearance; disguise*
And hither come in't. Go; hence with diligence!   *Exit* [ARIEL]
Awake, dear heart, awake! Thou hast slept well;
Awake.
MIRANDA [*awaking*] The strangeness of your story put
Heaviness° in me.   *Sleepiness*
310 PROSPERO   Shake it off. Come on;

---

2. *For . . . life:* Only because she got pregnant. Capital
sentences were commuted for pregnant women; ordi-
narily, condemned witches were either hanged or burned
at the stake.
3. Blue eyelids were thought to be a sign of pregnancy.
4. Difficult for Ariel, whose element is air.

5. You dullard, that's just what I said.
6. Prospero reduces this to within two days at line 425
and actually releases Ariel in about four hours' time.
7. *Be . . . else:* Ariel may wear a conventional costume,
indicating his invisibility to other characters onstage.

We'll visit Caliban my slave, who never
Yields us kind answer.
MIRANDA   'Tis a villain, sir,
I do not love to look on.
PROSPERO   But as 'tis,
We cannot miss° him. He does make our fire,   avoid; do without
315 Fetch in our wood, and serves in offices°   capacities, duties
That profit us.—What ho! Slave, Caliban!
Thou earth, thou, speak!
CALIBAN (within)   There's wood enough within.
PROSPERO   Come forth, I say! There's other business for thee.
Come, thou tortoise! When?
          Enter ARIEL, *like a water-nymph*
320 Fine apparition! My quaint[8] Ariel,
Hark in thine ear.
          [*He whispers*]
ARIEL   My lord, it shall be done.   *Exit*
PROSPERO   Thou poisonous slave, got° by the devil[9] himself   begot
Upon thy wicked dam,° come forth!   harmful, foul mother
          Enter CALIBAN
CALIBAN   As wicked dew as e'er my mother brushed[1]
325 With raven's feather from unwholesome fen°   bog
Drop on you both! A southwest[2] blow on ye,
And blister you all o'er!
PROSPERO   For this be sure tonight thou shalt have cramps,
Side-stitches that shall pen thy breath up. Urchins[3]
330 Shall forth at vast of° night, that they may work   during the boundless
All exercise on thee.[4] Thou shalt be pinched
As thick as honeycomb,[5] each pinch more stinging
Than bees that made 'em.°   (honeycomb cells)
CALIBAN   I must eat my dinner.
This island's mine, by Sycorax my mother,
335 Which thou tak'st from me. When thou cam'st first,
Thou strok'st° me and made much of me, wouldst give me   stroked
Water with berries in't, and teach me how
To name the bigger light, and how the less,[6]
That burn by day and night; and then I loved thee,
340 And showed thee all the qualities o'th' isle,
The fresh springs, brine-pits, barren place and fertile—
Cursed be I that did so! All the charms°   spells
Of Sycorax, toads, beetles, bats, light on you;
For I am all the subjects that you have,
345 Which first was mine own king, and here you sty me°   pen me up
In this hard rock, whiles you do keep from me
The rest o'th' island.
PROSPERO   Thou most lying slave,
Whom stripes° may move, not kindness! I have used° thee,   lashes / treated

8. The term could simultaneously mean "ingenious," "curious in appearance," and "elegant."
9. Not merely an insult, but also an allusion to Caliban's birth from the devil (incubus) and witch; pronounced as one syllable.
1. Brushed up, collected. Dew was a common ingredient of magical potions.
2. A southerly wind was considered plague-bearing.
3. Hedgehogs; but here indicates spirits disguised as hedgehogs.
4. *that ... thee:* in order that they may perform their habitual activity.
5. *Thou ... honeycomb:* The pinch marks will be as closely packed as, and of similar texture to, the cells of a honeycomb.
6. Recalls Genesis 1:16: "God then made two great lights: the greater light to rule the day, and the less light to rule the night."

Filth as thou art, with human[7] care, and lodged thee
350 In mine own cell, till thou didst seek to violate
The honour of my child.
CALIBAN   O ho, O ho! Would't had been done!
Thou didst prevent me; I had peopled else
This isle with Calibans.
MIRANDA[8] [Prospero]   Abhorrèd slave,
355 Which any print° of goodness wilt not take,   impression
Being capable of° all ill! I pitied thee,   susceptible to
Took pains to make thee speak, taught thee each hour
One thing or other. When thou didst not, savage,
Know thine own meaning, but wouldst gabble like
360 A thing most brutish, I endowed thy purposes
With words that made them known. But thy vile race,°   hereditary nature
Though thou didst learn, had that in't which good natures
Could not abide to be with; therefore wast thou
Deservedly confined into this rock,
365 Who hadst deserved more than a prison.
CALIBAN   You taught me language, and my profit on't
Is I know how to curse. The red plague rid you[9]
For learning me your language!
PROSPERO   Hag-seed,° hence!   Offspring of a hag
Fetch us in fuel. And be quick, thou'rt best,
370 To answer other business.°—Shrug'st thou, malice?   perform other tasks
If thou neglect'st or dost unwillingly
What I command, I'll rack thee with old[1] cramps,
Fill all thy bones with aches,[2] make thee roar,
That beasts shall tremble at thy din.
CALIBAN   No, pray thee.
375 [Aside] I must obey. His art is of such power
It would control my dam's god Setebos,[3]
And make a vassal of him.
PROSPERO   So, slave, hence!   Exit CALIBAN
Enter FERDINAND and ARIEL, invisible, playing and
singing.[4] [PROSPERO and MIRANDA stand aside]

                              Song

ARIEL   Come unto these yellow sands,
                       And then take hands;
380   Curtsied when you have and kissed—
                       The wild waves whist[5]—
                   Foot it featly° here and there,   Dance nimbly
                       And, sweet sprites, bear°   sing
                   The burden.° Hark, hark.   refrain
385 SPIRITS (dispersedly [within])[6]   Bow-wow!
ARIEL   The watch-dogs bark.
SPIRITS [within]   Bow-wow!

---

7. Accented on the first syllable, as usual, with secondary
meaning being "humane."
8. Many editors assign this speech to Prospero, believing
it to be out of character for Miranda.
9. The plague that gives red sores destroy, kill you.
1. As of aged people; long-accustomed.
2. As a noun, this was probably pronounced "aitches."
3. A name found in travel narratives as a god of the Pata-

gonians.
4. This probably does not imply that Ferdinand enters
first, though such a staging is possible if Ferdinand is
bewildered as to where this music is coming from. Ariel
is invisible to all but Prospero and the audience. He is
probably still dressed as a water nymph.
5. Become hushed and attentive.
6. From several directions offstage.

ARIEL   Hark, hark, I hear
               The strain of strutting Chanticleer
390   Cry 'cock-a-diddle-dow'.
FERDINAND   Where should this music be? I'th' air or th'earth?
It sounds no more; and sure it waits° upon   *attends*
Some god o'th' island. Sitting on a bank,
Weeping again the King my father's wreck,
395 This music crept by me upon the waters,
Allaying both their fury and my passion°   *grief*
With its sweet air.° Thence I have followed it—   *melody*
Or it hath drawn me rather. But 'tis gone.
No, it begins again.

Song

400 ARIEL   Full fathom five thy father lies.
               Of his bones are coral made;
               Those are pearls that were his eyes;
               Nothing of him that doth fade
               But doth suffer a sea-change
405   Into something rich and strange.
               Sea-nymphs hourly ring his knell:
SPIRITS [*within*]   Ding dong.
ARIEL   Hark, now I hear them.
SPIRITS [*within*]   Ding-dong bell. [*etc.*]
FERDINAND   The ditty does remember[7] my drowned father.
410 This is no mortal° business, nor no sound   *human; of death*
That the earth owes.°   *owns*
       [*Music*]
               I hear it now above me.
PROSPERO [*to* MIRANDA]   The fringèd curtains of thine eye advance,°   *raise*
And say what thou seest yon.
MIRANDA   What is't? A spirit?
Lord, how it looks about!° Believe me, sir,   *around*
415 It carries a brave° form. But 'tis a spirit.   *splendid, gallant*
PROSPERO   No, wench, it eats and sleeps, and hath such senses
As we have, such. This gallant° which thou seest   *fine gentleman*
Was in the wreck, and but° he's something° stained   *except that / somewhat*
With grief, that's beauty's canker,[8] thou mightst call him
420 A goodly person. He hath lost his fellows,
And strays about to find 'em.
MIRANDA   I might call him
A thing divine, for nothing natural
I ever saw so noble.
PROSPERO [*aside*][9]   It° goes on, I see,   *(My plan)*
As my soul prompts it. [*To* ARIEL] Spirit, fine spirit, I'll free thee
Within two days for this.
425 FERDINAND [*aside*]   Most sure the goddess
On whom these airs attend.[1] [*To* MIRANDA] Vouchsafe° my prayer   *Grant*
May know if you remain° upon this island,   *dwell*

---

7. Commemorate. *ditty*: the words of the song.
8. Cankerworm; caterpillar ("beauty" being seen as a flower); spreading sore.
9. Prospero's asides here and at lines 442, 454, and 497 may be either private utterances or addressed to Ariel. If the former, Ariel may nevertheless hear them; Prospero

speaks to Ariel after all these instances. Their import may well be purposefully enigmatic.
1. *Most . . . attend*: probably spoken aside, but possibly an invocation. *Most sure the goddess*: echoes Aeneas's reaction to seeing Venus after his shipwreck, "o dea certe" (*Aeneid* l. 328). *airs*: Ariel's melodies.

And that you will some good instruction give
How I may bear me° here. My prime request,   *conduct myself*
430   Which I do last pronounce, is—O you wonder²—
       If you be maid³ or no?

MIRANDA   No wonder, sir,
       But certainly a maid.
FERDINAND   My language! Heavens!
       I am the best⁴ of them that speak this speech,
       Were I but where 'tis spoken.
PROSPERO   How, the best?
435   What wert thou if the King of Naples heard thee?
FERDINAND   A single⁵ thing, as I am now that wonders
       To hear thee speak of Naples. He does hear me,⁶
       And that he does I weep. Myself am Naples,°   *King of Naples*
       Who with mine eyes, never since at ebb,° beheld   *ceasing to flow*
       The King my father wrecked.
440   MIRANDA   Alack, for mercy!
FERDINAND   Yes, faith, and all his lords, the Duke of Milan
       And his brave son⁷ being twain.
PROSPERO [*aside*]   The Duke of Milan
       And his more braver daughter could control⁸ thee,
       If now 'twere fit to do't. At the first sight
445   They have changed eyes.⁹—Delicate° Ariel,   *Graceful; artful*
       I'll set thee free for this. [*To* FERDINAND] A word, good sir.
       I fear you have done yourself some wrong.¹ A word.
MIRANDA [*aside*]   Why speaks my father so ungently?° This   *discourteously*
       Is the third man that e'er I saw, the first
450   That e'er I sighed for. Pity move my father
       To be inclined my way.
FERDINAND   O, if a virgin,
       And your affection not gone forth,² I'll make you
       The Queen of Naples.
PROSPERO   Soft, sir! One word more.
       [*Aside*] They are both in either's powers. But this swift business
455   I must uneasy° make, lest too light³ winning   *difficult*
       Make the prize light. [*To* FERDINAND] One word more. I charge thee
       That thou attend me. Thou dost here usurp
       The name thou ow'st° not; and hast put thyself   *own*
       Upon this island as a spy, to win it
       From me the lord on't.°   *of it*
460   FERDINAND   No, as I am a man.
MIRANDA   There's nothing ill can dwell in such a temple.⁴
       If the ill spirit have so fair a house,
       Good things will strive to dwell with't.
PROSPERO [*to* FERDINAND]   Follow me.
       [*To* MIRANDA] Speak not you for him; he's a traitor. [*To* FERDINAND] Come!

---

2. Miracle, punning on the meaning of Miranda's name.
3. Unmarried virgin; made (human).
4. Highest in rank, assuming he has succeeded his father.
5. Weak and helpless; solitary; one and the same.
6. "He" and "me" both refer to Ferdinand. Presuming his father to be dead, Ferdinand takes himself to be the new King of Naples (and as such, he hears himself speaking).
7. The only instance in which Antonio is mentioned as having a son.

8. Challenge, take to task; exercise power over.
9. Exchanged loving glances; fallen in love at first sight.
1. Euphemistic for "told a lie about yourself."
2. Given over to someone else.
3. Easy; playing on the meanings of "little valued" and also "promiscuous" in line 456.
4. A common metaphor for the body; also a conventional Renaissance notion that moral qualities were physically manifest.

465 I'll manacle thy neck and feet together.
     Sea-water shalt thou drink; thy food shall be
     The fresh-brook mussels,⁵ withered roots, and husks
     Wherein the acorn cradled. Follow!
FERDINAND   No.
     I will resist such entertainment° till   *treatment*
     Mine enemy has more power.
                He draws, and is charmed from moving
470 MIRANDA   O dear father,
     Make not too rash a trial of him, for
     He's gentle, and not fearful.⁶
PROSPERO   What, I say,
     My foot° my tutor? Put thy sword up, traitor,   *inferior*
     Who mak'st a show but dar'st not strike, thy conscience
475 Is so possessed with guilt. Come from thy ward,°   *defensive stance*
     For I can here disarm thee with this stick°   *magician's wand*
     And make thy weapon drop.
MIRANDA   Beseech you, father!
PROSPERO   Hence! Hang not on my garments.
MIRANDA   Sir, have pity.
     I'll be his surety.
PROSPERO   Silence! One word more
480 Shall make me chide thee, if not hate thee. What,
     An advocate for an impostor? Hush!
     Thou think'st there is no more such shapes° as he,   *forms; men*
     Having seen but him and Caliban. Foolish wench!
     To° th' most of men this is a Caliban,   *Compared to*
     And they to him are angels.
485 MIRANDA   My affections
     Are then most humble. I have no ambition
     To see a goodlier man.
PROSPERO [*to* FERDINAND] Come on; obey.
     Thy nerves° are in their infancy again,   *sinews*
     And have no vigour in them.
FERDINAND   So they are.
490 My spirits,° as in a dream, are all bound up.   *mental powers*
     My father's loss, the weakness which I feel,
     The wreck of all my friends, nor this man's threats
     To whom I am subdued, are but light to me,
     Might I but through my prison once a day
495 Behold this maid. All corners else° o'th' earth   *All other places*
     Let liberty make use of; space enough
     Have I in such a prison.
PROSPERO [*aside*]   It works. [*To* ARIEL] Come on.—
     Thou hast done well, fine Ariel. [*To* FERDINAND] Follow me.
     [*To* ARIEL] Hark what thou else shalt do me.
MIRANDA [*to* FERDINAND]   Be of comfort.
500 My father's of a better nature, sir,
     Than he appears by speech. This is unwonted°   *unusual*
     Which now came from him.
PROSPERO [*to* ARIEL]   Thou shalt be as free
     As mountain winds; but then° exactly do   *until then*
     All points of my command.

---

5. Freshwater mussels are inedible.   6. He's noble, and therefore not cowardly.

505 ARIEL To th' syllable.
   PROSPERO [to FERDINAND] Come, follow. [To MIRANDA] Speak
       not for him.   *Exeunt*

2.1

Enter ALONSO, SEBASTIAN, ANTONIO, GONZALO, ADRIAN,
   and FRANCISCO

GONZALO [to ALONSO] Beseech you, sir, be merry. You have cause,
   So have we all, of joy; for our escape
   Is much beyond our loss. Our hint° of woe   occasion
   Is common; every day some sailor's wife,
5 The masters of some merchant, and the merchant,[1]
   Have just° our theme of woe. But for the miracle,   exactly
   I mean our preservation, few in millions
   Can speak like us. Then wisely, good sir, weigh
   Our sorrow with° our comfort.   against
ALONSO   Prithee, peace.[2]
10 SEBASTIAN [to ANTONIO] He receives comfort like cold porridge.° broth
ANTONIO The visitor[3] will not give him o'er so.°   leave him alone
SEBASTIAN Look, he's winding up the watch of his wit. By and
   by it will strike.
GONZALO [to ALONSO] Sir—
15 SEBASTIAN [to ANTONIO] One: tell.°   keep count
GONZALO [to ALONSO] When every grief is entertained° that's   harbored
       offered,
   Comes to th'entertainer[4]—
SEBASTIAN A dollar.
GONZALO Dolour° comes to him indeed. You have spoken truer   Sorrow
20   than you purposed.
SEBASTIAN You have taken it wiselier than I meant you should.
GONZALO [to ALONSO] Therefore my lord—
ANTONIO [to SEBASTIAN] Fie, what a spendthrift is he of his
       tongue!
25 ALONSO [to GONZALO] I prithee, spare.°   spare your words
GONZALO Well, I have done. But yet—
SEBASTIAN [to ANTONIO] He will be talking.
ANTONIO Which of he or Adrian, for a good wager, first begins
       to crow?[5]
30 SEBASTIAN The old cock.
ANTONIO The cockerel.[6]
SEBASTIAN Done. The wager?
ANTONIO A laughter.[7]
SEBASTIAN A match!
35 ADRIAN [to GONZALO] Though this island seem to be desert°—   uninhabited
ANTONIO [to SEBASTIAN] Ha, ha, ha!
SEBASTIAN So, you're paid.[8]
ADRIAN Uninhabitable, and almost inaccessible—
SEBASTIAN [to ANTONIO] Yet—
40 ADRIAN Yet—

2.1
1. The owners of some merchant ship and the owner of
its cargo.
2. Sebastian takes this as "pease," as in "pease porridge."
3. Antonio compares Gonzalo with one who visits and
comforts the sick and distressed.
4. There comes to the person who accepts that grief.

5. Which of the two will first begin to speak ("crow")?
6. "The young cock crows as the old hears" was prover-
bial. "Old cock" refers to Gonzalo and "cockerel" to
Adrian.
7. From the proverb "He laughs that wins."
8. Antonio's laugh is his prize.

ANTONIO [*to* SEBASTIAN]   He could not miss't.

ADRIAN   It must needs be of subtle, tender, and delicate[9] temperance.°   *climate*

ANTONIO [*to* SEBASTIAN]   Temperance was a delicate wench.[1]

45 SEBASTIAN   Ay, and a subtle, as he most learnedly delivered.[2]

ADRIAN [*to* GONZALO]   The air breathes upon us here most sweetly.

SEBASTIAN [*to* ANTONIO]   As if it had lungs, and rotten ones.

ANTONIO   Or as 'twere perfumed by a fen.°   *bog*

50 GONZALO [*to* ADRIAN]   Here is everything advantageous to life.

ANTONIO [*to* SEBASTIAN]   True, save° means to live.   *except*

SEBASTIAN   Of that there's none, or little.

GONZALO [*to* ADRIAN]   How lush and lusty° the grass looks!   *tender and luxuriant* How green!

55 ANTONIO   The ground indeed is tawny.

SEBASTIAN   With an eye[3] of green in't.

ANTONIO   He misses not much.

SEBASTIAN   No, he doth but mistake the truth totally.

GONZALO [*to* ADRIAN]   But the rarity[4] of it is, which is indeed

60 almost beyond credit—

SEBASTIAN [*to* ANTONIO]   As many vouched° rarities are.   *alleged, accepted*

GONZALO [*to* ADRIAN]   That our garments being, as they were, drenched in the sea, hold notwithstanding their freshness and glosses, being rather new-dyed than stained with salt water.

65 ANTONIO [*to* SEBASTIAN]   If but one of his pockets[5] could speak, would it not say he lies?

SEBASTIAN   Ay, or very falsely pocket up his report.[6]

GONZALO [*to* ADRIAN]   Methinks our garments are now as fresh as when we put them on first in Afric, at the marriage of the

70 King's fair daughter Claribel to the King of Tunis.

SEBASTIAN   'Twas a sweet marriage, and we prosper well in our return.

ADRIAN   Tunis was never graced before with such a paragon to°   *for* their queen.

75 GONZALO   Not since widow Dido's[7] time.

ANTONIO [*to* SEBASTIAN]   Widow?[8] A pox o'that! How came that 'widow' in? Widow Dido!

SEBASTIAN   What if he had said 'widower Aeneas' too? Good Lord, how you take° it!   *fuss about*

80 ADRIAN [*to* GONZALO]   'Widow Dido' said you? You make me study of° that: she was of Carthage, not of Tunis.   *examine*

GONZALO   This Tunis, sir, was Carthage.[9]

ADRIAN   Carthage?

GONZALO   I assure you, Carthage.

---

9. Exquisite, but in Antonio's usage (line 44), "given to pleasure." *subtle*: fine, but in Sebastian's usage (line 45), "sexually expert" or "crafty."

1. Antonio takes "Temperance" to be the name of a girl. *delicate*: voluptuous, given to pleasure.

2. "Learnedly delivered" was a popular phrase among Puritans who wanted to appear pious.

3. A tinge. In Antonio's reply, an "eye of green" refers to Gonzalo's optimistic capacity to see green.

4. Exceptional quality; but in Sebastian's usage (line 61), "uncommon thing."

5. Seen as the garments' "mouth"; also implying that

Gonzalo's pockets are stained.

6. The evidence of stained pockets would confute Gonzalo's words and reputation for honesty. *to pocket up*: to suppress, or keep silent; also, to receive unprotestingly.

7. Queen of ancient Carthage, whose tragic love affair with Aeneas is related in Virgil's *Aeneid*.

8. Antonio picks on this designation for a woman abandoned by her lover as being either irrelevant or conspicuously prudish. Dido, however, was in fact a widow when she met Aeneas.

9. The city of Tunis was actually built ten miles from the site of Carthage.

85 ANTONIO [to SEBASTIAN] His word is more than the miraculous
 harp.[1]
 SEBASTIAN He hath raised the wall, and houses too.
 ANTONIO What impossible matter will he make easy next?
 SEBASTIAN I think he will carry this island home in his pocket,
90 and give it his son for an apple.
 ANTONIO And sowing the kernels° of it in the sea, bring forth   seeds
 more islands.
 GONZALO [to ADRIAN] Ay.[2]
 ANTONIO [to SEBASTIAN] Why, in good time.
95 GONZALO [to ALONSO] Sir, we were talking that our garments
 seem now as fresh as when we were at Tunis, at the marriage
 of your daughter, who is now queen.
 ANTONIO And the rarest that e'er came there.
 SEBASTIAN Bate,[3] I beseech you, widow Dido.
100 ANTONIO O, widow Dido? Ay, widow Dido.
 GONZALO [to ALONSO] Is not, sir, my doublet as fresh as the first
 day I wore it? I mean in a sort.[4]
 ANTONIO [to SEBASTIAN] That 'sort' was well fished for.
 GONZALO [to ALONSO] When I wore it at your daughter's
105 marriage.
 ALONSO You cram these words into mine ears against
 The stomach of my sense.[5] Would I had never
 Married my daughter there! For, coming thence,
 My son is lost; and, in my rate,° she too,   consideration
110 Who is so far from Italy removed
 I ne'er again shall see her. O thou mine heir
 Of Naples and of Milan, what strange fish
 Hath made his meal on thee?
 FRANCISCO   Sir, he may live.
 I saw him beat the surges under him
115 And ride upon their backs. He trod the water,
 Whose enmity he flung aside, and breasted
 The surge, most swoll'n, that met him. His bold head
 'Bove the contentious waves he kept, and oared
 Himself with his good arms in lusty° stroke   vigorous
120 To th' shore, that o'er his wave-worn basis bowed,[6]
 As° stooping to relieve him. I not° doubt   As if / do not
 He came alive to land.
 ALONSO   No, no; he's gone.
 SEBASTIAN [to ALONSO] Sir, you may thank yourself for this great loss,
 That would not bless our Europe with your daughter,
125 But rather loose° her to an African,   lose; release
 Where she, at least, is banished from your eye,
 Who° hath cause to wet the grief° on't.   (Claribel) / weep
 ALONSO   Prithee, peace.
 SEBASTIAN You were kneeled to and importuned otherwise[7]
 By all of us, and the fair soul herself
130 Weighed between loathness and obedience at

---

1. Referring to Amphion's harp, to the music of which
the walls (but not the houses) of Thebes arose.
2. Affirming his belief that Tunis was Carthage; Antonio
mocks the length of time this took.
3. Except (as a verb); don't mention.
4. Comparatively speaking; Antonio plays on "drawing
lots."

5. *You ... sense:* the image is of one being force-fed
words against the appetite ("stomach") for hearing them.
6. *that ... bowed:* that extended out and drooped over
the foot of the cliff, which had been eroded by waves.
7. *otherwise:* to act differently. "Importuned" is accented
on the second syllable.

Which end o'th' beam should bow.[8] We have lost your son,
I fear, for ever. Milan and Naples have
More widows in them of this business' making
Than we bring men to comfort them. The fault's your own.
ALONSO So is the dear'st o'th' loss.[9]
GONZALO   My lord Sebastian,
The truth you speak doth lack some gentleness
And time to speak it in. You rub the sore[1]
When you should bring the plaster.
SEBASTIAN [*to* ANTONIO] Very well.
ANTONIO And most chirurgeonly.°   *surgeon-like*
GONZALO [*to* ALONSO] It is foul weather in us all, good sir,
   When you are cloudy.
SEBASTIAN [*to* ANTONIO] Fowl weather?[2]
ANTONIO   Very foul.
GONZALO [*to* ALONSO] Had I plantation[3] of this isle, my lord—
ANTONIO [*to* SEBASTIAN] He'd sow't with nettle-seed.
SEBASTIAN   Or docks,
      or mallows.[4]
GONZALO And were the king on't, what would I do?
SEBASTIAN [*to* ANTONIO] Scape being drunk, for want of wine.
GONZALO I'th' commonwealth I would by contraries
   Execute all things.[5] For no kind of traffic°   *commerce*
   Would I admit, no name of magistrate;
   Letters° should not be known; riches, poverty,   *Writing; erudition*
   And use of service,° none; contract, succession,[6]   *servants*
   Bourn,° bound of land, tilth,° vineyard, none;   *Boundary / tillage*
   No use of metal, corn,° or wine, or oil;   *grain*
   No occupation, all men idle, all;
   And women too—but innocent and pure;[7]
   No sovereignty—
SEBASTIAN [*to* ANTONIO] Yet he would be king on't.
ANTONIO The latter end of his commonwealth forgets the
   beginning.
GONZALO [*to* ALONSO] All things in common° nature should   *for communal use*
      produce
   Without sweat or endeavour. Treason, felony,
   Sword, pike, knife, gun, or need of any engine,°   *weapon*
   Would I not have; but nature should bring forth
   Of it° own kind all foison,° all abundance,   *its / plenty*
   To feed my innocent people.
SEBASTIAN [*to* ANTONIO] No marrying[8] 'mong his subjects?
ANTONIO None, man, all idle: whores and knaves.
GONZALO [*to* ALONSO] I would with such perfection govern, sir,
   T'excel the Golden Age.[9]

8. Weighed . . . *bow*: Weighed loathness to marry against obedience to her father to find out which end of the scales' beam would sink.
9. That is the most grievous, or costliest part of the loss.
1. "To rub the sore" was proverbial. *plaster* (line 138): a soothing remedy.
2. Perhaps recalling lines 28–31.
3. Had I responsibility for colonization of the island, but also interpreted as "planting" by Antonio and Sebastian.
4. Cited as wild plants prone to grow on uncultivated land, but dock is a traditional soother of nettle stings, and mallow roots were used to make soothing ointment.

5. *I would . . . things*: I would advance the opposite to what would be usual. This speech is based on a passage in John Florio's translation of Montaigne's essay "Of the Cannibals."
6. Inheritance of property.
7. Idleness proverbially begets lust.
8. Seen as irrelevant to sexually innocent people; also a form of contract (line 151).
9. In classical mythology, the earliest of the ages—a time without strife, labor, or injustice, when abundant food grew without cultivation.

SEBASTIAN   Save° his majesty!   *God save*
ANTONIO   Long live Gonzalo!
GONZALO [*to* ALONSO]   And—do you mark me, sir?
170 ALONSO   Prithee, no more. Thou dost talk nothing to me.
GONZALO   I do well believe your highness, and did it to minister
   occasion[1] to these gentlemen, who are of such sensible° and   *sensitive*
   nimble lungs that they always use° to laugh at nothing.   *are accustomed*
ANTONIO   'Twas you we laughed at.
175 GONZALO   Who, in this kind of merry fooling, am nothing to
   you. So you may continue, and laugh at nothing still.
ANTONIO   What a blow was there given!
SEBASTIAN   An it had not fallen flat-long.[2]
GONZALO   You are gentlemen of brave mettle.[3] You would lift
180   the moon out of her sphere, if she would continue in it five
   weeks without changing.[4]
        Enter ARIEL, [*invisible,*] *playing solemn music*
SEBASTIAN   We would so, and then go a-bat-fowling.[5]
ANTONIO [*to* GONZALO]   Nay, good my lord, be not angry.
GONZALO   No, I warrant you, I will not adventure my discretion
185   so weakly.[6] Will you laugh me asleep? For I am very heavy.°   *tired; serious*
ANTONIO   Go sleep, and hear us.
        [GONZALO, ADRIAN, *and* FRANCISCO *sleep*]
ALONSO   What, all so soon asleep? I wish mine eyes
   Would, with themselves, shut up my thoughts.—I find
   They are inclined to do so.
SEBASTIAN   Please you, sir,
190 Do not omit° the heavy offer° of it.   *neglect / opportunity*
   It seldom visits sorrow; when it doth,
   It is a comforter.
ANTONIO   We two, my lord,
   Will guard your person while you take your rest,
   And watch your safety.
ALONSO   Thank you. Wondrous heavy.
        [*He sleeps. Exit* ARIEL]
195 SEBASTIAN   What a strange drowsiness possesses them!
ANTONIO   It is the quality o'th' climate.
SEBASTIAN   Why
   Doth it not then our eyelids sink? I find
   Not myself disposed to sleep.
ANTONIO   Nor I; my spirits are nimble.
   They fell together all, as by consent;°   *consensus*
200 They dropped as by a thunderstroke. What might,
   Worthy Sebastian, O, what might—? No more!—
   And yet methinks I see it in thy face.
   What thou shouldst be th'occasion speaks° thee, and   *opportunity reveals to*
   My strong imagination sees a crown
   Dropping upon thy head.
205 SEBASTIAN   What, art thou waking?°   *awake*
ANTONIO   Do you not hear me speak?

---

1. *minister occasion:* afford opportunity.
2. If it had not fallen on the flat, harmless side of the sword.
3. Courage; punning on "metal," as of a sword blade.
4. *You would ... changing:* If the moon were to remain in her orbit ("sphere") one week longer than usual (five weeks), you would steal her from her place.
5. Trapping birds by using light to attract them and bats to strike them down; may also mean swindling and victimizing the simple.
6. I will not put my sound judgment at risk so foolishly.

SEBASTIAN   I do, and surely
It is a sleepy language, and thou speak'st
Out of thy sleep. What is it thou didst say?
This is a strange repose, to be asleep
210 With eyes wide open; standing, speaking, moving,
And yet so fast asleep.
ANTONIO   Noble Sebastian,
Thou letst thy fortune sleep, die rather; wink'st°   *shut your eyes*
Whiles thou art waking.
SEBASTIAN   Thou dost snore distinctly;°   *meaningfully*
There's meaning in thy snores.
215 ANTONIO I am more serious than my custom. You
Must be so too if heed° me, which to do   *if you heed*
Trebles thee o'er.
SEBASTIAN   Well, I am standing water.[7]
ANTONIO I'll teach you how to flow.
SEBASTIAN   Do so; to ebb
Hereditary sloth[8] instructs me.
ANTONIO   O,
220 If you but knew how you the purpose cherish
Whiles thus you mock it;[9] how in stripping it
You more invest° it! Ebbing° men, indeed,   *clothe / Declining*
Most often do so near the bottom run
By their own fear or sloth.
SEBASTIAN   Prithee, say on.
225 The setting° of thine eye and cheek proclaim   *fixed look*
A matter° from thee, and a birth, indeed,   *Something important*
Which throes[1] thee much to yield.
ANTONIO   Thus, sir.
Although this lord° of weak remembrance,° this, *(Gonzalo) / memory*
Who shall be of as little memory°   *remembered*
230 When he is earthed,° hath here almost persuaded— *buried*
For he's a spirit of persuasion, only
Professes[2] to persuade—the King his son's alive,
'Tis as impossible that he's undrowned
As he that sleeps here swims.
SEBASTIAN   I have no hope
That he's undrowned.
235 ANTONIO   O, out of that 'no hope'
What great hope have you! No hope that way° is *(that he's not drowned)*
Another way so high a hope that even
Ambition cannot pierce a wink° beyond,   *catch a glimpse*
But doubt discovery there.[3] Will you grant with me
That Ferdinand is drowned?
SEBASTIAN   He's gone.
240 ANTONIO   Then tell me,
Who's the next heir of Naples?
SEBASTIAN   Claribel.

---

7. Between tides, and thus open to suggestion; also associated with being slothful. *Trebles thee o'er:* Makes you three times as great.
8. Inherited laziness, or the slowness to attain prosperity arising from being born a younger brother.
9. *If . . . it:* If you only understood that your mockery reveals how great your aspirations really are; also, the

hereditary position you mock is actually to your advantage. *cherish:* hold dear; cultivate.
1. Which puts in agony, as in childbirth.
2. *only / Professes:* his sole vocation is.
3. Doubt that there is anything to achieve beyond the high hope of the crown.

ANTONIO   She that is Queen of Tunis; she that dwells
Ten leagues beyond man's life;° she that from Naples   *lifetime journey*
Can have no note°—unless the sun were post°—   *information / messenger*
245   The man i'th' moon's too slow—till new-born chins
Be rough and razorable; she that from° whom   *returning from*
We all were sea-swallowed, though some cast again⁴—
And by that destiny, to perform an act
Whereof what's past is prologue, what to come
In yours and my discharge.°   *performance*
250   SEBASTIAN   What stuff is this? How say you?
'Tis true my brother's daughter's Queen of Tunis;
So is she heir of Naples; 'twixt which regions
There is some space.
ANTONIO   A space whose every cubit°   *about 18–22 inches*
Seems to cry out 'How shall that Claribel
255   Measure us° back to Naples? Keep° in Tunis,   *(the cubits) / Stay*
And let Sebastian wake.'° Say this were death   *(to his opportunity)*
That now hath seized them; why, they were no worse
Than now they are. There be that° can rule Naples   *those that*
As well as he that sleeps, lords that can prate
260   As amply and unnecessarily
As this Gonzalo; I myself could make
A chough of as deep chat.⁵ O, that you bore
The mind that I do, what a sleep were this
For your advancement! Do you understand me?
SEBASTIAN   Methinks I do.
265   ANTONIO   And how does your content
Tender° your own good fortune?   *Regard; care for*
SEBASTIAN   I remember
You did supplant your brother Prospero.
ANTONIO   True;
And look how well my garments sit upon me,
Much feater° than before. My brother's servants   *more trimly*
270   Were then my fellows; now they are my men.
SEBASTIAN   But for your conscience.
ANTONIO   Ay, sir, where lies that? If 'twere a kibe⁶
'Twould put me to° my slipper; but I feel not   *make me wear*
This deity in my bosom. Twenty consciences
275   That stand 'twixt me and Milan, candied⁷ be they,
And melt° ere they molest. Here lies your brother,   *melted; dissolved*
No better than the earth he lies upon
If he were that which now he's like—that's dead;
Whom I with this obedient steel,° three inches of it,   *sword*
280   Can lay to bed for ever; whiles you, doing thus,
To the perpetual wink for aye° might put   *sleep forever*
This ancient morsel, this Sir Prudence, who
Should not upbraid our course. For all the rest,
They'll take suggestion° as a cat laps milk;   *prompting to evil*
285   They'll tell the clock° to any business that   *chime; agree*
We say befits the hour.
SEBASTIAN   Thy case, dear friend,

---

4. Regurgitated, cast ashore; also, possibly, theatrical role-
playing.
5. *I . . . chat:* I could train a jackdaw (known for imitating

speech) to speak as profoundly.
6. Chilblain; sore on the heel.
7. Turned to sugar; crystallized in sugar.

Shall be my precedent. As thou got'st Milan,
I'll come by Naples. Draw thy sword. One stroke
Shall free thee from the tribute which thou payest,
And I the King shall love thee.

290 ANTONIO   Draw together,
And when I rear my hand, do you the like
To fall it on Gonzalo.
           [*They draw*]
SEBASTIAN   O, but one word.
           Enter ARIEL, [*invisible,*] *with music and song*
ARIEL [*to* GONZALO]   My master through his art foresees the danger
That you his friend are in—and sends me forth,
295 For else° his project dies, to keep them[8] living.   *otherwise*
           [*He*] *sings in Gonzalo's ear*
                    While you here do snoring lie,
                    Open-eyed conspiracy
                         His time° doth take.   *opportunity*
                    If of life you keep a care,
300   Shake off slumber, and beware.
                         Awake, awake!
ANTONIO [*to* SEBASTIAN]   Then let us both be sudden.
GONZALO [*awaking*]   Now good angels
Preserve the King!
ALONSO [*awaking*]   Why, how now? Ho, awake!
           [*The others awake*]
           [*To* ANTONIO *and* SEBASTIAN]   Why are you° drawn?   *your weapons*
           [*To* GONZALO] Wherefore this ghastly° looking?   *fearful*
305 GONZALO   What's the matter?
SEBASTIAN   Whiles we stood here securing° your repose,   *guarding*
Even now we heard a hollow burst of bellowing,
Like bulls, or rather lions. Did't not wake you?
It struck mine ear most terribly.
ALONSO   I heard nothing.
310 ANTONIO   O, 'twas a din to fright a monster's ear,
To make an earthquake! Sure it was the roar
Of a whole herd of lions.
ALONSO   Heard you this, Gonzalo?
GONZALO   Upon mine honour, sir, I heard a humming,
And that a strange one too, which did awake me.
315 I shaked you, sir, and cried.° As mine eyes opened   *called out*
I saw their weapons drawn. There was a noise,
That's verily.° 'Tis best we stand upon our guard,   *the truth*
Or that we quit this place. Let's draw our weapons.
ALONSO   Lead off this ground, and let's make further search
For my poor son.
320 GONZALO   Heavens keep him from these beasts!
For he is sure i'th' island.
ALONSO   Lead away.   [*Exeunt all but* ARIEL][9]
ARIEL   Prospero my lord shall know what I have done.
So, King, go safely on to seek thy son.   *Exit*

---

8. Gonzalo and Alonso.
9. Ariel's following lines are spoken as the other characters depart; he probably exits in another direction.

2.2

Enter CALIBAN, [*wearing a gaberdine,*[1] *and*] *with a bur-*
den of wood

CALIBAN [*throwing down his burden*]   All the infections that the
    sun sucks up
From bogs, fens, flats,° on Prosper fall, and make him   *marshes*
By inch-meal° a disease!   *inch by inch*
    [*A noise of thunder heard*][2]
                His spirits hear me,
And yet I needs must curse. But they'll nor pinch,
5 Fright me with urchin-shows,[3] pitch me i'th' mire,
Nor lead me like a fire-brand in the dark
Out of my way, unless he bid 'em. But
For every trifle are they set upon me;
Sometime like apes, that mow° and chatter at me   *grimace*
10 And after bite me; then like hedgehogs, which
Lie tumbling in my barefoot way and mount
Their pricks at my footfall; sometime am I
All wound with° adders, who with cloven tongues   *entwined by*
Do hiss me into madness.
    Enter TRINCULO[4]
             Lo now, lo!
15 Here comes a spirit of his, and to torment me
For bringing wood in slowly. I'll fall flat.
Perchance he will not mind° me.   *notice*
    [*He lies down*]
TRINCULO   Here's neither bush nor shrub to bear off° any   *ward off*
    weather at all, and another storm brewing. I hear it sing i'th'
20   wind. Yon same black cloud, yon huge one, looks like a foul
    bombard[5] that would shed his liquor. If it should thunder as it
    did before, I know not where to hide my head. Yon same cloud
    cannot choose but fall by pailfuls. [*Seeing* CALIBAN] What have
    we here, a man or a fish? Dead or alive?—A fish, he smells
25   like a fish; a very ancient and fish-like smell; a kind of not-of-
    the-newest poor-john.[6] A strange fish! Were I in England now,
    as once I was, and had but this fish painted,[7] not a holiday-fool
    there but would give a piece of silver. There would this mon-
    ster make a man.[8] Any strange beast there makes a man. When
30   they will not give a doit° to relieve a lame beggar, they will lay   *small coin*
    out ten to see a dead Indian.[9] Legged like a man, and his fins
    like arms! Warm, o'my troth! I do now let loose my opinion,
    hold it no longer. This is no fish, but an islander that hath
    lately suffered° by a thunderbolt.   *perished*
    [*Thunder*]
35   Alas, the storm is come again. My best way is to creep under
    his gaberdine; there is no other shelter hereabout. Misery
    acquaints a man with strange bedfellows. I will here shroud°   *take cover*
    till the dregs[1] of the storm be past.

2.2
1. A loose smock made of coarse material.
2. Caliban takes this as a response to his curse; in F, the direction comes before Caliban speaks.
3. With the sight of hedgehog-like spirits.
4. Trinculo is probably dressed in traditional fool's motley (many-colored garment).
5. Large leather drinking vessel; stone-throwing military engine.
6. Dried hake, a poor person's staple.
7. On a sign to attract spectators.
8. Make a fortune for a man; become a man.
9. An allusion to exhibitions of American Indians in London.
1. Drinks, as from a "bombard" of wine.

[He hides under Caliban's gaberdine.][2]
Enter STEFANO, *singing [with a wooden bottle in his hand]*

STEFANO   I shall no more to sea, to sea,
40   Here shall I die ashore—
This is a very scurvy tune to sing at a man's funeral.
Well, here's my comfort.
    [He] drinks, [then] sings
    The master, the swabber, the boatswain, and I,
      The gunner and his mate,
45   Loved Mall, Meg, and Marian, and Margery,
      But none of us cared for Kate.
       For she had a tongue with a tang,°   *sting*
       Would cry to a sailor 'Go hang!'
    She loved not the savour of tar nor of pitch,
50   Yet a tailor might scratch her where'er she did itch.[3]
       Then to sea, boys, and let her go hang!
       Then to sea *[etc.]*.
This is a scurvy tune, too. But here's my comfort.
    [He] drinks

CALIBAN *[to* TRINCULO*]*   Do not torment me! O!
55 STEFANO   What's the matter?° Have we devils here? Do you put   *What's going on*
tricks upon's with savages and men of Ind,° ha? I have not   *India*
scaped drowning to be afeard now of your four legs. For it hath
been said: 'As proper a man as ever went on four legs[4] cannot
make him give ground.' And it shall be said so again, while
60 Stefano breathes at° nostrils.   *at the*
CALIBAN   The spirit torments me. O!
STEFANO   This is some monster of the isle with four legs, who
hath got, as I take it, an ague.° Where the devil should he learn   *a fit of fever*
our language? I will give him some relief, if it be but for that.
65 If I can recover° him and keep him tame and get to Naples   *cure*
with him, he's a present for any emperor that ever trod on neat's
leather.°   *cowhide; shoes*
CALIBAN *[to* TRINCULO*]*   Do not torment me, prithee! I'll bring
my wood home faster.
70 STEFANO   He's in his fit now, and does not talk after° the wisest.   *in the manner of*
He shall taste of my bottle. If he have never drunk wine afore,
it will go near to° remove his fit. If I can recover him and keep   *almost*
him tame, I will not take too much for him.[5] He shall pay for
him that hath° him, and that soundly.   *gets*
75 CALIBAN *[to* TRINCULO*]*   Thou dost me yet but little hurt. Thou
wilt anon, I know it by thy trembling. Now Prosper works upon
thee.
STEFANO   Come on your ways.° Open your mouth. Here is that   *Come on*
which will give language to you, cat.[6] Open your mouth. This
80 will shake° your shaking, I can tell you, and that soundly. You   *dislodge*
cannot tell who's your friend. Open your chaps again.
    *[*CALIBAN *drinks]*

---

2. Caliban probably lies face down, and Trinculo creeps under the gaberdine so as to lie on Caliban's back, head to feet.
3. Implying sexual desire and gratification. Tailors were often mocked for supposed lack of virility.

4. Comically varying "on two legs" (upright); also suggesting "on crutches."
5. No sum can be too high for him.
6. "Ale will make a cat speak" was proverbial.

TRINCULO I should know that voice. It should be—but he is
drowned, and these are devils. O, defend me!

STEFANO Four legs and two voices—a most delicate° monster!   *exquisitely made*
His forward voice now is to speak well of his friend; his back-
ward voice is to utter foul speeches and to detract. If all the
wine in my bottle will recover him,[7] I will help his ague.
Come.

[CALIBAN *drinks*]

Amen.° I will pour some in thy other mouth.   *Enough*

TRINCULO Stefano!

STEFANO Doth thy other mouth call me? Mercy, mercy! This
is a devil, and no monster. I will leave him. I have no long
spoon.[8]

TRINCULO Stefano! If thou beest Stefano, touch me and speak
to me, for I am Trinculo. Be not afeard. Thy good friend Trin-
culo.

STEFANO If thou beest Trinculo, come forth. I'll pull thee by the
lesser legs. If any be Trinculo's legs, these are they.

[*He pulls out* TRINCULO *by the legs*]

Thou art very° Trinculo indeed! How cam'st thou to be the   *actual*
siege° of this moon-calf?[9] Can he vent° Trinculos?   *excrement / defecate*

TRINCULO [*rising*] I took him to be killed with a thunderstroke.
But art thou not drowned, Stefano? I hope now thou art not
drowned. Is the storm overblown? I hid me under the dead
moon-calf's gaberdine for fear of the storm. And art thou living,
Stefano? O Stefano, two Neapolitans scaped!

[*He dances* STEFANO *round*]

STEFANO Prithee, do not turn me about. My stomach is not
constant.

CALIBAN These be fine things, an if° they be not spirits.   *an if = if*
That's a brave° god, and bears celestial liquor.   *an excellent, a fine*
I will kneel to him.

[*He kneels*]

STEFANO [*to* TRINCULO] How didst thou scape? How cam'st thou
hither? Swear by this bottle how thou cam'st hither. I escaped
upon a butt of sack[1] which the sailors heaved o'erboard, by this
bottle—which I made of the bark of a tree with mine own
hands since I was cast ashore.

CALIBAN I'll swear upon that bottle to be thy true subject, for the
liquor is not earthly.

STEFANO [*offering* TRINCULO *the bottle*] Here. Swear then how
thou escapedst.

TRINCULO Swum ashore, man, like a duck. I can swim like a
duck, I'll be sworn.

STEFANO Here, kiss the book.[2]

[TRINCULO *drinks*]

Though thou canst swim like a duck, thou art made like a
goose.[3]

---

7. If it takes all the wine in my bottle to cure him.
8. From the proverbial "He should have a long spoon
that sups with the devil."
9. Deformed creature; miscarriage, owing to the sup-
posed detrimental influence of the moon.
1. Cask of Spanish or Canary wine.

2. Confirming an oath by kissing the Bible; or the prover-
bial "Kiss the cup" ("Drink").
3. Probably alluding to Trinculo's outstretched neck with
the bottle as a beak; also a byword for giddiness and
unsteadiness on the feet.

125   TRINCULO   O Stefano, hast any more of this?
      STEFANO   The whole butt, man. My cellar is in a rock by th'
      seaside, where my wine is hid.
            [CALIBAN *rises*]
      How now, moon-calf? How does thine ague?
      CALIBAN   Hast thou not dropped from heaven?
130   STEFANO   Out o'th' moon, I do assure thee. I was the man i'th'   *once upon a time*
      moon when time was.°
      CALIBAN   I have seen thee in her, and I do adore thee.
      My mistress° showed me thee, and thy dog and thy bush.   *(Miranda)*
      STEFANO   Come, swear to that. Kiss the book. I will furnish it
135   anon with new contents. Swear.
            [CALIBAN *drinks*]
      TRINCULO   By this good light,° this is a very shallow monster! I   *sun*
      afeard of him? A very weak monster! The man i'th' moon? A
      most poor, credulous monster! Well drawn,° monster, in good   *drunk*
      sooth!
140   CALIBAN [*to* STEFANO]   I'll show thee every fertile inch o'th' island,
      And I will kiss thy foot. I prithee, be my god.
      TRINCULO   By this light, a most perfidious and drunken monster!
      When's god's asleep, he'll rob his bottle.
      CALIBAN [*to* STEFANO]   I'll kiss thy foot. I'll swear myself thy subject.
145   STEFANO   Come on then; down, and swear.
            [CALIBAN *kneels*]
      TRINCULO   I shall laugh myself to death at this puppy-headed
      monster. A most scurvy monster! I could find in my heart to
      beat him—
      STEFANO [*to* CALIBAN]   Come, kiss.
            [CALIBAN *kisses his foot*]
150   TRINCULO   But that the poor monster's in drink.° An abominable   *drunk*
      monster!
      CALIBAN   I'll show thee the best springs; I'll pluck thee berries;
      I'll fish for thee, and get thee wood enough.
      A plague upon the tyrant that I serve!
155   I'll bear him no more sticks, but follow thee,
      Thou wondrous man.
      TRINCULO   A most ridiculous monster, to make a wonder of a
      poor drunkard!
      CALIBAN [*to* STEFANO]   I prithee, let me bring thee where crabs°   *crab apples*
      grow,
160   And I with my long nails will dig thee pig-nuts,°   *edible tubers*
      Show thee a jay's nest, and instruct thee how
      To snare the nimble marmoset. I'll bring thee
      To clust'ring filberts, and sometimes I'll get thee
      Young seamews° from the rock. Wilt thou go with me?   *seagulls*
165   STEFANO   I prithee now, lead the way without any more talk-
      ing.—Trinculo, the King and all our company else being
      drowned, we will inherit here.—Here, bear my bottle.[4]—Fel-
      low Trinculo, we'll fill him° by and by again.   *it*
      CALIBAN (*sings drunkenly*)[5]   Farewell, master, farewell, farewell!
170   TRINCULO   A howling monster, a drunken monster!

---

4. Probably spoken to Caliban.
5. This stage direction may be misplaced and may actually refer to the following song, "No more dams."

CALIBAN [*sings*]   No more dams I'll make for° fish,   *to trap*
                        Nor fetch in firing°   *firewood*
                        At requiring,
                    Nor scrape trenchering,[6] nor wash dish.
175   'Ban, 'ban, Cacaliban
                    Has a new master.—Get a new man![7]
        Freedom, high-day!° High-day, freedom! Freedom, high-day,   *holiday*
        freedom!
STEFANO   O brave° monster! Lead the way.   *Exeunt*   *excellent, fine*

3.1

Enter FERDINAND, *bearing a log*
FERDINAND   There be some sports are painful, and their labour
    Delight in them sets off.[1] Some kinds of baseness
    Are nobly undergone, and most poor matters
    Point to rich ends. This my mean° task   *lowly*
5   Would be as heavy to me as odious, but°   *except that*
    The mistress which I serve quickens° what's dead,   *enlivens*
    And makes my labours pleasures. O, she is
    Ten times more gentle than her father's crabbed,
    And he's composed of harshness. I must remove
10 Some thousands of these logs and pile them up,
    Upon a sore° injunction. My sweet mistress   *harsh*
    Weeps when she sees me work, and says such baseness
    Had never like executor. I forget,°   *I forget to work*
    But these sweet thoughts do even refresh my labours,
    Most busil'est[2] when I do it.°   *(labor)*
        Enter MIRANDA, *and* PROSPERO [*following at a distance*]
15 MIRANDA   Alas now, pray you
    Work not so hard. I would the lightning had
    Burnt up those logs that you are enjoined to pile.
    Pray set it down, and rest you. When this burns
    'Twill weep[3] for having wearied you. My father
20 Is hard at study. Pray now, rest yourself.
    He's safe° for these three hours.   *We are safe from him*
FERDINAND   O most dear mistress,
    The sun will set before I shall discharge
    What I must strive to do.
MIRANDA   If you'll sit down
    I'll bear your logs the while. Pray give me that;
    I'll carry it to the pile.
25 FERDINAND   No, precious creature.
    I had rather crack my sinews, break my back,
    Than you should such dishonour undergo
    While I sit lazy by.
MIRANDA   It would become me
    As well as it does you; and I should do it
30 With much more ease, for my good will is to it,
    And yours it is against.

6. Trenchers, or wooden plates.
7. Addressed to the old master, Prospero.
3.1
1. *their . . . off*: the greater effort invested amounts to
more pleasure; the labor of painful activities ("sports") is
offset by whatever delight we take in them.
2. Most busily (giving a double superlative).
3. By exuding drops of resin.

PROSPERO [*aside*]   Poor worm, thou art infected.[4]
This visitation[5] shows it.

MIRANDA [*to* FERDINAND]   You look wearily.

FERDINAND   No, noble mistress, 'tis fresh morning with me
When you are by at night. I do beseech you,
35 Chiefly that I might set it in my prayers,
What is your name?

MIRANDA   Miranda. O my father,
I have broke your hest° to say so!   disobeyed your command

FERDINAND   Admired[6] Miranda!
Indeed the top of admiration, worth
What's dearest to the world. Full many a lady
40 I have eyed with best regard, and many a time
Th'harmony of their tongues hath into bondage
Brought my too diligent° ear. For several virtues   attentive
Have I liked several° women; never any   various
With so full soul but some defect in her
45 Did quarrel with the noblest grace she owed°   owned
And put it to the foil.[7] But you, O you,
So perfect and so peerless, are created
Of every creature's best.

MIRANDA   I do not know
One of my sex, no woman's face remember
50 Save from my glass° mine own; nor have I seen   mirror
More that I may call men than you, good friend,
And my dear father. How features are abroad[8]
I am skilless° of; but, by my modesty,°   ignorant / virginity
The jewel in my dower,° I would not wish   dowry
55 Any companion in the world but you;
Nor can imagination form a shape
Besides° yourself to like of. But I prattle   Equal to
Something° too wildly, and my father's precepts   Somewhat
I therein do forget.

FERDINAND   I am in my condition°   rank
60 A prince, Miranda, I do think a king—
I would° not so—and would no more endure   wish it were
This wooden slavery[9] than to suffer
The flesh-fly[1] blow my mouth. Hear my soul speak.
The very instant that I saw you did
65 My heart fly to your service; there resides
To make me slave to it. And for your sake
Am I this patient log-man.

MIRANDA   Do you love me?

FERDINAND   O heaven, O earth, bear witness to this sound,
And crown what I profess with kind event°   favorable outcome
70 If I speak true! If hollowly,° invert   falsely
What best is boded° me to mischief!° I,   foretold to / misfortune
Beyond all limit of what° else i'th' world,   whatsoever
Do love, prize, honour you.

---

4. Inflicted with love sickness. *worm*: an expression of tenderness; but a worm was often thought to carry disease.
5. Suggesting a pastoral or charitable visit to the sick; or may indicate a visit by the plague, here love-sickness.
6. Playing on the meaning of Miranda's name.
7. Foiled it, or made it ineffectual; challenged it, as in a fencing match (compare "quarrel" in line 45).
8. What people look like elsewhere.
9. The log as a symbol of Prospero's oppression.
1. Species of fly that deposits its eggs ("blows") in dead flesh.

MIRANDA [*weeping*]　　　　　I am a fool
　　To weep at what I am glad of.
PROSPERO [*aside*]　　　　　Fair encounter
75　　Of two most rare affections! Heavens rain grace
　　On that which breeds between 'em.
FERDINAND [*to* MIRANDA]　　　　Wherefore weep you?
MIRANDA　At mine unworthiness, that dare not offer
　　What I desire to give, and much less take
　　What I shall die to want.² But this is trifling,
80　　And all the more it seeks to hide itself
　　The bigger bulk it shows.³ Hence, bashful cunning,°　　　　*artful shyness*
　　And prompt me, plain and holy innocence.
　　I am your wife, if you will marry me.
　　If not, I'll die your maid.° To be your fellow°　　　*virgin; servant / equal*
85　　You may deny me, but I'll be your servant
　　Whether you will or no.
FERDINAND [*kneeling*]　　My mistress,° dearest;　　　　*sweetheart*
　　And I thus humble ever.
MIRANDA　My husband then?
FERDINAND　Ay, with a heart as willing°　　　　*desirous*
90　　As bondage e'er of freedom. Here's my hand.⁴
MIRANDA　And mine, with my heart in't. And now farewell
　　Till half an hour hence.
FERDINAND　　　　　A thousand thousand.
　　　　　Exeunt [*severally*° MIRANDA *and* FERDINAND]　　　*separately*
PROSPERO　So glad of this as they I cannot be,
　　Who are surprised with all;° but my rejoicing　　　*overwhelmed by all*
95　　At nothing can be more. I'll to my book,°　　　*book of magic*
　　For yet ere supper-time must I perform
　　Much business appertaining.　　　　　*Exit*

3.2

Enter CALIBAN, STEFANO, *and* TRINCULO¹
STEFANO [*to* CALIBAN]　Tell not me. When the butt is out we will
　　drink water, not a drop before. Therefore bear up and board
　　'em.² Servant monster, drink to me.
TRINCULO　Servant monster? The folly° of this island! They say　　　*absurdity*
5　　there's but five upon this isle. We are three of them; if th'other
　　two be brained° like us, the state totters.　　　*have brains*
STEFANO　Drink, servant monster, when I bid thee. Thy eyes are
　　almost set° in thy head.　　　*fixed by drunkenness*
TRINCULO　Where should they be set° else? He were a brave　　　*placed*
10　　monster indeed if they were set in his tail.
STEFANO　My man-monster hath drowned his tongue in sack.
　　For my part, the sea cannot drown me. I swam, ere I could
　　recover the shore, five and thirty leagues,° off and on.³ By this　　　*about 100 miles*

2. *At . . . want:* Miranda withdraws from the implications
of what she says when she calls it "trifling." *to want:* from
lacking.
3. *all . . . shows:* an image of secret pregnancy.
4. *I am your wife . . . hand:* such an exchange could actu-
ally have constituted a marriage ceremony. In Shake-
speare's time, weddings did not need to be witnessed and
performed in a church to be valid (compare 4.1.14–19).
3.2
1. As Caliban, Stefano, and Trinculo are drunk, it is

impossible to say how far their actions conform to the
hints in the text. Caliban may or may not manage to drink
at line 7; Stefano and Caliban may collapse at line 17,
but so may Trinculo before line 38; Caliban kneels for an
indefinite length of time after line 39; Ariel might but
need not imitate Trinculo's voice (lines 42ff.); and so on.
2. Force a way aboard, continuing the naval warfare ter-
minology; take on board (drink). *bear up:* sail to the
attack.
3. Tacking away from and toward the shore.

light, thou shalt be my lieutenant, monster, or my standard.[4]

15 TRINCULO Your lieutenant if you list;° he's no standard.   *wish*

STEFANO We'll not run, Monsieur Monster.

TRINCULO Nor go° neither; but you'll lie[5] like dogs, and yet say   *walk*
nothing neither.

STEFANO Moon-calf, speak once in thy life, if thou beest a good
20 moon-calf.

CALIBAN How does thy honour? Let me lick thy shoe.
I'll not serve him; he is not valiant.

TRINCULO Thou liest, most ignorant monster! I am in case° to   *prepared*
jostle a constable. Why, thou debauched fish, thou, was there
25 ever man a coward that hath drunk so much sack as I today?
Wilt thou tell a monstrous lie, being but half a fish and half a
monster?

CALIBAN [*to* STEFANO] Lo, how he mocks me! Wilt thou let him,
my lord?

30 TRINCULO 'Lord' quoth he? That a monster should be such a
natural!⁶

CALIBAN [*to* STEFANO] Lo, lo, again! Bite him to death, I prithee.

STEFANO Trinculo, keep a good tongue in your head. If you
prove a mutineer, the next tree.° The poor monster's my sub-   *(for a gallows)*
35 ject, and he shall not suffer indignity.

CALIBAN I thank my noble lord. Wilt thou be pleased
To hearken once again to the suit I made to thee?[7]

STEFANO Marry, will I. Kneel and repeat it. I will stand, and so
shall Trinculo.[8]

[CALIBAN *kneels.*]
Enter ARIEL, *invisible*

40 CALIBAN As I told thee before, I am subject to a tyrant, a sor-
cerer, that by his cunning hath cheated me of the island.

ARIEL Thou liest.

CALIBAN [*to* TRINCULO] Thou liest, thou jesting monkey, thou.
I would my valiant master would destroy thee.
45 I do not lie.

STEFANO Trinculo, if you trouble him any more in's tale, by this
hand, I will supplant° some of your teeth.   *uproot*

TRINCULO Why, I said nothing.

STEFANO Mum, then, and no more. [*To* CALIBAN] Proceed.

50 CALIBAN I say by sorcery he got this isle;
From me he got it. If thy greatness will
Revenge it on him—for I know thou dar'st,
But this thing⁹ dare not—

STEFANO That's most certain.

55 CALIBAN Thou shalt be lord of it, and I'll serve thee.

STEFANO How now shall this be compassed?° Canst thou bring   *accomplished*
me to the party?°   *person concerned*

CALIBAN Yea, yea, my lord. I'll yield him thee asleep
Where thou mayst knock a nail into his head.¹

60 ARIEL Thou liest, thou canst not.

---

4. Standard-bearer, but in Trinculo's reply "one who can stand up."
5. Lie (down); tell lies; excrete.
6. An idiot, punning on the idea that monsters were unnatural.
7. Caliban's prose here seems to take on the rhythm of verse.

8. This and most of the remainder of Stefano's speeches in 3.2 are set up as very approximate verse in F; most but not all of these lines are unmetrical.
9. Trinculo; or perhaps Caliban himself.
1. As Jael murdered sleeping Sisera in Judges 4:21 and 5:26.

CALIBAN　What a pied ninny's° this! [*To* TRINCULO] Thou scurvy 　　*fool in motley*
　　patch!° 　　*jester; idiot*
　　[*To* STEFANO] I do beseech thy greatness give him blows,
　　And take his bottle from him. When that's gone
　　He shall drink naught but brine, for I'll not show him
65　Where the quick freshes° are. 　　*fast-flowing springs*
STEFANO　Trinculo, run into no further danger. Interrupt the
　　monster one word further, and, by this hand, I'll turn my mercy
　　out o'doors and make a stockfish of thee.[2]
TRINCULO　Why, what did I? I did nothing. I'll go farther off.
70　STEFANO　Didst thou not say he lied?
ARIEL　Thou liest.
STEFANO　Do I so? [*Striking* TRINCULO] Take thou that. As you
　　like this, give me the lie° another time. 　　*call me a liar*
TRINCULO　I did not give the lie. Out o'your wits and hearing
75　too? A pox o'your bottle! This can sack and drinking do. A
　　murrain° on your monster, and the devil take your fingers. 　　*plague*
CALIBAN　Ha, ha, ha!
STEFANO　Now forward with your tale. [*To* TRINCULO] Prithee,
　　stand further off.
80　CALIBAN　Beat him enough; after a little time
　　I'll beat him too.
STEFANO [*to* TRINCULO]
　　　　　　Stand farther. [*To* CALIBAN] Come, proceed.
CALIBAN　Why, as I told thee, 'tis a custom with him
　　I'th' afternoon to sleep. There° thou mayst brain him, 　　*Then*
　　Having first seized his books; or with a log
85　Batter his skull, or paunch° him with a stake, 　　*disembowel*
　　Or cut his weasand° with thy knife. Remember 　　*windpipe*
　　First to possess his books, for without them
　　He's but a sot° as I am, nor hath not 　　*stupid fool*
　　One spirit to command—they all do hate him
90　As rootedly as I. Burn but his books.
　　He has brave utensils,[3] for so he calls them,
　　Which when he has a house he'll deck withal.
　　And that most deeply to consider is
　　The beauty of his daughter. He himself
95　Calls her a nonpareil.° I never saw a woman 　　*one without equal*
　　But only Sycorax my dam and she,
　　But she as far surpasseth Sycorax
　　As great'st does least.
STEFANO　　　　　　Is it so brave° a lass? 　　*excellent, fine*
CALIBAN　Ay, lord. She will become thy bed, I warrant,
100　And bring thee forth brave brood.
STEFANO　Monster, I will kill this man. His daughter and I will
　　be king and queen—save° our graces!—and Trinculo and thy- 　　*God save*
　　self shall be viceroys. Dost thou like the plot, Trinculo?
TRINCULO　Excellent.
105　STEFANO　Give me thy hand. I am sorry I beat thee. But while
　　thou liv'st, keep a good tongue in thy head.

---

2. Proverbial allusion to the beating of dried fish before　　hold goods. Word is accented on the first and third sylla-
cooking it.　　bles.
3. Perhaps confusing implements for magic and house-

CALIBAN   Within this half hour will he be asleep.
      Wilt thou destroy him then?
STEFANO   Ay, on mine honour.
110 ARIEL [*aside*]   This will I tell my master.
CALIBAN   Thou mak'st me merry; I am full of pleasure.
      Let us be jocund. Will you troll° the catch°   sing / round, song
      You taught me but while-ere?°   a short time ago
STEFANO   At thy request, monster, I will do reason, any rea-
115   son.°—Come on, Trinculo, let us sing.   anything reasonable
      (*Sings*)   Flout 'em and cout[4] 'em,
                  And scout° 'em and flout 'em.   mock
                  Thought is free.
CALIBAN   That's not the tune.
      ARIEL *plays the tune on a tabor and pipe*[5]
120 STEFANO   What is this same?
TRINCULO   This is the tune of our catch, played by the picture of
      Nobody.[6]
STEFANO [*calls towards* ARIEL]   If thou beest a man, show thyself
      in thy likeness. If thou beest a devil, take't as thou list.°   wish
125 TRINCULO   O, forgive me my sins!
STEFANO   He that dies pays all debts.[7] [*Calls*] I defy thee.—
      Mercy upon us![8]
CALIBAN   Art thou afeard?
STEFANO   No, monster, not I.
130 CALIBAN   Be not afeard. The isle is full of noises,
      Sounds, and sweet airs,° that give delight and hurt not.   tunes
      Sometimes a thousand twangling instruments
      Will hum about mine ears, and sometime voices
      That if I then had waked after long sleep
135   Will make me sleep again; and then in dreaming
      The clouds methought would open and show riches
      Ready to drop upon me, that when I waked
      I cried to dream again.
STEFANO   This will prove a brave kingdom to me, where I shall
140   have my music for nothing.[9]
CALIBAN   When Prospero is destroyed.
STEFANO   That shall be by and by.° I remember the story.   very soon
                  [*Exit* ARIEL, *playing music*]
TRINCULO   The sound is going away. Let's follow it, and after do
      our work.
145 STEFANO   Lead, monster; we'll follow.—I would I could see this
      taborer. He lays it on.[1]
TRINCULO [*to* CALIBAN]   Wilt come? I'll follow Stefano.   *Exeunt*

4. Probably a dialectal form of "colt" (cheat). The stage direction ("Sings") suggests that the others cannot manage the catch and remain in bewildered silence. But Trinculo, and perhaps Caliban, may attempt to join in.
5. The tabor was a small drum slung on the left-hand side of the body; the tabor pipe was a long narrow pipe played with the left hand. The combination was associated with rustic dances and merrymaking.
6. "Nobody" was a character in a comedy who was depicted on the title page of the printed text. Large breeches up to his neck made him appear to have no trunk.
7. Varying the proverbial "Death pays all debts."
8. Stefano's defiance comically collapses.
9. James I spent large sums on court music, but not typically of the popular kind Ariel now plays.
1. He sets himself to his music vigorously. Stefano deserts Caliban in order to follow the music. Trinculo and Caliban in turn follow Stefano (line 147).

3.3

Enter ALONSO, SEBASTIAN, ANTONIO, GONZALO, ADRIAN,
and FRANCISCO

GONZALO [*to* ALONSO]   By'r la'kin,[1] I can go no further, sir.
  My old bones ache. Here's a maze trod indeed
  Through forthrights and meanders.° By your patience,   *direct and winding paths*
  I needs must rest me.

ALONSO   Old lord, I cannot blame thee,
5   Who am myself attached° with weariness   *seized*
  To th' dulling of my spirits. Sit down and rest.
  Even° here I will put off my hope, and keep it   *Exactly*
  No longer for° my flatterer. He is drowned   *as*
  Whom thus we stray to find, and the sea mocks
10   Our frustrate° search on land. Well, let him go.   *vain*
  [*They sit*]

ANTONIO [*aside to* SEBASTIAN]   I am right glad that he's so out of hope.
  Do not for° one repulse forgo the purpose   *on account of*
  That you resolved t'effect.

SEBASTIAN [*aside to* ANTONIO] The next advantage
  Will we take throughly.°   *thoroughly*

ANTONIO [*aside to* SEBASTIAN] Let it be tonight,
15   For now they are oppressed with travel.° They   *journey; travail*
  Will not nor cannot use such vigilance
  As when they are fresh.

SEBASTIAN [*aside to* ANTONIO] I say tonight. No more.
      Solemn and strange music. [*Enter*] PROSPERO *on the
      top,*[2] *invisible*

ALONSO   What harmony is this? My good friends, hark.

GONZALO   Marvellous sweet music.
      Enter [*spirits, in*] *several strange shapes, bringing in* [*a
      table and*] *a banquet, and dance about it with gentle
      actions of salutations, and, inviting the King and* [*his
      companions*] *to eat, they depart*

20 ALONSO   Give us kind keepers,° heavens! What were these?   *guardian angels*

SEBASTIAN   A living drollery.[3] Now I will believe
  That there are unicorns; that in Arabia
  There is one tree, the phoenix' throne, one phoenix[4]
  At this hour reigning there.

ANTONIO   I'll believe both;
25   And what does else want credit° come to me,   *lack belief*
  And I'll be sworn 'tis true. Travellers ne'er did lie,[5]
  Though fools at home condemn 'em.

GONZALO   If in Naples
  I should report this now, would they believe me—
  If I should say I saw such islanders?
30   For certes° these are people of the island,   *certainly*
  Who though they are of monstrous shape, yet note
  Their manners are more gentle-kind than of
  Our human generation you shall find
  Many, nay, almost any.

3.3
1. Ladykin: a colloquial form of reference to the Virgin
Mary.
2. A small acting area above the upper stage.
3. A puppet show with live actors.

4. The unicorn and phoenix were two mythological
beings that sometimes figured in travelers' tales. The
phoenix, a bird, was supposed to regenerate itself by rising
up from the ashes of its own funeral pyre.
5. Proverbially, "A traveler may lie with authority."

PROSPERO [*aside*]   Honest lord,
35 Thou hast said well, for some of you there present
    Are worse than devils.

ALONSO   I cannot too much muse.°   *marvel*
    Such shapes, such gesture, and such sound, expressing—
    Although they want the use of tongue°—a kind   *language*
    Of excellent dumb discourse.

PROSPERO [*aside*]   Praise in departing.[6]

FRANCISCO   They vanished strangely.

40 SEBASTIAN   No matter, since
    They have left their viands° behind, for we have stomachs.°   *food / good appetites*
    Will't please you taste of what is here?

ALONSO   Not I.

GONZALO   Faith, sir, you need not fear. When we were boys,
    Who would believe that there were mountaineers°   *mountain dwellers*
45 Dewlapped like bulls, whose throats had hanging at 'em
    Wallets° of flesh? Or that there were such men   *Pouches*
    Whose heads stood in their breasts? Which now we find
    Each putter-out of five for one[7] will bring us
    Good warrant of.

ALONSO [*rising*]   I will stand to and feed,°   *begin eating*
50 Although my last—no matter, since I feel
    The best is past. Brother, my lord the Duke,
    Stand to, and do as we.

              [ALONSO, SEBASTIAN, *and* ANTONIO *approach the table.*]
              Thunder and lightning. Enter ARIEL [*descending*] *like a*
              harpy,[8] *claps his wings upon the table, and, with a*
              quaint device,° *the banquet vanishes*[9]   *an ingenious mechanism*

ARIEL   You are three men of sin, whom destiny—
    That hath to° instrument this lower world   *as its*
55 And what is in't—the never-surfeited sea
    Hath caused to belch up you, and on this island
    Where man doth not inhabit, you 'mongst men
    Being most unfit to live. I have made you mad,
    And even with suchlike valour[1] men hang and drown
    Their proper selves.°   *Themselves*

              [ALONSO, SEBASTIAN, *and* ANTONIO *draw*][2]
60   You fools! I and my fellows
    Are ministers of fate. The elements
    Of whom your swords are tempered[3] may as well
    Wound the loud winds, or with bemocked-at stabs
    Kill the still-closing[4] waters, as diminish
65 One dowl° that's in my plume.° My fellow ministers   *featherlet / plumage*
    Are like° invulnerable. If you could hurt,   *similarly*

---

6. Reserve your praise until the end of the event.
7. A traveler could profit from a voyage by laying down a sum with a broker before departing and undertaking to bring back evidence of having reached his destination; if successful, he was repaid fivefold.
8. A mythological monster with a vulture's wings and claws and a woman's face. Aeneas and his companions encountered these harpies, who stole their meals and threatened to punish them with slow starvation. *Thunder and lightning:* both spectacular and functional for disguising the mechanics of the "quaint device."
9. The simplest effective staging is by means of a rotating tabletop with the vessels of the banquet fixed to its surface. Leg-to-leg planks supporting the tabletop or a hang-

ing cloth would conceal the vanished banquet. The harpy's wings would hide the mechanics from the audience, and clapping them would provide a visual distraction.
1. *suchlike valour:* fearlessness that comes from madness.
2. Ariel perhaps ascends beyond their reach here. Aeneas's companions, like Alonso here, similarly attempted to kill the harpies with swords.
3. Compounded and hardened. Metal was sometimes thought of as being compounded of earth and fire, here contrasted with winds and waters.
4. Self-healing, since they close immediately once parted.

Your swords are now too massy° for your strengths   *heavy*
And will not be uplifted.
    [ALONSO, SEBASTIAN, *and* ANTONIO *stand amazed*°]   *crazed, bewildered*
                  But remember,
For that's my business to you, that you three
70 From Milan did supplant good Prospero;
Exposed unto the sea, which hath requit it,
Him and his innocent child; for which foul deed,
The powers, delaying not forgetting,[5] have
Incensed the seas and shores, yea, all the creatures,[6]
75 Against your peace. Thee of thy son, Alonso,
They have bereft, and do pronounce by me
Ling'ring perdition[7]—worse than any death
Can be at once—shall step by step attend
You and your ways; whose[8] wraths to guard you from—
80 Which here in this most desolate[9] isle else falls
Upon your heads—is nothing° but heart's sorrow   *there is no alternative*
And a clear life° ensuing.   *a life innocent of sin*
        He [ascends and] vanishes[1] *in thunder. Then, to soft*
        music, enter the [spirits] again, and dance with mocks
        and mows,° *and [they depart,] carrying out the table*   *grimaces*
PROSPERO   Bravely the figure of this harpy hast thou
Performed, my Ariel; a grace it had devouring.[2]
85 Of my instruction hast thou nothing bated°   *omitted*
In what thou hadst to say. So with good life[3]
And observation strange[4] my meaner ministers°   *lesser spirits*
Their several kinds° have done.° My high charms work,   *various roles / performed*
And these mine enemies are all knit up
90 In their distractions. They now are in my power;
And in these fits I leave them, while I visit
Young Ferdinand, whom they suppose is drowned,
And his and mine loved darling.   [*Exit*]
    [GONZALO, ADRIAN, *and* FRANCISCO *go towards the*
    others]
GONZALO   I'th' name of something holy, sir, why stand you
In this strange stare?
95 ALONSO   O, it is monstrous, monstrous!
Methought the billows spoke and told me of it,
The winds did sing it to me, and the thunder,
That deep and dreadful organ-pipe, pronounced
The name of Prosper. It did bass my trespass.[5]
100 Therefor° my son i'th' ooze is bedded, and   *For that*
I'll seek him deeper than e'er plummet sounded,
And with him there lie mudded.   *Exit*
SEBASTIAN   But one fiend at a time,
I'll fight their legions o'er.°   *from beginning to end*

---

5. Related to the proverb "God stays long but strikes at last."
6. Compare Genesis 1:21: "Their God created . . . every thing living and moving."
7. Slow starvation; hell on earth of spiritual suffering. The phrase is first the object of "pronounce" and then the subject of "shall . . . attend."
8. Refers to "the powers" in line 73.
9. Joyless, wretched; barren, deserted.

1. Ariel is raised out of sight into the canopy.
2. In clapping his wings, Ariel has created the illusion of having devoured the banquet.
3. Convincingly; with vitality. So: In the same way.
4. Remarkable attention to the requirements of their parts, or instructions.
5. The thunder proclaimed my sin ("trespass") in a bass voice, or with a bass background; perhaps wordplay on the "utter baseness" of trespass.

ANTONIO   I'll be thy second.

Exeunt [SEBASTIAN *and* ANTONIO]

GONZALO   All three of them are desperate.° Their great guilt,   *in despair; reckless*
105   Like poison given to work° a great time after,   *take effect*
Now 'gins to bite the spirits. I do beseech you
That are of suppler joints, follow them swiftly,
And hinder them from what this ecstasy°   *madness*
May now provoke them to.

ADRIAN   Follow, I pray you.   *Exeunt*

4.1

Enter PROSPERO, FERDINAND, *and* MIRANDA

PROSPERO [*to* FERDINAND]   If I have too austerely punished you,
Your compensation makes amends, for I
Have given you here a third[1] of mine own life —
Or that for which I live — who° once again   *whom*
5   I tender° to thy hand. All thy vexations   *offer*
Were but my trials of thy love, and thou
Hast strangely° stood the test. Here, afore heaven,   *wonderfully*
I ratify this my rich gift. O Ferdinand,
Do not smile at me that I boast of her,
10   For thou shalt find she will outstrip all praise,
And make it halt° behind her.   *limp*

FERDINAND   I do believe it
Against an oracle.[2]

PROSPERO   Then, as my gift and thine own acquisition
Worthily purchased,° take my daughter. But   *Gained by effort*
15   If thou dost break her virgin-knot° before   *virginity*
All sanctimonious° ceremonies may   *holy*
With full and holy rite be ministered,
No sweet aspersion° shall the heavens let fall   *shower of grace*
To make this contract grow; but barren hate,
20   Sour-eyed disdain, and discord, shall bestrew
The union of your bed with weeds[3] so loathly
That you shall hate it both. Therefore take heed,
As Hymen's[4] lamps shall light you.

FERDINAND   As I hope
For quiet days, fair issue,° and long life   *children*
25   With such love as 'tis now, the murkiest den,°   *cave*
The most opportune[5] place, the strong'st suggestion°   *temptation*
Our worser genius can,[6] shall never melt
Mine honour into lust to take away
The edge° of that day's celebration;   *unblunted desire*
30   When I shall think or° Phoebus' steeds are foundered[7]   *either*
Or night kept chained below.

PROSPERO   Fairly spoke.

4.1
1. Miranda. The usual poetic conceit was a half; commentators variously conjecture the other third to be his dukedom, his books, or his late wife.
2. *I . . . oracle*: I would believe it even if an oracle said otherwise.
3. Weeds in place of the flowers traditionally strewn on the marriage bed; wordplay on both "marriage bed" and "seed-bed."
4. Classical god of marriage.

5. Accented on the second syllable.
6. Is capable of. *worser genius*: evil spirit corresponding to a guardian angel.
7. Collapsed and made lame by overriding. *Phoebus' steeds*: the mythological horses that drew the chariot of the sun. Ferdinand anticipates that on his wedding day he will in his impatience think that the night will never come.

Sit, then, and talk with her. She is thine own.
    [FERDINAND *and* MIRANDA *sit and talk together*]
What,° Ariel, my industrious servant Ariel!   *Now, then*
    Enter ARIEL
ARIEL   What would my potent master? Here I am.
35 PROSPERO   Thou and thy meaner° fellows your last service   *lesser*
   Did worthily perform, and I must use you
   In such another trick. Go bring the rabble,[8]
   O'er whom I give thee power, here to this place.
   Incite them to quick motion, for I must
40   Bestow upon the eyes of this young couple
   Some vanity[9] of mine art. It is my promise,
   And they expect it from me.
ARIEL   Presently?°   *At once*
PROSPERO   Ay, with a twink.[1]
ARIEL   Before you can say 'Come' and 'Go',
45   And breathe twice, and cry 'So, so',
          Each one tripping on his toe
          Will be here with mop and mow.[2]
          Do you love me, master? No?
PROSPERO   Dearly, my delicate Ariel. Do not approach
   Till thou dost hear me call.
50 ARIEL   Well; I conceive.°   *Exit*   *understand*
PROSPERO [*to* FERDINAND]   Look thou be true.[3] Do not give dalliance
   Too much the rein.[4] The strongest oaths are straw
   To th' fire i'th' blood. Be more abstemious,
   Or else, good night your vow.
FERDINAND   I warrant[5] you, sir,
55   The white cold virgin snow upon my heart
   Abates the ardour of my liver.[6]
PROSPERO   Well.—
   Now come, my Ariel! Bring a corollary°   *surplus*
   Rather than want° a spirit. Appear, and pertly.°   *lack / briskly*
    Soft music
   [*To* FERDINAND *and* MIRANDA] No tongue, all eyes! Be silent.
    Enter IRIS[7]
60 IRIS   Ceres, most bounteous lady, thy rich leas[8]
   Of wheat, rye, barley, vetches,[9] oats, and peas;
   Thy turfy mountains where live nibbling sheep,
   And flat meads° thatched with stover,[1] them to keep;   *meadows*
   Thy banks with peonied and twillèd[2] brims
65   Which spongy° April at thy hest betrims[3]   *wet*
   To make cold nymphs chaste crowns; and thy broom-groves,[4]
   Whose shadow the dismissèd bachelor° loves,   *rejected suitor*

8. Troupe of lesser spirits: *trick:* theatrical device, or clever artifice.
9. Trifle; conceit; illusion; display.
1. In the twinkling of an eye.
2. With derisive and grimacing gestures.
3. Look, be faithful to your promise. Prospero may have caught the lovers just indulging in dalliance.
4. To "give the rein" is to make a horse gallop.
5. Pronounced as one syllable.
6. *The . . . liver:* The thought of Miranda's ideal chastity (she may be in Ferdinand's arms, hence "upon my heart") is cold enough to allay any lustful passion. The liver was held to be the seat of passion.

7. Goddess of the rainbow and messenger of Juno; her apparel is in the colors of the rainbow, and she wears "saffron wings" (line 78).
8. Arable land. Ceres was the goddess of agriculture and generative nature.
9. Pea-like plants grown for fodder.
1. Hay for winter fodder.
2. Reinforced with entwined branches to prevent riverbank erosion. *peonied:* covered with peonies.
3. Adorns with flowers; recalls the colloquial "April showers bring forth May flowers."
4. Thickets of gorse, yellow-flowered shrubs. *cold:* chaste.

Being lass-lorn; thy pole-clipped vineyard,[5]
And thy sea-marge,° sterile and rocky-hard,   *seashore*
70 Where thou thyself dost air:° the Queen o'th' Sky,°   *take fresh air / Juno*
Whose wat'ry arch° and messenger am I,   *rainbow*
Bids thee leave these, and with her sovereign grace
      JUNO [*appears in the air*][6]
Here on this grass-plot,[7] in this very place,
To come and sport.—Her peacocks fly amain.[8]
75 Approach, rich Ceres, her to entertain.
      Enter [ARIEL *as*] CERES[9]
CERES   Hail, many-coloured messenger, that ne'er
Dost disobey the wife of Jupiter;°   *Juno*
Who with thy saffron wings upon my flowers
Diffusest honey-drops, refreshing showers,
80 And with each end of thy blue bow dost crown
My bosky[1] acres and my unshrubbed down,
Rich scarf[2] to my proud earth. Why hath thy queen
Summoned me hither to this short-grassed green?
IRIS   A contract of true love to celebrate,
85 And some donation freely to estate°   *bestow*
On the blest lovers.
CERES   Tell me, heavenly bow,°   *rainbow*
If Venus or her son,[3] as° thou dost know,   *as far as*
Do now attend the Queen. Since they did plot
The means that dusky Dis[4] my daughter got,
90 Her and her blind boy's scandalled° company   *scandalous, notorious*
I have forsworn.
IRIS   Of her society
Be not afraid. I met her deity
Cutting the clouds towards Paphos,[5] and her son
Dove-drawn[6] with her. Here thought they to have done
95 Some wanton charm upon[7] this man and maid,
Whose vows are that no bed-right[8] shall be paid
Till Hymen's torch be lighted[9]—but in vain.
Mars's hot minion° is returned again.   *lover; Venus*
Her waspish-headed[1] son has broke his arrows,
100 Swears he will shoot no more, but play with sparrows,[2]
And be a boy right out.°   *an ordinary boy*
    [*Music.* JUNO *descends to the stage*][3]
CERES   Highest queen of state,
Great Juno, comes; I know her by her gait.°   *majestic bearing*

---

5. Vineyard with vines embracing, twined around, their
supporting poles; pruned vineyard. "Vineyard" was pro-
nounced as three syllables. *lass-lorn:* abandoned by the
girl he wooed.
6. Juno was queen of the heavens and goddess of women,
held to protect marriages and preside over childbirth. Her
chair is ornamented with a peacock motif. She descends
by a "flight" mechanism to a position suspended in the
air above the stage. Music may be played. Juno remains
in view aloft until line 101. If, however, F's direction here
is misplaced, she may not appear until line 101.
7. Compare "this short-grassed green" (line 83) and "this
green land" (line 130): a green carpet on the acting area
is indicated.
8. In haste. Peacocks, sacred to Juno, drew her chariot.
9. Her part is probably played by Ariel (see line 167).
1. Covered with bushes and thickets.
2. Ornamental and hung across the body rather than

around the neck.
3. Cupid, proverbially blind.
4. King of the underworld in classical mythology. Venus
and her son Cupid made him fall in love with Ceres'
daughter Proserpine, whom he abducted (Ovid, *Meta-
morphoses* 5.395ff.).
5. City in Cyprus: associated with Venus.
6. Doves were sacred to Venus and drew her chariot.
7. *done . . . upon:* cast a lustful spell upon.
8. Right to consummate the marriage; also suggesting a
rite, as in line 17.
9. Until the wedding ceremony is performed.
1. Peevish, irritable, and with arrows like the wasp's sting.
2. Sparrows were associated with Venus because they
were proverbially lustful.
3. This completes Juno's flight to the stage; again, music
may be played.

JUNO   How does my bounteous sister? Go with me
　　To bless this twain, that they may prosperous be,
105　And honoured in their issue.
　　　　　　[CERES *joins* JUNO, *and*] *they sing*[4]
　JUNO　　　　Honour, riches, marriage-blessing,
　　　　　　Long continuance and increasing,
　　　　　　Hourly joys be still° upon you!　　　　　　　　　　*always*
　　　　　　Juno sings her blessings on you.
110　CERES　　Earth's increase, and foison° plenty,　　　　　　*abundance*
　　　　　　Barns and garners° never empty,　　　　　　　　*granaries*
　　　　　　Vines with clust'ring bunches growing,
　　　　　　Plants with goodly burden bowing;
　　　　　　Spring come to you at the farthest,
115　　　　　In the very end of harvest.[5]
　　　　　　Scarcity and want shall shun you,
　　　　　　Ceres' blessing so is on you.
　FERDINAND　This is a most majestic vision, and
　　Harmonious charmingly.[6] May I be bold°　　　　　*Would I be right*
　　To think these spirits?
120　PROSPERO　　　　　　　Spirits, which by mine art
　　I have from their confines[7] called to enact
　　My present fancies.
　FERDINAND　　　　　　Let me live here ever!
　　So rare a wondered° father and a wise　　　　*endowed with wonders*
　　Makes this place paradise.
　　　　　　JUNO *and* CERES *whisper, and send* IRIS *on employment*
　PROSPERO　　　　　　　Sweet° now, silence.　　　　　*Softly*
125　Juno and Ceres whisper seriously.
　　There's something else to do. Hush, and be mute,
　　Or else our spell is marred.
　IRIS　You nymphs called naiads of the wind'ring[8] brooks,
　　With your sedged crowns° and ever-harmless looks,　　*garlands of reeds*
130　Leave your crisp channels,° and on this green land　　*rippling streams*
　　Answer your summons; Juno does command.
　　Come, temperate nymphs, and help to celebrate
　　A contract of true love. Be not too late.
　　　　　Enter certain nymphs
　　You sunburned sicklemen,° of August weary,　　　　　*harvesters*
135　Come hither from the furrow and be merry;
　　Make holiday, your rye-straw hats put on,
　　And these fresh nymphs encounter every one
　　In country footing.
　　　　　Enter certain reapers, properly habited.[9] *They join with*
　　　　　the nymphs in a graceful dance; towards the end whereof
　　　　　PROSPERO *starts suddenly, and speaks*
　PROSPERO [*aside*]　I had forgot that foul conspiracy
140　Of the beast Caliban and his confederates
　　Against my life. The minute of their plot

---

4. Ceres and Juno might be raised together in the flight apparatus and sing suspended above the stage. They would then vanish (line 142 stage direction) by being raised into the heavens.
5. *Spring . . . harvest:* that spring should come six months ("the farthest") after harvest suggests the absence of winter; Ceres was held to have originally caused this by neglecting the earth when seeking Proserpine.
6. Delightfully; magically; harmoniously.
7. Regions of dwelling. Word is accented on the second syllable.
8. Perhaps a portmanteau of "wandering" and "winding." The naiads were mythical river nymphs.
9. Either properly or finely dressed.

Is almost come. [*To the spirits*] Well done! Avoid;° no more!   Begone
    To a strange, hollow, and confused noise, the [*spirits in*
    the pageant] *heavily vanish.*[1]
      [FERDINAND *and* MIRANDA *rise*]
FERDINAND [*to* MIRANDA]   This is strange. Your father's in some passion
    That works° him strongly.   agitates
MIRANDA   Never till this day
145   Saw I him touched with anger so distempered.°   troubled, distracted
PROSPERO   You do look, my son, in a moved sort,°   disturbed manner
    As if you were dismayed. Be cheerful, sir.
    Our revels[2] now are ended. These our actors,
    As I foretold you,° were all spirits, and   told you before
150   Are melted into air, into thin air;
    And like the baseless fabric[3] of this vision,
    The cloud-capped towers, the gorgeous palaces,
    The solemn temples, the great globe[4] itself,
    Yea, all which it inherit,[5] shall dissolve;
155   And, like this insubstantial pageant faded,
    Leave not a rack° behind. We are such stuff   wisp of cloud
    As dreams are made on,° and our little life   of
    Is rounded[6] with a sleep. Sir, I am vexed.
    Bear with my weakness. My old brain is troubled.
160   Be not disturbed with my infirmity.
    If you be pleased, retire into my cell,
    And there repose. A turn or two I'll walk
    To still my beating mind.
FERDINAND *and* MIRANDA   We wish your peace.
              Exeunt [FERDINAND *and* MIRANDA]
PROSPERO   Come with a thought![7] I thank thee, Ariel. Come!
     Enter ARIEL
ARIEL   Thy thoughts I cleave to. What's thy pleasure?
165 PROSPERO   Spirit,
    We must prepare to meet with Caliban.
ARIEL   Ay, my commander. When I presented[8] Ceres
    I thought to have told thee of it, but I feared
    Lest I might anger thee.
170 PROSPERO   Say again: where didst thou leave these varlets?°   ruffians
ARIEL   I told you, sir, they were red-hot with drinking;
    So full of valour that they smote the air
    For breathing in their faces, beat the ground
    For kissing of their feet; yet always bending°   aiming
175   Towards their project. Then I beat my tabor,°   side drum
    At which like unbacked° colts they pricked their ears,   never-ridden
    Advanced° their eyelids, lifted up their noses   Opened
    As° they smelt music. So I charmed their ears   As if
    That calf-like they my lowing° followed, through   mooing
180   Toothed briars, sharp furzes, pricking gorse,° and thorns,   prickly shrubs
    Which entered their frail shins. At last I left them
    I'th' filthy-mantled[9] pool beyond your cell,

1. Sorrowfully depart (probably not implying a trick of staging).
2. Entertainment, in both festive and theatrical senses.
3. An edifice or substance without foundations; insubstantial, alluding to buildings in masque scenery.
4. World; also with a passing allusion to the Globe theater.
5. All who come into possession of it.
6. Rounded off; surrounded; or, possibly, crowned.
7. Come as fast as thought, a colloquial simile.
8. Acted; produced the masque of; introduced while playing Iris.
9. Covered with filthy scum.

There dancing up to th' chins, that° the foul lake   *so that*
  O'er-stunk¹ their feet.
PROSPERO   This was well done, my bird.°   *chick; dear*
185   Thy shape invisible retain thou still.
  The trumpery° in my house, go bring it hither   *cheap goods*
  For stale° to catch these thieves.   *decoy; bait*
ARIEL   I go, I go.   *Exit*
PROSPERO   A devil, a born devil, on whose nature
  Nurture can never stick; on whom my pains,
190   Humanely taken, all, all lost, quite lost,
  And, as with age his body uglier grows,
  So his mind cankers.° I will plague them all,   *festers*
  Even to roaring.
      Enter ARIEL, *laden with glistening apparel, etc.*
        Come, hang them on this lime.²
      [ARIEL *hangs up the apparel. Exeunt* PROSPERO *and*
                                   ARIEL]
    Enter CALIBAN, STEFANO, *and* TRINCULO, *all wet*
CALIBAN   Pray you, tread softly, that the blind mole may
195   Not hear a foot fall. We now are near his cell.
STEFANO   Monster, your fairy, which you say is a harmless fairy,
  has done little better than played the Jack° with us.   *knave; will-o'-the-wisp*
TRINCULO   Monster, I do smell° all horse-piss, at which my nose   *smell of*
  is in great indignation.
200 STEFANO   So is mine. Do you hear, monster? If I should take a
  displeasure against you, look you—
TRINCULO   Thou wert but a lost monster.
CALIBAN   Good my lord, give me thy favour still.
  Be patient, for the prize° I'll bring thee to   *booty*
205   Shall hoodwink³ this mischance. Therefore speak softly.
  All's hushed as midnight yet.
TRINCULO   Ay, but to lose our bottles in the pool!
STEFANO   There is not only disgrace and dishonour in that, mon-
  ster, but an infinite loss.
210 TRINCULO   That's more to me than my wetting. Yet this is your
  harmless fairy, monster.
STEFANO   I will fetch off⁴ my bottle, though I be o'er ears° for   *drowned*
  my labour.
CALIBAN   Prithee, my king, be quiet. Seest thou here;
215   This is the mouth o'th' cell. No noise, and enter.
  Do that good mischief which may make this island
  Thine own for ever, and I thy Caliban
  For aye° thy foot-licker.   *ever*
STEFANO   Give me thy hand.
  I do begin to have bloody thoughts.
220 TRINCULO [*seeing the apparel*]   O King Stefano, O peer! O wor-
  thy Stefano, look what a wardrobe here is for thee!⁵
CALIBAN   Let it alone, thou fool, it is but trash.
TRINCULO [*putting on a gown*]   O ho, monster, we know what
  belongs to a frippery!° O King Stefano!   *old-clothes shop*

---

1. Made smelly; smelled worse than.
2. Lime tree, indicating a stage property.
3. Blind with a hood, as was done to pacify a hawk—
hence, make harmless; also, put out of sight.

4. Recover; rescue; drink off.
5. Recalling "King Stephen was a worthy peer, / His
breeches cost him but a crown," a popular ballad about
King Stephen, sung in part in *Othello* 2.3.

225 STEFANO Put off that gown, Trinculo. By this hand, I'll have that
gown.
TRINCULO Thy grace shall have it.
CALIBAN The dropsy[6] drown this fool! What do you mean
To dote thus on such luggage?° Let't alone,   *encumbrances*
230 And do the murder first. If he awake,
From toe to crown he'll fill our skins with pinches,
Make us° strange stuff.   *Turn us into*
STEFANO Be you quiet, monster.—Mistress lime, is not this my
jerkin?° Now is the jerkin under the line.[7] Now, jerkin, you are   *leather jacket*
235 like to lose your hair and prove a bald jerkin.[8]
        [STEFANO *and* TRINCULO *take garments*]
TRINCULO Do, do! We steal by line and level,[9] an't like° your   *if it please*
grace.
STEFANO I thank thee for that jest. Here's a garment for't. Wit
shall not go unrewarded while I am king of this country. 'Steal
240 by line and level' is an excellent pass of pate.[1] There's another
garment for't.
TRINCULO Monster, come, put some lime upon your fingers,[2]
and away with the rest.
CALIBAN I will have none on't. We shall lose our time,
245 And all be turned to barnacles,[3] or to apes
With foreheads villainous° low.   *wretchedly*
STEFANO Monster, lay to° your fingers. Help to bear this away   *apply*
where my hogshead of wine is, or I'll turn you out of my king-
dom. Go to, carry this.
250 TRINCULO And this.
STEFANO Ay, and this.
        [*They load* CALIBAN *with apparel.*]
        A noise of hunters heard. Enter divers° spirits in shape of   *various*
        dogs and hounds, hunting them about; PROSPERO *and*
        ARIEL *setting them on*
PROSPERO Hey, Mountain, hey!
ARIEL   Silver! There it goes, Silver!
PROSPERO Fury, Fury! There, Tyrant, there! Hark, hark!
        [*Exeunt* STEFANO, TRINCULO, *and* CALIBAN, *pursued by spirits*]
        [*To* ARIEL] Go, charge my goblins that they grind their joints
255 With dry convulsions,[4] shorten up their sinews
With agèd cramps, and more pinch-spotted[5] make them
Than pard or cat o'mountain.[6]
        [*Cries within*]
ARIEL   Hark, they roar!
PROSPERO Let them be hunted soundly.° At this hour   *thoroughly*
Lies at my mercy all mine enemies.

---

6. A disease characterized by the accumulation of fluid
in connective tissue.
7. Below the lime tree; south of the equator; below the
waist. Also a possible allusion to the proverb "Thou hast
stricken the ball under the line," meaning "You have
cheated." Stefano has taken the jerkin from the lime tree.
8. Baldness caused either through tropical disease or by
sailors who customarily shaved the heads of passengers
when they crossed the line of the equator for the first
time. "Under the [waist]line" (line 234) could also be an
allusion to baldness from syphilis.
9. An idiomatic expression for "properly, by the rules"—
literally, "by plumb line and carpenter's level"; also pun-

ning on "lime." Do, do: an expression of approval.
1. Thrust of wit (fencing term).
2. Be "lime-fingered," sticky-fingered (alluding to bird-
lime, a gluey substance used to catch birds).
3. Barnacle geese, also known as "tree geese" and sup-
posed to begin life as barnacle shells.
4. Afflicting "sapless," or old, people.
5. Spotted with bruises from pinches. *agèd cramps:* the
convulsions of old age.
6. Both terms are synonymous with "leopard"; the second
is from Jeremiah 13:23: "May a man of Ind change his
skin, and the cat of the mountain her spots?" (Bishops'
Bible).

260   Shortly shall all my labours end, and thou
    Shalt have the air at freedom. For a little,
    Follow, and do me service.   *Exeunt*

5.1

Enter PROSPERO, *in his magic robes, and* ARIEL
PROSPERO   Now does my project gather to a head.[1]
    My charms crack not, my spirits obey, and time
    Goes upright with his carriage.[2] How's the day?
  ARIEL   On the sixth hour; at which time, my lord,
    You said our work should cease.
5 PROSPERO   I did say so
    When first I raised the tempest. Say, my spirit,
    How fares the King and's° followers?   *and his*
  ARIEL   Confined together
    In the same fashion as you gave in charge,
    Just as you left them; all prisoners, sir,
10   In the lime-grove which weather-fends[3] your cell.
    They cannot budge till your release.° The King,   *you release them*
    His brother, and yours, abide all three distracted,°   *out of their wits*
    And the remainder mourning over them,
    Brimful of sorrow and dismay; but chiefly
15   Him that you termed, sir, the good old lord Gonzalo:
    His tears run down his beard like winter's drops
    From eaves of reeds.° Your charm so strongly works 'em *thatched roofs*
    That if you now beheld them your affections°   *feelings*
    Would become tender.
  PROSPERO   Dost thou think so, spirit?
  ARIEL   Mine would, sir, were I human.°   *mortal; humane*
20 PROSPERO   And mine shall.
    Hast thou, which art but air, a touch,° a feeling   *sense*
    Of their afflictions, and shall not myself,
    One of their kind, that relish all as sharply
    Passion as they,[4] be kindlier[5] moved than thou art?
25   Though with their high° wrongs I am struck to th' quick, *great*
    Yet with my nobler reason 'gainst my fury
    Do I take part.° The rarer action is   *side*
    In virtue than in vengeance. They being penitent,
    The sole drift of my purpose doth extend
30   Not a frown further. Go release them, Ariel.
    My charms I'll break, their senses I'll restore,
    And they shall be themselves.
  ARIEL   I'll fetch them, sir.   *Exit*
    [PROSPERO *draws a circle with his staff*][6]
  PROSPERO[7] Ye elves of hills, brooks, standing lakes and groves,
    And ye that on the sands with printless foot
35   Do chase the ebbing Neptune, and do fly him
    When he comes back; you demi-puppets[8] that

5.1
1. Draw to its fulfillment. "Project" suggests an alchemical projection or "experiment."
2. Because his carriage, or burden, is now light.
3. Which protects from the weather.
4. *that . . . they*: who feel as much strong emotion as they do.
5. More tenderly; more naturally.
6. The original text does not indicate when the circle is drawn. Other possibilities are at the beginning of the scene or before the entry at line 57.
7. Prospero's speech closely follows Ovid's *Metamorphoses* 7.265–77, in Arthur Golding's translation (1567); the speaker in Ovid is the sorceress Medea, who uses her witchcraft to vengeful ends.
8. Puppets; elves; quasi-puppets.

By moonshine do the green sour ringlets⁹ make
Whereof the ewe not bites; and you whose pastime
Is to make midnight° mushrooms, that rejoice   *springing up overnight*
40 To hear the solemn curfew;¹ by whose aid,
Weak masters² though ye be, I have bedimmed
The noontide sun, called forth the mutinous winds,
And 'twixt the green sea and the azured vault°   *the sky*
Set roaring war—to the dread rattling thunder
45 Have I given fire, and rifted° Jove's stout oak   *split*
With his own bolt;° the strong-based promontory   *lightning bolt*
Have I made shake, and by the spurs° plucked up   *roots*
The pine and cedar; graves at my command
Have waked their sleepers, oped, and let 'em forth
50 By my so potent art. But this rough³ magic
I here abjure. And when I have required°   *summoned*
Some heavenly music—which even now I do—
To work mine end upon their senses that°   *the senses of whom*
This airy⁴ charm is for, I'll break my staff,
55 Bury it certain° fathoms in the earth,   *several*
And deeper than did ever plummet sound
I'll drown my book.
          Solemn music. Here enters [first] ARIEL *[invisible]; then*
          ALONSO, *with a frantic gesture, attended by* GONZALO;
          SEBASTIAN *and* ANTONIO, *in like manner, attended by*
          ADRIAN *and* FRANCISCO. *They all enter the circle which*
          PROSPERO *had made, and there stand charmed; which*
          PROSPERO *observing, speaks*
[*To* ALONSO]⁵ A solemn air,° and° the best comforter   *song / which is*
To an unsettled fancy,° cure thy brains,   *imagination*
Now useless, boiled within thy skull.
60 [*To* SEBASTIAN *and* ANTONIO]⁶   There stand,
For you are spell-stopped.—
Holy Gonzalo, honourable man,
Mine eyes, ev'n sociable° to the show° of thine,   *sympathetic / appearance*
Fall fellowly drops. [*Aside*] The charm dissolves apace,
65 And as the morning steals upon the night,
Melting the darkness, so their rising senses
Begin to chase the ignorant fumes⁷ that mantle°   *envelop*
Their clearer° reason.—O good Gonzalo,   *growing clearer*
My true preserver, and a loyal sir°   *gentleman*
70 To him thou follow'st, I will pay° thy graces   *requite*
Home° both in word and deed.—Most cruelly   *Fully*
Didst thou, Alonso, use me and my daughter.
Thy brother was a furtherer° in the act.—   *an accomplice*
Thou art pinched° for't now, Sebastian.   *tortured; afflicted*
[*To* ANTONIO]   Flesh and blood,
75 You, brother mine, that entertained ambition,
Expelled remorse and nature,⁸ whom,° with Sebastian—   *who*

---

9. Fairy rings: distinctive circles of grass supposed to be
caused by dancing fairies, but actually caused by mush-
rooms.
1. The bell rung at nightfall, indicating the time when
spirits are abroad.
2. Ineffectual when acting independently; without super-
natural power; subordinate spirits.
3. Violent; discordant; crudely approximate.

4. Wrought by spirits of the air.
5. Prospero remains invisible and inaudible to Alonso
and his party until he greets Alonso at line 108.
6. Or perhaps to all the shipwrecked lords.
7. Fogs of ignorance; the image is of the sun ("rising
senses") dissipating morning mist.
8. Pity and brotherly affection.

Whose inward pinches therefore are most strong,—
Would here have killed your king, I do forgive thee,
Unnatural though thou art. [*Aside*] Their understanding
80 Begins to swell,° and the approaching tide   *(as does a tide)*
Will shortly fill the reasonable shores
That now lie foul and muddy. Not° one of them   *There is not*
That yet looks on me, or would know me.—Ariel,
Fetch me the hat and rapier⁹ in my cell.
85 I will discase° me, and myself present   *undress*
As I was sometime Milan.¹ Quickly, spirit!
Thou shalt ere long be free.
        ARIEL *sings and helps to attire him* [*as Duke of Milan*]
ARIEL   Where the bee sucks, there suck I:
        In a cowslip's bell I lie;
90   There I couch when owls do cry.
        On the bat's back I do fly
        After summer merrily.
        Merrily, merrily shall I live now
        Under the blossom that hangs on the bough.
95   Merrily, merrily shall I live now
        Under the blossom that hangs on the bough.
PROSPERO   Why, that's my dainty Ariel! I shall miss thee,
But yet thou shalt have freedom.—So, so, so.²—
To the King's ship, invisible as thou art!
100 There shalt thou find the mariners asleep
Under the hatches. The Master and the Boatswain
Being awake, enforce them to this place,
And presently,° I prithee.   *immediately*
ARIEL   I drink the air before me, and return
105 Or ere° your pulse twice beat.   *Exit*   *Before*
GONZALO   All torment, trouble, wonder, and amazement°   *bewilderment*
Inhabits here. Some heavenly power guide us
Out of this fearful country!
PROSPERO   Behold, sir King,
The wrongèd Duke of Milan, Prospero.
110 For more assurance that a living prince
Does now speak to thee, I embrace thy body;
And to thee and thy company I bid
A hearty welcome.
        [*He embraces* ALONSO]
ALONSO   Whe'er° thou beest he or no,   *Whether*
Or some enchanted trifle³ to abuse° me,   *delude; maltreat*
115 As late I have been, I not know. Thy pulse
Beats as of flesh and blood; and since I saw thee
Th'affliction of my mind amends, with which
I fear a madness held me. This must crave°—   *requires explanation*
An if this be at all⁴—a most strange story.
120 Thy dukedom⁵ I resign, and do entreat

---

9. Elements of normal aristocratic dress.   tion."
1. Formerly, when Duke of Milan.   4. If this is really happening.
2. Prospero arranges his attire approvingly.   5. Alonso's rights of homage and tribute from it.
3. With a suggestion of the old sense of "trifle" as "decep-

Thou pardon me my wrongs. But how should Prospero
Be living and be here?
PROSPERO [*to* GONZALO] First, noble friend,
　Let me embrace thine age,° whose honour cannot　　　　　　　　　　*old body*
　Be measured or confined.
　　　　　[*He embraces* GONZALO]
GONZALO　　　　　　　　Whether this be
　Or be not, I'll not swear.
125 PROSPERO　　　　　　　　You do yet taste
　Some subtleties⁶ o'th' isle that will not let you
　Believe things certain.—Welcome, my friends all.
　[*Aside to* SEBASTIAN *and* ANTONIO]
　But you, my brace° of lords, were I so minded,　　　　　　　　　*pair*
　I here could pluck his highness' frown upon you
130 And justify° you traitors. At this time　　　　　　　　　　　　　*prove*
　I will tell no tales.
SEBASTIAN [*to* ANTONIO] The devil speaks in him.
PROSPERO　　　　　　　　　　　　　No.
　[*To* ANTONIO]　For you, most wicked sir, whom° to call brother　　*who*
　Would even infect my mouth, I do forgive
　Thy rankest fault, all of them, and require
135 My dukedom of thee, which perforce° I know　　　　　　　　　*necessarily*
　Thou must restore.
ALONSO　　　　　　　　If thou beest Prospero,
　Give us particulars of thy preservation,
　How thou hast met us here, whom three hours since
　Were wrecked upon this shore, where I have lost—
140 How sharp the point of this remembrance is!—
　My dear son Ferdinand.
PROSPERO　　　　　　　　I am woe° for't, sir.　　　　　　　　　*I grieve*
ALONSO　Irreparable is the loss, and patience
　Says it is past her cure.
PROSPERO　　　　　　　　I rather think
　You have not sought her help, of° whose soft grace°　　　　　*by / mercy*
145 For the like loss I have her sovereign aid,
　And rest myself content.
ALONSO　　　　　　　　You the like loss?
PROSPERO　As great to me as late;° and supportable　　　　　　　*recent*
　To make the dear loss⁷ have I means much weaker
　Than you may call to comfort you, for I
　Have lost my daughter.⁸
150 ALONSO　　　　　　　　A daughter?
　O heavens, that they were living both in Naples,
　The king and queen there! That they were, I wish
　Myself were mudded in that oozy bed
　Where my son lies. When did you lose your daughter?
155 PROSPERO　In this last tempest. I perceive these lords
　At this encounter do so much admire°　　　　　　　　　　　　*wonder*
　That they devour their reason,⁹ and scarce think
　Their eyes do offices of truth,° these words　　　　　　　*function accurately*

---

6. *You . . . subtleties:* You still experience some of the illusions. "Subtleties" were also sweet confections shaped like castles, temples, beasts, allegorical figures, etc., and arranged like a pageant.
7. *supportable . . . loss:* in order to make the heartfelt loss bearable.
8. Prospero apparently means that Alonso still has a child, his daughter Claribel, to comfort him.
9. "Reason" has the additional sense of "discourse"; hence the phrase is an extension of "swallow their words."

Are natural breath. But howsoe'er you have
160 Been jostled from your senses, know for certain
That I am Prospero, and that very Duke
Which was thrust forth of Milan, who most strangely,
Upon this shore where you were wrecked, was landed
To be the lord on't. No more yet of this,
165 For 'tis a chronicle of day by day,
Not a relation for a breakfast, nor
Befitting this first meeting. Welcome, sir.
This cell's my court. Here have I few attendants,
And subjects none abroad.¹ Pray you, look in.
170 My dukedom since you have given me again,
I will requite you with as good a thing;
At least bring forth a wonder to content ye
As much as me my dukedom.

> Here PROSPERO discovers² FERDINAND and MIRANDA,
> playing at chess

MIRANDA   Sweet lord, you play me false.°   trick me
175 FERDINAND   No, my dearest love,
I would not for the world.
MIRANDA   Yes, for a score of kingdoms you should wrangle,
An I would call it fair play.³
ALONSO   If this prove
A vision of the island, one dear son
Shall I twice lose.
180 SEBASTIAN   A most high miracle.
FERDINAND [coming forward]   Though the seas threaten, they are merciful.
I have cursed them without cause.
> [He kneels]
ALONSO   Now all the blessings
Of a glad father compass thee about.°   surround you
Arise and say how thou cam'st here.
> [FERDINAND rises]
MIRANDA [coming forward]   O wonder!
185 How many goodly creatures are there here!
How beauteous mankind is! O brave new world
That has such people in't!
PROSPERO   'Tis new to thee.
ALONSO [to FERDINAND]   What is this maid with whom thou
        wast at play?
Your eld'st° acquaintance cannot be three hours.   longest
190 Is she the goddess that hath severed us,
And brought us thus together?
FERDINAND   Sir, she is mortal;
But by immortal providence she's mine.
I chose her when I could not ask my father
For his advice, nor thought I had one. She
195 Is daughter to this famous Duke of Milan,
Of whom so often I have heard renown,
But never saw before; of whom I have

---

1. Elsewhere about the island; beyond the cell.
2. Reveals by drawing back a curtain hanging in front of the discovery space.

3. for . . . play: you would quarrel for twenty kingdoms if I would not accuse you of cheating. Other editions read "And" for "An."

Received a second life; and second father
This lady makes him to me.

ALONSO   I am hers.[4]

200   But O, how oddly will it sound, that I
Must ask my child° forgiveness!   *(Miranda)*

PROSPERO   There, sir, stop.
Let us not burden our remembrance with
A heaviness° that's gone.   *sorrow*

GONZALO   I have inly wept,
Or should have spoke ere this. Look down, you gods,

205   And on this couple drop a blessèd crown,
For it is you that have chalked forth° the way   *marked out*
Which brought us hither.

ALONSO   I say amen, Gonzalo.

GONZALO   Was Milan° thrust from Milan, that his issue   *the Duke of Milan*
Should become kings of Naples? O rejoice

210   Beyond a common joy! And set it down
With gold on lasting pillars:[5] in one voyage
Did Claribel her husband find at Tunis,
And Ferdinand her brother found a wife
Where he himself was lost; Prospero his dukedom

215   In a poor isle; and all of us ourselves,
When no man was his own.[6]

ALONSO [*to* FERDINAND *and* MIRANDA] Give me your hands.
Let grief and sorrow still° embrace his heart   *always*
That° doth not wish you joy.   *Who*

GONZALO   Be it so! Amen!

Enter ARIEL, *with the* MASTER *and* BOATSWAIN *amazedly
following*

O look, sir, look, sir, here is more of us!

220   I prophesied if a gallows were on land
This fellow could not drown. [*To the* BOATSWAIN] Now,
blasphemy,°   *blasphemer*
That swear'st grace o'erboard: not an oath on shore?
Hast thou no mouth by land? What is the news?

BOATSWAIN   The best news is that we have safely found

225   Our King and company. The next, our ship,
Which but three glasses° since we gave out° split,   *hourglasses / declared*
Is tight and yare[7] and bravely rigged, as when
We first put out to sea.

ARIEL [*aside to* PROSPERO] Sir, all this service
Have I done since I went.

PROSPERO [*aside to* ARIEL]   My tricksy° spirit!   *capricious; neat*

230   ALONSO   These are not natural events; they strengthen°   *increase*
From strange to stranger. Say, how came you hither?

BOATSWAIN   If I did think, sir, I were well awake
I'd strive to tell you. We were dead of° sleep,   *with*
And—how we know not—all clapped° under hatches,   *shut up*

235   Where but even now, with strange and several° noises   *various*
Of roaring, shrieking, howling, jingling chains,
And more diversity of sounds, all horrible,

---

4. I will be her second father: Alonso's assent to the
betrothal.
5. Suggesting, perhaps, the "triumphal arches" commis-

sioned to celebrate notable occasions.
6. When we all had lost our senses.
7. Is sound and ready to sail.

We were awaked; straightway at liberty;
Where we in all her trim freshly beheld
240 Our royal, good, and gallant ship, our Master
Cap'ring to eye° her. On° a trice, so please you,   *Dancing to see / In*
Even in a dream, were we divided from them,
And were brought moping° hither.   *dazed*
ARIEL [*aside to* PROSPERO]   Was't well done?
PROSPERO [*aside to* ARIEL]   Bravely, my diligence. Thou shalt be free.
245 ALONSO   This is as strange a maze as e'er men trod,
And there is in this business more than nature
Was ever conduct° of. Some oracle   *conductor*
Must rectify our knowledge.
PROSPERO   Sir, my liege,
Do not infest° your mind with beating on[8]   *trouble*
250 The strangeness of this business. At picked leisure,
Which shall be shortly, single° I'll resolve you,   *in private*
Which to you shall seem probable,° of every   *plausible*
These happened accidents;° till when be cheerful,   *incidents*
And think of each thing well. [*Aside to* ARIEL] Come hither, spirit.
255 Set Caliban and his companions free.
Untie the spell.   [*Exit* ARIEL]
[*To* ALONSO]   How fares my gracious sir?
There are yet missing of your company
Some few odd lads that you remember not.
      Enter ARIEL, *driving in* CALIBAN, STEFANO, *and* TRIN-
      CULO, *in their stolen apparel*
STEFANO   Every man shift for all the rest, and let no man take
260 care for himself,[9] for all is but fortune. Coragio, bully-monster,[1]
coragio!
TRINCULO   If these° be true spies which I wear in my head, here's   *these eyes*
a goodly sight.
CALIBAN   O Setebos, these be brave spirits indeed!
265 How fine° my master is! I am afraid   *splendidly dressed*
He will chastise me.
SEBASTIAN   Ha, ha! What things are these, my lord Antonio?
Will money buy 'em?
ANTONIO   Very like;° one of them   *likely*
Is a plain° fish, and no doubt marketable.   *mere*
270 PROSPERO   Mark but the badges[2] of these men, my lords,
Then say if they° be true. This misshapen knave,   *(the men); (the badges)*
His mother was a witch, and one so strong
That could control the moon, make flows and ebbs,
And deal in her command without her power.[3]
275 These three have robbed me, and this demi-devil,[4]
For he's a bastard one, had plotted with them
To take my life. Two of these fellows you
Must know and own.[5] This thing of darkness I
Acknowledge mine.
CALIBAN   I shall be pinched to death.
280 ALONSO   Is not this Stefano, my drunken butler?

---

8. With repeatedly worrying about.
9. Stefano drunkenly confuses the saying "Every man for himself."
1. Gallant monster. *Coragio:* Take courage (Italian).
2. Livery. Servants often wore their master's emblem, but

Prospero probably refers to the stolen apparel.
3. And wield her (the moon's) power without her authority, or beyond the reach of her might.
4. Being the offspring of Sycorax and the devil.
5. And acknowledge to be yours.

SEBASTIAN   He is drunk now. Where had he wine?

ALONSO   And Trinculo is reeling ripe.° Where should they   *drunk*
    Find this grand liquor that hath gilded[6] 'em?
    [*To* TRINCULO] How cam'st thou in this pickle?[7]

285   TRINCULO   I have been in such a pickle since I saw you last that,
    I fear me, will never out of my bones. I shall not fear fly-
    blowing.[8]

SEBASTIAN   Why, how now, Stefano?

STEFANO   O, touch me not! I am not Stefano, but a cramp.

290   PROSPERO   You'd be king o'the isle, sirrah?

STEFANO   I should have been a sore° one, then.   *an inept; severe; pained*

ALONSO   [*pointing to* CALIBAN]   This is a strange thing as e'er I
    looked on.

PROSPERO   He is as disproportioned in his manners[9]

295   As in his shape. [*To* CALIBAN] Go, sirrah, to my cell.
    Take with you your companions. As you look
    To have my pardon, trim° it handsomely.   *tidy; decorate*

CALIBAN   Ay, that I will; and I'll be wise hereafter,
    And seek for grace. What a thrice-double ass

300   Was I to take this drunkard for a god,
    And worship this dull fool!

PROSPERO   Go to, away!   [*Exit* CALIBAN]

ALONSO   [*to* STEFANO *and* TRINCULO]
    Hence, and bestow your luggage where you found it.

SEBASTIAN   Or stole it, rather.   [*Exeunt* STEFANO *and* TRINCULO]

PROSPERO   [*to* ALONSO]   Sir, I invite your highness and your train

305   To my poor cell, where you shall take your rest
    For this one night; which part of it° I'll waste°   *part of which / spend*
    With such discourse as I not doubt shall make it
    Go quick away: the story of my life,
    And the particular accidents° gone by   *events*

310   Since I came to this isle. And in the morn
    I'll bring you to your ship, and so to Naples,
    Where I have hope to see the nuptial
    Of these our dear-belovèd solemnized;[1]
    And thence retire me to my Milan, where
    Every third thought shall be my grave.

315   ALONSO   I long
    To hear the story of your life, which must
    Take° the ear strangely.   *Captivate*

PROSPERO   I'll deliver° all,   *relate*
    And promise you calm seas, auspicious gales,
    And sail so expeditious that shall° catch   *it will*

320   Your royal fleet far off. [*Aside to* ARIEL] My Ariel, chick,
    That is thy charge. Then to the elements
    Be free, and fare thou well.   [*Exit* ARIEL]
                Please you, draw near.°   *go in*
            Exeunt [*all but* PROSPERO][2]

---

6. Probably alluding to the alchemical elixir ("liquor") known as *aurum potabile* (drinkable gold); hence "gilded" (flushed).

7. Sorry plight; Trinculo takes up the literal sense of "preserving liquid," recalling both his drunkenness and his drenching in the lake.

8. Not fear being infested with flies, since he has been "pickled" (preserved).

9. Behavior; moral character.

1. Accented on second and fourth syllables.

2. The general exeunt is through Prospero's cell; Ariel departs in another direction.

Epilogue

PROSPERO   Now my charms are all o'erthrown,
　　　And what strength I have's mine own,
　　　Which is most faint. Now 'tis true
　　　I must be here confined by you
5　　Or sent to Naples. Let me not,
　　　Since I have my dukedom got,
　　　And pardoned the deceiver, dwell
　　　In this bare island° by your spell;　　　　　　　　*(the stage)*
　　　But release me from my bands°　　　　　　　　　*fetters*
10　With the help of your good hands.°　　　　　　　*(applause)*
　　　Gentle breath° of yours my sails　　　　　*Favorable comment*
　　　Must fill, or else my project fails,
　　　Which was to please. Now I want°　　　　　　　　　*lack*
　　　Spirits to enforce, art to enchant;
15　And my ending[1] is despair
　　　Unless I be relieved by prayer,
　　　Which pierces so, that it assaults
　　　Mercy itself, and frees all faults.
　　　As you from crimes would pardoned be,
20　Let your indulgence[2] set me free.

　　　　　　　　　　　[He awaits applause, then] exit

TEXTUAL VARIANTS

Control text: F

F: The Folio of 1623
Fa, Fb: Successive states of F incorporating various print-shop corrections and changes

1.1.18–19 councillor Councellor   **19–20 work peace** worke the peace   **31 wi'th'** with   **54 s.p. MARINERS** [not in F]   **57 wi'th'** with'   **59 broom** Browne   **furze** firrs
1.2.100 oft of it.   **112 wi'th'** with   **153 wast** was't   **174 princes** Princesse   **201 bowsprit** Bore-spritt   **230 Bermudas** *Bermoothes*   **262 Algiers** *Argier*   **284 she** he   **304 to** [not in F]   **330 forth at** for that   **349 human** humane   **383 sprites** *Sprights*   **385–88 s.p. SPIR-ITS ... ARIEL ... SPIRITS** [Only the last refrain, "Hark, hark, I hear," is assigned to *Ar⟨iel⟩.* in F.]   **390 cock-a-diddle-dow** *cockadidle-dowe*   **407 s.p. SPIRITS ... dong** Burthen ding dong   **408 s.p. SPIRITS** [*within*] [not in F]   **470 power** pow'r
2.1.37 s.p. ANTONIO ... Sebastian *Seb⟨astian⟩. .... Ant⟨onio⟩.*   **133 More** Mo   **140 chirurgeonly** Chirurgeonly   **253 every** eu'ry
2.2.52 Then to sea [etc.] [not in F]   **108 spirits** sprights   **120 Swum** Swom   **164 seamews** Scamels
3.1.2 sets set   **15 busil'est** busie lest   **47 peerless** peetlesse
3.2.24 debauched debosh'd   **30 s.p. TRINCULO** [F (text)] *Cal⟨iban⟩.* [F (catchword)]
3.3.2 ache akes   **15 travel** trauaile   **29 islanders** Islands   **33 human** humaine   **65 plume** plumbe   **99 bass** base
4.1.9 of her her   **13 gift** guest   **17 rite** right   **52 rein** raigne   **53 abstemious** abstenious   **61 vetches** Fetches   **peas** Pease   **64 peonied** pioned   **74 Her** here   **81 bosky** boskie   **83 short-grassed** short gras'd   **110 s.p. CERES** [not in F]   **and** [not in F]   **123 wise** wife   **136 holiday** holly day   **180 gorse** gosse   **193 them on** on them   **lime** line   **229 Let't alone** let's alone

---

Epilogue
1. Punning on the sense "death."

2. Approval; appeasement; remission for sin.

5.1.10 lime-grove *Line-groue* 16 run runs 60 boiled boile 72 **Didst** [F (catchword)]
Did [F (text)] 75 **entertained** entertaine 81 **shores** shore 93–96 **Merrily . . . bough**
[In F, these lines are not repeated.] 113 **Whe'er** Where 126 **not** nor 158 **these**
Their 178 **An** And 202 **remembrance** remembrances 230 **events** [Fb] euens
[Fa] 237 **more** mo 239 **her** our 288 **Why** [Fb] Who [Fa]

Cardenio

Many plays acted in Shakespeare's time have failed to survive; they may easily include some that he wrote. The mystery of *Love's Labour's Won* is discussed above. Certain manuscript records of the seventeenth century suggest that at least one other play in which he had a hand may have disappeared. On 9 September 1653 the London publisher Humphrey Moseley entered in the Stationers' Register a batch of plays including 'The History of Cardenio, by Mr Fletcher and Shakespeare'. Cardenio is a character in Part One of Cervantes' *Don Quixote*, published in English translation in 1612. Two earlier allusions suggest that the King's Men owned a play on this subject at the time that Shakespeare was collaborating with John Fletcher (1579–1625). On 20 May 1613 the Privy Council authorized payment of £20 to John Heminges, as leader of the King's Men, for the presentation at court of six plays, one listed as 'Cardenno'. On 9 July of the same year Heminges received £6 13s. 4d. for his company's performance of a play 'called Cardenna' before the ambassador of the Duke of Savoy.

No more information about this play survives from the seventeenth century, but in 1728 Lewis Theobald published a play based on the story of Cardenio and called *Double Falsehood, or The Distrest Lovers*, which he claimed to have 'revised and adapted' from one 'written originally by W. Shakespeare'. It had been successfully produced at Drury Lane on 13 December 1727, and was given thirteen times up to 1 May 1728. Other performances are recorded in 1740, 1741, 1767 (when it was reprinted), 1770, and 1847. In 1770 a newspaper stated that 'the original manuscript' was 'treasured up in the Museum of Covent Garden Playhouse'; fire destroyed the theatre, including its library, in 1808.

Theobald claimed to own several manuscripts of an original play by Shakespeare, and remarked that some of his contemporaries thought the style was Fletcher's, not Shakespeare's. When he himself came to edit Shakespeare's plays he did not include either *Double Falsehood* or the play on which he claimed to have based it; he simply edited the plays of the First Folio, not adding either *Pericles* or *The Two Noble Kinsmen*, though he believed they were partly by Shakespeare. It is quite possible that *Double Falsehood* is based (however distantly) on a play of Shakespeare's time; if so, the play is likely to have been the one performed by the King's Men and ascribed by Moseley in 1653 to Fletcher and Shakespeare.

Double Falsehood is a tragicomedy; the characters' names differ from those in *Don Quixote*, and the story is varied. Henriquez rapes Violante, then falls in love with Leonora, loved by his friend Julio. Her parents agree to the marriage, but Julio interrupts the ceremony. Leonora (who had intended to kill herself) swoons and later takes sanctuary in a nunnery. Julio goes mad with desire for vengeance on his false friend; and the wronged Violante, disguised as a boy, joins a group of shepherds, and is almost raped by one of them. Henriquez's virtuous brother, Roderick, ignorant of his villainy, helps him to abduct Leonora. Leonora and Violante both denounce Henriquez to Roderick. Finally Henriquez repents and marries Violante, while Julio (now sane) marries Leonora.

Some of the motifs of *Double Falsehood*, such as the disguised heroine wronged by her lover and, particularly, the reuniting and reconciliation of parents with children, recall Shakespeare's late plays. But most of the dialogue seems un-Shakespearean. Though the play deserved its limited success, it is now no more than an interesting curiosity.

The Oxford Editors

The Two Noble Kinsmen

When Prospero proclaims near the end of *The Tempest* (1611), "But this rough magic / I here abjure" (5.1.50–51), audiences often think they are hearing Shakespeare's farewell to the theater. The final passage Shakespeare wrote for the stage, though, is more likely to be found at the conclusion of *The Two Noble Kinsmen* (1613–14). Theseus, Duke of Athens, the play's highest-ranking character, attempts to grasp the ironic, paradoxical twists of fate he has witnessed:

> Never fortune
> Did play a subtler game—the conquered triumphs,
> The victor has the loss. Yet in the passage
> The gods have been most equal.
> . . . .
> Let us be thankful
> For that which is, and with you [the gods] leave dispute
> That are above our question. Let's go off
> And bear us like the time.
>
> (5.6.112–37)

It is thus tempting to interpret Theseus's resigned disillusionment as Shakespeare's last word—if not on life, then at least on *The Two Noble Kinsmen*. But the message of the play is not that easy to determine. Theseus's emphasis on the gods, his confidence in their justice (they "have been most equal"), and his counsel of an ambivalent mixture of joy and sorrow ("bear us like the time") underestimate the grim cynicism that accompanies the undeniable pathos of the play. Chivalric military and sexual norms give a touching nobility to the action; but arguably they also generate the misery and destruction to which the bewildered Theseus attempts to respond.

The problem of determining the work's tone parallels the question of authorship. Shakespeare probably wrote *The Two Noble Kinsmen* with John Fletcher, a younger contemporary who succeeded him as the leading playwright of Shakespeare's acting company, the King's Men. Almost one-third of Shakespearean drama may have resulted from collaborations. In Shakespeare's final years, he worked with Fletcher—on the lost *Cardenio* (1612–13), *All Is True* (*Henry VIII*, 1613), and *The Two Noble Kinsmen*. For *The Two Noble Kinsmen*, he probably wrote most of the first and last acts plus a few other scenes, while his colleague composed the rest (slightly more than half; see the Textual Note). The two dramatists differ in style, characterization, and outlook. The rhetorically knotty, ritualistic, near-tragic grandeur in Shakespeare's share contrasts with the syntactically simpler, dramatically more dynamic, near-absurd deflation in Fletcher's. The play as a whole is therefore neither simply Shakespearean nor simply Fletcherian. It is the product of their collaboration and is accordingly marked by dissonance as well as unity.

As the Prologue explains, "Chaucer, of all admired, the story gives" (line 13). The main plot is taken—with greater freedom by Shakespeare than by Fletcher—from *The Knight's Tale*, which immediately follows *The General Prologue* in *The Canterbury Tales*. Concerned with the mortal rivalry for the hand of Emilia between Palamon and Arcite, the two cousins referred to in the title, the play resembles other Shakespearean and Fletcherian tragicomic romances of the preceding six or seven years. Among Shakespeare's works in this genre—*Pericles*, *The Winter's Tale*, *Cymbeline*, and *The Tempest*—one finds parallels to *The Two Noble Kinsmen*'s medieval source, pseudo-historical ancient Greek setting, emphasis on spectacle and ceremony, defense of innocence in the midst of corruption,

The beginning of *The Knight's Tale*, from *Works of Our Ancient and Learned Poet, Geoffrey Chaucer* (1602).

striving for self-mastery, and transcendence of self-interest. There are further similarities in the insistence on death as a necessary price of the survivors' happiness, successful supplication to the gods for aid, and consequent sense of a controlling metaphysical presence that orders events in a way that is beyond human control. Although *The Two Noble Kinsmen* occurs exclusively on dry land, the work even replicates the trademark maritime imagery of Shakespearean romance, with its focus on peril and destruction: the dying Arcite "such a vessel 'tis that floats but for / The surge that next approaches" (5.6.83–84).

Yet *The Two Noble Kinsmen* has a very different feel from other romances of the time, and not simply because of its stylized chivalric ethos and accompanying acts of courtesy, acts that go beyond what is found in Chaucer. Its unusually somber outcome to the impossible choices of the plot sets it apart. Despite Theseus's assertions, the behavior of the gods does not restore confidence in a benevolent Providence. Indeed, Mars, whose intercession Arcite requests, and Venus, to whom Palamon prays, emblematize the chaos reigning in human affairs. When Arcite asks for a sign before his decisive battle with Palamon, he correctly takes Mars's answering thunder as a promise of victory. But this reassurance is no less duplicitous than the guarantee that "none of woman born / Shall harm Macbeth" (*Macbeth*, 4.1.96–97), with the important difference that Macbeth is a usurping mass murderer whereas Arcite is guilty only of desiring a woman his cousin saw first. The divine poetic justice often thought to be operating, however deviously, in *Macbeth* seems like little more than a dirty trick in *The Two Noble Kinsmen*. The play is also structurally distinctive. Shakespearean romance reveals the passage from suffering to serenity, the redemption of the older generation by the younger (and particularly by the virtuous daughter). But Shakespeare and Fletcher's play has no interest in the restorative workings of time. All relationships occur within a single generation, and the young woman (Emilia) incites violence rather than reconciliation.

The opening of *The Two Noble Kinsmen*, in which three widowed queens beg Theseus to come to their aid against Thebes, introduces the military dimension of chivalric conduct. Greatly expanded from the source, this scene reveals Theseus reluctantly yielding to Hippolyta's and Emilia's entreaties to defer his own pleasure (marriage to Hippolyta) to help dowagers in distress. His intervention pits him against Palamon and Arcite, who conclude that they must fight for their home city despite their hatred of its ruler, Creon. This initial sequence implicitly invokes Thebes' history of intrafamilial violence. According to Greek legend, Cadmus sowed the soil with serpent's teeth, from which armed men grew; these men slaughtered each other, and together with Cadmus the few survivors founded Thebes. Later, Oedipus unwittingly murdered his father, and as the play opens, his two sons have killed each other in a battle for the throne that widowed the three queens.

The two cousins are compelled to repeat this history. When Theseus catches them fighting each other, he orders their death, only to reverse his decision once again at Hippolyta's and Emilia's request. He ultimately proposes a chivalric combat in which each cousin is to be aided by three knights and all members of the losing side are to be executed. This plan increases the expected death toll beyond what is necessary and indeed beyond what is found in Chaucer. And it is thwarted by the accidental death of Arcite, a death that is hard to see as providential but that undeniably makes Theseus's strategy look bad by comparison. Earlier, Palamon laments "Mars's so-scorned altar" and yearns for war "to get the soldier work, that peace might purge / For her repletion" (1.2.20–24). This image of war as the virtuous means of purging the excesses of peace is echoed in Arcite's prayer to Mars, who

> heal'st with blood
> The earth when it is sick, and cur'st the world
> O'th' plurisy of people.
>
> (5.1.63–65)

Yet *The Two Noble Kinsmen* sees in war and chivalric combat less a cure for society than a loss of life.

The subplot, which has no known source and which dramatizes the unrequited love of the Jailer's Daughter for Palamon, is mainly the work of Fletcher, who borrowed the morris dance before Theseus and Hippolyta in 3.5 from a masque (an aristocratic theatrical emphasizing song, dance, and spectacle) that Francis Beaumont had composed for court performance in February 1613. (The morris dance itself is a rural folk form often performed on May Day by dancers in outlandish costumes who employ stock characters to partly mime traditional stories.) Echoes of Shakespeare's earlier plays are also pervasive, particularly in Fletcher's scenes. Palamon and Arcite's initial resignation in prison recalls *Richard II*; their conflict over Emilia, *The Two Gentlemen of Verona*; Emilia's comparison of pictures, *Hamlet*. Within the subplot, the Daughter's fall into madness when ignored by Palamon is modeled on Ophelia's in *Hamlet*, complete with an attempted suicide. Her willow song (4.1.79–80) was earlier sung by Desdemona in *Othello*. The Doctor who prescribes her cure earlier ministered to King Lear and rather more unsuccessfully to Lady Macbeth. When the Daughter joins the people whom "ruder tongues distinguish 'villager' " (3.5.106) in the morris dance, the allusion is to another play indebted to *The Knight's Tale*: in *A Midsummer Night's Dream*, "rude mechanicals" (artisans, 3.2.9) also perform before Theseus and Hippolyta on the occasion of their wedding, and unrequited lovers wander through the forest. But *The Two Noble Kinsmen* is *A Midsummer Night's Dream* with a difference. One of Shakespeare's previous romances, *The Winter's Tale*, might be understood as the tragic jealousy of *Othello* lightened and redeemed by the pastoral experience of a romantic comedy, *As You Like It*. By contrast, in *The Two Noble Kinsmen*, the comic tone of *A Midsummer Night's Dream* is darkened by the intervening experience of *Troilus and Cressida*, a work that also draws on Chaucerian narrative to depict a combination of chivalry and sensuality that leads to self-destructive violence and an indifference to the desires of the idealized woman.

Shakespeare and Fletcher's play stands alone, however, in blaming a compulsive sexuality for the havoc that is wreaked. As Theseus says, "Being sensually subdued / We lose our human title" (1.1.231–32). Arcite and especially Palamon are willing to kill and die for a woman about whom they know nothing except her appearance, and even that only at a distance. Indeed, Arcite seems partly motivated by competitive emulation, by a desire to spite Palamon. He tells his cousin that when he sees Emilia, he will "pitch between her arms to anger thee" (2.2.221). The kinsmen claim rights to Emilia while serving life sentences in prison and without her being aware of their existence, much less expressing any interest in them; her feelings don't matter to them. Hence, chivalric combat seems an appropriate mechanism for determining which cousin deserves her. In the event, this stance is validated by their society through the intervention of Theseus. Emilia really doesn't have the choice of rejecting them both. When, bowing to the inevitable, she temporarily is attracted to them, she is unable to decide between "two such young handsome men" (4.2.3). She too looks only to looks.

Palamon's prayer to Venus unwittingly reveals a simultaneous approval and denigration of sexuality:

> I knew a man
> Of eighty winters, this I told them, who

A lass of fourteen brided—'twas thy power
To put life into dust. The agèd cramp
Had screwed his square foot round,
The gout had knit his fingers into knots,
Torturing convulsions from his globy eyes
Had almost drawn their spheres, that what was life
In him seemed torture. This anatomy
Had by his young fair fere a boy, and I
Believed it was his, for she swore it was,
And who would not believe her?

(5.2.39–50)

The power of love is thus exalted through deliberately repellent description. The reference to the "boy" anticipates imagery of sexuality and reproduction at the conclusion—"consummation," "miscarry," "conceives," "deliver" (5.5.94, 101, 137, 138)—that is unremittingly associated with loss. And the account ends with an apparently rhetorical but actually open question that undermines both Venus's sovereignty and female chastity. The very celebration of love has the effect of raising anxieties about women's fidelity and childbirth.

The subplot develops along distinctive but compatible lines. The Daughter, whose first soliloquy immediately follows some frank sexual talk by the morris dancers in 2.3, frees Palamon from prison in the hope that he will then satisfy her sexual desire for him. Though the genders are reversed, the situation is the same as in the main plot: the person in love knows little of the beloved, who in turn is almost completely oblivious of the lover. Palamon's indifference drives the Daughter to a madness that is cured pragmatically and amorally. On the advice of the Doctor and over the principled objections of her father (the

The imprisoned Palamon and Arcite gazing at Emilia in the garden below. From a c.1455 French translation of Giovanni Boccaccio's *Teseida* (the source of Chaucer's *Knight's Tale*), by René of Anjou.

Jailer), the Wooer pretends to be Palamon and makes love with her. Tricked into losing a virginity she was not trying to preserve, "she's well restored / And to be married shortly" (5.6.27–28) to the man who is socially and emotionally right for her. (Earlier, he foils her attempted suicide.) This outcome makes perfect sense in light of Renaissance medicine, which believed hysteria was caused by a wandering womb that could be returned to its proper place by intercourse. More cynically, however, one might conclude that the only thing women really need is sex and that any man will do.

The Daughter's madness is arguably no more deviant than the suicidal and homicidal behavior of Palamon and Arcite. Yet the two noble kinsmen are taken seriously in a way that she is not. Either because she is a woman or because she is from the lower class, she has no right to expect her feelings to be reciprocated, even though she has done more for Palamon than either of the cousins has for Emilia. It is unclear, however, whether the play aims to call attention to this obvious double standard. Ironically, her service to Palamon leads to Arcite's death after earlier bringing Palamon within a hair's breadth of the executioner's axe. On his way to the block, he meets the Jailer, graciously acknowledges his gratitude to "your gentle daughter" (5.6.24), and "gives his purse" (5.6.32 stage direction) as part of the dowry for her impending marriage. His generosity infects the other knights slated to die with him:

> FIRST KNIGHT   Nay, let's be offerers all.
> SECOND KNIGHT   Is it a maid?
> PALAMON   Verily, I think so.
>   (5.6.32–33)

Thus, with the play's characteristic irony, "they give their purses" (5.6.35 stage direction) on a doubly false assumption—that they are doomed and that they are contributing to a virgin's dowry. But in another sense, the Daughter is bought off. Palamon speaks with greater accuracy than he knows in saying she is "more to me deserving / Than I can quit [requite] or speak of" (5.6.34–35).

The Daughter thinks she is marrying one man only to end up with another. Similarly, as Emilia settles into her fate, fate forces her to resettle her affections. Neither woman is given a choice—which is just as well, since neither is capable of making distinctions. The generic names in the subplot—Daughter, Jailer, Wooer, Doctor, Brother, Friends—highlight lack of individuality while pointing toward a similar absence in the main plot. The critical effort to discriminate between Palamon and Arcite inadvertently reaffirms what it seeks to deny: that it takes an effort to tell the cousins apart.

Heterosexual desire is rendered even more unappealing in The Two Noble Kinsmen by the extended representation of what it destroys. This positive alternative is same-sex attachment, whether understood as the Renaissance ideal of male friendship, as girlish intimacy, or as homoerotic attraction. In a romantic comedy such as Much Ado about Nothing, the rejection of heterosexual bonding is seen as an immature foible to be overcome. Here, however, the movement from same-sex innocence to heterosexual experience is figured primarily as loss—comically in the Prologue, with its comparison of "new plays and maidenheads" (line 1), more grimly thereafter. Though in no other respect an Amazon, Emilia emphatically does prefer virginity and the company of females to the prospect of marriage. She tells Theseus that if he does not grant her petition, she will not "be so hardy / Ever to take a husband" (1.1.203–4). In her sexual joking with her Woman, she says that "men are mad things" (2.2.126) and praises the rose above all other flowers because "it is the very emblem of a maid" (2.2.137). Even after coming to admire the cousins, she still prays to Diana either that the more loving and deserving win her or that she be allowed to continue a virgin "in thy band" (5.3.26). When Theseus tells her, "If you can love, end this difference" by choosing one of the kinsmen, she evasively replies, "I cannot, sir. They are both too excellent" (3.6.277, 285).

This stance is explained by Emilia's earlier touching recollection of her intimacy with Flavina, who died when each was eleven. Her account of two girls who "loved for [simply because] we did" culminates in this exchange:

> EMILIA   the true love 'tween maid and maid may be
> More than in sex dividual.
> HIPPOLYTA   You're out of breath,
> And this high-speeded pace is but to say
> That you shall never, like the maid Flavina,
> Love any that's called man.
> EMILIA   I am sure I shall not.
>
> (1.3.81–86)

Neither she nor the play repudiates this position.

Palamon and Arcite do so, however, choosing to kill and die—and hence to ruin the most precious thing in their lives, their love for each other—out of desire for Emilia. This resolution of the standard Renaissance debate over the respective claims of love and friendship has a paradoxical effect. The very depreciation of the cousins' attachment, which is not emphasized in Chaucer, only highlights its value. When they are first imprisoned, though they regret that life imprisonment precludes marriage and family, their thoughts quickly turn to each other. Arcite recommends "the enjoying of our griefs together" (2.2.60) and misogynistically notes the danger of freedom, which "might, like women / Woo us to wander from" "the ways of honour" (lines 73–76). "Were we at liberty / A wife might part us lawfully," but in prison "we are one another's wife, ever begetting / New births of love" (lines 80–89).

As they boast of their loving friendship, Palamon's first sight of Emilia undermines their resolution. She is talking to her Woman about the narcissus flower. This leads her to reflect upon the myth of Narcissus, who fell in love with his own beautiful reflection in a pool and died pining for it: "That was a fair boy, certain, but a fool / To love himself. Were there not maids enough?" (2.2.120–21). This implicit connection between Palamon and Narcissus is made explicit when Emilia remarks that Palamon shows

> not a smile.
> Yet these that we count errors may become him:
> Narcissus was a sad boy, but a heavenly.
>
> (4.2.30–32)

Palamon's suggested autoeroticism and preference for males over females is anticipated in Emilia's immediately preceding, unequivocally homosexual description of Arcite:

> Just such another wanton Ganymede
> Set Jove afire once, and enforced the god
> Snatch up the goodly boy and set him by him.
>
> (4.2.15–17)

Similarly, as the cousins prepare to arm and then battle each other, Arcite admiringly remarks, "Defy me in these fair terms, and you show / More than a mistress to me" (3.6.25–26). And most strikingly of all, when Arcite is released from prison, Palamon imagines what would happen if the roles were reversed:

> Were I at liberty I would do things
> Of such a virtuous greatness that this lady,
> This blushing virgin, should take manhood to her
> And seek to ravish me.
>
> (2.2.260–63)

Even the thought of the woman he loves becomes a fantasy of homosexual rape.

If the play anywhere offers an ideal balance between same-sex and other-sex bonding, it is in Theseus, whose friendship with Pirithous coexists comfortably with his impending marriage to Hippolyta. As suggested earlier, however, Theseus's conduct is open to ques-

A joust celebrating the marriage of Henry IV of England to Joan of Navarre. From the Beauchamp Pageant (1485–90).

tion. Moreover, it is at least suggested that marriage to Hippolyta will never measure up to friendship with Pirithous. Most important, the catastrophic experience of Emilia and the kinsmen carries far more weight than Theseus's greater success in negotiating potentially antagonistic emotional and sexual attachments. Nonetheless, the figure of Theseus may be crucial to an extended allusion to the Jacobean court in *The Two Noble Kinsmen*. Theseus is perhaps an idealized image of King James, who combined marriage with homosexual behavior. In this interpretation, Arcite's death corresponds to the death of James's oldest son, Prince Henry, in the fall of 1612, and the concluding, bittersweet union of Emilia with Palamon parallels the marriage a few months later of James's daughter Elizabeth with the elector Palatine. The probable revivals of 1619–20 and 1625–26, as well as the publication of the First Quarto in 1634, may also have resonated with court life. On the other hand, the evidence is not overwhelming for a direct connection of the play to the Jacobean court, whose members in any case might not have been flattered by the comparison.

Such questions could not much matter to subsequent audiences, however, and with the exception of an adaptation in the late 1660s, *The Two Noble Kinsmen* seems to have remained unstaged until 1928. Twentieth-century performances have tended to be effective when they eschew realism for ritual. In a 1979 production, the decision to employ an all-male cast emphasized the work's homoerotic motifs. But beginning with the late seventeenth-century adaptation, the most consistently successful feature of the staging has been the Jailer's Daughter, who often emerges as the drama's central figure. Her four successive soliloquies in the middle of the play (2.4, 2.6, 3.2, 3.4) are marked by exclamations, questions, and a consequent intimacy with the audience denied the other characters. This position is characteristically reserved for a lower-class male character, especially the clown or fool, with whom the groundlings might identify. The Daughter's special stage position thus helps win sympathy for her openly sexual desire for the aristocratic Palamon. When she later joins the morris dance, she is appropriately cast as the "She-fool" (3.5.138 stage direction). In a dramaturgical sense, she *is* the female equivalent of the fool, and by this time Palamon's indifference has driven her mad. In the remainder of the play, having moved from one form of folly to another, she appears only in dialogue scenes and hence partly loses her unique contact with the audience. Yet even here her vigorous language and stage presence produce an immediacy that effectively combines with the pathos of her predicament. It is, finally, a pathos she shares with the characters in the main plot, who watch in bewildered incomprehension as their most cherished ideals fail them when it matters most.

WALTER COHEN

TEXTUAL NOTE

The Two Noble Kinsmen dates from between February 20, 1613, and October 31, 1614. The mention of "our losses" in the Prologue (line 32) has sometimes been taken as a reference to the burning of the Globe Theatre on June 29, 1613. If so, this is Shakespeare's final play, perhaps performed at Blackfriars, the King's Men's indoor theater, in the fall of 1613, or at the opening of the rebuilt Globe, their outdoor theater, a year after the fire. Both the only substantive text, the Quarto of 1634 (Q), and an entry from earlier the same year in the Stationers' Register (a listing of books approved for publication), which calls the play a "TragiComedy," attribute it to John Fletcher and Shakespeare. The exclusion of *The Two Noble Kinsmen* from the First Folio of 1623 (F) has sometimes led to doubts about Shakespeare's authorship, but most scholars accept the attribution, which is supported by other internal and external evidence. Although the exact division of labor between the two playwrights cannot be determined with certainty, Shakespeare probably wrote a little less than half the play: 1.1–2.1, 3.1–3.2, 5.1.34–5.3, and 5.5–5.6 (in other words, the beginning and end plus some of the middle).

Q is based either on the authors' manuscript or on a scribal transcript. It shows some sign of revision, possibly by an author, perhaps in the Prologue, more probably in 4.2, and especially in 4.3. Whether authorial or scribal, the manuscript was annotated with stage directions and other indications (for instance, about props) in preparation for performance, perhaps more than once—for the original production and again for a revival in 1625–26 by Edward Knight, who worked for the King's Men at the time. (There may also have been a revival at court in roughly 1619–20.) Q seems likely to have been printed from the resulting promptbook, though it may derive from a manuscript that merely served as the basis for the promptbook. If Q is in fact based on a scribal transcript, Knight is the most likely scribe.

Two compositors probably set the type for Q, alternating work quite frequently. The printed text is a good one, but it contains two scenes headed 2.4 (followed by 2.6); editors routinely convert the second 2.4 to 2.5. Q also follows 3.4 with 3.6 and 3.7—perhaps a sign of an original 3.5 that was cut without the subsequent scenes being renumbered, as they are here (as 3.5 and 3.6). In addition, it missets verse as prose and, more often (2.1, 4.3), prose as verse. Some editors have ignored Q's scene break between 2.1 and 2.2 on the grounds that the scene is continuous. As the notes explain, the present edition proposes a staging for the two scenes that justifies the scene division. On the other hand, though again for reasons of staging, this edition expands Q's 5.1 into three scenes: the final three scenes in the play are therefore converted from 5.2–4 to 5.4–6.

SELECTED BIBLIOGRAPHY

Abrams, Richard. "Gender Confusion and Sexual Politics in *The Two Noble Kinsmen*." *Drama, Sex, and Politics*. Ed. James B. Redmond. Cambridge: Cambridge University Press, 1985.

Berggren, Paula S. " 'For what we lack / We laugh': Incompletion and *The Two Noble Kinsmen*." *Modern Language Studies* 14, no. 4 (1984): 3–17.

Bertram, Paul. *Shakespeare and "The Two Noble Kinsmen."* New Brunswick, N.J.: Rutgers University Press, 1965.

Donaldson, E. Talbot. *The Swan at the Well: Shakespeare Reading Chaucer*. New Haven: Yale University Press, 1985. 50–73.

Edwards, Philip. "On the Design of *The Two Noble Kinsmen*." *Review of English Literature* 5 (1964): 89–105.

Frey, Charles, ed. *Shakespeare, Fletcher, and "The Two Noble Kinsmen."* Columbia: University of Missouri Press, 1989.

Potter, Lois. "Topicality or Politics? *The Two Noble Kinsmen*, 1613–34." *The Politics of Tragicomedy: Shakespeare and After*. Ed. Gordon McMullan and Jonathan Hope. London: Routledge, 1992. 77–91.

Spencer, Theodore. "*The Two Noble Kinsmen*." *Modern Philology* 36 (1939): 255–76.

Thompson, Ann. *Shakespeare's Chaucer: A Study in Literary Origins*. Liverpool: Liverpool University Press, 1978. 166–215.

Wickham, Glynne. "*The Two Noble Kinsmen* or *A Midsummer Night's Dream, Part II?*" *The Elizabethan Theatre*, VII. Ed. G. R. Hibbard. Hamden, Conn.: Archon Books, University of Waterloo, 1980. 167–96.

The Two Noble Kinsmen

THE PERSONS OF THE PLAY

PROLOGUE
THESEUS, Duke of Athens
HIPPOLYTA, Queen of the Amazons, later wife of Theseus
EMILIA, her sister
PIRITHOUS, friend of Theseus
PALAMON ⎤ the two noble kinsmen, cousins, nephews of
ARCITE ⎦ Creon, the King of Thebes
Hymen, god of marriage
A BOY, who sings
ARTESIUS, an Athenian soldier
Three QUEENS, widows of kings killed in the siege of Thebes
VALERIUS, a Theban
A HERALD
WOMAN, attending Emilia
An Athenian GENTLEMAN
MESSENGERS
Six KNIGHTS, three attending Arcite and three Palamon
A SERVANT
A JAILER in charge of Theseus' prison
The JAILER'S DAUGHTER
The JAILER'S BROTHER
The WOOER of the Jailer's daughter
Two FRIENDS of the Jailer
A DOCTOR
Six COUNTRYMEN, one dressed as a babion, or baboon
Gerald, a SCHOOLMASTER
NELL, a country wench
Four other country wenches: Friz, Madeline, Luce, and
 Barbara
Timothy, a TABORER
EPILOGUE
Nymphs, attendants, maids, executioner, guard

Prologue

Flourish.° [*Enter* PROLOGUE]   *Trumpet call*
PROLOGUE   New plays and maidenheads are near akin:
    Much followed both, for both much money giv'n
    If they stand sound and well. And a good play,
    Whose modest scenes blush on his marriage day
5   And shake to lose his honour,[1] is like her
    That after holy tie° and first night's stir   *marriage*
    Yet still is modesty, and still retains
    More of the maid to sight than husband's pains.[2]

Prologue
1. *Whose . . . honour:* Whose previously unwatched scenes are "modest" and shy (they "blush") on opening night and "shake" with fear at the thought of being viewed (losing their virginity).

2. *still . . . pains:* still looks more like a virgin ("maid") than like a married woman who has experienced her husband's sexual exertions.

We pray our play may be so,° for I am sure   (modest)
10   It has a noble breeder° and a pure,   begetter
A learnèd, and a poet never went
More famous yet 'twixt Po and silver Trent.[3]
Chaucer, of° all admired, the story gives: by
There° constant to eternity it lives.   In his words
15   If we let fall° the nobleness of this°   demean / (the poem)
And the first sound this child° hear be a hiss,   play
How will it shake the bones of that good man,°   (Chaucer)
And make him cry from under ground, 'O fan
From me the witless chaff of such a writer,
20   That blasts my bays and my famed works makes lighter
Than Robin Hood'?[4] This is the fear we bring,
For to say truth, it were an endless° thing   never-ending; impossible
And too ambitious to aspire to him,°   (Chaucer)
Weak as we are, and almost breathless swim
25   In this deep water. Do but you hold out
Your helping hands and we shall tack about
And something do to save us.[5] You shall hear
Scenes, though below his art, may yet appear
Worth two hours' travail.[6] To his bones, sweet sleep;
30   Content to you. If this play do not keep
A little dull time from us,[7] we perceive
Our losses fall so thick we must needs leave.[8]   *Flourish.* [*Exit*]

1.1

Music. Enter Hymen° with a torch burning, a BOY *in a*   god of marriage
white robe before, singing and strewing flowers. After
Hymen, a nymph encompassed in her tresses, bearing a
wheaten garland.[1] Then THESEUS *between two other*
nymphs with wheaten chaplets° on their heads. Then HIP-   wreaths
POLYTA,[2] *the bride, led by* [PIRITHOUS] *and another hold-*
ing a garland over her head, her tresses likewise hanging.
After her, EMILIA *holding up her train.* [*Then* ARTESIUS
and other attendants]
BOY [*sings during procession*]
            Roses, their sharp spines being gone,
            Not royal in their smells alone,
                But in their hue;
            Maiden pinks, of odour faint,

---

3. *a poet . . . Trent:* there has never been a more famous
poet from Italy to England. The Po is a river in Italy, the
Trent an English waterway.
4. *That . . . Hood:* Who disgraces my fame as a poet (gar-
lands of bay or laurel were awarded to great poets, hence
the name "poet laureate") and makes my renowned cre-
ations seem more trivial than a popular tale or ballad
(such as Robin Hood).
5. *Do but . . . us:* Help us by applauding, and we will turn
like a sailboat in the breeze produced by your clapping
hands, thereby saving our reputation.
6. *two hours' travail:* the actors' exertions ("travail") for
two hours in performing the play (standard length was
two to three hours); or, possibly, the audience will travel
("travail") on a two-hour imaginative journey while
watching the play. "Travail" continues the metaphor of
childbirth and rearing begun in line 10, which itself

develops from the image of the loss of virginity on the
marriage night.
7. *keep . . . us:* keep us amused.
8. Our losses will be so great we will need to quit the
theater. The "losses" refer to the decline in reputation
from a poorly received play and perhaps also to the burn-
ing of the Globe Theatre on June 29, 1613, during a per-
formance of *All Is True* (*Henry VIII*).
1.1 Location: Athens, near the temple where Hippolyta
and Theseus are to be married.
1. The young woman's hair hangs loose, indicating vir-
ginity; her garland signifies fertility.
2. According to legend, Hippolyta was Queen of the
Amazons before Theseus conquered her race of women
warriors and brought her to Thebes as his captive and
bride.

5   Daisies smell-less, yet most quaint,°   *beautiful*
      And sweet thyme true;

     Primrose, first-born child of Ver,°   *spring*
      Merry springtime's harbinger,
       With harebells dim;°   *pale*
10   Oxlips,° in their cradles growing,   *Flowering herbs*
      Marigolds, on deathbeds blowing,°   *flowering on graves*
       Lark's-heels° trim;   *Larkspur*
      All dear nature's children sweet,
      Lie fore bride and bridegroom's feet,
     [*He*] *strew*[*s*] *flowers*
15   Blessing their sense.
      Not an angel of the air,°   *good-luck bird*
      Bird melodious, or bird fair,
       Is absent hence.

     The crow, the sland'rous[3] cuckoo, nor
20   The boding° raven, nor chough hoar,[4] *ominous*
       Nor chatt'ring pie,°   *magpie*
      May on our bridehouse° perch or sing, *wedding venue*
      Or with them any discord bring,
       But from it fly.
     Enter three QUEENS *in black, with veils stained,° with* *dyed black*
     imperial crowns. The FIRST QUEEN *falls down at the foot*
     of THESEUS; *the* SECOND *falls down at the foot of* HIPPO-
     LYTA; *the* THIRD, *before* EMILIA
25 FIRST QUEEN [*to* THESEUS] For pity's sake and true gentility's,
  Hear and respect° me.   *attend to*
 SECOND QUEEN [*to* HIPPOLYTA] For your mother's sake,
  And as you wish your womb may thrive with fair ones,
  Hear and respect me.
 THIRD QUEEN [*to* EMILIA] Now for the love of him whom Jove
  hath marked°   *singled out for*
30 The honour of your bed, and for the sake
  Of clear° virginity, be advocate   *unspotted*
  For us and our distresses. This good deed
  Shall raze you out o'th' Book of Trespasses
  All you are set down there.[5]
 THESEUS [*to* FIRST QUEEN] Sad lady, rise.
 HIPPOLYTA [*to* SECOND QUEEN]   Stand up.
35 EMILIA [*to* THIRD QUEEN]   No knees to me.
  What woman I may stead° that is distressed   *assist*
  Does bind me to her.
 THESEUS [*to* FIRST QUEEN] What's your request? Deliver° you *Speak*
  for all.
 FIRST QUEEN [*kneeling still*] We are three queens whose sovereigns
  fell before
40 The wrath of cruel Creon;[6] who° endured   *(the sovereigns)*

---

3. Because it yelled out "cuckold" (husband of an adul-
terous wife), impugning faithful wives.
4. A small, rare, gray-headed ("hoar"), red-beaked, cliff-
dwelling crow.
5. *Shall . . . there*: Will expunge your sins from the divine
ledger.
6. Brother to Jocasta and hence both brother-in-law and

uncle to Oedipus, Creon succeeded Oedipus's son
Eteocles as King of Thebes following the siege known as
the "Seven against Thebes," in which both Eteocles and
all the attackers, led by Eteocles' brother Polynices, were
killed. Creon refused to bury any of the seven, including
the husbands of the Three Queens.

The beaks of ravens, talons of the kites,
And pecks of crows in the foul fields° of Thebes.   *battlefields*
He will not suffer us to burn their bones,
To urn their ashes, nor to take th'offence
45   Of mortal loathsomeness from the blest eye
Of holy Phoebus,° but infects the winds   *the sun*
With stench of our slain lords. O pity, Duke!
Thou purger of the earth,[7] draw thy feared sword
That does good turns to'th' world; give us the bones
50   Of our dead kings that we may chapel° them;   *entomb*
And of° thy boundless goodness take some note   *in*
That for our crownèd heads we have no roof,
Save this,° which is the lion's and the bear's,   *(the sky)*
And vault° to everything.   *ceiling*
THESEUS   Pray you, kneel not:
55   I was transported with° your speech, and suffered   *moved by*
Your knees to wrong themselves.° I have heard the fortunes   *(by kneeling)*
Of your dead lords, which gives me such lamenting
As wakes my vengeance and revenge for 'em.
King Capaneus was your lord: the day
60   That he should° marry you—at such a season   *was about to*
As now it is with me—I met your groom
By Mars's altar. You were that time fair,
Not Juno's mantle fairer than your tresses,
Nor in more bounty spread her.[8] Your wheaten wreath
65   Was then nor° threshed nor blasted;° fortune at you   *neither / withered*
Dimpled her cheek with smiles; Hercules our kinsman—
Then weaker than° your eyes—laid by his club.   *overwhelmed by*
He tumbled down upon his Nemean hide
And swore his sinews thawed.[9] O grief and time,
70   Fearful° consumers, you will all devour.   *Terrifying*
FIRST QUEEN [*kneeling still*]   O, I hope some god,
Some god hath put his mercy in your manhood,
Whereto he'll infuse power and press you forth
Our undertaker.°   *champion*
THESEUS   O no knees, none, widow:
[*The* FIRST QUEEN *rises*]
75   Unto the helmeted Bellona° use them   *Roman goddess of war*
And pray for me, your soldier. Troubled I am.
[*He*] *turns away*
SECOND QUEEN [*kneeling still*]   Honoured Hippolyta,
Most dreaded Amazonian, that hast slain
The scythe-tusked boar,[1] that with thy arm, as strong
80   As it is white, wast near to° make the male   *almost managed to*
To thy sex captive, but that this, thy lord—
Born to uphold creation in that honour
First nature styled it in[2]—shrunk thee into

---

7. Like his cousin Hercules (see 1.1.66, 3.6.175), Theseus was known for ridding the world of monsters and evildoers.
8. Nor is Juno (goddess of marriage) more luxuriantly wrapped in her mantle than you were in your hanging tresses.
9. *He . . . thawed:* He (Hercules) flopped down on the hide of the Nemean lion (which he wore after killing it as one of his twelve labors) and swore his muscles were

turned to water by your beauty. Most powerful of Greek mythological heroes, performer of "twelve strong labours" set for him by his cousin (3.6.175), Hercules was typically portrayed armed with a club.
1. *Honored . . . boar:* Hippolyta is here confused with Atalanta, another Amazon, who participated with Meleager in the hunt for the Calydonian boar. See note to 3.5.18.
2. *Born . . . in:* Born to sustain the natural order of creation—the order of man over woman.

The bound thou wast o'erflowing,[3] at once subduing
85 Thy force and thy affection; soldieress,
That equally canst poise° sternness with pity,   *balance*
Whom now I know hast much more power on° him   *over*
Than ever he had on thee, who ow'st° his strength,   *owns*
And his love too, who is a servant for
90 The tenor of thy speech;[4] dear glass of° ladies,   *mirror for*
Bid him that we, whom flaming war doth scorch,
Under the shadow of his sword may cool us.
Require him he° advance it o'er our heads.   *Command him to*
Speak't in a woman's key,° like such a woman   *tone*
95 As any of us three. Weep ere you fail.
Lend us a knee:
But touch the ground for us no longer time
Than a dove's motion when the head's plucked off.
Tell him, if he i'th' blood-sized° field lay swoll'n,   *blood-soaked*
100 Showing the sun his teeth, grinning at the moon,
What you would do.
HIPPOLYTA   Poor lady, say no more.
I had as lief trace[5] this good action with you
As that° whereto I am going, and never yet   *(marriage)*
Went I so willing way. My lord is taken°   *affected*
105 Heart-deep with your distress. Let him consider.
I'll speak anon.°   *soon*
    [*The* SECOND QUEEN *rises*]
THIRD QUEEN (*kneel*[*ing still*] *to* EMILIA)   O, my petition was
Set down in ice,[6] which by hot grief uncandied°   *thawed*
Melts into drops; so sorrow, wanting form,
Is pressed with deeper matter.[7]
EMILIA   Pray stand up:
Your grief is written in your cheek.
110 THIRD QUEEN   O woe,
You cannot read it there; there,° through my tears,   *in my eye*
Like wrinkled pebbles in a glassy stream,
You may behold 'em.°   *(my sorrows)*
    [*The* THIRD QUEEN *rises*]
                          Lady, lady, alack—
He that will all the treasure know o'th' earth
115 Must know° the centre too; he that will fish   *dig deep throughout*
For my least minnow, let him lead° his line   *weight with lead*
To catch one at my heart. O, pardon me:
Extremity, that sharpens sundry wits,
Makes me a fool.[8]
EMILIA   Pray you, say nothing, pray you.
120 Who cannot feel nor see the rain, being in't,
Knows neither wet nor dry. If that you were
The ground-piece of some painter,[9] I would buy you
T'instruct me 'gainst a capital° grief, indeed   *deadly*

---

3. *shrunk . . . o'erflowing*: returned you to the limits of
your sex, which you had previously exceeded.
4. *who is . . . speech*: who, like a good lover, obeys your
every spoken desire.
5. I would as willingly follow through.
6. *my . . . ice*: my former speech was cold and formal.
7. *so . . . matter*: so sorrow, lacking a way to express itself,

is made yet more oppressive by its inarticulateness; or,
perhaps, receives the stamp of "deeper" impulses.
8. *Extremity . . . fool*: Extreme suffering, which makes
some minds more clear, has made me speak inappropri-
ately.
9. *If . . . painter*: If you were merely the subject (model;
preliminary sketch?) of a painting.

Such heart-pierced° demonstration; but, alas,   *heartrending*
125 Being a natural sister of our sex,[1]
Your sorrow beats so ardently° upon me   *burningly*
That it shall make a counter-reflect 'gainst[2]
My brother's heart, and warm it to some pity,
Though it were made of stone. Pray have good comfort.
130 THESEUS   Forward to th' temple.° Leave not out a jot   *(for the wedding)*
O'th' sacred ceremony.
FIRST QUEEN   O, this celebration
Will longer last and be more costly than
Your suppliants' war. Remember that your fame
Knolls° in the ear o'th' world: what you do quickly   *Tolls like a bell*
135 Is not done rashly; your first thought is more
Than others' laboured meditance;° your premeditating   *careful meditation*
More than their actions. But, O Jove, your actions,
Soon as they move, as ospreys do the fish,[3]
Subdue before they touch. Think, dear Duke, think
What beds our slain kings have.
140 SECOND QUEEN   What griefs our beds,
That our dear lords have none.
THIRD QUEEN   None fit for th' dead.
Those that with cords, knives, drams,° precipitance,°   *poisons / leaps*
Weary of this world's light, have to themselves
Been death's most horrid agents, human grace°   *mercy*
Affords them dust and shadow.
145 FIRST QUEEN   But our lords
Lie blist'ring fore the visitating° sun,   *inspecting*
And were good kings, when living.
THESEUS   It is true,
And I will give you comfort to give° your dead lords graves,   *by giving*
The which to do must make some work with Creon.
150 FIRST QUEEN   And that work presents itself to th' doing.[4]
Now 'twill take form, the heats are gone tomorrow.[5]
Then, bootless° toil must recompense itself   *fruitless*
With its own sweat; now he's secure,°   *unaware of danger*
Not dreams we stand before your puissance°   *power*
155 Rinsing our holy begging in our eyes
To make petition clear.°   *pure; manifest*
SECOND QUEEN   Now you may take him,
Drunk with his victory.
THIRD QUEEN   And his army full
Of bread and sloth.
THESEUS   Artesius, that best knowest
How to draw out,° fit to this enterprise   *select*
160 The prim'st° for this proceeding and the number   *best soldiers*
To carry° such a business: forth and levy   *conduct; win*
Our worthiest instruments, whilst we dispatch
This grand act of our life, this daring deed
Of fate[6] in wedlock.

---

1. Since you are actually a live woman (rather than a representation of a grieving wife).
2. That, like a mirror, I'll reflect your (sunlike) sorrow back toward.
3. According to popular legend, ospreys had the power to compel fish to rise to the surface and turn over, making themselves available for capture.
4. And that work needs to be done as soon as possible.
5. While the plan, like molten metal, is still hot, it can be transformed into something—once it grows cold, it can no longer be shaped.
6. *this daring deed / Of fate*: this act (marriage) that challenges fate.

FIRST QUEEN [*to the other two* QUEENS]   Dowagers,° take hands;   *Widows*
165 Let us be widows to our woes; delay
Commends us to a famishing hope.[7]
ALL THREE QUEENS   Farewell.
SECOND QUEEN   We come unseasonably,° but when could grief   *at a bad time*
Cull forth,° as unpanged° judgement can, fitt'st time   *Choose / untormented*
For best solicitation?
THESEUS   Why, good ladies,
170 This is a service whereto I am going
Greater than any war—it more imports me°   *means more to me*
Than all the actions that I have foregone,°   *done to date*
Or futurely can cope.°   *achieve*
FIRST QUEEN   The more proclaiming°   *Clearly showing that*
Our suit shall be neglected when her arms,
175 Able to lock Jove from a synod,[8] shall
By warranting° moonlight corslet thee![9] O when   *authorizing*
Her twinning cherries° shall their sweetness fall°   *lips / let fall*
Upon thy tasteful° lips, what wilt thou think   *tasting*
Of rotten kings or blubbered° queens? What care   *tear-soaked*
180 For what thou feel'st not, what thou feel'st being able
To make Mars spurn his drum?° O, if thou couch   *(battle signal)*
But one night with her, every hour in't will
Take hostage of thee° for a hundred,° and   *Commit you / (more)*
Thou shalt remember nothing more than what
That banquet bids° thee to.   *invites*
185 HIPPOLYTA [*to* THESEUS]   Though much unlike
You should be so transported, as much sorry
I should be such a suitor[1]—yet I think
Did I not by th'abstaining of my joy,
Which breeds a deeper longing, cure their surfeit°   *excess of grief*
190 That craves a present medicine,° I should pluck   *an immediate relief*
All ladies' scandal° on me. [*Kneels*]   Therefore, sir,   *reproach*
As I shall here make trial of my prayers,
Either presuming them to have some force,
Or sentencing for aye their vigour dumb,[2]
195 Prorogue° this business we are going about, and hang   *Delay*
Your shield afore your heart—about that neck
Which is my fee,° and which I freely lend   *property*
To do these poor queens service.
ALL THREE QUEENS [*to* EMILIA]   O, help now,
Our cause cries for your knee.
EMILIA [*kneels to* THESEUS]   If you grant not
200 My sister her petition in that force°   *with that energy*
With that celerity and nature° which   *spontaneous speed*
She makes it in, from henceforth I'll not dare
To ask you anything, nor be so hardy°   *bold*
Ever to take a husband.
THESEUS   Pray stand up.

---

7. *Let . . . hope:* Let us mourn our misfortunes as we
mourned our husbands (or, let us, widow-like, part from
our woes), since by delaying the battle until his marriage
is completed, Theseus consigns us to failure.
8. Able to keep Jupiter from a meeting of the gods.
9. Encircle you like a "corslet," close-fitting defensive
armor. Theseus has traded arms (armor) for arms

(embraces).
1. *Though . . . suitor:* Although it's highly unlikely you'd
be so carried away, and just as unlikely I'd now request
you to postpone the wedding.
2. Or forever "sentencing" my prayers to silence, than
which they are no more effectual.

[*They rise*]

205   I am entreating of myself to do
    That which you kneel to have me.°—Pirithous,   *have me do*
    Lead on the bride: get you° and pray the gods   *go*
    For success and return; omit not anything
    In the pretended° celebration.—Queens,   *intended*
210   Follow your soldier.° [*To* ARTESIUS]   As before, hence you,   *Theseus*
    And at the banks of Aulis[3] meet us with
    The forces you can raise, where we shall find
    The moiety of a number for a business
    More bigger looked.[4]   [*Exit* ARTESIUS]
    [*To* HIPPOLYTA]   Since that our theme is haste,
215   I stamp this kiss upon thy current lip—
    Sweet, keep it as my token.[5] [*To the wedding party*] Set you
        forward,
    For I will see you gone.
    [*To* EMILIA] Farewell, my beauteous sister.—Pirithous,
    Keep the feast full:° bate° not an hour on't.°   *fully / abate / of it*
PIRITHOUS   Sir,
220   I'll follow you at heels. The feast's solemnity°   *ceremonial splendor*
    Shall want° till your return.   *be lacking*
THESEUS   Cousin,° I charge you   *Friend*
    Budge not from Athens. We shall be returning
    Ere you can end this feast, of which, I pray you,
    Make no abatement.°—Once more, farewell all.   *reduction*
        Exeunt [HIPPOLYTA, EMILIA, PIRITHOUS, *and train*]
                           towards the temple
FIRST QUEEN   Thus dost thou still make good the tongue o'th'
225   world.[6]
SECOND QUEEN   And earn'st a deity equal with Mars—
THIRD QUEEN   If not above him, for
    Thou being but mortal mak'st affections bend
    To godlike honours;[7] they themselves, some say,
    Groan under such a mast'ry.[8]
230 THESEUS   As we are men,
    Thus should we do; being sensually subdued°   *overcome by appetites*
    We lose our human title.° Good cheer, ladies.   *claim to humanity*
    Now turn we towards your comforts.   *Flourish. Exeunt*

1.2

Enter PALAMON *and* ARCITE

ARCITE   Dear Palamon, dearer in love than blood,
    And our prime cousin,° yet unhardened in   *nearest kin*
    The crimes of nature,[1] let us leave the city,

---

3. Port where the Greek troops assembled before sailing
for Troy.
4. *where . . . looked:* where we shall find part of an army
already assembled for a larger campaign than this one.
5. *I . . . token:* puns on coining and engraving. *stamp:*
press (a kiss); make a coin by impressing an image on
metal. *current:* flowing away (like a stream); red (currant);
genuine, not counterfeit. *token:* memento (often of love);
metal stamped and used as a coin.
6. In this way, you (Theseus) prove true everything the
world says of you.
7. *mak'st . . . honours:* subordinate your human passions

to godlike deeds.
8. *they . . . mast'ry:* the gods themselves complain of such
self-restraint; suffer because their passions master them.
1.2 Location: Thebes.
1. *unhardened . . . nature:* inexperienced in the natural
vices of man. In this scene, a number of the most
important themes of the play are introduced: that matu-
rity and experience necessitate a loss of innocence; that
friendship constitutes a stronger tie than either marriage /
love relations or blood; and that duty to the knightly vir-
tue of honor is stronger than duty to human laws and
sovereigns (except in times of war).

Thebes, and the temptings° in't, before we further *temptations*
5 Sully our gloss of° youth. *Tarnish our pristine*
  And here to keep in abstinence we shame
As in incontinence;[2] for not to swim
I'th' aid o'th' current° were almost to sink— *With the flow*
At least to frustrate striving;[3] and to follow
10 The common stream 'twould bring us to an eddy
Where we should turn° or drown; if labour through, *spin endlessly*
Our gain but life and weakness.[4]
PALAMON   Your advice
Is cried up with example.[5] What strange ruins° *ruined men*
Since first we went to school may we perceive
15 Walking in Thebes? Scars and bare weeds° *tattered clothes*
The gain o'th' martialist° who did propound *soldier*
To his bold ends[6] honour and golden ingots,
Which though he won, he had not;[7] and now flirted° *(is) mocked*
By peace for whom he fought. Who then shall offer
20 To Mars's so-scorned altar? I do bleed
When such I meet, and wish great Juno[8] would
Resume her ancient° fit of jealousy *former*
To get the soldier work, that peace might purge
For her repletion[9] and retain° anew *take into service*
25 Her° charitable heart, now hard and harsher *(Juno's); (peace's)*
Than strife or war could be.
ARCITE   Are you not out?° *off the point*
Meet you no ruin but the soldier in
The cranks and turns° of Thebes? You did begin *winding streets*
As if you met decays of many kinds.
30 Perceive you none that do arouse your pity
But th'unconsidered° soldier? *neglected*
PALAMON   Yes, I pity
Decays where'er I find them, but such most
That, sweating in an honourable toil,
Are paid with ice° to cool 'em. *treated coldly*
ARCITE   'Tis not this
35 I did begin to speak of. This is virtue,
Of no respect in Thebes. I spake of Thebes,
How dangerous, if we will keep our honours,
It is for our residing where every evil
Hath a good colour,° where every seeming good's *appearance*
40 A certain evil, where not to be ev'n jump° *exactly*
As they are here were to be strangers,° and *foreigners*
Such things to be,° mere monsters. *to be like them*
PALAMON   'Tis in our power,
Unless we fear that apes can tutor's,° to *that we're mere mimics*
Be masters of our manners. What need I
45 Affect another's gait, which is not catching° *infectious; attractive*

---

2. *here . . . incontinence*: we incur as much shame here (in a corrupt city) by remaining innocent as we would elsewhere by debauching ourselves.
3. And at least renders our exertions (on behalf of goodness) pointless.
4. *if . . . weakness*: if we were to pass through such a whirlpool ("eddy"), we would gain only our lives in a weakened state.

5. Is borne out by numerous examples.
6. *propound . . . ends*: propose as recompense for his courage.
7. Which, though victorious in battle, he didn't receive.
8. Juno's jealousy led to the Trojan War and other conflicts.
9. *purge / For her repletion*: take medicine to alleviate her (peace's) overeating (the indulgent life of peacetime).

Where there is faith?[1] Or to be fond° upon   *to dote*
Another's way of speech, when by mine own
I may be reasonably conceived°—saved, too—   *understood*
Speaking it° truly? Why am I bound   *If I speak*
50 By any generous° bond to follow him   *noble*
Follows° his tailor, haply° so long until   *Who heeds / at least*
The followed make pursuit?° Or let me know *(for unpaid bills)*
Why mine own barber is unblest—with him
My poor chin, too—for 'tis not scissored just
55 To such a favourite's glass?° What canon° is there   *image / law*
That does command my rapier from my hip
To dangle't in my hand? Or to go tiptoe
Before the street be foul?[2] Either I am
The fore-horse in the team or I am none
60 That draw i'th' sequent trace.[3] These poor slight sores
Need not a plantain.[4] That which rips my bosom
Almost to th' heart's—
ARCITE   Our uncle Creon.
PALAMON   He,
A most unbounded° tyrant, whose successes   *unrestrained*
Makes heaven unfeared and villainy assured°   *assured that*
65 Beyond its power there's nothing; almost puts
Faith in a fever,[5] and deifies alone
Voluble chance;° who only attributes   *Variable fortune*
The faculties of other instruments
To his own nerves and act;[6] commands men's service,
70 And what they win in't, boot° and glory; one   *booty; gain*
That fears not to do harm, good dares not.° Let *dares not do good*
The blood of mine that's sib° to him be sucked   *related*
From me with leeches. Let them break° and fall   *burst*
Off me with that° corruption.   *(Creon's)*
ARCITE   Clear-spirited° cousin, *Noble-spirited*
75 Let's leave his court that we may nothing share
Of his loud° infamy: for our milk   *well-known*
Will relish of the pasture,[7] and we must
Be vile or disobedient; not his kinsmen
In blood unless in quality.[8]
PALAMON   Nothing truer.
80 I think the echoes of his shames have deafed
The ears of heav'nly justice. Widows' cries
Descend again into their throats and have not
  Enter VALERIUS
Due audience of° the gods—Valerius.   *Proper notice from*
VALERIUS The King calls for you; yet be leaden-footed° *go slowly*
85 Till his great rage be off him. Phoebus, when
He broke his whipstock and exclaimed against
The horses of the sun,[9] but whispered to°   *compared to*

---

1. Self-reliance. Palamon's speech echoes familiar criticisms of the contrived, "effeminate" manners of courtiers and men of fashion, here contrasted with implicit religious norms ("faith"; "saved," line 48; "canon," line 55).
2. *go . . . foul:* tiptoe on a clean street.
3. *Either . . . trace:* I will not pull behind the lead ("fore-") horse (follow fashion).
4. Herb used for treating wounds.
5. *puts . . . fever:* undermines religion.
6. *attributes . . . act:* takes credit for others' successes.
7. Like cows whose milk absorbs the taste of whatever they eat.
8. *not . . . quality:* we ought not to act like his kinsmen unless we're willing to act like him; we're not his kinsmen unless we act like him.
9. After his son Phaeton died driving the horses of the sun, Phoebus (the sun) vented his grief at the horses—hence the broken whip handle ("whipstock").

The loudness of his fury.

PALAMON   Small winds shake him.
But what's the matter?

90 VALERIUS Theseus, who where he threats, appals, hath sent
Deadly defiance to him° and pronounces   (Creon)
Ruin to Thebes, who° is at hand to seal   (Theseus)
The promise of his wrath.[1]

ARCITE   Let him approach.
But that we fear the gods in him,° he brings not   justness of his cause
95 A jot of terror to us. Yet what man
Thirds his own worth—the case is each of ours—
When that his action's dregged with mind assured
'Tis bad he goes about.[2]

PALAMON   Leave that unreasoned.°   Forget that
Our services stand now for Thebes, not Creon,
100 Yet to be neutral to him were dishonour,
Rebellious° to oppose. Therefore we must   Treasonable
With him stand to the mercy of° our fate,   submit to
Who hath bounded our last minute.[3]

ARCITE   So we must.
Is't said this war's afoot? Or it shall be
On fail of° some condition?   If Thebes rejects
105 VALERIUS   'Tis in motion,
The intelligence of state° came in the instant   official announcement
With the defier.°   herald of Theseus

PALAMON   Let's to the King, who, were he
A quarter carrier of that honour which
His enemy come in, the blood we venture
110 Should be as for our health,[4] which were not spent,°   wasted
Rather laid out for purchase.° But, alas,   invested for profit
Our hands advanced before° our hearts, what will   beyond
The fall o'th' stroke do damage?[5]

ARCITE   Let th'event°—   outcome
That never-erring arbitrator—tell us
115 When we know all ourselves,[6] and let us follow
The becking° of our chance.   *Exeunt*   calling

1.3

Enter PIRITHOUS, HIPPOLYTA, *and* EMILIA
PIRITHOUS No further.

HIPPOLYTA   Sir, farewell. Repeat my wishes
To our great lord, of whose success I dare not
Make any timorous question; yet I wish him
Excess and overflow of power, an't might be,°   if possible
5 To dure° ill-dealing fortune. Speed to him;   endure
Store[1] never hurts good governors.

PIRITHOUS   Though I know
His ocean needs not my poor drops, yet they
Must yield their tribute there. [*To* EMILIA] My precious maid,

---

1. *seal . . . wrath:* turn anger to action.
2. *Yet . . . about:* Yet any man reduces his worth by two-thirds—as we do—when he knows the action he undertakes is unworthy.
3. *Who . . . minute:* Which has determined when we die.
4. *the blood . . . health:* our loss of blood in combat would

be equivalent to a therapeutic bloodletting.
5. *what . . . damage:* what harm will "the fall o'th' stroke" do?
6. *tell . . . ourselves:* speak for itself.
1.3 Location: The outskirts of Athens.
1. Abundant resources (here, good men like Pirithous).

Those best affections° that the heavens infuse   *inclinations*
10   In their best-tempered pieces° keep enthroned   *greatest creations*
In your dear heart.
EMILIA   Thanks, sir. Remember me
To our all-royal brother, for whose speed°   *success*
The great Bellona I'll solicit; and
Since in our terrene state° petitions are not   *earthly condition*
15   Without gifts understood, I'll offer to her
What I shall be advised she likes. Our hearts
Are in his army, in his tent.
HIPPOLYTA   In's bosom.
We have been soldiers,° and we cannot weep   *(as Amazons)*
When our friends don their helms,° or put to sea,   *helmets*
20   Or tell of babes broached° on the lance, or women   *speared*
That have sod° their infants in—and after eat them—   *boiled*
The brine they wept at killing 'em:[2] then if
You stay to see of us such spinsters, we
Should hold you here forever.[3]
PIRITHOUS   Peace be to you
25   As I pursue this war, which° shall be then   *(peace)*
Beyond further requiring.°   *Exit* PIRITHOUS   *In no need of prayer*
EMILIA   How his longing
Follows his friend! Since his depart,° his sports,   *Theseus's departure*
Though craving° seriousness and skill, passed slightly   *requiring*
His careless execution,[4] where nor° gain   *neither*
30   Made him regard or loss consider, but
Playing one business in his hand, another
Directing in his head, his mind nurse equal
To these so diff'ring twins.[5] Have you observed him
Since our great lord departed?
HIPPOLYTA   With much labour;°   *diligence*
35   And I did love him for't. They two have cabined°   *shared quarters*
In many as dangerous as poor a corner,
Peril and want contending;[6] they have skiffed°   *sailed across*
Torrents whose roaring tyranny and power
I'th' least of these° was dreadful, and they have   *At the weakest point*
40   Fought out together where death's self was lodged;
Yet fate hath brought them off. Their knot of love,
Tied, weaved, entangled with so true, so long,
And with a finger of so deep a cunning,°   *skill*
May be outworn,° never undone. I think   *worn out (in death)*
45   Theseus cannot be umpire to himself,
Cleaving his conscience into twain and doing
Each side like° justice, which[7] he loves best.   *equal*
EMILIA   Doubtless
There is a best, and reason has no manners
To say it is not you. I was acquainted
50   Once with a time when I enjoyed a playfellow;
You were at wars when she the grave enriched,

2. Miriam killed, cooked, and ate her son during the   5. *his . . . twins:* his attention divided equally between
Roman siege of Jerusalem, adding her own tears for sauce.   sports and Theseus.
3. *then if . . . forever:* if you wait long enough for us to turn   6. Contending for which was the greater hardship.
into spinners (housewives), you'll wait forever.   7. Pirithous or Hippolyta.
4. *passed . . . execution:* were pursued carelessly.

Who made too proud the bed;° took leave o'th' moon[8]—   *grave*
Which then looked pale at parting—when our count°   *age*
Was each eleven.
HIPPOLYTA   'Twas Flavina.
EMILIA   Yes.
55   You talk of Pirithous' and Theseus' love:
Theirs has more ground,° is more maturely seasoned,   *a stronger base*
More buckled° with strong judgement, and their needs   *joined together*
The one of th'other may be said to water
Their intertangled roots of love; but I
60   And she I sigh and spoke of were things innocent,
Loved for° we did, and like the elements,[9]   *simply because*
That know not what, nor why, yet do effect°   *create*
Rare issues° by their operance, our souls   *Amazing results*
Did so to one another. What she liked
65   Was then of° me approved; what not, condemned—   *by*
No more arraignment.° The flower that I would pluck   *inquiry*
And put between my breasts—O then but beginning
To swell about the blossom—she would long°   *desire*
Till she had such another, and commit it
70   To the like innocent cradle, where, phoenix-like,
They died in perfume.[1] On my head no toy°   *trifle*
But was her pattern.° Her affections—pretty,   *model*
Though happily her careless wear—I followed
For my most serious decking.[2] Had mine ear
75   Stol'n some new air,° or at adventure° hummed one,   *tune / by chance*
From musical coinage,° why, it was a note   *improvisation*
Whereon her spirits would sojourn—rather dwell on—
And sing it in her slumbers. This rehearsal—
Which, seely innocence wots well, comes in
80   Like old emportment's bastard[3]—has this end:
That the true love 'tween maid and maid may be
More than in sex dividual.[4]
HIPPOLYTA   You're out of breath,
And this high-speeded pace is but to say
That you shall never, like the maid Flavina,
85   Love any that's called man.
EMILIA   I am sure I shall not.
HIPPOLYTA   Now alack, weak sister,
I must no more believe thee in this point—
Though in't I know thou dost believe thyself—
90   Than I will trust a sickly appetite
That loathes even as it longs. But sure, my sister,
If I were ripe for your persuasion,° you   *open to your views*
Have said enough to shake me from the arm

---

8. Diana (the moon goddess), who watched over virgins and Amazons; hence Emilia's (equivocal) patron.
9. Air, fire, earth, and water—constituents of all matter.
1. The phoenix died by being burned on aromatic wood, only to be reborn from its own ashes.
2. *Her affections . . . decking*: Whatever she wore—though she wasn't aware of how appealing it was—I'd imitate with utmost seriousness. For "happily" Q has "happely," which could also mean "haply" (by chance).
3. *This . . . bastard*: This narrative, which, as any happy innocent well knows, is an illegitimate descendant (poor likeness) of my former passion (or, the former significance of the relationship). For "seely innocence" Q has "fury-innocent" (innocent, passionate love), which may be correct.
4. *in sex dividual*: between two sexes. Q has "individuall," which in the seventeenth century could mean the indivisible unity of male and female, and hence may be correct.

Of the all-noble Theseus, for whose fortunes
95 I will now in and kneel, with great assurance
That we more than his Pirithous possess
The high throne in his heart.
EMILIA   I am not
Against your faith, yet I continue mine.   *Exeunt*

1.4

Cornetts. A battle struck within. Then a retreat.
Flourish.[1] *Then enter* THESEUS, *victor. The three* QUEENS
meet him and fall on their faces before him. [Also enter
a HERALD, *and attendants bearing]* PALAMON *and*
ARCITE [*on*] *two hearses°*   biers
FIRST QUEEN [*to* THESEUS]   To thee no star be dark.°   unfavorable
SECOND QUEEN [*to* THESEUS]   Both heaven and earth
Friend thee for ever.
THIRD QUEEN [*to* THESEUS]   All the good that may
Be wished upon thy head, I cry 'Amen' to't.
THESEUS   Th'impartial gods, who from the mounted° heavens   high
5 View us their mortal herd, behold who err
And in their time chastise. Go and find out
The bones of your dead lords and honour them
With treble ceremony: rather than a gap
Should be in their dear° rites we would supply't.   valued
10 But those we will depute which shall invest°   clothe
You in your dignities, and even° each thing   rectify
Our haste does leave imperfect. So adieu,
And heaven's good eyes look on you.   *Exeunt* [*the*] QUEENS
                                    What are those?
HERALD   Men of great quality,° as may be judged   rank
15 By their appointment.° Some of Thebes have told's   armor and weapons
They are sisters' children, nephews to the King.
THESEUS   By th' helm° of Mars I saw them in the war,   helmet
Like to a pair of lions smeared with prey,
Make lanes in troops aghast. I fixed my note°   attention
20 Constantly on them, for they were a mark°   striking sight
Worth a god's view. What prisoner was't that told me
When I enquired their names?
HERALD   Wi' leave, they're called
Arcite and Palamon.
THESEUS   'Tis right: those, those.
They are not dead?
25 HERALD   Nor in a state of life. Had they been taken
When their last hurts were given, 'twas possible
They might have been recovered.° Yet they breathe,   healed
And have the name of men.
THESEUS   Then like men use 'em.
The very lees of such, millions of rates
30 Exceed the wine of others.[2] All our surgeons
Convent° in their behoof;° our richest balms,   Assemble / behalf
Rather than niggard,° waste. Their lives concern us   use stingily

---

1.4 Location: On the outskirts of Thebes.
1. Small horns sound offstage, signaling the start of bat-
tle, a retreat, and then a triumphal entrance.

2. *The very . . . others:* The dregs of such men far exceed
the best that others can offer.

Much more than Thebes is worth. Rather than have 'em
Freed of this plight and in their morning° state—   *former (healthy)*
35   Sound and at liberty—I would 'em dead;
But forty-thousandfold we had rather have 'em
Prisoners to us, than death. Bear 'em speedily
From our kind air, to them unkind,[3] and minister
What man to man may do—for our sake, more,
40   Since I have known frights, fury, friends' behests,
Love's provocations, zeal, a mistress' task,
Desire of liberty, a fever, madness,
Hath set a mark which nature could not reach to
Without some imposition, sickness in will
45   O'er-wrestling strength in reason.[4] For our love
And great Apollo's° mercy, all our best   *god of healing*
Their best skill tender.—Lead into the city
Where, having bound things scattered,° we will post°   *reimposed order / hurry*
To Athens fore our army.   *Flourish. Exeunt*

                                1.5
                Music. Enter the [three] QUEENS *with the hearses of*
                their [lords] in a funeral solemnity [with attendants]
                                Song
                Urns and odours, bring away,
                Vapours, sighs, darken the day;
                    Our dole° more deadly looks than dying.   *mourning*
                Balms and gums[1] and heavy cheers,°   *sad countenances*
5   Sacred vials filled with tears,
                    And clamours through the wild air flying:

                Come all sad and solemn shows,
                That are quick-eyed pleasure's foes.
                We convent naught else but woes,
10   We convent naught else but woes.
THIRD QUEEN   This funeral path brings° to your household's   *leads*
    grave—
Joy seize on you again, peace sleep with him.
SECOND QUEEN   And this to yours.
FIRST QUEEN   Yours this way. Heavens lend
A thousand differing ways to one sure end.°   *death*
15   THIRD QUEEN   This world's a city full of straying streets,
And death's the market-place where each one meets.
                                Exeunt severally°   *separately*

                                2.1
                Enter [the] JAILER *and [the]* WOOER
JAILER   I may depart with° little, while I live; something I may   *may spare*
    cast° to you, not much. Alas, the prison I keep, though it be for   *give (as a dowry)*
    great ones, yet they seldom come; before one salmon you shall
    take a number of minnows. I am given out to be better lined°   *said to be richer*
5   than it can appear to me report° is a true speaker. I would I   *rumor*

---

3. Fresh air was thought dangerous to wounds.
4. *Since ... reason:* Since compelling incentives can
impel men to perform beyond their normal abilities,
whereas otherwise weak will triumphs over strong reason.
mark: target. *imposition:* command.

1.5 Scene continues.
1. Aromatic substances used in mourning rituals.
2.1 Location: The palace garden in Athens, perhaps with
the second, or higher, gallery above representing the win-
dow of the cell where Palamon and Arcite are being held.

were really that° I am delivered° to be. Marry[1], what I have— *what / reported*
be it what it will—I will assure upon° my daughter at the day *bequeath to*
of my death.

WOOER Sir, I demand no more than your own offer, and I will
10   estate° your daughter in what I have promised. *settle*

JAILER Well, we will talk more of this when the solemnity[2] is
past. But have you a full promise of her?

     Enter [the JAILER'S*]* DAUGHTER *[with rushes]°* *(as floor coverings)*
When that shall be seen, I tender my consent.

WOOER I have, sir. Here she comes.

15 JAILER *[to* DAUGHTER*]* Your friend and I have chanced to name
you here, upon the old business—but no more of that now. So
soon as the court hurry is over we will have an end of it. I'th'
mean time, look tenderly° to the two prisoners. I can tell you *carefully*
they are princes.

20 JAILER'S DAUGHTER These strewings° are for their chamber. 'Tis *rushes*
pity they are in prison, and 'twere pity they should be out. I do
think they have patience to make any adversity ashamed; the
prison itself is proud of 'em, and they have all the world in their
chamber.[3]

25 JAILER They are famed° to be a pair of absolute° men. *reputed / perfect*

JAILER'S DAUGHTER By my troth, I think fame but stammers° *underrates*
'em—they stand a grece° above the reach of report. *step*

JAILER I heard them reported in the battle to be the only doers.° *supreme achievers*

JAILER'S DAUGHTER Nay, most likely, for they are noble suffer-
30 ers.[4] I marvel how they would have looked had they been vic-
tors, that with such a constant nobility enforce a freedom out of
bondage, making misery their mirth, and affliction a toy° to jest at. *trifle*

JAILER Do they so?

JAILER'S DAUGHTER It seems to me they have no more sense of
35 their captivity than I of ruling Athens. They eat well, look mer-
rily, discourse of many things, but° nothing of their own *but say*
restraint° and disasters. Yet sometime a divided° sigh—martyred *captivity / half-audible*
as 'twere i'th' deliverance—will break from one of them, when
the other presently° gives it so sweet a rebuke that I could wish *immediately*
40 myself a sigh to be so chid, or at least a sigher to be comforted.

WOOER I never saw 'em.

JAILER The Duke himself came privately in the night,

     PALAMON *and* ARCITE *[appear at a window] above*
and so did they.[5] What the reason of it is I know not. Look,
yonder they are. That's Arcite looks out.

45 JAILER'S DAUGHTER No, sir, no—that's Palamon. Arcite is the
lower° of the twain—*[pointing at* ARCITE*]* you may perceive a *shorter*
part of him.

JAILER Go to,° leave your pointing. They would not make us *Come now*
their object.[6] Out of their sight.

50 JAILER'S DAUGHTER It is a holiday to look on them. Lord, the
difference of° men! *Exeunt* *between*

---

1. To be sure (originally, by the Virgin Mary).
2. Theseus and Hippolyta's wedding.
3. They have everything they need in their prison cell, because they have each other. See 2.2.60.
4. For they endure nobly what others do to them. To do

and to suffer are antithetical.
5. Theseus brought them secretly at night.
6. They would not be so rude as to point at us; they don't want to look at us.

2.2

Enter PALAMON *and* ARCITE *in prison* [*in shackles, above*]

PALAMON How do you, noble cousin?

ARCITE   How do you, sir?

PALAMON Why, strong enough to laugh at misery
And bear the chance° of war. Yet we are prisoners,   *uncertainties*
I fear, for ever, cousin.

ARCITE   I believe it,
5   And to that destiny have patiently
Laid up my hour to come.°   *Consigned my future*

PALAMON   O, cousin Arcite,
Where is Thebes now?[1] Where is our noble country?
Where are our friends and kindreds? Never more
Must we behold those comforts, never see
10 The hardy youths strive for° the games of honour,   *in*
Hung with the painted favours° of their ladies,   *love tokens*
Like tall ships under sail; then start amongst 'em
And, as an east wind, leave 'em all behind us,
Like lazy clouds, whilst Palamon and Arcite,
15 Even in the wagging of a wanton leg,[2]
Outstripped the people's praises, won the garlands
Ere they have time to wish 'em ours. O never
Shall we two exercise, like twins of honour,
Our arms again and feel our fiery horses
20 Like proud seas under us. Our good swords, now—
Better° the red-eyed god of war ne'er wore—   *Better swords*
Ravished° our sides, like age must run to rust   *Torn from*
And deck the temples of those gods that hate us.
These hands shall never draw 'em out like lightning
To blast° whole armies more.   *annihilate*
25 ARCITE   No, Palamon,
Those hopes are prisoners with us. Here we are,
And here the graces of our youths must wither,
Like a too-timely° spring. Here age must find us   *buds in a premature*
And, which is heaviest,° Palamon, unmarried—   *what is saddest*
30 The sweet embraces of a loving wife
Loaden with kisses, armed with thousand Cupids,
Shall never clasp our necks; no issue° know us;   *offspring*
No figures° of ourselves shall we e'er see   *images*
To glad our age, and, like young eagles, teach 'em
35 Boldly to gaze against bright arms[3] and say,
'Remember what your fathers were, and conquer.'
The fair-eyed maids shall weep our banishments,
And in their songs curse ever-blinded fortune,
Till she for shame see what a wrong she has done
40 To youth and nature. This is all our world.
We shall know nothing here but one another,

2.2 Location: The prison in Athens, perhaps represented by the principal upper stage, located on the first, or lower, gallery; as in 2.1, the garden is located on the main stage. The shift of Palamon and Arcite from the higher to the lower gallery is implied by the stage directions and start of a new scene here in Q.

1. The kinsmen's view of Thebes in 1.2 is very different, perhaps because Shakespeare probably wrote the earlier scene and Fletcher this one.
2. *Even . . . leg*: Effortlessly.
3. Eagles supposedly could gaze at the sun without being blinded.

Hear nothing but the clock that tells° our woes.   *counts*
The vine shall grow, but we shall never see it;
Summer shall come, and with her all delights,
45 But dead-cold winter must inhabit here still.
PALAMON 'Tis too true, Arcite. To our Theban hounds
That shook the agèd forest with their echoes,
No more now must we holler; no more shake
Our pointed javelins whilst the angry swine°   *the wild boar*
50 Flies like a Parthian quiver[4] from our rages,
Struck with our well-steeled darts. All valiant uses°—   *activities*
The food and nourishment of noble minds—
In us two here shall perish; we shall die—
Which is the curse of honour—lastly,°   *at last*
Children of grief and ignorance.°   *Sad and unknown*
55 ARCITE   Yet, cousin,
Even from the bottom of these miseries,
From all that fortune can inflict upon us,
I see two comforts rising—two mere° blessings,   *pure*
If the gods please, to hold here a brave patience
60 And the enjoying of our griefs together.
Whilst Palamon is with me, let me perish
If I think this our prison.
PALAMON   Certainly
'Tis a main° goodness, cousin, that our fortunes   *the greatest*
Were twined together. 'Tis most true, two souls
65 Put in two noble bodies, let 'em suffer
The gall of hazard,° so° they grow together,   *bitterest luck / if*
Will never sink;° they must not, say° they could.   *succumb / even if*
A willing man dies sleeping[5] and all's done.
ARCITE Shall we make worthy uses of this place
That all men hate so much?
70 PALAMON   How, gentle cousin?
ARCITE Let's think this prison holy sanctuary,
To keep us from corruption of worse men.
We are young, and yet desire the ways of honour
That liberty and common conversation,°   *worldly acquaintances*
75 The poison of pure spirits, might, like women,
Woo us to wander from. What worthy blessing
Can be, but our imaginations
May make it ours? And here being thus together,
We are an endless mine° to one another: *resource*
80 We are one another's wife, ever begetting
New births of love; we are father, friends, acquaintance;
We are in one another, families—
I am your heir, and you are mine; this place
Is our inheritance: no hard oppressor
85 Dare take this from us. Here, with a little patience,
We shall live long and loving. No surfeits° seek us—   *diseases from excess*
The hand of war hurts none here, nor the seas
Swallow their youth. Were we at liberty

---

4. During the era of ancient Rome's supremacy, the Par-   5. A man resigned to his fate dies in peace, as if merely
thians were renowned archers, famous for shooting   falling asleep.
behind them at their enemies as they pretended to flee.

A wife might part us lawfully, or business;
90   Quarrels consume us; envy of ill men
Crave our acquaintance.⁶ I might sicken, cousin,
Where you should never know it, and so perish
Without your noble hand to close mine eyes,
Or prayers to the gods. A thousand chances,
Were we from hence, would sever us.

95   PALAMON   You have made me—

I thank you, cousin Arcite—almost wanton°   *delighted*
With my captivity. What a misery
It is to live abroad,° and everywhere!   *out of captivity*
'Tis like a beast, methinks. I find the court here;
100   I am sure, a more content;° and all those pleasures   *greater happiness*
That woo the wills of men to vanity
I see through now, and am sufficient
To tell the world 'tis but a gaudy shadow,
That old Time, as he passes by, takes with him.
105   What had we been, old° in the court of Creon,   *grown old*
Where sin is justice, lust and ignorance
The virtues of the great ones? Cousin Arcite,
Had not the loving gods found this place for us,
We had died as they do, ill° old men, unwept,   *wicked*
110   And had° their epitaphs, the people's curses.   *had for*
Shall I say more?

ARCITE   I would hear you still.°   *forever*
PALAMON   Ye shall.

Is there record of any two that loved
Better than we do, Arcite?

ARCITE   Sure there cannot.
PALAMON   I do not think it possible our friendship

Should ever leave us.

115   ARCITE   Till our deaths it cannot,

Enter EMILIA *and her* WOMAN [*below.*° PALAMON *sees*   *(in the garden)*
  EMILIA *and is silent*]

And after death our spirits shall be led
To those that love eternally.° Speak on, sir.   *(in Elysium)*

EMILIA [*to her* WOMAN]   This garden has a world of pleasure in't.

What flower is this?

WOMAN   'Tis called narcissus, madam.
120   EMILIA   That was a fair boy, certain, but a fool

To love himself.⁷ were there not maids enough?

ARCITE [*to* PALAMON]   Pray forward.°   *go on speaking*
PALAMON   Yes.
EMILIA [*to her* WOMAN]   Or were they all hard-hearted?
WOMAN   They could not be to one so fair.
EMILIA   Thou wouldst not.
WOMAN   I think I should not, madam.
EMILIA   That's a good wench—

But take heed to your kindness, though.

125   WOMAN   Why, madam?
EMILIA   Men are mad things.

---

6. *envy . . . acquaintance:* the malice (or, our envy) of evil men might infect us.
7. Narcissus fell in love with his own reflection in a pool and drowned trying to embrace it. After his death, he was turned into a flower.

ARCITE [*to* PALAMON]   Will ye go forward, cousin?
EMILIA [*to her* WOMAN]   Canst not thou work° such flowers in   *embroider*
    silk, wench?
WOMAN   Yes.
EMILIA   I'll have a gown full of 'em, and of these.
    This is a pretty colour—will't not do
    Rarely° upon a skirt, wench?   *Beautifully*
130 WOMAN   Dainty, madam.
ARCITE [*to* PALAMON]   Cousin, cousin, how do you, sir? Why,
    Palamon!
PALAMON   Never till now was I in prison, Arcite.
ARCITE   Why, what's the matter, man?
PALAMON   Behold and wonder!
        [ARCITE *sees* EMILIA]
    By heaven, she is a goddess!
ARCITE   Ha!
PALAMON   Do reverence.
    She is a goddess, Arcite.
135 EMILIA [*to her* WOMAN]   Of all flowers
    Methinks a rose is best.
WOMAN   Why, gentle madam?
EMILIA   It is the very emblem of a maid—
    For when the west wind courts her gently,
    How modestly she blows,° and paints the sun[8]   *blooms*
140 With her chaste blushes! When the north° comes near her,   *north wind*
    Rude and impatient, then, like chastity,
    She locks her beauties in her bud again,
    And leaves him to base briers.°   *thorns*
WOMAN   Yet, good madam,
    Sometimes her modesty will blow° so far   *open*
145 She falls for't°—a maid,   *because of it*
    If she have any honour, would be loath
    To take example by her.
EMILIA   Thou art wanton.
ARCITE [*to* PALAMON]   She is wondrous fair.
PALAMON   She is all the beauty extant.
EMILIA [*to her* WOMAN]   The sun grows high—let's walk in.
    Keep these flowers.
150 We'll see how close art can come near their colours.
    I am wondrous merry-hearted—I could laugh now.
WOMAN   I could lie down, I am sure.[9]
EMILIA   And take one° with you?   *(a rose); (a lover)*
WOMAN   That's as we bargain, madam.
EMILIA   Well, agree° then.   *let's bargain*
                Exeunt EMILIA *and* [*her*] WOMAN
PALAMON   What think you of this beauty?
ARCITE   'Tis a rare one.
PALAMON   Is't but a rare one?
155 ARCITE   Yes, a matchless beauty.
PALAMON   Might not a man well lose himself and love her?
ARCITE   I cannot tell what you have done; I have,
    Beshrew mine eyes° for't. Now I feel my shackles.   *Curse me (an oath)*

8. Tints the sunlight pink; the inside of a rose looks like   9. "Laugh and lie down" was an Elizabethan card game;
an image of the sun.   sexual allusion.

PALAMON You love her then?
160 ARCITE Who would not?
PALAMON And desire her?
ARCITE Before my liberty.
PALAMON I saw her first.
ARCITE   That's nothing.
PALAMON   But it shall be.
ARCITE I saw her too.
PALAMON   Yes, but you must not love her.
165 ARCITE I will not, as you do, to worship her
    As she is heavenly and a blessèd goddess!
    I love her as a woman, to enjoy her—
    So both may love.
PALAMON   You shall not love at all.
ARCITE Not love at all—who shall deny me?
170 PALAMON I that first saw her, I that took possession
    First with mine eye of all those beauties
    In her revealed to mankind. If thou¹ lov'st her,
    Or entertain'st a hope to blast my wishes,
    Thou art a traitor, Arcite, and a fellow°   (contemptuous)
175 False as thy title to° her. Friendship, blood,   claim to possess
    And all the ties between us I disclaim,
    If thou once think upon her.
ARCITE   Yes, I love her—
    And if the lives of all my name lay° on it,   my family depended
    I must do so. I love her with my soul—
180 If that will lose ye, farewell, Palamon!
    I say again,
    I love her, and in loving her maintain
    I am as worthy and as free° a lover,   noble
    And have as just a title to her beauty,
185 As any Palamon, or any living
    That is a man's son.
PALAMON   Have I called thee friend?
ARCITE Yes, and have found me so. Why are you moved° thus?   incensed
    Let me deal coldly° with you. Am not I   dispassionately
    Part of your blood, part of your soul? You have told me
    That I was Palamon and you were Arcite.
190 PALAMON   Yes.
ARCITE Am not I liable to those affections,°   passions
    Those joys, griefs, angers, fears, my friend shall suffer?
PALAMON Ye may be.
ARCITE   Why then would you deal so cunningly,
    So strangely, so unlike a noble kinsman,
195 To love alone? Speak truly. Do you think me
    Unworthy of her sight?
PALAMON   No, but unjust
    If thou pursue that sight.
ARCITE   Because another
    First sees the enemy, shall I stand still,
    And let mine honour down, and never charge?
PALAMON Yes, if he be but one.°   be alone

---

1. The contemptuous "thou" replaces the more polite "you." Arcite follows suit at line 218.

200	ARCITE But say that one	

ARCITE   But say that one
    Had rather combat me?
PALAMON   Let that one say so,
    And use thy freedom; else, if thou pursuest her,
    Be as that cursèd man that hates his country,
    A branded villain.
ARCITE   You are mad.
PALAMON   I must be.
205   Till thou art worthy, Arcite, it concerns me;
    And in this madness if I hazard° thee   *endanger*
    And take thy life, I deal but truly.°   *fairly*
ARCITE   Fie, sir.
    You play the child extremely. I will love her,
    I must, I ought to do so, and I dare—
    And all this justly.
210 PALAMON   O, that now, that now
    Thy false self and thy friend had but this fortune—
    To be one hour at liberty and grasp
    Our good swords in our hands! I would quickly teach thee
    What 'twere to filch affection from another.
215   Thou art baser in it than a cutpurse.°   *thief*
    Put but thy head out of this window more
    And, as I have a soul, I'll nail thy life to't.°   *to the window frame*
ARCITE   Thou dar'st not, fool; thou canst not; thou art feeble.
    Put my head out? I'll throw my body out
220   And leap° the garden when I see her next,   *jump down to*
        Enter [*the* JAILER *above*]
    And pitch° between her arms to anger thee.   *hurl myself*
PALAMON   No more—the keeper's coming. I shall live
    To knock thy brains out with my shackles.
ARCITE   Do.
JAILER   By your leave, gentlemen.
PALAMON   Now, honest keeper?
225 JAILER   Lord Arcite, you must presently to th' Duke.
    The cause I know not yet.
ARCITE   I am ready, keeper.
JAILER   Prince Palamon, I must a while bereave you
    Of your fair cousin's company.
        Exeunt ARCITE *and* [*the* JAILER]
PALAMON   And me, too,
    Even when you please, of life. Why is he sent for?
230   It may be he shall marry her—he's goodly,°   *handsome*
    And like enough the Duke hath taken notice
    Both of his blood° and body. But his falsehood!   *noble family*
    Why should a friend be treacherous? If that
    Get him a wife so noble and so fair,
235   Let honest men ne'er love again. Once more
    I would but see this fair one. Blessèd garden,
    And fruit and flowers more blessèd, that still° blossom   *perpetually*
    As her bright eyes shine on ye! Would I were,
    For all the fortune of my life hereafter,
240   Yon little tree, yon blooming apricot—
    How I would spread and fling my wanton arms
    In at her window! I would bring her fruit
    Fit for the gods to feed on; youth and pleasure

Still as° she tasted should be doubled on her;   *Whenever*
245 And if she be not heavenly, I would make her
So near the gods in nature they should fear her—
    Enter [*the* JAILER *above*]
And then I am sure she would love me. How now, keeper,
Where's Arcite?

JAILER   Banished—Prince Pirithous
Obtained his liberty; but never more,
250 Upon his oath and life, must he set foot
Upon this kingdom.

PALAMON [*aside*]   He's a blessèd man.
He shall see Thebes again, and call to arms
The bold young men that, when he bids 'em charge,
Fall on like fire. Arcite shall have a fortune,°   *chance*
255 If he dare make himself a worthy lover,
Yet in the field to strike a battle for her;
And if he lose her then, he's a cold coward.
How bravely may he bear himself to win her
If he be noble Arcite; thousand ways!
260 Were I at liberty I would do things
Of such a virtuous greatness that this lady,
This blushing virgin, should take manhood to her
And seek to ravish me.

JAILER   My lord, for you
I have this charge° to—   *order*

PALAMON   To discharge my life.
265 JAILER   No, but from this place to remove your lordship—
The windows are too open.

PALAMON   Devils take 'em
That are so envious° to me—prithee kill me.   *spiteful*

JAILER   And hang for't afterward?

PALAMON   By this good light,
Had I a sword I would kill thee.

JAILER   Why, my lord?
270 PALAMON   Thou bring'st such pelting° scurvy news continually,   *paltry*
Thou art not worthy life. I will not go.

JAILER   Indeed you must, my lord.

PALAMON   May I° see the garden?   *Will I be able to*

JAILER   No.

PALAMON   Then I am resolved—I will not go.

JAILER   I must constrain you, then; and for° you are dangerous,   *because*
I'll clap more irons on you.
275 PALAMON   Do, good keeper.
I'll shake 'em so ye shall not sleep:
I'll make ye a new morris.[2] Must I go?

JAILER   There is no remedy.

PALAMON   Farewell, kind window.
May rude wind never hurt thee. O, my lady,
280 If ever thou hast felt what sorrow was,
Dream how I suffer. Come, now bury me.[3]
    Exeunt PALAMON *and* [*the* JAILER]

---

2. Morris dancers wore bells on their clothes.
3. Palamon's new cell will be like a grave because he will be banished from Emilia.

2.3

Enter ARCITE

ARCITE Banished the kingdom? 'Tis a benefit,
A mercy I must thank 'em for; but banished
The free enjoying of that face I die for—
O, 'twas a studied° punishment, a death   *deliberate*
5   Beyond imagination; such a vengeance
That, were I old and wicked, all my sins
Could never pluck upon me. Palamon,
Thou hast the start° now—thou shalt stay and see   *advantage*
Her bright eyes break° each morning 'gainst thy window,   *(like dawn)*
10 And let in life into thee. Thou shalt feed
Upon the sweetness of a noble beauty
That nature ne'er exceeded, nor ne'er shall.
Good gods! What happiness has Palamon!
Twenty to one he'll come to speak to her,
15 And if she be as gentle as she's fair,
I know she's his—he has a tongue will tame
Tempests and make the wild rocks wanton.°   *full of joy*
Come what can come,
The worst is death. I will not leave the kingdom.
20 I know mine own° is but a heap of ruins,   *(Thebes)*
And no redress there. If I go he has her.
I am resolved another shape° shall make me,   *a disguise*
Or end my fortunes. Either way I am happy—
I'll see her and be near her, or no more.°   *or die*

Enter four COUNTRY[MEN], *one [of whom carries] a gar-*
land before them. [ARCITE *stands apart*]

25 FIRST COUNTRYMAN My masters, I'll be there—that's certain.
SECOND COUNTRYMAN And I'll be there.
THIRD COUNTRYMAN And I.
FOURTH COUNTRYMAN Why then, have with ye,° boys! 'Tis but   *I'll come too*
a chiding[1]—
Let the plough play° today, I'll tickle't out   *be idle*
Of the jades' tails tomorrow.[2]
30 FIRST COUNTRYMAN   I am sure
To have my wife as jealous as a turkey[3]—
But that's all one. I'll go through, let her mumble.°   *grumble*
SECOND COUNTRYMAN Clap her aboard tomorrow night and
stow her,[4]
And all's made up again.
THIRD COUNTRYMAN   Ay, do but put
35 A fescue° in her fist and you shall see her   *teacher's pointer*
Take a new lesson out° and be a good wench.   *Learn a new lesson*
Do we all hold against the maying?[5]
FOURTH COUNTRYMAN Hold? What should ail us?°   *prevent us*
THIRD COUNTRYMAN   Arcas will be there.
SECOND COUNTRYMAN And Sennois, and Rycas, and three better
40 lads ne'er danced under green tree; and ye know what
wenches, ha? But will the dainty dominie,° the schoolmaster,   *fussy teacher*

2.3 Location: The countryside outside Athens.
1. The worst punishment I'll get (for not working) is a scolding.
2. *I'll ... tomorrow:* I'll whip extra work out of the horses ("jades") tomorrow.

3. Thought to be jealously territorial.
4. Sexual metaphor: board her (like a ship) and fill up her cargo hold.
5. Are we still going to participate in the May Day celebrations (of fertility and the coming of spring)?

keep touch,° do you think? For he does all,[6] ye know.   *keep this promise*

THIRD COUNTRYMAN   He'll eat a hornbook[7] ere he fail. Go to, the

matter's too far driven° between him and the tanner's daughter   *affair's gone too far*

45   to let slip now, and she must see the Duke, and she must dance too.

FOURTH COUNTRYMAN   Shall we be lusty?°   *lively*

SECOND COUNTRYMAN   All the boys in Athens blow wind i'th'

breech on's![8] And here I'll be and there I'll be, for our town,

and here again and there again—ha, boys, hey for the weavers![9]

50 FIRST COUNTRYMAN   This must be done i'th' woods.

FOURTH COUNTRYMAN   O, pardon me.

SECOND COUNTRYMAN   By any° means, our thing of learning°   *all / our teacher*

said so; where he himself will edify the Duke most parlously°   *cleverly*

in our behalfs— he's excellent i'th' woods, bring him to th'

55 plains, his learning makes no cry.°   *falls silent*

THIRD COUNTRYMAN   We'll see the sports, then every man to's

tackle°—and, sweet companions, let's rehearse, by any means,   *morris-dancing gear*

before the ladies see us, and do sweetly, and God knows what

may come on't.

60 FOURTH COUNTRYMAN   Content—the sports once ended, we'll

perform. Away boys, and hold.°   *keep your word*

ARCITE [*coming forward*]   By your leaves, honest friends, pray

    you whither go you?

FOURTH COUNTRYMAN   Whither? Why, what a° question's that?   *what sort of a*

ARCITE   Yet 'tis a question

  To me that know not.

65 THIRD COUNTRYMAN   To the games, my friend.

SECOND COUNTRYMAN   Where were you bred, you know it not?

ARCITE   Not far, sir—

  Are there such games today?

FIRST COUNTRYMAN   Yes, marry, are there,

  And such as you never saw. The Duke himself

  Will be in person there.

ARCITE   What pastimes are they?

SECOND COUNTRYMAN   Wrestling and running. [*To the others*]

70   'Tis a pretty fellow.

THIRD COUNTRYMAN [*to* ARCITE]

  Thou wilt not go along?

ARCITE   Not yet, sir.

FOURTH COUNTRYMAN   Well, sir,

  Take your own time. [*To the others*] Come, boys.

FIRST COUNTRYMAN   My mind misgives me—

  This fellow has a vengeance trick o'th' hip:[1]

  Mark how his body's made for't.

SECOND COUNTRYMAN   I'll be hanged though

75 If he dare venture; hang him, plum porridge![2]

He wrestle? He roast eggs![3] Come, let's be gone, lads.

              Exeunt [*the*] *four* [COUNTRYMEN]

ARCITE   This is an offered° opportunity   *unsought*

  I durst not° wish for. Well I could have wrestled[4]—   *would not have dared*

6. For he arranges everything.
7. A primer or tablet, protected by a translucent plate of horn, inscribed with the alphabet.
8. Will try—and fail—to keep up with us.
9. Hooray for the weavers (the profession to which the speaker apparently belongs).
1. *My . . . hip*: I fear that this man may be a skillful wres-

tler.
2. Contemptuous, suggesting that Arcite is out of shape. Plum porridge was a heavy dessert of stewed dried fruits eaten at Christmas.
3. He'd be a better cook than wrestler (?); he probably can't cook an egg (?).
4. I knew how to wrestle.

The best men called it excellent—and run
80 Swifter than wind upon a field of corn,°   *wheat*
    Curling the wealthy° ears, never° flew. I'll venture,   *abundant / ever*
    And in some poor disguise be there. Who knows
    Whether my brows may not be girt with garlands,
    And happiness prefer° me to a place   *good fortune promote*
85 Where I may ever dwell in sight of her?   *Exit*

2.4

Enter [the] JAILER'S DAUGHTER
JAILER'S DAUGHTER Why should I love this gentleman? 'Tis
    odds°   *Chances are*
    He never will affect° me. I am base,   *love*
    My father the mean° keeper of his prison,   *lowly*
    And he a prince. To marry him is hopeless,
5   To be his whore is witless. Out upon't,
    What pushes° are we wenches driven to   *extremities*
    When fifteen° once has found us? First, I saw him;   *(the age)*
    I, seeing, thought he was a goodly man;
    He has as much to please a woman in him—
10 If he please to bestow it so—as ever
    These eyes yet looked on. Next, I pitied him,
    And so would any young wench, o'my conscience,
    That ever dreamed or vowed her maidenhead
    To a young handsome man. Then, I loved him,
15 Extremely loved him, infinitely loved him—
    And yet he had a cousin fair as he, too.
    But in my heart was Palamon, and there,
    Lord, what a coil he keeps!° To hear him   *turmoil he makes*
    Sing in an evening, what a heaven it is!
20 And yet his songs are sad ones. Fairer spoken
    Was never gentleman. When I come in
    To bring him water in a morning, first
    He bows his noble body, then salutes° me, thus: *greets*
    'Fair, gentle maid, good morrow. May thy goodness
25 Get thee a happy husband.' Once he kissed me—
    I loved my lips the better ten days after.
    Would he would do so every day! He grieves much,
    And me as much to see his misery.
    What should I do to make him know I love him?
30 For I would fain° enjoy him. Say I ventured   *eagerly*
    To set him free? What says the law then? Thus much
    For law or kindred! I will do it,
    And this night; ere tomorrow he shall love me.   *Exit*

2.5

Short flourish of cornetts and shouts within. Enter THES-
EUS, HIPPOLYTA, PIRITHOUS, EMILIA, ARCITE *[disguised]*
with a garland [and attendants]
THESEUS You have done worthily. I have not seen
    Since Hercules a man of tougher sinews.°   *muscles*
    Whate'er you are, you run the best and wrestle°   *wrestle the best*
    That these times can allow.°   *show*

2.4 Location: The prison in Athens.   2.5 Location: Athens, near the site of the athletic games.

ARCITE   I am proud to please you.
THESEUS   What country bred you?
5   ARCITE   This—but far off, prince.
THESEUS   Are you a gentleman?
ARCITE   My father said so,
      And to those gentle uses gave me life.[1]
THESEUS   Are you his heir?
ARCITE   His youngest, sir.
THESEUS   Your father
      Sure is a happy sire, then. What proves you?°   (a gentleman)
10 ARCITE   A little of all noble qualities.°   accomplishments
      I could have kept° a hawk and well have hollered   I knew how to keep
      To a deep° cry of dogs; I dare not praise   loud
      My feat in horsemanship, yet they that knew me
      Would say it was my best piece;° last and greatest,   attribute
      I would° be thought a soldier.   used to
15 THESEUS   You are perfect.
PIRITHOUS   Upon my soul, a proper° man.   handsome
EMILIA   He is so.
PIRITHOUS [to HIPPOLYTA]   How do you like him, lady?
HIPPOLYTA   I admire° him.   am amazed at
      I have not seen so young a man so noble—
      If he say true—of his sort.°   rank
EMILIA   Believe°   Be sure
20   His mother was a wondrous handsome woman—
      His face methinks goes that way.°   demonstrates that
HIPPOLYTA   But his body
      And fiery mind illustrate° a brave father.   indicate; copy
PIRITHOUS   Mark how his virtue,° like a hidden sun,   excellence
      Breaks through his baser garments.
HIPPOLYTA   He's well got,° sure.   wellborn
THESEUS [to ARCITE]   What made you seek this place, sir?
25 ARCITE   Noble Theseus,
      To purchase name° and do my ablest service   get a reputation
      To such a well-found° wonder as thy worth,   well-deserved
      For only in thy court of all the world
      Dwells fair-eyed honour.
PIRITHOUS   All his words are worthy.
30 THESEUS [to ARCITE]   Sir, we are much indebted to your travel,°   journey; effort
      Nor shall you lose your wish.—Pirithous,
      Dispose of° this fair gentleman.   Place
PIRITHOUS   Thanks, Theseus.
      [To ARCITE] Whate'er you are, you're mine, and I shall give you
      To a most noble service, to this lady,
35   This bright young virgin; pray observe° her goodness.   respect
      You have honoured her fair birthday with your virtues,
      And as your due you're hers. Kiss her fair hand, sir.
ARCITE   Sir, you're a noble giver. [To EMILIA] Dearest beauty,
      Thus let me seal my vowed faith.
            [He kisses her hand]
                              When your servant,
40   Your most unworthy creature, but offends you,
      Command him die, he shall.

---

1. And raised me for those genteel pursuits.

EMILIA   That were too cruel.
  If you deserve well, sir, I shall soon see't.
  You're mine, and somewhat better than your rank° I'll use you.   position
PIRITHOUS [*to* ARCITE]   I'll see you furnished,° and, because you   equipped
  say
45 You are a horseman, I must needs entreat you
  This afternoon to ride—but 'tis a rough one.°   (horse)
ARCITE   I like him better, prince—I shall not then
  Freeze in my saddle.
THESEUS [*to* HIPPOLYTA]   Sweet, you must be ready—
  And you, Emilia, [*to* PIRITHOUS] and you, friend—and all,
50 Tomorrow by the sun,° to do observance   by sunrise
  To flow'ry May in Dian's wood. [*To* ARCITE] Wait well, sir,
  Upon your mistress.—Emily, I hope
  He shall not go afoot.
EMILIA   That were a shame, sir,
  While I have horses. [*To* ARCITE] Take your choice, and what
55 You want,° at any time, let me but know it.   lack
  If you serve faithfully, I dare assure you,
  You'll find a loving mistress.
ARCITE   If I do not,
  Let me find that° my father ever hated—   that which
  Disgrace and blows.
THESEUS   Go, lead the way—you have won it.[2]
60 It shall be so: you shall receive all dues
  Fit for the honour you have won. 'Twere wrong else.
  [*To* EMILIA] Sister, beshrew my heart, you have a servant
  That, if I were a woman, would be master.
  But you are wise.
EMILIA   I hope too wise for that, sir. *Flourish. Exeunt*

2.6

Enter [the] JAILER'S DAUGHTER
JAILER'S DAUGHTER   Let all the dukes and all the devils roar—
  He is at liberty! I have ventured° for him,   taken a risk
  And out I have brought him. To a little wood
  A mile hence I have sent him, where a cedar
5 Higher than all the rest spreads like a plane,°   plane tree
  Fast° by a brook—and there he shall keep close°   Close / shall hide
  Till I provide him files and food, for yet
  His iron bracelets° are not off. O Love,°   shackles / Cupid
  What a stout-hearted child thou art! My father
10 Durst better have endured cold iron than done it.[1]
  I love him beyond love and beyond reason
  Or wit° or safety. I have made him know it—   sense
  I care not, I am desperate. If the law
  Find me and then condemn me for't, some wenches,
15 Some honest-hearted maids, will sing my dirge
  And tell to memory my death was noble,
  Dying almost a martyr. That way he takes,
  I purpose, is my way too. Sure, he cannot

---

2. Won the honor of leading the procession.
2.6 Location: Near the prison in Athens.

1. *My . . . it:* My father would sooner have been run through than have freed a prisoner.

Be so unmanly as to leave me here.
20 If he do, maids will not so easily
Trust men again. And yet, he has not thanked me
For what I have done—no, not so much as kissed me—
And that, methinks, is not so well. Nor scarcely
Could I persuade him to become a free man,
25 He made such scruples of the wrong he did
To me and to my father. Yet, I hope
When he considers more, this love of mine
Will take more root within him. Let him do
What he will with me—so he use me kindly.[2]
30 For use me,° so he shall, or I'll proclaim him,   (sexually)
And to his face, no man. I'll presently
Provide him necessaries and pack my clothes up,
And where there is a patch of ground I'll venture,
So he be with me. By him, like a shadow,
35 I'll ever dwell. Within this hour the hubbub
Will be all o'er the prison—I am then
Kissing the man they look for. Farewell, father:
Get° many more such prisoners and such daughters,   Catch; beget
And shortly you may keep yourself.[3] Now to him.   [Exit]

3.1

[A bush in place.] Cornetts in sundry° places. Noise and   various (offstage)
hollering as [of] people a-Maying.[1]
Enter ARCITE

ARCITE   The Duke has lost Hippolyta—each took°   went to
A several laund.° This is a solemn rite   A different clearing
They owe bloomed May, and the Athenians pay° it   observe
To th' heart of° ceremony. O, Queen Emilia,   With the utmost
5 Fresher than May, sweeter
Than her gold buttons° on the boughs, or all   buds
Th'enamelled knacks° o'th' mead° or garden—yea,   flowers / meadow
We challenge too the bank of any nymph
That makes the stream seem flowers;[2] thou, O jewel
10 O'th' wood, o'th' world, hast likewise blessed a pace°   path through the woods
With thy sole presence in thy [
]³ rumination
That I, poor man, might eftsoons come between
And chop on some cold thought.[4] Thrice blessèd chance
15 To drop on° such a mistress, expectation   run into
Most guiltless on't!° Tell me, O Lady Fortune,   unexpectedly
Next after Emily my sovereign, how far
I may be proud. She takes strong note of me,
Hath made me near her, and this beauteous morn,

2. Provided that he treat me gently; naturally; nobly, in a manner befitting a man of his kind.
3. You yourself may use the jail, since everyone else will either have escaped or been freed.
3.1 Location: All of Act 3 takes place in a forest near Athens.
1. May Day celebrations included feasts, hunting, music, entertainments (such as the morris dance of 3.5.139), and dancing around the maypole. See note to 2.3.37.
2. We ... flowers: Emilia surpasses in beauty even a

nymph's flowered riverbank, whose reflection makes the river itself seem covered with flowers.
3. Q has a comma after "presence" and lacks this gap. Editors often strengthen the punctuation by starting a new sentence with "In thy rumination." It is unclear how Arcite could "come between" (line 13) a "rumination," however—hence the hypothesis of a missing line.
4. might ... thought: might soon come upon you and seize some chaste thought.

20 The prim'st° of all the year, presents me with   *best*
 A brace° of horses—two such steeds might well   *pair*
 Be by a pair of kings backed,° in a field   *ridden*
 That their crowns' titles tried.[5] Alas, alas,
 Poor cousin Palamon, poor prisoner—thou
25 So little dream'st upon my fortune that
 Thou think'st thyself the happier thing to be
 So near Emilia. Me thou deem'st at Thebes,
 And therein wretched, although free. But if
 Thou knew'st my mistress breathed on me, and that
30 I eared her language,° lived in her eye—O, coz,   *listened to her*
 What passion would enclose° thee!   *rage would possess*
     Enter PALAMON *as out of a bush with his shackles.* [*He*]
     bends° his fist at ARCITE   *shakes*
 PALAMON   Traitor kinsman,
 Thou shouldst perceive my passion if these signs
 Of prisonment[6] were off me, and this hand
 But owner of a sword. By all oaths in one,
35 I and the justice of my love would make thee
 A confessed traitor. O thou most perfidious
 That ever gently looked,° the void'st of honour   *seemed gentlemanly*
 That e'er bore gentle token,° falsest cousin   *wore noble emblems*
 That ever blood made kin—call'st thou her thine?
40 I'll prove it in my shackles, with these hands,
 Void of appointment,° that thou liest and art   *Devoid of weapons*
 A very thief in love, a chaffy° lord   *worthless*
 Not worth the name of villain. Had I a sword
 And these house-clogs° away—   *fetters*
 ARCITE   Dear cousin Palamon—
45 PALAMON   Cozener° Arcite, give me language such   *Cheater (punning)*
 As thou hast showed me feat.[7]
 ARCITE   Not finding in
 The circuit of my breast any gross stuff
 To form me like your blazon holds me to
 This gentleness of answer[8]—'tis your passion
50 That thus mistakes, the which, to you being enemy,
 Cannot to me be kind.[9] Honour and honesty
 I cherish and depend on, howsoe'er
 You skip° them in me, and with them, fair coz,   *ignore*
 I'll maintain my proceedings. Pray be pleased
55 To show in generous° terms your griefs,° since that   *genteel / grievances*
 Your question's° with your equal, who professes   *dispute is*
 To clear his own way[1] with the mind and sword
 Of a true gentleman.
 PALAMON   That thou durst,° Arcite!   *You wouldn't dare*
 ARCITE   My coz, my coz, you have been well advertised°   *informed*
60 How much I dare; you've seen me use my sword
 Against th'advice° of fear. Sure, of° another   *warning / by*

5. *in . . . tried:* on a battlefield where they were fighting
for each other's kingdoms.
6. *signs / Of prisonment:* shackles.
7. *give . . . feat:* use words that accord better with your
(perfidious) actions.
8. *Not . . . answer:* Since I find nothing in me that fits
your description of me, I answer gently. *blazon:* (descrip-

tion of a) coat of arms.
9. *'tis . . . kind:* your anger ("passion") is your enemy (dis-
torts your judgment) and thus to me cannot be kind
(because you are my kinsman—"kind" also means
"kin"—and friend, and hence we share all enemies).
1. To justify; to make his own way.

You would not hear me doubted, but your silence
Should break out, though i'th' sanctuary.[2]
PALAMON   Sir,
I have seen you move in such a place° which well   *battle; tournament*
65   Might justify your manhood; you were called
A good knight and a bold. But the whole week's not fair
If any day it rain: their valiant temper°   *attitude*
Men lose when they incline to treachery,
And then they fight like compelled bears[3]—would fly
Were they not tied.
70   ARCITE   Kinsman, you might as well
Speak this and act it in your glass° as to   *mirror*
His ear which now disdains you.
PALAMON   Come up to me,
Quit° me of these cold gyves,° give me a sword,   *Free / chains*
Though it be rusty, and the charity
75   Of one meal lend me. Come before me then,
A good sword in thy hand, and do but say
That Emily is thine—I will forgive
The trespass° thou hast done me, yea, my life,   *wrong*
If then thou carry't;° and brave souls in shades°   *beat me / Hades*
80   That have died manly, which will seek of me
Some news from earth, they shall get none but this—
That thou art brave and noble.
ARCITE   Be content,
Again betake you to° your hawthorn house.   *go back into*
With counsel of the night[4] I will be here
85   With wholesome viands.° These impediments°   *food / shackles*
Will I file off. You shall have garments and
Perfumes to kill the smell o'th' prison. After,
When you shall stretch yourself and say but 'Arcite,
I am in plight',° there shall be at your choice   *I am ready*
Both sword and armour.
90   PALAMON   O, you heavens, dares any
So noble bear a guilty business!° None   *act shamefully*
But only Arcite, therefore none but Arcite
In this kind is so bold.
ARCITE   Sweet Palamon.
PALAMON   I do embrace you and your offer—for
95   Your offer do't I only, sir; your person,
Without hypocrisy, I may not wish
      Wind° horns [within]   *Sound*
More than my sword's edge on't.
ARCITE   You hear the horns—
Enter your muset° lest this match between's   *gap in a thicket*
Be crossed ere met.° Give me your hand, farewell. *prevented before begun*
100   I'll bring you every needful thing—I pray you,
Take comfort and be strong.
PALAMON   Pray hold your promise,
And do the deed with a bent brow.° Most certain   *stern countenance*
You love me not—be rough with me and pour

---

2. **your . . . sanctuary:** you would speak to defend me
even if you were hiding in a safe place (or in a church).
3. In bearbaiting competitions (a popular pastime with
connections to the theater), bears were tied to a stake.
4. With darkness to assist (and hide) me.

This oil° out of your language. By this air,   *smoothness; flattery*
105   I could for each word give a cuff, my stomach°   *anger*
    Not reconciled by reason.
ARCITE   Plainly spoken,
    Yet—pardon me—hard language: when I spur
        Wind horns [within]
    My horse I chide him not. Content and anger
    In me have but one face.° Hark, sir, they call   *the same expression*
110   The scattered to the banquet. You must guess
    I have an office° there.   *assigned duty*
PALAMON   Sir, your attendance
    Cannot please heaven, and I know your office
    Unjustly is achieved.°   *Was earned unfairly*
ARCITE   'Tis a good title.°   *It was won justly*
    I am persuaded this question, sick between's,
115   By bleeding must be cured.[5] I am a suitor°   *I beg*
    That to your sword you will bequeath this plea°   *lawsuit*
    And talk of it no more.
PALAMON   But this one word:
    You are going now to gaze upon my mistress—
    For note you, mine she is—
ARCITE   Nay then—
PALAMON   Nay, pray you—
120   You talk of feeding me to breed me strength—
    You are going now to look upon a sun
    That strengthens what it looks on. There you have
    A vantage o'er me, but enjoy it till
    I may enforce my remedy. Farewell.
        Exeunt [severally, PALAMON as into the bush]

3.2

Enter [the] JAILER'S DAUGHTER [with a file]
JAILER'S DAUGHTER   He has mistook the brake° I meant, is gone   *thicket*
    After[1] his fancy. 'Tis now wellnigh morning.
    No matter—would it were perpetual night,
    And darkness lord o'th' world. Hark, 'tis a wolf!
5   In me hath grief slain fear, and, but for one thing,
    I care for nothing—and that's Palamon.
    I reck° not if the wolves would jaw° me, so°   *care / gnaw / if*
    He had this file. What if I hollered for him?
    I cannot holler. If I whooped, what then?
10   If he not answered, I should call a wolf
    And do him but that service.[2] I have heard
    Strange howls this livelong night—why may't not be
    They have made prey of him? He has no weapons;
    He cannot run; the jangling of his gyves°   *fetters*
15   Might call fell° things to listen, who have in them   *wild*
    A sense to know a man unarmed, and can
    Smell where resistance is. I'll set it down°   *take it as fact*
    He's torn to pieces: they howled many together

---

5. *I am . . . cured:* I am convinced that the dispute between us (here, imagined as a sick person) can only be settled (cured) by a bloodletting.

3.2
1. *is gone / After:* is led by (only).
2. I would at least serve him by calling a wolf to attack him (ironic).

And then they fed on him. So much for that.
20 Be bold to ring the bell.° How stand I then?   *ring his death knell*
All's chared° when he is gone. No, no, I lie: *My work is all done*
My father's to be hanged for his escape,
Myself to beg, if I prized life so much
As to deny my act—but that I would not,
25 Should I try death by dozens.[3] I am moped°—   *dazed*
Food took I none these two days,
Sipped some water. I have not closed mine eyes
Save when my lids scoured off their brine.[4] Alas,
Dissolve, my life; let not my sense unsettle,°   *reason come unhinged*
30 Lest I should drown or stab or hang myself.
O state of nature,° fail together° in me,   *life / entirely*
Since thy best props° are warped. So which way now?   *supports*
The best way is the next° way to a grave,   *nearest*
Each errant step beside[5] is torment. Lo,
35 The moon is down, the crickets chirp, the screech-owl
Calls in the dawn. All offices are done
Save what I fail in:[6] but the point is this,
An end,° and that is all.   *Exit*   *A death*

3.3

Enter ARCITE *with* [*a bundle containing*] *meat, wine,*
and files

ARCITE I should be near the place. Ho, cousin Palamon!
Enter PALAMON [*as from the bush*]
PALAMON Arcite.
ARCITE   The same. I have brought you food and files.
Come forth and fear not, here's no Theseus.
PALAMON Nor none so honest, Arcite.
ARCITE   That's no matter—
5 We'll argue that hereafter. Come, take courage—
You shall not die thus beastly.° Here, sir, drink;   *like an animal*
I know you are faint. Then I'll talk further with you.
PALAMON Arcite, thou mightst now poison me.
ARCITE   I might—
But I must° fear you first. Sit down and, good now,   *should need to*
10 No more of these vain parleys.° Let us not,   *pointless comments*
Having our ancient[1] reputation with us,
Make talk for[2] fools and cowards. To your health, sir.
PALAMON Do.°   *You drink first*
[ARCITE *drinks*]
ARCITE   Pray sit down, then, and let me entreat you,
By all the honesty and honour in you,
15 No mention of this woman—'twill disturb us.
We shall have time enough.
PALAMON   Well, sir, I'll pledge you.°   *drink your health*
[PALAMON *drinks*]
ARCITE Drink a good hearty draught; it breeds good blood,° man. *makes you strong*

3. Even if I had to die dozens of times (ways).   herself).
4. Except when I blinked to clear my eyes of tears.   **3.3**
5. Each step that wanders from the direct path to the   1. Of long standing; former (now reestablished through
grave.   escape).
6. *All . . . in*: All tasks are done, except the one I've failed   2. Talk as though we were; make ourselves the talk of.
to complete (either giving the file to Palamon or killing

Do not you feel it thaw you?
PALAMON   Stay, I'll tell you
  After a draught or two more.
      [PALAMON *drinks*]
ARCITE   Spare it not—
  The Duke has more, coz. Eat now.
PALAMON   Yes.
      [PALAMON *eats*]

20 ARCITE   I am glad
  You have so good a stomach.°   an appetite; an anger
PALAMON   I am gladder
  I have so good meat° to't.   (to feed my anger)
ARCITE   Is't not mad,° lodging   strange; maddening
  Here in the wild woods, cousin?
PALAMON   Yes, for them
  That have wild° consciences.   uncivilized
ARCITE   How tastes your victuals?
  Your hunger needs no sauce, I see.
25 PALAMON   Not much.
  But if it did, yours is too tart,³ sweet cousin.
  What is this?
ARCITE   Venison.
PALAMON   'Tis a lusty° meat—   hearty
  Give me more wine. Here, Arcite, to the wenches
  We have known in our days. [*Drinking*] The lord steward's
    daughter.
  Do you remember her?
30 ARCITE   After you,⁴ coz.
PALAMON   She loved a black-haired man.
ARCITE   She did so; well, sir.
PALAMON   And I have heard some call him Arcite, and—
ARCITE   Out with't, faith.
PALAMON   She met him in an arbour—
  What did she there, coz? Play o'th' virginals?⁵
ARCITE   Something° she did, sir—   To some extent
35 PALAMON   Made her groan a month for't—
  Or two, or three, or ten.°   (in pregnancy)
ARCITE   The marshal's sister
  Had her share too, as I remember, cousin,
  Else there be tales° abroad. You'll pledge her?   false rumors
PALAMON   Yes.
      [*They drink*]
ARCITE   A pretty brown wench 'tis. There was a time
40 When young men went a-hunting, and a wood,
  And a broad beech, and thereby hangs a tale—
  Heigh-ho!°   (a sigh)
PALAMON   For Emily, upon my life! Fool,
  Away with this strained mirth. I say again,
  That sigh was breathed for Emily. Base cousin,
  Dar'st thou break⁶ first?
ARCITE   You are wide.°   wide of the mark

---

3. Your insolence ("sauce," line 25) is too bitter ("tart").
4. Finish your toast first, before I propose mine.
5. Small keyboard instrument; (sexual).
6. Break our agreement (not to refer to Emilia).

45 PALAMON   By heaven and earth,
  There's nothing in thee honest.
ARCITE   Then I'll leave you—
  You are a beast° now.   *behaving savagely*
PALAMON   As thou mak'st me, traitor.
ARCITE [*pointing to the bundle*]   There's all things needful: files
  and shirts and perfumes—
  I'll come again some two hours hence and bring
  That that shall quiet° all.   *silence*
50 PALAMON   A sword and armour.
ARCITE   Fear° me not. You are now too foul.° Farewell.   *Doubt / beastly*
  Get off your trinkets:° you shall want naught.   *shackles*
PALAMON   Sirrah°—   *(an insult)*
ARCITE   I'll hear no more.   *Exit*
PALAMON   If he keep touch°, he dies for't.   *keeps his promise*
                        Exit [*as into the bush*]

3.4

Enter [*the*] JAILER'S DAUGHTER
JAILER'S DAUGHTER   I am very cold, and all the stars are out too,
  The little stars and all, that look like aglets°—   *shiny ornaments*
  The sun has seen my folly. Palamon!
  Alas, no, he's in heaven. Where am I now?
5 Yonder's the sea and there's a ship—how't tumbles!
  And there's a rock lies watching under water—
  Now, now, it° beats upon it—now, now, now,   *(the ship)*
  There's a leak sprung, a sound° one—how they cry!   *large*
  Open her¹ before the wind—you'll lose all else.
10 Up with a course° or two and tack° about, boys.   *lower sail / turn*
  Good night, good night, you're gone. I am very hungry.
  Would I could find a fine frog—he would tell me
  News from all parts o'th' world, then would I make
  A carrack° of a cockle-shell, and sail   *cargo ship*
15 By east and north-east to the King of Pygmies,
  For he tells fortunes rarely.° Now my father,   *wonderfully*
  Twenty to one, is trussed up in a trice°   *to be hanged quickly*
  Tomorrow morning. I'll say never a word.
  [*She*] *sing*[*s*]
  For I'll cut my green coat, a foot above my knee,
20 And I'll clip my yellow locks, an inch below mine eye,
    Hey nonny, nonny, nonny,
  He s'buy° me a white cut,² forth for to ride,   *He shall buy*
  And I'll go seek him, through the world that is so wide,
    Hey nonny, nonny, nonny.
25 O for a prick now, like a nightingale,
  To put my breast against.³ I shall sleep like a top° else.   *Exit*   *soundly*

3.4
1. Open her sails (so she can run).
2. Horse (called a "cut" because it was a gelding or had a cropped tail).
3. O . . . *against*: nightingales supposedly pricked them-

selves to stay awake at night. "Prick" also carries a sexual meaning; compare the sexual punning here with that in Ophelia's "mad" speeches in *Hamlet*.

3.5

Enter [Gerald] a SCHOOLMASTER, *[five]* COUNTRYMEN, *[one of whom is dressed as a]* BABION, *[five] Wenches, [and Timothy,] a* TABORER. *[All are attired as morris dancers]*[1]

SCHOOLMASTER Fie, fie,
What tediosity and disinsanity[2]
Is here among ye! Have my rudiments°   *lessons; rehearsals*
Been laboured so long with ye, milked unto ye,
5   And, by a figure,° even the very plum-broth   *figure of speech*
And marrow[3] of my understanding laid upon ye?
And do you still cry 'where?' and 'how?' and 'wherefore?'
You most coarse frieze capacities, ye jean judgements,[4]
Have I said, 'thus let be', and 'there let be',
10   And 'then let be', and no man understand me?
Proh deum, medius fidius[5]—ye are all dunces.
Forwhy, here stand I. Here the Duke comes. There are you,
Close° in the thicket. The Duke appears. I meet him,   *Hidden*
And unto him I utter learnèd things
15   And many figures. He hears, and nods, and hums,°   *murmurs approval*
And then cries, 'Rare!', and I go forward.° At length   *continue*
I fling my cap up—mark there—then do you,
As once did Meleager and the boar,[6]
Break comely out° before him, like true lovers,[7]   *Appear decorously*
20   Cast yourselves in a body decently,[8]
And sweetly, by a figure, trace° and turn, boys.   *follow the steps*
FIRST COUNTRYMAN   And sweetly we will do it, master Gerald.
SECOND COUNTRYMAN   Draw up the company. Where's the
taborer?
THIRD COUNTRYMAN   Why, Timothy!
TABORER   Here, my mad boys, have at ye!°   *go ahead; I'm ready*
SCHOOLMASTER   But I say, where's these women?
25   FOURTH COUNTRYMAN   Here's Friz and Madeline.
SECOND COUNTRYMAN   And little Luce with the white legs, and
bouncing° Barbara.   *robust*
FIRST COUNTRYMAN   And freckled Nell, that never failed her
master.°   *(with sexual overtone)*
SCHOOLMASTER   Where be your ribbons,[9] maids? Swim° with   *Dance gracefully*
your bodies
And carry it° sweetly and deliverly,°   *move / nimbly*
30   And now and then a favour° and a frisk.°   *kiss; bow / leap*
NELL   Let us alone,° sir.   *Leave it to us*
SCHOOLMASTER   Where's the rest o'th' music?°   *musicians*
THIRD COUNTRYMAN   Dispersed° as you commanded.   *Placed here and there*
SCHOOLMASTER   Couple,° then,   *Pair up*
And see what's wanting.° Where's the babion?   *who's missing*

3.5
1. The morris dance was a rural folk dance of north English origin, performed in costume. *babion*: one morris dancer, who took the part of the fool, always wore the costume of an ape or baboon. *taborer*: drummer.
2. What tedium and folly (pedantic).
3. "Plum-broth" (hearty stew of dried fruits and suet) and "marrow" both suggest essence or fortifying sustenance.
4. *You . . . judgements:* You people of rudimentary intellects. "Frieze" and "jean" were coarse fabrics worn by

laborers.
5. O God, heaven help me (Latin).
6. Meleager was a Greek warrior who killed the great Calydonian boar and brought its head to the Amazon warrior Atalanta.
7. Like loving subjects of Theseus; in couples, as lovers do.
8. Position yourselves appropriately for the dance.
9. Morris dancers carried ribbons or streamers as props.

[*To the* BABION] My friend, carry your tail without offence°   *sexual offense*
35 Or scandal to the ladies; and be sure
You tumble with audacity and manhood,°   *bravery*
And when you bark, do it with judgement.
BABION   Yes, sir.
SCHOOLMASTER   *Quousque tandem?*[1] Here is a woman wanting!
FOURTH COUNTRYMAN   We may go whistle—all the fat's i'th'
    fire.[2]
40 SCHOOLMASTER   We have,
As learnèd authors utter, washed a tile;°   *worked in vain*
We have been *fatuus,*° and laboured vainly.   *foolish*
SECOND COUNTRYMAN   This is that scornful piece, that scurvy
    hilding°   *worthless woman*
That gave her promise faithfully she would be here—
45 Cicely, the seamstress' daughter.
The next gloves that I give her shall be dogskin.°   *cheap leather*
Nay, an° she fail me once—you can tell, Arcas,   *if*
She swore by wine and bread she would not break.°   *(her solemn oath)*
SCHOOLMASTER   An eel and woman,
50 A learnèd poet says, unless by th' tail
And with thy teeth thou hold, will either° fail—   *both*
In manners this was false position.[3]
FIRST COUNTRYMAN   A fire-ill take her!° Does she flinch now?   *A pox infect her*
THIRD COUNTRYMAN   What
Shall we determine,° sir?   *decide to do*
SCHOOLMASTER   Nothing;
55 Our business is become a nullity,
Yea, and a woeful and a piteous nullity.
FOURTH COUNTRYMAN   Now, when the credit of our town lay on it,
Now to be frampold, now to piss o'th' nettle![4]
Go thy ways—I'll remember thee, I'll fit thee!°   *get even with you*
    Enter [the] JAILER'S DAUGHTER
JAILER'S DAUGHTER [*sings*]
60   The *George Alow*[5] came from the south,
      From the coast of Barbary-a;
    And there he met with brave gallants of war,°   *warships*
      By one, by two, by three-a.
    'Well hailed, well hailed, you jolly gallants,
65   And whither now are you bound-a?
    O let me have your company
      Till I come to the sound-a.'

There was three fools fell out about an owlet—

    The one he said it was an owl,
70   The other he said nay,
    The third he said it was a hawk,
    And her bells were cut away.[6]

---

1. How much longer (must I wait)? (Latin, as throughout the scene). Expression of impatience that opens the ancient Roman writer Cicero's first oration against Catiline but here indicates the Schoolmaster's pomposity.
2. We may as well give up, since all our work has produced nothing. Both phrases were proverbial, although the second has a different meaning today.
3. A false (pro)position is a logical fallacy. The School-master compares Cicely's flawed manners to faulty logic.
4. Now to be temperamental, to lose her temper.
5. Probably taken from "The George Aloe and the Sweepstake," a ballad published in 1611. The *George Aloe* was a ship.
6. Hawks used for falconry wore bells in order to make them easier to catch.

THIRD COUNTRYMAN   There's a dainty° madwoman, master,   *fine*
 Comes i'th' nick,° as mad as a March hare.   *nick (of time)*
75 If we can get her dance, we are made again.°   *all will be well*
 I warrant her, she'll do the rarest gambols.°   *finest capers*
FIRST COUNTRYMAN   A madwoman? We are made, boys.
SCHOOLMASTER [*to the* JAILER'S DAUGHTER]   And are you mad,
 good woman?
JAILER'S DAUGHTER   I would be sorry else.
 Give me your hand.
SCHOOLMASTER   Why?
JAILER'S DAUGHTER   I can tell your fortune.
 [*She examines his hand*]
80 You are a fool. Tell ten—I have posed him.[7] Buzz!°   *Silence*
 Friend, you must eat no white bread—if you do,
 Your teeth will bleed extremely. Shall we dance, ho?
 I know you—you're a tinker.° Sirrah tinker,   *mender of kettles*
 Stop no more holes but what you should.°   *(sexual)*
SCHOOLMASTER   *Dii boni*°—   *Good gods*
 A tinker, damsel?
85 JAILER'S DAUGHTER   Or a conjurer°—   *magician*
 Raise me a devil now and let him play
 Qui passa o'th' bells and bones.[8]
SCHOOLMASTER   Go, take her,
 And fluently persuade her to a peace.°   *to do what we want*
 Et opus exegi, quod nec Iovis ira, nec ignis[9]—
 Strike up, and lead her in.
90 SECOND COUNTRYMAN   Come, lass, let's trip it.° *let's dance*
JAILER'S DAUGHTER   I'll lead.
THIRD COUNTRYMAN   Do, do.
SCHOOLMASTER   Persuasively and cunningly°—   *skillfully*
 Wind horns [*within*]   away, boys,
 I hear the horns. Give me some meditation,°   *time to think*
 And mark° your cue.   *don't forget*
   Exeunt all but [*Gerald the*] SCHOOLMASTER
95   Pallas° inspire me.   *goddess of wisdom*
 Enter THESEUS, PIRITHOUS, HIPPOLYTA, EMILIA, ARCITE,
 and train
THESEUS   This way the stag took.
SCHOOLMASTER   Stay and edify.°   *be edified*
THESEUS   What have we here?
PIRITHOUS   Some country sport, upon my life, sir.
THESEUS [*to the* SCHOOLMASTER]   Well, sir, go forward—we will
100 edify.
 Ladies, sit down—we'll stay it.°   *stay to watch*
 [*They sit:* THESEUS *in a chair, the others on stools*]
SCHOOLMASTER   Thou doughty Duke, all hail! All hail, sweet
 ladies.
THESEUS   This is a cold° beginning.   *(punning on "hail")*

---

7. *Tell . . . him:* Count to ten (a common test for insanity or idiocy)—I have stumped ("posed") him. The Jailer's Daughter tests the Schoolmaster for idiocy and fails him.
8. *Chi passa* (Italian: who passes) were the first words of a common dance tune. Bones were used as percussion instruments, along with bells.
9. "And I have created a work which neither Jove's anger nor fire [can destroy]." Slightly misquoted from Ovid's *Metamorphoses* 15.871.

SCHOOLMASTER   If you but favour,[1] our country pastime made is.

105 We are a few of those collected here,
     That ruder tongues distinguish° 'villager';   *call*
     And to say verity, and not to fable,
     We are a merry rout, or else a rabble,
     Or company, or, by a figure,° chorus,   *figure of speech*
110 That fore thy dignity will dance a morris.
     And I, that am the rectifier° of all,   *director; connector*
     By title *pedagogus,*° that let fall   *teacher*
     The birch upon the breeches of the small ones,
     And humble with a ferula° the tall ones,   *cane*
115 Do here present this machine, or this frame;[2]
     And dainty Duke, whose doughty dismal° fame   *awe-inspiring*
     From Dis to Daedalus,[3] from post to pillar,
     Is blown abroad, help me, thy poor well-willer,°   *well-wisher*
     And with thy twinkling eyes, look right and straight
120 Upon this mighty 'Moor'—of mickle° weight—   *much*
     'Ice' now comes in,[4] which, being glued together,
     Makes 'morris', and the cause that we came hither.
     The body of our sport, of no small study,[5]
     I first appear, though rude, and raw, and muddy,
125 To speak, before thy noble grace, this tenor[6]
     At whose great feet I offer up my penner.°   *pen case*
     The next,° the Lord of May and Lady bright;   *next to appear*
     The Chambermaid and Servingman, by night
     That seek out silent hanging;[7] then mine Host
130 And his fat Spouse, that welcomes, to their cost,
     The gallèd° traveller, and with a beck'ning   *tired*
     Informs the tapster° to inflame the reck'ning;°   *bartender / overcharge*
     Then the beest-eating Clown;[8] and next, the Fool;
     The babion with long tail and eke long tool,°   *penis*
135 *Cum multis aliis*° that make a dance—   *With many others*
     Say 'ay', and all shall presently° advance.   *at once*

THESEUS   Ay, ay, by any means, dear dominie.°   *teacher*

PIRITHOUS   Produce.°   *Put on (your show)*

SCHOOLMASTER   *(knock[s] for the dance)*
     Intrate filii,[9] come forth and foot it.
     [*He flings up his cap.*] *Music.*
     [*The* SCHOOLMASTER *ushers in*
     May Lord,   May Lady.
     Servingman,   Chambermaid.
     A Country Clown,
     or Shepherd,   Country Wench.

---

1. Approve. Compare Quince's speech to Theseus in A *Midsummer Night's Dream* 5.1.126–50.
2. Both "machine" and "frame" mean "structure" or "production."
3. Dis was god of the underworld; Daedalus was creator of the Cretan labyrinth and inventor of wings for human flight. Theseus triumphed over both the underworld and the labyrinth. Daedalus is invoked for the sake of alliteration and, because of his association with flight and hence the heavens, for contrast to Dis.
4. The Schoolmaster displays the word "morris" from two placards, possibly held by the dancers. In Q, the word is split into two syllables, "Morr" and "Is" (here emended to "Moor" and "Ice"). They may have been spelled out, or perhaps pictograms were used, with the first placard depicting a Moor and the second the allegorical figure Winter.
5. The main part in our entertainment, carefully prepared.
6. Argument; tenner (ten-syllable line).
7. Curtain behind which they can make love.
8. Clown or country shepherd (see stage direction at line 138) who likes "beest," the thick milk produced by a cow for the first few days after calving.
9. Come in, my sons (children). The masculine *filii* is especially appropriate, since the women's parts were played by boy actors.

An Host,	*Hostess.*
A He-babion,	*She-babion.*
A He-fool,	*The* JAILER'S DAUGHTER *as*
	She-fool.

All these persons apparelled to the life,° the men issuing   *in lifelike costume*
out of one door and the wenches from the other. They
dance a morris]

       Ladies, if we have been merry,
140   And have pleased ye with a derry,
       And a derry, and a down,°   *(song refrain words)*
       Say the schoolmaster's no clown.
       Duke, if we have pleased thee too,
       And have done as good boys should do,
145   Give us but a tree or twain
       For a maypole, and again,
       Ere another year run out,
       We'll make thee laugh, and all this rout.°   *company*
THESEUS   Take twenty, dominie. [*To* HIPPOLYTA] How does my
   sweetheart?
HIPPOLYTA   Never so pleased, sir.
150 EMILIA   'Twas an excellent dance,
   And for a preface,° I never heard a better.   *as for the prologue*
THESEUS   Schoolmaster, I thank you. One see 'em all rewarded.
PIRITHOUS   And here's something to paint your pole withal.
       [*He gives them money*]
THESEUS   Now to our sports again.
SCHOOLMASTER
155   May the stag thou hunt'st stand long,°   *give a good chase*
       And thy dogs be swift and strong;
       May they kill him without lets,°   *obstacles*
       And the ladies eat his dowsets.°   *testicles (a delicacy)*
       [*Exeunt* THESEUS *and train.*] *Wind horns* [*within*]
   Come, we are all made. *Dii deaeque omnes,°*   *Gods and goddesses all*
160   Ye have danced rarely, wenches.   *Exeunt*

3.6

Enter PALAMON *from the bush*
PALAMON   About this hour my cousin gave his faith°   *word*
   To visit me again, and with him bring
   Two swords and two good armours;° if he fail,   *suits of armor*
   He's neither man nor soldier. When he left me,
5   I did not think a week could have restored
   My lost strength to me, I was grown so low
   And crest-fall'n with my wants. I thank thee, Arcite,
   Thou art yet a fair foe, and I feel myself,
   With this refreshing, able once again
10   To out-dure° danger. To delay it longer   *endure*
   Would make the world think, when it comes to hearing,
   That I lay fatting, like a swine, to fight,
   And not a soldier.[1] Therefore this blest morning

3.6
1. *fatting . . . soldier:* being fattened like a swine for the slaughter, rather than preparing myself like a warrior for the fight.

Shall be the last; and that sword he refuses,°   *(in choosing first)*
15   If it but hold,° I kill him with; 'tis justice.   *Unless it breaks*
So, love and fortune for me!
          Enter ARCITE *with [two] armours and [two] swords*
                              O, good morrow.
ARCITE   Good morrow, noble kinsman.
PALAMON   I have put you
To too much pains, sir.
ARCITE   That too much, fair cousin,
Is but a debt to honour, and my duty.
20   PALAMON   Would you were so in all, sir—I could wish ye
As kind a kinsman, as you force me find
A beneficial foe, that my embraces
Might thank ye, not my blows.
ARCITE   I shall think either,
Well done, a noble recompense.
PALAMON   Then I shall quit° you.   *repay*
25   ARCITE   Defy me in these fair terms, and you show°   *show youself to be*
More than a mistress to me—no more anger,
As you love anything that's honourable.
We were not bred to talk, man. When we are armed
And both upon our guards, then let our fury,
30   Like meeting of two tides, fly strongly from us;
And then to whom the birthright° of this beauty   *rightful possession*
Truly pertains°—without upbraidings, scorns,   *belongs*
Despisings of our persons, and such poutings
Fitter for girls and schoolboys—will be seen,
35   And quickly, yours or mine. Will't please you arm, sir?
Or, if you feel yourself not fitting° yet,   *ready*
And furnished with your old strength, I'll stay,° cousin,   *wait*
And every day discourse you into health,
As I am spared.° Your person I am friends with,   *In my spare time*
40   And I could wish I had not said I loved her,
Though I had died;[2] but loving such a lady,
And justifying° my love, I must not fly from't.   *affirming*
PALAMON   Arcite, thou art so brave an enemy
That no man but thy cousin's fit to kill thee.
I am well and lusty°—choose your arms.   *eager to do battle*
45   ARCITE   Choose you, sir.
PALAMON   Wilt thou exceed in all,[3] or dost thou do it
To make me spare thee?
ARCITE   If you think so, cousin,
You are deceived, for as I am a soldier,
I will not spare you.
PALAMON   That's well said.
ARCITE   You'll find it.°   *find it so*
50   PALAMON   Then as I am an honest man, and love
With all the justice of affection,[4]
I'll pay thee soundly.°   *punish you properly*
          [He chooses one armour]
                    This I'll take.

---

2. Although it would have killed me to keep silent.
3. Will you always outdo me in courtesy (as here, by let-
ting me choose my arms first)?

4. Palamon's love of Emilia is just; Palamon will deal
justly (honorably) with Arcite because he loves him.

ARCITE [*indicating the remaining armour*]   That's mine, then.
  I'll arm you first.
PALAMON   Do.
        [ARCITE *arms* PALAMON]
                       Pray thee tell me, cousin,
  Where gott'st thou this good armour?
ARCITE   'Tis the Duke's,
  And to say true, I stole it. Do I pinch you?
55 PALAMON   No.
ARCITE   Is't not too heavy?
PALAMON   I have worn a lighter—
  But I shall make it serve.
ARCITE   I'll buckle't close.°   *tightly*
PALAMON   By any means.
ARCITE   You care not for a grand guard?[5]
PALAMON   No, no, we'll use no horses. I perceive
  You would fain be at that fight.°   *rather fight mounted*
60 ARCITE   I am indifferent.
PALAMON   Faith, so am I. Good cousin, thrust the buckle
  Through far enough.
ARCITE   I warrant you.°   *Trust me*
PALAMON   My casque° now.   *helmet*
ARCITE   Will you fight bare-armed?
PALAMON   We shall be the nimbler.
ARCITE   But use your gauntlets, though—those are o'th' least.°   *too small*
  Prithee take mine, good cousin.
65 PALAMON   Thank you, Arcite.
  How do I look? Am I fall'n much away?°   *much thinner*
ARCITE   Faith, very little—love has used you kindly.
PALAMON   I'll warrant thee, I'll strike home.
ARCITE   Do, and spare not—
  I'll give you cause, sweet cousin.
PALAMON   Now to you, sir.
        [PALAMON *arms* ARCITE]
70 Methinks this armour's very like that, Arcite,
  Thou wor'st that day the three kings fell, but lighter.
ARCITE   That was a very good one, and that day,
  I well remember, you outdid me, cousin.
  I never saw such valour. When you charged
75 Upon the left wing of the enemy,
  I spurred hard to come up,° and under me   *keep up with you*
  I had a right good horse.
PALAMON   You had indeed—
  A bright bay, I remember.
ARCITE   Yes. But all
  Was vainly laboured in me—you outwent me,
80 Nor could my wishes reach you.[6] Yet a little
  I did by imitation.
PALAMON   More by virtue°—   *your own carriage*
  You are modest, cousin.
ARCITE   When I saw you charge first,
  Methought I heard a dreadful clap of thunder
  Break from the troop.

---

5. Chest plate for fighting on horseback.   6. My wishes to keep up with you were not answered.

PALAMON   But still before that flew
85   The lightning of your valour. Stay a little,
      Is not this piece too strait?°   *tight*
ARCITE   No, no, 'tis well.
PALAMON   I would have nothing hurt thee but my sword—
      A bruise would be dishonour.
ARCITE   Now I am perfect°.   *ready*
PALAMON   Stand off,° then.   *Step back*
ARCITE   Take my sword; I hold° it better.   *consider*
90   PALAMON   I thank ye. No, keep it—your life lies° on it.   *depends*
      Here's one—if it but hold,° I ask no more   *holds together*
      For all my hopes. My cause and honour guard me.
ARCITE   And me, my love.
              They bow several ways,[7] then advance and stand
                       Is there aught else to say?
PALAMON   This only, and no more. Thou art mine aunt's son,
95   And that blood we desire to shed is mutual:
      In me, thine, and in thee, mine. My sword
      Is in my hand, and if thou kill'st me,
      The gods and I forgive thee. If there be
      A place prepared for those that sleep in honour,
100   I wish his weary soul that falls may win it.
      Fight bravely, cousin. Give me thy noble hand.
ARCITE   Here, Palamon. This hand shall never more
      Come near thee with such friendship.
PALAMON   I commend thee.°   *(to God)*
ARCITE   If I fall, curse me, and say I was a coward—
105   For none but such dare die in these just trials.
      Once more farewell, my cousin.
PALAMON   Farewell, Arcite.
              Fight. Horns within; they stand
ARCITE   Lo, cousin, lo, our folly has undone us.
PALAMON   Why?
ARCITE   This is the Duke a-hunting, as I told you.
      If we be found, we are wretched. O, retire,
110   For honour's sake, and safely, presently,
      Into your bush again. Sir, we shall find
      Too many° hours to die. In, gentle cousin—   *More than enough*
      If you be seen, you perish instantly
      For breaking prison, and I, if you reveal me,
115   For my contempt.[8] Then all the world will scorn us,
      And say we had a noble difference,
      But base disposers of it.°   *settled it ignobly*
PALAMON   No, no, cousin,
      I will no more be hidden, nor put off
      This great adventure° to a second trial.   *undertaking*
120   I know your cunning and I know your cause°—   *motive (for delay)*
      He that faints° now, shame take him! Put thyself   *is fainthearted*
      Upon thy present guard°—   *At once on guard*
ARCITE   You are not mad?
PALAMON   Or° I will make th'advantage of this hour   *Either I'm mad or*

---

7. They make ceremonial bows in various directions, as   8. For my disobedience to Theseus's order that I be ban-
if they were jousting in a tournament.   ished.

Mine own, and what to come shall threaten me
125   I fear less than my fortune.° Know, weak cousin,   *(in this fight)*
    I love Emilia, and in that I'll bury
    Thee and all crosses else.°   *all other obstacles*

ARCITE   Then come what can come,
    Thou shalt know, Palamon, I dare as well
    Die as discourse or sleep. Only this fears° me,   *frightens*
130   The law will have the honour of our ends.[9]
    Have at thy life!

PALAMON   Look to thine own well, Arcite!
       [They] fight again.
       Horns. Enter THESEUS, HIPPOLYTA, EMILIA, PIRITHOUS,
       *and train. [*THESEUS *separates* PALAMON *and* ARCITE]

THESEUS   What ignorant and mad malicious° traitors   *evil-minded*
    Are you, that 'gainst the tenor° of my laws   *purport*
    Are making battle, thus like knights appointed,°   *armed*
135   Without my leave and officers of arms?[1]
    By Castor,[2] both shall die.

PALAMON   Hold° thy word, Theseus.   *Keep*
    We are certainly both traitors, both despisers°   *disobedient*
    Of thee and of thy goodness. I am Palamon,
    That cannot love thee, he that broke thy prison —
140   Think well what that deserves. And this is Arcite;
    A bolder traitor never trod thy ground,
    A falser ne'er seemed friend. This is the man
    Was begged° and banished; this is he contemns thee,   *petitioned for*
    And what thou dar'st do; and in this disguise,
145   Against thine own edict, follows thy sister,°   *sister-in-law*
    That fortunate bright° star, the fair Emilia,   *luck-bringing*
    Whose servant° — if there be a right in seeing   *courtly lover*
    And first bequeathing of the soul to — justly
    I am; and, which is more, dares think her his.
150   This treachery, like a most trusty lover,
    I called him now to answer. If thou be'st
    As thou art spoken,° great and virtuous,   *reported to be*
    The true decider of all injuries,
    Say, 'Fight again', and thou shalt see me, Theseus,
155   Do such a justice thou thyself wilt envy.
    Then take my life — I'll woo thee to't.

PIRITHOUS   O heaven,
    What more than man is this!

THESEUS   I have sworn.

ARCITE   We seek not
    Thy breath of mercy, Theseus. 'Tis to me
    A thing as soon to die as thee to say it,
160   And no more moved. Where this man calls me traitor
    Let me say thus much — if in love be treason,
    In service of so excellent a beauty,
    As I love most, and in that faith will perish,
    As I have brought my life here to confirm it,
165   As I have served her truest, worthiest,
    As I dare kill this cousin that denies it,

---

9. We will die by execution rather than combat.
1. Overseers of chivalric combat.

2. Common Roman oath. Castor and Pollux, twins, were
sons of Jupiter.

So let me be most traitor and ye please me.
For° scorning thy edict, Duke, ask that lady   *As for*
Why she is fair, and why her eyes command me
170 Stay here to love her, and if she say, 'Traitor',
I am a villain fit to lie unburied.
PALAMON   Thou shalt have pity of° us both, O Theseus,   *on*
If unto neither thou show mercy. Stop,
As thou art just, thy noble ear against us;
175 As thou art valiant, for thy cousin's° soul,   *(Hercules')*
Whose twelve strong labours crown his memory,
Let's die together, at one instant, Duke.
Only a little let him fall before me,
That I may tell my soul he shall not have her.
180 THESEUS   I grant your wish; for to say true, your cousin
Has ten times more offended, for I gave him
More mercy than you found, sir, your offences
Being no more than his. None here speak for 'em,
For ere the sun set both shall sleep for ever.
185 HIPPOLYTA [*to* EMILIA]   Alas, the pity! Now or never, sister,
Speak, not to be denied. That face of yours
Will bear the curses else of after ages
For these lost cousins.
EMILIA   In my face, dear sister,
I find no anger to 'em, nor no ruin.
190 The misadventure of their own eyes kill° 'em.   *kills*
Yet that° I will be woman and have pity,   *to show that*
[*She kneels*]
My knees shall grow to th' ground, but° I'll get mercy.   *unless*
Help me, dear sister—in a deed so virtuous
The powers of all women will be with us.
[HIPPOLYTA *kneels*]
Most royal brother—
195 HIPPOLYTA   Sir, by our tie of marriage—
EMILIA   By your own spotless honour—
HIPPOLYTA   By that faith,
That fair hand, and that honest heart you gave me—
EMILIA   By that you would have pity in another,[3]
By your own virtues infinite—
HIPPOLYTA   By valour,
200 By all the chaste° nights I have ever pleased you—   *faithful only to you*
THESEUS   These are strange conjurings.°   *incantations*
PIRITHOUS   Nay, then, I'll in too.
[*He kneels*]
By all our friendship, sir, by all our dangers,
By all you love most: wars, and this sweet lady—
EMILIA   By that° you would have trembled to deny   *(chivalric aid)*
A blushing maid—
205 HIPPOLYTA   By your own eyes, by strength—
In which you swore I went beyond° all women,   *I excelled*
Almost all men—and yet I yielded, Theseus—
PIRITHOUS   To crown all this, by your most noble soul,
Which cannot want° due mercy, I beg first—   *lack*

3. By whatever you would expect someone else to pity.

HIPPOLYTA Next hear my prayers—
210 EMILIA   Last let me entreat, sir—
PIRITHOUS For mercy.
HIPPOLYTA   Mercy.
EMILIA   Mercy on these princes.
THESEUS Ye make my faith reel.[4] Say I felt
  Compassion to 'em both, how would you place° it?   *have me bestow*
  [*They rise*]
EMILIA Upon their lives—but with their banishments.
215 THESEUS You are a right° woman, sister: you have pity,   *typical*
  But want the understanding where to use it.
  If you desire their lives, invent a way
  Safer than banishment. Can these two live,
  And have the agony of love about 'em,
220 And not kill one another? Every day
  They'd fight about you, hourly bring your honour
  In public question with their swords.[5] Be wise, then,
  And here forget 'em. It concerns your credit°   *reputation*
  And my oath equally. I have said—they die.
225 Better they fall by th' law than one another.
  Bow not my honour.[6]
EMILIA   O my noble brother,
  That oath was rashly° made, and in your anger.   *impulsively*
  Your reason will not hold° it. If such vows   *sustain*
  Stand for express will,° all the world must perish.   *steadfast resolve*
230 Beside, I have another oath 'gainst yours,
  Of more authority, I am sure more love—
  Not made in passion, neither, but good heed.°   *thoughtfulness*
THESEUS What is it, sister?
PIRITHOUS [*to* EMILIA]   Urge it home, brave lady.
EMILIA That you would ne'er deny me anything
235 Fit for my modest suit and your free granting.
  I tie you to your word now; if ye fail in't,
  Think how you maim your honour—
  For now I am set a-begging, sir. I am deaf
  To all but your compassion—how their lives
240 Might breed the ruin of my name, opinion.°   *my reputation*
  Shall anything that loves me perish for° me?   *because of*
  That were a cruel wisdom: do men prune
  The straight young boughs that blush with thousand blossoms
  Because they may be° rotten? O, Duke Theseus,   *become*
245 The goodly mothers that have groaned for these,°   *(in childbirth)*
  And all the longing maids that ever loved,
  If your vow stand,° shall curse me and my beauty,   *holds*
  And in their funeral songs for these two cousins
  Despise my cruelty and cry woe worth° me,   *befall*
250 Till I am nothing but the scorn of women.
  For heaven's sake, save their lives and banish 'em.
THESEUS On what conditions?
EMILIA   Swear 'em never more
  To make me their contention, or to know me,°   *think of me*

---

4. You make my constancy to my own oath (to kill the kinsmen) waver.
5. *They'd . . . swords:* They'd fight publicly over you, thus compromising your honor.
6. Don't force me to lower (bend) my standards of honor.

To tread upon thy dukedom; and to be,
255 Wherever they shall travel, ever strangers
To one another.
PALAMON   I'll be cut a-pieces
Before I take this oath—forget I love her?
O all ye gods, despise me, then. Thy banishment
I not mislike, so we may fairly carry
260 Our swords and cause along—else, never trifle,
But take our lives, Duke. I must love, and will;
And for that love must and dare kill this cousin
On any piece° the earth has.   spot of ground
THESEUS   Will you, Arcite,
Take these conditions?
PALAMON   He's a villain then.
PIRITHOUS   These are men!
265 ARCITE   No, never, Duke. 'Tis worse to me than begging,
To take° my life so basely. Though I think   value
I never shall enjoy her, yet I'll preserve
The honour of affection and die for her,
Make death a devil.°   Even horribly
270 THESEUS   What may be done? For now I feel compassion.
PIRITHOUS   Let it not fall° again, sir.   diminish
THESEUS   Say, Emilia,
If one of them were dead—as one must—are you
Content to take the other to your husband?
They cannot both enjoy you. They are princes
275 As goodly as your own eyes, and as noble
As ever fame yet spoke of. Look upon 'em,
And if you can love, end this difference.
I give consent. [To PALAMON and ARCITE] Are you content too,
      princes?
PALAMON and ARCITE   With all our souls.
THESEUS   He that she refuses
Must die, then.
280 PALAMON and ARCITE   Any death thou canst invent, Duke.
PALAMON   If I fall from that mouth,° I fall with favour,   (because of her decision)
And lovers yet unborn shall bless my ashes.
ARCITE   If she refuse me, yet my grave will wed me,
And soldiers sing my epitaph.
THESEUS [to EMILIA]   Make choice, then.
285 EMILIA   I cannot, sir. They are both too excellent.
For° me, a hair shall never fall of these men.   On account of
HIPPOLYTA [to THESEUS]   What will become of 'em?
THESEUS   Thus I ordain it,
And by mine honour once again it stands,
Or both shall die. [To PALAMON and ARCITE] You shall both to your country,
290 And each within this month, accompanied
With three fair knights, appear again in this place,
In which I'll plant° a pyramid; and whether,°   fix / whichever
Before us that are here, can force his cousin,
By fair and knightly strength, to touch the pillar,
295 He shall enjoy her; the other lose his head,
And all his friends; nor shall he grudge to fall,[7]

7. And all his friends will die with him; nor should he consider his execution unjust.

Nor think he dies with interest in° this lady.   *a rightful claim to*
Will this content ye?
PALAMON   Yes. Here, cousin Arcite,
I am friends again till that hour.
ARCITE   I embrace ye.
THESEUS [*to* EMILIA] Are you content, sister?
300 EMILIA   Yes, I must, sir,
Else both miscarry.°   *perish*
THESEUS [*to* PALAMON *and* ARCITE]
     Come, shake hands again, then,
And take heed, as you are gentlemen, this quarrel
Sleep till the hour prefixed, and hold your course.° *keep your resolve*
PALAMON We dare not fail thee, Theseus.
THESEUS   Come, I'll give ye
305 Now usage like to princes and to friends.
When ye return, who wins I'll settle here,°   *set up in Athens*
Who loses, yet I'll weep upon his bier.
    Exeunt. [*In the act-time the bush is removed*]

4.1

Enter [*the*] JAILER *and his* FRIEND
JAILER Hear you no more? Was nothing said of me
Concerning the escape of Palamon?
Good sir, remember.
FRIEND   Nothing that I heard,
For I came home before the business
5 Was fully ended. Yet I might perceive,
Ere I departed, a great likelihood
Of both their pardons: for Hippolyta
And fair-eyed Emily upon their knees
Begged with such handsome pity that the Duke,
10 Methought, stood staggering° whether he should follow *wavering as to*
His rash oath or the sweet compassion
Of those two ladies; and to second them
That truly noble prince, Pirithous—
Half his own heart[1]—set in too, that° I hope   *so that*
15 All shall be well. Neither heard I one question
Of your name or his scape.
   Enter [*the*] SECOND FRIEND
JAILER   Pray heaven it hold° so.   *continue*
SECOND FRIEND Be of good comfort, man. I bring you news,
Good news.
JAILER   They are welcome.
SECOND FRIEND   Palamon has cleared you,
And got your pardon, and discovered° how   *exposed*
20 And by whose means he scaped—which was your daughter's,
Whose pardon is procured too; and the prisoner,
Not to be held ungrateful to her goodness,
Has given a sum of money to her marriage—
A large one, I'll assure you.
JAILER   Ye are a good man,
And ever bring good news.
25 FIRST FRIEND   How was it ended?

4.1 Location: The prison
1. Hippolyta is (has) the other half.

SECOND FRIEND   Why, as it should be: they that ne'er begged,
But° they prevailed, had their suits fairly granted—   *Still*
The prisoners have their lives.
FIRST FRIEND   I knew 'twould be so.
SECOND FRIEND   But there be new conditions which you'll hear of
At better time.
JAILER   I hope they are good.
30   SECOND FRIEND   They are honourable—
How good they'll prove I know not.
        Enter [the] WOOER
FIRST FRIEND   'Twill be known.
WOOER   Alas, sir, where's your daughter?
JAILER   Why do you ask?
WOOER   O, sir, when did you see her?
SECOND FRIEND   How he looks!
JAILER   This morning.
WOOER   Was she well? Was she in health?
Sir, when did she sleep?
35   FIRST FRIEND   These are strange questions.
JAILER   I do not think she was very well: for now
You make me mind° her, but this very day   *remind me of*
I asked her questions and she answered me
So far from what she was,° so childishly,   *her usual manner*
40   So sillily, as if she were a fool,
An innocent°—and I was very angry.   *idiot*
But what of her, sir?
WOOER   Nothing, but my pity²—
But you must know it, and as good by me
As by another that less loves her—
JAILER   Well, sir?
FIRST FRIEND   Not right?°   *in her right mind*
WOOER   No, sir, not well.
45   SECOND FRIEND   Not well?
WOOER   'Tis too true—she is mad.
FIRST FRIEND   It cannot be.
WOOER   Believe, you'll find it so.
JAILER   I half suspected
What you told me—the gods comfort her!
Either this was her love to Palamon,
50   Or fear of my miscarrying on³ his scape,
Or both.
WOOER   'Tis likely.
JAILER   But why all this haste, sir?
WOOER   I'll tell you quickly. As I late was angling°   *fishing*
In the great lake that lies behind the palace,
From the far shore, thick set with reeds and sedges,
55   As patiently I was attending sport,°   *awaiting a fish*
I heard a voice—a shrill one—and attentive
I gave my ear, when I might well perceive
'Twas one that sung, and by the smallness° of it   *high pitch*
A boy or woman. I then left my angle°   *fishing rod*
60   To his own skill,° came near, but yet perceived not   *To fish by itself*
Who made the sound, the rushes and the reeds

---

2. My pity for you and her makes me speak.   3. My being punished because of.

Had so encompassed it.° I laid me down   *overgrown the place*
And listened to the words she sung, for then,
Through a small glade cut by the fishermen,
I saw it was your daughter.

65   JAILER   Pray go on, sir.
    WOOER   She sung much, but no sense; only I heard her
      Repeat this often—'Palamon is gone,
      Is gone to th' wood to gather mulberries;
      I'll find him out tomorrow.'
    FIRST FRIEND   Pretty soul!
70   WOOER   'His shackles will betray him—he'll be taken,
      And what shall I do then? I'll bring a bevy,°   *company*
      A hundred black-eyed maids that love as I do,
      With chaplets° on their heads of daffodillies,   *wreaths*
      With cherry lips and cheeks of damask roses,
75   And all we'll dance an antic° fore the Duke   *a grotesque dance*
      And beg his pardon.'[4] Then she talked of you, sir—
      That you must lose your head tomorrow morning,
      And she must gather flowers to bury you,
      And see the house made handsome.° Then she sung   *neat*
80   Nothing but 'willow, willow, willow',[5] and between
      Ever was 'Palamon, fair Palamon',
      And 'Palamon was a tall° young man'. The place   *valiant*
      Was knee-deep° where she sat; her careless tresses   *(in rushes)*
      A wreath of bull-rush rounded;° about her stuck   *encircled*
85   Thousand freshwater flowers of several° colours—   *various*
      That° she appeared, methought, like the fair nymph   *Such that*
      That feeds the lake with waters, or as Iris[6]
      Newly dropped down from heaven. Rings she made
      Of rushes that grew by,[7] and to 'em spoke
90   The prettiest posies[8]—'Thus our true love's tied',
      'This you may lose, not me', and many a one.
      And then she wept, and sung again, and sighed—
      And with the same breath smiled and kissed her hand.
    SECOND FRIEND   Alas, what pity it is!
    WOOER   I made in to° her: *approached*
95   She saw me and straight sought the flood°—I saved her,   *at once jumped in*
      And set her safe to land, when presently
      She slipped away and to the city made,
      With such a cry and swiftness that, believe me,
      She left me far behind her. Three or four
100   I saw from far off cross° her—one of 'em   *intercept*
      I knew to be your brother, where she stayed°   *stopped*
      And fell, scarce to be got away. I left them with her,

          Enter [the JAILER'S] BROTHER, *[the* JAILER'S] DAUGHTER,*
          and others

      And hither came to tell you—here they are.
    JAILER'S DAUGHTER [*sings*]   'May you never more enjoy the
        light . . .'°—   *(unknown song)*
      Is not this a fine song?
105   JAILER'S BROTHER   O, a very fine one.

---

4. Beg Duke Theseus to pardon Palamon.
5. Refrain of a popular song, also sung by Desdemona in *Othello* 4.3.
6. Goddess of the rainbow and Juno's messenger.

7. *Rings . . . by*: sometimes used as wedding rings in rural (or mock) wedding ceremonies.
8. Mottoes and aphorisms, sometimes engraved on the inside of rings.

JAILER'S DAUGHTER   I can sing twenty more.
JAILER'S BROTHER   I think you can.
JAILER'S DAUGHTER   Yes, truly can I—I can sing 'The Broom'
  And 'Bonny Robin'⁹—are not you a tailor?
JAILER'S BROTHER   Yes.
JAILER'S DAUGHTER   Where's my wedding gown?
JAILER'S BROTHER   I'll bring it tomorrow.
110   JAILER'S DAUGHTER   Do, very rarely°—I must be abroad else,°   *early / or I'll be out*
  To call the maids and pay the minstrels,
  For I must lose my maidenhead by cocklight,°   *before dawn*
  'Twill never thrive else.¹ *(Sings)* 'O fair, O sweet . . .'²
JAILER'S BROTHER [*to the* JAILER]   You must e'en take it
        patiently.
JAILER   'Tis true.
JAILER'S DAUGHTER   Good ev'n, good men. Pray, did you ever
115   hear
  Of one young Palamon?
JAILER   Yes, wench, we know him.
JAILER'S DAUGHTER   Is't not a fine young gentleman?
JAILER   'Tis, love.
JAILER'S BROTHER   By no mean cross her, she is then distempered
  Far worse than now she shows.³
FIRST FRIEND [*to the* JAILER'S DAUGHTER]   Yes, he's a fine man.
JAILER'S DAUGHTER   O, is he so? You have a sister.
120   FIRST FRIEND   Yes.
JAILER'S DAUGHTER   But she shall never have him, tell her so,
  For° a trick that I know. You'd best look to her,   *Because of*
  For if she see him once, she's gone—she's done
  And undone in an hour. All the young maids
125   Of our town are in love with him, but I laugh at 'em
  And let 'em all alone. Is't not a wise course?
FIRST FRIEND   Yes.
JAILER'S DAUGHTER   There is at least two hundred now with
           child by him,
  There must be four;° yet I keep close⁴ for all this,   *four hundred*
  Close as a cockle;° and all these° must be boys—   *clam / (the offspring)*
130   He has the trick on't°—and at ten years old   *of producing boys*
  They must be all gelt for musicians⁵
  And sing the wars of Theseus.
SECOND FRIEND   This is strange.
JAILER'S BROTHER   As ever you heard, but say nothing.
FIRST FRIEND   No.
JAILER'S DAUGHTER   They come from all parts of the dukedom
           to him.
135   I'll warrant ye, he had not so few last night
  As twenty to dispatch. He'll tickle't up°   *do the (sexual) job*
  In two hours, if his hand be in.°   *if he's in good shape*
JAILER   She's lost
  Past all cure.

---

9. "The Broom" and "Bonny Robin" were popular songs
(Ophelia sings a line of the latter in *Hamlet* 4.5). "Robin"
could mean "penis."
1. Otherwise things (or possibly the marriage) won't pros-
per for me.
2. A song adapted from the seventh of Sir Philip Sidney's

Certain Sonnets (1598).
3. *By . . . shows:* Don't contradict her in any way, or she'll
become far more deranged than she is now.
4. Keep my mouth (and thighs) closed.
5. They must all be castrated so that their voices do not
break and they can become singers.

JAILER'S BROTHER   Heaven forbid, man!
JAILER'S DAUGHTER [*to the* JAILER]   Come hither—you are a
    wise man.
FIRST FRIEND   Does she know him?°   *recognize her father*
SECOND FRIEND   No—would she did.
140 JAILER'S DAUGHTER   You are master of a ship?
    JAILER   Yes.
    JAILER'S DAUGHTER   Where's your compass?
    JAILER   Here.
    JAILER'S DAUGHTER   Set it to th' north.
    And now direct your course to th' wood where Palamon
    Lies longing for me. For the tackling,°   *rigging*
    Let me alone.° Come, weigh,° my hearts, cheerly all.   *I'll do it / (anchor)*
145 Uff, uff, uff!⁶ 'Tis up. The wind's fair. Top° the bowline.   *Tighten*
    Out with the mainsail. Where's your whistle, master?
    JAILER'S BROTHER   Let's get her in.°   *inside (an aside)*
    JAILER   Up to the top,° boy!   *top of the mast*
    JAILER'S BROTHER   Where's the pilot?
    FIRST FRIEND   Here.
    JAILER'S DAUGHTER   What kenn'st thou?°   *What do you see*
    SECOND FRIEND   A fair wood.
    JAILER'S DAUGHTER   Bear for° it, master. *Steer toward*
150 Tack about!
    (*Sings*)   'When Cynthia° with her borrowed light . . .'⁷   *the moon*
                         Exeunt

4.2
    Enter EMILIA, *with two pictures*°   *(Palamon and Arcite)*
EMILIA   Yet I may bind those wounds up that must open
    And bleed to death for my sake else—I'll choose,
    And end their strife. Two such young handsome men
    Shall never fall for° me; their weeping mothers   *die because of*
5 Following the dead cold ashes of their sons,
    Shall never curse my cruelty. Good heaven,
    What a sweet face has Arcite! If wise nature,
    With all her best endowments, all those beauties
    She sows into the births of noble bodies,
10 Were here a mortal woman and had in her
    The coy° denials of young maids, yet doubtless   *modest*
    She would run mad for this man. What an eye,
    Of what a fiery sparkle and quick° sweetness   *lively*
    Has this young prince! Here° love himself sits smiling!   *In his eye*
15 Just such another wanton Ganymede
    Set Jove afire once, and enforced the god
    Snatch up the goodly boy and set him by him,
    A shining constellation.¹ What a brow,
    Of what a spacious majesty, he carries!
20 Arched like the great-eyed Juno's, but far sweeter,
    Smoother than Pelops' shoulder!° Fame and honour,   *(made of ivory)*

---

6. Grunts of exertion; possibly the sound of the wind in
the sails.
7. Line from an unknown song.

4.2 Location: Theseus's palace in Athens.
1. Ganymede was a beautiful youth whom Jupiter
became enamored of and carried off to be his cupbearer
on Mt. Olympus. In the end, Ganymede was transformed
into the constellation Aquarius.

Methinks, from hence,° as from a promontory   *his brow*
Pointed° in heaven, should clap their wings and sing   *Reaching its peak*
To all the under world° the loves and fights   *the earth*
25   Of gods, and such men near 'em.° Palamon   *men most like gods*
Is but his foil;[2] to him a mere dull shadow;
He's swart and meagre,° of an eye as heavy°   *dark and thin / sad*
As if he had lost his mother; a still temper,°   *lethargic disposition*
No stirring in him, no alacrity,
30   Of all this° sprightly sharpness, not a smile.°   *(Arcite's) / trace*
Yet these° that we count errors may become him: *these qualities*
Narcissus was a sad° boy, but a heavenly.°   *serious / beautiful*
O, who can find the bent of woman's fancy?[3]
I am a fool, my reason is lost in me,
35   I have no choice,[4] and I have lied so lewdly°   *wickedly*
That women ought to beat me. On my knees
I ask thy pardon, Palamon, thou art alone°   *uniquely*
And only beautiful, and these the eyes,
These the bright lamps of beauty, that command
40   And threaten love—and what young maid dare cross° 'em?   *oppose*
What a bold gravity, and yet inviting,
Has this brown manly face? O, love, this only
From this hour is complexion.[5] Lie there, Arcite,
Thou art a changeling to him, a mere gypsy,[6]
45   And this the noble body. I am sotted,°   *made stupid*
Utterly lost—my virgin's faith[7] has fled me.
For if my brother, but even now, had asked me
Whether I loved, I had run mad for Arcite;
Now if my sister, more for Palamon.
50   Stand both together.° Now come ask me, brother—   *(comparing portraits)*
Alas, I know not; ask me now, sweet sister—
I may go look.° What a mere child is fancy,   *seek further*
That having two fair gauds° of equal sweetness,   *toys*
Cannot distinguish,° but must cry for both!   *choose*
      Enter [a] GENTLEMAN
How now, sir?
55 GENTLEMAN   From the noble Duke your brother,
Madam, I bring you news. The knights are come.
EMILIA   To end the quarrel?
GENTLEMAN   Yes.
EMILIA   Would I might end first!
What sins have I committed, chaste Diana,[8]
That my unspotted youth must now be soiled°   *defiled*
60   With blood of princes, and my chastity
Be made the altar where the lives of lovers—
Two greater and two better never yet
Made mothers joy—must be the sacrifice
To my unhappy beauty?

---

2. Piece of thin, reflective metal in which a jewel was set, enhancing the jewel's brilliance (setting it off by contrast).
3. Who can discern which way a woman's affections will tend?
4. I am incapable of choosing.
5. *this only . . . complexion:* the only "complexion" I'll appreciate from now on is a dark one.
6. A changeling was an ugly or deformed child left by fairies in exchange for one they stole. Gypsies were also thought to steal children; otherwise the meaning is unclear, since the word generally referred to a swarthy person and Palamon has the dark complexion. Perhaps if a dark complexion is "fair," Arcite's fair skin will be considered the "gypsy" one.
7. My prior oath (1.3.86ff.) to remain a virgin.
8. Virgin goddess of the moon and of the Amazons. See 1.3.52 and note.

Enter THESEUS, HIPPOLYTA, PIRITHOUS, *and attendants*

THESEUS   Bring 'em in
65   Quickly, by any means, I long to see 'em.   [*Exit one or more*]
     [*To* EMILIA] Your two contending lovers are returned,
     And with them their fair knights. Now, my fair sister,
     You must love one of them.
EMILIA   I had rather both,
     So° neither for my sake should fall untimely.°   *So that / prematurely*
                Enter [*a*] MESSENGER
THESEUS   Who saw 'em?
PIRITHOUS   I a while.
70   GENTLEMAN   And I.
THESEUS [*to the* MESSENGER]
     From whence come you, sir?
MESSENGER   From the knights.
THESEUS   Pray speak,
     You that have seen them, what they are.
MESSENGER   I will, sir,
     And truly what I think. Six braver spirits
     Than these they have brought, if we judge by the outside,
75   I never saw nor read of.[9] He that stands
     In the first place with Arcite, by his seeming,°   *appearance*
     Should be a stout° man; by his face, a prince.   *brave*
     His very looks so say° him: his complexion,   *declare*
     Nearer a brown than black, stern and yet noble,
80   Which shows him hardy, fearless, proud° of dangers.   *scornful*
     The circles of his eyes show fire within him,
     And, as a heated° lion, so he looks.   *an angry*
     His hair hangs long behind him, black and shining,
     Like ravens' wings. His shoulders, broad and strong;
85   Armed long and round;[1] and on his thigh a sword
     Hung by a curious baldric, when he frowns
     To seal his will with.[2] Better,° o' my conscience,   *A better sword*
     Was never soldier's friend.
THESEUS   Thou hast well described him.
90   PIRITHOUS   Yet a great deal short,
     Methinks, of him that's first with Palamon.
THESEUS   Pray speak° him, friend.   *describe*
PIRITHOUS   I guess he is a prince too,
     And, if it may be, greater—for his show°   *appearance*
     Has all the ornament of honour in't.
95   He's somewhat bigger than the knight he° spoke of,   *(the messenger)*
     But of a face far sweeter. His complexion
     Is as a ripe grape, ruddy. He has felt,
     Without doubt, what he fights for,° and so apter   *(love)*
     To make this cause his own. In's face appears
100 All the fair hopes of° what he undertakes,   *confidence about*
     And when he's angry, then a settled° valour,   *steady*
     Not tainted with extremes, runs through his body
     And guides his arm to brave things. Fear he cannot—

---

9. *nor read of*: possibly a joke on the playwright's part; the following descriptions closely follow Chaucer's *Knight's Tale* 2129–78.
1. With long, well-muscled arms.

2. *Hung . . . with*: Hung from an artfully crafted ("curious") sword belt ("baldric"), which he uses to carry out his will when he is angry.

He shows no such soft temper. His head's yellow,
105 Hard-haired[3] and curled, thick twined: like ivy tods,° *bushes*
Not to undo with° thunder. In his face *Not destroyed by*
The livery of the warlike maid[4] appears,
Pure red and white—for yet no beard has blessed him—
And in his rolling eyes sits victory,
110 As if she ever° meant to court his valour. *(victory) always*
His nose stands high, a character° of honour; *distinguishing mark*
His red lips, after fights, are fit for ladies.

EMILIA   Must these men die too?

PIRITHOUS   When he speaks, his tongue
Sounds like a trumpet. All his lineaments° *body parts*
115 Are as a man would wish 'em—strong and clean.° *perfectly shaped*
He wears a well-steeled° axe, the staff° of gold. *well-honed / handle*
His age, some five-and-twenty.

MESSENGER   There's another—
A little man, but of a tough soul, seeming
As great° as any. Fairer promises *noble*
120 In such a body yet I never looked on.

PIRITHOUS   O, he that's freckle-faced?

MESSENGER   The same, my lord.
Are they° not sweet ones? *(the freckles)*

PIRITHOUS   Yes, they are well.

MESSENGER   Methinks,
Being so few and well disposed,° they show *arranged*
Great and fine art in nature. He's white-haired°— *blond*
125 Not wanton white,° but such a manly colour *effeminately fair*
Next to an auburn, tough and nimble set,° *and lithe*
Which shows an active soul. His arms are brawny,
Lined with strong sinews—to the shoulder piece
Gently they swell, like women new-conceived,° *starting pregnancy*
130 Which speaks him prone to labour, never fainting
Under the weight of arms; stout-hearted, still,° *when motionless*
But when he stirs, a tiger. He's grey-eyed,[5]
Which yields compassion where he conquers; sharp
To spy advantages, and where he finds 'em,
135 He's swift to make 'em his. He does no wrongs,
Nor takes none.° He's round-faced, and when he smiles *tolerates any*
He shows° a lover; when he frowns, a soldier. *looks like*
About his head he wears the winner's oak,[6]
And in it stuck the favour of his lady.
140 His age, some six-and-thirty. In his hand
He bears a charging staff° embossed with silver. *lance*

THESEUS   Are they all thus?

PIRITHOUS   They are all the sons of honour.

THESEUS   Now as I have a soul, I long to see 'em.
[*To* HIPPOLYTA] Lady, you shall see men fight now.

HIPPOLYTA   I wish it,
145 But not the cause, my lord. They would show

3. Perhaps influenced by Thomas Speght's 1602 edition
of Chaucer's *Knight's Tale*, where King Emetrius's hair
"was of yron" (was made of iron) instead of "yronne"
(curled).
4. *The . . . maid*: His allegiance to Bellona, goddess of
war (or possibly to Athena, also associated with warlike

powers).
5. With eyes of blue or blue-gray. Eyes of this color sup-
posedly implied compassion.
6. Valiant soldiers received a wreath of oak leaves, partic-
ularly if they saved their friends in battle.

Bravely about the titles of two kingdoms⁷—
'Tis pity love should be so tyrannous.
[*To* EMILIA] O my soft-hearted sister, what think you?
Weep not till they weep blood. Wench, it must be.
THESEUS [*to* EMILIA]
    You have steeled 'em° with your beauty.   *made them determined*
150   [*To* PIRITHOUS]   Honoured friend,
    To you I give the field:° pray order it   *charge of the combat*
    Fitting the persons that must use it.
PIRITHOUS   Yes, sir.
THESEUS   Come, I'll go visit 'em—I cannot stay,°   *wait*
    Their fame° has fired me so. Till they appear,   *This account of them*
    Good friend, be royal.°   *treat them royally*
155 PIRITHOUS   There shall want no bravery.°   *splendor*
EMILIA [*aside*]   Poor wench, go weep—for whosoever wins
    Loses a noble cousin for thy sins.   *Exeunt*

4.3

Enter [*the*] JAILER, [*the*] WOOER, [*and the*] DOCTOR
DOCTOR   Her distraction is more at some time of the moon than
    at other some,° is it not?   *at others*
JAILER   She is continually in a harmless distemper:° sleeps little;   *state of confusion*
    altogether without appetite, save often drinking; dreaming of
5   another world, and a better; and what broken piece of matter
    soe'er she's about, the name 'Palamon' lards it,¹ that she farces°   *stuffs*
    every business
        Enter [*the* JAILER'S] DAUGHTER
    withal,° fits it to every question. Look where she comes—you   *with it*
    shall perceive her behaviour.
        [*They stand apart*]
10 JAILER'S DAUGHTER   I have forgot it quite—the burden on't° was   *refrain of the song*
    'Down-a, down-a', and penned by no worse man than Giraldo,
    Emilia's schoolmaster. He's as fantastical,° too, as ever he may   *fanciful*
    go upon's legs°— for in the next world will Dido see Palamon,   *as any man*
    and then will she be out of love with Aeneas.²
15 DOCTOR   What stuff's here? Poor soul.
JAILER   E'en thus all day long.
JAILER'S DAUGHTER   Now for this charm that I told you of—you
    must bring a piece of silver on the tip of your tongue, or no
    ferry:³ then, if it be your chance to come where the blessed
20   spirits are—there's a sight now! We maids that have our livers
    perished,⁴ cracked to pieces with love, we shall come there and
    do nothing all day long but pick flowers with Proserpine.⁵ Then
    will I make Palamon a nosegay, then let him mark me,° then—   *notice me*
DOCTOR   How prettily she's amiss! Note her a little further.
25 JAILER'S DAUGHTER   Faith, I'll tell you: sometime we go to

---

7. *They ... kingdoms*: It would be more appropriate if
they were fighting for each other's kingdoms.
4.3 Location: The prison.
1. Whatever disjointed piece of business she tries to do
(or discuss), Palamon's name is inserted into it (like a
piece of fat into lean meat in order to make it cook
better).
2. Presumably the Schoolmaster has written a song about
Dido and her lover Aeneas, who abandons her in Virgil's
Aeneid. The Jailer's Daughter imagines a new ending in
which Dido falls in love with Palamon rather than Aeneas

in the afterworld.
3. Charon demanded payment for ferrying dead souls
across the river Styx to the underworld. Hence the custom
of placing a coin on the tongues of the dead.
4. Shrivel up from unrequited love. The liver was sup-
posed to be the seat of the passions.
5. One day while she was picking flowers, Proserpine was
spotted by Pluto, who carried her off to the underworld to
be his queen. Her mother, Demeter, got Zeus to allow
her to spend six months on earth each year.

barley-break,[6] we of the blessed. Alas, 'tis a sore life they have
i'th' other place—such burning, frying, boiling, hissing, howl-
ing, chattering, cursing—O they have shrewd measure°—take   *harsh retribution*
heed! If one be mad or hang or drown themselves, thither they
30 go, Jupiter bless us, and there shall we be put in a cauldron of
lead and usurers' grease,[7] amongst a whole million of cut-
purses, and there boil like a gammon° of bacon that will never   *side*
be enough.°   *cooked enough*
DOCTOR How her brain coins!°   *invents*
35 JAILER'S DAUGHTER Lords and courtiers that have got maids with
child—they are in this place. They shall stand in fire up to the
navel and in ice up to th' heart, and there th'offending part
burns, and the deceiving part freezes—in truth a very grievous
punishment as one would think for such a trifle. Believe me,
40 one would marry a leprous witch to be rid on't, I'll assure you.
DOCTOR How she continues this fancy! 'Tis not an engrafted
madness, but a most thick and profound melancholy.[8]
JAILER'S DAUGHTER To hear there a proud° lady and a proud city   *an aristocratic*
wife° howl together! I were a beast an° I'd call it good sport.   *merchant's wife / if*
45 One cries, 'O this smoke!', th'other, 'This fire!'; one cries, 'O
that ever I did it behind the arras!',° and then howls—th'other   *wall hanging*
curses a suing fellow and her garden-house.[9]
(Sings) 'I will be true, my stars, my fate . . .'°   Exit DAUGHTER   *(unknown song)*
JAILER [to the DOCTOR] What think you of her, sir?
50 DOCTOR I think she has a perturbed mind, which I cannot min-
ister to.
JAILER Alas, what then?
DOCTOR Understand you she ever affected° any man ere she   *loved*
beheld Palamon?
55 JAILER I was once, sir, in great hope she had fixed her liking on
this gentleman, my friend.
WOOER I did think so too, and would account I had a great
penn'orth° on't to give half my state° that both she and I, at this   *bargain / property*
present, stood unfeignedly on the same terms.
60 DOCTOR That intemperate surfeit of her eye hath distempered
the other senses.[1] They may return and settle again to execute
their preordained faculties, but they are now in a most extrava-
gant vagary.° This you must do: confine her to a place where   *errant wandering*
the light may rather seem to steal in than be permitted; take
65 upon you, young sir her friend, the name of Palamon; say you
come to eat with her and to commune of love. This will catch
her attention, for this her mind beats upon°—other objects that   *is obsessed with*
are inserted 'tween her mind and eye become the pranks and
friskins° of her madness. Sing to her such green songs[2] of love   *tricks and frolics*
70 as she says Palamon hath sung in prison; come to her stuck in°   *decorated with*
as sweet flowers as the season is mistress of, and thereto make
an addition of some other compounded odours° which are   *blended perfumes*

---

6. A game played with male-female couples: one couple
assigned to a place in the field called "hell" attempted to
entrap the other couples.
7. The traditional punishment for avarice was boiling in
oil (here, imagined as the sweat, "grease," given off by
usurers).
8. It is not a rooted ("an engrafted"), true madness, but a
deep depression (what today might be called love sick-

ness).
9. *a suing . . . garden-house:* the persuasive Wooer who
lured her into a garden house, a site notorious for amo-
rous trysts.
1. Her excessive gazing at Palamon has thrown her other
senses off.
2. Songs typical of youth.

grateful° to the sense. All this shall become° Palamon, for Pala-   *pleasant / befit*
mon can sing, and Palamon is sweet and every good thing.
75 Desire to eat with her, carve° her, drink to her, and still among³   *carve for*
intermingle your petition of grace and acceptance into her
favour. Learn what maids have been her companions and play-
feres,° and let them repair to her, with Palamon in their mouths,   *playmates*
and appear with tokens as if they suggested° for him. It is a   *interceded*
80 falsehood° she is in, which is with falsehoods to be combated.   *delusion*
This may bring° her to eat, to sleep, and reduce what's now out   *induce*
of square° in her into their former law and regiment.° I have   *disordered / rule*
seen it approved,⁴ how many times I know not, but to make the
number more I have great hope in this. I will between the
85 passages° of this project come in with my appliance.⁵ Let us   *stages*
put it in execution, and hasten the success,° which doubt not   *outcome*
will bring forth comfort.   *Exeunt*

5.1

[*An altar prepared.*] *Flourish. Enter* THESEUS, PIRI-
THOUS, HIPPOLYTA, *attendants*
THESEUS Now let 'em enter and before the gods
Tender their holy prayers. Let the temples
Burn bright with sacred fires, and the altars
In hallowed clouds commend° their swelling incense   *deliver*
5   To those above us. Let no due° be wanting.   *proper ritual*
            Flourish of cornetts
They have a noble work in hand, will° honour   *which will*
The very powers that love 'em.
            Enter PALAMON [*with his three*] *Knights* [*at one door*],
            and ARCITE [*with his three Knights at the other door*]
PIRITHOUS   Sir, they enter.
THESEUS You valiant and strong-hearted enemies,
You royal german° foes that this day come   *closely related*
10   To blow that nearness° out that flames between ye,   *close kinship*
Lay by your anger for an hour and, dove-like,
Before the holy altars of your helpers,
The all-feared gods, bow down your stubborn bodies.
Your ire° is more than mortal—so° your help be;   *anger / so may*
15   And as the gods regard° ye, fight with justice.   *are watching*
I'll leave you to your prayers, and betwixt ye
I part my wishes.°   *divide my hopes*
PIRITHOUS   Honour crown the worthiest.
            Exit THESEUS *and his train*
PALAMON [*to* ARCITE] The glass° is running now that cannot   *hourglass*
    finish
Till one of us expire. Think you but thus,
20   That were there aught in me which strove to show°   *to expose itself as*
Mine enemy in this business, were 't one eye
Against another, arm oppressed by arm,
I would destroy th'offender—coz, I would,

---

3. Among these pastimes.
4. I have seen this type of treatment successfully carried
out.
5. My final mode of treatment (see 5.4).
5.1 Location: The forest. A single altar is probably visible
upstage, perhaps on the inner stage, for this scene (at least

from line 34) and the next two. Here, it is dedicated to
Mars. Q treats these first three scenes as a single one. This
makes sense if there are three altars onstage, rather than,
as assumed here, only one, which successively represents
three different altars, presumably in different locations.

Though parcel° of myself. Then from this gather   *it were a piece*
How I should tender° you.   *treat*

25 ARCITE   I am in labour
To push your name, your ancient love, our kindred,°   *kinship*
Out of my memory, and i'th' selfsame place
To seat something I would confound.° So hoist we   *destroy*
The sails that must these vessels port even where°   *carry wherever*
The heavenly limiter° pleases.   *(of life)*

30 PALAMON   You speak well.
Before I turn,° let me embrace thee, cousin—   *turn away*
This I shall never do again.

ARCITE   One farewell.

PALAMON   Why, let it be so—farewell, coz.

ARCITE   Farewell, sir.

Exeunt PALAMON *and his [three] Knights*

Knights, kinsmen, lovers—yea, my sacrifices,[1]
35 True worshippers of Mars, whose spirit in you
Expels the seeds of fear and th'apprehension
Which still is father of it,[2] go with me
Before the god of our profession.° There   *god we worship*
Require of him the hearts of lions and
40 The breath° of tigers, yea, the fierceness too,   *endurance*
Yea, the speed also—to go on,° I mean,   *go forward*
Else° wish we to be snails. You know my prize   *Otherwise (in retreat)*
Must be dragged out of blood—force and great feat
Must put my garland on me, where she sticks,
45 The queen of flowers.[3] Our intercession, then,
Must be to him° that makes the camp a cistern   *(Mars)*
Brimmed with the blood of men—give me your aid,
And bend your spirits towards him.

They kneel [before the altar, fall on their faces, then on
their knees again]

[*Praying to Mars*]   Thou mighty one,
That with thy power hast turned green Neptune° into purple;[4]   *god of the sea*
50 Whose havoc in vast field comets prewarn,°   *forecast*
Unearthèd° skulls proclaim; whose breath blows down   *As yet unburied*
The teeming Ceres' foison;[5] who dost pluck°   *pull down*
With hand armipotent° from forth blue clouds   *powerful in arms*
The masoned° turrets, that both mak'st and break'st   *stone*
55 The stony girths° of cities; me thy pupil,   *walls*
Youngest follower of thy drum, instruct this day
With military skill, that to thy laud°   *praise*
I may advance my streamer,° and by thee   *banner*
Be styled° the lord o'th' day. Give me, great Mars,   *named*
60 Some token of thy pleasure.

Here they fall on their faces, as formerly, and there is
heard clanging of armour, with a short thunder, as the
burst of a battle, whereupon they all rise and bow to the
altar

---

1. The three knights may literally become human sacrifices from Arcite to Mars if Arcite loses the battle.
2. *th'apprehension . . . it*: the anticipation of a daunting situation, which always breeds fear.
3. *Must put . . . flowers*: Will win for my head (where Emilia already resides) the victor's laurels, of which she,

as the most beautiful of flowers, is part.
4. Red with blood.
5. *whose breath . . . foison*: whose breath (wind) destroys the plenty of the fields produced by Ceres, goddess of agriculture.

O great corrector of enormous° times,   *disordered*
  Shaker of o'er-rank° states, thou grand decider   *overripe*
  Of dusty and old titles, that heal'st with blood°   *through bloodletting*
  The earth when it is sick, and cur'st the world
65 O'th' plurisy° of people, I do take   *excess*
  Thy signs auspiciously, and in thy name,
  To my design, march boldly. [*To his Knights*] Let us go.

                        Exeunt

5.2

Enter PALAMON *and his Knights with the former
  observance*
PALAMON [*to his Knights*]   Our stars must glister° with new fire,   *fortunes must glisten*
    or be
  Today extinct.° Our argument is love,   *extinguished*
  Which if the goddess of it grant, she gives
  Victory too. Then blend your spirits with mine,
5 You whose free nobleness° do make my cause   *generous nobility*
  Your personal hazard. To the goddess Venus
  Commend° we our proceeding, and implore   *Commit*
  Her power unto our party.
    *Here they kneel [before the altar, fall on their faces then
      on their knees again*]
  [*Praying to Venus*] Hail, sovereign queen of secrets,[1] who hast
    power
10 To call the fiercest tyrant from his rage
  And weep unto a girl;[2] that hast the might,
  Even with an eye-glance, to choke° Mars's drum   *silence*
  And turn th'alarum° to whispers; that canst make   *call to arms*
  A cripple flourish with° his crutch, and cure him   *brandish*
15 Before Apollo;[3] that mayst force the king
  To be his subject's vassal, and induce
  Stale gravity° to dance; the polled° bachelor   *old men / bald*
  Whose youth, like wanton boys through bonfires,
  Have skipped° thy flame, at seventy thou canst catch   *Has escaped*
20 And make him to the scorn° of his hoarse throat   *(by listeners)*
  Abuse young lays of love.[4] What godlike power
  Hast thou not power upon? To Phoebus° thou   *the sun*
  Add'st flames hotter than his—the heavenly fires
  Did scorch his mortal son,[5] thine him. The huntress,
25 All moist and cold, some say, began to throw
  Her bow away and sigh.[6] Take to thy grace
  Me, thy vowed soldier, who do bear thy yoke
  As 'twere a wreath of roses, yet is° heavier   *though the yoke is*
  Than lead itself, stings more than nettles.
30 I have never been foul-mouthed against thy law;
  Ne'er revealed secret, for I knew none; would not,
  Had I kenned° all that were. I never practised   *known*
  Upon[7] man's wife, nor would the libels° read   *(against love)*

5.2 Location: The altar, here dedicated to Venus.
1. As the rest of the speech (lines 31ff.) indicates, secrecy
and discretion were essential components of the chivalric
love code.
2. Make him weep for a girl (or, weep so much that he
becomes like a girl).
3. Even more quickly than Apollo, the god of medicine.

4. Botch young lovers' love songs.
5. See note to 1.2.85–87.
6. *The huntress . . . sigh*: Diana, notwithstanding her vow
of chastity, fell in love with the shepherd Endymion. *cold*:
chaste.
7. *practised/Upon*: wooed.

Of liberal° wits. I never at great feasts   *licentious*
35   Sought to betray° a beauty, but have blushed   *expose the affairs of*
At simp'ring sirs that did. I have been harsh
To large confessors,[8] and have hotly asked them
If they had mothers—I had one, a woman,
And women 'twere they wronged. I knew a man
40   Of eighty winters, this I told them, who
A lass of fourteen brided°—'twas thy power   *wedded*
To put life into dust. The agèd cramp°   *cramp of old age*
Had screwed° his square foot round,   *twisted*
The gout had knit his fingers into knots,
45   Torturing convulsions from his globy eyes°   *swollen sockets*
Had almost drawn their spheres,° that° what was life   *eyeballs / so that*
In him seemed torture. This anatomy°   *skeleton*
Had by his young fair fere° a boy, and I   *mate*
Believed it was his, for she swore it was,
50   And who would not believe her? Brief°—I am   *In short*
To those that prate and have done,[9] no companion;
To those that boast and have not,° a defier;   *have done nothing*
To those that would and cannot, a rejoicer.
Yea, him I do not love that tells close offices°   *secret matters*
55   The foulest way, nor names concealments[1] in
The boldest language. Such a one I am,
And vow that lover never yet made sigh
Truer than I. O, then, most soft sweet goddess,
Give me the victory of this question,° which   *conflict*
60   Is true love's merit,° and bless me with a sign   *just deserts*
Of thy great pleasure.
    Here music is heard, doves° are seen to flutter. They fall   *(sacred to Venus)*
    again upon their faces, then on their knees
O thou that from eleven to ninety reign'st
In mortal bosoms, whose chase° is this world   *hunting ground*
And we in herds thy game, I give thee thanks
65   For this fair token, which, being laid unto
Mine innocent true heart, arms in assurance
My body to this business. [*To his Knights*] Let us rise
And bow before the goddess.
    They [rise and] bow

               Time comes on.   *Exeunt*

5.3

Still° music of record[er]s. Enter EMILIA *in white, her*   *Soft*
hair about her shoulders, [with] a wheaten wreath; one
in white holding up her train, her hair stuck with flow-
ers; one before her carrying a silver hind° in which is con-   *(sacred to Diana)*
veyed incense and sweet odours, which being set upon
the altar, her maids standing [apart], she sets fire to it.
Then they curtsy and kneel
EMILIA [*praying to Diana*]   O sacred, shadowy, cold,[1] and con-
    stant queen,
Abandoner of revels, mute contemplative,

---

8. To those who boast of their love conquests.
9. To those who talk of deeds they have actually done.
1. Nor exposes what should remain hidden.
5.3 Location: The altar, here dedicated to Diana.

1. *shadowy*: a goddess of the moon, Diana was associated with the night. *cold*: chaste. See 1.3.52, 4.2.58, and notes to these lines.

Sweet, solitary, white as chaste, and pure
As wind-fanned° snow, who to thy female knights   *windblown*
Allow'st no more blood° than will make a blush,   *sexual desire*
Which is their order's robe: I here, thy priest,
Am humbled fore thine altar. O, vouchsafe
With that thy rare green eye, which never yet
Beheld thing maculate,° look on thy virgin;   *tainted*
And, sacred silver mistress, lend thine ear—
Which ne'er heard scurril° term, into whose port°   *scurrilous / opening*
Ne'er entered wanton° sound—to my petition,   *lewd*
Seasoned with holy fear.° This is my last   *pious awe*
Of vestal office.² I am bride-habited,°   *dressed as a bride*
But maiden-hearted. A husband I have 'pointed,°   *have been assigned*
But do not know him. Out of two, I should
Choose one and pray for his success, but I
Am guiltless of election.³ Of mine eyes
Were I to lose one, they are equal precious—
I could doom neither: that which perished should
Go to't unsentenced. Therefore, most modest queen,
He of the two pretenders° that best loves me   *suitors*
And has the truest title in't,° let him   *claim to me*
Take off my wheaten garland,° or else grant   *Take my virginity*
The file and quality I hold I may
Continue in thy band.⁴

> *Here the hind vanishes under the altar and in the place*
> *ascends a rose tree having one rose° upon it*   *(symbol of virginity)*

[*To her women*] See what our general of ebbs and flows⁵
Out from the bowels of her holy altar,
With sacred act, advances—but one rose!
If well inspired,⁶ this battle shall confound°   *destroy*
Both these brave knights, and I a virgin flower
Must grow alone, unplucked.

> *Here is heard a sudden twang of instruments and the*
> *rose falls from the tree*

The flower is fall'n, the tree descends. [*To Diana*] O mistress,
Thou here dischargest me—I shall be gathered.⁷
I think so, but I know not thine own will.
Unclasp thy mystery.° [*To her women*] I hope she's pleased;   *Reveal your meaning*
Her signs were gracious.   *They curtsy and exeunt*

5.4

Enter [the] DOCTOR, *[the]* JAILER, *and [the]* WOOER *in*
[the] habit of° Palamon   *dressed as*

DOCTOR   Has this advice I told you done any good upon her?
WOOER   O, very much. The maids that kept her company have
   half persuaded her that I am Palamon. Within this half-hour
   she came smiling to me, and asked me what I would eat, and
   when I would kiss her. I told her presently,° and kissed her   *at once*
   twice.

---

2. *my . . . office;* my last duty as your virginal devotee.
3. Am not guilty of having made a choice (and hence of
having betrayed my vows).
4. *grant . . . band:* grant that I may continue to hold the
rank and condition (of virginity) as one of your devotees.

5. Our ruler of the moon and hence of tides.
6. If this is a true omen.
7. I shall be married; I shall lose my virginity.
5.4 Location: The prison.

DOCTOR 'Twas well done—twenty times had been far better,
For there° the cure lies mainly.   *(in kissing)*
WOOER   Then she told me
She would watch° with me tonight, for well she knew   *stay up*
What hour my fit° would take me.   *urgent inclination*
10 DOCTOR   Let her do so,
And when your fit comes, fit her home,[1]
And presently.
WOOER   She would have me sing.
DOCTOR   You did so?
WOOER   No.
DOCTOR   'Twas very ill done, then.
You should observe° her every way.   *accommodate*
WOOER   Alas,
15 I have no voice, sir, to confirm° her that way.   *assure*
DOCTOR   That's all one,° if ye make a noise.   *That doesn't matter*
If she entreat° again, do anything—   *beg*
Lie with her if she ask you.
JAILER   Ho there, Doctor.
DOCTOR   Yes, in the way of cure.
JAILER   But first, by your leave,
I'th' way of honesty.°   *(after marriage)*
20 DOCTOR   That's but a niceness°—   *an excessive scruple*
Ne'er cast your child away for honesty.[2]
Cure her first this way, then if she will° be honest,   *wants to*
She has the path° before her.   *(of marriage)*
JAILER   Thank ye, Doctor.
DOCTOR   Pray bring her in and let's see how she is.
25 JAILER   I will, and tell her her Palamon stays° for her.   *waits*
But, Doctor, methinks you are i'th' wrong still.   *Exit* JAILER
DOCTOR   Go, go. You fathers are fine fools—her honesty?
An we should give her physic till we find that[3]—
WOOER   Why, do you think she is not honest, sir?
DOCTOR   How old is she?
WOOER   She's eighteen.
30 DOCTOR   She may be—
But that's all one. 'Tis nothing to our purpose.°   *It makes no difference*
Whate'er her father says, if you perceive
Her mood inclining that way that I spoke of,
Videlicet,° the way of flesh—you have me?   *Namely*
WOOER   Yes, very well, sir.
35 DOCTOR   Please her appetite,
And do it home°—it cures her, *ipso facto,*[4]   *completely*
The melancholy humour° that infects her.   *mood (medical)*
WOOER   I am of your mind, Doctor.
          Enter [the] JAILER *and [his]* DAUGHTER *[mad]*
DOCTOR   You'll find it so—she comes: pray humour her.
          [The DOCTOR *and the* WOOER *stand apart]*
JAILER *[to his* DAUGHTER*]*   Come, your love Palamon stays for
40   you, child,

---

1. Fully serve her needs (have sex with her).
2. A paradox: don't lose your daughter (to her madness) in order to keep her (honest).
3. If we were to treat her until we could be sure of her virginity (the obvious continuation of the unfinished thought being, we'd be treating her forever).
4. By the very act (*ipso facto*) of having sex, she'll be cured. The Doctor assumes, correctly in the event, that the Daughter suffers from hysteria, thought to be caused by a wandering womb and cured by intercourse.

And has done this long hour, to visit you.

JAILER'S DAUGHTER I thank him for his gentle patience.
  He's a kind gentleman, and I am much bound° to him.   *obliged*
  Did you ne'er see the horse he gave me?

JAILER   Yes.

JAILER'S DAUGHTER How do you like him?

45 JAILER   He's a very fair° one.   *beautiful*

JAILER'S DAUGHTER You never saw him dance?

JAILER   No.

JAILER'S DAUGHTER   I have, often.
  He dances very finely, very comely,
  And, for a jig, come cut and long-tail to him,[5]
  He turns ye like a top.

JAILER   That's fine, indeed.

50 JAILER'S DAUGHTER He'll dance the morris twenty mile an hour,
  And that will founder the best hobbyhorse,[6]
  If I have any skill,° in all the parish—   *judgment*
  And gallops to the tune of 'Light o' love'.[7]
  What think you of this horse?

JAILER   Having these virtues
55 I think he might be brought to play at tennis.

JAILER'S DAUGHTER Alas, that's nothing.

JAILER   Can he write and read too?

JAILER'S DAUGHTER A very fair hand, and casts himself th'accounts[8]
  Of all his hay and provender. That ostler
  Must rise betime that cozens° him. You know   *get up early to cheat*
  The chestnut mare the Duke has?

60 JAILER   Very well.

JAILER'S DAUGHTER She is horribly in love with him, poor beast,
  But he is like his master—coy° and scornful.   *aloof*

JAILER What dowry has she?

JAILER'S DAUGHTER   Some two hundred bottles°   *bales of hay*
  And twenty strike° of oats, but he'll ne'er have her.   *bushels*
65 He lisps in's neighing, able to entice
  A miller's mare.[9] He'll be the death of her.

DOCTOR What stuff she utters!

JAILER Make curtsy—here your love comes.

WOOER [coming forward] Pretty soul,
  How do ye?
             [She curtsies]
70   That's a fine maid, there's a curtsy.

JAILER'S DAUGHTER Yours to command, i'th' way of honesty—
  How far is't now to th' end o'th' world, my masters?

DOCTOR Why, a day's journey, wench.

JAILER'S DAUGHTER [to WOOER]   Will you go with me?

WOOER What shall we do there, wench?

---

5. He . . . him: He dances finely no matter what horse he is compared with. cut: a horse with a docked tail (see note to 3.4.22). There is sexual wordplay throughout this scene.
6. That will lame ("founder") the best morris dancer. hobbyhorse: one extremely agile morris dancer was dressed as a horse and imitated its movements.
7. Popular ballad also referred to in Much Ado About

Nothing 3.4.39 and The Two Gentlemen of Verona 1.2.83. The title means "inconstant in love."
8. He has beautiful penmanship and reckons his own expenses.
9. He . . . mare: He's such a smooth talker he could seduce even a miller's mare—a workhorse renowned for its steadfast, circular plodding and hence least likely to be distracted.

JAILER'S DAUGHTER   Why, play at stool-ball[1] —
    What is there else to do?
75 WOOER   I am content
    If we shall keep our wedding° there.   *As long as we marry*
JAILER'S DAUGHTER   'Tis true —
    For there, I will assure you, we shall find
    Some blind priest for the purpose that will venture
    To marry us, for here they are nice,° and foolish.   *too scrupulous*
80   Besides, my father must be hanged tomorrow,
    And that would be a blot i'th' business.
    Are not you Palamon?
WOOER   Do not you know me?
JAILER'S DAUGHTER   Yes, but you care not for me. I have nothing
    But this poor petticoat and two coarse smocks.°   *undergarments*
WOOER   That's all one — I will have you.
85 JAILER'S DAUGHTER   Will you surely?
WOOER   Yes, by this fair hand, will I.
JAILER'S DAUGHTER   We'll to bed then.
WOOER   E'en when you will.°   *Whenever you like*
    [*He kisses her*]
JAILER'S DAUGHTER [*rubbing off the kiss*]
                   O, sir, you would fain be nibbling.
WOOER   Why do you rub my kiss off?
JAILER'S DAUGHTER   'Tis a sweet one,
    And will perfume me finely against° the wedding.   *in preparation for*
    [*Indicating the* DOCTOR] Is not this your cousin Arcite?
90 DOCTOR   Yes, sweetheart,
    And I am glad my cousin Palamon
    Has made so fair a choice.
JAILER'S DAUGHTER   Do you think he'll have me?
DOCTOR   Yes, without doubt.
JAILER'S DAUGHTER [*to the* JAILER]   Do you think so too?
JAILER   Yes.
JAILER'S DAUGHTER   We shall have many children. [*To the* DOCTOR]
        Lord, how you're grown!
95   My Palamon, I hope, will grow too,[2] finely,
    Now he's at liberty. Alas, poor chicken,
    He was kept down with hard meat° and ill lodging,   *coarse food*
    But I'll kiss him up again.
        Enter a MESSENGER
MESSENGER   What do you here? You'll lose the noblest sight
    That e'er was seen.
JAILER   Are they i'th' field?
100 MESSENGER   They are —
    You bear a charge° there too.   *have a duty*
JAILER   I'll away straight.
    [*To the others*] I must e'en leave you here.
DOCTOR   Nay, we'll go with you —
    I will not lose the sight.
JAILER   How did you like her?
DOCTOR   I'll warrant you, within these three or four days

---

1. A game, somewhat like cricket, played with ball and   2. Get fat; have an erection.
bat by women or by men and women together.

I'll make her right again.
                    [*Exit the* JAILER *with the* MESSENGER]
105 [*To the* WOOER] You must not from her,
But still preserve° her in this way.   *keep treating*
WOOER   I will.
DOCTOR Let's get her in.
WOOER [*to the* JAILER'S DAUGHTER]
                    Come, sweet, we'll go to dinner,
And then we'll play at cards.
JAILER'S DAUGHTER   And shall we kiss too?
WOOER A hundred times.
JAILER'S DAUGHTER   And twenty.
WOOER   Ay, and twenty.
JAILER'S DAUGHTER And then we'll sleep together.
110 DOCTOR [*to the* WOOER]   Take her offer.
WOOER [*to the* JAILER'S DAUGHTER]
Yes, marry, will we.
JAILER'S DAUGHTER   But you shall not hurt me.
WOOER I will not, sweet.
JAILER'S DAUGHTER   If you do, love, I'll cry.   *Exeunt*

5.5

Flourish. Enter THESEUS, HIPPOLYTA, EMILIA, PIRITHOUS,
and some attendants
EMILIA I'll no step further.
PIRITHOUS   Will you lose this sight?
EMILIA I had rather see a wren hawk at° a fly   *attack in midair*
Than this decision. Every blow that falls
Threats a brave life; each stroke laments
5 The place whereon it falls, and sounds more like
A bell° than blade. I will stay here.   *death knell*
It is enough my hearing shall be punished
With what shall happen, 'gainst the which there is
No deafing, but to hear;[1] not taint mine eye
With dread sights it may shun.
10 PIRITHOUS [*to* THESEUS]   Sir, my good lord,
Your sister will no further.
THESEUS   O, she must.
She shall see deeds of honour in their kind,°   *true nature*
Which sometime show well pencilled.° Nature now   *even when just drawn*
Shall make and act° the story, the belief   *invent and perform*
Both sealed with eye and ear.[2] [*To* EMILIA] You must be
15 present—
You are the victor's meed,° the price and garland   *reward*
To crown the question's title.[3]
EMILIA   Pardon me,
If I were there I'd wink.°   *keep my eyes closed*
THESEUS   You must be there—
This trial is, as 'twere, i'th' night, and you
The only star to shine.
20 EMILIA   I am extinct.°   *extinguished*

5.5 Location: The forest, near the tournament field.   2. *the belief . . . ear:* the story will be rendered credible
1. *there . . . hear:* there is no way to block out the noise   by all that is seen and heard.
in order not to hear.   3. To crown the rightful victor in the dispute.

There is but envy° in that light which shows malice
The one the other. Darkness, which ever was
The dam° of horror, who does stand accursed mother
Of many mortal millions, may even now,
25 By casting her black mantle over both,
That° neither could find other, get herself So that
Some part of a good name, and many a murder
Set off whereto° she's guilty. Atone for of which
HIPPOLYTA   You must go.
EMILIA   In faith, I will not.
THESEUS   Why, the knights must kindle
30 Their valour at your eye. Know, of this war
You are the treasure, and must needs be by° nearby
To give the service pay.° reward the winner
EMILIA   Sir, pardon me—
The title of a kingdom may be tried
Out of itself.° Outside the kingdom
THESEUS   Well, well—then at your pleasure.
35 Those that remain with you could wish their office
To any of their enemies.
HIPPOLYTA   Farewell, sister.
I am like to know your husband fore yourself,
By some small start of time. He whom the gods
Do of the two know° best, I pray them he know to be
40 Be made your lot.   Exeunt [all but EMILIA]
        [EMILIA takes out two pictures, one from her right side,
        and one from her left]
EMILIA   Arcite is gently visaged,° yet his eye has a gentle expression
Is like an engine bent[4] or a sharp weapon
In a soft sheath. Mercy and manly courage
Are bedfellows in his visage. Palamon
45 Has a most menacing aspect. His brow
Is graved° and seems to bury what it frowns on, frowned
Yet sometime 'tis not so, but alters to° according to
The quality° of his thoughts. Long time his eye nature
Will dwell upon his object. Melancholy
50 Becomes° him nobly—so does Arcite's mirth. Suits
But Palamon's sadness is a kind of mirth,
So mingled as if mirth did make him sad
And sadness merry. Those darker humours° that moods
Stick misbecomingly° on others, on them Seem misplaced
55 Live in fair dwelling.[5]
        Cornetts. Trumpets sound as to a charge
Hark, how yon spurs to spirit° do incite bravery
The princes to their proof.° Arcite may win me, to prove themselves
And yet may Palamon wound Arcite to
The spoiling of his figure.° O, what pity (so as to cripple him)
60 Enough for such a chance![6] If I were by° near
I might do hurt, for they would glance their eyes
Toward my seat, and in that motion might
Omit a ward or forfeit an offence

4. Is like a weapon, such as a bow, ready to be released.   6. Would be sufficient for such a (sad) turn of events.
5. *on them . . . dwelling:* suit them well.

Which craved that very time.[7] It is much better
    Cornetts. A great cry and noise within, crying, 'A
    Palamon'
65 I am not there. O better never born,
Than minister to such harm.
    Enter SERVANT
                        What is the chance?°   *Who won*
SERVANT   The cry's 'A Palamon'.
EMILIA   Then he has won. 'Twas ever likely—
He looked all grace and success, and he is
70 Doubtless the prim'st° of men. I prithee run   *most perfect*
And tell me how it goes.
    Shout and cornetts, crying, 'A Palamon'
SERVANT   Still 'Palamon'.
EMILIA   Run and enquire.   [*Exit* SERVANT]
    [*She speaks to the picture in her right hand*]
                      Poor servant,° thou hast lost.   *lover (Arcite)*
Upon my right side still I° wore thy picture,   *I always*
Palamon's on the left. Why so, I know not.
75 I had no end° in't, else chance would have it so.   *purpose*
    Another cry and shout within and cornetts
On the sinister side the heart lies—Palamon
Had the best-boding chance.[8] This burst of clamour
Is sure the end o'th' combat.
    Enter SERVANT
SERVANT   They said that Palamon had Arcite's body
80 Within an inch o'th' pyramid—that the cry
Was general 'A Palamon'. But anon
Th'assistants° made a brave redemption,° and   *knights / rescue*
The two bold titlers° at this instant are   *fighters for the title*
Hand to hand at it.
EMILIA   Were they° metamorphosed   *I wish they were*
85 Both into one! O why? There were no woman
Worth so composed a man:[9] their single share,
Their nobleness peculiar to them, gives
The prejudice of disparity, value's shortness,
To any lady breathing[1]—
    Cornetts. Cry within, 'Arcite, Arcite'
                  More exulting?
'Palamon' still?
90 SERVANT   Nay, now the sound is 'Arcite'.
EMILIA   I prithee, lay attention to the cry.
    Cornetts. A great shout and cry, 'Arcite, victory!'
Set both thine ears to th' business.
SERVANT   The cry is
'Arcite' and 'Victory'—hark, 'Arcite, victory!'
The combat's consummation° is proclaimed   *conclusion*
By the wind instruments.
95 EMILIA   Half sights saw°   *Mere glimpses showed*
That Arcite was no babe. God's lid,° his richness   *By God's eyelid*

---

7. *might . . . time:* might miss the perfect moment for a
defensive parry or an offensive move.
8. *On . . . chance:* The location of Palamon's picture—
on Emilia's left ("sinister") side, where her heart is—por-
tended victory, since the contest is about love.

9. *There . . . man:* No woman could be worthy of this
composite man made up of both Palamon and Arcite.
1. *their single . . . breathing:* no woman could have as
much nobility as either one of them. *their single share:*
each one's value.

And costliness of spirit looked through him—it could
No more be hid in him than fire in flax,°   *straw*
Than humble banks can go to law with° waters   *can battle*
100   That drift° winds force to raging. I did think   *driving*
Good Palamon would miscarry, yet I knew not
Why I did think so. Our reasons are not prophets
When oft our fancies are. They are coming off°—   *leaving the field*
Alas, poor Palamon.
    [She puts away the pictures.]
    Cornetts. Enter THESEUS, HIPPOLYTA, PIRITHOUS, ARCITE
    as victor, and attendants
105 THESEUS   Lo, where our sister is in expectation,
    Yet quaking and unsettled. Fairest Emily,
    The gods by their divine arbitrament
    Have given you this knight. He is a good one
    As ever struck at head. *[To* ARCITE *and* EMILIA*]* Give me your
        hands.
    [To ARCITE*]* Receive you her, *[to* EMILIA*]* you him: *[to both]*
110   be plighted with
    A love that grows as you decay.
  ARCITE   Emilia,
    To buy you I have lost what's dearest to me
    Save what is bought,° and yet I purchase cheaply   *(Emilia)*
    As I do rate your value.
  THESEUS *[to* EMILIA*]*   O lovèd sister,
115   He speaks now of as brave a knight as e'er
    Did spur a noble steed. Surely the gods
    Would have him die a bachelor lest his race
    Should show i'th' world too godlike. His behaviour
    So charmed me that, methought, Alcides° was   *Hercules*
120   To him a sow[2] of lead. If I could praise
    Each part of him to th'all I have spoke,[3] your Arcite
    Did° not lose by't; for he that was thus good,   *Would*
    Encountered yet his better. I have heard
    Two emulous Philomels[4] beat the ear o'th' night
125   With their contentious throats, now one the higher,
    Anon the other, then again the first,
    And by and by out-breasted, that the sense[5]
    Could not be judge between 'em—so it fared
    Good space° between these kinsmen, till heavens did   *For a good while*
130   Make hardly° one the winner. *[To* ARCITE*]* Wear the garland   *Barely make*
    With joy that you have won.—For the subdued,°   *losers*
    Give them our present° justice, since I know   *immediate*
    Their lives but pinch° 'em. Let it here be done.   *torment*
    The scene's not for our seeing; go we hence
135   Right joyful, with some sorrow. *[To* ARCITE*]* Arm° your prize;   *Give your arm to*
    I know you will not lose her. Hippolyta,
    I see one eye of yours conceives a tear,
    The which it will deliver.
    Flourish

2. Smelted metal taken from a furnace.
3. *to . . . spoke*: in the same way I have praised Palamon
as a whole.
4. Two rival nightingales. In Greek mythology, Philo-
mela was raped by her sister's husband, who cut out her
tongue so she couldn't accuse him. By weaving the story
into cloth, she nonetheless informed her sister, who fed
her husband their son. The gods turned the sister into a
nightingale and Philomela into a swallow.
5. And by and by outsung, so that the sense of hearing.

EMILIA   Is this winning?
O all you heavenly powers, where is your mercy?

140   But that your wills have said it must be so,
And charge me live to comfort this unfriended,°   *deprived of his friend*
This miserable prince, that cuts away
A life more worthy from him than all women,
I should and would die too.
HIPPOLYTA   Infinite pity

145   That four such eyes should be so fixed on one°   *one woman*
That two must needs be blind for't.⁶
THESEUS   So it is.   *Exeunt*

5.6

Enter [guarded] PALAMON *and his [three]* KNIGHTS *pin-
ioned; [enter with them the]* JAILER *[and an] executioner
[with block and axe]*

PALAMON   There's many a man alive that hath outlived
The love o'th' people; yea, i'th' selfsame state
Stands many a father with his child: some comfort
We have by so considering. We expire,

5   And not without men's pity; to live still,
Have their good wishes.¹ We prevent°   *avoid*
The loathsome misery of age, beguile°   *cheat*
The gout and rheum° that in lag° hours attend   *coughing / final*
For grey approachers;° we come towards the gods   *(to death)*

10   Young and unwappered,° not halting under crimes   *untired*
Many and stale°—that sure shall please the gods   *long gone*
Sooner than such,° to give us nectar with 'em,   *(sinful old men)*
For we are more clear° spirits. My dear kinsmen,   *innocent*
Whose lives for this poor comfort are laid down,
You have sold 'em° too too cheap.   *(your lives)*

15   FIRST KNIGHT   What ending could be
Of more content? O'er us the victors have
Fortune, whose title° is as momentary   *claim*
As to us death is certain—a grain of honour
They not o'erweigh us.²
SECOND KNIGHT   Let us bid farewell,

20   And with our patience anger tott'ring° fortune,   *unstable*
Who at her certain'st reels.³
THIRD KNIGHT   Come, who begins?
PALAMON   E'en he that led you to this banquet shall
Taste to you all.⁴ *[To the* JAILER*]* Aha, my friend, my friend,
Your gentle daughter gave me freedom once;

25   You'll see't done° now for ever. Pray, how does she?   *see me set free*
I heard she was not well; her kind of ill°   *illness*
Gave me some sorrow.
JAILER   Sir, she's well restored
And to be married shortly.
PALAMON   By my short life,

---

6. That two eyes must be blinded (in death); that two
men could be so blind as to fight to the death for one
woman.
5.6 Location: Scene continues.
1. *We expire . . . wishes:* Even though we are to die, we
have men's good wishes that we might go on living.

2. *a grain . . . us:* they have no more honor than we do.
3. Who, when she seems most certain, suddenly changes
direction.
4. Taste (death) first, like the servant at a state banquet
who was required to taste the food before the king and
guests to make sure it wasn't poisoned.

I am most glad on't. 'Tis the latest° thing   *last*
30 I shall be glad of. Prithee, tell her so;
Commend me to her, and to piece her portion°   *increase her dowry*
Tender her this.
    [*He gives his purse*]
FIRST KNIGHT   Nay, let's be offerers all.
SECOND KNIGHT   Is it a maid?°   *virgin*
PALAMON   Verily, I think so—
A right good creature more to me° deserving   *from me*
Than I can quit° or speak of.   *requite*
35 ALL THREE KNIGHTS   Commend us to her.
    They give their purses
JAILER   The gods requite you all, and make her thankful.
PALAMON   Adieu, and let my life be now as short
As my leave-taking.
    [*He*] *lies on the block*
FIRST KNIGHT   Lead, courageous cousin.
SECOND AND THIRD KNIGHTS We'll follow cheerfully.
    A great noise within: crying, 'Run! Save! Hold!'
    Enter in haste a MESSENGER
40 MESSENGER   Hold! Hold! O, hold! Hold! Hold!
    Enter PIRITHOUS *in haste*
PIRITHOUS   Hold, ho! It is a cursèd haste you made
If you have done° so quickly! Noble Palamon,   *finished*
The gods will show their glory in a life
That thou art yet to lead.
PALAMON   Can that be,
45 When Venus, I have said, is false? How do things fare?
PIRITHOUS   Arise, great sir, and give the tidings ear
That are most rarely sweet and bitter.
PALAMON   What
Hath waked us from our dream?
PIRITHOUS   List,° then: your cousin,   *Listen*
Mounted upon a steed that Emily
50 Did first bestow on him, a black one owing°   *owning*
Not a hair-worth of white—which some will say
Weakens his price[5] and many will not buy
His goodness with this note;° which superstition   *distinctive mark*
Here finds allowance°—on this horse is Arcite   *gains support*
55 Trotting the stones of Athens, which the calkins
Did rather tell than trample;[6] for the horse
Would make his length° a mile, if't pleased his rider   *length of stride*
To put pride in him. As he thus went counting
The flinty pavement, dancing, as 'twere, to th' music
60 His own hooves made—for, as they say, from iron
Came music's origin[7]—what envious flint,°   *cobblestone*
Cold as old Saturn[8] and like him possessed
With fire malevolent, darted a spark,

5. Makes him less valuable, because dark horses were considered vicious or ill-omened.
6. *which ... trample*: the horse's gait was so long and light that its feet seemed more to count ("tell") the cobbles one by one than to trample them. *calkins*: turned-down edges of a horseshoe.
7. Pythagoras is supposed to have discovered music when walking through a blacksmith's forge.
8. According to Chaucer's *Knight's Tale*, Saturn, father of Jupiter, was responsible for the reversal of fortune described here, because he had promised Venus that Palamon would win Emilia. Shakespeare and Fletcher limit Saturn's responsibility to a simile.

Or what fierce sulphur else, to this end made,[9]
65 I comment not—the hot horse, hot as fire,
Took toy° at this and fell to what disorder   *a capricious dislike*
His power could give his will; bounds; comes on end;
Forgets school-doing,° being therein trained   *school training*
And of kind manège;° pig-like he whines   *well disciplined*
70 At the sharp rowel,° which he frets at rather   *spur*
Than any jot obeys; seeks all foul means
Of boist'rous and rough jad'ry° to disseat   *behavior like a nag*
His lord, that kept it° bravely. When naught served,   *who kept his seat*
When neither curb would crack, girth break, nor diff'ring°   *various*
     plunges
75 Disroot his rider whence he grew,° but that   *was fixed*
He kept him 'tween his legs, on his hind hooves—
On end he stands—
That Arcite's legs, being higher than his head,
Seemed with strange art to hang. His victor's wreath
80 Even then fell off his head; and presently
Backward the jade comes o'er and his full poise°   *weight*
Becomes the rider's load. Yet is he living;
But such a vessel 'tis that floats but for
The surge that next approaches.[1] He much desires
85 To have some speech with you—lo, he appears.
     Enter THESEUS, HIPPOLYTA, EMILIA, [*and*] ARCITE *in a*
     chair [*borne by attendants*]
PALAMON   O miserable end of our alliance!
     The gods are mighty. Arcite, if thy heart,
     Thy worthy manly heart, be yet unbroken,
     Give me thy last words. I am Palamon,
     One that yet loves thee dying.
90 ARCITE   Take Emilia,
     And with her all the world's joy. Reach° thy hand—   *Give me*
     Farewell—I have told° my last hour. I was false,   *counted*
     Yet never treacherous.[2] Forgive me, cousin—
     One kiss from fair Emilia—[*they kiss*] 'tis done.
     Take her; I die.   [*He dies*]
95 PALAMON   Thy brave soul seek Elysium.
EMILIA [*to Arcite's body*]   I'll close thine eyes, Prince. Blessèd
     souls be with thee.
     Thou art a right good man, and, while I live,
     This day I give to tears.
PALAMON   And I to honour.
THESEUS   In this place first you fought, e'en very here
100 I sundered you.° Acknowledge to the gods   *separated your fight*
     Our thanks that you are living.
     His part is played, and, though it were too short,
     He did it well. Your day is lengthened and
     The blissful dew of heaven does arrouse° you.   *sprinkle*
105 The powerful Venus well hath graced her altar,
     And given you your love; our master, Mars,

---

9. Or some spark of hellfire made for this purpose.
1. *But such . . . approaches:* But he can live only until the
next onslaught (like a boat that can stay afloat only until
the next wave hits).

2. *I was . . . treacherous:* I was "false" to our friendship
(because Palamon did see Emilia first) but "never treach-
erous" in vying for Emilia's love.

Hath vouched° his oracle, and to Arcite gave   *made good on*
The grace of the contention.° So the deities   *victory in the battle*
Have showed due justice.—Bear this hence.

[*Exeunt attendants with Arcite's body*]

PALAMON   O cousin,
110   That we should things desire which do cost us
The loss of our desire! That naught could buy
Dear love, but loss of dear love!

THESEUS   Never fortune
Did play a subtler game—the conquered triumphs,
The victor has the loss. Yet in the passage°   *proceedings*
115   The gods have been most equal.° Palamon,   *impartial*
Your kinsman hath confessed the right o'th' lady°   *the right to Emilia*
Did lie in you,° for you first saw her and   *Was yours*
Even then proclaimed your fancy. He restored her
As your stol'n jewel, and desired your spirit
120   To send him hence forgiven. The gods my justice
Take from my hand, and they themselves become
The executioners.° Lead your lady off,   *executors of justice*
And call your lovers from the stage of death,°   *friends from the scaffold*
Whom I adopt my friends. A day or two
125   Let us look sadly and give grace unto
The funeral of Arcite, in whose end°   *after which*
The visages of bridegrooms we'll put on
And smile with Palamon, for whom an hour,
But one hour since, I was as dearly sorry
130   As glad of Arcite, and am now as glad
As for him sorry. O you heavenly charmers,°   *gods who enchant us*
What things you make of us! For what we lack
We laugh, for what we have, are sorry; still
Are children in some kind. Let us be thankful
135   For that which is, and with you leave dispute
That are above our question.³ Let's go off
And bear us like° the time.   *Flourish. Exeunt*   *act in accordance with*

Epilogue

[*Enter* EPILOGUE]

EPILOGUE   I would now ask ye how ye like the play,
But, as it is with schoolboys, cannot say.°   *speak*
I am cruel fearful.° Pray yet stay awhile,   *horribly afraid*
And let me look upon ye. No man smile?
5   Then it goes hard, I see. He that has
Loved a young handsome wench, then, show his face—
'Tis strange if none be here—and, if he will,
Against his conscience let him hiss and kill
Our market.° 'Tis in vain, I see, to stay ye.   *Our chance of success*
10   Have at the worst can come,° then! Now, what say ye?   *Do your worst*
And yet mistake me not—I am not bold—
We have no such cause.° If the tale we have told—   *purpose*
For 'tis no other—any way content° ye,   *please*
For to that honest purpose it was meant ye,°   *intended for you*
15   We have our end;° and ye shall have ere long,   *achieved our aim*
I dare say, many a better to prolong

---

3. *with . . . question:* cease to dispute with you, who are beyond our questioning.

Your old loves to us. We and all our might°   *all we can do*
Rest at your service. Gentlemen, good night.   *Flourish. [Exit]*

TEXTUAL VARIANTS

Control text: Q

Q: The Quarto of 1634
Qa, Qb: The uncorrected (Qa) and corrected (Qb) states of Q

Title: *The Two Noble Kinsmen* [Q] a TragiComedy called the two noble kinsmen [Stationers' Register]

s.p. PROLOGUE, EPILOGUE [Q simply titles each section "PROLOGVE" and "EPILOGVE," which could be interpreted either as speech prefixes or as section headings.]
s.p. JAILER [Q alternates between *Jailer* and *Keeper*. Standardized throughout.]
s.p. JAILER'S DAUGHTER [Q's consistent use of *Daughter* is expanded throughout.]
s.p. JAILER'S BROTHER [Q's consistent use of *Brother* is expanded throughout.]
s.p. COUNTRYMEN [Q uses only numbers to refer to the Countrymen, except in 3.5, when one of the Countrymen, who is dressed as a baboon, is referred to as *Baum* or *Bavian* ("babion," old form of "baboon") in Q and "babion" in this edition.]

Prologue s.d. *Enter* PROLOGUE / s.p. PROLOGUE PROLOGVE. 26 **tack** take
1.1. s.d. PIRITHOUS Theseus 1 s.p. BOY The Song. [In Q, the song is not assigned to a particular character. It is clear from the preceding stage direction, however, that it is the boy who sings.] 7 **born** borne 9 **harebells** *her bels* 13–14 **children sweet,** / Lie *children: sweete-* / *Ly* 20 **chough hoar** *Clough hee* 68 **Nemean** Nenuan 90 **thy** the 112 **glassy** glasse 132 **longer** long 138 **move** mooves 155 **Rinsing** Wrinching 158 **Artesius** *Artesuis* 166 s.p. ALL THREE QUEENS *All.* 171 **war** was 177 **twinning** twyning. ["Twined" remains a possible alternative modernization. Compare 2.2.64.] 211 **Aulis** Anly
1.2.55 **canon** Cannon 69 **men's service** men service 70 **glory; one** glory on
1.3.31 **one** ore 54 **eleven** a eleven 54 **Flavina** Flauia 73 **happily** happely 73 **wear** were 75 **one** on 79 **seely innocence** fury-innocent 82 **dividual** individuall 82 **out** ont
1.4.18 **smeared** [Qb] succard [Qa] 22 **Wi'leave** We leave 45 **O'erwrestling** Or wrastling 49 **fore** for
1.5. s.d. **Song** [not in Q] 9–10 **woes,** / **We . . . woes.** woes. We convent, &c.
2.2.21 **wore** were 22 **Ravished** Bravishd 64 **twined** twyn'd 118–19 s.p. EMILIA **This . . . in't.** / **What** This . . . in't. / *Emil.* What [In Q, Arcite continues speaking until the end of line 118.] 132 **was I** I was 150 **close** neere 182 **love her** love 189 **your blood** you blood 264 **to** too 272 **you** yon
2.3.6 **sins** [Qb] fins [Qa] 24 s.d. **garland** garlond [Qb] *Garlon* [Qa] 40 **ye** yet 53 **said** sees 64 **Yet** Yes
2.4.33 **night; ere tomorrow** night, or to morrow
2.5 Scaena 4 28 **For** Fo
2.6.33 **patch** path
3.1.2 **laund** land 11–12 **With . . . rumination** [Q prints as one line with no lacuna marked.] 37 **looked, the void'st** lookd the voydes 43 **Not** Nor 96 s.d. *within of Cornets.* [In Q's "*Winde hornes of Cornets,*" "*Cornets*" may be a playhouse addition; "*of*" could mean "off," or "offstage," here rendered as "within."] 98 **muset** Musicke 108 **not** nor 113 **'Tis** If 123 **enjoy it** enjoy't
3.2.1 **mistook the brake** mistooke; the Beake 7 **reck** wreake 19 **fed** feed 28 **brine** bine

3.3.12 sir &c.   23 them then   52 Sirrah— Sir ha:
3.4.9 Open Vpon   10 tack take   19 a foot *afoote*
3.5 Scaena 6 s.d. BABION Baum   8 jean jave   25 these their   33, 134 babion *Bavian*   67
I [not in Q]   68 There . . . owlet— *There . . . howlet* [Q's italics appear to derive from
the compositor mistakenly interpreting this line as part of the song.]   69 he [not in
Q]   100 s.p. THESEUS *Per.* [Pirithous]   120 'Moor' Morr   121 'Ice' Is   125 tenor ten-
ner   133 beest-eating beast eating   138 s.p. SCHOOLMASTER [not in Q]   139–48 Ladies
. . . rout [italics in Q. The compositor possibly misinterpreted this speech as a
song.]   140 ye *thee*   143 thee *three*   152 you yon
3.6 Scaena 7   145 thine this   236 fail fall   272 must muff   273 the other th'other   279,
280 s.p. PALAMON *and* ARCITE *Both.*
4.1.11 oath o'th   20 he scaped he escapt   45 WOOER No, Sir, not well. SECOND FRIEND
Not well? 2 Fr. Not well?——*Wooer, No Sir not well.*   63 sung song   84 wreath
wreake   86 she appeared, methought, me thought she appeard   104 light . . .' *light,
&c.* [Here and at 4.1.113 and 151 and 4.3.48, Q's "&c." suggests that more than the
single line of the song printed in the text was sung.]   113 sweet . . .' *sweete, &c.*   119 Far
For   133 s.p. JAILER'S BROTHER *Daugh.* [Jailer's Daughter]   140 s.p. SECOND FRIEND *I.
Fr.* [First Friend]   144–45 Cheerly all. / Uff cheerely. / All. Owgh [In Q, the "All" pre-
tend to join in.]   150 Tack Take   151 light . . .' *light, &c.*
4.2.16 Jove afire once Loue a fire with   54–55 both! / s.d. *Enter [a]* GENTLEMAN How
both. / s.d. *Enter Emil⟨ia⟩ and Gent⟨leman⟩:* s.p. *Emil⟨ia⟩.* How [Q's superfluous refer-
ences to Emilia in the s.d. and s.p. are omitted.]   76 first fitst   81 fire faire   105 tods
tops   110 court corect
4.3.20 spirits are spirits, as   27 i'th' other i'th / Thother   41 engrafted engraffed   45
th'other another   46 behind [Qb] behold [Qa]   48 fate . . .' *fate, &c.*   75 carve crave
5.1.37 father of farther off   44 me [not in Q]   49–50 purple; / Whose havoc in vast field
comets prewarn, purple. / Comets prewarne, whose havocke in vaste Feild   53 armipo-
tent armenypotent
5.2, 5.3 [Q continues as part of 5.1]
5.4 Scaena 2   34 Yes, Yet   38 s.d. *mad Maide*   39 humour honour   53 tune turne   103
lose the sight loose the Fight
5.5 Scaena 3   78 the end th'end   111 Emilia *Emily*   139 your you
5.6 Scaena 4   1 s.p. PALAMON [not in Q]   39 s.p. SECOND *and* THIRD KNIGHTS *I.2.
K⟨nights⟩.*   47 rarely early   79 victor's [Qb] victoros [Qa]   107 Hath Hast
Epilogue s.d. *Enter* EPILOGUE / s.p. EPILOGUE EPILOGVE.

POEMS

Venus and Adonis

When Shakespeare wrote the narrative poem *Venus and Adonis*, he was already an up-and-coming playwright; but he called his poem "the first heir of my invention" because, in 1593, it was his earliest work to see print. While plays were considered the property of the theater company and found their way to the printing house erratically if at all, an author could publish nondramatic works like *Venus and Adonis* and *The Rape of Lucrece* without impediment. It was customary to dedicate such published poems to aristocrats who might provide financial support or other form of patronage. Shakespeare dedicated *Venus and Adonis* to Henry Wriothesley, Earl of Southampton, a handsome nineteen-year-old aristocrat with sophisticated literary tastes, who was soon to come into a substantial fortune. But despite the conventionally flattering language of the dedication, Shakespeare intended to appeal to a larger audience than merely the patron to whom the poem was nominally addressed. Indeed, *Venus and Adonis* was exceedingly popular in Shakespeare's lifetime: it went through nine editions, and his contemporaries quote passages from it more often than they quote from any other Shakespearean play or poem.

Shakespeare found the story of Venus and Adonis in Ovid's *Metamorphoses*, a poem in fifteen books that retells, in beautiful, witty Latin, more than two hundred pagan myths of transformation. Since Elizabethan schoolboys were required to memorize long passages from the *Metamorphoses*, many of Shakespeare's readers knew Ovid in the original; others read him in a popular 1567 English translation by Arthur Golding. Shakespeare would have been aware that the cult of Adonis was widespread in antiquity, a cult that involved rites of fertility and seasonal renewal and was associated with the adoration of a mother goddess variously identified as Venus, Aphrodite, Astoreth, Isis, or Cybele. In the Old Testament, the Israelites are periodically chastised for abandoning their male divinity for the worship of this heathen goddess; her cult thus seems, at least for Jews, to have constituted an alluring alternative to patriarchal monotheism. For Christian interpreters, the myth of the mutilated, transformed Adonis resembles the story of Christ closely enough to be read, on the one hand, as a pagan analogue to Christ's death and resurrection and, on the other hand, as a demonstration of the superior power of the Judeo-Christian God, who, unlike Venus, can confer true immortality.

Shakespeare was not the only Elizabethan writer to adapt Ovid's stories to an English idiom. *Venus and Adonis* is an erotic narrative poem of a type that had become popular in the 1580s and grew even more so in the 1590s, partly because of the success of Shakespeare's poem and of Christopher Marlowe's roughly contemporaneous *Hero and Leander*. The writers of such poems acquired their plots from classical sources, but they got their idea of how to treat those plots from a medieval and Renaissance tradition of erotic poetry, deriving from the Italian poet Petrarch and developed in English by such poets as Thomas Wyatt, Henry Howard Earl of Surrey, Philip Sidney, and Edmund Spenser. In *Venus and Adonis*, Shakespeare reconceives his mythological protagonists so that his poem might in some respects more closely approximate a Petrarchan norm. When Ovid's Venus is dazzled by Adonis, she resolves to appeal to him by feigning an interest in his favorite sport. By donning hunting gear and resolutely chasing rabbits, she successfully captures the gorgeous huntsman, her true quarry. Shakespeare's Venus declares herself in a much more forthright fashion, but his Adonis, unlike Ovid's, remains unresponsive to her charms. Thus *Venus and Adonis* reproduces a dynamic that Petrarch and his followers had made familiar by the late sixteenth century, in which a yearning lover pleads endlessly with a chilly love object.

Two horses mating. From Antonio Tempesta, *Horses of Different Lands.*

The enduring fascination of this scenario for Renaissance poets lay in their recognition that the absence of sexual gratification can enhance erotic desire: "An oven that is stopped, / river stayed, / Burneth more hotly, swelleth with more rage" (lines 331–32). In Petrarchan poetry, little of consequence seems to happen, but the apparent lack of momentum is actually a prime stimulus to creativity. Frustration hones techniques of erotic persuasion; it energizes lament; it interestingly complicates the poet-lover's state of mind. The sophisticated pleasure of intense self-awareness replaces the straightforward, even mindless pleasure of the sex act itself. In *Venus and Adonis,* Shakespeare's concentration on psychological detail produces an extraordinary slowing-down and drawing-out of the action. Ovid spends about eighty-five lines on Adonis, beginning with a brisk description of his birth and ending with an equally succinct account of his metamorphosis into an anemone flower. Shakespeare manages to devote almost twelve hundred lines to the last twenty-four hours of Adonis's life.

In some important respects, however, Shakespeare departs from his Petrarchan precedents. The Ovidian retelling of the story of Venus and Adonis appears in *Metamorphoses* 10, a book that, as Ovid's translator Arthur Golding writes, "chiefly doth contain one kind of argument / Reproving most prodigious lusts." Taken together, the stories of Book 10 treat necrophilia, homosexuality, bestiality, fetishism, and incest; in this context, the story of Venus and Adonis seems relatively tame. But the "prodigiousness" of the Venus and Adonis story becomes clear when it is compared with similar Ovidian tales, which usually involve gods—Jove, Neptune, Apollo, or Pluto—who rape or attempt to rape beautiful young women. The story of Venus and Adonis reverses the "normal" gender of eager divinity and reluctant mortal.

Shakespeare's revisions of the story exaggerate the effects of this transposition. He attributes some conventionally "masculine" traits to his heroine and some conventionally "feminine" ones to his hero. His Venus is experienced, immensely strong, and apparently quite a bit larger than the Adonis whom she effortlessly tucks under one arm. Shakespeare's Adonis is dimpled, tender, coy, and virginal. At the same time, a female, even one as formidable as Venus, is imagined to be incapable of rape, so Venus cannot simply overpower her beloved as Apollo or Jove might do. Anatomical constraints force her to play a quite different but also conventionally masculine part: the pleading, unsatisfied role conventionally assigned to the male lover in Petrarchan poetry.

Since in Renaissance erotic poetry the positions of actively desiring, rhetorically fluent male and passive, unwilling female are ordinarily rather strictly demarcated, the sexual transpositions in the Venus and Adonis story have immediate consequences for Shakespeare's use of poetic conventions. Obviously they give those conventions a fresh twist: as the journalist's maxim has it, "Dog Bites Man" is not news, but "Man Bites Dog" is. In Shakespeare's hands, such novelty is often comic: the aggressive, rhetorically hyperbolic Venus and the fastidious Adonis are funny, because now as then they violate conventional notions of appropriate gender-specific behavior. Some of these reversals are obvious to a modern reader, since our courtship rituals retain vestiges of the assumption that males are naturally dominant and inclined to take the sexual initiative. Other reversals are more specific to the poetic tradition in which Shakespeare wrote. In traditional love poetry, for instance, the enamored man "blazons," or elaborately describes, the features of the woman he desires, dwelling on the incomparable beauty of her eyes, hair, lips, hands, voice, gestures, and so forth. But in *Venus and Adonis*, Venus is compelled to blazon her own charms, because Adonis will not do it for her.

> Mine eyes are grey, and bright, and quick in turning.
> My beauty as the spring doth yearly grow.
> My flesh is soft and plump, my marrow burning.
>
> . . . .
>
> Bid me discourse, I will enchant thine ear;
> Or like a fairy, trip upon the green;
> Or like a nymph, with long, dishevelled hair,
> Dance on the sands, and yet no footing seen.
>   (lines 140–48)

While in the conventional love situation the blazon is a man's cry of yearning for an exquisite object, here it becomes a woman's calculated, but unsuccessful, advertising campaign.

Shakespeare also dwells on the comic quality of Venus's divine attributes, such as the miraculous weightlessness of her robust body. At one point, Venus describes herself as a kind of giant balloon: "Witness this primrose bank whereon I lie: / These forceless flowers like sturdy trees support me" (lines 151–52). Her physical strength contrasts vividly with her quintessentially feminine body: when Venus "locks her lily fingers one in one" (line 228), she turns out to have a grip of steel. Shakespeare's interest in such apparent incongruities foreshadowed his much more elaborate exploration of the effects of transvestism and sexual reversal in such plays as *As You Like It*, *Twelfth Night*, *All's Well That Ends Well*, *Macbeth*, and *Antony and Cleopatra*. The humor of *Venus and Adonis* is two-edged, however, for it implicitly mocks not merely the aberrant protagonists but the standards from which they deviate. In what sense are particular traits or behaviors "naturally" masculine or feminine if actual males and females do not possess them?

The upending of gender stereotypes in *Venus and Adonis* is only one of the strategies of reversal that structure the imagery of the poem. Again and again, its metaphors and similes insist on the similarity of what seems different, the difference in what seems the same. Hunting is and is not like sexual pursuit; killing is and is not like loving; female sexual desire is and is not like maternal nurture; the boar, savagely rooting in Adonis's groin, is and is not like Venus; Adonis is and is not like the sun god or the flower into which he eventually transforms. Many of these comparisons or implied comparisons are quite traditional ones; Shakespeare's virtuosity is evident not so much in the originality of

Cupid taking aim. From George Wither, *A Collection of Emblems* (1635). The motto reads "Be wary, whosoe're thou be, / For from Love's arrows, none are free."

his individual conceits as in their extraordinary profusion and in the surprising way in which apparently incompatible images are tellingly juxtaposed.

The handling of imagery corresponds with the poem's abrupt reversals of mood and with the unpredictable, accidental quality of the story. The frank comedy of the beginning swerves into tragedy, or at least pathos, at the close, as the immortal goddess confronts the death of her reluctant beloved. Over the course of the poem, our estimation of both characters undergoes dizzying shifts. Venus—goddess, whore, cradle robber, and queen—is funny, scary, eloquent, and pitiable by turns. Adonis's sexual diffidence at first seems as ridiculous to the readers as it does to Venus; but he suddenly seems less absurd when he replies, gravely even if rather too sanctimoniously, to Venus's importunities.

Venus's frank joy in the pleasures of sex suggests an uninhibited pagan universe, in which gods, animals, and human beings all are ruled by the same laws of generation and sensual enjoyment. Shakespeare's lavish attention to the forest setting in which the poem takes place suggests his keen appreciation of the sensuous possibilities of a purely natural world. The bodies of animals—Adonis's splendid courser, inflamed by lust; the ferocious boar, bursting through the thorniest thickets; the zigzagging hunted hare—all are accorded blazons of their own, as if they, not merely the human lovers, were full participants in the story of love and death. At such moments, the poem seems enthusiastically to endorse the original religious significance of the Venus and Adonis story, which linked human lives with the rhythms of a natural environment.

But Shakespeare's poem hardly evokes a sexual utopia. Even though the pagan setting of the poem presumably frees the characters from the sexually abstemious culture of Christianity, the heroine and hero still disagree vehemently about the value of sexual indulgence. Chastity has its attractions even apart from whatever supernatural reinforcement Christian faith might lend to it—especially, as Adonis notes, for those who are not yet fully adult. The immortal Venus thinks of experience as an endless series of pleasurable present-tense moments; the mortal Adonis wants to conceive of his life in terms of narrative development, building slowly and coherently to a future maturity. His untimely death suggests the risks of thinking of one's life in this fashion; he seems unwisely to have forgone present satisfaction in the hope of a reward that never materializes.

On the other hand, why should Adonis, the victim of a sexual attack, enjoy caresses he has neither invited nor encouraged? Just as Shakespeare's reversal of gender stereotypes calls into question the adequacy of those stereotypes, so Adonis's recoil from Venus calls into question the naturalness of reproductive sexuality. Venus, the goddess of love, is supposed to be the apex of heterosexual desirability, both source and goal of every man's desire. Adonis, however, does not desire her even when she presses herself upon him. The congress of male and female thus seems simultaneously natural—what Adonis's palfrey and a passing mare know without tutelage—and optional, a possibility that some males, at any rate, may be willing to do without.

Shakespeare writes almost entirely from Venus's perspective: the boy, not the woman, is the sex object of *Venus and Adonis*. In an age lacking our comparatively rigid conception of sexual orientation, lovely androgynous boys were assumed to be attractive to adult men and women alike. Shakespeare returned to the subject of the adolescent boy's ambiguous, half-conscious sexiness in his transvestite comedies, and to the adult man's reluctance to commit himself to exclusively heterosexual alliances in those plays as well as in *The Merchant of Venice*. *Venus and Adonis* can thus be read both as a narrative of frustrated heterosexual desire and, perhaps, as a parable of desire for a beautiful, aloof boy by a male poet—a scenario also sketched in many of Shakespeare's sonnets.

The boar attacking Adonis. From Henry Peacham, *Minerva Britanna* (1612).

What is the meaning of sexuality? *Venus and Adonis* suggests a wide variety of possibilities: it is both a joke and a cosmic principle, a function of stern reproductive necessity and of sheer animal exuberance, a link with the animal world and an escape from it, a necessity and an option, a reminder of mortality and an intimation of immortality, a celebration of personal uniqueness and a threat to the formation of an individual identity. The shifting perspectives of the poem exploit the ambivalence with which Shakespeare's culture, as well as our own, treats sexual matters as simultaneously comical and deeply serious matters. The language of *Venus and Adonis* is especially good at capturing the confusing, contradictory array of sensations produced by another person's unfamiliar body close to one's own, a sensation simultaneously grand, comic, oppressive, arousing, and repellant. The sweating, reeking, melting, and liquefying that at first seem specific to Venus's courtship of Adonis seem, by the end of the poem, to represent a principle of mortal existence and moral evaluation, as one thing merges unsteadily, unexpectedly, into another.

Biographical critics have found in *Venus and Adonis* ample grounds for speculation. Does the sexual dynamic of this poem reflect Shakespeare's experience with the older Anne Hathaway, hauling him into some bosky nook outside Stratford, or alternatively an infatuation with Henry Wriothesley, the gorgeous youth to whom, some speculate, the early sonnets are devoted in both senses of the word? Given the scanty biographical data that have come down to us, it is impossible to know. What is clear is that *Venus and Adonis* inaugurates many of the distinctive features of Shakespeare's later work: a fascination with, and capacity to sympathize with, sexually assertive women and self-contained, immature young men; an erotic energy that is both exuberant and hard to pin down; a complex moral sensibility capable of apprehending contradictory ethical imperatives at the same time; and an uncanny ability to combine comic, tragic, pathetic, and sensuous effects in a single work, even in a single poetic moment.

KATHARINE EISAMAN MAUS

TEXTUAL NOTE

The textual history of *Venus and Adonis* is much less tangled than that of most of the plays. Critics have theorized that Shakespeare wrote the narrative poems in 1592 and 1593, when an epidemic of bubonic plague forced the London theaters to close. At the time, it was unclear whether the playhouses would be allowed to reopen, so Shakespeare may have had not merely plenty of time on his hands but an urgent practical motive for establishing his credentials as a nondramatic writer. *Venus and Adonis* was first published in quarto in 1593 by the printer Richard Field, who was, like Shakespeare, a native of Stratford-upon-Avon. Only one copy of this edition survives. It contains very few obvious misprints and was presumably prepared from Shakespeare's manuscript, perhaps under his direct supervision. *Venus and Adonis* was frequently reprinted during Shakespeare's lifetime, but there is little substantive variation from one printing to another.

SELECTED BIBLIOGRAPHY

Bate, Jonathan. "Sexual Perversity in *Venus and Adonis*." *Yearbook of English Studies* 23 (1993): 80–92.

Hughes, Ted. "Conception and Gestation of the Equation's Tragic Myth." *Shakespeare and the Goddess of Complete Being*. London: Faber and Faber, 1992. 49–92.

Hulse, Clark. *Metamorphic Verse: The Elizabethan Minor Epic*. Princeton: Princeton University Press, 1981. 143–75.

Kahn, Coppélia. "Self as Eros in *Venus and Adonis*." *Man's Estate: Masculine Identity in Shakespeare*. Berkeley: University of California Press, 1981. 21–46.

Keach, William. "*Venus and Adonis*." *Elizabethan Erotic Narratives: Irony and Pathos in the Ovidian Poetry of Shakespeare, Marlowe, and Their Contemporaries*. New Brunswick, N.J.: Rutgers University Press, 1977. 52–84.

Venus and Adonis

Vilia miretur vulgus; mihi flavus Apollo
Pocula Castalia plena ministret aqua.[1]

TO THE RIGHT HONOURABLE
HENRY WRIOTHESLEY,
EARL OF SOUTHAMPTON, AND
BARON OF TITCHFIELD[2]

Right Honourable, I know not how I shall offend in dedicating my
unpolished lines to your lordship, nor how the world will censure°   *judge*
me for choosing so strong a prop to support so weak a burden. Only,
if your honour seem but pleased, I account myself highly praised,
and vow to take advantage of all idle hours till I have honoured you
with some graver labour. But if the first heir[3] of my invention prove
deformed, I shall be sorry it had so noble a godfather, and never after
ear° so barren a land for fear it yield me still° so bad a harvest. I leave   *cultivate / always*
it to your honourable survey, and your honour to your heart's content,
which I wish may always answer your own wish and the world's hope-
ful expectation.

YOUR HONOUR'S IN ALL DUTY,
WILLIAM SHAKESPEARE

Even as the sun with purple-coloured face
Had ta'en his last leave of the weeping morn,[1]
Rose-cheeked Adonis hied him° to the chase.   *hurried*
Hunting he loved, but love he laughed to scorn.
5   Sick-thoughted° Venus makes amain° unto him,   *Lovesick / speedily*
    And like a bold-faced suitor 'gins to woo him.

'Thrice fairer than myself,' thus she began,
'The fields' chief flower, sweet above compare,
Stain to all nymphs,° more lovely than a man,   *Eclipsing all women*
10   More white and red than doves or roses are—
    Nature that made thee with herself at strife
    Saith that the world hath ending with thy life.[2]

'Vouchsafe, thou wonder, to alight thy steed
And rein his proud head to the saddle-bow;

Dedication
1. "Let vile people admire vile things; may fair-haired
Apollo serve me goblets filled with Castalian water"
(Ovid, *Amores* 1.15.35–36). Apollo is the god of poetry;
the Castalian spring is sacred to the Muses.
2. Prominent courtier, nineteen years old at the time of
Venus and Adonis's publication. Shakespeare also dedi-
cated *The Rape of Lucrece* to him.

3. *Venus and Adonis* was Shakespeare's first published
work.
Poem
1. Aurora, goddess of the dawn, weeps tears of dew when
forsaken each morning by her lover, the sun.
2. *Nature . . . life*: Nature, who strove to surpass herself in
making you, says that if you die, the world will end.

15 If thou wilt deign this favour, for thy meed°   *reward*
A thousand honey secrets shalt thou know.
    Here come and sit where never serpent hisses;
    And, being sat, I'll smother thee with kisses,

'And yet not cloy thy lips with loathed satiety,
20 But rather famish them amid their plenty,
Making them red, and pale, with fresh variety;
Ten kisses short as one, one long as twenty.
    A summer's day will seem an hour but short,
    Being wasted° in such time-beguiling sport.'   *spent*

25 With this, she seizeth on his sweating palm,
The precedent of pith and livelihood,[3]
And, trembling in her passion, calls it balm—
Earth's sovereign° salve to do a goddess good.   *potent*
    Being so enraged, desire doth lend her force
30   Courageously to pluck him from his horse.

Over one arm, the lusty courser's rein;
Under her other was the tender boy,
Who blushed and pouted in a dull disdain
With leaden appetite, unapt to toy.[4]
35   She red and hot as coals of glowing fire;
    He red for shame, but frosty in desire.

The studded bridle on a ragged bough
Nimbly she fastens—O, how quick is love!
The steed is stallèd° up, and even now   *fastened*
40 To tie the rider she begins to prove.°   *try*
    Backward she pushed him, as she would be thrust,
    And governed him in strength, though not in lust.

So soon was she along° as he was down,   *alongside him*
Each leaning on their elbows and their hips.
45 Now doth she stroke his cheek, now doth he frown
And 'gins to chide, but soon she stops his lips,
    And, kissing, speaks, with lustful language broken:°   *interrupted*
    'If thou wilt chide, thy lips shall never open.'

He burns with bashful shame; she with her tears
50 Doth quench the maiden burning of his cheeks.
Then, with her windy sighs and golden hairs,
To fan and blow them dry again she seeks.
    He saith she is immodest, blames her miss;°   *misbehavior*
    What follows more she murders with a kiss.

55 Even as an empty eagle, sharp by fast,°   *hungry from fasting*
Tires° with her beak on feathers, flesh, and bone,   *Tears*
Shaking her wings, devouring all in haste
Till either gorge° be stuffed or prey be gone,   *stomach*
    Even so she kissed his brow, his cheek, his chin,
60   And where she ends she doth anew begin.

---

3. The evidence of strength and liveliness.   4. Uninterested in sex play.

Forced to content,° but never to obey,°   *acquiesce / respond*
Panting he lies and breatheth in her face.
She feedeth on the steam as on a prey
And calls it heavenly moisture, air of grace,
65   Wishing her cheeks were gardens full of flowers,
        So they were dewed with such distilling° showers.   *gently dropping*

Look how a bird lies tangled in a net,
So fastened in her arms Adonis lies.
Pure shame and awed° resistance made him fret,   *overpowered*
70   Which bred more beauty in his angry eyes.
        Rain added to a river that is rank°   *full*
        Perforce will force it overflow the bank.

Still she entreats, and prettily entreats,
For to a pretty ear she tunes her tale.
75   Still is he sullen, still he lours° and frets   *frowns*
     'Twixt crimson shame and anger ashy-pale.
        Being red, she loves him best; and being white,
        Her best is bettered with a more delight.

Look how he can, she cannot choose but love;
80   And by her fair immortal hand she swears
     From his soft bosom never to remove
     Till he take truce° with her contending tears,   *come to terms*
        Which long have rained, making her cheeks all wet;
        And one sweet kiss shall pay this countless debt.

85   Upon this promise did he raise his chin,
     Like a divedapper⁵ peering through a wave
     Who, being looked on, ducks as quickly in—
     So offers he to give what she did crave.
        But when her lips were ready for his pay,
90   He winks,° and turns his lips another way.   *shuts his eyes*

Never did passenger° in summer's heat   *traveler*
More thirst for drink than she for this good turn.
Her help she sees, but help she cannot get.
She bathes in water, yet her fire must burn.
95   'O pity,' gan she cry, 'flint-hearted boy!
        'Tis but a kiss I beg—why art thou coy?

'I have been wooed as I entreat thee now
Even by the stern and direful god of war,°   *Mars*
Whose sinewy neck in battle ne'er did bow,
100 Who conquers where he comes in every jar.°   *conflict*
        Yet hath he been my captive and my slave,
        And begged for that which thou unasked shalt have.

'Over my altars hath he hung his lance,
His battered shield, his uncontrollèd° crest,   *unvanquished*
105 And for my sake hath learned to sport and dance,
     To toy, to wanton, dally, smile, and jest,

5. Grebe (small English waterbird).

Scorning his churlish drum and ensign red,
Making my arms° his field, his tent my bed.   *(a pun)*

'Thus he that over-ruled I oversEprecationwayed,
110   Leading him prisoner in a red-rose chain.
Strong-tempered steel his stronger strength obeyed,
Yet was he servile to my coy disdain.
    O, be not proud, nor brag not of thy might,
    For mast'ring her that foiled° the god of fight.   *conquered*

115   'Touch but my lips with those fair lips of thine—
Though mine be not so fair, yet are they red—
The kiss shall be thine own as well as mine.
What seest thou in the ground? Hold up thy head.
    Look in mine eyeballs: there thy beauty lies.°   *lies reflected*
120   Then why not lips on lips, since eyes in eyes?

'Art thou ashamed to kiss? Then wink again,
And I will wink. So shall the day seem night.
Love keeps his revels where there are but twain.
Be bold to play—our sport is not in sight.°   *unobserved*
125   These blue-veined violets whereon we lean
    Never can blab, nor know not⁶ what we mean.

'The tender spring° upon thy tempting lip   *growth of new beard*
Shows thee unripe; yet mayst thou well be tasted.
Make use of time; let not advantage slip.
130   Beauty within itself should not be wasted.
    Fair flowers that are not gathered in their prime
    Rot, and consume themselves in little time.

'Were I hard-favoured,° foul, or wrinkled-old,   *ugly*
Ill-nurtured, crooked, churlish, harsh in voice,
135   O'er-worn,° despisèd, rheumatic, and cold,   *Worn out*
Thick-sighted,° barren, lean, and lacking juice,   *Partly blind*
    Then mightst thou pause, for then I were not for thee.
    But having no defects, why dost abhor me?

'Thou canst not see one wrinkle in my brow.
140   Mine eyes are grey,⁷ and bright, and quick in turning.
My beauty as the spring doth yearly grow.°   *rejuvenate*
My flesh is soft and plump, my marrow° burning.   *vital spirits*
    My smooth moist hand, were it with thy hand felt,
    Would in thy palm dissolve, or seem to melt.

145   'Bid me discourse, I will enchant thine ear;
Or like a fairy, trip upon the green;
Or like a nymph, with long, dishevelled hair,
Dance on the sands, and yet no footing° seen.   *footprint*
    Love is a spirit all compact° of fire,   *made up*
150   Not gross° to sink, but light, and will aspire.°   *heavy / rise*

6. The double negative ("nor . . . not") was acceptable in   7. Considered the best eye color by medieval and Renais-
Elizabethan English.   sance love poets.

'Witness this primrose bank whereon I lie:
These forceless flowers like sturdy trees support me.
Two strengthless doves[8] will draw me through the sky
From morn till night, even where I list° to sport me.   *wherever I wish*
155   Is love so light, sweet boy, and may it be
     That thou should think it heavy unto thee?

'Is thine own heart to thine own face affected?°   *attracted*
Can thy right hand seize love upon thy left?°   *by clasping the left*
Then woo thyself, be of thyself rejected;
160   Steal thine own freedom,° and complain on theft.   *Capture your affections*
     Narcissus[9] so himself himself forsook,
     And died to kiss his shadow in the brook.

'Torches are made to light, jewels to wear,
Dainties to taste, fresh beauty for the use,
165   Herbs for their smell, and sappy plants to bear.
Things growing to themselves° are growth's abuse.   *only for themselves*
     Seeds spring from seeds, and beauty breedeth beauty:
     Thou wast begot; to get° it is thy duty.   *beget*

'Upon the earth's increase why shouldst thou feed
170   Unless the earth with thy increase be fed?
By law of nature thou art bound to breed,
That thine° may live when thou thyself art dead;   *(your children)*
     And so in spite of death thou dost survive,
     In that thy likeness still is left alive.'

175   By this,° the lovesick queen began to sweat,   *By this time*
For where they lay the shadow had forsook them,
And Titan,° tired in the midday heat,   *the sun god*
With burning eye did hotly overlook them,
     Wishing Adonis had his team° to guide   *(of sun horses)*
180   So he° were like him,° and by Venus' side.   *(Titan) / (Adonis)*

And now Adonis, with a lazy sprite°   *dull spirit*
And with a heavy, dark, disliking eye,
His louring brows o'erwhelming° his fair sight,   *overhanging*
Like misty vapours when they blot the sky,
185   Souring his cheeks,° cries, 'Fie, no more of love!   *Frowning*
     The sun doth burn my face; I must remove.'°   *leave*

'Ay me,' quoth Venus, 'young, and so unkind?°   *unnatural*
What bare° excuses mak'st thou to be gone?   *poor*
I'll sigh celestial breath, whose gentle wind
190   Shall cool the heat of this descending sun.
     I'll make a shadow for thee of my hairs;
     If they burn too, I'll quench them with my tears.

'The sun that shines from heaven shines but warm,°   *merely warms me*
And lo, I lie between that sun and thee.

8. Traditionally, Venus's chariot was drawn by swans or doves; see lines 1190–92.
9. In classical mythology, a young man who fell in love with his own image reflected in the water; after he pined to death, he was turned into a flower.

195 The heat I have from thence doth little harm;
Thine eye darts forth the fire that burneth me,
  And were I not immortal, life were done°   *destroyed*
  Between this heavenly and earthly sun.

'Art thou obdurate, flinty, hard as steel?
200 Nay, more than flint, for stone at rain relenteth.°   *wears away*
Art thou a woman's son, and canst not feel
What 'tis to love, how want of love° tormenteth? *being denied love*
  O, had thy mother borne so hard a mind,
  She had not brought forth thee, but died unkind.

205 'What am I, that thou shouldst contemn° me this?   *deny; scorn*
Or what great danger dwells upon my suit?
What were thy lips the worse for one poor kiss?
Speak, fair; but speak fair words, or else be mute.
  Give me one kiss, I'll give it thee again,
210   And one for int'rest, if thou wilt have twain.

'Fie, lifeless picture, cold and senseless° stone,   *insensible*
Well painted idol, image dull and dead,
Statue contenting but the eye alone,
Thing like a man, but of no woman bred:
215   Thou art no man, though of a man's complexion,° *appearance*
  For men will kiss even by their own direction.'° *inclination*

This said, impatience chokes her pleading tongue,
And swelling passion doth provoke a pause.
Red cheeks and fiery eyes blaze forth° her wrong. *display; flame out*
220 Being judge in love, she cannot right her cause;[1]
  And now she weeps, and now she fain° would speak, *gladly*
  And now her sobs do her intendments° break. *intended words*

Sometime she shakes her head, and then his hand;
Now gazeth she on him, now on the ground.
225 Sometime her arms enfold him like a band;°   *fetter*
She would, he will not in her arms be bound.
  And when from thence he struggles to be gone,
  She locks her lily fingers one in one.

'Fondling,'° she saith, 'since I have hemmed thee here *Foolish one; beloved*
230 Within the circuit of this ivory pale,°   *fence*
I'll be a park, and thou shalt be my deer.
Feed where thou wilt, on mountain or in dale;
  Graze on my lips, and if those hills be dry,
  Stray lower, where the pleasant fountains lie.

235 'Within this limit is relief[2] enough,
Sweet bottom-grass,[3] and high delightful plain,
Round rising hillocks, brakes obscure and rough,° *dark, shaggy thickets*
To shelter thee from tempest and from rain.

1. Although (or because) she is love's arbiter, she cannot win her own case.
2. Pasture; variety of landscape; sexual gratification.
3. Valley grass (pubic hair); Venus's body-landscape is intentionally suggestive throughout.

Then be my deer, since I am such a park;
240   No dog shall rouse thee,° though a thousand bark.'   *drive you from cover*

At this Adonis smiles as in disdain,
That in each cheek appears a pretty dimple.
Love made those hollows, if° himself were slain,   *so that if*
He might be buried in a tomb so simple,
245   Foreknowing well, if there he came to lie,
    Why, there love lived, and there he could not die.

These lovely caves, these round enchanting pits,
Opened their mouths to swallow Venus' liking.°   *to engulf her desire*
Being mad before, how doth she now for wits?[4]
250   Struck dead at first, what needs a second striking?
    Poor queen of love, in thine own law forlorn,°   *condemned to suffer*
    To love a cheek that smiles at thee in scorn!

Now which way shall she turn? What shall she say?
Her words are done, her woes the more increasing.
255   The time is spent; her object will away,
And from her twining arms doth urge releasing.
    'Pity,' she cries; 'some favour, some remorse!'°   *compassion*
    Away he springs, and hasteth to his horse.

But lo, from forth a copse° that neighbours by   *thicket*
260   A breeding jennet,° lusty, young, and proud,   *mare in heat*
Adonis' trampling courser doth espy,
And forth she rushes, snorts, and neighs aloud.
    The strong-necked steed, being tied unto a tree,
    Breaketh his rein, and to her straight goes he.

265   Imperiously he leaps, he neighs, he bounds,
And now his woven girths he breaks asunder.
The bearing[5] earth with his hard hoof he wounds,
Whose hollow womb resounds like heaven's thunder.
    The iron bit he crusheth 'tween his teeth,
270   Controlling what he was controllèd with.

His ears up-pricked, his braided hanging mane
Upon his compassed crest° now stand on end;   *arched neck*
His nostrils drink the air, and forth again,
As from a furnace, vapours doth he send.
275   His eye, which scornfully glisters like fire,
    Shows his hot courage° and his high desire.   *lust*

Sometime he trots, as if he told° the steps,   *counted*
With gentle majesty and modest pride.
Anon he rears upright, curvets,[6] and leaps,
280   As who° should say, 'Lo, thus my strength is tried,°   *one who / tested*
    And this I do to captivate the eye
    Of the fair breeder that is standing by.'

---

4. How does she keep her sanity now?   6. Bounds on his hind legs with raised forelegs.
5. Supporting; suffering; generative.

What recketh he° his rider's angry stir,°　　　　　　*cares he about / noise*
His flattering° 'Holla', or his 'Stand, I say!'?　　　　　　*cajoling*
285　What cares he now for curb° or pricking spur,　　　　　　*bit*
For rich caparisons or trappings gay?
　　He sees his love, and nothing else he sees,
　　For nothing else with his proud sight agrees.

Look when° a painter would surpass the life　　　　　　*Just as*
290　In limning out° a well proportioned steed,　　　　　　*depicting*
His art with nature's workmanship at strife,
As if the dead the living should exceed:
　　So did this horse excel a common one
　　In shape, in courage, colour, pace, and bone.°　　　　　　*frame*

295　Round-hoofed, short-jointed, fetlocks shag and long,[7]
Broad breast, full eye, small head, and nostril wide,
High crest, short ears, straight legs, and passing° strong;　　　　　　*extremely*
Thin mane, thick tail, broad buttock, tender hide—
　　Look what° a horse should have he did not lack,　　　　　　*Whatever*
300　　Save a proud rider on so proud a back.

Sometime he scuds far off, and there he stares;
Anon he starts at stirring of a feather.
To bid the wind a base[8] he now prepares,
And whe'er° he run or fly they know not whether;°　　　　　　*whether / which*
305　　For through his mane and tail the high wind sings,
　　Fanning the hairs, who wave like feathered wings.

He looks upon his love, and neighs unto her;
She answers him as if she knew his mind.
Being proud, as females are, to see him woo her,
310　She puts on outward strangeness,° seems unkind,　　　　　　*reserve*
　　Spurns at° his love, and scorns the heat he feels,　　　　　　*Repels; kicks*
　　Beating his kind° embracements with her heels.　　　　　　*amorous; natural*

Then, like a melancholy malcontent,
He vails° his tail that, like a falling plume,　　　　　　*lowers*
315　Cool shadow to his melting buttock lent.
He stamps, and bites the poor flies in his fume.°　　　　　　*anger*
　　His love, perceiving how he was enraged,
　　Grew kinder, and his fury was assuaged.

His testy° master goeth about° to take him,　　　　　　*angry / tries*
320　When lo, the unbacked breeder,[9] full of fear,
Jealous of catching,° swiftly doth forsake him,　　　　　　*Fearful of being caught*
With her the horse, and left Adonis there.
　　As they were mad unto the wood they hie them,
　　Outstripping crows that strive to overfly them.

325　All swoll'n with chafing,° down Adonis sits,　　　　　　*anger*
Banning° his boist'rous and unruly beast;　　　　　　*Cursing*

---

7. *short-jointed . . . long:* with short pasterns (the bone just above the horse's hoof) and shaggy joints above the hooves.

8. To dare the wind to run (from a children's game, prisoner's base).

9. Mare without mount (rider or stallion).

And now the happy season once more fits°   *is suited*
That lovesick love by pleading may be blessed;
    For lovers say the heart hath treble wrong
330   When it is barred the aidance of the tongue.

An oven that is stopped, or river stayed,°   *dammed*
Burneth more hotly, swelleth with more rage.
So of concealèd sorrow may be said
Free vent of words love's fire doth assuage.
335   But when the heart's attorney° once is mute,   *pleader (the tongue)*
    The client breaks,[1] as desperate in his suit.

He sees her coming, and begins to glow,
Even as a dying coal revives with wind,
And with his bonnet° hides his angry brow,   *hat*
340   Looks on the dull earth with disturbèd mind,
    Taking no notice that she is so nigh,
    For all askance he holds her in his eye.

O, what a sight it was wistly° to view   *intently*
How she came stealing to the wayward boy,
345   To note the fighting conflict of her hue,
How white and red each other did destroy!
    But now her cheek was pale; and by and by
    It flashed forth fire, as lightning from the sky.

Now was she just before him as he sat,
350   And like a lowly lover down she kneels;
With one fair hand she heaveth up his hat;
Her other tender hand his fair cheek feels.
    His tend'rer cheek receives her soft hand's print
    As apt as new-fall'n snow takes any dint.°   *dent*

355   O, what a war of looks was then between them,
Her eyes petitioners to his eyes suing!
His eyes saw her eyes as they had not seen them;
Her eyes wooed still; his eyes disdained the wooing;
    And all this dumb play had his° acts made plain   *its*
360   With tears which, chorus-like, her eyes did rain.[2]

Full gently now she takes him by the hand,
A lily prisoned in a jail of snow,
Or ivory in an alabaster band;
So white a friend engirds so white a foe.
365   This beauteous combat, wilful and unwilling,
    Showed° like two silver doves that sit a-billing.   *Looked*

Once more the engine of her thoughts began:
'O fairest mover on this mortal round,°   *earth*
Would thou wert as I am, and I a man,
370   My heart all whole as thine, thy heart my wound;°   *suffering my wound*

---

1. Breaks apart; goes bankrupt.
2. Venus's tears interpret her mute gestures as the chorus in a play explains a dumbshow.

For one sweet look thy help I would assure thee,
Though nothing but my body's bane° would cure thee.'   *destruction*

'Give me my hand,' saith he. 'Why dost thou feel it?'
'Give me my heart,' saith she, 'and thou shalt have it.
375 O, give it me, lest thy hard heart do steel it,³
And, being steeled, soft sighs can never grave° it;   *engrave*
    Then love's deep groans I never shall regard,
    Because Adonis' heart hath made mine hard.'

'For shame,' he cries, 'let go, and let me go!
380 My day's delight is past; my horse is gone,
And 'tis your fault I am bereft him so.
I pray you hence, and leave me here alone;
    For all my mind, my thought, my busy care
    Is how to get my palfrey° from the mare.'   *riding horse*

385 Thus she replies: 'Thy palfrey, as he should,
Welcomes the warm approach of sweet desire.
Affection° is a coal that must be cooled,   *Passion*
Else, suffered,° it will set the heart on fire.   *allowed to persist*
    The sea hath bounds, but deep desire hath none;
390   Therefore no marvel though thy horse be gone.

'How like a jade° he stood tied to the tree,   *nag*
Servilely mastered with a leathern rein!
But when he saw his love, his youth's fair fee,°   *reward*
He held such petty bondage in disdain,
395   Throwing the base thong from his bending crest,
    Enfranchising his mouth, his back, his breast.

'Who sees his true-love in her naked bed,
Teaching the sheets a whiter hue than white,
But when his glutton eye so full hath fed
400 His other agents° aim at like delight?   *faculties*
    Who is so faint that dares not be so bold
    To touch the fire, the weather being cold?

'Let me excuse thy courser, gentle boy;
And learn of him, I heartily beseech thee,
405 To take advantage on° presented joy.   *of*
Though I were dumb, yet his proceedings teach thee.
    O, learn to love! The lesson is but plain,
    And, once made perfect,° never lost again.'   *learned by heart*

'I know not love,' quoth he, 'nor will not know it,
410 Unless it be a boar, and then I chase it.
'Tis much to borrow, and I will not owe it.
My love to love is love but to disgrace it;⁴
    For I have heard it is a life in death,
    That laughs and weeps, and all but with a breath.

---

3. Turn my heart to steel; steal my heart.   4. My only interest in love is in discrediting it.

415 'Who wears a garment shapeless and unfinished?
Who plucks the bud before one leaf put forth?
If springing° things be any jot diminished,   *immature*
They wither in their prime, prove nothing worth.
    The colt that's backed° and burdened being young,   *ridden*
420   Loseth his pride, and never waxeth strong.

'You hurt my hand with wringing. Let us part,
And leave this idle° theme, this bootless° chat.   *useless / pointless*
Remove your siege from my unyielding heart;
To love's alarms° it will not ope the gate.   *assaults*
425   Dismiss your vows, your feignèd tears, your flatt'ry;
    For where a heart is hard they make no batt'ry.'°   *breach*

'What, canst thou talk?' quoth she. 'Hast thou a tongue?
O, would thou hadst not, or I had no hearing!
Thy mermaid's voice[5] hath done me double wrong.
430 I had my load before, now pressed° with bearing: *oppressed*
    Melodious discord, heavenly tune harsh sounding,
    Ears' deep-sweet music, and heart's deep-sore wounding.

'Had I no eyes but ears, my ears would love
That inward beauty and invisible;
435 Or were I deaf, thy outward parts would move
Each part in me that were but sensible.°   *perceiving*
    Though neither eyes nor ears to hear nor see,
    Yet should I be in love by touching thee.

'Say that the sense of feeling were bereft me,
440 And that I could not see, nor hear, nor touch,
And nothing but the very smell were left me,
Yet would my love to thee be still as much;
    For from the stillitory[6] of thy face excelling°   *incomparable*
    Comes breath perfumed, that breedeth love by smelling.

445 'But O, what banquet wert thou to the taste,
Being nurse and feeder of the other four!
Would they not wish the feast might ever last
And bid suspicion° double-lock the door   *wariness*
    Lest jealousy, that sour unwelcome guest,
450   Should by his stealing-in disturb the feast?'

Once more the ruby-coloured portal° opened   *threshold (mouth)*
Which to his speech did honey passage yield,
Like a red morn that ever yet betokened
Wrack° to the seaman, tempest to the field,   *Shipwreck*
455   Sorrow to shepherds, woe unto the birds,
    Gusts and foul flaws° to herdmen and to herds.   *winds*

This ill presage advisedly she marketh.[7]
Even as the wind is hushed before it raineth,
Or as the wolf doth grin° before he barketh,   *show his teeth*

5. Which, irresistible in song, was supposed to lure sailors onto rocks.
6. Apparatus used to distill perfume.
7. She notices this bad omen carefully.

460   Or as the berry breaks before it staineth,
     Or like the deadly bullet of a gun,
     His meaning struck her ere his words begun,

   And at his look she flatly falleth down,
   For looks kill love, and love by looks reviveth;
465   A smile recures° the wounding of a frown,   *cures*
   But blessèd bankrupt that by loss so thriveth!
     The silly° boy, believing she is dead,   *naive*
     Claps her pale cheek till clapping makes it red,

   And, all amazed,° brake° off his late intent,   *perplexed / broke*
470   For sharply he did think to reprehend her,
   Which cunning love did wittily prevent.
   Fair fall[8] the wit that can so well defend her!
     For on the grass she lies as she were slain,
     Till his breath breatheth life in her again.

475   He wrings her nose, he strikes her on the cheeks,
   He bends her fingers, holds her pulses hard;°   *takes her pulse*
   He chafes her lips; a thousand ways he seeks
   To mend the hurt that his unkindness marred.°   *caused to injure her*
     He kisses her; and she, by her good will,°   *consent*
480   Will never rise, so he will kiss her still.°   *keep kissing her*

   The night of sorrow now is turned to day.
   Her two blue windows° faintly she upheaveth,   *(her eyes)*
   Like the fair sun when, in his fresh array,
   He cheers the morn, and all the earth relieveth;
485   And as the bright sun glorifies the sky,
     So is her face illumined with her eye,

   Whose beams upon his hairless face are fixed,
   As if from thence they borrowed all their shine.
   Were never four such lamps together mixed,
490   Had not his clouded with his brow's repine.°   *discontent*
     But hers, which through the crystal tears gave light,
     Shone like the moon in water seen by night.

   'O, where am I?' quoth she; 'in earth or heaven,
   Or in the ocean drenched,° or in the fire?   *submerged*
495   What hour is this: or° morn or weary even?°   *either / evening*
   Do I delight to die, or life desire?
     But now I lived, and life was death's annoy;°   *deathly pain*
     But now I died, and death was lively° joy.   *living*

   'O, thou didst kill me; kill me once again!
500   Thy eyes' shrewd° tutor, that hard heart of thine,   *stern*
   Hath taught them scornful tricks, and such disdain
   That they have murdered this poor heart of mine,
     And these mine eyes, true leaders° to their queen,   *guides*
     But for thy piteous° lips no more had seen.   *pitying*

---

8. Good luck befall (with wordplay on "fall down").

505 'Long may they kiss each other, for this cure!
O, never let their crimson liveries wear,°   *wear out*
And as they last, their verdure⁹ still endure
To drive infection from the dangerous year,
That the star-gazers, having writ on death,°   *predicted plague*
510   May say the plague is banished by thy breath!

'Pure lips, sweet seals in my soft lips imprinted,
What bargains may I make still to be sealing?°   *kissing; making deals*
To sell myself I can be well contented,
So° thou wilt buy, and pay, and use good dealing;   *If*
515   Which purchase if thou make, for fear of slips°   *fraud*
     Set thy seal manual° on my wax-red lips.   *identifying stamp*

'A thousand kisses buys my heart from me;
And pay them at thy leisure, one by one.
What is ten hundred touches° unto thee?   *(of the lips)*
520 Are they not quickly told,° and quickly gone?   *counted*
     Say for non-payment that the debt should double,
     Is twenty hundred kisses such a trouble?'

'Fair queen,' quoth he, 'if any love you owe me,
Measure my strangeness° with my unripe years.   *Explain my coldness*
525 Before I know myself, seek not to know me.
No fisher but the ungrown fry forbears.¹
     The mellow plum doth fall, the green sticks fast,
     Or, being early plucked, is sour to taste.

'Look, the world's comforter° with weary gait   *(the sun)*
530 His day's hot task hath ended in the west.
The owl, night's herald, shrieks 'tis very late;
The sheep are gone to fold, birds to their nest,
     And coal-black clouds, that shadow heaven's light,
     Do summon us to part and bid good night.

535 'Now let me say good night, and so say you.
If you will say so, you shall have a kiss.'
'Good night,' quoth she; and ere he says adieu
The honey° fee of parting tendered° is.   *sweet / given*
     Her arms do lend his neck a sweet embrace.
540   Incorporate° then they seem; face grows to face,   *United in one body*

Till breathless he disjoined, and backward drew
The heavenly moisture, that sweet coral mouth,
Whose precious taste her thirsty lips well knew,
Whereon they surfeit, yet complain on drought.
545   He with her plenty pressed, she faint with dearth,
     Their lips together glued, fall to the earth.

Now quick desire hath caught the yielding prey,
And glutton-like she feeds, yet never filleth.
Her lips are conquerors, his lips obey,

9. Literally, greenness; here, freshness. The lips ward off   1. Every fisherman spares the young fish.
disease as fresh parsley was believed to do.

550   Paying what ransom the insulter° willeth,   *conqueror*
        Whose vulture° thought doth pitch the price so high   *ravenous*
        That she will draw his lips' rich treasure dry,

        And, having felt the sweetness of the spoil,
        With blindfold fury she begins to forage.
555   Her face doth reek° and smoke, her blood doth boil,   *steam*
        And careless° lust stirs up a desperate courage,   *reckless*
          Planting° oblivion, beating reason back,   *Implanting*
          Forgetting shame's pure blush and honour's wrack.°   *ruin*

        Hot, faint, and weary with her hard embracing,
560   Like a wild bird being tamed with too much handling,
        Or as the fleet-foot roe that's tired with chasing,
        Or like the froward° infant stilled with dandling,   *fretful*
          He now obeys, and now no more resisteth,
          While she takes all she can, not all she listeth.°   *desires*

565   What wax so frozen but dissolves with temp'ring°   *fingering*
        And yields at last to every light impression?
        Things out of° hope are compassed° oft with vent'ring,   *beyond / accomplished*
        Chiefly in love, whose leave° exceeds commission.°   *liberty / warrant*
          Affection faints° not, like a pale-faced coward,   *Passion relents*
570   But then woos best when most his choice is froward.

        When he did frown, O, had she then gave over,
        Such nectar from his lips she had not sucked.
        Foul° words and frowns must not repel a lover.   *Harsh*
        What though the rose have prickles, yet 'tis plucked!
575   Were beauty under twenty locks kept fast,
          Yet love breaks through, and picks them all at last.

        For pity now she can no more detain him.
        The poor fool° prays her that he may depart.   *(term of affection)*
        She is resolved no longer to restrain him,
580   Bids him farewell, and look well to° her heart,   *take good care of*
          The which, by Cupid's bow she doth protest,
          He carries thence encagèd in his breast.

        'Sweet boy,' she says, 'this night I'll waste in sorrow,
        For my sick heart commands mine eyes to watch.
585   Tell me, love's master, shall we meet tomorrow?
        Say, shall we, shall we? Wilt thou make the match?'
          He tells her no, tomorrow he intends
          To hunt the boar with certain of his friends.

        'The boar!' quoth she; whereat a sudden pale,
590   Like lawn° being spread upon the blushing rose,   *fine linen*
        Usurps her cheek. She trembles at his tale,
        And on his neck her yoking arms she throws.
          She sinketh down, still hanging by his neck.
          He on her belly falls, she on her back.

595 Now is she in the very lists[2] of love,
Her champion mounted for the hot encounter.
All is imaginary she doth prove.[3]
He will not manage her,° although he mount her,   *ride her (like a horse)*
That worse than Tantalus' is her annoy,[4]
600 To clip Elysium,[5] and to lack her joy.

Even so poor birds, deceived with painted grapes,
Do surfeit by the eye, and pine the maw;[6]
Even so she languisheth in her mishaps
As° those poor birds that helpless° berries saw.   *Like / unusable*
605 The warm effects° which she in him finds missing   *outward signs*
She seeks to kindle with continual kissing.

But all in vain, good queen! It will not be.
She hath assayed° as much as may be proved;°   *attempted / tried*
Her pleading hath deserved a greater fee:[7]
610 She's Love; she loves; and yet she is not loved.
'Fie, fie,' he says, 'you crush me. Let me go.
You have no reason to withhold me so.'

'Thou hadst been gone,' quoth she, 'sweet boy, ere this,
But that thou told'st me thou wouldst hunt the boar.
615 O, be advised; thou know'st not what it is
With javelin's point a churlish swine to gore,
Whose tushes,° never sheathed, he whetteth still,°   *tusks / continually*
Like to a mortal° butcher, bent° to kill.   *deadly / intending*

'On his bow-back° he hath a battle[8] set   *arched back*
620 Of bristly pikes that ever threat his foes.
His eyes like glow-worms shine; when he doth fret
His snout digs sepulchres where'er he goes.
Being moved,° he strikes, whate'er is in his way,   *angered*
And whom he strikes his crooked tushes slay.

625 'His brawny sides with hairy bristles armed
Are better proof° than thy spear's point can enter.   *armor*
His short thick neck cannot be easily harmed.
Being ireful,° on the lion he will venture.   *angry*
The thorny brambles and embracing bushes,
630 As° fearful of him, part; through whom° he rushes.   *As if / which*

'Alas, he naught esteems that face of thine,
To which love's eyes pays tributary gazes,
Nor thy soft hands, sweet lips, and crystal eyne,°   *eyes (archaic)*
Whose full perfection all the world amazes;
635 But having thee at vantage°—wondrous dread!—   *his mercy*
Would root° these beauties as he roots the mead.°   *root up / meadow*

---

2. Enclosed tournament arena.
3. The hot encounter is only imaginary, she finds.
4. Torment. In classical mythology, Tantalus was punished by eternal hunger and thirst; food and water were always visible but receded at his approach.
5. In classical mythology, the abode of the blessed dead.

clip: embrace.
6. Starve the stomach. The ancient Greek artist Zeuxis painted grapes so realistic that birds pecked at them.
7. A legal metaphor: Venus, acting as an attorney, deserves a better payment.
8. Row of armed soldiers.

'O, let him keep° his loathsome cabin° still.   *stay in / lair*
Beauty hath naught to do with such foul fiends.
Come not within his danger by thy will.
640   They that thrive well take counsel of their friends.
        When thou didst name the boar, not to dissemble,[9]
        I feared thy fortune, and my joints did tremble.

'Didst thou not mark my face? Was it not white?
Saw'st thou not signs of fear lurk in mine eye?
645   Grew I not faint, and fell I not downright?
Within my bosom, whereon thou dost lie,
        My boding heart pants, beats, and takes no rest,
        But like an earthquake shakes thee on my breast.

'For where love reigns, disturbing jealousy°   *apprehension*
650   Doth call himself affection's sentinel,
Gives false alarms, suggesteth mutiny,°   *incites rebellion*
And in a peaceful hour doth cry, "Kill, kill!",°   *(a battle cry)*
        Distemp'ring° gentle love in his desire,   *Quenching*
        As air and water do abate the fire.

655   'This sour informer, this bate-breeding° spy,   *conflict-breeding*
This canker° that eats up love's tender spring,°   *cankerworm / sprout*
This carry-tale, dissentious jealousy,
That sometime true news, sometime false doth bring,
        Knocks at my heart, and whispers in mine ear
660   That if I love thee, I thy death should fear;

'And, more than so, presenteth to mine eye
The picture of an angry chafing boar,
Under whose sharp fangs on his back doth lie
An image like thyself, all stained with gore,
665   Whose blood upon the fresh flowers being shed
        Doth make them droop with grief, and hang the head.

'What should I do, seeing thee so indeed,
That tremble at th'imagination?
The thought of it doth make my faint heart bleed,
670   And fear doth teach it divination.
        I prophesy thy death, my living sorrow,
        If thou encounter with the boar tomorrow.

'But if thou needs wilt hunt, be ruled by me:
Uncouple° at the timorous flying° hare,   *Unleash the dogs / fleeing*
675   Or at the fox which lives by subtlety,
Or at the roe which no encounter dare.
        Pursue these fearful° creatures o'er the downs,   *timid*
        And on thy well-breathed horse keep with thy hounds.

'And when thou hast on foot the purblind° hare,   *dim-sighted*
680   Mark the poor wretch, to overshoot° his troubles,   *run past*
How he outruns the wind, and with what care
He cranks and crosses° with a thousand doubles.   *twists and turns*

9. *not to dissemble:* to tell the truth.

The many musits° through the which he goes   *hedge gaps*
Are like a labyrinth to amaze° his foes.   *confuse*

685 'Sometime he runs among a flock of sheep
To make the cunning hounds mistake their smell,
And sometime where earth-delving conies° keep,   *rabbits*
To stop the loud pursuers in their yell;
     And sometime sorteth° with a herd of deer.   *consorts*
690   Danger deviseth shifts;° wit waits on fear.   *tricks*

'For there his smell with others being mingled,
The hot scent-snuffing hounds are driven to doubt,
Ceasing their clamorous cry till they have singled,
With much ado, the cold fault° cleanly out.   *lost scent*
695   Then do they spend their mouths.° Echo replies,   *give tongue*
     As if another chase were in the skies.

'By this, poor Wat,° far off upon a hill,   *(name for a hare)*
Stands on his hinder legs with list'ning ear,
To hearken if his foes pursue him still.
700 Anon their loud alarums he doth hear,
     And now his grief may be comparèd well
     To one sore sick that hears the passing-bell.[1]

'Then shalt thou see the dew-bedabbled wretch
Turn, and return, indenting° with the way.   *zigzagging*
705 Each envious° brier his weary legs do scratch;   *malicious*
Each shadow makes him stop, each murmur stay;
     For misery is trodden on by many,
     And, being low, never relieved by any.

'Lie quietly, and hear a little more;
710 Nay, do not struggle, for thou shalt not rise.
To make thee hate the hunting of the boar
Unlike myself thou hear'st me moralize,[2]
     Applying° this to that, and so to so,   *Showing the pertinence of*
     For love can comment upon every woe.

715 'Where did I leave?'° 'No matter where,' quoth he;   *leave off*
'Leave me, and then the story aptly ends.
The night is spent.' 'Why what of that?' quoth she.
'I am,' quoth he, 'expected of° my friends,   *by*
     And now 'tis dark, and going I shall fall.'
720   'In night,' quoth she, 'desire sees best of all.

'But if thou fall, O, then imagine this:
The earth, in love with thee, thy footing trips,
And all is but to rob thee of a kiss.
Rich preys° make true° men thieves; so do thy lips   *spoils / honest*
725   Make modest Dian[3] cloudy and forlorn
     Lest she should steal a kiss, and die forsworn.[4]

---

1. Bell tolled for one who has just died.
2. Although I (the goddess of love) do not usually make moral points, I do so now.
3. Goddess of the moon, hunting, and virginity, also called "Cynthia" (line 728); "cloudy" because covered with clouds, and because made sorrowful by her love of Adonis.
4. Die having violated her oath of chastity.

'Now of this dark night I perceive the reason.
Cynthia, for shame, obscures her silver shine
Till forging° nature be condemned of treason   *counterfeiting*
730   For stealing moulds from heaven, that were divine,
     Wherein she framed thee, in high heaven's despite,°   *defiance*
     To shame the sun by day and her by night.

'And therefore hath she bribed the destinies
To cross the curious° workmanship of nature,   *elaborate*
735   To mingle beauty with infirmities,
     And pure perfection with impure defeature,°   *disfigurement*
     Making it subject to the tyranny
     Of mad mischances and much misery;

'As burning fevers, agues pale and faint,
740   Life-poisoning pestilence, and frenzies wood,°   *insane fits*
     The marrow-eating sickness[5] whose attaint°   *infection*
     Disorder breeds by heating of the blood;
     Surfeits, impostumes,° grief, and damned despair   *abscesses*
     Swear nature's death for framing° thee so fair.   *making*

745   'And not the least of all these maladies
But in one minute's fight brings beauty under.
Both favour, savour,° hue, and qualities,   *beauty; smell*
     Whereat th'impartial gazer late did wonder,
     Are on the sudden wasted,° thawed, and done,   *wasted away*
750   As mountain snow melts with the midday sun.

'Therefore, despite of fruitless° chastity,   *defying barren*
Love-lacking vestals and self-loving nuns,
That on the earth would breed a scarcity
And barren dearth of daughters and of sons,
755   Be prodigal. The lamp that burns by night
     Dries up his oil to lend the world his light.

'What is thy body but a swallowing grave,
Seeming to bury that posterity
Which, by the rights of time, thou needs must have
760   If thou destroy them not in dark obscurity?
     If so, the world will hold thee in disdain,
     Sith° in thy pride so fair a hope is slain.   *Since*

'So in thyself thyself art made away,°   *destroyed*
A mischief° worse than civil, home-bred strife,   *An evil*
765   Or theirs whose desperate hands themselves do slay,
     Or butcher sire that reaves° his son of life.   *robs*
     Foul cank'ring rust the hidden treasure frets,°   *eats away*
     But gold that's put to use more gold begets.'

'Nay, then,' quoth Adon, 'You will fall again
770   Into your idle,° over-handled theme.   *unprofitable*
     The kiss I gave you is bestowed in vain,
     And all in vain you strive against the stream;

---

5. Syphilis, which attacks the bones.

For, by this black-faced night, desire's foul nurse,
Your treatise° makes me like you worse and worse.   *discussion; plea*

775 'If love have lent you twenty thousand tongues,
And every tongue more moving than your own,
Bewitching like the wanton mermaid's songs,
Yet from mine ear the tempting tune is blown;
 For know, my heart stands armèd in mine ear,
780 And will not let a false sound enter there,

'Lest the deceiving harmony should run
Into the quiet closure° of my breast,   *enclosure*
And then my little heart were quite undone,
In his bedchamber to be barred of rest.
785 No, lady, no. My heart longs not to groan,
 But soundly sleeps, while now it sleeps alone.

'What have you urged that I cannot reprove?
The path is smooth that leadeth on to danger.
I hate not love, but your device° in love,   *tactics*
790 That lends embracements unto every stranger.
 You do it for increase—O strange excuse,
 When reason is the bawd to lust's abuse!

'Call it not love, for love to heaven is fled
Since sweating lust on earth usurped his name,
795 Under whose simple° semblance he hath fed   *innocent*
Upon fresh beauty, blotting it with blame;
 Which the hot tyrant stains, and soon bereaves,
 As caterpillars do the tender leaves.

'Love comforteth, like sunshine after rain,
800 But lust's effect is tempest after sun.
Love's gentle spring doth always fresh remain;
Lust's winter comes ere summer half be done.
 Love surfeits not; lust like a glutton dies.
 Love is all truth, lust full of forgèd lies.

805 'More I could tell, but more I dare not say;
The text is old, the orator too green.
Therefore in sadness° now I will away;   *truly*
My face is full of shame, my heart of teen.°   *grief*
 Mine ears that to your wanton talk attended
810 Do burn themselves for having so offended.'

With this he breaketh from the sweet embrace
Of those fair arms which bound him to her breast,
And homeward through the dark laund° runs apace,   *glade*
Leaves love upon her back, deeply distressed.
815 Look how a bright star shooteth from the sky,
 So glides he in the night from Venus' eye,

Which after him she darts, as one on shore
Gazing upon a late-embarkèd friend
Till the wild waves will have him seen no more,

820 Whose ridges with the meeting clouds contend.
    So did the merciless and pitchy night
    Fold in the object that did feed her sight.

Whereat amazed,° as one that unaware   *shocked*
Hath dropped a precious jewel in the flood,
825 Or stonished,° as night wand'rers often are,   *confused*
Their light blown out in some mistrustful° wood: *anxiety-producing*
    Even so, confounded in the dark she lay,
    Having lost the fair discovery of her way.[6]

And now she beats her heart, whereat it groans,
830 That all the neighbour caves, as seeming troubled,
Make verbal repetition of her moans;
Passion° on passion deeply is redoubled.   *Lamentation*
    'Ay me,' she cries, and twenty times 'Woe, woe!'
    And twenty echoes twenty times cry so.

835 She, marking them, begins a wailing note,
And sings extemporally a woeful ditty,
How love makes young men thrall,° and old men dote,   *enslaved*
How love is wise in folly, foolish-witty.
    Her heavy° anthem still concludes in woe,   *sorrowful*
840   And still the choir of echoes answer so.

Her song was tedious, and outwore the night;
For lovers' hours are long, though seeming short.
If pleased themselves, others, they think, delight
In such-like circumstance, with such-like sport.
845   Their copious stories oftentimes begun
    End without audience, and are never done.

For who hath she to spend the night withal°   *with*
But idle sounds resembling parasites,°   *flattering hangers-on*
Like shrill-tongued tapsters° answering every call,   *tavern keepers*
850 Soothing the humour of fantastic wits?[7]
    She says ' 'Tis so'; they answer all ' 'Tis so',
    And would say after her, if she said 'No'.

Lo, here the gentle lark, weary of rest,
From his moist cabinet° mounts up on high   *nest*
855 And wakes the morning,° from whose silver breast   *(Aurora)*
The sun ariseth in his majesty,
    Who doth the world so gloriously behold
    That cedar tops and hills seem burnished gold.

Venus salutes him with this fair good-morrow:
860 'O thou clear° god, and patron of all light,   *bright*
From whom each lamp and shining star doth borrow
The beauteous influence[8] that makes him bright:

---

6. *the fair . . . way:* a clear view of her path; a beautiful guide.
7. Catering to the moods of erratic people.

8. The ethereal stream that in Renaissance astrology was supposed to flow from stars and planets.

There lives a son° that sucked an earthly mother   (Adonis)
May° lend thee light, as thou dost lend to other.'   Who may

865   This said, she hasteth to a myrtle grove,
      Musing° the morning is so much o'erworn°   Wondering / spent
      And yet she hears no tidings of her love.
      She hearkens for his hounds, and for his horn.
          Anon she hears them chant it lustily,°   sing out heartily
870   And all in haste she coasteth° to the cry.   rushes

      And as she runs, the bushes in the way
      Some catch her by the neck, some kiss her face,
      Some twine about her thigh to make her stay.
      She wildly breaketh from their strict° embrace,   restricting
875   Like a milch° doe whose swelling dugs° do ache,   milk / udders
          Hasting to feed her fawn hid in some brake.°   thicket

      By this° she hears the hounds are at a bay,[9]   By now
      Whereat she starts, like one that spies an adder
      Wreathed up in fatal folds just in his way,
880   The fear whereof doth make him shake and shudder;
          Even so the timorous yelping of the hounds
          Appals her senses, and her spirit confounds.

      For now she knows it is no gentle chase,
      But the blunt° boar, rough bear, or lion proud,   rude
885   Because the cry remaineth in one place,
      Where fearfully the dogs exclaim aloud.
          Finding their enemy to be so curst,°   vicious
          They all strain court'sy[1] who shall cope° him first.   contend with

      This dismal cry rings sadly in her ear,
890   Through which it enters to surprise° her heart,   assault
      Who, overcome by doubt and bloodless fear,
      With cold-pale weakness numbs each feeling part;°   sense organ
          Like soldiers when their captain once doth yield,
          They basely fly, and dare not stay° the field.   remain in

895   Thus stands she in a trembling ecstasy,°   stupor
      Till, cheering up her senses all dismayed,
      She tells them 'tis a causeless fantasy
      And childish error that they are afraid;
          Bids them leave quaking, bids them fear no more;
900   And with that word she spied the hunted boar,

      Whose frothy mouth, bepainted all with red,
      Like milk and blood being mingled both together,
      A second fear through all her sinews spread,
      Which madly hurries her, she knows not whither.
905   This way she runs, and now she will no further,
          But back retires to rate° the boar for murder.   berate

9. Stopped by the quarry, which is making a stand.   1. Politely defer to one another.

A thousand spleens° bear her a thousand ways.   *impulses*
She treads the path that she untreads again.
Her more than haste is mated° with delays,   *counteracted*
910   Like the proceedings of a drunken brain,
    Full of respects,° yet naught at all respecting;   *considerations*
    In hand with all things, naught at all effecting.[2]

Here kennelled in a brake she finds a hound,
And asks the weary caitiff° for his master;   *wretch*
915   And there another licking of his wound,
    'Gainst venomed sores the only sovereign plaster.°   *effective remedy*
    And here she meets another, sadly scowling,
    To whom she speaks; and he replies with howling.

When he hath ceased his ill-resounding noise,
920   Another flap-mouthed mourner, black and grim,
Against the welkin° volleys out his voice.   *sky*
Another, and another, answer him,
    Clapping their proud tails to the ground below,
    Shaking their scratched ears, bleeding as they go.

925   Look how the world's poor people are amazed
At apparitions, signs, and prodigies,°   *strange occurrences*
Whereon with fearful eyes they long have gazed,
Infusing them with° dreadful prophecies: *Reading into them*
    So she at these sad signs draws up her breath,
930   And, sighing it again, exclaims on° death.   *berates*

'Hard-favoured tyrant, ugly, meagre, lean,
Hateful divorce of love'—thus chides she death;
'Grim-grinning° ghost, earth's worm: what dost thou mean   *(like a skull)*
To stifle beauty, and to steal his breath
935   Who, when he lived, his breath and beauty set
    Gloss on the rose, smell to the violet?

'If he be dead—O no, it cannot be,
Seeing his beauty, thou shouldst strike at it.
O yes, it may; thou hast no eyes to see,[3]
940   But hatefully, at random dost thou hit.
    Thy mark° is feeble age; but thy false dart   *target*
    Mistakes that aim, and cleaves an infant's heart.

'Hadst thou but bid beware, then he° had spoke,   *(Adonis)*
And, hearing him, thy power had lost his° power.   *its*
945   The destinies will curse thee for this stroke.
They bid thee crop a weed; thou pluck'st a flower.
    Love's golden arrow at him should have fled,°   *flown*
    And not death's ebon dart to strike him dead.

'Dost thou drink tears, that thou provok'st such weeping?
950   What may a heavy groan advantage° thee?   *benefit*
Why hast thou cast into eternal sleeping
Those eyes that taught all other eyes to see?

---

2. Full of notions, yet actually attending to nothing.   3. Death's eye sockets are empty, like a skull's.

Now nature cares not for thy mortal vigour,[4]
Since her best work is ruined with thy rigour.'

955 Here overcome, as one full of despair,
She vailed° her eyelids, who like sluices stopped   *lowered*
The crystal tide that from her two cheeks fair
In the sweet channel of her bosom dropped.
　　But through the flood-gates breaks the silver rain,
960 　And with his strong course opens them again.

O, how her eyes and tears did lend and borrow!°   *(by reflection)*
Her eye seen in the tears, tears in her eye,
Both crystals, where they viewed each other's sorrow:
Sorrow, that friendly° sighs sought still to dry,   *consoling; like-minded*
965 　But, like a stormy day, now wind, now rain,
　　Sighs dry her cheeks, tears make them wet again.

Variable passions throng her constant woe,
As striving who should best become° her grief.   *fit*
All entertained,° each passion labours so   *permitted to enter*
970 That every present sorrow seemeth chief,
　　But none is best. Then join they all together,
　　Like many clouds consulting° for foul weather.   *gathering*

By this, far off she hears some huntsman hollo;°   *(hunting call)*
A nurse's song ne'er pleased her babe so well.
975 The dire imagination° she did follow   *train of thought*
This sound of hope doth labour to expel;
　　For now reviving joy bids her rejoice
　　And flatters her it is Adonis' voice.

Whereat her tears began to turn their tide,°   *to ebb*
980 Being prisoned in her eye like pearls in glass;
Yet sometimes falls an orient° drop beside,   *a glistening*
Which her cheek melts, as° scorning it should pass   *as if*
　　To wash the foul° face of the sluttish ground,   *dirty*
　　Who is but drunken when she seemeth drowned.

985 O hard-believing love—how strange it seems
Not to believe, and yet too credulous!
Thy weal° and woe are both of them extremes.   *prosperity*
Despair, and hope, makes thee ridiculous.
　　The one doth flatter thee in thoughts unlikely;
990 　In likely thoughts the other kills thee quickly.

Now she unweaves the web that she hath wrought.
Adonis lives, and death is not to blame.
It was not she that called him all to naught.[5]
Now she adds honours to his hateful name.
995 　She clepes° him king of graves, and grave for kings,   *calls (archaic)*
　　Imperious supreme° of all mortal things.   *Imperial ruler*

4. Nature does not heed your lethal power.　　5. She who called Death everything bad.

'No, no,' quoth she, 'sweet death, I did but jest.
Yet pardon me, I felt a kind of fear
Whenas I met the boar, that bloody beast,
1000 Which knows no pity, but is still severe.
    Then, gentle shadow—truth I must confess—
    I railed on thee, fearing my love's decease.

' 'Tis not my fault; the boar provoked my tongue.
Be wreakèd° on him, invisible commander.   *revenged*
1005 'Tis he, foul creature, that hath done thee wrong.
I did but act;° he's author of thy slander.   *(as an agent)*
    Grief hath two tongues,° and never woman yet   *is doubly loud*
    Could rule them both, without ten women's wit.'

Thus, hoping that Adonis is alive,
1010 Her rash suspect° she doth extenuate,   *suspicion*
And, that his beauty may the better thrive,
With death she humbly doth insinuate;°   *curry favor*
    Tells him of trophies, statues, tombs; and stories
    His victories, his triumphs, and his glories.

1015 'O Jove,' quoth she, 'how much a fool was I
To be of such a weak and silly mind
To wail his death who lives, and must not die
Till mutual° overthrow of mortal kind!   *universal*
    For he being dead, with him is beauty slain,
1020 And beauty dead, black chaos comes again.

'Fie, fie, fond° love, thou art as full of fear   *foolish; affectionate*
As one with treasure laden, hemmed with thieves.
Trifles unwitnessèd with eye or ear
Thy coward heart with false bethinking° grieves.'   *imagination*
1025 Even at this word she hears a merry horn,
    Whereat she leaps,° that was but late° forlorn.   *(for joy) / lately*

As falcons to the lure, away she flies.
The grass stoops not, she treads on it so light;
And in her haste unfortunately spies
1030 The foul boar's conquest on her fair delight;
    Which seen, her eyes, as murdered with the view,
    Like stars ashamed of° day, themselves withdrew.°   *put to shame by / shut*

Or as the snail, whose tender horns being hit
Shrinks backward in his shelly cave with pain,
1035 And there, all smothered up, in shade doth sit,
Long after fearing to creep forth again;
    So at his bloody view her eyes are fled
    Into the deep dark cabins of her head,

Where they resign their office and their light
1040 To the disposing of her troubled brain,
Who bids them still consort with° ugly night,   *always accompany*
And never wound the heart with looks again,
    Who,° like a king perplexèd° in his throne,   *(the heart) / troubled*
    By their suggestion° gives a deadly groan,   *(the eyes') incitement*

1045 Whereat each tributary subject[6] quakes,
As when the wind, imprisoned in the ground,
Struggling for passage, earth's foundation shakes,[7]
Which with cold terror doth men's minds confound.
    This mutiny each part doth so surprise°   *assail*
1050   That from their dark beds once more leap her eyes,

And, being opened, threw unwilling light
Upon the wide wound that the boar had trenched
In his soft flank, whose wonted° lily-white   *usual*
With purple tears that his wound wept was drenched.
1055   No flower was nigh, no grass, herb, leaf, or weed,
    But stole his blood, and seemed with him to bleed.

This solemn sympathy poor Venus noteth.
Over one shoulder doth she hang her head.
Dumbly° she passions,° franticly she doteth.   *Mutely / suffers*
1060 She thinks he could not die, he is not dead.
    Her voice is stopped, her joints forget to bow,°   *cannot bend*
    Her eyes are mad that they have wept till° now.   *before*

Upon his hurt she looks so steadfastly
That her sight, dazzling,° makes the wound seem three;   *blurring*
1065 And then she reprehends her mangling eye,
That makes more gashes where no breach should be.
    His face seems twain; each several limb is doubled;
    For oft the eye mistakes, the brain being troubled.

'My tongue cannot express my grief for one,
1070 And yet,' quoth she, 'behold two Adons dead!
My sighs are blown away, my salt tears gone,
Mine eyes are turned to fire, my heart to lead.
    Heavy heart's lead, melt at mine eyes' red fire!
    So shall I die by drops of hot desire.

1075 'Alas, poor world, what treasure hast thou lost,
What face remains alive that's worth the viewing?
Whose tongue is music now? What canst thou boast
Of things long since, or anything ensuing?
    The flowers are sweet, their colours fresh and trim;
1080   But true sweet beauty lived and died with him.

'Bonnet nor veil henceforth no creature wear:°   *(to preserve complexion)*
Nor sun nor wind will ever strive to kiss you.
Having no fair° to lose, you need not fear.   *beauty*
The sun doth scorn you, and the wind doth hiss you.
1085   But when Adonis lived, sun and sharp air
    Lurked like two thieves to rob him of his fair;

'And therefore would he put his bonnet on,
Under whose brim the gaudy sun would peep.
The wind would blow it off, and, being gone,

---

6. Each inferior organ of Venus's body.   7. Sixteenth-century explanation of earthquakes.

1090 Play with his locks; then would Adonis weep,
And straight,° in pity of his tender years,   *immediately*
They both would strive who first should dry his tears.

'To see his face the lion walked along
Behind some hedge, because he would not fear° him.   *frighten*
1095 To recreate° himself° when he hath sung,   *entertain / (Adonis)*
The tiger would be tame, and gently hear him.
If he had spoke, the wolf would leave his prey,
And never fright the silly° lamb that day.   *innocent*

'When he beheld his shadow in the brook,
1100 The fishes spread on it their golden gills.
When he was by, the birds such pleasure took
That some would sing, some other in their bills
Would bring him mulberries and ripe-red cherries.
He fed them with his sight, they him with berries.

1105 'But this foul, grim, and urchin-snouted° boar,   *hedgehog-snouted*
Whose downward eye still looketh for a grave,
Ne'er saw the beauteous livery⁸ that he wore:
Witness the entertainment° that he gave.   *reception*
If he did see his face, why then, I know
1110 He thought to kiss him, and hath killed him so.

' 'Tis true, 'tis true; thus was Adonis slain;
He ran upon the boar with his sharp spear,
Who did not whet his teeth at him again,°   *in return*
But by a kiss thought to persuade him° there,   *win him over*
1115 And, nuzzling in his flank, the loving swine
Sheathed unaware the tusk in his soft groin.

'Had I been toothed like him, I must confess
With kissing him I should have killed him first;
But he is dead, and never did he bless
1120 My youth with his, the more am I accursed.'
With this she falleth in the place she stood,
And stains her face with his congealèd blood.

She looks upon his lips, and they are pale.
She takes him by the hand, and that is cold.
1125 She whispers in his ears a heavy tale,
As if they heard the woeful words she told.
She lifts the coffer-lids° that close his eyes,   *treasure chest lids*
Where lo, two lamps burnt out in darkness lies;

Two glasses, where herself herself beheld
1130 A thousand times, and now no more reflect,
Their virtue° lost, wherein they late excelled,   *power*
And every beauty robbed of his° effect.   *its*
'Wonder of time,' quoth she, 'this is my spite,°   *torment*
That, thou being dead, the day should yet be light.

8. His appearance (literally, garment).

1135 'Since thou art dead, lo, here I prophesy
Sorrow on love hereafter shall attend.
It° shall be waited on with jealousy,   *(Love)*
Find sweet beginning, but unsavoury end;
Ne'er settled equally, but high or low,[9]
1140   That all love's pleasure shall not match his woe.

'It shall be fickle, false, and full of fraud,
Bud, and be blasted,° in a breathing-while:°   *blighted / moment*
The bottom poison, and the top o'erstrawed°   *strewn over*
With sweets that shall the truest sight beguile.
1145   The strongest body shall it make most weak,
Strike the wise dumb,° and teach the fool to speak.   *mute*

'It shall be sparing,° and too full of riot,°   *miserly / excess*
Teaching decrepit age to tread the measures.[1]
The staring° ruffian shall it keep in quiet,   *glaring*
1150 Pluck down the rich, enrich the poor with treasures;
It shall be raging-mad, and silly-mild;
Make the young old, the old become a child.

'It shall suspect where is no cause of fear;
It shall not fear where it should most mistrust.
1155 It shall be merciful, and too severe,
And most deceiving when it seems most just.°   *honest*
Perverse it shall be where it shows most toward,[2]
Put fear to valour, courage to the coward.

'It shall be cause of war and dire events,
1160 And set dissension 'twixt the son and sire;
Subject and servile to all discontents,[3]
As dry combustious matter is to fire.
Sith° in his prime death doth my love destroy,   *Since*
They that love best their loves shall not enjoy.'

1165 By this, the boy that by her side lay killed
Was melted like a vapour from her sight,
And in his blood that on the ground lay spilled
A purple flower sprung up, chequered with white,°   *(the anemone)*
Resembling well his pale cheeks, and the blood
1170   Which in round drops upon their whiteness stood.

She bows her head the new-sprung flower to smell,
Comparing it to her Adonis' breath,
And says within her bosom it shall dwell,
Since he himself is reft° from her by death.   *torn*
1175   She crops the stalk, and in the breach appears
Green-dropping sap, which she compares to tears.

'Poor flower,' quoth she, 'this was thy father's guise°—   *habit*
Sweet issue° of a more sweet-smelling sire—   *offspring; emission*

---

9. Ne'er . . . low: love shall involve extremes of happiness
and grief rather than equanimity; lovers shall come from
different social stations.

1. To dance (inappropriately).
2. It shall be stubborn where it seems most compliant.
3. Cause and slave of all discontentedness.

For every little grief to wet his eyes.
1180 To grow unto himself° was his desire,   *mature independently*
     And so 'tis thine; but know it is as good
     To wither in my breast as in his blood.

'Here was thy father's bed, here in my breast.
Thou art the next of blood,° and 'tis thy right.   *heir (with wordplay)*
1185 Lo, in this hollow cradle take thy rest;
My throbbing heart shall rock thee day and night.
     There shall not be one minute in an hour
     Wherein I will not kiss my sweet love's flower.'

Thus, weary of the world, away she hies,
1190 And yokes her silver doves, by whose swift aid
Their mistress, mounted, through the empty skies
In her light chariot quickly is conveyed,
     Holding their course to Paphos,[4] where their queen
     Means to immure° herself, and not be seen.   *confine*

TEXTUAL VARIANTS

Control text: Q1

Q1: The Quarto of 1593
Q2, Q3, Q7: Successive printings of Q1 that incorporate various corrections.

466 loss loue
680 overshoot ouer-shut [The Oxford editors point out that "shut" is a spelling variant of
    "shoot" in the early modern period.]
748 th'impartial [Q2] the th'impartiall
1031 as [Q3] are
1054 was [Q7] had

---

4. Venus's abode in Cyprus.

The Rape of Lucrece

In the dedication to *Venus and Adonis* in 1593, Shakespeare promised his patron the Earl of Southampton a "graver labor"; a year later, *The Rape of Lucrece* delivered on his pledge. The two poems have much in common: their classical inspiration; their lush, highly rhetorical narrative verse; their interest in the dynamic of a one-sided sexual passion. And like *Venus and Adonis*, *The Rape of Lucrece* was a popular success, reprinted at least six times during Shakespeare's lifetime. But whereas *Venus and Adonis*, despite its sad end, remains playful even in its pathos, *The Rape of Lucrece* treats a tragic subject of political as well as sexual consequence. Shakespeare's contemporary Gabriel Harvey captures the difference in the two poems when he comments that *Venus and Adonis* pleases "the younger sort," while *The Rape of Lucrece*, like *Hamlet*, pleases "the wiser sort."

Today *The Rape of Lucrece* is commonly regarded far less highly than the play with which Harvey classifies it. The change in estimation suggests that Shakespeare's original readers came to the poem with generic expectations, literary tastes, and interpretive equipment rather different from our own. One important difference is the greater familiarity many Renaissance readers would have had with Shakespeare's sources, a familiarity that left them free to concentrate on the ways in which the poet was varying or amplifying on well-known prototypes. Slightly different versions of the tale of Tarquin and Lucretia were available in Livy's history of Rome and in Ovid's *Fasti*, both commonly read in Elizabethan grammar schools. In 509 B.C., Rome's king was Tarquin the Proud, a good military leader but an oppressive ruler over his own subjects. Tarquinius Sextus, the king's son, raped Lucretia, the wife of Collatinus, one of his aristocratic retainers. Lucretia committed suicide after revealing the crime to her male relatives and exhorting them to revenge her. After her corpse was exhibited in the Roman Forum, a wholesale revolt against the Tarquins erupted, led by the king's nephew Lucius Junius Brutus. The royal family was exiled, and Rome became a republic, ruled by a senate and administered by one or more elected "consuls," of which Lucius Junius Brutus was the first.

For the Renaissance as well as for its original Roman audience, the story of Tarquin and Lucrece displayed vividly the inextricability of domestic and civic order, of public and private realms, of sexual and political violence. As a political fable, it suggested circumstances in which subjects were permitted, even obliged, to challenge the authority of their sovereign. In the late sixteenth century, when monarchies in western Europe were strengthening their power at the expense of parliaments and the higher aristocracy, the story could be cited as a precedent for resisting tyranny.

Purely as a sexual melodrama too, the story had wide appeal. Again and again, Renaissance painters portrayed Tarquin stealing into Lucretia's bed, Lucretia stabbing herself, and Lucius Junius Brutus exhorting over her body in the marketplace, often incorporating all three scenes into the same picture. Lucretia became a focus of especially fierce debate. On the one hand, she seemed a model of wifely duty, a woman to whom marital fidelity was not merely a matter of social respectability but a fundamental life principle. On the other hand, suicide by the sword—the traditional last, defiant gesture of heroic Roman men—could seem improperly self-assertive in a woman. Moreover, some Christian writers considered Lucretia's suicide not merely indecorous but sinful. In *The City of God*, Augustine argued that since virtues are properties of the will and not the body, Lucretia was innocent of unchastity. But ironically, her sexual blamelessness rendered her suicide completely inexcusable; Augustine considered her a murderess who had taken her own life out of unchristian pride. By Shakespeare's time, therefore, Lucretia could be held up, variously, as a model of female propriety and as an example of pagan willfulness, as a

Lucretia. Raphael.

woman who both upholds and breaks from the usual constraints upon her sex.

Adapting the story to his own purposes, Shakespeare makes interesting changes of detail and emphasis. As Ovid and Livy recount it, the story of violation, suicide, and revolution is full of turbulent physical action and unexpected revelations: and in Livy especially, the political consequences of the rape receive much more attention than the sexual assault itself. Shakespeare's version downplays— though it does not eliminate—the political aspects of the story, and it contains most of the feverish momentum of the original story in the prefatory "Argument": "The same night he treacherously stealeth into her chamber, violently ravished her, and early in the morning speedeth away. Lucrece, in this lamentable plight, hastily dispatcheth messengers." The poem itself, by contrast, concentrates not upon moments of violence or haste but upon what precedes and follows those moments: what Tarquin thinks on his way to Lucrece's bedchamber, how Lucrece occupies herself between the time she sends off her messenger and Collatine's return.

Like *Venus and Adonis, The Rape of Lucrece* eschews eventfulness for elaborate psychological analysis, attempting to capture in verse the uneven surge and flow of troubled, self-divided consciousnesses. In Shakespeare's hands, the story of Tarquin and Lucrece becomes a story about how people make choices that lead to violence. Everything in the poem is the consequence of a decision, not an accident of fate, and nothing seems inevitable. The poem teases the reader with alternative possibilities. What if Collatine had kept his marital happiness to himself? What if Tarquin's conscience had overcome his lust? What if Lucrece's beauty had blinded Tarquin permanently instead of temporarily? What if Collatine had arrived to save Lucrece at the last moment? What if Lucrece had resolved to kill Tarquin rather than herself?

In large part, these alternatives receive so much attention because both Tarquin and Lucrece make decisions that fail to reflect their best interests. The poem is constantly suggesting that they would be better off doing something else, and interestingly, the characters themselves at times seem lucidly aware of that fact. Tarquin tells himself that his assault will desecrate the very virtue he admires in Lucrece, destroy his own self-respect, and bring dishonor upon his family. Then he rapes Lucrece. Lucrece argues to herself what her husband and father will tell her later: that she cannot incur guilt by a sexual act to which she has not consented, and that therefore she need not take her own life. Then she commits suicide.

In both cases, the characters' stubborn refusal to acknowledge the obvious seems to follow from their tendency to conceive of themselves in terms of a few crucial metaphors. In Tarquin's case, the metaphors are military: "Affection is my captain, and he leadeth, / . . . My heart shall never countermand mine eye" (lines 271, 276). Such images attract Tarquin because they portray a rash, grossly disorderly act in terms of strict discipline. Even as he overturns the proper subordination of passion to reason, he elaborates a clear, if perverse, hierarchy of priorities. Moreover, by casting himself as a warrior and Lucrece as an enemy territory, Tarquin minimizes the blame that attaches to rape, an act conventionally associated with (and often excused in) soldiers pillaging an enemy town.

Of course, as Lucrece reminds him, she is not his foe, and Tarquin's actions violate not only her bodily integrity but her husband's trust in a friend and superior. Her pleas show how tendentious are Tarquin's interpretations of the metaphors he attaches to himself. When Tarquin describes himself as an "uncontrollèd tide," and therefore intractable to entreaties, Lucrece attempts to modify the sense of the metaphor:

> 'Thou art,' quoth she, 'a sea, a sovereign king,
> And lo, there falls into thy boundless flood
> Black lust, dishonour, shame, misgoverning,
> Who seek to stain the ocean of thy blood.'
>   (lines 652–55)

Likewise, her account of his psychological state replaces the military metaphor of battle against an enemy with one of civil order temporarily disrupted:

> I sue for exiled majesty's repeal;
> Let him return, and flatt'ring thoughts retire.
> His true respect will prison false desire.
>   (lines 640–42)

Eventually, the rape that Tarquin tries to think of as an orderly military maneuver leads not only to his psychological fragmentation and self-torment but to literal exile, an exile Lucrece describes as already having occurred metaphorically.

After the rape and Tarquin's departure, the narrative focus shifts to Lucrece. Although she knows that she is not intentionally guilty of breaking her marital vows, she nonetheless construes herself as culpable. Like her violator, Lucrece thinks of herself and her body in symbolic terms, although in her case the governing metaphors are fortress, house, mansion, temple, tree. By emphasizing the protective function of the body, these metaphors make it easy for Lucrece to think of herself as irreparably damaged once her body has been assaulted by Tarquin's lust:

> Ay me, the bark peeled from the lofty pine
> His leaves will wither and his sap decay;
> So must my soul, her bark being peeled away.
>   (lines 1167–69)

Once Tarquin sacks and batters Lucrece's fortress, she suffers regardless of her innocence, like the inhabitant of a plundered town. Of course, like Tarquin, Lucrece interprets such metaphors tendentiously: she could just as well think of the "bark" or the "house" that shelters her soul as a morally insignificant excrescence. Instead, when the condition of her body seems to conflict with the condition of her soul, she desperately attempts to resolve the inconsistency by declaring herself irredeemably contaminated. In doing so, she endorses—indeed, almost celebrates—a literally fatal ambivalence in the definition of female chastity. For despite Augustine's objections, female chastity ordinarily refers to a physical condition as well as to a mental attitude in cultures that value female bodily intactness; this ambivalence still haunts rape survivors today, who often blame themselves for their own victimization.

Comprehensible though Lucrece's suicide may be in these terms, however, it is ironically fraught with the very contradictions she seeks to avoid. She "revenges" herself upon Tarquin by completing the assault he began, plunging the phallic blade into what Shakespeare calls the "sheath" of her breast (the Latin word for "sheath" is *vagina*). She insists that she is acting in Collatine's interests even while she ignores his wishes; she proves her innocence by demanding of herself that she pay the penalty for guilt; she validates her version of the rape story by silencing herself more effectively than Tarquin had with the bedclothes.

Although the metaphors Tarquin and Lucrece use to think about their respective situations are, therefore, highly problematic, they are definitely not arbitrary. Both protagonists derive their figures of speech from the same medieval and Renaissance poetic tradition

Tarquino e Lucrezia. Titian.

Shakespeare had already drawn upon in *Venus and Adonis*. The configuration of characters—the warrior-lover desperately pursuing his passion, the beautiful woman whose chastity makes her irresistibly desirable—is likewise conventional. Shakespeare suggests the importance of this poetic mentality for *The Rape of Lucrece* by anachronistically importing the language of chivalry into a poem about ancient Rome: Tarquin agonizes about the consequences of his transgression for his family's coat of arms, and Lucrece accuses him of breaking "knighthood, gentry, and sweet friendship's oath" (line 569). This is closer to the world of Thomas Malory's Arthurian romances, Thomas Wyatt's sonnets, Philip Sidney's *Arcadia*, or Edmund Spenser's *Faerie Queene* than it is to the world of Livy or Ovid.

In fact, it is possible to see *The Rape of Lucrece*, like *Venus and Adonis*, as attempting to renovate a rhetoric of sexual passion that had begun to seem trite by Shakespeare's time. But the two poems employ almost exactly opposite strategies of renewal. *Venus and Adonis* surprises the reader by turning conventional expectations of gendered behavior upside down, assigning the aggressive, desiring role to the woman and casting the male as an uncorrupted fortress of virtue. *The Rape of Lucrece*, on the other hand, pushes the conventional language of love poetry in a relentlessly literal direction, making it interesting by unleashing the latent ferocity and misogyny of a courtly love aesthetic. Lovers in the poetry of Spenser and Sidney, Petrarch and Wyatt, think of themselves as soldiers of desire, but they are so awed by their mistresses that aggressive thoughts are quenched by a mere glance from their imperious beloveds. Shakespeare's Tarquin, in contrast, more consistent and less exquisitely sensitive, uses the implicitly coercive rhetoric of love poetry as a pretext for rape.

Given the poem's intense concern with the use and misuse of language, it is not surprising that *The Rape of Lucrece* is also attentive to the relationship of rhetoric to other forms of representation. Again and again, the poem pauses to consider the relative power and conviction of linguistic and visual experience, of the ear and the eye. At some points in the poem, vision seems the privileged sense, giving immediate access to the unquestionably real. "Beauty itself doth of itself persuade / The eyes of men without an orator," the narrator declares; "To see sad sights moves more than hear them told" (lines 29–30, 1324). Yet Shakespeare alters his sources to have Tarquin provoked to lust not by the sight of Lucrece but by Collatine's report of her; and he dwells too on Lucrece's inability to divine Tarquin's motives from his appearance.

This persistent concern with the relative adequacy of different representational modes culminates in a long passage in which Lucrece contemplates a tapestry of Troy. In multiple ways, the tapestry is relevant to her own case, for the Trojan War was the consequence of a rape, and after the city's destruction, Trojan exiles were supposed to have founded Rome. After Lucrece's suicide, the account of her rape will provide the pretext for another founding, that of the Roman Republic. Eventually, her story will be displayed by artists in the same way that the legend of Troy is illustrated here—a series of chronologically distinct episodes represented simultaneously on the same panel. As Lucrece gazes at the painter's

The death of Lucretia. From Jost Amman, *Icones Livianae* (1572).

vast panorama of violation, the poet emphasizes both the vivid realism of the depiction and the artificial means by which that realism is produced: "Here one man's hand leaned on another's head, / His nose being shadowed by his neighbour's ear" (lines 1415–16). Portraying people according to the laws of perspective makes them look "natural," but it also reduces them to a collection of grotesquely amputated shapes. Like *Venus and Adonis*, *The Rape of Lucrece* invokes nature as a category of value and then subverts it; but whereas the earlier poem undermines "nature" by suggesting that its supposed precepts are inadequate, the later poem undermines "nature" by suggesting that its effect is only achieved by extraordinary artifice. Shakespeare will consider the issue again in such plays as *A Midsummer Night's Dream*, *The Winter's Tale*, *The Tempest*, and, of course, *Hamlet*. Perhaps Gabriel Harvey was right after all.

KATHARINE EISAMAN MAUS

TEXTUAL NOTE

Richard Field was the printer for *The Rape of Lucrece*, published in 1594, as he had been for *Venus and Adonis* the previous year. Like *Venus and Adonis*, *Lucrece* in its printed state probably derives directly from Shakespeare's manuscript, and it presents relatively few textual difficulties. Some editors question whether Shakespeare wrote the prefatory "Argument." A few variations among surviving copies of the first quarto represent proof corrections; in Elizabethan times, proofreading was done while the work was in the process of being printed, so corrections could appear in some copies but not in others.

SELECTED BIBLIOGRAPHY

Donaldson, Ian. *The Rapes of Lucretia: A Myth and Its Transformations.* Oxford: Oxford University Press, 1982.

Fineman, Joel. "Shakespeare's Will: The Temporality of Rape." *Representations* 20 (Fall 1987): 25–76.

Kahn, Coppélia. "The Rape in Shakespeare's *Lucrece.*" *Shakespeare Studies* 9 (1976): 45–72.

Kramer, Jerome, and Kaminsky, Judith. " 'These Contraries Such Unity Do Hold': Structure in *The Rape of Lucrece.*" *Mosaic* 10 (1977): 143–55.

Maus, Katharine Eisaman. "Taking Tropes Seriously: Language and Violence in Shakespeare's *Rape of Lucrece.*" *Shakespeare Quarterly* 37 (1986): 66–82.

Vickers, Nancy. "The Blazon of Sweet Beauty's Best: Shakespeare's *Lucrece.*" *Shakespeare and the Question of Theory.* Ed. Patricia Parker and Geoffrey Hartman. New York: Methuen, 1985. 95–115

The Rape of Lucrece

TO THE RIGHT HONOURABLE
HENRY WRIOTHESLEY,
EARL OF SOUTHAMPTON AND
BARON OF TITCHFIELD[1]

The love I dedicate to your lordship is without end, whereof this pamphlet° without beginning[2] is but a superfluous moiety.° The warrant° I have of your honourable disposition, not the worth of my untutored lines, makes it assured of acceptance. What I have done is yours; what I have to do is yours, being part in all I have, devoted yours. Were my worth greater my duty would show greater, meantime, as it is, it is bound to your lordship, to whom I wish long life still° lengthened with all happiness.

                      YOUR LORDSHIP'S IN ALL DUTY,
                      WILLIAM SHAKESPEARE

short work / part
assurance

continually

THE ARGUMENT°

plot

Lucius Tarquinius (for his excessive pride surnamed Superbus),° after he had caused his own father-in-law Servius Tullius to be cruelly murdered, and, contrary to the Roman laws and customs, not requiring[3] or staying for the people's suffrages° had possessed himself of the kingdom, went accompanied with his sons and other noblemen of Rome to besiege Ardea,[4] during which siege the principal men of the army meeting one evening at the tent of Sextus Tarquinius, the King's son, in their discourses after supper everyone commended the virtues of his own wife, among whom Collatinus extolled the incomparable chastity of his wife, Lucretia. In that pleasant humour° they all posted° to Rome, and, intending by their secret and sudden arrival to make trial of that which everyone had before avouched, only Collatinus finds his wife (though it were late in the night) spinning amongst her maids. The other ladies were all found dancing, and revelling, or in several disports.° Whereupon the noblemen yielded Collatinus the victory and his wife the fame. At that time Sextus Tarquinius, being enflamed with Lucrece' beauty, yet smothering his passions for the present, departed with the rest back to the camp, from whence he shortly after privily° withdrew himself and was, according to his estate,° royally entertained and lodged by Lucrece at Collatium.[5] The same night he treacherously stealeth into her chamber, violently ravished her, and early in the morning speedeth away. Lucrece, in this lamentable plight, hastily dispatcheth messengers—

"the Proud"

approval

merry mood
hurried

diversions

secretly
rank

Dedication and **Argument**
1. See *Venus and Adonis*, note 2 to Dedication.
2. *The Rape of Lucrece* begins *in medias res* (in the middle of the story), as the Latin poet Horace recommends in *The Art of Poetry.*

3. Not asking for.
4. City twenty-five miles south of Rome.
5. Town ten miles east of Rome; the ancestral home of Collatinus's family.

one to Rome for her father, another to the camp for Collatine. They
came, the one accompanied with Junius Brutus, the other with
Publius Valerius, and, finding Lucrece attired in mourning habit,
demanded the cause of her sorrow. She, first taking an oath of them
for her revenge, revealed the actor° and whole manner of his dealing,   *doer*
and withal° suddenly stabbed herself. Which done, with one consent   *moreover*
they all vowed to root out the whole hated family of the Tarquins,
and, bearing the dead body to Rome, Brutus acquainted the people
with the doer and manner of the vile deed, with a bitter invective
against the tyranny of the King; wherewith the people were so moved
that with one consent and a general acclamation the Tarquins were
all exiled and the state government changed from kings to consuls.[6]

    From the besieged Ardea all in post,°   *haste*
    Borne by the trustless wings of false desire,
    Lust-breathèd° Tarquin leaves the Roman host   *Lust-inspired*
    And to Collatium bears the lightless° fire   *smoldering*
5   Which, in pale embers hid, lurks to aspire°   *rise up*
        And girdle with embracing flames the waist
        Of Collatine's fair love, Lucrece the chaste.

    Haply° that name of chaste unhapp'ly° set   *Perhaps / unfortunately*
    This bateless° edge on his keen appetite,   *unbluntable*
10   When Collatine unwisely did not let°   *forbear*
    To praise the clear unmatchèd red and white
    Which triumphed in that sky of his delight,°   *(Lucrece's face)*
        Where mortal stars° as bright as heaven's beauties   *(her eyes)*
        With pure aspects[1] did him peculiar° duties.   *exclusive*

15   For he the night before in Tarquin's tent
    Unlocked the treasure of his happy state,
    What priceless wealth the heavens had him lent
    In the possession of his beauteous mate,
    Reck'ning his fortune at such high-proud rate
20   That kings might be espousèd to more fame,
      But° king nor peer to such a peerless dame.   *But neither*

    O happiness enjoyed but of° a few,   *only by*
    And, if possessed, as soon decayed and done
    As is the morning's silver melting dew
25   Against the golden splendour of the sun,
    An expired date° cancelled ere well begun!   *time limit*
      Honour and beauty in the owner's arms
      Are weakly fortressed from a world of harms.

    Beauty itself doth of° itself persuade   *by*
30   The eyes of men without an orator.
    What needeth then apology be made
    To set forth that which is so singular?°   *unique*

6. Chief magistrates, elected for one-year terms.   **Poem**
                                      1. Looks; astral influences.

Or why is Collatine the publisher° *publicizer*
  Of that rich jewel he should keep unknown
35   From thievish ears, because it is his own?

Perchance his boast of Lucrece' sov'reignty° *superiority*
Suggested° this proud issue° of a king, *Tempted / offspring*
For by our ears our hearts oft tainted be.
Perchance that envy of so rich a thing,
40 Braving compare,° disdainfully did sting *Defying comparison*
    His high-pitched thoughts, that meaner° men should vaunt° *inferior / boast*
    That golden hap° which their superiors want.° *luck / lack*

But some untimely thought did instigate
His all-too-timeless° speed, if none of those. *untimely; rapid*
45 His honour, his affairs, his friends, his state° *rank*
Neglected all, with swift intent he goes
To quench the coal which in his liver° glows. *(seat of lust)*
    O rash false heat, wrapped in repentant cold,
    Thy hasty spring still blasts° and ne'er grows old! *is always frostbitten*

50 When at Collatium this false lord arrived,
  Well was he welcomed by the Roman dame,
  Within whose face beauty and virtue strived
  Which of them both should underprop her fame.
  When virtue bragged, beauty would blush for shame;
55   When beauty boasted blushes, in despite° *defiance*
    Virtue would stain° that or° with silver white. *dye / gold*

But beauty, in that white entitulèd° *claiming title*
From Venus' doves, doth challenge that fair field.[2]
Then virtue claims from beauty beauty's red,
60 Which virtue gave the golden age to gild[3]
Their silver cheeks, and called it then their shield,
    Teaching them thus to use it in the fight:
    When shame assailed, the red should fence° the white. *defend*

This heraldry in Lucrece' face was seen,
65 Argued° by beauty's red and virtue's white. *Demonstrated; disputed*
Of either's colour was the other queen,
Proving from world's minority° their right. *earliest age*
Yet their ambition makes them still to fight,
    The sovereignty of either being so great
70   That oft they interchange each other's seat.

This silent war of lilies and of roses
Which Tarquin viewed in her fair face's field
In their pure ranks his traitor eye encloses,
Where, lest between them both it should be killed,
75 The coward captive vanquishèd doth yield
    To those two armies that would let him go
    Rather than triumph in° so false a foe. *over*

2. Territory; battlefield; surface on which a coat of arms is displayed. *Venus' doves*: white turtledoves draw the chariot of Venus, the love goddess.
3. Coat with gold; cover with red (as in a blush). *the golden age*: a mythical, ideal era of innocence and plenty.

Now thinks he that her husband's shallow tongue,
The niggard prodigal that praised her so,
80 In that high task hath done her beauty wrong,
Which far exceeds his barren skill to show.°   *describe*
Therefore that praise which Collatine doth owe°   *fail to render*
    Enchanted Tarquin answers° with surmise   *compensates for*
    In silent wonder of still-gazing eyes.

85 This earthly saint adorèd by this devil
Little suspecteth the false worshipper,
For unstained thoughts do seldom dream on evil.
Birds never limed° no secret bushes fear,   *trapped*
So guiltless she securely° gives good cheer[4]   *unsuspectingly*
90   And reverent welcome to her princely guest,
    Whose inward ill no outward harm expressed,

For that he coloured° with his high estate,   *disguised*
Hiding base sin in pleats° of majesty,   *folds*
That° nothing in him seemed inordinate   *So that*
95 Save sometime too much wonder of his eye,
Which, having all, all could not satisfy,
    But poorly rich so wanteth in his store°   *plenty*
    That, cloyed with much, he pineth still for more.

But she that never coped with stranger° eyes   *strangers'*
100 Could pick no meaning from their parling° looks,   *persuasive*
Nor read the subtle shining secrecies
Writ in the glassy margins[5] of such books.
She touched no unknown baits nor feared no hooks,
    Nor could she moralize° his wanton sight°   *interpret / looking*
105   More than his eyes were opened to the light.[6]

He stories to her ears her husband's fame
Won in the fields of fruitful Italy,
And decks with praises Collatine's high name
Made glorious by his manly chivalry
110 With bruisèd arms° and wreaths of victory.   *dented weapons*
    Her joy with heaved-up hand she doth express,
    And wordless so greets heaven for his success.

Far from the purpose of his coming thither
He makes excuses for his being there.
115 No cloudy show of stormy blust'ring weather
Doth yet in his fair welkin° once appear   *sky (face)*
Till sable° night, mother of dread and fear,   *black*
    Upon the world dim darkness doth display
    And in her vaulty prison stows the day.

120 For then is Tarquin brought unto his bed,
Intending° weariness with heavy sprite;°   *Pretending / spirit*
For after supper long he questionèd°   *conversed*
With modest Lucrece, and wore out the night.

4. Hospitable entertainment.   placed.
5. Where summaries and interpretive remarks were often   6. Were made obvious.

Now leaden slumber with life's strength doth fight,
125   And everyone to rest himself betakes
       Save thieves, and cares, and troubled minds that wakes.

As one of which doth Tarquin lie revolving°   *considering*
The sundry dangers of his will's obtaining,°   *gratifying his desire*
Yet ever to obtain his will resolving,
130 Though weak-built hopes[7] persuade him to abstaining.
Despair to gain doth traffic oft for gaining,[8]
       And when great treasure is the meed° proposed,   *prize*
       Though death be adjunct,[9] there's no death supposed.°   *thought of*

Those that much covet are with gain so fond°   *infatuated*
135 That what° they have not, that which they possess,   *That for what*
They scatter and unloose it from their bond,°   *ownership*
And so by hoping more they have but less,
Or, gaining more, the profit° of excess   *advantage*
       Is but to surfeit and such griefs[1] sustain
140   That they° prove bankrupt in this poor-rich gain.   *(the covetous)*

The aim of all is but to nurse the life
With honour, wealth, and ease in waning age,
And in this aim there is such thwarting strife
That one for all, or all for one, we gage,°   *risk*
145 As° life for honour in fell° battle's rage,   *For instance / cruel*
       Honour for wealth; and oft that wealth doth cost
       The death of all, and all together lost.

So that, in vent'ring ill,[2] we leave to be
The things we are for that which we expect,
150 And this ambitious foul infirmity
In having° much, torments us with defect   *While we have*
Of that we have; so then we do neglect
       The thing we have, and all for want of wit°   *lack of sense*
       Make something nothing by augmenting it.

155 Such hazard now must doting Tarquin make,
Pawning his honour to obtain his lust,
And for himself himself he must forsake.
Then where is truth if there be no self-trust?°   *truth to oneself*
When shall he think to find a stranger just
160   When he himself himself confounds, betrays
       To sland'rous tongues and wretched hateful days?

Now stole upon the time the dead of night
When heavy sleep had closed up mortal eyes.
No comfortable star did lend his° light,   *its*
165 No noise but owls' and wolves' death-boding cries
Now serves the season, that they may surprise
       The silly° lambs. Pure thoughts are dead and still,   *innocent*
       While lust and murder wakes to stain° and kill.   *defile*

---

7. The fact that his hopes are flimsy.
8. Despair of gaining her (rightfully) often encourages him to gain her (by any means possible).
9. Be joined with it.
1. That is, the ills that accompany excess.
2. In taking serious risks; in undertaking evil deeds.

And now this lustful lord leapt from his bed,
170 Throwing his mantle rudely o'er his arm,
Is madly tossed between desire and dread.
Th'one sweetly flatters, th'other feareth harm,
But honest fear, bewitched with lust's foul charm,
    Doth too-too oft betake him to retire,°   *retreat*
175   Beaten away by brainsick rude desire.

His falchion° on a flint he softly smiteth,   *curved sword*
That from the cold stone sparks of fire do fly,
Whereat a waxen torch forthwith he lighteth,
Which must be lodestar° to his lustful eye,   *guiding light*
180 And to the flame thus speaks advisedly:°   *deliberately*
    'As from this cold flint I enforced this fire,
    So Lucrece must I force to my desire.'

Here pale with fear he doth premeditate
The dangers of his loathsome enterprise,
185 And in his inward mind he doth debate
What following sorrow may on this arise.
Then, looking scornfully, he doth despise
    His naked armour of still-slaughtered lust,[3]
    And justly thus controls° his thoughts unjust: *rebukes; restrains*

190 'Fair torch, burn out thy light, and lend it not
To darken her whose light excelleth thine;
And die, unhallowed thoughts, before you blot
With your uncleanness that which is divine.
Offer pure incense to so pure a shrine.
195   Let fair humanity abhor the deed
    That spots and stains love's modest snow-white weed.° *attire (chastity)*

'O shame to knighthood and to shining arms!
O foul dishonour to my household's grave!°   *ancestral tomb*
O impious act including° all foul harms!   *encompassing*
200 A martial man to be soft fancy's° slave!   *love's*
True valour still a true respect[4] should have;
    Then my digression° is so vile, so base,   *error*
    That it will live engraven in my face.

'Yea, though I die the scandal will survive
205 And be an eyesore in my golden coat.°   *(of arms)*
Some loathsome dash[5] the herald will contrive
To cipher me how fondly° I did dote,   *To show how foolishly*
That my posterity, shamed with the note,°   *stigma*
    Shall curse my bones and hold it for no sin
210   To wish that I their father had not been.

'What win I if I gain the thing I seek?
A dream, a breath, a froth of fleeting joy.
Who buys a minute's mirth to wail a week,

---

3. His ineffective defense against his lust, always quenched in the moment of fulfillment; his not-yet-erect penis.
4. A suitable awareness of virtue.
5. Bar in a coat of arms, indicating a dishonorable action by an ancestor.

Or sells eternity to get a toy?°   *trifle*

215 For one sweet grape who will the vine destroy?
    Or what fond beggar, but to touch the crown,
    Would with the sceptre straight be strucken down?

'If Collatinus dream of my intent
Will he not wake, and in a desp'rate rage
220 Post hither this vile purpose to prevent?—
This siege that hath engirt° his marriage,   *surrounded*
This blur° to youth, this sorrow to the sage,   *blot*
    This dying virtue, this surviving shame,
    Whose crime will bear an ever-during° blame.   *everlasting*

225 'O what excuse can my invention° make   *ingenuity*
When thou shalt charge me with so black a deed?
Will not my tongue be mute, my frail joints shake,
Mine eyes forgo their light,° my false heart bleed?   *power of vision*
The guilt being great, the fear doth still exceed,
230   And extreme fear can neither fight nor fly,
    But coward-like with trembling terror die.

'Had Collatinus killed my son or sire,
Or lain in ambush to betray my life,
Or were he not my dear friend, this desire
235 Might have excuse to work upon his wife
As in revenge or quittal° of such strife.   *requital*
    But as he is my kinsman, my dear friend,
    The shame and fault finds no excuse nor end.

'Shameful it is—ay, if the fact° be known.   *deed*
240 Hateful it is—there is no hate in loving.
I'll beg her love—but she is not her own.
The worst is but denial and reproving;
My will is strong past reason's weak removing.
    Who fears a sentence° or an old man's saw°   *maxim / proverb*
245   Shall by a painted cloth be kept in awe.'[6]

Thus graceless holds he disputation
'Tween frozen conscience and hot-burning will,
And with good thoughts makes dispensation,°   *dispenses*
Urging the worser sense for vantage still;
250 Which in a moment doth confound and kill
    All pure effects,° and doth so far proceed   *tendencies*
    That what is vile shows like a virtuous deed.

Quoth he, 'She took me kindly by the hand,
And gazed for tidings in my eager eyes,
255 Fearing some hard news from the warlike band
Where her belovèd Collatinus lies.
O how her fear did make her colour rise!
    First red as roses that on lawn° we lay,   *fine linen*
    Then white as lawn, the roses took away.

---

6. Will be awed by a tapestry (often depicting morally significant narratives, as in lines 1366ff.).

260 'And how her hand, in my hand being locked,
Forced it to tremble with her loyal fear,
Which struck her sad, and then it faster rocked
Until her husband's welfare she did hear,
Whereat she smilèd with so sweet a cheer°   *an expression*
265   That had Narcissus[7] seen her as she stood
Self-love had never drowned him in the flood.'

'Why hunt I then for colour° or excuses?   *pretext*
All orators are dumb when beauty pleadeth.
Poor wretches have remorse in poor abuses;°   *regret minor lapses*
270 Love thrives not in the heart that shadows° dreadeth;   *illusory scruples*
Affection° is my captain, and he leadeth,   *Passion*
And when his gaudy banner is displayed,
The coward fights, and will not be dismayed.

'Then childish fear avaunt,° debating die,   *begone*
275 Respect° and reason wait on° wrinkled age!   *Circumspection / attend*
My heart shall never countermand mine eye,
Sad° pause and deep regard beseems the sage.   *Serious*
My part is youth, and beats these from the stage.[8]
Desire my pilot is, beauty my prize.°   *pirate's booty*
280   Then who fears sinking where such treasure lies?'

As corn° o'ergrown by weeds, so heedful fear   *grain*
Is almost choked by unresisted lust.
Away he steals, with open list'ning ear,
Full of foul hope and full of fond° mistrust,   *foolish; passionate*
285 Both which as servitors to the unjust
So cross him with their opposite persuasion
That now he vows a league, and now invasion.

Within his thought her heavenly image sits,
And in the selfsame seat sits Collatine.
290 That eye which looks on her confounds his wits,
That eye which him beholds, as° more divine,   *because it is*
Unto a view so false will not incline,
But with a pure appeal seeks° to the heart,   *applies*
Which once corrupted, takes the worser part,

295 And therein heartens up his servile powers[9]
Who, flattered by their leader's jocund show,
Stuff up his lust as minutes fill up hours,
And as their captain, so their pride doth grow,
Paying more slavish tribute than they owe.[1]
300   By reprobate desire thus madly led
The Roman lord marcheth to Lucrece' bed.

The locks between her chamber and his will,
Each one by him enforced, retires his ward;°   *withdraws its bolt*
But as they open they all rate° his ill,   *berate (by squeaking)*

---

7. In classical mythology, a youth who fell in love with his reflection in a pool; in some versions of the tale, he drowned attempting to kiss the image.
8. Like the Vice character in the medieval morality play.
9. Appetites or passions, imagined as servants of the heart, the seat of conscience.
1. That is, debasing themselves by collaborating and encouraging the corrupted heart.

305 Which drives the creeping thief to some regard.°   *caution*
    The threshold grates the door to have him heard,
      Night-wand'ring weasels[2] shriek to see him there.
      They fright him, yet he still pursues his fear.°   *what makes him fear*

    As each unwilling portal yields him way,
310 Through little vents and crannies of the place
    The wind wars with his torch to make him stay,
    And blows the smoke of it into his face,
    Extinguishing his conduct° in this case.   *guide; behavior*
      But his hot heart, which fond desire doth scorch,
315   Puffs forth another wind that fires the torch,

    And being lighted, by the light he spies
    Lucretia's glove wherein her needle sticks.
    He takes it from the rushes where it lies,
    And gripping it, the needle his finger pricks,
320 As who should say 'This glove to wanton tricks
      Is not inured. Return again in haste.
      Thou seest our mistress' ornaments are chaste.'

    But all these poor forbiddings could not stay him;
    He in the worst sense consters° their denial.   *construes*
325 The doors, the wind, the glove that did delay him
    He takes for accidental things of trial,°   *tests of resolve*
    Or as those bars which stop the hourly dial,[3]
      Who with a ling'ring stay his course doth let°   *hinder; permit*
      Till every minute pays the hour his debt.

330 'So, so,' quoth he, 'these lets attend the time,
    Like little frosts that sometime threat the spring
    To add a more rejoicing to the prime,°   *spring*
    And give the sneapèd° birds more cause to sing.   *pinched with cold*
    Pain pays the income° of each precious thing.   *is the price of*
335   Huge rocks, high winds, strong pirates, shelves,° and sands   *reefs*
      The merchant fears, ere rich at home he lands.'

    Now is he come unto the chamber door
    That shuts him from the heaven of his thought,
    Which with a yielding latch, and with no more,
340 Hath barred him from the blessèd thing he sought.
    So from° himself impiety hath wrought°   *unlike / made him*
      That for his prey to pray he doth begin,
      As if the heavens should countenance his sin.

    But in the midst of his unfruitful prayer
345 Having solicited th'eternal power
    That his foul thoughts might compass° his fair fair,[4]   *obtain; embrace*
    And they would stand auspicious to the hour,
    Even there he starts.° Quoth he, 'I must deflower.   *is startled*
      The powers to whom I pray abhor this fact;°   *deed*
350   How can they then assist me in the act?

2. Weasels were kept to catch vermin.   before jerking forward.
3. The marks on a clock face, where the hands pause   4. His virtuous and beautiful one.

'Then love and fortune be my gods, my guide!
My will is backed with resolution.
Thoughts are but dreams till their effects be tried;
The blackest sin is cleared with absolution.
355   Against love's fire fear's frost hath dissolution.
      The eye of heaven is out,° and misty night   *extinguished*
      Covers the shame that follows sweet delight.'

This said, his guilty hand plucked up the latch,
And with his knee the door he opens wide.
360   The dove sleeps fast that this night-owl will catch.
Thus treason works ere traitors be espied.
Who sees the lurking serpent steps aside,
      But she, sound sleeping, fearing no such thing,
      Lies at the mercy of his mortal° sting.   *lethal*

365   Into the chamber wickedly he stalks,°   *steals*
And gazeth on her yet-unstainèd bed.
The curtains being close,° about he walks,   *shut*
Rolling his greedy eye-balls in his head.
By their high treason is his heart misled,
370   Which gives the watchword to his hand full soon
      To draw the cloud° that hides the silver moon.   *(the bed curtain)*

Look as° the fair and fiery-pointed sun   *See how*
Rushing from forth a cloud bereaves our sight,
Even so, the curtain drawn, his eyes begun
375   To wink,° being blinded with a greater light.   *close*
Whether it is that she reflects so bright
      That dazzleth them, or else some shame supposed,
      But blind they are, and keep themselves enclosed.

O had they in that darksome prison died,
380   Then had they seen the period° of their ill.   *end*
Then Collatine again by Lucrece' side
In his clear° bed might have reposèd still.   *undefiled*
But they must ope, this blessèd league° to kill,   *marriage*
      And holy-thoughted Lucrece to their sight
385   Must sell her joy, her life, her world's delight.

Her lily hand her rosy cheek lies under,
Coz'ning° the pillow of a lawful kiss,   *Cheating*
Who therefore angry seems to part in sunder,°   *in two*
Swelling on either side to want his bliss;[5]
390   Between whose hills her head entombèd is,
      Where like a virtuous monument she lies
      To be admired of lewd unhallowed eyes.

Without the bed her other fair hand was,
On the green coverlet, whose perfect white
395   Showed like an April daisy on the grass,
With pearly sweat resembling dew of night.

---

5. Because it is denied its pleasure (of her lips touching its surface).

Her eyes like marigolds[6] had sheathed their light,
    And canopied in darkness sweetly lay
    Till they might open to adorn the day.

400 Her hair like golden threads played with her breath—
    O modest wantons, wanton modesty!—
    Showing life's triumph in the map° of death,   *image*
    And death's dim look in life's mortality.
    Each° in her sleep themselves so beautify   *(life and death)*
405   As if between them twain there were no strife,
    But that life lived in death, and death in life.

Her breasts like ivory globes circled with blue,
    A pair of maiden[7] worlds unconquerèd,
    Save of their lord no bearing yoke they knew,
410 And him by oath they truly honourèd.
    These worlds in Tarquin new ambition bred,
        Who like a foul usurper went about
        From this fair throne to heave the owner out.

What could he see but mightily he noted?
415 What did he note but strongly he desired?
    What he beheld, on that he firmly doted,
    And in his will° his wilful eye he tired.[8]   *lust*
    With more than admiration he admired
        Her azure veins, her alabaster skin,
420   Her coral lips, her snow-white dimpled chin.

As the grim lion fawneth° o'er his prey,   *shows delight*
    Sharp hunger by the conquest satisfied,
    So o'er this sleeping soul doth Tarquin stay,
    His rage of lust by gazing qualified,°   *mollified*
425 Slaked not suppressed for standing by her side.
        His eye which late this mutiny restrains
        Unto a greater uproar tempts his veins,

And they like straggling slaves° for pillage fighting,   *lowborn soldiers*
    Obdurate vassals fell° exploits effecting,   *fierce*
430 In bloody death and ravishment delighting,
    Nor children's tears nor mothers' groans respecting,
    Swell in their pride, the onset still° expecting.   *at any moment*
        Anon his beating heart, alarum° striking,   *signal to attack*
        Gives the hot charge, and bids them do their liking.

435 His drumming heart cheers up his burning eye,
    His eye commends° the leading to his hand.   *entrusts*
    His hand, as proud of such a dignity,
    Smoking with pride marched on to make his stand
    On her bare breast, the heart of all her land,
440   Whose ranks of blue veins as his hand did scale°   *climb*
    Left their round turrets destitute and pale.

---

6. The pot marigold folds up its flowers at day's end.   8. Wearied; fed greedily (as a hawk tears flesh with its
7. Used of an unconquered citadel.   beak).

They, must'ring° to the quiet cabinet°   *gathering / room (heart)*
Where their dear governess° and lady lies,   *ruler*
Do tell her she is dreadfully beset,
445 And fright her with confusion of their cries.
She much amazed breaks ope her locked-up eyes,
    Who, peeping forth this tumult to behold,
    Are by his flaming torch dimmed and controlled.°   *overwhelmed*

Imagine her as one in dead of night
450 From forth dull sleep by dreadful fancy waking,
That thinks she hath beheld some ghastly sprite
Whose grim aspect sets every joint a-shaking.
What terror 'tis! But she in worser taking,°   *plight*
    From sleep disturbèd, heedfully doth view
455   The sight which makes supposèd terror true.

Wrapped and confounded in a thousand fears,
Like to a new-killed bird she trembling lies.
She dares not look, yet, winking,° there appears   *shutting her eyes*
Quick-shifting antics,° ugly in her eyes.   *grotesque shapes*
460 Such shadows are the weak brain's forgeries,
    Who, angry that the eyes fly from their lights,
    In darkness daunts them with more dreadful sights.

His hand that yet remains upon her breast—
Rude ram,° to batter such an ivory wall—   *battering ram*
465 May feel her heart, poor citizen, distressed,
Wounding itself to death, rise up and fall,
Beating her bulk,° that his hand shakes withal.°   *chest / as well*
    This moves in him more rage and lesser pity
    To make the breach and enter this sweet city.

470 First like a trumpet doth his tongue begin
To sound a parley[9] to his heartless° foe,   *terrified*
Who o'er the white sheet peers her whiter chin,
The reason of this rash alarm to know,
Which he by dumb demeanour° seeks to show.   *mute gesture*
475   But she with vehement prayers urgeth still
    Under what colour° he commits this ill.   *pretext*

Thus he replies: 'The colour in thy face,
That even for anger makes the lily pale
And the red rose blush at her own disgrace,
480 Shall plead for me and tell my loving tale.
Under that colour° am I come to scale   *pretext; hue; flag*
    Thy never-conquered fort. The fault is thine,
    For those thine eyes betray thee unto mine.

'Thus I forestall thee, if thou mean to chide:
485 Thy beauty hath ensnared thee to this night,
Where thou with patience must my will abide,
My will that marks thee for my earth's° delight,   *earthly; bodily*
Which I to conquer sought with all my might.

9. A call to a negotiation.

But as reproof and reason beat it° dead,   *(my lust)*
490 By thy bright beauty was it newly bred.

'I see what crosses° my attempt will bring,   *misfortunes*
I know what thorns the growing rose defends;
I think° the honey guarded with a sting;   *know*
All this beforehand counsel° comprehends.   *wisdom*
495 But will is deaf, and hears no heedful friends.
      Only he hath an eye to gaze on beauty,
      And dotes on what he looks, 'gainst law or duty.

'I have debated even in my soul
What wrong, what shame, what sorrow I shall breed;
500 But nothing can affection's° course control,   *passion's*
Or stop the headlong fury of his speed.
I know repentant tears ensue° the deed,   *follow*
      Reproach, disdain, and deadly enmity,
      Yet strive I to embrace mine infamy.'

505 This said, he shakes aloft his Roman blade,
Which like a falcon tow'ring in the skies
Coucheth the fowl° below with his wings' shade   *Makes the prey crouch*
Whose crooked beak threats, if he° mount he dies.   *(the fowl)*
So under his insulting° falchion lies   *triumphantly exulting*
510   Harmless Lucretia, marking what he tells
      With trembling fear, as fowl hear falcons' bells.[1]

'Lucrece,' quoth he, 'this night I must enjoy thee.
If thou deny, then force must work my way,
For in thy bed I purpose to destroy thee.
515 That done, some worthless slave of thine I'll slay
To kill thine honour with thy life's decay;[2]
      And in thy dead arms do I mean to place him,
      Swearing I slew him seeing thee embrace him.

'So thy surviving husband shall remain
520 The scornful mark of every open eye,°   *observer*
Thy kinsmen hang their heads at this disdain,
Thy issue blurred with nameless bastardy,[3]
And thou, the author of their obloquy,
      Shalt have thy trespass cited up in rhymes°   *described in ballads*
525 And sung by children in succeeding times.

'But if thou yield, I rest thy secret friend.
The fault unknown is as a thought unacted.
A little harm done to a great good end
For lawful policy remains enacted.[4]
530 The poisonous simple° sometime is compacted°   *ingredient / mixed*
      In a pure° compound; being so applied,   *benign*
      His venom in effect is purified.

---

1. Hunting falcons had bells attached to their legs.   father's name is unknown.
2. To destroy your reputation along with your life.   4. *For . . . enacted:* Is allowed as proper statesmanship.
3. Your children suspected of being bastards whose

'Then for thy husband and thy children's sake
Tender my suit;° bequeath not to their lot   *Regard my plea*
535   The shame that from them no device⁵ can take,
The blemish that will never be forgot,
Worse than a slavish wipe or birth-hour's blot;⁶
    For marks descried in men's nativity
    Are nature's faults, not their own infamy.'

540   Here with a cockatrice'⁷ dead-killing eye
He rouseth up himself, and makes a pause,
While she, the picture of pure piety,
Like a white hind° under the gripe's° sharp claws,   *doe / griffin*
Pleads in a wilderness where are no laws
545   To the rough beast that knows no gentle right,°   *law of gentility*
    Nor aught obeys but his foul appetite.

But when a black-faced cloud the world doth threat,
In his dim mist th'aspiring mountains hiding,
From earth's dark womb some gentle gust doth get
550   Which blows these pitchy vapours from their biding,°   *place*
Hind'ring their present° fall by this dividing;   *immediate*
    So his unhallowed haste her words delays,
    And moody Pluto winks while Orpheus plays.⁸

Yet, foul night-waking cat, he doth but dally
555   While in his holdfast foot the weak mouse panteth.
Her sad behaviour feeds his vulture folly,°   *ravenous insanity*
A swallowing gulf° that even in plenty wanteth.   *whirlpool; belly*
His ear her prayers admits, but his heart granteth
    No penetrable entrance to her plaining.°   *lament*
560   Tears harden lust, though marble wear with raining.

Her pity-pleading eyes are sadly fixed
In the remorseless wrinkles of his face.
Her modest eloquence with sighs is mixed,
Which to her oratory adds more grace.
565   She puts the period often from his° place,   *its*
    And midst the sentence so her accent breaks
    That twice she doth begin ere once she speaks.

She conjures him by high almighty Jove,
By knighthood, gentry,° and sweet friendship's oath,   *noble birth*
570   By her untimely tears, her husband's love,
By holy human law and common troth,⁹
By heaven and earth and all the power of both,
    That to his borrowed° bed he make retire,   *(guest)*
    And stoop¹ to honour, not to foul desire.

---

5. Ingenuity; heraldic emblem.
6. A slave's brand or birthmark.
7. Legendary monster whose glance was deadly.
8. When Orpheus, a legendary musician and poet, attempted to regain his dead wife from the underworld, he charmed Pluto, god of the underworld, by playing on

the lyre.
9. *common troth*: the good faith that binds communities together.
1. Swoop down to a lure (in falconry); lie down; subject himself.

575 Quoth she, 'Reward not hospitality
With such black payment as thou hast pretended.°   *offered*
Mud not the fountain that gave drink to thee;
Mar not the thing that cannot be amended;
End thy ill aim before thy shoot be ended.
580   He is no woodman° that doth bend his bow   *sportsman*
   To strike a poor unseasonable° doe.   *out-of-season*

'My husband is thy friend; for his sake spare me.
Thyself art mighty; for thine own sake leave me;
Myself a weakling; do not then ensnare me.
585 Thou look'st not like deceit; do not deceive me.
My sighs like whirlwinds labour hence to heave thee.
   If ever man were moved with woman's moans,
   Be movèd with my tears, my sighs, my groans.

'All which together, like a troubled ocean,
590 Beat at thy rocky and wreck-threat'ning heart
To soften it with their continual motion,
For stones dissolved to water do convert.
O, if no harder than a stone thou art,
   Melt at my tears, and be compassionate.
595   Soft pity enters at an iron gate.

'In Tarquin's likeness I did entertain thee.
Hast thou put on his shape to do him shame?
To all the host of heaven I complain me.
Thou wrong'st his honour, wound'st his princely name.
600 Thou art not what thou seem'st, and if the same,
   Thou seem'st not what thou art, a god, a king,
   For kings like gods should govern everything.

'How will thy shame be seeded° in thine age   *ripened*
When thus thy vices bud before thy spring?
605 If in thy hope° thou dar'st do such outrage,   *If not yet in power*
What dar'st thou not when once thou art a king?
O be remembered, no outrageous thing
   From vassal actors° can be wiped away;   *lowborn criminals*
   Then kings' misdeeds cannot be hid in clay.°   *(even after death)*

610 'This deed will make thee only loved for° fear,   *obeyed out of*
But happy monarchs still° are feared for love.   *always*
With foul offenders thou perforce must bear
When they in thee the like offences prove.
If but for fear of this, thy will remove;
615   For princes are the glass,° the school, the book   *mirror*
   Where subjects' eyes do learn, do read, do look.

'And wilt thou be the school where lust shall learn?
Must he in thee read lectures of such shame?
Wilt thou be glass wherein it shall discern
620 Authority for sin, warrant for blame,
To privilege° dishonour in thy name?   *justify*
   Thou back'st° reproach against long-living laud,°   *support / praise*
   And mak'st fair reputation but a bawd.

'Hast thou command?° By him° that gave it thee,   *authority / (God)*
625 From a pure heart command thy rebel will.
Draw not thy sword to guard iniquity,
For it was lent thee all that brood° to kill.   *kind of thing*
Thy princely office how canst thou fulfil
     When, patterned° by thy fault, foul sin may say   *given a precedent*
630   He learned to sin, and thou didst teach the way?

'Think but how vile a spectacle it were
To view thy present trespass in another.
Men's faults do seldom to themselves appear;
Their own transgressions partially they smother.°   *hide (from themselves)*
635 This guilt would seem death-worthy in thy brother.
     O, how are they wrapped in with infamies
     That from their own misdeeds askance° their eyes!   *turn away*

'To thee, to thee my heaved-up hands appeal,
Not to seducing lust, thy rash relier.²
640 I sue for exiled majesty's repeal;°   *recall from exile*
Let him return, and flatt'ring thoughts retire.
His true respect° will prison false desire,   *judgment*
     And wipe the dim mist from thy doting eyne,°   *eyes (archaic)*
     That thou shalt see thy state, and pity mine.'

645 'Have done,' quoth he; 'my uncontrollèd tide
Turns not, but swells the higher by this let.°   *restraint*
Small lights are soon blown out; huge fires abide,
And with the wind in greater fury fret.
The petty streams, that pay a daily debt
650   To their salt sovereign,° with their fresh falls' haste   *(the sea)*
     Add to his flow, but alter not his taste.'

'Thou art,' quoth she, 'a sea, a sovereign king,
And lo, there falls into thy boundless flood
Black lust, dishonour, shame, misgoverning,
655 Who seek to stain the ocean of thy blood.°   *disposition; birthright*
If all these petty ills shall change thy good,
     Thy sea within a puddle's womb is hearsèd,°   *enclosed*
     And not the puddle in thy sea dispersed.

'So shall these slaves° be king, and thou their slave;   *(lust, dishonor, etc.)*
660 Thou nobly base, they basely dignified;
Thou their fair life, and they thy fouler grave;
Thou loathèd in their shame, they in thy pride.
The lesser thing should not the greater hide.
     The cedar stoops not to the base shrub's foot,
665   But low shrubs wither at the cedar's root.

'So let thy thoughts, low vassals to thy state' —
'No more,' quoth he, 'by heaven, I will not hear thee.
Yield to my love. If not, enforcèd hate
Instead of love's coy° touch shall rudely tear thee.   *gentle*
670 That done, despitefully° I mean to bear thee   *maliciously*

_____
2. *thy rash relier:* on which you rashly rely.

Unto the base bed of some rascal groom°   *servant*
To be thy partner in this shameful doom.'

This said, he sets his foot upon the light;
For light and lust are deadly enemies.
675 Shame folded up in blind concealing night
When most unseen, then most doth tyrannize.
The wolf hath seized his prey, the poor lamb cries,
    Till with her own white fleece° her voice controlled°   *(bedclothes) / overpowered*
    Entombs her outcry in her lips' sweet fold.°   *crevice; sheep pen*

680 For with the nightly linen that she wears
He pens her piteous clamours in her head,
Cooling his hot face in the chastest tears
That ever modest eyes with sorrow shed.
O that prone° lust should stain so pure a bed,   *headlong; eager*
685   The spots whereof could weeping purify,
    Her tears should drop on them perpetually!

But she hath lost a dearer thing than life,
And he hath won what he would lose again.
This forcèd league doth force a further strife,
690 This momentary joy breeds months of pain;
This hot desire converts to cold disdain.
    Pure chastity is rifled of her store,
    And lust, the thief, far poorer than before.

Look° as the full-fed hound or gorgèd hawk,   *Just*
695 Unapt for tender° smell or speedy flight,   *delicate*
Make slow pursuit, or altogether balk°   *turn from*
The prey wherein by nature they delight,
So surfeit-taking Tarquin fares° this night.   *behaves; feeds*
    His taste delicious, in digestion souring,
700   Devours his will that lived by foul devouring.

O deeper sin than bottomless conceit°   *unlimited fantasy*
Can comprehend in still imagination!
Drunken desire must vomit his receipt°   *what he swallowed*
Ere he can see his own abomination.
705 While lust is in his pride, no exclamation
    Can curb his heat or rein his rash desire,
    Till like a jade° self-will himself doth tire.   *recalcitrant horse*

And then with lank and lean discoloured cheek,
With heavy eye, knit brow, and strengthless pace,
710 Feeble desire, all recreant,[3] poor, and meek,
Like to a bankrupt beggar wails his case.
The flesh being proud, desire doth fight with grace,
    For there it revels, and when that decays,°   *subsides*
    The guilty rebel for remission° prays.   *pardon*

715 So fares it with this faultful lord of Rome
Who this accomplishment so hotly chased;

3. Cowardly; faithless; exhausted.

For now against himself he sounds° this doom,°   *pronounces / sentence*
That through the length of times he stands disgraced.
Besides, his soul's fair temple is defaced,
720 To whose weak ruins muster troops of cares
  To ask the spotted princess° how she fares.   *(the defiled soul)*

She says her subjects with foul insurrection
Have battered down her consecrated wall,
And by their mortal° fault brought in subjection   *deadly*
725 Her immortality, and made her thrall
To living death and pain perpetual,
  Which° in her prescience she controllèd still,   *(the soul's subjects)*
  But her foresight could not forestall their will.

Ev'n in this thought through the dark night he stealeth,
730 A captive victor that hath lost in gain,
Bearing away the wound that nothing healeth,
The scar that will, despite of cure, remain;
Leaving his spoil° perplexed in greater pain.   *prey*
  She bears the load of lust he left behind,
735 And he the burden of a guilty mind.

He like a thievish dog creeps sadly thence;
She like a wearied lamb lies panting there.
He scowls, and hates himself for his offence;
She, desperate, with her nails her flesh doth tear.
740 He faintly flies, sweating with guilty fear;
  She stays, exclaiming on° the direful night.   *denouncing*
  He runs, and chides his vanished loathed delight.

He thence departs, a heavy convertite;°   *sad penitent*
She there remains, a hopeless castaway.
745 He in his speed looks for the morning light;
She prays she never may behold the day.
'For day,' quoth she, 'night's scapes° doth open lay,   *sins*
  And my true eyes have never practised how
  To cloak offences with a cunning brow.

750 'They think not but that every eye can see
The same disgrace which they themselves behold,
And therefore would they still in darkness be,
To have their unseen sin remain untold.
For they their guilt with weeping will unfold,
755 And grave,° like water that doth eat in steel,[4]   *engrave*
  Upon my cheeks what helpless shame I feel.'

Here she exclaims against repose and rest,
And bids her eyes hereafter still be blind.
She wakes her heart by beating on her breast,
760 And bids it leap from thence where it may find
Some purer chest to close° so pure a mind.   *enclose*
  Frantic with grief, thus breathes she forth her spite°   *reproach*
  Against the unseen secrecy of night:

---

4. *Aqua fortis* (literally, "strong water"), nitric acid.

'O comfort-killing night, image of hell,
765 Dim register° and notary of shame,   *recorder*
Black stage for tragedies and murders fell,
Vast sin-concealing chaos, nurse of blame!
Blind muffled bawd, dark harbour for defame,°   *infamy*
    Grim cave of death, whisp'ring conspirator
770   With close-tongued treason and the ravisher!

'O hateful, vaporous, and foggy night,
Since thou art guilty of my cureless crime,
Muster thy mists to meet the eastern light,
Make war against proportioned° course of time.   *orderly*
775 Or if thou wilt permit the sun to climb
    His wonted height, yet ere he go to bed
    Knit poisonous clouds about his golden head.

'With rotten damps° ravish the morning air,   *vapors*
Let their exhaled unwholesome breaths make sick
780 The life of purity, the supreme fair,°   *(the sun)*
Ere he arrive his weary noon-tide prick;°   *mark on a clock*
And let thy musty vapours march so thick
    That in their smoky ranks his smothered light
    May set at noon, and make perpetual night.

785 'Were Tarquin night, as he is but night's child,
The silver-shining queen[5] he would distain;°   *stain*
Her twinkling handmaids° too, by him defiled,   *(the stars)*
Through night's black bosom should not peep again.
So should I have co-partners in my pain,
790   And fellowship in woe doth woe assuage,
    As palmers'° chat makes short their pilgrimage.   *pilgrims'*

'Where now I have no one to blush with me,
To cross their arms[6] and hang their heads with mine,
To mask their brows and hide their infamy,
795 But I alone, alone must sit and pine,
    Seasoning the earth with showers of silver brine,
        Mingling my talk with tears, my grief with groans,
        Poor wasting monuments° of lasting moans.   *short-lived tokens*

'O night, thou furnace of foul reeking smoke,
800 Let not the jealous° day behold that face   *suspicious*
Which underneath thy black all-hiding cloak
Immodestly lies martyred with disgrace!
Keep still possession of thy gloomy place,
    That all the faults which in thy reign are made
805   May likewise be sepulchred in thy shade.

'Make me not object° to the tell-tale day: *manifest*
The light will show charactered° in my brow   *written*
The story of sweet chastity's decay,
The impious breach of holy wedlock vow.
810 Yea, the illiterate that know not how

5. The moon, symbol of chastity.   6. This is a conventional gesture of melancholy.

To cipher° what is writ in learnèd books   *decipher*
Will quote° my loathsome trespass in my looks.   *note*

'The nurse to still her child will tell my story,
And fright her crying babe with Tarquin's name.
815 The orator to deck his oratory
Will couple my reproach to Tarquin's shame.
Feast-finding minstrels[7] tuning my defame
   Will tie the hearers to attend° each line,   *listen to*
   How Tarquin wrongèd me, I Collatine.

820 'Let my good name, that senseless° reputation,   *intangible*
For Collatine's dear love be kept unspotted;
If that be made a theme for disputation,
The branches of another root are rotted,[8]
And undeserved reproach to him allotted
825   That is as clear from this attaint° of mine   *stain*
   As I ere this was pure to Collatine.

'O unseen shame, invisible disgrace!
O unfelt sore, crest-wounding[9] private scar!
Reproach° is stamped in Collatinus' face,   *Reproof; dishonor*
830 And Tarquin's eye may read the mot° afar,   *motto*
How he in peace is wounded, not in war.
   Alas, how many bear such shameful blows,
   Which not themselves but he that gives them knows!

'If, Collatine, thine honour lay in me,
835 From me by strong assault it is bereft;
My honey lost, and I, a drone-like bee,
Have no perfection of my summer left,[1]
But robbed and ransacked by injurious theft.
   In thy weak hive a wandering wasp hath crept,
840   And sucked the honey which thy chaste bee kept.

'Yet am I guilty of thy honour's wrack;°   *ruin*
Yet for thy honour did I entertain him.
Coming from thee, I could not put him back,
For it had been dishonour to disdain him.
845 Besides, of weariness he did complain him,
   And talked of virtue—O unlooked-for evil,
   When virtue is profaned in such a devil!

'Why should the worm intrude the maiden bud,
Or hateful cuckoos hatch in sparrows' nests,
850 Or toads infect fair founts with venom° mud,   *venomous*
Or tyrant folly° lurk in gentle breasts,   *cruel lewdness*
Or kings be breakers of their own behests?°   *commands*
   But no perfection is so absolute
   That some impurity doth not pollute.

---

7. Minstrels were paid to perform at banquets.
8. That is, Collatine's reputation is also destroyed.
9. Damaging the coat of arms, hence family honor (cf.

lines 204–10).
1. Have nothing left of what I made in the summer; have none of the purity of my prime remaining.

855 'The agèd man that coffers up his gold
Is plagued with cramps, and gouts, and painful fits,
And scarce hath eyes his treasure to behold,
But like still-pining Tantalus[2] he sits,
And useless barns° the harvest of his wits,   *hoards*
860   Having no other pleasure of his gain
    But torment that it cannot cure his pain.

'So then he hath it when he cannot use it,
And leaves it to be mastered° by his young,°   *possessed / children*
Who in their pride do presently° abuse it.   *immediately*
865 Their father was too weak and they too strong
To hold their cursèd-blessèd fortune long.
    The sweets we wish for turn to loathèd sours
    Even in the moment that we call them ours.

'Unruly blasts wait on the tender spring,
870 Unwholesome weeds take root with precious flowers,
The adder hisses where the sweet birds sing,
What virtue breeds, iniquity devours.
We have no good that we can say is ours
    But ill-annexèd opportunity[3]
875   Or° kills his life or else his quality.   *Either*

'O opportunity, thy guilt is great!
'Tis thou that execut'st the traitor's treason;
Thou sets the wolf where he the lamb may get;
Whoever plots the sin, thou point'st° the season.   *appoint*
880 'Tis thou that spurn'st at right, at law, at reason;
    And in thy shady cell where none may spy him
    Sits sin, to seize the souls that wander by him.

'Thou mak'st the vestal[4] violate her oath,
Thou blow'st the fire when temperance is thawed,
885 Thou smother'st honesty, thou murd'rest troth,
Thou foul abettor, thou notorious bawd;°   *procurer*
Thou plantest scandal and displacest laud.
    Thou ravisher, thou traitor, thou false thief,
    Thy honey turns to gall, thy joy to grief.

890 'Thy secret pleasure turns to open shame,
Thy private feasting to a public fast,
Thy smoothing° titles to a ragged name,   *flattering*
Thy sugared tongue to bitter wormwood taste.
Thy violent vanities can never last.
895   How comes it then, vile opportunity,
    Being so bad, such numbers seek for thee?

'When wilt thou be the humble suppliant's friend,
And bring him where his suit may be obtained?
When wilt thou sort° an hour great strifes to end,   *select*

---

2. A mythological figure who was punished in Hades by
eternal hunger and thirst; food and water were always visi-
ble but receded at his approach.
3. Bad circumstances joined to or following from the

good.
4. The priestess of Vesta, Roman goddess of the heath
and household; vestals were sworn to lifelong virginity.

900 Or free that soul which wretchedness hath chained,
　 Give physic° to the sick, ease to the pained?　　　　　　　　　*medicine*
　　 The poor, lame, blind, halt,° creep, cry out for thee,　　　　　*limp*
　　 But they ne'er meet with opportunity.

　 'The patient dies while the physician sleeps,
905 The orphan pines while the oppressor feeds,
　 Justice is feasting while the widow weeps,
　 Advice° is sporting while infection breeds.　　　　　　　　*(medical advice)*
　 Thou grant'st no time for charitable deeds.
　　 Wrath, envy, treason, rape, and murder's rages,
910 　 Thy heinous hours wait on them as their pages.

　 'When truth and virtue have to do with thee
　 A thousand crosses° keep them from thy aid.　　　　　　*impediments*
　 They buy° thy help, but sin ne'er gives a fee;　　　　　*(must pay for)*
　 He gratis comes, and thou art well appaid°　　　　　　　*satisfied*
915 As well to hear as grant what he hath said.
　　 My Collatine would else have come to me
　　 When Tarquin did, but he was stayed by thee.

　 'Guilty thou art of murder and of theft,
　 Guilty of perjury and subornation,[5]
920 Guilty of treason, forgery, and shift,°　　　　　　　　*fraud*
　 Guilty of incest, that abomination:
　 An accessory by thine inclination°　　　　　　　　　　*nature*
　　 To all sins past and all that are to come
　　 From the creation to the general doom.

925 'Misshapen time, copesmate° of ugly night,　　　　　　*comrade*
　 Swift subtle post,° carrier of grisly care,　　　　　　*messenger*
　 Eater of youth, false slave to false delight,
　 Base watch° of woes, sin's pack-horse, virtue's snare,　　*town crier, announcer*
　 Thou nursest all, and murd'rest all that are.
930 　 O hear me then, injurious shifting° time;　　　　　*changing; traitorous*
　　 Be guilty of my death, since° of my crime.　　　　　*as thou art*

　 'Why hath thy servant opportunity
　 Betrayed the hours thou gav'st me to repose,
　 Cancelled my fortunes, and enchainèd me
935 To endless date° of never-ending woes?　　　　　　　*duration*
　 Time's office is to fine° the hate of foes,　　　　　　*end; punish*
　　 To eat up errors by opinion° bred,　　　　　　　　　*rumor*
　　 Not spend the dowry of a lawful bed.

　 'Time's glory is to calm contending kings,
940 To unmask falsehood and bring truth to light,
　 To stamp the seal of time in agèd things,
　 To wake the morn and sentinel° the night,　　　　　　*guard*
　 To wrong the wronger till he render right,
　　 To ruinate proud buildings with thy hours
945 　 And smear with dust their glitt'ring golden towers;

———

5. Bribing others to give false testimony.

'To fill with worm-holes stately monuments,
To feed oblivion with decay of things,
To blot old books and alter their contents,
To pluck the quills from ancient ravens' wings,
950   To dry the old oak's sap and blemish° springs,   *contaminate*
      To spoil antiquities of hammered steel,
      And turn the giddy round of fortune's wheel;

'To show the beldame° daughters of her daughter,   *old woman*
To make the child a man, the man a child,
955   To slay the tiger that doth live by slaughter,
To tame the unicorn and lion wild,
To mock the subtle in themselves beguiled,[6]
      To cheer the ploughman with increaseful crops,
      And waste huge stones with little water drops.

960 'Why work'st thou mischief in thy pilgrimage,
Unless thou couldst return to make amends?
One poor retiring[7] minute in an age
Would purchase thee a thousand thousand friends,
Lending him wit that to bad debtors lends.
965   O this dread night, wouldst thou one hour come back,
      I could prevent this storm and shun thy wrack!

'Thou ceaseless lackey° to eternity,   *eternal servant*
With some mischance cross Tarquin in his flight.
Devise extremes beyond extremity
970   To make him curse this cursèd crimeful night.
Let ghastly shadows his lewd eyes affright,
      And the dire thought of his committed evil
      Shape every bush a hideous shapeless devil.

'Disturb his hours of rest with restless trances;°   *dreams; seizures*
975 Afflict him in his bed with bedrid groans;
Let there bechance him pitiful mischances
To make him moan, but pity not his moans.
Stone him with hardened hearts harder than stones,
      And let mild women to him lose their mildness,
980   Wilder to him than tigers in their wildness.

'Let him have time to tear his curlèd hair,
Let him have time against himself to rave,
Let him have time of time's help to despair,
Let him have time to live a loathèd slave,
985 Let him have time a beggar's orts° to crave,   *scraps*
      And time to see one that by alms doth live
      Disdain to him disdainèd scraps to give.

'Let him have time to see his friends his foes,
And merry fools to mock at him resort.°   *gather*
990 Let him have time to mark how slow time goes
In time of sorrow, and how swift and short

---

6. The cunning, taken in by their own schemes.
7. Returning (thus permitting people to do things differently).

His time of folly and his time of sport;
  And ever let his unrecalling crime[8]
  Have time to wail th'abusing of his time.

995 'O time, thou tutor both to good and bad,
  Teach me to curse him that thou taught'st this ill;
  At his own shadow let the thief run mad,
  Himself himself seek every hour to kill;
  Such wretched hands such wretched blood should spill,
1000   For who so base would such an office have
    As sland'rous deathsman° to so base a slave?   *detested executioner*

'The baser is he, coming from a king,
  To shame his hope with deeds degenerate.
  The mightier man, the mightier is the thing
1005 That makes him honoured or begets him hate,
  For greatest scandal waits on greatest state.[9]
    The moon being clouded presently° is missed,   *immediately*
    But little stars may hide them when they list.°   *wish*

'The crow may bathe his coal-black wings in mire
1010 And unperceived fly with the filth away,
  But if the like the snow-white swan desire,
  The stain upon his silver down will stay.
  Poor grooms° are sightless° night, kings glorious day.   *servants / dark*
    Gnats are unnoted wheresoe'er they fly,
1015   But eagles gazed upon with every eye.

'Out, idle words, servants to shallow fools,
  Unprofitable sounds, weak arbitrators!
  Busy yourselves in skill-contending schools,°   *(of rhetoric)*
  Debate where leisure serves with dull debaters,
1020 To trembling clients be you mediators;
    For me, I force° not argument a straw,   *value*
    Since that my case is past the help of law.

'In vain I rail at opportunity,
  At time, at Tarquin, and uncheerful night.
1025 In vain I cavil with° mine infamy,   *object to*
  In vain I spurn at my confirmed despite.°   *irreparable injury*
  This helpless° smoke of words doth me no right;   *unhelpful; weak*
    The remedy indeed to do me good
    Is to let forth my foul defilèd blood.

1030 'Poor hand, why quiver'st thou at this decree?
  Honour thyself to rid me of this shame,
  For if I die, my honour lives in thee,
  But if I live, thou liv'st in my defame.°   *infamy*
  Since thou couldst not defend thy loyal dame,
1035   And wast afeard to scratch her wicked foe,
    Kill both thyself and her for yielding so.'

8. Crime that cannot be undone.   9. Attends those of highest rank.

This said, from her betumbled couch she starteth,
To find some desp'rate instrument of death.
But this, no slaughterhouse, no tool imparteth°   *furnishes*
1040   To make more vent° for passage of her breath,   *a bigger hole*
Which thronging through her lips so vanisheth
        As smoke from Etna that in air consumes,
        Or that which from dischargèd cannon fumes.

'In vain,' quoth she, 'I live, and seek in vain
1045   Some happy mean to end a hapless life.
I feared by Tarquin's falchion to be slain,
Yet for the selfsame purpose seek a knife.
But when I feared I was a loyal wife;
        So am I now—O no, that cannot be,
1050   Of that true type° hath Tarquin rifled me.   *pattern of virtue*

'O, that is gone for which I sought to live,
And therefore now I need not fear to die.
To clear this spot by death, at least I give
A badge of fame to slander's livery,°   *servant's uniform*
1055   A dying life to living infamy.
        Poor helpless help, the treasure stol'n away,
        To burn the guiltless casket where it lay!

'Well, well, dear Collatine, thou shalt not know
The stainèd taste of violated troth.
1060   I will not wrong thy true affection so
To flatter thee with an infringèd oath.
This bastard graft[1] shall never come to growth.
        He shall not boast, who did thy stock pollute,
        That thou art doting father of his fruit,

1065   'Nor shall he smile at thee in secret thought,
Nor laugh with his companions at thy state.
But thou shalt know thy int'rest° was not bought   *property*
Basely with gold, but stol'n from forth thy gate.
For me, I am the mistress of my fate,
1070   And with my trespass never will dispense°   *dispense with = excuse*
        Till life to death acquit° my forced offence.   *atone for*

'I will not poison thee with my attaint,°   *contamination*
Nor fold° my fault in cleanly coined excuses.   *envelop*
My sable ground[2] of sin I will not paint
1075   To hide the truth of this false night's abuses.
My tongue shall utter all; mine eyes, like sluices,
        As from a mountain spring that feeds a dale
        Shall gush pure streams to purge my impure tale.'

By this, lamenting Philomel[3] had ended
1080   The well-tuned warble of her nightly sorrow,

---

1. Lucrece assumes that Tarquin has made her pregnant. Her image is from the grafting of plants, in which two different kinds of plants are artificially forced to grow as one; a "bastard slip" is an unwanted shoot.
2. Black background (a heraldic term).

3. The nightingale. In classical mythology, Philomela was raped by King Tereus, her sister's husband, and with her sister took vengeance on him. All three were changed into birds (see Ovid, *Metamorphoses* 6).

And solemn night with slow sad gait descended
To ugly hell, when lo, the blushing morrow
Lends light to all fair eyes that light will borrow.
　　But cloudy° Lucrece shames° herself to see,   *melancholy / is ashamed*
1085 　　And therefore still in night would cloistered be.

Revealing day through every cranny spies,
And seems to point her out where she sits weeping;
To whom she sobbing speaks, 'O eye of eyes,
Why pry'st thou through my window? Leave thy peeping,
1090 　Mock with thy tickling beams eyes that are sleeping,
　　Brand not my forehead with thy piercing light,
　　For day hath naught to do what's done by night.'

Thus cavils she with everything she sees:
True grief is fond° and testy as a child   *foolish*
1095 　Who, wayward once,° his mood with naught agrees;   *once out of sorts*
Old woes, not infant sorrows, bear them mild.°   *bear themselves mildly*
Continuance tames the one; the other wild,
　　Like an unpractised swimmer plunging still,°   *constantly*
　　With too much labour drowns for want of skill.

1100 　So she, deep drenchèd in a sea of care,
Holds disputation with each thing she views,
And to herself all sorrow doth compare;
No object but her passion's strength renews,
And as one shifts,° another straight° ensues.   *moves / immediately*
1105 　　Sometime her grief is dumb° and hath no words,   *mute*
　　Sometime 'tis mad and too much talk affords.

The little birds that tune their morning's joy
Make her moans mad with their sweet melody,
For mirth doth search° the bottom of annoy;°   *probe / vexation*
1110 　Sad souls are slain° in merry company;   *overcome with distress*
Grief best is pleased with grief's society.
　　True sorrow then is feelingly sufficed°   *properly contented*
　　When with like semblance it is sympathized.°   *matched*

'Tis double death to drown in ken° of shore;   *sight*
1115 　He ten times pines° that pines beholding food;   *starves*
To see the salve doth make the wound ache more;
Great grief grieves most at that would do it good;
Deep woes roll forward like a gentle flood
　　Who, being stopped, the bounding° banks o'erflows.   *confining*
1120 　　Grief dallied° with nor° law nor limit knows.   *trifled / neither*

'You mocking birds,' quoth she, 'your tunes entomb
Within your hollow-swelling feathered breasts,
And in my hearing be you mute and dumb;
My restless discord loves no stops nor rests;
1125 　A woeful hostess brooks° not merry guests.   *tolerates*
　　Relish° your nimble notes to pleasing ears;   *Warble; make pleasing*
　　Distress likes dumps° when time is kept with tears.   *sad songs*

'Come, Philomel, that sing'st of ravishment,
Make thy sad grove in my dishevelled hair.
1130 As the dank earth weeps at thy languishment,°   *lamentation*
So I at each sad strain will strain a tear,
And with deep groans the diapason° bear;   *bass accompaniment*
    For burden-wise[4] I'll hum on Tarquin still,
    While thou on Tereus descants better skill.[5]

1135 'And whiles against a thorn[6] thou bear'st thy part
To keep thy sharp woes waking, wretched I,
To imitate thee well, against my heart
Will fix a sharp knife to affright mine eye,
Who° if it wink° shall thereon fall and die.   *(I) / (my eye) close*
1140   These means, as frets° upon an instrument,   *(punning on "vexation")*
    Shall tune our heart-strings to true languishment.

'And for, poor bird, thou sing'st not in the day,
As shaming any eye should thee behold,
Some dark deep desert seated from the way,[7]
1145 That knows not parching heat nor freezing cold,
Will we find out, and there we will unfold
    To creatures stern sad tunes to change their kinds.°   *natures*
    Since men prove beasts, let beasts bear gentle minds.'

As the poor frighted deer that stands at gaze,
1150 Wildly determining which way to fly,
Or one encompassed with a winding maze,
That cannot tread the way out readily,
    So with herself is she in mutiny,
    To live or die which of the twain were better
1155   When life is shamed and death reproach's debtor.°   *will incur reproach*

'To kill myself,' quoth she, 'alack, what were it
But with my body my poor soul's pollution?[8]
They that lose half with greater patience bear it
Than they whose whole is swallowed in confusion.°   *ruin*
1160 That mother tries a merciless conclusion°   *experiment*
    Who, having two sweet babes, when death takes one
    Will slay the other and be nurse to none.

'My body or my soul, which was the dearer,
When the one pure the other made divine?
1165 Whose love of either to myself was nearer,
When both were kept for heaven and Collatine?
    Ay me, the bark peeled from the lofty pine
    His leaves will wither and his sap decay;
    So must my soul, her bark being peeled away.

1170 'Her house is sacked, her quiet interrupted,
Her mansion battered by the enemy,
Her sacred temple spotted, spoiled, corrupted,

---

4. Like a bass line; playing on "burden" as sorrow, weight.
5. Sings the treble part more skillfully.
6. The nightingale was imagined to press against a thorn to keep itself awake during the night.
7. Some uninhabited place located far from the road.
8. To pollute my poor soul, as my body has already been polluted.

Grossly engirt with daring° infamy.   *unrestrained*
Then let it not be called impiety
1175 If in this blemished fort° I make some hole   *(my body)*
Through which I may convey° this troubled soul.   *steal away*

'Yet die I will not till my Collatine
Have heard the cause of my untimely death,
That he may vow in that sad hour of mine
1180 Revenge on him that made me stop my breath.
My stainèd blood to Tarquin I'll bequeath,
Which by him tainted shall for him be spent,
And as his due writ° in my testament.°   *written / last will*

'My honour I'll bequeath unto the knife
1185 That wounds my body so dishonourèd.
'Tis honour to deprive° dishonoured life;   *take away*
The one° will live, the other° being dead.   *(honor) / (life)*
So of shame's ashes shall my fame be bred,[9]
For in my death I murder shameful scorn;
1190 My shame so dead, mine honour is new born.

'Dear lord of that dear jewel° I have lost,   *(chastity)*
What legacy shall I bequeath to thee?
My resolution, love, shall be thy boast,
By whose example thou revenged mayst be.
1195 How Tarquin must be used, read it in me.
Myself, thy friend, will kill myself, thy foe;
And for my sake serve° thou false Tarquin so.   *treat*

'This brief abridgement of my will I make:
My soul and body to the skies and ground;
1200 My resolution, husband, do thou take;
Mine honour be the knife's that makes my wound;
My shame be his that did my fame confound;
And all my fame that lives disbursèd be°   *that remains be paid out*
To those that live and think no shame of me.

1205 'Thou, Collatine, shalt oversee° this will.   *execute*
How was I overseen° that thou shalt see it!   *deluded*
My blood shall wash the slander of mine ill;
My life's foul deed my life's fair end shall free it.
Faint not, faint heart, but stoutly say "So be it".
1210 Yield to my hand, my hand shall conquer thee;
Thou dead, both die, and both shall victors be.'

This plot of death when sadly she had laid,
And wiped the brinish° pearl from her bright eyes,   *salty*
With untuned° tongue she hoarsely calls her maid,   *inharmonious*
1215 Whose swift obedience to her mistress hies;°   *hastens*
For fleet-winged duty with thought's feathers flies.
Poor Lucrece' cheeks unto her maid seem so
As winter meads when sun doth melt their snow.

9. My honor will be like the mythological phoenix, consumed in fire only to be reborn from the ashes.

Her mistress she doth give demure good-morrow
1220 With soft slow tongue, true mark of modesty,
And sorts° a sad look to her lady's sorrow,   *suits*
For why° her face wore sorrow's livery;°   *Because / attire*
But durst not ask of her audaciously
    Why her two suns were cloud-eclipsèd so,
1225   Nor why her fair cheeks over-washed with woe.

But as the earth doth weep, the sun being set,
Each flower moistened like a melting eye,
Even so the maid with swelling drops gan wet
Her circled° eyne, enforced° by sympathy   *rounded / compelled*
1230 Of those fair suns set in her mistress' sky,
    Who in a salt-waved ocean quench their light;
    Which makes the maid weep like the dewy night.

A pretty while° these pretty creatures stand,   *fair amount of time*
Like ivory conduits coral cisterns filling.
1235 One justly weeps, the other takes in hand°   *acknowledges*
No cause but company of her drops' spilling.
Their gentle sex to weep are often willing,
    Grieving themselves to guess at° others' smarts,°   *conjecture / pains*
    And then they drown their eyes or break their hearts.

1240 For men have marble, women waxen minds,
And therefore are they formed as marble will.
The weak oppressed, th'impression of strange kinds°   *alien natures*
Is formed in them by force, by fraud, or skill.
Then call them not the authors of their ill,
1245   No more than wax shall be accounted evil
    Wherein is stamped the semblance of a devil.

Their smoothness like a goodly champaign plain°   *open field*
Lays open° all the little worms that creep;   *Reveals*
In men as in a rough-grown grove remain
1250 Cave-keeping° evils that obscurely° sleep.   *Concealed / unseen*
Through crystal walls each little mote° will peep;   *speck*
    Though men can cover crimes with bold stern looks,
    Poor women's faces are their own faults' books.

No man° inveigh against the withered flower,   *Let no man*
1255 But chide rough winter that the flower hath killed.
Not that devoured, but that which doth devour
Is worthy blame. O, let it not be held
Poor women's faults that they are so full-filled
    With men's abuses. Those proud lords, to blame,
1260   Make weak-made women tenants to their shame.

The precedent° whereof in Lucrece view,   *proof*
Assailed by night with circumstances strong
Of present° death, and shame that might ensue   *immediate*
By that her death, to do her husband wrong.
1265 Such danger to resistance did belong
    That dying fear through all her body spread;
    And who cannot abuse a body dead?

By this,° mild patience bid fair Lucrece speak   *this time*
To the poor counterfeit of her complaining.°   *(the weeping maid)*
1270 'My girl,' quoth she, 'on what occasion break
Those tears from thee that down thy cheeks are raining?
If thou dost weep for grief of my sustaining,°   *borne by me*
   Know, gentle wench, it small avails° my mood.   *little helps*
   If tears could help, mine own would do me good.

1275 'But tell me, girl, when went'—and there she stayed,
Till after a deep groan—'Tarquin from hence?'
'Madam, ere I was up,' replied the maid,
'The more to blame my sluggard negligence.
Yet with the fault I thus far can dispense:°   *excuse*
1280   Myself was stirring ere the break of day,
   And ere I rose was Tarquin gone away.

'But lady, if your maid may be so bold,
She would request to know your heaviness.'°   *sorrow*
'O, peace,' quoth Lucrece, 'if it should be told,
1285 The repetition cannot make it less;
For more it is than I can well express,
   And that deep torture may be called a hell
   When more is felt than one hath power to tell.

'Go, get me hither paper, ink, and pen;
1290 Yet save that labour, for I have them here.
What should I say? One of my husband's men
Bid thou be ready by and by to bear
A letter to my lord, my love, my dear.
   Bid him with speed prepare to carry it;
1295   The cause craves° haste, and it will soon be writ.'   *requires*

Her maid is gone, and she prepares to write,
First hovering o'er the paper with her quill.
Conceit° and grief an eager combat fight;   *Imagination*
What wit° sets down is blotted straight with will;°   *thought / passion*
1300 This is too curious-good,° this blunt and ill.   *elaborate*
   Much like a press° of people at a door   *crowd*
   Throng her inventions, which shall go before.°   *first*

At last she thus begins: 'Thou worthy lord
Of that unworthy wife that greeteth thee,
1305 Health to thy person! Next, vouchsafe t'afford—
If ever, love, thy Lucrece thou wilt see—
Some present° speed to come and visit me.   *immediate*
   So I commend me,° from our house in grief;   *ask to be remembered*
   My woes are tedious, though my words are brief.'

1310 Here folds she up the tenor° of her woe,   *gist*
Her certain sorrow writ uncertainly.
By this short schedule° Collatine may know   *summary*
Her grief, but not her grief's true quality.
She dares not thereof make discovery,°   *revelation*
1315   Lest he should hold it her own gross abuse,°   *trespass*
   Ere she with blood had stained her stain's excuse.

Besides, the life and feeling of her passion
She hoards, to spend when he is by to hear her,
When sighs and groans and tears may grace the fashion°   appearance; fashioning
1320   Of her disgrace, the better so to clear her
From that suspicion which the world might bear her.
    To shun this blot she would not blot the letter
    With words, till action might become° them better.   suit

To see sad sights moves more than hear them told,
1325   For then the eye interprets to the ear
The heavy motion° that it doth behold,   sad action
When every part a part of woe doth bear.
'Tis but a part of sorrow that we hear;
    Deep sounds make lesser noise than shallow fords,
1330   And sorrow ebbs, being blown with wind of words.

Her letter now is sealed, and on it writ
'At Ardea to my lord with more than haste'.
The post attends,° and she delivers it,   messenger waits
Charging the sour-faced groom to hie as fast
1335   As lagging fowls before the northern blast.
    Speed more than speed° but dull and slow she deems;   Even unusual speed
    Extremity still urgeth such extremes.

The homely villain° curtsies to her low,   unpolished menial
And blushing on her with a steadfast eye
1340   Receives the scroll without or° yea or no,   either
And forth with bashful innocence doth hie.
But they whose guilt within their bosoms lie
    Imagine every eye beholds their blame,
    For Lucrece thought he blushed to see her shame,

1345   When, silly groom,° God wot,° it was defect   simple servant / knows
Of spirit, life, and bold audacity.
Such harmless creatures have a true respect
To talk in deeds,[1] while others saucily
Promise more speed, but do it leisurely.
1350   Even so this pattern of the worn-out age°   old-fashioned model
    Pawned° honest looks, but laid no words to gage.°   Offered / as a pledge

His kindled duty[2] kindled her mistrust,
That two red fires in both their faces blazed.
She thought he blushed as knowing Tarquin's lust,
1355   And blushing with him, wistly° on him gazed.   attentively
Her earnest eye did make him more amazed.°   bewildered
    The more she saw the blood his cheeks replenish,
    The more she thought he spied in her some blemish.

But long she thinks° till he return again,   she thinks it long
1360   And yet the duteous vassal scarce is gone.
The weary time she cannot entertain,°   while away
For now 'tis stale to sigh, to weep, and groan.

1. *have . . . deeds*: rightly express their deference by their   2. His blushing bow; his ardent loyalty.
actions (rather than merely by their words).

So woe hath wearied woe, moan tired moan,
   That she her plaints a little while doth stay,
1365   Pausing for means to mourn some newer way.

At last she calls to mind where hangs a piece
   Of skilful painting made for° Priam's Troy,   *representing*
   Before the which is drawn the power° of Greece,   *army*
   For Helen's rape the city to destroy,
1370   Threat'ning cloud-kissing Ilion° with annoy;°   *high-built Troy / injury*
     Which the conceited° painter drew so proud   *ingenious*
     As heaven, it seemed, to kiss the turrets bowed.

A thousand lamentable objects there,
   In scorn of° nature, art gave lifeless life.   *Defying*
1375   Many a dry drop seemed a weeping tear
   Shed for the slaughtered husband by the wife.
   The red blood reeked° to show the painter's strife,[3]   *smoked*
     And dying eyes gleamed forth their ashy lights
     Like dying coals burnt out in tedious nights.

1380   There might you see the labouring pioneer°   *trench digger*
   Begrimed with sweat and smearèd all with dust,
   And from the towers of Troy there would appear
   The very eyes of men through loop-holes thrust,
   Gazing upon the Greeks with little lust.°   *pleasure*
1385   Such sweet observance° in this work was had   *verisimilitude*
     That one might see those far-off eyes look sad.

In great commanders grace and majesty
   You might behold, triumphing in their faces;
   In youth, quick° bearing and dexterity;   *lively*
1390   And here and there the painter interlaces
   Pale cowards marching on with trembling paces,
     Which heartless° peasants did so well resemble   *dejected*
     That one would swear he saw them quake and tremble.

In Ajax and Ulysses, O what art
1395   Of physiognomy might one behold!
   The face of either ciphered° either's heart;   *represented*
   Their face their manners most expressly told.
   In Ajax' eyes blunt° rage and rigour rolled,   *rude*
     But the mild glance that sly Ulysses lent
1400   Showed deep regard° and smiling government.°   *judgment / self-control*

There pleading° might you see grave Nestor stand,   *persuading*
   As 'twere encouraging the Greeks to fight,
   Making such sober action with his hand
   That it beguiled attention, charmed the sight.
1405   In speech it seemed his beard all silver-white
     Wagged up and down, and from his lips did fly
     Thin winding breath which purled° up to the sky.   *curled*

---

3. Conflict between Trojans and Greeks; conflict between nature and art.

About him were a press of gaping faces
Which seemed to swallow up his sound advice,
1410 All jointly list'ning, but with several graces,° — *various attitudes*
As if some mermaid did their ears entice;
Some high, some low, the painter was so nice.° — *skillful; subtle*
   The scalps of many, almost hid behind,
   To jump up higher seemed, to mock the mind.° — *(by artistic illusion)*

1415 Here one man's hand leaned on another's head,
His nose being shadowed by his neighbour's ear;
Here one being thronged bears° back, all boll'n° and red; — *crowded pushes / swollen*
Another, smothered, seems to pelt° and swear, — *scold*
And in their rage such signs of rage they bear
1420   As but for loss of° Nestor's golden words — *That except they might miss*
   It seemed they would debate with angry swords.

For much imaginary° work was there; — *creative*
Conceit deceitful, so compact,° so kind,° — *efficient / natural*
That for Achilles' image stood his spear
1425 Gripped in an armèd hand; himself behind
Was left unseen save to the eye of mind;
   A hand, a foot, a face, a leg, a head,
   Stood for the whole to be imaginèd.

And from the walls of strong-besiegèd Troy
1430 When their brave hope, bold Hector, marched to field,
Stood many Trojan mothers sharing joy
To see their youthful sons bright weapons wield;
And to their hope they such odd action° yield — *contrary gestures*
   That through their light joy seemèd to appear,
1435   Like bright things stained, a kind of heavy fear.

And from the strand° of Dardan where they fought — *shore*
To Simois'° reedy banks the red blood ran, — *Trojan river*
Whose waves to imitate the battle sought
With swelling ridges, and their ranks began
1440 To break upon the gallèd° shore, and then — *eroded; injured*
   Retire again, till meeting greater ranks
   They join, and shoot their foam at Simois' banks.

To this well painted piece is Lucrece come,
To find a face where all distress is stelled.° — *engraved*
1445 Many she sees where cares have carvèd some,
But none where all distress and dolour dwelled
Till she despairing Hecuba° beheld — *Queen of Troy*
   Staring on Priam's° wounds with her old eyes, — *King of Troy*
   Which bleeding under Pyrrhus' proud foot lies.

1450 In her the painter had anatomized° — *laid open*
Time's ruin, beauty's wreck, and grim care's reign.
Her cheeks with chaps° and wrinkles were disguised;° — *cracks / disfigured*
Of what she was no semblance did remain.
Her blue blood changed to black in every vein,
1455   Wanting° the spring that those shrunk pipes had fed, — *Lacking*
   Showed life imprisoned in a body dead.

On this sad shadow Lucrece spends her eyes,
And shapes her sorrow to the beldame's° woes,   *old woman's*
Who nothing wants to answer her[4] but cries
1460   And bitter words to ban° her cruel foes.   *curse*
The painter was no god to lend her those,
    And therefore Lucrece swears he did her wrong
    To give her so much grief, and not a tongue.

'Poor instrument,' quoth she, 'without a sound,
1465   I'll tune° thy woes with my lamenting tongue,   *sing*
And drop sweet balm in Priam's painted wound,
And rail on Pyrrhus that hath done him wrong,
And with my tears quench Troy that burns so long,
    And with my knife scratch out the angry eyes
1470   Of all the Greeks that are thine enemies.

'Show me the strumpet° that began this stir,°   *(Helen) / dispute*
That with my nails her beauty I may tear.
Thy heat of lust, fond Paris, did incur
This load of wrath that burning Troy doth bear;
1475   Thine eye kindled the fire that burneth here,
    And here in Troy, for trespass of thine eye,
    The sire, the son, the dame and daughter die.

'Why should the private pleasure of someone
Become the public plague of many moe?°   *more*
1480   Let sin alone° committed light alone   *by one person*
Upon his head that hath transgressèd so;
Let guiltless souls be freed from guilty woe.
    For one's offence why should so many fall,
    To plague a private sin in general?°   *collectively*

1485 'Lo, here weeps Hecuba, here Priam dies,
Here manly Hector faints, here Troilus swoons,
Here friend by friend in bloody channel° lies,   *gutter*
And friend to friend gives unadvisèd° wounds,   *unintended*
And one man's lust these many lives confounds.
1490   Had doting Priam checked his son's desire,
    Troy had been bright with fame, and not with fire.'

Here feelingly she weeps Troy's painted woes;
For sorrow, like a heavy hanging bell
Once set on ringing, with his° own weight goes;   *its*
1495   Then little strength rings out the doleful knell.
So Lucrece, set a-work, sad tales doth tell
    To pencilled pensiveness and coloured sorrow.
    She lends them words, and she their looks doth borrow.

She throws her eyes about the painting round,
1500   And who she finds forlorn she doth lament.
At last she sees a wretched image bound,
That piteous looks to Phrygian shepherds lent.[5]

4. Who lacks nothing to resemble her.
5. That made Phrygian shepherds look on in pity (Phrygia was the area around Troy).

His face, though full of cares, yet showed content.
Onward to Troy with the blunt swains° he goes,   *rough rustics*
1505 So mild that patience° seemed to scorn his woes.   *his patience*

In him the painter laboured with his skill
To hide deceit and give the harmless show°   *appearance*
An humble gait, calm looks, eyes wailing still,°   *weeping continually*
A brow unbent that seemed to welcome woe;
1510 Cheeks neither red nor pale, but mingled so
That blushing red no guilty instance° gave,   *sign*
Nor ashy pale the fear that false hearts have.

But like a constant and confirmèd devil
He entertained° a show so seeming just,   *maintained*
1515 And therein so ensconced° his secret evil   *concealed*
That jealousy° itself could not mistrust°   *suspicion / suspect*
False creeping craft and perjury should thrust
Into so bright a day such blackfaced storms,
Or blot with hell-born sin such saint-like forms.

1520 The well skilled workman this mild image drew
For perjured Sinon,[6] whose enchanting° story   *deluding*
The credulous old Priam after slew;
Whose words like wildfire[7] burnt the shining glory
Of rich-built Ilion, that the skies were sorry,
1525 And little stars shot from their fixèd places
When their glass° fell wherein they viewed their faces.   *mirror (Troy)*

This picture she advisedly° perused,   *carefully*
And chid° the painter for his wondrous skill,   *scolded*
Saying some shape° in Sinon's was abused,   *(other person's shape)*
1530 So fair a form lodged not a mind so ill;
And still on him she gazed, and gazing still,
Such signs of truth in his plain° face she spied   *open*
That she concludes the picture was belied.°   *shown to be false*

'It cannot be,' quoth she, 'that so much guile' —
1535 She would have said 'can lurk in such a look',
But Tarquin's shape came in her mind the while,
And from her tongue 'can lurk' from 'cannot' took.
'It cannot be' she in that sense forsook,
And turned it thus: 'It cannot be, I find,
1540 But such a face should bear a wicked mind.

'For even as subtle Sinon here is painted,
So sober-sad, so weary, and so mild,
As if with grief or travail he had fainted,
To me came Tarquin armèd, too beguiled°   *disguised*
1545 With outward honesty, but yet defiled
With inward vice. As Priam him did cherish,
So did I Tarquin, so my Troy did perish.

---

6. Sinon was a Greek who pretended to have fled from
his own people; once "rescued" and brought to Troy, he
persuaded the Trojans to receive the wooden horse into
their city.
7. A mixture of sulfur, tar, and other combustible sub-
stances, used to set fires during battle.

'Look, look, how list'ning Priam wets his eyes
To see those borrowed° tears that Sinon sheds.   *inauthentic*
Priam, why art thou old and yet not wise?
For every tear he falls° a Trojan bleeds.   *(Sinon) lets fall*
His eye drops fire, no water thence proceeds.
   Those round clear pearls of his that move thy pity
   Are balls of quenchless fire to burn thy city.

'Such devils steal effects° from lightless hell,   *illusions*
For Sinon in his fire doth quake with cold,
And in that cold hot-burning fire doth dwell.
These contraries such unity do hold
Only to flatter° fools and make them bold;   *encourage*
   So Priam's trust false Sinon's tears doth flatter
   That he finds means to burn his Troy with water.'

Here, all enraged, such passion her assails
That patience is quite beaten from her breast.
She tears the senseless° Sinon with her nails,   *unfeeling*
Comparing him to that unhappy° guest   *misfortune-bringing*
Whose deed hath made herself herself detest.
   At last she smilingly with this gives o'er:
   'Fool, fool,' quoth she, 'his wounds will not be sore.'

Thus ebbs and flows the current of her sorrow,
And time doth weary time with her complaining.
She looks for night, and then she longs for morrow,
And both she thinks too long with her remaining.
Short time seems long in sorrow's sharp sustaining.°   *painful enduring*
   Though woe be heavy, yet it seldom sleeps,
   And they that watch° see time how slow it creeps.   *remain awake*

Which all this time hath overslipped her thought
That she with painted images hath spent,
Being from the feeling of her own grief brought
By deep surmise° of others' detriment,°   *contemplation / suffering*
Losing her woes in shows of discontent.°   *pictures of sorrow*
   It easeth some, though none it ever cured,
   To think their dolour others have endured.

But now the mindful° messenger come back   *dutiful*
Brings home his lord and other company,
Who finds his Lucrece clad in mourning black,
And round about her tear-distainèd° eye   *tear-stained*
Blue circles streamed, like rainbows in the sky.
   These water-galls° in her dim element°   *rainbow fragments / sky*
   Foretell new storms to° those already spent.   *in addition to*

Which when her sad beholding husband saw,
Amazedly in her sad face he stares.
Her eyes, though sod° in tears, looked red and raw,   *sodden*
Her lively colour killed with deadly cares.
He hath no power to ask her how she fares.
   Both stood like old acquaintance in a trance,
   Met far from home, wond'ring each other's chance.°   *fortune*

At last he takes her by the bloodless hand,
And thus begins: 'What uncouth° ill event   *strange*
Hath thee befall'n, that thou dost trembling stand?
1600 Sweet love, what spite° hath thy fair colour spent?   *harm*
Why art thou thus attired in discontent?[8]
    Unmask,° dear dear, this moody heaviness,   *Disclose*
    And tell thy grief, that we may give redress.'

Three times with sighs she gives her sorrow fire[9]
1605 Ere once she can discharge one word of woe.
At length addressed° to answer his desire,   *ready*
She modestly prepares to let them know
Her honour is ta'en prisoner by the foe,
    While Collatine and his consorted° lords   *accompanying*
1610   With sad attention long to hear her words.

And now this pale swan in her wat'ry nest
Begins the sad dirge of her certain ending.[1]
'Few words,' quoth she, 'shall fit the trespass best,
Where no excuse can give the fault amending.
1615 In me more woes than words are now depending,°   *weighing; belonging*
    And my laments would be drawn out too long
    To tell them all with one poor tired tongue.

'Then be this all the task it hath to say:
Dear husband, in the interest° of thy bed   *claiming possession*
1620 A stranger came, and on that pillow lay
Where thou wast wont to rest thy weary head;
And what wrong else may be imaginèd
    By foul enforcement might be done to me,
    From that, alas, thy Lucrece is not free.

1625 'For in the dreadful dead of dark midnight
With shining falchion in my chamber came
A creeping creature with a flaming light,
And softly cried, "Awake, thou Roman dame,
And entertain° my love; else lasting shame   *receive*
1630   On thee and thine this night I will inflict,
    If thou my love's desire do contradict.

'"For some hard-favoured° groom of thine," quoth he,   *ugly*
"Unless thou yoke thy liking to my will,
I'll murder straight,° and then I'll slaughter thee,   *immediately*
1635 And swear I found you where you did fulfil
The loathsome act of lust, and so did kill
    The lechers in their deed. This act will be
    My fame, and thy perpetual infamy."

'With this I did begin to start and cry,
1640 And then against my heart he set his sword,
Swearing unless I took all patiently

---

8. Black; see line 1585.
9. As sixteenth-century gunners lighted firearms with matches.

1. Swans were supposed to sing only when they were on the point of death.

I should not live to speak another word.
So should my shame still rest upon record,
  And never be forgot in mighty Rome
1645 Th'adulterate° death of Lucrece and her groom.   *adulterous*

'Mine enemy was strong, my poor self weak,
And far the weaker with so strong a fear.
My bloody judge forbade my tongue to speak;
No rightful plea might plead for justice there.
1650 His scarlet lust came° evidence to swear   *gave*
  That my poor beauty had purloined his eyes;
  And when the judge is robbed, the prisoner dies.

'O teach me how to make mine own excuse,
Or at the least this refuge let me find:
1655 Though my gross blood be stained with this abuse,
Immaculate and spotless is my mind.
  That was not forced, that never was inclined
    To accessory yieldings,² but still pure
    Doth in her poisoned closet yet endure.'

1660 Lo, here the hopeless merchant° of this loss,   *owner (Collatine)*
With head declined° and voice dammed up with woe,   *bent*
With sad set eyes and wreathèd arms across,³
From lips new waxen° pale begins to blow   *newly grown*
The grief away that stops his answer so;
1665   But wretched as he is, he strives in vain.
    What he breathes out, his breath drinks up again.

As through an arch° the violent roaring tide   *(under a bridge)*
Outruns the eye that doth behold his haste,
Yet in the eddy boundeth in his pride
1670 Back to the strait that forced him on so fast,
In rage sent out, recalled in rage being past;
  Even so his sighs, his sorrows, make a saw,⁴
  To push grief on, and back the same grief draw.

Which speechless woe of his poor she attendeth,°   *poor Lucrece notes*
1675 And his untimely frenzy° thus awaketh: *delirium*
'Dear lord, thy sorrow to my sorrow lendeth
Another power;° no flood by raining slaketh.   *Greater strength*
My woe too sensible° thy passion maketh,   *acutely felt*
  More feeling-painful. Let it then suffice
1680 To drown on woe one pair of weeping eyes.

'And for my sake, when I might charm thee so,⁵
For she that was thy Lucrece, now attend me.
Be suddenly revengèd on my foe—
Thine, mine, his own. Suppose thou dost defend me
1685 From what is past. The help that thou shalt lend me

---

2. To yielding that would make me an accessory to the
crime. See line 793 and note.
3. See line 793 and note.

4. Go back and forth (inhaling and exhaling), like a saw
cutting wood.
5. As I used to be when I charmed you (before the rape).

Comes all too late, yet let the traitor die,
For sparing° justice feeds° iniquity.   *lenient / encourages*

'But ere I name him, you fair lords,' quoth she,
Speaking to those that came with Collatine,
1690 'Shall plight° your honourable faiths to me   *pledge*
With swift pursuit to venge this wrong of mine;
For 'tis a meritorious fair design°   *intention*
    To chase injustice with revengeful arms.
    Knights, by their oaths, should right poor ladies' harms.'

1695 At this request with noble disposition°   *purpose*
Each present lord began to promise aid,
As bound in knighthood to her imposition,°   *imposed task*
Longing to hear the hateful foe bewrayed.°   *revealed*
But she that yet her sad task hath not said°   *completed*
1700   The protestation stops. 'O speak,' quoth she;
    'How may this forcèd stain be wiped from me?

'What is the quality of my offence,
Being constrained with dreadful circumstance?
May my pure mind with the foul act dispense,
1705 My low-declinèd honour to advance?°   *raise*
May any terms acquit me from this chance?°   *mishap*
    The poisoned fountain clears itself again,
    And why not I from this compellèd stain?'

With this they all at once began to say
1710 Her body's stain her mind untainted clears,
While with a joyless smile she turns away
The face, that map which deep impression bears
Of hard misfortune, carved in it with tears.
    'No, no,' quoth she, 'no dame hereafter living
1715   By my excuse shall claim excuse's giving.'

Here with a sigh as if her heart would break
She throws forth Tarquin's name. 'He, he,' she says—
But more than he her poor tongue could not speak,
Till after many accents° and delays,   *sighs*
1720 Untimely breathings, sick and short essays,°   *attempts*
    She utters this: 'He, he, fair lords, 'tis he
    That guides this hand to give this wound to me.'

Even here she sheathèd in her harmless° breast   *innocent*
A harmful knife, that thence her soul unsheathed.
1725 That blow did bail° it from the deep unrest   *liberate*
Of that polluted prison where it breathed.
Her contrite sighs unto the clouds bequeathed
    Her wingèd sprite,° and through her wounds doth fly   *spirit*
    Life's lasting date[6] from cancelled destiny.

---

6. Eternal duration. The line is difficult, and could mean that Lucrece's immortal soul separates from her earthly life and body (canceled destiny), or that Lucrece, by tak-ing her fate into her own hands (canceling her destiny), makes her fame eternal.

1730 Stone-still, astonished° with this deadly deed   *stunned*
Stood Collatine and all his lordly crew,
Till Lucrece' father that beholds her bleed
Himself on her self-slaughtered body threw;
And from the purple fountain Brutus[7] drew
1735   The murd'rous knife; and as it left the place
   Her blood in poor revenge held it in chase,

And bubbling from her breast it doth divide
In two slow rivers, that the crimson blood
Circles her body in on every side,
1740 Who like a late-sacked° island vastly° stood,   *just-looted / devastated*
Bare and unpeopled in this fearful° flood.   *fearsome*
   Some of her blood still pure and red remained,
   And some looked black, and that false Tarquin-stained.

About the mourning and congealèd face
1745 Of that black blood a wat'ry rigol° goes,   *circle*
Which seems to weep upon the tainted place;
And ever since, as pitying Lucrece' woes,
Corrupted blood some watery token shows;
   And blood untainted still doth red abide,
1750   Blushing at that which is so putrefied.

'Daughter, dear daughter,' old Lucretius cries,
'That life was mine which thou hast here deprived.
If in the child the father's image lies,
Where shall I live now Lucrece is unlived?°   *slain*
1755 Thou wast not to this end from me derived.
   If children predecease progenitors,
   We are their offspring, and they none of ours.

'Poor broken glass,° I often did behold   *mirror*
In thy sweet semblance my old age new born;
1760 But now that fair fresh mirror, dim and old,
Shows me a bare-boned death° by time outworn.   *skull*
   O, from thy cheeks my image thou hast torn,
   And shivered all the beauty of my glass,
   That I no more can see what once I was.

1765 'O time, cease thou thy course and last no longer,
If they surcease° to be that should survive!   *cease*
Shall rotten death make conquest of the stronger,
And leave the falt'ring feeble souls alive?
The old bees die, the young possess their hive.
1770   Then live, sweet Lucrece, live again and see
   Thy father die, and not thy father thee.'

By this starts Collatine as from a dream,
And bids Lucretius give his sorrow place;
And then in key-cold° Lucrece' bleeding stream   *cold as metal*
1775 He falls, and bathes the pale fear in his face,

7. Lucius Junius Brutus. Tarquin the Proud, the rapist's father, had killed Brutus's brother, but Brutus, whose name means "stupid," escaped royal suspicion by pretending to be mentally retarded. After Lucrece's rape, he led the coup that overthrew the Tarquins and established republican government in Rome.

And counterfeits to die with her a space,
  Till manly shame bids him possess his breath,
  And live to be revengèd on her death.

The deep vexation of his inward soul
1780 Hath served a dumb arrest° upon his tongue,   *silent injunction*
  Who, mad that sorrow should his use control,°   *prevent*
  Or keep him from heart-easing words so long,
  Begins to talk; but through his lips do throng
    Weak words, so thick come in his poor heart's aid
1785   That no man could distinguish what he said.

Yet sometime 'Tarquin' was pronouncèd plain,
  But through his teeth, as if the name he tore.
  This windy tempest, till it blow up rain,
  Held back his sorrow's tide to make it more.
1790 At last it rains, and busy winds give o'er.
    Then son and father weep with equal strife
    Who should weep most, for daughter or for wife.

The one doth call her his, the other his,
  Yet neither may possess the claim they lay.
1795 The father says 'She's mine'; 'O, mine she is,'
  Replies her husband, 'do not take away
  My sorrow's interest;° let no mourner say   *title of possession*
    He weeps for her, for she was only mine,
    And only must be wailed by Collatine.'

1800 'O,' quoth Lucretius, 'I did give that life
  Which she too early and too late hath spilled.'
  'Woe, woe,' quoth Collatine, 'she was my wife.
  I owed° her, and 'tis mine that she hath killed.'   *owned*
  'My daughter' and 'my wife' with clamours filled
1805   The dispersed air, who, holding Lucrece' life,[8]
    Answered° their cries, 'my daughter' and 'my wife'.   *Echoed*

Brutus, who plucked the knife from Lucrece' side,
  Seeing such emulation° in their woe   *competition*
  Began to clothe his wit in state° and pride,   *dignity*
1810 Burying in Lucrece' wound his folly's show.°   *pretended stupidity*
  He with the Romans was esteemèd so
    As silly jeering idiots° are with kings,   *court jesters*
    For sportive words and utt'ring foolish things.

But now he throws that shallow habit° by   *foolish appearance*
1815 Wherein deep policy° did him disguise,   *shrewdness*
  And armed his long-hid wits advisedly°   *prudently*
  To check the tears in Collatinus' eyes.
  'Thou wrongèd lord of Rome,' quoth he, 'arise.
    Let my unsounded° self, supposed a fool,   *of unknown depth*
1820   Now set thy long-experienced wit to school.

'Why, Collatine, is woe the cure for woe?
  Do wounds help wounds, or grief help grievous deeds?

8. See lines 1727ff.

Is it revenge to give thyself a blow
For his foul act by whom thy fair wife bleeds?
1825 Such childish humour° from weak minds proceeds;   *silly behavior*
    Thy wretched wife mistook the matter so
    To slay herself, that should have slain her foe.

'Courageous Roman, do not steep thy heart
In such relenting dew of lamentations,
1830 But kneel with me, and help to bear thy part
To rouse our Roman gods with invocations
    That they will suffer° these abominations—   *allow*
    Since Rome herself in them doth stand disgraced—
    By our strong arms from forth her fair streets chased.°   *to be chased*

1835 'Now by the Capitol that we adore,
And by this chaste blood so unjustly stained,
By heaven's fair sun that breeds the fat° earth's store,°   *fertile / plenty*
By all our country° rights in Rome maintained,   *civic*
And by chaste Lucrece' soul that late complained
1840   Her wrongs to us, and by this bloody knife,
    We will revenge the death of this true wife.'

This said, he struck his hand upon his breast,
And kissed the fatal knife to end his vow,
And to his protestation urged the rest,
1845 Who, wond'ring at him, did his words allow.°   *approve*
Then jointly to the ground their knees they bow,
    And that deep vow which Brutus made before
    He doth again repeat, and that they swore.

When they had sworn to this advisèd doom°   *considered judgment*
1850 They did conclude to bear dead Lucrece thence,
To show her bleeding body thorough° Rome,   *throughout*
And so to publish° Tarquin's foul offence;   *publicize*
Which being done with speedy diligence,
    The Romans plausibly° did give consent   *with applause*
1855   To Tarquin's everlasting banishment.

TEXTUAL VARIANTS

Control text: Q1

Q1: The Quarto of 1594

The poem is called "Lucrece" on the title page but *"The Rape of Lucrece"* in the head title and running titles.

550 blows blow
950 blemish cherish
1316 stain's stain'd
1475 Thine Thy
1544 armèd, too armed to
1662 wreathèd wretched
1713 in it it in

The Sonnets and
"A Lover's Complaint"

Shakespeare's plays have always been noted for their indifference to the rules of construction promoted by classically oriented dramatic theorists. His sonnets apparently fall at the opposite end of the spectrum: they faithfully conform to a highly structured set of formal requirements that often seem to constrain artistic creativity. But this adherence to convention provides the basis for a striking verbal and thematic originality organized around the daring representation of the speaker's homoerotic and adulterous passions.

What we now call the sonnet originated in thirteenth-century Italy. There, in the following century, the poetry of Francesco Petrarch inspired the internationalization of the form. Fourteen lines long and divided by the rhyme scheme (abbaabba cdecde) into an octave and a sestet, Petrarch's sonnets address an unapproachable, beloved woman in a sequence chronicling the author's passionate suffering, his self-absorption, his idealization of the beloved, his exquisitely modulated expressions of longing and frustration. The Petrarchan mode reached England by the early sixteenth century in the works of Sir Thomas Wyatt and Henry Howard, Earl of Surrey, whose sonnets were first published in what is known today as *Tottel's Miscellany* (1557). Wyatt and Surrey modified the form by developing the rhyme scheme later adopted by Shakespeare (abab cdcd efef gg), which divides the poem into three quatrains and a couplet.

The English enthusiasm for sonnet sequences, which was also influenced by the sixteenth-century French poets Ronsard and du Bellay, was triggered by the posthumous printing of Sir Philip Sidney's collection *Astrophel and Stella* (1591) and sustained by the publication of Samuel Daniel's *Delia* (1591, 1592) and Edmund Spenser's *Amoretti* (1595), among many others. Sonnets also circulated in manuscript form, since print culture was often considered beneath the dignity of the (would-be) gentleman or courtier-poet. This vogue for sonnet sequences responded to poets' literary, social, and economic ambitions as well as to the gender politics of the late Elizabethan court. Middle-class writers, for instance, sought protection and financial assistance for their work by praising their aristocratic patrons. Expressions of love in this hierarchical relationship may be less indications of deep feeling than competitive strategies of advancement. The group of Shakespeare's sonnets (78–80, 82–86) complaining that a rival poet is winning favor with the male youth the speaker loves seems to convert this competition into literary theme. In general, then, it is often hard to determine where authentic sentiment ends and professional calculation begins. *Love's Labour's Lost* (1594–95) includes two sonnets spoken by ardent lovers whose motives are treated with extreme skepticism by the women they woo.

The interest in love sonnets continued in the early seventeenth century, but the form also acquired greater thematic breadth. The deaths of Queen Elizabeth in 1603 (see sonnet 107) and of King James's son Prince Henry in 1612 inspired many individual memorial sonnets as well as whole sonnet sequences. Some poets, most notably John Donne, adapted the sonnet sequence to religious purposes (see sonnet 146). Always sensitive to literary and theatrical trends, Shakespeare composed sonnets on all of these themes as well as many others. Although traditionally the majority of his sonnets have been dated to the early or mid-1590s, recent scholarship has argued that most, perhaps nearly all were revised or initially composed no earlier than the late 1590s and that Shakespeare continued working on the sequence almost until its publication in 1609. (See the Textual Note.)

When the sonnets appeared in print, they were followed in the same collection by "A Lover's Complaint" (begun c. 1602–5, completed 1608–9). This work obviously belongs to the genre of complaint poetry, in which a woman laments her (usually) sexual ruin amid generally doleful reflections on life. Spenser's *Complaints* (1591) provided one of the models, but in the juxtaposition of sonnet sequence and complaint the collection recalls Daniel's *Delia*, whose three parts—sonnet sequence, short poem in anacreontics (an ancient Greek poetic meter), and complaint in rhyme royal (seven-line stanzas rhyming ababbcc)—comment on each other. Between 1593 and 1596, five other poets published works consisting of a sonnet sequence, a brief intermediate piece usually anacreontic in form or subject matter (Cupid, for example), and a concluding complaint. The sonnets section of one of these five works, Richard Barnfield's *Cynthia* (1595), from which Shakespeare probably borrowed, is addressed to an attractive male youth. Shakespeare follows suit: his first 126 sonnets also recount the speaker's homoerotic love for a beautiful, well-born male youth. Another work, Thomas Lodge's *Phillis* (1593), divides the sonnets section of his volume into two main groups. So does Shakespeare: sonnets 127–52 are organized around not the relationship with the youth but the speaker's adulterous affair with his mistress. (The final two sonnets concern Cupid.) Thus, Shakespeare's 1609 Quarto—a sonnet sequence divided into two parts, the first concerning a beautiful male youth and the second a woman; two concluding sonnets on Cupid; and a complaint in rhyme royal—is less miscellaneous collection than well-established multigeneric form.

That form is characterized by its links between the sonnets and the concluding complaint. In Shakespeare's collection, the voyeurism of some of the poems dealing with the affair between the male youth and the speaker's mistress (40–42, 133–34, 144) anticipates "A Lover's Complaint." In a conventional pastoral landscape, the narrator of the latter poem overhears a distraught young woman tell an old man of her seduction and abandonment by an attractive young man, whose features she stereotypically chronicles and whose duplicitous method of wooing she quotes at length. Except for the old man, the characters bear some resemblance to the three central figures in the sonnet sequence. Yet the similarities should not be overstressed. In "A Lover's Complaint" but not in the sonnets, the male youth seduces the woman, and both seemingly get to speak for themselves. The first-person voice—the only one heard in the sonnets—is not allowed even the concluding comment prepared for by the opening frame. In the narrative world of "A Lover's Complaint," the intensity of the more lyrical form is left behind. Similarly, the longer poem's ornamental, archaic diction, intensified by coinages designed to evoke bygone days, complements the dramatic setting and contrasts with the sonnets' mixture of down-to-earth colloquialism and metaphorical density.

In the sonnets, one finds a similar combination of the conventional and the innovative. Shakespeare does not experiment a great deal with meter, rhyme scheme, or the usual subdivisions internal to the poem (three quatrains and a couplet). Though a few sonnets develop a single image (sonnet 7, for example), most progress cumulatively by line (1) or quatrain (73) before being capped by the concluding couplet, which epigrammatically summarizes, generalizes, reverses, or draws inferences from the preceding argument. Shakespeare eschews dialogue, anagrams, and other variations introduced by earlier poets. His speaker almost always addresses or discusses the beloved. His frequent deployment of paired sonnets, though relatively anomalous in previous collections, does have a precedent in *Delia*. Again like his immediate predecessors, Shakespeare shows less interest in plot and character than in the occasion they provide for reflection on love and related topics—seasonal rhythms, human mortality, and artistic immortality. Even the rejection of Petrarchan stereotypes in favor of authentic emotion (130), including the speaker's desperation, had itself become a stereotype.

On the other hand, the sonnets are marked by an unusual linguistic inventiveness that produces elaborate verbal patterns. Syntax may play off against rhyme scheme. For instance, most of the sonnets link the first two quatrains into an octave; more striking, in sonnet 81, almost any two consecutive lines form a complete sentence. Equally complex effects are produced by the poems' alliteration and assonance, neologisms, wordplay, and especially metaphorical elaboration. Consider sonnet 73:

That time of year thou mayst in me behold
When yellow leaves, or none, or few, do hang
Upon those boughs which shake against the cold,
Bare ruined choirs where late the sweet birds sang.
5 In me thou seest the twilight of such day
As after sunset fadeth in the west,
Which by and by black night doth take away,
Death's second self, that seals up all in rest.
In me thou seest the glowing of such fire
10 That on the ashes of his youth doth lie
As the death-bed whereon it must expire,
Consumed with that which it was nourished by.
This thou perceiv'st, which makes thy love more strong,
To love that well which thou must leave ere long.

The evocation of fall in the opening quatrain communicates the sadness of aging with physical vividness, while the seasonal cycle works against the irreversibility of natural decay. "Yellow leaves" has the secondary meaning of leaves of a book, "bare ruined choirs" of quires (manuscript gatherings). Similarly, the birds' recent song, now no longer heard, seems to refer to the speaker's own poetic voice and hence to suggest a loss of confidence in his literary creativity. The fourth line may also link the inevitability of bodily decline with a hardly inevitable human act of violence—Henry VIII's dissolution of the monasteries. In short, the experience of aging is compared to the annual movement toward colder seasons, to the decline of artistic inspiration, and perhaps to the pillaging of the Catholic Church in the interest of monarchical centralization.

In the second quatrain, the unit of time constricts: "That time of year" is replaced by "the twilight of such day" as a metaphor for aging. But these lines also move forward in time in a way the first quatrain does not. Twilight is taken away by "black night . . . , / Death's second self, that seals up all in rest." Night is compared with death, and the syntax, at odds with the literal meaning, suggests that it is death rather than night "that seals up all in [eternal] rest." As in the opening lines, however, the cyclical character of nature works against the unidirectional finality of death—night follows day, but day also follows night.

The third quatrain opens like the second, with "In me thou seest," a phrase that partly occurs in the first line of the poem as well. This repetition reinforces the parallelism among the quatrains already implied by the rhyme scheme and suggests that the poem proceeds less by narrative progression than by variations on a single theme. Yet this quatrain seems to narrow time further, to the dying of a fire, while making the transition from aging to mortality still more explicit. The ashes are what is left of the fire's and, by implication, the speaker's "youth" (line 10); they are the fire's and the speaker's "death-bed" (line 11). In other words, the metaphorical relationship has been reversed. The dying fire is a metaphor for human aging, but that aging becomes a metaphor for the dying of the fire. Unlike seasons and days, fires are not cyclical; but the same hint of rebirth is achieved here through an allusion to the legendary phoenix, a self-resurrecting bird that died in flames and was reborn from the ashes. In the final line of the quatrain, the fire dies along with the ashes. Alternatively, the fire is "consumed" (choked) by the very ashes that, as fuel, previously "nourished" it. Both "consumed" and "nourished" are metaphorical explanations of the already metaphorical fire itself, which the two words implicitly connect back to humanity through their allusions to eating. The concealed reference seems to be to the speaker's fiery passion for the youth he is addressing, a passion that nourished him when he was young but that consumes him now that he is old.

The concluding couplet moves away from metaphor and toward generalization. Recognizing the speaker's literally consuming passion makes the youth's "love more strong" (line 13). The youth therefore loves well what he "must leave ere long" (line 14)—explicitly the speaker; implicitly, in a final generalizing step, his own life. The destructive power of time is partly counteracted by love. But the Christian belief in eternal life, perhaps weakly invoked in the quatrains' natural and mythological references to cyclical regeneration, is absent from this final couplet.

Shakespeare's reversing of the metaphorical relationship in sonnet 73 removes any fixed point of reference, any stable ground. This phenomenon is also apparent in the economic imagery of the first seventeen sonnets, in which the speaker tries to convince the youth to marry and thus produce an heir. That imagery frequently turns on usury. Long the subject of widespread denunciation, usury in Renaissance England was just beginning its conversion into the respectable financial category of interest, essential to capitalism. Shakespeare generally shared the prevailing repugnance at the idea that money could or should be made out of money. Thus, condemning his mistress for her affair with the young man, which is represented as collecting a debt, the speaker says,

> The statute of thy beauty thou wilt take,
> Thou usurer that putt'st forth all to use.
> (134.9–10)

She will "take" the full amount owed to her financially (sexually) because, like a "usurer," she employs "all" her wealth (her body) for profit ("use" means both "engage in usury" and "engage in sexual activity"). More ambivalently, the youth is criticized for being, paradoxically, both "unthrifty" and a "niggard" (4.1, 5):

> Profitless usurer, why dost thou use
> So great a sum of sums yet canst not live?
> (4.7–8)

Here, "use" antithetically means both "use up" and "lend at interest." Literally, how can the young man lend vast "sums" for profit and be unable to support himself? Metaphorically, he acts in a "profitless" manner in wasting his endowments. Hence, he cannot "live" on in his children. By implication, a usurer is always without value.

But the lines also imagine a thriving usurer. If there is a profitless usurer, there might also be a profitable one. It is this good usurer who predominates in the sonnets.

> That use is not forbidden usury
> Which happies those that pay the willing loan.
> (6.5–6)

Once again, there is an ambiguity: is "forbidden" an attribute of all, or just unallowable, usury? When "use" occurs in an economic context but without the presence of the word "usury," the valence is positive. For example, keeping one's "treasure" to oneself merits only "thriftless praise"; "beauty's use" deserves "much more praise" if a child results (2.6–9). At least "an unthrift" allows the world to enjoy his wealth; "beauty's waste" is indefensible—"kept unused, the user so destroys it" (9.9–12). And since nature made the speaker's beloved male, thus precluding a sexual relationship between them, "mine be thy love and thy love's use their treasure" (20.14). The speaker gets the youth's love, whereas women's "treasure" is merely the "use" (metaphorically, children) of that love. The poetic voice gets the principal, women the interest. (Alternatively, the youth uses women sexually while loving only the speaker.) These passages activate the multiple meanings of "use" for the metaphorical purpose of promoting marriage and family. But in so doing, they implicitly connect beauty with usury, which comes to be understood as the economic equivalent of human reproduction, the early sonnets' highest ideal. The traditional, almost feudal celebration of lineage smuggles in a defense of economic behavior often felt to be destructive of tradition. Employed as a metaphor to persuade the youth to marry and have children, usury is itself transformed into a potentially noble activity. Through metaphor, then, Shakespeare is able to entertain ideas that might have been literally unthinkable to him as bald statements.

Looming over the sonnets concerning the youth is the figure of time, to which the poet offers deeply meditated but increasingly desperate and not entirely convincing responses. These include the organic metaphors of recurrence—in sonnet 73, the seasons as well as day and night; elsewhere, plants and flowers, especially the rose. The admonitions to the youth to breed in the first seventeen sonnets come with the promise of immortality through marriage and childbirth. When the advice apparently goes unheeded, Shakespeare seemingly falls back on the immortality conferred by the speaker's verse: "Not marble nor the gilded monuments / Of princes shall outlive this powerful rhyme" (55.1–2). The evolution in the sonnets of the poet's argument about time and immortality is part of a more general movement toward pessimism that rehearses in miniature Shakespeare's shift in the theater from comedy to tragedy. The sonnets' two main sections—the poems on the youth and those on the mistress—can be seen as affirmation and negation, praise and blame, or main plot and subplot.

Yet the vast majority of the poems are not explicitly about either the youth or the mistress and do not even designate the sex of the person discussed. Only their relative position in the collection has produced the standard simplification adopted here. Similarly, though the sonnets' order makes the speaker's two relationships seem successive, these sections must be simultaneous if the love triangle described in each part refers to the same event (40–42, 133–34, and especially 144). The poems to the mistress in particular show little sign of process, instead expressing occasional affection combined with a dominant sense of chaos, bitterness, self-abasement, shame and self-loathing. But the first 126 sonnets too evince only intermittent interest in linear movement, emphasizing jealousy, longing, and a fear of separation, while anticipating both the desire and the anguish of the subsequent poems.

The intensity of these feelings, the psychological complexity with which they are scrutinized, the originality of this subject matter, the consistent use of the first person, and the speaker's self-conscious identification of himself with Shakespeare ("*Will*" in the quarto versions of 135–36), all encourage a biographical interpretation of the sonnets. So too does the feeling some of the verse gives the reader of overhearing snatches of conversation. For two centuries, such interpretation has proven risky either to undertake or to avoid. Shakespeare's unorthodox material is particularly difficult to assimilate because it is about Shakespeare rather than, as in the plays, fictional or historical figures. In 1780, Shakespearean editor George Steevens complained of sonnet 20, "It is impossible to read this fulsome panegyrick [excessive praise], addressed to a male object, without an equal mixture of disgust and indignation." For Steevens, the apostrophe to the young man in the second line—"thou, the master-mistress of my passion"—endorsed what we now call homosexuality. His revulsion extended to the sonnets as a whole, which he declined to publish in his 1793 edition of the plays. Even an ostensible foe of Steevens and friend of the sonnets, writing in 1840, found sonnet 20 "painful and . . . disagreeable"; the speaker's love for another male left this critic with a "disagreeable feeling, bordering on disgust."

The flip side of this response—to deny the homoeroticism of the relationship—is more common. The object of the poetic voice's desire, who is consistently called a "youth" (for instance, at 2.3), is converted into a young man, though he is actually referred to as a man only once—exactly as

"Thy beauty's form in table of my heart" (24.2). Here a man is holding a "table" (tablet) in front of his heart while another man engraves the first man's portrait on it. From Geffrey Whitney, A *Choice of Emblemes* (1586).

often as he is addressed as a boy. This tampering with age removes the possible embarrassment of pedophilia and allows the relationship to be seen as a version of Renaissance male friendship. Even the notorious sonnet 20 has been offered in support of this approach. There, the speaker seems to deny that his relationship with the youth was sexually consummated, "since [nature] pricked thee out for women's pleasure" (20.13). This interpretation, however, must ignore or explain away the many explicit expressions of love as well as the powerful evocation of a range of feelings ordinarily associated with love. It also cannot do justice to the repeated comparison of the youth to a "rose"—a traditional symbol of female genitalia and arguably the speaker's name for his object of desire. (See the note to 1.2.)

Since the poems to the speaker's mistress have also seemed scandalous, the sordid, adulterous affair they depict has been socially elevated and hence cleaned up by critics who name the mistress the "dark lady," thus giving her a rank comparable to the youth's. Yet she is never referred to as a lady and is called "dark" only once. On the other hand, she is repeatedly associated with blackness, and this has on occasion promoted racist anxieties. In 1861, the German writer Wilhelm Jordan concluded that the mistress came "from the West Indian colonies, was of creole descent with an admixture of African blood." Early twentieth-century critics found in her an "Ethiope," "a negress," or a "Creole type." The supposed discovery in the 1930s of the real historical personage, a London prostitute named Lucy Negro, inspired a 1964 demonstration that Lucy Negro was not a Negro and the denunciation of the "discredit of believing Shakespeare's fair enslaver a blackamoor."

The praise of blackness in the early sonnets to the mistress, as in other poetry of the time, echoes the biblical Song of Songs as well as sixteenth-century continental and English poetry, including that of Sir Philip Sidney. That praise is often part of a misogynistic denunciation of the use of cosmetics to produce artificial beauty (for example, 127). Blackness of hair and eyes (127.9, 130.4) gained prestige in the 1590s through a shift in fashion from blond hair to dark. Thus when Shakespeare writes, "In the old age black was not counted fair" (127.1), he records a social rather than merely personal change. There is no evidence of a racial reference in these poems, however. Even the information that "her breasts are dun" (130.3) contrasts the mistress with falsely idealized women or with aristocratic ladies who were able to avoid the sun. Nonetheless, the sonnets to the mistress may be metaphorically related to the racialized discourse of the period. Shakespeare recurrently features actual or threatened interracial coupling—in *Titus Andronicus*, *Othello*, *Antony and Cleopatra*, *The Tempest*, and, somewhat more surprisingly, *Love's Labour's Lost*. Despite the recent enthusiasm for black hair, the mistress's combination of blackness and promiscuity may provoke both the desire and the fear of a powerfully exotic female sexuality. The speaker's bitterness over the affair, then, produces the equation of blackness with immorality. Blackness is thus moralized in contradictory ways within this section of the sonnets.

The plausible belief that the poems are autobiographical has also inspired a major but unsuccessful scholarly effort to discover the real people whom Shakespeare discusses but does not name. Christopher Marlowe and George Chapman are among those suggested as the rival poet. The youth has most often been identified with Henry Wriothesley, Earl of Southampton, and William Herbert, Earl of Pembroke. The sonnets' dedication is to "M^r. W. H.," Pembroke's initials and the reverse of Southampton's. But neither is likely to have been addressed as "Mr.," there may well be chronological problems with the attributions, and "W. H." could be a misprint for "W. SH." (William Shakespeare). Suggestions about the mistress are even shakier. Candidates have included Lucy Negro; Mary Fitton, who had a child with Pembroke and was a lady-in-waiting at court; and Emilia Lanier, a dark-skinned woman who was supposedly Lord Hunsdon's mistress. Partly in response to these inconclusive speculations, mid-twentieth-century criticism of the sonnets focused on formal concerns. But the advances critics produced in this field often came at the expense of evading the disconcerting biographical material the poems do seem to provide. Both the sonnets and Shakespeare's plays combine verbal artistry with psychological exploration. It is harder to integrate these two concerns in the poetry than in the drama, however. The fascination and the challenge of the sonnets are that their language is of almost unequaled complexity, while the soul they examine is apparently Shakespeare's own.

WALTER COHEN

TEXTUAL NOTE

The sonnets and "A Lover's Complaint" were printed for the first time in "SHAKE-SPEARES SONNETS," a quarto that appeared in 1609. The type for the volume was set by two compositors, who probably worked from a scribal transcript of an authorial manuscript. Since the compositors punctuated in different ways, the quarto's punctuation cannot be regarded as authorial. Most editors have also doubted that Shakespeare had anything to do with the printing of the quarto; but this conclusion is probably wrong. The publisher, Thomas Thorpe, was a reputable figure who obtained the copyright for his book in the standard fashion—by having it entered in the Stationers' Register. He had good professional relations with Shakespeare's acting company and perhaps friendly personal relations with Shakespeare himself. Unauthorized publication would have jeopardized those connections. Moreover, a publisher did not have the right to include the author's name without the author's permission, and hardly any texts of the time that were registered for copyright violated this regulation. If Thorpe had done so, he would have risked a significant financial penalty that he could ill afford. In short, it is very likely that Shakespeare arranged and authorized the publication of the volume.

The quarto was reprinted in *Poems: Written by W. Shakespeare, Gent.* (1640), in which the sonnets (with eight omitted) and "A Lover's Complaint" were joined by additional poetry of Shakespeare and other writers, individual sonnets were run together to produce longer works, the sonnets were titled, their order was rearranged, and a few pronouns were changed or (in the titles) invented so as to make the speaker's beloved female rather than male. This collection has no independent textual value. *The Passionate Pilgrim* (first edition, 1599 or earlier; second edition, 1599–1600), an unauthorized volume attributed to Shakespeare by its publisher, is a different matter. The second edition includes twenty poems—three from *Love's Labour's Lost* (the 1598 Quarto of which presumably had already appeared in print), four others more reliably attributed to other writers, eleven pieces by unknown authors, and versions of sonnets 138 and 144 that seem to be both erroneous and unrevised. These two sonnets are included in the Alternative Versions printed after "A Lover's Complaint" in this edition.

Another dozen of the sonnets survive in various manuscripts, all from 1620 or later. Although many derive from the quarto, a few probably preserve—amid mistakes in transcription—authentically Shakespearean phrasing that seems earlier than the versions in the 1609 edition. It is possible that one or more of these transcripts derive directly from an authorial manuscript and in that sense are closer to what Shakespeare wrote than is the quarto. The Alternative Versions include manuscript renditions of sonnets 2 (the most popular, judging by the number of extant copies) and 106, as well as sonnets 138 and 144 as they appeared in *The Passionate Pilgrim*. Sonnets 8 and 128 could also possibly derive from authorial manuscripts. From the four included in the Alternative Versions, one may, with caution, learn something of Shakespeare's process of revision.

The date of original composition of the poems remains controversial. *The Passionate Pilgrim* and, more inferentially, some of the manuscripts show that Shakespeare composed a number of the sonnets in the 1590s at the latest. So too does Francis Meres's reference in 1598 to Shakespeare's "sugred Sonnets among his priuate friends." The circulation of manuscripts was a common form of "publication" at the time. It should be noted, however, that a "sonnet" could be any short lyric poem. The best candidate for early composition is probably 145, on the basis of its vocabulary, its use of tetrameters rather than pentameters, and the words "hate away" (line 13)—a possible pun on the name of the poet's wife, Anne Hathaway. The boom in love-sonnet sequences during the 1590s and parallels in vocabulary to plays of 1594–95 (including *Love's Labour's Lost*) led most scholars in the past to conclude that the majority of the sonnets were drafted between 1592 and 1596, with some additional writing and revision in the following decade.

As was stated in the Introduction, however, more recent work on the vocabulary of the poems points to a later chronology for most, perhaps nearly all of them. One study argues that 104–26 were composed in 1597–1603 and that 1–60 were revised shortly before publication in 1609. Another plausible reconstruction goes even further, placing the writing of roughly two-thirds of the poems in 1599–1600. These include 127–52, which concern the speaker's mistress, and 19–96, which are to or about the male youth to whom the speaker is attracted. On this hypothesis, most of the rest are from 1601 to 1605. Among them are 97–115 (107 apparently alludes to Elizabeth's death in 1603), 153–54, and some or all of 1–18 (which mainly urge the male youth to marry and have children). According to the same argument, shortly before publication Shakespeare revised many of the sonnets. The initial eighteen poems fall into this category, though several of them as well as 60 and 116–26 may have first been composed around 1608 as part of the work of organizing the individual sonnets into a sequence. A similar chronological pattern probably holds for "A Lover's Complaint," which Shakespeare apparently began in 1602–5 and substantially revised or augmented for the 1609 edition.

SELECTED BIBLIOGRAPHY

Booth, Stephen. *An Essay on Shakespeare's Sonnets.* New Haven: Yale University Press, 1969.

——, ed. *Shakespeare's Sonnets.* New Haven: Yale University Press, 1977.

De Grazia, Margreta. "The Scandal of Shakespeare's Sonnets." *Shakespeare Survey* 47 (1994): 35–49.

Fineman, Joel. *Shakespeare's Perjured Eye: The Invention of Poetic Subjectivity in the Sonnets.* Berkeley: University of California Press, 1986.

Herrnstein, Barbara, ed. *Discussions of Shakespeare's Sonnets.* Boston: Heath, 1964.

Marotti, Arthur F. " 'Love Is Not Love': Elizabethan Sonnet Sequences and the Social Order." *ELH* 49 (1982): 396–428.

Smith, Bruce R. *Homosexual Desire in Shakespeare's England: A Cultural Poetics.* Chicago: University of Chicago Press, 1991. 228–70.

Stallybrass, Peter. "Editing as Cultural Formation: The Sexing of Shakespeare's Sonnets." *Modern Language Quarterly* 54.1 (March 1993): 91–103.

Underwood, Richard Allan. *Shakespeare on Love: The Poems and the Plays. Prolegomena to a Variorum Edition of "A Lover's Complaint."* Salzburg: Institut für Anglistik und Amerikanistik Universität Salzburg, 1985.

Willen, Gerald, and Victor B. Reed, eds. *A Casebook on Shakespeare's Sonnets.* New York: Crowell, 1964.

Sonnets

1

From fairest creatures we desire increase,°	*offspring*
That thereby beauty's rose[1] might never die,	
But as the riper should by time decease,	
His tender[2] heir might bear his memory;	
5 But thou, contracted° to thine own bright eyes,	*engaged; reduced*
Feed'st thy light's flame with self-substantial fuel,[3]	
Making a famine where abundance lies,	
Thyself thy foe, to thy sweet self too cruel.	
Thou that art now the world's fresh ornament	
10 And only herald to the gaudy° spring	*brilliant*
Within thine own bud buriest thy content,°	*substance; happiness*
And, tender churl,° mak'st waste in niggarding.	*young old miser*
Pity the world, or else this glutton be:	
To eat the world's due, by the grave and thee.[4]	

2[1]

When forty winters shall besiege thy brow
And dig deep trenches in thy beauty's field,

Dedication

1. The identity of W. H. has generated much speculation. As "the only begetter of these ensuing sonnets," "W. H." is probably a misprint for "W. S." or "W. SH." (William Shakespeare). Other candidates include the person who obtained the manuscript for the publisher and the youth who apparently inspired most of the poems. For biographical speculation about the sonnets, see the Introduction.

2. God, literally "ever-living," who promises eternity to Shakespeare (if, as suggested in the previous note, "W. H." refers to Shakespeare); or, less probably, Shakespeare, who promises "eternity" to the young man.

3. Thomas Thorpe, the printer, is the "well-wishing adventurer."

Sonnet 1

1. In Q, "rose," unlike most other nouns, is always capitalized (35.2; 54.3, 6, 11; 67.8; 95.2; 98.10; 99.8; 109.14; and 130.5, 6). Here, it is also italicized. These printing conventions, combined with the placement of the word

near the beginning of the first sonnet and its frequent repetition thereafter, suggest that "rose" is the poet's name for the object of his desire, on the model of, for instance, Stella in Sir Philip Sidney's influential sonnet sequence *Astrophel and Stella* (published 1591). The rose had long been associated with female genitalia, most notably in the thirteenth-century French narrative poem *The Romance of the Rose*, by Guillaume de Lorris and Jean de Meun. In Shakespeare's case, however, the object of desire is male. He is most frequently referred to as "youth," almost never as "boy" or "man." Shakespeare's "mistress" in the later sonnets is contrasted with "roses" (130.5, 6).

2. The rose's (the youth's) young.

3. Are consuming yourself like a candle.

4. *this . . . thee*: be a glutton by causing what is due to the world (your posterity) to be consumed both by the grave and within yourself.

Sonnet 2

1. See *Spes Altera* in the Alternative Versions.

Thy youth's proud livery,° so gazed on now,   *uniform; appearance*
Will be a tattered weed,° of small worth held.   *clothing; plant*
5 Then being asked where all thy beauty lies,
Where all the treasure of thy lusty days,
To say within thine own deep-sunken eyes
Were an all-eating shame and thriftless praise.[2]
How much more praise deserved thy beauty's use[3]
10 If thou couldst answer 'This fair child of mine
Shall sum my count, and make my old excuse',[4]
Proving his beauty by succession thine.°   *inherited from you*
   This were° to be new made when thou art old,   *would be*
   And see thy blood warm when thou feel'st it cold.

3

Look in thy glass,° and tell the face thou viewest   *mirror*
Now is the time that face should form another,
Whose fresh repair° if now thou not renewest   *state*
Thou dost beguile° the world, unbless° some mother.   *swindle / leave childless*
5 For where is she so fair whose uneared° womb   *unplowed*
Disdains the tillage of thy husbandry?[1]
Or who is he so fond will be the tomb
Of his self-love to stop posterity?[2]
Thou art thy mother's glass, and she in thee
10 Calls back the lovely April of her prime;
So thou through windows of thine age[3] shalt see,
Despite of wrinkles, this thy golden time.
   But if thou live remembered not to be,[4]
   Die single, and thine image dies with thee.

4

Unthrifty loveliness, why dost thou spend
Upon thyself thy beauty's legacy?
Nature's bequest gives nothing, but doth lend,
And being frank, she lends to those are free.[1]
5 Then, beauteous niggard, why dost thou abuse
The bounteous largess given thee to give?
Profitless usurer, why dost thou use°   *lend for profit; spend*
So great a sum of sums yet canst not live?[2]
For having traffic° with thyself alone,   *(commercial); (sexual)*
10 Thou of thyself thy sweet self dost deceive.°   *defraud*
Then how when nature calls thee to be gone:
What acceptable audit canst thou leave?
   Thy unused[3] beauty must be tombed with thee,
   Which usèd, lives th'executor to be.

2. Would be a shameful admission of gluttony and boast
of excessive expenditure.
3. How much more would the use (employment; invest-
ment or usurious lending) of your beauty merit.
4. Shall make my accounts balance and defend (absolve)
me in my age.
Sonnet 3
1. Cultivation; acting as a husband.
2. *who . . . posterity:* who is so foolish that he will selfishly

deny posterity a child?
3. Eyes weakened by old age; your children.
4. But if you live to be forgotten.
Sonnet 4
1. And being generous, she lends to those who (also) are
generous.
2. Make a living; live on in your children.
3. Not put to use; not interest-bearing.

5

Those hours that with gentle work did frame°   *form*
The lovely gaze° where every eye doth dwell   *face*
Will play the tyrants to the very same,
And that unfair which fairly doth excel;[1]
5   For never-resting time leads summer on
To hideous winter, and confounds° him there,   *destroys*
Sap checked with frost, and lusty leaves quite gone,
Beauty o'er-snowed, and bareness everywhere.
Then were not summer's distillation left
10   A liquid prisoner pent in walls of glass,
Beauty's effect with beauty were bereft,[2]
Nor° it nor no remembrance what it was.   *Neither*
     But flowers distilled, though they with winter meet,
     Lose[3] but their show; their substance still lives sweet.

6[1]

Then let not winter's ragged° hand deface   *rough*
In thee thy summer ere thou be distilled.
Make sweet some vial,° treasure° thou some place   *womb / enrich*
With beauty's treasure ere it be self-killed.
5   That use° is not forbidden usury   *lending for profit*
Which happies those that pay the willing loan:[2]
That's for thyself° to breed another thee,   *So you would do*
Or ten times happier, be it ten for one;°   *1,000% interest*
Ten times thyself were happier than thou art,
10   If ten of thine ten times refigured° thee.   *copied*
Then what could death do if thou shouldst depart,
Leaving thee living in posterity?
     Be not self-willed,[3] for thou art much too fair
     To be death's conquest and make worms thine heir.

7

Lo, in the orient° when the gracious light°   *east / sun*
Lifts up his burning head, each under° eye   *earthly*
Doth homage to his new-appearing sight,
Serving with looks his sacred majesty,
5   And having climbed the steep-up heavenly hill,
Resembling strong youth in his middle age,°   *noon*
Yet mortal looks adore his beauty still,
Attending on his golden pilgrimage.
But when from highmost pitch, with weary car,°   *sun god's chariot*
10   Like feeble age he reeleth from the day,
The eyes, 'fore duteous, now converted° are   *turned*
From his low tract,° and look another way.   *path*
     So thou, thyself outgoing in thy noon,
     Unlooked on diest unless thou get° a son.°   *beget / (sun)*

Sonnet 5
1. Will make unattractive that which now excels in beauty.
2. *Then . . . bereft:* Then if there were no perfume distilled from flowers bottled in glass vials, both beauty and its effect would be lost.
3. Q has "Leese," understood in this edition as a cognate of "lose." This is Shakespeare's only use of "Leese," which

allows a pun on "lease." See 13.5.
Sonnet 6
1. This sonnet links with 5.
2. Which makes happy those who willingly lend, or who willingly repay the loan with interest (in the form of children).
3. Stubborn; leaving everything in a will to yourself alone.

8

Music to hear,[1] why hear'st thou music sadly?
Sweets° with sweets war not, joy delights in joy.   *Sweet things*
Why lov'st thou that which thou receiv'st not gladly,
Or else receiv'st with pleasure thine annoy?
5 If the true concord of well-tunèd sounds
By unions° married do offend thine ear,   *harmony*
They do but sweetly chide thee, who confounds°   *destroys*
In singleness the parts[2] that thou shouldst bear.
Mark how one string, sweet husband to another,
10 Strikes each in each° by mutual ordering,   *Resonates*
Resembling sire and child and happy mother,
Who all in one one pleasing note do sing;
   Whose speechless° song, being many, seeming one,   *The strings' wordless*
   Sings this to thee: 'Thou single wilt prove none.'[3]

9

Is it for fear to wet a widow's eye
That thou consum'st thyself in single life?
Ah, if thou issueless° shalt hap to die,   *childless*
The world will wail thee like a makeless° wife.   *widowed*
5 The world will be thy widow, and still° weep   *continually*
That thou no form of thee hast left behind,
When every private° widow well may keep   *individual*
By children's eyes her husband's shape in mind.
Look what° an unthrift in the world doth spend   *Whatever*
10 Shifts but his° place, for still the world enjoys it;   *its*
But beauty's waste hath in the world an end,
And kept unused, the user° so destroys it.   *spender; lender*
   No love toward others in that bosom sits
   That on himself such murd'rous shame commits.

10

For shame deny that thou bear'st love to any,
Who for thyself art so unprovident.
Grant, if thou wilt, thou art beloved of many,
But that thou none lov'st is most evident;
5 For thou art so possessed with murd'rous hate
That 'gainst thyself thou stick'st not to conspire,°   *don't balk at conspiring*
Seeking that beauteous roof to ruinate
Which to repair should be thy chief desire.
O, change thy thought, that I may change my mind!°   *judgment*
10 Shall hate be fairer lodged than gentle love?
Be as thy presence° is, gracious and kind,   *appearance*
Or to thyself at least kind-hearted prove.
   Make thee another self for love of me,
   That beauty still may live in thine or thee.

11

As fast as thou shalt wane, so fast thou grow'st
In one of thine from that which thou departest,[1]

Sonnet 8
1. You whose voice is music.
2. Musical parts; roles as husband and father.
3. Without an heir, death will render you nothing (allud-
ing to the proverb "One is no number").

Sonnet 11
1. In a child begotten in youth (with suggestions of sexual
intercourse and of death).

And that fresh blood which youngly thou bestow'st
Thou mayst call thine when thou from youth convertest.°   *turn away*
5 Herein lives wisdom, beauty, and increase;
Without this, folly, age, and cold decay.
If all were minded so, the times should cease,
And threescore year would make the world away.
Let those whom nature hath not made for store,°   *breeding*
10 Harsh,° featureless,° and rude,° barrenly perish.   *ugly (all 3 words)*
Look whom she best endowed she gave the more,[2]
Which bounteous gift thou shouldst in bounty° cherish.   *by using bountifully*
     She carved thee for her seal,[3] and meant thereby
     Thou shouldst print more, not let that copy die.

12

When I do count the clock° that tells the time,   *hours as they strike*
And see the brave° day sunk in hideous night;   *fine*
When I behold the violet past prime,
And sable° curls ensilvered o'er with white;   *black*
5 When lofty trees I see barren of leaves,
Which erst° from heat did canopy the herd,   *once*
And summer's green all girded up in sheaves
Borne on the bier with white and bristly beard:[1]
Then of thy beauty do I question make
10 That thou among the wastes of time must go,
Since sweets° and beauties do themselves forsake,   *sweet things*
And die as fast as they see others grow;
     And nothing 'gainst time's scythe can make defence
     Save breed to brave him° when he takes thee hence.   *children to defy time*

13

O that you were yourself![1] But, love, you are
No longer yours than you yourself here live.
Against° this coming end you should prepare,   *For*
And your sweet semblance to some other give.
5 So should that beauty which you hold in lease
Find no determination;° then you were°   *never end / would be*
Yourself again after your self's decease,
When your sweet issue your sweet form should bear.
Who lets so fair a house fall to decay,
10 Which husbandry[2] in honour might uphold
Against the stormy gusts of winter's day,
And barren rage of death's eternal cold?
     O, none but unthrifts,° dear my love, you know.   *spendthrifts*
     You had a father; let your son say so.

14

Not from the stars do I my judgement pluck,
And yet methinks I have astronomy;°   *astrological knowledge*

2. To whomever nature gave most (made best-looking) she gave even more (extra reproductive abilities). The near circularity of "best endowed" and "more" alludes to Matthew 25:29, the paradoxical parable of the talents: "For unto every man that hath, it shall be given."
3. Literally, a stamp of authority.

Sonnet 12
1. *And ... beard:* And sheaves of mature ("bearded") grain carried away on the harvest cart; old man borne on a funeral bier.
Sonnet 13
1. If only you could remain your (eternal) self.
2. Stewardship; being a husband.

But not to tell of good or evil luck,
Of plagues, of dearths, or seasons' quality.
5   Nor can I fortune to brief minutes° tell,   *precisely*
'Pointing to each his thunder, rain, and wind,
Or say with princes if it shall go well
By oft predict° that I in heaven find;   *numerous signs*
But from thine eyes my knowledge I derive,
10 And, constant stars, in them I read such art
As¹ truth and beauty shall together thrive
If from thyself to store thou wouldst convert.²
    Or else of thee this I prognosticate:
    Thy end is truth's and beauty's doom and date.°   *final judgment and end*

15

When I consider every thing that grows
Holds° in perfection but a little moment,   *Remains*
That this huge stage presenteth naught but shows
Whereon the stars in secret influence° comment;   *(astrologically)*
5   When I perceive that men as plants increase,
Cheerèd and checked even by the selfsame sky;
Vaunt° in their youthful sap,° at height decrease,   *Gloat / strength*
And wear their brave state out of memory:¹
Then the conceit° of this inconstant stay°   *imagination / (on earth)*
10 Sets you most rich in youth before my sight,
Where wasteful time debateth° with decay   *competes*
To change your day of youth to sullied night;
    And all in war with time for love of you,
    As he takes from you, I engraft you new.²

16¹

But wherefore do not you a mightier way
Make war upon this bloody tyrant, time,
And fortify yourself in your decay
With means more blessèd than my barren rhyme?
5   Now stand you on the top of happy hours,°   *in your prime*
And many maiden gardens yet unset°   *unplanted*
With virtuous wish would bear your living flowers,
Much liker than your painted counterfeit.°   *image in art or poetry*
So should the lines of life² that life repair°   *restore*
10 Which this time's pencil or my pupil pen³
Neither in inward worth nor outward fair
Can make you live yourself° in eyes of men.   *as yourself*
    To give away yourself keeps yourself still,°   *(as children)*
    And you must live drawn by your own sweet skill.

17

Who will believe my verse in time to come
If it were filled with your most high deserts? —
Though yet, heaven knows, it is but as a tomb

Sonnet 14
1. *such art / As*: such predictions as that.
2. *If you would provide for the future.*
Sonnet 15
1. Wear their splendid clothing until they are forgotten
(with a sense of "wearing out").
2. *And . . . new*: And I, in competition with time because

I love you, restore you with my verse.
Sonnet 16
1. This sonnet links with 15.
2. Lineage; living lines (unlike those of poet or painter).
3. Neither today's painters ("pencil" means "paintbrush")
nor I, who imitate painting in my verse.

Which hides your life, and shows not half your parts.°   *attributes*
5 If I could write the beauty of your eyes
And in fresh numbers° number all your graces,   *lively verses*
The age to come would say 'This poet lies;
Such heavenly touches ne'er touched earthly faces.'
So should my papers, yellowed with their age,
10 Be scorned, like old men of less truth than tongue,
And your true rights° be termed a poet's rage°   *praises / hyperbole*
And stretchèd metre° of an antique song.   *overwrought poetry*
    But were some child of yours alive that time,
    You should live twice: in it, and in my rhyme.

18

Shall I compare thee to a summer's day?
Thou art more lovely and more temperate.
Rough winds do shake the darling buds of May,
And summer's lease° hath all too short a date.   *fixed span of time*
5 Sometime too hot the eye of heaven shines,
And often is his gold complexion dimmed,
And every fair from fair[1] sometime declines,
By chance or nature's changing course untrimmed;°   *rendered ordinary*
But thy eternal summer shall not fade
10 Nor lose possession of that fair thou ow'st,°   *own*
Nor shall death brag thou wander'st in his shade
When in eternal lines to time thou grow'st.[2]
    So long as men can breathe or eyes can see,
    So long lives this, and this gives life to thee.

19

Devouring time, blunt thou the lion's paws,
And make the earth devour her own sweet brood;
Pluck the keen teeth from the fierce tiger's jaws,
And burn the long-lived phoenix[1] in her blood.°   *alive*
5 Make glad and sorry seasons as thou fleet'st,
And do whate'er thou wilt, swift-footed time,
To the wide world and all her fading sweets.°   *sweet things*
But I forbid thee one most heinous crime:
O, carve not with thy hours my love's fair brow,
10 Nor draw no lines there with thine antique° pen.   *old; capricious*
Him in thy course untainted do allow
For beauty's pattern to succeeding men.
    Yet do thy worst, old time; despite thy wrong
    My love shall in my verse ever live young.

20

A woman's face with nature's own hand° painted   *(without cosmetics)*
Hast thou, the master-mistress of my passion;
A woman's gentle heart, but not acquainted
With shifting change as is false women's fashion;
5 An eye more bright than theirs, less false in rolling,°   *wandering*

Sonnet 18
1. Lovely thing from loveliness.
2. When in immortal poetry you become engrafted to time.

Sonnet 19
1. Legendary, self-resurrecting bird believed to live in cycles of several centuries, dying in flames and reborn from the ashes. See also 73.9–12.

Gilding the object whereupon it gazeth;
A man in hue, all hues in his controlling,[1]
Which steals men's eyes and women's souls amazeth.°   *overwhelms*
And for° a woman wert thou first created,   *to be*
10   Till nature as she wrought thee fell a-doting,°   *behaved foolishly*
And by addition me of thee defeated°   *took you away*
By adding one thing to my purpose nothing.[2]
     But since she pricked° thee out for women's pleasure,   *chose (sexual)*
     Mine be thy love and thy love's use their treasure.[3]

21

So is it not with me as with that muse°   *poet*
Stirred by a painted° beauty to his verse,   *(with cosmetics)*
Who heaven itself for ornament° doth use,   *poetic imagery*
And every fair with his fair doth rehearse,[1]
5   Making a couplement of proud compare[2]
With sun and moon, with earth, and sea's rich gems,
With April's first-born flowers, and all things rare
That heaven's air in this huge rondure hems.°   *globe surrounds*
O let me, true in love, but truly write,
10   And then believe me my love is as fair
As any mother's child, though not so bright
As those gold candles° fixed in heaven's air.   *(the stars)*
     Let them say more that like of hearsay° well;   *clichés*
     I will not praise that purpose not° to sell.   *since I don't intend*

22

My glass° shall not persuade me I am old   *mirror*
So long as youth and thou are of one date;°   *While you're young*
But when in thee time's furrows I behold,
Then look I° death my days should expiate.°   *I expect / conclude*
5   For all that beauty that doth cover thee
Is but the seemly° raiment of my heart,   *fitting*
Which in thy breast doth live, as thine in me;
How can I then be elder than thou art?
O therefore, love, be of thyself so wary
10   As I, not for myself, but for thee will,
Bearing thy heart, which I will keep so chary°   *cautiously*
As tender nurse her babe from faring ill.
     Presume not on[1] thy heart when mine is slain:
     Thou gav'st me thine not to give back again.

23

As an unperfect actor on the stage
Who with his fear is put besides° his part,   *forgets*
Or some fierce thing replete with too much rage
Whose strength's abundance weakens his own heart,
5   So I, for fear of trust,° forget to say   *lack of confidence*

Sonnet 20
1. A man whose looks enable him to attract and domi-
nate all others; a man whose looks encompass all other
appearances (both male and female). See "A Lover's
Complaint," lines 124–33. For "hues," Q has *Hews*, the
normal Renaissance spelling for the surname "Hughes"
and hence a possible punning allusion.
2. *one . . . nothing:* something (a penis) of no use to me.

3. I'll have the main part of your love (the capital or prin-
cipal), while women get just the "use" (interest; pleasure;
children) of it (or, while you use women sexually).
Sonnet 21
1. And compares every beautiful thing with his beloved.
2. Making a link in proud comparison.
Sonnet 22
1. Do not expect to get back.

The perfect ceremony of love's rite,[1]
And in mine own love's strength seem to decay,
O'er-charged with burden of mine own love's might.
O let my books be then the eloquence

10 And dumb presagers° of my speaking breast,   *mute presenters*
Who plead for love, and look for recompense
More than that tongue that more hath more expressed.[2]
    O learn to read what silent love hath writ;
    To hear with eyes belongs to love's fine wit.

24

Mine eye hath played the painter,[1] and hath steeled[2]
Thy beauty's form in table° of my heart.   *the painted tablet*
My body is the frame wherein 'tis held,
And perspective[3] it is best painter's art;

5 For through the painter must you see his skill
To find where your true image pictured lies,
Which in my bosom's shop° is hanging still,   *heart's workshop*
That hath his windows glazèd with thine eyes.[4]
Now see what good turns eyes for eyes have done:

10 Mine eyes have drawn thy shape, and thine for me
Are windows to my breast, wherethrough the sun
Delights to peep, to gaze therein on thee.
    Yet eyes this cunning want° to grace their art: *lack this talent*
    They draw but what they see, know not the heart.

25

Let those who are in favour with their stars
Of public honour and proud titles boast,
Whilst I, whom fortune of such triumph bars,
Unlooked-for joy in that I honour most.[1]

5 Great princes' favourites their fair leaves spread°   *bloom*
But as the marigold at the sun's eye,[2]
And in themselves their pride lies° burièd,   *will lie*
For at a frown they in their glory die.
The painful warrior famousèd for might,

10 After a thousand victories once foiled
Is from the book of honour razèd° quite,   *deleted*
And all the rest forgot for which he toiled.
    Then happy I, that love and am beloved
    Where I may not remove nor be removed.

26

Lord of my love, to whom in vassalage°   *feudal allegiance*
Thy merit hath my duty strongly knit,

Sonnet 23
1. Q reads "right," suggesting love's due as well as ritual.
2. More than that (rival) speaker who has more often said more.
Sonnet 24
1. The running conceit is of the speaker and addressee looking into one another's eyes, seeing both the other and himself reflected.
2. Engraved. Editors often emend Q's "steeld" to "stell'd" (fixed, placed) for a better fit with "painter."
3. Seen from the proper angle, through the painter's eyes. A "perspective" was a distorted painting that looked right only if viewed from the correct angle.
4. The addressee looks into the speaker's eyes ("windows"), which seem fitted with glass ("glazèd") by the reflection there of the addressee's own eyes. The eyes are the heart's ("his" [its], referring to "bosom's," line 7) windows, through which the addressee can therefore see his own image in the speaker's heart.
Sonnet 25
1. Unexpectedly (privately) take pleasure in what I most esteem (the youth).
2. Only at the prince's pleasure or whim.

To thee I send this written embassage°   *missive*
To witness duty, not to show my wit;
5 Duty so great which wit so poor as mine
May make seem bare in wanting° words to show it,   *lacking*
But that I hope some good conceit° of thine   *opinion*
In thy soul's thought, all naked,[1] will bestow° it,   *provide a place for*
Till whatsoever star that guides my moving°   *actions*
10 Points on me graciously with fair aspect,°   *astrological influence*
And puts apparel on my tattered loving
To show me worthy of thy sweet respect.
     Then may I dare to boast how I do love thee;
     Till then, not show my head where thou mayst prove° me.   *test*

27

Weary with toil I haste me to my bed,
The dear repose for limbs with travel tired;
But then begins a journey in my head
To work my mind when body's work's expired;
5 For then my thoughts, from far where I abide,
Intend a zealous pilgrimage to thee,
And keep my drooping eyelids open wide,
Looking on darkness which the blind do see:
Save that my soul's imaginary sight
10 Presents thy shadow° to my sightless view,   *picture*
Which like a jewel hung in ghastly night
Makes black night beauteous and her old face new.
     Lo, thus by day my limbs, by night my mind,
     For° thee, and for myself, no quiet find.   *Because of*

28[1]

How can I then return in happy plight,°   *condition*
That am debarred the benefit of rest,
When day's oppression is not eased by night,
But day by night and night by day oppressed,
5 And each, though enemies to either's° reign,   *each other's*
Do in consent shake hands to torture me,
The one by toil, the other to complain[2]
How far I toil, still farther off from thee?
I tell the day to please him thou art bright,
10 And do'st him grace when clouds do blot the heaven;[3]
So flatter I the swart°-complexioned night   *dark*
When sparkling stars twire not thou gild'st the even.[4]
     But day doth daily draw my sorrows longer,
     And night doth nightly make grief's strength seem stronger.

29

When, in disgrace with fortune and men's eyes,
I all alone beweep my outcast state,
And trouble deaf heaven with my bootless° cries,   *unavailing*

Sonnet 26
1. Refers to his "bare"-seeming "duty."
Sonnet 28
1. This sonnet links with 27.

2. *one:* day. *other:* night, making me "complain."
3. And confer beauty on him as a substitute for the sun.
4. By saying that when stars aren't twinkling, you brighten the evening.

And look upon myself and curse my fate,
5   Wishing me like to one more rich in hope,
Featured like him, like him with friends possessed,[1]
Desiring this man's art° and that man's scope,°   *skill / range*
With what I most enjoy° contented least: *like; own*
Yet in these thoughts myself almost despising,
10 Haply[2] I think on thee, and then my state,°   *mood; fortunes*
Like to the lark at break of day arising
From sullen earth, sings hymns at heaven's gate;
    For thy sweet love remembered such wealth brings
    That then I scorn to change my state with kings'.

30

When to the sessions° of sweet silent thought   *court sittings*
I summon up remembrance of things past,
I sigh° the lack of many a thing I sought,   *mourn*
And with old woes new wail my dear time's waste.[1]
5 Then can I drown an eye unused to flow
For precious friends hid in death's dateless° night,   *endless*
And weep afresh love's long-since-cancelled° woe,   *repaid (with sorrow)*
And moan th'expense° of many a vanished sight.   *passing*
Then can I grieve at grievances foregone,°   *bygone*
10 And heavily° from woe to woe tell° o'er   *sadly / say; count*
The sad account° of fore-bemoanèd moan,   *story; finances*
Which I new pay as if not paid before.
    But if the while I think on thee, dear friend,
    All losses are restored, and sorrows end.

31

Thy bosom is endearèd with° all hearts   *loved by; enriched by*
Which I by lacking have supposèd dead,
And there reigns love, and all love's loving parts,
And all those friends which I thought burièd.
5 How many a holy and obsequious° tear   *dutifullly mourning*
Hath dear religious° love stol'n from mine eye   *devoted*
As interest of° the dead, which° now appear   *due payment to / who*
But things removed° that hidden in thee lie!   *absent*
Thou art the grave where buried love doth live,
10 Hung with the trophies° of my lovers gone,   *memorials*
Who all their parts° of me to thee did give: *shares*
That due of many[1] now is thine alone.
    Their images I loved I view in thee,
    And thou, all they,[2] hast all the all of me.

32

If thou survive my well-contented day[1]
When that churl death my bones with dust shall cover,
And shalt by fortune° once more resurvey   *chance*
                                         darken

Sonnet 29
1. *Wishing . . . possessed:* Three people he wants to be like—"like to one" with better prospects, better looking "like him," and having friends "like him."
2. By chance; also, pun on "happily."
Sonnet 30
1. *my . . . waste:* the frittering or wasting away of my pre-

cious time.
Sonnet 31
1. What was owed to many (myself).
2. And you, who are made up of all of them.
Sonnet 32
1. Day of my death, which I shall willingly accept.

These poor rude° lines of thy deceasèd lover, | rough
5 Compare them with the bett'ring° of the time, | progress; better art
And though they be outstripped by every pen,
Reserve them for my love, not for their rhyme
Exceeded by the height of happier men.²
O then vouchsafe me but this loving thought:
10 'Had my friend's muse grown with this growing age,
A dearer birth° than this his love had brought | worthier poem
To march in ranks of better equipage;° | poems
But since he died, and poets better prove,° | have improved
Theirs for their style I'll read, his for his love.'

33

Full many a glorious morning have I seen
Flatter the mountain tops with sovereign eye,° | sunlight
Kissing with golden face the meadows green,
Gilding pale streams with heavenly alchemy;
5 Anon° permit the basest° clouds to ride | (But) soon / darkest
With ugly rack° on his celestial face, | cloudy mask
And from the forlorn world his visage hide,
Stealing unseen to west with this disgrace.
Even so my sun one early morn did shine
10 With all triumphant splendour on my brow;
But out, alack,° he was but one hour mine; | alas
The region° cloud hath masked him from me now. | high
Yet him for this my love no whit disdaineth:
Suns of the world may stain° when heaven's sun staineth. | darken

34¹

Why didst thou promise such a beauteous day
And make me travel forth without my cloak,
To let base clouds o'ertake me in my way,
Hiding thy brav'ry° in their rotten smoke?° | finery / noxious mists
5 'Tis not enough that through the cloud thou break
To dry the rain on my storm-beaten face,
For no man well of such a salve can speak
That heals the wound and cures not the disgrace.²
Nor can thy shame° give physic to° my grief; | remorse / cure
10 Though thou repent, yet I have still the loss.
Th'offender's sorrow lends but weak relief
To him that bears the strong offence's cross.° | consequences
Ah, but those tears are pearl which thy love sheds,
And they are rich, and ransom° all ill deeds. | atone for

35

No more be grieved at that which thou hast done:
Roses have thorns, and silver fountains mud.
Clouds and eclipses stain° both moon and sun, | darken
And loathsome canker° lives in sweetest bud. | (worm)
5 All men make faults, and even I in this,

2. *Reserve . . . men:* Keep them because you love me, not for their value as poetry, which is surpassed by poets more fortunate in their talent than I.

Sonnet 34
1. This sonnet links with 33.
2. Disfigurement; dishonor done the poet by the youth's neglect.

Authorizing thy trespass with compare,[1]
Myself corrupting salving thy amiss,[2]
Excusing thy sins more than thy sins are;[3]
For to thy sensual fault I bring in sense[4]—
10 Thy adverse party is thy advocate—
And 'gainst myself a lawful plea commence.
　　Such civil war is in my love and hate
　　　That I an accessory needs must be
　　　To that sweet thief which sourly robs from me.

36

Let me confess that we two must be twain[1]
Although our undivided loves are one;
So shall those blots° that do with me remain ⟶ *flaws; sources of shame*
Without thy help by me be borne alone.
5 In our two loves there is but one respect,° ⟶ *focus of attention*
Though in our lives a separable spite[2]
Which, though it alter not love's sole° effect, ⟶ *single-minded*
Yet doth it steal sweet hours from love's delight.
I may not evermore acknowledge thee
10 Lest my bewailèd guilt should do thee shame,
Nor thou with public kindness honour me
Unless thou take° that honour from thy name. ⟶ *lose*
　　But do not so. I love thee in such sort° ⟶ *such a way*
　　　As, thou being mine, mine is thy good report.[3]

37

As a decrepit father takes delight
To see his active child do deeds of youth,
So I, made lame by fortune's dearest° spite, ⟶ *direst*
Take all my comfort of° thy worth and truth; ⟶ *in*
5 For whether beauty, birth, or wealth, or wit,
Or any of these all, or all, or more,
Entitled in thy parts[1] do crownèd sit,
I make my love engrafted to this store.[2]
So then I am not lame, poor, nor despised,
10 Whilst that this shadow° doth such substance give ⟶ *idea*
That I in thy abundance am sufficed
And by a part of all thy glory live.
　　Look what° is best, that best I wish in thee; ⟶ *whatever*
　　　This° wish I have, then ten times happy me. ⟶ *When this*

38

How can my muse want subject to invent° ⟶ *lack subject matter*
While thou dost breathe, that pour'st into my verse
Thine own sweet argument,° too excellent ⟶ *theme*

Sonnet 35
1. Justifying your offense with comparisons.
2. Corrupting myself in minimizing your transgression.
3. Excusing you (overindulgently) from worse sins than the ones you've committed.
4. I use reason to defend your sensual offense.
Sonnet 36
1. Separated; but also, paradoxically, two of a kind or bound together.

2. Separation that causes vexation; vexation that causes separation.
3. Reputation. This couplet also ends 96.
Sonnet 37
1. Enrolled among your good qualities.
2. I engraft my love onto this abundance (of good qualities).

For every vulgar paper to rehearse?[1]
5 O, give thyself the thanks if aught in me
Worthy perusal stand against thy sight;[2]
For who's so dumb that cannot write to thee,
When thou thyself dost give invention light?
Be thou the tenth muse, ten times more in worth
10 Than those old nine which rhymers invocate,
And he that calls on thee, let him bring forth
Eternal numbers° to outlive long° date.   *verses / a distant*
    If my slight muse do please these curious° days,   *finicky*
    The pain° be mine, but thine shall be the praise.   *pains; effort*

39

O, how thy worth with manners° may I sing   *modesty*
When thou art all the better part of me?
What can mine own praise to mine own self bring,
And what is't but mine own when I praise thee?
5 Even for° this let us divided live,   *Because of*
And our dear love lose name of single one,°   *the reputation of unity*
That by this separation I may give
That due to thee which thou deserv'st alone.
O absence, what a torment wouldst thou prove
10 Were it not thy sour leisure gave sweet leave
To entertain° the time with thoughts of love,   *enliven*
Which time and thoughts so sweetly doth deceive,
    And that thou teachest how to make one twain
    By praising him here° who doth hence remain!   *in this poem*

40[1]

Take all my loves, my love, yea, take them all:
What hast thou then more than thou hadst before?
No love, my love, that thou mayst true love call—
All mine was thine before thou hadst this more.
5 Then if for my love thou my love receivest,[2]
I cannot blame thee for my love thou usest;[3]
But yet be blamed if thou this self[4] deceivest
By wilful taste of what thyself° refusest.   *your better nature*
I do forgive thy robb'ry, gentle thief,
10 Although thou steal thee all my poverty;°   *what little I own*
And yet love knows it is a greater grief
To bear love's wrong than hate's known injury.
    Lascivious grace,° in whom all ill well shows,   *Charming wanton*
    Kill me with spites,° yet we must not be foes.   *offenses*

41

Those pretty° wrongs that liberty° commits   *minor / licentiousness*
When I am sometime absent from thy heart
Thy beauty and thy years full well befits,

Sonnet 38
1. Every ordinary, commonplace piece of writing to set forth.
2. *if . . . sight*: if you see anything in my writing worth reading.
Sonnet 40
1. Sonnets 40–42 concern a situation that may be identi-cal to the love triangle described in 133–34 and 144.
2. Then if for love of me you take my beloved.
3. *for . . . usest*: because you use my beloved (sexually).
4. The poet (often emended, perhaps rightly, to "thy-self").

For still° temptation follows where thou art.   *continually*
5 Gentle° thou art, and therefore to be won;   *Tender; upper-class*
Beauteous thou art, therefore to be assailed;
And when a woman woos, what woman's son
Will sourly leave her till he have prevailed?[1]
Ay me, but yet thou mightst my seat[2] forbear,
10 And chide thy beauty and thy straying youth
Who lead thee in their riot° even there   *depraved conduct*
Where thou art forced to break a two-fold troth:
    Hers, by thy beauty tempting her to thee,
    Thine, by thy beauty being false to me.

42

That thou hast her, it is not all my grief,
And yet it may be said I loved her dearly;
That she hath thee is of my wailing chief,°   *chief reason*
A loss in love that touches me more nearly.
5 Loving offenders, thus I will excuse ye:
Thou dost love her because thou know'st I love her,
And for my sake even so doth she abuse° me,   *mistreat*
Suff'ring my friend for my sake to approve her.[1]
If I lose thee, my loss is my love's gain,
10 And losing° her, my friend hath found that loss: *I losing*
Both find each other, and I lose both twain,
And both for my sake lay on me this cross.°   *affliction*
    But here's the joy: my friend and I are one.
    Sweet flattery!° Then she loves but me alone.   *Pleasing delusion*

43

When most I wink,° then do mine eyes best see,   *shut my eyes*
For all the day they view things unrespected;°   *unheeded; unworthy*
But when I sleep, in dreams they look on thee,
And, darkly bright, are bright in dark directed.[1]
5 Then thou, whose shadow shadows doth make bright,[2]
How would thy shadow's form° form happy show°   *substance / sight*
To the clear day with thy much clearer light,
When to unseeing eyes[3] thy shade shines so!
How would, I say, mine eyes be blessèd made
10 By looking on thee in the living day,
When in dead night thy fair imperfect° shade   *incorporeal*
Through heavy sleep on sightless eyes doth stay!
    All days are nights to see till I see thee,
    And nights bright days when dreams do show thee me.°   *to me*

44

If the dull° substance of my flesh were thought,   *heavy*
Injurious distance should not stop my way;
For then, despite of space, I would be brought

Sonnet 41
1. Until he has had his way. But Q's "he" could easily be a misprint for "she."
2. Rightful place (my mistress).
Sonnet 42
1. To put her to the test (sexually).

Sonnet 43
1. (My eyes) seeing in the dark turn toward your bright eyes in the dark.
2. Whose image lightens darkness.
3. Because closed in sleep.

From limits° far remote where° thou dost stay.   *places / to where*
5 No matter then although my foot did stand
Upon the farthest earth removed from thee;
For nimble thought can jump both sea and land
As soon as think the place where he° would be.   *(thought)*
But ah, thought kills me that I am not thought,
10 To leap large lengths of miles when thou art gone,
But that, so much of earth and water wrought,[1]
I must attend time's leisure[2] with my moan,
  Receiving naught by elements so slow
  But heavy tears, badges of either's woe.[3]

45[1]

The other two,[2] slight° air and purging fire,   *light*
Are both with thee wherever I abide;
The first my thought, the other my desire,
These present-absent[3] with swift motion slide;
5 For when these quicker° elements are gone   *livelier*
In tender embassy of love to thee,
My life, being made of four, with two alone
Sinks down to death, oppressed with melancholy,
Until life's composition be recured°   *renewed*
10 By those swift messengers returned from thee,
Who even but now come back again assured
Of thy fair health, recounting it to me.
  This told, I joy; but then no longer glad,
  I send them back again and straight° grow sad.   *suddenly*

46

Mine eye and heart are at a mortal° war   *lethal*
How to divide the conquest of thy sight.[1]
Mine eye my heart thy picture's sight would bar,
My heart, mine eye the freedom° of that right.   *free enjoyment*
5 My heart doth plead that thou in him dost lie,
A closet° never pierced with crystal eyes;   *room*
But the defendant doth that plea deny,
And says in him thy fair appearance lies.
To 'cide° this title is empanellèd°   *decide / enrolled*
10 A quest° of thoughts, all tenants to the heart,   *jury*
And by their verdict is determinèd
The clear eye's moiety° and the dear heart's part,   *share*
  As thus: mine eye's due is thy outward part,
  And my heart's right thy inward love of heart.

47[1]

Betwixt mine eye and heart a league is took,°   *truce is made*
And each doth good turns now unto the other.

Sonnet 44
1. Being compounded of so much earth and water (the heavy elements).
2. I must wait humbly (as if on a great man) for time to reunite us.
3. Emblems of the grief of each of the poet's elements (of earth because heavy [sad], of water because wet).
Sonnet 45
1. This sonnet links with 44.

2. Of the poet's four elements. See 44.11.
3. Now present, now absent; constantly coming and going.
Sonnet 46
1. The spoils of the sight of you (possibly in a painting; see 47.5–14).
Sonnet 47
1. This sonnet links with 46.

When that mine eye is famished for a look,
Or heart in love with sighs himself doth smother,[2]
5 With my love's picture then my eye doth feast,
And to the painted banquet bids my heart.
Another time mine eye is my heart's guest
And in his thoughts of love doth share a part.
So either by thy picture or my love,
10 Thyself away art present still with me;
For thou no farther than my thoughts canst move,
And I am still° with them, and they with thee;   *constantly*
  Or if they sleep, thy picture in my sight
  Awakes my heart to heart's and eye's delight.

48

How careful was I when I took my way°   *set off*
Each trifle under truest° bars to thrust,   *most reliable*
That to my use° it might unusèd stay   *benefit*
From hands of falsehood, in sure wards° of trust.   *safe places*
5 But thou, to° whom my jewels trifles are,   *compared to*
Most worthy comfort, now my greatest grief,[1]
Thou best of dearest and mine only care
Art left the prey of every vulgar thief.
Thee have I not locked up in any chest
10 Save where thou art not, though I feel thou art—
Within the gentle closure of my breast,
From whence at pleasure thou mayst come and part;°   *go*
  And even thence thou wilt be stol'n, I fear,
  For truth° proves thievish for a prize so dear.   *even honesty*

49

Against° that time—if ever that time come—   *In preparation for*
When I shall see thee frown on my defects,
Whenas thy love hath cast his utmost sum,[1]
Called to that audit by advised respects;°   *judicious reasons*
5 Against that time when thou shalt strangely° pass   *as a stranger*
And scarcely greet me with that sun, thine eye,
When love converted from the thing it was
Shall reasons find of settled gravity:[2]
Against that time do I ensconce me° here   *secure myself*
10 Within the knowledge of mine own desert,[3]
And this my hand against myself uprear°   *testify against myself*
To guard the lawful reasons on thy part.°   *defend your case*
  To leave poor me thou hast the strength of laws,
  Since why to love° I can allege no cause.   *why you should love*

50

How heavy° do I journey on the way,   *wearily*
When what I seek—my weary travel's end—
Doth teach that ease and that repose to say[1]

2. Or when my loving heart smothers itself with sighs.
Sonnet 48
1. Because absent and in danger of being stolen.
Sonnet 49
1. When your love has calculated the bottom line.
2. Shall find reasons for a dignified reserve; shall find rea-

sons of well-established seriousness (for leaving me).
3. My (lack of?) worthiness to be loved.
Sonnet 50
1. Teach the comforts at the end of the road to remind
me that.

'Thus far the miles are measured from thy friend.'
5 The beast that bears me, tired with my woe,
Plods dully on to bear° that weight in me,   *while bearing*
As if by some instinct the wretch did know
His rider loved not speed, being made² from thee.
The bloody spur cannot provoke him on
10 That sometimes anger thrusts into his hide,
Which heavily he answers with a groan
More sharp to me than spurring to his side;
    For that same groan doth put this in my mind:
    My grief lies onward and my joy behind.

51¹

Thus can my love excuse the slow offence°   *offense of slowness*
Of my dull bearer when from thee I speed:
From where thou art why should I haste me thence?
Till I return, of posting° is no need.   *riding quickly*
5 O what excuse will my poor beast then find
When swift extremity° can seem but slow?   *extreme (return) speed*
Then should I spur, though mounted on the wind;
In wingèd speed no motion shall I know.²
Then can no horse with my desire keep pace;
10 Therefore desire, of perfect'st love being made,
Shall rein° no dull flesh in his fiery race;   *curb*
But love, for love,° thus shall excuse my jade: *on love's behalf*
    Since from thee going he went wilful-slow,
    Towards thee I'll run and give him leave to go.°   *walk*

52

So am I as the rich° whose blessèd key   *rich man*
Can bring him to his sweet up-lockèd treasure,
The which he will not ev'ry hour survey,
For° blunting the fine point of seldom° pleasure. *To avoid / occasional*
5 Therefore are feasts° so solemn° and so rare   *feast days / dignified*
Since, seldom coming, in the long year set
Like stones of worth they thinly placèd are,
Or captain° jewels in the carcanet.°   *chief / jeweled collar*
So is the time that keeps you as° my chest,°   *like / jewel case*
10 Or as the wardrobe which the robe doth hide,
To make some special instant special blest
By new unfolding his imprisoned pride.
    Blessèd are you whose worthiness gives scope,
    Being had, to triumph; being lacked, to hope.¹

53

What is your substance, whereof are you made,
That millions of strange shadows on you tend?°   *attend*
Since every one hath, every one, one shade,¹

2. *speed, being made*: hastening away; haste, when and because it is.
Sonnet 51
1. This sonnet links with 50.
2. I will feel no motion when desire carries me back through the air. See line 11 and sonnets 44–45 for the association of fire and air with desire and thought, and of earth and water with dull, slow flesh.
Sonnet 52
1. *gives . . . hope*: allows me to exult when with you and to hope when not with you.
Sonnet 53
1. Since each person has an individual shadow.

And you, but one, can every shadow lend.[2]
5 Describe° Adonis, and the counterfeit°   *Draw / likeness*
   Is poorly imitated after you.
   On Helen's cheek all art of beauty set,
   And you in Grecian tires are painted new.[3]
   Speak of the spring and foison° of the year: *harvest time*
10 The one doth shadow of your beauty show,
   The other as your bounty doth appear;
   And you in every blessèd shape we know.°   *recognize*
      In all external grace you have some part,
      But you like none, none you, for constant heart.

54

   O how much more doth beauty beauteous seem
   By° that sweet ornament which truth doth give!   *Because of*
   The rose looks fair, but fairer we it deem
   For that sweet odour which doth in it live.
5 The canker blooms[1] have full as deep a dye
   As the perfumèd tincture° of the roses,   *color*
   Hang on such thorns, and play as wantonly°   *flatter as playfully*
   When summer's breath their maskèd buds discloses;
   But for° their virtue only is° their show   *since / lies wholly in*
10 They live unwooed and unrespected° fade,   *unappreciated*
   Die to themselves.° Sweet roses do not so;   *alone; without influence*
   Of their sweet deaths are sweetest odours made:
      And so of you, beauteous and lovely youth,
      When that° shall fade, by verse distils your truth.[2]   *beauty*

55

   Not marble nor the gilded monuments
   Of princes shall outlive this powerful rhyme,
   But you shall shine more bright in these contents
   Than unswept stone besmeared with sluttish° time.   *slovenly*
5 When wasteful war shall statues overturn,
   And broils° root out the work of masonry,   *battles*
   Nor Mars his° sword nor war's quick fire shall burn   *Neither Mars's*
   The living record of your memory.
   'Gainst death and all oblivious enmity
10 Shall you pace forth; your praise shall still find room
   Even in the eyes of all posterity
   That wear this world out to the ending doom.[1]
      So, till the judgement that yourself arise,
      You live in this, and dwell in lovers' eyes.

56

   Sweet love,[1] renew thy force. Be it not said
   Thy edge should blunter be than appetite,
   Which but° today by feeding is allayed,   *merely for*

2. Can cast all shadows (are visible in every image).
3. *On . . . new:* If one were to use every art to reproduce the beauty of Helen of Troy (or use artful cosmetics on Helen's cheek) it would look like you in Grecian headgear.
Sonnet 54
1. Dog roses (having little scent).
2. See sonnet 5. Q's "vade" is a variant of "fade," the read-

ing adopted here, but it probably has the secondary meaning of "depart," from the Latin *vadere.*
Sonnet 55
1. Doomsday: in Christianity, the Day of Judgment, when dead bodies are supposed to "arise" (line 13) from the grave and be united with their souls.
Sonnet 56
1. The feeling (not the beloved).

Tomorrow sharpened in his former might.
5 So, love, be thou; although today thou fill
Thy hungry eyes even till they wink° with fullness,   *close (to sleep)*
Tomorrow see again, and do not kill
The spirit of love with a perpetual dullness.
Let this sad int'rim like the ocean be
10 Which parts the shore where two contracted new
Come daily to the banks, that when they see
Return of love, more blessed may be the view;²
    Or call it winter, which, being full of care,
    Makes summer's welcome, thrice more wished, more rare.°   *valuable*

57

Being your slave, what should I do but tend°   *wait*
Upon the hours and times of your desire?
I have no precious time at all to spend,
Nor services to do, till you require;
5 Nor dare I chide the world-without-end° hour   *endless*
Whilst I, my sovereign, watch the clock for you,
Nor think the bitterness of absence sour
When you have bid your servant once adieu.
Nor dare I question with my jealous thought
10 Where you may be, or your affairs suppose,°   *speculate on*
But like a sad slave stay and think of naught
Save, where you are, how happy you make those.
    So true a fool is love that in your will,¹
    Though you do anything, he thinks no ill.

58¹

That god forbid, that made me first your slave,
I should in thought control your times of pleasure,
Or at your hand th'account of hours to crave,²
Being your vassal° bound to stay° your leisure.   *slave / wait upon*
5 O let me suffer, being at your beck,
Th'imprisoned absence of your liberty,³
And patience, tame to sufferance, bide each check,⁴
Without accusing you of injury.
Be where you list,° your charter° is so strong   *wish / freedom*
10 That you yourself may privilege° your time   *allocate*
To what you will; to you it doth belong
Yourself to pardon of self-doing° crime.   *commited by you*
    I am to wait, though waiting so be hell,
    Not blame your pleasure, be it ill or well.

59

If there be nothing new, but that which is
Hath been before, how are our brains beguiled,°   *cheated*

2. *Let . . . view:* The "sad" interval between periods of
feeling love is like an ocean dividing shores where two
lovers come daily hoping for the (emotionally renewing)
sight of a boat bringing the other. *contracted new:* newly
betrothed.
Sonnet 57
1. Desire (including sexual desire); capitalized in Q, per-
haps punning on Shakespeare's name. See 135–36.

Sonnet 58
1. This sonnet links with 57.
2. Or should seek an account of how you pass your time.
3. The imprisoned feeling caused by your licentiousness
when you're away.
4. And (let me) patient, acquiescent in suffering, endure
each setback.

Which, labouring° for invention, bear amiss   *working; giving birth*
The second burden of a former child!¹
5   O that record° could with a backward look   *recollection*
Even of five hundred courses of the sun
Show me your image in some antique book
Since mind at first in character was done,²
That I might see what the old world could say
10 To this composèd wonder of your frame;³
Whether we are mended° or whe'er better they,   *improved*
Or whether revolution be the same.⁴
    O, sure I am the wits° of former days   *clever writers*
    To subjects worse have given admiring praise.

60

Like as the waves make towards the pebbled shore,
So do our minutes hasten to their end,
Each changing place with that which goes before;
In sequent toil all forwards do contend.¹
5   Nativity,° once in the main of light,°   *A newborn / in the world*
Crawls to maturity, wherewith being crowned
Crookèd° eclipses 'gainst his glory fight,   *Pernicious*
And time that gave doth now his gift confound.°   *ruin*
Time doth transfix the flourish² set on youth,
10 And delves the parallels° in beauty's brow;   *carves the wrinkles*
Feeds on the rarities of nature's truth,³
And nothing stands but for his scythe to mow.
    And yet to times in hope° my verse shall stand,   *future days*
    Praising thy worth despite his cruel hand.

61

Is it thy will thy image should keep open
My heavy eyelids to the weary night?
Dost thou desire my slumbers should be broken
While shadows° like to thee do mock my sight?   *visions*
5   Is it thy spirit that thou send'st from thee
So far from home into my deeds to pry,
To find out shames and idle hours in me,
The scope and tenor of thy jealousy?¹
O no; thy love, though much, is not so great.
10 It is my love that keeps mine eye awake,
Mine own true love that doth my rest defeat,
To play the watchman ever for thy sake.
    For thee watch I° whilst thou dost wake elsewhere,   *I remain awake*
    From me far off, with others all too near.

62

Sin of self-love possesseth all mine eye,
And all my soul, and all my every part;
And for this sin there is no remedy,

Sonnet 59
1. *bear . . . child:* mistakenly ("amiss") give birth for a second time to a child that has already been born.
2. Since writing was invented.
3. To the wonderful composition of your form (perhaps referring to the sonnet itself as well).
4. Whether the revolving of the ages makes no difference.

Sonnet 60
1. Toiling one after the other, all seek to move forward.
2. Time pierces and destroys the ornament (beauty).
3. On the most precious products of nature's perfection.

Sonnet 61
1. The object and intent of your distrust (that is, "shames and idle hours," line 7).

It is so grounded inward in my heart.
5   Methinks no face so gracious is as mine,
No shape so true,° no truth of such account,   *perfect*
And for myself mine own worth do define
As° I all other° in all worths surmount.   *As if / others*
But when my glass° shows me myself indeed,   *mirror*
10   Beated and chapped with tanned antiquity,
Mine own self-love quite contrary I read;
Self so self-loving were iniquity.
    'Tis thee, my self,° that for° myself I praise,   *you, my other self / as*
    Painting my age with beauty of thy days.

63

Against° my love shall be as I am now,   *Preparing for when*
With time's injurious hand crushed and o'erworn;
When hours have drained his blood and filled his brow
With lines and wrinkles; when his youthful morn
5   Hath travelled° on to age's steepy[1] night,   *progressed; toiled*
And all those beauties whereof now he's king
Are vanishing, or vanished out of sight,
Stealing away the treasure of his spring:
For such a time do I now fortify
10   Against confounding° age's cruel knife,   *devastating*
That he shall never cut from memory
My sweet love's beauty, though° my lover's life.   *though he will sever*
    His beauty shall in these black lines be seen,
    And they shall live, and he in them still green.°   *perpetually youthful*

64

When I have seen by time's fell° hand defaced   *fierce*
The rich proud cost° of outworn buried age;   *expense*
When sometime°-lofty towers I see down razed,   *once*
And brass eternal slave to mortal rage;[1]
5   When I have seen the hungry ocean gain
Advantage on the kingdom of the shore,
And the firm soil win of° the wat'ry main,   *win ground from*
Increasing store with loss and loss with store;[2]
When I have seen such interchange of state,
10   Or state[3] itself confounded to decay,°   *reduced to ruins*
Ruin hath taught me thus to ruminate:
That time will come and take my love away.
    This thought is as a death, which° cannot choose   *since thought*
    But weep to have° that which it fears to lose.   *at having*

65

Since° brass, nor stone, nor earth, nor boundless sea,   *Since there is neither*
But sad mortality o'ersways their power,
How with this rage shall beauty hold a plea,[1]

Sonnet 63
1. Precipitous (like the path of the setting sun).
Sonnet 64
1. And eternal brass forever succumbs to death's violence.
2. Adding to the stock of one by loss of the other, and

vice versa.
3. *state* (line 9): condition; sovereign territory. *state* (line 10): pomp.
Sonnet 65
1. How can beauty make a (legal) case against such a power to destroy?

Whose action is no stronger than a flower?
5 O how shall summer's honey breath hold out
Against the wrackful° siege of battering days   *damaging*
When rocks impregnable are not so stout,
Nor gates of steel so strong, but time decays?°   *decays them*
O fearful meditation! Where, alack,
10 Shall time's best jewel° from time's chest[2] lie hid,   *(the beloved)*
Or what strong hand can hold his swift foot back,
Or who his spoil° of beauty can forbid?   *destruction*
　　O none, unless this miracle have might:
　　That in black ink my love may still shine bright.

66

Tired with all these°, for restful death I cry: *(the ensuing wrongs)*
As,° to behold desert° a beggar born,   *For example / merit*
And needy nothing trimmed in jollity,[1]
And purest faith unhappily forsworn,°   *betrayed; perjured*
5 And gilded honour shamefully misplaced,
And maiden virtue rudely strumpeted,
And right perfection wrongfully disgraced,
And strength by limping sway° disablèd,   *feeble leaders*
And art made tongue-tied° by authority,   *learning silenced*
10 And folly, doctor-like, controlling skill,[2]
And simple truth miscalled simplicity,°   *naiveté*
And captive good attending° captain ill.   *serving*
　　Tired with all these, from these would I be gone,
　　Save that to die I leave my love alone.

67

Ah, wherefore with infection[1] should he live
And with his presence grace impiety,
That° sin by him advantage should achieve   *So that*
And lace° itself with his society?   *decorate*
5 Why should false painting imitate his cheek,
And steal dead seeming of[2] his living hue?
Why should poor° beauty indirectly seek   *lesser*
Roses of shadow,° since his rose is true?   *Cosmetic beauty*
Why should he live now nature bankrupt is,
10 Beggared of blood to blush through lively veins,
For she hath no exchequer° now but his,   *treasury*
And proud of many, lives upon his gains?[3]
　　O, him she stores° to show what wealth she had   *keeps*
　　In days long since, before these last so bad.

68[1]

Thus is his cheek the map° of days outworn,   *image*
When beauty lived and died as flowers do now,
Before these bastard signs of fair° were borne°   *cosmetics / worn; born*

---

2. Treasure chest; coffin.
Sonnet 66
1. And ungifted (or impoverished) worthlessness adorned with finery.
2. And folly, feigning erudition, dominating true wisdom or ability. Before modern medicine, doctors were often portrayed as fools or con artists.
Sonnet 67
1. The world's ills (as in 66).

2. *dead seeming of:* an inanimate outward resemblance from.
3. Though (falsely) taking pride in her abundance (of offspring?), lives off the interest he earns (from his endowment of beauty).
Sonnet 68
1. This sonnet links with 67.

Or durst inhabit on a living brow;
5   Before the golden tresses of the dead,
The right of sepulchres,[2] were shorn away
To live a second life on second head;
Ere beauty's dead fleece made another gay.
In him those holy antique hours° are seen   *good old days*
10 Without all ornament, itself and true,
Making no summer of another's green,
Robbing no old to dress his beauty new;
   And him as for a map doth nature store,°   *keep*
   To show false art what beauty was of yore.

69

Those parts of thee that the world's eye doth view
Want° nothing that the thought of hearts can mend.°   *Lack / imagine better*
All tongues, the voice of souls, give thee that due,
Utt'ring bare truth even so as foes commend.[1]
5   Thy outward thus with outward praise is crowned,
But those same tongues that give thee so thine own°   *your due*
In other accents° do this praise confound°   *words / undermine*
By seeing farther than the eye hath shown.
They look into the beauty of thy mind,
10 And that in guess they measure by thy deeds.
Then, churls, their thoughts—although their eyes were kind—
To thy fair flower add the rank smell of weeds.
   But why thy odour matcheth not thy show,°   *appearance*
   The soil is this: that thou dost common grow.[2]

70[1]

That thou are blamed shall not be thy defect,
For slander's mark° was ever yet the fair.   *target*
The ornament of beauty is suspect,°   *suspicion*
A crow that flies in heaven's sweetest air.
5   So° thou be good, slander doth but approve   *So long as*
Thy worth the greater, being wooed of time;[2]
For canker vice[3] the sweetest buds doth love,
And thou present'st a pure unstainèd prime.°   *youth*
Thou hast passed by the ambush of young days
10 Either not assailed, or victor being charged;
Yet this thy praise cannot be so° thy praise   *enough*
To tie up envy, evermore enlarged.°   *forever at large*
   If some suspect of ill masked not thy show,°   *appearance*
   Then thou alone kingdoms of hearts shouldst owe.°   *own*

71

No longer mourn for me when I am dead
Than you shall hear the surly sullen bell
Give warning to the world that I am fled

---

2. Properly belonging to tombs (wigs were made from the hair of corpses).
Sonnet 69
1. Uttering minimal truth, in the way that enemies praise.
2. The ground (reason; also, stain) is this: you are becoming low (promiscuous).

Sonnet 70
1. This sonnet links with 69.
2. *slander . . . time:* the gossip merely proves that you're so popular ("wooed of time") that you're worth even more.
3. Slander, like a cankerworm.

From this vile world with vilest[1] worms to dwell.
5   Nay, if you read this line, remember not
The hand that writ it; for I love you so
That I in your sweet thoughts would be forgot
If thinking on me then should make you woe.
O, if, I say, you look upon this verse
10   When I perhaps compounded am° with clay,   *am mixed*
Do not so much as my poor name rehearse,°   *repeat*
But let your love even with my life decay,
    Lest the wise world should look into your moan
    And mock you with me° after I am gone.   *for loving me*

72

O, lest the world should task you to recite
What merit lived in me that you should love,
After my death, dear love, forget me quite;
For you in me can nothing worthy prove—
5   Unless you would devise some virtuous lie
To do more for me than mine own desert,
And hang more praise upon deceasèd I
Than niggard truth would willingly impart.
O, lest your true love may seem false in this,
10   That you for love speak well of me untrue,°   *untruthfully*
My° name be buried where my body is,   *Let my*
And live no more to shame nor me nor you;
    For I am shamed by that which I bring forth,[1]
    And so should you,° to love things nothing worth.   *you be*

73

That time of year thou mayst in me behold
When yellow leaves, or none, or few, do hang
Upon those boughs which shake against the cold,
Bare ruined choirs where late the sweet birds sang.[1]
5   In me thou seest the twilight of such day
As after sunset fadeth in the west,
Which by and by black night doth take away,
Death's second self, that seals up all in rest.
In me thou seest the glowing of such fire
10   That° on the ashes of his youth[2] doth lie   *As*
As the death-bed whereon it must expire,
Consumed with that which it was nourished by.[3]
    This thou perceiv'st, which makes thy love more strong,
    To love that° well which thou must leave ere long.   *(the speaker); (life)*

Sonnet 71
1. Q's "vildest" is an archaic form of "vilest" that may also carry the connotation of "most reviled."
Sonnet 72
1. Presumably alluding to the writer's poems or to his profession as actor and playwright.
Sonnet 73
1. *choirs*: the area in a church where the choir ("sweet birds") sings; gatherings of manuscript "leaves" (line 2), or quires ("quiers" in Q)—hence, the poet's own voice.

There may also be a reference to the dissolution of the monasteries during the Reformation, but "late" (formerly, but with an emphasis on recently) doesn't fit that context. See the Introduction.
2. Referring to the phoenix, a legendary self-resurrecting bird believed to live in cycles of several centuries, dying in flames and being reborn from the ashes. See also 19.4.
3. Ironically, the fire is choked ("consumed") by (at the same time as) the ashes, which are the residue of the fuel the fire previously fed upon ("was nourished by").

74[1]

But be contented when that fell arrest°   *fearful death*
Without all bail shall carry me away.
My life hath in this line° some interest,°   *verse / legal claim*
Which for memorial still with thee shall stay.
5 When thou reviewest° this, thou dost review   *reread*
The very part° was consecrate to thee.   *part of me that*
The earth can have but earth, which is his due;
My spirit is thine, the better part of me.
So then thou hast but lost the dregs of life,
10 The prey of worms, my body being dead,
The coward conquest of a wretch's knife,[2]
Too base of° thee to be rememberèd.   *by*
    The worth of that° is that which it contains,   *(the body)*
    And that is this,° and this with thee remains. *this spirit (his poetry)*

75

So are you to my thoughts as food to life,
Or as sweet-seasoned° showers are to the ground;   *spring*
And for the peace of you° I hold such strife   *you provide*
As 'twixt a miser and his wealth is found:
5 Now proud as an enjoyer, and anon
Doubting the filching age[1] will steal his treasure;
Now counting° best to be with you alone,   *estimating*
Then bettered° that the world may see my pleasure; *better contented*
Sometime all full with feasting on your sight,
10 And by and by clean° starvèd for a look;   *wholly*
Possessing or pursuing no delight
Save what is had or must from you be took.
    Thus do I pine and surfeit day by day,
    Or° gluttoning on all, or all away.°   *Either / having nothing*

76

Why is my verse so barren of new pride,°   *adornments*
So far from variation or quick° change?   *lively*
Why, with the time,° do I not glance aside   *following the fashion*
To new-found methods and to compounds[1] strange?
5 Why write I still all one, ever the same,
And keep invention in a noted weed,[2]
That every word doth almost tell my name,
Showing their birth and where° they did proceed?   *whence*
O know, sweet love, I always write of you,
10 And you and love are still my argument;°   *always my topic*
So all my best is dressing old words new,
Spending again what is already spent;
    For as the sun is daily new and old,
    So is my love, still telling what is told.

Sonnet 74
1. This sonnet links with 73.
2. The cowardly conquest of a wretch such as Death (who was thought to carry a scythe).
Sonnet 75
1. Fearing that these dishonest times.

Sonnet 76
1. *compounds*: stylistic or formal mixtures; compound words; elaborate medicines (with "methods," which also refers to both literary and medical treatments).
2. And keep literary creativity in such familiar clothing.

77[1]

Thy glass° will show thee how thy beauties wear,[2]   *mirror*
Thy dial° how thy precious minutes waste,   *sundial*
The vacant leaves thy mind's imprint° will bear,   *written ideas*
And of this book this learning mayst thou taste:
5 The wrinkles which thy glass will truly show
Of mouthèd° graves will give thee memory;°   *gaping / remind you*
Thou by thy dial's shady stealth° mayst know   *stealing shadow*
Time's thievish progress to eternity;
Look what° thy memory cannot contain   *Whatever*
10 Commit to these waste blanks,° and thou shalt find *empty pages*
Those children nursed,° delivered from thy brain, *preserved*
To take a new acquaintance of thy mind.°   *strike you afresh*
  These offices° so oft as thou wilt look   *functions*
  Shall profit thee and much enrich thy book.

78[1]

So oft have I invoked thee for my muse
And found such fair assistance in my verse
As every alien pen hath got my use,[2]
And under thee° their poesy disperse.   *with you as patron*
5 Thine eyes, that taught the dumb on high° to sing *aloud*
And heavy ignorance aloft to fly,
Have added feathers to the learned's wing[3]
And given grace° a double majesty.   *excellence*
Yet be most proud of that which I compile,°   *write*
10 Whose influence° is thine and born of thee.   *power to move*
In others' works thou dost but mend° the style,   *improve*
And arts° with thy sweet graces gracèd be;   *(their) artistry*
  But thou art all my art, and dost advance
  As high as learning my rude ignorance.

79

Whilst I alone did call upon thy aid
My verse alone had all thy gentle grace;
But now my gracious numbers are decayed,
And my sick muse doth give another place.°   *way to another poet*
5 I grant, sweet love, thy lovely argument[1]
Deserves the travail° of a worthier pen,   *labor*
Yet what of thee thy poet doth invent
He robs thee of, and pays it thee again.
He lends thee virtue, and he stole that word
10 From thy behaviour; beauty doth he give,
And found it in thy cheek: he can afford°   *extend*
No praise to thee but what in thee doth live.
  Then thank him not for that which he doth say,
  Since what he owes thee thou thyself dost pay.

Sonnet 77
1. This sonnet appears to have accompanied the gift of a notebook.
2. Last; wear away; "were" (Q's spelling).
Sonnet 78
1. This sonnet begins the rival poet sequence (78–80, 82–86).
2. That every other poet imitates me.
3. Have improved the poetic "flights" of even accomplished poets.
Sonnet 79
1. The subject of your loveliness.

80

O, how I faint° when I of you do write,   *get discouraged*
Knowing a better spirit° doth use your name,   *(the rival poet)*
And in the praise thereof spends all his might,
To make me tongue-tied, speaking of your fame!
5 But since your worth, wide as the ocean is,
The humble as° the proudest sail doth bear,   *as well as*
My saucy barque,° inferior far to his,   *impudent boat*
On your broad main° doth wilfully appear.   *waters*
Your shallowest help will hold me up afloat
10 Whilst he upon your soundless° deep doth ride;   *bottomless*
Or, being wrecked, I am a worthless boat,
He of tall building[1] and of goodly pride.°   *magnificence*
    Then if he thrive and I be cast away,
    The worst was this: my love was my decay.

81[1]

Or° I shall live your epitaph to make,   *Whether*
Or you survive when I in earth am rotten.
From hence° your memory death cannot take,   *the world; my poetry*
Although in me each part° will be forgotten.   *each of my attributes*
5 Your name from hence° immortal life shall have,   *henceforth; my poetry*
Though I, once gone, to all the world must die.
The earth can yield me but a common grave
When you entombèd in men's eyes shall lie.
Your monument shall be my gentle verse,
10 Which eyes not yet created shall o'er-read,
And tongues to be° your being shall rehearse°   *future tongues / recite*
When all the breathers of this world are dead.
    You still shall live—such virtue° hath my pen—   *power*
    Where breath most breathes, even in° the mouths of men.   *right in*

82

I grant thou wert not married to my muse,
And therefore mayst without attaint o'erlook°   *dishonor read*
The dedicated[1] words which writers° use   *other writers*
Of their fair subject, blessing every book.
5 Thou art as fair in knowledge as in hue,°   *appearance*
Finding thy worth a limit° past my praise,   *region*
And therefore art enforced to seek anew
Some fresher stamp of these time-bettering days.[2]
And do so, love; yet when they have devised
10 What strainèd touches rhetoric can lend,
Thou, truly fair, wert truly sympathized[3]
In true plain words by thy true-telling friend;
    And their gross painting° might be better used   *cosmetics; flattery*
    Where cheeks need blood: in thee it is abused.°   *used wrongly*

Sonnet 80
1. Tall, strong build.
Sonnet 81
1. Except for lines 2–3 and 10–11, any two consecutive
lines in this sonnet form a complete sentence.

Sonnet 82
1. Devoted; referring to a prefatory dedication.
2. Some more recent imprint (commendation) of these
culturally progressive times.
3. Would be accurately represented.

83

I never saw that you did painting° need,   *cosmetics*
And therefore to your fair° no painting set.   *beauty*
I found—or thought I found—you did exceed
The barren tender° of a poet's debt;   *payment*
5 And therefore have I slept in your report:[1]
That° you yourself, being extant, well might show *So that*
How far a modern° quill doth come too short,   *trite; fashionable*
Speaking of worth, what worth[2] in you doth grow.
This silence for° my sin you did impute,   *to be*
10 Which shall be most my glory, being dumb;
For I impair not beauty, being mute,
When others would give life, and bring a tomb.[3]
  There lives more life in one of your fair eyes
  Than both your poets can in praise devise.

84

Who is it that says most which[1] can say more
Than this rich praise: that you alone are you,[2]
In whose confine immurèd is the store
Which should example where your equal grew?[3]
5 Lean penury within that pen doth dwell
That to his subject lends not some small glory;
But he that writes of you, if he can tell
That you are you, so dignifies his story.
Let him but copy what in you is writ,
10 Not making worse what nature made so clear,°   *purely excellent*
And such a counterpart shall fame° his wit, *copy will make famous*
Making his style admirèd everywhere.
  You to your beauteous blessings add a curse,[4]
  Being fond on praise, which makes your praises worse.[5]

85

My tongue-tied muse in manners holds her still° *tactfully says nothing*
While comments of° your praise, richly compiled, *commentaries in*
Reserve thy character° with golden quill   *Hoard up your features*
And precious phrase by all the muses filed.°   *polished*
5 I think good thoughts whilst other° write good words, *others*
And like unlettered clerk still cry 'Amen'
To every hymn[1] that able spirit affords°   *offers*
In polished form of well-refinèd pen.
Hearing you praised I say ' 'Tis so, 'tis true,'
10 And to the most° of praise add something more; *highest*
But that is in my thought,° whose love to you, *unspoken*

Sonnet 83
1. Neglected to sing your praises.
2. In speaking of value of the worth that.
3. When others who try to make you live in their writings only end up burying you.
Sonnet 84
1. *Who . . . which:* What hyperbolical enthusiast.
2. The line is a poetical in-joke, echoing a passage in Gervase Markham's *Devoreux* (published 1597) that addresses and praises Penelope Rich, a famous beauty of the Elizabethan court. Like *Devoreux*, Q has "Rich" rather than "rich." See also 85.2.

3. *In . . . grew:* Within whom is contained the stock that would be needed to produce your equal?
4. Personality flaw; vexation (for those who would praise you).
5. Being (too) fond of praise, which makes the praise seem like flattery; being (too) fond of the sort of praise that detracts from you.
Sonnet 85
1. *like . . . hymn:* like an illiterate parish clerk reflexively approve ("cry 'Amen' " after) every poem ("hymn") of praise.

Though words come hindmost, holds his rank before.°   *before all others*
Then others for the breath of words respect,°   *regard*
Me for my dumb thoughts, speaking in effect.°   *in reality*

86

Was it the proud full sail of his° great verse   *(a rival poet's)*
Bound for the prize° of all-too-precious you   *pirate's spoils*
That did my ripe thoughts in my brain inhearse,°   *bury*
Making their tomb the womb wherein they grew?
5   Was it his spirit, by spirits taught to write
Above a mortal pitch,° that struck me dead?   *height*
No, neither he nor his compeers[1] by night
Giving him aid my verse astonishèd.°   *made silent*
He nor that affable familiar ghost°   *spirit*
10 Which nightly gulls° him with intelligence,°   *fools / ideas*
As victors, of my silence cannot boast;
I was not sick of any fear from thence.
    But when your countenance filled up[2] his line,
    Then lacked I matter; that enfeebled mine.

87

Farewell—thou art too dear° for my possessing,   *costly*
And like° enough thou know'st thy estimate.°   *it is likely / value*
The charter of thy worth gives thee releasing;[1]
My bonds in thee are all determinate.°   *terminated*
5   For how do I hold thee but by thy granting,
And for that riches where is my deserving?
The cause of this fair gift in me is wanting,
And so my patent back again is swerving.[2]
Thyself thou gav'st, thy own worth then not knowing,
10 Or me to whom thou gav'st it else mistaking;°   *overestimating*
So thy great gift, upon misprision growing,°   *based on error*
Comes home again, on better judgement making.[3]
    Thus have I had thee as a dream doth flatter:°   *creates an illusion*
    In sleep a king, but waking no such matter.

88

When thou shalt be disposed to set me light°   *value me little*
And place my merit in the eye of scorn,
Upon thy side against myself I'll fight,
And prove thee virtuous though thou art forsworn.
5   With mine own weakness being best acquainted,
Upon thy part I can set down a story
Of faults concealed wherein I am attainted,
That thou in losing me shall win much glory;
And I by this will be a gainer too;
10 For bending all my loving thoughts on thee,
The injuries that to myself I do,
    Doing thee vantage, double vantage me.

Sonnet 86
1. Colleagues (the "spirits" in line 5).
2. Your features gave subject matter to; your approval made up for any lack in.

Sonnet 87
1. The privilege you derive from your worth releases you from love's bonds.
2. My rights of possession revert to you.
3. *on . . . making*: when you realize your error.

Such is my love, to thee I so belong,
That for thy right myself will bear all wrong.

89

Say that thou didst forsake me for some fault,
And I will comment° upon that offence;   *elaborate*
Speak of my lameness, and I straight will halt,[1]
Against thy reasons making no defence.
5 Thou canst not, love, disgrace me half so ill,
To set a form upon desirèd change,[2]
As I'll myself disgrace, knowing thy will.
I will acquaintance strangle and look strange,[3]
Be absent from thy walks,° and in my tongue   *familiar places*
10 Thy sweet belovèd name no more shall dwell,
Lest I, too much profane, should do it wrong,
And haply° of our old acquaintance tell.   *by chance*
  For thee, against myself I'll vow debate;°   *combat*
  For I must ne'er love him whom thou dost hate.

90[1]

Then hate me when thou wilt, if ever, now,
Now while the world is bent my deeds to cross,°   *foil*
Join with the spite of fortune, make me bow,
And do not drop in for an after-loss.[2]
5 Ah do not, when my heart hath scaped this sorrow,
Come in the rearward of a conquered woe;[3]
Give not a windy night a rainy morrow
To linger out a purposed overthrow.[4]
If thou wilt leave me, do not leave me last,
10 When other petty griefs have done their spite,
But in the onset come; so shall I taste
At first the very worst of fortune's might,
  And other strains° of woe, which now seem woe, *types; burdens*
  Compared with loss of thee will not seem so.

91

Some glory in their birth, some in their skill,
Some in their wealth, some in their body's force,
Some in their garments (though new-fangled ill),° *fashionably ugly*
Some in their hawks and hounds, some in their horse,° *horses*
5 And every humour hath his° adjunct pleasure *temperament has its*
Wherein it finds a joy above the rest.
But these particulars are not my measure;°   *(of joy)*
All these I better° in one general best.   *exceed*
Thy love is better than high birth to me,
10 Richer than wealth, prouder than garments' cost,
Of more delight than hawks or horses be,
And having thee of all men's pride[1] I boast,

Sonnet 89
1. Talk of my disability (perhaps alluding to the lame meter of line 2), and I at once will limp (stop objecting).
2. To lend justification to the change you seek.
3. I will end our familiarity and act like a stranger.
Sonnet 90
1. This sonnet links with 89.

2. Do not fall upon me to inflict a later disaster.
3. Assault me again after I have overcome my present grief.
4. To . . . *overthrow:* By protracting or delaying your intended assault.
Sonnet 91
1. Of everything in which others take pride.

Wretched in this alone: that thou mayst take
All this away, and me most wretched make.

92[1]

But do thy worst to steal thyself away,
For term of° life thou art assurèd mine,   *the duration of my*
And life no longer than thy love will stay,
For it depends upon that love of thine.
5   Then need I not to fear the worst of wrongs
When in the least of them[2] my life hath end.
I see a better state to me belongs
Than that which on thy humour doth depend.
Thou canst not vex me with inconstant mind,
10   Since that my life on thy revolt doth lie.[3]
O, what a happy title[4] do I find—
Happy to have thy love, happy to die!
     But what's so blessèd fair that fears no blot?
     Thou mayst be false, and yet I know it not.

93[1]

So shall I live supposing thou art true
Like a deceivèd husband; so love's face°   *appearance*
May still seem love to me, though altered new—
Thy looks with me, thy heart in other place.
5   For there can live no hatred in thine eye,
Therefore in that I cannot know thy change.
In many's looks the false heart's history
Is writ in moods and frowns and wrinkles strange,[2]
But heaven in thy creation did decree
10   That in thy face sweet love should ever dwell;
Whate'er thy thoughts or thy heart's workings be,
Thy looks should nothing thence but sweetness tell.
     How like Eve's apple doth thy beauty grow
     If thy sweet virtue answer not thy show![3]

94

They that have power to hurt and will do none,
That do not do the thing they most do show,[1]
Who moving others are themselves as stone,
Unmovèd, cold,° and to temptation slow—   *composed*
5   They rightly° do inherit heaven's graces,   *truly*
And husband nature's riches from expense;[2]
They are the lords and owners of their faces,
Others but stewards° of their excellence.   *hired managers*
The summer's flower is to the summer sweet
10   Though to itself it only live and die,[3]
But if that flower with base infection meet

Sonnet 92
1. This sonnet links with 91.
2. In the slightest sign of your displeasure.
3. Since change in your affections would kill me.
4. What a claim to be considered happy.
Sonnet 93
1. This sonnet links with 92.
2. In signs of anger and frowns and displeased expres-
sions.
3. Does not correspond to your looks.
Sonnet 94
1. *they most do show:* that their appearance implies.
2. And protect nature's rich endowment from waste.
3. *is . . . die:* emits its sweetness to others even though it
lives and dies in apparent isolation (unpollinated: com-
pare 54.5–11).

The basest weed outbraves his dignity;[4]
    For sweetest things turn sourest by their deeds:
    Lilies that fester smell far worse than weeds.[5]

95

How sweet and lovely dost thou make the shame
Which, like a canker° in the fragrant rose,   *cankerworm*
Doth spot the beauty of thy budding name!°   *fame*
O, in what sweets dost thou thy sins enclose!
5 That tongue that tells the story of thy days,
Making lascivious comments on thy sport,°   *amorous adventures*
Cannot dispraise, but in a kind of praise,
Naming thy name, blesses° an ill report.   *makes positive*
O, what a mansion have those vices got
10 Which for their habitation chose out thee,
Where beauty's veil doth cover every blot
And all things turns to fair that eyes can see!
    Take heed, dear heart, of this large privilege:
    The hardest knife ill used doth lose his° edge.   *its*

96

Some say thy fault is youth, some wantonness;°   *promiscuity; frivolity*
Some say thy grace is youth and gentle sport.[1]
Both grace and faults are loved of more and less;°   *by people of all ranks*
Thou mak'st faults graces that to thee resort.
5 As on the finger of a thronèd queen
The basest jewel will be well esteemed,
So are those errors that in thee are seen
To truths translated° and for true things deemed.   *converted*
How many lambs might the stern° wolf betray   *vicious*
10 If like° a lamb he could his looks translate!   *into*
How many gazers mightst thou lead away
If thou wouldst use the strength of all thy state!°   *power*
    But do not so: I love thee in such sort°   *such a way*
    As, thou being mine, mine is thy good report.[2]

97

How like a winter hath my absence been
From thee, the pleasure of the fleeting year!
What freezings have I felt, what dark days seen,
What old December's bareness everywhere!
5 And yet this time removed° was summer's time,   *away*
The teeming autumn big° with rich increase,   *pregnant*
Bearing the wanton burden of the prime°   *harvest of wanton spring*
Like widowed wombs after their lords' decease.
Yet this abundant issue seemed[1] to me
10 But hope of orphans and unfathered fruit,
For summer and his pleasures wait° on thee,   *attend*
And thou away, the very birds are mute;

---

4. Exceeds the flower in magnificence.
5. This line also occurs in *The Reign of King Edward III*, a play printed anonymously in 1596 and sometimes attributed, in whole or in part, to Shakespeare.

Sonnet 96
1. A gentleman's sexual prerogative.
2. Reputation. The same couplet ends 36.
Sonnet 97
1. Offspring seemed in prospect, before the beloved's absence.

Or if they sing, 'tis with so dull a cheer°   *perfume*
That leaves look pale, dreading the winter's near.   *such a dismal mood*

98

From you have I been absent in the spring
When proud-pied° April, dressed in all his trim,°   *multicolored / finery*
Hath put a spirit of youth in everything,
That heavy Saturn[1] laughed and leapt with him.
5 Yet nor the lays° of birds nor the sweet smell   *not the songs*
Of different flowers° in odour and in hue   *flowers differing*
Could make me any summer's story tell,°   *speak (write) happily*
Or from their proud lap° pluck them where they grew;   *(the ground)*
Nor did I wonder at the lily's white,
10 Nor praise the deep vermilion in the rose.
They were but sweet, but figures° of delight   *merely emblems*
Drawn after you, you pattern of all those;
    Yet seemed it winter still, and, you away,
    As with your shadow I with these did play.[2]

99[1]

The forward° violet thus did I chide: *early*
Sweet thief, whence didst thou steal thy sweet° that smells,   *perfume*
If not from my love's breath? The purple pride°   *beauty*
Which on thy soft cheek for complexion dwells
5 In my love's veins thou hast too grossly° dyed.   *obviously*
The lily I condemnèd for thy hand,[2]
And buds of marjoram[3] had stol'n thy hair;
The roses fearfully on thorns did stand,
One blushing shame, another white despair;
10 A third, nor red nor white, had stol'n of both,°   *(making it pink)*
And to° his robb'ry had annexed thy breath;   *in addition to*
But for his theft in pride of all his growth
A vengeful canker° ate him up to death.   *cankerworm*
    More flowers I noted, yet I none could see
    But sweet° or colour it had stol'n from thee.   *perfume*

100

Where are thou, muse, that thou forget'st so long
To speak of that which gives thee all thy might?
Spend'st thou thy fury[1] on some worthless song,
Dark'ning° thy power to lend base subjects light?   *Debasing*
5 Return, forgetful muse, and straight° redeem   *immediately*
In gentle numbers° time so idly spent;   *noble poetry*
Sing to the ear that doth thy lays esteem
And gives thy pen both skill and argument.°   *substance*
Rise, resty° muse, my love's sweet face survey   *lazy*
10 If° time have any wrinkle graven there.   *To see if*
If any, be a satire to° decay   *satirist of*
And make time's spoils despisèd everywhere.

Sonnet 98
1. The planet Saturn was regarded as cold and slow, exerting a melancholy influence.
2. As if with your image I played with these flowers.

Sonnet 99
1. This sonnet has an extra opening line.
2. For stealing whiteness from your (the beloved's) hand.
3. The herb, sweet of scent and auburn in color.
Sonnet 100
1. Inspiration (the "poet's rage" of 17.11).

Give my love fame faster than time wastes life;
So, thou prevene'st° his scythe and crookèd knife. *impede*

101[1]

O truant muse, what shall be thy amends
For thy neglect of truth in beauty dyed?
Both truth and beauty on my love depends;
So dost thou too, and therein° dignified. *therein are you*
5 Make answer, muse. Wilt thou not haply° say *perhaps*
'Truth needs no colour with his colour fixed,[2]
Beauty no pencil beauty's truth to lay,[3]
But best is best if never intermixed'?° *(with cosmetics)*
Because he needs no praise wilt thou be dumb?
10 Excuse not silence so, for't lies in thee
To make him much outlive a gilded tomb,
And to be praised of° ages yet to be. *by*
  Then do thy office,° muse; I teach thee how *duty*
  To make him seem long° hence as he shows° now. *a long time / appears*

102

My love is strengthened, though more weak in seeming.° *appearance*
I love not less, though less the show appear.
That love is merchandized[1] whose rich esteeming° *appraisal*
The owner's tongue doth publish everywhere.
5 Our love was new and then but in the spring° *just beginning*
When I was wont to greet it with my lays,
As Philomel[2] in summer's front° doth sing, *beginning*
And stops her pipe in growth of riper days—
Not that the summer is less pleasant now
10 Than when her mournful hymns did hush the night,
But that wild music burdens[3] every bough,
And sweets grown common lose their dear delight.
  Therefore like her I sometime hold my tongue,
  Because I would not dull° you with my song. *overfeed*

103

Alack, what poverty my muse brings forth
That, having such a scope to show her pride,[1]
The argument all bare° is of more worth *subject by itself*
Than when it hath my added praise beside!
5 O blame me not if I no more can write!
Look in your glass° and there appears a face *mirror*
That overgoes my blunt invention[2] quite,
Dulling° my lines and doing me disgrace. *(by contrast)*
Were it not sinful then, striving to mend,° *improve*
10 To mar the subject that before was well?—
For to no other pass° my verses tend *end*

Sonnet 101
1. This sonnet links with 100.
2. Truth needs no artificial color to be added to his natural coloring.
3. True beauty need apply no (cosmetic) brush.
Sonnet 102
1. (Debased by being) turned into merchandise for sale.
2. Nightingale; with ambiguous hints of the myth of Philomel, whose brother-in-law raped her and ripped out her

tongue to ensure her silence. See Book 6 of Ovid's *Metamorphoses*.
3. Loads; provides a musical refrain (probably from many other poets) on.
Sonnet 103
1. Considering that she has such opportunity (in you) to display her skill (her pride in you).
2. That surpasses my dull powers of invention.

Than of your graces and your gifts to tell;
And more, much more, than in my verse can sit
Your own glass shows you when you look in it.

104

To me, fair friend, you never can be old;
For as you were when first your eye I eyed,
Such seems your beauty still. Three winters cold
Have from the forests shook three summers' pride;°   *splendor*
5 Three beauteous springs to yellow autumn turned
In process° of the seasons have I seen,   *the progress*
Three April perfumes in three hot Junes burned
Since first I saw you fresh, which yet° are green.   *who still*
Ah yet doth beauty, like a dial hand,
10 Steal from his figure and no pace perceived;[1]
So your sweet hue,° which methinks still doth stand,   *appearance*
Hath motion, and mine eye may be deceived.
    For fear of which, hear this, thou age unbred:°   *future age*
    Ere you were born was beauty's summer dead.

105

Let not my love be called idolatry,
Nor my belovèd as an idol show,
Since all alike my songs and praises be
To one, of one, still° such, and ever so.   *continually*
5 Kind is my love today, tomorrow kind,
Still constant in a wondrous excellence.
Therefore my verse, to constancy confined,
One thing expressing, leaves out difference.°   *diversity (of theme)*
'Fair, kind, and true' is all my argument,
10 'Fair, kind, and true' varying to other words,
And in this change is my invention spent,[1]
Three themes in one, which wonderous scope affords.
    Fair, kind, and true have often lived alone,°   *separately*
    Which three till now never kept seat° in one.   *dwelt permanently*

106[1]

When in the chronicle of wasted° time   *past*
I see descriptions of the fairest wights,°   *people*
And beauty making beautiful old rhyme
In praise of ladies dead and lovely knights;
5 Then in the blazon[2] of sweet beauty's best,
Of hand, of foot, of lip, of eye, of brow,
I see their antique pen would have expressed
Even such a beauty as you master° now.   *possess*
So all their praises are but prophecies
10 Of this our time, all you prefiguring,
And for° they looked but with divining° eyes   *as / prophetic*
They had not skill enough your worth to sing;   *want to*

Sonnet 104
1. *doth . . . perceived*: beauty imperceptibly "steals" (departs stealthily from; robs from) the youthful appearance ("figure") of the beloved as the hand of the watch ("dial") stealthily progresses ("steals") away from the number ("figure") on the watch face.

Sonnet 105
1. And in varying the words alone my inventiveness is expended.

Sonnet 106
1. See "On his Mistress' Beauty" in the Alternative Versions.
2. Poetic catalogue of virtues.

For we° which now behold these present days   *even we*
Have eyes to wonder, but lack tongues to praise.

107

Not mine own fears nor the prophetic soul
Of the wide world dreaming on things to come
Can yet the lease° of my true love control,   *allotted term*
Supposed as forfeit to a confined doom.[1]
5   The mortal moon hath her eclipse endured,[2]
And the sad augurs mock their own presage;[3]
Incertainties now crown themselves assured,[4]
And peace proclaims olives of endless age.[5]
Now with the drops[6] of this most balmy time
10 My love looks fresh, and death to me subscribes,°   *submits*
Since spite of him I'll live in this poor rhyme
While he insults° o'er dull and speechless tribes,[7]   *prevails*
    And thou in this shalt find thy monument
    When tyrants' crests and tombs of brass are spent.°   *ruined*

108

What's in the brain that ink may character°   *express*
Which hath not figured° to thee my true spirit?   *shown*
What's new to speak, what now to register,°   *record*
That may express my love or thy dear merit?
5   Nothing, sweet boy; but yet like prayers divine
I must each day say o'er the very same,
Counting no old thing old, thou mine, I thine,
Even as when first I hallowed thy fair name.
So that eternal love in love's fresh case°   *covering*
10 Weighs not° the dust and injury of age,   *Overlooks*
Nor gives to necessary° wrinkles place,°   *inevitable / priority*
But makes antiquity for aye his page,[1]
    Finding the first conceit of love there bred[2]
    Where time and outward form would° show it dead.   *want to*

109

O never say that I was false of heart,
Though absence seemed my flame to qualify°—   *reduce*
As easy might I from myself depart
As from my soul, which in thy breast doth lie.
5   That is my home of love. If I have ranged,
Like him that travels I return again,
Just to the time,° not with the time exchanged,°   *Punctually / changed*
So that myself bring water for my stain.[1]

Sonnet 107
1. Imagined as limited to a finite term.
2. Survived. The line is variously taken to refer to an eclipse of the moon, to an event in the life (or, more likely, to the death in 1603) of Queen Elizabeth (often known as Diana, the moon goddess), or, less probably, to the defeat of the Spanish Armada (1588).
3. And prophets of doom now ridicule their own prophecies.
4. Desired but doubtful possibilities now celebrate their realization; uncertainty is now unavoidable.
5. And peace declares the olive branches that symbolize it to be everlasting. Perhaps a reference to the peace treaty with Spain signed by King James, who succeeded Elizabeth.
6. Soothing drops of dew, rain, or balm. Balm was used in the coronation ceremony.
7. Over those legions of dead who have no poetic legacy.
Sonnet 108
1. But makes (old) age forever the (youthful) servant to love; perhaps referring to the pages of poetry written when the "sweet boy" (line 5) was still young.
2. The first feeling (poetic expression) of love generated in that place (the beloved; the poem).
Sonnet 109
1. *for my stain:* to cleanse the stain of my absence.

Never believe, though in my nature reigned
10   All frailties that besiege all kinds of blood,°   *disposition*
That it could so preposterously be stained
To leave for° nothing all thy sum of good;   *exchange for*
   For nothing this wide universe I call
   Save thou my rose; in it thou art my all.

110

Alas, 'tis true, I have gone here and there
And made myself a motley to the view,°   *clown to the world*
Gored° mine own thoughts, sold cheap what is most dear,   *Injured*
Made old offences of affections new.[1]
5   Most true it is that I have looked on truth°   *fidelity*
Askance and strangely.° But, by all above,   *coldly*
These blenches° gave my heart another youth,   *alterations*
And worse essays° proved thee my best of love   *experiments*
Now all is done, have what shall have no end;[2]
10   Mine appetite I never more will grind
On newer proof to try[3] an older friend,
A god in love, to whom I am confined.
   Then give me welcome, next my heaven the best,°   *next best to heaven*
   Even to thy pure and most most loving breast.

111

O, for my sake do you with[1] fortune chide,
The guilty goddess of my harmful deeds,
That did not better for my life provide
Than public means which public manners breeds.[2]
5   Thence comes it that my name receives a brand,°   *stigma*
And almost thence my nature is subdued
To what it works in, like the dyer's hand.
Pity me then, and wish I were renewed,°   *cured*
Whilst like a willing patient I will drink
10   Potions of eisel° 'gainst my strong infection;   *medicinal vinegar*
No° bitterness that I will bitter think,   *There is no*
Nor double penance to correct correction.°   *correct me twice over*
   Pity me then, dear friend, and I assure ye
   Even that your pity is enough to cure me.

112[1]

Your love and pity doth th'impression fill°   *eliminates the scar*
Which vulgar° scandal stamped upon my brow;   *public*
For what care I who calls me well or ill,
So you o'er-green my bad, my good allow?[2]
5   You are my all the world, and I must strive
To know my shames and praises from your tongue—
None else to me, nor I to none alive,

Sonnet 110
1. Repeated traditional misbehavior (infidelity)—or offended old friends—in (my treatment of) new attachments.
2. *have . . . end:* take that (my love) which will not expire.
3. *grind . . . try:* sharpen with new experience to test.
Sonnet 111
1. Q has "wish," which gives a more problematic array of

alternative meanings.
2. Probably: Than employment as an actor, which requires one to curry favor with the public.
Sonnet 112
1. This sonnet links with 111.
2. So long as you allow new growth to cover what is bad in me, and give credit for what is good.

That my steeled sense or changes, right or wrong.[3]
In so profound abyss I throw all care
10 Of others' voices that my adder's sense°   *deaf ears*
To critic and to flatterer stoppèd are.
Mark how with my neglect I do dispense:[4]
   You are so strongly in my purpose bred[5]
   That all the world besides, methinks, they're dead.

113

Since I left you mine eye is in my mind,[1]
And that which governs me to go about°   *And my real sight*
Doth part his° function and is partly blind,   *Divides its*
Seems seeing, but effectually is out;°   *blind*
5 For it no form delivers to the heart
Of bird, of flower, or shape which it doth latch.°   *catch sight of*
Of his quick objects° hath the mind no part,   *fleeting impressions*
Nor his own vision holds[2] what it doth catch;
For if it see the rud'st or gentlest° sight,   *coarsest or noblest*
10 The most sweet favour[3] or deformèd'st creature,
The mountain or the sea, the day or night,
The crow or dove, it shapes them to your feature.[4]
   Incapable of more, replete with you,
   My most true mind thus makes mine eye untrue.

114[1]

Or whether doth my mind, being crowned with you,[2]
Drink up the monarch's plague, this flattery,
Or whether shall I say mine eye saith true,
And that your love taught it this alchemy,[3]
5 To make of monsters and things indigest°   *chaotic*
Such cherubins° as your sweet self resemble,   *angels*
Creating every° bad a perfect best   *from every*
As fast as objects to his beams assemble?[4]
O, 'tis the first, 'tis flatt'ry in my seeing,
10 And my great° mind most kingly drinks it up.   *pompous*
Mine eye well knows what with his gust is 'greeing,[5]
And to his palate doth prepare the cup.
   If it be poisoned, 'tis the lesser sin
   That mine eye loves it and doth first begin.[6]

115

Those lines that I before have writ do lie,
Even those that said I could not love you dearer;
Yet then my judgement knew no reason why

---

3. *None . . . wrong*: perhaps, There being no one else to influence me, and no one else's influence being capable of positively or negatively affecting my hardened disposition.
4. How I excuse my neglect (of "other's voices," line 10).
5. Nurtured in all my plans.
Sonnet 113
1. I see with my mind's eye.
2. Nor does the eye's vision hold on to.
3. Face; perhaps Q's "sweet-favor" means "sweet-favored," or "good-looking."
4. It makes them look like you.

Sonnet 114
1. This sonnet links with 113.
2. Being made a king by having you. "Or whether" introduces alternatives.
3. And that love of you taught my eye how thus to transform things.
4. As fast as objects come before its gaze. (The eye was thought to emit beams of light).
5. What pleases the mind's appetite.
6. And drinks first (like a king's taster).

My most full flame should afterwards burn clearer.
5   But reckoning time,[1] whose millioned accidents
Creep in 'twixt vows° and change decrees of kings,   *(and their performance)*
Tan° sacred beauty, blunt the sharp'st intents,   *Darken*
Divert strong minds to th' course of alt'ring things—
Alas, why, fearing of time's tyranny,
10 Might I not then say[2] 'Now I love you best',
When I was certain o'er° incertainty,   *beyond*
Crowning° the present, doubting of the rest?   *Exalting*
Love is a babe; then might I not say so,[3]
To give° full growth to that which still doth grow.   *Thereby giving*

116

Let me not to the marriage of true minds
Admit impediments.[1] Love is not love
Which alters when it alteration finds,
Or bends with the remover to remove.[2]
5   O no, it is an ever fixèd mark[3]
That looks on tempests and is never shaken;
It is the star to every wand'ring barque,
Whose worth's unknown although his height be taken.[4]
Love's not time's fool,° though rosy lips and cheeks   *plaything*
10 Within his bending sickle's compass[5] come;
Love alters not with his brief hours and weeks,
But bears it out even to the edge of doom.[6]
If this be error and upon° me proved,   *against*
I never writ, nor no man ever loved.

117

Accuse me thus: that I have scanted° all   *neglected*
Wherein I should your great deserts repay,
Forgot upon your dearest love to call
Whereto all bonds do tie me day by day;
5   That I have frequent° been with unknown minds,°   *friendly / strangers*
And given to time your own dear-purchased right;[1]
That I have hoisted sail to all the winds
Which should° transport me farthest from your sight.   *were likely to*
Book both my wilfulness and errors down,
10 And on just proof surmise accumulate;[2]
Bring me within the level° of your frown,   *aim*
But shoot not at me in your wakened hate,
Since my appeal says I did strive to prove[3]
The constancy and virtue of your love.

Sonnet 115
1. But taking time into account; but time, which settles
accounts.
2. Was I not then right to have said.
3. Thus I shouldn't say, "Now I love you best" (line 10).
Sonnet 116
1. *Let . . . impediments*: echoing the traditional marriage
service.
2. Or abandons the relationship when the loved one is
unfaithful or has departed or died, or when time ("the
remover") alters things for the worse.
3. An unmoving sea mark, such as a lighthouse or a bea-
con, which provides a constant reference point for sailors.

4. *Whose . . . taken*: The star's (great) intrinsic value can-
not be assessed, although navigators at sea can measure
height above the horizon.
5. Within range of time's curved (and hostile) scythe.
"Compass" also recalls the imagery of the second qua-
train.
6. But endures till the eve of doomsday.
Sonnet 117
1. And wasted idly what should have been your right
(rite) because acquired by your great worth and affection
(because acquired at your great cost).
2. And pile suspicion on top of your proof.
3. Since my defense is that I was trying to test.

118

Like° as, to make our appetites more keen,   *Just*
With eager° compounds we our palate urge;°   *sharp / stimulate*
As to prevent° our maladies unseen   *forestall*
We sicken to shun sickness when we purge:[1]
5 Even so, being full of your ne'er cloying sweetness,
To bitter sauces did I frame° my feeding,   *adjust*
And, sick of welfare,[2] found a kind of meetness°   *suitability*
To be diseased ere that there was true needing.
Thus policy° in love, t'anticipate   *strategy*
10 The ills that were not, grew to faults assured,
And brought to[3] medicine a healthful state
Which, rank of goodness, would by ill be cured.[4]
    But thence I learn, and find the lesson true:
    Drugs poison him that so° fell sick of you.   *thus; so badly*

119

What potions have I drunk of siren[1] tears
Distilled from limbecks° foul as hell within,   *stills*
Applying° fears to hopes and hopes to fears,   *(as a medicine)*
Still° losing when I saw myself° to win!   *Always / expected*
5 What wretched errors hath my heart committed
Whilst it hath thought itself so blessèd never!
How have mine eyes out of their spheres been fitted[2]
In the distraction° of this madding° fever!   *delirium / fit-inducing*
O benefit of ill! Now I find true
10 That better is by evil still made better,
And ruined love when it is built anew
Grows fairer than at first, more strong, far greater.
    So I return rebuked to my content,
    And gain by ills thrice more than I have spent.

120

That you were once unkind befriends me now,
And for° that sorrow which I then did feel   *because of*
Needs must I under my transgression bow,
Unless my nerves° were brass or hammered steel.   *sinews*
5 For if you were by my unkindness shaken
As I by yours, you've past a hell of time,
And I, a tyrant, have no leisure taken
To weigh° how once I suffered in° your crime.   *contemplate / from*
O that our night of woe[1] might have remembered°   *reminded*
10 My deepest sense how hard true sorrow hits,
And soon to you as you to me then tendered°   *offered*
The humble salve which wounded bosoms fits![2]

Sonnet 118
1. We make ourselves sick with medicine that causes vomiting or bowel movements so as to prevent greater illness.
2. Made ill by good food.
3. Treated with; brought to the need of.
4. Overfull with goodness (health, the beloved), sought to be cured by disease (evil).
Sonnet 119
1. Deceitfully and dangerously alluring. Sirens were mythological creatures, part bird, part woman, said to lure sailors to their death with the sound of their irresistible songs.
2. Been driven convulsively out of their sockets.
Sonnet 120
1. Our earlier time of suffering (caused by the youth's unfaithfulness).
2. The salve of apology that is just the thing for an injured heart.

But that your trespass° now becomes a fee;°   *offense / compensation*
Mine ransoms° yours, and yours must ransom me.   *absolves*

121

'Tis better to be vile than vile esteemed°   *reputed vile*
When not to be receives reproach of being,°   *being so (vile)*
And the just pleasure lost, which is so deemed
Not by our feeling but by others' seeing.[1]
5 For why should others' false adulterate° eyes   *corrupted*
Give salutation to my sportive blood?[2]
Or on my frailties why are frailer spies,
Which in their wills[3] count bad what I think good?
No, I am that I am, and they that level°   *aim*
10 At my abuses reckon up their own.
I may be straight, though they themselves be bevel;°   *crooked*
By their rank° thoughts my deeds must not be shown,°   *foul / measured*
  Unless this general evil they maintain:
  All men are bad and in their badness reign.°   *thrive*

122

Thy gift, thy tables,° are within my brain   *notebook*
Full charactered° with lasting memory,   *written*
Which shall above that idle rank[1] remain
Beyond all date, even to eternity;
5 Or at the least so long as brain and heart
Have faculty° by nature to subsist,   *power*
Till each to razed° oblivion yield his part   *destroying*
Of thee, thy record never can be missed.°   *lost*
That poor retention[2] could not so much hold,
10 Nor need I tallies thy dear love to score;[3]
Therefore to give them° from me was I bold,   *(the "tables")*
To trust those tables° that receive thee more.   *memory*
  To keep an adjunct° to remember thee   *aid*
  Were to import° forgetfulness in me.   *imply*

123

No, time, thou shalt not boast that I do change!
Thy pyramids built up with newer might[1]
To me are nothing° novel, nothing strange,   *in no way*
They are but dressings of a former sight.[2]
5 Our dates° are brief, and therefore we admire   *lives*
What thou dost foist upon us that is old,
And rather make them born to our desire[3]

Sonnet 121
1. *And . . . seeing:* And we are denied the appropriate, innocent pleasure (or, we don't even get to enjoy the sin we've supposedly committed), which is considered sinful not by us but by others.
2. Wink knowingly at my lustful behavior.
3. *Or . . . wills:* Why should my failings be pried into by even more culpable people, who wilfully (who licentiously; who in Will Shakespeare).
Sonnet 122
1. Trivial status (of the "tables" as opposed to "memory").
2. That inadequate container (the "tables"); that faulty

memory.
3. Nor do I need the notched sticks used in calculating sums (to which the "tables" are contemptuously compared) to reckon up your precious love.
Sonnet 123
1. Grand buildings constructed by more modern means. Possibly referring to structures erected in Rome in 1586 or in London in 1603 (for James's coronation), but retaining a sense of almost timeless Egyptian antiquity.
2. Replicas of what's been seen before.
3. And consider them made just for us.

Than think that we before have heard them told.°   *described*
Thy registers° and thee I both defy,   *records*
10 Not wond'ring at the present nor the past;
For thy records and what we see doth lie,
Made more or less by thy continual haste.[4]
  This I do vow, and this shall ever be:
  I will be true despite thy scythe and thee.

124

If my dear love° were but the child of state[1]   *(for you)*
It might for fortune's bastard be unfathered,[2]
As subject to time's love or to time's hate,
Weeds among weeds or flowers with flowers gathered.[3]
5 No, it was builded far from accident;°   *chance*
It suffers° not in smiling pomp, nor falls   *changes*
Under the blow of thrallèd° discontent   *captive*
Whereto th'inviting time our fashion calls.[4]
It fears not policy,° that heretic   *expediency*
10 Which works on leases of short-numbered hours,°   *short-term contracts*
But all alone stands hugely politic,°   *prudent*
That it nor° grows with heat° nor drowns with showers.   *neither / prosperity*
  To this I witness call the fools of time,
  Which die for goodness, who have lived for crime.[5]

125

Were't aught to me I bore the canopy,[1]
With my extern° the outward honouring,   *exterior action*
Or laid great bases for eternity[2]
Which proves more short than waste° or ruining?   *decay*
5 Have I not seen dwellers on form and favour[3]
Lose all and more by paying too much rent,°   *overdoing homage*
For compound sweet forgoing simple savour,[4]
Pitiful thrivers in their gazing spent?[5]
No, let me be obsequious° in thy heart,   *dutiful*
10 And take thou my oblation,° poor but free,°   *offering / freely given*
Which is not mixed with seconds,[6] knows no art°   *artifice*
But mutual render,° only me for thee.   *exchange*
  Hence, thou suborned informer![7] A true soul
  When most impeached° stands least in thy control.   *accused*

4. Raised and destroyed by time's swift passage; made to seem more or less majestic by virtue of newness or antiquity and the tastes of the times.
Sonnet 124
1. Were simply the result of circumstances; of your high position.
2. It might be disinherited as a passing fancy, a product of fortune (chance, wealth).
3. *As . . . gathered:* Regarded as useless or valuable as time and fortune decide.
4. To which ("pomp" and "discontent") we are driven by the latest trend ("fashion").
5. *To . . . crime:* I call as witness those playthings of time

who, having lived wicked lives, reform or repent at death.
Sonnet 125
1. Would I care if I enhanced my status by carrying a ceremonial canopy for a royal person?
2. Laid foundations for eternal monuments.
3. Seen those who depend (linger) on ceremony and appearance.
4. For obsequious praise giving up plain candor.
5. Pitiful in their empty achievements, ruined by love of show.
6. The second-rate.
7. Paid spy: jealousy or the detractor whose charges the poem answers.

126[1]

O thou my lovely boy, who in thy power
Dost hold time's fickle glass,[2] his sickle-hour;[3]
Who hast by waning grown,[4] and therein show'st
Thy lovers withering as thy sweet self grow'st—
5   If nature, sovereign mistress over wrack,°   *decay*
As thou goest onwards still° will pluck thee back,   *constantly*
She keeps thee to this purpose: that her skill
May time disgrace, and wretched minutes kill.
Yet fear her, O thou minion° of her pleasure!   *darling*
10 She may detain but not still keep her treasure.
    Her audit,° though delayed, answered° must be,   *debt (to time) / paid*
    And her quietus° is to render° thee.   *settlement / relinquish*

127[1]

In the old age° black was not counted fair,[2]   *old days*
Or if it were, it bore not beauty's name;
But now is black beauty's successive heir,°   *heir by succession*
And beauty slandered with a bastard shame:[3]
5   For since each hand hath put on° nature's power,   *usurped*
Fairing° the foul with art's false borrowed face,   *Beautifying*
Sweet beauty hath no name, no holy bower,
But is profaned, if not lives in disgrace.
Therefore my mistress' eyes are raven-black,
10 Her brow so suited,[4] and they mourners seem
At such who, not born fair, no beauty lack,
Sland'ring creation with a false esteem.[5]
    Yet so° they mourn, becoming of° their woe,   *in such a way / adorning*
    That every tongue says beauty should look so.

128

How oft, when thou, my music, music play'st
Upon that blessèd wood whose motion° sounds   *mechanism*
With thy sweet fingers when thou gently sway'st°   *govern*
The wiry concord that mine ear confounds,°   *amazes (with delight)*
5   Do I envy those jacks[1] that nimble leap
To kiss the tender inward of thy hand
Whilst my poor lips, which should that harvest reap,
At the wood's boldness by thee blushing stand!
To be so tickled they would change their state
10 And situation with those dancing chips

Sonnet 126
1. This "sonnet" or envoi, of six couplets, concludes the part of the sequence apparently addressed to the youth and formally signals a change in tone and subject matter in the remaining sonnets.
2. Capricious, treacherous hourglass (?); mirror showing changing images (?).
3. Reaping time. "Sickle-hour" emends Q's "sickle, hower," which may be an error for "sickle o'er." A familiar emblem for time placed the hourglass below and the sickle above.
4. Become more beautiful with age. As the sand in the top half of an hourglass wanes, the sand in the bottom part grows.
Sonnet 127
1. Sonnets 127–52 have been traditionally known as the "dark lady" group, though their subject matter is not uniform and their object is only once called "dark" (147.14)

and never a "lady." She is referred to as the poet's "mistress" (127.9; 130.1, 8, 12), however, and often described as "black" (127.1, 3, 9; 130.4; 131.12, 13; 132.3, 13; 147.14). The celebration of black beauty goes back to the biblical Song of Songs, 1:4: "I am blacke . . . but comelie." See the Introduction.
2. Beautiful; light-colored.
3. And (fair) beauty accused of illegitimacy (by use of cosmetics).
4. Her brow dressed (matched) in an eyebrow black like her eyes (and for the same reason).
5. *At . . . esteem:* Because of those who, not being fair, make up for it with cosmetics, so that even natural beauty is presumed artificial.
Sonnet 128
1. Keys of the virginal, a harpsichord-like instrument; fellows.

O'er whom thy fingers walk with gentle gait,
Making dead wood more blessed than living lips.
    Since saucy° jacks so happy are in this,   *impudent*
    Give them thy fingers, me thy lips to kiss.

129

Th'expense of spirit in a waste of shame
Is lust in action;[1] and till action, lust
Is perjured, murd'rous, bloody, full of blame,
Savage, extreme, rude,° cruel, not to trust,°   *harsh / be trusted*
5 Enjoyed no sooner but despisèd straight,°   *immediately*
Past reason° hunted, and no sooner had   *Madly*
Past reason hated as a swallowed bait
On purpose laid to make the taker mad;
Mad in pursuit and in possession so,°   *(mad)*
10 Had, having, and in quest to have, extreme;
A bliss in proof and proved,[2] a very woe;
Before, a joy proposed; behind, a dream.
    All this the world well knows, yet none knows well
    To shun the heaven that leads men to this hell.

130

My mistress' eyes are nothing like the sun;
Coral is far more red than her lips' red.
If snow be white, why then her breasts are dun;°   *grayish brown*
If hairs be wires,[1] black wires grow on her head.
5 I have seen roses damasked,° red and white,   *dappled*
But no such roses see I in her cheeks;
And in some perfumes is there more delight
Than in the breath that from my mistress reeks.°   *issues; smells*
I love to hear her speak, yet well I know
10 That music hath a far more pleasing sound.
I grant I never saw a goddess go:°   *walk*
My mistress when she walks treads on the ground.
    And yet, by heaven, I think my love as rare
    As any she belied with false compare.[2]

131

Thou art as tyrannous so as thou art[1]
As those whose beauties proudly make them cruel,
For well thou know'st to my dear° doting heart   *fond(ly)*
Thou art the fairest and most precious jewel.
5 Yet, in good faith, some say that thee behold
Thy face hath not the power to make love groan.
To say they err I dare not be so bold,
Although I swear it to myself alone;
And, to be sure° that is not false I swear,   *for proof; surely*
10 A thousand groans but thinking on° thy face   *just thinking about*
One on another's neck° do witness bear   *In quick succession*

Sonnet 129
1. *Th'expense . . . action:* The expenditure of vital energy (semen) in a shameful waste (waist) is consummated lust.
2. *in proof:* while being experienced. *proved:* having been experienced.
Sonnet 130
1. Elizabethan poets often compared women's hair to golden wires.
2. As any woman misrepresented by false comparison.
Sonnet 131
1. As cruel as you are dark (hence not conventionally beautiful).

Thy black° is fairest in my judgment's place.[2]   *dark appearance*
In nothing art thou black° save in thy deeds,   *ugly*
And thence this slander,[3] as I think, proceeds.

132

Thine eyes I love, and they, as° pitying me—   *as if*
Knowing thy heart torment° me with disdain—   *to torment*
Have put on black, and loving mourners be,
Looking with pretty ruth° upon my pain;   *pity*
5 And truly, not the morning sun of heaven
Better becomes° the gray cheeks° of the east,   *beautifies / clouds*
Nor that full star that ushers in the even° *Venus, the evening star*
Doth° half that glory to the sober west,   *Imparts*
As those two mourning° eyes become thy face. *(pun on "morning")*
10 O, let it then as well beseem° thy heart   *become*
To mourn for me, since mourning doth thee grace,
And suit thy pity like in every part.[1]
  Then will I swear beauty herself is black,
  And all they foul° that thy complexion lack.   *ugly*

133

Beshrew° that heart that makes my heart to groan *Curse (a mild term)*
For that deep wound it gives my friend and me!
Is't not enough to torture me alone,
But slave to slavery° my sweet'st friend must be? *utterly enslaved*
5 Me from myself thy cruel eye hath taken,
And my next self thou harder hast engrossed.[1]
Of him, myself, and thee I am forsaken—
A torment thrice threefold thus to be crossed.°   *afflicted*
Prison° my heart in thy steel bosom's ward,°   *Imprison / cell*
10 But then my friend's heart let my poor heart bail;
Whoe'er keeps° me, let my heart be his guard;[2]   *guards*
Thou canst not then use rigour° in my jail.   *severity*
  And yet thou wilt; for I, being pent° in thee,   *locked up*
  Perforce am thine, and° all that is in me.   *as is*

134[1]

So, now° I have confessed that he is thine,   *now that*
And I myself am mortgaged to thy will,° *intent; sexual desire*
Myself I'll forfeit, so that other mine[2]
Thou wilt restore to be my comfort still.
5 But thou wilt not, nor he will not° be free,   *doesn't want to*
For thou art covetous, and he is kind.
He learned but surety-like° to write° for me *as guarantor / sign*
Under that bond° that him as fast[3] doth bind. *(of infatuation)*
The statute[4] of thy beauty thou wilt take,
10 Thou usurer that putt'st forth all to use,°   *at interest; for sex*
And sue a friend came° debtor for my sake;   *who became*

---

2. In my opinion.
3. See line 6 for "this slander."
Sonnet 132
1. And dress your pity similarly, in heart as well as eyes.
Sonnet 133
1. And my second self, or closest friend, you have even more cruelly monopolized.

2. My friend's prison.
Sonnet 134
1. This sonnet links with 133.
2. So long as my other self.
3. As firmly as myself.
4. The total guaranteed by the bond.

So him I lose through my unkind abuse.[5]
    Him have I lost; thou hast both him and me;
    He pays the whole,° and yet am I not free.   *(pun on "hole")*

135[1]

Whoever hath her wish, thou hast thy Will,
And Will to boot,° and Will in overplus.   *in addition*
More than enough am I that vex thee still,°   *always (by wooing)*
To thy sweet will making addition thus.
5 Wilt thou, whose will is large and spacious,
Not once vouchsafe to hide my will in thine?
Shall will in others° seem right gracious,   *others' wills*
And in my will no fair acceptance shine?[2]
The sea, all water, yet receives rain still,
10 And in abundance addeth to his° store;   *its*
So thou, being rich in Will, add to thy Will
One will of mine to make thy large Will more.
    Let no unkind no fair beseechers kill;[3]
    Think all but one,° and me in that one Will.   *one suitor*

136[1]

If thy soul check° thee that I come so near,[2]   *chide*
Swear to thy blind soul that I was thy Will,[3]
And will, thy soul knows, is admitted there;
Thus far for love my love-suit, sweet, fulfil.°   *grant*
5 Will will fulfill the treasure° of thy love,   *fill up the treasury*
Ay, fill it full with wills, and my will one.°   *one of them*
In things of great receipt° with ease we prove   *volume*
Among a number one is reckoned none.[4]
Then in the number let me pass untold,°   *uncounted*
10 Though in thy store's account° I one must be;   *tally (of lovers)*
For nothing hold me, so it please thee hold
That nothing me a something, sweet, to thee.[5]
    Make but my name thy love,[6] and love that still,°   *always*
    And then thou lov'st me for my name is Will.

137

Thou blind fool love, what dost thou to mine eyes
That they behold and see not what they see?
They know what beauty is, see where it lies,
Yet what the best is take the worst to be.[1]
5 If eyes corrupt° by over-partial° looks   *corrupted / overly doting*

---

5. Through your ill treatment of me.
Sonnet 135
1. This sonnet, as well as 136, 143, and "A Lover's Complaint," lines 126–33, puns elaborately on different senses of "will": wishes, sexual desire, futurity, testament, the name "Will" (applied to one or more persons, including Shakespeare, and capitalized and sometimes italicized in Q), and the male and female sexual organs. See also 57.13 and note.
2. And my will not be greeted with a kind reception.
3. Let no unkindness of yours kill any of your worthy suitors.

Sonnet 136
1. This sonnet links with 135.
2. I am so forthright; I am so physically close.
3. See sonnet 135, note 1.
4. Proverbially, one is no number.
5. For . . . *thee*: Think me worthless so long as, my darling, you treasure worthless me. Q's punctuation, "something sweet to thee," emphasizes the sexual implications. Through your ill treatment of me.
Sonnet 137
1. Yet take the worst to be the best.

Be anchored in the bay where all men ride,[2]
Why of eyes' falsehood hast thou forgèd hooks
Whereto the judgement of my heart is tied?
Why should my heart think that a several plot°   *private land*
10 Which my heart knows the wide world's common place?[3]—
Or° mine eyes, seeing this, say this is not,   *Or why should*
To put fair truth upon so foul a face?
   In things right true my heart and eyes have erred,
   And to this false plague[4] are they now transferred.

138[1]

When my love swears that she is made of truth
I do believe her though I know she lies,
That° she might think me some untutored youth   *So that*
Unlearnèd in the world's false subtleties.
5 Thus vainly° thinking that she thinks me young,   *in vain; with vanity*
Although she knows my days are past the best,
Simply I credit[2] her false-speaking tongue;
On both sides thus is simple truth suppressed.
But wherefore says she not she is unjust,°   *unfaithful*
10 And wherefore say not I that I am old?
O, love's best habit is in seeming trust,[3]
And age in love loves not to have years told.°   *counted*
   Therefore I lie° with her, and she with me,   *tell lies; lie down*
   And in our faults by lies we flattered be.

139

O, call° not me to justify° the wrong   *ask / approve*
That thy unkindness° lays upon my heart.   *infidelity*
Wound me not with thine eye[1] but with thy tongue;
Use power with power,[2] and slay me not by art.°   *by deceit*
5 Tell me thou lov'st elsewhere, but in my sight,
Dear heart, forbear to glance thine eye aside.
What° need'st thou wound with cunning when thy might   *Why*
Is more than my o'erpressed defence can bide?°   *endure*
Let me excuse thee: 'Ah, my love well knows
10 Her pretty looks have been mine enemies,
And therefore from my face she turns my foes
That they elsewhere might dart their injuries.'
   Yet do not so; but since I am near slain,
   Kill me outright with looks, and rid° my pain.   *put an end to*

140

Be wise as thou art cruel; do not press
My tongue-tied patience with too much disdain,
Lest sorrow lend me words, and words express

---

2. Harbor for general use (suggesting a promiscuous woman).
3. *the wide . . . place*: common land, open to all (suggesting promiscuity); a commonplace known by all.
4. This plague of false perception; this deceitful woman.
Sonnet 138
1. Another version of this sonnet appears in *The Passionate Pilgrim*. See the Textual Note and the Alternative Version.

sions.
2. Naively (foolishly; giving the appearance of folly) I (pretend to) believe.
3. Love is best dressed in apparent fidelity (apparent trust).
Sonnet 139
1. By looking elsewhere, at other men (see line 6).
2. Use power frankly; fairly.

The manner° of my pity-wanting° pain.

5 If I might teach thee wit,° better it were,   *wisdom*
Though not to love, yet, love, to tell me so—
As testy sick men when their deaths be near
No news but health from their physicians know.°   *learn*
For if I should despair I should grow mad,
10 And in my madness might speak ill of thee.
Now this ill-wresting world[1] is grown so bad
Mad slanderers by mad ears believèd be.
   That I may not be so, nor thou belied,°   *maligned*
   Bear thine eyes straight,[2] though thy proud heart go wide.° *astray*

141

In faith, I do not love thee with mine eyes,
For they in thee a thousand errors note;
But 'tis my heart that loves what they despise,
Who in despite of view° is pleased to dote.   *despite what it sees*
5 Nor are mine ears with thy tongue's tune delighted,
Nor tender feeling to base touches prone;[1]
Nor taste nor smell desire to be invited
To any sensual feast with thee alone;
But my five wits[2] nor my five senses can
10 Dissuade one foolish heart from serving thee,
Who leaves unswayed the likeness of a man.[3]
Thy proud heart's slave and vassal-wretch to be.
   Only my plague thus far° I count my gain: *to this extent*
   That she that makes me sin awards me pain.[4]

142[1]

Love is my sin, and thy dear virtue hate,
Hate of my sin grounded on sinful loving.[2]
O, but with mine compare thou thine own state,
And thou shalt find it° merits not reproving;   *(my state)*
5 Or if it do, not from those lips of thine
That have profaned their scarlet ornaments[3]
And sealed[4] false bonds of love as oft as mine,
Robbed others' beds' revenues of their rents.[5]
Be it lawful° I love thee as thou lov'st those   *let it be lawful that*
10 Whom thine eyes woo as mine importune thee.
Root pity in thy heart, that when it grows
Thy pity may deserve to pitied be.°   *make you pitiable*
   If thou dost seek to have what thou dost hide,°   *(pity)*
   By self example mayst thou be denied!

Sonnet 140
1. Now this world, that tends to interpret in the worst light.
2. Keep looking only at me (see 139).

Sonnet 141
1. Nor is my keen sense of touch susceptible to "base" sexual contact.
2. Mental faculties (common sense, imagination, fancy, judgment, memory).
3. Which (the heart, serving you) leaves without a commander the mere semblance of a man.
4. By making me sin, she causes me to suffer punitive penance, which will reduce my sufferings after death.

Sonnet 142
1. This sonnet links with 141.
2. *Love . . . loving:* My only sin is love, and your most valuable virtue is hatred, hatred of my sin in loving you (but also, your most valuable virtue is the haughty rejection of my wooing) based on (your) immoral sexual affairs.
3. Lips, which are scarlet, like a cardinal's robe.
4. "Sealed" with a kiss: comparing the mistress's lips to the red wax used to seal official documents.
5. Stolen the sexual and emotional intimacy ("rents" paid by a tenant) from others' marriages by committing adultery, thus reducing the possibility that these marriages will result in children ("revenues," estates that yield income).

143

Lo, as a care-full° housewife runs to catch   *busy*
One of her feathered creatures broke away,
Sets down her babe and makes all swift dispatch°   *hurries*
In pursuit of the thing she would have stay,
5 Whilst her neglected child holds her in chase,
Cries to catch her whose busy care is bent
To follow that which flies before her face,
Not prizing° her poor infant's discontent: *regarding*
So runn'st thou after that which flies from thee,
10 Whilst I, thy babe, chase thee afar behind;
But if thou catch thy hope, turn back to me
And play the mother's part: kiss me, be kind.
  So will I pray that thou mayst have thy Will[1]
  If thou turn back and my loud crying still.

144[1]

Two loves I have, of comfort and despair,
Which like two spirits do suggest° me still.   *entice*
The better angel is a man right fair,
The worser spirit a woman coloured ill.°   *darkly*
5 To win me soon to hell my female evil
Tempteth my better angel from my side,
And would corrupt my saint to be a devil,
Wooing his purity with her foul pride;
And whether that my angel be turned fiend
10 Suspect I may, yet not directly tell;
But being both from me, both to each friend,[2]
I guess one angel in another's hell.[3]
  Yet this shall I ne'er know, but live in doubt
  Till my bad angel fire my good one out.[4]

145[1]

Those lips that love's own hand did make
Breathed forth the sound that said 'I hate'
To me that languished for her sake;
But when she saw my woeful state,
5 Straight in her heart did mercy come,
Chiding that tongue that ever sweet
Was used in giving gentle doom,°   *judgment*
And taught it thus anew to greet:
'I hate' she altered with an end
10 That followed it as gentle day
Doth follow night who, like a fiend,
From heaven to hell is flown away.

Sonnet 143
1. A pun; see sonnet 135, note 1.
Sonnet 144
1. Another version of this sonnet appears in *The Passionate Pilgrim*. See the Textual Note and the Alternative Versions.
2. Both away from me and lovers to one another.
3. Each torments the other; they are in the "hell," or middle den, of a (sexually) boisterous game called barleybreak; the man occupies the sex organ ("hell") of the woman.
4. Until my bad angel expels my good one, who has become an animal to be smoked out of a burrow; until my bad angel infects my good one with venereal disease; until bad money ("angel" was a gold coin) drives out good.
Sonnet 145
1. Unlike the other sonnets, which are in iambic pentameter, 145 is composed of eight-syllable (iambic tetrameter) lines.

'I hate' from hate away she threw,[2]
And saved my life, saying 'not you.'

146

Poor soul, the centre of my sinful earth,
[   ] these rebel powers that thee array;[1]
Why dost thou pine within and suffer dearth,
Painting thy outward walls so costly gay?
5 Why so large cost, having so short a lease,
Dost thou upon thy fading mansion° spend?   *(the body)*
Shall worms, inheritors of this excess,
Eat up thy charge?° Is this thy body's end?   *expense*
Then, soul, live thou upon thy servant's° loss,   *(the body's)*
10 And let that pine to aggravate thy store.[2]
Buy terms divine° in selling hours of dross;°   *eternal life / waste*
Within be fed, without be rich no more.
    So shalt thou feed on death, that feeds on men,
    And death once dead, there's no more dying then.

147

My love is as a fever, longing still°   *continually*
For that which longer nurseth° the disease,   *nourishes*
Feeding on that which doth preserve° the ill,   *prolong*
Th'uncertain° sickly appetite to please.   *capricious*
5 My reason, the physician to my love,
Angry that his prescriptions are not kept,
Hath left me, and I desperate now approve
Desire is death, which physic did except.[1]
Past cure I am, now reason is past care,[2]
10 And frantic mad with evermore° unrest.   *constant*
My thoughts and my discourse as madmen's are,
At random from° the truth vainly° expressed;   *unconnected to / idly*
    For I have sworn thee fair, and thought thee bright,
    Who art as black as hell, as dark as night.

148

O me, what eyes hath love put in my head,
Which have no correspondence with true sight!
Or if they have, where is my judgement fled,
That censures falsely[1] what they see aright?
5 If that be fair whereon my false eyes dote,
What means the world to say it is not so?
If it be not, then love doth well denote[2]
Love's eye is not so true as all men's. No,[3]

---

2. She converted the normal meaning of the phrase "I hate" away from "hate." A pun on "hate away" and "(Anne) Hathaway," Shakespeare's wife, is possible.
Sonnet 146
1. This rebellious body that clothes you (lines you up for battle). At the beginning of the line, Q repeats "My sinful earth" from the previous line. There is no way of discovering what Shakespeare wrote; among the guesses are "Starved by" and "Foiled by."
2. And let the body dwindle to add to your wealth.
Sonnet 147
1. *now . . . except:* now discover that desire, which

rejected medicine, is fatal.
2. Medical care: inverting the proverb "Past cure, past care" (don't worry about what you can't control). In the proverb, you don't care because you can't cure; here, because you don't care, you can't cure.
Sonnet 148
1. That judges inaccurately (dishonestly). "False" (line 5) has similar meanings.
2. Then my self-delusion in love proves that.
3. Not so true as all other men's eye. On the contrary. Q's "all men's, no" is often emended to "all men's 'No,' " suggesting a pun on "eye/aye" (yes).

How can it, O, how can love's eye be true,
10 That is so vexed with watching° and with tears?   *staying awake*
No marvel then though I° mistake my view: *that I (eye)*
The sun itself sees not till heaven clears.
    O cunning love, with tears thou keep'st me blind
    Lest eyes, well seeing, thy foul faults should find!

149

Canst thou, O cruel, say I love thee not
When I against myself with thee partake?°   *take sides*
Do I not think on thee when I forgot
Am of myself, all-tyrant,[1] for thy sake?
5 Who hateth thee that I do call my friend?
On whom frown'st thou that I do fawn upon?
Nay, if thou lour'st° on me, do I not spend°   *scowl / wreak*
Revenge upon myself with present moan?°   *instant anguish*
What merit do I in myself respect°   *value; note*
10 That is so proud thy service to despise,[2]
When all my best° doth worship thy defect,°   *best qualities / flaws*
Commanded by the motion of thine eyes?
    But, love, hate on; for now I know thy mind.
    Those that can see thou lov'st, and I am blind.[3]

150

O, from what power hast thou this powerful might
With insufficiency° my heart to sway,   *By your flaws*
To make me give the lie to my true sight
And swear that brightness doth not grace the day?[1]
5 Whence hast thou this becoming of things ill,[2]
That in the very refuse of thy deeds°   *your basest behavior*
There is such strength and warrantise° of skill   *guarantee*
That in my mind thy worst all best exceeds?
Who taught thee how to make me love thee more
10 The more I hear and see just cause of hate?
O, though I love what others do abhor,
With others thou shouldst not abhor my state.
    If thy unworthiness raised love in me,
    More worthy I to be beloved of thee.

151

Love is too young° to know what conscience is,   *(Cupid being a boy)*
Yet who knows not conscience[1] is born of love?
Then, gentle cheater, urge° not my amiss,°   *stress / fault*
Lest guilty of my faults thy sweet self prove.
5 For, thou betraying me, I do betray
My nobler part° to my gross body's treason.   *soul*
My soul doth tell my body that he may

Sonnet 149
1. *when . . . all-tyrant:* when I tyrannically neglect myself.
2. So proud as to scorn to serve you.
3. You love those who see you accurately and thus admire you, but I am blinded (by love and thus, from your point of view, unworthy of being loved). The first clause may have the opposite sense, however: you love those who see your defects well enough not to love you.

Sonnet 150
1. *To . . . day:* the speaker is so blindly in love that he finds beauty only in the blackness he associates with his mistress.
2. This capacity to render the ugly attractive.
Sonnet 151
1. Moral sense; carnal knowledge.

Triumph in love; flesh stays no farther reason,[2]
But rising at thy name doth point out thee
10 As his triumphant prize. Proud of this pride,[3]
He is contented thy poor drudge to be,
To stand° in thy affairs, fall by thy side.   *assist; be erect*
    No want of conscience hold it that I call
    Her 'love' for whose dear love I rise and fall.

152

In loving thee thou know'st I am forsworn,[1]
But thou art twice forsworn to me love swearing:
In act thy bed-vow° broke, and new faith torn   *to husband (or lover)*
In vowing new hate after new love bearing.[2]
5 But why of two oaths' breach do I accuse thee
When I break twenty? I am perjured most,
For all my vows are oaths but to misuse° thee,   *deceive*
And all my honest faith in thee is lost.
For I have sworn deep oaths of thy deep kindness,
10 Oaths of thy love, thy truth, thy constancy,
And to enlighten thee gave eyes to blindness,[3]
Or made them swear against the thing they see.
    For I have sworn thee fair—more perjured eye°   *(punning on "I")*
    To swear against the truth so foul a lie.

153[1]

Cupid laid by his brand° and fell asleep.   *torch*
A maid of Dian's[2] this advantage found,°   *seized*
And his love-kindling fire did quickly steep
In a cold valley-fountain of that ground,
5 Which borrowed from this holy fire of love
A dateless° lively heat, still° to endure,   *An endless / always*
And grew a seething bath which yet men prove
Against strange maladies a sovereign cure.[3]
But at my mistress' eye love's brand new fired,°   *being newly lit*
10 The boy for trial° needs would touch my breast.   *to test it*
I, sick withal,° the help of bath desired,   *from it*
And thither hied, a sad distempered° guest,   *seriously ill*
    But found no cure; the bath for my help lies
    Where Cupid got new fire: my mistress' eyes.

154[1]

The little love-god lying once asleep
Laid by his side his heart-inflaming brand,°   *torch*
Whilst many nymphs that vowed chaste life to keep

2. Flesh, specifically the sexual organ, needs no further encouragement.
3. Swelling with pride (and lust).
Sonnet 152
1. Forsworn presumably in breaking loving vows—perhaps to his wife, to the youth to whom he promised unswerving devotion in earlier sonnets, or to both.
2. *new faith ... bearing:* the "new faith" followed by "new hate" may be addressed either to the speaker's young friend or to the speaker himself.
3. And to make you fair (give you insight), I looked blindly on your failings (pretended to see what I couldn't).

Sonnet 153
1. This and the following sonnet derive indirectly from classical fifth-century Greek epigrams.
2. Diana, goddess of chastity.
3. *And grew ... cure:* And became a boiling-hot medicinal bath (used, among other purposes, for the treatment of venereal disease), which men still find to be an outstanding remedy for foreign illnesses (venereal diseases were associated with foreigners). There may be an allusion here and in 154 to the town of Bath, which became a famous health spa in the eighteenth century.
Sonnet 154
1. This sonnet varies the topic of 153.

Came tripping by; but in her maiden hand
5   The fairest votary took up that fire
Which many legions of true hearts had warmed,
And so the general° of hot desire   *commander (Cupid)*
Was sleeping by a virgin hand disarmed.
This brand she quenchèd in a cool well by,°   *close by*
10 Which from love's fire took heat perpetual,
Growing a bath and healthful remedy
For men diseased; but I, my mistress' thrall,°   *slave*
   Came there for cure; and this° by that I prove: *the following*
   Love's fire heats water, water cools not love.

A Lover's Complaint

From off a hill whose concave womb re-worded°   *hollow side echoed*
A plaintful story from a sist'ring° vale,   *nearby*
My spirits t'attend° this double voice accorded,°   *hear / agreed*
And down I laid to list° the sad-tuned tale;   *listen to*
5 Ere long espied a fickle° maid full pale,   *a disturbed*
Tearing of papers, breaking rings a-twain,°   *in two*
Storming her world with sorrow's wind and rain.

Upon her head a plaited hive° of straw   *hat*
Which fortified° her visage from the sun,   *protected*
10 Whereon the thought° might think sometime it saw   *imagination*
The carcass of a beauty spent and done.
Time had not scythèd all that youth begun,
Nor youth all quit; but spite° of heaven's fell° rage, *in spite / fierce*
Some beauty peeped through lattice of seared° age.   *withered*

15 Oft did she heave her napkin to her eyne,[1]
Which on it had conceited characters,°   *imaginative designs*
Laund'ring the silken figures in the brine
That seasoned° woe had pelleted in tears,   *experienced; salted*
And often reading what contents it bears;
20 As often shrieking undistinguished° woe   *inarticulate*
In clamours of all size, both high and low.

Sometimes her levelled eyes their carriage ride[2]
As° they did batt'ry to the spheres° intend;   *As if / planets*
Sometime diverted their poor balls° are tied   *eyeballs; cannonballs*
25 To th'orbèd° earth; sometimes they do extend   *spherical*
Their view right on;° anon their gazes lend   *straight*
To every place at once, and nowhere fixed,
The mind and sight distractedly commixed.°   *confused*

Her hair, nor° loose nor tied in formal plait,   *neither*
30 Proclaimed in her a careless hand of pride;[3]
For some, untucked, descended her sheaved° hat, *fell from her straw*
Hanging her pale and pinèd cheek beside.
Some in her threaden fillet° still did bide,   *headband*
And, true to bondage, would not break from thence,
35 Though slackly braided in loose negligence.

A thousand favours° from a maund° she drew   *love tokens / basket*
Of amber, crystal, and of beaded jet,°   *beads of black stone*
Which one by one she in a river threw
Upon whose weeping margin she was set;°   *seated*
40 Like usury applying wet to wet,[4]

1. Often did she raise her handkerchief to her eyes.
2. Sometimes her eyes, aimed (like a cannon), glare (are mounted on a swivel).
3. A hand careless of pride; a hand proud in its care-lessness (knowing that she could attract with no effort).
4. Like usury making wealth wealthier (by adding tears to the stream).

Or monarch's hands that lets not bounty fall
Where want cries some, but where excess begs all.[5]

Of folded schedules° had she many a one   *letters*
Which she perused, sighed, tore, and gave the flood;
45 Cracked many a ring of posied gold and bone,[6]
Bidding them find their sepulchres in mud;
Found yet more letters sadly penned in blood,
With sleided silk feat and affectedly
Enswathed[7] and sealed to curious° secrecy.   *careful*

50 These often bathed she in her fluxive° eyes,   *flowing*
And often kissed, and often 'gan to tear;
Cried 'O false blood, thou register° of lies,   *record*
What unapprovèd° witness dost thou bear!   *unreliable*
Ink would have seemed more black and damnèd here!'
55 This said, in top of rage the lines she rents,°   *rips*
Big° discontent so breaking their contents.   *Powerful*

A reverend man that grazed his cattle nigh
Sometime a blusterer that the ruffle knew[8]
Of court, of city, and had let go by
60 The swiftest hours observèd as they flew,[9]
Towards this afflicted fancy fastly[1] drew,
And, privileged by age, desires to know
In brief the grounds and motives of her woe.

So slides he down upon his grainèd bat,[2]
65 And comely° distant sits he by her side,   *politely*
When he again desires her, being sat,
Her grievance with his hearing to divide.°   *share*
If that from him there may be aught applied
Which may her suffering ecstasy° assuage,   *grief*
70 'Tis promised in the charity of age.

'Father,' she says, 'though in me you behold
The injury of many a blasting° hour,   *disfiguring*
Let it not tell your judgement I am old;
Not age, but sorrow over me hath power.
75 I might as yet have been a spreading° flower,   *blooming*
Fresh to myself, if I had self-applied
Love to myself, and to no love beside.

'But, woe is me, too early I attended
A youthful suit—it was° to gain my grace°—   *was designed / favor*
80 O, one by nature's outwards° so commended   *external appearance*
That maidens' eyes stuck over all° his face.   *were glued to*
Love lacked a dwelling and made him her place,

5. *Or . . . all:* Or like the monarch who, rather than give a little to the truly needy, gives a great deal to those who already have plenty.
6. A ring of gold and ivory inscribed with messages (of love).
7. *With . . . / Enswathed:* Delicately and affectionately wrapped in strands of separated ("sleided") silk.
8. Once a man of the world who was accustomed to the busier life.
9. *had . . . flew:* was past the prime of life, but had learned from experience.
1. Toward this person afflicted by love rapidly (close by).
2. So he comes down the bank with the help of his forked herdsman's staff.

And when in his fair parts she did abide
She was new-lodged and newly deified.

85 'His browny locks did hang in crookèd curls,
And every light occasion° of the wind   *chance stirring*
Upon his lips their silken parcels° hurls.   *(of hair)*
What's sweet to do, to do will aptly find.[3]
Each eye that saw him did enchant the mind,
90 For on his visage was in little° drawn   *miniature*
What largeness thinks in paradise was sawn.[4]

'Small show of man was yet upon his chin;
His phoenix° down began but to appear,   *singularly lovely*
Like unshorn velvet, on that termless skin[5]
95 Whose bare outbragged the web[6] it seemed to wear;
Yet showed his visage by that cost more dear,[7]
And nice affections° wavering stood in doubt   *discriminating tastes*
If best were as it was, or best without.°   *(shaven)*

'His qualities were beauteous as his form,
100 For maiden-tongued° he was, and thereof free.°   *modest / well-spoken*
Yet if men moved° him, was he such a storm   *angered*
As oft twixt May and April is to see
When winds breathe sweet, unruly though they be.
His rudeness so with his authorized youth
105 Did livery falseness in a pride of truth.[8]

'Well could he ride, and often men would say
"That horse his mettle from his rider takes;
Proud of subjection, noble by the sway,°   *control*
What rounds, what bounds, what course,° what stop he makes!" *gallop*
110 And controversy hence a question takes,
Whether the horse by him became his deed,
Or he his manège by th' well-doing steed.[9]

'But quickly on this side the verdict went:
His real habitude° gave life and grace   *disposition*
115 To appertainings° and to ornament,   *external attributes*
Accomplished in himself, not in his case.°   *mere appearance*
All aids, themselves made fairer by their place,
Came for additions;[1] yet their purposed trim
Pieced not[2] his grace, but were all graced by him.

120 'So on the tip of his subduing tongue
All kind of arguments and question deep,
All replication prompt,° and reason strong,   *quick reply*

---

3. Ways are easily found to do pleasant things (look,
love).
4. What one would imagine seeing on a larger scale in
paradise.
5. Like velvet with its nap unclipped, on that indescrib-
able (invulnerable to time) skin.
6. Whose naked surface showed more beautiful than the
down covering.
7. Yet his face looked more precious (attractive) because

of its rich clothing.
8. His . . . truth: His roughness, sanctioned by his "youth,"
employed falseness in truth's uniform.
9. Whether . . . steed: Whether he performed so well be-
cause of his horsemanship or because his grace in horse-
manship (French: manège) was a result of the horse's skill.
1. Attempted to increase his worth.
2. their . . . not: their anticipated decorative effect did not
increase.

For his advantage still did wake and sleep.[3]
To make the weeper laugh, the laugher weep,
125 He had the dialect and different skill,[4]
Catching all passions in his craft of will,[5]

'That° he did in the general bosom reign   *So that*
Of young, of old, and sexes both enchanted,
To dwell with him in thoughts, or to remain
130 In personal duty, following where he haunted.°   *often went*
Consents[6] bewitched, ere he desire,° have granted,   *before he asks*
And dialogued for him what he would say,
Asked their own wills, and made their wills obey.

'Many there were that did his picture get
135 To serve their eyes, and in it put their mind,
Like fools that in th'imagination set
The goodly objects° which abroad° they find   *sights / traveling*
Of lands and mansions, theirs in thought assigned,
And labour in more pleasures to bestow them[7]
140 Than the true gouty landlord which doth owe° them.   *own*

'So many have, that never touched his hand,
Sweetly supposed them mistress of his heart.
My woeful self, that did in freedom stand,
And was my own fee-simple,[8] not in part,
145 What with his art in youth, and youth in art,
Threw my affections in his charmèd° power,   *magical*
Reserved the stalk and gave him all my flower.

'Yet did I not, as some my equals° did,   *young girls of my rank*
Demand of him, nor being desired yielded.°   *yielded sexual favors*
150 Finding myself in honour so forbid,
With safest distance I mine honour° shielded.   *chastity*
Experience° for me many bulwarks builded   *(of "my equals")*
Of proofs new bleeding, which remained the foil[9]
Of this false jewel and his amorous spoil.

155 'But ah, who ever shunned by precedent
The destined ill she must herself assay,°   *try out*
Or forced examples 'gainst her own content
To put the by-past perils in her way?[1]
Counsel may stop a while what will not stay,°   *stop for good*
160 For when we rage,° advice is often seen,   *(with lust)*
By blunting° us, to make our wills more keen.   *repressing*

---

3. *For . . . sleep*: (Like servants) adjusted their waking and
sleeping hours for the benefit of their master.
4. The manner of speech and versatile skill.
5. His faculty of persuasion. Here and in the next stanza,
there are suggestions of other senses of "will." See sonnets
135–36.
6. Powers of (sexual) consent; consenting people.
7. *theirs . . . them*: imagining the "lands and mansions"
their own, they try harder to use them pleasurably.
8. And had absolute control of myself (as of land in free-
hold).

9. *Of . . . foil*: Fresh examples of seduction, which
remained the defense (or sword—picking up the military,
specifically fencing, imagery of "distance," "shielded,"
"bulwarks," "bleeding," lines 151–53). But "foil" as the
dark material in which gems are set to make them look
more brilliant also works with "false jewel" in the follow-
ing line, to suggest that the young man's sexual escapades
made him more attractive.
1. *Or . . . way*: Or reminded herself, to counter her pres-
ent inclinations, of bygone dangers. *forced*: urged.

'Nor gives it satisfaction to our blood°   *sexuality*
That we must curb it upon others' proof,°   *experience*
To be forbod° the sweets that seems so good   *forbidden*
165 For fear of harms that preach in our behoof.°   *for our benefit*
O appetite, from judgement stand aloof!
The one a palate hath that needs will taste,
Though reason weep, and cry it is thy last.

'For further I could say this man's untrue,[2]
170 And knew the patterns° of his foul beguiling;   *instances*
Heard where his plants in others' orchards° grew,   *(wombs)*
Saw how deceits were gilded in his smiling,
Knew vows were ever brokers° to defiling,   *go-betweens*
Thought characters and words merely but art,[3]
175 And bastards of his foul adulterate heart.

'And long upon these terms I held my city°   *chastity*
Till thus he gan° besiege me: "Gentle maid,   *began to*
Have of my suffering youth some feeling pity,
And be not of my holy vows afraid.
180 That's° to ye sworn to none was ever said;   *What is*
For feasts of love I have been called unto,
Till now did ne'er invite nor never woo.

' "All my offences that abroad° you see°   *in the world / learn of*
Are errors of the blood,° none of the mind.   *sexual passion*
185 Love made them not; with acture they may be,[4]
Where neither party is nor true nor kind.°   *faithful or loving*
They sought their shame that so their shame did find,
And so much less of shame in me remains
By how much of me their reproach contains.[5]

190 ' "Among the many that mine eyes have seen,
Not° one whose flame my heart so much as warmèd   *There is not*
Or my affection put to th' smallest teen,°   *pain*
Or any of my leisures° ever charmèd.   *hours of leisure*
Harm have I done to them, but ne'er was harmèd;
195 Kept hearts in liveries,° but mine own was free,   *in uniform (service)*
And reigned commanding in his monarchy.

' "Look here what tributes wounded fancies° sent me   *lovers*
Of pallid pearls and rubies red as blood,
Figuring° that they their passions likewise lent me   *Showing*
200 Of grief and blushes, aptly understood
In bloodless white and the encrimsoned mood°—   *form (of rubies)*
Effects of terror and dear modesty,
Encamped in hearts, but fighting outwardly.[6]

---

2. I am able to say more about this man's perfidy.
3. Written and spoken words were merely instruments of skill (in seduction).
4. *with . . . be:* by a mere physical act they may be performed.

5. *By . . . contains:* The more they name me in their reproaches (thus revealing that they are unchaste and hence, by this logic, to blame).
6. *Effects . . . outwardly:* White ("terror") and red (blushing "modesty") fighting on their faces.

' "And lo, behold, these talents° of their hair,   *riches*
205 With twisted mettle amorously impleached,[7]
I have received from many a several fair,°   *a different beauty*
Their kind acceptance weepingly beseeched,
With th'annexations° of fair gems enriched,   *additions*
And deep-brained sonnets that did amplify°   *expound; increase*
210 Each stone's dear nature, worth, and quality.

' "The diamond?—why, 'twas beautiful and hard,
Whereto his invised[8] properties did tend;
The deep-green em'rald, in whose fresh regard
Weak sights their sickly radiance do amend;[9]
215 The heaven-hued sapphire and the opal blend[1]
With objects manifold; each several° stone,   *distinct*
With wit well blazoned,° smiled or made some moan.   *described*

' "Lo, all these trophies of affections° hot,   *passions*
Of pensived° and subdued desires the tender,°   *saddened / gifts*
220 Nature hath charged me that I hoard them not,
But yield them up where I myself must render—
That is to you, my origin and ender;°   *alpha and omega; all*
For these of force must your oblations[2] be,
Since I their altar, you enpatron me.[3]

225 ' "O then advance of yours that phraseless° hand   *beyond description*
Whose white weighs down the airy scale of praise.[4]
Take all these similes[5] to your own command,
Hallowed with sighs that burning° lungs did raise.   *(with love)*
What me, your minister for you, obeys,
230 Works under you,[6] and to your audit° comes   *account*
Their distract parcels° in combinèd sums.   *component parts*

' "Lo, this device was sent me from a nun,
A sister sanctified of holiest note,°   *reputation*
Which late her noble suit° in court did shun,   *attendance; suitors*
235 Whose rarest havings° made the blossoms° dote;   *qualities / young nobles*
For she was sought by spirits of richest coat,°   *coat of arms*
But kept cold distance, and did thence remove
To spend her living° in eternal love.°   *life / (of God)*

' "But O, my sweet, what labour is't to leave
240 The thing we have not, mast'ring what not strives,°   *does not resist*
Planing° the place which did no form[7] receive,   *Smoothing*
Playing patient sports in unconstrainèd gyves![8]
She that her fame so to herself contrives[9]

7. With misdirected courage (confused spirit?) lovingly
intertwined. Many editors emend "mettle" to "metal."
8. Its unseen—referring to the diamond but also, per-
haps, to the equally "beautiful and hard" young man.
9. in . . . amend: which, when looked at, can heal weak
vision.
1. Blended: many-colored; accompanying other "ob-
jects" (line 216).
2. For these necessarily must be offerings at your altar.
3. Since I am the altar (on which they were offered), you
must necessarily be the patron saint of the altar (me).

4. Whose white exceeds any measure of praise.
5. These emblematic gifts and the sonnets that explain
them.
6. What . . . under you: Whatever pays homage to me,
your agent, serves you.
7. No impression (of love, on the heart).
8. Patiently enduring shackles ("gyves") that have not
been forced upon one and that can be removed (or that
do not constrain). (The entire sentence is ironic.)
9. She who thus contrives for herself the reputation of
disinterest in love.

The scars of battle scapeth by the flight,
245 And makes her absence valiant, not her might.[1]

‘ “O, pardon me, in that my boast is true!
The accident which brought me to her eye
Upon the moment° did her force° subdue,   *Immediately / resolve*
And now she would the cagèd cloister fly.
250 Religious° love put out religion's eye.   *Devoted (sexual)*
Not to be tempted would she be immured,°   *walled up*
And now, to tempt, all liberty procured.

‘ “How mighty then you are, O hear me tell!
The broken bosoms° that to me belong   *hearts*
255 Have emptied all their fountains in my well,
And mine I pour° your ocean all among.   *pour into*
I strong o'er them, and you o'er me being strong,
Must for your victory us all congest,°   *gather*
As compound° love to physic° your cold breast.   *medicinal / treat*

260 ‘ “My parts° had power to charm a sacred nun,   *attributes*
Who disciplined, ay dieted in° grace,   *sustained by*
Believed her eyes when they t' assail begun,[2]
All vows and consecrations giving place.°   *yielding*
O most potential love: vow, bond, nor space
265 In thee hath neither sting, knot, nor confine,[3]
For thou art all, and all things else are thine.

‘ “When thou impressest,[4] what are precepts worth
Of stale example? When thou wilt inflame,
How coldly those impediments stand forth
270 Of wealth, of filial fear, law, kindred, fame.
Love's arms are° peace, 'gainst rule, 'gainst sense, 'gainst shame; *Love's power compels*
And° sweetens in the suff'ring pangs it bears   *And love*
The aloes° of all forces, shocks, and fears.   *bitterness*

‘ “Now all these hearts that do on mine depend,
275 Feeling it break, with bleeding groans they pine,[5]
And supplicant° their sighs to you extend   *as supplicants*
To leave° the batt'ry that you make 'gainst mine,   *cease*
Lending soft audience to my sweet design,[6]
And credent° soul to that strong-bonded oath   *trustful*
280 That shall prefer and undertake° my troth.”   *advance and guarantee*

'This said, his wat'ry eyes he did dismount,°   *lower (military)*
Whose sights till then were levelled° on my face.   *aimed*
Each cheek a river running from a fount
With brinish current downward flowed apace.
285 O, how the channel° to the stream° gave grace,   *cheeks / tears*

---

1. And achieves a reputation for valor by avoiding the temptation of love, not by strongly resisting it.
2. When my attributes (“parts”) began to assail her heart.
3. *potential . . . confine:* powerful love: a “vow” has no force (“sting”), a “bond” does not tie (“knot”), and “space” does not restrain (“confine”).
4. When you draft someone into your (military) service; make an impression on the heart.
5. Because each sigh supposedly robbed the heart of a drop of blood.
6. Looking favorably on my intentions.

Who glazed with crystal gate the glowing roses
That flame through water which their hue encloses.[7]

'O father, what a hell of witchcraft lies
In the small orb of one particular° tear!　　　　　　　*single*
290　But with the inundation of the eyes
What rocky heart to water will not wear?°　　　　　　*wear away*
What breast so cold that is not warmèd here?
O cleft° effect! Cold modesty, hot wrath,°　　　　　*divided / passion*
Both fire from hence and chill extincture hath.[8]

295　'For lo, his passion,° but an art of craft,　　　　　*passionate speech*
Even there resolved° my reason into tears.　　　　　　　*dissolved*
There my white stole of chastity I daffed,°　　　　　　*took off*
Shook off my sober guards and civil° fears;　　　　　　*seemly*
Appear to him as he to me appears,
300　All melting, though our drops this diff'rence bore:
His poisoned me, and mine did him restore.

'In him a plenitude of subtle matter,°　　　　　*raw material; cunning*
Applied to cautels,° all strange forms receives,[9]　　*tricky devices*
Of burning blushes or of weeping water,
305　Or swooning paleness; and he takes and leaves,°　*uses this and shuns that*
In either's aptness,° as it best deceives,　　　　*As each is appropriate*
To blush at speeches rank,° to weep at woes,　　　　　*offensive*
Or to turn white and swoon at tragic shows,

'That not a heart which in his level° came　　　　　*range (of fire)*
310　Could scape the hail of his all-hurting aim,
Showing fair nature is[1] both kind and tame,
And, veiled in them,° did win whom he would maim.　*(kindness and tameness)*
Against the thing he sought he would exclaim;
When he most burned in heart-wished luxury,°　　　　　*lust*
315　He preached pure maid° and praised cold chastity.　*virginal purity*

'Thus merely with the garment of a grace°　　　*with external appeal*
The naked and concealèd fiend he covered,
That th'unexperient° gave the tempter place,°　*inexperienced / entry*
Which like a cherubin above them hovered.°　　　*(as if protectively)*
320　Who, young and simple, would not be so lovered?[2]
Ay me, I fell, and yet do question make°　　　　　*wonder*
What I should do again for such a sake.°　　　　*person; pleasure*

'O that infected° moisture of his eye,　　　　　*tainted*
O that false fire which in his cheek so glowed,
325　O that forced thunder from° his heart did fly,　　*that from*
O that sad breath his spongy lungs bestowed,°　　　*emitted*
O all that borrowed motion seeming owed[3]
Would yet again betray the fore-betrayed,
And new pervert a reconcilèd° maid.'　　　　　*penitent*

---

7. *Who . . . encloses*: the river is seen as a kind of glass covering ("crystal gate") over the cheeks ("roses"), whose color shines through the "water," like a jewel enclosed in glass. *Who*: (the stream).
8. *Both . . . hath*: Tears heat up cold modesty and extin-

guish hot passion (as the following stanza elaborates).
9. *all . . . receives*: is shaped into novel forms.
1. Pretending his nature is.
2. Would not desire such a lover.
3. That emotion apparently his own.

Alternative Versions

Each of the four sonnets below exists in an alternative version. The text on top is the version as it appeared in the 1609 Quarto. *"Spes Altera"* and *"On his Mistress' Beauty"* derive from seventeenth-century manuscripts. The alternative versions of sonnets 138 and 144 are from *The Passionate Pilgrim* (1599).

2

When forty winters shall besiege thy brow
And dig deep trenches in thy beauty's field,
Thy youth's proud livery, so gazed on now,
Will be a tattered weed, of small worth held.
5   Then being asked where all thy beauty lies,
Where all the treasure of thy lusty days,
To say within thine own deep-sunken eyes
Were an all-eating shame and thriftless praise.
How much more praise deserved thy beauty's use
10 If thou couldst answer 'This fair child of mine
Shall sum my count, and make my old excuse',
Proving his beauty by succession thine.
    This were to be new made when thou art old,
    And see thy blood warm when thou feel'st it cold.

Spes Altera°   *Another Hope*

When forty winters shall besiege thy brow
And trench deep furrows in that lovely field,
Thy youth's fair liv'ry, so accounted° now,   *esteemed*
Shall be like rotten weeds of no worth held.
5   Then being asked where all thy beauty lies,
Where all the lustre of thy youthful days,
To say 'Within these hollow sunken eyes'
Were an all-eaten truth[1] and worthless praise.
O how much better were thy beauty's use
10 If thou couldst say 'This pretty child of mine
Saves my account[2] and makes my old excuse',
Making his beauty by succession thine.
    This were to be new born when thou art old,
    And see thy blood warm when thou feel'st it cold.

106

When in the chronicle of wasted time
I see description of the fairest wights,
And beauty making beautiful old rhyme
In praise of ladies dead and lovely knights;
5   Then in the blazon of sweet beauty's best,
Of hand, of foot, of lip, of eye, of brow,
I see their antique pen would have expressed
Even such a beauty as you master now.
So all their praises are but prophecies
10 Of this our time, all you prefiguring,
And for they looked but with divining eyes
They had not skill enough your worth to sing;

Spes Altera
1. An accurate statement that you had been gluttonous.   2. Preserves (increases) my wealth (my moral record).

For we which now behold these present days
Have eyes to wonder, but lack tongues to praise.

On his Mistress' Beauty

When in the annals of all-wasting time
I see descriptions of the fairest wights,
And beauty making beautiful old rhyme
In praise of ladies dead and lovely knights;
5   Then in the blazon of sweet beauty's best,
Of face, of hand, of lip, of eye, or brow,
I see their antique pen would have expressed
E'en such a beauty as you master now.
So all their praises were but prophecies
10 Of these our days, all you prefiguring,
And for they saw but with divining eyes
They had not skill enough your worth to sing;
   For we which now behold these present days
   Have eyes to wonder, but no tongues to praise.

138

When my love swears that she is made of truth
I do believe her though I know she lies,
That she might think me some untutored youth
Unlearnèd in the world's false subtleties.
5   Thus vainly thinking that she thinks me young,
Although she knows my days are past the best,
Simply I credit her false-speaking tongue;
On both sides thus is simple truth suppressed.
But wherefore says she not she is unjust,
10 And wherefore say not I that I am old?
O, love's best habit is in seeming trust,
And age in love loves not to have years told.
   Therefore I lie with her, and she with me,
   And in our faults by lies we flattered be.

138

When my love swears that she is made of truth
I do believe her though I know she lies,
That she might think me some untutored youth
Unskilful in the world's false forgeries.
5   Thus vainly thinking that she thinks me young,
Although I know my years be past the best,
I, smiling, credit her false-speaking tongue,
Outfacing° faults in love with love's ill rest.[1]   *Defying*
But wherefore says my love that she is young,
10 And wherefore say not I that I am old?
O, love's best habit's in a soothing tongue,
And age in love loves not to have years told.
   Therefore I'll lie with love,° and love with me,   *my lover; lovingly*
   Since that our faults in love thus smothered be.

Sonnet 138
1. With the "rest" of what's bad in love; restlessness.

144

Two loves I have, of comfort and despair,
Which like two spirits do suggest me still.
The better angel is a man right fair,
The worser spirit a woman coloured ill.
5 To win me soon to hell my female evil
Tempteth my better angel from my side,
And would corrupt my saint to be a devil,
Wooing his purity with her foul pride;
And whether that my angel be turned fiend
10 Suspect I may, yet not directly tell;
But being both from me, both to each friend,
I guess one angel in another's hell.
    Yet this shall I ne'er know, but live in doubt
    Till my bad angel fire my good one out.

144

Two loves I have, of comfort and despair,
That like two spirits do suggest me still.
My better angel is a man right fair,
My worser spirit a woman coloured ill.
5 To win me soon to hell my female evil
Tempteth my better angel from my side,
And would corrupt my saint to be a devil,
Wooing his purity with her fair pride;
And whether that my angel be turned fiend,
10 Suspect I may, yet not directly tell;
For being both to me, both to each friend,
I guess one angel in another's hell.
    The truth I shall not know, but live in doubt
    Till my bad angel fire my good one out.

TEXTUAL VARIANTS

Control text: Q

Q: The Quarto of 1609
Qa, Qb: Qa is the uncorrected version, Qb the corrected version
Other texts cited:
B1—British Library Add. MS 10309, fol. 143 (c. 1630; Margaret Bellasys)
B2—British Library Add. MS 21433, fol. 114ᵛ (c. 1630; Inns of Court)
B3—British Library Add. MS 25303, fol. 119ᵛ (c. 1620s–30s; Inns of Court)
M—Pierpont Morgan MA 1057, p. 96 (c. 1630s)
MS—St. John's, Cambridge, MS S. 23 (James 416), fols. 38ʳ–38ᵛ (c. 1630s–40s)
Passionate Pilgrim, c. 1599
R—Rosenbach MS 1083 / 16, p. 256 (c. 1630)
W—Westminster Abbey, MS 41, fol. 49 (1619–30s; George Morley)

Sonnets
1 [number not in Q]

2 [For another version of this sonnet, present in eleven manuscripts, see the Alternative Versions.] 4 **tattered** [MS] totter'd
5.14 **Lose** Leese
12.4 **ensilvered o'er** or siluer'd ore
13.7 **Yourself** You selfe
20.7 **hues** *Hews*
23.14 **with . . . wit** wit . . . wiht
25.9 **might** worth
26.12 **thy** their
27.10 **thy** their
28.12 **gild'st the even** guil'st th'eauen 14 **strength** length
31.8 **thee** there
34.12 **cross** losse
35.8 **thy . . . thy** their . . . their
37.7 **thy** their
39.12 **doth** dost
41.12 **troth** truth
43.11 **thy** their
44.13 **naught** naughts
45.12 **thy** their
46.3, 8, 13, 14 **thy** their 9 **'cide** side
47.10 **art** are 11 **no** nor
50.6 **dully** duly
51.10 **perfect'st** perfects 11 **rein** naigh
54.14 **fade** vade
55.1 **monuments** monument
56.13 **Or** As
61.8 **tenor** tenure
62.10 **chapped** chopt
63.5 **travelled** trauaild
65.12 **of** or
67.6 **seeming** seeing
69.3 **due** end 5 **Thy** Their 14 **soil** solye
70.6 **Thy** their
71.4 **vilest** vildest
73.4 **ruined choirs** rn'wd quiers
76.7 **tell** fel
77.10 **blanks** blacks
82.8 **these** the
85.3 **thy** their
86.13 **filled** fild
89.11 **profane** prophane [Qb]; proface [Qa]
90.11 **shall** stall
91.9 **better** bitter
99.9 **One** Our 13 **ate** eate
100.14 **prevene'st** preuenst
102.8 **her** his
106 [For another version of this sonnet, present in two manuscripts, see the Alternative Versions.] 12 **skill** [MSS] still
111.1 **with** wish
112.14 **they're dead** y'are dead
113.6 **latch** lack 14 **makes mine eye** maketh mine
116 119 [all but one extant copy of Q]
126.2 **sickle-hour** sickle, hower 8 **minutes** mynuit 12 [After this line, Q prints parentheses for each line of an imagined couplet.]
127.10 **brow** eyes

128.11, 14 **thy** their
129.9 **Mad** Made 11 **proved** proud **a** and
132.6 **the east** th'East 9 **mourning** morning
135.1, 2, 11, 12, 14 **Will** *Will*
136.2, 5, 14 **Will** *Will* 6 **Ay** I
138 [For another version of this sonnet, see the Alternative Versions.] **12 to have** [*Passionate Pilgrim*] t'haue
140.13 **belied** be lyde
143.13 **Will** *Will*
144 [For another version of this sonnet, see the Alternative Versions.] **6 side** [*Passionate Pilgrim*] sight 9 **fiend** finde
146.2 **[   ] My** sinfull earth
153.8 **strange** strang 14 **eyes** eye

A Lover's Complaint
7 **sorrow's** sorrowes,
37 **beaded** bedded
51 **'gan** gaue
112 **manège** mannad'g
118 **Came** Can
131 **Consents** Consent's
139 **labour** labouring
161 **wills** wits
182 **woo** vovv
198 **pallid** palyd [sometimes interpreted as "palèd," which properly means "having grown pale"]
204 **hair** heir
208 **th'annexations** th'annexions
228 **Hallowed** Hollowed
233 **A** Or
241 **Planing** Playing
251 **immured** enur'd
252 **procured** procure
260 **nun** Sunne
261 **ay** I
270 **kindred,** kindred
293 **O** Or

Alternative Versions

Spes Altera
Control text: W
Spes Altera [B1, B2, B3] To one y[t] would dye a Mayd
3 **liv'ry** [B1] liuery
5 **lies** lye [cropped control-text ms.]
8 **praise** prays [cropped control-text ms.]

On his Mistress' Beauty
Control text: M
2 **descriptions** [R] discription
3 **rhyme** [R] mine [but with "rime" written in the margin as a correction]
6 **hand** [R] hands
8 **E'en** Ev'n [M] Euen [R]
10 **these** [R] those
12 **your** thy

Various Poems

The short poems included here are occasional pieces. That is, they were written not as part of a longer work by a single author but for specific occasions. They were composed from the early 1590s until shortly before Shakespeare's death and are arranged in the following pages in possible chronological order. In this respect, they differ from the sonnets, which collectively possess a far greater coherence. Part of that coherence results from the almost unvarying use of the sonnet form. These poems, by contrast, employ a number of meters, line lengths, rhyme schemes, and stanzaic forms. Scholarly discussion has generally focused on the relationship of the poems to Shakespeare's biography and on the question of whether Shakespeare actually wrote them. Modern editions of the complete works routinely exclude many of them—in most instances wrongly, it seems. (See the Textual Note.) Ironically, the major exceptions are the poems from *The Passionate Pilgrim* (1599), some or all twenty of which are often included, presumably on the strength of the original publisher's assertion of Shakespeare's authorship. Nonetheless, Shakespeare is likely to have written only the five pieces in that collection that are lifted from his other works (the sonnets and *Love's Labour's Lost*). At least four poems in the collection are clearly by other writers. Among the other eleven, which remain anonymous and are accordingly printed here, numbers 4, 6, and 9—all sonnets—are noteworthy for their focus on the theme of *Venus and Adonis*, to which they may be a response.

Several of the other poems are elegies—compositions in memory of the dead, though sometimes written while the subject was still alive. The first of the two epitaphs on the usurer John Combe, of uncertain authorship, reveals a conventional hostility to usury. The second, however, deploys the complex, sometimes positive, metaphorical relation between usury and breeding characteristic of the early sonnets. Combe

> did gather [wealth from usury]
> To make the poor his issue [heirs]; he, their father,
> . . . [made] record of his tilth and seed.
> (lines 3–5)

Urging marriage and a family, sonnet 3 speaks of "the tillage of thy husbandry" (line 6). And sonnet 6 argues:

> That use is not forbidden usury
> Which happies those that pay the willing loan:
> That's for thyself to breed another thee,
> Or ten times happier, be it ten for one.
> (lines 5–8)

Thus, in the sonnets, the language of usury helps clarify paternity, whereas in the second epitaph, the language of paternity helps clarify usury. In both, however, the two terms are mutually illuminating. The last line quoted from sonnet 6 is also reminiscent of the opening of the first epitaph: "Ten in the hundred here lies engraved; / A hundred to ten his soul is not saved." Both refer to the highest legal interest rate—ten in a hundred, or 10 percent—though only the sonnet converts the allusion into a positive image.

Similarly, the "Verses upon the Stanley Tomb at Tong" closely parallel the language of some of Shakespeare's sonnets concerned with the destructive power of time. The "register" of the first of the two poems (1.3) and the "sky-aspiring pyramids" of the second (2.2) also appear in sonnet 123 ("pyramids built up," "registers," lines 2, 9). Closer still is the connection to sonnet 55: "Not marble nor the gilded monuments / Of princes shall outlive this powerful rhyme" (lines 1–2). Stanley's "fame is more perpetual than these stones" (1.4); "Not monumental stone preserves our fame" (2.1). Stanley's "memory," however, "shall outlive marble and defacers' hands" as well as "time's consumption" (2.3, 4, 5), just as "memory" need not worry that "war shall statues overturn" and is not dependent on "unswept stone besmeared with sluttish time" in sonnet 55 (lines 8, 5, 4). Although the guarantee of immortality seems to be Stanley's life rather than the "powerful rhyme" of the sonnet (line 2), the end is the same: Stanley "is not dead; he doth but sleep" (1.2), while in the sonnet, "gainst death and all oblivious enmity / Shall you pace forth" (lines 9–10). Ultimately, poetic fame in the sonnet lasts only "till the judgment that yourself arise" (on Judgment Day; line 13); analogously, "Stanley for whom this stands shall stand in heaven" (2.6). The pun on the name in this concluding line ("Stanley / stands / stand") is similar to the sign of the author's hand left in "Upon a pair of gloves that master sent to his mistress," where "the will is all" recalls Shakespeare's emphatic references to his first name in sonnets 135 and 136.

If "Upon a pair of gloves" seems to reveal Shakespeare intruding into a poem ostensibly from Alexander Aspinall to his (future?) wife, the "Epitaph on Himself" is strikingly impersonal. The lack of specificity may in this case be a poetic signature, however. By 1616, only Shakespeare could have written about Shakespeare without reference to his theatrical or literary career. This modesty coincides with an open threat: "cursed be he that moves my bones" (line 4). The apparently conventional warning was designed to forestall the very real danger of his body being dug up to make room for fresh corpses; in this case, it proved successful.

Of the two longer poems printed here, "A Song" is noteworthy mainly as a virtuoso display of rhyming: there are usually eight pairs of rhyme words in each ten-line stanza, with the rhymes occurring as often as every three syllables and on occasion every two syllables ("Being set, lips met," line 39). "The Phoenix and Turtle" is another matter. The one work in this section whose literary quality has been widely admired, it was one of several poems—others were by George Chapman, Ben Jonson, and John Marston—appended to Robert Chester's *Love Martyr* (1601). An abstruse philosophical work, "The Phoenix and Turtle" is divided into three sections. In the first five quatrains, which may be indebted to Chaucer's *Parliament of Fowls*, a language of elaborate circumlocution merely calls the birds together to mourn the deaths of two remarkably constant lovers—the proverbially faithful turtledove (here, male) and the legendary phoenix (here, female). Supposedly, only one phoenix was alive at any given moment, and the bird died only to be reborn from its own ashes. Neither of the two birds is named yet, however. The anthem, which constitutes the next eight stanzas, is presumably intoned by the birds. In a reversal of the procedure of the opening twenty lines, this epithalamion, or marriage hymn, turns to a deceptively simple vocabulary that conceals dense argumentation. Behind the emphasis on the paradoxical unity of two separate beings lies the mystery of the Christian Trinity as understood in Scholastic theology—medieval Europe's assimilation of the recently translated writings of Aristotle, which began in the twelfth century. The ideal love of the two birds ultimately defies the efforts at comprehension by Reason, which cannot understand how

> love in twain
> Had the essence but in one,
> Two distincts, division none,

or how

> the self was not the same.
> Single nature's double name
> Neither two nor one was called.
> (lines 25–27, 38–40)

In other words, the rationalist vocabulary of this section ultimately undermines its own legitimacy. Perhaps the lines vindicate the more mystical understanding of ideal love that Renaissance thought derived from Plato, whose doctrines Aristotle had sought to answer. In any case, the heterosexual love praised in this self-contradictory fashion parallels the celebration of homoerotic love in the sonnets to the young man: "Let me confess that we two must be twain / Although our undivided loves are one" (36.1–2). Following the anthem, Reason delivers the concluding section of the poem, the *threnos*, or mourning song, in which Shakespeare returns to the central genre of his occasional poetry—the elegy. Retaining the straightforwardly abstract diction of the anthem and the trochaic tetrameter meter of both of the first two parts, but abandoning quatrains (rhyming *abba*) for tercets (rhyming *aaa*), the last five stanzas emphasize the finality of the death of the couple, which apparently excludes both rebirth (even on the part of the immortal phoenix) and "posterity"—the latter as a result of a "married chastity" (lines 59, 61) that has the same (lack of) consequences as the love for the young man in the sonnets. The result is the diminution of life: the only authentic or perhaps ideal "truth and beauty buried be" (line 64).

"The Phoenix and Turtle" raises all sorts of interpretive problems. Since the *threnos* is spoken by Reason, who has been defeated by the phoenix and turtle, should the concluding stanzas be seen not as authorial statement but as the position of a fallible character who lets fly a crow of triumph at the couple's death? Moreover, the concluding summons of all "that are either true or fair" (line 66) sits oddly with the immediately preceding insistence that genuine truth and beauty no longer exist: perhaps now they exist only separately. And why does Shakespeare, through Reason, insist on the lack of offspring and, apparently rejecting a central feature of the legend, on the mortality of the phoenix? This last question is only emphasized by the occasion of publication. All of the poems with which "The Phoenix and Turtle" were printed are on the subject of the phoenix and turtle, and all but Shakespeare's deny the finality of the phoenix's death. "The Phoenix and Turtle" alone forgoes the possibility of exploiting the standard treatment of the phoenix as the intersection of the temporal and the timeless.

The title page of the volume advertises Chester's long poem as "allegorically shadowing the truth of Love, in the constant Fate of the Phoenix and Turtle." This claim, the abstract language of "The Phoenix and Turtle," and the avowed purpose of the volume—to honor Sir John Salusbury of Lleweni, knighted by the queen in June 1601—have all encouraged a search in Shakespeare's poem for allegorical meaning (beyond the praise of ideal human union through a tale of two birds). The marriage of phoenix and turtle has been seen as the joining of the literal and the metaphorical in poetry, so that the poem self-referentially becomes a metaphor for metaphor itself. Historical readings have found candidates for the parts of the turtle and the phoenix in Salusbury and his wife, as well as in the Earl of Essex, Salusbury, or the English people in relation to Queen Elizabeth. Though none of these theories is convincing, in part because of a failure to explain what real "tragic scene" is being allegorically represented by the couple's deaths (line 52), all testify to the poem's ability to hint at hidden meanings. Perhaps it is safer to explain the poem's suggestiveness simply by saying that "The Phoenix and Turtle" labors to construct an ideal image of love while simultaneously circumscribing the real utility of that ideal. Marriage and funeral, celebration and dirge, ideal affirmation and pragmatic denial, the poem is a characteristically Shakespearean venture in having it both ways.

WALTER COHEN

TEXTUAL NOTE

"A Song" (1592–95) survives in two related manuscript collections of poetry by different authors, dating from 1637 and 1639. It is untitled in both manuscripts, unattributed in the later collection, and ascribed to Shakespeare in the earlier one. The text printed here is based on the earlier version, though the choice between the two is not very important. Both manuscripts of "A Song" derive from a scribal transcript of the writer's original version, but it is impossible to determine how many intermediate copies there may have been. The poem was first assigned in print to Shakespeare in 1985, a claim that has aroused considerable skepticism. The name in the 1637 manuscript and the independent analysis of the poem's language carried out by statisticians make attribution to Shakespeare possible, though not particularly likely.

"Upon a pair of gloves" is found in a manuscript compiled by Sir Francis Fane of Bulbeck (1611–80). The poem supposedly accompanied gloves presented by Alexander Aspinall, a Stratford schoolmaster, to his second wife, whom he married in 1594.

The eleven poems from *The Passionate Pilgrim* (1599) printed here may well not be by Shakespeare. This collection of twenty lyrics published under Shakespeare's name includes five pieces that are clearly his. Three come from *Love's Labour's Lost*; the other two are sonnets 138 and 144 and are included in this edition as Alternative Versions at the end of the section on the sonnets and "A Lover's Complaint." Four poems are apparently by other writers—Richard Barnfield, Christopher Marlowe, Sir Walter Ralegh, and Thomas Deloney. The other eleven are of uncertain authorship.

All but one of the remaining pieces included in this edition are probably by Shakespeare. "The Phoenix and Turtle" was printed in 1601, untitled and ascribed to Shakespeare, among the "Poeticall Essaies" that follow Robert Chester's *Loves Martyr: or Rosalins Complaint*. The remaining poems are about specific people, and in each instance, as in "Upon a pair of gloves," there is a plausible London or Stratford connection between Shakespeare and the person(s) in question. The "Verses upon the Stanley Tomb at Tong" (c. 1600–3) are first attributed to Shakespeare in a manuscript from around 1630. It is not clear whether the lines constitute one poem or two, whether they are addressed to one member of the Stanley family or two, and which member or members are referred to. If they are intended as a single poem, it is not certain which group of six lines should come first. "On Ben Jonson," presumably written while Jonson was alive, is first attributed to Shakespeare in a manuscript from roughly 1650. "An Epitaph on Elias James" was published in the 1633 edition of John Stow's *Survey of London*. James died in 1610. "An extemporary epitaph on John Combe," who died in 1614, employs a joke about usurers that became popular starting in 1608. There is an ambiguous attribution to Shakespeare in 1634 and an unambiguous ascription of the last one and a half lines in a manuscript from around 1650, but Shakespeare may not have written the poem. "Another Epitaph on John Combe" is first attributed to Shakespeare in the same manuscript (c. 1650); the case for Shakespearean authorship of this poem is stronger, however. "Upon the King" was printed, unattributed, beneath an engraving of King James that was the frontispiece to the 1616 edition of the king's *Works*. The earliest ascription is found in a manuscript of c. 1633–34, where the poem is entitled "Shakespeare on the King." "Epitaph on Himself" appears on Shakespeare's gravestone in Stratford. The earliest other attribution occurs in a manuscript compiled by Sir Francis Fane, c. 1655–56.

SELECTED BIBLIOGRAPHY

Adams, Joseph Quincy. "Shakespeare as a Writer of Epitaphs." *The Manly Anniversary Studies in Language and Literature.* 1923. Reprint, Freeport, N.Y.: Books for Libraries Press, 1968. 78–89.

Cunningham, V. J. " 'Essence' and 'The Phoenix and Turtle.' " *ELH* 19 (1952): 265–76.

Foster, Donald. " 'Shall I Die' Post Mortem: Defining *Shakespeare.*" *Shakespeare Quarterly* 38 (1987): 58–77.

Garber, Marjorie. "Two Birds with One Stone: Lapidary Re-Inscription in *The Phoenix and Turtle.*" *The Upstart Crow* 5 (Fall 1984): 5–19.

Hobday, C. H. "Shakespeare's Venus and Adonis Sonnets." *Shakespeare Survey* 26 (1973): 103–9.

Honigmann, E. A. J. *Shakespeare: The "Lost" Years.* Totowa, N.J.: Barnes and Noble, 1985. 77–83, 90–113.

Hume, Anthea. "*Love's Martyr,* 'The Phoenix and the Turtle,' and the Aftermath of the Essex Rebellion." *Review of English Studies,* n.s., 40 (1989): 48–71.

Kolata, Gina. "Shakespeare's New Poem: An Ode to Statistics." *Science* 86 (1986): 335–36.

Underwood, Richard Allan. *Shakespeare's "The Phoenix and Turtle": A Survey of Scholarship.* Salzburg Studies in English Literature 15. Salzburg: Institut für Englische Sprache und Literatur, Universität Salzburg, 1974.

Various Poems

A Song[1]

1

Shall I die? Shall I fly
Lovers' baits and deceits,
   sorrow breeding?
Shall I tend?° Shall I send?   *wait passively*
5 Shall I sue, and not rue
   my proceeding?[2]
In all duty her beauty
Binds me her servant for ever.
  If she scorn, I mourn,
10 I retire to despair, joining never.

2

Yet I must vent my lust
And explain inward pain
   by my love conceiving.[3]
If she smiles, she exiles
15 All my moan; if she frown,
   all my hopes deceiving—
Suspicious doubt,° O keep out,   *fear (of rejection)*
For thou art my tormentor.
  Fie away, pack away;
20 I will love, for hope bids me venture.

3

'Twere abuse to accuse
My fair love, ere I prove°   *test*
   her affection.
Therefore try! Her reply
25 Gives thee joy—or annoy,
   or affliction.[4]
Yet howe'er, I will bear
Her pleasure with patience, for beauty
  Sure will not seem to blot
30 Her deserts, wronging him doth her duty.[5]

4

In a dream it did seem—
But alas, dreams do pass
   as do shadows—
I did walk, I did talk
35 With my love, with my dove,

---

1. This poem may or may not have been set to music.
2. Both "sue" (line 5) and "proceeding" refer to lawsuits.
3. Yet I must give expression to my lust by explaining (in poetry) the pain caused by my love. "Conceiving" may also refer to conceiving a child (line 13).

4. "Affliction" may also suggest a sexually transmitted disease.
5. *for beauty . . . duty:* for true beauty will not allow her reputation to appear tarnished by wronging him who serves her faithfully.

through fair meadows.
Still° we passed till at last   *Continually*
We sat to repose us for pleasure.
Being set, lips met,
40   Arms twined, and did bind my heart's treasure.

5

Gentle wind sport did find
Wantonly° to make fly   *Capriciously*
  her gold tresses.
As they shook I did look,
45   But her fair° did impair   *beauty*
  all my senses.
As amazed, I gazed
On more than a mortal complexion.
You that love can prove[6]
50   Such force in beauty's inflection.°   *bending*

6

Next° her hair, forehead fair,   *Next to*
Smooth and high; neat doth lie
  without wrinkle,
Her fair brows;° under those,   *forehead*
55   Star-like eyes win love's prize
  when they twinkle.
In her cheeks who° seeks   *whoever*
Shall find there displayed beauty's banner;°   *(a blush)*
O admiring desiring
60   Breeds, as I look still upon her.

7

Thin lips red, fancy's[7] fed
With all sweets when he meets,
  and is granted
There to trade,[8] and is made
65   Happy, sure, to endure
  still undaunted.
Pretty chin doth win
Of all their culled commendations;[9]
Fairest neck, no speck;
70   All her parts merit high admirations.

8

Pretty bare, past compare,
Parts those plots which besots
  still asunder.[1]
It is meet naught but sweet
75   Should come near that so rare
  'tis a wonder.[2]
No mis-shape, no scape°   *transgression*

---

6. You who are in love are able to test.
7. Affection is; imagination is.
8. *granted / There to trade:* allowed to kiss there.
9. Wins from all people their specially chosen praises.
1. *Pretty . . . asunder:* Incomparably pretty "bare" skin
and breasts (exposed above a low neckline) separate the nipples ("plots") that, always separated, (always) cause infatuation.
2. It is proper that nothing but good should come near that which is so wonderfully valuable.

Inferior to nature's perfection;
  No blot, no spot:
80 She's beauty's queen in election.

9

Whilst I dreamt, I exempt
From all care, seemed to share
  pleasure's plenty;
But awake, care take—
85 For I find to my mind
  pleasures scanty.
Therefore I will try
To compass° my heart's chief contenting.   *accomplish*
  To delay, some say,
90 In such a case causeth repenting.

'Upon a pair of gloves that master sent to his mistress'

The gift is small,
The will is all:[3]
Alexander Aspinall[4]

Poems from *The Passionate Pilgrim*

4

Sweet Cytherea,[5] sitting by a brook
With young Adonis, lovely, fresh, and green,°   *young; inexperienced*
Did court the lad with many a lovely look,
Such looks as none could look but beauty's queen.
5 She told him stories to delight his ear,
She showed him favours to allure his eye;
To win his heart she touched him here and there—
Touches so soft still° conquer chastity.   *always*
But whether unripe years did want conceit,°   *lack understanding*
10 Or he refused to take her figured° proffer,   *implied*
The tender nibbler would not touch the bait,
But smile and jest at every gentle offer.
    Then fell she on her back, fair queen and toward:°   *ready*
    He rose and ran away—ah, fool too froward!°   *obstinate*

6

Scarce had the sun dried up the dewy morn,
And scarce the herd gone to the hedge for shade,
When Cytherea, all in love forlorn,
A longing tarriance° for Adonis made   *waiting*
5 Under an osier° growing by a brook,   *a willow*
A brook where Adon used to cool his spleen.°   *hot temper*
Hot was the day, she hotter, that did look
For his approach that often there had been.
Anon he comes and throws his mantle by,

---

3. With a characteristic pun on the poet's name: the goodwill behind the gift is all-encompassing; it's the thought that counts.
4. Stratford schoolmaster from 1582 to 1624.

5. Sonnets 4, 6, and 9 all treat the unsuccessful wooing of the beautiful but unresponsive young man Adonis by Venus ("Cytherea"), the goddess of love.

10 And stood stark naked on the brook's green brim.
     The sun looked on the world with glorious eye,
     Yet not so wistly° as this queen on him.   *eagerly; longingly*
        He, spying her, bounced in whereas he stood.[6]
        'O Jove,' quoth she, 'why was not I a flood?'°   *body of water*

7

     Fair is my love, but not so fair as fickle,
     Mild as a dove, but neither true nor trusty,°   *trustworthy*
     Brighter than glass, and yet, as glass is, brittle;
     Softer than wax, and yet as iron rusty;°   *corrupt (morally)*
5   A lily pale, with damask° dye to grace her,   *red*
      None fairer, nor none falser to deface her.[7]

     Her lips to mine how often hath she joined,
     Between each kiss her oaths of true love swearing.
     How many tales to please me hath she coined,°   *invented*
10   Dreading my love, the loss whereof still fearing.[8]
      Yet in the midst of all her pure protestings
      Her faith, her oaths, her tears, and all were jestings.

     She burnt with love as straw with fire flameth,
     She burnt out love as soon as straw out burneth.
15   She framed° the love, and yet she foiled° the framing,   *built / ruined*
     She bade love last, and yet she fell a-turning.°   *(to another lover)*
      Was this a lover or a lecher whether,°   *which of the two*
      Bad in the best, though excellent in neither?[9]

9

     Fair was the morn when the fair queen of love,°   *Venus*
     [   ]¹
     Paler for sorrow than her milk-white dove,
     For Adon's sake, a youngster proud and wild,
5   Her stand she takes upon a steep-up hill.
     Anon° Adonis comes with horn and hounds.   *Soon*
     She, seely° queen, with more than love's good will   *foolish*
     Forbade the boy he should not pass those grounds.°   *cross those valleys*
     'Once,' quoth she, 'did I see a fair sweet youth
10   Here in these brakes° deep-wounded with° a boar,   *thickets / by*
     Deep in the thigh, a spectacle of ruth.°   *pity*
     See in my thigh,' quoth she, 'here was the sore.'
      She showèd hers; he saw more wounds than one,°   *(sexual)*
      And blushing fled, and left her all alone.

10

     Sweet rose, fair flower, untimely plucked, soon faded—
     Plucked in the bud and faded in the spring;
     Bright orient pearl, alack, too timely shaded;[2]
     Fair creature, killed too soon by death's sharp sting,

---

6. Jumped in from where he stood.
7. Nor is anyone more false, to her discredit; with a possible reference to cosmetics in "falser" and "deface."
8. Continually being anxious about losing my love.
9. Bad in romance, but not outstanding merely as a sex- ual partner either.
1. A line is missing here in the original edition.
2. Darkened too soon. "Orient" pearls were valued as more lustrous than their European counterparts.

5   Like a green plum that hangs upon a tree
And falls through wind before the fall should be.

I weep for thee, and yet no cause I have,
For why:° thou left'st me nothing in thy will,   *Because*
And yet thou left'st me more than I did crave,
10   For why: I cravèd nothing of thee still.[3]
    O yes, dear friend, I pardon crave of thee:[4]
    Thy discontent° thou didst bequeath to me.   *unhappiness*

12

Crabbèd° age and youth cannot live together: *Harsh*
Youth is full of pleasance, age is full of care;
Youth like summer morn, age like winter weather;
Youth like summer brave,° age like winter bare.   *well-dressed*
5   Youth is full of sport, age's breath is short.
Youth is nimble, age is lame,
Youth is hot and bold, age is weak and cold.
Youth is wild and age is tame.
    Age, I do abhor thee; youth, I do adore thee.
10   O my love, my love is young.
    Age, I do defy thee. O sweet shepherd, hie thee,°   *hurry up*
    For methinks thou stay'st° too long.   *delay*

13

Beauty is but a vain and doubtful good,
A shining gloss that fadeth suddenly,
A flower that dies when first it 'gins to bud,
A brittle glass that's broken presently.°   *immediately*
5   A doubtful good, a gloss, a glass, a flower,
Lost, faded, broken, dead within an hour.
And as goods lost are seld° or never found,   *seldom*
As faded gloss no rubbing will refresh,
As flowers dead lie withered on the ground,
10   As broken glass no cement can redress,°   *repair*
    So beauty blemished once, for ever lost,
    In spite of physic,° painting, pain,° and cost.   *medicine / labor*

14

Good night, good rest—ah, neither be my share.
She bade good night that kept my rest away,
And daffed° me to a cabin hanged° with care   *dismissed / adorned*
To descant on the doubts° of my decay.   *expand upon the fears*
5   'Farewell,' quoth she, 'and come again tomorrow.'
Fare well I could not, for I supped with sorrow.

Yet at my parting sweetly did she smile,
In scorn or friendship nill I conster whether.[5]
'Tmay be she joyed to jest at my exile,

---

3. "Nothing" (lines 8, 10) evokes the tangibility of absence caused by death. But "nothing" also may denote female sexual organs. In line 8, it would go with "will" (testament; lust) to suggest that the dead woman's desire (formerly) made her sexually available to the speaker. In line 10, the speaker would be saying that he always ("still") desired her.
4. This line seems to contradict the previous one by claiming that the speaker did, after all, "crave" something—"pardon."
5. I will not guess which of the two.

10 'Tmay be, again to make me wander thither.
  'Wander'—a word for shadows like myself,
  As take the pain but cannot pluck the pelf.°   *reward*

  Lord, how mine eyes throw gazes to the east!
  My heart doth charge the watch, the morning rise[6]
15 Doth cite° each moving° sense from idle rest,   *summon / living*
  Not daring trust the office of mine eyes.
     While Philomela° sings I sit and mark,°   *the nightingale / listen*
     And wish her lays were tunèd like the lark.[7]

  For she doth welcome daylight with her dite,°   *song*
20 And daylight drives away dark dreaming night.
  The night so packed,° I post° unto my pretty;   *sent off / hasten*
  Heart hath his hope, and eyes their wishèd sight,
     Sorrow changed to solace, and solace mixed with sorrow,
     Forwhy° she sighed and bade me come tomorrow.   *Because*

25 Were I with her, the night would post too soon,
  But now are minutes added to the hours.
  To spite me now each minute seems a moon,
  Yet not for me, shine sun[8] to succour flowers!
     Pack night, peep day; good day, of night now borrow;
30   Short night tonight, and length thyself tomorrow.[9]

Sonnets
to Sundry Notes of Music

15

  It was a lording's° daughter, the fairest one of three,   *lord's*
  That likèd of her master° as well as well might be,   *tutor*
  Till looking on an Englishman,° the fairest that eye could see,
     Her fancy fell a-turning.°   *(to another lover)*

5 Long was the combat doubtful° that love with love did fight: *uncertain*
  To leave the master loveless, or kill the gallant knight.
  To put in practice either, alas, it was a spite°   *would be a vexation*
     Unto the seely° damsel.   *helpless*
  But one must be refusèd, more mickle° was the pain   *great*
10 That nothing could be usèd° to turn them both to gain.   *done*
  For of the two the trusty knight was wounded with disdain—
     Alas, she could not help it.

  Thus art° with arms contending was victor of the day,   *learning*
  Which by a gift of learning did bear the maid away.
15 Then lullaby, the learned man hath got the lady gay;
     For now my song is ended.

---

6. Perhaps: My heart orders the "eyes" (line 13) to watch
for morning; my heart urges the night watch to hurry or
proclaim morning.
7. And wish her (nighttime) songs were the songs of the
(morning) lark.
8. Let the sun shine, not for my sake, but.
9. The speaker is asking night to shorten now and to
lengthen tomorrow, when he's with his mistress.

17

My flocks feed not, my ewes breed not,
　My rams speed° not, all is amiss.　　　　　　　　　　　　*thrive*
Love is dying, faith's defying,[1]
　Heart's denying causer of this.
5　All my merry jigs are quite forgot,
　All my lady's love is lost, God wot.°　　　　　　　　　　*knows*
Where her faith was firmly fixed in love,
There a nay is placed without remove.°　　　　　　　　　　*immovably*
　One seely cross° wrought all my loss—　　　　　　　　　*foolish mishap*
10　O frowning fortune, cursèd fickle dame!
　For now I see inconstancy
　More in women than in men remain.

In black mourn I, all fears scorn I,
　Love hath forlorn me, living in thrall.°　　　　　　　　*enslaved (to love)*
15　Heart is bleeding, all help needing—
　O cruel speeding,° freighted with gall.　　　　　　　　　*fortune*
My shepherd's pipe can sound no deal,°　　　　　　　　　　*not at all*
My wether's[2] bell rings doleful knell,
My curtal dog[3] that wont to° have played　　　　　　　*formerly liked to*
20　Plays not at all, but seems afraid,
　With sighs so deep procures to weep
　In howling wise° to see my doleful plight.　　　　　　　*fashion*
　How sighs resound through heartless ground,
　Like a thousand vanquished men in bloody fight!

25　Clear wells spring not, sweet birds sing not,
　Green plants bring not forth their dye.
Herd stands weeping, flocks all sleeping,
　Nymphs back peeping fearfully.
All our pleasure known to us poor swains,
30　All our merry meetings on the plains,
All our evening sport from us is fled,
All our love is lost, for love is dead.
　Farewell, sweet lass, thy like ne'er was
　For as sweet content, the cause of all my moan.
35　Poor Corydon[4] must live alone,
　Other help for him I see that there is none.

18

Whenas° thine eye hath chose the dame　　　　　　　　　　*When*
And stalled° the deer that thou shouldst strike,　　　　　*entrapped*
Let reason rule things worthy blame
As well as fancy, partial might.[5]
5　Take counsel of some wiser head,
　Neither too young nor yet unwed,
And when thou com'st thy tale to tell,
Smooth not thy tongue with filèd° talk　　　　　　　　*rehearsed; scheming*

1. Faith's rejection; "de-fying" means de-faithing.
2. A male sheep castrated while still immature. The "bell-wether" is the lead sheep of the flock.
3. Dog with a cut tail.
4. Conventional name for a shepherd (from one of Vir-
gil's *Eclogues*, which were pastoral poems).
5. Let reason as well as desire (fancy), which is biased and by itself inadequate, govern your potentially blame-worthy love affairs.

Lest she some subtle practice° smell: *deception*
10 A cripple soon can find a halt.[6]
    But plainly say thou lov'st her well,
    And set her person forth to sale,[7]

And to her will° frame all thy ways.°   *desire / habits*
    Spare not to spend, and chiefly there
15 Where thy desert may merit praise
    By ringing in thy lady's ear.[8]
      The strongest castle, tower, and town,
      The golden bullet beats it down.

Serve always with assurèd trust,°   *reliability*
20 And in thy suit be humble-true;
    Unless thy lady prove unjust,°   *unfaithful*
    Press never thou to choose anew.[9]
      When time° shall serve, be thou not slack   *occasion*
      To proffer, though she put thee back.[1]

25 What though° her frowning brows be bent,   *Although*
    Her cloudy looks will calm ere night,
    And then too late she will repent
    That thus dissembled her delight,[2]
      And twice desire,° ere it be day,   *(sexual gratification)*
30   That which with scorn she put away.°   *rejected*

What though she strive to try her strength,
    And ban,° and brawl,° and say thee nay,   *curse / shout*
    Her feeble force will yield at length
    When craft° hath taught her thus to say: *craftiness*
35   'Had women been so strong as men,
      In faith you had not had it then.'

The wiles and guiles that women work,°   *employ*
    Dissembled with an outward show,
    The tricks and toys° that in them lurk   *whims*
40 The cock that treads them[3] shall not know.
      Have you not heard it said full oft
      A woman's nay doth stand for nought?[4]

Think women still to strive with men,
    To sin and never for to saint.[5]
45 There is no heaven; be holy then
    When time with age shall them attaint.[6]
      Were kisses all the joys in bed,
      One woman would another wed.

---

6. Those practiced in deceit can easily sense deception. *find a halt:* detect a limp.
7. Like a salesman, start praising her qualities. One of the manuscript versions of this poem has "& set thy body forth to sell."
8. Don't be stingy about spending your money in ways that will draw your lady's attention to your merit.
9. Don't make attempts to choose someone else (?)
1. Even if she resists you. The "proffer," at first an offer, becomes outright rape here and in the following stanzas.
2. She who in this way concealed her desire.
3. The man who copulates with them.
4. Nothing; (sexual) naughtiness; a vulva.
5. Expect women always to engage (compete) with men in sin but not in saintliness, or chastity.
6. There is no thought of heaven (purity) in women seeking sexual pleasure. Let them be holy when they're old and unattractive.

But soft, enough—too much, I fear,
50 Lest that my mistress hear my song
    She will not stick to round me on th'ear[7]
    To teach my tongue to be so long.
    Yet will she blush (here be it said)
    To hear her secrets so bewrayed.°   *revealed*

The Phoenix and Turtle[8]

Let the bird of loudest lay[9]
On the sole Arabian tree[1]
Herald sad and trumpet be,
To whose sound chaste wings° obey.   *virtuous birds*

5   But thou shrieking harbinger,°   *the screech owl*
    Foul precurrer of the fiend,[2]
    Augur of the fever's end°—   *Prophet of death*
    To this troupe[3] come thou not near.

    From this session interdict°   *forbid*
10 Every fowl of tyrant wing°   *bird of prey*
    Save the eagle, feathered king.
    Keep the obsequy° so strict.   *funeral rite*

    Let the priest in surplice white°   *the swan*
    That defunctive music can,[4]
15 Be the death-divining swan,
    Lest the requiem lack his right.°   *its due; its rite*

    And thou treble-dated° crow,   *long-lived*
    That thy sable gender mak'st
    With the breath thou giv'st and tak'st,[5]
20 'Mongst our mourners shalt thou go.

    Here the anthem doth commence:
    Love and constancy is dead,
    Phoenix and the turtle fled
    In a mutual flame from hence.

25 So they loved as° love in twain   *that*
    Had the essence but in one,
    Two distincts, division none.
    Number there in love was slain.[6]

7. She won't refrain from scolding me (boxing me) on the ear.
8. *Phoenix*: a legendary, self-resurrecting bird believed to live in cycles of several centuries, dying in flames and reborn from its own ashes—here, regarded as female. *Turtle*: turtledove, symbol of constancy—here, regarded as male.
9. *Song*. It is unclear which bird this refers to—possibly the phoenix, unless one reads "Death is now the phoenix' nest" (line 56) not as part of a cycle but as a final resting place. Alternately, it is some other bird (the rooster?) known for its loud voice.
1. Supposedly, a unique tree on which sits the phoenix, which is similarly unique: only one exists at any given time.

2. Precursor of the devil: screech owls were thought to foretell death.
3. The troupe of mourning birds called forth by "the bird of loudest lay" (line 1).
4. That is skilled in funereal music. Swans were thought to sing beautifully just before (their own) death (hence the phrase "swan song").
5. *That . . . tak'st*: crows were believed to conceive by billing (kissing)—hence, "With the breath." *sable gender*: black offspring.
6. The stanza toys with the commonplace paradox of lovers' simultaneous unity and separateness, ending with the hyperbolic claim that being neither one nor two, the love of the phoenix and the turtle killed the very notion of "number" (line 28).

Hearts remote° yet not asunder, *separate*
30 Distance and no space was seen
'Twixt this turtle and his queen.
But in them it were a wonder.[7]

So° between them love did shine *So much*
That the turtle saw his right° *due; possession; nature*
35 Flaming in the Phoenix' sight.° *eyesight; appearance*
Either was the other's mine.° *self; wealth*

Property was thus appalled
That the self was not the same.[8]
Single nature's double name[9]
40 Neither two nor one was called.

Reason, in itself confounded,° *thoroughly destroyed*
Saw division grow together
To themselves, yet either neither,[1]
Simple were so well compounded[2]

45 That it cried 'How true° a twain *faithful; truly*
Seemeth this concordant one!
Love hath reason, reason none,
If what parts can so remain.'[3]

Whereupon it made this threne[4]
50 To the phoenix and the dove,
Co-supremes° and stars of love, *Joint rulers*
As chorus to their tragic scene.

Threnos

Beauty, truth,° and rarity, *fidelity*
Grace in all simplicity,
55 Here enclosed in cinders lie.

Death is now the phoenix' nest,[5]
And the turtle's loyal breast
To eternity doth rest.[6]

Leaving no posterity
60 'Twas not their infirmity,° *sterility*
It was married chastity.

Truth may seem but cannot be,
Beauty brag, but 'tis not she.[7]
Truth and beauty buried be.

---

7. It would have seemed extraordinary in any creatures but them.
8. The notion of an essential self was thus weakened by the fact that the self was not identical to itself.
9. An indivisible essence with two separate names.
1. Saw separate entities paradoxically become one, but each one was neither single nor united.
2. Single elements were so perfectly combined (appearing to remain "simple" rather than "compounded").
3. Love represents a higher reason than reason itself because of this embodiment of the paradox of unity of separate elements.
4. Reason made this threnody (a mourning song or epitaph).
5. The phoenix's nest, ordinarily a site of regeneration, is finally a place of death; alternatively, the regenerative qualities of the phoenix's nest will overcome death.
6. Rests eternally; endures forever.
7. Any appearances of fidelity or beauty will only be illusions.

65   To this urn let those repair°   *go*
      That are either true or fair.
      For these dead birds sigh a prayer.

Verses upon the Stanley Tomb[8] at Tong

Written upon the east end of the tomb

Ask who lies here, but do not weep.
He is not dead; he doth but sleep.
This stony register° is for his bones;   *record*
His fame is more perpetual than these stones,
5 And his own goodness, with himself being gone,
   Shall live when earthly monument is none.

Written upon the west end thereof

Not monumental stone preserves our fame,
Nor sky-aspiring pyramids[9] our name.
The memory of him for whom this stands
Shall outlive marble and defacers' hands.
5 When all to time's consumption shall be given,
   Stanley for whom this stands shall stand in heaven.

On Ben Jonson[1]

Master Ben Jonson and master William Shakespeare being merry
at a tavern, Master Jonson having begun this for his epitaph:

Here lies Ben Jonson
That was once one,°   *alive*

he gives it to Master Shakespeare to make up who presently
writes:

Who while he lived was a slow thing,[2]
And now, being dead, is nothing.

An Epitaph on Elias James[3]

When God was pleased, the world unwilling yet,[4]
Elias James to nature paid his debt,
And here reposeth. As he lived, he died,
The saying strongly in him verified:
5 'Such life, such death'.° Then, a known truth to tell,   *One dies as one lives*
   He lived a godly life, and died as well.

---

8. Shakespeare had various connections to the Stanley family. It is unclear whether these verses, still visible on the tombstone, memorialize Sir Edward Stanley, Sir Thomas Stanley, or both (with one verse devoted to each).
9. Grand buildings constructed by more modern means. Possibly referring to structures erected in Rome in 1586 or in London in 1603 (for James's coronation), but retaining from their association with Egypt a sense of almost timeless antiquity.
1. One of the best-known of Shakespeare's fellow playwrights (1572–1637).
2. Jonson was a notoriously slow writer.
3. A London brewer of Shakespeare's acquaintance who gave ten pounds to the parish poor when he died. His tomb was destroyed in the Great Fire of London (1666).
4. Though the world was still unwilling.

An extemporary epitaph on John Combe,[5] a noted usurer

Ten in the hundred[6] here lies engraved;
A hundred to ten his soul is not saved.
If anyone ask who lies in this tomb,
'O ho!' quoth the devil, ' 'tis my John-a-Combe.'

Another Epitaph on John Combe

He being dead, and making the poor his heirs,[7] William
Shakespeare after writes this for his epitaph:

Howe'er he livèd judge not,
John Combe shall never be forgot
While poor hath memory, for he did gather[8]
To make the poor his issue;° he, their father,   *offspring; heirs*
5 As record of his tilth and seed[9]
Did crown him° in his latter deed.   *himself*

Upon the King
At the foot of the effigy of King James I, before his *Works* (1616)[1]

Crowns have their compass;° length of days, their date;°   *boundaries / limit*
Triumphs, their tombs; felicity, her fate.
Of more than earth can earth make none partaker,[2]
But knowledge makes the king most like his maker.

Epitaph on Himself[3]

Good friend, for Jesus' sake forbear
To dig the dust enclosèd here.
Blessed be the man that spares these stones,
And cursed be he that moves my bones.

TEXTUAL VARIANTS

Title variants are not included in the lists below.

A Song
Control text: B
B: Bodleian MS Rawlinson poet. 160, fols. 108ʳ–109ᵛ
Y: Yale Osborn b. 197
5 sue shewe   **10 joining** [Y] Ioying   **13 conceiving** breeding   **19 Fie** [Y] Fly   **29 will** [Y]

5. Combe, a wealthy Stratford bachelor, left Shakespeare five pounds—a fairly generous sum—in his will.
6. A slang term for "usurer," suggesting one who lends money at 10 percent interest.
7. Combe left generous bequests to the poor of Stratford in his will, including a provision that a hundred pounds continue to be lent out, with the interest given as alms.
8. Accumulate wealth (through usury).
9. Tillage and planting (offspring).
1. These lines appear below a picture of James that was the frontispiece to the 1616 edition of his works.
2. No earthly power (not even a king) has power over the afterlife.
3. Carved above Shakespeare's grave in Stratford.

wit **30** stanza number 4 [Y] [no number in B] **38 pleasure** [Y] our pleasure **49 You**
[Y] Then **52 neat** next **68 their culled** thats cald **commendations** [B may instead
read "commendatious."] **71 Pretty** [Y] A pretty **77 mis-shape** mishap **82 From**
For **83 plenty** [Y] in plenty

Upon a pair of gloves
Control text: Shakespeare Birthplace Trust Record Office (MS ER.93)

Poems from *The Passionate Pilgrim*
Control text, poems 4, 17, 18: O1; remaining poems: O2
O1: The First Octavo of 1599
O2: The Second Octavo of 1599
Fo2: Folger Library MS V.a.339, fol. 203
Madrigals: Thomas Weelkes, *Madrigals* (1597)
Helicon: England's Helicon (1600)
4.5 ear [Fo2] eares **10 her** [O2] his
10.1, 2 faded vaded **8, 9 left'st** leftts
12.12 stay'st staies
13.2, 6, 8 fadeth . . . faded . . . faded vadeth . . . vaded . . . vaded
14.17 Philomela sings Philomela sits and sings **19 dite** ditte **20 daylight** [not in O2] **24
sighed** sight **27 a moon** an houre
17.3 faith's Faithes **4 Heart's** harts **16 freighted** fraughted **27 Herd** Heards **28 back**
[*Madrigals*] blacke **33 lass** [*Madrigals*] loue **34 moan** [*Helicon*] woe
18.45 be [Fo2] by

The Phoenix and Turtle
Control text: Robert Chester, *Loves Martyr: or Rosalins Complaint. Allegorically shadowing
the truth of Loue, in the constant Fate of the Phoenix and Turtle* (1601), sigs. Z3ᵛ–Z4ᵛ

Verses upon the Stanley Tomb at Tong
Control text: Inscription on the Stanley tomb at Tong

On Ben Jonson
Control text: Bodleian MS Ashmole 38, p. 181 (c. 1650), a transcript, probably in the hand
of Nicholas Burgh

An Epitaph on Elias James
Control text: John Stow, *Survey of London* (1633), p. 825
B: Bodleian MS Rawlinson poet. 160, fol. 41
3 reposeth [B] reposes

An extemporary epitaph on John Combe, a noted usurer
Control text: Fo1
Fo1: Folger MS V.a. 147, fol. 72ʳ (1673), a transcript, probably in the hand of Robert
Dobyns
Fo2: Folger MS V.a. 345, p. 232
1 here lies here lyeth **2 not** now **3 lies** [Fo2] lyeth

Another Epitaph on John Combe
Control text: Bodleian MS Ashmole 38, p. 180 (c. 1650), a transcript, probably in the hand
of Nicholas Burgh
William Shakespeare hee [The epitaph is attributed at the end to "W. Shak."]

Upon the King
Control text: King James I, *Works* (1616), beneath the engraving of the king on the frontispiece

Epitaph on Himself
Control text: Shakespeare's grave at Stratford

APPENDICES

The Shakespearean Stage
by
ANDREW GURR

Publication by Performance

The curt exchange between the sentries in the first six lines of *Hamlet* tells us that it is very late at night (" 'Tis now struck twelve") and that " 'tis bitter cold." This opening was staged originally at the Globe in London in broad daylight, at 2 o'clock probably on a hot summer's afternoon. The words required the audience, half of them standing on three sides of the stage platform and all of them as visible to one another as the players were, to imagine themselves watching a scene quite the opposite of what they could see and feel around them. The original mode of staging for a Shakespearean play was utterly different from the cinematic realism we are used to now, where the screen gives us close-ups on a simulacrum of reality, an even more privileged view of the actors' facial twitches than we get in ordinary life. Eloquence then was in words, not facial expressions.

The playgoers of Shakespeare's own time knew the plays in forms at which we can only now guess. It is a severe loss. Shakespeare's own primary concept of his plays was as stories "personated" onstage, not as words on a page. He himself never bothered to get his playscripts into print, and more than half of them were not published until seven years after his death, in the First Folio of his plays published as a memorial to him in 1623. His fellow playwright Francis Beaumont called the printing of plays "a second publication"; the first was their showing onstage. Print recorded a set of scripts, written for the original players to teach them what they should speak in the ensemble of the play in production. The only technology then available to record the performances was the written word. If video recordings had existed at that time, our understanding of Shakespeare would be vastly different from what it is today.

Since the texts were composed only to be a record of the words the players were to memorize, we now have to infer how the plays were originally staged largely by guesswork. Shakespeare was himself a player and shareholder in his acting company, and he expected to be present at rehearsals. Consequently, the stage directions in his scripts are distinctly skimpy compared with some of those provided by his fellow playwrights. He was cursory even in noting entrances and exits, let alone how he expected his company to stage the more complex spectacles, such as heaving Antony up to Cleopatra on her monument. There are sometimes hints in the stage directions and more frequently in the words used to describe some of the actions, and knowing what the design of the theater was like is a help as well. Knowing more about how Shakespeare expected his plays to be staged can transform how we think about them. But gaining such knowledge is no easy matter. One of the few certainties is that Shakespeare's plays in modern performance are even more different from the originals than modern printed editions are from the first much-thumbed manuscripts.

The Shakespearean Mindset

The general mindset of the original playgoers, the patterns of thinking and expectation that Tudor culture imposed on Shakespeare's audiences, is not really difficult to identify. It is less easy, though, to pin it down in the sort of detail that tells us what the original concept of staging the plays would have been like. We know that all the original playgoers paid for the privilege of attending the plays and committed themselves willingly to suspend their disbelief in what they were to see. They knew as we do that they were paying to be entertained by fictions. Beyond that, we need reminding today that going to open-air performances in daylight in Shakespeare's time meant being constantly aware that one was in a theater, a place designed to offer illusions. On the one hand, this consciousness of oneself and where one was meant that the players had to do more to hold attention than is needed now, when audiences have nothing but the stage to look at and armchairs to sit in. On the other hand, it made everyone more receptive to extratheatrical tricks, such as Hamlet's reference to "this distracted globe," or Polonius's claim in the same play to have taken the part of Julius Caesar at the university and been killed by Brutus. The regular playgoers at the Globe who recognized Polonius as the man who had played Caesar in Shakespeare's play of the year before, and who recognized Hamlet as the man who had played Brutus, would laugh at this theatrical in-joke. But two scenes later, when Hamlet kills Polonius, they would think of it again, in a different light.

Features of the original mindset such as these are quite readily identifiable. For others, though, we need to look further, into the design of the theaters and into the staging traditions that they housed and that Shakespeare exploited. Invisibility has a part to play in A Midsummer Night's Dream that we can easily underrate, for instance. Invisibility onstage is a theatrical in-joke, an obvious privileging of the audience, which is allowed to see what the characters onstage can't. The impresario Philip Henslowe's inventory of costumes used at the Rose theater in 1597, which lists "a robe for to go invisible," indicates a fictional device that openly expects the willing suspension of the audience's disbelief. In A Midsummer Night's Dream, the ostensible invisibility of all the visible fairies emphasizes the theatricality of the whole presentation while pandering to the audience's self-indulgent superiority, the feeling that it knows what is going on better than any character, whether he be Bottom or even Duke Theseus. That prepares us for the mockery of stage realism we get later, in the mechanicals' play in Act 5, and even for the doubt we as willing audience might feel over Theseus's own skepticism about the dangers of imagination that he voices in his speech at the beginning of Act 5.

More to the point, though, it throws into question our readiness to be an audience, since we have ourselves been indulging in just the games of suspending disbelief that the play staged by the mechanicals enters into so unsuccessfully. When Theseus disputes with Hippolyta about the credibility of the lovers' story, he voices the very skepticism—about the lover, the lunatic, and the poet—that any sensible realist in the audience would have been feeling for most of the previous three acts in the forest. The play starts and ends at the court in broad daylight, while the scenes of midsummer madness take place at night in a forest. At the early amphitheaters, all the plays were staged in broad daylight, between 2 and 5 o'clock in the afternoon, and without any persuasive scenery: the two stage posts served as trees onstage. So the play, moving as it does from daylight realism to nocturnal fantasy and back again, with a last challenge to credulity in the mechanicals' burlesque of how to stage a play, has already thoroughly challenged the willing suspension of the viewers' disbelief. A Midsummer Night's Dream is a play about nocturnal dreams and fictions that are accepted as truths in broad daylight. It was only a small extension of this game to have the women's parts played by boys, as well as plots in which the girls dressed as boys, to the point where in As You Like It Rosalind was played by a boy playing a girl pretending to be a boy playing a girl.

The Shakespeare plays were written for a new and unique kind of playhouse, the Elizabethan amphitheater, which had a distinctive design quite different from modern theaters. Elizabethans knew what the standard features in their theaters stood for, and Shakespeare drew on that knowledge for the staging of his plays. The physical features of the playhouses were a potent element in the ways that the plays were designed for the Elizabethan mindset. When Richard III, the archdeceiver and playactor, appears "aloft between two Bishops" to claim the crown in Richard III 3.7, his placing on the stage balcony literally above the crowd on the stage would, even without the accompanying priests, have signified his ironic claim to a social and moral superiority that ought to have matched his elevation. When Richard II comes down from the wall of Flint Castle to the "base court" in *Richard II* 3.3, Elizabethans would have seen his descent as a withdrawal from power and status. These theaters were still new when Shakespeare started to write for them, and their novelty meant that the plays were written more tightly to fit their specific design than the plays of later years, when theatergoing had become a more routine social activity and different kinds of theater were available.

London Playgoing and the Law

This heightened sense of theatricality, or "metatheater," in Shakespearean audiences was far from the only difference in their mindset from that of all modern audiences. Regular playgoing in London only started in the 1570s, and through Shakespeare's earlier years it was always a perilous and precarious activity. The Lord Mayor of London and the mayors of most of England's larger towns hated playgoing and tried to suppress it whenever and wherever it appeared. Playgoing was exciting not only because it was new but because it was dangerous. The hostility of so many authorities to plays meant that they were seen almost automatically as subversive of authority. Paradoxically, the first London companies were only able to establish themselves in London through the active support of Queen Elizabeth and her Privy Council, which tried hard, in the face of constant complaints from the lord mayor, to ensure that the best companies would be on hand every Christmas to entertain the queen's leisure hours. Popular support for playgoing depended on royal protection for the leading companies.

London was by far the largest city in England. Within a few years of Shakespeare's death, it became the largest in Europe. It was generally an orderly place to live, especially in the city itself. Even in the suburbs, where the poorer people had to live, there were not many of the riots and other disorders that preachers always associated with the brothels, animal-baiting arenas, and playhouses clustering there. The reputation that the playhouses gained for promoting riots was not well justified. Any crowd of people was seen by the authorities as a potential riot, and playhouses regularly drew some of the largest crowds that London had yet seen. The city's government was not designed to control large crowds of people. There was no paid police force, and the lord mayor was held responsible by the Privy Council, the queen's governing committee, for any disorders that did occur. So the city authorities found that playgoing challenged their control over their people.

The rapid growth of London did not help the situation. Officially, the city was governed by the lord mayor and his council. But he had authority only inside the city, and London now spread through a large suburban area in the adjacent counties of Middlesex to the north and Surrey across the river to the south. Because the court and the national government were housed in London, the Privy Council often intervened in city affairs in its own interests, as well as when orders were needed that covered broader zones than the city itself. The periodic outbreaks of bubonic plague were one clear instance of such a need, because the plague took no notice of parish or city boundaries. The intrusion of the professional companies to play in London provided another. In the early years, they were chronic travelers and London was simply one of many stopovers. But the queen enjoyed seeing plays at Christmas, and her council accordingly supported the best companies so that they could perform for her. It protected the playing companies against the hatred of successive lord mayors, except when a national emergency such as a plague epidemic erupted. The Privy Council took control then by ordering the 126 parishes in and around London to list all deaths from plague separately from ordinary deaths. Each Thursday, the parish totals were added together. When the total number of deaths from plague in these lists rose above thirty in any one week, the Privy Council closed all places of public assembly. This meant especially the playhouses, which created by far the largest gatherings. When the theaters were closed, the playing companies had to revert to their traditional practice of going on tour to play in the towns through the country, provided that the news of plague did not precede them.

Plague was not the only reason for the government to lay its controlling hand on the companies. From the time the post was inaugurated in 1578, the Master of the Revels controlled all playing. He was executive officer to the lord chamberlain, the Privy Council officer responsible for the annual season of royal entertainment and thus by extension for the professional playing companies. The Master of the Revels licensed each company and censored its plays. He was expected to cut out any references to religion or affairs of state, and he tried to prevent other offenses by banning the depiction of any living person on-stage. After 1594, he issued licenses to the approved London playhouses too. Later still, the printing of any playbook was allowed only if he gave authority for it. The companies had to accept this tight control because the government was its only protector against the hostile municipal authorities, who included not only the Lord Mayor of London but also the mayors of most of the major towns in the country.

Most mayors had the commercial interest of keeping local employees at work to justify their hostility to playgoing. But across the country, the hostility went much deeper. A large proportion of the population disliked the very idea of playacting. Their reasons, ostensibly religious, were that for actors to pretend to be characters they were unlike in life was a deception and that for boys to dress as women was contrary to what the Bible said. Some-where beneath this was a more basic fear of pretense and deceit, of people not acting honestly. It put actors into the same category as con men, cheats, and thieves. That was probably one reason why companies of boys acting men's parts were thought rather more tolerable than men pretending to be other kinds of men. The deception involved in boys playing men was more transparent than when men played characters other than them-selves. There was also a strong Puritan suspicion about shows of any kind, which looked too much like the Catholic ceremonial that the new Church of England had renounced. Playgoing found much better favor on the Catholic side of English society than on the Puritan side. Different preachers took different positions over the new phenomenon of playgoing. But few would speak in its favor, and most of them openly disapproved of it. Playgoing was an idle pastime, and the devil finds work for idle hands.

In the 1590s, when *Romeo and Juliet* and Shakespeare's histories and early comedies were exciting audiences, only two playhouses and two companies were officially approved by the queen's Privy Council for the entertainment of London's citizens. The other main forms of paid entertainment were bear- and bullbaiting, which were much harder on the performers than was playing and so could be staged less frequently. The hostility to plays meant that the right to perform was confined to only a few of the most outstanding compa-nies. These few companies were in competition with one another, and this led to a rapid growth in the quality of their offerings. But playacting was always a marginal activity. Paying to enter a specially built theater in order to see professional companies perform plays was still a new phenomenon, and it still met with great opposition from the London authorities. The open-air theaters like the Globe were built out in the suburbs. London as a city had no centrally located playhouses until after the civil war and the restoration of the monarchy, in 1661. And even playing in the city's suburbs, where they were free from the lord mayor's control, the companies had to work under the control of the Privy Coun-cil. All the great amphitheaters were built either in Middlesex, to the north of the city walls, or in Surrey across the river from the city, on the south bank of the Thames. At the height of their success, in the years after Shakespeare's death, the Privy Council never licensed more than four or five playhouses in London.

Playgoing in London was viewed even by the playgoers as an idle occupation. The largest numbers who went to the Globe were apprentices and artisans taking time off work, often surreptitiously, and law students from the Inns of Court doing the same. These fugitives were linked with the wealthier kind of idler, "gallants" or rich gentlemen and other men of property, along with soldiers and sailors on leave from the wars, people visiting London from the country on business or pleasure (usually both), and above all the women of London. Women were not expected to be literate, but one did not need to be able to read and write to enjoy hearing and seeing a play. A respectable woman had to make sure she was escorted by a man. He might be a husband or a friend, or her page if she was rich, or her husband's apprentice if she was a middle-class citizen. She might have

The city of London and its suburbs in 1572.

a mask on, part of standard women's wear outdoors to protect the face against the weather and to assert modesty, and perhaps anonymity. Market women (applewives and fishwives) went to plays in groups. Whores were expected to be there looking for business, especially from the gallants, but they usually had male escorts too.

The social range of playgoers at the two playhouses approved for use in 1594 was almost complete, stretching from the aristocracy to the poorest workmen and boys. Many people disapproved of plays, but at peak times up to 25,000 a week flocked to see the variety of plays being offered. Prices for playgoing remained much the same throughout the decades up to 1642, when the parliamentary government that was fighting the king closed all the theaters for eighteen years. Until then, one could get standing room at an amphitheater for one penny (1/240th of a modern pound, roughly one cent), or a seat on a bench in the roofed galleries for twopence. A seat in a lord's room cost sixpence, which was not much less than a day's wage for a skilled artisan in 1600. The smaller roofed theaters that opened in 1599 were much more expensive. They were called "private" theaters to distinguish them from the "public" open-air amphitheaters, though the claim to privacy was mainly a convenient fiction to escape the controls imposed on the "public" theaters. At the Blackfriars hall theater, sixpence only gained you a seat in the topmost gallery, while a seat in the pit near the stage cost three times that amount and a seat in a box five times, or half a skilled worker's weekly wage.

It was not only the plays and players that were the sights at the playhouses. The richest lords and gallants went to be seen as much as they went to see. At the Globe, the costliest rooms were positioned alongside the balcony "above," over the stage. They were called "lords' rooms," and the playgoers who chose to sit there had a limited view of what went on beneath them. They saw no "discoveries," for instance, such as Portia's three caskets in *The Merchant of Venice*, which were uncovered underneath them inside the alcove in the center of the *frons scenae*, nor anything other than the backs of the players when they entered. But as audience they were themselves highly visible, and that was what they paid for. In the hall, or "private," playhouses, with much higher admission prices than at the Globe, there were boxes flanking the stage for the gentry, which gave them a better view of the "discoveries." But at these "select" (because costlier) hall playhouses, where unlike the Globe everyone had a seat, some of the most colorful and exhibitionistic gallants could go one better. Up to fifteen gallants could pay for a stool to sit and watch the play on the stage itself, sitting in front of the boxes that flanked the stage. Each would enter from the players' dressing room (the "tiring-house") with his stool in hand before the play started. This gave them the best possible view of the play and easily the most conspicuous place in the audience's eye. Playgoing was a public occasion in which the visibility of audience members allowed them to play almost as large a part as the players.

Through the 1590s, the only permanent and custom-made playhouses were the large open-air theaters. Paying sixpence for a ferry across the river, as the richer playgoers did, or walking across London Bridge to the Rose or the Globe, or else trudging north through the mud of Shoreditch and Finsbury Fields or Clerkenwell to the Theatre or the Fortune in order to see a play, did not have great appeal when it was raining. Consequently, the companies were always trying to secure roofed halls nearer the city center. Up to 1594, they could use city inns, especially in winter, but the lord mayor's hostility to playing never made them reliable places for performing. Two constant problems troubled the players throughout these first years of professional theater in London: the city officials' chronic hatred of plays and the periodic visitations of the plague, which always led the government to close the theaters as soon as the number of plague deaths rose to dangerously high levels.

Playgoing was not firmly established in London until the Privy Council chose to protect it in 1594 and to approve specific playhouses for the two companies that it officially sanctioned. By then, Shakespeare had already made his mark. He became a player, a shareholder, and the resident playwright for one of these two companies. That status gained him a privileged place in the rapidly growing new world of playgoing. From then on, although his theater was still located only in the suburbs of the city, his work had the law behind it. That status was amply confirmed in 1603, when the new king made himself the company's patron. The King's Men held their status until the king himself lost power in 1642.

The Design of the Globe

The Globe was Shakespeare's principal playhouse. He put up part of the money for its construction and designed his best plays for it. It was built on the south side of the Thames in 1599, fashioned out of the framing timbers of an older theater. Essentially, it was a polygonal scaffold of twenty bays or sections, nearly one hundred feet in outside diameter, making a circle of three levels of galleries that rose to more than thirty feet high, with

The second Globe, from Wenceslas Hollar's engraving of the "Long View" of London (1647).

wooden bench seating and cushions for those who could afford them. This surrounded an open "yard," into which the stage projected.

The yard was over seventy feet in diameter. Nearly half the audience stood on their feet to watch the play from inside this yard, closest to the stage platform. The stage extended out nearly to the middle of the yard, so the actors could stand in the center of the crowd. The uncertain privilege of having standing room in the open air around the stage platform could be bought with the minimal price for admission, one penny (about a cent). It had the advantage of proximity to the stage and the players; its disadvantage was keeping you on your feet for the two or three hours of the play, as well as leaving you subject to the weather. If you wanted a seat, or if it rained and you wanted shelter, you paid twice as much to sit in the three ranks of roofed galleries that circled behind the crowd standing in the yard. With some squeezing, the theater could hold over three thousand people. It was an open-air theater because that gave it a larger capacity than a roofed hall. The drawback of its being open to the weather was more than outweighed by the gain in daylight that shone on stage and spectators alike.

The stage was a great square platform as much as forty feet wide. It had over it a canopied roof, or "heavens," to protect the players and their expensive costumes from rain. This canopy was held up by two pillars rising through the stage. The stage platform was about five feet high, and without any protective rails, so that the eyes of the audience in the yard were at the level of the players' feet. At the back of the stage, a wall, or *frons scenae*, stretched across the front of the players' tiring-house, the attiring or dressing room. It had a door on each flank and a wider curtained space in the center, which was used for major entrances and occasionally for set-piece scenes. Above these entry doors was a gallery or balcony, most of which was partitioned into rooms for the wealthiest spectators. A central room "above" was sometimes used in staging: for example, as Juliet's balcony, as the place for Richard III to stand between the bishops, as the wall of Flint Castle in *Richard II*, and as the wall over the city gates of Harfleur in *Henry V*. After 1608, when Shakespeare's company acquired the Blackfriars consort of musicians, this central gallery room

A photograph of the interior framework of the "new" Globe on the south bank of the Thames in London, showing the general dimensions of the yard and the surrounding galleries.

was turned into a curtained-off music room that could double as an "above" when required. Fewer than half of Shakespeare's plays need an "above."

The Original Staging Techniques

Shakespearean staging was emblematic. The "heavens" that covered the stage was the colorful feature from which gods descended to the earth of the stage platform. When Jupiter made his appearance in *Cymbeline*, in clouds of "sulphurous breath" provided by fireworks, he was mounted on an eagle being lowered through a trapdoor in the heavens. The other trapdoor, set in the stage platform itself, symbolized the opposite, a gateway to hell. The large stage trap was the place where the Gravedigger came to work at the beginning of Act 5 of *Hamlet*. It was the cell where Malvolio was imprisoned in *Twelfth Night*. The Shakespearean mindset accepted such conventions automatically.

Shakespeare inherited from Marlowe a tradition of using the stage trap as the dreaded hell's mouth. Barabbas plunges into it in *The Jew of Malta*, and the demons drag the screaming Faustus down it at the end of *Dr. Faustus*. Hell was not a fiction taken lightly by Elizabethans. Edward Alleyn, by far the most famous player of Faustus in the 1590s, wore a cross on his breast while he played the part, as insurance—just in case the fiction turned serious. Tracking the Elizabethan mindset about the stage trapdoor can give us a few warnings of what we might overlook when we come fresh to the plays today.

In the original staging of *Hamlet* at the Globe, the stage trap had two functions. Besides serving as Ophelia's grave, it was the distinctive entry point, not used by any other character, for the Ghost in Act 1. When he tells his son that he is "for the day confined to fast in fires," the first audiences would have already taken the point that he had come up from the underworld. His voice comes from under the stage, telling the soldiers to swear the oath of secrecy that Hamlet lays upon them. The connection between that original entry by the Ghost through the trap and the trap's later use for Ophelia is one we might easily miss. At the start of Act 5, the macabre discussion between the Gravediggers about whether

The Globe as reconstructed in Southwark near the original site in London.

she committed suicide and is therefore consigned to hell gets its sharpest edge from the association of the trap, here the grave being dug for her, with the Ghost's purgatorial fires. More to the point, though, Hamlet, as he eavesdrops on the curtailed burial ceremony, makes the same connection when he discovers that it is the body of Ophelia being so neglectfully interred. He remembers the other apparition that came up through the trap

The *frons scenae* of the new Globe.

A gesture using the language of hats, as shown by the man attending the brothers Browne.

and springs forward in a grotesque parody of the Ghost, crying, "This is I, Hamlet the Dane!" It is a melodramatic claim to be acting a new role, that of his father the dead King. The first audiences would have remembered the ghost of dead King Hamlet using the stage trap at this point more readily than we do now. Hamlet's private knowledge of the Ghost and the trapdoor sets him, as so often in the play, at odds with his audience. Consequently, centuries of editors, like the characters onstage, have misread this claim as a declaration that young Hamlet ought to be king.

Since his own name is Hamlet, and since he alone could have made the connection between the Ghost and the trapdoor, he was all too likely to be misunderstood. In the next scene, Osric certainly shows that he understands Hamlet's graveside claim that he is his father's ghost to be a claim that he should now be King of Denmark. That explains why Osric insists on keeping his hat in his hand when he comes to invite Hamlet to duel with Laertes. With equals, an Elizabethan gentleman would doff his hat in greeting and then put it back on. Only in the presence of your master, or as a courtier in the presence of the king, did you keep it in your hand. Osric is trying tactfully to acknowledge what he thinks is Hamlet's lunatic claim to be king. He missed the private connection that Hamlet had made with the trapdoor and his father's ghost. Tudor body language, with its wordless gestures and signals that defined human relations, was an aspect of social life so widely understood that it needed no stage direction. The language of hats was a part of the Shakespearean mindset that we now have to register in footnotes.

Other signifiers are necessarily more elusive. We might take heart from the range of the comments made in *Much Ado About Nothing* 4.1 when Hero is accused and is seen to go red. Each of the viewers—Claudio, Leonato, and Friar Francis—gives a different reading (or "noting") of her blush. Different mindsets lead to visual indicators being read in different ways. Each reading tells as much about the observer as about the thing observed. We might add that since the blush is commented on so extensively, Shakespeare must have been concerned to save the boy playing Hero from the necessity of holding his breath long enough to produce the right visual effect.

Costume was a vital element in the plays, a mute and instant signifier of the scene. If a character entered carrying a candle and dressed in a gown with a nightcap on his head, he had evidently just been roused from bed. Characters who entered wearing cloaks and riding boots and possibly holding a whip had just ended a long journey. York, entering in *Richard II* with a gorget (a metal neck plate, the "signs of war about his agèd neck" [2.2.74]), was preparing for battle. Even the women's wigs that the boys wore could be used to indicate the wearer's state of mind. Hair worn loose and unbound meant madness, whether in *Hamlet's* Ophelia or *Troilus's* Cassandra.

Comparable audience expectations could be roused by other visual features. Charac-

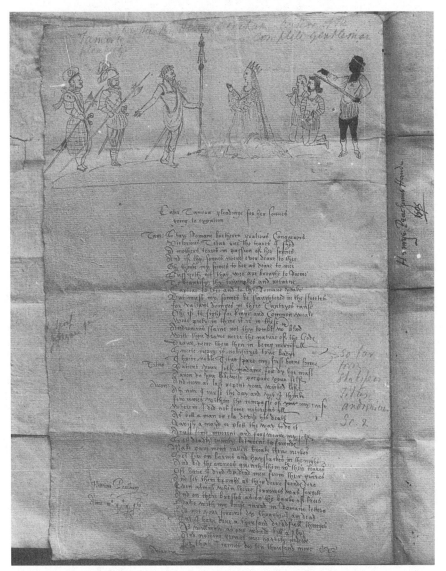

A sketch by Henry Peacham of an early staging of *Titus Andronicus* by Shakespeare's company (1595). Note the attempt at Roman costume for Titus but not for his soldiers, who carry Tudor halberds, and note Aaron's makeup and wig.

ters with faces blackened and wigs of curly black wool were recognized as Moors, alien and dangerous non-Christians. Aaron the Moor in *Titus Andronicus* and the Prince of Morocco in *The Merchant of Venice* acquire that character as soon as they come in view. Othello, by Iago's report and by his own first appearance, takes on the same stereotype. By contrast, Iago is dressed like a simple and honest soldier. Only in the course of Act 1 does it become apparent that it is Othello who is the honest soldier, Iago the un-Christian alien. The play neatly reverses the visual stereotypes of Elizabethan staging. Twentieth-century playgoers miss most of these signals and the ways that the original players used them to

A detail from Johannes De Witt's drawing of the Swan theater in 1596, showing two boys playing women greeted by a chamberlain.

show the discrepancy between outward appearance and inner person. As King Lear said, robes and furred gowns hide all.

For *The Merchant of Venice*, Shylock wore his "Jewish gabardine" and may also have put on a false nose, as Alleyn was said to have done for the title role in *The Jew of Malta*. Other national characteristics were noted by features of dress, such as the Irish "strait strossers" (tight trousers) that Macmorris would have worn in *Henry V*. The dress of the women in the plays, who were usually played by boys with unbroken voices, was always a special expense. The records kept by Philip Henslowe, owner of the Rose playhouse and impresario for the rival company to Shakespeare's, show that he paid the author less for the script of *A Woman Killed with Kindness* than he paid the costumer for the heroine's gown.

Women's clothing and the decorums and signals that women's costume contained were very different from those of men and men's clothing. Men frequently used their hats, doffing them to signal friendship and holding them in their hands while speaking to anyone in authority over them. Women's hats were fixed to their heads and were rarely if ever taken off in public. The forms and the language of women's clothes reflected the silent modesty and the quiet voices that men thought proper for women. Women had other devices to signal with, including handkerchiefs, fans, and face masks, and the boys playing the women's parts in the theaters exploited such accessories to the full. A lady out of doors commonly wore a mask to protect her complexion. When Othello is quizzing Emilia in 4.2 about his wife's behavior while she spoke to Cassio, he asks Emilia, who should have been chaperoning her mistress, whether Desdemona had not sent her away "to fetch her fan, her gloves, her mask nor nothing?" There is little doubt that the boys would have routinely worn masks when they played gentlewomen onstage, and not just at the masked balls in *Romeo and Juliet*, *Love's Labour's Lost*, and *Much Ado About Nothing*.

Other features of the original staging stemmed from the actor–audience relationship, which differs radically in daylight, when both parties can see one another, from what we are used to in modern, darkened, theaters. An eavesdropping scene onstage, for instance, works rather on the same basis as the "invisible" fairies in *A Midsummer Night's Dream*, where the audience agrees to share the pretence. At the Globe, it also entailed adopting the eavesdropper's perspective. In *Much Ado*, the two games of eavesdropping played on Benedict and Beatrice are chiefly done around the two stage posts. In these scenes, the posts that held up the stage cover, or "heavens," near what we now think of as the front of the stage were round, like the whole auditorium, and their function was to allow things to be seen equally by all of the audience, wherever people might be standing or sitting. Members of the audience, sitting in the surrounding galleries or standing around the stage itself at the Globe or its predecessors, had the two tall painted pillars in their sight all the time, wherever they were in the playhouse. And since the audience was in a complete circle all around the stage, if the stage posts were used for concealment there was always a large proportion of the audience who could see the player trying to hide behind a post. It was a three-dimensional game in which the audience might find itself behind any of the game players, victims or eavesdroppers, complicit in either role.

The first of *Much Ado*'s eavesdropping scenes, 2.3, starts as usual in Shakespeare with a verbal indication of the locality. Benedict tells his boy, "Bring it hither to me in the orchard." So we don't need stage trees to tell us where we are supposed to be. He later hides "in the arbour" to listen to what Don Pedro and the others have set for him; this means concealing himself behind a stage post, closer to the audience than the playactors who are talking about him. Don Pedro asks, "See you where Benedict hath hid himself?," a self-contradiction that confirms the game. When it is Beatrice's turn in her arbor scene, 3.1, she slips into a "bower" behind "this alley," which again signals a retreat behind the prominent stage post. These games are played with both of the eavesdroppers hiding behind the post at the stage edge, while the others do their talking at center stage between the two posts.

Such games of eavesdropping, using the same bits of the stage structure, make a strong visual contrast with all that goes on at what we two-dimensional thinkers, used to the pictorial staging of the cinema, call the "back" of the stage, or upstage—where, for instance, the Friar starts the broken-off wedding and where Claudio and Don Pedro later figure at Leonato's monument. These events are more distant from the audience, less obviously comic and intimate. The close proximity of players to audience in such activities as eavesdropping strongly influenced the audience's feeling of kinship with the different groupings of players.

A multitude of other staging differences can be identified. Quite apart from the fact that the language idioms were more familiar to the playgoers at the original Globe than they are now, all playgoers in 1600, many of them illiterate, were practiced listeners. The speed of speech, even in blank verse, was markedly higher then than the recitation of Shakespeare is today. The original performances of *Hamlet*, if the Folio version reflects what was usually acted, would have run for not much more than two and a half hours (the time quoted by Ben Jonson for a play as long as *Hamlet*), compared with the more than four hours that the full Folio or 1605 Quarto text with at least one intermission would take today. Quicker speaking, quicker stage action, no intermissions, and the audience's ability to grasp the language more quickly meant that the plays galloped along. The story, not the verse, carried the thrust of the action. Occasional set speeches, like Hamlet's soliloquies or Gaunt's "sceptred isle" speech in *Richard II*, would be heard, familiar as they already were to many in the audience, like a solo aria in a modern opera. In theory if not in practice, the business of hearing, as "audience" (from the Latin *audire*, "to hear"), was more important than the business of seeing, as "spectators" (from the Latin *spectare*, "to see"). The visual aspects of acting, like scenic staging, are inherently two-dimensional and do not work well when the audience completely surrounds the actors. Most of Shakespeare's fellow writers, notably Jonson, understandably set a higher priority on the audience's hearing their verse than on their seeing what the players did with the lines. The poets wanted listeners, although the players did try to cater to the viewers. Yet for all the games with magic tricks and devils spouting fireworks that were part of the Shakespearean staging tradition, spectacle was a limited resource on the scene-free Elizabethan stage. Shakespeare in this was a poet more than a player. Even in his last and most richly staged plays, *Cymbeline*, *The Winter's Tale*, and *The Tempest*, he made notably less use of such "spectacles" than did his contemporaries.

One piece of internal evidence about the original staging is Hamlet's advice to the visiting players. In 3.2, before they stage the *Mousetrap* play that he has rewritten for them, he lectures them on what a noble student of the theater then considered to be good acting. He objects first to overacting and second to the clown who ad libs with his own jokes and does not keep to the script. How far this may have been Shakespeare's own view it is impossible to say. Hamlet is an amateur lecturing professionals about how they should do their job. His views are what we would expect an amateur playwright with a liking for plays that are "caviar to the general" to hold. His objections to the clown are noteworthy, because once the original performances ended, the clown would conclude the afternoon's entertainment with a comic song-and-dance jig. Thomas Platter, a young German-speaking Swiss student, went to the Globe in 1599 to see *Julius Caesar*. He reported back home that

> on 21 September after lunch I and my party crossed the river, and there in the playhouse with the thatched roof witnessed an excellent performance of the tragedy of the first emperor Julius Caesar with a cast of about fifteen people. When the play was over they danced marvellously and gracefully together as their custom is, two dressed as men and two as women.[1]

The script for one jig survives, probably played by Will Kemp, who was the Shakespeare company clown until he left just before *Hamlet* came to the Globe. Its story is a bawdy knockabout tale of different men trying to seduce a shopkeeper's wife in rhyming couplets, hiding in a chest from her husband, and beating one another up. There is nothing to say

---

1. *Thomas Platter's Travels in England* (1599), rendered into English from the German, and with introductory matter by Clare Williams (London: Cape, 1937), p. 166.

The hall screen in the Middle Temple Hall, built in 1574. Shakespeare's company staged *Twelfth Night* in this hall in February 1602.

what the audience reaction to such a jig might have been after they had seen a performance of *Julius Caesar* or *Hamlet*. It is possible that the Globe players stopped offering that kind of coda when they acquired the clown who played Feste in *Twelfth Night* in 1601. The song with which Feste ends that play might have become an alternative form of closure, replacing the traditional bawdy jig.

Vigorous and rapid staging was inevitable when the half of the audience closest to the stage had to stand throughout the performance. Shakespeare's plays were distinctive among the other plays of the time for their reliance on verbal sparkle over scenes of battle and physical movement, but even the soliloquies raced along. There was little occasion for long pauses and emoting. Dumb shows, like the players' prelude to the *Mousetrap* play in *Hamlet*, were the nearest that the players came to silent acting. There were no intermissions—apples, nuts, and drink were peddled in the auditorium throughout the performance—and the only "comfort stations" were, for the men, the nearest blank wall; for the women, whatever convenient pots or bottles they might be carrying under their long skirts.

Nor were there any pauses to change scenes. There was no static scenery apart from an emblematic candle to signify a night scene, a bed "thrust out" onto the stage, or the canopied chair of state on which the ruler or judge sat for court scenes. Usually any special locality would be signaled in the first words of a new scene, but unlocalized scenes were routine. Each scene ended when all the characters left the stage and another set entered. No act breaks appear in the plays before *The Tempest*. *Henry V* marked each act with a Chorus, but even he entered on the heels of the characters from the previous scene. Blue-coated stagehands were a visibly invisible presence onstage. They would draw back the central hangings on the *frons scenae* for a discovery scene, carry on the chair of state on its dais for courtroom scenes, or push out the bed with Desdemona on it for the last act of *Othello*. They served the stage like the house servants with whom the nobility peopled every room in their great houses, silent machines ready to spring into action when needed.

There has been a great deal of speculation about the tiring-house front at the rear of the stage platform: did it look more like an indoor set or an outdoor one, like the hall screen of a great house or palace or like a house front exterior? In fact, it could easily be either. The upper level of the *frons*, the balconied "above," might equally represent a musicians' gallery, like those in the main hall of a great house, or a city wall under which the central discovery space served as the city gates, as it did for York in *Richard Duke of York (3 Henry VI)* 4.8, or *Henry V*'s Harfleur (3.3.78). The "above" could equally be an indoor gallery or an outdoor balcony. The appearance of the stage was everything and nothing, depending on what the play required. Players and playwrights expected the audience members to use their imagination, as they had to with the opening lines of *Hamlet*, or, as the Prologue to *Henry V* put it, to "piece out our imperfections with your thoughts."

Shakespeare's Companies and Their Playhouses

Shakespeare's plays were written for a variety of staging conditions. Until 1594, when he joined a new company under the patronage of the lord chamberlain, the queen's officer responsible for licensing playing companies, poets had written their plays for any kind of playhouse. The Queen's Men, the largest and best company of the 1580s, is on record as playing at the Bell, the Bel Savage, and the Bull inns inside the city, and at the Theatre and the Curtain playhouses in the suburbs. Early in 1594, it completed this sweep of all the available London venues by playing at the Rose. But in that year, the system of playing changed. The lord mayor had always objected to players using the city's inns, and in May 1594 he succeeded in securing the lord chamberlain's agreement to a total ban. From then on, only the specially built playhouses in the suburbs were available for plays.

The Queen's Men had been set up in 1583, drawn from all the then-existing major companies with the best players. This larger and favored group at first monopolized playing in London. But it was in decline by the early 1590s, and the shortage of companies to perform for the queen at Christmas led the lord chamberlain and his son-in-law, the lord admiral, to set up two new companies in its place as a duopoly in May 1594. Shakespeare became a "sharer," or partner, in one of these companies. As part of the same new establishment, his company, the Lord Chamberlain's Men, was allocated the Theatre to perform in, while its partner company in the duopoly, the Lord Admiral's Men, was assigned to the Rose. This was the first time any playing company secured a playhouse officially authorized for its use alone.

The Theatre, originally built in 1576 by James Burbage, father of the leading player of the Lord Chamberlain's company, was in Shoreditch, a suburb to the north of the city. The Rose, built in 1587 by Philip Henslowe, father-in-law of the Lord Admiral's leading player, Edward Alleyn, was in the suburb of Southwark, on the south bank of the Thames. Henslowe's business papers, his accounts, some lists of costumes and other resources, and his "diary," a day-by-day listing of each day's takings and the plays that brought the money in, have survived for the period from 1592 until well into the next decade. Together they provide an invaluable record of how one of the two major companies of the later 1590s, the only rival to Shakespeare's company, operated through these years.[2] Some of Shakespeare's earlier plays, written before he joined the Lord Chamberlain's Men, including *1 Henry VI* and *Titus Andronicus*, were performed at the Rose. After May 1594, the new company acquired all of his early plays; every Shakespeare play through the next three years was written for the Theatre. Its familiarity supplied one sort of resource to the playwright. But the repertory system laid heavy demands on the company.

Henslowe's papers give a remarkable record of the company repertory for these years. Each afternoon, the same team of fifteen or so players would stage a different play. With

---

2. See *Henslowe's Diary*, ed. R. A. Foakes and R. T. Rickert (Cambridge: Cambridge University Press, 1961).

only two companies operating in London, the demand was for constant change. No play at the Rose was staged more than four or five times in any month, and it was normal to stage a different play on each of the six afternoons of each week that they performed. A new play would be introduced roughly every three weeks—after three weeks of transcribing and learning the new parts; preparing the promptbook, costumes, and properties; and rehearsing in the mornings—while each afternoon, whichever of the established plays had been advertised around town on the playbills would be put on. The leading players had to memorize on average as many as eight hundred lines for each afternoon. Richard Burbage, who played the first Hamlet in 1601, probably had to play Richard III, Orlando in *As You Like It*, and Hamlet on successive afternoons while at the same time learning the part of Duke Orsino and rehearsing the new *Twelfth Night*—and still holding at least a dozen other parts in his head for the rest of the month's program. In the evenings, he might be called on to take the company to perform a different play at court, or at a nobleman's house in the Strand. The best companies made a lot of money, but not without constant effort.

The companies were formed rather like guilds, controlled by their leading "sharers." Each senior player shared the company's profits and losses equally with his fellows. Most of the plays have seven or eight major speaking parts for the men, plus two for the boys playing the women. A normal London company had eight or ten sharers, who collectively chose the repertory of plays to be performed, bought the playbooks from the poets, and put up the money for the main company resource of playbooks and costumes (not to mention the wagon and horses for touring when plague forced the London theaters to close). Shakespeare made most of his fortune from his "share," first in his company and later in its two playhouses.

As a playhouse landlord, Henslowe took half of the takings from the galleries each afternoon for his rent, while the players shared all the yard takings and the other half of the gallery money. From their takings, the sharers paid hired hands to take the walk-on parts and to work as stagehands, musicians, bookkeeper or prompter, and "gatherers" at the different entry gates. The leading players also kept the boys who played the women's parts, housing and feeding them as "apprentices" in an imitation of the London livery companies and trades, which ran apprenticeships to train boys to become skilled artisans, or "journeymen." City apprenticeships ran for seven years from the age of seventeen, but the boy players began much younger, because unbroken voices were needed. They graduated to become adult players at an age when the city apprentices were only beginning their training. Most of the "extras," apart from the playing boys, would be left in London whenever the company had to go on tour.

Because the professional companies of the kind that Shakespeare joined all started as traveling groups rather than as companies settled at a single playhouse in London, the years up to 1594 yielded plays that could be staged anywhere. The company might be summoned to play at court, at private houses, or at the halls of the Inns of Court as readily as at inns or innyards or the custom-built theaters themselves. They traveled the country with their plays, using the great halls of country houses, or town guildhalls and local inns, wherever the town they visited allowed them. Consequently, the plays could not demand elaborate resources for staging. In this highly mobile tradition of traveling companies, they were written in the expectation of the same basic but minimal features being available at each venue. Besides the stage platform itself, the basic features appear to have been two entry doors, usually a trap in the stage floor, a pair of stage pillars, sometimes a discovery space, and very occasionally a heavens with descent machinery. Apart from these fixtures, properties such as chairs and a table, a canopied throne on a dais, and sometimes a bed were also in regular use, though in a pinch these could be as mobile as the players themselves. The only essential traveling properties were players, playbooks, and costumes.

Once the two authorized companies settled permanently at the Theatre and the Rose in 1594, they slowly lost some of this mobility. The demands of versatility and readiness to make rapid changes now had to be switched from the venues to the plays themselves. A traveling company needed very few plays, since the locations and audiences were always changing. When the venues became fixed, it was the plays that had to keep changing. The Henslowe papers record that the Lord Admiral's Men staged an amazingly varied repertory of plays at the Rose. Shakespeare's company must have been equally versatile. The practice of giving popular plays long runs did not begin until the 1630s, by which time the number of London playhouses had grown to as many as five, all offering their plays each afternoon. Shakespeare's company in London had only the one peer from 1594 until 1600; and only two from then until 1608, aside from the once-weekly plays by the two boy companies, the "little eyases" mentioned in *Hamlet*, that started with the new century.

In the years from May 1594 to April 1597 at the Theatre, in addition to all his earlier plays that he brought to his new company, Shakespeare gave them possibly *Romeo and Juliet* and *King John*, and certainly *Richard II*, *A Midsummer Night's Dream*, *1 Henry IV*, and *The Merchant of Venice*. But then they ran into deep trouble, because they lost the Theatre. In April 1597, its original twenty-one-year lease expired, and the landlord, who disliked plays, refused to let them renew it. Anticipating this, the company's impresario James Burbage had built a new theater for them, a roofed place in the Blackfriars near St. Paul's Cathedral. The Blackfriars precinct was a "liberty," free from the lord mayor's jurisdiction. But the plan proved a disaster. The rich residents of Blackfriars objected, and the Privy Council stopped the theater from opening. From April 1597, Shakespeare's company had to rent the Curtain, an old neighbor of their now-silent Theatre, and it was there that the next four of Shakespeare's plays—*2 Henry IV*, *Much Ado About Nothing*, *The Merry Wives of Windsor*, and probably *Henry V*—were first staged.

In December 1598, losing hope of a new lease for the old Theatre, the Burbage sons had it pulled down and quietly transported its massive framing timbers across the Thames to make the scaffold for the Globe on the river's south bank, near the Rose. Most of their capital was sunk irretrievably into the Blackfriars theater, and they could afford only half the cost of rebuilding. So they raised money as best they could. Some of the company's more popular playbooks were sold to printers, including *Romeo and Juliet*, *Richard III*, *Richard II*, and *1 Henry IV*. More to the point, the Burbage brothers raised capital for the building by cutting in five of the leading players, including Shakespeare, and asking them to put up the other half of its cost. The Globe, its skeleton taken from the old Theatre, thus became the first playhouse to be owned by its players, and, within the limits set by the old frame, the first one built to their own design.

For this theater, one-eighth of which he personally owned, Shakespeare wrote his greatest plays: *Julius Caesar*, *As You Like It*, *Hamlet*, *Twelfth Night*, *Othello*, *All's Well That Ends Well*, *Measure for Measure*, *King Lear*, *Macbeth*, *Pericles*, *Antony and Cleopatra*, *Coriolanus*, *Cymbeline*, *The Winter's Tale*, and most likely *Troilus and Cressida* and *Timon of Athens*. As the first playhouse to be owned by the players who expected to use it, its fittings must have satisfied all the basic needs of Shakespearean staging. At one time or another, the company staged every one of Shakespeare's plays there.

In 1600, a company consisting entirely of boys started using the Blackfriars playhouse that Richard Burbage's father had tried to open four years before. Companies of boy players had a higher social status than the adult professionals, and, playing only in halls, they commanded a more affluent clientele. The boys performed only once a week, and the relative infrequency of their crowds, plus their skills as trained singers (they were choir-school children turned to making money for their choirmasters), proved less offensive to the local residents than a noisy adult company with its drums and trumpets. Leasing the Blackfriars to the boy company made a minor profit for the Burbages, who took the rent for eight years.

In the longer run, though, this arrangement provided a different means for the Burbage–Shakespeare company to advance its career. The boys' eight years of playing in their rented hall playhouse eventually made it possible for the company of adult players to renew Burbage's old plan of 1596. Shakespeare's company had been made the King's Men when James came to the throne in 1603, and their new patron gave them a status that made it impossible for the residents of Blackfriars to prevent them from implementing the original plan. During a lengthy closure of all the theaters because of a plague epidemic in

A section from Hollar's "Long View" of London. Drawn from a standpoint on the tower of the church that is now Southwark Cathedral, Hollar's view shows the roof of the great hall in which the Blackfriars playhouse was built. It can be seen as the long angled roof with a central turret, below and to the east of St. Bride's Church.

1608, the boys' manager surrendered his lease of the hall playhouse to the Burbages. They then took possession for their own company of the playhouse that their father had built for them twelve years before. They divided the new playhouse property among the leading players as they had done in 1599 with the Globe. They were the King's Men, the leading company in the country, and their status after ten years of playing at the Globe was matched by their wealth. By the time theaters reopened late in 1609, the company had established a new system of playing.

The King's Men now had two playhouses, a large open amphitheater and a much smaller roofed hall. Instead of selling or renting one out and using the other for themselves, they decided to use both in turn, for half of each year. It was a reversion to the old system with the city inns, where through the summer they played in the large open yards and in the winter played at inns with big indoor rooms. This time, though, the company owned both playhouses. Their affluence and their high status are signaled by the fact that they chose to keep one of their playhouses idle while they used the other, despite there now being a shortage of playhouses in London. That affluence was needed in 1613 when the Globe burned down at a performance of *All Is True (Henry VIII)*, and the company chose the much more expensive option of rebuilding it instead of reverting to the Blackfriars for both winter and summer. That decision, in its way, was the ultimate gesture of affection for their original playhouse. It was a costly gesture, but it meant that the Globe continued in use by the company until all the theaters were closed down by Parliament in 1642.

In 1609, when they reopened after the closure for plague, Shakespeare's company had made several changes in their procedures. The restart was at the Blackfriars, and although they offered the same kind of plays, they began to alter their style of staging. Along with the Blackfriars playhouse, they acquired a famous consort of musicians who played on strings and woodwinds in a music room set over the stage. The new consort was a distinct enhancement of the company's musical resources, which until then had been confined to song, the occasional use of recorders or hautboys, and military drums and trumpets for the scenes with soldiery. In 1608, a central room on the Globe's stage balcony was taken over to serve as a music room like the one at the Blackfriars. From this time on, the King's Men's performances began with a lengthy overture or concert of music before the play.

With that change, the plays themselves now had music to back their singers and provide other sorts of atmospheric effects. Some of the songs and music that appear in the plays not printed until the First Folio of 1623, such as the song that Mariana hears in *Measure for Measure* 4.1, may have been added after Shakespeare's time to make use of this new resource. Shakespeare did use songs, sometimes with string accompaniment, quite regularly in the early plays, but instrumental music hardly ever appears. The last play that he wrote alone, *The Tempest*, was the only one in which he made full use of this new resource.

All the plays containing soldiers and battles used the military drums that in war conveyed signals to infantry formations, as well as the trumpets that were used for signaling to cavalry. These were usually employed for offstage noises, sound effects made from "within" (inside the dressing room or tiring-house behind the stage). Soldiers marching in procession, as in the dead march at the close of *Hamlet*, would have the time marked by an onstage drum. Shakespeare never calls for guns to be fired onstage, though other writers did, but he did have other noises at his command. A small cannon or "chamber" might be used, fired from the gable-fronted heavens over the stage, as Claudius demands in *Hamlet* and as the Chorus to Act 3 of *Henry V* notes. It was wadding from a ceremonial cannon shot that set the gallery thatch alight at a performance of *All Is True* in July 1613 and burned the Globe to the ground. Stage battles such as Shrewsbury at the end of *1 Henry IV*, written for the Theatre, were accompanied by sword fights that were not the duels of *Hamlet*'s finale but exchanges with broadswords or "foxes" slammed against metal shields or "targets." That action guaranteed emphatic sound effects. The drums and trumpets, with clashes of swords and a great deal of to-ing and fro-ing onto and off the stage, were highlighted in between the shouted dialogue by some hard fighting between the protagonists. The leading players were practiced swordsmen, who knew they were being watched by experts. These were the scenes of "four or five most vile and ragged foils" that the fourth Chorus self-consciously derided in *Henry V* at the Curtain.

The second great reason for noise in the amphitheaters was to mark storm and tempest. Stagehands used the kind of device that Jonson mocked in the Prologue to *Every Man in His Humour*, written for its 1616 publication. His play, wrote Jonson, was free from choruses that wafted you over the seas, "nor rolled bullet heard / To say, it thunders; nor tempestuous drum / Rumbles, to tell you when the storm doth come." For centuries, lead balls rolling down a tin trough were a standard way of making thunder noises in English theaters. The tempest in Act 3 of *King Lear* is heralded several times in the text before a stage direction, "Storm and tempest" (Folio 2.2.450), tells us that it has at last arrived. In 2.2, Cornwall notes its coming twice (Folio 2.2.452, 473). Kent comments on the "Foul weather" in his first line in Act 3, prefaced by the entry stage direction for Act 3, "Storm still," which is repeated for 3.2. Such stage directions appear in both texts (Q has "Storm" for the equivalent Scenes 8, 9, and also at 11, F's 3.4, where F omits any further reference to these noises). These explicit signals indicate that the stagehands provided offstage noises, for all that Lear himself outstorms them with his violent speeches in 3.2.

The main question about the storm scenes in *King Lear* is this: with such consistent emphasis on storm in the language, what was the design behind the stage directions? In the centuries that *Lear* has been restaged, the tempest has been made to roar offstage in a wide variety of ways, often with so much effect that, in the face of complaints that the storm noises made it difficult for the audience to hear the words, some modern productions reduced the storm to solely visual effects, or even left Lear's own raging language to express it unsupported. But the two stage directions indicate that in the original performances the "storm in nature" was not left to Lear himself to convey. The two "Storm still" directions in the Folio suggest a constant rumbling, not the intermittent crashes that might allow Lear to conduct a dialogue with the occasional outbursts of storm noises, as some modern productions have done.

Shakespeare left regrettably few stage directions to indicate the special tricks or properties that he wanted. Curtained beds are called for in *Othello* 5.2 and *Cymbeline* 2.2, and there is the specification "Stocks brought out" in *King Lear* 2.2.132. Small and portable things like papers were a much more common device, from the letters in *The Two Gentlemen of Verona* 1.2.46, 1.3.44, and 2.1.95 to Lear's map at 1.1.35. Across the whole thirty-eight plays, though, there are very few such directions. Shakespeare's economy in preparing his scripts is a major impediment to the modern reader. He hardly ever bothered to note the standard physical gestures, such as kneeling or doffing a hat, and did little more to specify any special effects. Nonetheless, it is important not to imagine elaborate devices or actions where the text does not call for them. On the whole, the demands Shakespeare made of his fellows for staging his plays appear to have been remarkably modest. Since he was a company shareholder, his parsimony may have had a simple commercial motive. Stage properties cost the company money, and one had to be confident of a new play's popularity before investing much in its staging.

There may have been other reasons for avoiding extravagant staging spectacles. Shakespeare made little use of the discovery space until the last plays, for instance, for reasons that we can only guess at. The few definite discoveries in the plays include Portia's caskets in *The Merchant of Venice*, Falstaff sleeping off his sack in *1 Henry IV* 2.5.482, the body of Polonius in *Hamlet*, Hermione's statue in *The Winter's Tale* 5.3.20, and the lovers in *The Tempest* 5.1.173, who are found when discovered to be playing chess. The audience's shock when Hermione moves and comes out of the discovery space onto the main stage is rare in Shakespeare: in every other play, whether comedy or tragedy, the audience knows far more than the characters onstage about what is going on. Shakespeare matched this late innovation in *The Winter's Tale* with his last play, *The Tempest*. After the preliminary and soothing concert by the resident Blackfriars musicians, it opens with a storm at sea so realistic that it includes that peculiarly distinctive stage direction "Enter Mariners, wet" (1.1.46). That startling piece of stage realism turns out straightaway to be not real at all but a piece of stage magic.

A Funeral Elegy

William Peter (b. 1582) spent most of his adult life as a university student. Competent but hardly zealous, he took several extended leaves from school. In the winter of 1608–9, a year after "his father's death had freed his will" (*A Funeral Elegy*, line 68), Peter returned to his native Exeter, where he met and married Margaret Brewton (b. 1591). And on January 25, 1612, while riding home from a day of revels in the city of Exeter, he was murdered, stabbed in the back of the head by his friend and junior kinsman Edward Drew.

Word of the slaying traveled quickly. *A Funerall Elegye in memory of the late Vertuous Maister William Peeter*, a poem of 578 lines, was completed within days of the murder and registered to be printed in London. Observing a convention of modesty in Jacobean memorial verse, the author withheld his name, signing his text as he signed his dedication: "W. S." Issued privately and presented to Peter's elder brother John, the elegy was soon forgotten. Like other printed pamphlets memorializing private citizens, the Peter elegy appears never to have been marketed for public sale; and it remained outside the pale of traditional literary studies, attracting scarcely any notice until January 1996, when it became global news in response to mounting evidence that the W. S. who wrote it was William Shakespeare.

Thomas Thorp, who arranged for W. S.'s elegy to be printed, was closely associated with Shakespeare's dramatic company, the Lord Chamberlain's Men, later the King's Men. Active from 1600 to 1625, he published Shakespeare's Sonnets, plays by Ben Jonson, John Marston, and George Chapman, prose pamphlets by friends of Jonson, and, posthumously, nondramatic texts by Christopher Marlowe. William Peter and his killer, Edward Drew, also had friends and family within Shakespeare's circle of acquaintance. But the case for Shakespearean authorship of *A Funeral Elegy* rests largely on internal and intertextual evidence. W. S.'s vocabulary has been tested against a comprehensive cross sample of early modern texts in electronic form — an archive of more than twelve million words (from A.D. 1500 to 1700). Among hundreds of contemporaneous texts and writers, W. S.'s diction most closely matches that of Shakespeare, including more than a dozen rare words for which there is no precedent except Shakespeare. The lexical match extends also to more common words. Both W. S. and Shakespeare use conjunctions that were falling out of use by 1612 — for example, "for that" (because), "sith" (since), "whiles." Both prefer the same auxiliary verbs ("hath," "doth," and "wert" for the alternatives "has," "does," and "wast"). Both poets coin compound words on the same pattern, most often with a participle ("best-speaking," "low-level'd," "clean-temper'd," "close-lurking" [W. S.]; "false-speaking," "low-declined," "clean-timber'd," "fell-lurking" [Shakespeare]). Both coin nouns from adjectives ("vain" for "vanity") or verbs from nouns ("necessitied" [Shakespeare], "possibilited" [W. S.]). And so on.

W. S. and Shakespeare use even the most ordinary function words with corresponding frequency ("and," "but," "like," "not," "so," "that"), and the two poets share quirky habits of grammar and syntax that were not identified as distinctively "Shakespearean" until 1880 or later. Examples include the exceptional and frequent use of "who" for inanimate, unpersonified antecedents ("embracements . . . who," "orbs . . . in whom," etc.), which is typical of W. S. and Shakespeare but rare elsewhere. W. S. also makes habitual use of the "Shakespearean hendiadys," or false doublet. The elegy's dozen examples include "the By-path and the Ridgeway . . . leads" (lines 41–42), "the candle and the body's light / Darkens" (261–62), "the world and heat of sin entices" (280). Equally rare is W. S.'s extraordinarily high rate of enjambment (with run-on lines approaching 50 percent), unequaled in 1612 except by Shakespeare, among known poets. The only contemporaries whose verse regularly approaches W. S. and Shakespeare in this respect are Cyril Tourneur and John Webster, Jacobean playwrights who (like Shakespeare) overcame a beginner's reliance on end-stopped lines by writing verse-dialogue for the public stage.

W. S. and Shakespeare draw on the same published texts, including Samuel Daniel's *Poems*, Sir Philip Sidney's *Arcadia*, and plays by Jonson and Marston. Significantly, W. S. appears also to have read at least two private manuscripts that circulated within Shakespeare's theatrical company, Thomas Shelton's translation of *Don Quixote* (published 1612) and Elizabeth Cary's *Mariam* (published 1613). Shelton's manuscript was used by Middleton, Fletcher, and Shakespeare in 1611. Cary scholars have suggested that *Mariam* was consulted in manuscript by Middleton in 1611 and by Shakespeare in 1607 or later. We find W. S. borrowing material from these same two manuscripts in January 1612.

Nothing is known of the personal history to which W. S. alludes, a troubled friendship that entailed slander and misunderstanding. These matters were presumably known to the elegy's immediate audience, John Peter and family, who could not have believed that Shakespeare wrote this largely autobiographical poem if Shakespeare had not, in fact, been friends with the deceased. Yet W. S. implies that he is Shakespeare: his prefatory epistle is closely modeled on the dedication to Southampton in *The Rape of Lucrece*, and the elegy draws freely on such texts as *Richard II*, the Sonnets, and *The Winter's Tale*. If W. S. is not Shakespeare, he must have wished for his readers to think so.

But if Shakespeare wrote *A Funeral Elegy*, why did he not write it *better*? One's experience of reading the elegy is hardly to be reconciled with the attributional evidence. In a first reading, perhaps in every reading, *A Funeral Elegy* seems repetitive and rather dull, with only brief flashes of figurative brilliance. If we were to discover a "lost" Shakespeare, this is hardly the one we would have hoped for. That W. S.'s elegy should be aesthetically disappointing and yet distinctively Shakespearean is a paradox that raises a question about its literary value. As W. S. remarks,

> When all shall turn to dust from whence we came
> And we low-level'd in a narrow grave,
> What can we leave behind us but a name?
>
> (193–95)

Without Shakespeare's name attached to it, the Peter elegy had (for nearly four hundred years) a narrow grave indeed. Transfigured as a Shakespeare poem, that same elegy has gained worldwide attention, receiving, perhaps, more credit than it deserves while threatening to unsettle our very notions of what we mean by the cultural term "Shakespeare." These problems, which have yet to be fully negotiated, have a direct bearing on the poem's meaning. When read as a text by W. S., the elegy is a competent funeral poem memorializing a person of no consequence. But if W. S. is Shakespeare, then the elegy is his final composition (apart from collaborative work), and one of the few texts in which Shakespeare speaks to us in the first person. Richard Abrams has argued persuasively that the elegy represents the final valediction of a Shakespeare who has grown weary of "vain conceit," of "popular applause and power's commission" and the stage's "empty sound of overweening passion" (230, 450, 276). If so, then *A Funeral Elegy* may be a text of consummate importance.

When Shakespeare's Sonnets, long neglected, were at last resurrected for English readers in the latter eighteenth century, the poems were greeted with initial disdain. Editor George Steevens remarked of the Sonnets in 1793 that "the strongest act of Parliament that could be framed, would fail to compel readers into their service." William Wordsworth, in a first acquaintance, found many of the Sonnets to be "abominably harsh, obscure, and worthless," and the rest marred by "sameness, tediousness, quaintness, and elaborate obscurity." *A Funeral Elegy* invites similar complaints, though it is not without critical interest. W. S.'s tribute to William Peter lacks the cleverness and sheer exuberance of most Shakespearean texts, but as we come to study it more closely, we may find that the poem has its surprises and that it can make us better readers not just of the Shakespeares that we already knew, but of this one as well.

W. S. introduces the life of William Peter as a text abridged by time and misconstrued by unworthy readers (1–6). The poet condemns those who would generate a false version of Peter's life by supposing that the man's bad end presupposes a life badly lived. This moralistic reading is said to be a "text of malice," construed with "corrupt commentaries" by blind and ignorant men who would "[pick] out matter to inform the worst" (256–67). Yet W. S. implicates even his own text in Peter's misinterpreted life. Much of the elegist's language of praise tends, in a close reading, to undermine itself with ambiguities that wed compliment to damaging innuendo (for example, 12, 60, 93–96, 294–95, 321–24, 328, 511–14). As a result, W. S.'s elegy facilitates the sinister misreading of Peter's life that the poet condemns.

That W. S. wishes to honor his slain friend seems beyond doubt—but the elegy is a text fraught with deep ambivalence and colored with resentment over a past injury. The poet recalls being cast down in "days of youth" when envious men "sifted to embane / [His] reputation with a witless sin," leaving him with a "taste / Of knowing shame" (137–48). W. S. protests his innocence, contrasting his silent love for Peter with the "invitements strange" of those who praised his friend only to gratify their own "prompt desires" or the "sensual aptness of [their] disunion'd vices" (278–90). W. S. hopes that his "country's thankless misconstruction" can be buried along with Peter, thereby to free himself and Peter's name from the "spleenful sense / And spite of malice" (33–34; compare 399–414). Working against that hope, however, is the poet's sense that all hope may come to nought—even, perhaps, a hope in the resurrection. What finally matters is that the poet loved Will Peter, loved him in silence, in death as in life (553–78).

DONALD W. FOSTER

TEXTUAL NOTE

The text of the elegy is provided by the quarto: *A Funerall Elegye in memory of the late Vertuous Maister William Peeter. By W. S.* (London: G[eorge] Eld [for Thomas Thorp], 1612). Although the edition appears to have had a small private printing, two copies survive, both at Oxford, one at the Bodleian Library and one in the Balliol College Library. The quarto (Q) is badly printed, with botched punctuation throughout. The print-shop compositors—often bewildered, it seems, by the poet's highly enjambed verse and light pointing (punctuation)—heavily overpunctuated the text, often confusing the sense. In this conservatively normalized edition, the pointing is kept light. Obvious misprints ("Sot" for "Sat," "goood" for "good," "witnesles" for "witnesses," etc.) are quietly corrected. There is one substantive emendation, following a suggestion of G. Blakemore Evans: at line 8, the quarto reads, "Sith as it euer hee maintain'd the same," which is ungrammatical and makes little sense. Where "it" appears, one should expect to find "that," since this word in Elizabethan verse was frequently used as a conjunctional affix following "as." It seems likely that the compositor simply misread the author's "yᵗ" (that) for "yᵗ" (it). Common nouns that are capitalized and italicized in the quarto (signaling personification or punning—for example, *"Ridg-way," "Drew," "Rock"*) are here not italicized, but remain capitalized to preserve something of the original emphasis. Italicized quotations in the quarto are here rendered in quotation marks. Spelling conforms with modern usage, though archaic variants are retained where they represent Jacobean alternatives in the form of words, not merely in the spelling. Examples are "sith," "conster," "disgest," "adventers," "strook," and the frequent elided participles ("Rememb'ring," "sund'red").

SELECTED BIBLIOGRAPHY

Abrams, Richard. "W[illiam] S[hakespeare]'s 'Funeral Elegy' and the Turn from the Theatrical." *Studies in English Literature* 36.2 (1996): 435–60.

Foster, Donald W. *Elegy by W. S.: A Study in Attribution.* Cranbury, N.J.: Associated University Presses, 1989.

——. "*A Funeral Elegy*: W[illiam] S[hakespeare]'s 'Best-Speaking Witnesses." *PMLA* 111.5 (1996): 1080–105.

A Funeral Elegy

TO MASTER JOHN PETER
of Bowhay in Devon, Esq.

The love I bore to your brother, and will do to his memory, hath crav'd from me this last duty of a friend; I am herein but a second to the privilege of Truth, who can warrant more in his behalf than I undertook to deliver. Exercise in this kind I will little affect, and am less addicted to,[1] but there must be miracle in that labor which, to witness my remembrance to this departed gentleman, I would not willingly undergo.[2] Yet whatsoever is here done, is done to him, and to him only. For whom and whose sake I will not forget to remember any friendly respects to you, or to any of those that have lov'd him for himself, and himself for his deserts.

W. S.

Since Time, and his predestinated end,
Abridg'd the circuit of his hopeful days,
Whiles both his Youth and Virtue did intend
The good endeavors of deserving praise,
5   What memorable monument can last
Whereon to build his never-blemish'd name
But his own worth, wherein his life was grac'd—
Sith as that ever he maintain'd the same?[3]
Oblivion in the darkest day to come,
10   When sin shall tread on merit in the dust,
Cannot rase out the lamentable tomb
Of his short-liv'd deserts; but still they must,
Even in the hearts and memories of men,
Claim fit Respect, that they, in every limb
15   Rememb'ring what he was, with comfort then
May pattern out one truly good, by him.[4]
For he was truly good, if honest care
Of harmless conversation may commend
A life free from such stains as follies are,[5]
20   Ill recompensed only in his end.[6]
Nor can the tongue of him who lov'd him least
(If there can be minority of love
To one superlative above the rest
Of many men in steady faith) reprove
25   His constant temper, in the equal weight[7]
Of thankfulness and kindness: Truth doth leave
Sufficient proof, he was in every right[8]
As kind to give, as thankful to receive.
The curious eye of a quick-brain'd survey

---

1. The writing of funeral verses is an exercise that I scarcely care for and rarely aspire to.
2. But in memorializing William Peter, I would undertake any labor short of the miraculous (see lines 499–501, 541–47).
3. In that he always sustained his own worthiness. *Sith as:* Since.
4. May take him as a standard of human goodness.

5. A life free from the blemish of foolish vices.
6. Only in his death was he badly requited for his goodness.
7. Nor . . . *weight:* His well-tempered behavior was beyond rebuke even from those who least loved him (if one can even make distinctions of a lesser love when speaking of this superlative human being).
8. In every way; by any right standard.

30   Could scantly find a mote amidst the sun[9]
      Of his too-short'ned days, or make a prey[1]
      Of any faulty errors he had done—
      Not that he was above the spleenful sense[2]
      And spite of malice, but for that° he had   *but because*
35   Warrant enough in his own innocence
      Against the sting of some in nature bad.
      Yet who is he so absolutely blest
      That lives encompass'd in a mortal frame,
      Sometime in reputation not oppress'd
40   By some in nothing famous but defame?[3]
      Such in the By-path and the Ridgeway[4] lurk
      That leads to ruin, in a smooth pretense
      Of what they do to be a special work
      Of singleness, not tending to offense;
45   Whose very virtues are, not to detract
      Whiles hope remains of gain (base fee of slaves),
      Despising chiefly men in fortunes wrack'd—
      But death to such gives unrememb'red graves.
         Now therein liv'd he happy, if to be
50   Free from detraction happiness it be.
      His younger years gave comfortable hope
      To hope for comfort in his riper youth,
      Which, harvest-like, did yield again the crop
      Of Education, better'd in his truth.°   *constancy; truthfulness*
55   Those noble twins of heaven-infused races,°   *of heavenly descent*
      Learning and Wit,° refined in their kind   *intelligence*
      Did jointly both in their peculiar graces
      Enrich the curious[5] temple of his mind;
      Indeed a temple, in whose precious white[6]
60   Sat Reason by Religion oversway'd,[7]
      Teaching his other senses, with delight,
      How Piety and Zeal should be obey'd—
      Not fruitlessly in prodigal expense
      Wasting his best of time, but so content
65   With Reason's golden Mean to make defense
      Against the assault of youth's encouragement;
      As not° the tide of this surrounding age   *So that not even*
      (When now his father's death[8] had freed his will[9])
      Could make him subject to the drunken rage
70   Of such whose only glory° is their ill.°   *boast / wrongdoing*
      He from the happy knowledge of the wise
      Draws virtue to reprove secured° fools   *certified; self-assured*
      And shuns the glad sleights of ensnaring vice
      To spend his spring of days in sacred schools.

---

9. *The curious . . . sun:* an allusion to Matthew 7:1–5: "Judge not, that ye be not judged. . . . And why seest thou the mote that is in thy brothers eye, and perceivest not the beam that is in thine own eye," etc. *a quick-brain'd:* an ingenious.

1. Or seize (upon); or find fault (with).

2. He was not immune to spiteful insinuations or inference.

3. *Yet . . . defame:* Yet who in a mortal body can escape the calumny of those whose only claim to fame is their skill in defaming others?

4. The Exeter-London road on which Peter died was a causeway known as "the Ridgeway"; but there may also be a disapproving glance at Peter's fiercely Protestant uncle Sir Thomas Ridgeway (then secretary of wars in Ireland) or other members of Ridgeway family.

5. Studious; beautifully wrought.

6. *temple of . . . white:* the mind as a temple of purity; but also, the "precious white" (fair) temples of his head.

7. Guided (but perhaps, overmastered). It is unclear whether religion swayed his reason or vice versa.

8. Otho Peter died in June 1607.

9. With an apparent pun on "Will" (compare lines 246, 291, 338).

75 Here gave he diet to the sick desires
That day by day assault the weaker man
And with fit moderation still retires
From what doth batter virtue now and then.
But that I not intend in full discourse
80 To progress out his life, I could display
A good man in each part exact[1] and force
The common voice[2] to warrant what I say.
For if his fate and heaven had decreed
That full of days he might have liv'd to see
85 The grave in peace, the times that should succeed
Had been best-speaking witnesses with me;[3]
Whose conversation so untouch'd did move[4]
Respect most in itself, as who would° scan   *so that whoever might*
His honesty and worth, by them might prove
90 He was a kind, true, perfect gentleman—
Not in the outside of disgraceful folly,
Courting opinion with unfit disguise,[5]
Affecting fashions,[6] nor addicted wholly
To unbeseeming blushless° vanities,   *To uncomely shameless*
95   But suiting[7] so his habit[8] and desire
  As that his Virtue was his best Attire.
Not in the waste of many idle words
Car'd he to be heard talk, nor in the float°   *flood, current*
Of fond conceit,° such as this age affords,   *Of foolish wit*
100 By vain discourse upon himself to dote;
For his becoming silence gave such grace
To his judicious parts, as what he spake
Seem'd rather answers which the wise embrace
Than busy questions such as talkers[9] make.
105 And though his qualities might well deserve
Just commendation, yet his furnish'd mind
Such harmony of goodness did preserve
As nature never built in better kind;
Knowing the best, and therefore not presuming
110 In knowing, but for that it was the best,
Ever within himself free choice resuming
Of true perfection, in a perfect breast;
So that his mind and body made an inn,
The one to lodge the other,[1] both like fram'd
115 For fair conditions, guests that soonest win
Applause; in generality, well fam'd,
If trim behavior, gestures mild, discreet
Endeavors, modest speech, beseeming mirth,
True friendship, active grace, persuasion sweet,[2]

1. Consummately, in each personal trait; in each acted theatrical role, if his life were narrated or "progressed out" (line 80), as in a stage play (Abrams, pp. 440–41).
2. Popular opinion (compare *All Is True* [*Henry VIII*] 5.2.208–9: "The common voice, I see, is verified / Of thee").
3. *the times . . . me:* succeeding generations would have been able with eloquence to join me in affirming his goodness.
4. Whose spotless interaction with others motivated.
5. Seeking favorable opinion, fame, popular applause with unsuitable disguise.

6. Not pretentiously adopting trendy manners or clothing.
7. Dressing; fitting the one to the other.
8. Garb; customary behavior; disposition.
9. Such as mere talkers (compare *All Is True* 2.2.78).
1. *So . . . other:* The body serving as an inn, and hence as a provincial theater, for his mind and for his virtues, the playerlike guests in lines 115–28 that "soonest win / Applause."
2. *persuasion sweet:* sound religious belief; graceful persuasiveness in his speech.

120　Delightful love innated[3] from his birth,
　　　Acquaintance unfamiliar, carriage just,[4]
　　　Offenceless resolution, wish'd sobriety,[5]
　　　Clean-temper'd[6] moderation, steady trust,
　　　Unburthen'd conscience, unfeign'd piety;
125　If these, or all of these, knit fast in one
　　　Can merit praise, then justly may we say,
　　　Not any° from this frailer stage° is gone　　　　　　　*No one / our mortal world*
　　　Whose name is like to live a longer day—
　　　Though not in eminent courts or places great
130　For popular concourse,° yet in that soil　　　　　　　　*public gatherings*
　　　Where he enjoy'd his birth, life, death, and seat°　　　*estate*
　　　Which now sits mourning his untimely spoil.°　　　　　*wrack*
　　　And as much glory is it to be good
　　　For private persons, in their private home,
135　As those descended from illustrious blood
　　　In public view of greatness, whence they come.
　　　Though I, rewarded with some sadder taste
　　　Of knowing shame, by feeling it have prov'd
　　　My country's thankless misconstruction cast
140　Upon my name and credit,[7] both unlov'd
　　　By some whose fortunes, sunk into the wane
　　　Of plenty and desert, have strove to win
　　　Justice by wrong, and sifted to embane
　　　My reputation with a witless sin;[8]
145　Yet time, the father of unblushing truth,
　　　May one day lay ope malice which hath cross'd it,
　　　And right the hopes of my endangered youth,
　　　Purchasing credit in the place I lost it.[9]
　　　Even in which place the subject of the verse
150　(Unhappy matter of a mourning style
　　　Which now that subject's merits doth rehearse)
　　　Had education and new being; while
　　　By fair demeanor he had won repute
　　　Amongst the all of all[1] that lived there,°　　　　　　*(in Oxford)*
155　For that° his actions did so wholly suit　　　　　　　　*In that*
　　　With worthiness, still memorable here.°　　　　　　　　*(in this poem)*
　　　The many hours till the day of doom
　　　Will not consume his life and hapless end,
　　　For should he° lie obscur'd without a tomb,　　　　　　*even if he should*
160　Time would to time his honesty commend;[2]
　　　Whiles parents to their children will make known,
　　　And they to their posterity impart,
　　　How such a man was sadly overthrown

3. Inherent, part of his very constitution.
4. Discriminating and circumspect in his friendships and having honorable comportment.
5. Gracious but resolute, with all desired gravity.
6. Thoroughly self-controlled (compare *Julius Caesar* 4.2.169, 170); purely fashioned (compare "Hector was not so clean-timbered," *Love's Labour's Lost* 5.2.628; "Those best affections that the heavens infuse / In their best-tempered pieces," *The Two Noble Kinsmen* 1.3.9–10; "Strong-tempered steel," *Venus and Adonis* 111).
7. *by . . . credit:* have proved my innocence by feeling shame (unlike the shameless friends noted in lines 283– 90). *prov'd:* experienced; made manifest. *country's:* probably the English midlands, but perhaps also, the nation.

credit: honorable reputation.
8. *both unlov'd . . . sin:* envious of my name and renown, certain unsuccessful and undeserving persons sought to poison my reputation by accusing me of a foolish vice.
9. *Yet . . . it:* Yet truth may prevail in time, redeeming the hopes of my vulnerable past, so that I obtain renown even in Oxford (the apparent site of the scandal mentioned here and in lines 557–60). *cross'd it:* obstructed the truth. *endangered:* controlled by the will of another; liable to censure or punishment.
1. The unanimous accord of all; the best-deserving of all (compare sonnet 31.14, *Love's Labour's Lost* 5.1.92).
2. Time would commend his honesty to each succeeding generation.

By a hand guided by a cruel heart,
165   Whereof as many as shall hear that sadness
      Will blame the one's hard fate, the other's madness;
Whiles such as do recount that tale of woe,
Told by remembrance of the wisest heads,
Will in the end conclude the matter so,
170 As they will all go weeping to their beds.
For when the world lies winter'd in the storms
Of fearful consummation, and lays down
Th' unsteady change of his fantastic forms,[3]
Expecting ever to be overthrown;
175 When the proud height of much affected sin
Shall ripen to a head, and in that pride
End in the miseries it did begin
And fall amidst the glory of his° tide;   *its (sin's)*
Then in a book[4] where every work is writ
180 Shall this man's actions be reveal'd, to show
The gainful fruit of well-employed wit,
Which paid to heaven the debt that it did owe.
Here shall be reckon'd up the constant faith,
Never untrue, where once he love profess'd;
185 Which is a miracle in men, one saith,°   *as one might say*
Long sought though rarely found, and he is best
    Who can make friendship, in those times of change,
      Admired more for being firm than strange.[5]
When those weak houses of our brittle flesh
190 Shall ruin'd be by death, our grace and strength,
Youth, memory and shape that made us fresh
Cast down, and utterly decay'd at length;
When all shall turn to dust from whence we came
And we low-level'd in a narrow grave,
195 What can we leave behind us but a name,
Which, by a life well led, may honor have?
Such honor, O thou youth untimely lost,
Thou didst deserve and hast; for though thy soul
Hath took her flight to a diviner coast,
200 Yet here on earth thy fame lives ever whole,
In every heart seal'd up, in every tongue
Fit matter to discourse,[6] no day prevented°   *excepted*
That pities not thy sad and sudden wrong,
Of all alike beloved and lamented.
205 And I here to thy memorable worth,
In this last act of friendship, sacrifice°   *offer up*
My love to thee, which I could not set forth[7]
In any other habit of disguise.[8]
Although I could not learn, whiles yet thou wert,°   *were alive*
210 To speak the language of a servile breath,
My truth stole from my tongue into my heart,
Which° shall not thence be sund'red, but in death.   *(my truth); (constancy)*

3. The vicissitudes of this world's ("his") elaborate but insubstantial creations.
4. The Book of Life (Revelation 3.5, 22.19, etc.); perhaps also anticipating the poet's own collected works (see "here," lines 156, 183).
5. More wondered at for its steadiness than for a sudden show of aloofness (in a friend's time of misfortune).
6. *In every . . . discourse:* in contrast with the poet, whose tongue has been sealed while his heart discourses (see lines 209–28).
7. Publish or issue as a printed literary text; narrate; adorn or embellish.
8. In any other outward form of public display; under the guise of my customary (theatrical?) mode.

And I confess my love was too remiss
That had not made thee know how much I priz'd thee,
215   But that mine error was, as yet it is,
To think love best in silence: for I siz'd thee
By what I would have been,[9] not only ready
In telling I was thine, but being so,
By some effect to show it. He is steady
220   Who seems less than he is in open show.°[1]   resolved
Since then I still reserv'd° to try the worst
Which hardest fate and time thus can lay on me.
T' enlarge my thoughts[2] was hindered at first,
While thou hadst life; I took this task upon me,
225   To register with mine unhappy pen
Such duties as it owes to thy desert,
And set thee as a precedent to men,
And limn thee to the world but as thou wert[3]—
Not hir'd, as heaven can witness in my soul,
230   By vain conceit to please such ones as know it,
Nor servile to be lik'd, free from control,
Which, pain to many men, I do not owe it.[4]
But here I trust I have discharged now
(Fair lovely branch too soon cut off) to thee,
235   My constant and irrefragable° vow,   unbreakable
As, had it chanc'd, thou mightst have done to me—
But that no merit strong enough of mine
Had yielded store to thy well-abled quill
Whereby t'enroll my name, as this of thine,
240   How s'ere enriched[5] by thy plenteous skill.
Here, then, I offer up to memory
The value of my talent, precious man,
Whereby if thou live to posterity,
Though't be not as I would, 'tis as I can:[6]
245   In minds from whence endeavor doth proceed,
       A ready will is taken for the deed.[7]
Yet ere I take my longest last farewell
From thee, fair mark of sorrow,[8] let me frame
Some ampler work of thank, wherein to tell
250   What more thou didst deserve than in thy name,
And free thee from the scandal° of such senses   gossip; disgrace
As in the rancor of unhappy spleen°   malice
Measure thy course of life, with false pretenses
Comparing by thy death what thou hast been.[9]
255   So in his° mischiefs is the world accurs'd: its
       It picks out matter to inform the worst.[1]

9. By what I *myself* wished to be (not just telling, but showing, love); also, by what I *would* have been (had I not been "hindered" in my show of love [lines 223ff.]).
1. Who in outward show (or public shows) seems less loving than he really is.
2. To express my love fully, without inhibition.
3. And depict you to the world simply as you were.
4. *Not hir'd . . . it:* I will not obligate myself by writing for patronage (a painful servility). *vain conceit:* worthless artifice in my verse; conceited vanity.
5. No matter how greatly augmented.
6. Though my memorial tribute is not as valuable as I could wish, it is the best that I can do. But if " 't" (it) *refers* to a manner of living, to "posterity" and not only to "the

value of my talent," then: Though literary immortality is no substitute for actual life, you may live to posterity insofar as I (as your poet) am able to do so.
7. Possibly a nominal pun on the poet's name and elegiac project: a well-prepared Will undertakes the labor.
8. William Peter ("thee") as a fair scar/sign of grief, or as the target/aim of the poet's lament; but also (as an appositive, not as a term of address), the poem itself, the poet's own "last farewell" (line 247) as the visible trace or marking of sorrow.
9. Taking your bad end to be the sign of a life badly lived.
1. The world selects ill matter to construct the worst possible text of your life.

The willful blindness that hoodwinks the eyes
Of men enwrapped in an earthy veil
Makes them most ignorantly exercise
260 And yield to humor° when it doth assail,   *unreasonable caprice*
Whereby the candle and the body's light
Darkens the inward eyesight of the mind,
Presuming still it sees, even in the night
Of that same ignorance which makes them blind.
265 Hence conster they with corrupt commentaries,
Proceeding from a nature as corrupt,
The text of malice,[2] which so often varies
As 'tis by seeming reason underpropp'd.
O, whither tends the lamentable spite
270 Of this world's teenful apprehension,[3]
Which understands all things amiss, whose light
Shines not amidst the dark of their dissension?
True 'tis, this man, whiles yet he was a man,
Sooth'd not[4] the current[5] of besotted° fashion   *excessive; crazed*
275 Nor could disgest,[6] as some loose mimics[7] can,
An empty sound of overweening passion,
So much to be made servant to the base
And sensual aptness of disunion'd vices,[8]
To purchase commendation by disgrace,
280 Whereto the world and heat of sin entices.
But in a safer contemplation,
Secure in what he knew, he ever chose
The ready way to commendation,
By shunning all invitements strange, of those
285 Whose illness is, the necessary praise
Must wait upon their actions;[9] only rare°   *extraordinary*
In being rare in° shame (which strives to raise   *devoid of*
Their name by doing what they do not care),
As if the free commission of their ill
290 Were even as boundless as their prompt desires;
Only like lords, like subjects to their will,[1]
Which their fond dotage ever more admires.
He was not so: but in a serious awe,
Ruling the little ordered commonwealth
295 Of his own self, with honor to the law
That gave peace to his bread, bread to his health;
Which ever he maintain'd in sweet content
And pleasurable rest, wherein he joy'd°   *enjoyed*
A monarchy of comfort's government,
300 Never until his last to be destroy'd.
For in the Vineyard° of heaven-favored learning   *Oxford University*
Where he was double-honor'd in degree,[2]

---

2. *Hence . . . malice:* Thus have ignorant persons construed ("conster") your life, relying on the corrupt commentary of malicious detractors (compare *All Is True* 5.1.132–36).
3. Deplorable sensibility; spiteful misapprehension.
4. Did not praise; did not subject himself to.
5. Currency, trendiness.
6. Could stomach; could bring slowly to a state of perfection.
7. Players; by extension, dissipated flatterers.
8. *base . . . vices:* vulgar and lustful inclination of disorderly vices.
9. *By . . . actions:* Peter refused commendation that depended on the perverse inducements ("invitements strange") of shameless men who (by flattering Peter) sought only to gratify their "prompt desires" (line 290).
1. Always acting lordly, yet like slaves to their desires; perhaps also, like servants to Will (Peter), or likely topical material for Will (the poet).
2. Peter received his bachelor's degree in 1603, his master's degree in 1606.

His observation and discreet discerning
Had taught him in both fortunes° to be free;   *good and bad fortune*
305   Whence now[3] retir'd home, to a home indeed
The home of his condition and estate,
He well provided 'gainst the hand of need,
Whence young men sometime grow unfortunate;
His disposition, by the bonds of unity,
310   So fast'ned to his reason that it strove
With understanding's grave immunity
To purchase from all hearts a steady love;
Wherein not any one thing comprehends
Proportionable note of what he was,
315   Than that he was so constant to his friends
As he would no occasion overpass
Which might make known his unaffected° care,   *sincere*
In all respects of trial, to unlock
His bosom and his store, which did declare
320   That Christ was his, and he was Friendship's Rock:
A Rock[4] of Friendship figured in his name,
Fore-shewing what he was, and what should be,
Most true presage; and he discharg'd the same
In every act of perfect amity—
325   Though in the complemental[5] phrase of words
He never was addicted to the vain[6]
Of boast, such as the common breath affords;
He was in use most fast,[7] in tongue most plain,
Nor amongst all those virtues that forever
330   Adorn'd his reputation will be found
One greater than his Faith, which did persever,
 'Where once it was protested, alway sound.[8]
Hence sprung the deadly fuel that reviv'd
The rage which wrought his end, for had he been
335   Slacker in love, he had been longer liv'd
And not oppress'd by wrath's unhappy sin—
By wrath's unhappy sin, which unadvis'd
Gave death for free good will, and wounds[9] for love.
Pity it was that° blood had not been priz'd   *his*
340   At higher rate, and reason set above
Most unjust choler, which untimely Drew
Destruction[1] on itself; and most unjust,
Robb'd virtue of a follower so true
As time can boast of, both for love and trust:
345   So henceforth all (great glory to his blood)
Shall be but seconds° to him, being good.   *followers*
The wicked end their honor with their sin
In death, which only then the good begin.[2]
Lo, here a lesson by experience taught°   *is taught*

---

3. That is, after receiving his M.A. (Peter returned to Devon in 1608 and was married in January 1609.)
4. The name "Peter" (from the Greek *Petros*) means "rock."
5. Ceremonious; complimentary.
6. Vein; vanity (compare *Troilus and Cressida* 2.3.189, *Measure for Measure* 2.4.12).
7. In his daily practice or exercise most steadfast.
8. *which . . . sound:* once affirmed, his faithfulness en-dured, always healthy and stable.
9. *unadvised . . . wounds:* compare "Here friend by friend in bloody channel lies, / And friend to friend gives unad-visèd wounds," *The Rape of Lucrece* 1487–88. *unadvised:* injudicious, unconsidered.
1. *Drew / Destruction:* punning on the name of Peter's killer. (Q has "*Drew*.")
2. Good men only begin to be honored at death.

350 For men whose pure simplicity[3] hath drawn
Their trust to be betray'd by being caught
Within the snares of making truth a pawn;
Whiles it,° not doubting whereinto it enters,   *(their trust)*
Without true proof and knowledge of a friend,
355 Sincere in singleness of heart, adventers°   *ventures*
To give fit cause, ere love begin to end:
   His unfeign'd friendship where it least was sought,
   Him to a fatal timeless ruin brought;
Whereby the life that purity adorn'd
360 With real merit, by this sudden end
Is in the mouth of some in manners scorn'd,
Made questionable, for they do intend,
According to the tenor of the saw[4]
Mistook° (if not observ'd, writ long ago   *Wrongly applied*
365 When men were only led by Reason's law),[5]
That "Such as is the end, the life proves so."
Thus he,° who to the universal lapse   *(Christ)*
Gave sweet redemption, off'ring up his blood
To conquer death by death, and loose the traps
370 Of hell,[6] even in the triumph that it stood:
He thus, for that his guiltless life was split
By death, which was made subject to the curse,
Might in like manner be reprov'd of guilt
In his pure life, for that his end was worse.
375 But O far be it, our unholy lips
Should so profane the deity above
As thereby to ordain revenging whips
Against the day of Judgment and of Love.[7]
The hand that lends us honor in our days
380 May shorten[8] when it please, and justly take
Our honor from us many sundry ways,
As best becomes that wisdom did us make.[9]
The second brother,° who was next begot   *Abel*
Of all that ever were begotten yet,
385 Was by a hand in vengeance rude and hot
Sent innocent to be in heaven set—
Whose fame the angels in melodious quires°   *choirs*
Still witness to the world. Then why should he,[1]
Well-profited in excellent desires,
390 Be more rebuk'd, who had like destiny?
Those saints before the everlasting throne
Who sit with crowns of glory on their heads,
Wash'd white in blood,[2] from earth hence have not gone
All to their joys in quiet on their beds,

---

3. Untainted sincerity; honest naiveté.
4. The import of the old proverb.
5. *writ . . . law:* written in the Golden Age, when men were guided by reason (but perhaps not observed even then).
6. *loose . . . hell:* break open the gates; open up the snares; containing, perhaps, a suggestion that Christ provides a release from sinful ensnarements, including the poet's own past attachment to the stage—a symbolic bursting of the trapdoors to the understage, called "Hell."
7. *to ordain . . . Love:* to justify God's scourge prepared for the coming day of eternal judgment and salvation; to

sanction whips of punishment against those "days of youth" (line 559) in which the poet's love was misconstrued, and wrongly judged, as sinful.
8. Draw back; withdraw its support.
9. As best suits the wise God that made us.
1. William Peter, a younger brother who like Abel was slain by a kinsman, though innocent.
2. *saints . . . blood:* saints whose souls were redeemed by Christ ("washed . . . white in the blood of the Lamb," Revelation 7:14); martyrs whose pallid corpses were steeped in their own blood.

395 But tasted of the sour-bitter scourge
Of torture and affliction ere they gained
Those blessings which their sufferance did urge,
Whereby the grace fore-promis'd they attained.
Let then the false suggestions of the froward,[3]
400 Building large castles in the empty air,
By suppositions fond° and thoughts untoward°   *foolish / perverse*
(Issues of discontent and sick despair)
Rebound gross arguments upon their heart
That may disprove their malice, and confound
405 Uncivil loose opinions which insert
Their souls into the roll[4] that doth unsound[5]
Betraying policies, and show their brains,
Unto their shame, ridiculous; whose scope
Is envy,[6] whose endeavors° fruitless pains,   *endeavors are*
410 In nothing surely prosperous, but hope°—   *but in hope*
And that same hope, so lame, so unprevailing,
It buries self-conceit in weak opinion;
Which being cross'd, gives matter of bewailing
Their vain designs, on whom[7] want hath dominion.
415 Such, and of such condition, may devise
Which way to wound with defamation's spirit
(Close-lurking whisper's hidden forgeries)
His° taintless goodness, his desertful merit.   *(William Peter's)*
But whiles the minds of men can judge sincerely,
420 Upon assured knowledge, his repute
And estimation shall be rumor'd clearly
In equal worth—time shall to time renew 't.
The Grave—that in his ever-empty womb
Forever closes up the unrespected
425 Who, when they die, die all[8]—shall not entomb
His pleading best perfections as neglected.[9]
They to his notice in succeeding years
Shall speak for him when he shall lie below;
When nothing but his memory appears
430 Of what he was, then shall his virtues grow.
His being but a private man in rank
(And yet not rank'd beneath a gentleman)
Shall not abridge the commendable thank°   *thankfulness*
Which wise posterity shall give him then;[1]
435 For Nature, and his therein happy Fate,
Ordain'd that by his quality of mind
T' ennoble that best part, although his state°   *social rank*
Were to a lower blessedness[2] confin'd.
Blood, pomp, state, honor, glory and command,
440 Without fit ornaments of disposition,

---

3. The insinuations of the impudent.
4. Q has "roule," a frequent Jacobean spelling for both "roll" and "role".
5. Prove as unsound; silence.
6. *whose . . . envy:* (slanderers) who are motivated only by their envy.
7. On which; an instance of Shakespearean "who," having an inanimate, unpersonified antecedent (rare outside Shakespeare); again at lines 516, 520, 563.
8. Utterly expire, even from human memory.

9. *shall . . . neglected:* Peter's virtues shall successfully plead (with the voracious grave) for continued life, though Peter has himself perished.
1. *abridge . . . then:* in Q, which has "abridge . . . thanke . . . than," this makes an orthographic pun known as an *antanaclasis*; compare "end, / Abridg'd . . . endeavors" (lines 1–4).
2. That is, the blessings of ordinary private life (compare Cardinal Wolsey, who after his fall "found the blessèdness of being little," *All Is True* 4.2.66).

Are in themselves but heathenish and profane,[3]
And much more peaceful is a mean condition
Which, underneath the roof of safe content,
Feeds on the bread of rest, and takes delight
445 To look upon the labors it hath spent
For its own sustenance, both day and night;
Whiles others, plotting which way to be great,
How to augment their portion and ambition,
Do toil their giddy brains, and ever sweat
450 For popular applause and power's commission.[4]
But one in honors, like a seeled dove[5]
Whose inward eyes are dimm'd with dignity,°   *by glamour and prestige*
Does think most safety doth remain above
And seeks to be secure by mounting high:
455 Whence, when he falls, who did erewhile aspire,
Falls deeper down, for that° he climbed higher.   *because*
Now men who in a lower region live
Exempt from danger of authority[6]
Have fittest times in Reason's rules to thrive,
460 Not vex'd with envy of priority,
 And those are much more noble in the mind
 Than many that have nobleness by kind.°   *by birth*
Birth, blood, and ancestors, are none of ours,[7]
Nor can we make a proper challenge to them,
465 But virtues and perfections in our powers
Proceed most truly from us, if we do them.
Respective titles or a gracious style,
With all what men in eminence possess,
Are, without ornaments to praise them, vile:
470 The beauty of the mind is nobleness.
And such as have that beauty, well deserve
Eternal characters,° that after death   *Everlasting inscriptions*
Remembrance of their worth we may preserve
So that their glory die not with their breath.
475 Else what avails it in a goodly strife
Upon this face of earth here to contend,
The good t' exceed the wicked in their life,
Should both be like obscured in their end?
Until which end, there is none rightly can
480 Be termed happy, since the happiness
Depends upon the goodness of the man,
Which afterwards his praises will express.
Look hither then, you that enjoy the youth
Of your best days, and see how unexpected
485 Death can betray your jollity to ruth°   *remorse*

---

3. Q reads, "prophane," possibly a misprint for "pro-
phand" (that is, "profan'd").
4. *Do . . . commission:* possibly with a note of self-mock-
ery from a poet who, with his own "plotting" (plot mak-
ing, line 447), seeks not only figurative but literal
applause from the masses.
5. In falconry, a pigeon with its eyes stitched shut so as to
make it climb higher; compare lines 451–56 with Sidney:

> Like as the Dove which seeled up doth flie,
> . . . .
> But hopes to gaine some helpe by mounting hie,

Till want of force do force her fall to ground.
Right so my minde, caught by his guiding eye
And thence cast off, where his sweet hurt he found,
Hath neither leave to live, nor doome to dye.
      (*Certaine Sonets* 15.1–7)

6. *live . . . authority:* live free from the corrupting influ-
ence of power; live private lives not vulnerable to author-
ity's censure.
7. High birth, noble blood, distinguished ancestors (nei-
ther Peter nor the poet are of noble descent).

When death you think is least to be respected!
The person of this model here set out
Had all that youth and happy days could give him,
Yet could not all-encompass him about
490 Against th'assault of death, who to relieve him
Struck home but to the frail and mortal parts
Of his humanity,[8] but could not touch
His flourishing and fair long-liv'd deserts,
Above fate's reach, his singleness was such—
495 So that he dies but once, but doubly lives,
Once in his proper self, then in his name;
Predestinated Time, who all deprives,
Could never yet deprive him of the same.
And had the Genius[9] which attended on him
500 Been possibilited[1] to keep him safe
Against the rigor that hath overgone him,
He had been to the public use a staff,
Leading by his example in the path
Which guides to doing well, wherein so few
505 The proneness of this age to error hath
Informed rightly in the courses true.[2]
As then the loss of one, whose inclination
Strove to win love in general, is sad,
So specially his friends, in soft compassion
510 Do feel the greatest loss they could have had.
Amongst them all, she who those nine of years[3]
Liv'd fellow to his counsels and his bed[4]
Hath the most share in loss: for I in hers[5]
Feel what distemperature[6] this chance hath bred.
515 The chaste embracements of conjugal love,
Who° in a mutual harmony consent,   *Which (embracements)*
Are so impatient of a strange remove
As meager[7] death itself seems to lament,
And weep upon those cheeks° which nature fram'd   *(of Peter's widow)*
520 To be delightful orbs in whom° the force   *which*
Of lively sweetness plays, so that asham'd
Death often pities his unkind divorce.
Such was the separation here constrain'd
(Well-worthy to be termed a rudeness° rather),   *unruliness; violence*
525 For in his life his love was so unfeign'd
As he was both an husband and a father[8]—
The one in firm affection and the other

8. *Yet ... humanity*: Assailed by death, inadequately shielded by his youth, Peter was partly relieved by death's inability to destroy him utterly.
9. Tutelary god or attendant spirit; possibly also the poet himself as Peter's attendant friend (compare lines 541ff.).
1. Enabled (compare "Necessitied," *All's Well That Ends Well* 5.3.86).
2. *so few ... true*: the general inclination in our time toward error has guided few persons in a proper course.
3. This allusion is a puzzle. In 1602–3, Peter's wife, Margaret Brewton, was an eleven-year-old girl living with her parents in Exeter while Peter was in Oxford; she and Peter had been married for three years at the time of his death (January 1609–January 1612). A contrast is perhaps implied between Peter's chaste conjugal love (lines 515–29) and an overheated relationship with another woman

(lines 509–14), a friend (line 509) during his nine years away from home (June 1599 to autumn 1608).
4. Compare John Ford's *Funeral Poem*, in which he speaks of William Godolphin's love for Charles Blount (1606): "So mayest thou, knightly youth, who wert his friend, / Companion to his chamber and his bed" (lines 259–60).
5. For I, by sharing in that loss.
6. Distempered condition; perhaps also, ironically, loss of sexual heat.
7. Emaciated, skeletal; unsatisfied (compare death's "meagre, lean, / Hateful divorce of love," *Venus and Adonis* 931–32).
8. Peter was survived by a daughter, Rose, aged two; a second daughter, Margaret, was born posthumously.

In careful providence, which ever strove
With joint assistance to grace one another[9]
530 With every helpful furtherance of love.
But since the sum of all that can be said
Can be but said that[1] "He was good" (which wholly
Includes all excellence can be display'd
In praise of virtue and reproach of folly).
535   His due deserts, this sentence on him gives,[2]
"He died in life, yet in his death he lives."
Now runs the method of this doleful song[3]
In accents brief[4] to thee, O thou deceas'd!
To whom those pains do only all belong[5]
540 As witnesses I did not love thee least.
For could my worthless brain find out but how
To raise thee from the sepulcher of dust,
Undoubtedly thou shouldst have partage° now   *portion, share*
Of life with me, and heaven be counted just
545 If to a supplicating soul it would
Give life anew, by giving life again[6]
Where life is miss'd; whereby discomfort should
Right his old griefs, and former joys retain
Which now with thee are leap'd into thy tomb
550 And buried in that hollow vault of woe,
Expecting yet a more severer doom°   *an even harsher judgment*
Than time's strict flinty[7] hand will let 'em know.
And now if I have level'd mine account°   *paid my debt*
And reckon'd up in a true measured score
555 Those perfect graces which were ever wont°   *accustomed*
To wait on thee alive, I ask no more
(But shall hereafter in a poor content[8]
Immure those imputations I sustain,[9]
Learning my days of youth so to prevent[1]
560 As not to be cast down by them again)—
Only those hopes which fate denies to grant
In full possession to a captive heart[2]
Who, if it were in plenty,[3] still would want
Before it° may enjoy his° better part;   *(my heart) / (my friend's)*
565 From which detain'd, and banish'd in th' exile
Of dim misfortune, has none other prop
Whereon to lean and rest itself the while
But the weak comfort of the hapless, Hope.[4]
And Hope must in despite of fearful change

---

9. which . . . another: his roles as husband and father lent grace each to the other.
1. the sum. . . that: the sum of all one can say of him can only be expressed in the simple thought.
2. His deservings fully justify this epigrammatic thought or verdict; compare *Richard Duke of York* 5.1.56–57, *Romeo and Juliet* 2.2.79–80, *All's Well That Ends Well* 1.3.66–69.
3. The course of this elegiac verse.
4. In brief speech ("brief" as adjective); in poetry's epistle ("brief" as noun).
5. To whom alone my poetic labor is devoted.
6. Give renewed life to the poet by giving life again to the deceased.
7. Unyielding, ungenerous (perhaps also suggesting the

precise, flintlike hands of a clock).
8. Satisfaction; matter contained in writing.
9. Bury (with Peter) those accusations leveled against me in my "days of youth" (line 559).
1. Remedy, thwart, counteract (compare sonnet 118.3, 2 *Henry IV* 1.2.211, *The Tragedy of King Lear* 3.4.147, *Timon of Athens* 5.2.88).
2. Only . . . heart: I ask (line 556) only for a fuller hope in the resurrection (which fate has not granted to me).
3. Who . . . plenty: That (a captive heart), even if my hopes were plentiful.
4. Except for hope, the poor consolation of hapless persons; except for the thin comfort of my hapless hope in our mutual salvation (Q omits the comma).

570 Play in the strongest closet⁵ of my breast,
Although perhaps I ignorantly range
And court opinion⁶ in my deep'st unrest.
But whether° doth the stream of my mischance   *even if; whither*
Drive me beyond myself, fast friend, soon lost,
575 Long may thy worthiness thy name advance
Amongst the virtuous and deserving most,
  Who° herein hast forever happy prov'd: *You who*
  In life thou liv'dst, in death thou died'st belov'd.⁷

FINIS

---

5. Chamber (as for a private theatrical performance by "Hope"); also, strongbox for valuables.
6. *range . . . opinion:* compare line 92; also sonnets 109–110.

7. That is, not as in the familiar epitaph "In life you died, in death you live," but simply: Though dead now, you lived and died beloved.

Documents

This selection of documents provides a range of contemporary testimony about Shakespeare's character, his work, and the social and institutional conditions under which it was produced. In the absence of newspapers and reviewers, few references to the theater survive. The availability of such hints and fragments as are presented here serves as a mark of Shakespeare's distinction, for the theater was perceived by much of the literate population as ephemeral popular entertainment. The reports of spectators whose accounts we have are more like reviews than any other texts the period has to offer; hence the importance even of brief notes such as Nashe's or Platter's, and the particular value of extended accounts such as those of Simon Forman. The government documents included here offer a vivid glimpse of the institutional procedures by which the theater was regulated. The legal documents—a contract for the construction of a theater modeled on the Globe, and Shakespeare's will—provide the most detailed account available of the material conditions of his life and work. The poems, extracts from criticism, and other literary texts show the diversity of contemporary response to his art.

The source for each text is given at the end of the introductory headnote.

WS: E. K. Chambers, *William Shakespeare: A Study of Facts and Problems*. 2 vols. Oxford: Clarendon Press, 1930.
ES: E. K. Chambers, *The Elizabethan Stage*. 4 vols. Oxford: Clarendon Press, 1923.

Robert Greene on Shakespeare (1592)

[Robert Greene (1560–1592), a prolific author of plays, romances, and pamphlets, attacked Shakespeare in his *Greenes Groats-worth of Wit, bought with a million of Repentaunce*. Greene had studied at Cambridge, and his "M.A." was prominently displayed on his title pages. Shakespeare's lack of a university education is clearly one motive for the professional resentment of the following excerpt. Another is probably that Greene was poor and very ill and felt forsaken while writing the *Groats-worth of Wit*; the preface refers to it as his "Swanne-like song," and the narrative is framed as the repentance of a dying man. (Some scholars have held that the posthumously published work contains fabrications by a publisher attempting to capitalize on Greene's name.) The three colleagues Greene addresses are likely to be Christopher Marlowe, Thomas Nashe, and George Peele. The text is that of 1596, as printed in Alexander B. Grosart's edition of Greene's *Life and Complete Works*, vol. 12 (New York: Russell and Russell).]

> To those Gentlemen his *Quondam* acquaintance,
> that spend their wits in making Plaies, R. G.
> wisheth a better exercise, and wisdome
> to prevent his extremities. . . .

Base minded men al three of you, if by my miserie ye be not warned: for unto none of you (like me) fought those burres to cleave: those Puppits (I meane) that speake from our mouths, those Anticks garnisht in our colours. Is it not strange that I, to whom they al have beene beholding: is it not like that you, to whome they all have beene beholding, shall (were ye in that case that I am now) be both at once of them forsaken? Yes trust them not: for there is an upstart Crow, beautified with our feathers, that with his *Tygers heart wrapt in a Players hide*,[1] *supposes he is as well able to bumbast out a blanke verse as the best of you: and being an absolute Johannes fac totum*,[2] is in his owne conceit the onely Shake-scene in a countrie. O that I might intreate your rare wits to be imployed in more profitable courses: & let those Apes imitate your past excellence, and never more acquaint them with your admired inventions. I know the best husband[3] of you all will never prove an Usurer, and the kindest of them / all will never proove a kinde nurse: yet whilst you may, seeke you better Maisters; for it is pittie men of such rare wits, should be subject to the pleasures of such rude groomes.

Thomas Nashe on *1 Henry VI* (1592)

[Thomas Nashe (1567–1601), Greene's fellow playwright and pamphleteer, protests the attribution to himself of the *Groats-worth of Wit* in the preface to the 1592 edition of a pamphlet of his own, *Pierce Penilesse his Supplication to the Divell*. The satire of *Pierce Penilesse* is more general and political than that of the *Groats-worth*, attacking the manners of the middle class. The allusion to the Talbot scenes of *1 Henry VI* (4.2–7) comes in a section subtitled "The defence of Playes." Talbot is supposed to have been played by Richard Burbage, later the leading actor of the Lord Chamberlain's and King's Men. The text is from McKerrow's 1904 edition of Nashe's *Works*, vol. 1 (London: Bullen).]

How would it have joyed brave *Talbot* (the terror of the French) to thinke that after he had lyne two hundred yeares in his Tombe, hee should triumphe againe on the Stage, and have his bones newe embalmed with the teares of ten thousand spectators at least (at severall times), who, in the Tragedian that represents his person, imagine they behold him fresh bleeding.

Henry Chettle on Greene and Shakespeare (1592)

[Henry Chettle was involved in publishing Greene's *Groats-worth of Wit* and saw fit several months afterward to offer an apology for Greene's unfavorable treatment of Shakespeare. Chettle's willingness to serve as a kind of character witness for Shakespeare ("the other" playwright of whom he writes) may testify to Shakespeare's growing reputation. The first playwright Chettle mentions, of whom he writes more unfavorably, is Christopher Marlowe. The text is from Chettle's introductory epistle to a literary work of his own, entitled *Kind-Harts Dreame*, as reprinted in WS, vol. 2.]

About three moneths since died M. *Robert Greene*, leaving many papers in sundry Booke sellers hands, among other his Groatsworth of wit, in which a letter written to divers play-makers, is offensively by one or two of them taken; and because on the dead they cannot be avenged, they wilfully forge in their conceites[1] a living Author: and after tossing it to and fro, no remedy, but it must light on me. How I have all the time of my conversing in printing hindered the bitter inveying against schollers, it hath been very well knowne; and how in that I dealt, I can sufficiently proove. With neither of them that take offence was I acquainted, and with one of them I care not if I never be: The other, whome at that time I did not so much spare, as since I wish I had, for that as I have moderated the heate of living writers, and might have usde my owne discretion (especially in such a case) the Author beeing dead, that I did not, I

---

1. A parody of *Richard Duke of York (3 Henry VI)* 1.4.138: "O tiger's heart wrapped in a woman's hide!" This obvious allusion and the following pun on Shakespeare's name make it certain that Shakespeare is the

"crow" described here.
2. Jack-of-all-trades. *conceit*: imagination.
3. Steward.
1. Imaginations.

am as sory as if the originall fault had beene my fault, because my selfe have seene his demeanor no lesse civill than he exelent in the qualitie he professes: Besides, divers of worship[2] have reported his uprightnes of dealing, which argues his honesty, and his facetious grace in writting, that aprooves[3] his Art.

Gesta Grayorum on The Comedy of Errors (December 28, 1594)

[Gesta Grayorum is the title of an account of the holiday revels conducted by the law students of Gray's Inn. It was first published in 1688 (hence the modern spelling) from a manuscript that apparently had been handed down since the previous century. The subtitle of the book, "History of the High and mighty Prince, Henry Prince of Purpoole," alludes to the ceremonial ruler chosen for the occasion, the "Prince of State" referred to in the excerpt below. The performance of The Comedy of Errors was evidently part of the entertainment for the second night of revels. The text is from the 1968 reprint of Desmond Bland (Liverpool: Liverpool University Press).]

The next grand Night was intended to be upon Innocents-Day at Night; at which time there was a great Presence of Lords, Ladies, and worshipful Personages, that did expect some notable Performance at that time; which, indeed, had been effected, if the multitude of Beholders had not been so exceeding great, that thereby there was no convenient room for those that were Actors; by reason whereof, very good Inventions and Conceipts could not have opportunity to be applauded, which otherwise would have been great Contentation to the Beholders. Against which time, our Friend, the Inner Temple,[1] determined to send their Ambassador to our Prince of State, as sent from Frederick Templarius, their Emperor, who was then busied in his Wars against the Turk. The Ambassador came very gallantly appointed, and attended by a great number of brave Gentlemen, which arrived at our Court about Nine of the Clock at Night. . . . He was received very kindly of the Prince, and placed in a Chair besides His Highness, to the end that he might be Partaker of the Sports intended. . . .

When the Ambassador was placed, as aforesaid, and that there was something to be performed for the Delight of the Beholders, there arose such a disordered Tumult and Crowd upon the Stage, that there was no Opportunity to effect that which was intended: There came so great a number of worshipful Personages upon the Stage, that might not be displaced; and Gentlewomen, whose Sex did privilege them from Violence, that when the Prince and his Officers had in vain, a good while, expected and endeavoured a Reformation, at length there was no hope of Redress for that present. The Lord Ambassador and his Train thought that they were not so kindly entertained, as was before expected, and thereupon would not stay any longer at that time, but, in a sort,[2] discontented and displeased. After their Departure the Throngs and Tumults did somewhat cease, although so much of them continued, as was able to disorder and confound any good Inventions whatsoever. In regard whereof, as also for that the Sports intended were especially for the gracing of the Templarians, it was thought good not to offer any thing of Account, saving Dancing and Revelling with Gentlewomen; and after such Sports, a Comedy of Errors (like to Plautus his Menechmus) was played by the Players. So that Night was begun, and continued to the end, in nothing but Confusion and Errors; whereupon, it was ever afterwards called, The Night of Errors. . . .

The next Night upon this Occasion, we preferred Judgments thick and threefold, which were read publicly by the Clerk of the Crown, being all against a Sorcerer or Conjurer that was supposed to be the Cause of that confused Inconvenience. Therein

---

2. divers of worship: various men of rank. qualitie he professes: his vocation.
3. Demonstrates. facetious: polished, agreeable.

1. Another of the Inns of Court.
2. Departed.

was contained, How he had caused the Stage to be built, and Scaffolds to be reared to the top of the House, to increase Expectation. Also how he had caused divers Ladies and Gentlewomen, and others of good Condition, to be invited to our Sports; also our dearest Friend, the State of *Templaria*, to be disgraced, and disappointed of their kind Entertainment, deserved and intended. Also that he caused Throngs and Tumults, Crowds and Outrages, to disturb our whole Proceedings. And Lastly, that he had foisted a Company of base and common Fellows,[3] to make up our Disorders with a Play of Errors and Confusions; and that that Night had gained to us Discredit, and it self a Nickname of Errors. All which were against the Crown and Dignity of our Sovereign Lord, the Prince of *Purpoole*. . . .

The next grand Night was upon *Twelfth-day* at Night. . . . First, There came six Knights of the Helmet, with three that they led as Prisoners, and were attired like Monsters and Miscreants. The Knights gave the Prince to understand, that as they were returning from their Adventures out of *Russia*, wherein they aided the Emperor of *Russia*, against the *Tartars*, they surprized these three Persons, which were conspiring against His Highness and Dignity.[4] . . . Which being done, the Trumpets were commanded to sound, and then the King at Arms came in before the Prince, and told His Honour, that there was arrived an Ambassador from the mighty Emperor of *Russia* and *Moscovy*, that had some Matters of Weight to make known to His Highness. So the Prince willed that he should be admitted into his Presence; who came in Attire of *Russia*, accompanied with two of his own Country, in like Habit.

Francis Meres on Shakespeare (1598)

[Francis Meres (1565–1647) was educated at Cambridge and was active in London literary circles in 1597–98, after which he became a rector and schoolmaster in the country. The descriptions of Shakespeare are taken from a section on poetry in *Palladis Tamia, Wits Treasury*, a work largely consisting of translated classical quotations and *exempla*. Unlike the main body of the work, the subsections on poetry, painting, and music include comparisons of English artists to figures of antiquity. Meres goes on after the extract below to list Shakespeare among the best English writers for lyric, tragedy, comedy, elegy, and love poetry. The text is from D. C. Allen's 1933 edition of the section "Poetrie" (Urbana: University of Illinois).]

From XI

As the Greeke tongue is made famous and eloquent by *Homer, Hesiod, Euripedes, Aeschilus, Sophocles, Pindarus, Phocylides* and *Aristophanes*; and the Latine tongue by *Virgill, Ovid, Horace, Silius Italicus, Lucanus, Lucretius, Ausonius* and *Claudianus*: so the English tongue is mightily enriched, and gorgeouslie invested in rare ornaments and resplendent abiliments by Sir *Philip Sidney, Spencer, Daniel, Drayton, Warner, Shakespeare, Marlow* and *Chapman*.

From XIV

As the soule of *Euphorbus* was thought to live in *Pythagoras*: so the sweete wittie soule of Ovid lives in mellifluous & honytongued *Shakespeare*, witnes his *Venus* and *Adonis*, his *Lucrece*, his sugred Sonnets.

From XV

As *Plautus* and *Seneca* are accounted the best for Comedy and Tragedy among the Latines: so *Shakespeare* among ye English is the most excellent in both kinds for

---

3. That is, the actors.
4. This last paragraph has been included because of the theory that this ostensible visit of the Russian ambassa-

dor to the court of the Prince of Purpoole provided a model for the masque of Muscovites in *Love's Labour's Lost* 5.2.

the stage; for Comedy, witnes his *Gĕtlemĕ of Verona,* his *Errors,* his *Love labors lost,* his *Love labours wonne,*[1] his *Midsummers night dreame,* & his *Merchant of Venice:* for Tragedy his *Richard the 2. Richard the 3. Henry the 4. King John, Titus Andronicus* and his *Romeo* and *Juliet.*

As *Epius Stolo* said, that the Muses would speake with *Plautus* tongue, if they would speak Latin: so I say that the Muses would speak with *Shakespeares* fine filed phrase, if they would speake English.

Parnassus Plays on Shakespeare (1598–1601)

[The three *Parnassus* plays, *The Pilgrimage to Parnassus* and *The Return from Parnassus, Parts 1* and *2,* were performed at Christmastime, probably in 1598, 1599, and 1601, by students of St. John's College, Cambridge. The references to Shakespeare and other contemporary writers are frequently ironic or equivocal. In the excerpts from *The Return, Part 1,* Ingenioso is an aspiring poet and Gullio a fop. In the second excerpt, Ingenioso is presenting the verses requested in the previous excerpt, having begun with examples in the vein or style of Chaucer and Spenser. Ingenioso returns in *Part 2* to discuss the merits of contemporary poets with Judicio (a critic). In the last two excerpts, Richard Burbage and Will Kempe, famous actors and colleagues of Shakespeare, turn up to try recruiting students as actors for their company "at a low rate" of pay. Burbage auditions one of them for the part of Richard III. The text is from J. B. Leishman's edition of 1949 (London: Nicholson and Watson).]

The Return from Parnassus, Part 1
ACT 3, SCENE 1

GULLIO Suppose also that thou wert my M^ris, as somtime woodden statues represent the goddesses, thus I woulde looke amorously, thus I would pace, thus I woulde salute thee.

INGENIOSO It will be my lucke to dye noe other death than by hearinge of his follies, I feare this speach thats a comīnge will breede a deadly disease in my ears.

GULLIO Pardon faire lady, thoughe sicke thoughted Gullio maks a maine unto thee, & like a bould faced sutore gins to woo thee.[1]

INGENIOSO We shall have nothinge but pure Shakspeare, and shreds of poetrie that he hath gathered at the theators.

GULLIO Pardon mee moy mittressa, ast am a gentleman the moone in comparison of thy bright hue[2] a meere slutt, Anthonies Cleopatra a blacke browde milkmaide, Hellen a dowdie.[3]

INGENIOSO Marke Romeo and Juliet: o monstrous theft, I thinke he will runn throughe a whole booke of Samuell Daniells.[4]

GULLIO Thrise fairer than my selfe, thus I began,
The gods faire riches, sweete above compare,
Staine to all Nimphes, [m]ore lovely the[n][5] a man,
More white and red than doves and roses are:
Nature that made thee, with herselfe had strife,
Saith that the worlde hath ending with thy life.[6]

INGENIOSO Sweete Mr Shakspeare.

GULLIO As I am a scholler, these arms of mine are long and strong withall:
Thus elms by vines are compast ere they falle.

1. The play—or at least the title—has not survived; a bookseller's record of the title does survive, however.
1. *sicke . . . thee:* compare *Venus and Adonis,* lines 5–6. Of the numerous quotations and allusions, only those referring to Shakespeare are identified.
2. *Is. ast:* as I.
3. *Anthonies . . . dowdie:* compare *Romeo and Juliet*

2.3.37.
4. Probably Samuel Daniel's sonnet sequence *Delia.*
5. *more lovely then:* correction is based on *Venus and Adonis;* other slight errors or misquotations are left uncorrected.
6. *Thrise . . . life:* compare *Venus and Adonis,* lines 7–12. *had strife:* the phrase in Shakespeare is "at strife."

INGENIOSO   Faith gentleman, youre reading is wonderfull in our English poetts.

GULLIO   Sweet M^{ris}, I vouchsafe to take some of there wordes and applie them to mine owne matters by a scholasticall imitation. Report thou upon thy credit, is not my vayne in courtinge gallant & honorable?

INGENIOSO   Admirable sanes compare, never was soe mellifluous a witt joynet to so pure a phrase, such comly gesture, suche gentleman like behaviour.

GULLIO   But stay, its verie true, good wittes have badd memories: I had almoste forgotten the cheife pointe I cald thee out for: new years day approcheth, and wheras other gallants bestowe Jewells upon there Mistrisses (as I have done whilome), I now count it base to do as the comon people doe; I will bestow upon them the precious stons of my witt, a diamonde of Invention, that shall be above all value & esteeme; therfore, sithens I am employed in some weightie affayrs of the courte, I will have thee, Ingenioso, to make them, and when thou hast done, I will peruse, pollish, and correcte them.

INGENIOSO   My pen is youre bounden vassall to comande, but what vayne woulde it please you to have them in?

GULLIO   Not in a vaine veine (prettie y faith): make mee them in two or three divers vayns, in Chaucers, Gowers and Spencers, and Mr Shakspeares. Marry I thinke I shall entertaine[7] those verses which run like these:

   Even as the sunn with purple coloured face
   Had tane his laste leave on the weeping morne,[8] etc.

O sweet Mr Shakspeare, Ile have his picture in my study at the courte.

INGENIOSO   Take heede my maisters, hele kill you with tediousness ere I can ridd him of the stage.

ACT 4, SCENE 1

GULLIO   Youe schollers are simple felowes, men that never came where Ladies growe; I that have spente my life amonge them knowes best what becometh my pen, and theire Ladishipps ears. Let mee heare Mr Shakspears veyne.

INGENIOSO   Faire Venus, queene of beutie and of love,
Thy red doth stayne the blushinge of the morne,
Thy snowie neck shameth the milke white dove,
Thy presence doth this naked worlde adorne;
Gazinge on thee all other nymphes I scorne,
When ere thou dyest slowe shine that Satterday,
Beutie and grace muste sleepe with thee for aye.

GULLIO   Noe more, I am one that can judge accordinge to the proverbe *bovem ex unguibus*.[9] Ey marry S^r, these have some life in them: let this duncified worlde esteeme of Spēcer and Chaucer, Ile worshipp sweet Mr Shakspeare, and to honoure him will lay his *Venus and Adonis* under my pillowe, as wee reade of one[1] (I do not well remember his name, but I am sure he was a kinge) slept with Homer under his beds heade. Well, Ile bestowe a Frenche crowne in the faire writinge of them out, and then Ile instructe thee about the delivery of them. Meane while, Ile have thee make an elegant description of my M^{ris}; liken the worste part of her to Cynthia, make also a familiar Dialogue betwixt her and my selfe. Ile now in, and correct these verses.   *Exit.*

INGENIOSO   Why, who coulde endure this post put into a sattin sute, this haberdasher of lyes, this Bracchidochio,[2] this Ladye munger, this meere rapier and dagger, this cringer, this foretopp, but a man thats ordayned to miserie?

---

7. Accept; prefer.
8. *Euen . . . morne*: compare *Venus and Adonis*, lines 1–2.
9. [One may know] the bull by his hoof: Gullio's cor-

ruption of the proverb *Leonem ex unguibus æstimare* (The lion is known by his claws).
1. Alexander the Great.
2. Braggart.

The Return from Parnassus, Part 2
ACT 1, SCENE 2

INGENIOSO *Benjamin Johnson.*
JUDICIO The wittiest fellow of a Bricklayer in England.
INGENIOSO A meere Empyrick, one that getts what he hath by observation, and makes onely nature privy to what he endites; so slow an Inventor, that he were better betake himselfe to his old trade of Bricklaying; a bould whorson, as confident now in making of a booke, as he was in times past in laying of a brick.

William Shakespeare.
JUDICIO Who loves not *Adons* love, or *Lucrece* rape?
His sweeter verse contaynes hart robbing lines,
Could but a graver subject him content,
Without loves foolish lazy languishment.

ACT 4, SCENE 3

KEMPE Few of the uniuersity [men] pen plaies well, they smell too much of that writer *Ovid,* and that writer *Metamorphoses,*[3] and talke too much of *Proserpina &* *Juppiter.* Why heres our fellow *Shakespeare* puts them all downe, I and *Ben Jonson* too. O that *Ben Jonson* is a pestilent fellow, he brought up *Horace* giving the Poets a pill, but our fellow *Shakespeare* hath given him a purge that made him beray his credit.[4]
BURBAGE Its a shrewd fellow indeed. I wonder these schollers stay so long, they appointed to be here presently that we might try them: oh here they come.

ACT 4, SCENE 4

BURBAGE I like your face and the proportion of your body for *Richard* the 3., I pray [you] M. *Philomusus* let me see you act a little of it.
PHILOMUSUS Now is the winter of our discontent
Made glorious summer by the sonne of Yorke, [&c.]
BURBAGE Very well I assure you.

Epilogue to the Queen, possibly by Shakespeare (1599)

[This epilogue was copied into a commonplace book by Henry Stanford, a retainer of the household of the Lord Chamberlain, who was also the official patron of Shakespeare's company. Shakespeare was the chief writer for the company, and the epilogue could have followed a court performance by the Lord Chamberlain's Men recorded for Shrove Tuesday, February 20, 1599, matching the year (1598 by the old calendar) and period (Shrovetide, the three days preceding Lent) specified in the heading and the text, respectively. The scholars who discovered the manuscript argue that the poem matches Shakespeare's style more closely than that of other potential authors. The text is taken from the article in which its discovery was first announced, in *Modern Philology* 70 (1972): 138–39.]

3. The title of a work by Ovid, not another "writer." The playwright here mocks the supposed ignorance of a mere player.
4. *he brought . . . credit:* this is a reference to the so-called War of the Theaters, a polemic involving Jonson against fellow playwrights John Marston and Thomas Dekker.

to ye Q. by ye players 1598.

As the diall hand tells ore /
ye same howers yt had before
still beginning in ye ending /
circuler account still lending
So most mightie Q. we pray /
like ye diall day by day
you may lead ye seasons on /
making new when old are gon.
that the babe wch now is yong /
& hathe yet no use of tongue
many a shrovetyde here may bow /
to ye empresse I doe now
that the children of these lordes /
sitting at your counsell bourdes
may be grave & aeged seene /
of her ye was ther father Quene
once I wishe this wishe again /
heaven subscribe yt wth amen.

John Weever on Shakespeare (1599)

[This sonnet, which follows the "Shakespearean" rhyme scheme, was published in a col-
lection entitled *Epigrammes in the oldest Cut, and newest Fashion*. Like many of the other
references to Shakespeare's writings in this period, Weever's poem pays less attention to
the plays than to the narrative poems, which were of higher literary status and (to judge,
for example, from the *Parnassus* plays) popular among young men of fashion. Weever
(1576–1632) was himself a student at Cambridge not long before this poem was published.
The text is from *WS*, vol. 2.]

Ad Gulielmum Shakespeare.

Honie-tongued Shakespeare when I saw thine issue
I swore *Apollo* got them[1] and none other,
Their rosie-tainted features cloth'd in tissue,[2]
Some heaven born goddesse said to be their mother:
Rose-checkt[3] Adonis with his amber tresses,
Faire fire-hot *Venus* charming him to love her,
Chaste *Lucretia* virgine-like her dresses,
Prowd lust-stung *Tarquine* seeking still to prove[4] her:
Romea Richard; more whose names I know not,
Their sugred tongues, and power attractive beuty
Say they are Saints althogh that Sts they shew not
For thousands vowes to them subjective dutie:[5]
They burn in love thy children *Shakespear* het them,
Go, wo thy Muse more Nymphish brood beget them.[6]

1. *when ... them*: Shakespeare's poetic productions
("issue") are so perfect they seem to have been created
(begotten) by the patron of poets, Apollo, himself. The
identification of Shakespeare's muse as goddess (line 4)
or nymph (line 14) continues the trope of divine inspira-
tion.
2. Rich fabric. *tainted*: tinted.
3. Cheeked.
4. Attempt.
5. *Their ... dutie*: Shakespeare's characters are so com-
pelling that they have elicited the devotion ordinarily
given to saints. Their actions may not be saintly ("Sts
they show not"), but "thousands" have given to them
the devotion a subject gives a sovereign.
6. *They burn ... them*: the antecedent for "they" is
"thousands" in line 12; with modern spelling and punc-
tuation, the couplet might read: "They burn in love; thy
children, Shakespeare, het [heated] them. / Go woo thy
muse, more nymphish brood beget them."

Thomas Platter on *Julius Caesar* (September 21, 1599)

[Thomas Platter (b. 1574), a Swiss traveler, recorded his experience at the Globe playhouse in an account of his travels. The German text is printed in WS 2:322.]

Den 21 Septembris nach dem Imbissessen, etwan umb zwey vhren, bin ich mitt meiner geselschaft v̇ber daz wasser gefahren, haben in dem streüwinen Dachhaus die Tragedy vom ersten Keyser Julio Caesare mitt ohngefahr 15 personen sehen gar artlich agieren; zu endt der Comedien dantzeten sie ihrem gebraucht nach gar v̇ber-ausz zierlich, ye zwen in mannes vndt 2 in weiber kleideren angethan, wunderbahr-lich mitt einanderen.

On the 21st of September after lunch, about two o'clock, I crossed the water [the Thames] with my party, and we saw the tragedy of the first emperor Julius Caesar acted very prettily in the house with the thatched roof, with about fifteen characters; at the end of the comedy, according to their custom, they danced with exceeding elegance, two each in men's and two in women's clothes, wonderfully together.

[Translated by Noah Heringman]

Gabriel Harvey on *Hamlet, Venus and Adonis,* and *The Rape of Lucrece* (1598–1603)

[Gabriel Harvey (c. 1550–1631), a scholar perhaps best remembered as the particular friend of Spenser, gave the following account of Shakespeare and other contemporaries in a long manuscript note in his copy of Speght's 1598 edition of Chaucer. The date of the note is uncertain, but internal evidence makes it highly unlikely to be later than 1603. The references to Shakespeare are brief but suggestive, and the note is useful both in providing a context for the appreciation of Shakespeare and for its characteristically keen assessment of the state of modern literature. The text is from G. C. Moore Smith's edition of *Gabriel Harvey's Marginalia* (Stratford-upon-Avon: Shakespeare Head Press, 1913).]

And now translated Petrarch, Ariosto, Tasso, & Bartas himself deserve curious comparison with Chaucer, Lidgate, & owre best Inglish, auncient & moderne. Amongst which, the Countesse of Pembrokes Arcadia, & the Faerie Queene ar now freshest in request: & Astrophil, & Amyntas ar none of the idlest pastimes of sum fine humanists. The Earle of Essex much commendes Albions England:[1] and not unwor-thily for diverse notable pageants, before, & in the Chronicle. Sum Inglish, & other Histories nowhere more sensibly described, or more inwardly discovered. The Lord Mountjoy makes the like account of Daniels peece of the Chronicle,[2] touching the Usurpation of Henrie of Bullingbrooke, which in deede is a fine, sententious, & poli-tique peece of Poetrie: as proffitable, as pleasurable. The younger sort takes much delight in Shakespeares Venus, & Adonis: but his Lucrece, & his tragedie of Hamlet, Prince of Denmarke, have it in them, to please the wiser sort. Or such poets: or better: or none.

Vilia miretur vulgus: mihi flavus Apollo
Pocula Castaliæ plena ministret aquæ:[3]

quoth Sir Edward Dier, betwene jest, & earnest. Whose written devises farr excell most of the sonets, and cantos in print. His Amaryllis, & Sir Walter Raleighs Cynthia,

---

1. By William Warner (1586).
2. *The Civil Wars Between the Two Houses of Lancaster and York* (1595).
3. "Let what is cheap excite the marvel of the crowd; for me may golden Apollo minister full cups from the Castalian fount" (Ovid, *Amores* 1.15.35–36, Loeb trans-lation). These lines also appear on the title page of Shakespeare's *Venus and Adonis* (1593).

how fine & sweet inventions? Excellent matter of emulation for Spencer, Constable, France, Watson, Daniel, Warner, Chapman, Silvester, Shakespeare, & the rest of owr florishing metricians. I looke for much, aswell in verse, as in prose, from mie two Oxford frends, Doctor Gager, & M. Hackluit: both rarely furnished for the purpose: & I have a phansie to Owens new Epigrams, as pithie as elegant, as plesant as sharp, & sumtime as weightie as breife: & amongst so manie gentle, noble, & royall spirits meethinkes I see sum heroical thing in the clowdes: mie soveraine hope. Axiophilus[4] shall forgett himself, or will remember to leave sum memorials behinde him: & to make an use of so manie rhapsodies, cantos, hymnes, odes, epigrams, sonets, & discourses, as at idle howers, or at flowing fitts he hath compiled. God knowes what is good for the world, & fitting for this age.

Contract for the Building of the Fortune Theatre (1600)

[This contract was drawn up between Philip Henslowe and Edward Alleyn, partners in the venture, and Peter Street, the carpenter (or general contractor) in charge of the construction. In fact, Alleyn seems to have put up all the money, £440 for the work specified in the contract in addition to £80 for decoration and considerable sums to acquire the lot and surrounding properties. Alleyn faced opposition from residents of the neighborhood, but he had secured the favor of key supporters, so that he was able to proceed with the construction. As the new home of the Lord Admiral's Men, the Fortune did in fact become a center of disturbances, with complaints coming to the Middlesex Bench of assaults, petty thefts, and riotous behavior. Alleyn had been the leading actor of the Lord Admiral's Men, chief competitors of the Lord Chamberlain's Men, and the Fortune was conceived to compete with the Globe, meanwhile replacing the decaying and poorly situated Rose Theatre. The contract's descriptions and frequent references to the Globe, given this background, can be seen as providing some of our best evidence on the nature of the Globe itself. The text is reprinted in *ES*, vol. 2.]

'This Indenture made the Eighte daie of Januarye 1599,[1] and in the Twoe and Fortyth yeare of the Reigne of our sovereigne Ladie Elizabeth, by the grace of god Queene of Englande, Fraunce and Irelande, defender of the Faythe, &c. betwene Phillipp Henslowe and Edwarde Allen of the parishe of S[te] Saviours in Southwark in the Countie of Surrey, gentlemen, on thone parte, and Peeter Streete, Cittizen and Carpenter of London, on thother parte witnesseth That whereas the saide Phillipp Henslowe & Edward Allen, the daie of the date hereof, have bargayned, compounded & agreed with the saide Peter Streete ffor the erectinge, buildinge & settinge upp of a new howse and Stadge for a Plaiehouse in and uppon a certeine plott or parcell of grounde appoynted oute for that purpose, scytuate and beinge nere Goldinge lane in the parishe of S[te] Giles withoute Cripplegate of London,[2] to be by him the saide Peeter Streete or somme other sufficyent woorkmen of his provideinge and appoyntemente and att his propper costes & chardges, for the consideracion hereafter in theis presentes expressed, made, erected, builded and sett upp in manner & forme followinge (that is to saie); The frame of the saide howse to be sett square[3] and to conteine ffowerscore foote of lawfull assize everye waie square withoutt and fiftie five foote of like assize square everye waie within, with a good suer and stronge foundacion of pyles, brick, lyme and sand bothe without & within, to be wroughte one foote of assize att the leiste above the grounde; And the saide fframe to conteine three Stories in heighth, the first or lower Storie to conteine Twelve foote of lawfull assize in

4. Probably Harvey himself.
1. 1600 (New Style).
2. *nere . . . London:* an area then in the northwest suburbs, literally outside Cripplegate and, like the Globe across the water, outside the jurisdiction of a City Coun-

cil often inimical to the theater.
3. This square shape was unusual; the outlines of comparable theaters of the period were round or polygonal (with more than four sides).

heighth, the second Storie Eleaven foote of lawfull assize in heigth, and the third or upper Storie to conteine Nyne foote of lawfull assize in heigth; All which Stories shall conteine Twelve foote and a halfe of lawfull assize in breadth througheoute, besides a juttey forwardes in either of the saide twoe upper Stories of Tenne ynches of lawfull assize, with ffower convenient divisions for gentlemens roomes,[4] and other sufficient and convenient divisions for Twoe pennie roomes, with necessarie seates to be placed and sett, aswell in those roomes as througheoute all the rest of the galleries of the saide howse, and with suchelike steares, conveyances & divisions withoute & within, as are made & contryved in and to the late erected Plaiehowse on the Banck in the saide parishe of S[te] Saviours called the Globe; With a Stadge and Tyreinge howse[5] to be made, erected & settupp within the saide fframe, with a shadowe or cover[6] over the saide Stadge, which Stadge shalbe placed & sett, as alsoe the stearecases of the saide fframe, in suche sorte as is prefigured in a plott[7] thereof drawen, and which Stadge shall conteine in length Fortie and Three foote of lawfull assize and in breadth to extende to the middle of the yarde[8] of the saide howse; The same Stadge to be paled in belowe with good, stronge and sufficyent newe oken bourdes, and likewise the lower Storie of the saide fframe withinside, and the same lower storie to be alsoe laide over and fenced with stronge yron pykes; And the saide Stadge to be in all other proporcions contryved and fashioned like unto the Stadge of the saide Plaie howse called the Globe; With convenient windowes and lightes glazed to the saide Tyreinge howse; And the saide fframe, Stadge and Stearecases to be covered with Tyle, and to have a sufficient gutter of lead to carrie & convey the water frome the coveringe of the saide Stadge to fall backwardes; And also all the saide fframe and the Stairecases thereof to be sufficyently enclosed withoute with lathe, lyme & haire, and the gentle-mens roomes and Twoe pennie roomes to be seeled[9] with lathe, lyme & haire, and all the fflowers of the saide Galleries, Stories and Stadge to be bourded with good & sufficyent newe deale bourdes of the whole thicknes, wheare need shalbe; And the saide howse and other thinges beforemencioned to be made & doen to be in all other contrivitions, conveyances, fashions, thinge and thinges effected, finished and doen according to the manner and fashion of the saide howse called the Globe, saveinge only that all the princypall and maine postes of the saide fframe and Stadge forwarde shalbe square and wroughte palasterwise,[1] with carved proporcions called Satiers[2] to be placed & sett on the topp of every of the same postes, and saveinge alsoe that the said Peeter Streete shall not be chardged with anie manner of pay[ntin]ge in or aboute the saide fframe howse or Stadge or anie parte thereof, nor rendringe[3] the walls within, nor seeling anie more or other roomes then the gentlemens roomes, Twoe pennie roomes and Stadge before remembred. Nowe theiruppon the saide Peeter Streete dothe covenant, promise and graunte ffor himself, his executours and administratours, to and with the saide Phillipp Henslowe and Edward Allen and either of them, and thexecutours and administratours of them and either of them, by theis presentes in manner & forme followeinge (that is to saie); That he the saide Peeter Streete, his executours or assignes, shall & will att his or their owne propper costes & chardges well, woorkmanlike & substancyallie make, erect, sett upp and fully finishe in and by all thinges, according to the true meaninge of theis presentes, with good, stronge and substancyall newe tymber and other necessarie stuff, all the saide fframe and other woorkes whatsoever in and uppon the saide plott or parcell of grounde (beinge not by anie aucthoretie restrayned, and haveinge ingres, egres & regres to doe the same) before the ffyve & twentith daie of Julie next commeinge after the date hereof; And

4. Something like the V.I.P. boxes of the present day.
5. "Attiring house," a dressing room and backstage area extending onto the rear of the stage.
6. A roof (known as "the heavens") partially covering the stage, supported by the pillars that also served as ver-satile pieces of scenery.
7. Plan.
8. *in breadth . . . yarde:* the stage would then extend

about twenty-seven feet into the yard, specified earlier as fifty-five feet square.
9. Coated both on the "ceiling" (a related word) and the walls.
1. Finished in the form of pilasters, ornamental col-umns in the classical style.
2. Satyrs. *proporcions:* figures.
3. Plastering.

shall alsoe at his or theire like costes and chardges provide and finde all manner of
woorkmen, tymber, joystes, rafters, boordes, dores, boltes, hinges, brick, tyle, lathe,
lyme, haire, sande, nailes, lade, iron, glasse, woorkmanshipp and other thinges whatso-
ever, which shalbe needefull, convenyent & necessarie for the saide fframe &
woorkes & everie parte thereof; And shall alsoe make all the saide fframe in every
poynte for Scantlinges[4] lardger and bigger in assize then the Scantlinges of the timber
of the saide newe erected howse called the Globe; And alsoe that he the saide Peeter
Streete shall furthwith, aswell by himself as by suche other and soemanie woorkmen
as shalbe convenient & necessarie, enter into and uppon the saide buildinges and
woorkes, and shall in reasonable manner proceede therein withoute anie wilfull
detraccion untill the same shalbe fully effected and finished. In consideracion of all
which buildinges and of all stuff & woorkemanshipp thereto belonginge, the saide
Phillipp Henslowe & Edward Allen and either of them, ffor themselves, theire, and
either of theire executours & administratours, doe joynctlie & severallie covenante &
graunte to & with the saide Peeter Streete, his executours & administratours by theis
presentes, that they the saide Phillipp Henslowe & Edward Allen or one of them, or
the executours administratours or assignes of them or one of them, shall & will well &
truelie paie or cawse to be paide unto the saide Peeter Streete, his executours or
assignes, att the place aforesaid appoynted for the erectinge of the saide fframe, the
full somme of Fower hundred & Fortie Poundes of lawfull money of Englande in
manner & forme followeinge (that is to saie), att suche tyme and when as the Tymber-
woork of the saide fframe shalbe rayzed & sett upp by the saide Peeter Streete his
executours or assignes, or within seaven daies then next followeinge, Twoe hundred &
Twentie poundes, and att suche time and when as the saide fframe & woorkes shalbe
fullie effected & ffynished as is aforesaide, or within seaven daies then next follow-
einge, thother Twoe hundred and Twentie poundes, withoute fraude or coven.[5] Pro-
vided allwaies, and it is agreed betwene the saide parties, that whatsoever somme or
sommes of money the saide Phillipp Henslowe & Edward Allen or either of them, or
thexecutours or assignes of them or either of them, shall lend or deliver unto the saide
Peter Streete his executours or assignes, or anie other by his appoyntemente or con-
sent, ffor or concerninge the saide woorkes or anie parte thereof or anie stuff thereto
belonginge, before the raizeinge & setttinge upp of the saide fframe, shalbe reputed,
accepted, taken & accoumpted in parte of the firste paymente aforesaid of the saide
some of Fower hundred & Fortie poundes, and all suche somme & sommes of
money, as they or anie of them shall as aforesaid lend or deliver betwene the razeinge
of the saide fframe & finishinge thereof and of all the rest of the saide woorkes, shalbe
reputed, accepted, taken & accoumpted in parte of the laste pamente aforesaid of the
same somme of Fower hundred & Fortie poundes, anie thinge abovesaid to the con-
trary notwithstandinge. In witnes whereof the parties abovesaid to theis presente
Indentures Interchaungeably have sett theire handes and seales. Geoven[6] the daie and
yeare ffirste abovewritten.

P S

Sealed and delivered by the saide Peter Streete in the presence of me William Harris
Pub[lic] Scr[ivener] And me Frauncis Smyth appr[entice] to the said Scr[ivener]
        [Endorsed:] Peater Streat ffor The Building of the Fortune.

Augustine Phillips, Francis Bacon, et al. on *Richard II* (1601)

[These extracts from testimony submitted at the Earl of Essex's trial for treason, and related
documents, show that some of Essex's supporters had contracted with the Lord Chamber-
lain's Men to revive *Richard II*, apparently in order to provide a model for the justified
deposition of a monarch and thus propitiate the coup in which Essex planned to depose

4. Prescribed dimensions of the beams.   6. Given.
5. Deceit.

Elizabeth. The play was performed on February 7, and "it was on the same day," according to E. K. Chambers, "that Essex received a summons to appear before the Privy Council. This interrupted his plans for securing possession of the Queen's person and arresting her ministers, and precipitated his futile outbreak of February 8." Augustine Phillips was one of Shakespeare's colleagues in the Lord Chamberlain's Men. Sir Edward Coke was, for a time, chief justice under King James. The last excerpt is a contemporary record of a conversation between the queen and her archivist several months after Essex was executed. The texts are from WS, vol. 2.]

From the Abstract of Evidence

The Erle of Essex is charged with high Treason, namely, That he plotted and practised with the Pope and king of Spaine for the disposing and settling to himself Aswell the Crowne of England, as of the kingdom of Ireland.

From the Examination of Augustine Phillips, February 18, 1601

The Examination of Augustyne Phillypps servant unto the L Chamberlyne and one of hys players taken the xviij^th of Februarij 1600 upon hys oth

He sayeth that on Fryday last was sennyght or Thursday Sr Charles Percy Sr Josclyne Percy and the L. Montegle with some thre more spak to some of the players in the presans of thys examinate to have the play of the deposyng and kyllyng of Kyng Rychard the second to be played the Saterday next promysyng to gete them xls. more then their ordynary to play yt. Wher thys Examinate and hys fellowes were determyned to have played some other play, holdyng that play of Kyng Richard to be so old & so long out of use as that they shold have small or no Company at yt. But at their request this Examinate and his fellowes were Content to play yt the Saterday and had their xls. more then their ordynary for yt and so played yt accordyngly

Augustine Phillipps

From the speech of Sir Edward Coke at Essex's trial, February 19

I protest upon my soul and conscience I doe beleeve she should not have long lived after she had been in your power. Note but the precedents of former ages, how long lived Richard the Second after he was surprised in the same manner? The pretence was alike for the removing of certain counsellors, but yet shortly after it cost him his life.

From [Francis Bacon's] "A Declaration of the . . . Treasons . . . by Robert late Earle of Essex"

The afternoone before the rebellion, Merricke,[1] with a great company of others, that afterwards were all in the action, had procured to bee played before them, the play of deposing King Richard the second. Neither was it casuall, but a play bespoken by Merrick. And not so onely, but when it was told him by one of the players, that the play was olde, and they should have losse in playing it, because fewe would come to it: there was fourty shillings extraordinarie given to play it, and so thereupon playd it was. So earnest hee was to satisfie his eyes with the sight of that tragedie which hee thought soone after his lord should bring from the stage to the state, but that God turned it upon their owne heads.

From a Memorandum in the Lambard family manuscript, August 4

. . . so her Majestie fell upon[2] the reign of King Richard II. saying, 'I am Richard II. know ye not that?'

---

1. Sir Gilly Merrick, one of Essex's supporters, was later tried separately for treason.

2. Came across (in reading). The memorandum describes a scene in which the queen is reading over the

W.L. 'Such a wicked imagination was determined and attempted by a most unkind Gent. the most adorned creature that ever your Majestie made.'

Her Majestie. 'He that will forget God, will also forget his benefactors; this tragedy was played 40^tie times in open streets and houses.'

John Manningham on *Twelfth Night* and *Richard III* (1602)

[John Manningham (d. 1622) kept a diary during his time as a law student at the Middle Temple, recording the witticisms of his colleagues and a rich variety of anecdotes. The vibrant and boisterous life of the Inns of Court is also illustrated by the *Gesta Grayorum* (see above). The February entry describes the festivities organized for Candlemas Day at the Middle Temple, while the second recounts an anecdote related to Manningham by one Mr. Touse (this name is difficult to read in the manuscript). As with all the documents in this section, any date before March 25 is assigned to the following year according to our calendar, so that 1601 here becomes 1602 (New Style). The text is from the 1976 edition of Robert Sorlien (Hanover, N.H.: University Press of New England).]

Febr. 1601

2. At our feast wee had a play called "Twelve night, or what you will"; much like the commedy of errores, or Menechmi[1] in Plautus, but most like and neere to that in Italian called Inganni.[2] A good practise in it to make the steward beleeve his Lady widdowe[3] was in Love with him, by counterfayting a letter, as from his Lady, in generall termes, telling him what shee liked best in him, and prescribing his gesture in smiling, his apparraile, &c., and then when he came to practise, making him beleeve they tooke him to be mad.

Marche. 1601

13. . . . Upon a tyme when Burbidge played Rich[ard] 3. there was a Citizen grewe soe farr in liking with him, that before shee went from the play shee appointed him to come that night unto hir by the name of Ri[chard] the 3. Shakespeare, overhearing their conclusion, went before, was intertained, and at his game ere Burbidge came. Then message being brought that Richard the 3^d. was at the dore, Shakespeare caused returne to be made that William the Conquerour was before Rich[ard] the 3. Shakespeare's name William. (Mr. Touse.)

Letters Patent formalizing the adoption of the Lord Chamberlain's Men as the King's Men (May 19, 1603)

[James I issued the warrant ordering this patent shortly after his coronation, enhancing the status of Shakespeare's company. As retainers of the royal household with the title of Grooms of the Chamber, they performed at the court with increasing frequency (177 times between 1603 and 1616) and assisted occasionally with other court functions, but more important, they acted throughout the kingdom under the authority of the royal patent, whose scope the forceful wording below makes clear. The patent, bearing the Great Seal, was issued May 19 as ordered in the warrant of May 17. There is some evidence to suggest that James was particularly taken with Shakespeare's poetry, and the playwright's valorization of James's ancestry (as originating with Banquo) in *Macbeth* certainly suggests that Shakespeare cultivated his esteem. The text is from *ES*, vol. 2.]

---

archives that have been in the keeping of her interlocutor, William Lambard.

1. Source for *The Comedy of Errors*.
2. The two plays with this exact title (1562 and 1592) seem less likely to be "most like" *Twelfth Night* than another Italian play, *Ingannati* (1537), which has char-

acters named Fabio and Malevolti and makes reference to Twelfth Night (Epiphany).
3. Olivia is not a widow in the version of Shakespeare's play that has come down to us, though she is so described in one of Shakespeare's principal sources for the play.

Commissio specialis James by the grace of god &c. To all Justices, Maiors, Sher-
pro Laurencio Fletcher iffes, Constables, hedborowes,[1] and other our Officers and
& Willelmo Shacke- lovinge Subjectes greetinge. Knowe yee that Wee of our spe-
speare et aliis[2] ciall grace, certeine knowledge, & mere motion[3] have
licenced and aucthorized and by theise presentes[4] doe licence and aucthorize theise
our Servauntes Lawrence Fletcher, William Shakespeare, Richard Burbage,
Augustyne Phillippes, John Heninges, Henrie Condell, William Sly, Robert Armyn,
Richard Cowly, and the rest of theire Assosiates freely to use and exercise the Arte and
faculty of playinge Comedies, Tragedies, histories, Enterludes, moralls,[5] pastoralls,
Stageplaies, and Suche others like as theie have alreadie studied or hereafter shall use
or studie, aswell for the recreation of our lovinge Subjectes, as for our Solace and
pleasure when wee shall thincke good to see them, duringe our pleasure. And the said
Commedies, tragedies, histories, Enterludes, Morralles, Pastoralls, Stageplayes, and
suche like to shewe and exercise publiquely to theire best Commoditie,[6] when the
infection of the plague shall decrease, aswell within theire nowe usual howse called
the Globe within our County of Surrey, as alsoe within anie towne halls or Moute
halls[7] or other conveniente places within the liberties and freedome of anie other
Cittie, universitie, towne, or Boroughe whatsoever within our said Realmes and
domynions. Willinge and Commaundinge you and everie of you, as you tender our
pleasure, not onelie to permitt and suffer them herein without anie your lettes hin-
drances or molestacions during our said pleasure, but alsoe to be aidinge and
assistinge to them, yf anie wronge be to them offered, And to allowe them such former
Curtesies as hath bene given to men of theire place and quallitie,[8] and alsoe what
further favour you shall shewe to theise our Servauntes for our sake wee shall take
kindlie at your handes. In wytnesse whereof &c. witnesse our selfe at Westminster the
nyntenth day of May

per breve de privato sigillo[9] &c.

Master of the Wardrobe's Account (March 1604)

[This entry offers us a rare glimpse of the players in the entourage of King James, sporting
festive regalia in their capacity as Grooms of the Chamber. The royal procession took
place March 15, 1604. The text is from WS, vol. 2.]

Red Clothe bought of sondrie persons and given by his Majestie to diverse persons
against[1] his Majesties sayd royall proceeding through the Citie of London, viz.:— . . .

The Chamber . . .	
Fawkeners[2] &c. &c.	Red cloth
William Shakespeare	iiii yardes di.
Augustine Phillipps	"
Lawrence Fletcher	"
John Hemminges	"
Richard Burbidge	"
William Slye	"
Robert Armyn	"
Henry Cundell	"
Richard Cowley	"

1. A parish officer similar to a petty constable.
2. *Commissio . . . aliis:* By special commission on
behalf of . . . and others.
3. Inclination, desire.
4. The present document.
5. Morality plays.
6. Advantage.
7. Council chambers.

8. Profession.
9. In sum, from the privy seal.
1. For.
2. Obsolete form of "falconers," very likely the men
who trained the falcons used for James's fowl-hunting
expeditions. The falconers might owe their place in the
retinue to James's well-known passion for hunting.

Henry Jackson on *Othello* (September 1610)

[Several excerpts from the letters of Henry Jackson (d. 1662) of Corpus Christi College, Oxford, were made, probably after Jackson's death, by William Fulman, Jackson's successor in the college living of Meysey Hampton. One of these letters reveals that the King's Men played at Oxford in 1610, probably in September when the letter was written (the specific days are not given). After expressing some shock at the "violation" of Holy Scripture occurring in Jonson's *The Alchemist*, also in the repertoire of the King's Men, Jackson proceeds in the excerpt below to a more favorable discussion of the company's "tragedies," singling out *Othello* for special praise. Geoffrey Tillotson reprinted Fulman's transcripts in the *Times Literary Supplement* for July 20, 1933. The original letters do not survive.]

Habuerunt et Tragœdias, quas decorè, et aptè agebant. In quibus non solùm, dicendo, sed etiam faciendo quædam lachrymas movebant. —
—At verò Desdemona illa apud nos a marito occisa, quanquam optimè semper causam egit, interfecta tamen magis movebat; cum in lecto decumbens spectantium misericordiam ipso vultu imploraret.—

Sept. 1610.

They also had some tragedies, which they performed beautifully and with propriety. Among those, a few aroused tears, not only through their words, but even their gestures.—
—But truly Desdemona, having been killed by her husband before our eyes, although she pleaded her cause superbly throughout, nevertheless she moved [us] more after she had been murdered, when, lying upon her bed, her face itself implored pity from the onlookers.

Simon Forman on *Macbeth, Cymbeline,* and *The Winter's Tale* (1611)

[Simon Forman (1552–1611) was a largely self-educated physician and astrologer who rose from humble beginnings to establish a successful London practice. A large parcel of his manuscripts, including scientific and autobiographical material as well as the diary from which this account of the plays is taken, has survived, making his life one of the best-documented Elizabethan lives. These manuscripts provide detailed information about Forman's many sidelines, such as the manufacture of talismans, alchemy, and necromancy, as well about his sex life. The text is from WS, vol. 2.]

The Bocke of Plaies and Notes therof per formane for Common Pollicie[1]

In Mackbeth at the Glob, 1610 ⟨1611⟩, the 20 of Aprill ♄ (Saturday), ther was to be observed, firste, howe Mackbeth and Bancko, 2 noble men of Scotland, Ridinge thorowe a wod, the ⟨r⟩ stode before them 3 women feiries or Nimphes, And saluted Mackbeth, sayinge, 3 tyms unto him, haille Mackbeth, king of Codon;[2] for thou shalt be a kinge, but shalt beget No kinges, &c. Then said Bancko, What all to Mackbeth And nothing to me. Yes, said the nimphes, haille to thee Bancko, thou shalt beget kinges, yet be no kinge. And so they departed & cam to the Courte of Scotland to Dunkin king of Scotes, and yt was in the dais of Edward the Confessor. And Dunkin bad them both kindly wellcome, And made Mackbeth forth with Prince of Northumberland,[3] and sent him hom to his own castell, and appointed Mackbeth to provid for

---

1. *Common Pollicie:* practical use. Forman's title for his notes on plays is not printed in Chambers, but interpolated here from G. Blakemore Evans's transcription in the *Riverside Shakespeare.*

2. Cawdor.
3. Probably Forman's error; Duncan gives Macbeth the title Thane of Cawdor. Duncan's son Malcolm is the Prince of Northumberland.

him, for he would sup with him the next dai at night, & did soe. And Mackebeth contrived to kill Dunkin, & thorowe the persuasion of his wife did that night Murder the kinge in his own Castell, beinge his guest. And ther were many prodigies seen that night & the dai before. And when Mack Beth had murdred the kinge, the blod on his handes could not be washed of by Any meanes, nor from his wives handes, which handled the bloddi daggers in hiding them, By which means they became both moch amazed & Affronted. The murder being knowen, Dunkins 2 sonns fled, the on to England, the ⟨other to⟩ Walles, to save them selves, they being fled, they were supposed guilty of the murder of their father, which was nothinge so. Then was Mackbeth crowned kinge, and then he for feare of Banko, his old companion, that he should beget kinges but be no kinge him selfe, he contrived the death of Banko, and caused him to be Murdred on the way as he Rode. The next night, beinge at supper with his noble men whom he had bid to a feaste to the which also Banco should have com, he began to speake of Noble Banco, and to wish that he wer ther. And as he thus did, standing up to drincke a Carouse to him, the ghoste of Banco came and sate down in his cheier behind him. And he turninge About to sit down Again sawe the goste of Banco, which fronted him so, that he fell into a great passion of fear and fury, Utterynge many wordes about his murder, by which, when they hard that Banco was Murdred they Suspected Mackbet.

Then MackDove fled to England to the kinges sonn, And soe they Raised an Army, And cam into Scotland, and at Dunston Anyse overthrue Mackbet. In the meantyme whille Macdovee was in England, Mackbet slewe Mackdoves wife & children, and after in the battelle Mackdove slewe Mackbet.

Observe Also howe Mackbetes quen did Rise in the night in her slepe, & walke and talked and confessed all, & the docter noted her wordes.

Of Cimbalin king of England.

Remember also the storri of Cymbalin king of England, in Lucius tyme, howe Lucius Cam from Octavus Cesar for Tribut, and being denied, after sent Lucius with a greate Arme of Souldiars who landed at Milford haven, and Affter wer vanquished by Cimbalin, and Lucius taken prisoner, and all by means of 3 outlawes, of the which 2 of them were the sonns of Cimbalim, stolen from him when they were but 2 yers old by an old man whom Cymbalin banished, and he kept them as his own sonns 20 yers with him in A cave. And howe ⟨one⟩ of them slewe Clotan, that was the quens sonn, goinge to Milford haven to sek the love of Innogen the kinges daughter, whom he had banished also for lovinge his daughter,[4] and howe the Italian that cam from her love conveied him selfe into A Cheste, and said yt was a chest of plate sent from her love & others, to be presented to the kinge. And in the depest of the night, she being aslepe, he opened the cheste, & cam forth of yt, And vewed her in her bed, and the markes of her body, & toke awai her braslet, & after Accused her of adultery to her love, &c. And in thend howe he came with the Romains into England & was taken prisoner, and after Reveled to Innogen, Who had turned her self into mans apparrell & fled to mete her love at Milford haven, & chanchsed to fall on the Cave in the wodes wher her 2 brothers were, & howe by eating a sleping Dram they thought she had bin deed, & laid her in the wodes, & the body of Cloten by her, in her loves apparrell that he left behind him, & howe she was found by Lucius, &c.

In the Winters Talle at the glob 1611 the 15 of maye ☿ ⟨Wednesday⟩.

Observe ther howe Lyontes the kinge of Cicillia was overcom with Jelosy of his wife with the kinge of Bohemia his frind that came to see him, and howe he contrived his death and wold have had his cup berer to have poisoned, who gave the king of Bohemia warning therof & fled with him to Bohemia.

Remember also howe he sent to the Orakell of Appollo & the Annswer of Apollo,

---

4. Morgan/Belarius is not banished in the version of the play that comes down to us.

that she was giltles and that the king was jelouse &c. and howe Except the child was found Again that was loste the kinge should die without yssue, for the child was caried into Bohemia & ther laid in a forrest & brought up by a sheppard And the kinge of Bohemia his sonn maried that wentch & howe they fled into Cicillia to Leontes, and the sheppard having showed the letter of the nobleman by whom Leontes sent a was ⟨away?⟩ that child and the jewells found about her, she was knowen to be Leontes daughter and was then 16 yers old.

Remember also the Rog[5] that cam in all tottered like coll pixci[6] and howe he feyned him sicke & to have bin Robbed of all that he had and howe he cosened the por man of all his money, and after cam to the shep sher[7] with a pedlers packe & ther cosened them Again of all their money And howe he changed apparrell with the kinge of Bomia his sonn, and then howe he turned Courtier &c. Beware of trustinge feined beggars or fawninge fellouss.

Chamber Account of Performances by the King's Men (May 1613)

[The performances of Shakespeare's company at court are especially well documented, because there were established systems of record keeping for the activities of the royal household. The players, as the King's Men, were officially Grooms of the Chamber, and it was this division of the royal household, under the supervision of the Lord Chamberlain, that organized entertainments, along with many other aspects of the operation of the court. The most significant item to the Treasurer of the Chamber who prepared the accounts was naturally the sum paid to the company on each occasion. In some instances, the titles of the plays given are also preserved, and the list given for May 20, when the company received payment (in two installments) for twenty plays given over the previous weeks, is especially complete. This list indicates the full range of the company's repertoire, which included many plays not by Shakespeare. The amount paid for the first group of plays was 93 pounds, 6 shillings, 8 pence, and for the second, smaller, group, 60 pounds. The text is from the first column of the accounts as reproduced under the heading "Payees" in *ES*, vol. 4.]

'To him [Hemynges] more'; 'fowerteene severall playes, viz: one playe called ffi-laster, One other called the knott of ffooles, One other Much adoe aboute nothinge, The Mayeds Tragedy, The merye dyvell of Edmonton, The Tempest, A kinge and no kinge, The Twins Tragedie, The Winters Tale, Sir John ffalstaffe,[1] The Moore of Venice,[2] The Nobleman, Caesars Tragedye, And on other called Love lyes a blee-dinge'.

'the sayd John Heminges'; 'Sixe severall playes, viz: one play called a badd begininge makes a good endinge, One other called y[e] Capteyne, One other the Alcumist. One other Cardenno, One other the Hotspur,[3] And one other called Benedicte and Betteris'.[4]

Sir Henry Wotton on *All Is True (Henry VIII)* and the Burning of the Globe (1613)

[Sir Henry Wotton (1568–1639), a highly educated poet and essayist, distinguished diplomat, and finally provost of Eton College, wrote to his nephew Sir Edmund Bacon shortly

5. Rogue (Autolycus).
6. Probably "colt-pixie," a mischievous sprite or fairy.
7. Sheep shearing.
1. *1* or *2 Henry IV*, or possibly *The Merry Wives of*

Windsor.
2. *Othello.*
3. *1 Henry IV.*
4. *Much Ado About Nothing.*

after the burning of the Globe. Chambers includes several other accounts of this incident in *The Elizabethan Stage*, vol. 2, pp. 419ff. The event is also recorded in John Stow's chronicles and was lamented by poets, including (several years later) Ben Jonson, and held up by Puritan divines like Prynne as an intimation of God's wrath. The excerpt below is from the earliest extant text, *Letters of Sir Henry Wotton to Sir Edmund Bacon* (London, 1661), p. 29.]

Now, to let matters of State sleep, I will entertain you at the present with what hath happened this week at the banks side. The Kings Players had a new Play, called *All is true*, representing some principall pieces of the raign of *Henry* 8, which was set forth with many extraordinary circumstances of Pomp and Majesty, even to the matting of the stage; the Knights of the Order, with their Georges and Garter, the Guards with their embroidered Coats, and the like: sufficient in truth within a while to make greatness very familiar, if not ridiculous. Now, King *Henry* making a Masque at the Cardinal, *Wolsey's* house, and certain Chambers[1] being shot off at his entry, some of the paper, or other stuff wherewith one of them was stopped, did light on the thatch, where being thought at first but an idle smoak, and their eyes more attentive to the show, it kindled inwardly, and ran round like a train, consuming within less then an hour the whole house to the very grounds.

This was the fatal period of that vertuous fabrique, wherein yet nothing did perish, but wood and straw, and a few forsaken cloaks; only one man had his breeches set on fire, that would perhaps have broyled him, if he had not by the benefit of a provident wit put it out with bottle Ale. The rest when we meet.

Ballad on the Burning of the Globe (June 30, 1613)

[The ballad reprinted here may be one of the ballads on the burning of the Globe entered in the Stationers' Register on June 30, 1613, the day after the fire occurred. It survives only in a nineteenth-century transcript. The fire was in any case a significant news item, and topical ballads were often turned out rapidly, as a means of disseminating news, and sold cheaply on the streets as single printed sheets, or broadsides. The burning of the Globe had the additional appeal of being a peculiarly literary topic. The text is from *ES*, vol. 2.]

A Sonnett upon the pittiful burneing of the Globe playhowse in London.

>Now sitt the downe, Melpomene,[1]
>   Wrapt in a sea-cole robe,
>And tell the dolefull tragedie,
>   That late was playd at Globe;
>For noe man that can singe and saye
>   [But?] was scard on St. Peters daye.[2]
>   Oh sorrow, pittifull sorrow, and yett all this is true.[3]

>All yow that please to understand,
>   Come listen to my storye,
>To see Death with his rakeing brand[4]
>   Mongst such an auditorye;
>Regarding neither Cardinalls might,
>Nor yett the rugged face of Henry the Eight.
>   Oh sorrow, &c.

1. Small pieces of artillery, used for firing salutes.
1. The muse of tragedy. *the:* thee.
2. June 29, the day of the fire. *scard:* Chambers's emendation; some such word appears to be missing.

3. Reference to the title of the "tragedie" being performed onstage at the time of the fire.
4. Torch; but also, blade—hence the traditional scythe of Death.

This fearfull fire beganne above,
    A wonder strange and true,
And to the stage-howse did remove,
    As round as taylors clewe;[5]
And burnt downe both beame and snagg,
And did not spare the silken flagg.[6]
    Oh sorrow, &c.

Out runne the knightes, out runne the lordes,
    And there was great adoe;
Some lost their hattes, and some their swordes;
    Then out runne Burbidge too;
The reprobates, though druncke on Munday,
Prayd for the Foole and Henry Condye.
    Oh sorrow, &c.

The perrywigges and drumme-heades frye,
    Like to a butter firkin;
A wofull burneing did betide
    To many a good buffe jerkin.
Then with swolne eyes, like druncken Flemminges,
Distressed stood old stuttering Heminges.[7]
    Oh sorrow, &c.

No shower his raine did there downe force
    In all that Sunn-shine weather,
To save that great renowned howse;
    Nor thou, O ale-howse, neither.[8]
Had itt begunne belowe, sans doubte,
Their wives for feare had pissed itt out.
    Oh sorrow, &c.

Bee warned, yow stage-strutters all,
    Least yow againe be catched,
And such a burneing doe befall,
    As to them whose howse was thatched;
Forbeare your whoreing, breeding biles,[9]
And laye up that expence for tiles.[1]
    Oh sorrow, &c.

Goe drawe yow a petition,
    And doe yow not abhorr itt,
And gett, with low submission,
    A licence to begg for itt
In churches, sans churchwardens checkes,
In Surrey and in Midlesex.
    Oh sorrow, pittifull sorrow, and yett all this is true.

---

5. A tailor's ball of thread. Probably a reference to the name "Globe" as well as the shape of the Globe, though not quite round.

6. A flag flying from the top of the theater to indicate that a performance was in progress.

7. John Heminges, Richard Burbadge, and Henry Condell were colleagues of Shakespeare in the King's Men.

8. Another report on the fire indicates that a house adjoining the Globe burned down as well. This house may be the same as the "ale-howse."

9. Boils.

1. Roof tiles, in place of the more flammable thatched roof. The rebuilt Globe, which opened a year after the fire, did in fact have a tile roof.

Ben Jonson on *The Tempest* (and *Titus Andronicus*) (1614)

[This extract from *Bartholomew Fair* contains one of several allusions to Shakespeare in the plays of his associate and sometime rival. The first paragraph alludes to the fashion for revenge plays such as Shakespeare's *Titus Andronicus* and Kyd's *Spanish Tragedy*, at its height roughly twenty-five years before *Bartholomew Fair* was written. The second paragraph refers disapprovingly to *The Tempest* (1613), first produced shortly before *Bartholomew Fair*. The text is that reprinted in WS, vol. 2, from the 1631 edition of Jonson's play (from the play's Induction).]

Hee that will sweare, *Jeronimo*, or *Andronicus* are the best playes, yet, shall passe unexcepted at,[2] heere, as a man whose Judgement shewes it is constant, and hath stood still, these five and twentie, or thirtie yeeres. . . .

If there bee never a *Servant-monster* i' the Fayre; who can helpe it? he[3] sayes; nor a nest of Antiques?[4] Hee is loth to make Nature afraid[5] in his *Playes*, like those that beget *Tales*, *Tempests*, and such like *Drolleries*, to mixe his head with other mens heeles; let the concupisence of *Jigges* and *Dances*, raigne as strong as it will amongst you.[6]

Francis Beaumont (?) on Shakespeare (c. 1615)

[Chambers was the first to print this poem in full, and the attribution to Francis Beaumont, a lawyer (not the playwright) who died in 1616, remains conjectural, though plausible. Not much is known about Beaumont's precise relationship to Jonson, but he had previously written a well-known verse-epistle to the poet, and theatrical allusions in this poem suggest a taste for the theater. The excerpted passage is remarkable as a precursor of the long-dominant view of Shakespeare as an untutored genius whose artistic accomplishment was due to the force of nature's gifts alone. In the lines preceding the excerpt, Beaumont amplifies the claim to authenticity of the love he wishes to express in the epistle by abjuring all stylistic refinement. The text is from WS, vol. 2.]

To Mr. B.J.

heere I would let slippe
(If I had any in mee) schollershippe,
And from all Learninge keepe these lines as ⟨cl⟩eere[7]
as Shakespeares best are, which our heires shall heare
Preachers apte to their auditors to showe
how farr sometimes a mortall man may goe
by the dimme light of Nature.

Shakespeare's Will (March 25, 1616)

[Shakespeare probably dictated this will sometime around January 1616. The first draft seems to have been dated in January, and 1616 is the most likely inference for the year (see note 1). The final revision was certainly made on the date given, but no clean copy was prepared, so the manuscript contains a substantial number of insertions and deletions.

2. Uncriticized.
3. The author.
4. Variant spelling of "antics," grotesque or ludicrous representations, or the actors (such as the clowns in *The Tempest*) playing such parts.
5. Make nature afraid by inexact imitation or too much fantasy.

6. *concupisence . . . you*: a reference to the dance generally incorporated into theatrical performance (see, for example, Platter's account above). Jonson suggests he is refusing to cater to the vulgar taste for more dancing in plays.
7. Chambers's emendation. The manuscript reads "deere," probably a scribal error.

The text here has been silently emended to assist in ease of reading. Deleted passages have been eliminated; the most significant of these is reproduced in the notes, where significant interlineations are also identified. Most of the altered passages, as Chambers writes, simply "correct slips, make the legal terminology more precise, or incorporate afterthoughts." The revision of the will was occasioned chiefly by the February marriage of Shakespeare's daughter Judith. Our text is adapted from E. A. J. Honigmann and Susan Brock, *Playhouse Wills, 1558–1642*. For a facsimile and thorough discussion of the will, see WS 2:169–80.]

Testamentum willelmij Shackspeare
Vicesimo Quinto die martij Anno Regni Domini nostri Jacobi nunc Regis Anglie &c decimo quarto & Scotie xlixo Annoque domini 1616[1]
In the name of god Amen I William Shackspeare of Stratford upon Avon in the countie of warrwick gentleman in perfect health & memorie god be praysed doe make & Ordayne this my last will & testament in manner & forme followeing That ys to saye ffirst I Comend my Soule into the handes of god my Creator hoping & assuredlie beleeving through thonelie merittes of Jesus Christe my Saviour to be made partaker of lyfe everlastinge And my bodye to the Earth whereof yt ys made Item I Gyve & bequeath unto my Daughter Judyth One Hundred & ffyftie poundes of lawfull English money to be paied unto her in manner & forme followeing That ys to saye One Hundred Poundes in discharge of her marriage porcion[2] within one yeare after my Deceas with consideracion[3] after the Rate of twoe shillinges in the pound for soe long tyme as the same shalbe unpaied unto her after my deceas & the ffyftie poundes Residewe thereof upon her Surrendring of or gyving of such sufficient securitie as the overseers of this my Will shall like of to Surrender or graunnte All her[4] estate & Right that shall discend or come unto her after my deceas or that shee nowe hath of in or to one Copiehold tenemente with thappurtenaunces lyeing & being in Stratford upon Avon aforesaied in the saied countie of warrwick being parcell or holden of the mannour of Rowington unto my Daughter Susanna Hall & her heires for ever Item I Gyve & bequeath unto my saied Daughter Judith One Hundred & ffyftie Poundes more if shee or Anie issue of her bodie be Lyvinge att thend of three Yeares next ensueing the daie of the Date of this my Will during which tyme my executours to paie her consideracion from my deceas according to the Rate afore saied And if she dye within the saied terme without issue of her bodye then my will ys & I doe gyve & bequeath One Hundred Poundes thereof to my Neece Elizabeth Hall & the ffiftie Poundes to be sett fourth by my executours during the lief of my Sister Johane Harte & the use & proffitt thereof Cominge shalbe payed to my saied Sister Jone & after her deceas the saied 1 li[5] shall Remaine Amongst the children of my saied Sister Equallie to be Devided Amongst them But if my saied Daughter Judith be lyving att thend of the saied three Yeares or anie yssue of her bodye then my Will ys & soe I devise & bequeath the saied Hundred & ffyftie poundes to be sett out by my executours & overseers for the best benefitt of her & her issue & the stock[6] not to be paied unto her soe long as she shalbe marryed & Covert Baron[7] but my will ys that she shall have the consideracon yearelie paied unto her during her lief & after her deceas the saied stock and consideracion to bee paied to her children if she have Anie & if not to her executours or assignes she lyving the saied terme after my deceas Provided that if such husbond as she shall att thend of the saied three Yeares be marryed unto or attaine after doe sufficientle Assure unto her & thissue of her bodie landes Awnswereable to the porcion by this my will gyven unto her & to be adjudged

---

1. *Testamentum . . . 1616*: The Will of William Shakespeare (marginal heading). On the twenty-fifth day of March, in the fourteenth year of the reign of our lord James now King of England, etc., and of Scotland the forty-ninth, in the year of our Lord 1616. (The abbreviation for "January" is crossed out in the manuscript, "March" having been substituted at the time the will was revised.)

2. The phrase "in discharge of her marriage porcion" was inserted during the course of revision.
3. Compensation, or interest.
4. Susanna Hall's. (The preceding "All" marks the beginning of a new sentence.)
5. *1 li*: fifty pounds.
6. Principal.
7. *Covert Baron*: under the protection of a husband.

soe by my executours & overseers then my will ys that the saied Cl li[8] shalbe paied to such husbond as shall make such assurance to his owne use Item I gyve & bequeath unto my saied sister Jone xx li & all my wearing Apparrell to be paied & Delivered within one yeare after my deceas And I doe Will & devise unto her the house with thappurtenaunces in Stratford wherein she dwelleth for her naturall lief under the yearelie Rent of xii d. Itm I gyve & bequeath unto her three sonns William Harte[9] hart & Michaell Harte ffyve poundes A peece to be payed within one Yeare after my deceas[1] Item I gyve & bequeath unto her the saied Elizabeth Hall All my Plate (except my brod silver & gilt bole)[2] that I nowe have att the Date of this my Will Itm I gyve & bequeath unto the Poore of Stratford aforesaied tenn poundes to mr Thomas Combe my Sword to Thomas Russell Esquier ffyve poundes & to ffrauncis Collins of the Borough of Warrwick in the countie of Warrwick gentleman thirteene poundes Sixe shillinges & Eight pence to be paied within one Yeare after my Deceas Itm I gyve & bequeath to Hamlett Sadler xxvi s viii d[3] to buy him A Ringe to William Raynoldes gentleman xxvi s viii d to buy him A Ringe to my godson William Walker xx s in gold to Anthonye Nashe gentleman xxvi s viii d & to mr John Nashe xx vi s viii d & to my fellows John Hemynnges Richard Burbage & Henry Cundell xxvi s viii d A peece to buy them Ringes[4] Item I Gyve Will bequeath & Devise unto my Daughter Susanna Hall for better enabling of her to performe this my will & towardes the performans thereof All that Capitall messuage or tenemente[5] with thappurtenaunces in Stratford aforesaied Called the newe place Wherein I nowe Dwell & twoe mes-suages or tenementes with thappurtenaunces scituat lyeing & being in Henley streete within the borough of Stratford aforesaied And all my barnes stables Orchardes gar-dens landes tenementes & hereditamentes[6] Whatsoever scituat lyeing & being or to be had Receyved perceyved or taken within the townes Hamlettes villages ffieldes & groundes of Stratford upon Avon Oldstratford Bushopton & Welcombe or in anie of them in the saied countie of warrwick And alsoe All that Messuage or tenemente with thappurtenaunces wherein one John Robinson dwelleth scituat lyeing & being in the blackfriers in London nere the Wardrobe & all other my landes tenementes & hereditamentes Whatsoever To Have & to hold All & singuler the saied premisses with their Appurtenaunces unto the saied Susanna Hall for & During the terme of her naturall lief & after her Deceas to the first sonne of her bodie lawfullie Issueing & to the heires males of the bodie of the saied first Sonne lawfullie Issueinge & for defalt of such issue to the second Sonne of her bodie lawfullie issueinge & to the heires males of the bodie of the saied Second Sonne lawfullie issueinge & for defalt of such heries to the third Sonne of the bodie of the saied Susanna Lawfullie issueing & of the heires males of the bodie of the saied third sonne lawfullie issueing And for defalt of such issue the same soe to be & Remaine to the ffourth ffyfth sixte & Seaventh sonnes of her bodie lawfullie issueing one after Another & to the heires[7] Males of the bodies of the saied ffourth fifth Sixte & Seaventh sonnes lawfullie issueing in such manner as yt ys before Lymitted to be & Remaine to the first second & third Sonns of her bodie & to their heires males And for defalt of such issue the saied premisses to

8. *Cl li:* One hundred fifty pounds.
9. A blank in the manuscript. Shakespeare appears to have forgotten the name of one of his nephews, Thomas.
1. *unto . . . deceas:* this passage was inserted at the top of the second page, probably when the will was revised. The following lines, with which the page originally began, are crossed out in the original: "to be sett out for her within one Yeare after my Deceas by my executours with thadvise & direccions of my overseers for her best proffitt untill her Marriage & then the same with the increase thereof to be paied unto her." These lines evi-dently referred to Judith Shakespeare as unmarried.
2. This parenthetical clause is an insertion, and has sparked some debate about Shakespeare's opinion of

Judith's marriage.
3. The "s" stands for "shillings," the "d" for "pence."
4. *to my fellows . . . Ringes:* Shakespeare's "fellows," or colleagues, Heminges, Burbage, and Condell, had worked with him in the Lord Chamberlain's Men and King's Men for many years. Many other wills and docu-ments of the period provide evidence of the practice of wearing mourning rings alluded to here.
5. Residence. *messuage:* dwelling house with its out-buildings or adjoining lands.
6. Heritable property.
7. In addition to the signature near the end, Shake-speare signed the will here, in the bottom right-hand corner of the second page.

be & Remaine to my sayed Neece Hall[8] & the heires Males of her bodie Lawfullie yssueing for Defalt of such issue to my Daughter Judith & the heires Males of her bodie lawfullie issueinge And for Defalt of such issue to the Right heires of me the saied William Shackspere for ever Itm I gyve unto my wief my second best bed[9] with the furniture Item I gyve & bequeath to my saied Daughter Judith my broad silver gilt bole All the Rest of my goodes Chattelles Leases plate Jewels & household stuffe Whatsoever after my dettes and Legasies paied & my funerall expences discharged I gyve Devise & bequeath to my Sonne in Lawe John Hall gentleman & my Daughter Susanna his wief Whom I ordaine & make executours of this my Last Will & testament And I doe intreat & Appoint the saied Thomas Russell Esquier & ffrauncis Collins gentleman to be overseers hereof And doe Revoke All former wills & publishe this to be my last Will & testament In Witnes Whereof I have here unto put my hand the Daie & Yeare first above Written. /　　　　By me William Shakespeare witnes to the publishing hereof Fra: Collyns Julyus Shawe John Robinson Hamnet Sadler Robert Whattcott[1]

William Basse's Elegy for Shakespeare (1616–23)

[This highly literary elegy was written sometime between 1616 and 1623 by William Basse (c. 1583–c. 1653), of whom Chambers reports that he "was an Oxford student and a retainer of Lord Wenman of Thame." In numerous manuscript sources, the poem is ascribed to Basse, and in the 1640 *Poems: Written by Wil. Shake-speare, Gent.*, it is subscribed "W. B.," but it was also published in the 1633 edition of John Donne's poetry. In one source, "comedian" is substituted for the "Tragœdian" of line 12. The text is from WS, vol. 2.]

On Mr. Wm. Shakespeare
he dyed in Aprill 1616.

Renowned Spencer, lye a thought more nye
To learned Chaucer, and rare Beaumont lye
A little neerer Spenser to make roome
For Shakespeare in your threefold fowerfold Tombe.
To lodge all fowre in one bed make a shift
Untill Doomesdaye, for hardly will a fift
Betwixt this day and that by Fate be slayne
For whom your Curtaines may be drawn againe.
If your precedency in death doth barre
A fourth place in your sacred sepulcher,
Under this carved marble of thine owne
Sleep rare Tragœdian Shakespeare, sleep alone,
Thy unmolested peace, unshared Cave,
Possesse as Lord not Tenant of thy Grave,
That unto us and others it may be
Honor hereafter to be layde by thee.

Wm. Basse

8. Susanna Hall's daughter Elizabeth, actually Shakespeare's granddaughter (the sense of "niece" is less restricted in early modern usage). Elizabeth proved to be Susanna's only surviving child, and since Susanna was already thirty-three in 1616, the hypothetical series of seven sons preceding this mention of Elizabeth is doubly remarkable.
9. This bequest to Shakespeare's wife, Anne, was inserted in the course of his revision of the will. She is not mentioned elsewhere in the will at least partly because, as Shakespeare's widow, she would be guaranteed a certain portion of the estate by law. The appearance of this inserted bequest is nevertheless strange enough to have evoked much speculation.
1. After Shakespeare's death, the will was endorsed here at the bottom of the third page with a Latin inscription indicating that the will had gone to probate before a magistrate on June 22, 1616.

Nicholas Richardson on *Romeo and Juliet* (1620)

[The following passage from *Romeo and Juliet*, together with the note describing its spiritual application, is recorded in an early seventeenth-century commonplace book. The recorder had evidently heard the sermons in which Richardson, a Church of England clergyman, used the passage (slightly misquoted here) from Shakespeare, and was impressed by them. Of Richardson it is known that he became a fellow of Magdalen College, Oxford, in 1614. The text is from *WS*, vol. 2.]

> 'Tis almost morning I would have thee gone
> And yet no farther then a wantons bird,
> That lets it hop a little from his hand,
> Like a poore prisoner, in his twisted gyves,
> Then with a silken thread plucks it back againe
> So jealous loving of his liberty. Tragedy of
> Romeo and Juliet. 40: pag. 84:
> Said by Juliet: pro eadem.[1]

this Mr Richard^{son} Coll. Magd: inserted hence into his Sermon, preached it twice a^t St Maries 1620. 1621. applying it to gods love to his Saints either hurt with sinne, or adversity never forsaking thè.[2]

Front Matter from the First Folio of Shakespeare's Plays (1623)

[John Heminges and Henry Condell, friends and colleagues of Shakespeare, organized this first publication of his collected (thirty-six) plays. Eighteen of the plays had not appeared in print before, and for these the First Folio is the sole surviving source. Only *Pericles*, *The Two Noble Kinsmen*, and *Sir Thomas More* are not included in the volume. The first twelve (printed) pages of the Folio are reproduced below in reduced facsimile, with a minimum of explanatory notes. This "front matter" includes Droeshout's portrait of Shakespeare, Jonson's brief address "To the Reader" along with four other commendatory poems, two epistles by Heminges and Condell, a table of contents, and a list of actors, followed by the first page of text from *The Tempest*.]

---

1. On her own behalf.   2. Them.

To the Reader.

This Figure, that thou here feeſt put,
    It vvas for gentle Shakeſpeare cut;
Wherein the Grauer had a ſtrife
    with Nature, to out-doo the life :
O, could he but haue dravvne his vvit
    As vvell in braſſe, as he hath hit
Hisface ; the Print vvould then ſurpaſſe
    All, that vvas euer vvrit in braſſe.
But, ſince he cannot, Reader, looke
    Not on his Picture, but his Booke.

                                      B. I.

Mr. WILLIAM
SHAKESPEARES

COMEDIES,
HISTORIES, &
TRAGEDIES.

Publifhed according to the True Originall Copies.

Martin Droeshout ſculpſit London.

LONDON.
Printed by Iſaac Iaggard, and Ed. Blount. 1623.

TO THE MOST NOBLE
AND
INCOMPARABLE PAIRE
OF BRETHREN.

WILLIAM
Earle of Pembroke, &c. Lord Chamberlaine to the
Kings most Excellent Maiesty.

AND

PHILIP
Earle of Montgomery, &c. Gentleman of his Maiesties
Bed-Chamber. Both Knights of the most Noble Order
of the Garter, and our singular good
LORDS.

Right Honourable,

*Hilst we studie to be thankful in our particular, for
the many fauors we haue receiued from your L.L.
we are falne vpon the ill fortune, to mingle
two the most diuerse things that can bee, feare,
and rashnesse ; rashnesse in the enterprize, and
feare of the succeffe. For, when we valew the places your H.H.
suftaine,we cannot but know their dignity greater,then to descend to
the reading of these trifles:and,vvhile we name them trifles,we haue
depriu'd our selues of the defence of our Dedication. But since your
L.L. haue beene plead'd to thinke these trifles some-thing, heereto-
fore; and haue prosequuted both them, and their Authour liuing,
vvith so much fauour : we hope,that (they out-liuing him,and he not
hauing the fate, common with some, to be exequutor to his owne wri-
tings) you will vfe the like indulgence toward them, you haue done*

A2

vnto

Line 2. *L.L.:* Lordships.
Line 6. *places:* rank(s), status. *H.H.:* Highnesses.

Line 11. *prosequuted:* pursued.

The Epiſtle Dedicatorie.

vnto their parent. There is a great difference, vvhether any Booke choose his Patrones, or finde them : This hath done both. For, so much were your L L. likings of the seuerall parts, vvhen they were acted, as before they vvere publiſhed, the Volume ask'd to be yours. We haue but collected them, and done an office to the dead, to procure his Orphanes, Guardians; vvithout ambition either of selfe-profit, or fame : onely to keepe the memory of so worthy a Friend, & Fellow aliue, as was our SHAKESPEARE, *by humble offer of his playes, to your most noble patronage. Wherein, as we haue iuſtly obſerued, no man to come neere your L.L. but vvith a kind of religious addreſſe; it hath bin the height of our care, vvho are the Preſenters, to make the preſent worthy of your H.H. by the perfection. But, there we muſt alſo craue our abilities to be conſiderd, my Lords. We cannot go beyond our owne powers. Country hands reach foorth milke, creame, fruites, or what they haue : and many Nations (we haue heard) that had not gummes & incenſe, obtained their requeſts with a leauened Cake. It vvas no fault to approch their Gods, by what meanes they could : And the moſt, though meaneſt, of things are made more precious, when they are dedicated to Temples. In that name therefore, we moſt humbly conſecrate to your H.H. theſe remaines of your ſeruant* Shakeſpeare ; *that what delight is in them, may be euer your L.L. the reputation his, & the faults ours, if any be committed, by a payre ſo carefull to ſhew their gratitude both to the liuing, and the dead, as is*

Your Lordſhippes moſt bounden,

IOHN HEMINGE.
HENRY CONDELL.

To the great Variety of Readers.

Rom the moſt able, to him that can but ſpell: There you are number'd. We had rather you were weighd. Eſpecially, when the fate of all Bookes depends vpon your capacities : and not of your heads alone, but of your purſes. Well! It is now publique, & you wil ſtand for your priuiledges wee know : to read, and cenſure. Do ſo, but buy it firſt. That doth beſt commend a Booke, the Stationer ſaies. Then, how odde ſoeuer your braines be, or your wiſedomes, make your licence the ſame, and ſpare not. Iudge your ſixe-pen'orth, your ſhillings worth, your fiue ſhillings worth at a time, or higher, ſo you riſe to the iuſt rates, and welcome. But, what euer you do, Buy. Cenſure will not driue a Trade, or make the Iacke go. And though you be a Magiſtrate of wit, and ſit on the Stage at *Black-Friers,* or the *Cock-pit,* to arraigne Playes dailie, know, theſe Playes haue had their triall alreadie, and ſtood out all Appeales; and do now come forth quitted rather by a Decree of Court, then any purchas'd Letters of commendation.

It had bene a thing, we confeſſe, worthie to haue bene wiſhed, that the Author himſelfe had liu'd to haue ſet forth, and ouerſeen his owne writings; But ſince it hath bin ordain'd otherwiſe, and he by death departed from that right, we pray you do not envie his Friends, the office of their care, and paine, to haue collected & publiſh'd them; and ſo to haue publiſh'd them, as where (before) you were abuſ'd with diuerſe ſtolne, and ſurreptitious copies, maimed, and deformed by the frauds and ſtealthes of iniurious impoſtors, that expoſ'd them: euen thoſe, are now offer'd to your view cur'd, and perfect of their limbes; and all the reſt, abſolute in their numbers, as he conceiued the. Who, as he was a happie imitator of Nature, was a moſt gentle expreſſer of it. His mind and hand went together: And what he thought, he vttered with that eaſineſſe, that wee haue ſcarſe receiued from him a blot in his papers. But it is not our prouince, who onely gather his works, and giue them you, to praiſe him. It is yours that reade him. And there we hope, to your diuers capacities, you will finde enough, both to draw, and hold you : for his wit can no more lie hid, then it could be loſt. Reade him, therefore; and againe, and againe : And if then you doe not like him, ſurely you are in ſome manifeſt danger, not to vnderſtand him. And ſo we leaue you to other of his Friends, whom if you need, can bee your guides : if you neede them not, you can leade your ſelues, and others. And ſuch Readers we wiſh him.

                    A 3   *Iohn Heminge.*
                                    Henrie Condell.

Line 8. *Stationer:* bookseller.

Line 13. *Iacke:* machine.

Lines 13–14. *And though . . . dailie:* addressed in particular to men of fashion who occupied seats onstage so they could be seen while watching the play.

Lines 15–17. *these Playes . . . commendation:* the legal puns that began with "Magistrate of wit" (fashionable playgoer) in line 13 continue here. The "purchas'd Letters of commendation" refer to escaping the conse-

quences of a crime by means of bribery or other undue influence; Shakespeare's plays, by contrast, have been acquitted after a proper and rigorous trial (approved by theater audiences and not insinuated into the public favor by some outside influence).

Line 27. *absolute in their numbers:* correct in their versification. *the:* them.

Line 28. *a happie:* an apt; a successful.

To the memory of my beloued,
The AVTHOR
MR. WILLIAM SHAKESPEARE:
AND
what he hath left vs.

TO draw no enuy (Shakespeare) on thy name,
　Am I thus ample to thy Booke, and Fame:
　While I confesse thy writings to be such,
　As neither Man, nor Muse, can praise too much.
'Tis true, and all mens suffrage. But these wayes
　Were not the paths I meant vnto thy praise:
For seeliest Ignorance on these may light,
　Which, when it sounds at best, but eccho's right;
Or blinde Affection, which doth ne're aduance
　The truth, but gropes, and vrgeth all by chance;
Or crafty Malice, might pretend this praise,
　And thinke to ruine, where it seem'd to raise.
These are, as some infamous Baud, or Whore,
　Should praise a Matron. What could hurt her more?
But thou art proofe against them, and indeed
　Aboue th'ill fortune of them, or the need.
I, therefore will begin. Soule of the Age!
　The applause! delight! the wonder of our Stage!
My Shakespeare, rise; I will not lodge thee by
　Chaucer, or Spenser, or bid Beaumont lye
A little further, to make thee a roome:
　Thou art a Moniment, without a tombe,
And art aliue still, while thy Booke doth liue,
　And we haue wits to read, and praise to giue.
That I not mixe thee so, my braine excuses;
　I meane with great, but disproportion'd Muses:
For, if I thought my iudgement were of yeeres,
　I should commit thee surely with thy peeres,
And tell, how farre thou didst our Lily out-shine,
　Or sporting Kid, or Marlowes mighty line.
And though thou hadst small Latine, and lesse Greeke,
　From thence to honour thee, I would not seeke
For names; but call forth thund'ring Æschilus,
　Euripides, and Sophocles to vs,
Paccuuius, Accius, him of Cordoua dead,
　To life againe, to heare thy Buskin tread,
And shake a Stage : Or, when thy Sockes were on,
　Leaue thee alone, for the comparison

of

Of all, that insolent Greece, *or haughtie* Rome
  sent forth, or since did from their ashes come.
Triumph, my Britaine, *thou hast one to showe,*
  To whom all Scenes of Europe *homage owe.*
He was not of an age, but for all time!
  And all the Muses still were in their prime,
when like Apollo *he came forth to warme*
  Our eares, or like a Mercury *to charme!*
Nature her selfe was proud of his designes,
  And ioy'd to weare the dressing of his lines!
which were so richly spun, and wouen so fit,
  As since, she will vouchsafe no other Wit.
The merry Greeke, *tart* Aristophanes,
  Neat Terence, *witty* Plautus, *now not please;*
But antiquated, and deserted lye
  As they were not of Natures family.
Yet must I not giue Nature all: Thy Art,
  My gentle Shakespeare, *must enioy a part.*
For though the Poets *matter, Nature be,*
  His Art doth giue the fashion. And, that he,
Who casts to write a liuing line, must sweat,
  (such as thine are) and strike the second heat
Vpon the Muses *anuile: turne the same,*
  (And himselfe with it) that he thinkes to frame;
Or for the lawrell, he may gaine a scorne,
  For a good Poet's *made, as well as borne.*
And such wert thou. Looke how the fathers face
  Liues in his issue, euen so, the race
Of Shakespeares *minde, and manners brightly shines*
  In his well torned, and true filed lines:
In each of which, he seemes to shake a Lance,
  As brandish't at the eyes of Ignorance.
Sweet Swan of Auon! *what a sight it were*
  To see thee in our waters yet appeare,
And make those flights vpon the bankes of Thames,
  That so did take Eliza, *and our* Iames!
But stay, I see thee in the Hemisphere
  Aduanc'd, and made a Constellation there!
Shine forth, thou Starre of Poets, *and with rage,*
  Or influence, chide, or cheere the drooping Stage;
Which, since thy flight frō hence, hath mourn'd like night,
  And despaires day, but for thy Volumes light.

BEN: IONSON.

Vpon the Lines and Life of the Famous
Scenicke Poet, Mafter WILLIAM
SHAKESPEARE.

Hofe hands, which you fo clapt, go now, and wring
You *Britaines* braue; for done are *Shakefpeares* dayes :
His dayes are done, that made the dainty Playes,
Which made the Globe of heau'n and earth to ring.
Dry'de is that veine, dry'd is the *Thefpian* Spring,
Turn'd all to teares, and *Phæbus* clouds his rayes :
That corp's, that coffin now befticke thofe bayes,
Which crown'd him *Poet* firft, then *Poets* King.
If *Tragedies* might any *Prologue* haue,
All thofe he made, would fcarfe make one to this :
Where *Fame*, now that he gone is to the graue
(Deaths publique tyring-houfe) the *Nuncius* is.
For though his line of life went foone about,
The life yet of his lines fhall neuer out.

HVGH HOLLAND.

Line 5. *Thespian:* the Greek poet Thespis was regarded as the originator of tragedy.

Line 6. *Phoebus:* Apollo; the sun.

Line 7. *besticke:* cover; infest. *bayes:* a crown of bay leaves was the traditional prize for the victors of Greek poetry contests.

Line 10. *All those:* All those tragedies. *this:* the great tragedy of Shakespeare's death.

Line 12. *publique tyring-house:* the tiring-house was the actors' dressing room; the grave is a public tiring-house because there every mortal prepares for Judgment Day.

Line 12. *Nuncius:* messenger.

A CATALOGVE

of the feuerall Comedies, Hiftories, and Tragedies contained in this Volume.

TO THE MEMORIE

of the deceafed Authour Maifter
W. SHAKESPEARE.

SHake-fpeare, *at length thy pious fellowes giue*
The world thy Workes: thy Workes,by which,out-liue
Thy Tombe, thy name muft · when that ftone is rent,
And Time diffolues thy Stratford *Moniment,*
Here we aliue fhall view thee ftill. This Booke,
When Braffe and Marble fade,fhall make thee looke
Frefh to all Ages: when Pofteritie
Shall loath what's new,thinke all' is prodegie
That is not Shake-fpeares*; eu'ry Line,each* Verfe
Here fhall reuiue,redeeme thee from thy Herfe.
Nor Fire,nor cankring Age,as Nafo *faid,*
Of his,thy wit-fraught Booke fhall once inuade.
Nor fhall I e're beleeue, or thinke thee dead
(Though mift)vntill our bankrout Stage be fped
(Jmpofsible) with fome new ftraine t'out-do
Pafsions of Iuliet,*and her* Romeo ;
Or till J heare a Scene more nobly take,
Then when thy half-Sword parlying Romans *fpake.*
Till thefe,till any of thy Volumes *reft*
Shall with more fire,more feeling be expreft,
Be fure,our Shake-fpeare, *thou canft neuer dye,*
But crown'd with Lawrell,liue eternally.

L. Digges.

To the memorie of M. *W.Shake-fpeare.*

VVEE *wondred* (Shake-fpeare) *that thou went'ft fo foone*
From the Worlds-Stage,*to the* Graues-Tyring-roome.
Wee thought thee dead, but this thy printed worth,
Tels thy Spectators,that thou went'ft but forth
To enter with applaufe. An Actors Art,
Can dye,and liue,to acte a fecond part.
That's but an Exit *of Mortalitie ;*
This, a Re-entrance to *a* Plaudite.

I. M.

Digges
Line 8. *prodegie:* freakish, deformed.
Line 11. *cankring age:* meddlesome or critical period of history. Naso is the Roman poet Ovid.
Line 14. *mist:* missed. *sped:* provided.

Line 15. *straine:* song or verse.
I. M.
Line 2. *Graves-Tyring-roome:* see note to Holland poem, line 12.
Line 8. *Plaudite:* accolade, applause.

The Workes of William Shakespeare,

containing all his Comedies, Histories, and

Tragedies: Truely set forth, according to their first
O R J G J N A L L.

The Names of the Principall Actors

in all these Playes.

William Shakespeare.	*Samuel Gilburne.*
Richard Burbadge.	*Robert Armin.*
John Hemmings.	*William Ostler.*
Augustine Phillips.	*Nathan Field.*
William Kempt.	*John Underwood.*
Thomas Poope.	*Nicholas Tooley.*
George Bryan.	*William Ecclestone.*
Henry Condell.	*Joseph Taylor.*
William Slye.	*Robert Benfield.*
Richard Cowly.	*Robert Goughe.*
John Lowine.	*Richard Robinson.*
Samuell Crosse.	*Iohn Shancke.*
Alexander Cooke.	*Iohn Rice.*

1

THE
TEMPEST.

Actus primus, Scena prima.

A tempestuous noise of Thunder and Lightning heard: Enter a Ship-master, and a Botefwaine.

Master.

OTe-fwaine.

Botef. Heere Mafter: What cheere?

Maft. Good : Speake to th'Mariners: fall too't, yarely, or we run our felues a ground, befurre, beftirre.   *Exit.*

Enter Mariners.

Botef. Heigh my hearts, cheerely, cheerely my harts: yare, yare: Take in the toppe-fale : Tend to th'Mafters whiftle : Blow till thou burft thy winde , if roome e- nough.

Enter Alonfo, Sebaftian, Anthonio, Ferdinando, Gonzalo, and others.

Alon. Good Botefwaine haue care : where's the Ma- fter ? Play the men.

Botef. I pray now keepe below.

Anth. Where is the Mafter, Bofon ?

Botef. Do you not heare him? you marre our labour, Keepe your Cabines : you do affift the ftorme.

Gonz. Nay, good be patient.

Botef. When the Sea is : hence, what cares thefe roa- rers for the name of King? to Cabine; filence : trouble vs not.

Gon. Good, yet remember whom thou haft aboord.

Botef. None that I more loue then my felfe. You are a Counfellor, if you can command thefe Elements to fi- lence, and worke the peace of the prefent, wee will not hand a rope more, vfe your authoritie : If you cannot, giue thankes you haue liu'd fo long, and make your felfe readie in your Cabine for the mifchance of the houre, if it fo hap. Cheerely good hearts : out of our way I fay.   *Exit.*

Gon. I haue great comfort from this fellow:methinks he hath no drowning marke vpon him, his complexion is perfect Gallowes : ftand faft good Fate to his han- ging, make the rope of his deftiny our cable, for our owne doth little aduantage : If he be not borne to bee hang'd, our cafe is miferable.   *Exit.*

Enter Botefwaine.

Botef. Downe with the top-Maft : yare, lower, lower, bring her to Try with Maine-courfe. A plague——

A cry within.   Enter Sebaftian, Anthonio & Gonzalo.

vpon this howling: they are lowder then the weather, or our office : yet againe ? What do you heere? Shal we giue ore and drowne, haue you a minde to finke ?

Sebaf. A poxe o'your throat, you bawling, blafphe- mous incharitable Dog.

Botef. Worke you then.

Anth. Hang cur, hang, you whorefon infolent Noyfe- maker, we are leffe afraid to be drownde, then thou art.

Gonz. I'le warrant him for drowning, though the Ship were no ftronger then a Nutt-fhell, and as leaky as an vnftanched wench.

Botef. Lay her a hold, a hold , fet her two courfes off to Sea againe, lay her off.

Enter Mariners wet.

Mari. All loft, to prayers, to prayers, all loft.

Botef. What muft our mouthes be cold ?

Gonz. The King, and Prince, at prayers, let's affift them, for our cafe is as theirs.

Sebaf. I'am out of patience.

An. We are meerly cheated of our liues by drunkards, This wide-chopt-rafcall, would thou mightft lye drow- ning the wafhing of ten Tides.

Gonz. Hee'l be hang'd yet, Though euery drop of water fweare againft it, And gape at widft to glut him. *A confufed noyfe within.* Mercy on vs. We fplit, we fplit, Farewell my wife, and children, Farewell brother : we fplit, we fplit, we fplit.

Anth. Let's all finke with' King

Seb. Let's take leaue of him.   *Exit.*

Gonz. Now would I giue a thoufand furlongs of Sea, for an Acre of barren ground : Long heath, Browne firs, any thing; the wills aboue be done, but I would faine dye a dry death.   *Exit.*

Scena Secunda.

Enter Profpero and Miranda.

Mira. If by your Art (my deereft father) you haue Put the wild waters in this Rore; alay them: The fkye it feemes would powre down ftinking pitch, But that the Sea, mounting to th' welkins cheeke, Dafhes the fire out. Oh ! I haue fuffered With thofe that I faw fuffer: A braue veffell

A   (Who

Leonard Digges on Shakespeare (1623–35)

[Leonard Digges (1588–1635) was a scholar apparently associated for most of his adult life with University College, Oxford. According to Chambers, he is remembered primarily as a translator, and G. Blakemore Evans adds that he was a scholar, traveler, and poet. It is impossible to date the following poem exactly, for Digges had been dead five years when it was printed as one of two commendatory poems in the opening pages of a 1640 edition of Shakespeare, *Poems: Written by Wil. Shake-speare, Gent.* He had written a shorter commendatory poem for the First Folio of 1623 (see above). The first forty lines of praise are quite conventional, but the discussion of specific plays and their impact on audiences is almost unique among such records of Shakespeare. The text is from the first edition (1640).]

Upon Master William Shakespeare, the Deceased Authour, and his Poems

Poets are borne not made,[1] when I would prove
This truth, the glad rememberance I must love
Of never dying *Shakespeare*, who alone
Is argument enough to make that one.
First, that he was a Poet none would doubt,
That heard th'applause of what he sees set out
Imprinted; where thou hast (I will not say
Reader his Workes for to contrive a Play:
To him twas none) the patterne of all wit,
Art without Art unparaleld as yet.
Next Nature onely helpt him, for looke thorow
This whole Booke, thou shalt find he doth not borrow,
One phrase from Greekes, nor Latines imitate,
Nor once from vulgar Languages Translate,
Nor Plagiari-like from others gleane,
Nor begges he from each witty friend a Scene
To peece his Acts with, all that he doth write,
Is pure his owne,[2] plot, language exquisite,
But oh! what praise more powerfull can we give
The dead, then that by him the Kings men live,
His Players, which should they but have shar'd the Fate,
All else expir'd within the short Termes date;
How could the Globe have prospered, since through want
Of change, the Plaies and Poems had growne scant.
But happy Verse thou shall be sung and heard,
When hungry quills shall be such honour bard,
Then vanish upstart Writers to each Stage,
You needy Poetasters of this Age,
Where *Shakespeare* liv'd or spake, Vermine forbeare,
Least with your froth you spot them, come not neere;
But if you needs must write, if poverty
So pinch, that otherwise you starve and die,
On Gods name may the Bull or Cockpit[3] have
Your lame blancke Verse, to keepe you from the grave
Or let new Fortunes younger brethren see,

---

1. A commonplace of the period, based on an anonymous Latin saying.
2. *Art without Art . . . owne:* another, more exaggerated view of Shakespeare's untutored genius and originality

(compare Beaumont's poem, above).
3. The Red Bull, the Cockpit, and the Fortune (below) were other public theaters. The Fortune was rebuilt in 1623 after being destroyed by fire.

What they can picke from your leane industry.
I doe not wonder when you offer at
Blacke-Friers,[4] that you suffer; tis the fate
Of richer veines, prime judgements that have far'd
The worse, with this deceased man compar'd.
So have I seene, when Cesar would appeare,
And on the Stage at halfe-sword parley were,
Brutus and *Cassius*:[5] oh how the Audience,
Were ravish'd, with what wonder they went thence,
When some new day they would not brooke a line,
Of tedious (though well laboured) *Catalines*;
Sejanus[6] too was irkesome, they priz'de more
Honest *Iago*, or the jealous Moore.[7]
And though the Fox and subtill alchimist,[8]
Long intermitted could not quite be mist,
Though these have sham'd all the Ancients, and might raise,
Their Authours merit with a crowne of Bayes.
Yet these sometimes, even at a friends desire
Acted, have scarce defrai'd the Seacoale fire
And doore-keepers: when let but *Falstaffe* come,
Hall, Poines,[9] the rest you scarce shall have a roome
All is so pester'd: let but *Beatrice*
And *Benedicke*[1] be seene, loe in a trice
The Cockpit Galleries,[2] Boxes, all are full
To heare *Malvoglio*[3] that crosse garter'd Gull.
Briefe, there is nothing in his wit fraught Booke,
Whose sound we would not heare, on whose worth looke
Like old coynd gold, whose lines, in every page,
Shall passe true currant to succeeding age.
But why do I dread *Shakespeares* praise recite,
Some second *Shakespeare* must of *Shakespeare* write;
For me tis needlesse, since an host of men,
Will pay to clap his praise, to free my Pen.

Richard James on Falstaff (c. 1625)

[The following is one of several surviving discussions of Shakespeare's great comic charac-
ter and his resemblance to the two actual personages for whom he was successively named,
Sir John Oldcastle and Sir John Falstaff. Richard James studied at Oxford and served as
librarian to Sir Robert Cotton. The text is an excerpt from the *Epistle* to Sir Harry Bour-
chier, as printed in WS, vol. 2.]

A young Gentle Lady of your acquaintance, having read y[e] works of Shakespeare,
made me this question. How S[r] John Falstaffe, or Fastolf, as he is written in y[e] Statute
book of Maudlin[1] Colledge in Oxford, where everye day that society were bound to
make memorie of his soul, could be dead in y[e] time of Harrie y[e] Fift and again live in
y[e] time of Harrie y[e] Sixt to be banished for cowardice: Whereto I made answear that

---

4. The indoor, "private" theater acquired by the King's
Men in 1608 and used afterward along with the Globe.
5. See *Julius Caesar* 4.3.
6. Ben Jonson's two poorly received tragedies.
7. In *Othello*.
8. Jonson's comedies *Volpone* and *The Alchemist*.

9. Characters in *1* and *2 Henry IV*.
1. Characters in *Much Ado About Nothing*.
2. Standing room around the stage, more often known
simply as "the pit."
3. Character in *Twelfth Night*.
1. Magdalen.

it was one of those humours[2] and mistakes for which Plato banisht all poets out of his commonwealth.[3] That Sr John Falstaffe was in those times a noble valiant souldier, as apeeres by a book in ye Heralds Office dedicated unto him by a Herald who had binne with him, if I well remember, for the space of 25 yeeres in ye French wars; that he seems also to have binne a man of learning, because, in a Library of Oxford, I find a book of dedicating Churches sent from him for a present unto Bishop Wainflete, and inscribed with his own hand. That in Shakespeares first shew of Harrie the fift, the person with which he undertook to playe a buffone was not Falstaffe, but Sir Jhon Oldcastle, and that offence beinge worthily taken by Personages descended from his title (as peradventure by many others allso whoe ought to have him in honourable memorie) the poet was putt to make an ignorant shifte of abusing Sir Jhon Falstophe, a man not inferior of Vertue, though not so famous in pietie as the other, who gave witnesse unto the truth of our reformation with a constant and resolute Martyrdom, unto which he was pursued by the Priests, Bishops, Moncks, and Friers of those days.

Milton on Shakespeare (1630)

[John Milton (1608–1674) was born in London and as a boy might conceivably have seen Shakespeare's company act. This poem first appeared prefixed to the Second Folio of Shakespeare's works in 1632, and again in the 1640 *Poems* of Shakespeare. The text is from the 1645 edition of Milton's *Poems*, as reprinted in WS, vol. 2, but the title given is from the Second Folio version.]

An Epitaph on the admirable Dramaticke Poet, W. Shakespeare

> What needs my *Shakespear* for his honour'd Bones,
> The labour of an age in piled Stones,
> Or that his hallow'd reliques should be hid
> Under a star-ypointing[1] *Pyramid?*
> Dear son of memory, great heir of Fame,
> What need'st thou such weak witnes of thy name?
> Thou in our wonder and astonishment
> Hast built thy self a live-long Monument.
> For whilst toth' shame of slow-endeavouring art,
> They easie numbers flow, and that each heart
> Hath from the leaves of thy unvalu'd[2] Book,
> Those Delphick[3] lines with deep impression took,
> Then thou our fancy of itself bereaving,[4]
> Dost make us Marble with too much conceaving;
> And so Sepulcher'd in such pomp dost lie,
> That Kings for such a Tomb would wish to die.

Ben Jonson on Shakespeare (1623–37)

[In addition to numerous allusions to Shakespeare in his plays, Ben Jonson (1573–1637) writes explicitly about his friend, colleague, and rival in a number of places, most significantly in the two commendatory poems prefixed to the First Folio (see above) and in the

---

2. Whims.
3. See the *Republic*, Books 2–3.
1. Pointing to the stars.
2. Invaluable.
3. Reference to Apollo, god of poetry, whose most

famous shrine was at Delphi.
4. *our . . . bereaving:* "our imaginations are rapt 'out of ourselves,' leaving behind our soulless bodies like statues"—Isabel MacCaffrey.

published extracts from his notebooks entitled *Timber: or, Discoveries; Made upon Men and Matter*, first published in his *Works* of 1640. It is impossible to date the original entries precisely; Chambers's conjecture is that the following entry on Shakespeare was made after 1630. The text is from the authoritative edition of Herford and Simpson, vol. 8 (Oxford: Clarendon Press, 1952).]

Indeed, the multitude commend Writers, as they doe Fencers, or Wrastlers; who if they come in robustiously, and put for it, with a deale of violence, are received for the *braver-fellowes*: when many times their owne rudenesse is a cause of their disgrace; and a slight touch of their Adversary, gives all that boisterous force the foyle. But in these things, the unskilfull are naturally deceiv'd, and judging wholly by the bulke, thinke rude things greater then polish'd; and scatter'd more numerous, then compos'd: Nor thinke this only to be true in the sordid multitude, but the neater sort of our *Gallants*: for all are the multitude; only they differ in cloaths, not in judgement or understanding.

I remember, the Players have often mentioned it as an honour to *Shakespeare*, that in his writing, (whatsoever he penn'd) hee never blotted out line.[1] My answer hath beene, Would he had blotted a thousand. Which they thought a malevolent speech. [I had not told posterity this,] but for their ignorance, who choose that circumstance to commend their friend by, wherein he most faulted. And to justifie mine owne candor, (for I lov'd the man, and doe honour his memory (on this side Idolatry) as much as any.) Hee was (indeed) honest, and of an open, and free nature: had an excellent *Phantsie*[2]; brave notions, and gentle expressions: wherein hee flow'd with that facility, that sometime it was necessary he should be stop'd: *Sufflaminandus erat;*[3] as *Augustus* said of *Haterius*.[4] His wit was in his owne power; would the rule of it had beene so too. Many times hee fell into those things, could not escape laughter: As when hee said in the person of *Cæsar*, one speaking to him; *Cæsar, thou dost me wrong*. Hee replyed: *Cæsar did never wrong, but with just cause*[5]: and such like; which were ridiculous. But hee redeemed his vices, with his vertues. There was ever more in him to be praysed, then to be pardoned.

John Aubrey on Shakespeare (1681)

[What Chambers calls "the Shakespeare-mythos" was already well under way by the time John Aubrey (1626–1697) collected these anecdotes for the biographies in his *Brief Lives*, first anthologized in 1692. Aubrey's chief sources were prominent figures of the Restoration stage, which had seen increasingly popular revivals and adaptations of *Hamlet*, *The Tempest*, and many other plays of Shakespeare. Numerous actors and critics in the latter part of the seventeenth century helped to "rehabilitate" Shakespeare; if at the time of the Restoration his plays had seemed terribly musty and old-fashioned, by the 1680s his reputation as an author of lasting value was well established, thanks to the enthusiasm of Restoration playgoers. Aubrey's first source, Christopher Beeston, was the son of a one-time member of Shakespeare's company. William Davenant was a formidable entrepreneur as well as a dramatist, and Thomas Shadwell a prolific playwright perhaps best remembered as Dryden's King of Dullness. The text is from Chambers's transcription (*WS*, vol. 2), with a few silent emendations for ease of reading. Some of the material is from the published version of *Brief Lives*, and some of it from manuscript notes apparently used in writing the *Lives*.]

1. Compare Heminges and Condell's address to the reader in the First Folio: "And what he thought, he uttered with that easinesse, that wee have scarse received from him a blot in his papers."
2. Imagination.

3. "He needed the drag-chain" (adapted from Marcus Seneca's *Controversiae* 4, Preface).
4. Quintus Haterius, Roman rhetorician (d. A.D. 26).
5. See *Julius Caesar* 3.1.47.

the more to be admired q[uia][1] he was not a company keeper[2] lived in Shoreditch, wouldnt be debauched, & if invited to writ; he was in paine.[3]

W. Shakespeare.

M[r]. William Shakespear. [*bay-wreath in margin*] was borne at Stratford upon Avon, in the County of Warwick; his father was a Butcher, & I have been told heretofore by some of the neighbours, that when he was a boy he exercised his father's Trade, but when he kill'd a Calfe, he would doe it in a *high style*, & make a Speech. There was at that time another Butcher's son in this Towne, that was held not at all inferior to him for a naturall witt, his acquaintance & coetanean,[4] but dyed young. This Wm. being inclined naturally to Poetry and acting, came to London I guesse about 18. and was an Actor at one of the Play-houses and did act exceedingly well: now B. Johnson was never a good Actor, but an excellent Instructor. He began early to make essayes at Dramatique Poetry, which at that time was very lowe; and his Playes tooke well: He was a handsome well shap't man: very good company, and of a very readie and pleasant smooth Witt. The Humour[5] of . . . the Constable in a Midsomersnight's Dreame, he happened to take at Grendon [*In margin,* 'I thinke it was Midsomer night that he happened to lye there'.] in Bucks[6] which is the roade from London to Stratford, and there was living that Constable about 1642 when I first came to Oxon.[7] M[r]. Jos. Howe is of that parish and knew him. Ben Johnson and he did gather Humours of men dayly where ever they came. One time as he was at the Tavern at Stratford super[8] Avon, one Combes an old rich Usurer was to be buryed, he makes there this extemporary[9] Epitaph

Ten in the Hundred[1] the Devill allowes
But *Combes* will have twelve, he sweares & vowes:
If any one askes who lies in this Tombe:
Hoh! quoth the Devill, 'Tis my John o' Combe.

He was wont to goe to his native Country once a yeare. I thinke I have been told that he left 2 or 300[li] per annum[2] there and therabout: to a sister. [*In margin,* 'V.[3] his Epitaph in Dugdales Warwickshire'.] I have heard S[r] Wm. Davenant and M[r]. Thomas Shadwell (who is counted the best Comœdian we have now) say, that he had a most prodigious Witt, and did admire his naturall parts beyond all other Dramaticall writers. He was wont to say, That he never blotted out a line in his life: sayd Ben: Johnson, I wish he had blotted out a thousand. [*In margin,* 'B. Johnsons Underwoods'.] His Comœdies will remaine witt, as long as the English tongue is understood; for that he handles mores hominum;[4] now our present writers reflect so much upon particular persons, and coxcombeities, that 20 yeares hence, they will not be understood. Though as Ben: Johnson sayes of him, that he had but little Latine and lesse Greek, He understood Latine pretty well: for he had been in his younger yeares a Schoolmaster in the Countrey. [*In margin,* 'from M[r] —— Beeston'.]

S[r] William Davenant Knight Poet Laureate was borne in ____ street in the City of Oxford, at the Crowne Tavern. His father was John Davenant a Vintner there, a very

---

1. Because.
2. "Company keeper" can mean "libertine" or "reveler"; the general sense of the passage is that Shakespeare is "the more to be admired" for his temperance and modesty.
3. The embarrassment ("paine") at being asked to write is presumably due to the same alleged modesty.
4. Contemporary.
5. Character, personality.
6. Buckinghamshire.

7. Oxford.
8. Upon.
9. Extemporaneous.
1. 10 percent interest. (Combe is damned because he charges 12 percent on his loans, 2 percent above the maximum allowed for usury not to be a mortal sin.)
2. 300 pounds a year.
3. See.
4. *for that . . . hominum:* because he treats of (general) human manners or customs.

grave and discreet Citizen: his mother was a very beautifull woman, & of a very good witt and of conversation extremely agreable. . . . Mr William Shakespeare was wont to goe into Warwickshire once a yeare, and did commonly in his journey lye at this house in Oxon: where he was exceedingly respected. I have heard parson Robert D[avenant] say that here Mr W. Shakespeare here gave him a hundred kisses. Now S^r Wm. would sometimes when he was pleasant over a glasse of wine with his most intimate friends e.g. Sam: Butler (author of Hudibras) &c. say, that it seemed to him that he writt with the very spirit that Shakespeare,[5] and seemed contented enough to be thought his Son: he would tell them the story as above. in which way his mother had a very light report, whereby she was called a whore.

5. A word such as "had" seems to be missing.

A Shakespearean Chronicle
1558–1616

Entries marked by • are from John Stow's *Abridgement of the English Chronicle* (1618). Stow, a member of the Merchant Tailor's Guild, published his first chronicle in 1565 and offered continued, expanded, and abridged versions constantly thereafter, sometimes as often as every year; after his death in 1605, the work was continued by Edmund Howes. Stow's chronicles give us a sense of how "history" was actually experienced from day to day by the citizens of London. Major political events share the page with developments in civic government and portentous signs of all kinds; Stow does not record the date of distant events like the Battle of Lepanto (1571), but he tells us when the news arrived in London and how the citizens responded.

Following Stow, marked by ■, are additional cultural and political details, and then, marked by ♦, information about (probable) first performances of Shakespeare's and others' works, Shakespeare's life and career, and stage history. While some years include all of the categories, most do not. Plays are listed under the year of their first performance; dates in parentheses are (probable) dates of composition, and those in brackets are dates of publication (in the case of Shakespeare's plays, quarto publication).

1558

• The 17 of November 1558 came certain news unto the Parliament house of the death of Queen Mary, whereat many rejoiced, and many lamented, and forthwith her death being generally known, they proclaimed the Lady Elizabeth second daughter to King Henry the eighth Queen of England, France, and Ireland, defender of the faith, &c.

♦ *Translation of Euripides' Iphigenia in Aulis by Jane Lumley.*

Mary I (1553–58), by John Master (fl. 1544–45).

1559

• The 20 of January began a Parliament . . . the Queen granted license for a free disputation to be held in Westminster Church, concerning some different points in Religion, but it came to no effect.

The 24 of June the Book of Common Prayer was established, and the Mass clean suppressed in all Churches.

In August following all ancient Church relics and new made Images in Queen Mary's reign, were beaten down and burned in the open streets.

■ **Acts of Uniformity and Supremacy passed. Elizabeth rejects a reluctant offer of marriage from Philip II of Spain.**

♦ *First account of Lord Robert Dudley's Men (later known as the Earl of Leicester's Men).*

Sources: Bentley, *Shakespeare: A Biographical Handbook*; Bullough, *Narrative and Dramatic Sources of Shakespeare*; Chambers, *The Elizabethan Stage* and *William Shakespeare: A Study of Facts and Problems*; Harbage, Schoenbaum, and Wagonheim, eds., *Annals of English Drama, 975–1700.*

1560

- In April the Lord Gray entered Scotland with ten thousand men, and besieged Leith, where between the French and the English were many hot skirmishes, and many slain on either part.

  The 5 of July through shooting of a Gun in a house in crooked lane, a barrel of powder was set on fire, which blew up four houses, shattered divers others, slew twenty persons outright, and hurt as many, besides great damage to houses and goods.

  This year the Queen by consent of her council, made Proclamation for the utter abolishing and suppression of all manner of base copper monies, which until this time had been current through out the Realm in divers Kings' reigns, and after this publication there was not any base metal coined in England.

- Treaty of Edinburgh: French withdraw from Scotland. Presbyterianism established in Scotland. Publication of the Geneva Bible.

♦ *Translation of Seneca's* Thyestes *by Jasper Heywood.*

Title page to the New Testament of the Geneva Bible (1560).

1561

- The 21st of March, the wardens and assistants of the Merchant-Tailors in London, founded the famous free school in the Parish of St. Lawrence Pountenay.

  The 10 of April W. Geffrey was whipped from the Marshalsea unto Bedlam, for publishing that one John Moore was Jesus Christ, which said John Moore after he had been well whipped, confessed himself a cozening knave.

  The 4 of June between 4 and 5 a clock in the afternoon, there chanced a terrible tempest of thunder and lightning, and chiefly about London, where amongst many harms, it fired the lofty spire of Paul's steeple.

- **Silver coinage reformed. Tulips brought to Europe. Rebellion in Ireland.**

- *Translation of pseudo-Seneca's* Hercules Oetaeus *by Elizabeth I.*

1562

- The 14 of May a man child was borne at Chichester in Sussex, the head, arms, and legs whereof, were like an Anatomy, the breast and belly big, from the navel a long string hanging about the neck, a collar of flesh like the ruff of a neckerchief, coming up about the ears.

- **French civil wars begin. Elizabeth sends an English force to occupy Le Havre. First slave-trading voyage of John Hawkins.**

- *Thomas Norton and Thomas Sackville, The Tragedy of Gorboduc [1565], the first English play in blank verse; shows strong influence of Seneca.*

1563

- The plague of pestilence being in the town of Newhaven [Le Havre], through the number of soldiers that returned into England, the infection thereof spread into divers parts of this realm, but especially the City of London.

  There was no term kept Michaelmas.

  An earthquake in the month of September, specially in Lincoln and Northhampton shires.

- **Church of England adopts the Thirty-Nine Articles.**

1564

- Peace proclaimed between England and France.

  The second of October was an obsequy at Pauls for Ferdinando late Emperor.

  The seventh of October at night all the North parts of the Element seemed to be covered with flames of fire, proceeding from the Northeast and Northwest toward the midst of the firmament, and descended West.

- *Birth of William, John Shakespeare's eldest son (christened April 26). John Shakespeare listed as a "capital burgess" of Stratford and contributes toward the relief of local plague victims.*

1565

• The third day of February, Henry Stuart Lord Darnley . . . took his journey toward Scotland, and in summer following married Mary Queen of Scotland.

✦ *John Shakespeare is made an alderman of Stratford.*

1566

• The 31 of August the Queen's Majesty in her Progress came to the University of Oxford, and was of all the Students honorably received.
  Charles James, the first of that name, son to Henry Stuart Lord Darnley and Mary, King and Queen of Scots, was born in Edinburgh Castle. . . . The Queen's Majesty of England was the Godmother, who gave a font of gold curiously wrought and enamelled, weighing 333 ounces.

▪ **Tobacco brought from the New World around this time.**

✦ *Ariosto's Il Suppositi, translated by George Gascoigne [1573]; first English comedy with significant amount of prose.*

1567

• The 10 of February in the morning, H. Stuart Lord of Darnley, before named King of Scots, was traitorously murdered, the revenge whereof remaineth in the mighty hands of God.
  Within the space of ten months last past, died seven Aldermen in London.
  The 29 of July Charles James the young Prince of Scotland, after a sermon made by John Knox, was crowned King of Scots [James VI] at Sterling Church, and at that time the Queen of Scots was prisoner at Loughleven.

▪ **Revolt against Spanish rule in the Netherlands. The Irish leader Shane O'Neill defeated by Lord Deputy Sir Henry Sidney and later murdered by "certain wild Scots."**

1568

• The 16 of May, Mary Q. of Scots after her escape made out of Loughleven, where she had been long imprisoned, arrived at Werkington in England . . . where she was stayed, and conveyed to Carlisle, and from thence to Bolton castle.
  The eleventh of October were taken in Suffolk at Downham Bridge, 17 monstrous fishes, some of them 27 foot in length, 2 miles from Ipswich.
  The 22 of December was the first day that the Marchants left their meeting in Lombard street, and came into the Burse in Cornhill, builded for that purpose.

▪ **Publication of the Bishops' Bible. Foundation of English College at Douai, to train Jesuits.**

✦ *John Shakespeare elected Bailiff of Stratford, the town's highest office. The Queen's Players and Earl of Worcester's Men perform at Stratford.*

1569

• The 27 of January a Frenchman & two Englishmen were drawn from Newgate to Tiburne, and there hanged, the French man quartered, who had coined gold counterfeit, the Englishmen, the one had clipped silver, the other cast testons of tin.

The 17 of August, an Ambassador from Muscovy, landed at Tower-wharf, and was there received by the Lord Mayor of London.

The 11 of October, Thomas Duke of Norfolk was brought to the Tower prisoner.

The 24 of November the Queen's Majesty caused the Earls of Northumberland and Westmerland, who rebelled in the north, to be proclaimed traitors, and forthwith prepared an Army for their suppression.

Two swordsmen. From "The Norfolke Gentleman," *Roxburghe Ballads.*

1570

- The fourth and fifth of January did suffer [for their part in the Northern Rebellion] at Durham to the number of sixty six Constables and other, amongst whom an Alderman of the towne, and a Priest called Parson Plomtree.

  The Lord Scrope Warden of the West Marches, entered Scotland the 18 of April, burnt and spoiled almost the Dumfries, took many prisoners, and returned safely. . . . There were razed and overthrown and burnt in this journey, above fifty strong Castles and piles, and above 3 thousand towns and villages.

- **Elizabeth excommunicated by Pope Pius V.**

1571

- The 16 of July Rebecca Chambers of Heriettesham, for poisoning T. Chambers her husband, was burnt at Maidstone in Kent.

  The 9 of November great rejoicing was made in London, for the late come news of a marvelous victory obtained against the Turks [The Battle of Lepanto].

1572

- It was enacted that all persons above the age of fourteen years, being taken, vagrant, and wandering misorderly, should be apprehended, whipped, and burnt through the right ear with a hot iron for the first time so taken, the second time to be hanged. [The order includes actors not under the protection of a patron.]

This year 1572, was the [St. Bartholomew's Day] Massacre in Paris.

The 2 of June Thomas Duke of Norfolk was beheaded on Tower Hill.

The 18 of November was seen a star Northward, very bright and clear in the constellation of Cassiopeia, which with three chief fixed stars of the said constellation made a Geometrical figure lozengewise, of the learned men called Rombus. ... The same star was found to be in place celestial, far above the Moon, otherwise than ever any comet hath been seen, or naturally can appear: therefore it is supposed, that the signification thereof is directed purposely, and specially to some matter not natural but celestial, or rather supercelestial, so strange, as from the beginning of the world never was the like.

✦ *The Earl of Leicester's Men perform at Stratford.*

1573

● The 18 of January William Lord Herbert Earl of Worcester, began his journey toward France, to the christening of the King's daughter there, in stead of the Queen's majesty of England. The said Earl with many of his company, were robbed upon the sea of much of their baggage, and three or four of their men slain.

1574

● The 7 of August, a solemn Obsequy was held in Paul's Church in London, for Charles the 9 King of France.

The 15 of August, being Sunday, Agnes Bridges, a maid about the age of 20 years, and Rachel Pinder, a wench about 12 years old, who both of them had counterfeited to be possessed by the devil, stood at Paul's Cross, where they acknowledged their hypocritical counterfeiting, requiring forgiveness of God, & the world: for they had made the people believe many things.

✦ *The Earl of Warwick's and Earl of Worcester's Men perform at Stratford. The Earl of Leicester's men are issued a patent by Queen Elizabeth permitting them to act in London and the provinces.*

1575

● The 16 of February, between four and five of the clock in the afternoon, great Earthquakes happened in the City of York, Worcester, Gloucester, Bristol, Hereford, and the Countries about, which caused the people to run out of their houses, for fear they should have fallen upon their heads.

On Easter day, the third of April, was disclosed a Congregation of Anabaptists, Dutchmen, in a house without the bars of Algate, at London, whereof 17 were taken, and sent to prison, and four of them bearing faggots, recanted at Paul's cross, on the 15 of May. [The rest were later banished or burned.]

✦ *Gascoigne (?) and Sir Henry Lee (?), The Queen's Entertainment at Woodstock.*

1576

- The 11 of February Anne Averies widow, forswearing herself for a little money, that she should have paid for six pounds of tow [rope] at a Shop in Woodstreet in London, fell immediately down speechless, casting up at her mouth, the same matter, which by Nature's course, should have been voided downwards, till she died.

■ Spanish sack Antwerp. Dutch provinces unite against Spain (Treaty of Ghent). Martin Frobisher makes his first voyage in search of the Northwest Passage to Asia.

♦ *James Burbage (father of Richard, the leading actor in Shakespeare's company) builds The Theatre (located in Shoreditch), London's first regular playhouse.*

Burning city under siege. From Raphael Holinshed, *Chronicles of England, Scotland, and Ireland* (1587).

1577

- The 31 of May, Martin Frobisher, with one Ship and two Barks, furnished for that purpose, sailed from Harwich, in Essex, towards Cathay, by the Northwest Seas, and entered his straits, beyond Queen Elizabeth's foreland, about thirty leagues, where he went on shore, and finding store of gold Ore (as he had been informed) fraught his Ship and Bark, caught a man, woman and child of that country, and then on the twenty four of August, returning, arrived at Milford haven on the twentieth of September.

  The stone tower of London Bridge, being decayed, was taken down, and a new foundation drawn.

■ Sir Francis Drake begins his voyage around the world.

♦ *Around this time, John Shakespeare begins his decline into debt.*
  The Curtain Theatre (Shoreditch) opens.

1578

- The 3 of February, John Nelson, for denying the Queen's supremacy, was drawn to Tyburn, and there hanged and quartered.

✦ *Mary Shakespeare pawns her estate, Asbyes at Wilmcote, and her lands at Snitterfield. Lord Strange's Men and Lord Essex's Men perform at Stratford. (Performances in Stratford continue at the rate of at least one a year.)*

1579

- This year Mark Scaliot, Blacksmith of London, for trial of his workmanship made one hanging lock of Iron, steel and brass of eleven several pieces, and a pipe key, all clean wrought, which weighed but one grain of gold. He also at the same time made a chain of gold of forty-three links, to which chain the lock and key being fastened and put about a fleas neck, she drew the same with ease. All which lock, key, chain, and flea, weighed but one grain and a half: a thing most incredible, but that I myself have seen it.

  This year John Fox of Woodbridge, William Wicnor, Robert Moore Englishmen, having been prisoners in Turkey about the space of thirteen years, with more than 260 other Christians of divers nations, by killing of their keeper, marvelously escaped, and returned to their native countries.

- Protestant northern provinces of Holland unite (Union of Utrecht). John Stubbs loses his right hand for attacking Elizabeth's proposed marriage to the Duke of Alençon.

1580

- About the 18 of July, the Lord Gray took his voyage towards Ireland, as Lord Deputy thereof, after whom were sent divers bands of lusty soldiers, both horsemen and footmen, under the leading of expert captains. [In November, Gray massacred several hundred Spanish and Italian mercenaries at Smerwick.]

  The 23 of September at Fennistanton in Huntingtonshire, one Agnes, wife to William Linsey, was delivered of an ugly and strange monster, with a face black, mouth and eyes like a Lion, and both male and female.

- Jesuit mission established in England. Return of Sir Francis Drake.

✦ *John Shakespeare unable to redeem Mary Shakespeare's pawned property.*

1581

- About the 11 of January proclamation was published at London, for revocation of sundry of the Queen's Majesty's subjects remaining beyond the seas under color of study, and yet living contrary to the laws of the Realm. And also against the retaining of Jesuits and massing Priests, sowers of sedition, and other treasonable attempts, &c.

  The first of November Monsieur the French King's brother Duke of Anjou, and other Nobles of France having lately arrived in Kent, came to London, and were honorably received and retained at the Court with great banqueting.

  The first of December, Edmund Campion Jesuit, Ralph Sherwin, and Alexander Brian Seminary Priests, having been arraigned and condemned for high treason, were drawn from the tower of London to Tyburn, and there hanged and quartered.

✦ *A new patent is issued to the Master of the Revels authorizing him to "reform, authorize and put down, as shall be thought meet or unmeet unto himself" any play to be performed in England.*

1582

● This year was first founded a public lecture in Surgery, to begin to be read in the College of Physicians in London.

Peter Morris free denizen, conveyed Thames water in pipes of Lead . . . up to the Northwest corner of Leaden Hall (the highest ground of London) . . . plentifully serving to the commodity of the inhabitants near adjoining in their houses, and also cleansing the kennels of the street towards Bishops gate, Algate, the Bridge, and the Stocks market. But now no such matter, private commodity being preferred, common commodity is neglected, and not reformed as was promised.

▪ Alençon departs from England. Plague in London. Pope Gregory XIII reforms calendar; Protestant countries retain old calendar.

✦ *Shakespeare marries Anne Hathaway (license issued November 27).*

1583

● This year 1583, William Prince of Orange was slain by John Jowrigny a Walloon Soldier, who notwithstanding sundry extreme torments inflicted upon his body and limbs in prison, as also having his flesh plucked off with hot pincers upon an open stage, yet he neither shrunk, nor craved any favor, neither repented him of the fact, but feared he had not slain him. [In fact, William was assassinated in 1584.]

This year 1583, the Queen being at Barne Elmes, at the earnest suit of Sir Francis Walsingham, she entertained twelve Players into her service, and allowed them wages and liveries, as Grooms of the Chamber, and until then she had none of her own, but divers Lords had Players [Queen Elizabeth's Men].

▪ Galileo discovers the principle governing the motion of the pendulum.

✦ *Birth of Shakespeare's older daughter, Susanna.*
Queen Elizabeth's Men established by royal order.

1584

● On the 10 of January, William Carter was arraigned and condemned of high treason, for printing a seditious and traitorous book, entitled, A Treatise of Schism, and was for the same on the next morrow, drawn from Newgate to Tyburn, and there hanged, boweled and quartered, and forthwith a book was published, entitled, A Declaration of the favorable dealing of her Majesty's Commissioners, &c.

▪ Failure of Sir Walter Ralegh's Virginia colony.

Indians gathering food in their Virginia village. From Thomas Hariot, *A Briefe and True Report of the New Found Land of Virginia* (1590).

1585

- The 26 of June, arrived at London, Deputies for the States of the Netherlands, who were lodged about the Tower street, and had their diet worshipfully appointed at the charges of her Majesty, in the Clothworkers hall. Those on the 29 of June, repaired to the Court then at Greenwich, where they presented to her Majesty the sovereignty of those countries.

- Elizabeth declines sovereignty of the Netherlands but sends an army to the Low Countries under the Earl of Leicester.

- *Birth of Shakespeare's twin son and daughter, Hamnet and Judith. John Shakespeare fined for not going to church.*

1586

- A Commission was erected from her Majesty, tending to the ratifying of a firm League of amity, between her Majesty and James King of Scots [confirmed July 1].
  In the month of July, divers traitorous persons were apprehended, and detected of most wicked conspiracy against her Majesty [the Babington Plot], and also of minding to have stirred up a general rebellion throughout the whole Realm. For joy of whose apprehension, the Citizens of London on the 15 of the same month at night, and on the next morrow caused the Bells to be rung, and bonfires to be made, and also banqueted every man according to his ability, some in their houses, some in the streets.

- Mary, Queen of Scots is implicated in the Babington Plot and sentenced to death. Sir Philip Sidney dies from wounds received at the Battle of Zutphen. Leicester is recalled to England.

- *Shakespeare may leave Stratford at about this time. A contemporary reports that he became a country schoolmaster. It is certain only that he is in London by 1592.*

1587

- The 8 of February being Wednesday according to sentence lately given by the nobility, Mary Stuart Queen of Scots, about ten of the Clock before noon, was executed and suffered death, by beheading. . . .
  This year was a late spring, and a cold Summer, so that at Midsummer Peas in the cods were sold at London for 8 pence the peck, yet after were plenty, no cherries ripe til Saint James's-tide or Lammas, and then such plenty that they were sold for a penny the pound.

- Drake defeats Spanish fleet at Cadiz.

- *Thomas Kyd, The Spanish Tragedy [c. 1592]. Christopher Marlowe, 1 Tamburlaine the Great [1590].*
  John Shakespeare loses his position as an alderman.
  The Rose Theatre (located at Bankside, on the Thames) built by Philip Henslowe.

1588

- Great provision was made this year both by Land and Sea, for withstanding the invasion by the Spanish Armada against the Realm.

The 19 of July, intelligence was brought to the Lord Admiral by a pirate Pinnace, whose captain was Thomas Fleming, that the Spanish Fleet was seen in the sea.

The 20 of July, the Lord Admiral made toward the Sea, and the same day had sight of the Spanish fleet, in number by estimation 158 sails. The Lord Admiral cast about toward the land to interrupt them from approaching, & having got the wind of them, prosecuted them all that night, and so continually, from place to place, until the second of August, in which space by the power of GOD having wonderfully overcome them, he returned to Margate in Kent.

- Death of Leicester. Puritan "Martin Marprelate" tracts ridicule the prelacy. African Company receives charter.

♦ John Lyly, Endymion, the Man in the Moon.

Naval battle. From Raphael Holinshed, *Chronicles of England, Scotland, and Ireland* (1587).

1589

- The first of February two soldiers were set on the Pillory at the Leadenhall, whereon they stood by the space of three hours, the one had his ear nailed, the other his tongue pierced with an awl, which awl remained in his tongue till he was taken from the Pillory, for abusing their captains and Governors with bad speeches.

In the month of September, the Citizens of London furnished 1000 men to be sent over into France, to the aiding of Henry late King of Navarre, then challenging the Crown of France.

This year 1589, was devised and perfected, the Art of knitting, or weaving of silk stockings, Wastcotes, Coverlets, and divers other things by engines, or steel Looms, by William Lee, sometime master of St. John's College in Cambridge: and sixteen years after this, he went into France, and taught it to the French, because he was not regarded in England.

- Henry III of France assassinated by a friar.

Medal of Henry III of France. From the *Shirburn Ballads*, no. 46.

✦ *Robert Greene*, Friar Bacon and Friar Bungay. *Thomas Kyd*, Hamlet *(1582–89, not extant; likely source of Shakespeare's* Hamlet). *John Lyly*, Midas *[1592]. Christopher Marlowe*, The Jew of Malta. *Anonymous*, The Taming of a Shrew *(c. 1588–93) [1594]; may be a "bad quarto" of Shakespeare's play.*

Shakespeare is probably affiliated with the amalgamated Lord Strange's and Lord Admiral's Men from about this time until 1594.

Master of the Revels obtains authority to censor and license all plays.

1590

• The 21 of September, being the Feast of Saint Matthew in the afternoon, was a great stir at Lincoln's Inn, by Prentices, and others, against young Gentlemen students at Law there, for some rude demeanors, late before by them done, against the inhabitants of Chancery Lane, which had like to have grown to great mischief, had not the same been by wise Magistrates soon appeased: for the uproar grew great and violent, suddenly.

■ **James VI returns to Scotland with his bride, Anne of Denmark. Beginning of witchcraft trials in Scotland.**

✦ *Translation of Garnier's* Tragedy of Antonius *by Mary Herbert, Countess of Pembroke. Anonymous,* Edward III *(the "Countess scenes" in this play have been attributed to Shakespeare). Anonymous,* The True Chronicle History of King Leir, and His Three Daughters.

1591

• The 16 of July, Edmund Coppinger, and Henry Arthington, Gentlemen, came into Cheap, and there in a car, proclaimed news from heaven, (as they said) to wit, that one William Hacket Yeoman, represented Christ, by partaking his glorified body, by his principal spirit, and that they were two Prophets, the one of mercy, the other of Judgment, called and sent of God, to assist him in his great work, &c. [Hacket

Three old witches with familiars. From *The Wonderful Discoverie of the Witchcrafts of Margaret and Phillip Flower* (1619).

was hanged and quartered; Coppinger starved himself to death in prison; Arthington repented and was set free.]

▪ **Robert Devereux, Earl of Essex, leads expedition to France in aid of Henry IV. Tea is first drunk in England.**

◆ 2 Henry VI *(1591)*; *quarto*, The First Part of the Contention of the Two Famous Houses of York and Lancaster *[1594]*. 3 Henry VI *(1591)*; *octavo*, The True Tragedy of Richard Duke of York and the Good King Henry the Sixth *[1595]*.

Acting is restricted on Sundays and Thursdays to provide for sufficient turnout at bearbaitings.

The bull- and bearbaiting arenas. Detail of *Civitas Londinum*, by Ralph Agas.

1592

● The 13 of December, a certain gentlewoman by the Council's commandment was whipped through the City of London, for affirming her self to be the daughter of Philip king of Spain, as she had been persuaded (by some accounted Soothsayers, after proved liars) for she was known to be a Butcher's daughter in Eastcheap.

▪ **Plague hits London.**

◆ 1 Henry VI *(1592)*. Richard III *(1592–93)* *[1597]*. Venus and Adonis *(1592–93)* *[1593]*. The Comedy of Errors *(1592–94)*.

Marlowe, The Tragical History of Dr. Faustus *and* The Troublesome Reign and Lamentable Death of Edward II.

Robert Greene attacks Shakespeare in his Groats-worth of Wit, *the earliest reference to Shakespeare's career in the theater.*

Philip Henslowe's records show a total of 105 performances between February 19 and June 22, 1592, in London by Lord Strange's Men, probably in the Rose Theatre. Of the plays listed, two are possibly by Shakespeare: Harey the vj *(1 Henry VI, 15 performances) and* Titus & Vespacia *(Titus Andronicus?, 7 performances). Other plays include Greene's* Friar Bacon and Friar Bungay *and Marlowe's* Jew of Malta.

Henslowe begins his diary (continued until 1604), an important source on the theater. From June 1592 until June 1594, London theaters are shut down because of the plague, and acting companies take to the provinces.

1593

- This year was no Bartholomew fair kept at London, for the avoiding of concourse of people, whereby the infection of the pestilence might have increased.

  The whole number this year buried within the City of London, the suburbs and other places adjoining, as well of the plague, as of the other diseases, from the 29 of December in the year 1592, until the 20 of December, 1593 was as followeth. Within the walls of all diseases, 8598, whereof the plague, 5390, without the walls & in the liberties, 9295, the plague 5285. So that within the City and Liberties, of all diseases 17863 [sic]. Whereof the Plague was 10675.

- **Decree requiring church attendance on pain of banishment. Henry of Navarre becomes Catholic.**

- *Sonnets (1593–1603) [1609].* The Rape of Lucrece *(1593–94) [1594].* Titus Andronicus *(1592) [1594].* The Taming of the Shrew *(1592).*

  Henslowe's records show 29 performances for December 29, 1592, to February 1, 1593, again including 1 Henry VI and Titus Andronicus. Lord Strange's Men are led at this time by Edward Alleyn (from the associated Lord Admiral's Men), and also include Will Kempe and John Heminges, Shakespeare's eventual colleagues in the Lord Chamberlain's Men. (There is no mention of Shakespeare himself, who may have traveled with another company or may not have acted at all during the plague years of 1592–94.)

Woodcut showing the plague in London.

1594

● The last of February, Roderigo Lopez a Portugal (as it was said) professing Physic, was arraigned in the Guild-hall of London, found guilty, and had judgment of high Treason, for conspiring her majesty's destruction by poison.
The 16 of April Ferdinando Earl of Derby deceased at Latham, in a very strange manner.

■ **Henry of Navarre crowned Henry IV of France. Birth of James VI's first son, Henry.**

◆ *Shakespeare dedicates* The Rape of Lucrece *to Henry Wriothesley, Earl of Southampton.* The Two Gentlemen of Verona *(1590–91).* Love's Labour's Lost *(1594–95) [1598].* Sir Thomas More *(1592–93; parts revised by Shakespeare, 1603–4).*
Francis Bacon, Thomas Campion, et al., Gesta Grayorum *(1594–95; contains the first surviving formal masque).*
Henslowe's record for the early part of this winter includes one play probably by Shakespeare, listed as Titus & Ondronicous, *suggesting a possible revision of the previous season's* Titus *play. On June 11,* The Tamynge of a Shrowe *enters the London record; this could be an early version of* The Taming of the Shrew, *similar to the bad quarto of this year bearing the same title. The repertoire of the united Lord Admiral's and Lord Chamberlain's Men at this time also includes* Hamlet *(the "Ur-Hamlet," not Shakespeare's), as well as* The Jew of Malta, Titus Andronicus, *and other plays. After June 15, however, the Lord Chamberlain's company re-forms as a separate entity, no longer involving Edward Alleyn.*

1595

● This year by means of the late transportation of grain into foreign Countries, the same was here grown to an excessive price, as in some parts of this Realm, from fourteen shillings to four marks the quarter.
On the 29 of June being Sunday in the afternoon, a number of unruly youths on the Tower hill, being blamed by the Warders of Towerstreet-ward to sever themselves and depart from thence, threw at them stones, and drave them back into Tower street, and were heartened thereunto by a late Soldier, sounding of a trumpet, but the trumpeter and many other of them being taken by the sheriffs of London, and committed to prison.
The two & twenty of July, in presence of the Earl of Essex, and other sent from the Queen, were arraigned in the Guild-hall of London, five of those unruly youths that were on the Tower hill apprehended, they were condemned, and had judgment to be drawn, hanged and quartered.

■ **Hugh O'Neill, Earl of Tyrone, rebels in Ireland. Sir Walter Ralegh sails to Guiana. Robert Southwell, Jesuit poet, is executed.**

◆ Richard II *(1595) [1597].* Romeo and Juliet *(1595) [1599; "bad quarto," 1597].* A Midsummer Night's Dream *(1594–96) [1600].*
Shakespeare living in St. Helen's Parish, Bishopsgate, in London. He apparently becomes a sharer in (provides capital for) the newly re-formed Lord Chamberlain's Men.
Evidence of the activity of the Lord Chamberlain's Men from 1595 to 1599, no longer reflected in Henslowe's records, is scanty. Records of payments in Cambridge and Ipswich indicate at least one provincial tour. Internal evidence suggests that A Midsummer Night's Dream *was the play performed at the court wedding of the Earl of Derby and Lady Elizabeth Vere on January 26, 1595.*
Swan Theatre (Bankside) built.

1596

- On the 11 of April being Easter day about ten of the clock came a new charge, so that all men being in the parish Churches ready to have received the Communion, the Aldermen, their deputies, and Constables, were fain to close up the Church-doors, till they had pressed so many to be soldiers, that by 12 of the Clock, they had in the whole City 1000 men, and they were forthwith furnished of armor and weapons &c. And they were for the most part that night and the rest on the next morning sent away, to Dover, as the like out of other parts of the Realm, but returned again about a week after, for the French had lost Calais, &c. [The Spanish held Calais until 1598.]

  This year, like as in the months of August, September, October, and November, fell great rains, whereupon high waters followed: wheat in meal was sold at London for ten shillings the bushel, Rye six shillings, and Oatmeal eight shillings.

- "League of amity" between England and France.

♦ King John *(1596)*. The Merchant of Venice *(1596–97)* *[1600]*. 1 Henry IV *(1596–97)* *[1598]*.

John Shakespeare is granted a coat of arms, hence the title of "gentleman." William Shakespeare's son Hamnet dies.

Court records list payments to the Lord Chamberlain's Men for several performances in the winter of 1596 and again a year later. Provincial records indicate extensive touring in 1596–97. Payments during this tour average about 20 shillings.

The Shakespeare coat of arms, drafted October 20, 1596.

1597

- This summer arrived here an Ambassador from the King of Polonia, and had audience the twenty five of July, whose Oration was presently answered by her Majesty in Latin.

  A Parliament began at Westminster, on the 24 of October: on the which day divers people were smuldered and crushed to death, pressing between White-hall, and the College Church, to have seen her Majesty, and Nobility riding in their Robes to the said Parliament.

♦ The Merry Wives of Windsor *(1597–98)* *[1602]*.

  James Burbage builds Second Blackfriars Theatre. Restraint on playing in London forces the Lord Chamberlain's Men to tour the provinces. They perform at the Curtain Theatre from late 1597 to 1599 while the Globe is under construction. The scene showing the deposition of Richard is cut from the First Quarto of Richard II, as Elizabeth perceives an analogy between Richard and herself.

1598

- On the third of April, Twiford Town in Devonshire was burnt by casualty of fire, beginning in a poor cottage, a woman there frying pancakes with straw, the same fired the house, and so to the Town, about one of the clock in the afternoon.
 The third of September, died Philip the second of that name, King of Spain.
 In the month of December, great frosts, the Thames nigh over-frozen at London.

- **Edict of Nantes ends French civil wars, granting toleration to Protestants.**

- ♦ 2 Henry IV *(1597–98) [1600]*. Much Ado About Nothing *(1598) [1600]*.
 Jonson, Every Man in His Humor.
 Shakespeare's name is first on the list of "principal Comedians" for Every Man in His Humor.
 Court records of 1598 and 1599 again show payments to the Lord Chamberlain's Men in late December, early January, and late February, specifying Shakespeare's colleagues "Thomas Pope and John Heminges servants to the Lord Chamberlain" as recipients.
 Materials from the demolished Theatre (at Shoreditch) are transported across the river and used in building the Globe as the "public," outdoor theater to replace it.

1599

- The 27 of March, about two of the clock in the afternoon, Robert Devereux, Earl of Essex, Lieutenant General, Lord High Marshal, &c. departed from his house in Seding lane, through Fenchurch street, Grace-street, Cornhill, Cheap, &c. toward Iseldone, High-gate, and rode that night to Saint Albans, towards Ireland.
 The City and Citizens kept unusual watch and ward, and all sorts of people were much amazed and frighted, as well by reason of preparation for wars, not knowing any cause, as also by the sudden strange, and terrible rumors and reports of the Spaniards fierce approach.
 On Michaelmas even, Robert, Earl of Essex, Lieutenant General for Ireland, having secretly returned into England, came to the Court at Nonsuch, & spake with the Queen, and on the second of October, was for contempt, &c. committed to the Lord Keeper.

- **Satires and other offensive books called in and burned by ecclesiastical order. Thomas Nashe and Gabriel Harvey forbidden to publish.**

- ♦ Henry V *(1598–99) [1600]*. Julius Caesar *(1599)*. As You Like It *(1599–1600)*.
 Drayton et al., The First Part of the True and Honorable History of the Life of Sir John Oldcastle, the Good Lord Cobham (response to Shakespeare's treatment of Oldcastle-Falstaff in the Henry IV plays; falsely attributed to Shakespeare).
 Globe playhouse opens as home of the Lord Chamberlain's Men. Will Kempe, the most famous comedian of his day, leaves the Lord Chamberlain's Men around the same time that he performs his famous dance from London to Norwich.

1600

- The fifth of June, the Earl of Essex was called before the Lords of the Council, at the Lord Keepers, where for matters laid to his charge, he was supended from use of divers offices, till her Majesty's pleasure to the contrary, to keep his house, as before: whereat the people still murmured.
 The 8 of August, 1600, came Ambassadors from Abdela Wayhetanow, King of

Barbary. . . . They were very bountifully entertained at the Queen's charges, during their five months abode, they were very subtle and unthankful, they abhorred to give any manner of Alms unto any poor Christians, they sold their broken meat unto those who would give most for it, they killed all their own meat in the Ambassador's house, as Lambs, and all kinds of Pullen, &c. which they usually killed, turning their faces toward the East, they used to wash their own feet twice or thrice a day, and sometimes to wash their bodies: they use beads, and pray to Turkish Saints: they diligently observed the manner of our weights and measures, and all things else that might avail their native Merchants, and prejudice the English Nation.

- **Birth of James VI's second son, Charles. Founding of East India Company.**

✦ Hamlet *(1600–1) [1604; "bad quarto," 1603].*
  Jonson, Cynthia's Revels.
  A letter of Rowland Whyte to Sir Robert Sidney describes a command performance of one of the Falstaff plays arranged by the lord chamberlain (Lord Hunsdon) to entertain a foreign dignitary on March 6: "Upon Thursday my Lord Chamberlain feasted him, and made him very great, and a delicate Dinner, and there in the Afternoon his Players acted, before Vereiken, Sir John Oldcastle [Falstaff], to his great Contentment."
  Edward Alleyn and Philip Henslowe build the Fortune Theatre for the Lord Admiral's Men, competing with the Globe.

Engraving of the Earl of Essex as Lord General.

1601

- Sunday the eight of February, about ten of the clock before noon, Robert Devereux Earl of Essex, assisted by sundry Noblemen and Gentlemen in warlike manner entered the City of London at the Temple Bar, crying for the Queen. [The rising failed, and Essex yielded to arrest the same day.]

  Ash Wednesday, the five and twenty of February, the Earl of Essex was beheaded in the Tower. . . . The Hangman was beaten as he returned thence, so that the Sheriffs of London were sent for, to assist and rescue him from such as would have murdered him.

  The 15 of March, in the night, a new Scaffold was carried from Leaden Hall in London to the Tower hill, and there set up by Torchlight.

  Lightning and thunder often before Christmas, and in the holy days, and an Earthquake at London on Christmas even at noon.

The execution of the Earl of Essex. From the *Shirburn Ballads*, no. 79.

- **New Poor Law places responsibility for relief for the poor on the local parish.**

♦ *"The Phoenix and Turtle" (1601) published in Robert Chester's Loves Martyr. Twelfth Night (1601).*
  Shakespeare's father, John, dies.
  Essex's followers arrange a staging of Richard II at the Globe, to incite rebellion. Culmination of the War of the Theaters, with Ben Jonson in opposition to John Marston and Thomas Dekker.

1602

- In the month of January news came out of Ireland, that on Christmas day the Spaniards and Irish were overcome and slain in great numbers, and the Englishmen were victors.

  The last of June, Atkenson a customer of Hull, was set on the Pillory in Cheap, and with him three other, who had been brought thither on horse back, with their faces toward the horses' tails, and papers on their heads. They were there whipped on the Pillory, and lost their ears by judgment of the Star-Chamber, for slanderous words by them spoken, against the Council.

◆ Troilus and Cressida *(1602) [1609].*
Anonymous, Timon *(its relationship to Shakespeare's* Timon of Athens *is unclear).*
Shakespeare receives a conveyance of land in Old Stratford (127 acres) for £320 and copyhold for a cottage in Stratford.
Salmon Pavy, a boy player referred to as "the stage's jewel" in his epitaph written by Ben Jonson, dies at the age of thirteen.
Opening of the Bodleian Library.

Sketch by George Vertue (1737) of Shakespeare's house in Stratford.

1603

● In the month of March, the Queen lying at Richmond, dangerously sick, straight watches were kept in London with warding at the gates, lanthorns with lights hanged out all night, at which news the people were sore perplexed.

Thursday the four and twenty of March, about two of the clock in the morning, deceased Queen Elizabeth. . . .

[James VI of Scotland declared King James I of England.] This change was very plausible, and well pleasing to the nobility and the Gentry, and generally to all the Commons of the Realm, among whom the name of a King was then so strange, as few could remember, or had seen a King before, except they were aged persons, considering that the government of the Realm had continued near the space of 50 years under the reign of two Queens, which is the far greater part of an old man's age.

Against this time of Coronation, the citizens had made wondrous great provision; but through the terrible increase of pestilence in the City and the Suburbs, their sumptuous Pageants, and other triumphant entertainments, stood like ruins, being not yet finished, and the King constrained to omit his former determination in riding through London, as Kings have accustomed, and all Londoners prohibited by Proclamation from coming at Court: there died that week of all diseases, eleven hundred and three: the twenty five of July being Monday, and the feast of St. James the Apostle, King James the first of that name, King of England, and the most noble Lady Queen Anne his wife, were both crowned and anointed at Westminster.

■ **Hugh O'Neill surrenders in Ireland.**

◆ *Shakespeare's name appears for the last time in Jonson's actors' lists, as a "principal Tragedian" in* Sejanus.
The average take during a provincial tour of this year by Shakespeare's company,

now the King's Men, seems to increase relative to earlier tours, approaching 30 shillings. A letter described by Lady Herbert in 1865 but never subsequently found alludes to a performance of As You Like It *that may have taken place in the fall 1603: "We have a letter, never printed, from Lady Pembroke to her son, telling him to bring James I from Salisbury to see* As You Like It; *'we have the man Shakespeare with us.'"*

Theaters closed again on account of the plague from mid-1603 until April 1604.

The coronation of Macbeth. From Raphael Holinshed, *Chronicles of England, Scotland, and Ireland* (1587).

1604

● The 5 of March was Proclamation made, for the authorizing the Book of Common Prayer.

In October, the Customs of Merchandise were raised both inward and outward, and then let to farm.

■ Peace with Spain. Tax on tobacco.

◆ Measure for Measure *(1603).* Othello *(1603–4) [1622].*

The Malcontent *(possible source for Gloucester's suicide attempt in* King Lear*).* Anonymous, The London Prodigal *(possibly influenced Edgar's use of dialect in* King Lear*).*

Shakespeare's status as a member of the King's Men is recognized in an allowance of four yards of red cloth to wear as a participant in James's coronation procession through London.

A nobleman's letter of January 15, 1604, states: "On New years night we had a play of Robin goodfellow," probably A Midsummer Night's Dream. *Records of eight performances at court during the winter season reflect the growing prominence of the King's Men. The first entry in the Revels Accounts, kept under the auspices of Edmund Tilney, for the 1604–5 season reads: "Hallowmas Day being the first of November A Play in the Banqueting house at Whitehall Called The Moor of Venice [*Othello*]." The* Merry Wives of Windsor *is performed on November 4. Shakespeare is listed several times under the category "the poets which made the plays," though in the unusual spelling "Shaxberd"; he is credited for the performance of* Measure for Measure *on December 26 and of* The Comedy of Errors *two days later.*

1605

- The twenty first of February was a Lion whelped in the Tower, which whelp was taken from the Dam, and brought up by hand, as the King had commanded.

  Upon May day last, Richard Haydocke, a Physician, asked forgiveness of the Lord Archbishop of Canterbury, for deluding the King and many others, under pretense of being inspired, and to preach in his sleep by night with which deceit he had so strongly possessed the vulgar, as it was hard to remove them, although he confessed the abuse.

  [Discovery of Gunpowder Plot] to undermine and blow up the Parliament House, at the instant when the King, Queen, Prince, Peers, and Commons were all assembled. [Guido ("Guy") Fawkes arrested.] The same day in the afternoon, the manner of the treason was by Proclamation made known unto the people, for joy whereof, there was that night as many bonfires as the streets could permit.

- ✦ All's Well That Ends Well *(1604–5).* King Lear *(1604–5) [1608].*

  Ben Jonson writes his first masque for the court.

  The Revels Accounts continue into the new year, listing Love's Labour's Lost *for early January,* Henry V *for January 7, and* The Merchant of Venice *for February 10. The Merchant of Venice is evidently a hit; the entry for February 12 states, "On Shrove Tuesday A play Called the Merchant of Venice Again Commanded By the Kings Majesty." The company also performs three plays not by Shakespeare, including Jonson's* Every Man in His Humour *(February 2).*

  Red Bull Theatre built.

1606

- A very great Whale came within eight miles of London whose length was divers times seen above the water, and the same was judged to be a great deal longer than the longest ship in the river.

  Friday the 28 of March 1606 in the Guildhall in London was arraigned and condemned Henry Garnet Provincial of the Jesuits in England, for being acquainted with the Gunpowder plot, and concealing the same, for the which he was adjudged to be drawn, hanged & quartered, and his head to be set upon London bridge. [The chief conspirators in the plot had been executed in January.]

  The 15 of July the wife of Richard Homwood of East Grimsted in Sussex without any known cause murdered her own three children, and threw them into a pit, and then cut her own throat likewise.

- ■ **London and Plymouth Companies receive charters to colonize Virginia.**

- ✦ Macbeth *(1606).* Antony and Cleopatra *(1606).*

  Jonson, Volpone, *or* The Fox. *Anonymous,* The Revenger's Tragedy.

  Provincial performances of the King's Men continue along with regular London engagements.

  Parliament passes "An Act to Restrain Abuses of Players" in order to purify the language in plays.

1607

- About the middle of May, certain common persons assembled themselves in Northamptonshire, Warwickshire, and Leicestershire: they cut and brake down hedges, filled up ditches, and laid open all such enclosures of commons and other grounds, which of ancient time had been open, and employed to tillage.

About the beginning of September, there fled out of Ireland into the parts beyond the Seas, Hugh Earl of Tyrone, Tyrconnel, Hugh Baron of Dongannon . . . with divers others their servants and followers.

■ Captain John Smith settles Jamestown, Virginia.

✦ Timon of Athens (1607–8). Pericles (1607–8) [1609].

Shakespeare's daughter Susanna married to John Hall. Shakespeare's brother Edmund (described as a player) dies.

1608

● From Sunday the tenth of January, until the fifteenth of the same, the frost grew extreme, so as the Ice [on the Thames] became firm, and removed not, & then all sorts of men, women, and children, went boldly upon the Ice in most parts; some shot at pricks, others bowled and danced, with other variable pastimes; by reason of which concourse of people, there were many that set up booths and standings upon the Ice, as Fruit sellers, Victuallers, that sold beer and wine, Shoemakers, & a Barber's tent, &c. Every of them had fire near their beings.

All the Hartichokes in gardens about London were killed with this frost.

✦ Coriolanus (1608).

William Rowley, The Birth of Merlin (Shakespeare mistakenly named as a collaborator on the title page). Documents mention performances in London of Pericles.

Birth of Shakespeare's granddaughter and death of his mother. Shakespeare obtains a one-seventh share in the Second Blackfriars Theatre.

Hamlet and Richard II (not performed by the King's Men) serve as entertainment on board an East India vessel, the Dragon, off the coast of Sierra Leone. On March 31, Captain Keeling records in his journal: "I invited Captain Hawkins to a fish dinner, and had Hamlet acted aboard me: which I permit to keep my people from idleness and unlawful games, or sleep."

The King's Men lease the Second Blackfriars as a second venue, for private indoor performances.

1609

● The last year, and this spring, according to his Majesty's express order, upon apparent reason and great likelihood of future good & utility to the common subjects of this land, there were many thousands of young Mulberry trees brought hither out of France . . . which were likewise by order sent into divers shires, and there planted for the feeding of Silkworms to make silk, like as it is made in France.

The first, second and third of June, the king in person royal heard the differences between the ecclesiastical and the temporal Judges argued, touching prohibitions out of the King's Bench, and Common Pleas.

■ Moors expelled from Spain.

✦ Publication of the Sonnets. Cymbeline (1609–10). A Lover's Complaint (1609).

1610

• Thursday the 3 of May, the French Queen, with all solemnity was crowned in Paris, having been ten years before married to the king: and the next day after the King was murdered in his coach as he rode through Paris by a base villain that stabbed him in the body with a long knife twice, that he died instantly, and his body was carried to the Louvre.

The Triumphs, Trophies, and pleasant devices at this time, in honor of the Lord Mayor and City of London, were extraordinary great, being in a manner twice so much as hath been usual within the City, and so likewise were the stately shows and ingenious devices upon the water, at the charges of the Company of Merchant-Tailors.

■ **Henry is made Prince of Wales. James dissolves Parliament.**

♦ The Winter's Tale *(1609).*
Jonson, The Alchemist.
Shakespeare probably returns to Stratford and settles there.
Documents mention performances in London of Othello *(Globe, April 30, 1610). There are also records of five provincial performances.*

1611

• The 6 of June the King by Proclamation straightly commanded the oath of Allegiance to be ministered unto all sorts of people, and a true certificate to be made thereof unto the great Lords of the Council.

At this time was concluded a double match between the young French King and the King of Spain's daughter, and the Prince of Spain and the French King's sister.

■ **Plantation of Ulster. Publication of the Authorized (King James) Version of the Bible.**

Inigo Jones's design for Oberon's palace in Ben Jonson's masque *Oberon, the Fairy Prince* (1611).

✦ The Revels Accounts are again available for 1611–12. Two of Shakespeare's last plays are given: The Tempest (November 1) and "ye winters nightes Tayle" (November 5). The series also includes Francis Beaumont and John Fletcher's A King and No King.

1612

● Barthelmew Legat an obstinate Arian Heretic was burned in Smithfield. . . . Edward Wightman, an other perverse Heretic, having refused more favor than he could either desire or deserve, was burned at Lichfield, this Heretic would fain have made the people believe, that he himself was the Holy Ghost and immortal, with sundry other most vile opinions, not fit to be mentioned among Christians.

At this time the corpse of Queen Mary late Queen of Scotland, was translated from Peterborough to Westminster . . . and there placed in a vault, upon the South-side whereof the King had made a Royal Tomb for her, where she now resteth.

Friday the sixth of October [actually November] died the most Noble and hopeful Prince Henry Prince of Wales.

■ **Execution of Lancashire Witches.**

✦ Cardenio, *with Fletcher (1612–13, lost).*

John Webster, The White Devil *(1609–12). Anonymous,* Thorney Abbey, *or* The London Maid *(1606–14; influenced by* Macbeth*).*

Henry, Prince of Wales (1610–11), by Isaac Oliver.

1613

● The 17 of April 1613 at Alington in Lancashire was born a maiden child, having four Legs, four Arms, two Bellies joined to one back, one head with two faces, the one before and the other behind, and this year likewise was great Shipwrack, by violent tempests, there happened also sundry Inundations, and strange accidents, and much damage done by fire in divers places, and upon Saint Peter's day the Globe on the bankside was burned.

■ **Princess Elizabeth married to Frederick, Elector Palatine.**

✦ All Is True (Henry VIII), *probably with John Fletcher (1613)*. The Two Noble Kinsmen, *with Fletcher (1613–14) [1634]*.
Shakespeare purchases Blackfriars Gatehouse.
The Chamber Accounts for 1612–13 indicate that the King's Men had given a total of twenty plays at court by May 20, including revivals of Much Ado About Nothing, 1 and 2 Henry IV, Othello, *and* Julius Caesar, *taking in £60. A further payment is recorded in compensation of a performance before a foreign dignitary in June.*

1614

• In September there was a general muster of horse and foot throughout the Land, and therewithal training of soliders, but chiefly in the City of London by the citizens themselves, many whereof by their former voluntary exercise of Armes and Military discipline, were now so ready and expert that they taught others.

▪ "Addled" Parliament is summoned and dissolved.

✦ Jonson, Bartholomew Fair. Webster, The Duchess of Malfi.
Philip Henslowe and Jacob Meade build the Hope Theatre (Bankside), a combination theater and bear garden. The Globe reopens.

1615

• At this time proclamation was made again, not only to stay, all further increase of buildings, which were daily erected in and about London, contrary to sundry former Edicts, and thereupon this Proclamation ratified and confirmed all former Proclamations, and straightly charged all Commissioners in that behalf, to look and search in to the depth of such offenders, and offenses, and to punish them accordingly. This Proclamation was dated the 16 of July 1615. And yet for all this, there was wondrous new increase of buildings round about London.

✦ *Lady Elizabeth's players draw up a series of articles of grievance against Philip Henslowe, concerning their considerable debt to him. The Privy Council orders the eight leading members of four London companies, including Richard Burbage and Christopher Beeston, to come before them for performing during Lent against the orders of the Master of the Revels.*

1616

• This Summer, and harvest was so dry, that passengers were annoyed with dust in the highways the 20 of November.

▪ William Harvey describes the circulation of blood.

✦ *Marriage of Shakespeare's daughter Judith. Shakespeare makes his will on March 25; he dies April 23.*
Ben Jonson, The Works of Benjamin Jonson, *the first collection of plays by an English author. His* Masque of Christmas *presented at court.*
Christopher Beeston builds the Phoenix Theatre.

James I (1603–25), by Simon de Passe.

1616–23

♦ *The First Folio of Shakespeare's plays is published by members of the King's Men in 1623.*

Records for the years immediately following Shakespeare's death show the continued popularity of Twelfth Night *and* A Winter's Tale, *among other plays. Both are performed at court by the King's Men in April 1618; a performance at court of* A Winter's Tale *is recorded for 1619–20 and of* Twelfth Night *for Candlemas (February 2), 1623. A letter of May 20, 1619, written by Sir Gerrard Herbert describes the entertainment of a visiting French nobleman: "In the kinges greate Chamber they went to see the play of*

Pirrocles, Prince of Tyre, which lasted till 2 aclocke. After two actes, the players ceased till the French all refreshed them with sweetmeates brought on Chinay voiders, & wyne & ale in bottells, after the players begann anewe." The new Master of the Revels, Sir Henry Herbert, notes on August 19, 1623: *"For the king's players. An olde playe called Winter's Tale, formerly allowed of by Sir George Bucke, and likewise by mee on M*^r* Hemminges his worde that there was nothing profane added or reformed, thogh the allowed booke was missinge; and therefore I returned it without a fee."*

General Bibliography

There is a huge and ever-expanding scholarly literature about Shakespeare and his culture. This general list and the ten-item lists accompanying the individual plays and poems in this volume are only a small sampling of the available resources. Journals devoted to Shakespeare studies include *Shakespeare Bulletin, Shakespeare Jahrbuch* (Germany), *Shakespeare Newsletter, Shakespeare Quarterly, Shakespeare Studies, Shakespeare Studies* (Tokyo), and *Shakespeare Survey* (England). The categories below are only approximate; many of the texts could properly belong in more than one category.

Shakespeare's World

Social, Political, and Economic History

Archer, Ian W. *The Pursuit of Stability: Social Relations in Elizabethan London.* Cambridge: Cambridge University Press, 1991.

Aries, Philippe, and Georges Duby, eds. *A History of Private Life: Passions of the Renaissance.* Vol. 3. Ed. Roger Chartier. Trans. Arthur Goldhammer. Cambridge: Belknap Press of Harvard University Press, 1989.

Barry, J., ed. *The Tudor and Stuart Town.* London: Longman, 1990.

Barry, Jonathan, and Christopher Brooks. *The Middling Sort of People.* New York: St. Martin's Press, 1994.

Barthelmey, Gerard. *Black Face, Maligned Race.* Baton Rouge: Louisiana State University Press, 1987.

Beier, A. L. *Masterless Men: The Vagrancy Problem in England, 1560–1640.* New York: Methuen, 1987.

——, and Roger Finlay, eds. *London 1500–1700: The Making of a Metropolis.* London: Longman, 1986.

Ben-Amos, Ilana Krausman. *Adolescence and Youth in Early Modern England.* New Haven: Yale University Press, 1994.

Bridenbaugh, Carl. *Vexed and Troubled Englishmen, 1590–1642.* New York: Oxford University Press, 1968.

Camden, Carroll. *The Elizabethan Woman.* Rev. ed. Mamaroneck, N.Y.: Appel, 1975.

Chew, Samuel. *The Crescent and the Rose.* New York: Octagon Books, 1965.

Clark, Alice. *Working Life of Women in the Seventeenth Century.* 1968. London: Routledge, 1992.

Clay, C. G. A. *Economic Expansion and Social Change.* 2 vols. Cambridge: Cambridge University Press, 1984.

Cruickshank, C. G. *Elizabeth's Army.* 2nd ed. Oxford: Clarendon Press, 1966.

Elliot, J. H. *The Old World and the New, 1492–1650.* Cambridge: Cambridge University Press, 1970.

Ellis, Steven G. *Tudor Ireland.* London: Longman, 1985.

Elton, G. R. *The Tudor Revolution in Government.* Cambridge: Cambridge University Press, 1959.

——. *England Under the Tudors.* London: Methuen, 1955.

Emmison, P. G. *Elizabethan Life: Disorder.* Chelmsford: Essex County Council, 1970.

Erickson, Amy Louise. *Women and Property in Early Modern England.* London: Routledge, 1993.

Finlay, Roger. *Population and Metropolis: The Demography of London, 1580–1650*. Cambridge: Cambridge University Press, 1979.

Fletcher, Anthony. *Gender, Sex, and Subordination in England, 1500–1800*. New Haven: Yale University Press, 1995.

——, and John Stevenson, eds. *Order and Disorder in Early Modern England*. Cambridge: Cambridge University Press, 1985.

Gittings, C. *Death, Burial and the Individual in Early Modern England*. London: Croom Helm, 1984.

Helgerson, Richard. *Forms of Nationhood: The Elizabethan Writing of England*. Chicago: University of Chicago Press, 1990.

Hirst, Derek. *Authority and Conflict: England, 1603–1658*. Cambridge: Harvard University Press, 1986.

Ingram, Martin. *Church Courts, Sex, and Marriage in England, 1570–1640*. Cambridge: Cambridge University Press, 1987.

James, Mervyn. *Society, Politics and Culture: Studies in Early Modern England*. Cambridge: Cambridge University Press, 1986.

Kantorowicz, E. H. *The King's Two Bodies*. Princeton: Princeton University Press, 1957.

King, J. N. *Tudor Royal Iconography*. Princeton: Princeton University Press, 1989.

Klein, Joan Larsen. *Daughters, Wives, and Widows: Writings by Men about Women and Marriage in England, 1500–1640*. Urbana: University of Illinois Press, 1992.

Laqueur, Thomas. *Making Sex: Body and Gender from the Greeks to Freud*. Cambridge: Harvard University Press, 1990.

Laslett, Peter. *The World We Have Lost: Further Explored*. 3rd ed. New York: Scribner, 1984.

Levin, Carole. *"The Heart and Stomach of a King": Elizabeth I and the Politics of Sex and Power*. Philadelphia: University of Pennsylvania Press, 1994.

Lockyer, Roger. *The Early Stuarts: A Political History of England*. London: Longman, 1989.

MacCaffrey, Wallace T. *Elizabeth I: War and Politics*. Princeton: Princeton University Press, 1992.

——. *The Shaping of the Elizabethan Regime*. Princeton: Princeton University Press, 1968.

Manning, Roger B. *Village Revolts: Social Protest and Popular Disturbances in England, 1509–1640*. Oxford: Clarendon Press, 1988.

Mattingly, Garrett. *The Armada*. Boston: Houghton Mifflin, 1959.

Mukerji, Chandra. *From Graven Images: Patterns of Modern Materialism*. New York: Columbia University Press, 1983.

Neale, J. E. *Queen Elizabeth I*. London: Cape, 1961.

Neale, John E. *Elizabeth I and Her Parliaments*. 2 vols. New York: St. Martin's Press, 1958.

Nichols, John, ed. *The Progresses and Public Processions of Queen Elizabeth*. 3 vols. London, 1823.

Notestein, Wallace. *The House of Commons, 1604–1610*. New Haven: Yale University Press, 1971.

Palliser, D. M. *The Age of Elizabeth*. 2nd ed. London: Longman, 1992.

Parry, G. *The Age of Reconnaissance: Discovery, Exploration, and Settlement, 1450–1650*. New York: Praeger, 1969.

Pearson, Lu Emily. *Elizabethans at Home*. Stanford: Stanford University Press, 1957.

Peck, Linda Levy. *Court Patronage and Corruption in Early Stuart England*. Boston: Unwin Hyman, 1990.

Pocock, J. G. A. *The Ancient Constitution and the Feudal Law*. Rev. ed. Cambridge: Cambridge University Press, 1987.

Quinn, David B. *The Elizabethans and the Irish*. Ithaca, N.Y.: Cornell University Press, 1966.

Scarisbrick, J. J. *Henry VIII*. Berkeley and Los Angeles: University of California Press, 1968.

Sharpe, J. A. *Crime in Seventeenth-Century England: A Country Study.* Cambridge: Cambridge University Press, 1983.
Slack, Paul. *The Impact of Plague in Tudor and Stuart England.* London: Routledge & Kegan Paul, 1985.
——, ed. *Rebellion, Popular Protest and the Social Order in Early Modern England.* Cambridge: Cambridge University Press, 1984.
Stone, Lawrence. *The Causes of the English Revolution, 1529–1642.* New York: Routledge & Kegan Paul, 1986.
——. *The Family, Sex and Marriage in England, 1500–1800.* New York: Harper & Row, 1977.
——. *The Crisis of the Aristocracy, 1558–1641.* Oxford: Clarendon Press, 1965.
Stow, John. *Survey of London.* Ed. C. L. Kingsford. Oxford: Clarendon Press, 1971.
Tawney, R. H. *Religion and the Rise of Capitalism.* 1926. New York: Peter Smith, 1962.
Thirsk, Joan. *Economic Policy and Projects: The Development of a Consumer Society in Early Modern England.* Oxford: Clarendon Press, 1978.
Thomas, Keith. *Religion and the Decline of Magic.* New York: Scribner, 1971.
Underdown, David. *Revel, Riot, and Rebellion: Popular Politics and Culture in England, 1603–1660.* Oxford: Clarendon Press, 1985.
Walvin, James. *The Black Presence: A Documentary History of the Negro in England, 1555–1860.* London: Orbach & Chambers, 1971.
Willson, David Harris. *King James VI & I.* 1956. London: Cape, 1972.
Wilson, F. P. *Elizabethan and Jacobean.* Oxford: Clarendon Press, 1945.
Yates, Frances. *Astraea: The Imperial Theme in the Sixteenth Century.* London: Routledge & Kegan Paul, 1975.
Zagorin, Perez. *Rebels and Rulers, 1500–1660.* 2 vols. Cambridge: Cambridge University Press, 1982.
——. *The Court and the Country: The Beginnings of the English Revolution.* New York: Atheneum, 1970.
Zeeveld, W. Gordon. *Foundations of Tudor Policy.* Cambridge: Harvard University Press, 1948.

Intellectual and Religious History

Baker, Herschel C. *The Race of Time: Three Lectures on Renaissance Historiography.* Toronto: University of Toronto Press, 1967.
Barkan, Leonard. *Nature's Work of Art: The Human Body as Image of the World.* New Haven: Yale University Press, 1975.
Bouwsma, William J. *John Calvin: A Sixteenth-Century Portrait.* New York: Oxford University Press, 1988.
Brower, Reuben A. *Hero and Saint: Shakespeare and the Graeco-Roman Tradition.* New York: Oxford University Press, 1971.
Cassirer, Ernst. *The Individual and the Cosmos in Renaissance Philosophy.* Trans. Mario Domandi. Philadelphia: University of Pennsylvania Press, 1972.
Collinson, Patrick. *The Elizabethan Puritan Movement.* New York: Oxford University Press, 1989.
——. *The Religion of Protestants: The Church in English Society, 1559–1625.* Oxford: Clarendon Press, 1982.
Dickens, A. G. *The English Reformation.* New York: Schocken Books, 1964.
Haydn, Hiram. *The Counter-Renaissance.* 1950. Gloucester, Mass.: P. Smith, 1966.
Hill, Christopher. *Society and Puritanism in Pre-Revolutionary England.* New York: Schocken Books, 1967.
Kelly, Henry Ansgar. *Divine Providence in the England of Shakespeare's Histories.* Cambridge: Harvard University Press, 1970.
Klaits, Joseph. *Servants of Satan: The Age of the Witch Hunts.* Bloomington: Indiana University Press, 1985.

Kocher, Paul. *Science and Religion in Elizabethan England.* 1953. New York: Octagon Books, 1969.

Kristeller, Paul Oskar. *Renaissance Thought: The Classic, Scholastic, and Humanistic Strains.* New York: Harper, 1961.

Levao, Ronald. *Renaissance Minds and Their Fictions.* Berkeley and Los Angeles: University of California Press, 1985.

Levin, Harry. *The Myth of the Golden Age in the Renaissance.* Bloomington: University of Indiana Press, 1969.

Levy, Fred J. *Tudor Historical Thought.* San Marino, Calif.: Huntington Library Press, 1967.

Lovejoy, A. O. *The Great Chain of Being: A Study of the History of an Idea.* Cambridge: Harvard University Press, 1936.

Mack, Peter, ed. *Renaissance Rhetoric.* New York: St. Martin's Press, 1994.

Popkin, Richard H. *The History of Skepticism from Erasmus to Spinoza.* Berkeley and Los Angeles: University of California Press, 1979.

Rossi, Paolo. *Francis Bacon: From Magic to Science.* London: Routledge & Kegan Paul, 1968.

Shuger, Debora Kuller. *Habits of Thought in the English Renaissance: Religion, Politics, and the Dominant Culture.* Berkeley and Los Angeles: University of California Press, 1990.

Sonnino, Lee A. *A Handbook to Sixteenth-Century Rhetoric.* London: Routledge & Kegan Paul, 1968.

Strong, Roy. *The Cult of Elizabeth.* London: Thames and Hudson, 1977.

———. *The English Icon: Elizabethan and Jacobean Portraiture.* London: Routledge & Kegan Paul, 1969.

Tillyard, E. M. W. *The Elizabethan World Picture.* London: Chatto & Windus, 1943.

Wind, Edgar. *Pagan Mysteries in the Renaissance.* 2nd ed. London: Faber, 1968.

Cultural History

Aers, David, Bob Hodge, and Gunther Kress. *Literature, Language and Society in England, 1589–1680.* Totowa, N.J.: Barnes & Noble, 1981.

Austern, Linda Phyllis. " 'Sing Againe Syren': The Female Musician and Sexual Enchantment in Elizabethan Life and Literature." *Renaissance Quarterly* 42 (1989): 420–48.

Bakhtin, Mikhail. *Rabelais and His World.* Cambridge: MIT Press, 1968.

Barkan, Leonard. *The Gods Made Flesh: Metamorphosis and the Pursuit of Paganism.* New Haven: Yale University Press, 1986.

Barker, Francis. *The Tremulous Private Body.* London: Methuen, 1994.

Beilin, Elaine V. *Redeeming Eve: Women Writers of the English Renaissance.* Princeton: Princeton University Press, 1987.

Bevington, David. *Tudor Drama and Politics: A Critical Approach to Topical Meaning.* Cambridge: Harvard University Press, 1968.

Bray, Alan. *Homosexuality in Renaissance England.* London: Gay Men's Press, 1982.

Briggs, K. M. *Pale Hecate's Team: An Examination of the Beliefs on Witchcraft and Magic among Shakespeare's Contemporaries and His Immediate Successors.* New York: Humanities Press, 1962.

———. *The Anatomy of Puck: An Examination of Fairy Beliefs among Shakespeare's Contemporaries and Successors.* London: Routledge & Kegan Paul, 1959.

Burke, Peter. *Popular Culture in Early Modern Europe.* New York: New York University Press, 1978.

Burt, Richard, and John Michael Archer, eds. *Enclosure Acts: Sexuality, Property, and Culture in Early Modern England.* Ithaca, N.Y.: Cornell University Press, 1994.

Buxton, John. *Elizabethan Taste.* London: Macmillan, 1963.

Caldwell, John. *The Oxford History of English Music.* Vol. 1. Oxford: Clarendon Press, 1991.

Cressy, David. *Literacy and the Social Order: Reading and Writing in Tudor and Stuart England.* Cambridge: Cambridge University Press, 1980.

Dolan, Frances. *Dangerous Familiars: Representations of Domestic Crime in England, 1550–1700.* Ithaca, N.Y.: Cornell University Press, 1994.

Eisenstein, Elizabeth. *The Printing Press as an Agent of Change.* 2 vols. Cambridge: Cambridge University Press, 1979.

Ferguson, Margaret W., Maureen Quilligan, and Nancy J. Vickers, eds. *Rewriting the Renaissance: The Discourses of Sexual Difference in Early Modern Europe.* Chicago: University of Chicago Press, 1986.

Fumerton, Patricia. *Cultural Aesthetics: Renaissance Literature and the Practice of Social Ornament.* Chicago: University of Chicago Press, 1991.

Garber, Marjorie, ed. *Cannibals, Witches, Divorce: Estranging the Renaissance.* Baltimore: Johns Hopkins University Press, 1987.

Gillies, John. *Shakespeare and the Geography of Difference.* New York: Cambridge University Press, 1994.

Goldberg, Jonathan. *Writing Matter: From the Hands of the English Renaissance.* Stanford: Stanford University Press, 1990.

——. *James I and the Politics of Literature: Jonson, Shakespeare, Donne and Their Contemporaries.* Baltimore: Johns Hopkins University Press, 1983.

——, ed. *Queering the Renaissance.* Durham, N.C.: Duke University Press, 1994.

Greenblatt, Stephen. *Learning to Curse: Essays in Early Modern Culture.* New York: Routledge, 1990.

——. *Renaissance Self-Fashioning: From More to Shakespeare.* Chicago: University of Chicago Press, 1980.

——, ed. *New World Encounters.* Berkeley and Los Angeles: University of California Press, 1993.

——, ed. *Representing the English Renaissance.* Berkeley and Los Angeles: University of California Press, 1988.

Grout, Donald Jay. *A Short History of Opera.* New York: Columbia University Press, 1988.

Hall, Kim F. *Things of Darkness: Economies of Race and Gender in Early Modern England.* Ithaca, N.Y.: Cornell University Press, 1996.

Haselkorn, Anne M., and Betty S. Travitsky, eds. *The Renaissance Englishwoman in Print: Counterbalancing the Canon.* Amherst: University of Massachusetts Press, 1990.

Henderson, Katherine Usher, and Barbara F. McManus. *Half Humankind: Contexts and Texts of the Controversy About Women in England, 1540–1640.* Urbana: University of Illinois Press, 1985.

Hendricks, Margo, and Patricia Parker, eds. *Women, "Race," and Writing in the Early Modern Period.* London: Routledge, 1994.

Hoeniger, F. David. *Medicine and Shakespeare in the English Renaissance.* Newark: University of Delaware Press, 1991.

Huizinga, Johan. *The Autumn of the Middle Ages.* Trans. Rodney J. Payton and Ulrich Mammitzsch. Chicago: University of Chicago Press, 1996.

Hull, Suzanne W. *Chaste, Silent and Obedient: English Books for Women, 1475–1640.* San Marino, Calif.: Huntington Library, 1982.

Jardine, Lisa. *Still Harping on Daughters: Women and Drama in the Age of Shakespeare.* 1983. 2nd ed. New York: Columbia University Press, 1989.

Javitch, Daniel. *Poetry and Courtliness in Renaissance England.* Princeton: Princeton University Press, 1978.

Jordan, Constance. *Renaissance Feminism: Literary Texts and Political Models.* Ithaca, N.Y.: Cornell University Press, 1990.

Kelso, Ruth. *Doctrine for the Lady of the Renaissance.* 1956. Urbana: University of Illinois Press, 1978.

——. *The Doctrine of the English Gentleman in the Sixteenth Century.* 1929. Gloucester, Mass.: P. Smith, 1964.

Manley, Lawrence. *Literature and Culture in Early Modern London.* Cambridge: Cambridge University Press, 1995.

Marcus, Leah. *The Politics of Mirth: Jonson, Herrick, Milton, Marvell, and the Defense of Old Holiday Pastimes.* Chicago: University of Chicago Press, 1986.

Miller, David Lee, Sharon O'Dair, and Harold Weber, eds. *The Production of English Renaissance Culture.* Ithaca, N.Y.: Cornell University Press, 1994.

Norbrook, David. *Poetry and Politics in the English Renaissance.* London: Routledge & Kegan Paul, 1984.

Orlin, Lena Cowen. *Private Matters and Public Culture in Post-Reformation England.* Ithaca, N.Y.: Cornell University Press, 1994.

Parry, G. *The Golden Age Restor'd: The Culture of the Stuart Court, 1603–1642.* Manchester: Manchester University Press, 1981.

Patterson, Annabel. *Censorship and Interpretation: The Conditions of Writing and Reading in Early Modern England.* Madison: University of Wisconsin Press, 1984.

Shapiro, James. *Shakespeare and the Jews.* New York: Columbia University Press, 1996.

Sharpe, K., and Lake, P., eds. *Culture and Politics in Early Stuart England,* Stanford: Stanford University Press, 1993.

Simon, Joan. *Education and Society in Tudor England.* Cambridge: Cambridge University Press, 1966.

Sinfield, Alan. *Literature in Protestant England, 1560–1660.* Totowa, N.J.: Barnes & Noble, 1983.

Smith, Bruce. *Homosexual Desire in Shakespeare's England.* Chicago: University of Chicago Press, 1991.

Spufford, Margaret. *Small Books and Pleasant Histories: Popular Fiction and Its Readership in Seventeenth-Century England.* Athens: University of Georgia Press, 1981.

Stallybrass, Peter, and Allon White. *The Politics and Poetics of Transgression.* Ithaca, N.Y.: Cornell University Press, 1986.

Turner, James Grantham, ed. *Sexuality and Gender in Early Modern Europe: Institutions, Texts, Images.* Cambridge: Cambridge University Press, 1993.

Whigham, Frank. *Ambition and Privilege: The Social Tropes of Elizabethan Courtesy Theory.* Berkeley and Los Angeles: University of California Press, 1984.

Woodbridge, Linda. *Women and the English Renaissance: Literature and the Nature of Womankind, 1540–1620.* Urbana: University of Illinois Press, 1986.

Wright, L. B. *Middle-Class Culture in Elizabethan England.* Chapel Hill: University of North Carolina Press, 1935.

Shakespeare's Literary and Theatrical Contexts

Agnew, Jean-Christophe. *Worlds Apart: The Market and the Theatre in Anglo-American Thought, 1550–1750.* Cambridge: Cambridge University Press, 1986.

Alpers, Paul. *What Is Pastoral?* Chicago: University of Chicago Press, 1996.

Altman, Joel. *The Tudor Play of Mind.* Berkeley and Los Angeles: University of California Press, 1978.

Barber, C. L. *Creating Elizabethan Tragedy: The Theater of Kyd and Marlowe.* Chicago: University of Chicago Press, 1988.

Barish, Jonas. *Ben Jonson and the Language of Prose Comedy.* Cambridge: Harvard University Press, 1960.

———. *The Antitheatrical Prejudice.* Berkeley and Los Angeles: University of California Press, 1981.

Bate, Jonathan. *Shakespeare and Ovid.* Oxford: Clarendon Press, 1993.

Bates, Catherine. *The Rhetoric of Courtship in Elizabethan Language and Literature.* Cambridge: Cambridge University Press, 1992.

Belsey, Catherine. *The Subject of Tragedy: Identity and Difference in Renaissance Drama.* London: Methuen, 1985.

Bentley, G. E. *The Profession of Player in Shakespeare's Time, 1590–1642.* Princeton: Princeton University Press, 1984.

———. *The Profession of Dramatist in Shakespeare's Time, 1590–1642.* Princeton: Princeton University Press, 1971.

———. *The Seventeenth-Century Stage: A Collection of Critical Essays.* Chicago: University of Chicago Press, 1968.

———. *The Jacobean and Caroline Stage.* 7 vols. Oxford: Clarendon Press, 1941–68.

Bevington, David. *From "Mankind" to Marlowe: Growth of Structure in the Popular Drama of Tudor England.* Cambridge: Harvard University Press, 1962.

Bowers, Fredson T. *Elizabethan Revenge Tragedy, 1587–1642.* Princeton: Princeton University Press, 1940.

Bradbrook, M. C. *The Rise of the Common Player: A Study of Actor and Society in Shakespeare's England.* London: Chatto & Windus, 1962.

Braden, Gordon. *Renaissance Tragedy and the Senecan Tradition.* New Haven: Yale University Press, 1985.

Briggs, Julia. *This Stage-Play World: English Literature and Its Background, 1580–1625.* Oxford: Oxford University Press, 1983.

Bristol, Michael D. *Carnival and Theater: Plebeian Culture and the Structure of Authority in Renaissance England.* New York: Methuen, 1985.

Bruster, Douglas. *Drama and the Market in the Age of Shakespeare.* Cambridge: Cambridge University Press, 1992.

Bullough, Geoffrey, ed. *Narrative and Dramatic Sources of Shakespeare.* 8 vols. New York: Columbia University Press, 1957–75.

Butler, Martin. *Theatre and Crisis, 1632–1642.* Cambridge: Cambridge University Press, 1984.

Clubb, Louise George. *Italian Drama in Shakespeare's Time.* New Haven: Yale University Press, 1989.

Cohen, Walter. *Drama of a Nation: Public Theater in Renaissance England and Spain.* Ithaca, N.Y.: Cornell University Press, 1985.

Dessen, Alan C. *Recovering Shakespeare's Theatrical Vocabulary.* Cambridge: Cambridge University Press, 1995.

———. *Elizabethan Stage Conventions and Modern Interpreters.* Cambridge: Cambridge University Press, 1984.

———. *Elizabethan Drama and the Viewer's Eye.* Chapel Hill: University of North Carolina Press, 1977.

Doran, Madeleine. *Endeavors of Art: A Study of Form in Elizabethan Drama.* Madison: University of Wisconsin Press, 1954.

Empson, William. *The Structure of Complex Words.* 1951. London: Chatto & Windus, 1970.

Farnham, Willard. *The Medieval Heritage of Elizabethan Tragedy.* 1936. New York: Barnes & Noble, 1956.

Foakes, R. A. *Illustrations of the English Stage, 1580–1642.* Stanford: Stanford University Press, 1985.

Gardiner, H. C. *Mysteries' End.* New Haven: Yale University Press, 1946.

Harbage, Alfred. *Shakespeare and the Rival Traditions.* 1952. New York: Barnes & Noble, 1968.

Hardison, O. B. Jr. *Christian Rite and Christian Drama in the Middle Ages.* Baltimore: Johns Hopkins University Press, 1965.

Hattaway, Michael. *Elizabethan Popular Theatre: Plays in Performance.* London: Routledge & Kegan Paul, 1982.

Heinemann, Margot. *Puritanism and Theatre: Thomas Middleton and Opposition Drama under the Early Stuarts.* Cambridge: Cambridge University Press, 1980.

Homan, Sidney, ed. *Shakespeare's "More Than Words Can Witness."* Lewisburg, Pa.: Bucknell University Press, 1980.

Hosley, Richard, ed. *Shakespeare's Holinshed: An Edition of Holinshed's Chronicles.* New York: Putnam, 1968.

Hunter, G. K. *John Lyly: The Humanist as Courtier.* Cambridge: Harvard University Press, 1962.

Jones, Emrys. *Scenic Form in Shakespeare.* Oxford: Clarendon Press, 1971.

Kernan, Alvin. *The Cankered Muse: Satire of the English Renaissance.* New Haven: Yale University Press, 1959.

Kolve, V. A. *The Play Called Corpus Christi.* Stanford: Stanford University Press, 1966.

Leggatt, Alexander. *Citizen Comedy in the Age of Shakespeare.* Toronto: University of Toronto Press, 1973.

Levin, Harry. *The Overreacher: A Study of Christopher Marlowe.* 1932. Cambridge: Harvard University Press, 1964.

Levin, Richard. *The Multiple Plot in English Renaissance Drama.* Chicago: University of Chicago Press, 1971.

Lomax, Marion. *Stage Images and Traditions: Shakespeare to Ford.* Cambridge: Cambridge University Press, 1987.

McLuskie, Kathleen. *Renaissance Dramatists.* New York: Harvester Wheatsheaf, 1989.

McMillin, Scott. *The Elizabethan Theatre and the Book of Sir Thomas More.* Ithaca, N.Y.: Cornell University Press, 1987.

Montrose, Louis. *The Purpose of Playing: Shakespeare and the Cultural Politics of the Elizabethan Theatre.* Chicago: University of Chicago Press, 1996.

Muir, Kenneth. *Shakespeare's Sources.* 2 vols. London, 1957.

Orgel, Stephen. *The Illusion of Power: Political Theater in the English Renaissance.* Berkeley and Los Angeles: University of California Press, 1975.

Rose, Mark. *Shakespearean Design.* Cambridge: Harvard University Press, 1972.

Rose, Mary Beth. *The Expense of Spirit: Love and Sexuality in English Renaissance Drama.* Ithaca, N.Y.: Cornell University Press, 1988.

Sanders, Wilbur. *The Dramatist and the Received Idea: Studies in the Plays of Marlowe and Shakespeare.* Cambridge: Cambridge University Press, 1968.

Spivack, Bernard. *Shakespeare and the Allegory of Evil.* New York: Columbia University Press, 1958.

Waith, Eugene. *The Herculean Hero in Marlowe, Chapman, Shakespeare, and Dryden.* New York: Columbia University Press, 1962.

Weimann, Robert. *Shakespeare and the Popular Tradition in the Theater: Studies in the Social Dimension of Dramatic Form and Function.* Ed. Robert Schwartz. Baltimore: Johns Hopkins University Press, 1978.

Woolf, Rosemary. *The English Mystery Plays.* Berkeley and Los Angeles: University of California Press, 1972.

The Playing Field: London Theaters and State Regulation

Astington, John H., ed. *The Development of Shakespeare's Theater.* New York: AMS Press, 1992.

Barrol, Leeds. *Politics, Plague, and Shakespeare's Theater: The Stuart Years.* Ithaca, N.Y.: Cornell University Press, 1991.

Beckerman, Bernard. *Shakespeare at the Globe, 1599–1609.* New York: Macmillan, 1962, 1967.

Berry, Herbert. *Shakespeare's Playhouses.* Illustrated by C. Walter Hodges. AMS Studies in the Renaissance 19. New York: AMS Press, 1987.

Chambers, E. K. *The Elizabethan Stage.* 4 vols. Oxford: Clarendon Press, 1923.

———. *The Medieval Stage.* 2 vols. Oxford: Clarendon Press, 1903.

Clare, Janet. *"Art Made Tongue-Tied by Authority": Elizabethan and Jacobean Dramatic Censorship.* New York: St. Martin's Press, 1990.

Cook, Ann Jennalie. *The Privileged Playgoers of Shakespeare's London: 1576–1642.* Princeton: Princeton University Press, 1981.

Gair, W. Reavley. *The Children of Paul's.* Cambridge: Cambridge University Press, 1982.

Gildersleeve, Virginia C. *Government Regulation of the Elizabethan Drama.* Westport, Conn.: Greenwood Press, 1975.

Greg, W. W., ed. *Dramatic Documents from the Elizabethan Playhouses: Stage Plots; Actor's Parts; Prompt Books.* 2 vols. 1931. Oxford: Clarendon Press, 1969.

Gurr, Andrew. *The Shakespearean Stage, 1574–1642.* 3rd ed. Cambridge: Cambridge University Press, 1992.

———. *Playgoing in Shakespeare's London.* Cambridge: Cambridge University Press, 1987.

———, and John Orrell. *Rebuilding Shakespeare's Globe.* London: Weidenfeld and Nicolson, 1989.

Harbage, Alfred. *Shakespeare's Audience.* New York: Columbia University Press, 1941.

Henslowe, Philip. *Henslowe's Diary.* Ed. R. A. Foakes and R. T. Rickert. Cambridge: Cambridge University Press, 1961.

Hodges, C. Walter. *The Globe Restored.* 1953. New York: Norton, 1968, 1973.

Ingram, William. *The Business of Playing: The Beginnings of Adult Professional Theater in Elizabethan London.* Ithaca, N.Y.: Cornell University Press, 1992.

Joseph, Bertram L. *Acting Shakespeare.* London: Routledge & Kegan Paul, 1960.

Kernodle, G. R. *From Art to Theatre: Form and Convention in the Renaissance.* 1944. Chicago: University of Chicago Press, 1965.

King, T. J. *Shakespearean Staging, 1599–1642.* Cambridge: Harvard University Press, 1971.

Knutson, Roslyn L. *The Repertory of Shakespeare's Company, 1594–1613.* Fayetteville: University of Arkansas Press, 1991.

Mullaney, Steven. *The Place of the Stage: License, Play and Power in Renaissance England.* Chicago: University of Chicago Press, 1987.

Orgel, Stephen. *Impersonations: The Performance of Gender in Shakespeare's England.* Cambridge: Cambridge UP, 1996.

Shapiro, Michael. *Children of the Revels: The Boy Companies of Shakespeare's Time and Their Plays.* New York: Columbia University Press, 1977.

Smith, Irwin. *Shakespeare's Blackfriars Playhouse.* New York: New York University Press, 1964.

———. *Shakespeare's Globe Playhouse.* New York: Scribner, 1956.

Wickham, Glynne. *Early English Stages: 1300 to 1660.* 4 vols. New York: Columbia University Press, 1959–81.

Shakespeare's Life

Alexander, Peter. *Shakespeare's Life and Art.* New ed. New York: New York University Press, 1961.

Baldwin, T. W. *William Shakspere's Small Latine and Lesse Greeke.* 2 vols. Urbana: University of Illinois Press, 1944.

Bentley, G. E. *Shakespeare: A Biographical Handbook.* New Haven: Yale University Press, 1961.

Bradbrook, Muriel. *Shakespeare: The Poet in His World.* London: Weidenfeld and Nicolson, 1978.

Burton, S. H. *Shakespeare's Life and Stage.* Edinburgh: W. & R. Chambers, 1989.

Chambers, E. K. *William Shakespeare: A Study of Facts and Problems.* 2 vols. Oxford: Clarendon Press, 1930.

Eccles, Mark. *Shakespeare in Warwickshire.* Madison: University of Wisconsin Press, 1961.

Fraser, Russell. *Shakespeare: The Later Years.* New York: Columbia University Press, 1992.

——. *Young Shakespeare*. New York: Columbia University Press, 1988.

Greer, Germaine. *Shakespeare*. New York: Oxford University Press, 1986.

Honigmann, E. A. J. *Shakespeare: The Lost Years*. Totowa, N.J.: Barnes & Noble, 1985.

——, ed. *Shakespeare and His Contemporaries: Essays in Comparison*. Manchester: Manchester University Press, 1986.

Hotson, Leslie. *Shakespeare Versus Shallow*. London: Nonesuch Press, 1931.

Levi, Peter. *The Life and Times of William Shakespeare*. New York: Holt, 1989.

Matus, Irvin Leigh. *Shakespeare: The Living Record*. New York: St. Martin's Press, 1991.

Reese, M. M. *Shakespeare: His World and His Work*. Rev. ed. New York: St. Martin's Press, 1980.

Rogers, Joyce. *The Second Best Bed: Shakespeare's Will in a New Light*. Westport, Conn.: Greenwood Press, 1993.

Sams, Eric. *The Real Shakespeare: Retrieving the Early Years, 1564–1594*. New Haven: Yale University Press, 1995.

Schmidgall, Gary. *Shakespeare and the Poet's Life*. Lexington: University Press of Kentucky, 1990.

Schoenbaum, Samuel. *Shakespeare's Lives*. New ed. New York: Oxford University Press, 1991.

——. *Shakespeare: His Life, His Language, His Theater*. New York: Signet, 1990.

——. *William Shakespeare: A Compact Documentary Life*. Rev. ed. Oxford: Oxford University Press, 1987.

Thomson, Peter. *Shakespeare's Professional Career*. Cambridge: Cambridge University Press, 1992.

Wells, Stanley. *Shakespeare: A Life in Drama*. New York: Norton, 1995.

Shakespearean Criticism

Founding Figures

Shakespeare: The Critical Heritage. Ed. Brian Vickers. Multiple volumes. London: Routledge & Kegan Paul, 1974–.

Coleridge, S. T. *Coleridge on Shakespeare: The Text of the Lectures of 1811–12*. Ed. R. A Foakes. Charlottesville: University of Virginia Press, 1971.

Coleridge, S. T. *Samuel Taylor Coleridge: Shakespearean Criticism*. 2 vols. 2nd ed. 1960. Ed. T. M. Raysor. Totowa, N.J.: Biblio Distribution Center, 1974, 1980.

Hazlitt, William. *Characters of Shakespear's Plays*. London, 1817.

Johnson, Samuel. *Johnson on Shakespeare*. Ed. Arthur Sherbo. Vol. 7 of The Yale Edition of the Works of Samuel Johnson. New Haven: Yale University Press, 1968.

Morgann, Maurice. *Shakespearean Criticism*. Ed. Daniel Fineman. Oxford: Clarendon Press, 1972.

Language and Style

Baxter, John. *Shakespeare's Poetic Styles*. London: Routledge & Kegan Paul, 1980.

Blake, N. F. *Shakespeare's Language: An Introduction*. New York: St. Martin's Press, 1983.

Cercignani, Fausto. *Shakespeare's Works and Elizabethan Pronunciation*. New York: Oxford University Press, 1981.

Clemen, Wolfgang. *The Development of Shakespeare's Imagery*. London: Methuen, 1951.

Danson, Lawrence. *Tragic Alphabet: Shakespeare's Drama of Language*. New Haven: Yale University Press, 1974.

Donawerth, Jane. *Shakespeare and the Sixteenth-Century Study of Language*. Urbana: University of Illinois Press, 1984.

Edwards, Philip, Inga-Stina Ewbank, and G. K. Hunter, eds. *Shakespeare's Styles.* Cambridge: Cambridge University Press, 1980.

Hussey, S. S. *The Literary Language of Shakespeare.* London: Longman, 1982.

Kökeritz, Helge. *Shakespeare's Pronunciation.* New Haven: Yale University Press, 1959.

Mahood, M. M. *Shakespeare's Wordplay.* London: Methuen, 1957.

Miriam Joseph, Sister. *Shakespeare's Use of the Arts of Language.* New York: Columbia University Press, 1947.

Parker, Patricia. *Shakespeare from the Margins: Language, Culture, Context.* Chicago: University of Chicago Press, 1996.

Partridge, Eric. *Shakespeare's Bawdy: A Literary and Psychological Essay and a Comprehensive Glossary.* 3rd ed. New York: Routledge, 1991.

Spurgeon, Caroline. *Shakespeare's Imagery and What It Tells Us.* 1935. Cambridge: Cambridge University Press, 1968.

Vickers, Brian. *"Shakespeare's Use of Rhetoric." A New Companion to Shakespeare Studies.* Ed. Kenneth Muir and S. Schoenbaum. Cambridge: Cambridge University Press, 1971. 83–98.

——. *The Artistry of Shakespeare's Prose.* London: Methuen, 1968.

Wright, George T. *Shakespeare's Metrical Art.* Berkeley and Los Angeles: University of California Press, 1988.

Critical Approaches

Adelman, Janet. *Suffocating Mothers: Fantasies of Maternal Origin in Shakespeare's Plays.* New York: Routledge, 1992.

Andrews, John F. *William Shakespeare: His World, His Work, His Influence.* 3 vols. New York: Scribner, 1985.

Bamber, Linda. *Comic Women, Tragic Men: A Study of Gender and Genre in Shakespeare.* Stanford: Stanford University Press, 1982.

Barber, C. L. *Shakespeare's Festive Comedy: A Study of Dramatic Form and Its Relation to Social Custom.* Princeton: Princeton University Press, 1959.

——, and Richard P. Wheeler. *The Whole Journey: Shakespeare's Power of Development.* Berkeley and Los Angeles: University of California Press, 1986.

Barker, Deborah E., and Ivo Kamps, eds. *Shakespeare and Gender: A History.* New York: Verso, 1995.

Barton, Anne. *Essays, Mainly Shakespearean.* Cambridge: Cambridge University Press, 1994.

Battenhouse, Roy, ed. *Shakespeare's Christian Dimension: An Anthology of Commentary.* Bloomington: Indiana University Press, 1994.

Berry, Ralph. *Shakespeare and Social Class.* Atlantic Highlands, N.J.: Humanities Press International, 1988.

——. *Shakespeare and the Awareness of the Audience.* New York: St. Martin's Press, 1985.

Boose, Lynda E. *"The Father and the Bride in Shakespeare." PMLA* 97 (1982): 325–47.

Booth, Stephen. *"King Lear," "Macbeth," Indefinition and Tragedy.* New Haven: Yale University Press, 1983.

Bradley, A. C. *Shakespearean Tragedy.* 1904. 3rd ed. New York: St. Martin's Press, 1992.

Bradshaw, Graham. *Misrepresentations: Shakespeare and the Materialists.* Ithaca, N.Y.: Cornell University Press, 1993.

——. *Shakespeare's Skepticism.* New York: St. Martin's Press, 1987.

Brissenden, Alan. *Shakespeare and the Dance.* Atlantic Highlands, N.J.: Humanities Press International, 1981.

Bristol, Michael. *Shakespeare's America, America's Shakespeare.* London: Routledge, 1990.

Burkhardt, Sigurd. *Shakespearean Meanings.* Princeton: Princeton University Press, 1968.

Calderwood, James. *Shakespeare and the Denial of Death.* Amherst: University of Massachusetts Press, 1987.

———. *Shakespearean Metadrama*. Minneapolis: University of Minnesota Press, 1971.

Callaghan, Dympna. *Woman and Gender in Renaissance Tragedy: A Study of "King Lear," "Othello," "The Duchess of Malfi," and "The White Devil."* Atlantic Highlands, N.J.: Humanities Press International, 1989.

Carroll, William C. *The Metamorphoses of Shakespearean Comedy*. Princeton: Princeton University Press, 1985.

Cavell, Stanley. *Disowning Knowledge in Six Plays of Shakespeare*. Cambridge: Cambridge University Press, 1987.

Charnes, Linda. *Notorious Identity: Materializing the Subject in Shakespeare*. Cambridge: Harvard University Press, 1993.

Clemen, Wolfgang H. *Shakespeare's Soliloquies*. Trans. Charity Scott Stokes. London: Methuen, 1987.

Cohen, Derek. *Shakespeare's Culture of Violence*. New York: St. Martin's Press, 1993.

Colie, Rosalie L. *Shakespeare's Living Art*. Princeton: Princeton University Press, 1974.

Colman, E. A. M. *The Dramatic Use of Bawdy in Shakespeare*. London: Longman, 1974.

Cox, John D. *Shakespeare and the Dramaturgy of Power*. Princeton: Princeton University Press, 1989.

Cunningham, J. V. *Woe or Wonder: The Emotional Effect of Shakespearean Tragedy*. Denver: University of Denver Press, 1951.

Dash, Irene. *Wooing, Wedding, and Power: Women in Shakespeare's Plays*. New York: Columbia University Press, 1981.

Dawson, Anthony. *Indirections: Shakespeare and the Art of Illusion*. Toronto: University of Toronto Press, 1978.

De Grazia, Margreta. "Homonyms before and after Lexical Standardization." *Deutsche Shakespeare Gesellschaft West (Jahrbuch)*. Bochum, Germany, 1990. 143–56.

Dollimore, Jonathan, and Alan Sinfield, eds. *Political Shakespeare: Essays in Cultural Materialism*. 2nd ed. Manchester: Manchester University Press, 1994.

———. *Radical Tragedy: Religion, Ideology, and Power in the Drama of Shakespeare and His Contemporaries*. Durham, N.C.: Duke University Press, 1993.

Drakakis, John, ed. *Alternative Shakespeares*. London: Methuen, 1985.

Dubrow, Heather, and Richard Strier. *The Historical Renaissance*. Chicago: University of Chicago Press, 1988.

Dusinberre, Juliet. *Shakespeare and the Nature of Women*. 2nd ed. Houndsmill, Basingstoke: Macmillan, 1996.

Eagleton, Terry. *William Shakespeare*. Oxford: Blackwell, 1987.

Edwards, Philip. *Shakespeare: A Writer's Progress*. Oxford: Oxford University Press, 1986.

Eliot, T. S. "Shakespeare and the Stoicism of Seneca." *Selected Essays, 1917–1932*. 1932. New York: Harcourt Brace Jovanovich, 1950.

Engle, Lars. *Shakespearean Pragmatism: Market of His Time*. Chicago: University of Chicago Press, 1993.

Erickson, Peter. *Patriarchal Structures in Shakespeare's Drama*. Berkeley and Los Angeles: University of California Press, 1985.

———, and Coppèlia Kahn, eds. *Shakespeare's Rough Magic: Essays in Honor of C. L. Barber*. Newark: University of Delaware Press, 1985.

Evans, Malcolm. *Signifying Nothing: Truth's True Contents in Shakespeare's Text*. Athens: University of Georgia Press, 1986.

Farrell, Kirby. *Play, Death, and Heroism in Shakespeare*. Chapel Hill: University of North Carolina Press, 1989.

Felperin, Howard. *Shakespearean Romance*. Princeton: Princeton University Press, 1972.

Fiedler, Leslie. *The Stranger in Shakespeare*. New York: Stein & Day, 1972.

French, Marilyn. *Shakespeare's Division of Experience*. London: Cape, 1981.

Frye, Northrop. *Fools of Time: Studies in Shakespearean Tragedy*. Toronto: University of Toronto Press, 1967.

———. *A Natural Perspective: The Development of Shakespearean Comedy and Romance*. New York: Columbia University Press, 1965.

Garber, Marjorie. *Coming of Age in Shakespeare.* London: Methuen, 1981.
———. *Shakespeare's Ghost Writers: Literature as Uncanny Causality.* New York: Methuen, 1987.
Girard, Rene. *A Theater of Envy: William Shakespeare.* New York: Oxford University Press, 1991.
Goldberg, Jonathan. *Sodometries: Renaissance Texts, Modern Sexualities.* Stanford: Stanford University Press, 1992.
Goldman, Michael. *Shakespeare and the Energies of Drama.* Princeton: Princeton University Press, 1972.
Grady, Hugh. *The Modernist Shakespeare: Critical Texts in a Material World.* Oxford: Clarendon Press, 1991.
Greenblatt, Stephen. *Shakespearean Negotiations: The Circulation of Social Energy in Renaissance England.* Berkeley and Los Angeles: University of California Press, 1988.
Hapgood, Robert. *Shakespeare: The Theatre-Poet.* Oxford: Oxford University Press, 1988.
Hawkes, Terence. *Meaning by Shakespeare.* London: Routledge, 1992.
———. *That Shakespeherian Rag.* London: Methuen, 1986.
Hibbard, G. R. *The Making of Shakespeare's Dramatic Poetry.* Toronto: University of Toronto Press, 1981.
Holderness, Graham, ed. *Shakespeare's History Plays: "Richard II" to "Henry V."* New York: St. Martin's Press, 1992.
———, ed. *The Shakespeare Myth.* Manchester: Manchester University Press, 1988.
Holland, Norman. *Psychoanalysis and Shakespeare.* New York: McGraw-Hill, 1966.
———, et al., eds. *Shakespeare's Personality.* Berkeley and Los Angeles: University of California Press, 1989.
Honigmann, E. A. J. *Myriad-Minded Shakespeare: Essays, Chiefly on the Tragedies and Problem Plays.* New York: St. Martin's Press, 1989.
———, ed. *Shakespeare's Impact on His Contemporaries.* London: Macmillan, 1982.
Hope, Jonathan. *The Authorship of Shakespeare's Plays.* Cambridge: Cambridge University Press, 1994.
Houston, John Porter. *Shakespearean Sentences: A Study in Style and Syntax.* Baton Rouge: Louisiana State University Press, 1988.
Howard, Jean. *The Stage and Social Struggle in Early Modern England.* New York: Routledge, 1994.
———, and Marion F. O'Connor, eds. *Shakespeare Reproduced: The Text in History and Ideology.* New York: Methuen, 1987.
Hughes, Ted. *Shakespeare and the Goddess of Complete Being.* London: Faber, 1992.
Hunt, Maurice. *Shakespeare's Labored Art: Stir, Work, and the Late Plays.* New York: Peter Lang, 1995.
Jones, Emrys. *The Origins of Shakespeare.* Oxford: Clarendon Press, 1977.
Kahn, Coppèlia. *Man's Estate: Masculine Identity in Shakespeare.* Berkeley and Los Angeles: University of California Press, 1981.
Kamps, Ivo, ed. *Materialist Shakespeare: A History.* New York: Verso, 1995.
Kastan, David Scott. *Shakespeare and the Shapes of Time.* Hanover: University Press of New England, 1982.
Kermode, Frank, ed. *Four Centuries of Shakespearean Criticism.* 1965. New York: Avon, 1974.
Kernan, Alvin. *Shakespeare, the King's Playwright: Theater in the Stuart Court, 1603–1613.* New Haven: Yale University Press, 1995.
Kirsch, Arthur. *Shakespeare and the Experience of Love.* Cambridge: Cambridge University Press, 1981.
Knapp, Jeffrey. *An Empire Nowhere: England, America, and Literature from "Utopia" to "The Tempest."* Berkeley and Los Angeles: University of California Press, 1992.
Knapp, Robert S. *Shakespeare—The Theater and the Book.* Princeton: Princeton University Press, 1989.

Knight, G. Wilson. *The Wheel of Fire*. 1930. 5th rev. ed. Cleveland: World Publishing, 1962.

Kott, Jan. *Shakespeare Our Contemporary*. Trans. Boleslaw Taborski. Garden City, N.Y.: Doubleday Anchor, 1966.

Laroque, François. *Shakespeare's Festive World: Elizabethan Seasonal Entertainment and the Professional Stage*. Cambridge: Cambridge University Press, 1993.

Lenz, Carolyn Ruth Swift, Gayle Greene, and Carol Thomas Neely, eds. *The Woman's Part: Feminist Criticism of Shakespeare*. Urbana: University of Illinois Press, 1980.

Levin, Harry. *Shakespeare and the Revolution of the Times*. New York: Oxford University Press, 1976.

Levith, Murray J. *Shakespeare's Italian Settings and Plays*. New York: St. Martin's Press, 1989.

Loomba, Ania. *Gender, Race, Renaissance Drama*. Manchester: Manchester University Press, 1989.

Lukacher, Ned. *Daemonic Figures: Shakespeare and the Question of Conscience*. Ithaca, N.Y.: Cornell University Press, 1994.

Mack, Maynard. *Everybody's Shakespeare: Reflections Chiefly on the Tragedies*. Lincoln: University of Nebraska Press, 1993.

Mahon, John W., and Thomas A. Pendleton, eds. *"Fanned and Winnowed Opinion": Shakespearean Essays Presented to Harold Jenkins*. London: Methuen, 1987.

Mallin, Eric S. *Inscribing the Time: Shakespeare and the End of Elizabethan England*. Berkeley and Los Angeles: University of California Press, 1995.

Marcus, Leah S. *Puzzling Shakespeare: Local Reading and Its Discontents*. Berkeley and Los Angeles: University of California Press, 1988.

Maus, Katharine. *Inwardness and Theater in the English Renaissance*. Chicago: University of Chicago Press, 1995.

McDonald, Russ. *The Bedford Companion to Shakespeare: An Introduction with Documents*. Boston: Bedford Books, 1996.

McMullan, Gordon, and Jonathan Hope, eds. *The Politics of Tragicomedy: Shakespeare and After*. London: Routledge, 1992.

Miola, Robert. *Shakespeare's Rome*. Cambridge: Cambridge University Press, 1983.

Mooney, Michael E. *Shakespeare's Dramatic Transactions*. Durham, N.C.: Duke University Press, 1990.

Mowat, Barbara. *The Dramaturgy of Shakespeare's Romances*. Athens: University of Georgia Press, 1976.

Muir, Kenneth. *The Sources of Shakespeare's Plays*. London: Methuen, 1977.

Neely, Carol Thomas. *Broken Nuptials in Shakespeare's Plays*. New Haven: Yale University Press, 1985.

Nevo, Ruth. *Tragic Form in Shakespeare*. Princeton: Princeton University Press, 1972.

Newman, Karen. *Fashioning Femininity and English Renaissance Drama*. Chicago: University of Chicago Press, 1991.

Novy, Marianne. *Love's Argument: Gender Relations in Shakespeare*. Chapel Hill: University of North Carolina Press, 1984.

——, ed. *Women's Re-Visions of Shakespeare*. Urbana: University of Illinois Press, 1990.

O'Brien, Peggy, ed. *Shakespeare Set Free*. 3 vols. New York: Washington Square, 1993–95.

Orkin, Martin. *Shakespeare against Apartheid*. Craighall, South Africa: Ad. Donker, 1987.

Parker, Patricia, and Geoffrey Hartman, eds. *Shakespeare and the Question of Theory*. London: Routledge & Kegan Paul, 1985.

Paster, Gail Kern. *The Body Embarrassed: Drama and the Disciplines of Shame in Early Modern England*. Ithaca, N.Y.: Cornell University Press, 1993.

Patterson, Annabel. *Shakespeare and the Popular Voice*. Oxford: Blackwell, 1989.

Pechter, Edward. *What Was Shakespeare?: Renaissance Plays and Changing Critical Practice*. Ithaca, N.Y.: Cornell University Press, 1995.

Pitt, Angela. *Shakespeare's Women*. Totowa, N.J.: Barnes & Noble, 1981.

Rabkin, Norman. *Shakespeare and the Problem of Meaning.* Chicago: University of Chicago Press, 1981.

——. *Shakespeare and the Common Understanding.* New York: Free Press, 1967.

Rackin, Phyllis. *Stages of History: Shakespeare's English Chronicles.* Ithaca, N.Y.: Cornell University Press, 1990.

Ranald, Margaret Loftis. *Shakespeare and His Social Context: Essays in Osmotic Knowledge and Literary Interpretation.* New York: AMS Press, 1987.

Ryan, Kiernan. *Shakespeare.* 2nd ed. London: Prentice Hall, 1995.

Salingar, Leo. *Dramatic Form in Shakespeare and the Jacobeans.* Cambridge: Cambridge University Press, 1986.

——. *Shakespeare and the Traditions of Comedy.* London: Cambridge University Press, 1974.

Schwartz, Murray, and Coppélia Kahn, eds. *Representing Shakespeare: New Psychoanalytic Essays.* Baltimore: Johns Hopkins University Press, 1980.

Shapiro, Michael. *Gender in Play on the Shakespearean Stage: Boy Heroines and Female Pages.* Ann Arbor: University of Michigan Press, 1994.

Shepard, Simon. *Amazons and Warrior Women: Varieties of Feminism in Seventeenth-Century Drama.* N.Y.: St. Martin's Press, 1981.

Siemon, James. *Shakespearean Iconoclasm.* Berkeley and Los Angeles: University of California Press, 1985.

Skura, Meredith Anne. *Shakespeare the Actor and the Purposes of Playing.* Chicago: University of Chicago Press, 1993.

——. *The Literary Use of the Psychoanalytic Process.* New Haven: Yale University Press, 1981.

Snyder, Susan. *The Comic Matrix of Shakespeare's Tragedies.* Princeton: Princeton University Press, 1979.

Sprengnether, Madelon, and Shirley Nelson Garner, eds. *Shakespearean Tragedy and Gender.* Bloomington: Indiana University Press, 1996.

Stockholder, Kay. *Dream Works: Lovers and Families in Shakespeare's Plays.* Toronto: University of Toronto Press, 1987.

Summers, Joseph H. *Dreams of Love and Power: On Shakespeare's Plays.* Oxford: Clarendon Press, 1984.

Tennenhouse, Leonard. *Power on Display: The Politics of Shakespeare's Genres.* New York: Methuen, 1986.

Thomas, Vivian. *The Moral Universe of Shakespeare's Problem Plays.* New York: Routledge, 1991.

Traub, Valerie. *Desire and Anxiety: Circulations of Sexuality in Shakespearean Drama.* London: Routledge, 1992.

Trousdale, Marion. *Shakespeare and the Rhetoricians.* Chapel Hill: University of North Carolina Press, 1982.

Watson, Robert. *The Rest Is Silence: Death as Annihilation in the English Renaissance.* Berkeley and Los Angeles: University of California Press, 1994.

——. *Shakespeare and the Hazards of Ambition.* Cambridge: Harvard University Press, 1984.

Wells, Robin Headlam. *Shakespeare: Politics and the State.* London: Macmillan, 1986.

Wheeler, Richard P. *Shakespeare's Problem Comedies: Turn and Counter Turn.* Berkeley and Los Angeles: University of California Press, 1981.

Wilson, Richard. *Will Power: Essays on Shakespearean Authority.* Detroit: Wayne State University Press, 1993.

Woodbridge, Linda, and Edward Berry, eds. *True Rites and Maimed Rites: Ritual and Anti-Ritual in Shakespeare and His Age.* Urbana: University of Illinois Press, 1992.

Young, David. *The Action to the Word: Structure and Style in Shakespearean Tragedy.* New Haven: Yale University Press, 1990.

Zimmerman, Susan, ed. *Erotic Politics: Desire on the Renaissance Stage.* New York: Routledge, 1992.

The Dream of the Master Text

Allen, Michael J. B., and Kenneth Muir, eds. *Shakespeare's Plays in Quarto*. Berkeley and Los Angeles: University of California Press, 1981.

Blayney, Peter W. M. *The First Folio of Shakespeare*. Washington: Folger Library Publications, 1991.

——. *The Texts of "King Lear" and Their Origins*. Vol. 1: *Nicholas Okes and the First Quarto*. Cambridge: Cambridge University Press, 1982.

Bower, Fredson. *On Editing Shakespeare*. Charlottesville: University of Virginia Press, 1966.

Crewe, Jonathan. *Trials of Authorship: Anterior Forms and Poetic Reconstruction from Wyatt to Shakespeare*. Berkeley and Los Angeles: University of California Press, 1990.

De Grazia, Margreta. *Shakespeare Verbatim: The Reproduction of Authenticity and the 1790 Apparatus*. Oxford: Oxford University Press, 1991.

——, and Peter Stallybrass. "The Materiality of the Shakespearean Text." *Shakespeare Quarterly* 44 (1993): 255–83.

Franklin, Colin. *Shakespeare Domesticated: The Eighteenth-Century Editions*. Brookfield, Vt.: Scolar Press, 1991.

Greg, W. W., ed. *The Merry Wives of Windsor, 1602*. Oxford: Clarendon Press, 1910.

Hinman, Charlton. *The Norton Facsimile: The First Folio of Shakespeare*. 2nd ed. New York: Norton, 1996.

——. *The Printing and Proof-Reading of the First Folio of Shakespeare*. 2 vols. Oxford: Clarendon Press, 1963.

Honigmann, E. A. J. *The Stability of Shakespeare's Text*. London: E. Arnold, 1965.

Ioppolo, Grace. *Revising Shakespeare*. Cambridge: Harvard University Press, 1991.

Irace, Kathleen O. *Reforming the "Bad" Quartos: Performance and Provenance of Six Shakespearean First Editions*. Newark: University of Delaware Press, 1994.

Maguire, Laurie E. *Shakespeare's Suspect Texts: The "Bad" Quartos and Their Contexts*. Cambridge: Cambridge University Press, 1996.

McKerrow, R. B. *Prolegomena for the Oxford Shakespeare*. Oxford: Clarendon Press, 1939.

Mcleod, Randall, ed. *Crisis in Editing: Texts of the English Renaissance*. New York: AMS Press, 1994.

Pollard, A. W. *Shakespeare's Fight with the Pirates*. Cambridge: Cambridge University Press, 1920.

——. *Shakespeare's Folios and Quartos*. London: Methuen, 1909.

Seary, Peter. *Lewis Theobald and the Editing of Shakespeare*. Oxford: Clarendon Press, 1990.

Taylor, Gary, and Michael Warren, eds. *The Division of the Kingdoms*. Oxford: Clarendon Press, 1983.

Urkowitz, Steven. *Shakespeare's Revision of "King Lear."* Princeton: Princeton University Press, 1980.

Walker, Alice. *Textual Problems of the First Folio*. Cambridge: Cambridge University Press, 1953.

Wells, Stanley. *Re-Editing Shakespeare for the Modern Reader*. New York: Oxford University Press, 1984.

——, and Gary Taylor. *William Shakespeare: A Textual Companion*. Oxford: Clarendon Press, 1987.

——, and Gary Taylor. *Modernizing Shakespeare's Spelling*. Oxford: Clarendon Press, 1979.

Werstine, Paul. "*Narratives About Printed Shakespeare Texts: 'Foul Papers' and 'Bad' Quartos.*" *Shakespeare Quarterly* 41 (1990): 65–86.

Williams, George Walton. *The Craft of Printing and the Publication of Shakespeare's Works*. Washington: Folger Books, 1985.

Wilson, J. Dover. *The Manuscript of Shakespeare's "Hamlet" and the Problems of Its Transmission.* 2 vols. Cambridge, Eng. 1934.

Shakespeare in Performance

Ball, Robert Hamilton. *Shakespeare on Silent Film.* New York: Theater Art Books, 1968.
Bartholomeusz, Dennis. *Macbeth and the Players.* Cambridge: Cambridge University Press, 1969.
Barton, John. *Playing Shakespeare.* London: Methuen, 1984.
Bate, Jonathan, and Russell Jackson, eds. *Shakespeare: An Illustrated Stage History.* New York: Oxford University Press, 1996.
Berger, Harry Jr. *Imaginary Audition: Shakespeare on Stage and Page.* Berkeley and Los Angeles: University of California Press, 1989.
Berry, Francis. *The Shakespeare Inset: Word and Picture.* London: Routledge & Kegan Paul, 1965.
Berry, Ralph. *Changing Styles in Shakespeare.* Boston: Allen & Unwin, 1981.
Bevington, David. *Action Is Eloquence: Shakespeare's Language of Gesture.* Cambridge: Harvard University Press, 1984.
Branam, George C. *Eighteenth-Century Adaptions of Shakespearean Tragedy.* Berkeley and Los Angeles: University of California Press, 1936, 1956, 1973.
Brennan, Anthony. *Onstage and Offstage Worlds in Shakespeare's Plays.* New York: Routledge, 1989.
——. *Shakespeare's Dramatic Structures.* Boston: Routledge & Kegan Paul, 1986.
Brockbank, Philip, ed. *Players of Shakespeare.* Cambridge: Cambridge University Press, 1985.
Brown, Ivor. *Shakespeare and the Actors.* London: Bodley Head, 1970.
Brown, John Russell. *Shakespeare's Dramatic Style.* London: Heineman, 1970.
——. *Shakespeare's Plays in Performance.* New York: St. Martin's Press, 1967.
Bulman, James C., and H. R. Coursen, eds. *Shakespeare on Television.* Hanover, N.H.: University Press of New England, 1988.
——, J. R. Mulryne, and Margaret Shewring. *Shakespeare in Performance Series.* Manchester: Manchester University Press, 1982.
Carlisle, Carol Jones. *Shakespeare from the Greenroom: Actors' Criticisms of Four Major Tragedies.* Chapel Hill, N.C.: University of North Carolina Press, 1969.
Cohn, Ruby. *Modern Shakespeare Offshoots.* Princeton: Princeton University Press, 1976.
Cook, Judith. *Shakespeare's Players.* London: Harrap, 1983.
Dawson, Anthony B. *Indirections—Shakespeare and the Art of Illusion.* Toronto: University of Toronto Press, 1978.
Dean, Winton. "Shakespeare in the Opera House." *Shakespeare Survey* 18 (1965): 75–93.
Donohue, Joseph W., Jr. *Dramatic Character in the English Romantic Age.* Princeton: Princeton University Press, 1970.
Downer, Alan S. *The Eminent Tragedian, William Charles Macready.* Cambridge: Harvard University Press, 1966.
Eckert, Charles W., ed. *Focus on Shakespearean Films.* Englewood Cliffs, N.J.: Prentice-Hall, 1972.
Goldman, Michael. *Acting and Action in Shakespearean Tragedy.* Princeton: Princeton University Press, 1985.
Hartwig, Joan. *Shakespeare's Analogical Scene: Parody as Structural Syntax.* Lincoln: University of Nebraska Press, 1983.
Hirsch, James F. *The Structures of Shakespearean Scenes.* New Haven: Yale University Press, 1981.
Hogan, Charles B., ed. *Shakespeare in the Theatre, 1701–1800.* 2 vols. Oxford: Clarendon Press, 1952–57.

Homan, Sidney, ed. *When the Theater Turns to Itself: The Aesthetic Metaphor in Shakespeare.* Lewiston, Pa.: Bucknell University Press, 1981.

———, ed. *Shakespeare's "More Than Words Can Witness": Essays on Visual and Nonverbal Enactment in the Plays.* Lewisburg, Pa.: Bucknell University Press, 1980.

Howard, Jean E. *Shakespeare's Art of Orchestration: Stage Technique and Audience Response.* Urbana: University of Illinois Press, 1984.

Jones, Emrys. *Scenic Form in Shakespeare.* Oxford: Clarendon Press, 1971.

Jorgens, Jack L. *Shakespeare on Film.* Bloomington: Indiana University Press, 1976.

Manvell, Roger. *Shakespeare and the Film.* London: Dent, 1971.

McGuire, Philip C. *Speechless Dialect: Shakespeare's Open Silences.* Berkeley and Los Angeles: University of California Press, 1983.

———, and David A. Samuelson. *Shakespeare: The Theatrical Dimension.* New York: AMS Press, 1979.

Odell, George C. D. *Shakespeare from Betterton to Irving.* 2 vols. New York: Scribner, 1920, 1966.

Poel, William. *Shakespeare in the Theatre.* 1913, 1968. New York: AMS Press, 1974.

Rosenberg, Marvin. *The Masks of Lear.* Berkeley and Los Angeles: University of California Press, 1972.

Rutter, Carol, et al. *Clamorous Voices: Shakespeare's Women Today.* London: Women's Press, 1988.

Shattuck, Charles H. *Shakespeare on the American Stage from the Hallams to Edwin Booth.* Washington, D.C.: Folger Shakespeare Library, 1976. . . . *from Booth and Barrett to Sothern and Marlowe.* Washington, D.C.: Folger Shakespeare Library, 1987.

———. *The Shakespeare Promptbooks: A Descriptive Catalogue.* Urbana: University of Illinois Press, 1965.

Slater, Ann Pasternak. *Shakespeare the Director.* Totowa, N.J.: Barnes & Noble, 1982.

Speaight, Robert. *Shakespeare on the Stage: An Illustrated History of Shakespearian Performance.* Boston: Little, Brown, 1973.

———. *William Poel and the Elizabethan Revival.* London: Heineman, 1954.

Spencer, Hazelton. *Shakespeare Improved: The Restoration Versions in Quarto and on the Stage.* Cambridge, Mass., 1927.

Sprague, Arthur Colby. *Shakespearian Players and Performances.* Cambridge: Harvard University Press, 1953.

———. *Shakespeare and the Actors.* Cambridge: Harvard University Press, 1944.

Styan, J. L. "Sight and Space: The Perception of Shakespeare on Stage and Screen." *Shakespeare, Pattern of Excelling Nature.* Ed. David Bevington and Jay L. Halio. Newark: University of Delaware Press, 1978.

———. *Shakespeare's Stagecraft.* Cambridge: Cambridge University Press, 1967.

Thaler, Alwin. *Shakespeare to Sheridan.* Cambridge, Mass.: Arno Press, 1922.

Thompson, Marvin and Ruth, eds. *Shakespeare and the Sense of Performance.* Newark: University of Delaware Press, 1989.

Trewin, J. C. *Shakespeare on the English Stage, 1900–1964.* London: Barrie & Rockliff, 1964.

Van den Berg, Kent. *Playhouse and Cosmos: Shakespearean Theater as Metaphor.* Newark: University of Delaware Press, 1985.

Wells, Stanley. *Royal Shakespeare: Four Major Productions at Stratford-upon-Avon.* Manchester: Manchester University Press, 1977.

Glossary

"Above" The gallery on the upper level of the *frons scenae*. In open-air theaters, such as the Globe, this space contained the lords' rooms. The central section of the gallery was sometimes used by the players for short scenes. Indoor theaters such as Blackfriars featured a curtained alcove for musicians above the stage.

"Aloft" See *"Above."*

Amphitheater An open-air theater, such as the Globe.

Arras See *Curtain.*

Cellerage See *Trap.*

Chorus In the works of Shakespeare and other Elizabethan playwrights, a single individual (not, as in Greek tragedy, a group) who speaks before the play (and often before each act), describing events not shown on stage as well as commenting on the action witnessed by the audience.

Curtain Curtains, or arras (hanging tapestries), covered a part of the *frons scenae,* thus concealing the discovery space, and may also have been draped around the edge of the stage to conceal the open area underneath.

Discovery space A central opening or alcove concealed behind a curtain in the center of the *frons scenae.* The curtain could be drawn aside to "discover" tableaux such as Portia's caskets, the body of Polonius, or the statue of Hermione. Shakespeare appears to have used this stage device only sparingly.

Doubling The common practice of having one actor play multiple roles, so that a play with a large cast of characters might be performed by a relatively small company.

Dumb shows Mimed scenes performed before a play (or before each act), summarizing or foreshadowing the plot. Dumb shows were popular in early Elizabethan drama, but although they already seemed old-fashioned in Shakespeare's time, they were employed by writers up to the 1640s.

Epilogue A brief speech or poem addressed to the audience by an actor after the play. In some cases, as in 2 *Henry IV*, the epilogue could be combined with, or could merge into, the jig.

Forestage The front of the stage, closest to the audience.

Frons scenae The wall at the back of the stage, behind which lay the players' tiring-house. The *frons scenae* of the Globe featured two doors flanking the central discovery space, with a gallery "above."

Gallery Covered seating areas surrounding the open yard of the public amphitheaters. There were three levels of galleries at the Globe; admission to these seats cost an extra penny (in addition to the basic admission fee of one penny to the yard), and seating in the higher galleries another penny yet. In indoor theaters such as Blackfriars, where there was no standing room, gallery seating was less expensive than seating in the pit; indeed, seats nearest the stage were the most expensive.

Gatherers Persons employed by the playing company to take money at the entrances to the theater.

Groundlings Audience members who paid the minimum price of admission (one penny) to stand in the yard of the open-air theaters; also referred to as "understanders."

Heavens Canopied roof over the stage in the open-air theaters, protecting the players and their costumes from rain. The "heavens" would be brightly decorated with sun, moon, and stars, and perhaps the signs of the zodiac.

Hut A structure on the top of the cover over the stage, where stagehands produced the effects of thunder and lightning and operated the machinery by which gods, such as Jupiter in *Cymbeline*, descended through the trapdoor in the "heavens."

Jig A song-and-dance performance by the clown and other members of the company at the conclusion of a play. These performances were frequently bawdy and were officially banned in 1612.

Lords' rooms Partitioned sections of the gallery "above," where the most prestigious and expensive seats in the public playhouses were located. These rooms were designed not to provide the best view of the action on the stage below, but to make their privileged occupants conspicuous to the rest of the audience.

Open-air theaters Unroofed public playhouses in the suburbs of London, such as the Theatre, the Rose, and the Globe.

Part The character played by an actor. In Shakespeare's theater, actors were given a roll of paper called a "part" containing all of the speeches and all of the cues belonging to their character. The term "role," synonymous with "part," is derived from such rolls of paper.

Patrons Important nobles and members of the royal family under whose protection the theatrical companies of London operated; players not in the service of patrons were punishable as vagabonds. The companies were referred to as their patrons' "Men" or "Servants." Thus the name of the company to which Shakespeare belonged for most of his career was first the Lord Chamberlain's Men, then was changed to the King's Men in 1603, when James I became their patron.

Pillars The "heavens" were supported by two tall painted pillars or posts near the front of the stage. These occasionally played a role in stage action, allowing a character to "hide" while remaining in full view of the audience.

Pit The area in front of the stage in indoor theaters such as Blackfriars, where the most expensive and prestigious bench seating was to be had.

Posts See *Pillars*.

Proscenium The space of the transparent "fourth wall," which divides the actors from the orchestra and audience in the standard modern theater. The stages on which Shakespeare's plays were first performed had no proscenium.

Rearstage The back of the stage, farthest from the audience.

Repertory The stock of plays a company had ready for performance at a given time. Companies generally performed a different play each day, often more than a dozen plays in a month and more than thirty in the course of the season.

Role See *Part*.

Sharers Senior actors holding shares in a joint-stock theatrical company; they paid for costumes, hired hands, and new plays, and they shared profits and losses equally. Shakespeare was not only a longtime "sharer" of the Lord Chamberlain's Men but, from 1599, a "housekeeper," the holder of a one-eighth share in the Globe playhouse.

Tiring-house The players' dressing (attiring) room, a structure located at the back of the stage and connected to the stage by two or more doors in the *frons scenae*.

Trap A trapdoor near the front of the stage that allowed access to the "cellarage" beneath and was frequently associated with hell's mouth. Another trapdoor in the "heavens" opened for the descent of gods to the stage below.

"Within" The tiring-house, from which offstage sound effects such as shouts, drums, and trumpets were produced.

Yard The central space in open-air theaters such as the Globe, into which the stage projected and in which audience members stood. Admission to the yard in the public theaters cost a penny, the cheapest admission available.

TEXTUAL TERMS

Aside See *Stage direction.*

Autograph Text written in the author's own hand. With the possible exception of a few pages of the collaborative play *Sir Thomas More*, no dramatic works or poems written in Shakespeare's hand are known to survive.

Canonical Of an author, the writings generally accepted as authentic. In the case of Shakespeare's dramatic works, only two plays that are not among the thirty-six plays contained in the First Folio, *Pericles* and *The Two Noble Kinsmen*, have won widespread acceptance into the Shakespearean canon. (This sense of "canonical" should not be confused with the use of "the canon" to denote the entire body of literary works, including but not limited to Shakespeare's, that have traditionally been regarded as fit objects of admiration and study.)

Catchword A word printed below the text at the bottom of a page, matching the first word on the following page. The catchword enabled the printer to keep the pages in their proper sequence. Where the catchword fails to match the word at the top of the next page, there is reason to suspect that something has been lost or misplaced.

Compositor Person employed in a print shop to set type. To speed the printing process, most of Shakespeare's plays were set by more than one compositor. Compositors frequently followed their own standards in spelling and punctuation. They inevitably introduced some errors into the text, often by selecting the wrong piece from the type case or by setting the correct letter upside-down.

Conflation A version of a play created by combining readings from more than one substantive edition. Since the early eighteenth century, for example, most versions of *King Lear* and of several other plays by Shakespeare have been conflations of quarto and First Folio texts.

Control text The text upon which a modern edition is based.

Dramatis personae A list of the characters appearing in the play. In the First Folio such lists were printed at the end of some but not all of the plays. The editor

Nicholas Rowe (1709) first provided lists of dramatis personae for all of Shakespeare's dramatic works.

Exeunt / Exit See *Stage direction.*

Fair copy A transcript of the "foul papers" made either by a scribe or by the playwright.

Folio A book-making format in which each large sheet of paper is folded once, making two leaves (four pages front and back). This format produced large volumes, generally handsome and expensive. The First Folio of Shakespeare's plays was printed in 1623.

Foul papers An author's first completed draft of a play, typically full of blotted-out passages and revisions. None of Shakespeare's foul papers is known to survive.

Licensing By an order of 1581, new plays could not be performed until they had received a license from the Master of the Revels. A separate license, granted by the Court of High Commission, was required for publication, though in practice plays were often printed without license. From 1610, the Master of the Revels had the authority to license plays for publication as well as for performance.

Manent / Manet See *Stage direction.*

Memorial reconstruction The conjectural practice of reconstructing the text of a play from memory. Companies touring in the provinces without access to promptbooks may have resorted to memorial reconstruction. This practice also provides a plausible explanation for the existence of the so-called bad quartos.

Octavo A book-making format in which each large sheet of paper is folded three times, making eight leaves (sixteen pages front and back). Only one of Shakespeare's plays, *Richard Duke of York* (*3 Henry VI*, 1595), was published in octavo format.

Playbook See *Promptbook.*

Press variants Minor textual variations among books of the same edition, resulting from corrections made in the course of printing or from damaged or slipped type.

Promptbook A manuscript of a play (either foul papers or fair copy) annotated and adapted for performance by the theatrical company. The promptbook incorporated stage directions, notes on properties and special effects, and revisions, sometimes including those required by the Master of the Revels. Promptbooks are usually identifiable by the replacement of characters' names with actors' names.

Quarto A book-making format in which each large sheet of paper is folded twice, making four leaves (eight pages front and back). Quarto volumes were smaller and less expensive than books printed in the folio format.

Scribal copy A transcript of a play produced by a professional scribe (or "scrivener"). Scribes tended to employ their own preferred spellings and abbreviations and could be responsible for introducing a variety of errors.

Speech prefix (s.p.) The indication of the identity of the speaker of the following line or lines. Early editions of Shakespeare's plays often use different prefixes at different points to designate the same person. On occasion, the name of the actor who was to play the role appears in place of the name of the character.

Stage direction (s.d.) The part of the text that is not spoken by any character but that indicates actions to be performed onstage. Stage directions in the earliest editions of Shakespeare's plays are sparse and are sometimes grouped together at the beginning of a scene rather than next to the spoken lines they should precede, accompany, or follow. By convention, the most basic stage directions were written in Latin. "Exit" indicates the departure of a single actor from the stage, "exeunt" the departure of more than one. "Manet" indicates that a single actor remains onstage, "manent" that more than one remains. Lines accompanied by the stage direction "aside" are spoken so as not to be heard by the others on stage. This stage direction appeared in some early editions of Shakespeare plays, but other means were also used to indicate such speech (such as placing the words within parentheses), and sometimes no indication was provided.

Stationers' Register   The account books of the Company of Stationers (of which all printers were legally required to be members), recording the fees paid for permission to print new works as well as the fines exacted for printing without permission. The Stationers' Register thus provides a valuable if incomplete record of publication in England.

Substantive text   The text of an edition based upon access to a manuscript, as opposed to a derivative text based only on an earlier edition.

Variorum editions   Comprehensive editions of a work or works in which the various views of previous editors and commentators are compiled.

ILLUSTRATION ACKNOWLEDGMENTS

General Introduction Plague death bill: By permission of the Folger Shakespeare Library Webbe: By permission of the British Library Amman: Spencer Collection, The New York Public Library, Astor, Lenox and Tilden Foundation *Swetnam* title page: By permission of The Huntington Library, San Marino, California Pope as Antichrist: By permission of the Folger Shakespeare Library de Heere: The National Museum of Wales Armada portrait: By kind permission of Marquess of Tavistock and Trustees of the Bedford Estate Boaistuau: By permission of The Huntington Library, San Marino, California Mandeville: By permission of the Houghton Library, Harvard University Funeral procession: Additional Ms. 35324, folio 37v. By permission of the British Library Gheeraerts: By permission of the Trustees of Dulwich Picture Gallery van den Broek: Fitzwilliam Museum, University of Cambridge Swimming: Bodleian Library, University of Oxford, 4 G.17.Art Panorama of London: By permission of the British Library Tarleton: Harley 3885, folio 19. By permission of the British Library Hanging: Pepys Library, Magdalene College, Cambridge Syphilis victim: By permission of The Huntington Library, San Marino, California *Spanish Tragedy* title page: By permission of the Folger Shakespeare Library Stratford-upon-Avon: By permission of City of York Libraries Cholmondeley sisters: Tate Gallery, London Alleyn: By permission of the Trustees of Dulwich Picture Library *If You Know Not Me* title page: By permission of The Huntington Library, San Marino, California van der Straet: By permission of the Folger Shakespeare Library

Venus and Adonis Tempesta: British Museum Wither: By permission of the Houghton Library, Harvard University Peacham: By permission of the Folger Shakespeare Library

The Rape of Lucrece Raphael: The Metropolitan Museum of Art, Purchase, Lila Acheson Wallace Gift, 1997. (1997. 153) Photograph 1997 The Metropolitan Museum of Art. Titian: Fitzwilliam Museum, University of Cambridge Amman: Rare Books and Manuscripts Division, The New York Public Library, Astor, Lenox and Tilden Foundations

Sonnets Whitney: By permission of the Folger Shakespeare Library

Pericles Gower title page: C.34.L.8. By permission of the British Library Inigo Jones: Devonshire Collection, Chatsworth. Reproduced by permission of the Duke of Devonshire and the Chatsworth Settlement Trustees. Photo credit: The Courtauld Institute of Art

The Winter's Tale *Bloudy Mother* title page: By permission of the Houghton Library, Harvard University Rüff: By permission of the Folger Shakespeare Library Pedlar: Pepys Library, Magdalene College, Cambridge

Cymbeline Camerarius: By permission of the Folger Shakespeare Library van de Pâsse: British Museum Alciati: By permission of the Folger Shakespeare Library

The Tempest Magnus: Reproduced by permission of The Huntington Library, San Marino, California Galle: The Burndy Library, Norwalk, Connecticut

The Two Noble Kinsmen "The Knight's Tale" extract: Division of Rare and Manuscript Collections, Cornell University Library René of Anjou: Österreichische Nationalbibliothek, Vienna Beauchamp Pageant: Cotton Julius E IV art 6, folio 3. By permission of the British Library

The Shakespearean Stage Braun and Hogenburg: 8.Tab.c.4. Bk.1.pl.1. By permission of the British Library Hollar: Guildhall Library, Corporation of London Interior of the "new" Globe: Courtesy of The International Shakespeare Globe Center Ltd. Photo: John Tramper Exterior of the "new" Globe: Courtesy of The International Shakespeare Globe Center Ltd. Photo: Richard Kalina *Frons scenae* of the "new" Globe: Courtesy of The International Shakespeare Globe Center Ltd. Photo: Richard Kalina Oliver: The Burghley House Collection. Photograph: Courtauld Institute of Art Peacham: Reproduced by permission of the Marquess of Bath, Longleat House, Warminster, Wiltshire, Great Britain. Photograph: Courtauld Institute of Art de Witt: University Library, Utrecht, MS 842, f.132r Middle Temple Hall: The Benchers of the Honorable Society of the Middle Temple, London Hollar: Guildhall Library, Corporation of London

Contemporary Documents

First Folio front matter: *The Norton Facsimile of the First Folio of Shakespeare*, 2nd ed. (1996)

A Shakespearean Chronicle, 1558–1616

Master John: By courtesy of the National Portrait Gallery, London Geneva Bible page: Bodleian Library, University of Oxford, Bibl.Eng.1560 Swordsmen: By permission of the Folger Shakespeare Library Holinshed (burning city): By permission of the Houghton Library, Harvard University Holinshed (naval battle): By permission of the Houghton Library, Harvard University Henri III: By permission of the Folger Shakespeare Library Witches: C.27.b.35. By permission of the British Library Agas: Guildhall Library, Corporation of London Plague woodcut: Ashley 617. By permission of the British Library Coat of Arms: Shakespeare Drafts (Vincent 157, no. 23). By permission of the College of Arms Earl of Essex: British Museum Execution of Essex: By permission of the Folger Shakespeare Library Vertue sketch: Additional Ms. 70438, folio 18. By permission of the British Library Holinshed (Macbeth's coronation): By permission of the Houghton Library, Harvard University Inigo Jones: Devonshire Collection, Chatsworth. Reproduced by permission of the Duke of Devonshire and the Chatsworth Settlement Trustees. Photo credit: The Courtauld Institute of Art Henry, Prince of Wales: Fitzwilliam Museum, University of Cambridge van de Passe (James I): Bodleian Library, University of Oxford, E 14 Th.Seld

Index of Poems: Titles
and First Lines